USEFUL CHECKLISTS, SUMMARIES, AND BOXES

Critical Thinking and *Critical Decisions* Boxes

Apostrophes: Tests for placement **480**
Arguments: Finding support **165**
Arguments: Responding to opposing views **175**
Comparative forms: A test for choices **277**
Comma use: Distinguish nonessential information **459–60**
Coordination vs. subordination: Knowing which to use **367–8**
Critical habits: Alertness to differences **3**
Critical habits: Setting issues in context **7**
Critical reading: Preview, read, & review **12–14**
Gender messages & pronouns in context **266**
Linking independent clauses: choosing methods **300**
Modifiers: Choosing their placement **321**
Paragraphs: Revising for coherence **137**
Parallelism: Matching content with phrasing **355**
Pronoun choice: Tests for *who* and *whom* **225**
Pronoun choice: Tests for *who, which, that* **312**
Quotations: When to incorporate them? **492**
Revision: Challenge thesis and structure **102**
Separating sentences: Use a semicolon, period, or comma & conjunction **471**
Sources: Forging relationships **55, 56**
Theses for Informative papers **84**
Theses for Argumentative papers **86**
Theses: Quizzing a working thesis **90–91**
Tone & register choices **403**
Writing analyses **48**
Writing evaluations **39, 40**
Writing from synthesized sources **58**
Writing summaries **34**

The Writing and Revising Process: Essays and Paragraphs

Arguments: An emotional appeal **174**
Arguments: Structures and options **176, 177**
Arguments: Gathering materials **179**
Audience analysis **68–9**
Drafting strategies **94**
Paragraphs: Essential features **143**
Paragraphs: Introductions **154** Conclusions **156**
Paragraphs: Transitional expressions **141**
Paragraphs: Unity, coherence, development **125**
Revising for unity **105**
Revising for balance **107**

Revising: Peer editing guidelines **110**
Revising: The revision process **99–100, 102**
Theses: Features of working theses **592**
Theses: Generating working theses **89–90**
Theses: Narrowing the subject **83**
Topics: Know your topic **62–3**
Topics: Narrow your topic **64**
Writing a section of a paper **97**
Writing process: An overview **61**

Revising Sentences, Words, Punctuation (see also *Critical Decisions* boxes)

Abbreviations in the disciplines **532**
Acronyms: Helping readers understand **529**
Clear, concise, direct writing **352**
Comma splices: Four ways to avoid them **465**
Dashes: When do writers need them? **503**
Homonyms commonly confused **430–1**
Pretentious language vs. technical terms **413**
Pronoun references: Revising to clarify **310**
Sentences: Basic patterns **202–3**
Sentences: Five ways to mark boundaries **293**
Sentence fragments: How to eliminate them **287**
Sexism & gender-specific nouns **410**
Subjects & verbs: Basic relationships **196**
Verb tense: Sequence in a sentence **244–5**
Verb tense in scientific writing **711**

Researching and Writing in the Disciplines

Document systems: An overview **621**
Eliminating plagiarism **586**
Focused reading **566**
General sources: When to use them **556–7**
Humanities references materials **682**
Interviewing checklist **569**
Laboratory notebooks: Guidelines **716–17**
Literary analysis: Key questions & topics **668, 675–6**
Social science: Manuscript form **698**
Social science reference materials **706**
Sources: Distinguishing facts from opinions **21**
Sources: Strategies for synthesizing **27, 56, 58**
Sources: Using authoritative sources **172**
Sources: Gathering material for an argument **179**
Sources: When to summarize, paraphrase, or quote **586**
Verbs to attribute quotations **585**

The first handbook built on the underlying themes of *Critical Thinking* and *Writing Across the Curriculum* is now revised with *attention to ESL* concerns integrated throughout!

THE ALLYN & BACON HANDBOOK
Second Edition

Leonard J. Rosen
Harvard University

Laurence Behrens
University of California, Santa Barbara

The NEW Second Edition offers

- ESL coverage throughout the text

- Expanded treatment of critical thinking

- "Spotlight on Common Errors" boxes

- Coverage of writing about literature

- Greater attention to the revision process

The Second Edition gives students even more help with learning to think, read, and write critically.

The handbook's foundational chapters — "Critical Thinking and Reading" and "Critical Thinking and Writing" — offer substantive instruction and common strategies for students. By working with this material, students become better prepared to evaluate and analyze their college reading and writing assignments.

NEW — Chapter 1 now begins with a section on "habits of the mind."

This new section prepares students to think critically about college-level materials and help them work with the source materials on which they base much of their writing.

Emphasizes the variety of CHOICES available to students in the writing process.

Throughout its treatment of the writing process, grammar, mechanics, and punctuation, the Allyn & Bacon Handbook emphasizes the *choices* that students face in developing sentences, paragraphs, and essays, and in solving problems with respect to audience and purpose.

NEW — "Critical Decision" Boxes

These new "Critical Decision" boxes show students how to think through and make judgments when writing.

The first handbook to consider writing as a fundamental skill for inquiry and expression in *all* college disciplines.

The text is based on the premise that the composition course is only the *first* course in college in which writing will be an essential and valuable skill. One of the book's primary goals, therefore, is to help students master the kinds of reading and writing assignments that are crucial to their college success. The *grammar, punctuation*, and *mechanics* coverage offers examples and exercises that are drawn from the type of reading students can expect to encounter in their college studies.

Three innovative and extensive chapters on Writing and Reading in the Humanities, Social Sciences, and Natural Sciences show how thinking, reading, and writing differ from one discipline area to another.

Each discipline chapter

- covers discipline-specific strategies for writing to inform and argue
- reviews typical reading and audience situations
- presents the common assignments students will encounter in each discipline, and
- provides a sample student paper and a guide to specialized reference materials for each of the discipline areas.

NEW SECTION on Writing about Literature appears in Ch. 37, Writing & Reading in the Humanities.

The most extensive coverage of Argument in any handbook!

The argument chapter introduces a clear and direct approch to the Toulmin model of argument, in order to provide students with ways to construct and support an argumentative thesis.

ADDED COVERAGE of Logical fallacies in Ch. 6, "Writing and Evaluating Arguments."

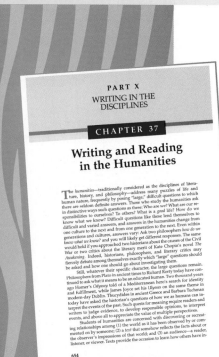

NEW — ESL coverage throughout addresses the particular needs of non-native speakers.

An entirely new Part XII "Writing English as a Second Language" has been added and includes these three chapters to provide supplementary help to students for whom English is a second language:

- Ch. 42 ESL — Using English Nouns, Pronouns, and Articles
- Ch. 43 ESL — Using English Verbs
- Ch. 44 ESL — Using Modifiers and Connectors in English Sentences

In addition, there are ESL Notes integrated throughout the remaining chapters of the book to give students extra help *as they need it.*

For the instructor, there are further suggestions in the margins of the Annotated Instructor's Edition:
- Teaching ideas geared specifically toward multicultural differences
- ESL Alerts that "red-flag" potential language problems for non-native speakers
- ESL Exercises that can be used as additional assignments for those students who would benefit from such exercises.

PART XII
ESL REFERENCE GUIDE

The next three chapters are designed to supplement the rest of the *Handbook.* They provide basic information on structural and idiomatic features of the English language that students from an English as a Second Language (ESL) background may need for reference.

These chapters assume that ESL students are now working in a basic English composition course alongside native speakers, and that they have already completed a college-level course of instruction (or its equivalent) in using English as a Second Language. The role of this material is not to provide primary ESL instruction but to give students help in three ways: (1) to identify key topics and problems that persistently cause difficulties for ESL students from many different backgrounds; (2) to propose standard usage guidelines and remedies for such problems (with the assistance of exercises); and (3) to refer ESL students to sections of chapters 1–41 that will give particular help with difficult language and usage issues in English. Students should also notice that chapters 7–33 have been furnished with topical "ESL Note" references, which briefly describe key issues and refer readers to pertinent sections of these supplementary chapters.

The following chapters cover topics in the three functional areas of English language usage: chapter 42—nouns and noun-related structures (including articles and determiners); chapter 43—verbs, verbals, and related structures (including particles with phrasal verbs); and chapter 44—usage for modifiers and modifying structures. Prepositions—perhaps the most troublesome feature of English—are treated in connection with the structures that determine them in each chapter of this part. (Prepositions determined by nouns are discussed in 42c; those determined by phrasal verbs are discussed in 43f; and those governed by adjectives are discussed in 44b.)

747

TEACHING IDEAS

You might demonstrate the value of noting and acting on differences by asking students to respond to these questions on the roles of men and women in various religions. Discussion will be generated. Five or ten minutes into the discussion, make the observation that the discussion was made possible by the discrepancies noted in the two newspaper accounts. Such discussion is, for the curious, the logical outgrowth of a difference. Your discussion in class will demonstrate for students that noting differences opens possibilities for research.

ESL ALERT

ESL students (as well as native speakers) might confuse "critical" with "negative criticism," and might feel uncomfortable with the idea of being openly confrontational or argumentative. Emphasizing the idea of noticing key differences and actively raising questions would be a positive and productive way to present "critical" thinking.

EXERCISE 1

Individual responses

ESL ALERT

The Western academic practice of teaching critical thinking through student-teacher class discussion is far from universal, with the majority of students (especially from Asia and the Middle East) viewing their role as more passive than U.S. instructors may be accustomed to: receiving and memorizing truths passed down by authority figures—without questioning such information. This concept of role affects classroom behavior, with the Japanese, for instance, believing that "the nail that sticks up gets hammered down." Such students often consider volunteering to answer or participating in class discussion a violation of the rules. This difference in cultural attitudes must be dealt with

4 **1b**   *Critical Thinking and Reading*

rabbis and that, only one week before the bishops' conference and after a heated debate, the Anglican church voted to ordain women as priests. Such knowledge of a difference between the views of Catholics and the views of some Jews and Anglicans could prompt questions such as these:

What are the relevant differences among Anglican, Catholic, and Jewish religious traditions?

What is the role of the priest or rabbi in these religions?

What is the role of women and men in these religions?

How will women priests change the Anglican church? Have they changed the Episcopal churches in America, or have women rabbis changed Jewish congregations?

What will be the effect of men continuing to dominate the priesthood in the Catholic church?

What were the key issues in the Catholic and Anglican debates, and how can these be compared and contrasted?

Option: Generate an action plan.

Questions that you pose suggest activity on your part. The preceding questions, for instance, might lead to an investigation of the roles of men and women in the Catholic church and in other denominations. With a more limited focus, you might decide to learn what happened at the bishops' conference by obtaining a draft of the bishops' policy statement on the role of women. Once you notice and develop questions based on a difference, you can undertake a research project. Indeed, in many disciplines, researchers begin their investigations by noticing a difference and speculating on causes. Of course, not every question you pose will lead to full-blown research. Be aware, though, that your questions can direct you to further work.

EXERCISE 1

Every day, for a week, read two or more newspapers—your town's local paper (s) and one or more of the following: the *New York Times,* the *Wall Street Journal,* and *USA Today.* Pay special attention to each paper's coverage of a single news event. Read the accounts and observe differences—among the three or between what any of the pieces report and your own experience. Pose questions based on these differences. Finally, outline a plan for potential research based on your questions.

1b Active, critical thinkers challenge, and are challenged by, sources.

Spotting a difference or discrepancy based on your reading gives you an entrance into a source. The word *entrance* suggests that reading selections and buildings share a certain quality: both have interiors. To know what's inside a building you open the door and step inside. What

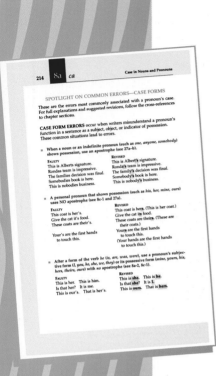

NEW —"Spotlight on Common Errors" boxes help students identify and solve those errors that writers make most frequently.

Rosen and Behrens identify eight subject areas and include nine "Spotlights" on those areas that give students the most trouble. Each "Spotlight" identifies the error, using a minimum of technical terminology, and then states the rules that should be followed, giving examples of faulty and revised sentences with referrals to chapter sections for full explanations.

The "Spotlights on Common Errors" include:
Case Form • Verbs • Agreement • Sentence Fragments and Comma Splices • Pronoun Reference • Modifiers • Parallelism • Comma Use

In addition, easy-reference endpages provide page number listings for all of the "Spotlights" throughout the handbook.

Coverage of *revision* has also been greatly expanded to provide even more help through the writing process.

Coverage now includes:
- More on rediscovering your main idea
- An extended section on thesis writing
- More student examples
- Three drafts of a student paper, with color highlights to show changes made with each revision

THE INSTRUCTOR'S ANNOTATED EDITION

Provides on-the-spot, in-text references and teaching aids.

Greatly expanded, the Instructor's Annotated Edition (IAE) facilitates your teaching efforts. Carefully designed to support you throughout the course, the IAE augments the student text with succinct marginal annotations related to key topics in each chapter. Each type of annotation, identified by a bold headline, appears on a wide margin page in a beige colored panel.

The following annotations are found in the Instructor's Annotated Edition:

Key Features, positioned at the beginning of each chapter, provide you with a quick overview of the forthcoming coverage. "Key Features" give you an at-a-glance preview of what students should learn from the chapter.

Looking Back and Looking Ahead appear at different points throughout all chapters in the text. Each relates to a specific concept covered in the chapter and connects it with material either covered earlier (Looking Back) or in an upcoming chapter (Looking Ahead). These annotations help you link important ideas quickly and integrate them from one chapter to another.

ESL Alerts identify for you the areas in which ESL students may have trouble with and provide suggestions on how to deal with them. Careful consideration has been given to addressing problems that students from a variety of language backgrounds might encounter.

Annotations appear only in the margins of the IAE. They are not printed in the student edition.

Group Activities are designed to assist you in encouraging collaborative learning in the classroom. Each annotation shows how students can work together on a specific aspect of the writing process, helping to reinforce major concepts and sharpen skills.

Teaching Ideas provide you with additional approaches to teaching specific chapter material, particularly in the areas of Critical Thinking, Writing Across the Curriculum, and Multicultural Differences. Each offers suggestions for effectively presenting key concepts to students, as well as providing additional readings and highly-focused assignments.

For Discussion sections precede select "Exercise" and "Additional Exercise" annotations within most chapters. Each recommends topics and approaches for classroom discussions that help examine skills reinforced in both sets of exercises.

Exercise annotations provide you with answers to the student exercises wherever appropriate.

Additional Exercises are provided as supplements to exercises located in the Student Edition. Ready for immediate assignment, these are designed to give students further practice honing their writing and grammatical skills.

Reference annotations support key points throughout the text, providing brief descriptions of and references for professional readings that can add new dimensions to your approach to teaching the subject matter.

NEW — ESL Exercises designed specifically for non-native speakers are now included.

INNOVATIVE PEDAGOGY —
Designed for Success.

Creating a text that offers students the most complete and current coverage of composition is only part of the story behind *The Allyn & Bacon Handbook*. Presenting this material in an efficient, highly-accessible manner is another.

This new book incorporates several features designed to enhance the presentation of key concepts — to make it easy for students to access information and easy for them to learn.

Among the many innovative pedagogical features integrated throughout this text are these:

Highlight Boxes
Throughout each chapter, key points are showcased in color-enhanced highlight boxes. These boxes feature short, succinct entries that summarize fundamental writing rules and troubleshooting techniques. Each is strategically placed in close proximity to pertinent material, making it easy for students to identify and link concepts.

Sub-Section Headings
Another feature that helps students locate writing guidelines quickly and easily are subsection headings. Within each chapter, these headings pinpoint appropriate usage in the writing process. Each is numbered for quick cross-reference and is followed by a clear, concise explanation of the proper usage guideline. The headings are linked to tab guides at the top of each page that include the appropriate correction symbol for common errors.

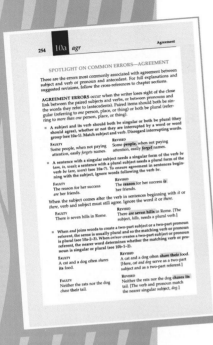

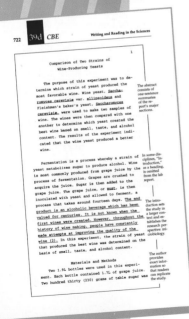

NEW
"Spotlight on Common Errors"
These special features give students a quick way to identify and correct the most frequently made mistakes. Errors are described with a minimum of technical terms for easy access.

NEW
"Critical Decision" Boxes
These boxes are designed to help students with choices they will need to make in developing sentences, paragraphs, and essays.

Examples and Illustrations have been expanded to include more work by students.
Within the text, carefully prepared and class-tested examples are used to illustrate concepts. Some examples demonstrate correct usage; most provide contrasting instances of faulty versus revised usage, asking students to make decisions as they gain skill in writing. Best of all, these examples are taken from a wide range of disciplines and are often presented as connected discourse, rather than disjointed sentences — making them more interesting and accessible to readers.

Exercises
Designed for in-class or independent assignment, all exercises are written to encourage greater student involvement and reinforce fundamental skills. The abundant exercises are often based on actual readings from across the curriculum to help build strong, broad-based writing skills.

ADDITIONAL SUPPLEMENTS —
Greater Resources for Better Learning

Instructor's Resource Manual
Designed as a guide for graduate assistant and adjunct faculty and providing additional suggestions for experienced faculty, the IRM includes:

- an expanded discussion of ways to use the text

- suggested syllabi and strategies for teaching writing across the curriculum and critical thinking

- background information on how to grade papers and conduct a peer classroom

- an annotated bibliography

- critical thinking articles and hints on integrating critical thinking, writing across the curriculum, and argument concepts into the composition course

- additional suggestions on teaching non-native speakers from different cultural backgrounds.

Allyn & Bacon Diagnostic Tests and Exercise Bank
Two 50-item grammar and mechanics diagnostics with error analysis, keyed to the Handbook. These can be used to make placement decisions or measure a student's progress.

The Exercise Bank consists of 600 additional exercise items, including fill-in-the-blank, multiple choice, and true/false items which provide extra practice for the grammar, mechanics, and punctuation sections in the Handbook. Also available in a computerized format (IBM and Macintosh).

The Allyn & Bacon Workbook
— *Now with ESL material and exercises* —
This student workbook contains unique critical thinking exercises as well as simplified versions of the explanations in the text. The workbook provides an abundance of additional exercise work on critical thinking, the writing process, and argumentation, as well as basic grammar, sentence faults, punctuation and mechanics, the writing process, effective sentence construction, vocabulary usage, and ESL concerns.

On-Line Handbook
This electronic version of the handbook provides a pop-up window for easy access to information while writing with a word processor. Words or topics can be accessed in three ways:
1. Through the Table of Contents
2. Through the Index
3. By a key word or topic search

Available in DOS, Windows, and Macintosh formats.

GrammarTeacher® Software
Ten interactive modules provide lessons for mastering the most common errors made in writing. Each lesson delivers questions to students on grammar and usage, along with basic guidelines and "help" frames with background information. The modules perform automatic scoring and record management for instructors. A grammar glossary for student reference is also included.

CLAST Study Guide

TASP Study Guide

Allyn & Bacon Video Grammar Library*
This series of 5 videotapes, free to adopters, includes 10 brief (12 minute) lessons on common grammar and mechanics problems such as subject-verb agreement, sentence fragments, and run-on sentences. Two special lessons discuss how to avoid sexist language and plagiarism.

* Some restrictions may apply. See your Allyn & Bacon representative for details. All information is accurate as of date of printing. Subject to change without notice.

Instructor's Annotated Edition

THE
Allyn & Bacon
HANDBOOK
Second Edition

LEONARD J. ROSEN

Harvard University

LAURENCE BEHRENS

University of California, Santa Barbara

Annotations Prepared by

Kathleen Shine Cain

Merrimack College

Allyn & Bacon

Boston   London   Toronto   Sydney   Tokyo   Singapore

Executive Editor: Joseph Opiela
Series Editorial Assistant: Brenda Conaway
Developmental Editor: Allen Workman
Production Administrator: Susan McIntyre
Editorial-Production Service: Kathy Smith
Cover Administrator: Linda Dickinson
Composition Buyer: Linda Cox
Manufacturing Buyer: Louise Richardson

Copyright © 1994, 1992 Allyn & Bacon
A Division of Paramount Publishing
160 Gould Street
Needham Heights, MA 02194

Printed in the United States of America

10   9   8   7   6   5   4   3   2   1   99   98   97   96   95   94

ISBN 0-205-15567-7

CONTENTS

The Instructor's Annotated Edition

Annotations for the instructor appear in the wide margins of this Instructor's Edition. They include overviews of chapter topics; cross-reference comments linking closely interrelated topics; "Teaching Ideas," "Discussion," and "Group Activities" suggesting class or collaborative learning activities and "ESL Alert" comments about distinctive features of English usage that may have an impact on international students. The annotations also include "Additional Exercises" and answers (or suggested answers) to the Exercises in the text. In addition, the annotations furnish bibliographical "References" for professional articles related to hand-

book chapter topics, with a descriptive sentence or abstract for each publication.

The Instructor's Resource Manual by Kathleen Shine Cain provides additional material for new and experienced instructors, including expanded suggestions for using the text and for teaching writing across the disciplines, suggested syllabi, grading procedures, and approaches to conducting a peer classroom. The manual also provides an extensive selection of reprinted articles on critical thinking and cross-curricular writing, and a section on working with ESL students.

Brief Contents of the Allyn & Bacon Handbook

THE
Allyn & Bacon
HANDBOOK
Second Edition

LEONARD J. ROSEN
Harvard University

LAURENCE BEHRENS
University of California, Santa Barbara

Allyn & Bacon

Boston   London   Toronto   Sydney   Tokyo   Singapore

To Linda, Jonathan, and Matthew—
teachers all.

Executive Editor: Joseph Opiela
Series Editorial Assistant: Brenda Conaway
Developmental Editor: Allen Workman
Production Administrator: Susan McIntyre
Editorial-Production Service: Kathy Smith
Designer: Deborah Schneck
Cover Administrator: Linda Dickinson
Composition Buyer: Linda Cox
Manufacturing Buyer: Louise Richardson

Allyn & Bacon
A Division of Paramount Publishing
160 Gould Street
Needham Heights, MA 02194

Library of Congress Cataloging-in-Publication Data

Rosen, Leonard J.
    The Allyn & Bacon handbook / Leonard J. Rosen, Laurence Behrens. -
- 2nd ed.
        p.   cm.
    Includes bibliographical references and index.
    ISBN 0-205-15327-5
        1. English language—Rhetoric—Handbooks, manuals, etc.
2. English language—Grammar—Handbooks, manuals, etc.   I. Behrens,
Laurence.   II. Title.   III. Title: Allyn and Bacon handbook.
PE1408.R677   1994
808'.042—dc20   93-39768
                                                                                        CIP

Printed in the United States of America
10 9 8 7 6 5 4 3 2 1   99 98 97 96 95 94

CONTENTS

PREFACE TO THE INSTRUCTOR

The Allyn & Bacon Handbook, First Edition, offered something new in the genre of handbooks: a strong focus on the interconnectedness of thinking, reading, and writing, both in the composition classroom and throughout the curriculum. We have been heartened by the praise our book has received, and we have sought in the second edition to build on the approach that classroom teachers have found useful. Specifically, we have expanded our coverage of critical thinking and its relation to the writing process; and we have improved accessibility by developing a comprehensive ESL component and by creating an alternate reference system for students whose knowledge of formal grammar is limited.

Critical thinking

With its opening chapters—"Critical Thinking and Reading" and "Critical Thinking and Writing"—*The Allyn & Bacon Handbook* continues to make a departure in the world of handbooks. We open with new strategies for developing critical skills and habits, for reading thoughtfully, and for thinking about sources *through* writing. This approach, based on a survey of current research in the field, follows our conviction that writing at the college level is most often based on reading. If students want to write well, they must also read well.

Writing as a process

Chapters 3 through 6 on the writing process are designed to serve both as a quick-reference tool and as a mini-rhetoric, with assignments that call on students to write and revise paragraphs and whole papers. Throughout Part II and extending to our discussion of sentence construction and word choice in Parts III through VI, we emphasize the role of revision in clarifying meaning and achieving a clean, spare style. In chapters 3 and 4, students observe a sample paper evolve from an initial assignment and meandering first thoughts through two stages of revision to a polished, final draft.

Because we have found that writing improves significantly when students give careful and sustained attention to a paper's governing sentence, **we have made our discussion of thesis far more extensive than is commonly found in handbooks.**

Writing across the curriculum and argumentation

Our comprehensive cross-curricular chapters (37, 38, and 39) orient students to the kinds of thinking, reading, and writing they will be called on to do in their various courses. After a general introduction devoted to characteristic assumptions and questions, each cross-curricular chapter reviews patterns for writing to inform and for making arguments in its discipline area; it reviews typical kinds of reading and audience situations; and it presents types of assignments found in the discipline, a complete student paper, and a listing of specialized reference materials. The sample papers in these chapters explore one topic—alcohol—from distinctive disciplinary points of view.

Argumentation in the disciplines. As an outgrowth of the attention given throughout the book to critical thinking, Chapter 6 focuses on both writing and evaluating arguments. Equally important, it introduces an approach to argument that provides a foundation for making claims in all disciplines across the curriculum, as shown in chapters 37–39. The *Allyn & Bacon Handbook*, the first handbook to adapt the **Toulmin model** of argument, uses basic terminology suited to composition students. In Chapter 6 we present the elements common to arguments in any discipline, and in Chapters 37 through 39 we discuss the discipline- (or context-) specific elements of argument.

The research paper

The research paper section of this handbook integrates critical thinking, the writing process, and writing across the curriculum. It draws heavily on critical thinking concepts from chapters 1 and 2 in the use of sources and incorporates phases of the writing process from chapters 3–6; it also looks ahead to research assignments in the three major discipline areas (chapters 37 through 39). The result is a strong treatment on the use and evaluation of sources and their integration into students' writing. In addition, the documentation coverage in chapter 36 treats four different conventions: the MLA system, the APA system, the footnote style (based on the *Chicago Manual of Style*), and the CBE systems used in the sciences. These sections, with the research paper samples from every discipline area, provide a comprehensive coverage on research.

Guidelines and choices in sentence revision

Any experienced writer knows that there is often more than one solution to a common sentence error. Therefore, when appropriate, we discuss alternative solutions and encourage students in their role as writers to make decisions. When usage is a matter of strict convention, we offer firm, clear guidelines for eliminating common errors and understanding key concepts of grammar, usage, and style. We have used student and professional writing from the disciplines as the basis for more than 90 percent of the exercises *and* example sentences. Both exercises *and* examples almost always feature connected discourse from a variety of disciplines—on topics as various as Van Gogh's life, Newton's separation of visible light into a spectrum, and the origins of the First World War. To make the book easy-to-use as a reference tool and visually appealing, we have created numerous boxes that summarize important information, provide useful lists, or apply critical thinking to decisions and choices.

New to This Edition

Critical thinking: Expanded coverage

We have expanded the coverage of critical thinking to include general, critical habits of mind that students can adopt before they bring specific strategies to their reading. In a new section beginning the first chapter, we show students how to be alert to differences, how to set issues in a broader context, how to challenge and be challenged by a text, and how to form and support opinions. Using these skills, students can bring specific strategies to bear on sources: reading to summarize, respond, evaluate, and synthesize.

Critical Decisions boxes have been added throughout the book to emphasize the ways in which these critical habits of mind can be applied throughout the writing process down to the level of sentences, words, and punctuation. These boxes form an explicit link for students between the foundational materials in Part I and the applied topics in over twenty-five locations in the rest of the book. See the the reverse side of the front endsheet for an index to the Critical Decisions boxes.

The "Spotlight" system: An alternative way to locate errors

To provide students with more help in identifying remedies for the most common errors, we have created an alternative to chasing errors in the index called "Spotlight on Common Errors." This new system for error recognition stresses examples, sentence patterns, and minimal formal terminology. Its aim is to help students who get limited use from handbook coverage because they are uncomfortable or unfamiliar with the formal terminology of grammar in a traditional index. The "Spotlight" system consists of three parts: (1) the Spotlight chart on the back endpaper, with its broad view of error patterns, refers students to (2) the "Spotlight" summary pages in selected chapters, which provide error recognition and brief remedies, in turn referring students to (3) chapter sections with detailed explanations and revisions. The "Spotlight" error-location system is based on these assumptions:

- The most common errors involving 90 percent or more of student mistakes have been widely recognized for many years both in texts and articles; these are clustered and hence "spotlighted" into groups closely identified with standard handbook treatments. For the purposes of spotting errors, we reduce the use of formal terminology to the barest minimum.

■ Since examples are usually more powerful recognition tools than abstract principles, error situations can be shown in the form of the basic sentence patterns in which common errors occur. These are offered as recognition examples (in addition to contextualized examples) throughout selected chapters.

The "Spotlight on Common Errors" feature is described in several places: See the back endpaper chart, the "How to Use This Book" section in the student preface that follows, and the tinted-page inserts in chapters 8–10, 12–15, 18, and 25 that give quick answers to common errors.

Writing about literature: Expanded coverage

A guiding assumption of both editions of this book is that college-level writing is for the most part based on reading. In some classrooms teachers assign a considerable amount of literature to create a context for writing, and we have acknowledged this by adding material on writing about literature. Chapter 33, while retaining its detail on argument in the humanities, now amplifies the principles for writing on literature to provide specific guidelines and examples, including annotated excerpts of Joyce's "Counterparts."

Comprehensive ESL coverage

Students whose native language is not English have been entering mainstream composition courses in increasing numbers, with varying degrees of prior preparation from specialized English as a Second Language (ESL) courses. As a result, composition instructors have been called upon to help ESL students cope with features of English that have not traditionally caused problems for native speakers. This edition of the handbook provides ESL students with unique help at three levels: through special "ESL Notes" in the main text; through substantial coverage of ESL language issues in the ESL section at the back of the book; and through instructor annotations ("ESL Alerts") in the Annotated Instructor's Edition.

ESL notes in the text: In appropriate chapters of the main text, special "ESL Notes" have been added to alert students to aspects of English that have proved difficult for non-native speakers. These notes briefly identify troublesome features before referring readers to pertinent units in ESL chapters 42–44.

Three ESL chapters: The chapters of the ESL section cover topics in three functional areas of English language usage: nouns and related structures (chapter 42); verbs, verbals, and related structures (chapter 43); and modifying structures (chapter 44). Prepositions and particles—especially troublesome forms for ESL students—are treated in appropriate structures *in all three chapters.* This section, developed with help from Will Van Dorp of Northern Essex Community College, offers a depth of coverage in verb forms and in modifying structures that is new in composition handbooks.

Notes to the instructor: Another dimension not previously offered in handbooks is ESL help for instructors who may have limited background in this specialized field. The notes were contributed by Professors Andrew and Gina Macdonald of Loyola University in New Orleans, who share insights from practical experience in both composition and ESL programs.

Supplements for the student

For students who need a self-help study workbook and for instructors who want to assign work that parallels the handbook, *The Allyn & Bacon Workbook,* 2nd Edition, by Kathleen Shine Cain of Merrimack College, continues to serve as a distinctive source for student supplementary work. With its abridged topical explanations keyed to handbook sections, it offers a new set of illustrative examples and an abundance of additional exercises. Most distinctively, these exercises include new readings and assignment materials suited to in-class or self-study work on critical thinking. Exercises also provide extensive supplementary work on the writing process, paragraph structure, sentence construction, punctuation and mechanics, and now entirely new material on ESL features.

Two self-help supplements are available for students working on computers: first, a new *On-line Handbook*; and second, *Grammar Teacher,* a new set of computer-based tutorial exercises. (These are described under "software" below.)

Finally, special workbooks are available to prepare students for writing and usage topics in English sections of the CLAST and TASP competency tests as given in Florida and Texas.

Supplements for the instructor

The *Instructor's Annotated Edition* of the handbook, by Kathleen Shine Cain of Merrimack College, features succinct annotations in the margins of each chapter; these offer a wide variety of useful information, suggested assignments, ESL topics, and references both on professional viewpoints and on resources for students needing special help.

The *Instructor's Resource Manual* provides background information for both new and experienced instructors. It contains suggested syllabi and exercise sequences, key professional readings on critical thinking, writing across the curriculum, and the writing process, as well as an extensive section of "Notes on Teaching Composition to ESL Students."

Testing and exercise instruments in computerized form and in booklet form are also available to support the instructor's composition program. Two fifty-item Diagnostic Tests are keyed to the text; a test analysis for every error item identifies a topic and handbook or workbook section to which students can be referred for specific help. Second, a computerized Exercise Bank contains hundreds of exercise examples keyed to grammar and usage topics in the handbook, providing extra material for students needing practice either independently or in a class or lab setting.

Software and audiovisual supplements

"The Allyn & Bacon On-Line Handbook" is available in Macintosh or IBM/DOS formats for students to install on word-processing software. It provides an easy-access window on the word-processing screen in which abridged sections of the handbook appear on request.

To help students with basic grammar and usage lessons, *Grammar Teacher,* a set of computer-based tutorial disks, has been authored by Professor Eva Thury of Drexel University. These tutorials, available in Macintosh and IBM/DOS formats, can serve as computer-based workbook lessons for use in the classroom or in a learning lab setting.

A package of twenty transparency masters presents key text diagrams and exhibits along with examples for lectures and demonstration pieces for use in focusing classroom discussions. A custom series of ten professionally produced video teaching lessons, forming *The Allyn & Bacon Video Grammar Library,* is also available free to adopters for use in classrooms or learning laboratories. These 10-minute lessons present separate topics in grammar, mechanics, sentence structure, and special topics such as sexist language and plagiarism.

From the smallest details to the broadest themes that motivated us to undertake this project, we have aimed to make *The Allyn & Bacon Handbook* a single, coherent text that both demonstrates and celebrates the rich variety of academic writing. We invite you to continue contacting us with your comments and suggestions. It is through such welcome conversations that we continue to refine our work.

Acknowledgments

In this revision, special thanks go to Kathleen Shine Cain of Merrimack College for her fine work on the *Instructor's Annotated Edition,* the companion *Allyn & Bacon Workbook,* and the *Instructor's Resource Manual.* We also appreciate and value the ESL annotations by Professors Andrew and Gina Macdonald of Loyola University of New Orleans, which reflect their years of experience in both composition and ESL programs. For work on Chapters 42–44 we are grateful for special help from Will Van Dorp of Bradford College and Northern Essex Community College, whose apt examples and descriptions have helped ESL students remedy problems in writing in English.

To the many reviewers who took time to critique our work, both in the first edition and in this revision, we give warm thanks. The following reviewers were both generous and realistic in their comments; we are grateful for the force and insight of their arguments, which led us to rethink and improve on countless dimensions of this text. For their reviews of the first edition, many thanks go to Chris Anson, University of Minnesota; Phillip Arrington, Eastern Michigan University; Kathleen Shine Cain, Merrimack College; Barbara Carson, University of Georgia; Thomas Copeland, Youngstown State University; Sallyanne Fitzgerald, University of Missouri, Saint Louis; Dale Gleason, Hutchinson Community College; Stephen Goldman, The University of Kansas; Donna Gorrell, St. Cloud State University; Patricia Graves, Georgia State University; John Hanes, Duquesne University; Kristine Hansen, Brigham Young University; Bruce Herzberg, Bentley College; Vicki Hill, Southern Methodist University; Jeriel Howard, Northeastern Illinois State University; Clayton Hudnall, University of Hartford; David Joliffe, University of Illinois at Chicago; Kate Kiefer, Colorado State University; Nevin Laib, Franklin and Marshall University; Barry Maid, University of Arkansas at Little Rock; Thomas Martinez, Villanova University; Mary McGann, University of Indianapolis; Walter Minot, Gannon University; Jack Oruch, University of Kansas; Twyla Yates Papay, Rollins College; Richard Ramsey, Indiana/Purdue University at Fort Wayne; Annette Rottenberg, University of Massachusetts, Amherst; Mimi Schwartz, Stockton State College; Louise Smith, University of Massachusetts, Boston; Sally Spurgin, Southern Methodist University; Judith Stanford, Rivier College; Barbara Stout, Montgomery College; Ellen Strenski, University of California, Los Angeles; Christopher Thaiss, George Mason University; Michael Vivion, University of Missouri, Kansas City; Barbara Weaver, Ball State University; and Richard Zbracki, Iowa State University.

And for their reviews of the second edition, thanks to Bruce Appleby, Southern Illinois University; Linda Bensel-Myers, University of Tennessee; Melody Brewer, University of Toledo; Therese Brychta, Truckee Meadow Community College; Christopher Burnham, New Mexico State University; Peter Carino, Indiana State University; Neil Daniel, Texas Christian University; Virginia Draper, Stevenson College; Ray Dumont, University of Massachusetts, Dartmouth; Kathy Evertz, University of Wyoming; Barbara Gaffney, University of New Orleans; Ruth Greenberg, Jefferson Community College; Stephen Hahn, William Paterson College; Kathleen Herndon, Weber State University; Maureen Hoag, Wichita State University; Ralph Jenkins, Temple University; Rodney Keller, Ricks College; Judith Kohl, Dutchess Community College; Douglas Krienke, Sam Houston State University; Wendell Mayo, Indiana University–Purdue University Fort Wayne; Charles Meyer, University of Massachusetts, Boston; Joan Mullin, University of Toledo; Patricia Murray, California State University, Northridge; Richard Nordquist, Armstrong State University; Jon Patton, University of Toledo; Randall Popken, Tarleton State University; Kirk Rasmussen, Utah Valley Community College;

Sally Barr Reagan, University of Missouri; David Roberts, Samford University; John Shea, Loyola University; Margot Soven, La Salle University; Ann Taylor, Salem State College; Elizabeth Tentarelli, Merrimack College; and Richard Zbaracki, Iowa State University.

Many others helped us along the way; their particular contributions are too numerous to list, but we gratefully acknowledge their assistance. From Bentley College, we thank Tim Anderson, Christy Bell, Lindsey Carpenter, Sarika Chandra, Robert Crooks, Nancy Esposito, Barbara Gottfried, Sherman Hayes, Tom Heeney, Richard Kyte, Donald McIntyre, Kathy Meade, and George Radford. We thank other colleagues as well: John Clarke of the University of Vermont, whose work on critical thinking aided the formulating of our pedagogy for the book, and Carol Gibbens of the University of California, Santa Barbara, for suggestions on the reference unit. Thanks go to Burke Brown, University of Southern Alabama; Eric Godfrey, Ripon College; Clarence Ivie, University of Southern Alabama; John Laucus, University Librarian, Boston University; William Leap, The American University; Larry Renbaum, Georgetown University Law School; Carol G. Schneider, Association of American Colleges; Alison Tschopp, Boston University Law School; and Arthur White, Western Michigan University.

As writers we are indeed fortunate to work with an editorial, production, marketing, and sales staff as fine as the team at Allyn & Bacon. Joe Opiela, Editor-in-Chief for Humanities, shared and helped to shape our vision for this book. Throughout the manuscript's writing and rewriting, Joe proved himself a tireless advocate and a steady source of helpful ideas. Allen Workman, with his more than twenty years of experience, is surely one of the industry's premier developmental editors. With his crisp line-by-line edits and his astonishingly detailed analysis of the features that make a handbook useful, Allen earned his last name with honesty and great distinction. Susan McIntyre and Kathy Smith shepherded the manuscript through production with an unfailing eye for detail.

Major support for this handbook has come from the Allyn & Bacon marketing team: Lisa Kimball, Marketing Manager; Sandi Kirshner, Vice President for Marketing; John Gilman, Vice President for Sales; and Allyn & Bacon's fifty resourceful sales representatives have all brought enormous enthusiasm and creativity to focusing attention on the themes that make this book distinctive. Bill Barke, President of Allyn & Bacon, has generously committed the editorial, production, and marketing resources needed to make this a project in which all concerned can take pride. Editorial Assistant Brenda Conaway, with brisk good humor, was able to help speed the writing and reviewing process cleanly and smoothly. To all we give hearty and warm thanks.

        Leonard Rosen, Expository Writing Program, Harvard University
        Laurence Behrens, University of California, Santa Barbara

PREFACE TO THE STUDENT

One of the underlying goals of *The Allyn & Bacon Handbook* is to make you aware of the connections between good writing and clear thinking. Successful writers are problem solvers: They are critical thinkers who pose questions about their own work, spot difficulties that block communication, and devise strategies for resolving those difficulties. To gain competence as a writer, a person must think critically about his or her performance, first by gaining distance from it and then by posing questions that help pinpoint difficulties and set corrective courses of action. Building upon these critical habits of mind, *The Allyn & Bacon Handbook* aims to help you analyze your written work and, if need be, take corrective action.

Writing and reading in the disciplines

On a typical day, as you take courses in and read about a number of different subjects, you will realize that certain features of good writing are essential to your success as a writer, whatever the context. For instance, all writing must be well organized. At the same time certain features of writing change as you move from one subject area to another. In Chapters 37, 38, and 39, *The Allyn & Bacon Handbook* encourages you to appreciate some of the significant ways in which the skills of writing, reading, and thinking can change for different parts of the curriculum. The early sections of the book will help you master skills that are common to all the disciplines.

How will this book help you?

As you become a more accomplished writer who makes decisions and solves problems, you can use *The Allyn & Bacon Handbook* as you would any familiar tool: to help fix what is broken and strengthen what is weak. While this handbook provides many ways to find your way through the writing process at any stage—as shown on the next pages—it will not give you any shortcuts for actually working through the process. Good writers write, and they revise. The more you know, the more you will want to revise, and the messier your papers will become as you work your way toward final drafts. For this effort you will produce letters, essays, and papers that communicate clearly and that earn the respect of your colleagues. Persevere and you *will* succeed.

Leonard Rosen, Expository Writing Program, Harvard University
Laurence Behrens, University of California, Santa Barbara

To find key terms and topics:

1   Use these information locators:

■ *Front endpapers:* The compact contents chart provides an overview of the section and page numbers of the major topics.

■ *Main contents:* This detailed listing shows sections and pages for all topics and usage guidelines.

■ *Index:* This alphabetical listing shows page and section numbers of every key term, word, or topic.

■ *Revision symbols—inside back endpaper:* This guide to common instructor markings will help locate discussions of revision topics.

■ *Useful checklists, summaries, and boxes—inside front endpaper:* Locates the special panels that provide rapid checklists of basic procedures.

■ *"Spotlight on Common Errors":* See the facing page.

2   To narrow the search, look for these features on each page:

■ *Header* briefly identifies chapter section topics.

■ *Tab* shows the section-number combination for every topic. A *symbol* next to the tab shows typical instructor markings used to call attention to the topic.

■ *Section number* gives chapter and section letter accompanying the *heading* that states or identifies a usage guideline.

■ *Subsection number* identifies subtopics.

■ *Explanations* describe how or why processes or usage guidelines operate. *Cross-references* lead to related background or definitions found elsewhere in the Handbook. *Bold type* identifies key terms being defined on location or in a cross-reference.

■ *Revision examples* are labeled to identify problems and the best revisions. In the nine chapters devoted to the most common errors, additional examples appear beneath the headings as an aid to spotting errors.

■ *Boxed checklists,* summaries or "critical decisions" boxes are in shaded panels.

218 | **8c** | *ca* | Case in Nouns and Pronouns

WITH INFINITIVE   His 60 home runs in 1927 helped *him* to reach a level of stardom unmatched by other athletes of his era. [The objective-form pronoun appears between the verb *helped* and the infinitive *to reach.*]

His home runs helped *him* reach stardom. [The subject of the infinitive *reach* uses the objective form, *him.*]

8c   Using nouns and pronouns in the possessive case

Use a possessive noun or pronoun before a noun to indicate ownership of that noun (or noun substitute).

Eleanor Roosevelt gave the Civil Works Administration *her* enthusiastic support for hiring 100,000 women by the end of 1933.

ESL NOTE   Many English nouns are made possessive either with the possessive case noun (*a woman's voice*) or with the noun as object of the preposition *of* (*voice of a woman*). With some inanimate nouns the prepositional form is standard and the possessive case form is seldom used (NOT *a house's color* BUT *color of a house*). See 42c-1.

Possessive Forms of Pronouns

	Singular	*Plural*
1st person	my, mine	our, ours
2nd person	your, yours	your, yours
3rd person	his, her, hers, its	their, theirs

1   Certain possessive pronouns are used as subjects or subject complements to indicate possession.

Yours are the first hands to touch this. These are *theirs*.

The possessive pronouns *mine, ours, yours, his, hers, theirs* are used in place of a noun as subjects or subject complements.

Ours is a country of opportunity for both men and women, Eleanor Roosevelt argued. This opportunity is *ours*. (*mine, yours, his, hers, theirs*)

2   Use a possessive noun or pronoun before a gerund to indicate possession.

The group argued for *her* getting the new position.

To spot-check for common errors:

1   Check the back endpaper chart. The nine sections in this chart cover over 90 percent of the most common sentence and punctuation errors you are likely to make. Look in these sections for sentence patterns and word forms close to what you have written. If any of the examples or explanations lead you to suspect an error in your work, follow the references to one of the text chapters.

SPOTLIGHT ON COMMON ERRORS

1. FORMS OF NOUNS AND PRONOUNS   See the SPOTLIGHT (page 214, Chapter 8).
Apostrophes can show possession or contraction. Never use an apostrophe with a possessive pronoun.

FAULTY FORMS
The scarf is *Chris*. It is *her's*.
Give the dog *it's* collar.
Its a difficult thing.

REVISED
The scarf is *Chris's*. It is *hers*.
Give the dog *its* collar.
It's [it is] a difficult thing.

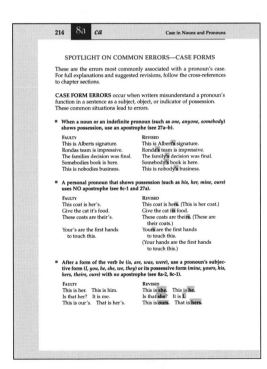

2   Go to the blue-tinted "spotlight" summary page that matches your situation. Colored "spotlight" pages in nine chapters give basic recognition patterns and sentences that fit common error situations.

3   Narrow the search. Find a sentence or situation that more closely resembles a sentence you have written. *Note* the revision suggested. Do you suspect a possible error? If so, *note* the reference to the chapter section where this revision is explained.

4   Go to the Handbook section; find a usage guideline and example that describes the possible error in your work. Challenge your sentence: Does it meet the Handbook's usage guideline? Make a decision about revising your sentence.

PART I
THINKING CRITICALLY

CHAPTER 1

Critical Thinking and Reading

Most writing that you do in college and beyond will be based on reading. Writing always involves acts of thinking, and writing based on what you read requires that you think carefully about what others have written. This chapter has a twofold purpose: first, to suggest habits of mind that will prepare you in a general way for thinking critically about college-level materials and, second, to provide *particular* strategies for understanding and responding to sources.[1] Practiced conscientiously, these strategies will give you confidence to work with what you read, in college and beyond.

ACTIVE, CRITICAL HABITS OF MIND

Turn your attention to habits of mind that promote critical thinking. You begin the process of careful, systematic understanding and response by being alert to differences and discrepancies; by challenging source materials and being challenged by them; by setting issues in broader contexts; and by forming and supporting opinions. Developing these critical habits of mind will prepare you for working with the source materials on which you will base much of your writing.

 1a | **Active, critical thinkers are alert to differences and discrepancies.**

As an active, critical thinker, you are alert to differences and discrepancies. Think of a difference as a disagreement between what you expect to see and what you see, or as a discrepancy between what two or

---

[1]We use the terms *source materials, sources,* and *texts* interchangeably to mean any reading selection.

TEACHING IDEAS

Given that much American education operates on what Paulo Freire calls the "banking concept" (instructors make "deposits" of knowledge into students' heads), critical thinking may be a foreign—and intimidating—notion to some students. A rather simple exercise can dispel some of their fears: Ask students to recall their favorite classes, especially those in which they feel they learned a great deal. As they discuss these classes, ask them to focus on how the class was conducted. Chances are, the most meaningful classes will be those in which teachers fostered a good deal of discussion and demanded thinking from the students. Simply reminding students that they've had positive experiences in the past with what these first two chapters call "critical thinking" should ease their minds about what lies ahead.

The material in this chapter relies on the following books:

CLARKE, John H. *Patterns of Thinking: Integrating Learning Skills in Content Teaching.* Boston: Allyn and Bacon, 1990.

BROWNE, NEIL M., and STUART M. KEELEY. *Asking the Right Questions.* 2nd ed. Englewood Cliffs, NJ: Prentice-Hall, 1986.

KURFISS, JOANNE G. *Critical Thinking: Theory, Research, and Possibilities.* ASHE-ERIC Higher Education Report No. 2. Washington, DC: Association for the Study of Higher Education, 1988.

MARZANO, ROBERT J., et al. *Dimensions of Thinking: A Framework for Curriculum and Instruction.* Alexandria, VA: ACSD. 1988.

JONES, BEAU FLY, et al., eds. *Strategic Teaching and Learning: Cognitive Instruction in the Content Areas.* Alexandria, VA: ASCD, 1987.

TOULMIN, STEPHEN, RICHARD RIEKE, and ALLAN JANIK. *An Introduction to Reasoning.* New York: Macmillan, 1979.

RORTY, RICHARD. *Philosophy and the Mirror of Nature.* Princeton: Princeton UP, 1979.

KUHN, THOMAS. *The Structure of Scientific Revolutions.* 2nd ed. Enlarged. Chicago: U Chicago P, 1970.

more people say about a single subject, issue, or problem. You will have many occasions to notice such differences, both in college and later on. Assume that in a government class, your professor gave you this assignment: to read two newspapers daily, a local paper and a national one. If you lived in Cleveland and were working on this assignment for November 19, 1992, you might have noticed a difference or discrepancy in the way two newspapers treated a single story:

Cleveland's *Plain Dealer*

Bishops leave door open for women

Washington

Catholic bishops yesterday chose dialogue over dogma, rejecting a controversial proposal on women's roles in the church.

The National Conference of Catholic Bishops, convening here this week, failed to muster the two-thirds vote needed to adopt the proposal, which would have firmly prohibited women's ordination, as a formal church statement. Instead, members accepted the committee report for further study and discussion.

"This does as much as we can do right now," said Cardinal Joseph Bernardin, who proposed keeping the document a committee report only.

USA Today

U.S. bishops reject wider women's role

U.S. Catholic bishops voted down a long-planned policy statement on women after a fractious debate over whether women can ever be priests.

After nine years of work and four separate drafts, the pastoral letter received 137 "yes" votes, 53 short of the two-thirds needed to make it the policy of the National Conference of Catholic Bishops.

Voting no: 110 bishops.

Auxiliary Bishop Austin Vaughn of New York said he considered the papal rule against ordaining women "infallible and unchangeable. Women priests are as impossible as me having a baby."

Differences lead to questions.

These articles present a difference: contrasting accounts of a national conference of Catholic bishops, called to discuss the roles of women and men in the church. Of the tens of thousands of people who glanced at both newspapers that day, how many noticed the contradictory headlines? How many noticed that two authoritative sources provided vastly different coverage of a single event? *You* would have noticed, if you had trained yourself to be alert to differences and discrepancies. And beyond noticing, you would have posed a question or two, because questions—primarily the question *why*—follow from observing such a difference. When you spot a difference, you naturally say: "What explains this?" Such a question can lead to fruitful lines of research. The following box presents a set of techniques for being alert to differences.

Be Alert to Differences

Before reading:

- Skim a text and identify its topic.
- Make a note, mental or written, on what you know about the topic or what you can remember others have written about it.

During reading:

- Compare what the author has written with your notes.
- Identify differences.
- Complete your reading by returning to each point of difference and using it to generate questions.

After reading:

- Option: Begin an investigation or create an action plan for doing so, guided by your questions.

Pose questions based on a difference between sources.

Having read and noticed differences or discrepancies between two accounts of a single subject, issue, or problem, you are in a position to pose some questions—the answers to which could help you to understand the difference. In the case of the bishops' conference, the following questions seem useful:

What happened at the conference?

What were the key elements of the debate?

What does the pastoral letter on women's roles actually say?

Why were the bishops meeting on this issue?

What did a "yes" or a "no" vote represent?

How have women's groups responded to the vote?

Pose questions based on a difference between a text and your experience.

Not only can you pose questions on differences you've observed between two or more sources, but you can pose questions based on differences between what an author presents and what you know to be true or likely, based on your experience. Return to the bishops' conference: perhaps on reading one of these articles you noticed a difference between what the Catholic bishops had decided concerning women in the priesthood and what you knew about the gender of priests in other denominations. Perhaps you knew that in the Jewish religion there are women

GROUP ACTIVITY

Working in groups of three, students can analyze the structure and content of the two newspaper accounts. Ask students to explain the purpose of the lead paragraph, the middle paragraph(s), and the final paragraph. To what extent is the information in the two newspaper accounts *structured* the same way? (Each piece has a lead paragraph, one or two context-setting paragraphs, and a paragraph devoted to a quotation.) Given this structure, students can then compare content. At which points do the accounts differ?

ADDITIONAL EXERCISE A

Ask students to analyze the structure of the first five paragraphs of any three front-page news accounts. Students could present their findings orally to the class. The assignment will help to develop in students an awareness that news stories have a structure, which can aid the student's general newspaper reading.

TEACHING IDEAS

ACROSS THE CURRICULUM In many disciplines, especially in the sciences, research projects begin with a researcher's noticing a difference or discrepancy: results of an experiment differ from what was expected. The difference leads naturally to a search for explanations. This search can be an important impetus to new experiments. Ask students to consult their textbooks in other disciplines for evidence that researchers are alert to and act on differences.

CRITICAL THINKING

Alverno College of Wisconsin has published a series of books on teaching critical thinking in the content areas. In their *Teaching Critical Thinking in Psychology* (1986), the editors present a theory that a discrepancy between observed events and the observer's "knowledge base" initiates critical thinking. Richard Kasschau of the University of Houston develops the model in Part I of the book. Parts II and III are devoted to a series of assignments in psychology that are designed to create for students discrepancies that launch critical thinking.

TEACHING IDEAS

You might demonstrate the value of noting and acting on differences by asking students to respond to these questions on the roles of men and women in various religions. Discussion *will* be generated. Five or ten minutes into the discussion, make the observation that the discussion was made possible by the discrepancies noted in the two newspaper accounts. Such discussion is, for the curious, the logical outgrowth of a difference. Your discussion in class will demonstrate for students that noting differences opens possibilities for research.

ESL ALERT

ESL students (as well as native speakers) might confuse "critical" with "negative criticism," and might feel uncomfortable with the idea of being openly confrontational or argumentative. Emphasizing the idea of noticing key differences and actively raising questions would be a positive and productive way to present "critical" thinking.

EXERCISE 1

Individual responses

ESL ALERT

The Western academic practice of teaching critical thinking through student-teacher class discussion is far from universal, with the majority of students (especially from Asia and the Middle East) viewing their role as more passive than U.S. instructors may be accustomed to: receiving and memorizing truths passed down by authority figures—without questioning such information. This concept of role affects classroom behavior, with the Japanese, for instance, believing that "the nail that sticks up gets hammered down." Such students often consider volunteering to answer or participating in class discussion a violation of the rules. This difference in cultural attitudes must be dealt with

rabbis and that, only one week before the bishops' conference and after a heated debate, the Anglican church voted to ordain women as priests. Such knowledge of a difference between the views of Catholics and the views of some Jews and Anglicans could prompt questions such as these:

> What are the relevant differences among Anglican, Catholic, and Jewish religious traditions?
>
> What is the role of the priest or rabbi in these religions?
>
> What is the role of women and men in these religions?
>
> How will women priests change the Anglican church? Have they changed the Episcopal churches in America, or have women rabbis changed Jewish congregations?
>
> What will be the effect of men continuing to dominate the priesthood in the Catholic church?
>
> What were the key issues in the Catholic and Anglican debates, and how can these be compared and contrasted?

Option: Generate an action plan.

Questions that you pose suggest activity on your part. The preceding questions, for instance, might lead to an investigation of the roles of men and women in the Catholic church and in other denominations. With a more limited focus, you might decide to learn what happened at the bishops' conference by obtaining a draft of the bishops' policy statement on the role of women. Once you notice and develop questions based on a difference, you can undertake a research project. Indeed, in many disciplines, researchers begin their investigations by noticing a difference and speculating on causes. Of course, not every question you pose will lead to full-blown research. Be aware, though, that your questions can direct you to further work.

EXERCISE 1

Every day, for a week, read two or more newspapers—your town's local paper (s) and one or more of the following: the *New York Times*, the *Wall Street Journal*, and *USA Today*. Pay special attention to each paper's coverage of a single news event. Read the accounts and observe differences—among the three or between what any of the pieces report and your own experience. Pose questions based on these differences. Finally, outline a plan for potential research based on your questions.

1b Active, critical thinkers challenge, and are challenged by, sources.

Spotting a difference or discrepancy based on your reading gives you an entrance into a source. The word *entrance* suggests that reading selections and buildings share a certain quality: both have interiors. To know what's inside a building you open the door and step inside. What are the "doors" to a text? *Questions.* When carefully posed, questions can lead you deep into a reading selection. The more questions you ask and the more times you turn to the text (or to others) seeking answers, the deeper and more informed your reading will be.

1   Asking questions of the text

Every reading invites specific questions, but the following basic questions can get you started in your effort to read any text critically:

- What central problem, issue, or subject does the text explore? What are the reasons for this problem? What are the effects of this problem?
- What is the most important, or the most striking, statement the author makes? Why is it important or striking?
- Who is the author, and what are the author's credentials for writing on this topic? What is the author's stake in writing this? What does the author have to gain?
- How can I use this selection? What can I learn from it?

> **Illustration: Responses to General Questions about the Newspaper Articles on the Bishops' Conference**

Central issue: Should women be priests in the Catholic church?

Reasons for the controversy: Over the last twenty years, women have demanded more control over institutions that affect their lives. The Catholic church is one such institution. In this conference, the debate in the larger culture was brought into the Catholic church for formal consideration.

Most striking statement: No single statement stands out; however, the sharply different coverage in the two newspaper accounts is startling.

The authors' stakes: The authors' personal biases seem to have entered the news reporting; for example, the first quotations that the authors use represent very different points of view, which happen to be consistent with the tone and information of the rest of each piece—including the differing headlines.

Using the selections: These pieces suggest that further research is needed to understand what happened at the bishops' conference. A research paper on the topic could begin with the two differing accounts of what happened.

early in the course with a discussion of what acceptable classroom behavior is; why Americans value critical commentary, particularly in give-and-take Socratic dialogue; how necessary it will be to success in an American college.

KOHLS, ROBERT. *Developing Intercultural Awareness.* Washington, DC: The Society for Intercultural Education, 1981.

HALL, EDWARD T. *The Silent Language.* Garden City, NY: Anchor Press, 1973.

HARRIS, P. R., and R. T. MORAN. *Managing Cultural Differences.* Houston, TX: Gulf Publishing Co., 1979.

2   Asking questions of yourself, based on the text

A critical reading points in two directions: to the text(s) you are reading, and to *you.* The questions you ask about what you read can prompt you to investigate your experience, values, and opinions. As part of any critical reading, allow the issues that are important to the text to *challenge* you. Question yourself and respond until you know your views about a topic. Pose the following questions to yourself:

- What can I learn from this text? Will this knowledge change me?
- What is my background on this topic? How will my experience affect my reading?
- What is the origin of my views on the topic?
- What new interest, or what new question or observation, does this text spark in me?
- If I turned the topic of this selection into a question on which people voted, how would I vote—and why?

> ### Illustration: Responses to Personal Questions Raised by the Articles on the Bishops' Conference

My background: I'm not Catholic, so I view the debate from the outside. I'm Anglican Episcopal, and the Anglican church in England just finished a fierce debate and voted to allow women to be priests.

My vote: The debate among Catholics and Anglicans is obviously intense. As an Anglican, it's easy for me to say that I'd vote as most of the Anglicans have. But rather than vote just yet, I'd want to find out more about the disagreement among Catholics.

New interests: I want to learn more about the roles of men and women in the Jewish and Muslim religions. How do these roles compare with those of Catholics and Anglicans? Why have gender roles been assigned as they have in various religions?

EXERCISE 2

Answers will vary.

EXERCISE 2

Reread the three newspaper pieces you selected for Exercise 1. Based on suggestions in the preceding section, pose questions that challenge underlying assumptions in each piece. Also, use one or two of the pieces as a basis on which to pose questions that challenge you.

1c   Active, critical thinkers set issues in a broader context.

To the extent that you can, identify issues and questions important to a single text and then think large: assume that every particular issue, concern, or problem that you read about exists in a larger context—in a larger cluster of related issues, concerns, or problems. (In the example that follows, you will see how the debate over women in the priesthood can be seen in the larger context of the history of debates in the Catholic church and in other organized religions.) Do not expect that this larger context will be obvious. Usually, you will have to work to discover it. The summary box shows a set of techniques for doing so.

Setting Issues in Their Broader Context

- Begin by identifying one or more issues you feel are important to a text.

- Assume that each issue is an instance, or example, of something larger. Your job is to speculate on this larger something.

- Write the name of the issue at the top of a page, or on the computer screen. Below this, write a question: "What's this a part of?" Then write a one-paragraph response.

- Reread your response, and briefly state the broader context.

- Use this broader context to stimulate more thought on the reading selection and to generate questions about issues of interest.

- Option: Begin an investigation or create an action plan for doing so, guided by your questions (optional).

Apply these techniques by returning to the newspaper accounts of the bishops' conference and the debate over the roles of women and men in organized religion (see 1a). What might be the broader context here?

Illustration: The Debate over Women as Priests
WHAT'S THIS A PART OF?

Following the advice in the summary box, you might write a paragraph that looks like this:

The debate about the role of women in the church is part of the larger debate about gender relations and power sharing in our society. The feminist revolution of the past three decades has made its way to the most conservative of our institutions: our religions. The "fractious debate" reported in *USA Today* is an instance in the Catholic church of the same debate in the larger culture: to what extent do women share power in institutions that affect their lives? This debate has probably taken place in other religious traditions as well. It is also an example of how the church responds to pressure from the outside. Over the centuries, the Catholic church has changed—but very slowly. How do social issues of the day become a subject of debate within the church? And what's the process by which the church changes as the result of such debate?

CRITICAL THINKING

In *Cultivating Thinking in English and the Language Arts* (NCTE, 1991), Robert Marzano discusses four principles of learning and thinking, one of which is that "learning involves the construction of meaning." A key to this constructive process, says Marzano, is that "the learner acquires new knowledge by attaching what she already knows to what she is about to learn." Attempting to identify larger contexts can be an important part of the student's linking what is known to what is not. Larger contexts provide a cognitive frame in which students operate. Often, students need only remind themselves that these larger frames exist; then these frames help students to link new knowledge to old.

Broader context: the feminist revolution
the history of debate in the Catholic church
the roles of women and men in the Jewish,
Muslim, Catholic, and Protestant traditions

In your search for broader contexts, you may find in a single text more than one key issue on which to write. In the case of the bishops' conference, at least two issues are important: the one just illustrated (the debate over the roles of men and women in organized religion) and the fact of conflicting news accounts. Both issues can be a source of questions, and both can be set in a larger context.

Option: Generate an action plan.

Every broader context that you define gives you opportunities for generating new questions about a source and, potentially, for launching a broader-scale investigation. For more on how critical reading and, in particular, the investigation of a broadened context can lead to good research projects, see 33a and 33b.

EXERCISE 3

Individual responses

EXERCISE 3

Explore the larger context suggested by the differing news accounts of the two articles that you found for Exercise 1. Create a phrase that summarizes one issue, subject, or problem that you think is important to these accounts. Place that phrase at the top of a page and the question "What's this a part of?" below it. Then write an answer in order to identify a broader context. Based on this broader context, generate an action plan: identify some research activity that could follow from your writing.

LOOKING AHEAD

This section of chapter 1 raises for students the importance of forming and supporting opinions, which at its root is a matter of making arguments. See chapter 6 for an extensive discussion of argumentation, following the Toulmin model. See also the cross-curricular chapters, 37–39, in which the authors discuss the important elements of argument—including claims and standards of evidence—in the humanities, social sciences, and sciences.

1d Active, critical thinkers will form, and support, opinions.

Know what you think about what you see and read. Have an opinion and be able to support it. Opinions generally follow from responses to questions such as these:

- Has the author explained things clearly?
- In what ways does this topic confuse me?
- Has the author convinced me of his or her main argument?
- What is my view on this topic?
- Would I recommend this source to others?

Whatever your opinion, be prepared to support it with comments that are based on details about what you have seen or read. Later in this chapter (see 1g), you will learn techniques for reading to evaluate a source; and in chapter 2 (see 2b), you will learn techniques for writing an evaluation—a type of writing in which you formally present your opinions and give reasons for holding them. It is not practical or necessary that you develop a formal response (oral or written) to every source you read. Just the same, as a critical and active thinker you should be able to offer reasons for believing as you do. Here's an illustration of an opinion based on the differing news accounts of the bishops' conference:

Illustration: Opinion and Support Concerning the Differing Articles on the Bishops' Conference

One or both of these authors are biased in their reporting. In support of this view, see the contrasting headlines: "Bishops leave door open for women" vs. "U.S. bishops reject wider women's roles." Here's a case of a glass being half empty or half full, depending on the point of view of the person who's making the judgment. Obviously, points of view in these two accounts differ.

You and your classmates may agree or disagree about particular ideas, as they are expressed in a source. In either case, you should be able to have an informed discussion about these ideas. For an extensive discussion on stating and supporting opinions, see chapter 6 on argumentation.

EXERCISE 4
Use the suggestions in the preceding section to develop an opinion based on one or more of the articles you selected for Exercise 1. In writing, state your opinion in a sentence or two. Then, in a brief paragraph, support your opinion by pointing to particular paragraphs or sentences in the news accounts.

COMPONENTS OF A CLOSE, CRITICAL READING

The habits of mind discussed in the first part of this chapter prepare you in a general way for thinking critically about what you see and hear. Noticing differences, challenging and being challenged by sources, setting issues in a broader context, and forming and supporting opinions— these habits of mind, so important to thinking critically, do not necessarily lead to formal statements on your part about the materials you encounter. When teachers and, later, employers ask that you read and use source materials as a basis for writing, you *will* need to formalize and systematize your skills of critical thinking. A close, critical reading requires that you read to understand, respond, evaluate, and synthesize as appropriate to your task. These are the component parts of a close, critical reading that you will find discussed in this section. The forms of writing associated with close reading—summary, evaluation, analysis, and synthesis—are discussed in chapter 2.

Reading and *rereading*

To a greater or lesser extent, you will naturally mix into a single reading the tasks of reading to understand, to respond, to evaluate, and to synthesize. The goal of a close, critical reading is to make sure you perform these tasks well. To do so, even the most experienced readers find they must read a text two or more times. For instructional purposes, we discuss the four types of close, critical reading in four sections (1e–1h). We do *not* mean to suggest by this arrangement that you read your sources four times. This is not practical, nor is it usually warranted. Still, you should commit yourself to reading however much is necessary to understand, respond, evaluate, and synthesize. In the sections that follow you will get a clearer idea of what each of these tasks entails.

1e   Critical reading (1): Reading to understand

Every use to which you can put a source is based on your ability to understand it. Without understanding you can do nothing, and so understanding must be your very first goal as a critical reader.

1   Setting goals for reading to understand

The steps in reading to understand can be summarized as follows:

- *Identify the author's purpose.* This will likely be to inform or to argue.
- *Identify the author's intended audience.* The text will be written with particular readers in mind. Determine if you are the intended audience.
- *Locate the author's main point.* Every competently written text has a main point that you should be able to express in your own words.
- *Understand the structure of the text.* If the author is arguing, locate the main point and supporting points; if the author is presenting information, locate the main point and identify the stages into which the presentation has been divided.
- *Identify as carefully as possible what you do not understand.*

Read the following example, which is typical of what you might encounter in one of your courses—say, in media studies. The passage is a defense of advertising written by James Playsted Wood for a text entitled *This is Advertising,* published in 1968. Throughout this chapter, we will add "layers" of highlighting and notes to this passage in order to demonstrate strategies for reading to understand, respond, evaluate, and synthesize. The highlighting and notes you see on the passage here illustrate how you might read to understand. Techniques for highlighting in this way follow the passage itself.

From **The Merits of Advertising**

Part 1:
Account of
what ad is

In its open declaration of intent [advertising] is perhaps the most honest form of major present-day journalism.

    On the face of it, an advertisement says what it is. It says: I am an advertisement. I have been bought and paid for. I make no pretense to objectivity. I am not a disinterested and impartial observer. I am a deeply interested and wholly partial pleader. My object is gain. I want to sell you something. I will persuade you by every means I can devise to buy what I have for sale.

    What an advertisement has to sell may be a jet airplane, a pen, an automobile, a lipstick, a new food, an old food, a fad, or a trip from wherever you are to wherever you can be persuaded to spend your money to go. It may try to sell you an idea, a dream, a fact, an opinion, or a prejudice. The advertisement may entice. It may soothe or excite. It may try to frighten you. It may order or coax. Whatever it does and in whatever way it tries to do it, it is directed at you.

    The advertisement wants to affect your mind or your emotions. It wants to separate you from your money. It offers delights for hard cash or the promise of hard cash. Come buy! Come buy! Always you are the target. You are the concern of giant corporations, big department stores, and little neighborhood shops—everybody who has something to sell. There is flattery in this. It is pleasant to be offered goodies, even when you know you have to pay. It is pleasant to be tempted. It is wonderful to be the center of attention, and you are the center of attention when you enjoy or detest a television commercial or look at a page of glamorous advertising in a slick magazine.

    This is an advertisement. You have been warned. It may have the dignity of the Declaration of Independence or the winsomeness of a small child telling Mummy he loves her, but it is an advertisement. You know you are flirting with danger when you stop, look, or listen. There is excitement in that. Be self-indulgent and buy yourself a diamond, an almost-Paris frock, a garden tractor, or a double-edged, triple-plated, 496 hp, all-weather guarantee of attractiveness to the other sex.

    Advertising in reputable media is honest in its declaration of intent. It is almost always honest in the claims it makes for the product or service it brings to

Thesis

Ads are honest

Ads will sell by any means necessary

Psychological & emotional tactics

Ads honest in intent: they want to separate you and your $.

REFERENCES

BROOKFIELD, STEPHEN D. *Developing Critical Thinkers.* San Francisco: Jossey-Bass, 1987. Describes how critical thinking skills learned in school can be applied to everyday life.

SCHLESINGER, MARK A. "The Road to Teaching Thinking." *JGE: The Journal of General Education* 36 (1984): 182–96. An evaluation of four current approaches to teaching thinking.

NEWKIRK, THOMAS, ed. *Only Connect: Uniting Reading and Writing.* Upper Montclair, NJ: Boynton/Cook, 1986. A collection of essays emphasizing the role interpretation plays in reading and writing.

SEIGEL, MARJORIE, and ROBERT CAREY. *Critical Thinking: A Semiotic Perspective.* Urbana: ERIC/RCE & NCTE, 1989. Critical thinking must be approached within the frame of reference provided by particular disciplines.

SCHOR, IRA. *Critical Thinking and Everyday Life.* 1980. Rpt. Chicago: U Chicago P, 1987. Based on Freirean principles, encourages critical thinking as part of a practical "liberatory pedagogy."

GOLUB, JEFF, and the NCTE Committee on Classroom Practices, eds. *Activities to Promote Critical Thinking.* Urbana: NCTE, 1986. A collection of essays containing practical advice on teaching critical thinking.

REFERENCES

DILLON, GEORGE. *Constructing Texts*. Bloomington: Indiana UP, 1981. Readers do more than simply decode texts; they make meaning from the text.

MEYERS, CHET. *Teaching Students to Think Critically*. San Francisco: Jossey-Bass, 1986. Teachers can develop visual models to represent critical thinking in various disciplines.

BUCKLER, PATRICIA PRONDINI. "Reading, Writing, and Psycholinguistics: An Integrated Approach Using Joyce's 'Counterparts.' " *Teaching English in the Two-Year College* 12 (1985): 22–31. Assignments in a freshman course follow Rosenblatt's reading model and Moffett's writing model.

BLACKMON, JO ANNE RAIFORD, and HOWARD I. BERRENT. "Open to Suggestion: OH RATS—A Note-taking Technique." *Journal of Reading* 27 (1984): 548–50. A system for note-taking during reading helps students understand material better.

ADDITIONAL EXERCISE B

Using the guidelines from this section, conduct a close reading of the passage from Herbert Fingarette's *Heavy Drinking: The Myth of Alcoholism as a Disease* (see 34f-4). After you have completed your reading, meet in groups of three or four and compare your notes and observations with fellow students. Are there any significant differences? How do you account for them? Do other students' responses cause you to rethink some of your own? Do other students note anything you missed (or vice versa)? Finally, see if the group can come to a consensus about the selection.

Part 2: Argument that ads are honest in own self-interest

what it hopes will be your favorable attention. Generally the nationally advertised item is all that it claims to be. Usually it is better and less expensive than a comparable product or service not advertised. Advertising is not masquerading propaganda or disguised publicity. It blazons its intent, and it offers sound value for your approval and purchase.

Why all this virtue? Advertising is not created and used just to provide a smug example of public morality. Advertising is honest because it has to be.

Advertising is subject to all of the laws against fraud. Advertisers can be found guilty and prosecuted if they are proven to have defrauded or attempted to defraud. Advertising is scrutinized continually by Better Business Bureaus, and it comes under the jurisdiction of the Federal Trade Commission, which was set up in 1915 to enforce prohibition of unfair methods of competition in interstate commerce. The Food and Drug Administration, the Federal Communications Commission, the Alcohol and Tobacco Tax Division of the Internal Revenue Service, and the United States Post Office also have some regulatory power over advertising.

Review of laws & agencies ads subject to

In 1906, with the strong backing of reputable advertisers and advertising media, the Food and Drug Act—the "Wiley Law"—was passed. This law made it a misdemeanor to make or sell misbranded or adulterated foods, drugs, medicines, or liquors. Control was greatly extended by the passage of the Pure Food and Drug Act of 1938, known as the Wheeler-Lea Act. This forbade dissemination of false advertising about foods, drugs, related products, and cosmetics.

Advertising is policed by government, but the strongest controls are exerted by advertisers and advertising media themselves. Like most other successful activities, advertising is largely self-regulatory. It has to be. Advertising is basically honest in its own self-interest. There is no satisfactory alternative.

Self-interest, not altruism, motivates ad companies.

2   Applying techniques for reading to understand

When you know that you must base later writing on a source you are reading, you should consciously adopt a system for reading to understand. There are many systems you can follow, but each commonly entails reading in three stages.

PREVIEW   Skim the text, reading quickly both to identify the author's purpose and to recall what you know about the topic.

READ   Read with pen in hand, making notes (on separate sheets or on photocopied pages) about the content and the structure of the text. Stop periodically to monitor your progress.

REVIEW   Skim the text a second time to consolidate your notes: jot down questions and highlight especially important passages.

What follows are techniques for highlighting information important to understanding a source. These same techniques led to the highlighting and note making on the previous passage by James Playsted Wood, above.

Preview the text.

- *Read titles, openings, and closings in full.* This preview will give you a sense of topic, audience, purpose, and main point. Read the title and guess the relationship between the title and text. If you are reading an article or a chapter of a book, read the opening and closing paragraphs in full. If you are reading a book, read the preface along with the first and last chapters.

- *Skim the rest of the text.* A brief look at the text will help you to understand the structure, or layout, of the source. When skimming an article, read all headings along with a few sentences from every second or third paragraph. When skimming a book, review the table of contents and then read the opening and closing paragraphs of each chapter.

- *Recall what you know about the topic.* A review of your previous exposure to a topic will prepare you to be interested and ready with questions as you begin reading. After skimming a text, think about the topic: reflect on your personal history with it.

- *Predict what you will learn from reading.* Based on your quick review of the text and on your knowledge of the topic, predict what you will learn. Predictions form an important part of a close, critical reading by keeping you focused on the content and alert to potential difficulties.

Read the text.

Read with a pen or pencil in hand and make notes that will help you understand.

- *Identify the author's purpose.* The author's purpose will likely be to inform or to argue. Locate passages that illustrate this purpose.

- *Underline important phrases and sentences.* Your underlining or highlighting of important information should work with your notes (see below) so that you can return to the text and spot the author's main topic at a glance.

- *Write notes that summarize your underlining.* You can summarize important points of an explanation or an argument by writing brief phrases in the margins; this will help you to understand as you read and to recall important information as you reread.

EXTRA HELP

The steps developed here in 1e-2 share some features with traditional "SQ3R" techniques, which go back to the 1940s; (Robinson, H. *Why Pupils Fail in Reading.* U Chicago P, 1946). Those methods place special emphasis on the student's effort in forming key "challenge" questions throughout the reading process, and then seeking the answers that will reinforce memory and comprehension. This stepwise questioning process has been repeatedly shown to be effective in helping students to improve comprehension at all levels from learning-deficient to near-proficiency. (Wong, B., and W. Jones, "Increasing metacomprehension in learning disabled and normally achieving students through self-questioning training." *Learning Disability Quarterly* 5.2 (1982): 228–38.) Idea-generating strategies such as "mapping" (3d-7) have also been shown to be effective as analytical tools to help in comprehension; (Kameeni, E. J. and D. C. Simmons, *Designing Instructional Strategies: The Prevention of Academic Learning Disabilities.* Columbus, OH: Charles Merrill, 1990).

Students with a history of difficulty in reading comprehension can usually get extra help from various developmental reading textbooks in study skill centers. In addition, a variety of remedial computer programs have been designed to build up comprehension skills by degree. These programs often emphasize sentence-completion exercises at graduated levels, focusing on such basic functions as those identified in the adjoining text. Some learning laboratories, study skill centers, or special education departments may have access to programs such as the following (or other more recent products in this rapidly developing technology):

The first two programs feature paragraphs with structured omissions for readers to fill in.

Cloze Plus. Millikin Publishing Co. Six levels of exercises (from a basic 5th-grade reading level). Reviewed by Boygo, J., and P. M. Hardiman. "Cloze." *Journal of Learning Disabilities* 18 (1985): 364–65.

Comprehension Power Program. Millikin Publishing Co. Twelve levels of exercises featuring vocabulary words as well as structural reading skills, suited for secondary level students. Reviewed by Lindemann, S. K. *Journal of Learning Disabilities* 18 (1985): 495–96.

(continued)

Critical Reading, Lesson Series A–H. Eight disks published by Borg-Warner Educational Systems. Lesson units instruct secondary-level readers in critical thinking and reasoning patterns; four units focus on contrasts/alternatives, inclusive categories, conditional statements, and inductive reasoning. Reviewed by Wilson, J. "Critical Reading." *Learning Disability Quarterly* 8 (1985): 64–66.

- *Identify sections.* A section of a text is a grouping of related paragraphs (see 5a). Sometimes, an author will provide section headings; at other times, you will need to write them. In either case, your awareness of sections will help you understand the structure of a text.

- *Identify difficult passages.* You can use a question mark to identify passages that confuse you, and circle unfamiliar words. Unless a particular word is repeated often and seems central to the meaning of a text, postpone using a dictionary until you complete your reading. Frequent interruptions to check the meaning of words will fragment your reading and disrupt your understanding (see 22e).

- *Periodically ask: Am I understanding?* You should stop at least once during your reading to ask yourself this question. If you are having trouble, change your plan for reading. For especially difficult selections, try dividing the text into small sections and reading one section at a sitting. Read until you understand each section, or until you can identify what you do not understand.

Review the text.

After reading and making notes, spend a few minutes consolidating what you have learned. Focus on the content of the passage and its structure. Understand the pattern by which the author has presented ideas and information. The additional minutes of review that you devote now will crystallize what you have learned and be a real help later on, when you are asked to refer to and *use* the selection, perhaps for an exam or paper.

- *Consolidate information.* Skim the passage and reread your notes. Clarify them, if necessary, so that they accurately represent the selection. Reread and highlight (with boxes or stars) what you consider to be the author's significant sentences or paragraphs.

- *Organize your questions.* Review the various terms and concepts you have had trouble understanding. Organize your questions concerning vocabulary and content. Use dictionaries; seek out fellow students or a professor to clarify especially difficult points. Even if you do not pursue these questions immediately, you should clarify what you do not understand. Your questions, gathered into one place, such as a journal, will be an excellent place to begin reviewing for an exam.

3   Practicing reading to understand

Many of the techniques just discussed are illustrated in the sample passage by James Playsted Wood, in 1e-1. Observe how the thesis is identified and how notes of summary correspond with underlined sentences and phrases. In addition, you will find notes highlighting the structure of the passage: Wood's first several paragraphs offer an extended definition of advertising; the remaining paragraphs argue that advertising agencies must regulate themselves. Based on such a close reading, you could summarize Wood's passage—and you will see an example of such a summary in 2a. Now it is your turn to practice close reading by completing the following exercise.

EXERCISE 5

Using the techniques discussed in the preceding section read to understand the following passage from Charles A. O'Neil's "The Language of Advertising." Underline what you consider to be important sentences and phrases, and make notes of summary. In addition, identify sections of the passage. You will return to O'Neil's discussion to complete other exercises in this chapter.

A Defense of Advertising

Some critics view the entire advertising business as a cranky, unwelcomed child of the free enterprise system, a noisy, whining, brash kid who must somehow be kept in line, but can't just yet be thrown out of the house. Because advertising mirrors the fears, quirks, and aspirations of the society that creates it (and is, in turn, sold by it), it is wide open to parody and ridicule.

Perhaps the strongest, most authoritative critic of advertising language in recent years is journalist Edwin Newman. In his book *Strictly Speaking*, he poses the question, "Will America be the death of English?" Newman's "mature, well thought out judgement" is that it will. As evidence, he cites a number of examples of fuzzy thinking and careless use of language, not just by advertisers, but by many people in public life, including politicians and journalists:

> The federal government has adopted the comic strip character Snoopy as a symbol and showed us Snoopy on top of his doghouse, flat on his back, with a balloon coming out of his mouth, containing the words, "I believe in conserving energy," while below there was this exhortation: savEnergy.
>
> savEnergy. An entire letter e at the end was savd. In addition, an entire space was savd. Perhaps the government should say onlYou can prevent forest fires. . . . Spelling has been assaulted by Duz, E-Z Off, Fantastik, Kool, Kleen . . . and by products that make you briter, so that you will not be left hi and dri at a parti, but made welkom. . . . Under this pressure, adjectives become adverbs; nouns become adjectives; prepositions disappear; compounds abound.[1]

In this passage, Newman presents three of the charges most often levied against advertising:

1. Advertising debases English.
2. Advertising downgrades the intelligence of the public.
3. Advertising warps our vision of reality, implanting in us groundless fears and insecurities. (He cites, as examples of these groundless fears, "tattletale grey," "denture breath," "morning mouth," "unsightly bulge," "ring around the collar.")

Other charges have been made from time to time. They include:

1. Advertising sells daydreams; distracting, purposeless visions of lifestyles beyond the reach of most of the people who are most exposed to advertising.

EXERCISE 5

Answers will vary.

2. Advertising feeds on human weaknesses and exaggerates the importance of material things, encouraging "impure" emotions and vanities.
3. Advertising encourages bad, even unhealthy habits like smoking.
4. Advertising perpetuates racial and sexual stereotypes.

What can be said in advertising's defense? Advertising is only a reflection of society; slaying the messenger (and just one of the messengers, at that) would not alter the fact—if it is a fact—that "America will be the death of English." A case can be made for the concept that advertising language is an acceptable stimulus for the natural evolution of language. (At the very least, advertising may stimulate debate about what current trends in language are "good" and "bad.") Another point: is "proper English" the language most Americans actually speak and write, or is it the language we are told we should speak and write, the language of *The Elements of Style* and *The Oxford English Dictionary?*

What about the charge that advertising debases the intelligence of the public? Those who support this particular criticism would do well to ask themselves another question: Exactly how intelligent is the public? How many people know the difference between adverbs and adjectives? How many people *want* to know? The fact is that advertisements are effective, not because agencies say they are effective, but because they sell products.

Advertising attempts to convince us to buy products; we are not forced to buy something because it is heavily advertised. Who, for example, is to be blamed for the success, in the mid-70s, of a nonsensical, nonfunctional product—"Pet Rocks"? The people who designed the packaging, those who created the idea of selling ordinary rocks as pets, or those who bought the product?

Perhaps much of the fault lies with the public, for accepting advertising so readily. S. I. Hayakawa finds "the uncritical response to the incantations of advertising . . . a serious symptom of a widespread evaluational disorder." He does not find it "beyond the bounds of possibility" that today's suckers for national advertising will be tomorrow's suckers for the master political propagandist who will, by playing up the 'Jewish menace,' in the same way as national advertisers play up the 'pink toothbrush menace,' and by promising us national glory and prosperity, sell fascism in America.[2]

Fascism in America is fortunately a far cry from Pet Rocks, but the point is well taken. In the end, advertising simply attempts to change behavior. It is a neutral tool, just as a gun is a neutral tool, but advertising at least has not been known to cause accidental deaths. Like any form of communication, it can be used for positive social purposes, neutral commercial purposes, or for the most pernicious kind of paranoid propaganda. Accepting, for the purpose of this discussion, that propaganda is, at heart, an extension of politics and therefore is materially different from commercial advertising as practiced in the United States of America, circa 1990, *do* advertisements sell distracting, purposeless visions? Occasionally. But perhaps such visions are necessary components of the process through which our society changes and improves.

And recognize this: advertising is a mirror. It is not perfect; sometimes it distorts. When we view ourselves in it, we're not always pleased with what we see. Perhaps, all things considered, that's the way it should be.

Source Notes for "A Defense of Advertising":

1. Edwin Newman, *Strictly Speaking* (Indianapolis: Bobbs-Merrill, 1974) 13.
2. S. I. Hayakawa, *Language in Action* (New York: Harcourt, Brace, 1941) 235.

1f Critical reading (2): Reading to respond

Your personal response to a text is the second component of a critical, comprehensive reading. If your responses are to be informed, you must understand what you have read—which is why your first job is to understand. This done, focus on yourself. Explore your responses to the text.

1 Setting goals for reading to respond

The overall goal of reading to respond is to identify and explore *your* reactions to a text. More specifically, these goals are as follows:

- Reflect on your experience and associations with the topic of a text.
- Know what you feel about a text—know your emotional response.
- Let the text challenge you.
- Use a text to spark new, imaginative thinking.

Following is the passage by James Playsted Wood, which you read in 1e-1 and saw underlined, with accompanying notes of summary. Reread a portion of the same passage, this time observing the second "layer" of notes in teal, which represent one reader's personal response to the passage. Recommended techniques for highlighting in this way follow. You will have a chance to practice these techniques on the passage you have read by Charles O'Neil (for Exercise 5).

From The Merits of Advertising

Part 1: Account of what ad is

In its open declaration of intent [advertising] is perhaps the most honest form of major present-day journalism. *Thesis*

On the face of it, an advertisement says what it is. It says: I am an advertisement. I have been bought and paid for. I make no pretense to objectivity. I am not a disinterested and impartial observer. I am a deeply interested and wholly partial pleader. My object is gain. I want to sell you something. I will persuade you by every means I can devise to buy what I have for sale. *Ads are honest*

out with my tears every little spot upon your happiness . . .

But, O Sarah! If the dead can come back to this earth and the unseen around those they loved, I shall always be near you; in the gladdest days and in the darkest nights . . . always, always, and if there be a soft breeze upon your cheek, it shall be my breath, as the cool air fans your throbbing temple, it shall be my spirit passing by. Sarah, do not mourn me dead; think I am gone and wait for thee, for we shall meet again.

I like W's claim: it's honest & direct. He describes my reactions to ads—excitement, pleasure, humor.

And what if you don't need these? Isn't that a problem?

I wonder: if regulations not present, would advertisers be so ethical?.

I doubt it. They'll get away with what they can.

This is an advertisement. You have been warned. It may have the dignity of the Declaration of Independence or the winsomeness of a small child telling Mummy he loves her, but it is an advertisement. You know you are flirting with danger when you stop, look, or listen. There is excitement in that. Be self-indulgent and buy yourself a diamond, an almost-Paris frock, a garden tractor, or a double-edged, triple-plated, 496 hp, all-weather guarantee of attractiveness to the other sex.

<u>Advertising in reputable media is honest in its declaration of intent.</u> It is almost honest in the claims it makes for the product or service it brings to what it hopes will be your favorable attention. Generally the nationally advertised item is all that it claims to be. . . .

Advertising is policed by government, but the strongest controls are exerted by advertisers and advertising media themselves. Like most other successful activities, advertising is largely self-regulatory. It has to be. Advertising is basically honest in its own self-interest. There is no satisfactory alternative.

Ads honest in intent: they want to separate you and your $.

Self-interest not altruism, motivates ad companies.

2 Applying techniques for reading to respond

You can achieve the goals of reading to respond when you approach a text with a set of questions that continually return your focus to *you* and *your* reactions. Here is a sampling of such questions.

Questions that promote a personal response

- *Which one or two sentences did I respond to most strongly in this text? What was my response?* Usually, you will read one or two sentences that will prompt reactions. Name these reactions. Explore your reasons for being excited, angry, thoughtful, surprised, or threatened. Keep the focus on you.

- *What is the origin of my views on this topic? Who else shares my views?* If you are reading on a controversial topic, explore where and under what circumstances you learned about the topic. For the sake of developing a response, criticize the views of people who believe as you do. Apply this criticism to yourself. What do you discover?

- *If I turned the subject of this text into a question on which people would vote, how would I vote—and why?* This question can help involve you with the text, since casting a vote requires some interest, if only self-interest, in a topic. Try getting involved with the text by locating a debate in the text and by taking sides.

- *What new interest, question, or observation does this text spark in me?* Use a text to spark your own thinking. Let the text help you pose new questions or make new observations. Use the text as a basis for speculation.

See 37d for a discussion on a special case of reading to respond: responding to literature.

3 Practicing reading to respond

Many of the techniques just discussed are illustrated in the sample passage by James Playsted Wood, in 1e-1. Observe the personal nature of the example notes. Comments such as "He describes my reactions to ads" differ from comments that summarize, such as "Part I—Account of what ad is." Responses, by definition, are personal matters. They will differ from one reader to the next, and you can expect your response to Wood's thesis (that advertising is an "honest" medium) will differ from those of your classmates.

> **EXERCISE 6**
> Reread the passage by Charles O'Neil in Exercise 5, this time to respond. Write notes and underline sentences and phrases, based on your response. Consider choosing a different color pen or pencil for your notes than the ones used while reading to understand so that you can recreate your various layers of reading.

1g Critical reading (3): Reading to evaluate

Evaluating a text is the third component of a close, critical reading. Having understood and responded to a text, you are in a position to investigate its strengths and weaknesses—that is, to evaluate it. You will not find every text to be of equal value: equally accurate, equally useful, equally convincing, equally well written. As a critical reader, you should determine the extent to which an author has succeeded or failed in presenting material; and you should be able to explain why you and the author agree or disagree.

1 Setting goals for reading to evaluate

Specifically, your goals in reading to evaluate are these:

- Distinguish between an author's use of facts and opinions.
- Distinguish between an author's assumptions (fundamental beliefs about the world) and your own.
- Judge the effectiveness of an explanation.
- Judge the effectiveness of an argument.

EXERCISE 6

Answers will vary.

ESL ALERT

ESL students from Asian and Middle Eastern countries may be disturbed by the concept of evaluation of a source. They will not take for granted the necessity to do so, and Middle Eastern students especially may have attitudes toward journalistic sources which diverge dramatically from Western attitudes.

REFERENCES

AARONS, VICTORIA. "Ethical Issues: A Rhetorical Methodology." *The Writing Instructor* 4 (1985): 83–88. Using ethical issues for discussion in composition class encourages critical thinking.

Following is the passage by James Playsted Wood, which you read in 1e-1, where you saw summary notes, and again in 1f-1, where you saw response notes. Reread the passage, this time observing a third "layer" of notes in burgundy, which represent one reader's notes on evaluating the passage. Recommended techniques for reading to evaluate follow. You will have a chance to practice these techniques on the passage by Charles O'Neil.

From The Merits of Advertising

This is an advertisement. You have been warned. It may have the dignity of the Declaration of Independence or the winsomeness of a small child telling Mummy he loves her, but it is an advertisement. You know you are flirting with danger when you stop, look, or listen. There is excitement in that. Be self-indulgent and buy yourself a diamond, an almost-Paris frock, a garden tractor, or a double-edged, triple-plated, 496 hp, all-weather guarantee of attractiveness to the other sex.

And what if you don't need these? Isn't that a problem?

Ads honest in intent: they want to separate you and your $.

<u>Advertising in reputable media is honest in its declaration of intent.</u> <u>It is almost honest in the claims it makes for the product</u> or service it brings to what it hopes will be your favorable attention. Generally the nationally advertised item is all that it claims to be. . . .

But this begs the question: what is the claim? And how is it made?

Advertising is policed by government, but the strongest controls are exerted by advertisers and advertising media themselves. Like most other successful activities, advertising is largely self-regulatory. It has to be. Advertising is basically honest in its own self-interest. <u>There is no satisfactory alternative.</u>

Faulty, either/or logic: I'm sure many advertisers--as well as businesses--cheat until they get caught. Also faulty cause & effect logic.

Self-interest, not altruism, motivates ad companies.

2 Applying techniques for reading to evaluate

When you are reading to evaluate, you want to be alert to an author's use of *facts, opinions,* and *definitions,* and his or her *assumed views of the world.* You will also want to know if an author's purpose is primarily to inform or to argue, so that you can pose specific questions accordingly.

ADDITIONAL EXERCISE D

Label each of the following statements as *fact* or *opinion.* Be prepared to defend your choice.

1. Socialism died with the fall of the Eastern European governments.
2. Improperly dumped toxic waste presents environmental hazards.
3. Socrates was the greatest philosopher in ancient Greece.
4. Large corporations have a social responsiblity to the communities in which they operate.
5. All humans are created equal.

Distinguish facts from opinions.

Before you can evaluate a statement, you should know whether it is being presented to you as a fact or an opinion. A **fact** is any statement that can be verified.

Nationwide, the cost of college tuition is rising.

New York lies at a more southerly latitude than Paris.

> ### Distinguishing Fact from Opinion
>
> **Fact:** A statement, the accuracy of which can be checked
> Ask: Is this fact dependable?
>   How could I check the accuracy of this fact?
>
> **Opinion:** An interpretation or judgment
> Ask: Is this opinion well supported?
>   If so, do I agree or disagree? Why?

Andrew Johnson was the seventeenth President of the United States.
The construction of the Suez Canal was completed in 1869.

These statements, if challenged, can be established as true or false through appropriate research. As a reader evaluating a selection, you might question the accuracy of a fact or how the fact was shown to be true. You might doubt, for instance, that Paris is a more northerly city than New York. The argument is quickly settled by reference to agreed-upon sources—in the case of Paris, a map.

An **opinion** is a statement of interpretation and judgment. Opinions are not true or false in the way that statements of fact will be. Opinions are more or less well supported. If a friend says, "That movie was terrible," this is an opinion. If you ask why and your friend responds, "Because I didn't like it," you are faced with a statement that is unsupported and that makes no claim on you for a response. Someone who writes that the majority of U.S. space missions should not have human crews is stating an opinion. Someone who refers to the *Challenger* disaster is referring to a fact, a matter of historical record. Opinions are judgments. If an opinion is supported by an entire essay, then the author is, in effect, demanding a response from you.

Identify the strongly stated opinions in what you read, and then write a **comment note:** in the margin, jot down a brief note summarizing your response to the opinion. Agree or disagree. Later, your note will help you crystallize your reactions to the selection.

Distinguish your assumptions from those of an author.

An assumption is a fundamental belief that shapes the way people see. If your friend says that a painting is "beautiful," she is basing that statement, which is an opinion, on another, more fundamental opinion—an assumed view of beauty. Whether or not your friend directly states to you what qualities make a painting beautiful, she is *assuming* these qualities and is basing her judgment on them. If the basis of her judgment is that the painting is "lifelike," this is an assumption. Perhaps she dislikes

ADDITIONAL EXERCISE E

Reproduce the following paragraph, written by Anna Freud and Dorothy Burlingham, and ask students to identify the authors' assumptions.

> Work in the War Nurseries is based on the idea that the care and education of young children should not take second place in wartime and should not be reduced to wartime level. Adults can live under emergency conditions and, if necessary, on emergency rations. But the situation in the decisive years of bodily and mental development is entirely different. It has already been generally recognised, and provision has been made accordingly, that the lack of essential foods, vitamins, etc., in early childhood will cause lasting bodily malformation in later years, even if harmful consequences are not immediately apparent. It is not generally recognised that the same is true for the mental development of the child. Whenever certain essential needs are not fulfilled, lasting psychological malformations will be the consequence. These essential elements are: the need for personal attachment, for emotional stability, and for permanency of educational influence.

Working with Brown and Keeley's classification (see the preceding Teaching Idea), we can observe that a value assumption and a descriptive assumption are explicitly made in this paragraph. On the basis of these directly stated assumptions, Freud and Burlingham, directors of three wartime nurseries in England during World War II, presented in their book several case studies on children and their reactions to war.

Value Assumption
(what an author wants the world to be like): "The care and education of young children should not take second place in wartime and should not be reduced to wartime level."

Descriptive Assumption
(how an author believes the world works): "Whenever certain needs are not fulfilled, lasting psychological malformations will be the consequence."

abstract paintings and you like them. If you challenged each other on the point or asked *why,* you both might answer: "I don't know why I think this way. I just do." Sometimes you will find that assumptions are based on clearly defined reasons, and other times (as in the painting example) you will find that they are based on ill-defined feelings. Either way, the opinions that people have (if they are not direct expressions of assumptions themselves) can be better understood by identifying the assumptions that guide them.

CONSIDER TWO SETS OF ASSUMPTIONS

When you read a source, two sets of assumed views about the world come into play: yours and the author's. The extent of your agreement with an author depends largely on the extent to which your assumptions coincide. Therefore, in evaluating a source, you want to understand the author's assumptions concerning the topic at hand, as well as your own. To do so, you must perform two related tasks: identify an author's opinions, and determine whether or not each opinion is based on some other opinion or assumed view.

IDENTIFY DIRECT AND INDIRECT ASSUMPTIONS

Assumptions may be stated directly or indirectly. In either case, your job as a critical reader is to identify and determine the extent to which you agree with them.

Assumption stated directly
#1 A nation is justified in going to war only when hostile forces threaten its borders.

#2 A nation is justified in going to war when hostile forces threaten its interests anywhere in the world.

At times, an author hints at, but does not directly state, an assumed view—as in this example:

Assumption not stated
#3 A conflict 7,000 miles from our border does not in any way threaten this nation, and we are therefore not justified in fighting a war that far from home.

Sentence #3 is based on the assumption expressed in sentence #1. Suppose you were reading an editorial and came across sentence #3. In a close, critical reading you would see in this statement an unexpressed assumption about the reasons nations *should* go to war. If you can show that an author's assumed views (whether directly or indirectly expressed) are flawed, then you can argue that all opinions based on them are flawed and should be rejected, or at least challenged.

Distinguish your definitions of terms from those of an author.

Consider this statement: *Machines can explore space as well as and in some cases better than humans.* What do the words *as well as* and *better than* mean? If an author defines these words one way and you define them another, you and the author are sure to disagree. In evaluating a source, identify the words important to the author's presentation. If the author does not define these words directly, then state what you believe the author's definitions to be. At times you will need to make educated guesses based on your close reading of the source.

Question sources that explain and sources that argue.

Outside of the literature classroom, you will read sources that are written primarily to inform or to argue. As a critical reader engaged in evaluating a source, determine the author's primary purpose and pose questions accordingly.

SOURCES THAT EXPLAIN

When a selection asks you to accept an explanation, a description, or a procedure as accurate, pose—and respond to—these questions:

- For whom has the author intended the description, explanation, or procedure? The general public—non-experts? Someone involved in the same business or process? An observer, such as an evaluator or a supervisor?
- What does the text define and explain? How successful is the presentation, given its intended audience?
- How trustworthy is the author's information? How current is it? If it is not current, are the points being made still applicable, assuming more recent information could be obtained?
- If the author presents a procedure, what is its purpose or outcome? Who would carry out this procedure? When? For what reasons? Does the author present the stages of the procedure?

SOURCES THAT ARGUE

When a selection asks you to accept an argument, pose—and respond to—these questions:

- What conclusion am I being asked to accept?
- What reasons and evidence has the author offered for me to accept this conclusion? Are the reasons logical? Is the evidence fair? Has the author acknowledged and responded to other points of view?
- To what extent is the author appealing to logic? to my emotions? to my respect for authorities?[2]

Practice reading to evaluate.

Many of the techniques just discussed are illustrated in highlighting and notes made for the sample passage by James Playsted Wood, in

---

[2]See 6h for a full discussion of evaluating arguments.

REFERENCE

DEANE, BARBARA. "Putting the Inferential Process to Work in the Classroom." *CCC* 27 (1976): 50–52. Classroom activities can assist students in developing the ability to make inferences.

ADDITIONAL EXERCISE F

Identify in the following statements value assumptions, descriptive assumptions, and definitional assumptions, and indicate whether the assumptions are explicitly stated or implied.

1. Only by experience can anyone realize how deep, and dark, and foul is that pit of abominations [slavery]. (Harriet A. Jacobs)
2. It is easier for a camel to go through the eye of a needle, than for a rich man to enter into the kingdom of God. (The Gospel according to St. Matthew)
3. I consider the written word inferior to the spoken. (Gloria Naylor)
4. The world must be made safe for democracy. (Woodrow Wilson)

1g-1. The third layer of comments that you see (in burgundy) would prepare a reader for writing a formal evaluation of the passage. You can prepare for writing an evaluation of the piece by Charles O'Neil by completing Exercise 7.

EXERCISE 7

Answers will vary.

GROUP ACTIVITY

To underscore the fact that different readers respond differently to the same text, have students share their responses to this exercise in small groups. Ask them to focus on the *evaluative* comments they've made, and to discuss differences with an eye toward clarifying their own responses rather than convincing others that their responses are "correct."

EXERCISE 7

Reread the passage by Charles O'Neil (1e-3, Exercise 5), this time to evaluate the success of his presentation. Write notes and underline phrases and sentences, based on the discussion in the preceding section. Consider choosing a different color pen or pencil for your notes than the ones used while reading to understand and reading to respond so that you can recreate your various layers of reading.

As an option, read the following passage by media critic Jean Kilbourne, a nationally recognized authority on the effects of gender stereotyping in advertising. As you read, make notes and highlight in ways that help you to understand, respond to, and evaluate the passage.

The Child as Sex Object[3]

We have been surrounded for years by images of grown women acting like little girls, often playing with dolls and wearing bows in their hair. Erving Goffman demonstrated in *Gender Advertisements* that women are often shown as children in advertisements via their body language, in addition to more obvious ways (Goffman, 1979). It is only recently, however, that the little girl herself has been presented as a grown woman, the sex object, the ideal.

Little girls are being sexually exploited today by everyone from Calvin Klein to the multi-billion dollar pornography industry. Sexual abuse of children seems to be increasing dramatically (or perhaps is just more often reported). An estimated one out of four girls and one out of ten boys is sexually molested during their childhood. Is there a connection? Is there a link between the images of very thin women that surround us and the rise in eating disorders?

It would be foolish to suggest that advertising is *the cause* of eating disorders or the sexual abuse of children. The problems are complex and have many causes and contributing factors. There is no doubt that flagrant sexism and sex role stereotyping abound in all forms of the media. There is abundant information about this (Butler and Paisley, 1980; Courtney and Whipple, 1983). It is far more difficult to document the effects of these sex role presentations on the individuals and institutions exposed to them, because it is difficult to separate media effects from other aspects of the socialization process and almost impossible to find a control group.

---

[3]Jean Kilbourne, excerpt pp. 40–46 from "The Child as Sex Object: Images of Children in the Media," reprinted with permission from *The Educator's Guide to Preventing Sexual Abuse*, edited by Mary Nelson and Kay Clark, 1986, ETR Associates, Santa Cruz, CA. For information about other related materials, call 1-800-321-4407.

The average American is exposed to over two thousand ads every day and will spend a year and a half of his or her life watching television commercials. Advertising is an over eighty-five billion dollar industry, and uses very sophisticated techniques for both research and production. The influence is pervasive, often subtle, and mostly unconscious (Fore, 1977; Gerbner, 1972; Leymore, 1975). The evidence indicates that the media perpetuate and reflect sex role stereotypes, but the precise effects are more difficult to determine. Research does show, however, that media users, especially children, are directly affected and influenced by media content (Comstock, 1978; Courtney and Whipple, 1983).

It is certainly safe to say that advertising is a powerful educational force in America. It is both a creator and perpetuator of the dominant attitudes, values and ideology of the culture, the social norms and myths by which most people govern their behavior (Ewen, 1976; Price, 1978; Williamson, 1978).

At the very least, advertising helps to create a climate in which certain attitudes and values flourish, such as the attitude that a woman's physical appearance is what is most important and valuable about her, that aging makes women unattractive and therefore less valuable, that women who are the victims of sexual assault "asked for it." This attitude applies now to females of all ages, as was evidenced by the recent remark of a Wisconsin judge that a five-year-old rape victim was "an unusually sexually permissive young lady" (*National Now Times*, 1982). This is a very dangerous attitude. The media do not cause this type of attitude but they do contribute to it by surrounding us with images of women and girls as passive, decorative, seductive and often as enjoying aggression and violence.

Advertising is partially a reflection of the culture that has created it. Because of its power, however, it does a great deal more than simply reflect the cultural attitudes and values. It plays an important role in shaping those values. Far from being a passive mirror of society, it is an effective medium of influence and persuasion.[4]

1h Critical reading (4): Reading to synthesize

Once you have understood, responded to, and evaluated a single source, you are in a position to link that source with others. By establishing links between one author and others (including yourself), you achieve a synthesis: an *integration* of sources. Synthesis is the fourth and in some ways the most complex component of a close, critical reading: it requires that you read and understand *all* your source materials and that you respond to and evaluate each one.

REFERENCE

ZELLER, ROBERT. "Developing the Inferential Reasoning of Basic Writers." CCC 38 (1987): 343–45. Asking students to infer relationships between photographs and writing encourages critical thinking.

[4]"References" for the works cited in this excerpt appear with "References and Works Cited" for chapter 1 at the end of this handbook.

Setting goals for reading to synthesize

You are the organizing force of a synthesis. Without your active involvement with source materials, without your creative and integrating ideas, synthesis is impossible. Specifically, your goals in reading to synthesize are these:

- Read to understand, respond to, and evaluate multiple sources on a subject, problem, or issue.
- Understand your own views on the subject, problem, or issue. Be able to state these views in a sentence or two.
- Forge relationships among source materials, according to your purpose. In a synthesis, *your* views should predominate. Use the work of various authors to support what you think.
- Generally, try to create a conversation among sources. Be sure that yours is the major voice in the conversation.

2 **Applying techniques for reading to synthesize**

When you are reading to synthesize, you want to be alert to the ways in which various sources "talk to" each other concerning a particular topic. Seek out relationships among sources. Be sure to consider yourself as a source—and a valuable one.

We will now discuss each element of this strategy for reading to synthesize in turn.

Read multiple sources on a topic.

Identifying relationships among lengthy selections may seem a formidable task. Realize, though, that as a critical reader you do not make relationships among whole articles, chapters of books, or entire books; you make relationships among *specific parts* of these works. In the same way, as a writer, you never write an entire essay or paper at any one time; you write *parts*. The key to your success lies in your ability to divide a topic into parts. When reading multiple sources, you will discover that authors discuss the same parts of the topic, although they may use different terms to do so. Once you begin to make cross-references and generate your own private index to your reading selections, you will be well on your way to developing a synthesis.

Divide the topic into parts.

Your ability to divide a topic into parts depends *entirely* on the quality of your reading. If you read selections with care and make notes in the margins, you can depend on those notes when the time comes to relate

ADDITIONAL EXERCISE G

Find a current topic covered in several newspapers or weekly newsmagazines. (In addition to local and city newspapers, you might consider *Time, Newsweek, U.S. News, The Christian Science Monitor.*) Using the strategy outlined in 1a, analyze the relationships among the sources.

A Strategy for Synthesizing Sources

1. *Read, respond to, and evaluate multiple sources on a topic.* It is very likely that the authors will have different observations to make. Because you are working with the different sources, you are in a unique position to draw relationships among them.

2. *Subdivide the topic into parts and give each a brief title.* Call the topic that the several authors discuss X. What are all the parts, or the subdivisions, of X that the authors discuss? List the separate parts, giving each a brief title.

3. *Write cross-references for each part.* For each subdivision of the topic, list *specific* page references to whichever sources discuss that part. This is called **cross-referencing.** Once you have cross-referenced each of the topic's parts, you will have created an index to your reading selections.

4. *Summarize each author's information or ideas about each part.* Now that you have generated cross-references that show you which authors discuss which parts of topic X, take up one part at a time and reread all passages you have cross-referenced. Summarize what each author has written on particular parts of the topic.

5. *Forge relationships among reading selections.* Study your notes and try to link sources. Here are several relationships that you might establish:

   Comparison: One author *agrees* with another.
   Contrast: One author *disagrees* with another.
   Example: Material in one source *illustrates* a statement in another.
   Definition: Material from several sources, considered together, may help you *define* or redefine a term.
   Cause and effect: Material from one source may allow you to *explain directly* why certain events occur in other sources.
   Personal response: You find yourself agreeing or disagreeing with points made in one or more sources. Ask yourself *why* and then develop an answer by referring to specific passages.

   *For ways to synthesize details you've observed in a work of literature, see 37d, 2–4.

the sources to one another. You have three sources on advertising available to you in chapter exercises: two defenses of advertising, one by James Playsted Wood (1e-1) and a second by Charles O'Neil (1e-3, Exercise 5) and an attack on the ways advertising perpetuates and promotes stereotypes, by Jean Kilbourne (1g-2, Exercise 7). Before continuing with the discussion here, read them and also read a fourth and final source, "The

EXERCISE 8

Answers will vary, but here are some suggestions:

1. The honesty or dishonesty of advertising

    Wood: Ads are honest in their intent—they acknowledge they will by all means necessary try to get you to part with your money.

    O'Neil: Ads are neither honest nor dishonest; they're neutral and can be used for good or ill, depending on the motives of the people paying for the ad.

    Kilbourne: Ads perpetuate and promote gender stereotypes—simplistic and ultimately dishonest views of gender.

    Schrank: Ads create illusions of superiority—they "balance on the narrow line between truth and falsehood."

2. Advertising as a reflection of society

    Wood:

    O'Neil: The mirror of advertising may distort, but it shows us to ourselves, warts and all.

    Kilbourne: Advertising does reflect, but the makers of the mirror glass have their own views (about gender, for instance) that become part of the reflection.

    Schrank:

3. The public's involvement with advertisements

    Wood: Ads may please, tempt, intrigue, endanger, or irritate the public; ultimately, the public is flattered by all the attention.

    O'Neil: Quoting Hayakawa, he says that the public is uncritical in response to ads; he feels this response is "a serious symptom of a widespread evaluation disorder."

    Kilbourne: Given advertising's repeated images of women as passive or seductive, the public is reinforced in its gender stereotypes.

    Schrank: The public is often duped because it is unaware of an ad's claims.

4. Protecting the public's interests

    Wood: Agencies and laws are created to protect the public interest; advertisers stay within the bounds of these for their own self-interest.

    O'Neil: The public is not forced to buy—it chooses to or not, presumably in its own best interest (though with the "pet rock" craze, one wonders).

    Kilbourne: The public interest is not served by sexually suggestive pictures of young

Language of Advertising Claims" by Jeffrey Schrank (2c-3). Schrank discusses the "pseudo-information" of advertisements and provides ten strategies for analyzing the claims that advertisers make.

If you have read these sources carefully, you will be able to divide the broad topic of advertising into at least four parts: (1) the honesty or dishonesty of advertising; (2) advertising as a reflection of society; (3) the public's involvement with advertisements; and (4) protecting the public's interests. Each of these topics is suggested, directly, by one or more of the sources. Not directly suggested but nonetheless common to all the sources is a fifth idea: (5) advertising as a lightning rod, or point of conflict, in our consumer society. Not all of the authors address each of the five parts into which we have divided the broad topic of advertising, but these five parts will allow you to forge connections between your views and those of the four authors.

Cross-reference each part and summarize.

In actual course work, your reading selections will come from different journals, newspapers, and books—and cross-referencing should prove a useful technique. Assume that you have identified parts of your topic and have listed page numbers from your sources that relate to each part. Following the page references, you would write a brief note summarizing the author's information or ideas. In Exercise 8 you are asked to do just this.

EXERCISE 8

The broad topic of advertising has been divided into five parts. Based on your careful reading of the selections by Wood (1e-1), O'Neil (1e-3, Exercise 5), Kilbourne (1g-2, Exercise 7), and Schrank (2c-3), complete the note making for these parts. For each there is a space for you to record your views as well as those of the authors. Be sure to jot down your views, since of all the sources you draw on in forging a synthesis, you are the most important. Remember: not all of the authors will necessarily have written something on each of these five parts.

1. *The honesty or dishonesty of advertising*

    Wood: Ads are honest in their intent—they acknowledge that by all means necessary they will try to get you to part with your money.
    O'Neil:
    Kilbourne:
    Schrank: Ads create illusions of superiority—they "balance on the narrow line between truth and falsehood."
    You:

2. *Advertising as a reflection of society*

    Wood:
    O'Neil: Advertising's mirror may distort, but it shows us to ourselves, warts and all.
    Kilbourne:

Schrank:
You:

3. *The public's involvement with advertisements*
Wood:
O'Neil:
Kilbourne: Given advertising's repeated images of women as passive or seductive, the public is reinforced in its gender stereotypes.
Schrank:
You:

4. *Protecting the public's interests*
Wood: Agencies and laws are created to protect the public interest; advertisers stay within the bounds of these for their own self-interest.
O'Neil:
Kilbourne:
Schrank:
You:

5. *Advertising as a point of conflict in our consumer society*
Wood: Ads scream their intention—"Come buy!" Ads are the speech of consumer society.
O'Neil: In the first part of his article, O'Neil reviews the general arguments against ads and then lists them.
Kilbourne:
Schrank:
You:

girls. The implicit message is that advertisers will subvert standards of decency and gains made by women to sell products. Young girls are exploited in these ads.

Schrank: The public can be protected by consciously analyzing the claims of advertisements.

5. Advertising as a point of conflict in a consumer society

Wood: Ads scream their intention: "Come buy!" Ads are the speech of consumer society.

O'Neil: In the first part of the article, he reviews the general arguments against ads and then lists them.

Kilbourne: She brings concerns from culture (sexism) and points to ads as partly responsible.

Schrank: He speaks of ads "attacking" consumers, using the language of warfare, of conflict, in which people win and lose.

Forge relationships among your sources.

Based on your close reading of each selection and on your cross-references and notes, you should be able to establish relationships among the readings. Five general questions should get you started.

1. Which authors agree?
2. Which authors disagree?
3. Are there examples in one source of statements or ideas expressed in another?
4. What definitions can you offer, based on the readings?
5. Do you detect a cause-and-effect relationship in any of the readings?

EXERCISE 9
Develop answers to the following questions, which are designed to get you thinking about your views and experience in relation to the sources you have read.

1. Which authors agree?
James Playsted Wood (1e-1), a defender of advertisements, writes that advertisements are honest in that they say, openly, "We will do

EXERCISE 9

See 2d-3 for possible answers to these questions.

anything necessary, within the law, to get you to buy." Jean Kilbourne (1g-2, Exercise 7), a critic of advertising, apparently agrees with this view. How so?

Kilbourne and Schrank agree on the potential of advertisements to do harm. How so?

2. Which authors disagree?

Schrank claims that advertisements work at a subconscious level. Wood argues that advertisements are honest and openly declare their intentions. Comment on this difference. Can you explain it?

Kilbourne and O'Neil both suggest that advertisements are reflections of society. Both use the language of mirrors and reflections—though in slightly different ways, and for differing purposes. Explain.

3. Are there examples in one source of statements or ideas expressed in another?

Wood writes that an "advertisement may entice. It may soothe or excite. It may try to frighten you. It may order or coax." Find examples of this view in the selections by Kilbourne and Schrank. Then answer this question: Do advertisements sometimes succeed too well?

4. What definitions can you offer, based on the readings?

Develop a definition of advertising that takes into account conflicting information in the selections you've read.

5. Do you detect a cause-and-effect relationship in any of the readings? The authors variously argue for and against cause-and-effect relationships concerning advertising. Review the selections and focus on these relationships. Decide on the extent to which you agree with the views of each author.

CHAPTER 2

Critical Thinking and Writing

You will frequently be asked to demonstrate your understanding of sources by writing summaries, evaluations, analyses, and syntheses—four forms of writing that are fundamental to college-level work. Each form emphasizes a particular way of thinking about texts,[1] and each is built upon particular skills in critical reading.

Forms of writing that build on reading

■ **Summary.** When you summarize, you briefly—and neutrally—restate the main points of a text. Summary draws on your skills of reading to understand (see 1e).

■ **Evaluation.** When you evaluate, you judge the effectiveness of an author's presentation and explain your agreement or disagreement. Evaluation draws on your skills of reading to understand (1e), reading to respond (1f), and reading to evaluate (1g).

■ **Analysis.** When you analyze, you use the clearly defined principles set out by one or more authors to investigate the work of other authors (or to investigate various situations in the world). Analysis draws on your skills of reading to understand (1e), reading to respond (1f), and reading to evaluate (1g).

■ **Synthesis.** When you synthesize texts, you gather the work of various authors according to *your* purpose. Synthesis draws on your skills of reading to understand (1e), reading to respond (1f), reading to evaluate (1g), and reading to synthesize (1h).

The cumulative layers of writing

The forms of writing discussed in this chapter are interrelated. You will write summaries as part of writing evaluations, analyses, and syntheses. Before you evaluate an author's presentation, you are obligated to demonstrate through summary that you understand the text. When you gather and synthesize multiple texts for a research paper, you will summarize *and* evaluate the texts as you forge relationships among them. When you conduct an analysis, you must have thoroughly understood and evaluated the principles you apply; this calls for written summary and evaluation as part of your analysis.

---

[1]We used the word *text* interchangeably with *source* to mean any reading selection.

KEY FEATURES

This chapter continues the discussion of critical thinking begun in chapter 1, presenting critical writing as progressing naturally from critical reading. The emphasis on questioning remains as students are introduced to four patterns of academic writing: summary, evaluation, analysis, and synthesis. Each pattern is explained in terms of specific goals; for each pattern, techniques are offered to help students begin to write, based on reading. Additionally, each pattern is shown to involve elements of other patterns: for instance, analysis, evaluation, and synthesis all involve elements of summary. To demonstrate the connections between reading and writing, the authors use selections that students have read in chapter 1 to illustrate summary, evaluation, and analysis. Several of the student exercises are also based on reading selections in chapter 1. The synthesis section of the chapter likewise builds on several of the readings in chapter 1. The example synthesis, based on this material, is found in chapter 6, on argumentation. For each of the patterns of writing presented in the chapter, students are given models and are then invited to practice the strategies themselves. With the foundation provided by chapters 1 and 2, students will be able to understand the links between reading and writing at the college level.

LOOKING AHEAD

ACROSS THE CURRICULUM While this section states that summary, evaluation, analysis, and synthesis are essentially the same regardless of the discipline, you may want to refer students to Part X for extensive treatment of writing, with particular emphasis on research in humanities, social sciences, and sciences. (See chapters 37, 38, and 39.) Writing in a business environment is covered in chapter 40.

31

LOOKING AHEAD

The material covered in the following sections will be useful in chapter 34 (Using Sources). Since students are sometimes assigned research papers in other courses before covering the topic in Composition, you may want to call attention to that chapter, as well as the chapters on writing research in the disciplines (chapters 37, 38, and 39).

The material in this chapter relies on the following books:

KURFISS, JOANNE G. *Critical Thinking: Theory, Research, and Possibilities.* ASHE-ERIC Higher Education Report No. 2. Washington, DC: Association for the Study of Higher Education, 1988.

MARZANO, ROBERT J., et al. *Dimensions of Thinking: A Framework for Curriculum and Instruction.* Alexandria, VA: ACSD, 1988.

JONES, BEAU FLY, et al., eds. *Strategic Teaching and Learning: Cognitive Instruction in the Content Areas.* Alexandria, VA: ASCD, 1987.

TOULMIN, STEPHEN, RICHARD RIEKE, and ALLAN JANIK. *An Introduction to Reasoning.* New York: Macmillan, 1979.

RORTY, RICHARD. *Philosophy and the Mirror of Nature.* Princeton: Princeton UP, 1979.

KUHN, THOMAS. *The Structure of Scientific Revolutions.* 2nd ed. Enlarged. Chicago: U Chicago P, 1970.

These forms of academic writing are cumulative: one builds on the next in much the same way that strategies for reading comprehensively are cumulative. For clarity of presentation, we discuss summary, evaluation, analysis, and synthesis in separate sections and as separate tasks. In practice—in the texts you read and in the papers you write—you will find that these forms of writing and thinking merge into one another.

2a Writing a summary

Fundamental to working with sources in any academic setting is the **summary,** a brief, neutral restatement of a text. You will read texts in every course; and before you can earn the right to comment on them or otherwise put them to use, you must first demonstrate an ability to understand authors on their own terms. Like any piece of writing, summary calls for you to make decisions and to plan, draft, and revise. While sometimes called for on exams, a summary more typically appears as part of evaluations, analyses, and syntheses. The following three assignments require summaries.

ASSIGNMENTS THAT EXPLICITLY CALL FOR A SUMMARY

MATHEMATICS — Read the article "Structuring Mathematical Proofs," by Uri Leron (*The American Mathematical Monthly,* 90, March 1983: 174–185). In two to four typed pages, summarize the concept of linear proof, giving one good example from the course.

FILM STUDIES — Summarize Harvey Greenberg's discussion of *The Wizard of Oz.*

SOCIAL PSYCHOLOGY — Write a summary of your textbook's discussion of the "realistic conflict theory." Make sure that you address the theory's explanation of prejudice as an intergroup conflict.

An assignment may not explicitly call for a summary but may require it just the same, as in the following example. In completing this assignment, a student would need to summarize (the Mary Shea argument) and then respond.

ASSIGNMENT THAT IMPLIES THE NEED FOR A SUMMARY

BUSINESS ETHICS — In "Good Riddance to Corporate America," Mary Shea argues that highly credentialed women MBAs are beginning to quit corporate America because of its "essential emptiness." How convinced are you by Shea's argument?

1 Setting goals for writing a summary

The focus of a summary is on a specific text, *not* on your reactions to it. Overall, your goal is to restate the text, as briefly as possible, in your own words. More specifically, you should aim to meet these goals:

- Understand the author's purpose for writing—for instance, to inform, explain, argue, justify, defend, compare, contrast, or illustrate. Most often, the author will have a single purpose; at times, an author may have two closely related purposes, such as to explain and justify.
- State the author's thesis in relation to this purpose.
- Identify the sections of the text and understand the ways in which they work together to support, or explain, the thesis.
- Distinguish information needed to explain the author's thesis from examples and less important information.
- Write the summary using your own words; avoid phrase-by-phrase "translations" from the original.

2 Understanding techniques for writing a summary

Summary begins with an application of the skills discussed in 1e, reading to understand. There you were advised to make notes as you previewed, read, and reviewed a text. Before you attempt to follow the guidelines below and write a summary, read 1e and apply the skills discussed there to any text you are about to summarize.

Techniques for summarizing an especially difficult text

When the topic of a text is completely new to you, or when you are reading a text intended for an audience that has more experience with a topic than you have, reading to understand—and writing a summary—will be especially difficult. In addition to the reading strategies discussed in 1e, try these reading strategies to promote understanding and to facilitate summary writing:

1. Identify every example in the text and ask: what point is being illustrated here? Make a list of these points. Considered together, they will reveal the author's thesis.
2. Look for repeated terms or phrases. Define them, consulting specialized dictionaries or encyclopedias, if necessary.
3. Read and reread the opening and closing paragraphs of the text. Look for a sentence or two—the thesis—that seems to summarize the whole. "Interrogate" that sentence, following advice in 3d-4. Link specific parts of the sentence to different parts (or sections) of the text. Understand what you can; identify what you cannot understand—and then take *specific* questions to a fellow student or your professor.

3 Applying techniques for writing summaries

The techniques for writing a summary can now be applied to an example passage found in chapter 1: "The Merits of Advertising" (section

REFERENCES

NEWKIRK, THOMAS, ed. *Only Connect: Uniting Reading and Writing.* Upper Montclair, NJ: Boynton/Cook, 1986. A collection of essays emphasizing the role interpretation plays in reading and writing.

MORRIS, BARBARA S. *Disciplinary Perspectives on Thinking and Writing.* Ann Arbor: English Composition Board, 1989. A collection of essays illustrating different modes of inquiry and approaches to writing among various disciplines.

MAIMON, ELAINE P., BARBARA F. NODINE, and FINBARR O'CONNOR. *Thinking, Reasoning, and Writing.* New York: Longman, 1989. Offers methods of teaching based on theories of reading and writing as social acts.

LANGER, JUDITH A. "Learning through Writing: Study Skills in the Content Areas." *Journal of Reading* 29 (1986): 400–406. Composing full essays about a reading promotes more effective learning than simply taking notes and responding to questions.

REFERENCES

SHERRARD, CAROL, "Summary Writing: A Topographical Study." *Written Communication* 3 (1986): 324–43. The longer the summary, the more likely an inexpert writer will use his or her own words instead of copying parts of the original.

BUCKLER, PATRICIA PRONDINI. "Reading, Writing, and Psycholinguistics: An Integrated Approach Using Joyce's 'Counterparts.' " *Teaching English in the Two-Year College* 12 (1985): 22–31. Assignments in a freshman course follow Rosenblatt's reading model and Moffett's writing model.

LAMBERT, JUDITH R. "Summaries: A Focus for Basic Writers." *Journal of Developmental Education.* 8 (1984): 10–12, 32. Describes various advantages of teaching students to summarize.

LOOKING BACK

The use of James Playsted Wood's piece on advertising in this section reinforces the interconnectedness of reading and writing. This section reminds students that what they are doing is a continuation of the process begun in chapter 1 (Critical Thinking and Reading).

Writing a Summary

- Read your source with care, putting into practice strategies discussed in 1e, reading to understand.

- Determine the purpose of the source—for instance, to inform, explain, argue, justify, defend, compare, contrast, or illustrate.

- Summarize the thesis. Based on the notes you have made and the phrases or sentences you have highlighted while reading, restate the author's main point in your own words. In this statement, refer to the author by name; indicate the author's purpose (e.g., to argue or inform); and refer to the title.

- Summarize the body of the text. STRATEGY 1: Write a one- or two-sentence summary of every paragraph. Summarize points important to supporting the author's thesis. Omit minor points and omit illustrations. Avoid the temptation to translate phrase for phrase from sentences in the text. STRATEGY 2: Identify sections (groupings of related paragraphs) and write a two- or three-sentence summary of each section.

- Study your paragraph or section summaries. Determine the ways in which the paragraphs or sections work together to support the thesis.

- Write the summary. Join your paragraph or section summaries with your summary of the thesis, emphasizing the relationship between the parts of the text and the thesis.

- Revise for clarity and for style. Quote sparingly. Provide transitions where needed.

1e), by James Playsted Wood. You may want to reread the selection so that you understand the preparations for summary that follow.

Prepare: Make notes for a summary.

The notes below are based on the advice offered in the preceding box, "Writing a Summary." Notice that the writer begins by observing the purpose of the selection—to argue—and then incorporates that purpose into a one-sentence summary of Wood's thesis. Notice, as well, that the writer prepares one-sentence summaries for each paragraph in sections 1 and 2.

PURPOSE   to argue

THESIS   In "The Merits of Advertising," James Playsted Wood argues that advertising is an honest form of communication because it openly announces its intentions and because advertisers wish to avoid government penalties for dishonesty.

IDENTIFY SECTIONS

Section 1 (¶s 1–6): Advertising, an honest form of communication

¶1: Advertising is an honest form of communication.

¶2: Advertising states its intentions openly—to persuade consumers to buy, by any means necessary.

¶3: Advertisers will sell anything, and they will use psychological tactics: they will "entice," "soothe or excite," "frighten," or "order or coax."

¶4: Advertising makes each consumer the object of attention, which is flattering.

¶5: Advertisements carry their own warning—beware, I'm trying to separate you from your money. Consumers enjoy the danger of ads.

¶6: Advertisements are generally honest in their claims for a product's superiority.

Section 2 (¶s 7–10): Regulations and agencies keep advertiser honest

¶7: Advertisers stay honest, not to provide an example of moral behavior but to avoid stiff penalties for illegal conduct.

¶8: Various agencies, including the Federal Trade Commission, set rigorous standards for advertisers, who face prosecution if they violate these standards.

¶9: Two laws—the Wiley Law and the Wheeler-Lea Act—extended federal oversight to advertisers' claims about food, drugs, and cosmetics.

¶10: Even with stringent standards governing their behavior, advertisers remain their own strictest regulators—not out of altruism but out of self-interest.

Write the summary.

Join paragraph- or section-summaries to the thesis and emphasize the relationship of parts.

In "The Merits of Advertising," James P. Wood argues that advertising is honest because it openly announces its intentions and because advertisers wish to avoid government penalties for dishonesty. According to Wood, an advertisement is in its very presence a warning to consumers, saying in effect: I am going to separate you from your money. Wood believes that consumers enjoy flirting with the danger implied by such a statement, and that consumers are flattered by the advertiser's lavish attentions. Advertising is honest for a second reason, as well: if it were dishonest, advertisers would find themselves in trouble. Wood claims that various laws (such as the Wiley Law and the Wheeler-Lea Act, for foods and drugs) along with various agencies (such as the Fed-

GROUP ACTIVITY

It can be extremely useful for students to compare summaries. Ask them to share their summaries in small groups, comparing them for *content*: length, main points, detail, and the like. When there are differences, each student should try to defend his or her choice. In articulating their reasons, students will come to a better understanding of what constitutes an effective summary.

ADDITIONAL EXERCISE A

ACROSS THE CURRICULUM Choose a brief section from a textbook in one of your other courses. (It would be doubly helpful if you chose something you're studying at the moment.) Using the guidelines from the box in section 2a-3, write a summary of the section. Then think about how you understood the section before you actually summarized it and how you understand it afterward. Write a brief paragraph explaining what you learned through summarizing.

eral Trade Commission) set standards for the work of advertisers, who face prosecution if they violate these standards. But even with stringent regulations governing their actions, advertisers remain their own strictest regulators, says Wood—not out of altruism but out of self-interest.

EXERCISE 1

Based on your close reading of Charles O'Neil's defense of advertising (1e-3, Exercise 5) and on the notes you made while reading that selection, write a summary. Follow the advice given in this section, particularly in the box in 2a-3. You might want to work with these section designations for O'Neil's discussion: Section 1: Criticisms of advertising; Section 2: A defense of advertising.

EXERCISE 2

Based on the advice given in this section, read and write a summary of Jeffrey Schrank's "The Language of Advertising Claims" (2c-3) in this chapter.

2b Writing an evaluation

In an **evaluation** you judge the effectiveness and reliability of a text and discuss the extent to which you agree or disagree with its author. Consider the following assignments, which call for evaluation.

SOCIOLOGY   Write a review of Christopher Lasch's *Culture of Narcissism.*

HISTORY   In "Everyman His Own Historian," Carl L. Becker argues for a definition of history as "the memory of things said and done." Based on your reading in this course, evaluate Becker's definition.

PHYSICS   Write a review of *Surely You're Joking, Mr. Feynman!*

Writing an evaluation formalizes the process of reading to evaluate, which, in turn, depends on reading to understand and to respond (see 1f, 1e). Evaluation will always entail summary writing (see 2a), since before you can reasonably agree or disagree with an author's work or can determine its effectiveness, you must show that you understand and can restate it.

1 Setting goals for writing an evaluation

You have two primary goals when writing to evaluate, and both depend on a critical, comprehensive reading:

EXERCISE 1

Individual answers

EXERCISE 2

Individual answers

TEACHING IDEAS

As students move from critical reading to critical writing, a journal can be most helpful. Anne Berthoff suggests (in the essay cited on page 39) that students keep a notebook in which they record initial observations, questions, comments on one side, and then *respond* to those notes on the other side. The result is a conversation of sorts—the right side in dialogue with the left. Such a journal is the ideal place for students to make the transition between reading and writing. In fact, in addition to the dialogue described above, the journal can also include summaries and evaluative notes. Keeping these notes in a designated notebook rather than on any available scrap of paper lends them an air of permanence.

ESL ALERT

ESL students from Asian and Middle Eastern countries may be disturbed by the concept of evaluation of a source. They will not take for granted the necessity to do so, and the latter, especially, may have attitudes toward journalistic sources which diverge dramatically from Western attitudes.

- Judge the effectiveness of the author's presentation. Your concern is on the quality of the presentation, not (for the moment) on your agreement or disagreement with the author.
- Agree and/or disagree with the author, and explain your responses.

2 Understanding techniques for writing an evaluation

The basic pattern of evaluation is: (1) offer a judgment about the text; (2) refer to a specific passage—summarize, quote, or paraphrase; and (3) explain your judgment in light of the passage referred to. If you can remember these components of evaluation, you will help to establish your authority as someone whose insights a reader can trust.

Prepare: Make notes on the effectiveness of the presentation.

You will evaluate the effectiveness and reliability of a presentation according to the author's purpose for writing. If the author is arguing a position, you bring one set of criteria, or standards of judgment, to bear on the text; if the author is informing—providing explanations or presenting procedures or descriptions—you bring to bear another set of criteria. You can use certain criteria for evaluating any text.

CRITERIA FOR TEXTS THAT INFORM *or* PERSUADE

Use the following criteria to judge the effectiveness of any text. Remember: when using criteria to evaluate a text, support your evaluation by referring to and discussing a specific passage.

ACCURACY   Are the author's facts accurate?

DEFINITIONS   Have terms important to the discussion been clearly defined—and if not, has lack of definition confused matters?

DEVELOPMENT   Does each part of the presentation seem well developed, satisfying to you in the extent of its treatment? Is each main point adequately illustrated and supported with evidence?

CRITERIA FOR TEXTS THAT INFORM

When an author writes to inform, you can evaluate the presentation based on any of the preceding criteria as well as on the ones discussed in this section. Remember: when using criteria to evaluate a text, support your evaluation by referring to and discussing a specific passage.

AUDIENCE   Is the author writing for a clearly defined audience who will know what to do with the information presented? Is the author consistent in presenting information to one audience?

CLARITY   How clear has the author been in defining and explaining? Is information presented in a way that is useful? Will readers be able to understand an explanation or follow a procedure?

ADDITIONAL EXERCISE B

Sometimes it's difficult to separate the content of a selection from its presentation; if you don't like or agree with what an author is saying, often you don't give the author credit for a well-written piece. In order to force yourself to consider presentation, scan some brief opinion pieces in current newspapers and magazines and find a selection with which you disagree—strongly, if possible. Then analyze the author's presentation based on the guidelines in section 2b-2.

PROCEDURE   Has the author presented the stages of a process? Is the reader clear about the purpose of the process, about who does it and why?

CRITERIA FOR TEXTS THAT PERSUADE

When an author writes to persuade, you can evaluate the presentation based on any of the preceding criteria as well as on the ones that follow. Remember: when using the following (or any) criteria to evaluate a text, support your evaluation by referring to and discussing specific passages.

FAIRNESS   If the issue being discussed is controversial, has the author presented opposing points of view? Has the author seriously considered and responded to these points? (See 6e.)

LOGIC   Has the author adhered to standards of logic? Has the author avoided, for instance, fallacies such as personal attacks and faulty generalization? (See 6h.)

EVIDENCE   Do facts and examples fairly represent the available data on the topic? Are the author's facts and examples current? Has the author included negative examples? (See 6h.)

AUTHORITY   Are the experts that the author refers to qualified to speak on the topic? Are the experts neutral? (See 6d-3 and 6h.)[2]

Prepare: Make notes on your agreement and disagreement with the author.

By applying the criteria above, you may decide that a selection is well written. Just the same, you may disagree with the author in part or in whole, or you may agree. In either case, you should examine the reasons for your reactions. For instance, in the upcoming example evaluation of James Playsted Wood's piece in chapter 1, the student writer will on the one hand admire, and agree with, Wood's statement that an advertisement "blazons its intent" by saying, "Come buy! Come buy!" On the other hand, the writer will disagree with Wood's argument that advertising is honest.

Whatever your reaction to a text, you should (1) identify an author's views, pointing out particular passages where these views are apparent; (2) identify your own views; and (3) examine the basis on which you and the author agree or disagree. For the most part, you can explain agreements and disagreements by examining both your assumptions and the author's. Recall from chapter 1 that an assumption is a fundamental belief that shapes the opinions people develop. Here is a format for distinguishing your views from an author's. (You will see an example of note making that follows this format in the next section.)

Author's view on topic X:

My view:

ADDITIONAL EXERCISE C

Using the newspaper or magazine selection you analyzed for presentation in Additional Exercise B, list the author's assumptions and your reactions according to the guidelines in section 2b-2.

---

[2]In 6h you will find an extended discussion of evaluating arguments.

Author's assumption:

My assumption:

Prepare: Organize your notes and gain a general impression.

Once you have prepared for writing an evaluation by making notes, review your material and try to develop an overall impression of the reading. In writing an evaluation, you will have space enough to review at least two, but probably not more than four or five, aspects of an author's work. Therefore, be selective in the points you choose to evaluate. Review your notes concerning quality of the presentation and extent of your agreement with the author; select the points that will best support your overall impression of the reading. As with any piece of formal writing, plan your evaluation with care. If you are going to discuss three points concerning a selection, do so in a particular order, for good reasons. Readers will expect a logical, well-developed discussion.

3 Applying techniques for writing evaluations

James Playsted Wood's "Merits of Advertising" (1e-1) provides an opportunity to practice evaluating a text. The first step of evaluation, writing a summary, was completed early in this chapter (2a-3). You may

CRITICAL DECISIONS

Challenge and be challenged: Writing evaluations

When you evaluate a text and particularly when you respond to the text, you can choose to have a moment of real contact with an author—or not. What distinguishes real contact from a pat, uninvolved response?

- Real contact with an author invites you to "suspend disbelief." You allow yourself for a moment to accept what the author is saying as true, probable, or desirable. For a moment, at least, you believe. Then you respond.

- In your moment of belief, what did you feel? How did the author's view affect you? Investigate your responses, especially the more volatile ones—these suggest that the author has touched a nerve.

- Reconsider your response. Might you allow the author's views to change yours? When you can entertain this question seriously, you are letting the text challenge you.

- Form your response into a challenge, and direct that challenge at the author. How do you imagine the author responding?

Devise an action plan: Accept a moment of real contact with an author whose work you are evaluating. Let your evaluation reflect this encounter.

REFERENCES

BERTHOFF, ANNE E. "A Curious Triangle and the Double-Entry Notebook: Or, How Theory Can Help Us Teach Reading and Writing." *The Making of Meaning: Metaphors, Models, and Maxims for Writing Teachers.* Upper Montclair, NJ: Boynton/Cook, 1981. In a double-entry notebook, or dialogic journal, students respond to readings and then respond at length to their original responses.

CARELLA, MICHAEL J. "Philosophy as Literacy: Teaching College Students to Read Critically and Write Cogently." *CCC* 34 (1983): 57–61. An approach to evaluating philosophical arguments without merely summarizing them.

MCCORMICK, KATHLEEN. "Teaching Critical Thinking and Writing." *The Writing Instructor* 2 (1983): 137–44. Critiquing flawed essays can help students develop skills of analysis and evaluation.

HAHN, STEPHEN. "Counter-Statement: Using Written Dialogue to Develop Critical Thinking and Writing." *CCC* 38 (1987): 97–100. Using debate can help students evaluate assumptions and opinions.

find it useful to reread Wood's discussion before continuing here. Two questions will help to organize your thinking for an evaluation: (1) How effective and reliable is the author's presentation? (2) Do I agree with the author? Answers to one or both of these questions can provide the basis on which to write an evaluation.

How effective and reliable is the author's presentation?

In 2b-2 you found ten criteria, or standards of judgment, on which to determine the effectiveness and reliability of a text: accuracy, definitions, development, audience, clarity, procedure, fairness, logic, evidence, and authority. What follows is an example of how one of these criteria—logic—applies to Wood's discussion. This evaluation assumes that Wood is arguing—trying to convince readers that advertising is honest for two reasons: because ads openly declare their intentions and because advertisers must follow government regulations.

DEFINITIONS

Wood argues that "advertising is honest." And inasmuch as advertisements openly declare their intention to separate our money from us, ads *are* honest. But Wood broadens his definition and wants to suggest that ads are honest in all respects. This simply isn't so: many ads consist of claims that are not supported with verifiable facts, and many aim at the subconscious mind, not directly—and openly—at the conscious mind. Wood twists the meaning of *honesty* in this selection.

Writing an Evaluation

■ Introduce the topic and author: one paragraph.

One sentence in the introduction should hint at your general impression of the piece.

■ Summarize the author's work: one to three paragraphs.

If brief, the summary can be joined to the introduction.

■ Briefly review the key points in the author's work that you will evaluate: one paragraph.*

■ Identify key points in the author's presentation; discuss each in detail: three to six paragraphs.

If you are evaluating the quality of the author's presentation, state your criteria for evaluation explicitly; if you are agreeing or disagreeing with opinions, try to identify assumptions (yours and the author's) underlying these.

■ Conclude with your overall assessment of the author's work.

*The order of parts in the written evaluation may not match the actual order of writing. You may be unable to write this third section of the evaluation without first having evaluated the author's key points—the next section. The evaluation will take shape over multiple drafts.

Do I agree with the author?

React to the texts that you read (see 1f). Point to specific passages that demonstrate the author's view; summarize that view and your response to it; and then explain the assumptions underlying both your view and the author's. Here's an example:

WOOD'S VIEW ¶s 1–6	Advertisements are an honest form of communication.
MY VIEW	Even though Wood is right that ads scream at you, "I'm going to make you buy," ads are not necessarily honest.
WOOD'S ASSUMPTION	An act that is honest in its intentions is honest, generally.
MY ASSUMPTION	A person's warning to harm someone does not make the act of inflicting harm honest or admirable.

Evaluation of James Wood's "Merits of Advertising"

Walk into a store or down a street, open a newspaper or a magazine, turn on the television: everywhere we look, we are overwhelmed by advertisements. Our consumer economy is based on selling, and in such an economy both producers and consumers depend on advertising as a medium that transmits information, along with an obvious message: BUY! Unless ads are blatantly false in the claims they make for a product, people expect a certain amount of overstatement. People also expect advertisers to sidestep discussions of a product's weaknesses.

We all understand the game: "You'll get mostly the truth here," an ad seems to say, "but perhaps not the whole truth." Magazines such as <u>Consumer Reports</u> have gained wide circulation, in part, because people value an independent ("honest") judgment of the worth and durability of various consumer goods. No one expects to find particularly honest claims in advertisements. It comes as something of a surprise, therefore, when James P. Wood calls advertisements "perhaps the most honest form of major present-day journalism."

Side notes (right margin):

Two-paragraph introduction: 1st ¶—ads in our society

Introduction of "honesty" as an element in the upcoming evaluation

Hint of criticism to come

In "The Merits of Advertising," Wood argues
that advertising is honest because it openly announces its intentions and because advertisers
wish to avoid government penalties for dishonesty. According to Wood, an advertisement is in
its very presence a warning to consumers, saying
in effect: I am going to separate you from your
money. Wood believes that consumers enjoy flirting with the danger implied by such a statement, and that consumers are flattered by the
advertiser's lavish attentions. Advertising is
honest for a second reason, as well: if it were
dishonest, advertisers would find themselves in
trouble. Wood claims that various laws (such as   Summary
the Wiley Law and the Wheeler-Lea Act, for
foods and drugs) along with various agencies
(such as the Federal Trade Commission) set standards for the work of advertisers, who face
prosecution if they violate these standards. But
even with stringent regulations governing their
actions, advertisers remain their own strictest
regulators, says Wood--not out of altruism but
out of self-interest.

Wood is correct to observe that advertise-
ments announce that they are going to persuade   Preview of
us to spend money. Wood assumes, however, that   key point in
this announcement alone qualifies advertisements   evaluation
as honest and renders the advertiser's efforts
to "entice," "soothe or excite," "frighten," or   Author's
"order or coax" consumers likewise honest. Ad-   assumption
vertisers must be careful to break no laws--they   noted
cannot make fraudulent claims, or they risk
legal action. But this side of outright lying,
is all the information that advertisers load
into their ads (as well as the information they
withhold) a demonstration of honesty? Based on
the view that a consumer who is forewarned is
forearmed, Wood seems to think so.

But this view is flawed. An ad that announces that it is going to take someone's
money--and then succeeds through devious psycho-

logical means--is <u>not</u> honest. So much depends on
<u>how</u> the money is gotten. Recently, some adver-
tisers have begun appealing to male consumers
with photos of five-year-old girls, posed sug-
gestively. Is this honest? Apparently it's
legal, but the appeal is vulgar and arguably
damaging to the children being posed as well as
being destructive to important social values.
The appeal is also based on a subconscious need
that advertisers feel some men have for seeing
women as young girls. Such ads do not state
these needs directly, but they nonetheless suggest them. Tactics like these seek to bury a
message rather than deliver it directly. Tactics
like these are <u>dis</u>honest.

> The evaluator's competing assumption is provided

    Wood claims too much for his definition of
honesty. He is right to say that advertisements
are honest when it comes to announcing their
motive. Yes--ads want to separate us from our
money. But Wood tries to broaden this one use
of the word <u>honesty</u> to include others: for instance, that honest communication is <u>direct</u> communication; or that an honest claim should be
supported by verifiable facts. Very often, advertisements ignore both types of honesty. For
instance, take two claims common to advertising:
can all gasolines advertised as "best" be best?
Does an aspirin manufacturer's claim that "we
give you more for your money" count as honest
when consumers are not told that "more" refers
to the starch in the aspirin pill, not to the
active ingredient? These are not big lies, but
they are lies and they are representative. Misleading words and phrases such as these are
commonplace in the world of advertising.

> Agreement—but mostly disagreement—with the author over the definition of *honesty*

    Much as I enjoy and agree with Wood's spir-
ited description of advertising's bold intentions and agree with his claim that advertisements scream "Come buy!" I do not accept his
calling advertisements <u>honest</u>. A consumer culture such as ours depends on advertising to

function. We are so used to advertisers stretching the truth to promote their products that we
no longer see the stretching as an offense to
honesty. But for Wood to claim that advertisements are honest is to ask too much of that
word. Advertisements are not honest. They are
"more or less" <u>honest</u> or, as Wood himself
writes, they are "basically" honest. Let's not
make advertising into a virtue. Advertising is
necessary, and it is no evil. But neither is it
particularly honest.

Conclusion

EXERCISE 3

Individual responses

GROUP ACTIVITY

Students who have yet to become entirely comfortable with active reading may find Exercise 3
a bit frustrating—it will look to them as though
every possible opinion and assumption that
could be mentioned already has been mentioned. To help such students along, turning this
exercise into a group endeavor might be helpful.
A group activity can also stimulate discussion of
opinions among those who are able to do the exercise on their own.

EXERCISE 4

Individual responses

NOTE TO THE INSTRUCTOR

This book reserves the term *analysis* to denote
what a writer generates (as in 2c) when applying
some theory or principle systematically to a text
or to an experience. Some teachers may also use
the term *analysis* to denote the reader's effort to
understand a text by studying its structure and
determining where the main point is placed and
exactly where that point is supported. Here that
effort is incorporated into the activity of reading
to understand (see 1e).

EXERCISE 3

Write an evaluation of Charles O'Neil's defense of advertising, which
you read in chapter 1, Exercise 5. If you have not already done so, you
should complete Exercises 5, 6, and 7 in chapter 1 so that in beginning
this exercise you will already have read to understand, respond to, and
evaluate O'Neil's discussion. In evaluating O'Neil, you may want to
consider these questions: (1) How effective is the defense that "advertising is a reflection of society"? (2) What is your view of the gun analogy—that like a gun, advertising is a neutral tool? (3) To what extent
does O'Neil acknowledge that advertisements might help to shape social behavior and values as well as reflect them? (4) According to
O'Neil, how gullible is the American public? Do you agree with O'Neil
on this point?

EXERCISE 4

Following the advice in this section, evaluate the essay by Jeffrey
Schrank (see 2c-3).

2c Writing an analysis

An **analysis** is an investigation that you conduct by applying a principle or definition to an activity or to an object in order to see how that activity or object works, what it might mean, or why it might be significant.
Analysis enables you to make interpretations. You might analyze, for instance, an event, condition, behavior, painting, novel, play, or television
show. As an illustration of the range of ways analysis can be used, read
the following four assignments from different disciplines. Notice how
each asks students to apply a principle or a definition.

SOCIOLOGY   Write an essay in which you place yourself in American
            society by locating both your absolute position and relative

rank on each single criterion of social stratification used by Lenski & Lenski. For each criterion, state whether you have attained your social position by yourself or if you have "inherited" that status from your parents.

LITERATURE Apply principles of Jungian psychology—that is, an Archetypal approach to literature—to Hawthorne's "Young Goodman Brown." In your reading of the story, apply Jung's concepts of the *shadow, persona,* and *anima.*

PHYSICS Use Newton's Second Law ($F = ma$) to analyze the acceleration of a fixed pulley, from which two weights hang: m_1 (.45 kg) and m_2 (.90 kg). Having worked the numbers, explain in a paragraph the principle of Newton's law and your method of applying it to solve a problem. Assume your reader is not comfortable with mathematical explanations: do not use equations in your paragraph.

FINANCE Using Guilford C. Babcock's "Concept of Sustainable Growth" [*Financial Analysts Journal* 26 (May–June 1970): 108–114], analyze the stock price appreciation of the XYZ Corporation, figures for which are attached.

In these assignments, students are asked to analyze themselves (their place in society), a short story, the acceleration of a pulley, and the stock performance of a corporation. In every discipline, certain principles and definitions play a key role in helping researchers to pose questions from a particular point of view, in order to better understand the activities and objects under study. Professors will assign analyses to determine the extent to which you have understood principles and definitions important to your coursework. A key test of understanding is *application:* can you apply what you have learned to new situations? By writing an analysis, you show that you can. Analysis builds on skills of reading to understand (1e) and writing summaries (2a).

1 Setting goals for writing an analysis

An analysis should show readers how an activity or object works, what it might mean, or why it is significant. The specific goals of analysis are to:

- Understand a principle or definition and demonstrate your understanding by using it to study an activity or an object.
- Thoroughly apply this principle or definition to all significant parts of the activity or object under study.
- Create for the reader a sense that your analysis makes the activity or object being studied understandable—if not for the first time, then at least in a new way.

TEACHING IDEAS

If your schedule permits, having students read the three full analyses of *The Wizard of Oz* cited on this page can be a good stimulus to class discussion. Even as they write their own analyses, students need to appreciate that other analyses of identical material are possible, given other criteria. Competing analyses of the same text, in this case Dorothy's dream journey to Oz, make this point explicitly.

ESL ALERT

All allusions to literature, films, history, current events, and the like are by definition culturally biased. What is meant by cultural literacy is so variant that the instructor would be well advised to confirm that students have see *The Wizard of Oz*.

TEACHING IDEAS

ACROSS THE CURRICULUM Ask students to investigate how analyses are conducted in a discipline they are studying. The point of the exercise is twofold: for students to discover that analysis is an activity fundamental to academic inquiry; and for students to see that material within any disciplinary setting can be analyzed in multiple ways. Depending on the method used, information generated by analyses will differ, not only in a writing classroom but in other classrooms as well. Students could report on their findings orally.

Different analyses lead to different interpretations.

What you discover through analysis depends entirely on which principles you apply to the activity or object under study. One event or text, analyzed according to different principles, will yield different interpretations. For example, over the years many writers have analyzed the L. Frank Baum classic, *The Wizard of Oz*, and the movie based on it. These writers have arrived at different interpretations, according to the different principles or definitions they applied to the story. Consider three specific insights into *The Wizard of Oz*, based on an application of three different principles.

PSYCHOLOGICAL ANALYSIS

At the dawn of adolescence, the very time she should start to distance herself from Aunt Em and Uncle Henry, the surrogate parents who raised her on their Kansas farm, Dorothy Gale experiences a hurtful reawakening of her fear that these loved ones will be rudely ripped from her, especially her Aunt (Em—M for Mother!). [Harvey Greenberg, *The Movies on Your Mind* (New York: Dutton, 1975).]

POLITICAL ANALYSIS

[*The Wizard of Oz*] was originally written as a political allegory about grass-roots protest. It may seem harder to believe than Emerald City, but the Tin Woodsman is the industrial worker, the Scarecrow [is] the struggling farmer, and the Wizard is the president, who is powerful only as long as he succeeds in deceiving the people. [Peter Dreier, "Oz Was Almost Reality," *Cleveland Plain Dealer* 3 Sept. 1989.]

LITERARY ANALYSIS

The Kansas described by Frank Baum is a depressing place. Everything in it is gray as far as the eye can see: the prairie is gray, and so is the house in which Dorothy lives. As for Auntie Em, "The sun and wind . . . had taken the sparkle from her eyes and left them a sober gray; they had taken the red from her cheeks and lips, and they were gray also. She was thin and gaunt, and never smiled now." And "Uncle Henry never laughed. . . . He was gray also, from his long beard to his rough boots." The sky? It was "even grayer than usual." [Salman Rushdie, "Out of Kansas," *New Yorker* 11 May 1992.]

Different analytical approaches yield different insights, and no analysis can be ultimately correct. There will be as many different interpretations of *The Wizard of Oz*, for instance, as there are principles of analysis; and each, potentially, has something to teach us. Not every analysis will be equally useful, however. An analysis is useful or authoritative to the extent that a writer (1) clearly defines a principle or definition to be applied; (2) applies this principle or definition thoroughly and systematically; and in so doing (3) reveals new and convincing insights into the activity or object being analyzed.

2   Understanding the techniques for writing an analysis

Prepare: Turn elements of a principle or definition into questions—and *probe*.

You can prepare for an analysis by developing questions based on the definition or principle you are going to apply, and then by directing these questions to the activity or object under study. Once you have posed questions and assembled notes, you are ready to select from your insights and organize your written analysis.

In an essay that analyzed television watching as a form of addiction, writer Marie Winn turned elements of her definition of addiction into questions.[3] Here is one element of that definition:

> [J]ust as alcoholics are only inchoately aware of their addiction, feeling that they control their drinking more than they really do . . . people similarly overestimate their control over television watching. Even as they put off other activities to spend hour after hour watching television, they feel they could easily resume living in a different, less passive style. But somehow or other while the television set is present in their homes, the click doesn't sound. With television pleasures available, those other experiences seem less attractive, more difficult somehow.

ELEMENT OF DEFINITION   An addict needs to repeat the addictive behavior.
QUESTION FOR ANALYSIS   Can television viewers stop watching the tube?

The author based a series of related questions on an extended definition of *addiction*. She then methodically directed these questions to the activity she wished to analyze. Just as this author has done, you can prepare for writing an analysis by turning the principles and definitions you are working with into questions and directing them to the activity or object you wish to study—regardless of the discipline in which you are working.

3   Applying techniques for writing analyses

The most common error in writing analyses is to present your readers with a summary only. Summary is naturally a *part* of analysis: you will need to summarize the object or activity you are examining and the principle or definition with which you are working, if this is not known to your readers. You must then take the next step and *apply* the principle or definition, using it as an investigative tool.

---

[3]Marie Winn, "The Plug-in Drug," *The Plug-in Drug* (New York: Viking, 1977) 21.

TEACHING IDEAS

Students can bring print advertisements to class. Using Schrank's criteria, groups of three or four can analyze selected ads and then present their analyses to the class for discussion. You may want to photocopy and distribute a single ad to several groups for their analysis. In a teacher-led discussion, groups would then share analyses and explore why different people using the same criteria might arrive at different analytical understandings of an object (in this case, the advertisement) under study.

Writing an Analysis

- Introduce and summarize the activity or object to be analyzed. Whatever parts of this activity or object you intend to analyze should be mentioned here.

- Introduce and summarize the key definition or principle that will form the basis of your analysis.

- Analyze. Systematically apply elements of this definition or principle to parts of the activity or object under study. Part by part, discuss what you find.

- Conclude by reviewing all the parts you have analyzed. To what extent has your application of the definition or principle helped you to explain how the object works, what it might mean, or why it is significant?

Prepare to write an analysis of advertising by reading Jeffrey Schrank's "The Language of Advertising Claims." Schrank believes that advertisers present consumers with "pseudo-information," and he discusses ten techniques that advertisers use to blur the line between truth and falsehood in their claims about products. Schrank suggests that readers who understand these techniques can use them as principles by which to analyze advertisements—which is what you will be asked to do in Exercise 5, following the article.

The Language of Advertising Claims

JEFFREY SCHRANK

High school students, and many teachers, are notorious believers in their immunity to advertising. These naive inhabitants of consumerland believe that advertising is childish, dumb, a bunch of lies, and influences only the vast hordes of the less sophisticated. Their own purchases are made purely on the basis of value and desire, with advertising playing only a minor supporting role. They know about Vance Packard and his "hidden persuaders" and the adwriter's psychosell and bag of persuasive magic. They are not impressed.

Advertisers know better. Although few people admit to being greatly influenced by ads, surveys and sales figures show that a well-designed advertising campaign has dramatic effects. A logical conclusion is that advertising works below the level of conscious awareness and it works even on those who claim immunity to its message. Ads are designed to have an effect while being laughed at, belittled, and all but ignored.

A person unaware of advertising's claim on him or her is precisely the one most defenseless against the adwriter's attack. Advertisers delight in an audience which believes ads to be harmless nonsense, for such an audience is rendered defenseless by its belief that there is no attack taking place. The purpose of a classroom study of advertising is to raise the level of awareness about the persuasive techniques used in ads. One way to do this is to analyze ads in microscopic detail. Ads can be studied to detect their psychological hooks, they can be used to gauge values and hidden desires of the common person, they can be studied for their use of symbols, color, and imagery. But perhaps the simplest and most direct way to study ads is through an analysis of the language of the advertising claim.

The "claim" is the verbal or print part of an ad that makes some claim of superiority for the product being advertised. After studying claims, students should be able to recognize those that are misleading and accept as useful information those that are true. A few of these claims are downright lies, some are honest statements about a truly superior product, but most fit into the category of neither bold lies nor helpful consumer information. They balance on the narrow line between truth and falsehood by a careful choice of words.

The reason so many ad claims fall into this category of pseudo-information is that they are applied to parity products, products in which all or most of the brands available are nearly identical. Since no one superior product exists, advertising is used to create the illusion of superiority. The largest advertising budgets are devoted to parity products such as gasoline, cigarettes, beer and soft drinks, soaps and various headache and cold remedies.

The first rule of parity involves the Alice in Wonderlandish use of the words "better" and "best." In parity claims, "better" means "best" and "best" means "equal to." If all the brands are identical they must all be equally good, the legal minds have decided. So "best" means that the product is as good as the other superior products in its category. When Bing Crosby declares Minute Maid Orange Juice "the best there is" he means it is as good as the other orange juices you can buy.

The word "better" has been legally interpreted to be a comparative and therefore becomes a clear claim of superiority. Bing could not have said that Minute Maid is "better than any other orange juice." "Better" is a claim of superiority. The only time "better" can be used is when a product does indeed have superiority over other products in its category or when the better is used to compare the product with something other than competing brands. An orange juice could therefore claim to be "better than a vitamin pill," or even "the better breakfast drink."

The second rule of advertising claim analysis is simply that if any product is truly superior, the ad will say so very clearly and offer some kind of convincing evidence of the superiority. If an ad hedges the least bit about a product's advantage over the competition you can strongly suspect it is not superior—maybe equal to but not better. You will never hear a gasoline company say "we will give you four miles per gallon more in your car than any other brand." They would love to make such a claim, but it would not be true. Gasoline is a parity product.

TEACHING IDEAS

Schrank writes that aside from studying the language of advertisements, one can study ads "to detect their psychological hooks, . . . to gauge values and hidden desires of the common person, . . . [and to study] symbols, color, and imagery." Schrank is observing that ads are susceptible to multiple analyses, and certainly a week or more of class might profitably be devoted to just this. One group of students could analyze an ad or series of ads using Schrank's criteria; a second group could work with Goffman's *Gender Advertisements* (New York: Harper, 1979); a third group could use Arthur Asa Berger's "Analyzing Signs and Sign Systems" in *Signs in Contemporary Culture* (Salem, WI: Sheffield, 1989); and a final group could conduct a gender-based analysis. (Other materials that provide criteria for analysis would work just as well.) Group work would lead to a series of presentations on the same material, and the exercise could help to reinforce the lesson that different analytical perspectives will yield different analytical insights.

TEACHING IDEAS

In his third paragraph, Schrank writes that "the purpose of a classroom study of advertising is to raise the level of awareness about the persuasive techniques used in ads." Schrank clearly believes that ads are insidious, that they undermine what should be rational discussions about a product's merit. Many students will be sympathetic, but there may be some in class who are more partial to James Playsted Wood's position (1e-1) that ads are honest in that they virtually scream to the consumer: "I will get you to buy this product." Wood believes that consumers do *not* mistake advertisements for rational discussion; therefore, Schrank's criticizing ads on the basis that they are not rational misses an important and obvious point about advertising. If only to play devil's advocate, you could adopt Wood's logic and challenge students on the assumptions underlying Schrank's piece. If one begins with the assumption that ads are not insidious "attacks" (Schrank's word), then how well do Schrank's principles of analysis hold up? You might ask students the extent to which, in their view, people are rational in their buying decisions. Is irrationality *caused* by persuasive ads?

To create the necessary illusion of superiority, advertisers usually resort to one or more of the following ten basic techniques. Each is common and easy to identify.

1. The Weasel Claim

A weasel word is a modifier that practically negates the claim that follows. The expression "weasel word" is aptly named after the egg-eating habits of weasels. A weasel will suck out the inside of an egg, leaving it appear intact to the casual observer. Upon examination, the egg is discovered to be hollow. Words or claims that appear substantial upon first look but disintegrate into hollow meaninglessness on analysis are weasels. Commonly used weasel words include "helps" (the champion weasel); "like" (used in a comparative sense); "virtual" or "virtually"; "acts" or "works"; "can be"; "up to"; "as much as"; "refreshes"; "comforts"; "tackles"; "fights"; "come on"; "the feel of"; "the look of"; "looks like"; "fortified"; "enriched"; and "strengthened."

Samples of Weasel Claims

"*Helps control* dandruff *symptoms* with *regular use.*" The weasels include "helps control," and possibly even "symptoms," and "regular use." The claim is not "stops dandruff."

"*Leaves dishes virtually* spotless." We have seen so many ad claims that we have learned to tune out weasels. You are supposed to think "spotless," rather than "virtually" spotless.

"Only half the price of *many* color sets." "Many" is the weasel. The claim is supposed to give the impression that the set is inexpensive.

"Tests confirm one mouthwash *best* against mouth odor."

"Hot Nestlé's cocoa is the very *best.*" Remember the "best" *and* "better" routine.

"Listerine *fights* bad breath." "Fights" not "stops."

"Lots of things have changed, but Hershey's *goodness* hasn't." This claim does not say that Hershey's chocolate hasn't changed.

"Bacos, the crispy garnish that tastes just *like* its name."

2. The Unfinished Claim

The unfinished claim is one in which the ad claims the product is better, or has more of something but does not finish the comparison.

Samples of Unfinished Claims

"Magnavox gives you more." More what?

"Anacin: Twice as much of the pain reliever doctors recommend most." This claim fits in a number of categories but it does not say twice as much of what pain reliever.

"Supergloss does it with more color, more shine, more sizzle, more!"

"Coffee-mate gives coffee more body, more flavor." Also note that "body" and "flavor" are weasels.

"You can be sure if it's Westinghouse." Sure of what?

"Scott makes it better for you."

3. The "We're Different and Unique" Claim

This kind of claim states that there is nothing else quite like the product advertised. For example, if Schlitz would add pink food coloring to its beer they could say "There's nothing like new pink Schlitz." The uniqueness claim is supposed to be interpreted by readers as a claim to superiority.

Samples of "We're Different and Unique" Claim

"There's no other mascara like it."
"Only Doral has the unique filter system."
"Cougar is like nobody else's car."
"Either way, liquid or spray, there's nothing else like it."
"If it doesn't say Goodyear, it can't be polyglas." "Polyglas" is a trade name owned by Goodyear. Goodrich or Firestone could make a tire exactly identical to the Goodyear one and yet couldn't call it "polyglas"—a name for fiberglass belts.
"Only Zenith has chromacolor." Same as the "polyglas" gambit. Admiral has solarcolor and RCA has accucolor.

4. The "Water Is Wet" Claim

"Water is wet" claims say something about the product that is true for any brand in that product category (e.g., "Schrank's water is really wet"). The claim is usually a statement of fact, but not a real advantage over the competition.

Samples of "Water Is Wet" Claim

"Mobil: the Detergent Gasoline." Any gasoline acts as a cleaning agent.
"Great Lash increases the diameter of every lash."
"Rheingold, the natural beer." Made from grains and water as are other beers.
"SKIN smells differently on everyone." As do all perfumes.

5. The "So What" Claim

This is the kind of claim to which the careful reader will react by saying "So What?" A claim is made which is true but which gives no real advantage to the product. This is similar to the "water is wet" claim except that it claims an advantage which is not shared by most of the other brands in the product category.

Samples of the "So What" Claim

"Geritol has more than twice the iron of ordinary supplements." But is twice as much beneficial to the body?
"Campbell's gives you tasty pieces of chicken and not one but two chicken stocks." Does the presence of two stocks improve the taste?
"Strong enough for a man but made for a woman." This deodorant claim says only that the product is aimed at the female market.

6. The Vague Claim

The vague claim is simply not clear. This category often overlaps with others. The key to the vague claim is the use of words that are colorful but meaningless, as well as the use of subjective and emotional opinions that defy verification. Most contain weasels.

Samples of the Vague Claim

"Lips have never looked so luscious." Can you imagine trying to prove or disprove such a claim?
"Lipsavers are fun—they taste good, smell good and feel good."
"Its deep rich lather makes hair feel good again."
"For skin like peaches and cream."
"The end of meatloaf boredom."

"Take a bite and you'll think you're eating on the Champs Elysées."
"Winston tastes good like a cigarette should."
"The perfect little portable for all around viewing with all the features of higher priced sets."
"Fleischmann's makes sensible eating delicious."

7. The Endorsement or Testimonial

A celebrity or authority appears in an ad to lend his or her stellar qualities to the product. Sometimes the people will actually claim to use the product, but very often they don't.

Samples of Endorsements or Testimonials

"Joan Fontaine throws a shot-in-the-dark party and her friends learn a thing or two."
"Darling, have you discovered Masterpiece? The most exciting men I know are smoking it." (Eva Gabor)
"Vega is the best handling car in the U.S." This claim was challenged by the FTC, but GM answered that the claim is only a direct quote from *Road and Track* magazine.

8. The Scientific or Statistical Claim

This kind of ad uses some sort of scientific proof or experiment, very specific numbers, or an impressive sounding mystery ingredient.

Samples of Scientific or Statistical Claims

"Wonder Bread helps build strong bodies 12 ways." Even the weasel "helps" did not prevent the FTC from demanding this ad be withdrawn. But note that the use of the number 12 makes the claim far more believable than if it were taken out.
"Easy-Off has 33% more cleaning power than another popular brand." "Another popular brand" often translates as some other kind of oven cleaner sold somewhere. Also the claim does not say Easy-Off works 33% better.
"Special Morning—33% more nutrition." Also an unfinished claim.
"Certs contains a sparkling drop of Retsyn."
"ESSO with HTA."
"Sinarest. Created by a research scientist who actually gets sinus headaches."

9. The "Compliment the Consumer" Claim

This kind of claim butters up the consumer by some form of flattery.

Samples of "Compliment the Consumer" Claim

"We think a cigar smoker is someone special."
"If you do what is right for you, no matter what others do, then RC Cola is right for you."
"You pride yourself on your good home cooking. . . ."
"The lady has taste."
"You've come a long way, baby."

10. The Rhetorical Question

This technique demands a response from the audience. A question is asked and the viewer or listener is supposed to answer in such a way as to affirm the product's goodness.

Samples of the Rhetorical Question

"Plymouth—isn't that the kind of car America wants?"
"Shouldn't your family be drinking Hawaiian Punch?"
"What do you want most from coffee? That's what you get most from Hills."
"Touch of Sweden: could your hands use a small miracle?"

EXERCISE 5

Use one or more of the techniques that Jeffrey Schrank offers as principles for understanding advertising claims to analyze an advertisement. To do so, follow the advice in the preceding section, especially the techniques for turning principles and definitions into questions, 2c-2, and the suggested steps for writing an analysis, 2c-3. Your analysis should (1) clearly define which of Schrank's techniques you will apply; (2) apply these techniques thoroughly and systematically to the advertisement being studied; and (3) reveal for your readers new insights into the advertisement.

2d Writing a synthesis

A **synthesis** is a written discussion in which you gather and present source materials according to a well-defined purpose. In the process of writing a synthesis you answer these questions: (1) Which authors have written on my topic? (2) In what ways can I link the work of these authors to one another and to my own thinking? (3) How can I best use the material I've gathered to create a discussion that supports *my* views? The following assignment calls for synthesis:

SOCIOLOGY   This semester we have read a number of books, articles, and essays on the general topic of marriage: its legal, religious, economic, and social aspects. In a 5-page paper, reflect on these materials and discuss the extent to which they have helped to clarify, or confuse, your understanding of this "sacred institution."

The word *synthesis* does not appear in this assignment; nonetheless, the professor is asking students to gather and discuss sources. Note the importance of the writer here. Given multiple sources, a dozen students working on this sociology assignment would produce a dozen different papers; what would distinguish one paper from the next and make each uniquely valuable is the *particular* insights of each student. You are the most important source in any synthesis. However much material you gather into a discussion, your voice should predominate.

No synthesis is possible without a critical, comprehensive reading of sources. The quality of a synthesis is tied directly to the quality of prior reading. You have the best possible chance of producing a meaningful synthesis when you have read sources to understand (1e), respond (1f), evaluate (1g), and synthesize (1h). At one point or another, a synthesis will draw on all your skills of critical reading and writing, discussed in this and the last chapter; synthesis therefore represents some of the most sophisticated and challenging writing you will do in college.

Ensuring that your voice is heard

When writing a synthesis, avoid letting sources dominate a discussion unless you are being asked to write a literature review (see 39c-2

ACROSS THE CURRICULUM Assume that you're writing papers about the topics that underlie the statements below. The statements are tentative opening lines, but the writer is invisible. Rewrite each statement so that the writer's voice can be heard. (Don't worry about whether or not you'd be able to follow through on the statement; the exercise is designed only to give you practice in making your voice heard among all the sources.)

1. Some corporate executives advocate a hierarchical model, with decisions being made at the top; others espouse a model in which decisions are made collaboratively.
2. Four top analysts have four different opinions on how long the current recession will last.
3. While one group of researchers believes that obesity is the result of specific eating disorders, another group cites studies indicating that heredity is responsible for obesity.
4. Critical opinion is divided on who is the best filmmaker of the eighties: Woody Allen, Francis Ford Coppola, or Bruce Beresford.

—though even in this case your point of view dominates in that you select the articles to be discussed and determine the principles that organize discussion). In its most extreme form, the error of allowing sources to dominate leads to a series of summaries in which the writer, making no attempt at merging sources, disappears. The problem can be avoided if you remember that a synthesis should draw on your insights first, and only then on the insights of others. *A paper organized as a series of summaries of separate sources, introduced by a statement such as "Many authors have discussed topic X," is* not *a synthesis because it makes no attempt to merge ideas.*

Do Not Become Invisible in Your Papers

The danger signs:

1. Your paragraphs are devoted wholly to the work of the authors you are synthesizing.
2. Virtually every sentence introduces someone else's ideas.
3. The impulse to use the first-person *I* never arises.

Instead of writing a string of paragraphs organized around the work of others, write paragraphs organized around your own statements. In the context of a paper on advertising, a discussion organized as summaries of separate sources would leave you invisible. Generally, one needs to read no further than a statement such as the one that follows to know that the writer will never appear.

Several authors have discussed the topic of advertising.

This statement, and the paper likely to be built upon it, is *source based* and exhibits all the danger signals mentioned in the preceding box. By contrast, a paper in which the author is present will show an active, interested mind engaged with the reading material and headed in some clear direction, with a purpose:

The topic of advertising is guaranteed to generate debate whenever it is discussed. It is rare to find a person who does not have strong, specific opinions about advertising and its effects on our culture.

This statement is *writer* based. The writer's purpose and direction are made known, and we sense the reading material will not overshadow the writer. If you find source materials monopolizing your work, reexamine your thesis and make it into a writer-based statement.

1 Setting goals for writing a synthesis

Your goal in writing a synthesis is to create and participate in a discussion, joining your views on a topic to the views of others. Specifically, you want to do the following:

- Understand your purpose for writing.
- Define your topic and your thesis (see 3d).
- Locate the work of others who have written on this topic and read to understand, respond to, and evaluate.
- Forge relationships among sources; link the thinking of others to your own thinking.
- Create a discussion governed by your views; draw on sources as contributors to a discussion that you design and control.

2 Understanding the techniques for writing a synthesis

In writing a synthesis, you will at one point or another write partial summaries, evaluations, and analyses. Synthesis draws on these forms and is larger and more ambitious than any one of them: summary and evaluation treat single sources; analysis is limited to an application of one source (or set of ideas) to a second source; but synthesis merges sources and looks for larger patterns of relation.

Cross-referencing ideas

A synthesis organized by *ideas* shows you to be intellectually present and involved with the material you have gathered. To organize a paper by ideas, you need first to divide the topic into the component parts that the various authors take up in their discussions. These com-

---

A Strategy for Forging Relationships among Sources

1. Read multiple sources on a topic.
2. Subdivide the topic into parts and give each a brief title.
3. Cross-reference your sources for each part.
4. Summarize authors' information or ideas about each part.
5. Identify connections among readings, which may be related by comparison, contrast, example, definition, cause and effect—or by the extent of your agreement or disagreement with particular selections.

---

ponent parts then become the key ideas around which you organize your paper. You can follow this method when your writing is based on library research. Cross-referencing is a necessary step in the process (see 1h-2), once you have identified a component part of a topic and cross-referenced authors' discussions, you are nearly ready to write. In response to Exercise 8 in chapter 1, you worked on completing a note sheet. If you have not completed this assignment, turn back to 1h-2, Exercise 8, and do so now.

Clarifying relationships among authors

Your cross-referenced notes enable you to lay out and examine what several authors have written about *particular* parts of a topic, in this case advertising. Working with what your sources say on a particular point, you can now forge relationships. Sources can be related in a variety of ways, but you will find that patterns emerge, which can be identified by asking several questions.

Which authors agree?

Which authors disagree?

Are there any examples in one source of statements made in another?

Can you offer any definitions?

Are any readings related by cause and effect?

LOOKING BACK

"Broader context" is one of the possible relationships that can be inferred among sources. See 1c for a discussion of how critical thinkers can set an idea in a broader context.

CRITICAL DECISIONS

Set issues in a broader context: Forging relationships

When forging relationships among sources, look for authors who provide a broad context in which to situate the topics you are studying.

- Be alert to historical backgrounds.
  Example: A labor dispute in the garment industry, read about in one source, might be viewed differently when seen in light of a general history of the garment industry, discussed in another source.

- Be alert to broader sets of problems.
  Example: The discussion of sex-role identity in America discussed in one source can be viewed differently when set in the context of cross-cultural studies.

Devise an action plan: Devote an hour or two of concentrated research to seeking out broader contexts in which to view your topic. Understanding broader contexts helps you to place the topic in relation to other topics—which you may or may not choose to investigate. This knowledge is always helpful, if only to let you know the boundaries of the topic you are researching.

In addressing these questions, you need not be limited by the parts of the topic you have already defined. Pose these questions to all the readings as well to see if any new relationships emerge. Refer to Exercise 9, chapter 1 for specific questions for the passages related to advertising. Your responses to these questions will help you prepare to write a paper based on sources.

A strategy for writing syntheses

A paper in which you draw on source materials will usually involve your forging a number of relationships among sources. When you know you will be referring to sources in a paper, consider carefully before you begin writing how various authors will contribute to the points you wish to make. Draw from your preparatory notes. Generally, you can use the guidelines in the box on page 58 for writing a paper that synthesizes source materials.

3   Applying techniques for writing syntheses

Since the writer's own views should predominate in a synthesis, no two syntheses, even if based on the same source materials, should look alike. Still, individuals reading the same sources should be able to agree on the basic ways in which those sources are related. In chapter 1, you read three texts with great care: James Playsted Wood's "The Merits of Advertising" (1e-1), Charles O'Neil's "A Defense of Advertising (1e-3, Exercise 5), and Jean Kilbourne's "The Child as Sex Object" (1g-2, Exercise 7). In this chapter, you read a fourth selection on advertising: Jeffrey Schrank's "The Language of Advertising Claims" (2c-3). Here are several relationships you could establish among these texts.

FORGING RELATIONSHIPS AMONG SOURCES

AGREEMENT   James P. Wood, a defender of advertisements, writes that advertisements are honest in that they say, openly, "We will do anything necessary, within the law, to get you to buy." Jean Kilbourne, a critic of advertising, apparently agrees with this view in the sense that advertisers will stop at nothing—even posing young girls—to secure a sale.

Kilbourne and Schrank agree on the potential of advertisements to do harm. Schrank believes that ads "attack" viewers with "psychological hooks." Kilbourne sees ads helping "to create a climate in which certain [damaging] attitudes and values flourish."

Both Wood and O'Neil believe that a consumer's right to say "No!" to an advertisement excuses advertisers from the charge that they manipulate consumers. Wood says that consumers are "warned" by the ad. O'Neil (quoting

Synthesis: Writing a Paper Based on Sources

- Read sources on the topic; subdivide the topic into parts and infer relationships among parts, cross-referencing sources when possible.
- Clarify relationships among authors by posing these questions:
  Which authors agree?
  Which authors disagree?
  Are there any examples in one source of statements made in another?
  Can I offer any definitions?
  Are any readings related by cause and effect?
- Write a thesis (see 3d) that ensures your voice is heard and that allows you to develop sections of the paper in which you refer to sources.
- Sketch an outline of your paper, organizing your discussion by *idea*, not by summary. Enter the names of authors into your outline along with notes indicating how these authors will contribute to your discussion.
- Write a draft of your paper and revise, following strategies discussed in chapter 4.

	S. I. Hayakawa) finds consumers at least partly responsible for their own behavior.
DISAGREEMENT	Schrank claims that advertisements work at a subconscious level. Wood argues that advertisements are honest and that they openly declare their intentions. Both authors seem to be right. At least as regards their motives, advertisers are open in their attempt to get consumers to buy. But then advertisers frequently employ subtle, even hidden, techniques for persuading consumers.
	Kilbourne and O'Neil suggest that ads are reflections of society. O'Neil does not see advertisers purposefully shaping values. He sees them understanding values as they already exist in society and then repackaging them in ads. Kilbourne believes that advertisers, as the people who reflect social values, also play "an important role in shaping those values." O'Neil believes the mirror of advertising is basically passive and accurate. Kilbourne believes the mirror is active and distorting.
DEFINITIONS	See the "disagreement," above. Wood sees advertising as basically "honest," and O'Neil sees it as a "neutral" tool. Kilbourne and Schrank see advertising as dishonest and as a tool for perpetuating damaging stereotypes. These

contrasting sets of definitions can be combined into one definition of advertising that would include a sense of its contradictions.

EXAMPLES   Wood writes that an "advertisement may entice. It may soothe or excite. It may try to frighten you. It may order or coax." Kilbourne, a critic of ads, agrees and cites the use of young girls as an example of the lengths to which advertisers will go to secure a sale.

CAUSE AND EFFECT   The selections do not establish a clear cause-and-effect link between advertising on the one hand and the changed behavior of consumers on the other. Certainly consumers have a say in whether or not they choose to part with their money. Yet advertisements do entice consumers. Cause and effect is complicated here.

The importance of the writer's views

What you do with the relationships you forge among source materials will depend on your purpose for writing and on the opinions you have come to hold concerning these sources. You and two of your classmates might be able to agree on the ways in which the views of Wood, O'Neil, Kilbourne, and Schrank are related. (You might agree, specifically, on the relationships summarized above.) But your papers, guided by different purposes and different theses, might look nothing alike. In chapter 6 you will find an example synthesis based on three of these sources, plus two others (see the end of 6g). Alison Tschopp, a student at Boston University who is planning to study law, has brought specific concerns to bear on the topic of advertising. Here is the thesis of her argument:

A parent's close involvement with children, not limiting the First Amendment, is the appropriate countermeasure to the power of advertisers.

Alison draws on the work of Wood, O'Neil, Kilbourne, and Schrank according to her own purpose. Based on this thesis you can see clearly that she, and not her source materials, will control the discussion that follows.

> EXERCISE 6
>
> Write a synthesis that draws on the writing of Wood, O'Neil, Kilbourne, and Schrank. Recall that the first goals of synthesis (2d-1) are to know your purpose for writing and to have a well-defined topic and thesis. If you need help getting started on the paper, you may want to write and revise in conjunction with the exercises in chapters 3 and 4, which follow from extended discussions on the writing process. See chapter 3, exercises 1–4, 6, 8, and 9.

EXERCISE 6

Individual answers

CHAPTER 3

Planning, Developing, and Writing a Draft

KEY FEATURES

This chapter introduces students to the practical applications of critical thinking and reading with respect to the writing process. Students will come to understand that it is only through trying out various ideas in drafts that they can develop a clear understanding of just what they want to say in a paper. Both the recursive nature of the writing process and the notion that ideas develop and change during the course of that process are emphasized in this chapter. Particularly helpful is the metaphor of the "writing wheel," which allows students to visualize the essential unity of the entire writing process. The more traditional prewriting concepts of purpose, audience, idea generation, organization, drafting, revising, and the like are covered with a fresh perspective provided by the writing wheel metaphor. In addition, strategies for analyzing audience, generating ideas, narrowing theses, organizing material, and providing unity and coherence are introduced. The development of a student paper on high school football from general ideas through rough draft is provided to illustrate the various stages in the writing process. Sean Hannan's paper—an analysis of the dehumanizing effects of football hero-worship—progresses from journal entries, idea-generating strategies, outlines, and thesis development drafts, offering students clear, relevant examples of precisely the processes they will find themselves going through as they work on their own papers. Reinforcing this focus on students' own writing, exercises throughout the

There may be as many strategies for planning, developing, and writing a draft as there are writers. Just the same, one principle holds true for all: a writer's thoughts take shape through the very act of writing and rewriting. That is, when you write you are also thinking; and when you revise you are thinking again about your topic and clarifying ideas for yourself—and, in the process, for your readers. Experienced writers produce a first draft and then revise at least once.

The three stages of writing are, broadly speaking, distinct. Different activities take place in each stage and the stages unfold more or less in this order: preparing to write, writing, and revising. But the stages also blend into each other. In the middle of a first draft, a writer may pause to revise an important sentence or paragraph, deciding to make one part of her document nearly finished while other parts remain rough or not yet written. In a first draft, the writer may discover new approaches to her topic and may stop to write new lists and make new outlines, activities associated with preparing to write. Typically, writers loop backward and forward through the three stages of writing—several times for any one document. The process of writing is **recursive**: it bends and it circles, and it is illustrated well with a wheel. (See the illustration on page 62.)

3a Discovering your topic, purpose, and audience

1 Understanding your topic

In both college and business, you can expect to be assigned topics for writing and to define topics for yourself. In either case, you will write most efficiently, and with greatest impact, when you write about what you know (or what you can learn in a reasonably brief time); when you

An Overview of the Writing Process

Preparing to write

3a   **Discovering your topic, purpose, and audience.** Know your topic and, if necessary, research it. Know your purpose for writing and use this to generate and organize ideas. Keep specific readers in mind as you write.

3b   **Generating ideas and information.** Use strategies like freewriting or reading to generate the ideas and information on the basis of which you will write your draft.

3c   **Reviewing and categorizing ideas and information.** Review the material you have generated and group like ideas and information into categories.

3d   **Writing a thesis and devising a sketch of your paper.** Study the material you have assembled and write a working thesis, a statement that will give your draft a single, controlling idea. Based on your thesis, sketch your draft.

Writing

3e   **Writing a draft.** Prepare a draft of your document by adopting a strategy suited to your temperament. As you write, expect to depart from your sketch.

Revising

4a   **Early revision: Rediscovering your main idea.** Refine your thesis; use it to revise for unity, coherence, and development. Be sure that the broad sections of your document and the sentences within your paragraphs are coherent and lead logically from one to the next.

4b   **Later revision: Bringing your main idea into focus.** Read and clarify individual sentences. Correct problems with grammar, usage, punctuation, and spelling.

chapter encourage students to work through the writing process using *their own ideas* rather than simply responding to material generated by others.

ESL ALERT

Writing as a process will be an unfamiliar concept to most international students, although teachers in some cultures do in fact "intervene" with help in the stages of composition. Many students, however, may expect instructors to be uninterested in the process, focusing only on the final product. It may be worth explaining clearly what a "draft" is supposed to be; what the responsibilities of teacher and student are in the improvement of early drafts; and what degree of dependency on the instructor (or tutors, peer editors, other readers) is proper. This last point is crucial if later plagiarism problems are to be forestalled.

REFERENCES

LINDEMANN, ERIKA. *A Rhetoric for Writing Teachers.* 2nd ed. New York: Oxford UP, 1987. 11–30. A thorough overview of the complexities involved in the writing process (includes bibliography).

GEBHARDT, RICHARD. "Initial Plans and Spontaneous Composition: Toward a Comprehensive Theory of the Writing Process." *CE* 44 (1982): 620–27. Whether a linear or recursive composing model is used, all writers discover as they write.

HILLOCKS, GEORGE, JR. *Research on Written Composition.* Urbana: ERIC, 1986. 1–62. A survey of studies on the writing process since 1963.

STOTSKY, SANDRA. "On Planning and Writing Plans—Or Beware of Borrowed Theories!" *CCC* 41 (1990): 57. Cautions that ambiguity with regard to key terms in research on planning can have serious implications for the teaching of writing.

TEDLOCK, DAVID. "The Case Approach to Composition." *CCC* 32 (1981): 253–62. Argues that cases provide useful assignments in writing courses.

SELZER, JACK. "Exploring Options in Composing." *CCC* 35 (1984): 276–84. Encourages experimentation to discover composing styles appropriate to individual students.

(continued)

find some way to own your topic; and when you sufficiently narrow your topic so that you can write on it fully within an allotted number of pages.

Know your topic.

Readers respect, and demand, authority in a writer. Since college writing and business writing are usually based on information or on the ideas of others, knowing your topic will usually require some investigation on your part.

BERLIN, JAMES A. "Contemporary Composition: The Major Pedagogical Theories." *CE* 44 (1982): 765–77. Instructors should pay close attention to the particular process approach they employ in the classroom.

MACKENZIE, NANCY. "Teaching the Composing Process: A Three-Part Project." *The Writing Instructor* 1 (1982): 103–111. Practical classroom strategies to make students aware of writing process.

PERL, SONDRA. "Understanding Composing." *CCC* 31 (1980): 363–69. Emphasizes the recursive nature of composing

TEACHING IDEAS

It's worth spending some time acquainting students with the writing wheel; the metaphor will recur throughout this chapter and chapter 4, and it will be tremendously helpful to students as they develop their own writing processes. Simply asking students to comment on their perceptions of the several points on the wheel will get them thinking about what terms like "organize" and "thesis" really mean. It's also useful to ask them how their concept of the writing process would change if the metaphor were a writing *line* instead of a wheel.

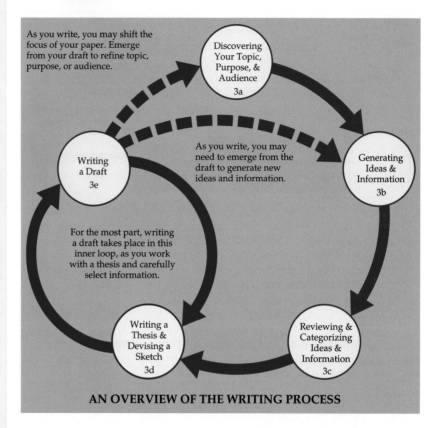

As you write, you may shift the focus of your paper. Emerge from your draft to refine topic, purpose, or audience.

Discovering Your Topic, Purpose, & Audience
3a

Writing a Draft
3e

As you write, you may need to emerge from the draft to generate new ideas and information.

Generating Ideas & Information
3b

For the most part, writing a draft takes place in this inner loop, as you work with a thesis and carefully select information.

Writing a Thesis & Devising a Sketch
3d

Reviewing & Categorizing Ideas & Information
3c

AN OVERVIEW OF THE WRITING PROCESS

Know Your Topic

Read: If you do not know a topic well, read sources and gather information: letters, photographs, articles, lecture notes—whatever is pertinent. Read until you understand all the aspects of your topic that you will be writing about.

Interview: Locate people who are knowledgeable about your topic and interview them. Read sufficiently before the interview so that you do not pose questions that can be answered with basic research. Develop pointed questions that yield information and ideas unique to this source. (See 1b for help on generating good questions.)

Reflect: Investigate your personal commitment to the topic. What experiences have you had that influence your thinking? How has your point of view been shaped by these experiences? Issues on which you might write may require that you take a stand. Know your position. (See 1b for strategies that can aid reflection.)

Illustration: Knowing Your Topic

Assignment: The Board of Trustees at your school has just voted to ban overnight guests in campus dormitory rooms. Write an essay responding to the decision. Assume that you will submit your work to the college newspaper for publication.

Before writing:

> *Read:* (1) Read the minutes of the trustees' meeting to determine exactly who supported the measure, who opposed it, and on what grounds. (2) In the library, locate as many college bulletins as you can to determine which other schools in the country have such a ban in place.
>
> *Interview:* (1) Interview administrators and trustees, based on your understanding of their positions (from the minutes you have read). Prepare specific questions for each trustee interviewed. (2) Interview by phone directors of dormitories and students at schools where a similar ban is in effect.
>
> *Reflect:* Recall experiences of entertaining guests in your dormitory room. Can you classify guests in any way: as family? friends from home? boyfriend/girlfriend? Does the category of guest affect how you, your friends, your parents, or the administration might feel about overnight visits?

Own your topic.

Effective writing is produced by those who understand *and* are committed to a topic. When you are committed, you are interested, and your interest will help to engage your readers. If you are assigned a topic that does not, at first, stimulate you, try these strategies.

Own Your Topic

Stretch the topic to fit your interests. Redefine the assignment in such a way that it touches on your experience and at the same time is acceptable to your professor.

Identify a debate concerning the topic and choose sides. Try to understand why the topic is debatable (if it is) and whom the topic affects, as well as the merits and limitations of each side of the debate. To stimulate interest, personalize the debate. Imagine yourself affected by it and take a position.

Talk with friends. Sometimes informal conversations will help you to identify elements of a topic that interest you. Get a conversation going, listen, and participate. What aspects of the topic interest other people? Become engaged yourself.

REFERENCE

ROHMAN, D. GORDON. "Pre-writing: The State of Discovery in the Writing Process." *CCC* 16 (1965): 106–12. Approaches invention from the perspective of meditation techniques.

ESL EXERCISE

Perceptions of time vary not just from person to person but from culture to culture. Address the following issues as a class exercise.

1. Discuss how late you can be for a serious appointment (a job interview, a visit to an academic counselor) before you are "too late" (you need the excuse of a major accident to get yourself back in good graces).
2. Make up a chart indicating how people from different cultures define "permissible lateness time." Your chart might need to allow for individual differences and for people who are early or late no matter what the rules of their culture.
3. Write up the results of your chart as a report.

ADDITIONAL EXERCISE B

Ask students to work with *any* writing assignment in your class or in another that they will be obliged to complete during the course of the semester. Working with that assignment, ask students to plan a strategy for knowing the topic, owning the topic, and narrowing the topic. Each student could present his or her plan in small groups. Presentations would turn into brainstorming sessions in which group mates would make suggestions for knowing, owning, and narrowing a topic. You might advise students that group brainstorming sessions are commonplace in industry, where workers frequently turn to colleagues in an effort to generate and refine ideas.

ADDITIONAL EXERCISE C

Use the strategies outlined in this section to produce two appropriately narrow topics for each of the broad topics listed below:

1. popular music
2. environmentalism
3. women in business
4. parent-child relationships

Illustration: Owning Your Topic

Assignment: Select three advertisements that describe similar products. Which ad is most effective? Why?

> *Stretch the topic to fit your interests:* (1) Compare ads for a product that you or someone you know buys or would like to buy. (2) Choose ads to study based on the product you would promote if given a large budget. (3) Choose a product category based on how you or someone you know has been *influenced* by a certain ad.
>
> *Identify a debate concerning the topic:* Identify ads that have stirred public controversy or comment, such as ads that use children to sell products to other children. Begin with the debate and then find examples of multiple ads for a common product.
>
> *Talk with friends:* Gather three ads for a product and show them to a small group of friends. Ask for their response. Get a discussion going by asking which ad is most effective—and why. Listen closely for comments that you might build on in an essay.

Narrow your topic.

Know how long your document is expected to be, and limit your writing accordingly. Avoid the frustration of choosing a broad topic (for example, the controversy over affirmative action) for a brief paper or report—a mistake that will guarantee a superficial product. The briefer your document is expected to be, the more narrowly directed your topic should be.

Narrow Your Topic

- *Divide the topic into constituent parts.* Ask yourself: What are the component parts of this topic? What parts (or subtopics) do I know most about? Can I link subtopics together in meaningful ways? In which subtopic am I most interested?
- *Ask a journalist's questions.* Narrow a topic to a subtopic that interests you by posing questions, as appropriate: who, what, where, when, why, how? Often, a response to one or more of these questions can become the focus for a paper.

Illustration: Narrowing Your Topic

Assignment: Choose a broad topic about which you know a great deal and narrow it, in preparation for beginning work on an essay.

Broad topic: my championship football season

Topic divided into parts:

the final game—our strategy for winning

team members' hopes for college scholarships

the intensity needed to win

pressure to devote whole life to football

the public's reaction to our winning season—they loved us

my reactions to our winning season—I hated myself

Narrowed topic: (a combination of the last two items above)

Reactions (mine and the public's) to our winning season

EXERCISE 1

List three topics with which you are intimately familiar and about which you can write for *public* view. Subdivide each topic into as many parts as you can. Eventually, you will select from these parts a focus for your paper.

EXERCISE 2

Of the topics you have narrowed in Exercise 1, which do you care most about? Write a brief paragraph in which you explain to yourself the *reasons* you are interested in one of these narrowed topics.

2   Identifying your purpose

Think of an object, an idea, an emotion, a relationship, or an institution: think of anything at all and you can probably explain it, argue about it, reflect on its significance, or make it the subject of an artistic work. There are four basic purposes or aims for writing: to *inform,* to *persuade,* to *express,* and to *entertain.* Since you will generally be asked to produce informative and persuasive pieces in college, this book is devoted primarily to these types of writing.

Informative writing

When writing to *inform,* your job is to present a topic and to explain, define, or describe it so that the reader understands its component parts, its method of operation, its uses, and so on. The following assignments call for informative writing.

REFERENCE

COE, RICHARD M. "If Not to Narrow, Then How to Focus: Two Techniques for Focusing." CCC 32 (1981): 272–77. Discusses value of techniques that emphasize focusing rather than simply narrowing a topic.

EXERCISE 1

Individual responses

EXERCISE 2

Individual responses

ESL EXERCISE

The "polite distance" we maintain with others is often described as a "bubble of space" used to keep strangers at a safe distance from us. Except in elevators and subways, people in North America keep a "nose-to-nose" distance of at least one foot (30.5 centimeters), and as much as two feet (61 centimeters). Address the following issues as a class exercise:

1. Discuss how many inches/centimeters your culture "recommends" as a polite distance to keep from others (you may have to experiment and measure this distance). What do people do when this rule is violated and the distance becomes either too close or too far?
2. Make up a chart indicating how people from different cultures define "politeness distance."
3. Write up the results of your chart as a report.

TEACHING IDEAS

Since students are often unaware of their own writing processes, much less the reasons for their choices, it's a good idea to ask them to keep a writer's log focusing on the details of their progress in composing a paper. If responses to the exercises dealing with their own writing can be kept separate from other exercises, they can trace the process they used to produce a final draft. While early log entries tend to be superficial (e.g., "I chose this topic because I know a lot about it"), gradually students begin to show more awareness of the reasons for their choices.

REFERENCES

KINNEAVY, JAMES L. *A Theory of Discourse*. Englewood Cliffs: Prentice, 1971. A classification of discourse based on purpose and emphasis.

KNOBLAUCH, C. H. "Intentionality in the Writing Process: A Case Study." *CCC* 331 (1980): 153–59. Argues that a writer's purpose shifts during the course of the writing process.

TEACHING IDEAS

The distinctions between informative and persuasive writing on the one hand and expressive writing on the other are in some sense arbitrarily drawn. Expressive writing can become an excellent means for a writer's understanding his or her personal commitment to a topic. The expressive writing may remain private, but some echo of it will often be found in an accomplished writer's public utterances. For this reason many teachers begin a writing sequence with a personal, expressive exercise. Students are encouraged to explore an idea privately. A second assignment might ask students to take a view articulated in an expressive, personal piece and to convert it to a public utterance—into an essay that informs or persuades.

LITERATURE — Cite three examples of metaphor in *Great Expectations* and explain how each works.

CHEMISTRY — Explain the chemical process by which water, when boiled, becomes steam.

PSYCHOLOGY — What is "cognitive dissonance" and in what ways does it contribute to the development of personality?

What the reader already knows about the topic will in large part determine the level of language you use and the difficulty of the information that you present. A professor of aeronautical engineering discussing the flight of planes would use one vocabulary with engineering students and another vocabulary with an audience that had no technical background. (See 3a-3.)

Persuasive writing

When you write to *persuade*, your job is to change a reader's views about a topic. As with informative writing, the persuasive writer must carefully consider the reader's prior knowledge in order to provide the background information necessary for understanding. If you lacked a background in international business, for instance, you might not be persuaded about the need to master a foreign language in college. The person urging you to learn Spanish or Japanese would need to inform you, first, of certain facts and trends. As a persuasive writer, you will provide information both to establish understanding and to provide a base for building an argument. (See chapter 6, which is devoted entirely to argumentation.) The following assignments call for persuasive writing.

ASTRONOMY — Given limited government money available for the construction and updating of astronomical observatories, which of the projects discussed this semester deserve continued funding? Argue for your choices based on the types of discoveries you expect the various projects to make in the next five years.

SOCIOLOGY — You have read two theories on emotions: the Cannon-Bard theory and the James-Lange theory. Which seems the more convincing to you? Why?

MARKETING — Select three ads that describe similar products. Which ad is most effective? Why?

Expressive writing and writing to entertain

Expressive writing—sometimes private and recorded as journal entries, sometimes written for public view—focuses on an exploration of your own ideas and emotions. When it is private, expressive writing can lead you to be more experimental, less guarded, perhaps even more honest than in a paper meant for others. When it is public, expressive writing will not be a journal entry, but rather an essay in which you reflect on your impressions. In many composition courses, the first part of a semester or an entire semester will be devoted to expressive writing. The least frequent purpose of academic writing is to *entertain*. Possibly you will write a poem, story, or play in your college career; and certainly you will read forms of writing that are intended to entertain readers. What makes a piece of writing entertaining is itself a subject for debate. It suffices to say here that writing to entertain need not be writing that evokes smiles.

Purposes for writing may overlap: in a single essay, you may inform, persuade, and entertain a reader. But if an essay is to succeed, you should identify a *single,* primary purpose for writing. Otherwise, you risk having a document that tries to do all things but does none well.

EXERCISE 3

Return to the writing you produced for Exercises 1 and 2, in which you divided broad topics into subtopics and then selected one narrowed topic as particularly interesting. This (or the topic suggested below) will become your topic for a five-page paper. Write a brief paragraph explaining your purpose for this paper. Although purposes may overlap to some extent, decide on one of two primary purposes for this paper: to inform *or* persuade your reader. If the topics in Exercises 1 and 2 left you uninspired, you may want to try this one:

The Board of Trustees at your school has just voted to ban overnight guests in campus dormitory rooms. Write an essay responding to the decision. Assume that you will submit your work to the college newspaper for publication. (For help getting started on this topic, see the illustration panel on page 63: "Knowing your topic.")

3 Defining your audience

Unless you are making a journal entry, you will write in order to communicate *with* someone: whether your intent is primarily to inform or persuade, you must know your audience since what you write will depend greatly on who will read it. With readers who understand your topic, you can assume a common base of knowledge. For instance, if you were preparing a paper on gene splicing for an audience of nonbiologists, you would be obliged to cover rudimentary concepts in language that nonspecialists would understand. In preparing a paper on the same topic for fellow biology majors, you would be free to use technical terms and to discuss higher level material. Questions that you ask about an audience *before you write a first draft* can help you make decisions concerning your paper's content and level of language.

Writing for an unspecified audience

If your audience is not clearly specified, then regard your professor as the main reader. Do not think that because he or she is an expert on the topic of your paper you are relieved of developing points thoroughly.

REFERENCES

Roth, Robert G. "The Evolving Audience: Alternatives to Audience Accommodation." *CCC* 38 (1987): 47–55. Student writers, rather than focusing on the attributes of an audience, should concentrate instead on how to claim an audience's attention.

Long, Russell C. "Writer-Audience Relationships: Analysis or Invention?" *CCC* 31 (1980): 221–26. Suggests strategies for creating audiences.

Park, Douglas. "Analyzing Audiences." *CCC* 37 (1986): 478–88. In order to invent an audience, writers must define the social context in which they are writing.

Flower, Linda. "Writer-Based Prose: A Cognitive Basis for Problems in Writing." *CE* 41 (1979): 19–37. Suggests that early drafts are written for the writer; only in later drafts do readers' needs become significant.

Ede, Lisa, and Andrea Lunsford. "Audience Addressed/Audience Invoked: The Role of Audience in Composition Theory and Pedagogy." *CCC* 35 (1984): 155–71. Suggests a theory of audience that balances a writer's power with effective communication of ideas to an audience.

Kroll, Barry. "Writing for Readers: Three Perspectives on Audience." *CCC* 35 (1984): 172–85. Overemphasis on audience can lead to neglect of a writer's voice, subject, or purpose.

Pfister, Fred R., and Joan Petrick. "A Heuristic Model for Creating a Writer's Audience." *CCC* 31 (1980): 213–20. The right questions can be helpful in creating audience.

Ong, Walter J., S. J. "The Writer's Audience is Always a Fiction." *PMLA* 90 (1975): 9–21. Readers should be aware that writers invent their own audiences.

TEACHING IDEAS

Uninitiated as they are in academic discourse, students have a difficult time understanding why some of their writing (e.g., "Shakespeare, a famous writer of plays . . .") strikes their teachers as comically inappropriate. To help students understand the teacher's view, ask students to think about some nonacademic subject on which they are experts. Have them imagine a group of similarly experienced experts, and then ask them to write a paragraph that

---

Audience Needs Analysis

Pose these general questions, regardless of your purpose:

- Who is the reader? What is the reader's age, sex, religious background, educational background, and ethnic heritage?
- What is my relationship with the reader?
- What impact on my presentation—on choice of words, level of complexity, and choice of examples—will the reader have?
- Why will the reader be interested in my paper? How can I best spark the reader's interest?

If you are writing to inform, pose these questions as well:

- What does the reader know about the topic's history?
- How well does the reader understand the topic's technical details?
- What does the reader need to know? want to know?
- What level of language and content will I use in discussing the topic, given the reader's understanding?

If you are writing to persuade, pose both sets of questions above as well as the following:

- What are the reader's views on the topic? Given what I know about the reader (from the preceding questions), is the reader likely to agree with my view on the topic? to disagree? to be neutral?
- What factors are likely to affect the reader's beliefs about the topic? What special circumstances (work, religious conviction, political views, etc.) should I be aware of that will affect the reader's views?
- How can I shape my argument to encourage the reader's support, given his or her present level of interest, level of understanding, and beliefs?

Many writing assignments are developed expressly to gauge what you know about a topic; in these instances, to omit information intentionally will prove disastrous.

Assume the professor functions as an expert editor who will review your paper before passing it on to another reader. This second reader is *not* an expert on your topic and must therefore rely fully on your powers of explanation. Assume this reader is skeptical and neutral regarding your topic. The reader will hear you out, but will probe with questions and will require that you develop general statements with specific illustrations and that you defend any assertions needing support.

When Does Your Audience Need to Know More?

Consider these points when deciding whether your audience needs to know more about a key term or person.

- Major personalities referred to in textbooks or in lectures will help constitute the general, shared knowledge of a discipline. In all cases, *refer to people in your papers either by their* last *names or by their first* and *last names.* Do not identify "giants of a field" with explanatory tags like *who was an important inventor in the early part of the 20th century.*

- Terms that have been defined at length in a textbook or lecture also constitute the general, shared knowledge of a discipline. Once you have understood these terms, use them in your papers—but do not define them. Demonstrate your understanding by using the terms accurately.

- The same people and terms not requiring definition in an academic context may well need to be defined in a nonacademic one. Base decisions about what information to include in a paper on a careful audience analysis.

EXERCISE 4

Return to the topic you selected in Exercise 3, where you wrote a paragraph explaining your purpose for a proposed five-page paper. Working with your topic and your purpose (to inform or persuade), answer questions in the Audience Needs Analysis box three times, once for each of three different audiences: a friend at another school, your parents, and some other audience of your choosing. Select one of these audiences as the one to whom you will direct your paper.

4 Analyzing topic, purpose, audience—and the writing occasion

Each new writing project constitutes a distinct **occasion for writing** and requires that you understand anew the relationship of topic, purpose, and audience. As a writer, you will analyze each occasion and decide on the tone you will adopt and the register.

Tone is a writer's general attitude toward the reader and the subject. Through an accumulation of signals, some subtle and others not, readers can tell whether you are interested in your topic and whether you are committed, engaged, humble, proud, irritable, irreverent, or defensive. Appreciate that a paper *will* have, and cannot help but have, a characteristic tone. English offers numerous ways of saying the same thing. For example, the most simple request can be worded to reflect a variety of tones.

May I have the salt?	Give me that salt!	Salt!
Pass the salt.	Pass the salt, please.	

vastly underestimates the degree of knowledge shared by the expert audience. Then the students should analyze what is wrong with their paragraph, specifying the errors that signaled to the audience that the writer was inexperienced.

Make the jump, now, to academic expertise. As freshmen and sophomores, students will be inexperienced in their various subjects of study. Invariably, they will make the errors they constructed in their example paragraphs. The best beginning students can make is to be aware of the question: What sorts of things do writers say or not say in this discipline? Student writers may be unable to answer the question, but it will help to keep them sensitive to the conventions of various disciplines. Entering a course with this sensitivity should prove a useful stance for any student.

GROUP ACTIVITY

Questions about how much to tell the audience should be particularly relevant to students taking introductory courses in areas other than composition. Dividing students into small groups, ask them to choose one introductory course and answer the following questions about it: What key terms, concepts, and names did you learn for the first time in this course? As the course continued, what terms, concepts, and names became so familiar that you no longer needed explanation? How are those terms, concepts, and names treated in the text as they become more familiar? In the instructor's lectures? In what situations do you find it necessary to explain or identify those terms, concepts, and names? Why do you have to explain them sometimes?

EXERCISE 4

Individual responses

ESL EXERCISE

Interview at least four American students about teacher expectations and classroom behavior. Write a short paper contrasting their attitudes of what is proper and improper with the attitudes of students from your culture. Speculate about the reasons for such differences.

For every writing occasion, choose a tone that you think is appropriate to your topic or that, in your judgment, your readers will think appropriate. Mismatching tone and topic can create problems. Imagine a writer's discussing some grim event with a lighthearted, devil-may-care tone. Readers would surely turn away, and thus the purpose of communication would be defeated.

Register is the degree of formality in your writing. In adopting a **formal register,** you adhere to all the rules and conventions of writing expected in the professional and academic worlds. Formal writing is precise and concise; it avoids colloquial expressions, and it is thorough in content and tightly structured. The **informal register** is common in personal correspondence and journals, and tends to be conversational. Word choice is freely colloquial and structure need not be as tightly reasoned as in a formal paper. Occasional lapses in grammar, usage, spelling, or punctuation matter little in personal correspondence and not at all in personal journal writing. The **popular register** is typical of most general interest magazines. It adheres to all conventions of grammar, usage, spelling, and punctuation; it is also carefully organized. The language, however, is more conversational than that found in formal writing. Heavy emphasis is placed on engaging readers and maintaining their interest. For suggestions on matching tone and register to the writing occasion, see 21e on the use of Formal English.

Versatile writers can shift register and tone as the writing occasion requires. You can inform or persuade a reader in *any* register or tone, but once chosen, register and tone should be used consistently (21e). This diagram suggests the need for a balanced, four-way relationship among the basic elements of the writing occasion.

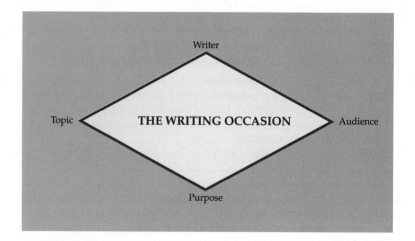

EXERCISE 5

Write a series of three brief letters to a mail-order business. Ask why you have not received the computer software you ordered and paid for.

The letters should show a change in tone, moving from a neutral inquiry in the first letter to annoyed concern in the second to controlled anger in the third. In each case, maintain a formal tone. Avoid using colloquial expressions.

EXERCISE 6

Given the audience and the purpose you have chosen for the paper you are planning (see your answers to Exercises 3 and 4), decide on the tone and register you should adopt.

3b Generating ideas and information

It is not easy to generate ideas about a topic. In most academic writing, a combination of efforts is usually needed: you will reflect on your own experience and think a topic through to get ideas for writing; and you will conduct research in a library, in a lab, or in the field. At times you may stare at your topic, a word on a blank page, and feel as though there is *nothing* to write about. However, there are proven strategies for generating ideas and information.

When you are generating material, try to put the critic in you to sleep and give yourself the freedom to have ideas—bad ones as well as good ones. As a writer, you will need to be both creator and critic. At this early stage in the process, avoid being too hard on yourself lest you dampen the creative impulses you will need to write a good paper. Create—and then *later* evaluate and choose. As you review the various strategies for generating ideas and information, bear in mind this "User's Manual":

- No one method will work for all topics.
- Some methods may not suit your style of discovery.
- Some methods work well when combined.
- Move quickly to a new strategy if one does not work.
- Tell your critic to take a vacation.

The invention strategies discussed in this section can complement each other; you will generate one type of information using one strategy and other types using others. When you examine *all* the material you have generated, you should find ample opportunities to advance to the next stage of writing. The work of a single student, Sean Hannan (whose completed paper appears on page 115), illustrates how you might put the various strategies to use.

1 Reading

Most academic writing is based on reading. Early in the writing process, when you are still not precisely sure of what your topic will be,

EXERCISE 6

Individual responses

REFERENCES

FLOWER, LINDA S., and JOHN R. HAYES. "Problem-Solving Strategies and the Writing Process." *CE* 39 (1977): 442–48. Techniques to assist in development of ideas.

CORBETT, EDWARD P. J. *Classical Rhetoric for the Modern Student.* New York: Oxford UP, 1965. 94–174. Discussion of classical schemes for invention.

YOUNG, RICHARD. "Recent Developments in Rhetorical Invention." *Teaching Composition: 12 Bibliographic Essays.* Ed. Gary Tate. Fort Worth: Texas Christian UP, 1987. 1–38. A survey of research on invention since 1973.

LAUER, JANICE. "Issues in Rhetorical Invention." *Essays on Classical Rhetoric and Modern Discourse.* Eds. Robert J. Connors, Lisa S. Ede, and Andrea A. Lunsford. Carbondale: Southern Illinois UP, 1984. 127–39. Assumptions writers make about the composing process inform the strategies used for prewriting.

TEACHING IDEAS

ACROSS THE CURRICULUM One of the most difficult things to get students to understand about higher education (especially liberal arts education) is the interrelatedness of their courses. Occasionally students have been known to apologize for introducing irrelevant material when they make a connection between what's being covered in one course and an issue that arises in another course. A brief discussion of the relevance of their courses to topics they've chosen to write about will help them shed that misconception.

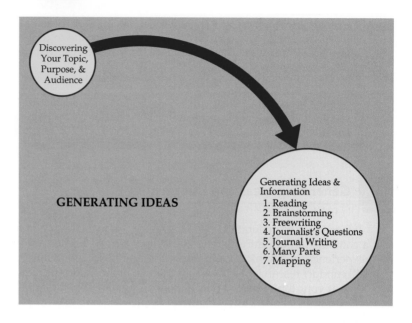

reading can be an excellent stimulus. Even if you do not plan to depend heavily on sources in a paper, reading about your tentative topic will help you to generate ideas. Source materials may present compelling facts or strongly worded opinions with which to agree or disagree. Above all, read to *respond.* Be alert to your responses and jot them down, for they may later become important to your paper. (See chapter 1 and the discussion of strategies for reading effectively.) If you are writing a paper that will not draw heavily on sources, use your reading mainly as a stimulus. If you are writing a research report, read to generate the information you will then use to write the paper. In this case, realize you will need to cite sources (see chapter 36).

At the time Sean Hannan was preparing to write, he was enrolled in an introductory social psychology course. He browsed through the index of his textbook and found that the entries on *aggression* and *compliance* sparked his interest. Sean's tentative topic was Reactions (mine and the public's) to my football team's championship season. Sean made the following notes, based on his initial reading.

Illustration: Sean Hannan's Paper
READING

    According to my textbook, human aggression is an intensely
studied problem and much on people's minds. Group members can
be particularly aggressive because few members of a group are
willing to speak up and call aggression wrong. There are

```
powerful psychological and social incentives in belonging to a
group. For a football team to be a team, everyone must
sacrifice for each other physically and emotionally. A close
bond forms that no one will break--even if his conscience
calls on him to do so. My problem on the football field was
not just my problem, I've discovered. Everyone is susceptible
to group pressures and can lose individuality.
```

2   Brainstorming

The object of **brainstorming** is to write quickly and, once finished, to return to your work with a critical eye. Place your topic at the top of a page, and then list any related phrase or word that comes to mind. Set a time limit of five or ten minutes, and list items as quickly as you can. All items are legitimate for your list, since even an allegedly bad idea can spark a good one. To brainstorm in a small group, a technique that allows the ideas of one person to build on those of another, write your topic on a board or sheet of easel paper. (If you have no topic, see "Freewriting," 3b-3). Sit in a circle and ask each member of the group to offer two or three words or phrases for your list. Work about the circle a second time, asking each member to add another one or two ideas, based on an item already mentioned. Finally, open the floor to anyone who can add more ideas. As a ground rule, urge each group member to understand that all ideas are equally useful.

After you have generated your list, group related items and set aside items that do not fit into a grouping. Groupings with the greatest number of items indicate areas that should prove fertile in developing your paper. Save the results of your brainstorming session for your next step in the planning process: selecting, organizing, and expanding information.

Sean divided his topic into three parts and brainstormed separately about each part (my reactions to the championship season, the public's reactions, the season).

| **Illustration: Sean Hannan's Paper** |
| **BRAINSTORMING** |

My reactions

```
elation--winning was a high
fear--about the person I was becoming
anger, hostility--about the person I was becoming
numbness--couldn't let these thoughts in during a game
coach--frightened me with his intensity sometimes
```

```
intensity--team's, coach's
winning--at all costs
media attention--I loved it
close bond with team, like we shared this secret, were
  brothers
loved the glory--made me feel important
tackle--broke a guy's thigh, terrible
tackle--wrecked a guy's knee, mean, felt like an animal
```

Sean grouped the list as follows. The question mark denotes the "leftover" category. Sean was unsure how to group "tackles."

My Reactions

Negatives	Positives	?
fear	elation	tackles
anger	winning	
numbness	bond with team	
intensity	glory	
winning	media	

REFERENCES

ELBOW, PETER. *Writing with Power: Techniques for Mastering the Writing Process.* New York: Oxford UP, 1981. Thorough description of the uses of freewriting.

—. *Writing without Teachers.* New York: Oxford UP, 1973. One of the earliest discussions of the value of freewriting.

REYNOLDS, MARK. "Make Free Writing More Productive." *CCC* 39 (1988): 81–82. Provides guidelines for generating useful freewriting.

SOUTHWELL, MICHAEL G. "Free Writing in Composition Classes." *CE* 38 (1977): 676–81. Freewriting can be used to strengthen skills and to develop formal papers.

3 Freewriting and focused freewriting

Freewriting is a technique to try when you are asked to write but have no topic. Think for a moment about the subject area in which you have been asked to write. Recall lectures or chapters read in textbooks. Choose a broad area of interest and then start writing for some predetermined amount of time—say, five or ten minutes. Alternately, you can write until you have filled a certain number of pages (typically one or two). As you write, do not stop to puzzle over a word choice or punctuation. Do not stop to cross words out because they do not capture your meaning. Push on to the next sentence. Freely change thoughts from one sentence to the next, if this is where your thinking takes you. Once you have reached your time limit or page allotment, read over what you have done. Circle ideas that lend themselves to possible paper topics. To generate ideas about these specific topics, you may then try a more focused strategy for invention: brainstorming, focused freewriting, or any of the other strategies that will be discussed in later sections.

Focused freewriting gives you the benefits of freewriting, but on a *specific* topic. The end result of this strategy is the same as brainstorming, and so the choice of invention strategies is one of style: do you prefer making lists or writing sentences? Begin with a definite topic. Write for five or ten minutes; reread your work; and circle any words, phrases, or sentences that look potentially useful. Draw lines that link circled words, and make notes to explain the linkage. Then clarify these linkages on a separate sheet of paper. The result will be a grouping of items, some in sentence form, that looks a great deal like the result of brainstorming.

Save your work for the next step in the planning process: selecting, organizing, and expanding information.

Following is a portion of Sean's focused freewrite around the second part of his topic: the public's reaction to his team's championship season.

Illustration: Sean Hannan's Paper
FOCUSED FREEWRITING

Winning only one game got the town all excited about how our team was going to win a league championship. I never realized how important winning was to my neighbors. We were only a high school team after all. Why should they be so excited? They were. After we had won a couple of games, it seemed we were holding more interviews than practices. And then there were the people erecting signs in storefront windows and the headlines, not just on the sports pages either, of our local paper. It was getting out of hand. At the end of the season, the coach was on a platform with us--the town gave us a banquet--and he spoke about the team like we were national heroes. Stuff that made no sense to me, about character, poise, dedication. To football, maybe. But what about the people who got hurt along the way--some not by accident? The town loved us. They loved the animals we became. I didn't. It scared me, to see the evil I was capable of and what scared me even more, I think, was that people on the outside didn't see it at all. They wanted heroes and they got them. But the cost was too high. We started the season as young men. I felt something like a criminal by the end of it.

Sean organized his freewriting into these notes:

Town excited	Why?
-people erecting signs	-wanted heroes
-headlines in local paper	-didn't see our ugly side
-banquet	
We became animals	
-hurt people intentionally	
-I was capable of evil	
-others didn't see, all the more frightening	

Select a classmate from a different language, cultural, or national group. Write down a series of questions to help you find out what your classmate's career goals are and what past experiences led to those goals. Ask your classmate the questions. Then write a short biography focused on those past events which brought your classmate to where she or he is today. Your audience will be a third classmate to whom you are introducing your new friend.

REFERENCE

Washington, Eugene. "WH-Questions in Teaching Composition." *CCC* 28 (1977): 54–56. Techniques for generating information using journalist's questions.

TEACHING IDEAS

Students who have never used journals before are often at a loss as to what to write; the result is often either a series of mini-essays clearly aimed at a professorial audience or a tedious, unproductive diary. It's a good idea to check journal entries periodically in the first few weeks of class to let students know if they're making good use of the journal as a writer's tool. Asking students with particularly good journals for permission to reproduce sample entries can help those who haven't yet "got the hang of it." (Privacy is a problem here, but it can be dealt with: Always ask permission; always maintain student anonymity; if possible, distribute sample entries to students in a different class; and ideally, build a collection of sample entries to be used in subsequent years.)

REFERENCES

Huff, Roland, and Charles R. Kline, Jr. *A Contemporary Writing Curriculum: Rehearsing, Composing, and Valuing.* New York: Columbia UP, 1987. 1–51. Describes a course with journal writing at its core.

Fulwiler, Toby. "The Personal Connection: Journal Writing across the Curriculum." *Language Connections.* Urbana: NCTE, 1982. Emphasizes use of journals as "writing to learn" in all content courses.

4   The journalist's questions

You have read or heard of the journalist's questions: *who, what, when, where, why,* and *how.* In answering the questions, you can define, compare, contrast, or investigate cause and effect. Again, the assumption is that by thinking about parts you will have more to write about than if you focused on a topic as a whole. The journalist's questions can help you to narrow a topic (see 3a-1), giving you the option to concentrate, say, on any three parts of the whole: perhaps the *who, what,* and *why* of the topic. Under the topic of mapping, you will find Sean Hannan's notes made in response to three of the journalist's questions.

5   Journal writing

You might keep a journal in conjunction with your writing course. A *journal* is a set of private, reflective notes that you keep, in which you describe your reactions to lectures, readings, discussions, films, current events—any topic touching on your course work. A journal borrows from both diary writing and course notebooks. As in a diary, your journal entries are private, reflective, and "safe" in the sense that you know no one is looking over your shoulder; thus, you are free to experiment with ideas and to express your thoughts honestly without fear of consequences. Unlike a diary, a journal focuses on matters relating to your course work and not on matters of your private life, unless such observations tie in with your course work. Journal writing gives you an opportunity to converse with yourself in your own language about what you have been studying. You pose questions, develop ideas, reflect on readings, speculate and explore, and try to pinpoint confusions. The more you write, the more you clarify what you know and, equally important, what you do not know. The language of your journal entries should reflect your voice: use the words, expressions, and rhythms of vocabulary that you use when you chat with friends. Punctuation is not important as long as you can reread your journal entries. Periodically review journal entries, looking for ideas in which you seemed particularly interested. As with freewriting, use these ideas as the basis for a more focused strategy of invention.[1]

6   The "many parts" strategy[2]

Another method for generating ideas about a topic is to list its parts. Number the items on your list. Then ask: "What are the uses of Number

---

[1]Discussion of journal writing here is based on Toby Fulwiler, ed. *The Journal Book* (Portsmouth, NH: Boynton/Cook-Heinemann, 1987) 1–7.

[2]This strategy is adapted from John C. Bean and John D. Ramage, *Form and Surprise in Composition: Writing and Thinking Across the Curriculum* (New York: Macmillan, 1986) 170–71.

1? Number 2? Number 3?" and so on. If *uses of* does not seem to work for the parts in question, try *consequences of:* "What are the consequences of Number 1?" The *many parts* strategy lets you be far more specific and imaginative in thinking about the topic as a whole than you might be ordinarily. Once you have responded to your questions about the uses or consequences of some part, you might pursue the one or two most promising responses in a focused freewrite.

Illustration: Sean Hannan's Paper
THE "MANY PARTS" STRATEGY

I. What are the parts of a championship season?

    1. student, teacher pride

    2. town pride

    3. something to talk about, besides weather

    4. way to divert attention from problems

    5. intense players

    6. coach keeps job and is known as winner

One part, explored:

II. What are the consequences of students' and teachers' showing pride?

    - focus on school as a positive place

    - increase students' awareness of behaving in ways that
      don't reflect poorly on school--good for administration
      & teachers

    - some students let pride go to their heads--they brag

    - pride also creates burden--students, teachers,
      administrators begin to cut us slack and we begin to
      think we're as great as everybody tells us

    - school's pride creates respect for players

---

7 Mapping

If you enjoy thinking visually, try **mapping** your ideas. Begin by writing your topic as briefly as possible (a single word is best). Circle the topic and draw three, four, or five short spokes from the circle. At the end of each spoke place one of the journalist's questions, making a major branch off the spoke for every answer to a question. Now, working with each answer individually, pose one of the six journalist's questions once again. After you have completed the exercise, you will have a page that places ideas in relation to one another. Notice how the "map" distinguishes between major points and supporting information.

—, ed. *The Journal Book.* Portsmouth, NH: Boynton/Cook-Heinemann, 1987. A collection of essays on journal use across the curriculum.

BERTHOFF, ANNE E. *Forming/Thinking/Writing: The Composing Imagination.* Rochelle Park, NJ: Hayden, 1978. Invaluable information on the role of journals in the composing process.

BLAU, SHERIDAN. "Invisible Writing: Investigating Cognitive Processes in Composition." *CCC* 34 (1983): 297–312. Suggests freewriting with an empty pen, removing temptation to review what's already written.

WHITEHILL, SHARON. "Using the Journal for Discovery: Two Devices." *CCC* 38 (1987): 472–74. Presents practical strategies for using journals to generate ideas.

TEACHING IDEAS

Both the "many parts" strategy and mapping attempt to get writers thinking about parts of a topic, as opposed to a monolithic and undifferentiated whole. Once students begin to see parts, they can begin to see relations; and it is the relationships that students create that sustain a paper. To help students appreciate the advantages of thinking about parts, begin class one day with the abrupt assignment: "Write on X— 15 minutes. Begin." Students will be lost and disgruntled—with reason! X might be ozone depletion, government bureaucracy, consumer electronics—any very broad, undifferentiated topic will do. After a minute or so (time enough to let students appreciate the futility of the assignment), tell them to stop, and ask them why they found making a beginning difficult. There might be several answers to this question: Who are we writing to? What is our purpose? What specifically about this topic are we supposed to address?

The writing occasion entails all three questions, and each must be answered precisely if writing is to succeed. For the moment, focus on the need for a writer to work with a carefully defined topic. That is, focus on the last question: What specifically about this topic are we supposed to address? Using the "many parts" strategy or mapping on the chalkboard, show students how they can take a broad, ill-defined topic and illuminate it for themselves by examining parts. Students will readily see that it is more profitable to talk about parts of a broad

(continued)

topic and the relation of parts than it is to talk in generalities about the whole.

ESL EXERCISE

The use of living space varies from culture to culture, with some groups valuing open space and "emptiness" and others preferring closeness and "filled" areas. For example, British fashion of a hundred years ago was to fill every possible area of a room with furniture and decoration, in marked contrast with modern Japanese or Scandinavian fashions. Address the following issues as a class exercise.

1. Discuss preferences for large living space as opposed to a small living space. OR discuss preferences for few furnishings and uncluttered space as opposed to much furniture and filled space.
2. Draw a diagram of a single room, labeling the kind of furniture you would typically expect to find in your culture.
3. Compare your diagram with those of other students and then make conclusions about how your culture regards the use of space. Write your observations up as a short report.

ESL ALERT

The concept of mapping and outlining may be new to some ESL students, who will need practice seeking unifying categories. Vocabulary limitations sometimes make brainstorming activities extremely difficult for ESL students.

TEACHING IDEAS

Students should be encouraged during this and similar exercises to try to distinguish between strategies that they find productive and those that don't yield satisfactory results. Since people process information differently, it's extremely helpful to understand early on the types of strategies that work best for the individual writer.

EXERCISE 7

Individual responses

EXERCISE 8

Individual responses

Illustration: Sean Hannan's Paper
MAPPING THE JOURNALIST'S QUESTIONS

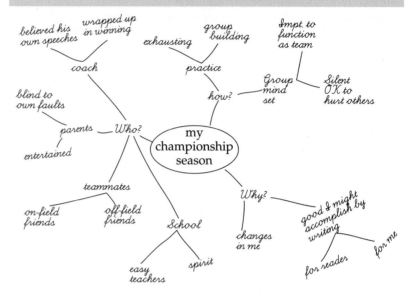

EXERCISE 7

Generate ideas about three of the following topics, using *two* of the previously mentioned methods of invention for each idea. The results of this exercise will provide the basis for your answer to Exercise 10.

river rafting   the symphony   dorm life
a cousin   compulsory draft   space flight

EXERCISE 8

If you are preparing a paper as you read this chapter, use any *three* methods of invention to generate ideas about your topic. The end result of your work should be several categories of grouped ideas.

3c   Reviewing and categorizing ideas and information

Not all of the information you have generated will be equally useful. Therefore, your next task in the writing process is to select those ideas that look most promising. *Promising* in this context is an inexact term, and at this stage of the writing process there is no way to be exact: Until you have completed a first draft, you cannot know for certain the content of your paper. Despite the plans you make when preparing to write, your actual writing is where you will discover much of your content. For this reason, the choices you make about which ideas and information to include in a paper must be based on hunches: informed guesses about what will work.

1   Reviewing ideas and making meaningful categories

Make sense of the information you have generated by creating categories. A category is akin to a file drawer into which you place related materials. Your job is to consolidate: take all the ideas and information you have generated; spread your notes out before you; and then take a clean sheet of paper and group ideas. Give each new grouping a general category name. Beneath each category name, list subordinate, or supporting, information.

Sean Hannan generated five categories of information on which he could base a paper. Following is one of these categories, with information

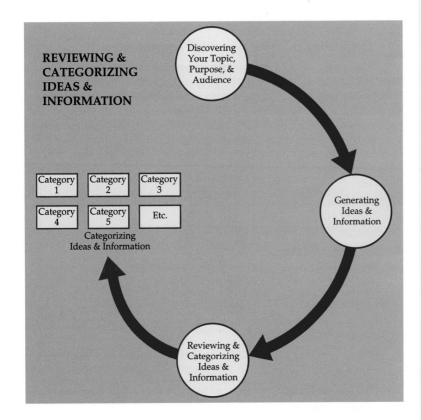

REVIEWING & CATEGORIZING IDEAS & INFORMATION

Discovering Your Topic, Purpose, & Audience

Generating Ideas & Information

Reviewing & Categorizing Ideas & Information

Category 1 Category 2 Category 3
Category 4 Category 5 Etc.

Categorizing Ideas & Information

ADDITIONAL EXERCISE F

THINKING CRITICALLY In order to practice distinguishing between major and supporting points, choose a brief article from the magazine you used for Additional Exercise B. Working backward from finished product to informal outline, list the major points and supporting points found in the article.

consolidated from the results of four different methods for generating information.

Illustration: Sean Hannan's Paper
SELECTING INFORMATION INTO CATEGORIES

<u>Playing has disadvantages.</u>
```
winning became a burden--we had to win league title
intensity: games, lockers, coach was hard to handle
fear of becoming an animal, a criminal
I broke a kid's leg on a tackle, unintentionally
I took one kid out of a game, intentionally--terrible
one teammate banged head on wall to prepare--scary
every game, pressure built to keep win streak alive
couldn't sleep before game nights, sometimes
```

2   Organizing information *within* categories

Organize information within categories to clarify your ideas and their relation to each other. First, you will need to identify main, or *general,* points within each category and the subordinate, or *specific,* points supporting them, which is exactly what you will do when writing a paper. Use an informal outline or a tree diagram to organize major and supporting points within a category.

Illustration: Sean Hannan's Paper
ORGANIZING INFORMATION WITHIN CATEGORIES

Organization by informal outline

<u>Playing has disadvantages.</u>
<u>Major point:</u> winning became a burden--we had to win league title
  <u>Supporting points:</u> (1) every game, pressure built to keep win streak alive; (2) couldn't sleep before game nights, sometimes
<u>Major point:</u> intensity--games, lockers, coach was hard to handle
  <u>Supporting points:</u> (1) one teammate banged his head on a wall to prepare--scary

```
Major point: fear of becoming an animal, a criminal
 Supporting points: (1) I broke a kid's leg on a tackle
 unintentionally; (2) I took one kid out of a game,
 intentionally--in retrospect, terrible
```

Organization by tree diagram

3 Expanding information: filling in gaps

Organizing material within a category is an excellent technique for revealing which of your main points will need further development once you begin writing a first draft. When Sean Hannan organized his category on the disadvantages of playing football, he realized that he had neglected to generate enough supporting materials for his point about the season's intensity. When Sean asked, "What other examples of intensity can I point to?" answers came quickly. An asterisk marks the two additions to the category.

```
Major point: intensity: games, lockers, coach was hard to
handle
 Supporting points: one teammate banged his head
  on a wall to prepare--scary
*coach gave inspiring speeches in which he ignored or
 downplayed the fact of kids getting seriously hurt
*during games, nothing else existed except playing football--I
 locked every other part of myself away
```

Look to each of your main points to see how you might add supporting points. You may need to read sources to fill in gaps. Developing categories fully at this stage will maximize the information you will have to work with when devising a thesis.

EXERCISE 9

Select the most promising information from your efforts to generate ideas about your topic, as defined in Exercise 8. *Form categories:* consolidate information that resulted from your using all three invention strategies. Write a brief sentence or phrase of definition for each category. *Organize each category* into a main point and supporting points. Finally, *expand information:* fill in gaps and if you are interested (or if your professor requires it) seek out source material that you can use in your paper. At the conclusion of this exercise, each category should have a main point supported by at least two specific, subordinate points.

3d   Writing a thesis and devising a sketch of your paper

A **thesis** is a general statement that you make about your topic, usually in the form of a single sentence that summarizes the controlling idea of your paper. You cannot produce a fully accurate **final thesis** until you have written down a complete draft. When sitting down to a first draft, you will at best have a **working thesis**: a statement that, based on everything you know about your topic, should prove to be a reasonably accurate summary of what you will write.

Like any sentence, a thesis consists of a subject and a predicate—that is, a verb and its associated words (see 7a-1). The *subject* of a thesis statement identifies the *subject* of your paper. The *predicate* represents the claim or assertion you will make about that subject.

Realize that your ideas for a paper and, consequently, for your thesis develop and change as your paper develops. Don't be bound by a single sentence at the beginning of your draft. Your working thesis *will* change. Nonetheless, you must depend on it to get you started.

1   Narrowing the subject of your thesis

As much as possible, you want the subject of your thesis statement to name something that is relatively narrowly defined; you want to name something you can discuss thoroughly within the allotted number of pages. How will you narrow your subject?

Build on the fact that you have organized your information into categories. To settle on a subject for your thesis, review your categories and select from among them your most promising and interesting material. Most likely, you will focus on only a fraction of this material in your actual paper.

EXERCISE 9

Individual responses

ADDITIONAL EXERCISE G

If you prefer to have students work inductively to understand how a thesis works, ask them to read any or all of the seven example student papers in this book located in chapters 4, 6, 35, and 36–39. For each paper, the thesis sentence is highlighted. In preparation for class discussion or possibly individual or group presentations ask students to explain the relation between the highlighted thesis and the paper that follows from it.

> ## Narrowing the Subject of a Thesis
>
> One useful way to narrow the subject of your thesis is to pose a journalist's questions: *who, what, when, where,* and *which aspects.*
>
> **Subject (too broad):** wilderness
> **Limiting questions:** which aspects?
> **Narrowed subject:** wilderness camping

2 Basing your thesis on a relationship you want to clarify

Once you have narrowed your subject, you must make an assertion about it; that is, you must complete the predicate part of your thesis. If you have ever written a paper before, you recognize this as the moment of chaos coalescing into order. If you have generated ideas on your own, you have several pages of notes; if you have conducted research, you have filled out perhaps fifty file cards. You cannot write until you have begun to make relationships among the ideas and information that you have generated. It is only *in the process* of making relationships—trying to make logical connections one way, seeing that a certain tactic does not work, trying other tactics, and constantly making adjustments—that sense emerges and you come to know what you think about your material. In examining the notes you have generated and organized into categories, ask yourself: What new statement can I make that helps to explain this material (if I am writing an informative paper) or to explain my reactions to this material (if I am writing a persuasive paper)? Think of a relationship that ties all—or part—of your material together. You will express this relationship in the predicate part of your thesis.

3 The thesis and your ambitions for a paper

Whether you intend to inform or persuade, the relationship that you assert in your thesis can be more or less ambitious: when the assertion is ambitious, your thesis and the paper that you build from it will be, too. The legal scholar and Supreme Court justice Oliver Wendell Holmes (1841–1935) once characterized intellectual ambition in terms of the number of levels, or stories, in a building. His description captures the qualities that distinguish barely adequate theses from competent and more challenging ones:

> There are one-story intellects, two-story intellects, and three-story intellects with skylights. All fact collectors who have no aim beyond their facts are one-story men. Two-story men compare, reason, generalize,

LOOKING AHEAD

Ask students to compare this Critical Decisions box and the related box on page 86. All example theses deal with the topic of creativity. Ask students to study the differences among example sentences. Students may well find that examples in this box are slightly argumentative, and certainly there is a familiar position in rhetorical studies that *all* claims are persuasive. If this is your view or that of your students, you may want to have the class compare *degrees* of persuasiveness entailed by each example thesis. At issue is the level of proof needed to substantiate the claim as true or probable.

LOOKING AHEAD

The discussion in chapter 5 of patterns of development refers specifically to the varieties of inference covered here. To further reinforce the interconnectedness of all phases of the writing process, you might inform students that this material will come in handy when they begin to revise paragraphs in their first drafts.

CRITICAL DECISIONS

Devise an action plan: Theses that lead to *informative* papers

A thesis is an action plan for the paper you intend to write. The predicate part of a thesis establishes a relationship that you believe brings meaning to the material that you are working with. Once you determine this relationship, your goal is to demonstrate it in your paper.

Certain relationships—sequential order, definition, classification, comparison, and contrast—lead to an informational thesis that says, in effect: "Here's how X works. Here are its distinctive features. Here are its parts. Here are its uses." This type of thesis results in a paper that informs. In the examples that follow, the key, informational relationship of each thesis is italicized.

Sequential order: You place your information and ideas in a logical order, or sequence—a pattern of first, second, third. . . .

> A creative thinker *will study a problem, arrive at a solution, and then delay accepting that solution until she has explored alternatives.*

Definition: Your information, considered as a whole, allows you to define a term.

> Creativity is *the act of recognizing problems and finding solutions.*

Classification: You find enough examples of something that you can recognize varieties.

> The four types of creativity *are visual, verbal, musical, and mathematical.*

Comparison: After studying two or more people, places, things, or ideas, you are able to demonstrate similarities.

> Of the four types of creativity, musical and mathematical *are most alike.*

Contrast: After studying two or more people, places, things, or ideas, you are able to demonstrate differences.

> Of the four types of creativity, visual and verbal *differ the most.*

using the labor of fact collectors as their own. Three-story men idealize, imagine, predict—their best illumination comes from above the skylight.[3]

One-story thesis

A one-story thesis leads to informative writing and demonstrates that you can gather and report facts. Any paper that follows from such a thesis requires little more than a stitching together of summaries. Strong papers do not use one-story theses. Only on some essay exams will a

---

[3]Oliver Wendell Holmes, cited in Esther Fusco, "Cognitive Levels Matching and Curriculum Analysis." *Developing Minds: A Resource Book for Teaching Thinking.* Ed. Arthur L. Costa. (Alexandria, VA: ASCD, 1985) 81.

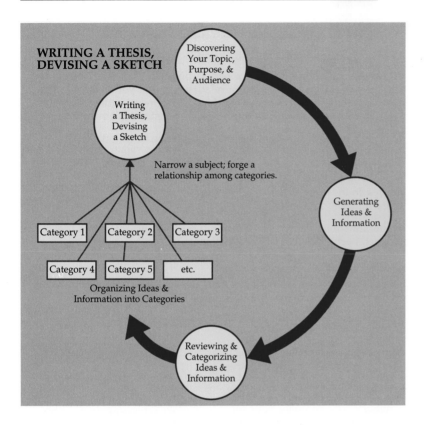

paper developed in support of a one-story thesis be appropriate in college writing.

Illustration: Examples of a One-Story Thesis

(1) Wilderness camping poses many challenges.
   —Challenge #1
   —Challenge #2, etc.
(2) Sean Hannan's one-story thesis:
   Football is a psychologically demanding sport.
   —Demands discipline
   —Demands identification with the team

Each one-story thesis requires little more than a summary of the topic's component elements. The writers make no attempt to forge relationships among these elements.

LOOKING AHEAD

With regard to the box on this page, see the instructor's annotation for the box on page 84. For much more on argumentative thesis, see chapter 6, sections b and d. The relationships here that lead to argumentative papers are identical to the lines of argument discussed in 6d.

REFERENCE

D'ANGELO, FRANK. *A Conceptual Theory of Rhetoric.* Cambridge: Winthrop, 1975. Patterns of development are also patterns of thought.

CRITICAL DECISIONS

Devise an action plan: Theses that lead to *argumentative* papers

A thesis is an action plan for the paper you intend to write. The predicate part of a thesis establishes a relationship that you believe brings meaning to the material you are working with. Once you determine this relationship, you set yourself the goal of demonstrating it in your paper.

Certain relationships—generalization, causation, sign, and analogy—lead to an argumentative thesis that says, in effect: "Here is my opinion on X. Here is my support and here are my reasons for thinking this way. I want you to agree with me." This type of thesis results in a paper that argues. In the examples that follow, the key, argumentative relationship of each thesis is italicized.

Generalization: Representative examples of a group allow you to infer a general principle that is true for all members of that group.

> Creative students *are essential to the success of any classroom.*

Causation: You can show that certain actions lead to certain effects or that certain effects follow from certain actions or conditions.

> The causes of creativity *are complex and involve a rich mixture of inheritance and learning.*

Sign: You can establish that one thing tends to occur in the presence of (and therefore is a sign of) another.

> Risk taking *is a sign of creativity.*

Analogy: You compare your topic to another topic, apparently unrelated, and can show an illuminating relation.

> In the same way that athletes who train vigorously for one sport may be out of shape for others, people who are creative in one sphere— visually, verbally, musically, or mathematically—*will not necessarily be creative in others.*

Two-story thesis

Holmes suggests that a thinker is someone who compares facts, generalizes from them, or reasons with them: that is, a thinker *argues* or *informs* with some degree of sophistication. Someone who reasons will define, order, classify, delineate a process, or establish cause and effect— all types of thinking and writing discussed in this book. When you can reason with facts, you are working with a two-story thesis because you are seeing facts *in relation to one another;* you are making inferences and seeing implications. By contrast, the writer of a one-story thesis sees and can write about only one set of facts at a time. A two-story thesis shows an engaged mind at work, *making connections* where none existed previously.

Illustration: Examples of a Two-Story Thesis

(1) Like holding a mirror to your personality, wilderness camping shows you to yourself—for better *and* worse.

—Wilderness camping described

—The camper in the wilderness, described

—Ways in which the wilderness elicits personal response, positive and negative

(2) Sean Hannan's two-story thesis:

A player who gives his allegiance and discipline to a winning football team must take care not to lose his soul in the process.

—Winning teams demand allegiance and discipline

—Allegiance and discipline, given unthinkingly, can create problems

—Taking care: striking a healthy balance between team life and individual life

Each two-story thesis forges a relationship between two previously unrelated elements: between wilderness camping and self-reflection and between team affiliation and self-destruction.

Three-story thesis

In addition to making connections where none existed previously, a three-story thesis shows a writer willing to take intellectual risks: that is, the writer is willing to expand the scope of the paper, widening its context in order to take up a broader, more complex, and (if executed well) more important discussion. A three-story thesis will create a paradox, a tension among its parts, by setting opposites against each other.[4] In a thesis with tension, you often find the conjunctions *although* and *even if*. The writer's job is to navigate between paradoxical opposites. The reader, sensing tension, wants to know what happens and why.

The three-story thesis, the most ambitious of the three types, can be enormously satisfying as you set out to "idealize, imagine, [or] predict." Holmes remarks that illumination for such a thinker comes "from above the skylight." The metaphor does not suggest someone waiting to be inspired by mysterious agents; rather, the skylight metaphor suggests a mind that is open to a world outside itself and is ready to question. The very best papers are built on three-story theses. These papers tend to be argumentative.

LOOKING BACK

In 3c, students were reviewing and categorizing ideas and information. The connection between that activity and formulating a thesis becomes clear with the two- and three-story theses, in which the student must forge a relationship between two previously unrelated elements. Again, the student's obligation, as writer, is to be *active*. In a three-story thesis, the writer must not only forge a relationship but show a willingness to go beyond the material in some original way.

---

[4]The term *tension,* as it relates to the thesis statement, is borrowed from John C. Bean and John D. Ramage, *Form and Surprise in Composition: Writing and Thinking Across the Curriculum* (New York: Macmillan, 1986) 168–69.

Illustration: Examples of a Three-Story Thesis

(1) Wilderness camping teaches that we must preserve what is brutal in Nature, even at the expense of public safety.
—Rigors of wilderness camping
—Potential danger to public
—Paradox: dangers notwithstanding, wilderness must be maintained

(2) Sean Hannan's three-story thesis:
Though belonging to a group has its benefits, the price of membership is steep: the loss of individual conscience.
—Group identity and its benefits
—What the individual sacrifices in order to belong
—Paradox: strength of group comes at the expense of individual's integrity

(3) Three-story thesis for the "curfew assignment."
By instituting a curfew and acting on what it believed was the students' behalf, the administration undermined the moral and educational principles it wanted to uphold.
—In setting a curfew, the administration said it was acting in the best interest of students
—"Best interests"defined, from student and administrative perspectives
—Paradox: in mandating morality through a curfew, the administration denied students a chance to grapple with moral issues and reach mature decisions on their own. The administration undermined its own educational aims.

Each three-story thesis broadens the scope of the paper and creates interest through paradoxical opposites. Each thesis promises a paper that will be argumentative.

What sort of paper are you writing?

As you create a working thesis, consider whether you are writing a one-, two-, or three-story thesis. By no means should you feel compelled to write a three-story thesis (and a three-story paper) for every assignment. Many writing tasks are one-story jobs: summaries, for instance, and responses to certain essay questions do not call for imaginative engagement on your part. Then again, you may not have time enough to develop a three-story thesis, or you may not know enough about the material to write ambitiously on it. When you have the opportunity, though, try at least for a two-story thesis.

Generating a Working Thesis

1. Narrow your subject so that you will be able to write specifically on it in the number of pages allotted.

2. Assemble the notes—arranged in categories—that you have generated for your paper.

3. Forge a relationship that clarifies the material you have assembled.

4. Devise a sentence—a working thesis—that links the relationship you have forged with your narrowed subject.

5. Determine how ambitious you will be with your thesis—and your paper.

Sometimes you will understand the ambition of your paper before you set out to write it; at other times you will not have a clear sense of how "large" a paper you are writing until you get mid-way or most of the way through a draft and discover your ideas. In any event, the point of the Holmes metaphor is for you to appreciate what sort of paper you are writing as you sit down to *revise* your first draft. Reread the draft; see what you have; and determine how ambitious your final draft should be. You will choose your final thesis, and shape your final paper, accordingly.

EXERCISE 10

Refer to your results of Exercise 7, where you chose three topics from a list and generated ideas about them. Choose one of these topics and narrow it by posing a journalist's questions, as described in 3b-4, so that it would be appropriate for a five-page paper. Then, given the ideas you generated in Exercise 7, write one-, two-, and three-story theses for this topic.

4 Devising a sketch of your paper, or developing a formal outline

Look to your working thesis for clues about the ideas you will need to develop in your essay. For an academic paper to succeed, you must develop all directly stated or implied ideas in the thesis. You may want to regard your thesis as a contract. In the final draft, the contract exists between you and your reader; the thesis promises the reader a discussion of certain material, and the paper delivers on that promise. As a tool used in writing a first draft, your working thesis is a provisional contract.

Identifying significant parts of your thesis

To create a sketch of your first draft, study your working thesis and identify all significant elements, stated directly or indirectly. In your

EXERCISE 10

Individual responses

GROUP ACTIVITY

A very simple group activity can generate healthy discussion of the thesis statements students have written so far. Using the same technique outlined in 3c-1, have students formulate questions for each other's thesis statements. Not only will writers have more productive questions to use toward an outline, but they'll also begin to appreciate that each reader looks at a thesis (or an entire essay) from a unique perspective.

REFERENCES

The following articles offer advice on specific patterns of development:

WILCOX, LANCE. "Time Lines in the Composing of Narratives: A Graphic Aid to Organization." *The Writing Instructor* 6 (1987): 162–73.

BERMAN, NEIL. "Language, Process, and Tinkertoys." CCC 26 (1975): 390–92.

(continued)

DEAN, TERRY. "Causal, Not Casual: An Advance Organizer for Cause-and-Effect Compositions." *Structuring for Success in the English Classroom.* Ed. Candy Carter. Urbana: NCTE, 1982. 92–97.

HAICH, GEORGE D. "If the Reader Never Saw One, How Would You Describe It?" *CCC* 26 (1975): 298–300.

LOOKING AHEAD

The quizzing technique discussed here is also a technique used to help students revise their work. See 4a-3 for a discussion on testing a paper or sections of a paper for unity and coherence.

paper, you are obliged to develop each of these elements and to explain how it is related to others. Write the working thesis at the top of a page and circle its significant words. You can then ask development questions of, or make comments about, each circled element. If you are thorough in quizzing your thesis, you will identify most of its significant parts. (You may not discover some parts until you write a first draft.) Having identified these significant parts, briefly sketch the paper you intend to write.

Question or Make Comments about Your Thesis in Order to Identify Major Sections of Your Paper

Questions

how does/will it happen?	what has prevented/will prevent it
how to describe?	from happening?
what are some examples?	who is involved?
what are the reasons for?	what are the key features?
what is my view?	what are the reasons against?
compared to what?	how often?
what is the cause?	possible to classify types or parts?
any stories to tell?	what is the effect of this?
how?	which ones?
when?	

Comments

define	review the reasoning
review the facts	explain the contrast or paradox

Option: Preparing a formal outline of your paper

Many writers feel that a rough sketch is sufficient for beginning the first draft of a paper. Others feel more comfortable with a formal plan of action—an outline with clearly delineated major and minor points. In collaborative writing situations, with different writers responsible for various sections of the project, a formal outline is probably the only way to reach agreement on what each writer will contribute.

Whatever your choice, be aware that before the first draft is written, any form of plan is, at best, *provisional* and subject to change. Outlines are sketches for getting started; they help you unify your paper and avoid discussing any topic not closely related to your thesis. They also help you to develop all significant points of your thesis, and they help you to achieve coherence—to ensure that all parts of the plan will lead logically from one to the next. Typically the parts of an outline are arranged in a logical order: the topic is divided into at least two constituent parts and each part is discussed separately. The order can be *spatial,* in terms of the location of the parts, or *chronological,* in terms of time sequence, or it can be based on some other criterion such as priority of importance to the issue at hand.

CRITICAL DECISIONS

Challenge and be challenged: Quizzing your working thesis to determine major sections of your paper

In writing a thesis, you compress a great deal of information into a single sentence; in writing a paper based on this thesis, you will need to "unpack" and discuss this information. Use the following technique as an aid to unpacking: challenge, or quiz, your thesis with questions (see box on p. 90). The technique will lead to a sketch of your paper.

Thesis   *define*   *what are / the key features?*   *why?*

Though belonging to a group has it benefits, the price of membership is steep: the loss of individual conscience. — *how does this happen?*

Sketching the paper
—Define group identity
—Discuss key benefits of belonging to a group
—Define individual conscience
—Review the process of how an individual sacrifices in order to belong to a group
—Explain the paradox: reasons that the strength of a group comes at the expense of an individual's integrity.

Thesis   *Review the reasoning*   *define "students' behalf" from students' and administration's point of view*

By instituting a curfew and acting on what it believed was the students' behalf, the administration undermined the moral and educational principles it wanted to uphold.   *how?*   *define both*

Sketching the paper
—Review the reasoning: in setting a curfew, the administration said it was acting in the best interest of students
—Define "students' behalf" from student and administrative perspectives
—Define moral issues and educational principles at issue
—Explain the paradox: in mandating morality through a curfew, the administration denied students a chance to grapple with moral issues and reach mature decisions on their own. The administration undermined its own educational aims.

Devise an action plan: A sketch based on your thesis is an action plan, a paper to be written. Depending on your preference, you can fill in the sketch, converting it to a detailed outline, or you can work with it as a sketch. In either case, this plan—closely connected to your thesis—sets an agenda for the paper to follow.

FOR DISCUSSION

A little extra time spent on these concepts now can make the job of evaluating drafts and final papers much easier on instructor and student alike: If students truly understand the meanings of *unity* and *coherence*, they'll understand instructors' comments that refer to the terms. A discussion of what students understand by the terms, with particular reference to paragraphs or essays they consider unified and coherent (see 5c and 5d), can serve to make paper evaluation a good deal more meaningful.

REFERENCES

Podis, Leonard A. "Teaching Arrangement: Defining a More Practical Approach." *CCC* 31 (1980): 197–204. Suggests strategies for teaching students to shape essays.

Podis, JoAnne M., and Leonard A. Podis. "Identifying and Teaching Rhetorical Plans for Arrangement." *CCC* 41 (1990): 430–42. Offers an alternative taxonomy to assist writers in arrangement of material in essays.

FOR DISCUSSION

Probably one of the most despised terms in student-dom is *outline*: some students may recall horror stories of being required to produce formal outlines prior to drafting a paper, while others may simply recall frustration with the whole concept. (Instructors have their share of stories as well.) During the course of a discussion of these stories, students might be asked to speculate on why the formal-outline-prior-to-draft assignment is so awful. If they read the section carefully, they should appreciate the purpose of an outline—and perhaps understand why the best outlines are produced only *after* at least one draft has been completed.

Useful as an outline can be, you will still need to discover the important elements of your paper during the process of writing and, necessarily, your outline or sketch will change as the writing takes shape.

Illustration: Formal Outline

What are the key features?   *What are the reasons for?*   *How will it happen?*

Thesis: (Establishing colonies on the moon)(will be possible by the early

Who's involved?   *What will prevent it from happening?*

21st century.)

I. Colonizing the moon
   A. Base
   B. Missions
      1. Science
         a. Astronomy
         b. Geology
      2. Industry
         a. Mining
         b. Crystal growth
   C. Inhabitants
      1. Specialists
      2. Nonspecialists

II. Designing and building the base
   A. Designers
      1. Architects
      2. Psychologists
      3. Engineers
   B. Construction
      1. Materials
      2. Methods
      3. Crews
      4. Dangers

A formal outline establishes the major sections and subsections of your paper. The outline shows how each section is supported by points you plan to discuss (see 18e). It also shows how these points are themselves supported. The goal of a formal outline is to make visible the material you plan to use in the paper. Standard outline form is as follows: uppercase roman numerals indicate the most general level of heading in the outline; these headings correspond with major sections of your paper. Uppercase letters mark the major points you will use in developing each heading. Arabic numbers mark the supporting points you will use in developing main points. Lowercase letters mark further subordination—support of supporting points. Note that the entries at each level of heading are grammatically parallel (see 18e); that each level of heading has at least two entries; and that only the first letter of an entry is capitalized. A formal outline need not show plans for your introduction or conclusion.

Illustration: Formal Outline with Sentences

Each item of a formal outline can also be written as a sentence, which you may prefer in your efforts to begin writing. The following is one section of the preceding outline, written in sentence form.

B. There will be two broad missions for a Moon Base.
   1. The first mission will be scientific.
      a. By setting up telescopes on the far side of the moon, astronomers will have an unparalleled view of the universe.
      b. Geologists studying samples of lunar soil will be able to learn both about earth's origin and about the origin of the solar system.
   2. The second mission will be industrial.
      a. Mining companies will be able to begin commercial operations almost immediately.
      b. In the light moon gravity, technicians will be able to grow superior crystals.

REFERENCE

HOLLOWAY, KARLA F. C. "Teaching Composition Through Outlining." *Teaching the Basics—Really!* Ed. Ouida Clapp. Urbana: NCTE, 1977. 36–39. Outlines can be a useful strategy in teaching the composing process.

EXERCISE 11

From the topic that you chose in Exercise 10 construct a two- or three-story thesis. Circle significant words or phrases, pose development questions, and prepare an informal or formal outline of your paper. Then expand your outline into a first draft of your paper.

EXERCISE 11

Individual responses

3e   Writing a draft

Your working thesis and your sketch or outline are essential for giving you the confidence to begin a first **draft.** Realize, however, that your final paper will *not* be identical to your original plans, even if they were carefully prepared. Once begun, writing will lead you to discard and revise your original ideas and will lead to new ideas as well. Through writing you will *explore* your subject. As you do, obstacles and opportunities will present themselves: by keeping your eyes open, you will be ready to avoid one and seize the other.

The object of a first draft is to get ideas down on paper, to explore them, and to establish the shape of your paper. The object is *not* to produce anything that is readable to anyone beside yourself. Finished, readable documents come through revision. When sitting down to write a draft, successful writers know they will be revising. They understand, in advance, that they will review *every* sentence and paragraph they produce and will rewrite many of them. This understanding can help you: If you can adopt the expert's attitude with regard to first and subsequent drafts, you will free yourself to write quickly—and imperfectly. You will give yourself permission to write in ways that you know will be imperfect but that will nonetheless be an essential step in your achieving a final product.

TEACHING IDEAS

This section will reinforce the notion that the "perfect" outline comes only *after* an essay has been written. Those students who rely too heavily on outlines may find the ideas put forth in this section daunting; rigid outlines have always provided a safety net for them. (Of course, slavish adherence to outlines has probably resulted in a string of mediocre papers as well.) If it is emphasized here that the drafting stage is where mistakes are okay, indeed where they're *supposed* to occur, the entire process of producing drafts might be made less painful for insecure students.

To get a sense of how different writers adopt different strategies for drafting, interview several people who write, either for a living or for their own enjoyment. (Professors are ideal candidates for such interviews; many write for both reasons. Writing Center staff are also accustomed to talking about their writing process.) Ask your subjects how they move from outline to draft. As you record their responses, note the differences between writers. Which of the processes most closely resembles yours? In what ways? Do the various responses offer any advice to you on your own movement from outline to draft? If so, what specific changes do you plan to make?

ESL ALERT

Writer's block is not the same for ESL students as for native speakers. ESL students might be unable to generate information because of a total lack of experience with the topic or understanding of its significance. For instance, an assignment asking ESL students to write on the cigarette smoking controversy may produce limited or poor papers because for much of the world cigarette smoking is an unquestioned way of life; in other words, our controversy is not an understandable controversy for them. Papers on topics like the military draft or AIDS may also produce skewed results. What we take for granted as being of universal concern is not necessarily so.

Strategies for Drafting
Working yourself through the draft

1. Write *one* section of the paper at a time: write a general statement that supports some part of your thesis, then provide details about the supporting statement. Once you have finished a section, take a break. Then return to write another section, working incrementally in this fashion until you have completed the draft.
   - Alternately, write one section of the paper and take a break. Then reread and revise that one section before moving to the next. Continue to work in this fashion, one section at a time, until you complete the draft.
2. Accept *two* drafts, minimum, as the standard for writing any formal paper. In this way, you give yourself permission to write a first draft that is not perfect.
3. If you have prepared adequately for writing, then trust that you will discover what to write *as* you write.
4. Save for later substantial revisions concerning grammar, punctuation, usage, and spelling. In your first drafts, focus on content.

1 Beating writer's block

Journalists, novelists, beginning writers, writing teachers, graduate students, business people, students in freshmen composition: *everybody* avoids writing at some point or another. Odd as it may seem, this information can be of comfort: for if you avoid writing, be assured that avoidance does *not* mean you have done things poorly or that you do not "have what it takes" to be a competent writer. Avoidance and the anxiety that causes it are natural parts of the writing process. By no means are they ever-present parts, and if you devote sufficient time to preparing yourself to write, you minimize the danger of writer's block. Still, preparing is not the same as writing a draft, and you inevitably face a moment in which you decide to take a step—or not. Think about the feelings you get when you do not want to write. When you are stuck as a writer, what might you be telling yourself? And how might you get unstuck?

STUCK *I cannot get started.* I am afraid of the blank page—or its electronic equivalent, the empty screen: However fully formed ideas for writing may come to me, I can only write one word after the next. And as I do, what I *have not* written seems so vast that I cannot make a beginning.

UNSTUCK *Prepare yourself mentally to write one section of the paper, not the entire paper.* Three-page papers, just like 500-page books, get written one section at a time. When you sit down to write a draft, identify a *section:* a grouping of related paragraphs that you can write in a single sitting.

STUCK   *I want my writing to be perfect.* My early attempts to express anything are messy. I get a sinking feeling when I reread my work and see how much revision is needed. Whenever I cannot think of the right word, I freeze up.

UNSTUCK   *Accept* two *drafts, minimum, as the standard for writing any formal paper.* When you understand that you will rewrite the first draft of all formal papers or letters, you can give yourself permission to write a first draft quickly and at times imprecisely.

STUCK   *Why advertise my problems?* I worry about grammar, punctuation, and spelling, and I do not want to embarrass myself.

UNSTUCK   *Use a writer's reference tools.* Many people are nervous about these errors. The fear is real. As long as you know how to use standard desk references—a dictionary and a handbook—there is no need to memorize rules of grammar, punctuation, and spelling. Of course, knowing the rules *does* save you time.

2   Working with your sketch or outline

Following are three strategies for using your sketch or outline as a basis for writing. None of these strategies is *correct* in the sense that one produces a better draft than the others. All will get you a first draft, and all have advantages and disadvantages. How you choose to use a sketch or outline is a matter of your temperament as a writer.

Adhering closely to your outline

One strategy for writing a draft is to follow closely the sketch or outline you made prior to actual drafting. To make full and frequent use of the detailed outline you have assembled makes a great deal of sense, as long as you are aware that your paper *will* deviate from the outline.

Advantages
By regularly consulting your outline, you will feel that you are making regular progress toward the completion of your paper.

Disadvantages
A comprehensive outline can so focus your vision that you will not allow yourself to stray and discover the territory of your paper. The paper planned will be the paper written, for better or worse.

Adhering loosely to your outline

Some writers prefer to use a sketch or outline exclusively as a strategy for preparing; in the actual drafting of the paper, they abandon their plan in favor of one that they generate *while* writing the draft. Examine your outline, studying its first section carefully, and then begin writing. The outline is set aside and, once writing is under way, a new outline for each section of the paper you are about to write is created, based on the material you have just written. As you complete each section, update and adjust your outline.

REFERENCES

ROSE, MIKE. "Rigid Rules, Inflexible Plans, and the Stifling of Language: A Cognitivist Analysis of Writer's Block." *CCC* 31 (1980): 389–401. Writers who use guidelines rather than rigid rules seldom experience blocking.

BLOOM, LYNN Z. "Research on Writing Blocks, Writing Anxiety, and Writing Apprehension." *Research in Composition and Rhetoric.* Eds. Michael G. Moran and Ronald F. Lunsford. Westport: Greenwood, 1984. 71–91. An examination of strategies for overcoming writer's block (includes research).

HILLOCKS, GEORGE, JR. *Research on Written Composition.* Urbana, ERIC, 1986. 39–49. A review of current research on revising, with emphasis on strategies.

ELBOW, PETER. "Quick Revising," "Thorough Revising," "Revising with Feedback," and "Cut and Paste Revising and the Collage." *Writing with Power: Techniques for Mastering the Writing Process.* New York: Oxford UP, 1981. Practical advice on all areas of revising.

SCHWARTZ, MIMI. "Revision Profiles: Patterns and Implications." *CE* 45 (1983): 549–58. Writers revise according to the category into which they fit.

LINDEMANN, ERIKA. *A Rhetoric for Writing Teachers.* 2nd ed. New York: Oxford UP, 1987. 171–88. A discussion of several revising strategies (includes bibliography).

MURRAY, DONALD. "Teaching the Motivating Force of Revision." *Learning by Teaching.* Upper Montclair, NJ: Boynton/Cook, 1982. The act of revising can itself motivate writers.

BRANNON, LIL, MELINDA KNIGHT, and VERA NEVEROW-TURK. *Writers Writing.* Upper Montclair, NJ: Boynton/Cook, 1983. Writing and revising are not discrete stages in the writing process.

HARRIS, MURIEL. "Composing Behaviors of One- and Multi-Draft Writers." *CE* 51 (1989): 174–91. A look at revising practices of student writers, emphasizing differences between those who do and those who do not write multiple drafts.

TEACHING IDEAS

It can be helpful for students to spend some time reacquainting themselves with the writing wheel at this point. Many student writers tend to consider a first draft a finished product; the wheel illustrates the occasions for revising that present themselves as writers encounter difficulty with the draft. Understanding that it's okay to move back to an earlier stage in the writing process will help students feel confident even when the draft doesn't seem to be progressing as it should. Many student writers need constant reassurance that their frustrations don't stem from their inadequacies, but rather provide evidence that they are indeed writers. The visual image of the wheel offers some of that reassurance.

ADDITIONAL EXERCISE I

Having recorded observations on your writing process in your writer's log, try to "plug in" your own process on the writing wheel. Using the labels provided in the diagram, offer more specific descriptions of what you do at each of the "loops" on the wheel. Compare your diagram to those of a few of your classmates. What similarities can you find? Differences?

TEACHING IDEAS

The suggested technique of writing at least three related paragraphs at a sitting can help to free students of writer's block. Students should first understand that their first-draft paragraphs *will* be revised; with this knowledge, students should be more free to investigate and experiment with their writing, secure in knowing that no other readers need see their preliminary work. By helping students to focus on producing *sections*, you simultaneously help them to think of their drafts structurally and to beat the often demoralizing habit of stopping after each sentence to labor over the next. The fine-tuning of sentences is a matter for second- and third-draft attention.

Advantages

This strategy gives you the best chance of discovering material, since each new section of the paper is based on the writing you have just completed and not on an outline prepared in advance.

Disadvantages

The same freedom that gives you room to be creative can result in paragraphs that do not lead logically from one to the next and whole groupings of paragraphs that drift away from the working thesis.

Combining strategies

Some writers like to give themselves more freedom than close adherence to a pre-draft outline allows; but at the same time they prefer more structure than the outline-as-you-go approach provides. These writers borrow from both methods. First, they carefully review their pre-draft outline for each section of the paper before writing it; then they write the section *without* further reference to the outline. At the end of each section, they compare their work against the outline and plan to add or delete material as needed. They also look ahead to the next section and revise the outline, if necessary.

3 Writing one section of your paper at a sitting

Unless you are writing an introduction, conclusion, or transition, every paragraph that you write will be situated in a grouping of paragraphs, or a **section** that constitutes part of the larger document. Think of the draft you are writing as a series of sections: typically groupings of three, four, or five related paragraphs. Plan to write *one* section of your paper at a sitting. Then take a break. Sooner than you realize, the pages will add up and you will have finished the draft.

As your draft develops, you will probably find yourself devoting a section to each major point you wish to develop. (Recall that you were able to identify these points, at least most of them, by "quizzing" your working thesis—see page 91.) Every section of your paper should have a dominant, controlling focus—a **section thesis** that explicitly announces the major point you will address in the grouping of paragraphs to follow. The section thesis will help you to write your draft and, eventually, will help your readers to follow your discussion.

4 Recalling the key relationship in your thesis

Once you express a relationship in the predicate part of your thesis, you will want to develop that relationship by giving examples and providing support. *The types of paragraphs you write in a paper are tied directly to the relationships that you express in your thesis.* For instance, if your thesis states that you have inferred a sequence concerning your subject, then

---

How to Write One Section of a Paper

1. **Prepare to write.** Identify purpose and define audience; generate and organize ideas and information; and devise a working thesis.

2. **Identify sections of the paper.** Ask of your thesis: What parts must I develop in order to deliver on the promise of this statement? Your answer of perhaps three or four points will identify the sections you need to write to complete that statement.

3. **Plan to write one section of your paper at a sitting.** If a section is long, divide it into manageable parts and write one part at a sitting.

4. **Write individual paragraphs.** Each paragraph will be related to others in the section. As you begin a second paragraph, clearly relate it to the first; relate the third paragraph to the second, and so on until you finish writing the section. Then take a break.

5. **Write other sections, one at a time.** Continue writing, building one section incrementally on the next, until you complete your first draft.

---

surely at least several of the paragraphs that you write will be introduced with *first, second, third,* and so on. If your thesis suggests a comparison, then surely you will organize a certain number of paragraphs in one of the two ways discussed under "comparison/contrast" in section 5e-6. Your papers will consist of many paragraphs, of course; and only certain ones will directly develop the relationship in the predicate part of your thesis, but these will be the key paragraphs in your paper. Others will prepare for or will lead away from these key paragraphs. Therefore, at some point in the writing of your draft, explicitly recall the key relationship of your thesis.

5   Identifying and resolving problems in mid-draft

It is likely that at some point in the writing process you will find yourself unable to steam ahead, one section after the next. You will encounter obstacles, which you can recognize as follows: You are aware that your work in one section of the paper is not as good as it is elsewhere, or you make several attempts at writing a section and find that you simply cannot do it. When you are feeling especially frustrated, stop. Step back from your work and decide how you will get past this obstacle. Ask: Why am I having trouble? Here are several possibilities:

Potential obstacles in writing a draft

1. You do not have enough information to write. You have not gathered the information or, if you have, you may not thoroughly understand it.

2. You do not understand the point you planned to make or its relation to the rest of your paper.

3. The point you planned to make no longer seems relevant or correct, given what you have discovered about your subject while writing.

4. You recognize a gap in the structure of your paper, and you suddenly see the need to expand an existing section or to write an entirely new section.

5. The material in the section seems inappropriate for your audience.

6. You have said everything you need to in a page, but the assignment calls for six to ten pages.

7. At the moment, you do not have the attention span to write.

Each of these obstacles can frustrate your attempts at writing, and only you can know what is for you a normal and abnormal level of frustration. Whatever your tolerance, develop sensors to let you know when things are not going well. Frustration usually occurs for a good reason, so you should trust the reaction and then act on it. You will come of age as a writer the moment you can realize you are having trouble and can then step away to name your problem and find a solution.

6   Working collaboratively

In assigning a writing project, your professor may ask you to work collaboratively—that is, in a group. The great advantage of creating and writing a document collaboratively is that you can put the power of several minds to work on a task that might prove overwhelming for one person. Both in content and in presentation, however, your group's work should read as though *one* person had written it even if several people have been involved in the actual writing.

- To minimize rewriting, meet with group members before any writing takes place. Agree on a structure for the overall document and then assign parts to individual group members. Agree on a consistent point of view for the paper.

- At a second meeting after writing has just begun, ask each group member to outline his or her section and to discuss its structure. As a group, think specifically of the ways in which one section will build from and lead to another. Also raise and address any problems encountered thus far in the writing.

- At the completion of a first draft, distribute the assembled document to the entire group and have each member revise for content and consistency of perspective.

- Incorporate all revisions in a single version of the document. *One* member of the group should then take responsibility for rewriting the paper so as to ensure continuity of style and voice.

CHAPTER 4

The Process of Revision

As much as a first draft, revision is in its own way an act of creation. The difference between your first and second efforts at creating a document is that in a first draft you work to give a document potential: the writing may be incomplete, hurried, or inexact; but you are working toward an important, controlling idea. In your second and subsequent drafts, you work to make an earlier draft's potential *real*: you revise, and through revision—by adding, altering, or deleting sentences and paragraphs—you clarify your main point for yourself and, on the strength of that, for your reader. Accomplished writers expect to revise. They know that good revision reaches deep; that it is not, for the most part, about cosmetic changes (a word scratched out here, another added there) but about fundamental changes and redirections that help you discover meaning. Above all, readers expect *clarity* of ideas in your writing. When you revise, you rethink and you clarify; you will serve your own interests and your reader's by committing yourself to meaningful revision.

The Process of Revision

Think of revision as occurring in three stages—early, later, and final:

4a **Early revision:** Reread your first draft and rediscover your main idea. What you *intended* to write is not always, or even usually, what you *in fact* have written.

4b **Later revision:** Make all significant parts of your document work together in support of your main idea.

4c **Final revision (editing):** Correct errors at the sentence level that divert attention from your main point.

4a Early revision: Rediscovering your main idea

When writing succeeds, it always works at the largest possible level by clearly communicating a single idea. When writing fails, it is very often because the writer has not understood his most important idea well enough to present it to others. A key difference between successful and unsuccessful writing is the commitment a writer makes to revision, since it is the process of revision that helps to clarify the writer's main idea. The important word here is *commitment,* not ability. You can and will learn techniques of revision. What you alone can provide is the commitment to

KEY FEATURES

This chapter continues the discussion of the writing process begun in chapter 3 and culminates with the final draft of Sean Hannan's essay on high school football. In the revising process, students are advised to consider both unity and coherence, first from the perspective of the entire paper, then individual sections or paragraphs, and then sentences. In discussing the use of instructors' and peer editors' comments, the chapter acknowledges the need for honesty, respect, and thoughtfulness on the part of both writer and reviewer. As in chapter 3, exercises are designed primarily to guide students through the process of drafting and revising their own papers.

ESL ALERT

ESL students will have learned to follow teacher instructions on the correction of "errors," but will probably not understand the process of writing/revising to improve, on their own, the structure and development of an argument. Some might be revising for the first time ever.

GROUP ACTIVITY

Sometimes students have difficulty getting distance from their writing, even when they've left it alone for a day or so. Other readers, on the other hand, can offer a fresh reading of the paper. Arrange students in groups according to the directions outlined in 3c-1. Readers then answer simple, nonjudgmental questions about each draft:

1. What is the working thesis of this paper? Where does it appear?
2. Is there evidence of any competing thesis? If so, where does it appear?
3. Which thesis seems more consistent with the body of the paper? Why?

In addition to helping writers hone their theses, this activity provides nonthreatening practice for later peer editing sessions in which students make judgments on each other's papers.

TEACHING IDEAS

Bring to class multiple drafts of a paper or essay you have recently finished. Or bring multiple drafts of a single paragraph. Students are often fascinated to learn that their composition teachers practice the very principles they teach. With various drafts of a page before you and the students, discuss how your early revisions of a paragraph or page differ from later revisions. Recreate for students your thinking as you moved closer to the final form of a passage. Then make the link to student writing and to your expectations for early and later revisions in their work.

ADDITIONAL EXERCISE A

Ask students to prepare a lesson on revision, to be presented in a small group. Students should make and distribute photocopies of their various rewrites of one page, or a particular set of paragraphs, beginning with the final draft. After students have reported in their groups on the process of revision, have the group summarize the various strategies for revision just presented. Groups could write major points on sheets of easel paper that would be taped on the walls of the room, and you could lead the class in examining similarities and differences in revision technique. Doubtless, the class will observe more than one strategy at work, which is just the point of the discussion in 4a-1.

rework drafts until they express your meaning *exactly*. Early revision involves adding, altering, or deleting entire paragraphs with the sole purpose of clarifying your main idea. Commit yourself to real and meaningful revision, and your writing will be good consistently; back away from this commitment, and your writing will fail to the degree that you back away.

Strategies for Early Revision

Pose three questions to get started on early revision. Your goal is to rediscover and clarify what you have written in a first draft. Here are some tactics to help discover a main idea:

■ What I *intended* to write in my first draft may not be what I have *in fact* written. What is the main idea of this first draft?

Underline one sentence in your draft in answer to this question; if you cannot find such a sentence, write one.

Choose a title for your second draft. The title will help you to clarify your main idea.

■ Does what I have written in this draft satisfy my original purpose for writing?

Review the assignment or set of instructions that began your writing project. Restate the purpose of that assignment. Reread your draft to determine the extent to which you have met this purpose. To the degree you have not, plan to revise.

■ Does my writing communicate clearly to my audience?

Think of your audience and reread your draft with this audience clearly in mind. If need be, revise your level of language, your choice of illustrations, and your general treatment of the topic in order to help your audience understand.

---

1 Choosing a revision strategy that suits you

There are as many different strategies for revising a paper as there are for writing one, and the strategy you choose will depend on your temperament. Some first-draft writers work on individual paragraphs, revising continually until they achieve their idea for that paragraph before they move on. Others write and revise one section of their paper at a time, revising a grouping of related paragraphs continually until that grouping functions as a single, seamless unit. Still other writers complete an entire first draft and then revise. The approach to revision advocated here is that a writer make several "passes" over a draft and on each pass revise with a different focus. First, revise the largest elements (the sections); on the next pass, revise paragraphs within sections; and on the final pass (or passes), revise individual sentences within paragraphs. Choose a revision strategy that suits your temperament.

2   Strategies for clarifying and developing your main idea

The overall objective of your first revision of a draft, which will be your major revision, is to rediscover your main idea. You began your first draft with a main idea that you wanted to develop. But what you intended to write may not be what you have in fact written. Now is the time to check. The Critical Decisions box on page 102 shows several techniques for rereading and evaluating your first draft. On the basis of your evaluation, you will plan a second draft.

Reread your first draft with care, looking for some sentence other than your working thesis that more accurately describes what you have written. Often, such a "competing" thesis appears near the end of the draft, the place where you force yourself to summarize. If you can find no competing thesis and are sure that your original working thesis does not fit the paper you have written, modify the existing working thesis or write a new one. Be prepared to quiz the new thesis as you did before. See the box in 3d-4 to review techniques for doing this.

Outline the sections of a revised paper.

Recall that a *section* of your paper is a group of related paragraphs (see 3e-3 and 5a-2). Based on your revised thesis and on your development questions and comments about that thesis, outline the sections of a revised paper.

Incorporate sections of your first draft into your revised outline.

The next step of the revision process is a simple one. Study your new outline. Reexamine your first draft to determine how much of it will fit, with or without changes, into your plans for the final paper. Then, using block commands, retrieve your first draft and cut and paste usable sections of this draft onto your final outline. Be sure to reread each sentence of first-draft writing that you move into the second draft. Every sentence must contribute toward developing the meaning of your newly conceived thesis.

Write new sections of the final outline, as needed.

The preceding step will leave you with a partial paper: a detailed outline, some of the sections of which (imported from your first draft) are close to complete, other sections of which are indicated in the sketchiest possible terms by a phrase in your outline. You will need to write these sections from scratch. Before beginning a new section of your paper, write a section thesis to help focus your efforts (see 3e-3 and 5a-2).

LOOKING AHEAD

For a list of transitional expressions categorized by purpose, see the box in 5d-3.

ADDITIONAL EXERCISE C

ACROSS THE CURRICULUM Sometimes it's helpful to look at paragraphs written by professionals in order to better understand the concepts of unity and coherence. Find a brief (two-to four-page) self-contained section in one of your textbooks, and analyze it for unity and coherence. Use strategies such as the following: find the thesis; outline the selection; relate sections or paragraphs to the thesis; identify the logic that underlies the arrangement of paragraphs; identify transitional words, phrases, sentences, and paragraphs.

LOOKING BACK

In revision, writers adopt something of an adversarial response to their own work. To perfect their work, they need to think critically about it, which entails challenging their assertions and their defenses of those assertions. The habit of challenging oneself promotes critical thinking at all stages of the writing process, particularly in revision. See the discussion at 1b, where many of the questions suggested for challenging source materials can be directed toward the student's own work.

CRITICAL DECISIONS

Challenge and be challenged: Early revision

Early revision is a crucial stage in the writing process; in some ways it is as important as generating a first draft, for in early revision you make a unified, coherent presentation out of your work and give it the shape readers will see. You can help the process by challenging key elements of your paper.

- **Challenge your thesis.** You began your first draft with a working thesis. The thesis that organized your actual draft may differ from this. Try two strategies for identifying the sentence that will become your final thesis.

  Underline the sentence you intended to be your thesis in the first draft. Ask: "Is this the sentence I wrote about?" For a moment, play a doubting game. Provisionally answer with a *no* and search for a competing thesis. Reread the draft's final paragraphs with special care. If you find no alternate thesis, return to the original.

  Study the sentence you now know to be your thesis, and revise repeatedly until it is both precise and concise: make the sentence say what it must in as few words as possible. Base all subsequent revisions of your paper on this new, leaner version of your thesis.

- **Challenge your paper's structure.** What often changes most from first draft to second is the structure of a paper. A first draft is *yours* in the sense that you are writing it, at least partly, to discover what you think about a topic. The second draft is more the *reader's* in the sense that you must consider how others will regard your work and how you might best present it to secure approval and understanding. Rethink the structure of your paper in light of the reader's needs. Challenge the structure of your draft in two ways:

  Consider locating your revised thesis in some different part of the paper. How would this change the order of presentation? Are there advantages to be gained?

  Consider beginning your paper not with your present first paragraph, but with some paragraph from the middle of the draft. How does the paper present itself differently, based on this change? What further changes would be needed to ensure coherence?

Devise an action plan: Based on your challenges to the paper's thesis and structure, set yourself a "to do" list. A new thesis may require that you write new sections. A revised structure will require careful attention to coherence and at least several new sentences of transition.

3 Reconsidering purpose and audience

Purpose

At some point in the process of revision you will want to reconsider your earliest reasons for writing. You may have been asked to explain, describe, argue, compare, analyze, summarize, define, discuss, illustrate, evaluate, or prove. (See explanations of these and other important word meanings in assignments in 41b.) With your purpose firmly in mind, evaluate your first draft to determine the extent to which you have met that purpose. Alter your revision plans, if necessary, to satisfy your reason for writing.

- Identify the key verb in the assignment and define that verb with reference to your topic. (See 41b.)
- If you have trouble understanding the purpose, seek out your professor or your professor's assistant. Bring your draft to a conference and explain the direction you've taken.
- Once you identify the parts of a paper that will achieve a stated purpose, incorporate those parts into your plans for a revised draft.

Audience

Revisit your initial audience analysis (see 3a-3); will your audience be classmates, fellow majors, or a professor? Take whatever conclusions you reached in your analysis and use them as a tool for evaluating your first draft. You may find it useful to pose these questions:

- How will this subject appeal to my readers?
- Is the level of difficulty with which I have treated this subject appropriate for my readers?
- Is my choice of language, in both its tone (see 3a-4) and its level of difficulty, appropriate for my readers?
- Are my examples appropriate in interest and complexity for my readers?

Make changes to your revision plans according to your analysis of the first draft.

4   Choosing and using a title

Before rewriting your paper, use your revised thesis to devise a title. A title creates a context for your readers; a title alerts readers to your topic and your intentions for treating it. Forcing yourself to devise a title before beginning your major revision will help you to clarify your main idea. A *descriptive* title directly announces the content of a paper and is appropriate for reports and write-ups of experiments: occasions when you are expected to be direct. An *evocative* title is a playful, intriguing, or otherwise indirect attempt to pique a reader's interest. Both descriptive and evocative titles should be brief (no longer than ten words).

Working with his revised thesis, Sean Hannan chose an evocative title for his second draft: "The Win Justifies the Means," which plays on the phrase "the end justifies the means." The phrasing of this title directly captures the sense of his paper. Sean gave his final draft a descriptive title: "Group Life and the Loss of Conscience." That title more accurately matched what Sean came to understand was his ultimate purpose in writing: to explore the effects of group life on individuals in any circumstance, not only on the football field.

EXERCISE 1
Individual responses

EXERCISE 1
Following advice offered in this section, revise the first draft of the paper you wrote in response to Exercise 11, in chapter 3. Your early revision may be a major one, requiring you to rework your thesis and to redefine major sections of the paper.

4b Later revision: Bringing your main idea into focus

Your first major revision of a draft (the revision you achieved if you completed Exercise 1) requires the courage to look deep into your paper and make fundamental changes in order to present a single idea clearly. Later revisions will not be dramatic or far-reaching, and will require for the most part that you understand and be able to apply systematically certain principles of organization. Three principles of organization important to a later revision are unity, coherence, and balance.

1 Focusing the paper through unity

A paper is unified when the writer discusses only those elements of the subject implied by its thesis. **Unity** is a principle of logic that applies equally to the whole paper, to sections, and to individual paragraphs. In a unified paper, you discuss only those topics that can be anticipated by someone who reads your thesis. Following is an example of a revised thesis by student Josefa Pinto (resulting in the paper shown in student paragraphs in chapter 5), showing the section of the paper that she generated by quizzing the thesis:

> *Thesis:*
> Although genetic engineering has been considered the biotechnological breakthrough of the century, there are still many doubts concerning its potential effects on our environment.

> *Sections implied by thesis:*
> Definition of genetic engineering
> History, this century
> Benefits of genetic engineering
> Dangers of genetic engineering
> Controversy over genetic engineering

A paper is *not* unified if the writer introduces any topic that strays from the thesis—that is, that strays from the list of topics generated by quizzing the thesis.

Unity at the Level of the Essay, the Section, and the Paragraph

Unity is a principle of logic that applies equally to the whole paper, to sections, and to individual paragraphs. A unified discussion will not stray from the sentence that organizes and focuses any one of these principal parts of a paper. Recall that a *thesis* announces and controls the content of an entire essay, and that a *section thesis* announces and controls the content of a section. Just so, a *topic sentence* announces and controls the content of sentences in a single paragraph. Think of the topic sentence as a paragraph-level *thesis*, and you will see the principle of unity at work at *all* levels of the paper. At each level of the essay, a general statement is used to guide you in assembling specific, supporting parts.

ESSAY-LEVEL UNITY	The thesis (the most general statement in the essay) governs your choice of sections in a paper.
SECTION-LEVEL UNITY	Section theses (the second-most general statements in the essay) govern your choice of paragraphs in a section.
PARAGRAPH-LEVEL UNITY	Topic sentences (the third-most general statements in the essay) govern your choice of sentences in a paragraph.

A unified section of a paper is a discussion of those topics implied by your section thesis (see 3d-3 and 5a-2). Every topic generated by quizzing the thesis will become a *section* of your final paper. You will devote at least one, and maybe more, paragraphs to developing each section, or subtopic, of the thesis. In a unified paragraph, you discuss only one topic, the one implied by your topic sentence (see 5c).

2 Focusing the paper through coherence

Coherence describes the clarity of the relationship between one unit of meaning and another: between sections of a paper; between paragraphs within sections; and between sentences within paragraphs. Like unity, coherence is a principle of logic that applies equally to the whole paper, to sections, and to individual paragraphs. A *whole paper* is coherent when its sections (groupings of related paragraphs) follow one another in a sensible order. A *section* of the paper is coherent when the individual paragraphs that constitute it follow one another in a sensible order. And a *paragraph* is coherent when individual sentences that comprise it follow one another in a sensible order. At every level of a paper, you establish coherence by building logical bridges, or transitions, between thoughts. A **transition** may be a word, a sentence, or a paragraph devoted to building a smooth, logical relationship. In all cases, a transition has a double function: to remind readers of what they have just read and then to forecast for them what they are about to read. Transitional expressions include *additionally, likewise, first, second (and so on), afterward, for example, of course, accordingly, however, in conclusion,* and *on the whole.* (See 5d-3 for a detailed discussion of transitions and a more complete list.)

Transitions serve to highlight relationships that already exist between sections, paragraphs, or sentences that you have placed in a particular order. If you have trouble finding a word or sentence to serve as an effective transition, reexamine the sentences, paragraphs, or sections that you are trying to link. You may not have arranged them coherently in the first place, and may need to rearrange them.

As you revise your paper, pause to analyze its sections *in relation* to each other. Rearrange sections, if need be, in order to improve the logical flow of ideas among the largest units of meaning, the paper's sections.

Illustration: Josefa Pinto's Paper
ARRANGING SECTIONS OF THE PAPER COHERENTLY

Thesis:

Although genetic engineering has been considered the biotechnological breakthrough of the century, there are still many doubts concerning its potential effects on our environment.

Sections implied by thesis:

Definition of genetic engineering; History, this century; Benefits of genetic engineering; Dangers of genetic engineering; Controversy over genetic engineering

Coherent arrangements:

Usually, several arrangements of sections will lead to a coherent paper. Choose an arrangement based on your evidence, your audience, and your thesis.

A. Definition of genetic engineering
    History, this century
    Benefits of genetic engineering
    Dangers of genetic engineering
    Controversy over genetic engineering

B. Definition of genetic engineering
    History, this century
    Controversy over genetic engineering (I)
    Benefits of genetic engineering
    Controversy over genetic engineering (II)
    Dangers of genetic engineering

3   Focusing the paper through balance

Balance is a principle of development that guides you in expanding, condensing, and cutting material as you revise. First drafts are typically uneven in the amount of attention given to each section of a paper. In revision, one of your jobs is to review the weight (the extent of development) you have given each of the topics you have discussed and to determine how appropriate that weight is to the importance of that particular point. At times, you will need to **expand:** to add material, in which case you will need to return to the notes you made in preparing to write. You may need to generate new information by reflecting on your subject, by conducting additional library research, or both. At times, you will need to **condense:** to take a lengthy paragraph, for example, and reduce it to two sentences. At other times you will need to **cut:** to delete sentences because they are off the point or because they give too much attention to a subordinate point.

Revise for Balance: Expand, Condense, and Cut

1. In conjunction with your revision for unity and coherence, reread your paper to determine how evenly you have developed each section.
2. Expand discussions that are underdeveloped.
3. Condense discussions that are overdeveloped.
4. Cut extraneous material or material that gives too much weight to minor points.

EXERCISE 2
Revise your first draft for unity, coherence, and balance following the guidelines discussed in this chapter.

4c   Final revision

1   Editing

Editing is revision at the sentence level: the level at which you attend to style, grammar, punctuation, and word choice. Depending on their preferences, writers will edit (just as they revise) throughout the writing process, from the first draft through to the last. It would be misleading to state flatly that the process of sentence-level rewriting should wait until all issues of unity and coherence are resolved. Still, to the extent

GROUP ACTIVITY

Checking drafts for balance offers yet another opportunity for students to practice peer editing. Ask groups to evaluate each other's drafts according to the guidelines in the box in section 4b-3.

EXERCISE 2

Individual responses

REFERENCES

WILLIAMS, JOSEPH. *Style: Ten Lessons in Clarity and Grace.* 2nd ed. Glenview: Scott Foresman, 1985. Practical advice on how to correct errors in style, covering words, sentences, and paragraphs.

LAIB, NEVIN. "Conciseness and Amplification." *CCC* 41 (1990): 443–58. Uses a historical approach to argue for balance between brevity and elaboration in prose.

that you *can* hold off, save editing until the later drafts, once you are relatively confident that your paper has a final thesis and that the major sections of the paper are in order. In any event, don't allow sentence-level concerns to block your writing process early on—especially since the sentence you are fretting over may not even make it to the final draft.

Matters of precision are not so easily held off, however. Precise wording means precise thinking; and no doubt your ability to think clearly at any point in the draft will affect your subsequent writing. Use your judgment. If you find yourself struggling with the wording of an especially important sentence, take the time to edit and get it right. But if you are groping for a word in a sentence that is not central to your thinking, hold off your editing. Later in the writing process you will have time enough to settle questions of style, grammar, punctuation, usage, and spelling. By no means must you memorize rules concerning these matters as long as you can recognize problems and seek help in a handbook and a dictionary.

A suggestion made in the preface is worth repeating here: take an hour to read the introductions to each of the chapters in the handbook. If such a review is not realistic, then read the introductions to the chapters on sentence errors (see 12–16), effective sentences (see 17–20), and punctuation (see 24–29). Your review will give you a sense of the types of errors to watch for when editing. In addition, you can use the "Spotlight on Common Errors" device in the endpapers and in key chapters of this book. Use the "Spotlight" pages as checklists for uncovering and revising the most common sentence and punctuation errors.

2   Proofreading

Before you call a paper finished, check for minor errors that may annoy readers and embarrass you. Reread your paper to identify and correct misspelled words; words (often prepositions) omitted from sentences; words that have been doubled; punctuation that you tend to forget; and homonyms (writing *there* instead of *their*). If you have trouble spotting these minor errors in your writing, find a way to disrupt your usual pattern of reading so that the errors will become visible to you. One technique is to photocopy your work and have a friend read it aloud. You read along and make corrections. Another technique is to read each line of your paper in reverse order, from the last word on the line to the first. This approach forces you to focus on one word at a time. Besides checking for minor errors, review your occasion for writing one last time to make sure you have prepared your manuscript in an appropriate form. (See Appendix B on Manuscript Form and Preparation.)

3   Determining when a final draft is *final*

At some point you must determine that your paper is finished. In the age of word processing, this is not always an easy decision since you can make that one last correction and have the computer print a new page with relative ease. If you work with a typewriter and not a computer, then the decision about your final draft is more clear-cut. At some point you will refuse to retype another page if the change you are making does not seem worth the effort.

When changes seem not to improve the product, then you have reached an end to revision and editing. To consider a draft final, you should be satisfied that your paper has met these standards:

- The paper has a clearly stated main point to communicate.
- It has met all requirements of unity and coherence at the levels of the paper, section, and paragraph.
- It is punctuated correctly and is free of errors in grammar and usage.

Stylistically, you could edit your papers *ad infinitum*. For especially important papers, take extra time to ensure that your writing is crisp and direct and that your sentence rhythms are pleasing. But once you have met your obligations in the final draft, any changes you make will amount to refinements of an already competent work. To be sure, stylistic editing can mean the difference between a good work and an excellent one. Eventually, however, you will reach a point at which changes do not improve the quality of your paper. When you reach this point, stop.

> **EXERCISE 3**
> Edit the draft of the paper you have revised for purpose, coherence, and balance. Realize that you may need to make several passes at your draft to put it into final form. Now proofread your final draft.

4d Responding to editorial advice from peers or professors

One of your jobs as a writer is to learn how to give and receive editorial advice. All writers can benefit from an editor, a person whose fresh perspective can identify trouble spots that escaped the writer's view. If you are working collaboratively with your peers you will discover this quickly. There are two basic ground rules for giving and receiving editorial advice: the first concerns ego and the second, honesty.

1 Receiving advice

Without question, it is difficult and sometimes painful to be told by an instructor or fellow student that your paper needs a major revision. As the writer of a paper that does not yet succeed, you should be aware that critical comments, provided they come from a responsible source, are being directed at your work and not at you. To the extent possible, disengage your ego from the editorial review and respond not according to

TEACHING IDEAS

One of the most rewarding—and most diffi-cult—activities that student writers engage in is peer editing. It's rewarding because students be-come adept at revising by looking closely at the work of others; they also develop a greater sense of being real writers when their audience is ex-panded beyond the instructor. But it's difficult for students to offer honest criticism; it's so much easier and more pleasant to praise what-ever drafts come their way. Perhaps the most ef-fective way to counter the tendency to "be nice and not hurt anyone's feelings" is to expose that attitude for the myth it is: It's not "nice" to re-main silent about an obvious problem when the writer faces grading by a demanding instructor. Students need to understand that refusing to be honest when evaluating each other's drafts is a selfish behavior. That being said, they also need to know how to phrase their comments so as not to "hurt anyone's feelings." One way instructors may facilitate tactful comments is to design an evaluation sheet that calls for responses to be phrased in nonjudgmental ways. The "group ac-tivities" guidelines throughout this chapter allow students to offer meaningful feedback in nonthreatening ways.

GROUP ACTIVITY

Sometimes it's easier for students to offer criti-cism of drafts when they don't have to face the writer. Before asking students to evaluate each other's drafts, you may wish to distribute anon-ymous drafts for students to practice on. These drafts may be from your files or drafts you've composed for the occasion. (Using genuine student drafts shouldn't be a problem if you've received permission and if you preserve anon-ymity by not using material that's less than three years old.) In groups, students can evaluate the sample drafts and discuss their responses.

Guidelines for Peer Editing

1. Understand your role as an editor. Disinvest your ego and work to improve the paper according to the author's needs, not your own.

2. Ask the writer to identify elements of the paper to which you should pay special attention.

3. Questions you might consider as you are reading:

   Is the writer helping me to become interested in this topic?

   Do all the parts of this paper seem to be present? Are general points backed up with specific examples?

   Is the writing at the sentence level sharp?

   How much help does the writer need with the nuts and bolts of gram-mar and punctuation?

4. Begin with the positive. Whether you are writing your editorial com-ments or are delivering them in conference, begin with the parts of the paper that you liked. If at all possible, find *something* that is wor-thy of a compliment.

5. Be specific with criticism. Identify sections or sentences that you par-ticularly like and state why you like them. When you see room for improvement, identify specific words, sentences, or paragraphs, and state specifically what you think needs changing and why. If possi-ble, build your constructive criticisms on earlier strengths:

   Avoid statements like "This is vague."

   Strive for statements like "Your sentences in this section don't have the same vivid detail as your earlier sentences."

6. End your editorial advice with a summary of what you have ob-served. Then suggest a point-by-point action plan for the writer. That is, advise the writer on specific steps to take that will lead to an im-proved paper.

---

your hurt feelings but to the substance of the comments directed at your paper.

As a writer, you have the absolute prerogative to accept, to accept partially, or to reject editorial advice. Of course, you will also bear the bur-den of rejecting advice. But if you truly disagree with your editor, even one who will at some point be grading you, then you should hold your ground and thoughtfully explain what you were trying to do in the paper, what you would like to do, and why you cannot accept a particular sug-gestion for revision. *Thoughtfully* is the key here. First, give your editor the benefit of any doubt and assume that the advice offered is well founded. If the advice seems wrong, say: "I don't understand . . . Could you ex-plain again. . . ." If you understand the editor's advice and continue to disagree, say so—and give your reasons. But remember that if the editor is responsible, he or she has the interests of your paper in mind and is making suggestions to improve your effort. These suggestions deserve an honest hearing.

2 Giving advice

As an editor, you will want to be similarly mindful of ego and honesty. First, you must allow the writer his or her topic and interest in it. Do not criticize because a topic does not interest you. Next, realize that this is not your paper that you are commenting on. Disinvest your ego from the job so that you do not attempt in your comments to make the paper yours. Realize as well the power of your criticism. Many people feel fragile about their writing, and when you must criticize, be respectful. Most writing has something good in it. Start there and be specific with your praise. State "I like this sentence," and say why. If possible, build your criticisms with your compliments. Say, for instance, "These sentences in the other part of the paper don't do what you did earlier. Here's why. . . ." You must be honest with your criticism.

The better you edit other people's work, the more proficient you will become at editing your own. Whatever your editorial skills, you still can benefit from the editorial advice of others precisely because they are not you and can therefore offer a fresh perspective. In developing your own guidelines for giving editorial advice, you may want to build on the notes in the box on page 110.

4e Revising a first draft

Here is the first clean draft of Sean Hannan's paper, preparations for which you followed in chapter 3. Sean revised as best he could to clarify matters of purpose, unity, coherence, and balance before submitting the draft to his instructor for review. You will find the instructor's comments written throughout.

```
                 Rough Draft
     Football is a challenging sport. To
win, players must sacrifice physically and
mentally. I know this because in my senior
year of high school, I played on a champi-
onship team. The raw emotion and violence
of the game which had dominated our lives        1
for four months had manifested into an evil
unparalleled by any good that could have
been derived from winning. Fans don't know
```

REFERENCES

BECK, JAMES P. "Asking Students to Annotate Their Own Papers." *CCC* 38 (1982): 322–23. Discusses effectiveness of students' evaluating the strategies used in their own papers.

GERE, ANN RUGGLES. *Writing Groups: History, Theory, and Implications.* Carbondale: Southern Illinois UP, 1987. A review of writing groups, including theory and practice. Includes annotated bibliography.

HERRINGTON, ANNE J., and DEBORAH CADMAN. "Peer Review and Revising in an Anthropology Course: Lessons for Learning." *CCC* 42 (1991): 184–99. Argues that a collaborative approach to writing is valuable in "content" courses as well as in writing classes.

GRIMM, NANCY. "Improving Students' Responses to Their Peers' Essays." *CCC* 37 (1986): 91–94. Practical advice on using response groups in the classroom.

TRIMBUR, JOHN. "Collaborative Learning and Teaching Writing." *Perspectives on Research and Scholarship in Composition.* Eds. Ben W. McLelland and Timothy R. Donovan. New York: MLA, 1985. 87–109. Analysis of collaborative learning, emphasizing implications for classrooms.

HARRIS, JEANNETTE. "Proofreading: A Reading/Writing Skill." *CCC* 38 (1987): 464–66. Highlights strategies students can use to proofread without getting caught up in content of a paper.

REFERENCES

SOMMERS, NANCY. "Responding to Student Writing." *CCC* 33 (1982): 148–56. An analysis of the problems involved in teachers' responses to students' texts.

HELLER, DANA A. "Silencing the Soundtrack: An Alternative to Marginal Comments." *CCC* 40 (1989): 210–15. Demonstrates an alternative method, based on post-structuralist theory, of responding to student papers.

HARRIS, MURIEL. *Teaching One-to-One.* Urbana, IL: NCTE, 1986. A practical discussion of the conference method of teaching writing.

SIEMINSKI, GREG C. "Couching Our Cutting the Compassion." *CCC* 42 (1991): 211–17. Using the analogy of surgery, argues that instructors must "cultivate a bedside manner" in student conferences.

SHAW, MARGARET L. "What Students Don't Say: An Approach to the Student Text." *CCC* 41 (1991): 45–54. Uses recent critical and literary theory to help instructors make responses that encourage students to think critically about their content and their writing/reading process.

LINDEMANN, ERIKA. *A Rhetoric for Writing Teachers.* 2nd. ed. New York: Oxford UP, 1987. 207–33. A discussion of meaningful comments on student texts (includes bibliography).

BUTTURF, DOUGLAS R., and NANCY I. SOMMERS. "Placing Revision in a Reinvented Rhetorical Tradition." *Reinventing the Rhetorical Tradition.* Eds. Aviva Freedman and Ian Pringle. Conway: L & S Books, 1980. 99–104. Instructors' comments should focus on revision.

ROBERTSON, MICHAEL. "Is Anybody Listening?" *CCC* 37 (1986): 87–91. Instructors should focus comments on text's content rather than its style or technique.

LOOKING BACK

If students have worked through chapter 3, they will have seen illustrations of Sean Hannan's preparing to write this draft. Before they read it, you might ask your students to review Hannan's various notes, his working thesis, and his sketch. See the various illustration panels in chapter 3, which present a realistic view of the effort entailed in preparing to write a first draft.

Expand. What about before the season?

You are planning to discuss how a football player can become an animal. Does the process begin on the first game of the year? before this?

Expand. A horrifying moment!

You must have been torn with conflicting emotions. How did you feel after breaking this player's leg?

Expand. How else did the town support you, and what were your reactions to this support?

Expand. You have me wanting more! What happened during the season? A process shows steps along the way, from beginning to end.

---

how the raw emotion and violence required of a football player can turn him into an animal.

The first game of the year served as introduction to both the horrors and advantages of winning. At the beginning of the second half we were beating the opposition handily. They were visibly fatigued and getting desperate, calling trick plays and misdirections. I was playing linebacker, when a reverse was run to my side. I had read the play from the snap and was waiting for the runner. My heart raced and adrenaline pumped as he ran directly at me. I lunged at him and planted my helmet into his thigh. Halfway through the tackle I felt his leg give under my helmet and heard the sound of bone breaking. We landed hard and were immediately covered by my teammates who were trying to make the same play. My arms were still wrapped around his knees and my helmet still laid against his crooked thigh, when he began crying.

After winning only one game the team and the media already talked of a league championship. What's more, our town which had been deprived of the title for thirty years began to vehemently support us. Signs were erected in store fronts to encourage us, and we made headlines in the local paper.

We had won all our games, and with each win the town's support grew until it reached a fever pitch at the last game. We were scheduled to play the league's only other undefeated team. Before the game, players were putting on their pads and taping their knees seemingly unaware of what they were about to go through. The coach soon entered and told us to be ready in a half hour. Immediately, as if in one mo-

2

3

4

Cut or condense? I'm concerned that your story of the season is becoming just—that is, only—a story. Your narration is compelling, but too much narration causes difficulties. See my note at the end.

tion, helmets went on, chin straps were tightened, and the stereo was turned on. The mood became deadly serious as players began to zombie about trying to unlock a rage within themselves. I focused on the words of the heavy metal music playing. I had my eyes closed thinking about the game when one of my teammates grabbed me and embraced me. Tears began to flow.

My heart was filled with absolute hatred when we took the field and I raged at the sight of our opponents. But, as the game began it became clear that our opposition wanted to win just as bad as we did. They matched us in intensity and will to win. On a kick-off one of our players named Jason had five ribs broken away from the play, and for the first time I feared being seriously hurt. The game was tied at 0 going into the fourth quarter. I was in charge of blocking their best player. His name was Hunter. He was over six feet tall and weighed about two hundred and fifty pounds. He was also the one responsible for injuring my teammate. Toward the end of the game we were able to get the ball inside their twenty. I was having trouble blocking Hunter. He made two big tackles that stalled our drive. It was third and seven and we called a time out. My teammates confronted me. Mark, who was apparently speaking for the whole group, looked directly into my eyes and asked: "Did you notice Hunter's knee brace." Nothing else was said, I knew what I had to do. On the next play I didn't even try to block Hunter. Instead, I stayed back. He stood up and exposed the weakness. When his leg was firmly planted I rushed him. I lowered my shoulder and planted it into the side of his right knee. It collapsed easier than I

5

TEACHING IDEAS

You may want to point out to students that the teacher's comments on Hannan's first draft are restricted to matters of content. Hannan has made various sentence-level errors, and students can assume the teacher has noted these. The teacher wants Hannan to reconsider *content*, primarily, and *structure* when thinking about a first major revision. At the appropriate point, late in the writing process, Hannan devotes time to revising sentences—see page 115. Early on, he focused on larger concerns.

thought, but he did not scream or cry or even fall. Instead he hobbled off the field squinting. The game had made Hunter tough and I respected him but I also knew that he wouldn't be back. In the huddle I was met with thankful nods and pats on the back. Everyone knew that what had happened was no accident. Revitalized, the team went on to score and eventually win. Elation was in the air as fans poured onto the field.

The intensity of this game and of our opponents had given us perspective, though. In playing, we were forced to look into a mirror. While the town celebrated, my teammates and I began to question what we were doing and why we were doing it. Throughout the next week I thought about the people that had been hurt in our climb to the league championship. I had also discovered what evil I was capable of. And now that we had achieved our goal, I could no longer rationalize the monster I had become. Winning, with all of its benefits, had created monsters out of us.

6

Have you discovered a new thesis here? I can't help but think that you've ended at a more significant place than where you began.

General comments: The writing here is immediate and forceful. You have a talent for describing violence with sensitivity. The essay tells a story of conversion, of how you changed. Two points to bear in mind that might improve the telling: Your story locks you into a strict time sequence in which you must present all information chronologically. A full accounting of how playing football turned you into an animal would therefore be very long. The second, related difficulty is that your "narrator" mode locks out your "observer" mode, and the observer has some shrewd things to say. To sum up: Compress the narration when you can; add comments and interpretations when you can. This is a strong beginning—speaking of which, your introduction could be more imaginative. And what about a title?

4f Sample paper: Final draft

Sean Hannan wrote three drafts of his paper, developing a successively more ambitious thesis in each. In early revisions, he settled large-scale matters of unity and coherence. Then, in a final effort he corrected errors in grammar, punctuation, and usage. As you will see, Sean spent time refining his sentences so that they would read effortlessly. You will find in his essay the paradox evident in all good writing: When sentences are clear and easy to read, they mask the considerable effort that went into their making. Good writing looks to a reader as though it took no work at all; but of course the writer knows otherwise.

Changes that Sean made in his second and third drafts of this paper are indicated by various screens. Lines of the paper left unscreened are more or less original to Sean's first draft. A teal screen indicates material that he added to his second draft; a burgundy screen indicates material that he added to the third (and final) draft. As you will see, Sean's second draft essentially fleshed out his original paper. The burgundy screen shows that in his final effort, Sean generalized the focus of his paper: he used his experiences on the football team to discuss the larger question of group membership and individual identity.

TEACHING IDEAS

Sean Hannan's final draft has been color-coded to show the evolution of the paper from first to final draft. Students who are particularly interested in this evolution can turn to the illustration panels in chapter 3 to see Hannan's earliest notes and his efforts to achieve a working thesis and sketch. Students might similarly code their own papers and demonstrate to themselves the extent to which material in a first draft persists into the final draft. Indeed, once during the semester you might formally ask students to document the evolution of their own papers. This will make the point that a writer's ideas evolve and that a final draft's clean, effortless presentation is the result of many prior (and messy) efforts.

Group Life and the Loss of Conscience

"This team has more character than any other team I've had the pleasure of working with." My football coach spoke honestly to the audience of players, parents and local officials, but hearing him filled me with disdain. I glanced across the table to catch a teammate's reactions. He simply shook his head, disgusted and shamed by how we were being made into heroes. All of the players understood that the traits referred to by our coach were nothing to be proud of, were nothing to celebrate, and certainly were nothing to cheer about. But the crowd gave us an ovation anyway. During the season, as fans had turned to us as a source of pride and entertainment, members of the team had turned to one another for different, darker reasons. We had become a tightly knit group. We stood up for each other: played together, won together. and as the season unfolded--lost our souls together. Though being a member of a group has its benefits, =but the price of membership can be steep--the loss of group life can usurp an individual's conscience--a lesson I learned all too well playing football.

Introduction frames the paper

Sean returns to the banquet in his conclusion

1

With this thesis, the point of the paper is generalized from football to group behavior

■ *material added to 2nd draft*   ■ *material added to 3rd draft*

What The social psychologist Solomon Asch ob-
~~served~~ *about* ~~that groups~~ *behavior certainly describes my football team:* ~~behave according to laws that have little resemblance to the laws governing individual behavior:~~

> [W]hen men live and act in groups there arise forces and phenomena that follow laws of their own and which cannot be described in terms of the properties of individuals composing them. (242)

Asch was describing the "Group Mind Thesis" here, the validity of which I proved to myself during the football season. I do not think of myself as a thug. In fact, people have described my manner as gentle. But as a member of my football team, I became something else. Before the season even started the team attended practices that conditioned both bodies and minds. These practices thoroughly stripped us of our personal identities, and we were taught like soldiers to be obedient and to define ourselves by becoming part of the team. In this way, the success of the team became my success, and the failure of the team became my failure. The team became my family and winning became my only goal.

Reference to a source that sets the discussion of football in a broader context

2

The first game of the year served as an introduction to both the horrors and advantages of winning. At the beginning of the second half we were beating the opposition handily. They were visibly fatigued and getting desperate, calling trick plays and misdirections. I was playing linebacker, when a reverse was run to my side. I had read the play from the snap and was waiting for the runner. My heart raced and adrenaline pumped as he ran directly at me. I lunged at him and planted my helmet into his thigh. Halfway through the tackle I felt his leg give under my helmet and heard the sound of bone breaking. We landed hard and were immediately covered by my teammates who were trying to make

Narration: the story of Sean's season

3

▨ *material added to 2nd draft*   ▧ *material added to 3rd draft*

the same play. My arms were still wrapped around his knees and my helmet still laid against his crooked thigh, when he began crying. I wanted to get up and away from what I had done, but the weight of my teammates held me down. When I was finally let up I stood with the team trying to disassociate myself from the scene. I felt sick. I didn't want to play football anymore. I wanted to tell the injured boy how sorry I was. But I didn't; instead I listened to a rabble-rousing speech from the coach ("That's the kind of hit that wins games!") and attempted to play. I was tentative; the whole team was. Luckily, the other team was just as disturbed as we were and made no attempt to come back.

My initiation into the group had been cemented by that tackle. In retrospect, I see that the team gained its identity that afternoon. No one stepped forward to say: "That was a lousy thing that happened." Publicly, at least, no one dared violate what was becoming the group ethic: hit hard, make opponents fear us, and win! Why didn't anyone object? According to recent research in social psychology, individuals become members of groups because of two strong desires. The first desire is to be liked. Known as "normative social influence," this desire causes people to agree because agreement brings approval. In the locker room, after the game, no one was willing to bring down the anger of the whole team on his head by saying what he and the rest of us felt. The second desire is to be right. Known as "informational social influence," this desire causes people to agree because agreement confirms the correctness of certain behaviors. I broke an opposing player's leg. If no one spoke against the injury, then the circumstances that caused it--circumstances in which we all played a part-- must have been acceptable (Baron and Byrne, 323).

Directly develops the end of ¶2 in 1st draft

Reference to a second subject

4

3rd draft effort to "enlarge" the paper

The violence of our first game was no doubt horrifying, but at the same time the glory of winning was monstrously pleasurable. After winning only one game the team and the media already talked of a league championship. What's more, our town, which had been deprived of the title for thirty years, began to vehemently support us. Signs were erected in store fronts to encourage us, and we made headlines in the local paper. As we continued to win, support for the team intensified. One game after the next we beat our opponents. Everywhere we went people stopped to wish us luck. At restaurants we got free food. At school, at least one key player who had been struggling academically was kept eligible to play by the generosity of understanding teachers. Gradually, we grew accustomed to our special treatment, until winning and its benefits became something we expected and needed--like a drug. Sadly, no one seemed to notice how our characters were being transformed.

Loyalty to the team became my passionate concern. That was the warning sign I should have heeded; for when a group's interests overwhelm an individual's, trouble is sure to follow. Our public life is filled with stories of an individual's conscience being usurped by a group. Two examples come to mind. In the Watergate scandal, John Dean and others lied and went to jail in order to protect President Nixon. In the E. F. Hutton check-kiting scandal, a major brokerage house regularly overdrew its accounts by as much as a million dollars in order to collect on the interest illegally earned. Numerous employees knew of the fraud, but no one dared speak up. In both cases, the need to be liked and the need to be right were

Transition returns reader to narration

5

Directly develops ¶3 in 1st draft

Two nonfootball examples of a group usurping an individual's conscience

Added to 3rd draft, then cut (as off the point)

▇ *material added to 2nd draft*　▇ *material added to 3rd draft*

operating--and were overwhelming individual conscience. These same needs were so strong in me
that by the end of the football season I knew I
would do anything to help my team win the championship.

Our obsession with winning and our popular-
ity peaked at the same time: the end of the
regular season when our team, in true movie-
script form, was scheduled to play the only
other undefeated team in the league. The night
before the game several members of the team
went out for dinner at a local restaurant. No
one mentioned the game during our meal, but we
seemed to prolong leaving as if waiting for
some significant thing to happen. Mark, who sat
across the table from me, raised his hand. My
hand met his. He gripped it tightly and said:
"I would do anything to win this game: this is
my only chance to do anything important."

The next day the game was to start at one
o'clock, but I went early to get ready. The
pregame ritual that had been developed over the
season aided in transforming young men into monsters whose sole purpose was winning, no matter
what the consequences. In our locker room, the
heavy metal music was loud and the mood, deadly
serious. One teammate began to knock his bare
head against a cinder block wall in order to
bang away whatever civilized parts of him remained. I kept my eyes closed, thinking about
the game, when one of my teammates grabbed and
embraced me. The others joined in, and as a
team we exited the locker room possessed by an
evil more powerful than any good that could
have come from winning a football game.

My heart was filled with absolute hatred
when we took the field, and I raged at the
sight of our opponents. But as the game began
it became clear that our opposition wanted to
win every bit as much as we did. They matched

Return to
narration

6

Narration
continued

7

us in intensity and will. On a kick-off one of our players named Jason had five ribs broken away from the play, and for the first time I feared being seriously hurt. The game was tied at 0 going into the fourth quarter. I was in charge of blocking their best player. His name was Hunter. He was over six feet tall and weighed about two hundred and fifty pounds. He was also the one responsible for injuring my teammate.

8

Toward the end of the game we were able to get the ball inside their twenty yard line. I was having trouble blocking Hunter. He made two big tackles that stalled our drive. It was third and seven and we called a time out. My teammates confronted me. Mark, who was apparently speaking for the whole group, looked directly into my eyes and asked: "Did you notice Hunter's knee brace?" Nothing else was said. I knew what I had to do. On the next play I didn't even try to block Hunter. Instead, I stayed back. He stood up and exposed the weakness. When his leg was firmly planted I rushed him. I lowered my shoulder and planted it into the side of his right knee. It collapsed easier than I thought, but he did not scream or cry or even fall. Instead he hobbled off the field squinting. The game had made Hunter tough and I respected him, but I also knew that he wouldn't be back. In the huddle I was met with thankful nods and pats on the back. Revitalized, the team went on to score and eventually win.

Narration
continued

9

By the evening of our victory banquet, I had thought a good deal about the intensity of that game and the intensity of our opponents. They craved that win every bit as much as we craved it. In Hunter's team we had met ourselves and were forced to look into a mirror. While the town celebrated, my teammates and I

Conclusion: ends the "banquet frame" begun in the introduction

■ *material added to 2nd draft*　　■ *material added to 3rd draft*

began to question what we were doing and why   10
we were doing it. Winning had become so fierce
an addiction that we would do anything, including hurting people, to win. We rationalized
our behavior with a dangerous philosophy--that
the end justifies the means. We had become
monsters, capable of inflicting great harm;
and for this, people cheered us as heroes.

An individual's conscience, it turns out, is
a fragile thing both on the football field and   11
off. This is what I learned in my championship   3rd draft
season, and this is what I remember whenever I   effort to set
look at my trophy. I have hurt people. But I   context
don't think I ever will again--not knowingly,   larger than
anyway, because my conscience is far stronger   football
now for having lost it once.

Works Cited

Asch, Solomon. <u>Social Psychology.</u> New York:
    Prentice, 1952.
Baron, Robert A., and Donn Byrne. <u>Social Psy-
    chology: Understanding Human Interaction.</u>
    6th ed. Boston: Allyn and Bacon, 1991.

CHAPTER 5

The Paragraph and the Paper

KEY FEATURES

In keeping with current scholarship, this chapter treats paragraphs as units in a larger text. Emphasis throughout is on paragraphs not only as individual units, but as parts of a *section*, which is itself part of a whole essay. Interspersed between examples of individual paragraphs, then, are examples of larger sections. This attention to context reinforces the advice given to students to work on their papers one section at a time. As the traditional features of topic sentence, unity, coherence, and development are covered, the student's attention is always focused on the "big picture," i.e., how the paragraph works both internally and within its context. Topic sentences, for example, are discussed with regard to the paragraph and to the thesis of the section in which the paragraph is found. The same is true for treatment of other essential features. Throughout the chapter, decisions on paragraphing are considered in light of the purpose of the paper, of the section, and of the paragraph itself. Coverage of introductions, conclusions, and paragraph length takes into consideration both purpose and audience: students are advised to consider the needs of readers when framing their papers and when dividing paragraphs. As in previous chapters, several exercises are designed for use with students' own writing. The use of one set of paragraphs for several exercises gives students the opportunity to analyze the same section with respect to several essential features. Using the chapter to revise their own essays and to analyze the work of others should help students understand paragraphs from both the writer's and the reader's perspectives.

A paragraph is a group of related sentences organized by a single, controlling idea. Marked with an indented first word (typically five spaces from the left margin), a paragraph can be as brief as a sentence or longer than a page. Paragraphs rarely stand in isolation: they are extended units of thought that, pieced carefully together, build the content of a paper. In this chapter you will learn about the characteristics of a well-written paragraph and the relationship of individual paragraphs to larger units of thought.[1]

5a The relationship of single paragraphs to a whole paper

At times, you may feel that generating a paragraph is easy enough, but that writing an entire essay, paper, or report lies beyond your abilities. (How will I *ever* write twenty pages?) In these moments, you need to rediscover that whole documents are written one paragraph at a time and whole paragraphs, one sentence at a time.

1 The relationship of paragraphs to sections

Just as sentences are the units that comprise individual paragraphs, paragraphs are the units that comprise whole letters, essays, and reports. Aside from specialized occasions for writing such as summaries and short-answer essay exams, you will seldom write a single, isolated paragraph. Usually, any paragraph will be situated in a grouping—a **section**—that constitutes part of the larger document. Except for the beginning of a paper and the end (see 5f), any one paragraph will be involved directly with at least two others: the one immediately preceding and the one that follows. If in a single sitting you can write a group of three related paragraphs, then you will be able to piece together an entire paper.

The paragraphs that follow form a section—one part of a chapter—of Helen Keller's autobiography. At the age of nineteen months, Keller was stricken by a disease that left her deaf and blind. Not until she was

---

[1]Example paragraphs from various sources are consecutively numbered throughout the chapter for ease of reference.

seven, with the arrival of her teacher Anne Sullivan, did Keller discover language. The moment described in these famous paragraphs is one of extraordinary awakening: the realization that things in the world have names. These paragraphs are related; they read as a carefully written section, as if they appeared from the pen of the author all at the same instant. Be assured, however, that Keller wrote this section of her autobiography one paragraph at a time, one sentence at a time. She was twenty-two and a sophomore at Radcliffe College when *My Life Story* was published.

1   The morning after my teacher came she led me into her room and gave me a doll. The little blind children at the Perkins Institution had sent it and Laura Bridgman had dressed it; but I did not know this until afterward. When I had played with it a little while, Miss Sullivan slowly spelled into my hand the word "d-o-l-l." I was at once interested in this finger play and tried to imitate it. When I finally succeeded in making the letters correctly I was flushed with childish pleasure and pride. Running downstairs to my mother I held up my hand and made the letters for doll. I did not know that I was spelling a word or even that words existed; I was simply making my fingers go in monkey-like imitation. In the days that followed I learned to spell in this uncomprehending way a great many words, among them *pin, hat, cup* and a few verbs like *sit, stand* and *walk*. But my teacher had been with me several weeks before I understood that everything has a name.

2   One day, while I was playing with my new doll, Miss Sullivan put my big rag doll into my lap also, spelled "d-o-l-l" and tried to make me understand that "d-o-l-l" applied to both. Earlier in the day we had had a tussle over the words "m-u-g" and "w-a-t-e-r." Miss Sullivan had tried to impress it upon me that "m-u-g" is *mug* and that "w-a-t-e-r" is *water,* but I persisted in confounding the two. In despair she had dropped the subject for the time, only to renew it at the first opportunity. I became impatient at her repeated attempts and, seizing the new doll, I dashed it upon the floor. I was keenly delighted when I felt the fragments of the broken doll at my feet. Neither sorrow nor regret followed my passionate outburst. I had not loved the doll. In the still, dark world in which I lived there was no strong sentiment or tenderness. I felt my teacher sweep the fragments to one side of the hearth, and I had a sense of satisfaction that the cause of my discomfort was removed. She brought me my hat, and I knew I was going out into the warm sunshine. This thought, if a wordless sensation may be called a thought, made me hop and skip with pleasure.

3   We walked down the path to the well-house, attracted by the fragrance of the honeysuckle with which it was covered. Someone was drawing water and my teacher placed my hand under the spout. As the cool stream gushed over one hand she spelled into the other the word *water,* first slowly, then rapidly. I stood still, my whole attention fixed upon the motions of her fingers. Suddenly I felt a misty consciousness as of something forgotten—a thrill of returning thought; and somehow the mystery of language was revealed to me. I knew then that "w-a-t-e-r" meant the wonderful cool something that was flowing over my hand. That living word awakened my soul, gave it light, hope, joy,

LOOKING BACK

Students will be able to make ample use of revision strategies covered in chapter 4 as they work through chapter 5. Throughout this chapter, paragraphs are treated as units in a larger whole, and decisions on composing and revising are always considered in context. Some linear-minded students may consider material in this chapter repetitive; use such observations as an opportunity to reinforce both the recursive nature of the writing process and the interrelatedness of all segments of a text.

REFERENCES

Moran, Michael G. "The English Paragraph." *Research in Rhetoric and Composition: A Bibliographic Sourcebook.* Eds. Michael G. Moran and Ronald F. Lunsford. Westport: Greenwood, 1984. 425–50. Discusses definitions of paragraphs that focus on the individual unit and on the relationship of the unit to the whole text.

Rogers, Paul, Jr. "A Discourse-Centered Rhetoric of the Paragraph." *CCC* 17 (1966): 2–11. Paragraphs can be understood fully only in terms of the purposes of the larger text.

Bamburg, Betty. "What Makes a Text Coherent?" *CCC* 34 (1983): 417–29. Paragraph coherence has as much to do with the entire essay as it does with the paragraph itself.

D'Angelo, Frank. "The Topic Sentence Revisited." *CCC* 37 (1986): 431–41. Topic sentences increase readability of prose.

Lindemann, Erika. *A Rhetoric for Writing Teachers.* 2nd. ed. New York: Oxford UP, 1987. 141–57. Advocates approach using various theories of teaching paragraphs.

Braddock, Richard. "The Frequency and Placement of Topic Sentences in Expository Prose." *Research in Teaching Writing* 8 (1974): 287–304. The topic-sentence-first paragraph is not commonly used by professional writers.

Popken, Randell L. "A Study of Topic Sentence Use in Academic Writing." *Written Communication* 4 (1987): 209–28. Study reveals that topic sentences are common in professional prose.

ADDITIONAL EXERCISE A

Students may find the following paragraphs of interest. They were written by Anne Sullivan and concern the same event that Keller describes.

April 5, 1887

I must write you a line this morning because something very important has happened. Helen has taken the second great step in her education. She has learned that *everything has a name, and that the manual alphabet is the key to everything she wants to know.*

In a previous letter I think I wrote you that "mug" and "milk" had given Helen more trouble than all the rest. She confused the nouns with the verb "drink." She didn't know the word for "drink," but went through the pantomime of drinking when-

set it free! There were barriers still, it is true, but barriers that could in time be swept away.

4   I left the well-house eager to learn. Everything had a name, and each name gave birth to a new thought. As we returned to the house every object which I touched seemed to quiver with life. That was because I saw everything with the strange, new sight that had come to me. On entering the door I remembered the doll I had broken. I felt my way to the hearth and picked up the pieces. I tried vainly to put them together. Then my eyes filled with tears; for I realized what I had done, and for the first time I felt repentance and sorrow.

5   I learned a great many new words that day. I do not remember what they all were; but I do know that *mother, father, sister, teacher* were among them—words that were to make the world blossom for me, "like Aaron's rod, with flowers." It would have been difficult to find a happier child than I was as I lay in my crib at the close of that eventful day and lived over the joys it had brought me, and for the first time longed for a new day to come.

—Helen Keller, *My Life Story*

2 The relationship of sections to the whole paper

A **thesis** explicitly states the topic you will address in a paper and either directly or indirectly suggests the points you will make about that topic (see 3d). You will probably devote one section of your paper to discussing each point you wish to develop. For each section of your paper you will write a **section thesis,** a statement that explicitly announces the point you will address in the section and either directly or indirectly suggests what you will discuss relating to this point. You will organize your discussion in paragraphs.

The section thesis organizing the paragraphs by Helen Keller appears at the end of ¶1: *"But my teacher had been with me several weeks before I understood that everything has a name."* The next four paragraphs focus on and develop various aspects of this statement.

¶2   Events leading to the moment of discovery: an account of Sullivan's frustrated attempts to teach Keller.

¶3   The moment of discovery: clearly the most famous in the autobiography, Keller realizing the mystery of language.

¶4   Consequence 1 of the discovery: objects quivering with life and Keller knowing repentance and sorrow for the first time.

¶5   Consequence 2 of the discovery: joy in having learned that everything has a name.

These five paragraphs form a distinct section of one chapter in Keller's autobiography. The section as a whole is *unified* and *well developed* in that all paragraphs focus on and amply discuss a single controlling idea: the section thesis highlighted previously. Each paragraph is unified and well developed; each focuses on and amply discusses its own more narrowly defined controlling idea. And because each paragraph builds

Unity, Coherence, and Development

Each *paragraph* of a paper consists of *sentences* that are

Unified: the sentences are all concerned with a central, controlling idea.

Coherent: the sentences are arranged in a clear order, according to a definite plan.

Well developed: the sentences provide details that explain and illustrate the paragraph's controlling idea.

Each *section* of a paper consists of *paragraphs* that are

Unified: the groups of paragraphs are devoted to one controlling idea, a section-thesis that develops some part of the thesis.

Coherent: the groups of paragraphs within a section are arranged in a clear order, according to a definite plan.

Well developed: the groups of paragraphs provide details that explain and illustrate the section's controlling idea.

Every *paper* consists of *sections* (groups of related paragraphs) that are

Unified: each section is devoted to developing one part of the thesis, the central organizing idea of the paper.

Coherent: the sections are arranged in a clear order, according to some definite plan.

Well developed: each section of the paper provides details important for developing the thesis.

on the one that precedes it and is positioned according to a clear plan, the whole section is *coherent.* In the same way, every paragraph in the section is itself coherent since the sentences of each lead from one to the next and establish a clear pattern of relation.

EXERCISE 1

Read the following section of a paper on genetically engineered organisms, written by student Josefa Pinto. Analyze Josefa's paragraphs as follows: (1) identify her controlling idea, or section thesis; (2) explain how the section is unified, developed, and coherent.

Student Example: Josefa Pinto

6

Although these experiments may seem beneficial, there are certain dangers and problems involved with the use and release of genetically engineered organisms into the environment. One such problem is the limited research into and knowledge about these organisms. As Francis Sharples, former member of the Recombinant DNA Advisory Committee, stated, "Knowledge of the biotic and antibiotic interactions of most species in mixed populations in natural ecosystems is extremely limited. Currently the unknowns far outweigh the knowns where the ecological properties of microbes are concerned" (44). Many scientists are concerned with marketing fruits, vegetables, and grains after such a

ever she spelled "mug" or "milk." This morning, while she was washing, she wanted to know the name for "water." When she wants to know the name of anything, she points to it and pats my hand. I spelled "w-a-t-e-r" and thought no more about it until after breakfast. Then it occurred to me that with the help of this new word I might succeed in straightening out the "mug-milk" difficulty. We went out to the pump-house, and I made Helen hold her mug under the spout while I pumped. As the cold water gushed forth, filling the mug, I spelled "w-a-t-e-r" in Helen's free hand. The word coming so close upon the sensation of cold water rushing over her hand seemed to startle her. She dropped the mug and stood as one transfixed. A new light came into her face. She spelled "water" several times. Then she dropped on the ground and asked for its name and pointed to the pump and the trellis, and suddenly turning round she asked for my name. I spelled "Teacher." Just then the nurse brought Helen's little sister into the pump-house, and Helen spelled "baby" and pointed to the nurse. All the way back to the house she was highly excited, and learned the name of every object she touched, so that in a few hours she had added thirty new words to her vocabulary. Here are some of them: *Door, open, shut, give, go, come,* and a great many more.

P.S.—I didn't finish my letter in time to get it posted last night; so I shall add a line. Helen got up this morning like a radiant fairy. She has flitted from object to object, asking the name of everything and kissing me for very gladness. Last night when I got in bed, she stole into my arms of her own accord and kissed me for the first time, and I thought my heart would burst, so full was it of joy.

—ANNE SULLIVAN

Students may be asked to analyze Sullivan's paragraphs as follows: (1) Identify the controlling idea (the section thesis). (2) Explain how the entire section is unified, developed, and coherent. Here are suggested responses:

1. Controlling idea: Sentences 2 and 3, ¶6.
2. Unity: ¶7 opens with reference to Helen's ability to distinguish between related concepts, then moves to the word for "water" for a breakthrough. Naming "water" leads to naming other things. ¶8 reveals that the naming continues into the next day.

(continued)

Development: Section is developed primarily through example—use of "mug," "milk," "drink," and "water" keeps section focused on names for things related to drinking. When this concept is established, words focus on people—"Teacher," "baby."

Coherence: The section coheres through the use of chronological order.

EXERCISE 1

Throughout this chapter, several example paragraphs from a single student paper will be presented. The first three of these paragraphs appear in Exercise 1.

(1) Section thesis: "Although these experiments may seem beneficial, there are certain dangers and problems involved with the use and release of genetically engineered organisms into the environment." (2) Josefa develops this section thesis in three paragraphs, each of which is devoted to a particular danger posed by genetically engineered organisms. Paragraph 6 concerns the "limited research into . . . these organisms." Paragraph 7 concerns the "potential health hazards." Paragraph 9 concerns our "inability to control organisms." By being narrowly focused on a particular danger, each paragraph is unified, and the three paragraphs, working together, form a unified section. The paragraphs also illustrate attention to coherence. The second paragraph builds on the first with the transition "also"; the third paragraph builds on the previous two with the transitional phrase "Perhaps the most dangerous problem associated with genetic engineering. . . ."

EXERCISE 2

Individual responses

limited amount of research. Ecologists such as Martin Alexander of Cornell feel that more research should be done before genetically altered bacteria are released. Not enough is known to guarantee the safety of these organisms.

7   There are also potential health hazards that may result from consumer use of these products. Studies have shown that "shuffling" genes has elevated plant toxins. This was the case in the 1960s when scientists bred a new kind of potato that caused human illness. The gene mixing had increased the plant's natural toxins to dangerous levels, thereby forcing the United States Department of Agriculture to recall the poisonous product from the market. Although some scientists argue that illness may be detected within two weeks of consumption, long-term effects are unknown. Other health concerns include potential risks of allergic reactions. Studies have shown that "some microorganisms with potential for extracting metals and oils from the earth such as *Sclerotium Rafi* and various species of *Aureobasidium* have been associated with lung disease and wound infections, respectively" (Office 122).

8   Perhaps the most dangerous problem associated with genetic engineering is the inability to control organisms or to predict their behavior, once released into the open environment. Some scientists argue that laboratory testing may not be an accurate prediction of an organism's behavior once it is released. According to Francis Sharples, "so many factors interact in the environment to determine where there will be trouble, that predictions of just which species introductions will cause ecological disruptions is nearly beyond the ability of ecologists and population biologists" (41). There is also the concern for the possibility of having weeds capture a gene for herbicide resistance to environmentally safe herbicides, thereby forcing scientists to use much harsher and more dangerous chemicals to control weed growth. As Cornell ecologist David Pimentel argues, "You can stop using pesticides, but once you put one of these microbes out there the damn thing will reproduce and grow and we'll never get rid of it" (16). Past experiences have left ecologists skeptical: experiments such as the release of the gypsy moth and the introduction of the Kudzu vine have caused ecological havoc and billions of dollars in damage. What happens if something goes wrong with an organism once it has been released into the environment? Once it has been released and found an appropriate habitat, the organism may not only reproduce and spread but might also evolve in ways that will benefit its existence—not ours (Sharples 40).

EXERCISE 2

Choose *one* section of a textbook chapter to study in depth. (Define a *section* as a group of related paragraphs preceded by a subheading.) Closely read each paragraph in this section, and prepare an analysis by responding to three points: (1) Identify the controlling idea (the section thesis) of the section. (2) Explain how the entire section is unified, developed, and coherent. (3) Discuss the way in which the section fits into the overall structure of the chapter.

5b The paragraph: Essential features

In important ways, a paragraph and an essay are essentially alike. Both must be *unified* if they are to be comprehensible: all sentences of a paragraph must refer to one organizing idea, just as all paragraphs of an essay must concern one organizing idea. Both an essay as a whole and its individual paragraphs must be *well developed*: sentences in a paragraph must amply explain or defend the main point of a paragraph just as paragraphs of an essay must explain or defend a thesis. As well, both a paragraph and an essay must be *coherent*: sentences of a paragraph must be arranged in some order, just as paragraphs in an essay must follow from one to the next according to some clear progression of ideas. If you can master the techniques necessary for making a single paragraph unified, well developed, and coherent, then by adapting these same techniques and by expanding your focus you will be able to write and organize an entire essay.

The following is an example of a well-written paragraph. It appears in a biology text.

> Life on this planet began in water, and today, almost wherever water is found, life is also present. There are one-celled organisms that eke out their entire existence in no more water than that which can cling to a grain of sand. Some species of algae are found only on the melting undersurfaces of polar ice floes. Certain species of bacteria and certain blue-green algae can tolerate the near-boiling water of hot springs. In the desert, plants race through an entire life cycle—seed to flower to seed—following a single rainfall. In the jungle, the water cupped in the leaves of a tropical plant forms a microcosm in which a myriad of small organisms are born, spawn, and die. We are interested in whether the soil of Mars and the dense atmosphere surrounding Venus contain water principally because we want to know whether life is there. On our planet, and probably on others where life exists, life and water have been companions since life first began.
>
> —HELENA CURTIS, "Water"

Examine the qualities that make this grouping of sentences a paragraph, a unit of thought. First, each of the six sentences constituting the body of Curtis's paragraph is narrowly focused by a single, controlling idea: *water* and its relation to life. Given this focus, the grouping of sentences is unified. Observe as well that Curtis develops her central idea with six sentences arranged according to a clear plan. In the first five of these, she associates water with life on earth. Notice how she moves from an extreme presented in one sentence to an opposite extreme presented in the next.

Curtis's next-to-last sentence about water on Mars or Venus extends observations made concerning water and life on earth to other planets, and once again she drives home her point, which she repeats by way of summary in the paragraph's last sentence. She has taken care to present

ADDITIONAL EXERCISE B

CRITICAL THINKING Find two interesting paragraphs from textbooks, magazines, or other collections. Using the analysis of the Curtis paragraph as a model, evaluate the unity, development, and coherence of these paragraphs. Then compare the two: Is one a better paragraph than the other? If so, why? How do the two differ in development and coherence?

ESL ALERT

Problems with paragraphing often reflect a difference in accepted patterns of representing thought rather than simple language difficulties. The concept of the paragraph differs greatly between cultures, with romance languages accepting and even encouraging what we would term "digression" as a way to create variety and interest, a sense of "fullness." Farsi speakers, for example, value such subtlety that the central idea may not become clear until the very end, with the development following a circular or looping pattern constructed of high-level abstractions. The straightforward, linear paragraph movement considered the norm in U.S. schools is actually typical only of English, and may even be valued less highly in British prose. See Robert B. Kaplan's discussion of paragraph differences in "Cultural Thought Patterns in Inter-Cultural Education," *Language Learning* 16 (1966): 1–20.

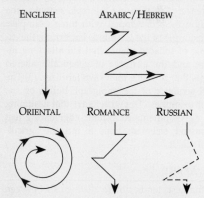

Paragraph conventions in different languages also vary greatly in their tolerance of digression. While frequent digression in the English paragraph is a decided fault, the practice may be viewed as a sign of fluency, knowledgeability,

(continued)

and confidence even in languages not greatly distant from English, such as Spanish and Russian.

The concept of paragraph development by patterns, for example from most common to least common or from general to particular, by consistent space or time order or degree, might seem obvious to English speakers, but is not so obvious in other languages where imperatives of content may be more important than sequences of order. Consequently, a clear explanation of differences between methods of paragraph development will be needed to supplement this handbook. ESL students will see the models, but may not understand them or believe their currency.

ESL ALERT

Spanish speakers may not have the concept of indentation and might use initial dashes instead: "—Another key concern is . . ."

Depending on the conventions of the country of origin, the paragraphs of Spanish speakers may be short, like newspaper paragraphs, or there may be no paragraphing at all. The idea of indentation and paragraph division might be lacking in ESL students from a number of different language groups.

EXERCISE 3

(1) The central idea is stated clearly in the first sentence. (2) Following the topic sentence, the paragraph is developed with three examples: the example of the ice-minus bacterium; the example of tobacco plants that kill attacking insects; and the example of genetically altered plants that produce their own fertilizer. (3) The final sentence of the paragraph builds on the prior examples. The writer says that assuming the developments in genetic engineering just discussed, scientists hope to increase agricultural yields.

ESL ALERT

Vietnamese tends not to distinguish between oral and written structures, so Vietnamese students writing in English may be highly informal with the lengthy rambling style of oral discourse.

eight *unified* sentences that *develop* a central idea and that are arranged in a meaningful, *coherent* order. Thus, Curtis has written a paragraph: a well-developed unit of thought organized around a single idea and arranged according to some definite plan.

EXERCISE 3

Read the following group of sentences and explain why it can justifiably be called a paragraph. In your explanation (1) identify the central, organizing idea that unifies the sentences, (2) identify the parts of the paragraph that explain or defend this central idea, and (3) explain how the sentences are organized according to a definite, coherent plan.

Student Example: Josefa Pinto

Scientists have discovered the benefits and uses of genetically engineered organisms in agriculture. One important example is the ice-minus bacterium created by Steve Lindow and Nicholas Panopoulos. Realizing a bacterium commonly found in plants produces a protein that helps ice to form, these scientists removed the unfavorable gene and thereby prevented ice from forming on greenhouse plants (Carey 18). Others have manipulated genetic materials to create tobacco that kills attacking insects and to produce plants that resist herbicides. Geneticists hope in 20 to 40 years to produce plants such as corn and other grains that "fix" their own nitrogen—that will be able to extract nitrogen from the atmosphere without relying on nitrifying bacteria. If such plants could be created, U.S. farmers would save $3 to $4 billion annually in fertilizer costs and could save one third of all crops lost each year to pests. Ultimately, geneticists hope to use the same amounts of land, fertilizer, and pesticide while producing greater yields; this method of increasing productivity could be most beneficial to countries with limited usable land (Pimentel 25).

5c Writing and revising to achieve paragraph unity

A unified paragraph will focus on, will develop, and will not stray from a paragraph's central, controlling idea or **topic sentence.** Recall that a *thesis* announces and controls the content of an entire essay, and that a *section thesis* announces and controls the content of a section. Just so, a *topic sentence* announces and controls the content of sentences in a single paragraph. Think of the topic sentence as a paragraph-level *thesis,* and you will see the principle of unity at work at *all* levels of the paper. At each level of the essay, a general statement is used to guide you in assembling specific, supporting parts.

| ESSAY-LEVEL UNITY | The thesis (the most general statement in the essay) governs your choice of sections in a paper. |

| SECTION-LEVEL UNITY | Section theses (the second-most general statements in the essay) govern your choice of paragraphs in a section. |
| PARAGRAPH-LEVEL UNITY | Topic sentences (the third-most general statements in the essay) govern your choice of sentences in a paragraph. |

Within a paragraph, a topic sentence can appear anywhere, provided that you recognize it and can lead up to and away from it with some method in mind. If you have read the example paragraphs in this chapter thus far, you have seen topic sentences placed at virtually all locations in a paragraph: at the beginning, one sentence after the beginning, the middle, the end, and both the beginning *and* end. The basic positions of a paragraph's topic sentence are discussed below.

1 Placing the topic sentence at the beginning of a paragraph

Very often, a topic sentence is placed first in a paragraph. You will want to open your paragraphs this way when your purpose is to inform or persuade a reader and you wish to be as direct as possible, as in the following example.

> 11 Factory farm animals need liberation in the most literal sense. Veal calves are kept in stalls five feet by two feet. They are usually slaughtered when about four months old, and have been too big to turn in their stalls for at least a month. Intensive beef herds, kept in stalls only proportionately larger for much longer periods, account for a growing percentage of beef production. Sows are often similarly confined when pregnant, which, because of artificial methods of increasing fertility, can be most of the time. Animals confined in this way do not waste food by exercising, nor do they develop unpalatable muscle.
> —PETER SINGER, "Animal Liberation"

Peter Singer begins the paragraph with a direct statement: *Factory farm animals need liberation in the most literal sense.* Every subsequent sentence focuses on and develops this topic sentence.

2 Placing the topic sentence in the middle of a paragraph

When you want to present material on two sides of an issue in your paragraph, consider placing the topic sentence in the middle of the paragraph. Lead up to the topic sentence with supporting material concerning its first part; lead away from the topic sentence with material concerning its second part, as in the following example:

Student Example: Josefa Pinto

Those in favor of genetic engineering argue that the exchange of genes taking place during laboratory experiments is merely an imitation of what is done in nature all the time. In other words, genetic engineer-

Choose a grammatical interference problem between your first language and English. "Grammatical interference" means that the mental habit involved in the grammatical form in the first language causes mistakes or confusion in the second language, English. In one well-organized paragraph, explain the grammatical interference problem, providing numerous examples to make it clear to your audience, which is teachers who do not speak your language and who do not understand why you make so many mistakes.

The order of your paragraph should be as follows: a clear topic sentence at the beginning expressing the problem and the reason for the problem; at least two supporting examples with explanations of each; and a concluding sentence or two clearly aimed at the teacher who is your audience.

Remember that your strategy is to make your mistake part of a general pattern, not a personal or private problem that other speakers of your language do not share.

ADDITIONAL EXERCISE C

Ask students to read any of the sample student papers in chapters 4, 6, 35, and 37 through 39. For any paper, have the student identify section theses and topic sentences as a check to ensure that the paragraphs and sections of the paper are unified. Groups of students could read the same paper and discuss their findings among themselves. Students could discuss placement of topic sentences and the degree to which variety (or lack of variety) contributes to (or detracts from) the paper.

ing is a natural process that is being reproduced by humans. Scientists are confident that strict regulation and principles of agreement between private companies and government agencies will ensure the safety and efficiency of any genetically engineered organism (Hanson 24). Furthermore, American molecular biologists fear that additional road blocks to their research will cause them to fall behind European competitors—and that the United States will lose its lead in yet another area of technology. The dilemmas over genetic engineering are, at their root, based on a struggle between the advancement of knowledge and competition on the one hand and the need for safety on the other. Ecologists who oppose the uses of genetically engineered organisms in the open environment argue that the genetic engineer, today, is a 20th-century sorcerer's-apprentice playing with a technology that is not fully understood (Pimentel 14). Others question the consequences of "playing God." They feel that humans do not know enough about life to manipulate its forms. Nor are they sure who would assume responsibility for any disruption or irreparable damage done to our environment.

Josefa's topic sentence is the pivot on which this paragraph turns: *The dilemmas over genetic engineering are, at their root, based on a struggle between the advancement of knowledge and competition on the one hand and the need for safety on the other.*

3 Placing the topic sentence at the end of a paragraph

When writing an informative or argumentative paper, you may in specific paragraphs want to postpone the topic sentence until the end. You would do this to ensure that readers would consider all the sentences in a paragraph before coming to your main point. The strategy works especially well when you are arguing, as in the following example.

The place of history in the world of learning and its relation to the various other fields of study can be argued without end. History is sometimes classed with the humanities, along with literature, the arts, and philosophy, as an aspect of the human achievement over the centuries. However, it differs from all of these subjects in being based on fact rather than on imagination and feeling. More often history is included among the social sciences, together with economics, political science, sociology, anthropology, and some branches of geography and psychology. One may question whether any of these fields deserves to be called a "science" in the sense we associate with the natural or exact sciences, but history is particularly resistant to a strictly scientific approach. It tries to explain by particular description rather than by general analysis and laws; its aim is to depict the significant historical individual or situation in all its living detail. History is defined by its focus on time, but it also has the characteristic of embracing all aspects of human activity as they occurred in the past. History, accordingly, is able to serve as the discipline that integrates the specialized work of the other fields of social science. (32)

—ROBERT V. DANIELS, *Studying History: How and Why*

If you place the last sentence of this paragraph first, you see that subsequent sentences support and develop the idea that *History . . . is able to serve as the discipline that integrates the specialized work of the other fields of social science*. This statement is debatable, which Daniels acknowledges at the beginning of the paragraph. By delaying his topic sentence, Daniels ensures that his audience will have read his survey of the debate, which is important to accepting Daniels's point. See ¶18 for another example of this arrangement.

4   Omitting the topic sentence from the paragraph

In narrative and descriptive papers, and much less frequently in informative and persuasive papers, writers will occasionally omit the topic sentence from a paragraph. In a narrative paragraph in which you are telling a story, including the topic sentence may be too heavy handed and may ruin an otherwise subtle effect. Descriptive writing may be so obvious that including a topic sentence seems redundant. When you decide to omit a topic sentence from a paragraph, take care to write the paragraph as though a topic sentence were present. With respect to unity, this means that you should focus each sentence on the implied topic and should not include any sentence that strays from that implied topic. Helen Keller does exactly this in ¶2 (page 123). Had she written a topic sentence for this paragraph, it might have read: *The events immediately leading up to my discovery of language showed how thoroughly difficult and insensitive a child I was.*

The following is an example of an informative paragraph with an implied topic sentence, rather than a directly stated one.

14   Etiquette books used to teach that if a woman had *Mrs.* in front of her name then the husband's name should follow because *Mrs.* is an abbreviated form of *Mistress* and a woman couldn't be a mistress of herself. As with many arguments about "correct" language usage, this isn't very logical because *Miss* is also an abbreviation of *Mistress*. Feminists hoped to simplify matters by introducing *Ms.* as an alternative to both *Mrs.* and *Miss*, but what happened is that *Ms.* largely replaced *Miss* to became a catch-all business title for women. Many married women still prefer the title *Mrs.*, and some resent being addressed with the term *Ms.* As one frustrated newspaper reporter complained, "Before I can write about a woman, I have to know not only her marital status but also her political philosophy." The result of such complications may contribute to the demise of titles which are already being ignored by many computer programmers who find it more efficient to simply use names; for example in a business letter: "Dear Joan Garcia," instead of "Dear Mrs. Joan Garcia," "Dear Ms. Garcia," or "Dear Mrs. Louis Garcia."

—ALLEEN PACE NILSEN, "Sexism in English: A 1990s Update"

TEACHING IDEAS

Students who have been carefully trained to include a topic sentence for every paragraph might try this experiment with one of their completed papers: Find one or two paragraphs from which the topic sentence could be removed without negatively affecting the reader's understanding of the material. Students may need to add transitional phrases. Have students, in groups, read over competing versions of the same paragraph, with and without a topic sentence, in the context of two or three neighboring paragraphs from the original paper. Students can discuss the extent to which the paragraph improves or is harmed by the omitted topic sentence.

The sentence that comes closest to being a topic sentence is the paragraph's long final sentence. But the opening of this sentence, "The result of such complications," assumes another sentence, not written: *There has been a great deal of confusion about the politically correct title of address for women.* Placed at the head of Nilsen's paragraph, this would function adequately as a topic sentence. The paragraph's final sentence is actually built on the validity of this implied topic sentence. Nilsen's choice of every sentence is governed by the implied topic sentence just as if that sentence had actually been included in the paragraph.

EXERCISE 4
Individual responses

EXERCISE 5
See suggested answers to Exercises 1 and 3.

EXERCISE 4
Reread several paragraphs you have recently written for one of your classes. Choose one paragraph to revise for unity: add, delete, or modify sentences as needed.

EXERCISE 5
Locate the topic sentence in paragraphs 6, 7, 8, and 10 of Josefa Pinto's paper on genetic engineering. Analyze each paragraph and be prepared to discuss how every sentence contributes to the paragraph's unity.

5d Writing and revising to achieve paragraph coherence

Your job in ensuring the overall coherence of a paragraph is to make clear the logic by which you position sentences in the paragraph. When your paragraphs are coherent, readers will understand the logic by which you move from one sentence to the next, toward or away from your topic sentence. When writing the first draft of a paper, you may not have a plan to ensure paragraph coherence; you may not even have a clear idea of every paragraph's main point. Revision is the time when you sort these matters out, when you can make certain that each paragraph has a clear purpose and a clear, coherent plan for achieving that purpose.

1 Arranging sentences to achieve coherence

There are standard patterns available to you for arranging paragraphs. The most common are arrangements by space, by time, and by importance. If it occurs to you as you are writing a first draft that one of these patterns lends itself to the particular point you are discussing, then by all means write your paragraph with the pattern in mind. It is not necessary, though, that you map out patterns of coherence ahead of time.

Arrangement by space

You can help readers visualize what you are describing by arranging a paragraph spatially. Start the reader at a well-defined position with

TEACHING IDEAS

ACROSS THE CURRICULUM Arrangement is a concept that can be illustrated by an analogy to film. Virtually all students are familiar with movies, so a discussion of arrangement in those terms can be useful. Ask students to think of the camera sweeping across a room or a landscape in a given scene in order to understand arrangement by space—after all, this kind of arrangement is more visual than literal. For arrangement by time they can think of scene sequences in films, parts of the film when the action seems most important. Arrangement by importance presents more of a challenge. But with a little prodding, some students should be able to recall movies in which the action is general and dispersed in certain scenes, only to move to specific, focused action in later scenes. As they realize that the filmmaker uses these techniques according to the needs of the plot, purpose, and audience, they'll come to understand the similar reasons for making arrangement decisions when writing paragraphs.

respect to the object being described, and then move him or her from that position to subsequent ones by taking systematic steps, one at a time, until your description is complete. In planning the paragraph, you might divide the object into the parts that you will describe; next, devise a definite plan for arranging these parts. Your description could proceed from front to back, right to left, top to bottom, outside to inside, and so on: the choice is yours. Once you choose a plan for organizing details, stick to the plan and you will help your readers to visualize your topic, as in this paragraph on the Brooklyn Bridge.

15   Brooklyn Bridge belongs first to the eye. Viewed from Brooklyn Heights, it seems to frame the irregular lines of Manhattan. But across the river perspective changes: through the narrow streets of lower Manhattan and Chinatown, on Water Street or South Street, the structure looms above drab buildings. Fragments of tower or cable compel the eye. The view changes once again as one mounts the wooden walk of the bridge itself. It is a relief, an open space after dim, crowded streets.

—ALAN TRACHTENBERG, *Brooklyn Bridge: Fact and Symbol*

This description of the bridge is arranged by the various perspectives from which it is viewed: from Brooklyn Heights, the bridge has one appearance; viewed from lower Manhattan, the structure "looms above drab buildings"; viewed from the wooden walkway of the bridge, the view provides a "relief."

Arrangement by time

You can arrange a paragraph according to a sequence of events. Start the paragraph with a particular event, and move forward or backward in time in some definite order. Give your readers signals in each sentence that emphasize the forward or backward movement. In this example paragraph on the history of genetic engineering, Josefa Pinto moves the reader forward in time with a series of phrases and single words, which are highlighted.

Student Example: Josefa Pinto

The movement of creating genetically engineered organisms began in the early 1900s based on the experiments and ideas of the Austrian monk Gregory Mendel. During the 1800s, through his cross-breeding experiments, Mendel laid the foundation for future experiments in genetic engineering. By the 1970s, American geneticists began developing techniques for isolating and altering genes. They discovered that a soil 16   bacterium known as *Agrobacterium* was nature's own genetic engineer and could exchange pieces of DNA (the raw material of genes) with startling frequency (Carey 18). On June 30, 1981, biologists Jack Kemp of the Department of Agriculture and Timothy Hall of the University of Wisconsin first harvested the bacterium's power. The first experiment consisted of using a microbe or microorganism to slip a bean plant gene

REFERENCES

HALLIDAY, M. A. K., and RUGAIYA HASAN. *Cohesion in English*. London: Longman, 1976. An extensive discussion of cohesion at the paragraph and essay level.

SLOAN, GARY. "The Frequency of Transitional Markers in Discursive Prose." *CE* 46 (1984): 158–79. Transitional markers are not used frequently by college writers or professionals.

WINTEROWD, W. ROSS. "The Grammar of Coherence." *CE* 31 (1971): 828–35. Discusses linkages between sentences and between paragraphs.

SMITH, ROCHELLE. "Paragraphing for Coherence: Writing as Implied Dialogue." *CE* 46 (1984): 8–21. Applies reader response theory to understanding paragraph coherence as implied dialogue between writer and reader.

WITTE, STEPHEN P., and LESTER FAIGLEY. "Coherence, Cohesion, and Writing Quality." *CCC* 32 (1981): 189–204. Questions classroom emphasis on cohesion over coherence.

BECKER, A. L. "A Tagmemic Approach to Paragraph Analysis." *CCC* 16 (1965): 237–42. Paragraphs are usually arranged according to a TRI (topic-restriction-illustration) pattern or a PS (problem-solution) pattern.

MARKELS, ROBIN BELL. *A New Perspective on Cohesion in Expository Paragraphs*. Carbondale: Southern Illinois UP, 1984. Cohesion should not be explained exclusively in syntactic terms; it involves semantics as well.

STOTSKY, SANDRA. "Types of Lexical Cohesion in Expository Academic Discourse." *CCC* 34 (1983): 430–46.

CHRISTENSEN, FRANCIS. "A Generative Rhetoric of the Paragraph." *CCC* 16 (1965): 144–56. Paragraphs can be understood by considering them in terms of sentence types (coordinate, subordinate, or a combination of the two).

BROSTOFF, ANITA. "Coherence: 'Next to' Is Not 'Connected To.'" *CCC* 32 (1981): 278–94. Teaching coherence should emphasize logical connections, sequencing, and clear relationships within paragraphs and larger texts.

TEACHING IDEAS

Just as with examinations of a paragraph's unity, a writer is more likely to profit most by examining a paragraph's coherence *in revision*. While producing a first draft, the writer is concerned foremost with generating ideas. The finely tuned progression of those ideas in a first draft is less important than getting ideas down on paper. It is in revision, typically, that a writer will craft a paragraph, attending to matters of unity by deleting sentences if they are off the topic or adding sentences in the interest of topic development. And it is in revision when the writer brings specific strategies for paragraph coherence to the draft. The movement of ideas from specific to general or vice versa depends on the strategic effects the writer wants to create. You can illustrate the crafting of paragraphs in revision by bringing a few of your own to class, in various draft forms. Especially useful would be a demonstration of how you altered the organization of a paragraph in order to achieve some rhetorical purpose, or in order to present specific material more efficiently.

into a sunflower plant. Later, in 1982, bacterially produced insulin became the first recombinant DNA drug approved by the Food and Drug Administration for use by people. By 1987 and 1988, genes were being transferred into higher organisms such as plants and animals (Scherfeas 87). Presently, genetic engineers have produced most of the economically important varieties of plants and animals, such as flowers, vegetables, grains, cows, horses, and dogs.

Arrangement by importance

Just as you discuss different parts of a thesis at different locations in a paper, you will discuss different parts of a topic sentence at different locations in a paragraph. When revising, be aware of a paragraph's component parts so that you can arrange these parts in the most logical, accessible order. Arrangement is largely determined by your positioning of the topic sentence. How will your sentences lead to and away from the topic sentence? You should be aware of two general patterns: general to specific and specific to general.

GENERAL TO SPECIFIC: WHEN THE TOPIC SENTENCE BEGINS THE PARAGRAPH

By far the most common method for arranging sentences in a paragraph is to begin with your topic sentence and follow with specific, supporting details. When beginning a paragraph this way, decide how to order the information that will follow. You might ask: What does this paragraph's topic sentence obligate me to discuss? What are the *parts* of this paragraph and in what order will I discuss them? Arthur C. Clarke discusses three parts of his topic, the portable electronic library—the library's top half, its bottom half, and its overall size—in the following paragraph.

17   The great development in your near future is the portable electronic library—a library not only of books, but of films and music. It will be about the size of an average book and will probably open in the same way. One half will be the screen with high-definition, full-color display. The other will be a keyboard, much like one of today's computer consoles, with the full alphabet, digits, basic mathematical functions, and a large number of special keys—perhaps 100 keys in all. It won't be as small as some of today's midget calculators, which have to be operated with toothpicks.

—ARTHUR C. CLARKE, "Electronic Tutors"

SPECIFIC TO GENERAL: WHEN THE TOPIC SENTENCE ENDS THE PARAGRAPH

When you are writing a description or narration and when you are arguing a point, you may want to delay your topic sentence until the final sentence of a paragraph. Here you reverse the standard arrangement of a paragraph and move from specific details to a general, concluding statement. The goal is to build one sentence on the next so securely that the final sentence strikes the reader as inevitable.

18

> We drink it, use it to wash, and use it to grow farm products and manufacture goods. We almost take for granted that rain will replenish whatever amount of water we may use up. Water, however, is no longer the infinitely renewable resource that we once thought it was. Consider the giant Ogallala aquifer, which stretches nearly 800 miles under eight states from the Texas panhandle to South Dakota. The aquifer provides about 30 percent of the total irrigation needs in the United States and serves as the water source for 200,000 wells in 180 counties and for 40 percent of the nation's beef cattle. Water is being drawn from the Ogallala aquifer eight times faster than nature can replenish the supply, creating huge sinkholes in the Texas panhandle. Economists believe that part of the problem is that water has traditionally been underpriced. The law of demand indicates that a higher price of water will reduce the quantity of water used. One solution for the rapidly decreasing water resources, therefore, would be to make it more expensive for consumers to use the water.
>
> —SEMOON CHANG, *Modern Economics*

In this paragraph, Chang makes an argument by moving from specific facts to a general conclusion, or topic sentence. Chang begins with facts concerning water use about which no one could disagree. His second sentence builds on the first by generalizing about attitudes concerning water use: we "almost take for granted" that water is an infinitely renewable resource. The third sentence builds on the second by making another, though debatable, statement of fact that (1) sets up a contrast with the second sentence and (2) is itself supported by several subsequent sentences about the Ogallala aquifer. Chang builds sentence on sentence, leading us to the paragraph's climax in which he applies economic theory to the problem of "decreasing water resources." The solution to this problem is the paragraph's final, topic sentence.

2 Achieving coherence with cues

When sentences are arranged with care, you need only to highlight this arrangement to ensure that readers will move easily through a paragraph. To highlight paragraph coherence, use **cues**: words and phrases that remind readers as they move from sentence to sentence (1) that they continue to read about the same topic and (2) that ideas are unfolding logically. Four types of cues help to highlight sentence-to-sentence connections: pronouns, repetition, parallel structures, and transitions (which will be discussed in the next section). Accomplished writers usually combine techniques in order to highlight paragraph coherence, often not adding cues to a paragraph until the revision stage, when they are better able to discern a paragraph's shape.

LOOKING AHEAD

Concepts covered in this section will be covered in greater depth in chapters 14 (Pronoun Reference), 18 (Maintaining Sentence Parallelism), and 19 (Building Emphasis—repetition section). Students having difficulty understanding any of these concepts can be referred to the appropriate chapters later in the book.

Pronouns

The most direct way to remind readers that they continue to examine a certain topic as they move from sentence to sentence is to repeat the most important noun, or the subject, of your topic sentence. To prevent repetition from becoming tiresome, use a pronoun to take the place of this important noun. Every time a pronoun is used, the reader is *cued*, or reminded, about the paragraph's main topic. In the following example, *he* and *his* take the place of the name *Herbert Hoover*. These pronouns are repeated eight times, tying the paragraph together without dulling the reader with repetition.

Illustration: Pronoun Substitution

19

Herbert Hoover was a perfect symbol of the ideals and hopes of the American business community in the 1920s. He showed that to succeed in the United States and to be elected President you did not have to come from a rich, upper-class family. His life proved that in America character, intelligence, and hard work could make a national leader. Born of Quaker parents on a small farm in Iowa in 1874, he had been orphaned at the age of ten. He worked his way through Stanford University, where he studied engineering. Then he made his fortune as a mining engineer—in Australia, Africa, China, Latin America, and Russia. He was a millionaire by the time he was 40.

—Daniel Boorstin and Brooks Mather Kelley, *A History of the United States*

Repetition

While unintentional repetition can make sentences awkward, planned repetition can contribute significantly to a paragraph's coherence. The strategy is to repeat identically or to use a substitute phrase to repeat an important word or words in a paragraph. As with pronoun use, repetition cues readers, reminding them of the paragraph's important information. In the example on the next page, concerning the word *meter*, combinations of the following four words are repeated sixteen times: *meter, define/definition, bar, standard*. Skillful use of repetition ties sentences together without boring the reader. Repetition helps to make this paragraph coherent.

LOOKING BACK

This chapter emphasizes the point that paragraphs do not stand in isolation but, rather, exist in a broader context of related paragraphs. See 5a and, more generally, for a discussion of how awareness of a broader context contributes to critical thinking, see 1c.

CRITICAL DECISIONS

Set issues in a broader context: Revising paragraphs for coherence

A sentence gains meaning from the sentences that come before and after it in a paragraph. A paragraph similarly gains meaning from the paragraphs that come before and after it in a paper. As a writer, you probably have too much to do in a first draft to monitor the relationship among sentences and paragraphs or to develop coherence: the smooth flow of ideas. In a second or third draft, however, once you are settled on your final thesis and on the structure of your paper, you should evaluate your sentences in the broader context of paragraphs, and paragraphs in the broader context of sections (groupings of related paragraphs).

■ **Revise every paragraph within its section.** To revise an individual paragraph, examine it in relation to the ones that come before and after. Develop the habit of including transitional words at the beginning or end of paragraphs to help readers move from one paragraph to the next. If you have difficulty writing a particular transition, rethink the logical connection between paragraphs. Transitions highlight a logic already present. A rough transition, always a disruption to the smooth flow of ideas, is a sign of faulty logic.

■ **Revise every sentence within its paragraph.** Once you are sure of a paragraph's place in your paper, revise its component sentences to ensure coherence. Evaluate each sentence in relation to the sentences that come before and after. Use cues—pronouns, parallelism, repetition and transitions—to help move the reader from one sentence to the next through a paragraph.

Illustration: Word Repetition

20   The fundamental unit of length in the (metric system) is the (meter.) Originally, the (meter) was (defined) to be 10^{-7} of the distance from the North Pole to the equator. Later, a platinum-iridium (bar) was constructed whose length was as close as possible to the original (definition.) (This bar,) which became known as the (standard meter,) is kept at the Bureau of Weights and Measures near Paris. A (similar bar) was installed at the U.S. Bureau of Standards in Washington, D.C. All rulers, (meter) sticks, and other length-measuring devices were in the past calibrated by comparison with the (standard meter bar.) An even more precise (standard) is currently being used. The (meter) is now (defined) to be a length equal to the distance light travels in a vacuum in 1/299,792,458

of a second. The number of digits in this figure shows the great precision with which such measurements can be made.

—PAUL S. COHEN AND MILTON A. ROTHMAN, *Basic Chemistry*

TEACHING IDEAS

ACROSS THE CURRICULUM A concerted effort has been made in this book to include examples of writing from across the curriculum because they illustrate to students that the principles of good writing discussed in the composition classroom generalize. In paragraph 20 we see repetition used to ensure paragraph coherence. In paragraph 21, student Josefa Pinto, writing on genetic engineering, demonstrates the use of parallelism.

As an exercise, ask students to photocopy a page from an article or a book being read for another course. Have them study one paragraph and point out the author's use of various techniques to ensure coherence. Students should watch for pronouns, repetition, parallel structures, and transitions.

Parallelism

Chapter 18 is devoted entirely to a discussion of **parallelism:** the use of grammatically equivalent words, phrases, and sentences to achieve coherence and balance in your writing. A sentence whose structure parallels that of an earlier sentence has an echo-like effect, linking the content of the second sentence to the content of the first. As with pronoun use and skillful repetition, parallel structures cue readers by highlighting the paragraph's important information.

Illustration: Student Example
JOSEFA PINTO

21   Not only have geneticists found beneficial uses of genetically engineered organisms in agriculture, but they have also found useful ways to use these organisms advantageously in the larger environment. According to the Monsanto company, a leader in genetic engineering research, recombinant DNA techniques may provide us with new ways to clean up our environment and with more efficient methods of producing chemicals (Monsanto 24). By using genetically engineered organisms, scientists have been able to produce natural gas. This process will decrease our dependence on the environment and will reduce the rate at which we deplete natural resources. In other processes, genetically engineered bacteria are being used both to extract metals from their geological setting and to speed the breakup of complex petroleum mixtures, which will help to clean oil spills. In addition, firms such as Flow Laboratories are selling genetically engineered microbes to be used in sewage systems for facilitating breakdown and detoxification (Office of Technology Assessment 124).

Josefa Pinto uses parallelism *within* sentences, for the most part.

Not only have geneticists found . . . but they have also found
may provide us with new ways . . . and with more efficient methods
This process will decrease . . . and will reduce

LOOKING AHEAD

Students may want to peruse chapter 19 (Coordination and Subordination) as they study this section. Considering the later chapter here could help students when they reach the editing stage of their own papers: they'll understand coordination and subordination in the context of paragraph coherence rather than simply rules of sentence structure.

bacteria are being used both to extract . . . and to speed
for facilitating breakdown and detoxification

In one case, Josefa uses parallel structures in adjacent sentences.

This process . . .
In other processes . . .

3 Highlighting coherence with transitions

Transitions are words that establish logical relationships between sentences, between paragraphs, and between whole sections of an essay. A transition can take the form of a single word, a phrase, a sentence, or an entire paragraph. In each case it functions the same way: first, it either directly summarizes the content of a preceding sentence (or paragraph) or it implies that summary. Having established a summary, transitions then move forward into a new sentence (or paragraph), helping the reader anticipate what is to come. For example, when you read the word *however*, you are immediately aware that the material you are about to read will contrast with the material you have just read. In so brief a transition, the summary of the preceding material is implied—but present. As the reader, *you* do the summarizing.

Transitions *within* paragraphs

Transitions act as cues by helping readers to anticipate what is coming *before* they read it. Within a paragraph, transitions tend to be single words.

Illustration: Transitions

The survival of the robin, (and indeed) of many other species (as well,) seems fatefully linked with the American elm, a tree that is part of the history of thousands of towns from the Atlantic to the Rockies, gracing their streets and their village squares (and) college campuses with majestic archways of green. (Now) the elms are stricken with a disease that afflicts them throughout their range, a disease so serious that many experts believe all efforts to save the elms will in the end be futile. It would be tragic to lose the elms, (but) it would be doubly tragic if, in vain

22

efforts to save them, we plunge vast segments of our bird populations into the night of extinction. (Yet) this is precisely what is threatened.

—RACHEL CARSON, *Silent Spring*

Transitions *between* paragraphs

Transitions placed between paragraphs help readers move through sections of your paper. If you have done a good job of arranging paragraphs so that the content of one leads logically to the next, then by using a transitional expression you are highlighting a relationship that already exists. By summarizing the previous paragraph and telegraphing something of the content of the paragraph that follows, a transition helps to move the reader through your paper. A transition between paragraphs can be a word or two—*however, for example, similarly*—a phrase, or a sentence. The following is a sentence-length transition used to join two sections of a chapter in a textbook.

> *Just as through* formal religion and civic life the Sumerians at the dawn of recorded history created a new kind of human experience, *so through* writing and figurative art they found a new way to represent that experience. Writing had been invented by the simplifying of pictures into signs, . . .
>
> —*Gardner's Art Through the Ages,* 5th ed.

The first half of this paragraph's lead sentence explicitly summarizes the preceding section of a chapter. The second half of the sentence is the paragraph's topic sentence and points the reader forward to a new discussion on writing and figurative art. If the relationship between sections of a paper is complex, you may want to take some time and write a paragraph-length transition, as in this example.

> 23
> So Grant and Lee were in complete contrast, representing two diametrically opposed elements in American life. Grant was the modern man emerging; beyond him, ready to come on the stage, was the great age of steel and machinery, of crowded cities and a restless burgeoning vitality. Lee might have ridden down from the old age of chivalry, lance in hand, silken banner fluttering over his head. Each man was the perfect champion of his cause, drawing both his strengths and his weaknesses from the people he led.
>
> 24
> Yet it was not all contrast, after all. Different as they were—in background, in personality, in underlying aspiration—these two great soldiers had much in common. Under everything else, they were marvelous fighters. Furthermore, their fighting qualities were really very much alike.
>
> Each man had, to begin with, the great virtue of utter tenacity and fidelity. Grant fought his way down the Mississippi Valley in spite of acute personal discouragement and profound military handicaps. Lee

25 hung on in the trenches at Petersburg after hope itself had died. In each man there was an indomitable quality . . . the born fighter's refusal to give up as long as he can still remain on his feet and lift his two fists.

—BRUCE CATTON, "Grant and Lee: A Study in Contrasts"

Whatever its length, a transition will establish a clear relationship between sentences, parts of sentences, paragraphs, or entire sections of an essay. Transitions serve to highlight relationships already present by virtue of a writer's having positioned sentences or paragraphs next to one another. Whenever you have trouble finding a word or sentence to serve as an effective transition, reexamine the sentences or paragraphs you are trying to link: it may well be that they are not arranged coherently, and thus are in need of revision. The following box lists the most common transitions, arranged by type of relationship.

Transitional Expressions

To show addition	additionally, again, also, and, as well, besides, equally important, further, furthermore, in addition, moreover, then
To show similarity	also, in the same way, just as . . . so too, likewise, similarly
To show an exception	but, however, in spite of, on the one hand . . . on the other hand, nevertheless, nonetheless, notwithstanding, in contrast, on the contrary, still, yet
To indicate sequence	first, second, third, . . . next, then, finally
To show time	after, afterwards, at last, before, currently, during, earlier, immediately, later, meanwhile, now, recently, simultaneously, subsequently, then
To provide an example	for example, for instance, namely, specifically, to illustrate
To emphasize a point	even, indeed, in fact, of course, truly
To indicate place	above, adjacent, below, beyond, here, in front, in back, nearby, there
To show cause and effect	accordingly, consequently, hence, so, therefore, thus
To conclude or repeat	finally, in a word, in brief, in conclusion, in the end, on the whole, thus, to conclude, to summarize

---

4 Combining techniques to achieve coherence

Experienced writers will often combine the four techniques just discussed to establish coherence within a paragraph. A skillful mix of pronouns, repeated words and phrases, parallel structures, and transitions will help to maintain the focus of a paragraph and to provide multiple cues, or signposts, that help readers find their way from one sentence to the next. The following paragraph on the settling of the Kansas frontier in the mid-nineteenth century illustrates the use of all four techniques for establishing paragraph coherence.

Illustration: Achieving Coherence

Beautiful and bountiful, the (land) was the great lure of Kansas. (Some settlers) sought freedom, (some) yearned for prosperity, (some) craved adventure, (but) in the end it was the promise of the (land) that drew them halfway across a continent. (Here) they could build their own homes, cultivate (their own fields) and develop their own communities. (Undoubtedly,) it took a special kind of fortitude to adjust to (this harsh terrain.) (Yet) with hard work, imagination and tenacity, the future was theirs to mold. In (this new land,) (God's own country,) they reached to the stars through the (wilderness.)

—Joanna Stratton, *Pioneer Women*

26

In this paragraph, the word *land* is repeated in six ways. As well, the term for the main actors of the paragraph—the *settlers*—is repeated with six pronouns. In three different sentences, Joanna Stratton makes effective use of parallel structures. Stratton also makes use of transitional expressions: *but, here, undoubtedly,* and *yet*.

EXERCISE 6

Individual responses

EXERCISE 6

Choose any four example paragraphs in this chapter. For each paragraph, identify the techniques that the author uses to establish coherence. Show the use of pronouns, repetition, parallel structures, and transitions. In addition, identify the use of transitions between paragraphs.

EXERCISE 7

Individual responses

EXERCISE 7

Reread a paragraph you have recently written, and circle all words that help to establish coherence. If few words suggest themselves to you for circling, this may be a sign that your paragraph lacks coherence. Photocopy your paragraph and then revise it for coherence, using the techniques discussed previously: arrange sentences according to a pattern and then highlight that arrangement with pronouns, repeated words, parallel structures, and transitions. When you are done revising, write a clean copy of the paragraph and make photocopies of both the original and the revision for classmates in a small-group discussion. Prepare a brief presentation in which you discuss the changes you have made.

5e Writing and revising to achieve well-developed paragraphs

One important element of effective writing is the level of detail you can offer in support of a paragraph's topic sentence. To *develop* a paragraph means to devote a block of sentences to a discussion of its core idea. Sentences that develop will explain or illustrate, and will support with reasons or facts. The various strategies presented here will help you to develop paragraphs that inform and persuade.

Developing Paragraphs: Essential Features

In determining whether a paragraph is well or even adequately developed, you should be able to answer three questions without hesitation:

- **What is the main point of the paragraph?**

- **Why should readers accept this main point?** (That is, what reasons or information have you provided that would convince a reader that your main point is accurate or reasonable?)

- **Why should readers care about the main point of this paragraph?**

When writing the first draft of a paper, you may not stop to think about how you are developing the central idea of every paragraph. There is no need in first-draft writing to be this deliberate. By the second draft, however, you will want to be conscious of developing your paragraphs. The most common technique is **topical development,** that is, announcing your topic in the opening sentence; dividing that topic into two or three parts (in the case of chronological arrangement, into various *times*); and then developing each part within the paragraph.

The patterns of paragraph development that follow mirror the varieties of relationship that can underlie a paper's thesis. You forge relationships among materials you have gathered in planning a paper, and these relationships become a key component of your working thesis (see 3d). The key paragraphs of any paper will be the ones that express and develop the patterns of relation that lie at the core of either the working thesis or a section thesis. In chapter 3 you saw that these relationships were of several types: sequential order, definition, classification, comparison and contrast, causation, and analogy. These same patterns of relation can be used to develop ideas in individual paragraphs.

ADDITIONAL EXERCISE E

Choose one set of general statements from the following list, and develop a paragraph by providing specific details related to the core idea. As you develop the paragraph, keep in mind the guidelines in the box.

1. Trying to hold down a job while caring for a family (*or* while pursuing a college degree) can pose many problems. Frequently, the individual trying to balance the two ends up shortchanging both.
2. The perfect vacation should offer equal amounts of relaxation, excitement, and enlightenment.
3. The kind of music played on radio stations in a given city can reveal a good deal about the inhabitants' ages, interests, and socioeconomic status.

REFERENCE

COHAN, CAROL. "Writing Effective Paragraphs." *CCC* 27 (1976): 363–65. Development can be taught by considering topic sentences to be questions requiring answers.

GROUP ACTIVITY

GROUP ACTIVITY

CRITICAL THINKING Actually covering each of the patterns of development in succession during class time can become tedious, no matter how interesting the model paragraphs may be. A group activity can make this section far more interesting to discuss, as well as help students understand the patterns better. Divide the class into groups (the number will depend on the class size and your own thoughts on whether to include topical development, whether to split classification and division, and other such considerations). Each group will be responsible for finding, reproducing, and analyzing one paragraph that illustrates a specific pattern of development. (If you're using an anthology that includes a rhetorical table of contents, you may want to simply refer students to that—although much of the challenge will be eliminated.) Groups will then present their paragraphs to the entire class. This activity encourages critical reading for style, invites evaluation of written material, and provides students the opportunity to teach themselves through their discussions.

TEACHING IDEAS

ACROSS THE CURRICULUM Students should not assume that narration is "merely" for personal (journal or letter) writing or for fiction. In the social sciences, particularly in reports on field studies, narration is an important skill.

Descriptions are also used widely across the curriculum. For an example of description in a qualitative field study, see "The Story of Edward," by Paul Rollinson, at 38b-1. Like any effective description, Rollinson's prose gives the reader a clear sense of a character and a place. For another example in the social sciences, see "Factors Influencing the Willingness to Taste Unusual Foods," by Laura P. Otis, at 38b-1. For an example of description in the sciences, see the "methods" section in the student paper on the fermentation of wine, at 39d. You might ask students how the descriptive qualities of these three pieces differ.

1   Narration and description

Stories that you tell (**narration**) and events or scenes that you describe (**description**) are two strategies for development that can give a paper vivid detail.

Narration

Narratives usually involve descriptions; a narrative's main purpose is to recount for readers a story that will have a point pertinent to the larger essay. Brief stories are often used as examples. Most often, narratives are sequenced chronologically and will occur in an essay either as a single paragraph or as a grouping of paragraphs. The challenge in writing a narrative is to keep readers involved both in the events you are relating and in the people involved in those events. In the example that follows, Annie Dillard manages to do both. These paragraphs appear in her autobiography, in a chapter devoted to joke telling in her family.

27   There was another very complicated joke, also in a select category, which required a long weekend with tolerant friends.

You had to tell a joke that was not funny. It was a long, pointless story about a construction job that ended with someone's throwing
28   away a brick. There was nothing funny about it at all, and when your friends did not laugh, you had to pretend you'd muffed it. (Your husband in the crowd could shill for you: " 'Tain't funny, Pam. You told it all wrong.")

A few days later, if you could contrive another occasion for joke telling, and if your friends still permitted you to speak, you set forth on another joke, this one an old nineteenth-century chestnut about angry passengers on a train. The lady plucks the lighted, smelly cigar from the man's mouth and flings it from the moving train's window. The man
29   seizes the little black poodle from her lap and hurls the poor dog from the same window. When at last the passengers draw unspeaking into the station, what do they see coming down the platform but the black poodle, and guess what it has in its mouth? "The cigar," say your friends, bored sick and vowing never to spend another weekend with you. "No," you say, triumphant, "the brick." This was Mother's kind of joke. Its very riskiness excited her. It wasn't funny, but it was interesting to set up, and it elicited from her friends a grudging admiration.
—ANNIE DILLARD, *An American Childhood*

Description

All writers must make observations and describe what they see. What counts as an accurate and worthwhile description will vary according to circumstance, but generally it can be said that a writer who can evoke in us a clear sense of sight, feeling, smell, hearing, or taste earns our admiration. Following is a description of the promenade—the walkway—on the Brooklyn Bridge. The author does a fine job of letting us see the bridge, even if we have never been there.

On most traffic bridges the only foot passage is a pavement along-side rushing vehicles. Here the walk is a promenade raised above the traffic; one can lean over the railing and watch cars speeding below. The promenade is wide enough for benches—for walkers and for cyclists.

30 Old-fashioned lamp posts remind the walker that it is, after all, a thoroughfare. But the walk is narrow enough for the promenader to reach over and touch the large, round cables, wrapped in wire casing, or the rough wire rope of the vertical suspenders. Crossing the verticals is a rigging of diagonal wire ropes—stays, attached somewhere below to the floor of the roadway.

—ALAN TRACHTENBERG, *Brooklyn Bridge: Fact and Symbol*

2 Example

An example is a particular case of a more general point. After topical development, development by example is probably the most common method of supporting the core idea of a paragraph. Examples *show* readers what you mean; if an example is vivid, readers will have a better chance of remembering your general point. The topic sentence of a paragraph may be developed with one extended example or several briefer ones. It is very common for writers to include an example along with other strategies for developing a paragraph. Several transitions are commonly used to introduce examples: *for example, for instance, a case in point, to illustrate.* In the following paragraph, Rachel Carson describes how methods of insect control can affect fish.

Wherever there are great forests, modern methods of insect control threaten the fishes inhabiting the streams in the shelter of the trees. One of the best-known examples of fish destruction in the United States took place in 1955, as a result of spraying in and near Yellowstone National

31 Park. By the fall of that year, so many dead fish had been found in the Yellowstone River that sportsmen and Montana fish-and-game administrators became alarmed. About 90 miles of the river were affected. In one 300-yard length of shoreline, 600 dead fish were counted, including brown trout, whitefish, and suckers. Stream insects, the natural food of trout, had disappeared.

—RACHEL CARSON, *Silent Spring*

3 Sequential order/process

If you have ever cooked a meal by following a recipe, you have read paragraphs patterned as a sequence of steps, as a process. Such a paragraph will not explain the causes of a particular outcome—it will not, for instance, explain the chemical reactions that cake batter undergoes when placed in an oven. A paragraph that presents a process will show carefully sequenced events. The range of possibilities is endless: what is the process by which people fall in love? by which children learn? by which a computer chip is manufactured? Each of these cases, different as they

LOOKING BACK, LOOKING FORWARD

An example by definition stands in relation to a larger point the writer wishes to make. On this point, see 1c, the discussion of larger contexts as it relates, generally, to critical thinking. In that discussion, students are urged to ask of particular cases: "What's this a part of?" In the present discussion, students are being urged to ask: "How can I support my general point by directing the reader to a particular instance?" The questions are inversions of one another, and students will do well to develop a facility in moving in their thinking from the general to the specific and from the specific to the general. Later, in 6d-1, students will see that the argument from generalization draws on this same relationship: Generalizations are made possible when one has studied a number of representative examples. The writer who makes a generalization is obliged to prove it by citing examples.

TEACHING IDEAS

ACROSS THE CURRICULUM For three examples of how a sequential order, or process, is presented differently in different curricular contexts, see the following examples in this book: Sean Hannan's paper (the process of becoming an animal), page 115; the "methods" section of the article by Laura P. Otis, page 691; the "materials and methods" section of the paper by Clarence Ivie, page 722.

FOR DISCUSSION

Often definitions can be stated simply, and writers can assume that readers will share their understanding of a term. But definitions will, at times, become an occasion for arguments. You may want to discuss with students Carl Becker's argument in defining the term "history."

[History is a word] that I wish to reduce to its lowest terms. In order to do that I need a very simple definition. I once read that "history is the knowledge of events that have occurred in the past." That is a simple definition, but not simple enough. It contains three words that require examination. The first is knowledge. Knowledge is a formidable word. I always think of knowledge as something that is stored up in the *Encyclopaedia Britannica* or the *Summa Theologica:* something difficult to acquire, something at all events that I have not. Resenting a definition that denies me the title of historian, I therefore ask what is most essential to knowledge. Well, memory, I should think (and I mean memory in the broad sense, the memory of events inferred as well as the memory of events observed); other things are necessary too, but memory is fundamental: without memory no knowledge. So our definition becomes, "History is the memory of events that have occurred in the past." But events—the word carries an implication of something grand, like the taking of the Bastille or the Spanish-American War. An occurrence need not be spectacular to be an event. If I drive a motor car down the crooked streets of Ithaca, that is an event—something done; if the traffic cop bawls me out, that is an event—something said; if I have evil thoughts of him for so doing, that is an event—something thought. In truth anything done, said, or thought is an event, important or not as may turn out. But since we do not ordinarily speak without thinking, at least in some rudimentary way, and since the psychologists tell us that we cannot think

are, requires a clear delineation of steps. In paragraphs organized as a process, you will typically use transitions that show sequence in time: *first, second, after, before, once, next, then,* and *finally.*

> Making a chip is a complex process. Most manufacturers now use what Heilmeier calls the "dip and wash" technique. A diagram of electronic circuitry is designed by a scientist on a computer terminal. Photographic machines produce hundreds of reproductions of the display and reduce them in size until their individual components are in the micron range. A photographic negative, or mask, is made of the patterns. Ultraviolet light is then projected through the mask onto a thin, 4-inch wafer of silicon that has been treated with photo resist, a light-sensitive material. Just like a film, the photo resist is developed, and the tiny patterns of the chips' circuitry emerge on the silicon's surface. The wafer is dipped in acid, which eats away the silicon where there is no photo resist. A layer of metal can be deposited for the interconnections between circuits, then another layer of photo resist. Some wafers take ten or more etched layers. Once all the layers are formed on the wafer, the chips are sawed out, fine wire leads are connected and they are ready for use in electronic devices.
>
> —MERRILL SHEILS, "And Man Created the Chip"

4   Definition

Paragraphs of definition are always important. In informative writing, readers can learn the meaning of terms needed for understanding difficult concepts. In essays intended to persuade, writers define terms in order to establish a common language with the reader, an important first step toward gaining the reader's agreement. Once a term is defined, it can be clarified with examples, comparisons, or descriptions. The paragraph that follows is informative in character—more or less announcing its definition.

Student Example: Josefa Pinto

> What exactly is genetic engineering? Genetic engineering is the name given techniques by which scientists alter or combine genes (hereditary material) in an organism. Genes, which are part of all living cells, carry chemical information that determines an organism's characteristics; genes have often been called "blueprints" of life. By changing an organism's genes, scientists can manipulate the organism's traits and the traits of its descendants. Ultimately, through manipulation of genetic material, scientists hope to produce flawless organisms—microorganisms, plants, and animals that exhibit greater productivity, lower cost, and more resistance to illnesses.

5   Division and classification

Division (also called *analysis*) and classification are closely related operations. A writer who divides a topic into parts to see what it is made of performs an analysis. Analysis is an act of critical thinking that can be put to several ends. A careful study of parts can be instrumental in comparing and contrasting, in understanding a process, and in inferring cause and effect. While a paragraph may emphasize a definition, comparison, process, or cause, in each case this emphasis is made meaningful at least in part through analysis.

A *classification* is a grouping of like items. The writer begins with what may appear at first to be bits of unrelated information. Gradually, patterns of similarity emerge and the writer is able to establish categories by which to group like items. In the example that follows, Brian Fagan considers the various locations at which archaeological digs are made and then classifies or groups the digs according to common features. Because establishing categories is a matter of judgment, another writer might well classify archaeological sites differently. Fagan's paragraph begins with his topic sentence. Notice that once he defines various classes, he devotes a sentence or two to developing each.

> Archaeological sites are most commonly classified according to the activities that occurred there. Thus, cemeteries and other sepulchers like Tutankhamun's tomb are referred to as **burial sites.** A 20,000-year-old Stone Age site in the Dnieper Valley of the Ukraine, with mammoth-bone houses, hearths, and other signs of domestic activity, is a **habitation site.** So too are many other sites, such as caves and rockshelters, early Mesoamerican farming villages, and Mesopotamian cities—in all, people lived and carried out greatly diverse activities. **Kill sites** consist of bones of slaughtered game animals and the weapons that killed them. They are found in East Africa and on the North American Great Plains.
>
> 34 **Quarry sites** are another type of specialist site, where people mined stone or metals to make specific tools. Prized raw materials, such as obsidian, a volcanic glass used for fine knives, were widely traded in prehistoric times and profoundly interest the archaeologist. Then there are such spectacular **religious sites** as the stone circles of Stonehenge in southern England, the Temple of Amun at Karnak, Egypt, and the great ceremonial precincts of lowland Maya centers in Central America at *Tikal,* Copán, and Palenque. **Art sites** are common in southwestern France, southern Africa, and parts of North America, where prehistoric people painted or engraved magnificent displays of art.
>
> BRIAN FAGAN, *Archaeology*

6   Comparison/contrast

To *compare* is to discuss the similarities between people, places, objects, events, or ideas. To *contrast* is to discuss differences. The writer developing such a paragraph conducts an analysis of two or more subjects, studying the parts of each and then discussing the subjects in relation to each other. Specific points of comparison and contrast make the discussion possible. Suppose you are comparing and contrasting a computer and the human brain. Two points you might use to make the discussion meaningful are the density with which information is packed

without speaking, or at least not without having anticipatory vibrations in the larynx, we may well combine thought events and speech events under one term; and so our definition becomes, "History is the memory of things said and done in the past." But the past—the word is both misleading and unnecessary: misleading, because the past, used in connection with history, seems to imply the distant past, as if history ceased before we were born; unnecessary, because after all everything said or done is already in the past as soon as it is said or done. Therefore I will omit that word, and our definition becomes, "History is the memory of things said and done." This is a definition that reduces history to its lowest terms, and yet includes everything that is essential to understanding what it really is.

—CARL BECKER, "Everyman His Own Historian"

LOOKING AHEAD

Defining terms is an important part of argumentation. See 6b-2 for more on defining terms in an argument. See also 38a-3 for an example of the rigor with which a definition can be presented in the social sciences. (B. F. Skinner is defining the term *conditioned reflex.*") See also Ludwig Wittgenstein's *definition of family resemblances* (37a-2), a term he defines by asking what is common to "the proceedings that we call 'games.'"

FOR DISCUSSION

Aside from being a technique for organizing paragraphs, comparison and contrast has long been used to organize entire essays. If you assign a book of readings in your class, most likely it will contain at least one example of a comparison-contrast essay. Students can get a hint of the larger uses of comparison and contrast by turning to paragraphs 23 through 25 in this chapter, where Bruce Catton is discussing the similarities and differences of Grant and Lee.

Organizing a Paragraph of Comparison and Contrast

Comparison and contrast is a type of analysis in which parts of two (or more) subjects are studied and then discussed in terms of one another. Particular points of comparison and contrast provide the means by which to observe similarities and differences between subjects. A comparative analysis is usually arranged in one of two ways.

Arrangement by subject

Topic sentence (may be shifted to other positions in the paragraph)

Introduce Subject A
   Discuss Subject A in terms of the first point
   Discuss Subject A in terms of the second point

Introduce Subject B
   Discuss Subject B in terms of the first point
   Discuss Subject B in terms of the second point

Conclude with a summary of similarities and differences.

Arrangement, point-by-point

Topic sentence (may be shifted to other positions in the paragraph)

Introduce the first point to be compared and contrasted
   Discuss Subject A in terms of this point
   Discuss Subject B in terms of this point

Introduce the second point to be compared and contrasted
   Discuss Subject A in terms of this point
   Discuss Subject B in terms of this point

and the speed with which information is processed. You could analyze a computer and a human brain in light of these two points, and presumably your analysis would yield similarities *and* differences.

Paragraphs of comparison and contrast should be put to some definite use in a paper. It is not enough to point out similarities and differences; you must *do* something with this information: three possibilities would be to classify, evaluate, or interpret. When writing your paragraph, consider two common methods of arrangement: by subject or point-by-point.

When the comparisons you want to make are relatively brief, arrangement by subject works well. Readers are able to hold in mind the first part of the discussion as they read the second. When comparisons are longer and more complex, a point-by-point discussion helps the reader to focus on specific elements of your comparative analysis. Paragraphs developed by comparison and contrast use transition words such as *similarly, also, as well, just so, by contrast, conversely, but, however, on the one hand/on the other,* and *yet*.

In the following paragraph, Carl Sagan uses a point-by-point arrangement to compare and contrast the human brain with a computer. First, he examines the two subjects with respect to the density with which their information is packed; next, he examines the two subjects with respect to the speed with which they process information.

> How densely packed is the information stored in the brain? A typical information density during the operation of a modern computer is about a million bits per cubic centimeter. This is the total information content of the computer, divided by its volume. The human brain contains, as we have said, about 10^{13} bits in a little more than 10^3 cubic centimeters, for an information content of $10^{13}/10^3 = 10^{10}$, about ten billion bits per cubic centimeter; the brain is therefore ten thousand times more densely packed with information than is a computer, although the computer is much larger. Put another way, a modern computer able to process the information in the human brain would have to be about ten thousand times larger in volume than the human brain. On the other hand, modern electronic computers are capable of processing information at a rate of 10^{16} to 10^{17} bits per second, compared to a peak rate ten billion times slower in the brain. The brain must be extraordinarily cleverly packaged and "wired," with such a small total information content and so low a processing rate, to be able to do so many significant tasks so much better than the best computer.
>
> —CARL SAGAN, *The Dragons of Eden*

35

In the following paragraph, John Morreall organizes his comparative discussion by subject. First, he discusses his Subject A: the person with a sense of humor and the traits associated with this view of the world. Then Morreall discusses his Subject B: the person who lacks a sense of humor and the traits associated with this view of the world. Morreall concludes the paragraph with a topic sentence that makes a general point about humor and places the comparison and contrast in a larger perspective.

> When the person with a sense of humor laughs in the face of his own failure, he is showing that his perspective transcends the particular situation he's in, and that he does not have an egocentric, overly precious view of his own endeavors. This is not to say that he lacks self-esteem—quite the contrary. It is because he feels good about himself at a fundamental level that this or that setback is not threatening to him. The person without real self-esteem, on the other hand, who is unsure of his own worth, tends to invest his whole sense of himself in each of his projects. Whether he fails or succeeds, he is not likely to see things in an objective way; because his ego rides on each of the goals he sets for himself, any failure will constitute personal defeat and any success personal triumph. He simply cannot afford to laugh at himself, whatever happens. So having a sense of humor about oneself is psychologically healthy. As A. Penjon so nicely said, it "frees us from vanity, on the one hand, and from pessimism on the other by keeping us larger than what we do, and greater than what can happen to us."
>
> —JOHN MORREALL, *Taking Laughter Seriously*

36

FOR DISCUSSION

Creative analogies can be helpful to an argument. You might share with students the following excerpt from Amitai Etzioni's "Children of the Universe" (Rpt. in *Utne Reader* May/June 1993, 53):

> Consider for a moment parenting as an industry. As farming declined, most fathers left to work away from home generations ago. Over the past 20 years, millions of American mothers have sharply curtailed their work in the "parenting industry" by moving to work outside the home. By 1991 two-thirds (66.7 percent) of all mothers with children under 18 were in the labor force, and more than half (55.4 percent) of women with children under the age of 3 were. At the same time, a much smaller number of child-care personnel moved into the parenting industry.
>
> If this were any other business, say, shoemaking, and more than half of the labor force had been lost and replaced with fewer, less-qualified hands and still we asked the shoemakers to produce the same number of shoes of the same quality, we would be considered crazy. But this is what happened to parenting. . . .

See 6d-1 to see the ways in which analogy can be used in an argument (as above). Note that there is a point at which any analogy breaks down. For instance, Etzioni's assumption that parenting is an industry, comparable to shoemaking, must be accepted for the analogy to work. If the assumption is questioned, the analogy loses force. The well-chosen analogy, however, can advance an argument.

LOOKING AHEAD

See 6d-1 for a discussion of cause-and-effect reasoning and its place in argumentation. For examples of how paragraphs arranged by cause and effect are used in actual papers, see the student essay in 6g, in which Alison Tschopp argues that the real cause of children's problems with advertisements is not advertising but lack of parental supervision. See also 38d, paragraph 2, in which Kristy Bell argues that one reason women alcoholics are invisible is that they are well protected by family and friends. The larger point to make in these examples is that the cause-and-effect paragraph forms *one* part of a larger argument. For an example of extended

7 Analogy

An **analogy** is a comparison of two topics that, on first appearance, seem unrelated. An analogy gains force by surprising a reader, by demonstrating that an unlikely comparison is not only likely but in fact is illuminating. Well-chosen analogies can clarify difficult concepts. In the following example, the process of learning is compared with a symphony orchestra. The words *like* and *analogous to* typically signal the beginning of an analogy. After describing the first of the two topics in the comparison, the writer follows with an expression such as *just so* or *similarly* and then continues with the second part of the comparison.

> In closing, we might describe learning with an analogy to a well-orchestrated symphony, aimed to blend both familiar and new sounds. A symphony is the complex interplay of composer, conductor, the repertoire of instruments, and the various dimensions of music. Each instrument is used strategically to interact with other instruments toward a rich construction of themes progressing in phases, with some themes recurring and others driving the movement forward toward a conclusion or resolution. Finally, each symphony stands alone in its meaning, yet has a relationship to the symphonies that came before and those that will come later. Similarly, learning is a complex interaction of the learner, the instructional materials, the repertoire of available learning strategies, and the context, including the teacher. The skilled learner approaches each task strategically toward the goal of constructing meaning. Some strategies focus on understanding the incoming information, others strive to relate the meaning to earlier predictions, and still others work to integrate the new information with prior knowledge.
>
> —BEAU FLY JONES, ET AL., "Learning and Thinking"

8 Cause and effect

Development by cause and effect shows how an event or condition has come to occur. Inferring a causal relationship between events requires careful analysis. As discussed elsewhere (see 6d-1), causes are usually complex, and a writer must avoid the temptation to oversimplify. In particular, avoid the mistake of suggesting that because one event precedes another in time, the first event causes the second. A causal relationship is not always so clear-cut, a point that James Watts and Alan Davis acknowledge in the following paragraph on the Depression of the 1930s. Paragraphs developed by cause and effect frequently use these transition words: *therefore, thus,* and *consequently.*

> The depression was precipitated by the stock market crash in October 1929, but the actual cause of the collapse was an unhealthy economy. While the ability of the manufacturing industry to produce consumer goods had increased rapidly, mass purchasing power had remained relatively static. Most laborers, farmers, and white-collar workers, therefore, could not afford to buy the automobiles and refrigerators

38   turned out by factories in the 1920s, because their incomes were too low. At the same time, the federal government increased the problem through economic policies that tended to encourage the very rich to over-save.

—JAMES WATTS AND ALAN F. DAVIS, *Your Family in Modern American History*

cause-and-effect thinking common to science writing, see the lab report in 39d. The report, in effect, is an argument in which Clarence Ivie proves that using a certain strain of yeast produces (i.e., *causes* the formation of) a superior wine.

Writers may combine methods of developing a paragraph's core idea, as needed. The same paragraph that shows an example may also show a comparison or contrast. No firm rules constrain you in developing a paragraph. Let your common sense and an interest in helping your reader understand your subject be your guides.

EXERCISE 8
Return to Exercise 2 (page 126) in which you selected one section of a textbook chapter to study in depth. If you have not done so, complete that exercise, and then for that same block of paragraphs analyze each paragraph and identify its pattern of development.

EXERCISE 8

Individual responses

EXERCISE 9
In one paragraph compare and contrast your first day as a student at your present school with your first day in any other circumstance. Take care to choose two or three points on the basis of which you will generate your comparison and contrast. Be sure your comparison and contrast is put to some purpose (perhaps you will classify, interpret, or evaluate). Express this purpose in your paragraph's topic sentence. See ¶s 35 and 36 for possible models.

EXERCISE 9

Individual responses

EXERCISE 10
Reread a paper you have recently written and select a paragraph to revise so that its topic sentence is thoroughly developed. Use any of the patterns of development presented here so that you are able, without hesitation, to answer the three questions in the box on page 143. Make photocopies of your original paragraph and your revision; plan to address a small group of classmates and explain the choices you have made in revision.

EXERCISE 10

Individual responses

5f Writing and revising paragraphs of introduction and conclusion

The introduction and conclusion to a paper can be understood as a type of transition. Transitions provide logical bridges in a paper: they help readers to move from one sentence to another, one paragraph to another, and one section to another (see 5d-3). At the beginning of a paper, the introduction serves as a transition by moving the reader from the world outside of your paper to the world within. At the end of the paper, the conclusion works in the opposite direction by moving readers from the world of your paper back to their own world—with, you hope, something useful gained by their effort.

1 Introductions

Writing an introduction is often easier once you know what you are introducing; for this reason many writers choose not to work seriously on an introduction until they have finished a draft and can see the overall shape and content of a paper. Other writers need to begin with a carefully written introduction. If this is your preference, remember not to demand perfection of a first draft, especially since the material you will be introducing has yet to be written. Once it is written, your introduction may well need to change.

The introduction as a frame of reference

Introductions establish frames of reference. On completing an introduction, readers know the general topic of your paper; they know the disciplinary perspective from which you will discuss this topic; and they know the standards they will use in evaluating your work. Readers quickly learn from an introduction if you are a laboratory researcher, a field researcher, a theorist, an essayist, a reporter, a student with a general interest, and so on. Each of these possible identities implies for readers different standards of evidence and reasoning by which they will evaluate your work. Consider the paragraph that follows, which introduces a paper that you will find in chapter 37, Writing and Reading in the Humanities. The introduction, explicitly in the thesis and implicitly in the writer's choice of vocabulary, establishes a frame of reference that alerts readers to the type of language, evidence, and logic that will be used in the subsequent paper. Thus situated, readers are better able to anticipate and evaluate what they will read.

FOR DISCUSSION

Reproduce several introductions that provide a frame of reference (these can be gathered from anthologies or student papers). Ask students to discuss what signals they pick up from the paragraphs—what they learn about the writer, the approach, the language, the type of evidence or detail that will be used, and the like.

TEACHING IDEAS

While it's always a bit dangerous to focus on negative examples, many students do need to be made aware of some taboos with regard to introductions. If you can frame your discussion in terms of the approach in this chapter, you can address the problem of the hesitant introduction—the "I don't really know much about this but here goes anyway" variety. If the introduction provides readers with their first impression of the writer, then certainly the writer doesn't want to sound ignorant or insecure. Similarly, if you focus on the differences between introductions from various disciplines, you can steer students away from using inappropriate introductions such as the "In this paper I will" for humanities or the introductory anecdote for sciences.

Illustration: Writing in the Humanities

James Joyce's "Counterparts" tells the story of a man, Farrington, who is abused by his boss for not doing his job right. Farrington spends a long time drinking after work; and when he finally arrives

39   home, he in turn abuses—he beats—his son Tom. In eleven pages, Joyce tells much more than a story of yet another alcoholic venting failures and frustrations on family members. In "Counterparts," Farring-

Language of literary analysis

Evidence: based on close reading of a story

Logic: generalization

Drinking and church going related to a need for power

ton turns to drink in order to gain power—in much the same way his wife and children turn to the Church.

Also comparison/contrast

By comparison, read the following introduction to a paper written from a sociological perspective. This paragraph introduces a paper you will find in chapter 38, Writing and Reading in the Social Sciences.

■

Illustration: Writing in the Social Sciences

40

Currently in the United States there are at least two million women alcoholics (Unterberger, 1989, p. 1150). Americans are largely unaware of the extent of this debilitating disease among women and the problems it presents. Numerous women dependent on alcohol remain invisible largely because friends, family, coworkers, and the women themselves refuse to acknowledge the problem. *This denial amounts to a virtual conspiracy of silence and greatly complicates the process of diagnosis and treatment.*

Language of sociology

Evidence: based on review of sociological literature

Logic: cause and effect. Will show how denial complicates diagnosis and treatment.

■

The introduction as an invitation to continue reading

Aside from establishing a frame of reference and set of expectations about language, evidence, and logic, an introduction also does—or does not— establish in your reader a desire to *continue* reading. A complete introduction provides background information needed to understand a paper. An especially effective introduction gains the reader's attention and gradually turns that attention toward the writer's thesis and the rest of the paper. Writers typically adopt specialized strategies for introducing their work. In the discussion that follows you will learn several of these strategies, all of which can be developed in one or two paragraphs, at the end of which you will place your thesis. These examples by no means exhaust the possible strategies available to you for opening your papers.

Student Example: Daniel Burke, "Defense of Fraternities"

A revolutionary event took place at Raleigh Tavern in 1776, an event that has added an important dimension to my life at college. In fact,

ADDITIONAL EXERCISE F

Assignment: Ask students to read any one of the sample student papers in chapters 4, 6, 35, and 37 through 39. In each case, students should study the writer's strategy used in the introduction. Students should then prepare themselves to argue that the introduction is or is not effective. One variation on the assignment would be to ask that students also prepare an alternate introduction to the paper. (See also the Additional Exercise on page 156, in which students are asked to do the same with the paper's conclusion.)

41   nearly all American undergraduates are affected in some way by the actions of several students from the College of William and Mary on December 5, 1776. The formation of the first Greek-letter fraternity, Phi Beta Kappa, started the American college fraternity-sorority tradition that today can be an important addition to your undergraduate education.

In this example, student writer Daniel Burke provides pertinent historical information that sets a context for the paper. By linking a "revolutionary event" in 1776 to his own life over two hundred years later, Burke captures the reader's interest.

The following example begins with a question, the response to which leads to the author's thesis. (The reference to "Valenti" is to Jack Valenti, head of the Motion Picture Production Association when Stephen Farber wrote his book.)

> How are [movie] ratings actually determined? Official brochures on the rating system provide only very brief general definitions of the four categories, and I do not believe the categories can or should be defined

Strategies for Writing Introductions

1. Announce your topic, using vocabulary that hints at the perspective from which you will be writing. On completing your introduction, readers should be able to anticipate the type of language, evidence, and logic you will use in your paper.

2. If readers lack the background needed to understand your paper, then provide this background. In a paragraph or two, choose and develop a strategy that will both orient readers to your subject and interest them in it:

    define terms
    present a brief history
    review a controversy

3. If readers know something of your subject, then devote less (or no) time to developing background information and more time to stimulating interest. In a paragraph or two, choose and develop a strategy that will gain the reader's attention:

    raise a question
    quote a source familiar to the reader
    tell a story
    begin directly with a statement of the thesis

4. Once you have provided background information and gained the reader's attention with an opening strategy, gradually turn that attention toward your thesis, which you will position as the last sentence of the introductory paragraph(s).

much more specifically. It is impossible to set hard-and-fast rules; every film is different from every other film, and no precise definition could possibly cover all films made. Valenti has frequently toyed with the idea of more detailed definitions, though any rigid demarcations between the categories inevitably seem hopelessly arbitrary.

42

—STEPHEN FARBER, *The Movie Rating Game*

See 5f-3 for two additional strategies for opening a paper: using a quotation and telling a story.

2 Conclusions

One important job in writing a paper is to explain to readers what you have accomplished and why your ideas are significant. Minimally, a conclusion will summarize your work, but often you will want to do more than write a summary. Provided you have written carefully and believe in what you have written, you have earned the right to expand on your paper's thesis in a conclusion: to point the reader back to the larger world and to suggest the significance of your ideas in that world. This is exactly what Josefa Pinto does in the conclusion of her paper, many paragraphs of which you've seen as illustrations in this chapter.

Student Example: Josefa Pinto

Having weighed the pros and cons of the debate, I feel that nature is too precious to be gambled with. We may be tempted to use the opportunities presented by the revolution in genetic engineering, but we should always exercise caution. As Albert Einstein once advised, "Concern for man himself and his fate must always form the chief interest of all technical endeavors, in order that the creations of our minds, and I would add, our laboratories, shall be a blessing and not a curse" (qtd. in Wickelgren 124). I hope that man's search for perfection will not blind him to the consequences and dangers that the search may bring.

43

A conclusion gives you an opportunity to answer a challenge that all readers raise—*So what? Why does this paper matter to me?* A well-written conclusion will answer these questions and will leave readers with a trace of your thinking as they turn away from your paper and back to their own business.

The example conclusions that follow do not exhaust the strategies for closing your papers; these examples should, however, give you a taste for the variety of techniques available. Here is a paragraph that presents the simplest possible conclusion: a summary.

One can see by the number of steps involved in the legislative process that the odds are very great against an average bill becoming law. At almost every turn a bill may be killed. Hundreds of bills may start out, but only a few survive to become law.

44

—KEVIN COSTELLO, "Long Odds: How a Bill Becomes Law"

TEACHING IDEAS

As with introductions, conclusions can also pose problems for students. Again framing your discussion in terms of the approach in this chapter, you can address the problem of the repetitive conclusion—the "In conclusion I have said" variety. By clarifying what's meant by "comment" you can steer students away from the conclusion that introduces an entirely new idea. Finally, again by focusing on the differences between disciplines, you can help students avoid producing conclusions inappropriate to the discipline in which they're writing.

ADDITIONAL EXERCISE H

Ask students to read any one of the sample student papers in chapters 4, 6, 35, and 37 through 39. In each case, students should study the writer's strategy used in the conclusion. Students should then prepare themselves to argue that the conclusion is or is not effective. One variation on the assignment would be to ask that students also prepare an alternate conclusion to the paper. (See also Additional Exercise F on page 153, in which students are asked to do the same with the paper's introduction.)

ADDITIONAL EXERCISE I

ACROSS THE CURRICULUM Find representative conclusions (of chapters, sections, essays) from the reading you're doing for courses in two different disciplines, using the categories found in Additional Exercise G. Using what you've learned about conclusions in this chapter, compare the two samples and explain the methods they use to signal that the paper is finished, as well as the message they leave with the reader.

Strategies for Writing Conclusions

1. **Summary.** The simplest conclusion is a summary, a brief restatement of your paper's main points. Avoid conclusions that repeat exactly material presented elsewhere in the paper.

2. **Summary and Comment.** More emphatic conclusions build on a summary in one of several ways. These conclusions will:
   set ideas in the paper in a larger context
   call for action (or research)
   speculate or warn
   purposefully confuse or trouble the reader
   raise a question
   quote a familiar or authoritative source
   tell a story

A more ambitious conclusion will move beyond a summary and call for involvement on the reader's part. For instance, you might ask the reader to address a puzzling or troubling question, to speculate on the future, or to reflect on the past. In this next example, the reader is asked to help resolve a problem plaguing college sports.

Student Example: Jenafer Trahar, "Athletes and Education"

We don't need to eliminate college sports. We probably couldn't anyway, what with all the money being made. Eliminating sports would do more harm than good, taking away both a source of pride in college life and an important source of revenue. Changing the admissions process to deny marginally prepared student-athletes would not be fair, since for many of these kids sports is their only avenue of exposure to college life and the possibility of a higher education. To eliminate the chance to attend college for marginal student-athletes would be heartless, because it places on them a burden they did not make, a burden that should and can be lifted with the proper approach. That's why a plan that modifies the present system, not destroys it, makes the most sense. Let's take advantage of all the money that college sports generates and use that money to *really* educate the student-athlete. The proposals I have made not only would allow student-athletes to gain access to college but also would increase the chances of their actually receiving an education.

Two additional strategies for concluding a paper are discussed next: using a quotation and telling a story.

3 The opening and closing frame

You might consider creating an introductory and concluding frame for your papers. The strategy is to use the same story, quotation, question—any device that comes to mind—as an occasion both to introduce your subject and, when the time is right, to conclude emphatically. Provided the body of a paper is unified, coherent, and well developed, an opening and closing frame will give the paper a pleasing symmetry. In the following example, Rachel L. Jones works with a quotation.

Introduction

46
William Labov, a noted linguist, once said about the use of black English, "It is the goal of most black Americans to acquire full control of the standard language without giving up their own culture." He also suggested that there are certain advantages to having two ways to express one's feelings. I wonder if the good doctor might also consider the goals of those black Americans who have full control of standard English but who are every now and then troubled by that colorful, grammar-to-the-winds patois that is black English. Case in point—me.

Conclusion

47
I would have to disagree with Labov in one respect. My goal is not so much to acquire full control of both standard and black English, but to one day see more black people less dependent on a dialect that excludes them from full participation in the world we live in. I don't think I talk white; I think I talk right.

—RACHEL L. JONES, "What's Wrong with Black English"

EXERCISE 11

Locate a collection of essays and or articles: any textbook that is an edited collection of readings will work. Read three articles and examine the strategies the authors use to introduce and conclude their work. Choose one article to analyze more closely. Examine the strategies for beginning and ending the selection and relate these strategies to the selection itself. Why has the writer chosen these *particular* strategies? Be prepared to discuss your findings in a small group.

EXERCISE 11

Individual responses

EXERCISE 12

In connection with a paper you are writing, draft *two* opening and *two* closing paragraphs, using different strategies. Set your work aside for a day or two and then choose which paragraphs appeal to you the most. Be prepared to discuss your choices in a small group.

EXERCISE 12

Individual responses

5g Determining paragraph length

Paragraphs vary greatly in length. As long as the governing idea of a paragraph remains clear, all sentences are unified, and the paragraph is coherent, then in theory a paragraph can be one sentence, five sentences, or twenty. This said, you should realize that readers will tire of a paper whose paragraphs are consistently one typewritten page or longer. If for no other reason than to give readers visual relief, keep paragraphs mod-

GROUP ACTIVITY

The following activity can be done more easily if students compose their essays on computers: Since paragraph length has a great deal to do with the needs of the reader, ask students to make two copies of a brief paper *without any paragraph divisions*. In groups of three, each student will mark the other two papers for paragraph divisions. The ensuing discussion of differences between each reader (and the writer's original divisions) will encourage students to analyze the relative demands that content, purpose, and audience place on a writer in determining paragraph length.

REFERENCES

STERN, ARTHUR A. "When Is a Paragraph?" *CCC* 27 (1976): 253–57. Calls into question descriptions of paragraphs as logical units.

EDEN, RICK, and RUTH MITCHELL. "Paragraphing for the Reader." *CCC* 37 (1986): 416–30. Various choices in paragraphing should be made with audience expectations in mind.

ADDITIONAL EXERCISE J

See the "For Discussion" annotation on page 146. Ask students to read the paragraph in which Carl Becker defines "history." Then have students mark the places that, for reasons of length, they would begin new paragraphs.

Suggested response:

Break between . . . *three words that require examination.* and *The first is knowledge.*

Break between . . . *events that have occurred in the past.* and *But events. . . .*

Break between . . . *things said and done in the past.* and *But the past. . . .*

erate in length. *Moderate* is a variable and personal term. Perhaps you decide that visually your paragraphs should average one-third to two-thirds of a typewritten page. If your sentences tend to be brief, then your average number of sentences per paragraph may be ten or twelve; if your sentences tend to be long, then the average of sentences per paragraph may drop to six.

Devote your energies to the content of your paragraphs first. Turn to paragraph length in the later stages of revision when you are relatively satisfied with your work. Then think of your reader and the way your paragraphs appear on the page. Visually, does the length of your paragraphs invite the reader into your paper? Consistently short paragraphs may send the signal that your ideas are not well developed. Consistently long paragraphs may give the impression that your writing is dense or that your ideas are not well differentiated. You should freely divide a long paragraph for reasons of length alone. A new paragraph created because of length does not need its own topic sentence, provided this paragraph is a clear continuation of the one preceding it.

Brief paragraphs of one, two, or three sentences can be useful for establishing transitions between sections of a paper (see ¶24) and, as illustrated in this next example, for creating emphasis.

> A coyote also eats avocados, oranges, melons, berries, chickens, small dogs, livestock and fowl with relish. The rare but rising number of attacks on small children indicates that once certain coyotes overcome their inherent fear of man, very young human specimens also look like food. And if his own offspring or mate is killed, he might well snack off the carcass. A meal's a meal.
>
> To Brother Coyote, it's truly a dog-eat-dog world.
>
> Coyotes, it was discovered, are so intelligent they can learn from their own mistakes and the mistakes of fellow coyotes. Remarkably, they also teach their young to avoid those mistakes.
>
> —MICHELLE HUNEVEN, "The Urban Coyote"

If in revising a first draft you find that your paragraphs are consistently two or three sentences, consider ways in which you can further develop each paragraph's topic sentence. Unless you are writing in a journalism class or in some other context where consistently brief paragraphs are valued, once again the advice is to maintain a moderate length and only rarely—for clear reasons—use very brief or very long paragraphs.

CHAPTER 6

Writing and Evaluating Arguments

Arguments provide a way of knowing about and participating in the world. Through argumentation, you exchange views with parents, friends, and associates; when differences arise, you try to influence others so that they will agree with you. In academic circles, researchers construct their views of the world through arguments. They experiment, read critically, and administer surveys; and then, observing patterns, they make statements—the truth, probability, or desirability of which they try to demonstrate through arguments. In this chapter you will learn the elements essential to arguing in *any* context. Later, in chapters 37–39, you will learn how these elements change according to the discipline in which you are writing.[1]

6a An overview of argument

An **argument** is a process of influencing others, of changing minds through reasoned discussion. Arguments consist of three parts: claim, support, and reasoning. The relationships among these parts give an argument its force. No argument is possible unless claim, support, and reasoning pull together to make a persuasive whole.

CLAIM   A claim is an argument's thesis, a statement about which people will disagree. There are three types of claim (see 6b); whichever you use, you need to define terms with care.

  ■ Claims about facts
  ■ Claims about what is valuable
  ■ Claims about policy

SUPPORT   Support consists of facts, opinions, and examples that you present to readers so that they will accept your claim. Usually, you will present several types of support for a claim. (6c)

REASONING   Reasoning is the pattern of thought that connects support to a claim. Each type of support involves a corresponding form of reasoning. Reasoning will be based on appeals to a reader's logic, respect for authority, or emotion.

---

[1]The approach to argument taken here is based on the work of Stephen Toulmin, as developed in *The Uses of Argument* (Cambridge: The University Press, 1958).

concept of argumentation will be alien to many Asian students for whom confrontation is an anathema. They will try to provide a balanced discussion on both sides of an issue, with a focus on compromise and conciliation. Indonesians in particular will find the concept of argumentation at odds with their culture's whole philosophy of behavior and human relationships, in which confrontation suggests chaos and hence must be avoided.

LOOKING FORWARD

ACROSS THE CURRICULUM The Toulmin model of argumentation, adopted here, suggests that certain features of argument, including claim, support, and reasoning, remain constant regardless of the discipline or "field" in which one happens to be arguing. What changes from one discipline to the next, says Toulmin, is the notion of what counts as a legitimate claim; what counts as acceptable support; and what counts as valid reasoning. This chapter introduces the overarching elements of argumentation: claim, support, and reasoning. The cross-curricular chapters on writing and reading in the humanities, the social sciences, and the sciences (chapters 37–39) address *directly* the defining features of argumentation in these discipline areas. Thus, chapter 6 and the cross-curricular chapters work in tandem. Students need not read them together; all chapters in this book are independent. But reading chapter 6 will provide useful background to the cross-curricular chapters.

GROUP ACTIVITY

In order to help students become aware of the various considerations necessary for an effective argument, you might ask them to work in small groups constructing an argument for a position that's relevant to them: convincing a teacher to make a final exam a take-home exam, for example, or getting parents' permission to spend a semester abroad. As they discuss what will and will not be effective, one student in the group records the reasons for acceptance and rejection of specific approaches. When the groups analyze these reasons, they'll become aware of such considerations as audience, understanding of the issue, and dealing with opposing views.

- Appeals to logic (6d-1)
- Appeals to authority (6d-2)
- Appeals to emotion (6d-3)

Sample argument

The arguments you write will usually be longer than the one that follows, but the principles involved will be the same. Note how three kinds of support are offered for the claim that a college education can help you to think critically. Each statement of support is connected to the claim by a specific type of reasoning. As in any argument, claim, support, and reasoning pull together to make a persuasive case.

Illustration: Argument

1st statement of support (Appeal to logic) Do not expect your undergraduate college education to prepare you for a *specific* job. Seventy percent of college graduates take jobs unrelated to their majors, and what is true of them is likely to be true of you. What, then, is the value of college? No single answer could satisfy everyone, but most would accept this *partial* answer: **Claim** a college education can help you to think critically. The importance of thinking critically cannot be overstated. Robert Ornstein of the Institute for the Study of Human Knowledge put it this way: "Solutions to the significant problems facing modern society demand a widespread, qualitative improvement in thinking and understanding. . . . We need a breakthrough in the *quality* of thinking employed both by decision-makers at all levels of society and by each of us in our daily affairs." **2nd statement of support (Appeal to authority)** Effective, strategic thinkers are needed urgently and are appreciated everywhere, and you will do well to make clear thinking an explicit goal of your studies. Specifically, you **Key term defined** should learn to identify and solve problems; to plan strategically; to challenge others and yourself; and to generate new ideas and information. **3rd statement of support (Appeal to emotion)**

Analysis: The example paragraph consists of three sets of statements that support the claim. Each is based on a corresponding type of reasoning. Claim, support, and reasoning function as one persuasive whole:

(1) **Support:** Fact (most students take jobs unrelated to their major)
Reasoning: Appeal to logic (a generalization—what's true of most will be true of you)

Claim: (about value):

> A college education can help you to think critically, and thinking critically is a good thing.

(2) **Support:** Opinion (statement by Robert Ornstein)
Reasoning: Appeal to authority (Ornstein is an expert on thinking and learning; his testimony is valuable)

(3) **Support:** Opinion (you will do well to make clear thinking a goal of college)
Reasoning: Appeal to emotion (self-interest will lead you to agree)

Key term defined: Critical thinking is the ability to identify and solve problems, to plan strategically, to challenge, and to generate. ∎

While writing an argument, you should aim to pull claim, support, and reasoning together so that you construct a persuasive whole. If you discover that the parts are not fitting together as expected, let your difficulty be a signal that you may need to modify your claim. Never alter your facts to fit the thesis.

EXERCISE 1

In a paragraph, recall an argument that you have had recently in which some issue of importance to you was being debated. With whom did you argue? What positions did you and the other person (people) argue? What was the outcome? To what extent did your powers of persuasion affect the argument's outcome?

6b   Making a claim (an argumentative thesis)

Any paper that you write in college will have a claim, a single statement that crystallizes your purpose for writing and governs the logic and development of the paper. The claim, also called an *argumentative thesis*, will express your view on a subject. Your goal in the argument is to defend your claim as being true, probable, or desirable. Because the claim thesis is a specialized case of thesis statements for all varieties of writing, the discussion here assumes that you have read chapter 3, section d.

1   Answering questions with your claim

Arguments provide answers to one of three types of questions: questions of *fact*, *value*, or *policy*.

REFERENCES

TOULMIN, STEPHEN. *The Uses of Argument*. New York: Cambridge UP, 1964. Characterizes effective arguments as consisting of "claim," or argument itself; "data," or evidence in support of argument; and "warrant," or general principles linking the two.

The Toulmin model used in this chapter is developed in the following works:

————, RICHARD RIEKE, and ALLAN JANIK. *An Introduction to Reasoning*. New York: Macmillan, 1979.

RIEKE, RICHARD, and MALCOLM SILLARS. *Argumentation and the Decision Making Process*. 2nd ed. Glenview: Scott, 1984.

ROTTENBERG, ANNETTE. *Elements of Argument*. 2nd ed. Boston: Bedford, 1988.

BROCKRIEDE, WAYNE, and DOUGLAS EHNINGER. "Toulmin on Argument: An Interpretation and Application." *Quarterly Journal of Speech* 46 (1960): 44–53.

MCCLEARY, WILLIAM J. "A Case Approach for Teaching Academic Writing." *CCC* 36 (1985): 203–12. Describes course in which students are asked to construct arguments based on a collection of legal evidence.

FRISCH, ADAM. "The Proposal to a Small Group: Learning to 'See Otherwise.'" ERIC, 1989. ED 303 796. Students should address arguments to small groups with clearly defined values.

PERELMAN, CHAIM. "The Premises of Argumentation." *The Realm of Rhetoric*. Notre Dame: U of Notre Dame P, 1982. 21–32. Emphasizes common ground as the basis for all discourse, including argument.

BRENT, DOUG. "Young, Becker and Pike's 'Rogerian' Rhetoric: A Twenty-Year Reassessment." *CE* 53 (1991): 452–65. While Young, Becker, and Pike's rhetoric has begun to "show its age," the Rogerian principle of consensus on which their rhetoric is based is still powerful.

FAHNESTOCK, JEANNE, and MARIE SECOR. "Teaching Argument: A Theory of Types." *CCC* 34 (1983): 20–30. A rhetorical/generative approach to argument is preferable to other approaches because of its applicability to various situations.

Claims that answer questions of fact

A *question of fact* can take the following forms:

Does X exist?

Does X lead to Y?

How can we define X?

The first question can be answered with a *yes* or *no*. The second question leads to an argument about cause and effect. If one thing leads to or causes another, the writer must show how this happens. The third question is an argument about definitions. At times, definitions can be presented without debate; at other times, writers will argue to define a term in a particular way and then will build an entire presentation based on that definition.

Once established as true, a statement of fact can be used as evidence in other arguments. For instance, in a problem-solution argument (see the box at 6f) the writer must establish that a problem exists; once this fact is established, the writer can make a second argument in support of a particular solution.

Example theses

Extrasensory perception does not exist.

Chronic fatigue syndrome *is* real, though its causes are not entirely understood.

Stories describing near-death experiences have not withstood scientific scrutiny.

Claims that answer a question of value

A *question of value* takes the form: *What is X worth?* You make an argument about values when at the conclusion of a hearty meal you pat your belly and smile. In more academic circumstances, scholars argue about value when they review and comment on one another's work—for instance, calling a theory *powerful* or elegant. Determinations of value are based on standards called *criteria* that are explicitly stated and then used to judge the worth of the object under review. (See 2b, "Writing an evaluation.")

Example theses

So-called "cold fusion," if it proves practical, will have tremendous economic and humanitarian value.

Though it raises useful questions, Eric Smith's research linking intelligence and birth order is flawed.

Nabokov's *Lolita* is a great novel.

Claims that answer a question of policy

A *question of policy* takes the form: *What action should we take?* Politics is a major arena for arguments of policy. In this arena, arguments help to determine which legislative actions are taken and how huge sums of money are spent. *Should the legislature raise taxes? Should the United States support totalitarian regimes?* These questions about what *ought* to be done prompt arguments based on claims of policy.

Example theses

Funding decisions for NASA should be based on a coherent, long-term approach to space exploration.

Eventually, taxes will have to be raised if the government cannot reduce our massive national debt.

More businesses should provide on-site daycare facilities.

EXERCISE 2

Choose two subjects and pose questions of fact, value, and policy about them. Of each topic, ask: Does X exist? (or Does X lead to Y? or How can we define X?) What is the value of X? and What should we do with regard to X? Answer these questions with statements that could serve as claims for later arguments. Possible topics: artificial intelligence, posttraumatic stress disorder, ozone holes, gene splicing.

2   Defining terms in the argumentative thesis

In order to provide the basis for a sound argument, all words of a claim must be carefully defined so that people are debating the same topic. Consider this claim, which answers a question of policy: *The United States should not support totalitarian regimes.* Unless the term *totalitarian regimes* is clearly defined (and distinguished, say, from authoritarian regimes), the argument could not succeed. The writer, the reader, and various experts referred to in the argument might define and use the word *totalitarian* differently. If this happened, a reader could not be sure about what is being argued and no meaningful exchange of ideas would take place. Take care to examine your claims and, if one term or another requires it, actually write a paragraph of definition into your argument. If you suspect that your audience will not accept your definition, then you will need to argue for it. Entire arguments are sometimes needed to define complex terms, such as *honor.* If a key term in your claim is not complicated, then a paragraph or even a sentence of definition will suffice. With terms well defined, argumentation can begin.

EXERCISE 3

Circle any terms needing definitions in the following claims. Choose any two of the terms you have circled and briefly define them.

FOR DISCUSSION

ACROSS THE CURRICULUM The examples provided here are from science and literature. Since many freshman composition courses are made up of students from different majors, a class discussion of examples of arguments found in different disciplines can be useful. Ask students to recall one argument from a course in their major, and list the topics on the board. After the topics are listed, the class can choose one and develop a claim, list sources for data, describe the logic, and speculate on a conclusion for that topic. Not only will this activity reinforce the treatment of basic academic argument in the text, but it will also allow students to practice argumentation in a relatively nonthreatening way.

LOOKING FORWARD

ACROSS THE CURRICULUM Following Toulmin, students should anticipate that as they move from one disciplinary area to another, what counts as a claim will differ. In the cross-curricular chapters of this book, students will read the following:

Chapter 37 (section a):

To make a claim about literature, make an interpretation. Then focus on an imaginative work and discuss how certain passages are related to your interpretation.

To make a claim in history, writers make interpretations of available records from the past and try to reconstruct them into a meaningful pattern.

In philosophy, writers make claims about "ideas and their relation to other ideas."

Chapter 38 (section a):

Claims in the social sciences will often commit you to observing the actions of individuals or groups and to stating how these actions are significant, both for certain individuals and for the people responding to them.

Chapter 39 (section a):

Scientific arguments often involve two sorts of claims: the first concerning a definition and the second a fact. In this pattern, the first claim takes the form *X is somehow puzzling....* The process continues when you make a second claim: *X can be explained as follows.*

(continued)

One of the underlying assumptions of this handbook is that as they move from one discipline to the next, students need to appreciate that patterns of claim, support, and reasoning change. Following the above statements about claims, each successive chapter demonstrates through multiple examples and a full research paper the uses of claim, support, and reasoning across the disciplines.

EXERCISE 2

Individual responses

REFERENCES

PORTER, JEFFREY. "The Reasonable Reader: Knowledge and Inquiry in Freshman English." *CE* 49 (1987): 332–44. A reader's "participation" in a text is organized by the enthymeme.

GAGE, JOHN T. "Teaching the Enthymeme: Invention and Arrangement." *Rhetoric Review* 2 (1983): 38–50. The importance of audience to the construction of an effective argument can best be taught by using the enthymeme.

EXERCISE 3

Words that might be circled:
1. *yuppie:* a young urban professional, usually upper middle-class and materialistic.

   chronic fatigue syndrome: a condition in which the sufferer is consistently lethargic.
2. *near-death experiences:* situations in which a person comes so close to death that the mind seems to separate from the body.

   scientific scrutiny: the careful experimentation to which scientists put theories or hypotheses.

   anecdotal evidence: evidence based on individual reports rather than experimentation or extensive research.
3. *cold fusion:* the process of fusing atoms at room temperature.

   economic: relating to the satisfaction of human beings' material needs.

   humanitarian: relating to the betterment of the human condition.
4. *great novel:* a novel that has withstood critical analysis, usually for a number of years.
5. *swamp gas:* gases given off in swampy areas, frequently resulting in visible vapors.

Funding decisions for NASA should be based on a (coherent,)(long-term) approach to space exploration.

A "coherent, long-term" approach would seek to define NASA's objectives for the next fifteen years and would commit funds to meet those objectives. NASA's funding should not be subject to a year-by-year review in which a year's political considerations can end up affecting scientific goals.

1. Far from being an imaginary "yuppie" disease, chronic fatigue syndrome *is* real.
2. Stories describing near-death experiences have not stood up to scientific scrutiny, although a great deal of anecdotal evidence for such experiences is mounting.
3. So-called "cold fusion," if it proves practical, will have tremendous economic and humanitarian value.
4. Nabokov's *Lolita* is a great novel, notwithstanding the opinion of one editor who, rejecting it, commented that the manuscript should be "buried under a stone for a thousand years."
5. The saucer-shaped flying object in the sky that thousands of New Jersey residents saw on the evening of July 18, 1988, was swamp gas.

6c Offering three types of support for a claim

You can offer facts, opinions, and examples as support for your claims. A **fact** is a statement that can be verified, proven true or false. As a writer you should be able to verify facts on demand, and most often you will do this by referring to an authoritative source. (This is one of the reasons for documenting your papers.) In most circumstances once facts are presented and accepted by experts in a given field, the rest of us can be content to accept them as well. Facts are constantly being updated and revised as a consequence of research. It is therefore essential that you refer to the most recent sources possible.

An **opinion** is a statement of interpretation and judgment. Opinions are themselves arguments and should be based on evidence in order to be convincing. Opinions are not true or false in the way that statements of fact are. Rather, opinions are more or less well supported. You do your own argument a service by referring to the opinions of experts who agree with you. An **example** is a particular instance of a statement you are trying to prove. The statement is a generalization, and by offering an example you are trying to demonstrate that the generalization is correct.

EXERCISE 4

Provide paragraph-length examples for two of the following general statements. If you feel that the statement is inaccurate, revise it to your liking. Then provide an example based on your own experience.

1. During the first weeks of a semester, freshmen are unsure of themselves socially.

CRITICAL DECISIONS

Form, and support, opinions: Finding support for your arguments

Once you have decided on a claim, turn your attention to gathering support. Question your claim vigorously: What will readers need to see in order to accept your view as true, probable, or desirable? Assemble support from the various categories available to you:

- **Facts:** Find sources on your topic. Take copious notes on any facts that you think are pertinent. Remember that the facts you gather should accurately represent the available data.

- **Statistics:** Again, find sources on your topic. Begin with the U.S. Government Printing Office, which publishes volumes of statistics on life in the United States. Locate other publications, particularly statistical studies.

- **Expert opinions:** Locate experts by reviewing source materials and checking for people whose work is referred to repeatedly. Also compare bibliographies and look for names in common. Within a week or so of moderately intensive research, you will identify acknowledged experts on a topic. Quote experts when their language is particularly powerful or succinct; otherwise, summarize or paraphrase.

- **Emotions:** Do not underestimate the power of emotions in swaying readers to your position. If you are arguing honestly and believe in your claim, then you can in good conscience appeal to the emotions of your readers. Discover their needs and explain, perhaps through an example, how the issues important to you affect them.

Devise an action plan: Take advantage of the various kinds of support available to you when arguing. To the extent it is appropriate for the context in which you are arguing, make appeals to logic, authority, *and* emotion. Think strategically about how best to position your facts, statistics, expert opinions, and appeals to emotion.

ESL EXERCISE

On the basis of talks with Americans, past readings about the United States, and discussions with classmates, non-native students might list some of the cultural assumptions of Americans. What concepts or values do Americans hold important?

Teachers might guide students to discover such values as individualism, competition, informality, directness, cause/effect logic, self-help, personal choice, a short-term view of the future, trouble-shooting/problem solving, and practicality.

TEACHING IDEAS

ACROSS THE CURRICULUM The notion that different disciplines require different kinds of evidence will probably be new to most students. Ask each student to interview a faculty member from a specific discipline, asking two questions: (1) What sort of evidence is usually required to support an argument in the discipline? (2) What sort of evidence does the instructor him- or herself find most convincing? When students report to the class, a picture should emerge illustrating the need to understand the requirements of different disciplines and different audiences within those disciplines.

2. Assignments at the college level are much more demanding than those in high school.
3. My friend _____ (you provide the name) usually offers sound advice.

EXERCISE 5

With pen in hand, reread the paragraphs you wrote in answer to Exercise 4. Circle your statements of opinion. Underline your statements of fact. Do any patterns emerge? (Instead of working with your own paragraphs, you might work with the paragraphs of a classmate.)

EXERCISE 4

Individual responses

EXERCISE 5

Individual responses

6d   Reasoning and lines of argument

Reasoning in an argument is the pattern of thinking you use to connect statements of support to your claim. Formally, types of reasoning are

GROUP ACTIVITY

Many students place too much weight on facts and opinions: Since facts are indisputable, some students fail to realize that they can be interpreted in different ways. And since "we're all entitled to our own opinions," some students don't understand the relative merits of well and poorly supported opinions. Ask small groups of students to find two opposing opinion pieces on the same topic. They might look at *The Nation* and *The National Review*, or they might look at two newspapers with opposing editorial viewpoints. Once the group has decided on the selections, they can list the facts that are used to support opposing views, and the opinions that are supported by those facts.

TEACHING IDEAS

ACROSS THE CURRICULUM Writers support arguments according to the conventions of a discipline. In the sciences, for instance, relatively little credence is given to expert opinions, while in the humanities writers are taught to call on authorities in support of a claim. Students can learn something of the uses of evidence across the curriculum by turning to the sample papers in 37d, 38d, and 39d. Each paper concerns the general topic of "alcohol"; each is written from a different disciplinary perspective—the humanities, the social sciences, and the sciences. Ask students to read these papers and make their observations concerning the use of evidence.

FOR DISCUSSION

In thinking about making arguments, students should know that this table summarizes potential strategies. Arguments cannot be assembled "cookbook fashion." The student writer must know his or her material and, above all, know the audience in order to understand whether appeals to logic, authority, or emotion are likely to be successful. Part of any preparation for argument should be a thorough audience analysis (see 6f and 3a-3.) Having made some strategic decisions about the type of appeal that will be made, the writer is still faced with a question of how to position particular appeals within the argument. Perhaps as an overview to reasoning in argumentation, students should read the example essay later in this chapter, in which two appeals to logic are made and one appeal to

referred to as **lines of argument.** There are three lines of argument available to you in presenting claims of fact, value, and policy. You can appeal to the reader's sense of logic, respect for authority, and emotion. The following chart summarizes the main lines of argument you can use when connecting supporting statements to a claim. To support a claim of fact, for instance, you would look to the chart and see that you could argue in any of six ways. There are five ways to argue for claims of value and five for claims of policy. In presenting a claim, you will typically offer several statements of support and, correspondingly, several lines of argument.

Matching lines of argument with types of claims

	Claims of Fact	Claims of Value	Claims of Policy
Appeals to Reason			
generalization	x	x	
causation	x		x
sign	x		
analogy	x	x	x
parallel case	x	x	x
Appeals to Authority	x	x	x
Appeals to Emotion		x	x

Adapted from Wayne Brockriede and Douglas Ehninger, "Toulmin on Argument: An Interpretation and Application," *Quarterly Journal of Speech* 46 (1960): 53.

1 Appealing to logic

An appeal to reason is by far the most common basis for arguing in the academic world. This section demonstrates five of the most common appeals to logic. You can argue from generalization, from causation, from sign, from analogy, or from parallel case.

Argument from generalization

Given several representative examples of a group (of people, animals, paintings, trees, washing machines, whatever), you can infer a general principle or **generalization**—a statement that applies to other examples of that group. In order for a generalization to be fair, you must select an adequate number of examples that are typical of the entire group; you must also acknowledge the presence of examples that apparently disprove the generalization. Arguments from generalization allow you to support claims that answer questions of fact and value.

Sample argument

As litter, plastic is unsightly and deadly. Birds and small animals die after getting stuck in plastic, six-pack beverage rings. Pelicans accidentally hang themselves with discarded plastic fishing line. Turtles choke on plastic bags or starve when their stomachs become clogged with hard-to-excrete, crumbled plastic. Sea lions poke their heads into plastic rings and have their jaws locked permanently shut. Authorities estimate that plastic refuse annually kills up to 2 million birds and at least 100,000 mammals.

—GARY TURBAK, "60 Billion Pounds of Trouble"

CLAIM   Plastic litter kills animals.

SUPPORT   Birds, turtles, sea lions, and various mammals have died from plastic litter.

REASONING   Generalization. Danger to the animals cited can be generalized to other animals that come into contact with plastic litter.

Argument from causation

In an argument from causation, you begin with a fact or facts about some person, object, or condition. (If readers are likely to contest these facts, then you must make an argument to establish them before pushing on with an argument from causation.) An argument from **causation** enables you to claim that an action created by that person, object, or condition leads to a specific result, or effect: Sunspots cause the aurora borealis. Dieting causes weight loss. Smoking causes lung cancer. Working in the opposite direction, you can begin with what you presume to be an effect of some prior cause: the swing of a pendulum, inattention among school children, tornadoes. Of this presumed effect, you ask: "What causes this?" If you are a scientist or social scientist, you might perform an experiment. Establishing a direct causal link is seldom easy, for usually multiple causes will lead to a single condition (think of the inattentive child at school). In arguing causation, therefore, you need to be sensitive to complexity. Arguments of causation allow you to support a claim that answers a question of fact or a claim that answers a question of policy. Cause-and-effect reasoning also allows you to use a problem-solution structure in your arguments. (See the box at 6f.)

Sample argument

Under primitive agricultural conditions the farmer had few insect problems. Those arose with the intensification of agriculture—the devotion of immense acreages to a single crop. Such a system set the stage for explosive increases in specific insect populations. Single-crop farming does not take advantage of the principles by which nature works; it is agriculture as an engineer might conceive it to be. Nature has introduced great variety into the landscape, but man has displayed a passion for simplifying it. Thus he undoes the built-in checks and balances by which nature holds the species within bounds. One important natural check is a limit on the amount of suitable habitat for each species. Obviously then, an insect that lives on wheat can build up its population to much higher levels on a farm devoted to wheat than on one in which wheat is intermingled with other crops to which the insect is not adapted.

—RACHEL CARSON, *Silent Spring*

authority. Some students do not understand that multiple appeals can be made within a single argument; the art of argumentation lies in making the appeals work in unison.

REFERENCES

DEANE, BARBARA. "Putting the Inferential Process to Work in the Classroom." *CE* 27 (1976): 50–52. Classroom activities can assist students in making accurate inferences.

KNEUPPER, CHARLES. W. "Teaching Argument: An Introduction to the Toulmin Model." *CCC* 29 (1978): 237–41. Students can improve their ability to write arguments by applying Toulmin's simplified model.

TRENT, JIMMIE D. "Toulmin's Model of an Argument: An Examination and Extension." *QJS* 54 (1968): 252–59. The Toulmin model should be considered a supplement to syllogism, not a substitute.

FULKERSON, RICHARD. "Technical Logic, Comp-Logic, and the Teaching of Writing." *CCC* 39 (1988): 436–52. Modern informal logic is preferable to technical or comp-logic.

LEVIN, GERALD. "On Freshman Composition and Logical Thinking." *CCC* 28 (1977): 359–64. Controversial essays can enhance the teaching of patterns of argument.

RAPKINS, ANGELA A. "The Uses of Logic in the College Freshman English Classroom." *Activities to Promote Critical Thinking: Classroom Practices in Teaching English.* Urbana: NCTE, 1986. Even when teaching argument toward the end of a semester, instructors should introduce students to logic early on.

EDE, LISA S., and ANDREA LUNSFORD. "On Distinctions between Classical and Modern Rhetoric." *Essays on Classical Rhetoric and Modern Discourse.* Ed. Robert J. Connors, Lisa S. Ede, and Andrea A. Lunsford. Carbondale, IL: Southern Illinois P, 1984. 37–49. Self-explanatory title.

KAUFER, DAVID S., and CHRISTINE M. NEUWIRTH. "Integrating Formal Logic and the New Rhetoric: A Four Stage Heuristic." *CE* 45 (1983): 380–89. The heuristic begins with a summary and ends with a final essay based on principles of formal logic.

LOOKING AHEAD

ACROSS THE CURRICULUM Have students compare the markedly different ways in which cause and effect is argued in the sciences (see the student paper at 39d) and in the humanities (see the student paper in this chapter at 6g).

ADDITIONAL EXERCISE A

A great many advertisements are based on implicit claims of sign and claims of cause and effect. Ask students to examine print ads and television ads, select one for close study, and prepare an analysis of the advertiser's claims. Students should be able to make explicit the claim based on sign or on cause and effect. Students should also be prepared to state whether or not the claim is supported by evidence in the ad.

CLAIM	Insect problems arose with the practice of intensive, single-crop farming.
SUPPORT	The variety of vegetation in natural habitats discourages infestation; natural habitats have "checks and balances."
REASONING	Cause and effect. By creating one-crop farms and eliminating the checks and balances of natural habitats, farmers caused their own insect problems.

Argument from sign

A sore throat and fever are signs of flu. Black smoke billowing from a window is a sign of fire. Risk taking is a sign of creativity. In an argument from **sign**, two things are correlated; that is, they tend to occur in the presence of one another. When you see one thing, you tend to see the other. A sign is *not* a cause, however. If your big toe aches at the approach of thunderstorms, your aching toe may be a sign of approaching storms, but it surely does not cause them. Economists routinely look to certain indexes (housing starts, for instance) as indicators, or signs, of the economy's health. Housing starts are *correlated with* economic health, often by means of a statistical comparison. If a sign has proven a particularly reliable indicator, then you can use it to support a claim that answers a question of fact.

Sample argument

> Anxiety over the body as a kind of wasteland is implicit in appeals in advertisements about retaining and restoring moisture. . . . Dry skin . . . [is] a sign of a woman who is all dried up and is not sexually responsive—and who may also be sterile. This is because water is connected, in our psyches, with birth. It is also tied to purity, as in baptismal rites when sin is cleansed from a person. All of this suggests that words and images that picture a body of a woman as being dehydrated and losing water have great resonance.
>
> —ARTHUR ASA BERGER, "Sex as Symbol in Fashion Advertising"

CLAIM	In advertisements, words and images of dehydration resonate for readers and viewers.
SUPPORT	Readers have profound psychological associations with dryness.
REASONING	Sign. Dry skin is a sign of sterility and infertility, deeply resonant themes for men and women.

Argument from analogy

An argument from **analogy** sets up a comparison between the topic you are arguing and another topic that initially appears unrelated. While suggestive and at times persuasive, an analogy actually proves nothing.

There is always a point at which an analogy will break down, and it is usually a mistake to build an argument on analogy alone. Use analogies as you would seasonings in cooking. As one of several attempts to persuade your reader, an analogy spices your argument and makes it memorable. You can use analogies in support of claims that answer questions of fact, value, or policy.

Sample argument

In closing, we might describe learning with an analogy to a well-orchestrated symphony, aimed to blend both familiar and new sounds. A symphony is the complex interplay of composer, conductor, the repertoire of instruments, and the various dimensions of music. Each instrument is used strategically to interact with other instruments toward a rich construction of themes progressing in phases, with some themes recurring and others driving the movement forward toward a conclusion or resolution. Finally, each symphony stands alone in its meaning, yet has a relationship to the symphonies that came before and those that will come later. Similarly, learning is a complex interaction of the learner, the instructional materials, the repertoire of available learning strategies, and the context, including the teacher. The skilled learner approaches each task strategically toward the goal of constructing meaning. Some strategies focus on understanding the incoming information, others strive to relate the meaning to earlier predictions, and still others work to integrate the new information with prior knowledge.

—BEAU FLY JONES, ET AL., "Learning and Thinking"

CLAIM   Learning involves a complex blending of learner, materials, and context.

SUPPORT   In a symphony orchestra, meaning (sound) is created through interaction of musicians, conductor, composer, and history.

REASONING   Analogy. The complex interactions needed to create symphonic music are analogous to the interaction needed to create meaning for a learner.

Argument from parallel case

While an analogy argues a relationship between two apparently unrelated people, objects, conditions, or events, an argument from **parallel case** argues a relationship between directly related people, objects, events, or conditions. The implicit logic is this: the way a situation turned out in a closely related case is the way it will (or should) turn out in this one. Lawyers argue from parallel case whenever they cite a prior criminal or civil case in which the legal question involved is similar to the question involved in a current case. Because the earlier case ended a certain way (with the conviction or acquittal of a defendant, or with a particular monetary award), so too should the present case have this outcome. An argument from parallel case requires that situations presented as parallel be alike in essential ways; if this requirement is not met, the argument loses

LOOKING BACK

In chapter 5, page 149 see another example of argument from analogy. In that passage, the author uses an analogy of the shoemaking industry to illustrate a point he is making about the "parenting industry."

LOOKING AHEAD

See the student essay in this chapter (second paragraph from the end, page 184, for an example of how an argument from parallel case can be used. Alison Tschopp is careful to cite a case that raises First Amendment issues similar to the ones raised in her paper about the legality and wisdom of limiting television advertisements directed at children. Note that Tschopp uses argument from cause and an appeal to authority as well.

force. The argument would also be weakened if someone could present a more nearly perfect parallel case than yours. You can use a parallel case in support of claims that answer questions of fact, value, or policy.

Sample argument

Would registry of handguns stop the criminal from carrying the unregistered gun? No, and it might afflict the householder with some extra red tape. However, there is a valid argument for registry. Such a law might have no immediate effect, but we have to begin somewhere. We license automobiles and drivers. That does not stop automobile deaths, but surely the highways would be even more dangerous if populated with unlicensed drivers and uninspected cars.

—ADAM SMITH, "Fifty Million Handguns"

CLAIM　　　Registration can mark a modest beginning to resolving the problem of handguns.

SUPPORT　　Cars and drivers are licensed.

REASONING　Parallel case. The registration of guns will have a limited effect on deaths caused by guns, just as the registration of drivers and automobiles has a limited effect on the number of traffic deaths. Both efforts, however minimal, show a willingness to manage a problem.

2　Appealing to authority

Two types of authority are important in arguments: the authority you bring as a writer and the authority of those who have expert knowledge on the topic that concerns you. Of the two types, *you* are the essential one, since you are present in every argument you make. From one argument to the next, you may or may not call on expert sources (according to your purpose and the needs of your audience).

Establishing yourself as an authority

Intangible elements such as trustworthiness, decency, thoroughness, and engagement are quite different from, but just as important as, the logical force you bring to an argument. An argument impinges on the will of your readers. It asks them to change their minds, and such a request will to some extent make anyone feel vulnerable. After all, you are asking the reader to admit: "I was wrong on that issue, or my thinking was unclear. I'll accept what *you* have to say." To make such a change requires something of an emotional submission ("I'll follow you on this point") as well as an intellectual one ("Your reasons are better than mine"). Before readers will agree, they need to trust the person who asks for their agreement; as a maker of arguments, you must therefore work to establish your trustworthiness—your authority to speak and make a claim. *Authority* in this sense is not the same as having expert knowledge;

it has to do, rather, with establishing a presence that readers can yield to in a self-respecting way.

How do you establish this trust? Be honest, first of all. The point is so obvious it hardly seems worth making; but readers generally have a good nose for dishonesty. One whiff and they will turn away—for good. Beyond honesty, which is the main thing, strike a reasonable tone (see 21e) and choose a level of language appropriate for the occasion (see 3a-4). Read thoroughly enough on your topic to establish that, although you are not an expert, you do know the important issues and are knowledgeable enough to have an opinion worth considering.

Referring readers to experts

As a writer, you greatly help your cause when you can quote experts on a subject who support your point of view. Realize, though, you are likely to find that experts disagree. For instance, in court cases both prosecution and defense present expert witnesses, sworn to tell the truth. One expert says a defendant is sane and competent to stand trial; a second expert says the opposite. No doubt, the experts *are* telling the truth. But expert *opinions* are just that: interpretations of facts. Facts usually lend themselves to multiple interpretations, and you should not be discouraged when authorities seem to contradict one another.

Whether you find contradictions or not, sources of authority must be authoritative. If they are not, any argument built on an appeal to authority will falter. One of your important challenges, then, both as a writer of arguments and as a critical reader, is to evaluate the worthiness of sources that you and others use. Is the expert testimony that you or others are drawing on truly expert? If you are not an expert in the field, how can you tell? A number of general guidelines should help you make this determination. (See the box on page 172.)

Once you have determined to the best of your ability that an expert whom you wish to quote is indeed expert, you must then identify those points in your discussion where appeals to authority will serve you well. You may want to mix appeals to authority with appeals to reason and, perhaps, to emotion. Appeals to authority can be used to support claims that answer questions of fact, value, and policy.

Sample argument
Leo Marx claims that Melville's "Bartleby the Scrivener" is autobiographical.

CLAIM   Herman Melville's "Bartleby the Scrivener" is a story about Melville.

SUPPORT   Leo Marx says so.

REASONING   Authority. Leo Marx is a respected literary critic who has taught at leading universities; his insights are valuable and are worth examining.

TEACHING IDEAS

CRITICAL THINKING Advertising is the most visible example of appeals to authority and emotion in our society. Ask students to peruse magazines and newspapers, as well as television commercials, for ads that illustrate these appeals. (If you have access to a VCR, students can tape commercials at home and replay them for the class.) Using the most appropriate student examples, ask students to analyze and evaluate the appeals in the ads—not only for the type of appeal but also for intended audience and effectiveness of argument.

Use *Authoritative* Sources

1. Prefer acknowledged authorities to self-proclaimed ones.

2. Prefer an authority working within his or her field of expertise to one who is reporting conclusions about another subject.

3. Prefer first-hand accounts over those from sources who were separated by time or space from the events reported.

4. Prefer unbiased and disinterested sources over those who can reasonably be suspected of having a motive for influencing the way others see the subject under investigation.

5. Prefer public records to private documents in questionable cases.

6. Prefer accounts that are specific and complete to those that are vague and evasive.

7. Prefer evidence that is credible on its own terms to that which is internally inconsistent or demonstrably false to any known facts.

8. In general, prefer a recently published report to an older one.

9. In general, prefer works by standard publishers to those of unknown or "vanity" presses.

10. In general, prefer authors who themselves follow [standard] report-writing conventions. . . .

11. When possible, prefer an authority known to your audience to one they have never heard of. . . .

Source: Thomas E. Gaston and Bret H. Smith, *The Research Paper: A Common-Sense Approach* (Englewood Cliffs: Prentice Hall, 1988) 31–33.

3   Appealing to emotion

Appeals to reason are based on the force of logic; appeals to authority are based on the reader's respect for the opinions of experts. By contrast, appeals to emotion are designed to tap the needs and values of an audience. Arguments based on appeals to reason and authority may well turn out to be valid; but validity does not guarantee that readers will *endorse* your position. For instance, you might establish with impeccable logic that the physical condition of your community's public schools has deteriorated badly, to the point of affecting the performance of students. While true, your claim may not carry force enough to persuade the Town Council to vote on a bond issue or to raise taxes—two actions that would generate the requisite money to renovate several buildings. To succeed in your effort or in any appeal to emotion, you must make your readers feel the same urgency to act that you do. The following includes an emotional appeal.

Sample argument

Our children are sitting in schools where paint is flaking off the walls, where the heating plant works sixty percent of the time, where plumbing backs up repeatedly, where windows are cracked or broken and covered by cardboard to keep out the winter. No member of the Town Council would for a moment consider working in an office with such appalling conditions. You each would be indignant and would claim that the environment endangered your welfare. Yet these are precisely the conditions our children contend with now. To vote against a tax hike will be to condemn our children to circumstances that you personally would find intolerable.

—Linda Cohen, "School Committee Hearing"

CLAIM   You should vote for the tax increase.

SUPPORT   Our children attend a school that is in deplorable condition.

REASONING   Emotion. The story of the conditions at the school is unsettling enough to convince town council members to vote for a tax increase, which will alleviate those conditions.

On the basis of an audience analysis (see 3a-3), you can sketch a profile of your readers and consider strategies suited to win their emotional support. Plan your emotional appeal by beginning with a claim that has already been supported by an appeal to reason. In your efforts to raise taxes for school renovation, you could show photographs, produce a list of items in need of repair, and quote expert witnesses who believe that children's learning suffers in deteriorating environments. Having argued by an appeal to reason, you can then plan an emotional appeal.

The limits of argument

In the real world, the best of arguments may sometimes fail to achieve its objective. Some subjects—for example, abortion or capital punishment—are so controversial or so tied to preexisting religious or moral beliefs that many people have long since made up their minds one way or the other and will never change them. Such subjects are so fraught with emotion that logical arguments are ineffective in persuading people to rethink their positions. Sometimes, also, your audience has a vested interest in *not* being persuaded by your arguments. (Perhaps your audience has a financial stake in holding to an opposing position.) When your audience feels significantly threatened by the prospect of your victory, you must realize that it is futile to continue insisting on the validity of your argument.

Making an Emotional Appeal

1. List the needs of your audience with respect to your subject: these needs might be physical, psychological, humanitarian, environmental, or financial.
2. Select the category of needs best suited to your audience and identify emotional appeals that you think will be persuasive.
3. In your appeal, place the issue you are arguing in your reader's lap. Get the reader to respond to the issue emotionally.
4. Call on the reader to agree with you on a course of action.

EXERCISE 6

Individual responses

TEACHING IDEAS

Uncertain of their own powers of persuasion, students sometimes try to ignore opposing arguments in hopes that those arguments will never arise. In order to provide students with practice in acknowledging the opposition, ask them to write out their positions on several controversial issues (preferably issues you've assigned as paper topics). Once they've articulated their positions, their task will be to argue for the *opposing* position. Thus before they've even begun to construct their own arguments, they're playing devil's advocate. When they do develop their own positions, they'll be well aware of the objections they might encounter.

EXERCISE 6

Write the sketch of an argument, your claim for which should be based on the following scenario:

> Imagine yourself a student at a college or university where the Board of Trustees has voted to institute a curfew on dormitory visitors. After 11 P.M. on weekdays and 1 A.M. on weekends, no student may have a guest in his or her dormitory room. The rule simply put: no overnight guests.

Decide on a claim, and determine whether it answers a question of fact, value, or policy. Consult the chart on "Matching Lines of Argument with Types of Claims," and plan a discussion in which you argue three ways in support of your claim. (Make sure these arguments are consistent with the type of claim you are making—see the chart.)

6e Making rebuttals

By definition, arguments are subject to challenge, or to counterarguments. Because reasonable people will disagree, you must be prepared when arguing to acknowledge differences of opinion and to address them—for two reasons. First, by raising a challenge to your own position you force yourself to see an issue from someone else's perspective. This can be a valuable lesson in that challenges can prompt you to reevaluate and refine your views. In addition, challenges pique a reader's interest. Research shows that when tension (that is, disagreement) exists in an argument, readers maintain interest: they want to know what happens or how the argument is resolved.

Once you acknowledge opposing views, respond with a **rebuttal,** an argument of opposition. One type of response is to reject the counterargument by challenging its logic. If the logic is flawed, the counterargument will not weaken the validity of your argument. When you are confident in the position you are arguing, raise the most damaging argu-

CRITICAL DECISIONS

Be alert to differences: Responding to opposing points of view

Expect opposition. When you have located opposing points of view, use the occasion to extend your thinking. Let disagreement enhance the quality of your argument.

- **The facts are in dispute.** When the facts you are relying on in an argument are disputed—a potentially serious challenge—then you must investigate both the validity of your facts and the opposition's.

  Check the credibility of sources. Be sure that your sources are reliable; if you discover some dispute about reliability, you must meet this challenge head on: raise it in your argument and, if you can, establish the trustworthiness of your information. If you have trouble doing so, abandon questionable sources and be grateful to your opposition.

  If both sources (yours and the opposition's) are equally reliable, ask: Through what process of investigation were these facts established? Different methods of investigation can lead to different perceptions of the facts. Acknowledge these methods in your argument and state clearly which methods you (or your sources) have relied on.

- **Expert opinions are in dispute.** Experts *will* disagree, and most writers can find experts, real or so-called, to support or attack an argument. Respond to differences of expert opinion by checking qualifications. Lacking expertise in a subject, you may have some trouble doing this. Try these strategies, both of which can help you to reaffirm, or discount, the usefulness of expert opinion:

  Strategy 1: To validate expertise, be sure that an author is referred to in several sources. If the author were a fringe personality, you would not find repeated, serious references to his or her work.

  Strategy 2: To validate expertise, locate a book written by the person in question. Locate two reviews, which will be written by someone at least familiar with the topic. From the reviews you will get a sense of a book's strengths and weaknesses, and you will learn something of the author's reputation.

  If the experts holding opposing views are reliable, you will need to acknowledge the disagreement in your argument. Determine its basis. If you find a conflict of assumptions, investigate and discuss these. If you find your assumptions still worth supporting, then support them—with reasons.

Devise an action plan: Use the differences you find to clarify your own thinking on a topic. When your opposition has a valid point, acknowledge it openly and adjust. Show that you expect differences and can incorporate them into your thinking.

LOOKING AHEAD

See the sample student paper in this chapter for an example of how an argument can open by posing a problem and rebutting unacceptable solutions. Following the rebuttal, the writer introduces another solution. The tactic is often referred to as "strawman."

REFERENCE

WINDER, BARBARA E. "The Delineation of Values in Persuasive Writing." *CCC* 29 (1978): 55–58. Students should articulate their opponent's position as well as their own in order to understand differences in values.

ment against your position that you can, and then neutralize that challenge. If you do not raise objections, your readers inevitably will; better that you raise them on your terms so that you can control the debate.

Of course, one response to an opposing argument is *to let it change you.* After all, if you are arguing honestly, you are by definition participating in a reasoned exchange. This is to say, when arguing you should be available to accepting the views of others. Readers will appreciate, and take as a sign of your reasonableness, your ability to concede at least some of your opposition's points.

6f Preparing to write an argument

Devising strategies for argument

There are two time-honored strategies for arranging arguments: the "problem-solution" structure and the classic "five-part" structure are summarized in the adjoining boxes. In these structures, each part of the argument may run as one paragraph or as a section consisting of several paragraphs.

Inductive and deductive arrangements

Inductive and deductive arrangements have to do with where you place your claim in an argument. Induction moves from support—particular facts, examples, and opinions—to a claim. A great deal of scientific and technological argument proceeds this way. The writer makes certain observations, finds patterns in those observations, and then makes a claim about those observations. Visually, the process could be represented as in the diagram on the left.

Deductive arrangement which is shown in the diagram on the right, moves from a claim to support—to particular facts, opinions, and examples. A good deal of writing in the humanities, in politics, and in law proceeds this way. The writer begins with a general principle or claim, the truth, likelihood, or desirability of which is then proven.

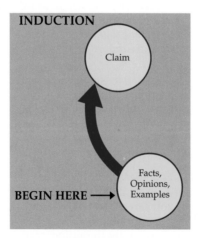

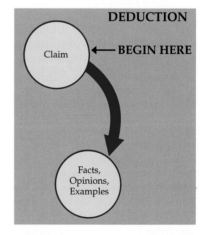

REFERENCE

KATULA, RICHARD A., and RICHARD W. ROTH. "A Stock Issues Approach to Writing Arguments." *CCC* 31 (1980): 183–96. Emphasizes the problem-solution approach to argument.

Writing an Argument: The Problem-Solution Structure

I. There is a serious problem.
    A. The problem exists and is growing.
        (Provide support for this statement.)
    B. The problem is serious.
        (Provide support.)
    C. Current methods cannot cope with the problem.
        (Provide support.)

II. There is a solution to the problem. (Your claim goes here.)
    A. The solution is practical.
        (Provide support.)
    B. The solution is desirable.
        (Provide support.)
    C. We can implement the solution.
        (Provide support.)
    D. Alternate solutions are not as strong as the proposed solution.
        (Review—and reject—competing solutions.)

Note: This six-part structure for argument does not suggest, necessarily, a six-paragraph argument. A problem-solution argument can be considerably longer than six paragraphs.

Source: Adapted from Richard D. Rieke and Malcolm O. Sillars, *Argumentation and the Decision Making Process* (Glenview: Scott, Foresman, 1984) 163.

What determines whether you will use an inductive or deductive arrangement for your argument? First, realize that in either approach you *begin* writing your argument with the identical information: in both cases, you know before the draft what your claim, support, and lines of reasoning will be. The decision to move inductively or deductively is a decision about strategy.

You can position the claim in your argument at the beginning, middle, or end of the presentation. In the problem-solution structure, you see that the claim is made only after the writer introduces a problem. Working with the five-part structure, you have more flexibility in positioning your claim. One factor that can help determine placement is considering the members of your audience and the likelihood of their agreeing with you. When an audience is likely to be neutral or supportive, you can make your claim early on with the assurance that you will not alienate readers. When an audience is likely to disagree, plan to move your claim toward the end of the presentation, in that way giving yourself space to build consensus with your readers, step by step, until you reach a conclusion.

Writing an Argument: The Classic Five-Part Structure

1. Introduce the topic to be argued. Establish its importance.

2. Provide background information so that readers will be able to follow your discussion.

3. State your claim (your argumentative thesis) and develop your argument by making a logical appeal based on the following factors (discussed in 6d-1, 6d-2, and 6d-3): generalization, causation, sign, analogy, parallel case, or authority. Support your claims with facts, opinions, and examples. If appropriate, mix an emotional appeal or an appeal to authority with your logical appeals.

4. Acknowledge counterarguments and treat them with respect. Rebut these arguments. Reject their evidence or their logic or concede some validity and modify your claim accordingly. Be flexible: you might split the counterarguments and rebut them one at a time at different locations in the paper; or you might begin the paper with a counterargument, rebut it, and then move on to your own claim.

5. A useful way to conclude is to summarize the main points of your argument. Then remind readers of what you want them to believe or do.

Note: This five-part structure for argument does not suggest, necessarily, a five-paragraph argument. Arguments can be considerably longer than five paragraphs.

Readers tend to remember most clearly what they read last. Thus, you may want to present your reasons in support of your claim in the order of least to most emphatic. Conversely, you may want to offer your most emphatic reasons in support of a claim at the very beginning of the argument. In one strong move you might gain the reader's agreement and then cement that agreement with reasons of secondary importance. Any argument can be arranged in a variety of ways. Decisions you make about placing your claim and arranging your points of support will depend on your assessment of the members of your audience and their probable reactions to your views.

EXERCISE 7

Individual responses

EXERCISE 7

In light of the discussion in this section, return to the argument you outlined in Exercise 6 and introduce at some point in the outline an argument counter to your own. In a paragraph, discuss how you would rebut the counterargument or accept it in part so as to neutralize any damage it could do to your own claim.

Gathering materials for argument

Writing an argument is more a re-creation of thinking than an exploration. Exploration—through writing or through talking with friends—comes prior to writing a first draft. Consider writing a *pre*draft: a brief paper, intended for your eyes only, in which you explore the position you want to take in your argument. Whatever your method for doing so, arrive at your views on a topic—your claim— *before* you sit down to write the draft. As you begin, you should understand the support you will present and the lines of reasoning you will use to link that support to your claim. You will flesh out the discussion as you write; but the backbone of your argument should be carefully thought out ahead of time.

Gathering Materials for Your Argument

1. Gather material on your subject. Generate information on your own—see 3b; if necessary, conduct research. See Part IX on library research.

2. Review the material you have gathered. Decide what you think about the topic, and in a single sentence answer a question of fact, value, or policy. Your one-sentence answer to the question will be the claim of your argument.

3. Understand your audience: What do they know about the topic? What do they need to know? To what sorts of appeals will they respond?

4. Plan out the lines of argument you will present in support of your claim.

5. Identify strong counterarguments and plan to rebut and neutralize them. Possibly concede some of your opposition's points.

6. Sketch your argument, deciding on placement of your claim and arrangement of your lines of argument.

7. Write a draft of your argument, realizing that you will need to backtrack on occasion to get new information or to rethink your strategy. As with the writing of any paper, writing an argument will be a messy, backward-looping activity that often requires mid-course corrections. See chapters 3 and 4 on the necessary uncertainties in preparing for and writing a first draft.

8. Revise two or three times. See chapter 4 for advice.

EXERCISE 8

Individual responses

EXERCISE 8

Based on your outline in Exercise 7, write the draft of a five-page argument.

6g A sample argument

The following argument, "Advertising to Children Should Not Be Banned," utilizes (with some modification) the classic five-part structure for writing arguments presented on page 178. Alison Tschopp, a student at Boston University, begins her argument by introducing her topic (the problem of television advertising directed at children) and then provides pertinent background information. But before stating her claim and developing an argument, she summarizes and rejects one proposed solution to the problem she has identified. Alison reverses steps #3 and #4 in the five-part structure, a strategy sometimes referred to as "strawman": the idea is to present one argument for the purpose of tearing it down, as a prelude to presenting your own reasonable alternative. When Alison introduces her own claim, a solution to the problem of advertising directed at children, she argues primarily from cause and from parallel case.

Advertising to Children Should Not Be Banned

Are television commercials rotting the minds and bodies of our children? Some people think so, especially when it comes to advertisements for expensive toys and foods of questionable nutritional value. Impressionable children are easy prey for marketers, say the critics (Charren 14). And advertisements can perpetuate attitudes and myths that are harmful to children's development, such as the myth that girls are not as aggressive as boys or that boys are not sensitive enough to care for a baby-doll (Kilbourne 45).

Introduction: statement of the problem

We know that advertisers are persuasive, and we know that the power of advertisements over children is directly related to the amount of television that children watch. According to a survey cited in a recent article by American Federation of Teachers President Albert Shanker, one-quarter of nine year olds in this country watch 42 hours of television each week (7)--

Background information

approximately eight hours of which is devoted to
advertisements. The most obvious way to eliminate the exposure to so much advertising is to
limit television viewing. Still, we are not
about to eliminate television from the American
household. In a best-case scenario, we might reduce viewing time by half. If we could return
our children to viewing a modest 25 hours of
weekly television (the 1977 level), they would
still be seeing nearly 260 hours of advertisements each year. Is this acceptable?

Peggy Charren, president of Action for Children's Television (ACT), a national consumer's
group, says no and recommends banning television
ads directed at children. Charren argues that
our constitution's First Amendment, which protects freedom of speech, should be suspended to
allow such a ban. She maintains that television
ads directed at children do not deserve First
Amendment protection on the grounds that, since
children cannot fully appreciate the persuasive
nature of advertisements, TV commercials are inherently unfair and deceptive (15).

A proposed solution to the problem

Charren begins her argument by discussing
the child consumer. She criticizes companies
that advertise to children for asking children
to "make complex and reasoned consumer judgments" (13). She explains that, since children
do not comprehend advertisers' motives, they are
not armed with the reasonable skepticism with
which adults evaluate advertisements--and that,
therefore, the advertisers' right to free
speech, at least with respect to children,
should be limited. The right of free speech in
our society is so important that anyone who
proposes that we limit it bears a heavy burden
of presenting a compelling argument. But Charren
does not. First, she assumes that the skepticism
portrayed by adult viewers of advertisements
protects them (and could likewise protect
children) from advertisers' power of persuasion.

Proposed solution rejected— 1st reason

But realistically, few people are immune to the advertiser's art. In his article "The Language of Advertising Claims," Jeffrey Schrank asserts that skepticism does not protect consumers because advertising works "below the level of conscious awareness and it works even on those who claim immunity to its message" (156).

Most adult viewers in this country watch advertisements and believe that "no attack is taking place" (Schrank 156), which is precisely the condition under which Charren claims that children watch televised advertising. Yet we hear no one arguing that because adults are being manipulated we should therefore ban television advertising. What we do hear--from the Supreme Court--is that when ads are blatantly deceptive or unfair, they are not protected by the First Amendment. Basically, the Court has said that it is never legal for an advertiser to lie--either to children or to adults.

But such protection is not enough for Charren, who believes that children make, and should be protected in making, important consumer decisions. She argues that advertisements aimed at affecting these decisions are unfair, and that children are being persuaded improperly. To illustrate, she claims that ads, specifically for sugared cereals, are deceptive and teach children to make unreasonable food choices. She feels that advertisers' reminders that cereal is "part of a balanced breakfast" do not give children information sufficient for judging the issues. In support of her argument, she cites a study where two-thirds of the preschoolers tested believed that a bowl of cereal alone constituted a balanced meal (15).

Most parents know that preschoolers and children in grades 1 through 4 (through age 11) cannot be depended upon to choose for themselves, for instance, a well-balanced diet or to

Proposed solution rejected—2nd reason

understand the principles of comparison shopping for price and quality. We do not expect that children make these decisions alone; parents are responsible for guiding their children's decisions. Young children do not have the resources to do the shopping. Parents do. Preschoolers do not make their own meals. Parents do. If children are not getting all their nutritional needs fulfilled, this is not caused by advertisers but by families that lack resources for making balanced choices. If children are duped into choosing poorly made or overpriced but cleverly advertised products, this is not the fault of advertisers but of a family situation that permits children to influence important consumer decisions without a counterbalancing influence from parents.

Parents play a key role in a child's development, nutritional and otherwise. <u>A parent's close involvement with children, not limiting the First Amendment, is the appropriate countermeasure to the power of advertisers.</u> Let parents interact with their children and begin their own persuasive campaign! Perhaps children are being confused when messages seen on television advertisements conflict with messages heard at home. But conflict in itself is not "bad." Parents must guide their children towards appropriate conclusions in making most decisions: what clothes to wear; what cereal to eat; what toys are worthwhile. As children mature they must learn to evaluate and resolve such questions for themselves. Keeping the world, with its sometimes harmful and often confusing messages, from children does not offer protection. If that were the case, how high would we need to build walls to block out the everyday assaults on the lives of our children? Do we ban the evening news because of its frequently upsetting content? Do we stop talking about the threat of drugs? No.

Claim (Argumentative thesis

Argument from cause (the real problem is lack of parental involvement, not advertisements)

What we do is acknowledge to our children that dangers exist, and then we exercise parental judgment: we <u>teach</u> children and hope they learn well enough to one day manage on their own.

Children receive conflicting messages from a variety of sources which cannot be silenced: teachers, books, friends, and television programs. We have, from time to time, experimented in this country with limiting access to potentially damaging or offensive materials, such as books and movies. But these experiments have not withstood legal challenges. The courts have decided that Americans have the right to choose what they see or hear and that writers and others have the right to create what they wish. Certain extreme instances, like child pornography, are so offensive and damaging to the children being filmed that as a society we <u>have</u> said that such products are repugnant and should not be supported by viewers who argue it is their right to see such material. And, in part, this is the argument that Charren is making about advertisements directed at children. But as a society we have agreed to limit speech only in the most extreme cases. There is nothing in the making of advertisements that is as purposefully vulgar or hurtful as there is in child pornography. If anything, advertising more closely resembles the language of our everyday speech: we live, after all, in a consumer society and advertising is the language of consumerism. In this sense, Charren's real argument is with America's values, and on this point she may be right. But values cannot be legislated. They must be taught.

The task of shaping children's values, like their diets, is better addressed through ongoing discussions between parents and children than through limiting the right of free speech. There is no need to silence advertisers in order to teach values or protect the innocent and unskep-

Argument from parallel case (other attempts made to limit materials)

Potential objection to proposed solution

Objection rebutted

Conclusion

tical. The right to free speech is protected by the Constitution because as a nation we believe that no one person is capable of determining which ideas are true and rational. Like media critic Jean Kilbourne, we may disagree with some of the messages being conveyed through advertising--say, the message that women are attractive only when they are young and thin (44). Like Peggy Charren, we can agree that advertisements can create stresses in a family's life (15). Nevertheless, we must allow all ideas a place in the market place. As Charles O'Neil, an advertiser and a defender of the medium, suggests, "[a]dvertising is only a reflection of society; slaying the messenger will not alter the fact" that potentially damaging or offensive ideas exist (196). If we disagree with the message sent in an ad, it is our responsibility to send children a different message.

Appeal to an authority

Works Cited

Charren, Peggy. "Should We Ban TV Advertising to Children? YES." <u>National Forum: The Phi Kappa Phi Journal</u> 59.4 (1979): 13-16.

Kilbourne, Jean. "The Child as Sex Object: Images of Children in the Media." <u>The Educator's Guide to Preventing Child Abuse.</u> Ed. Mary Nelson and Kay Clark. Santa Cruz: Network Publications, 1986. 40-46.

O'Neil, Charles A. "The Language of Advertising." <u>Exploring Language.</u> 6th ed. Ed. Gary Goshgarian. New York: HarperCollins, 1992. 186-97.

Schrank, Jeffrey. "The Language of Advertising Claims." <u>Teaching About Doublespeak</u>. Urbana, IL: National Council of Teachers of English, 1976. 156-62.

Shanker, Albert. "Where We Stand: TV Chastity Belt." <u>New York Times</u> 7 Mar. 1993, sec. 4: 7.

6h Evaluating arguments and avoiding common errors

Whether you are evaluating your own arguments or someone else's, there are several common errors to watch for. Correct these errors in your own writing, and raise a challenge when you find them in the writing of others.

1 Defining terms

Your evaluation of an argument should begin with its claim. Locate the claim and be sure that all terms are well defined. If they are not, determine whether the lack of definition creates ambiguities in the argument itself. For example, the term *generosity* might appear, without definition, in a claim. If that term and the claim itself were later illustrated with the example of a mall developer's "generously offering the main corridors of the mall for exhibitions, during the Christmas Season, of waste recycling demonstrations by Scouting troops," you might justifiably question the validity of the argument. If you define *generosity* as the giving of oneself freely and without any expectation of return, then you might wonder how generous the mall developer is really being. Certainly the increased traffic flow through the mall would boost business, and the supposed generosity might be an advertising ploy. As the reader of this argument, you would be entitled to raise a challenge; if you were the writer, you could by carefully defining terms avoid later challenges to your implied view of the word *generosity*. For instance, you could define the word as "any action, regardless of its motive, that results in the greatest good for the greatest number of people." This one sentence (specifically, the phrase *regardless of its motive*) lets you fend off the challenge, which you could rebut by saying: "Sure, the mall developer is increasing traffic to the mall, and probably profits as well; the developer is also educating an entire community about the importance of recycling. Here is a situation in which everyone wins. To be generous, you don't need to be a martyr."

2 Examining lines of reasoning

As you have seen, the lines of reasoning that a writer develops—generalization, causation, and so on—establish logical support for a claim. If you as the reader feel that the argument's reasoning is not valid, then you are entitled to raise a challenge because if this is flawed, the validity of the claim may be in doubt. Any of the following seven types of fallacies, or flaws, will undermine an argument's logic. The first four flaws specifically address the lines of reasoning you will use to make arguments from generalization, causation, sign, and analogy.

1. *Faulty generalization.* Generalizations may be flawed if they are offered on the basis of insufficient data. It would not be valid, for instance, to make the generalization that left-handed people are

clumsy because all three lefties of your acquaintance are clumsy. A more academic example: Assume you had administered a survey to students in your dorm. In studying the results you discovered that attitudes toward joining fraternities and sororities were evenly split. Slightly more than 50 percent wanted to join, a bit less than 50 percent did not. It would be a faulty generalization to claim on the basis of this one survey that students on your campus are evenly split on joining Greek organizations. In order for your generalization to be accurate, the survey would need to have been administered campus-wide, if not to every student, then at least to a representative cross-section.

2. *Faulty cause and effect.* Two fallacies can lead a writer to infer incorrectly that one event causes another. The first concerns the ordering of events in time. The fact that one event occurs before another does *not* prove that the first event caused the second. (In Latin, this fallacy is known as *post hoc*, a brief form of *post hoc, ergo propter hoc*—after this, therefore because of this.) If the planets Venus and Jupiter were in rare alignment on the morning of the Mt. St. Helens eruption, it would not be logical to argue that an alignment of two planets caused the volcano to erupt. The second flaw in thinking that leads to a faulty claim of causation is the belief that events must have *single* causes. Proving causation is often complicated, for many factors usually contribute to the occurrence of an event. What caused the layoff of production-line workers at the General Motors plant in Framingham, Massachusetts? An answer to this question would involve several issues, including increased competition from foreign auto manufacturers, a downturn in the economy, the cost of modernizing the Framingham assembly line, a need to show stockholders that there were fewer employees on the payroll, and a decision to build more cars out of the country. To claim that *one* of these is the sole cause of the plant shutdown would be to ignore the complexity of the event.

3. *Confusing correlation with causation.* There is a well-known saying among researchers that *correlation does not imply causation.* In one study on creativity, researchers correlated *risk taking* and *a preference for the unconventional* with groups of people classified as creative. It would not be logical to infer from this correlation that creativity *causes* risk taking or a preference for the unconventional or that these traits *cause* creativity. The most that can be said is that the traits are associated or correlated with—they tend to appear in the presence of—creative people. Arguments made with statistical evidence are usually subject to this limitation.

4. *Faulty analogy.* The key components of an analogy must very nearly parallel the issues central to the argument you are making. The wrong analogy not only will *not* clarify, but also will positively confuse. For instance, an attempt to liken the process of writing to climbing a flight of stairs would create some confusion. The anal-

ogy suggests that the writing process occurs in clearly delineated steps, when progress in actual writing is seldom so neat. The stages of writing do not progress "step by step" until a final draft is achieved. It is more accurate to say that the process of writing loops back on itself and that the process of revision takes place not just at the end of writing (the last step) but throughout. So the stairs analogy might confuse writers who, reflecting on their own practices, do not see neat linear progress and therefore assume they must be doing something wrong. Analogies should enhance, not obscure, understanding.

5. *Either/or reasoning.* Assume that someone is trying to persuade you that the United States ought to intervene militarily in a certain conflict many thousands of miles from U.S. territory. At one point in the argument you hear this: "Either we demonstrate through force that the United States continues to be a world power or we take a backseat, passive role in world affairs. The choice is clear." Actually, the choice is not at all clear. The person arguing has presented two options and has argued for one. But many possibilities for conducting U.S. foreign policy exist besides going to war or becoming passive. An argument will be flawed when its author pre-selects two possibilities from among many and then attempts to force a choice.

6. *Personal attacks.* Personal attacks, known in Latin as *ad hominem* arguments, challenge the person presenting a view rather than the view itself. You are entitled to object when you read or hear this type of attack: "The child psychologist on that talk show has no kids, so how can he recommend anything useful to me concerning my children?" Notice that the challenge is directed at the person who is presenting ideas, not at the ideas themselves. The psychologist's advice may well be excellent, but the *ad hominem* attack sidesteps the issues and focuses instead on personality. Here is a variant on the *ad hominem* argument: The speaker is giving what sounds like good advice on child rearing, but she is neither a psychologist nor an educator, so we really shouldn't base our actions on her views." In this case, the critic is dismissing a statement because the speaker is not an acknowledged expert. This kind of criticism can be legitimate if an argument is being directly based on the authority of that speaker's expertise, and you *should* give preference to sources that are authoritative. Nonetheless, it is sidestepping the other issues in an argument to dismiss an apparently useful observation by dismissing the person who holds it. At the very least, statements should be evaluated on their merits.

7. *The begged question.* Writers who assume the validity of a point that they should be proving by argument are guilty of begging the question. For instance, the statement "All patriotic Americans should support the President" begs a question of definition: what *is* a patriotic American? The person making this statement assumes a

definition that he should in fact be arguing. By making this as-sumption, the writer sidesteps the issue of definition altogether. The point you want to make must be addressed directly through careful argument.

3 Examining evidence

Arguments also can falter when they are not adequately or legiti-mately supported by facts, examples, statistics, or opinions. Refer to the following guidelines when using evidence.

Facts and examples

1. *Facts and examples should fairly represent the available data.* An exam-ple cannot be forced. If you find yourself needing to sift through a great deal of evidence *against* a point you wish to make in order to find one confirming fact or example, take your difficulty as a sign and rethink your point.

2. *Facts and examples should be current.* Facts and examples need to be current, especially when you are arguing about recent events or are drawing information from a field in which information is changing rapidly. If, for example, you are arguing a claim about the likelihood of incumbent politicians being reelected, you should find sources that report on the most recent elections. If in your argument you are trying to show a trend, then your facts and examples should also be drawn from sources going back several years, if not decades.

3. *Facts and examples should be sufficient to establish validity.* A general-ization must be based on an adequate number of examples and on representative examples. To establish the existence of a problem concerning college sports, for instance, it would not do to claim that because transcripts were forged for a handful of student-athletes at two schools a problem exists nationwide.

4. *Negative instances of facts and examples should be acknowledged.* If an ar-gument is to be honest, you should identify facts and examples that constitute evidence *against* your position. Tactically, you are better off being the one to raise the inconvenient example than having someone else do this for you in the context of a challenge. For ex-ample, an argument might conclude that a particular advertising company has consistently misrepresented facts about its products. The arguer would be less than ethical to omit from the discussion several advertisements that were entirely legitimate in their treat-ment of facts. The wiser strategy would be for the arguer to address these negative examples (negative in the sense that they apparently disprove the claim), either turning them to advantage or at the very least neutralizing them.

Statistics

5. *Use statistics from reliable and current sources.* Statistics are a numerical compression of information. Assuming you do not have the expertise to evaluate procedures by which statistics are generated, you should take certain commonsense precautions when selecting statistical evidence. First, cite statistics from reliable sources. If you have no other way of checking reliability, you can assume that the same source cited in several places is reliable. The U.S. government publishes volumes of statistical information and is considered a reliable source. Just as with facts and examples, statistics should be current when you are arguing about a topic of current interest.

6. *Comparative statistics should compare items of the same logical class.* If you found statistical information on housing starts in New England in one source and in a second source found information on housing starts in the Southwest, you would naturally want to compare the numbers. The comparison would be valid only if the term "housing starts" was defined clearly in both sources. Lacking a definition, you might plunge ahead and cite the statistics in a paper, not realizing that one figure included apartment buildings in its definition of "housing" while the other included only single-family homes. Such a comparison would be faulty.

Expert opinions

7. *"Experts" who give opinions should be qualified to do so.* Anyone can speak on a topic, but experts speak with authority by virtue of their experience. Cite the opinions of experts in order to support your claims. Of course you will want to be sure that your experts are, in fact, expert; and evaluating the quality of what they say can be troublesome when you do not know a great deal about a topic. You can trust a so-called expert as being an authority if you see that person cited as such in several sources. For experts who are not likely to be cited in academic articles or books, use your common sense. If you were arguing that birchbark canoes track better in the water than aluminum canoes, you would want to seek out a person who has considerable experience with both. (See the box in 6d-2 for more on evaluating expert opinions and choosing authoritative sources.)

8. *Experts should be neutral.* You can disqualify an expert's testimony for possible use in your argument if you find that the expert will profit somehow from the opinions or interpretations offered. Returning to the example of the birchbark canoe: you would want to cite as an authority in your paper the person who has paddled hundreds of miles in both aluminum and birchbark canoes, not the one who earns a living making birchbark canoes.

CHAPTER 7

Constructing Sentences

If you are a lifelong speaker of English, then you are an expert in the language—in its grammar, its vocabulary, its sentence structures, and the proper relationships among its words. When you speak, people understand. You *know* English, but in all likelihood your knowledge is *implicit*. That is to say, you can do just fine communicating verbally, and yet you may not know the textbook definition of *participle*, for instance—even though you use participles correctly every day. Although you will seldom need to talk of participles, you will gain confidence as a writer by making your implicit knowledge *explicit*.

7a Understanding sentence parts

The sentence is our basic unit of communication. Sentences, of course, are composed of words, each of which can be classified as a part of speech. As you review definitions of nouns, verbs, and the other parts of speech, remember that these are parts of a whole: meaning in language is built on the *relationship* among words.

1 The basics: Recognizing subjects and predicates

The fundamental relationship in a sentence is the one between a subject and its predicate. Every sentence has a **subject:** a noun or noun-like word group that engages in the main action of the sentence or is described by the sentence. In addition, every sentence has a **predicate:** a verb, and other words associated with it, that state the action undertaken by a subject or the condition in which the subject exists.

A **simple subject** is the single noun or pronoun that identifies what the sentence is about or produces the action of the sentence. The **simple**

KEY FEATURES

Opening on a note reassuring to students, this chapter emphasizes the difference between *implicit* and *explicit* knowledge of sentence structure. The chapter continues the movement from larger units of discourse (essays) through smaller units (paragraphs) to yet smaller units (sentences). While understanding sentence structure is discussed in the context of writing and revising, the initial discussion uses traditional grammatical terminology. It makes sense to use such terms as "subject" and "predicate," since most students are familiar with them. As students gain confidence in identifying not only the major parts of sentences but also the parts of speech that constitute those sentence parts, they are ready to move on to a study of sentence types. In keeping with the approach used in the previous section, the sections covering sentence types focus on meaning rather than rules. And as in the treatment of the rudiments of sentence structure, coverage of sentence types begins with basic types and moves on, using what students have learned in the first part of the chapter, to discuss expanding sentences by modifying them with increasingly complex phrases and clauses. All of the standard sentence patterns are covered in fairly traditional terms, but the emphasis remains on meaning, not rules. Even a brief discussion of punctuation is explained in terms of the meaning of the entire sentence. The last part of the chapter offers both functional and structural definitions of sentences. Exercises provide students with ample
(continued)

practice in identifying and composing various types of sentences.

TEACHING IDEAS

CRITICAL THINKING Some students with sentence-level writing problems have become so fearful of the specter of grammar and sentences that they're convinced they'll simply "never get it." For that reason, it's probably worth a few minutes of class time to ask them to write out any definition of a sentence they can recall learning. Then ask them how meaningful the definition is: Can they use it to identify a sentence? to identify something that isn't a sentence? How *do* they determine whether or not a group of words is a sentence? Most students, after some initial hesitation, will be able to provide some parameters for sentences. This chapter will reinforce the basic knowledge these students have. If they can begin the chapter with confidence, then they're far more likely to make use of the material in it.

ADDITIONAL EXERCISE A

This exercise is designed to show you just how much you really do know about sentences. In the following paragraph, mark off places where you'd end a sentence. (You can also supply commas where you think they're needed, but that's not necessary for the purposes of this exercise.) Then compare your response to other students' responses. As you discuss differences, try to explain why you divided the paragraph as you did. (There are several different ways of dividing the paragraph.)

> The Supreme Court hears about 125 to 130 cases during the seven months each year that it is in session these cases are chosen from over 5,000 petitions most of which are prepared by highly specialized law firms but every year 200 to 300 petitions are submitted by individuals on their own behalf these cases are called *pro se* the Latin words for "for himself" in most years no more than one or two *pro se* cases are heard and fewer result in a positive decision many of these petitions are prepared by prisoners who have given up on lawyers one of the most famous of these cases was that of Clarence Gideon a poor man who was convicted without having been represented by a lawyer Gideon's petition which he wrote out by hand was accepted by the Court and resulted in a land-

predicate is the main sentence verb. You can gain a great deal of confidence from your ability to divide a sentence into its subject and predicate parts; you will improve your ability to avoid fragments and to write sentences with varied, interesting structures. Again, recall that subjects and predicates consist of nouns, verbs, and other parts of speech. Learning these parts of speech and their functions will help you understand how sentences operate. In the sentences that follow, the simple subject is marked "ss" and the simple predicate, "sp."

Subject	Predicate
ss In small doses, alcohol	*sp* acts as a stimulant.
ss Large doses	*sp* act as a depressant.
ss Individuals under the influence	*sp* often become more aggressive.
ss Alcohol consumption	*sp* interferes with one's ability to foresee negative consequences.
ss A person's actions	*sp* can grow extreme in the presence of this drug.

2 Nouns

A **noun** (from the Latin *nomen*, or name) is the part of speech that names a person, place, thing, or idea.[1] Only nouns can be introduced by an **article** or a **determiner,** the words, *a, an,* and *the*: a rock; an animal; the truth. The **indefinite article,** *a* or *an,* introduces a generalized noun: *a* person can be any person. The indefinite article *a* appears before nouns beginning with a consonant; *an* is placed before nouns beginning with a vowel or unpronounced *h*—as in *hour*: *a* book, *an* hour. The **definite article,** *the,* denotes a specific noun: *the* book. Nouns can also be accompanied by certain classes of words that limit what they refer to. The most common limiting words (and their categories) are: *this, that, these, those* (demonstrative); *any, each, some* (indefinite); *one, two, first, second,* etc. (numerical); *which, that, whose,* etc. (relative).

ESL NOTE The use of articles or of various limiting, quantifying, or determining words indicates whether an English noun names a person or thing that is specific or definite. Nouns that name something generic, nonspecific, or abstract are used without these words or with indefinite limiting words like *some* or *any* (see 42a-2 and 42-b).

---

[1]We owe our discussions on the parts of speech to Hulon Willis, *Modern Descriptive English Grammar* (San Francisco: Chandler, 1972).

The use of a plural form or a numerical limiting word often indicates whether an English noun names a person or thing that can be counted—that is, a count noun (versus a mass or noncount noun that names uncountable quantities or abstractions). See the box on this page and 42a-1.

Nouns change their form to show **number;** they can be made singular or plural: *boy/boys, child/children, herd/herds.* They also undergo limited change in form to show **possession,** but, unlike pronouns (discussed next), they do this only with the addition of an apostrophe and usually an *s: girl's, children's, herd's.* Finally, nouns can be classified according to categories of meaning that affect the way they are used, as shown in the following box.

Classification of Nouns

Proper nouns, which are capitalized, name particular persons, places, or things:

> *Sandra Day O'Connor, Chevrolet, "To His Coy Mistress"*

Common nouns refer to general persons, places, or things and are not capitalized:

> *judge, automobile, poem*

Count nouns can be counted:

> *cubes, cups, forks, rocks*

Mass nouns cannot be counted:

> *sugar, water, air, dirt*

Concrete nouns name tangible objects:

> *lips, clock, dollar*

Abstract nouns name an intangible idea, emotion, or quality:

> *love, eternity, ambition*

Animate versus **inanimate nouns** differ according to whether they name something alive:

> *fox* and *weeds* versus *wall* and *honesty*

Collective nouns are singular in form but plural in sense:

> *crowd, family, group, herd*

Specific uses of nouns are addressed in several places in this handbook.

Nouns: as modifiers 11g	Nouns: as objects 7b
Nouns: agreement with verbs 10a	Nouns: phrases 7d-2 and 3
Nouns: as complements 7b	Nouns: showing
Nouns: as clauses 7e-3	possession 27a, 8c
Nouns with articles and	Nouns: as subjects 7b
determiners 42b	

mark ruling that people who can't afford lawyers must be given the opportunity to be represented by a court-appointed lawyer.

Possible response:

The Supreme Court hears about 125 to 130 cases during the seven months each year that it is in session. These cases are chosen from over 5,000 petitions, most of which are prepared by highly specialized law firms. But every year 200 to 300 petitions are submitted by individuals on their own behalf. These cases are called *pro se,* the Latin words for "for himself." In most years no more than one or two *pro se* cases are heard, and fewer result in a positive decision. Many of these petitions are prepared by prisoners who have given up on lawyers. One of the most famous of these cases was that of Clarence Gideon, a poor man who was convicted without having been represented by a lawyer. Gideon's petition, which he wrote out by hand, was accepted by the Court and resulted in a landmark ruling that people who can't afford lawyers must be given the opportunity to be represented by a court-appointed lawyer.

ESL ALERT

The following texts are useful references for ESL students having problems with English grammar:

COOK, MARY JANE. *Trouble Spots of English Grammar, a Test-Workbook for ESL.* 2 vols. New York: Harcourt Brace Jovanovich.

AZAR, BETTY. *Understanding and Using English Grammar.* 2 vols. Englewood Cliffs, NJ: Prentice-Hall.

FRANK, MARCELLA. *Modern English.* 2 vols. Englewood Cliffs, NJ: Prentice-Hall.

GRAHAM, SHEILA, and WYNN CURTIS,. *Harbrace ESL Workbook.* New York: Harcourt Brace Jovanovich.

HOLSCHUH, LOUIS. *The Elements of English Grammar.* 2 vols. New York: St. Martin's Press.

3 Verbs

A **verb,** the main word in the predicate of a sentence, expresses an action, describes an occurrence, or establishes a state of being.

ACTION	Eleanor *kicked* the ball.
OCCURRENCE	A hush *descended* on the crowd.
STATE OF BEING	Thomas *was* pious.

Verbs change form on the basis of their **principal parts.** Building from the **infinitive** or **base form** (often accompanied by **to**), these parts are the **past tense,** the **present participle,** and the **past participle.**

Base form	Past tense	Present participle	Past participle
to escape	escaped	am escaping	escaped
to ring	rang	am ringing	rung

The principal parts of a verb have a major role in how the verb shows **tense,** the change in form that expresses the verb's action in time relative to a present statement.

There are four varieties of verbs in English; each establishes a different relationship among sentence parts, as shown in the following box.

Classification of Verbs

Transitive verbs transfer action from an actor—the subject of the sentence—to a person, place, or thing receiving that action (see 9d-1).

> *buy, build, kick, kiss, write*
> Wanda *built* a snowman.

Intransitive verbs show action; yet no person, place, or thing is acted on (see 9d-1).

> *fall, laugh, sing, smile*
> Stock prices *fell.*

Linking verbs allow the word or words following the verb to complete the meaning of a subject (see 11d).

> *be (am, is, are, was, were, has/have been), look, remain, sound, seem, taste*
> Harold *seems* happy.

Helping or **auxiliary verbs** help to show the tense and mood of a verb (see 9c and 43d).

> *be (am, is, are, was, were) has, have, had, do, did, will*
> I *am* going. I *will* go. I *have* gone. I *did* go.

Modal auxiliaries such as *might, would, could,* and *must* help a verb to express urgency, obligation, and likelihood (see 9c-1 and 43d).

> I *should* go. I *might* go. I *could* go.

ESL NOTE To determine whether a word in a sentence is a verb, apply the test sequence described in 12a (on sentence fragments).

See chapter 9 for a detailed discussion of verbs. The following list provides a brief index to more information on verb use.

Verbs: active and passive
  voices   9g and 43a-1
Verbs: transitive and
  intransitive   9d-1 and 43a-1
Verbs: agreement with
  subjects   10a
Verbs versus
  verbals   7a-4 and 43e
Verbs: mood   9h and 43b-5–6
Verbs: modal auxiliaries
  9c-1 and 43d
Verbs: regular and
  irregular   9a, b

Verbs: linking   11d
Verbs: (avoiding) shifts   16a, b
Verbs: strong vs. weak
  9g–h, 17b
Verbs: tense   9e, f and 43b-1–4
Verbs: thesis statements
  3d-1, 2, 3

4   Verbals

A **verbal** is a verb form that functions in a sentence as an adjective, an adverb, or a noun. There are three types of verbals: gerunds, participles, and infinitives. A **gerund,** the -*ing* form of a verb without its helping verbs, functions as a noun.

Editing is both a skill and an art. [The gerund is the subject of the sentence.]

I am tired of *editing*. [The gerund is an object of a preposition.]

A **participle** is a verb form that modifies nouns and pronouns. Its present and past forms make up two of the verb's principal parts, as shown previously.

The *edited* manuscript was 700 pages. [The past participle modifies the noun *manuscript*.]

The man *editing* your manuscript is Max Perkins. [The present participle modifies the noun *man*.]

An **infinitive,** often preceded by **to,** is the base form of the verb (often called its *dictionary form*). An infinitive can function as a noun, adjective, or adverb.

To edit well requires patience. [The infinitive functions as the noun subject of the sentence.]

The person *to edit* your work is Max Perkins. [The infinitive functions as an adjective.]

He waited *to edit* the manuscript. [The infinitive functions as an adverb.]

TEACHING IDEAS

The concept of a verbal can be confusing to some students; they have difficulty understanding why a verbal cannot function as a verb in a sentence. It may be helpful to ask students to construct sentences using forms of *edit* in the predicate position. Or you may want to present them with the following sentences, asking them to distinguish between the use of *edit* as verb in these sentences and as a verbal in the sample sentences in the text:

She *is editing* the book with skill and art.
I *am editing* the essay even though I am tired.
Max Perkins *edited* that manuscript.
Max Perkins *was editing* the manuscript when I called.
Max Perkins *will edit* the manuscript.

ESL ALERT

Students should be reminded that because gerunds serve the function of nouns and may appear wherever a noun appears, one gerund equals one noun and therefore takes a singular verb. Gerunds often, though not always, refer to action in the past or action from the past to the present (in contrast to infinitives, which refer to the future). When gerunds are placed as objects of the verb, this distinction is vital to clear communication, as in the following.

> He stopped seeing her./He stopped to see her.
> He remembered going there./He must remember to go there.

Also, gerunds take the possessive pronoun.

> his book/his having done that.

Another helpful rule is that two- and three-part verbs always take a gerund instead of an infinitive object: "look forward to going" not "look forward to go."

Recognizing gerund and infinitive subjects may be difficult for ESL students, who might benefit from practice underlining subjects, as in "*Getting to know you* will be fun" and "*To be or not to be* was Hamlet's question."

REFERENCES

TRAUGOTT, ELIZABETH CLOSS. *A History of English Syntax: A Transformational Approach to the History of English Sentence Structure.* New York: Holt, 1972. Transformational grammar provides a meaningful perspective from which to study sentence structure.

GORRELL, DONNA. "Controlled Composition for Basic Writers." *CCC* 32 (1981): 308–16. Students who practice manipulating the writing of others can become skilled in producing their own sentences.

CHRISTENSEN, FRANCIS. "A Generative Rhetoric of the Sentence." *CCC* 14 (1963): 155–61. Adding to the basic sentence can help students become more fluent writers of cumulative sentences.

KOLLN, MARTHA. "Closing the Books on Alchemy." *CCC* 32 (1981): 139–51. Understanding grammatical terminology provides students with a means of controlling their own writing.

WILLIAMS, JOSEPH M. "The Phenomenology of Error." *CCC* 32 (1981): 152–68. Instructors

The following list is a brief index to other information on verbals.

Verbals: using verbal phrases   7d-2, 3
Verbals: choosing tense   9e, f
Verbals: tense with words   43e
Verbals: choosing pronouns   8b-2, 8c-2
Verbals: avoiding fragments   12a

Important Relationships between a Subject and Verb

A complete sentence must have both a subject and a verb. A word grouping that lacks a subject, a verb, or both is considered a fragment. See chapter 12 on fragments and chapter 16 for a special class of fragments—grammatically "mixed" constructions.

INCOMPLETE	At the beginning of the meeting. [There is no verb.]
REVISED	At the beginning of the meeting, the treasurer reported on recent news.
INCOMPLETE	The fact that this is an emergency meeting. [The use of *that* leaves the statement incomplete, without a verb.]
REVISED	This is an emergency meeting of the board.

A sentence must have a *logically compatible* subject and verb. A sentence in which a subject is paired with a logically incompatible verb is sure to confuse readers, as you will see in chapter 16.

INCOMPATIBLE	The meeting room is sweating. [A room does not normally sweat.]
REVISED	Those gathered in the meeting room are sweating.

A sentence must have a subject and verb that *agree in number.* A subject and verb must both be singular or plural. The conventions for ensuring consistency are found in chapter 10.

INCONSISTENT	The treasurer are a dynamic speaker. [The plural verb does not match the singular subject.]
REVISED	The treasurer is a dynamic speaker.

A sentence must have a subject close enough to the verb to ensure clarity. Meaning in a sentence can be confused if the subject/verb pairing is interrupted with a lengthy modifier. See chapter 15 for a discussion of misplaced modifiers.

INTERRUPTED	We because of our dire financial situation and our interests in maintaining employee welfare have called this meeting.
REVISED	We have called this meeting because of our dire financial situation and our interests in maintaining employee welfare.

---

5   Adjectives

By modifying or describing a noun or pronoun, an **adjective** provides crucial defining and limiting information in a sentence. It can also provide nonessential but compelling information to help readers see, hear, feel, taste, or smell something named. Adjectives include the present and past participle forms of verbs, such as *fighting* Irish, *flying* wing, *baked* potato, and *written* remarks. The single-word adjectives in the following sentences are italicized.

> Climate plays an *important* part in determining the *average* numbers of a species, and *periodical* seasons of *extreme* cold or drought I believe to be the most *effective* of *all* checks.
>
> —CHARLES DARWIN, *On the Origin of Species*

6 Adverbs

An **adverb** can modify a verb, an adjective, an adverb, or an entire sentence. Adverbs describe, define, or otherwise limit, generally answering these questions: *when, how, where, how often, to what extent,* and *to what degree.* Although many adverbs in English are formed by adding the suffix -*ly* to an adjective, some are not: *after, ahead, already, always, back, behind, here, there, up, down, inside, outside.* **Descriptive adverbs** describe individual words within a sentence.

> The poor *unwittingly* subsidize the rich. [The adverb modifies the verb *subsidize.*]

> Poverty *almost* always can be eliminated at a higher cost to the rich. [The adverb modifies the adverb *always.*]

> Widespread poverty imposes an *increasingly* severe strain on our social fabric. [The adverb modifies the adjective *severe.*]

Conjunctive adverbs establish adverb-like relationships between whole sentences. These words—*moreover, however, consequently, thus, therefore, furthermore,* and so on—play a special role in linking ideas and sentences. (See 7a-9 and 19a-3.) Chapter 11 provides a detailed discussion of adjectives and adverbs. The following is a brief index to more information on adjectives and adverbs.

7 Pronouns

Pronouns substitute for nouns. The word that a pronoun refers to and renames is called its **antecedent.** Like a noun, a pronoun shows **number**—it can be singular or plural. Depending on its function in a sentence, a pronoun will change form—that is, its **case:** it will change from **subjective,** to **objective,** to **possessive.** The following examples show this change in case for the pronoun *he,* which in each instance is a substitute for the noun *Jake.*

should look at sentence errors in terms of writing behavior that can be altered if given sufficient attention.

FOR DISCUSSION

In order to familiarize students with the function of adjectives and adverbs in a sentence, ask them to identify and discuss the role played by the various modifiers in the following passage.

> Female slaves seldom escaped harassment from owners. Nearly all young slave women —some of them only girls—regularly encountered the terrifying prospect of rape or attempted rape. The young slave Harriet Jacobs unwillingly endured the sexual attentions of her unscrupulous master, who continually pressured her to fulfill his desires. She refused adamantly. Consequently, she was occasionally subjected to severely painful beatings.

ADDITIONAL EXERCISE B

Compose a paragraph in which you use at least five of the classes of pronouns. Identify each pronoun you use by class, and where appropriate, by case and number.

    antecedent   pronoun
                    (subjective)
Jake reads a magazine. *He* reads a magazine.

                                    pronoun
                    antecedent   (objective)
The magazine was given to Jake. The magazine was given to *him.*

                        pronoun
    antecedent   (possessive)
Jake's subscription is running out. *His* subscription is running out.

There are eight classes of pronouns.

Personal pronouns (*I, me, you, us, his, hers*, etc.) refer to people and things.

> When sugar dissolves in water, the sugar molecules break *their* close connection within the sugar crystal.

Relative pronouns (*who, whose, which, that*, etc.) begin dependent clauses (see 7e) and refer to people and things.

> The presence of the sugar, *which* is now in solution, changes many of the properties of the water.

Demonstrative pronouns (*this, these, that, those*) point to the nouns they replace.

> *These* changes involve the water's density, boiling point, and more.

Interrogative pronouns (*who, which, what, whose*, etc.) form questions.

> *What* does boiling sugar water have to do with coating caramel apples?

Intensive pronouns (*herself, themselves*, and other compounds formed with *self* or *selves*) repeat and emphasize a noun or pronoun.

> The sugar *itself* can be recovered from the water by the simple act of boiling.

Reflexive pronouns (*herself, themselves*, and other compounds formed with *self* or *selves*) rename—reflect back to—a preceding noun or pronoun.

> The ease of recovery demonstrates that sugar molecules do not bind *themselves* strongly to water molecules.

Indefinite pronouns (*one, anyone, somebody, nobody, everybody*, etc.) refer to general, or nonspecific, persons or things.

> *Anyone* who has stained a shirt with salad dressing knows that water will not dissolve oil.

Reciprocal pronouns (*one another, each other*) refer to the separate parts of a plural noun.

> The many solvents available to chemists complement *one another.*

The following is a brief index to more information on pronouns.

8 Prepositions

A **preposition** links a noun (or word group substituting for a noun) to other words in a sentence—to nouns, pronouns, verbs, or adjectives. *In, at, of, for, on, by,* are all prepositions. Many common prepositions are shown in the following box. Along with the words that follow them, prepositions form **prepositional phrases,** which function as adjectives or adverbs. In the following sentence, an arrow leads from the (three) prepositional phrases to the (three) words modified. Note that the middle prepositional phrase modifies *evolution* in the first prepositional phrase.

The theory *of evolution by natural selection* was proposed *in the 1850s.*

Common Prepositions

Single-word prepositions

about	beyond	off
above	by	on
across	concerning	onto
after	despite	out
against	down	outside
along	during	over
among	except	through
around	for	to
as	from	toward
before	in	under
behind	into	until
below	like	up
beneath	near	with
between	of	

Multiword prepositions

according to	contrary to	on account of
along with	except for	on top of
apart from	in addition to	outside of
as for	in back of	owing to
because of	in case of	with regard to
by means of	in spite of	with respect to

ADDITIONAL EXERCISE C

ACROSS THE CURRICULUM Make a photocopy of a brief passage from a textbook in one of your other courses. In order to practice identifying sentence parts and parts of speech, mark off the simple subjects and simple predicates according to the instructions for Exercise 1, and then, using abbreviations (n-noun, v-verb, adj-adjective, adv-adverb, pro-pronoun, prep-preposition, con-conjunction, and—if there are any—int-interjection), try to identify as many parts of speech as you can.

ESL ALERT

Because their languages may not depend on word order to the degree that English does, many ESL students will be confused by English words that retain the same spelling even though they serve different grammatical functions, as exemplified by the Groucho Marx saying: "Time *flies like* an arrow; fruit *flies like* a banana."

Marking out prepositional phrases before determining subject and verb is a good rule of thumb to help students distinguish subjects and verbs: "~~In the back of the room behind the huge desk~~ stood an antique clock ~~of the type~~ revered ~~by his grandparents.~~"

In Japanese the object precedes the verb.

The following literal translation from Chinese makes clear the word order interference problems possible:

"he in/on/at here that daughter also to be very good looking"

The student speaking or writing in English must recast such statements in terms of their content and intent, finding English equivalents instead of translating literally; yet even students highly fluent in English who "think in" their new language will sooner or later stumble over localized word order interference problems. Sympathy and tolerance are appropriate.

ESL ALERT

There is little logic to English speakers' use of prepositions, and such use differs in British and American English. In fact, American usage can vary as well ("stand on line"—East Coast; "stand in line"—other regions). ESL students may *never* master English prepositions completely and *should not be expected to.* They can learn usage of some of the most common prepositions through rote memory, and there are some rules to help with prepositions of location, but even a seemingly bilingual student can be recognized as a non-native speaker by occasional preposition abuse.

Sometimes a helpful rule can be invented; for instance, most English words beginning with "co-," "col-" "com-" "con-" or "cor-," take the preposition "with," as in "cooperate with," "collaborate with," "communicate with," "connect with," "correspond with," because this prefix carries the idea of "together." "On" used for location frequently refers to the surface and "in" to the interior as in "on the desk" as opposed to "in the desk," but the difference between "on" the sofa and "in" the chair relates to the construction of those furnishings: the sofa without arms, the chair enclosing and enveloping. You use "on" if you must step up to board ("get on a bus," "get on a train," "get on a large ship") but "in" if you must step down ("get in a small boat," "get in a car"). Contrast *"in* a canoe" with *"on* a raft." The best rule for "on" and "in" contrasts "touching" (visual correlative: O) and "enclosed" (O): "Those who ride *on the back of a tiger are in danger of ending up* in the tiger" (with apologies to J. F. Kennedy).

Multiword prepositions will be the hardest ones for non-native speakers to recognize as prepositions, and prepositions used in two- and three-part verbs will confuse everyone.

ESL NOTE Prepositions occur in a very wide variety of English constructions that are often highly idiomatic. They are often followed by a noun or pronoun in the objective form or case (see 8b-1 and 42c) thus forming a modifying prepositional phrase (see 7d-1).

When used with certain verbs, prepositions (as well as certain adverbs like *down, out,* and *away*) are called *particles,* combining with the simple form of the verb into a *phrasal verb* that has a distinct new meaning (see 43f). These phrasal-verb meanings with their particles are listed in standard English dictionaries.

When used with an adjective and the verb *be* followed by an object, a preposition forms a distinctive idiomatic construction (see 44b). In this form, many adjectives must be used with very specific prepositions. (See also 16g-3 and 18a-1 for this usage in parallel constructions.) Such idiomatic usages are hard to find in standard English dictionaries.

The following is a brief index to more information on prepositions.

Prepositions: and
  fragments   12c-2
Prepositions: and mixed
  constructions   16g-3, 18a
Prepositions: using objective-
  case pronouns   8b-1
Prepositions: punctuating
  introductory phrases   25a

Prepositions: punctuating
  nonessential phrases   25d
Prepositions: with nouns   42c
Prepositions: with verbs   43f
Prepositions: with
  adjectives   44b

9 Conjunctions

Conjunctions join sentence elements or entire sentences in one of two ways: either by establishing a coordinate or *equal* relationship among joined parts or by establishing a subordinate *unequal* relationship. (Subordinating conjunctions are discussed in detail in 7e. Coordinating and correlative conjunctions are discussed in chapter 19.) Briefly, conjunctions are classified in four ways: as coordinating conjunctions, conjunctive adverbs, correlative conjunctions, or subordinating conjunctions.

Coordinating conjunctions join parallel elements from two or more sentences into a single sentence: *and, but, or, nor, for, so.* (For uses of coordinating conjunctions see 10a-2, 3, 19a-7, and 25b.)

> Infants only cry at birth, *but* within a few short years they speak in complete sentences.

Conjunctive adverbs create special logical relationships between the clauses or sentences joined: *however, therefore, thus, consequently,* etc. (For uses of conjunctive adverbs see 13b-4, 19a-3, and 26b.)

> Infants can only cry at birth. Within a few short years, *however,* they can speak in complete sentences.

Correlative conjunctions are pairs of coordinating conjunctions that place extra emphasis on the relationship between the parts of the coordinated construction: *both/and, neither/nor, not only/but also,* etc. (For uses of correlative conjunctions see 10a-3.)

> Three-year-olds *not only* speak in complete sentences, *but* they *also* possess vocabularies of hundreds or even thousands of words.

Subordinating conjunctions connect subordinate clauses to main clauses: *when, while, although, because, if, since, whereas,* etc. (For uses of subordinating conjunctions see 7e-1 and 19b-1.)

> *When* children reach the age of three, they can usually carry on complete conversations with their peers and with adults.

10 Interjections

An **interjection** is an emphatic word or phrase. When it stands alone, it is frequently followed by an exclamation point. As part of a sentence, the interjection is usually set off by commas.

> Oh, they're here.   Never!

11 Expletives

An **expletive** is a word that fills a slot left in a sentence that has been rearranged. *It* and *there* function as expletives—as filler words without meanings of their own—in the following examples.

BASIC SENTENCE   A sad fact is that too few Americans vote.

WITH EXPLETIVE   It is a sad fact that too few Americans vote.

BASIC SENTENCE   Millions of people are not voting.

WITH EXPLETIVE   There are millions of people not voting.

Expletives are used with the verb *be* in sentences with a delayed subject. Sentences with expletives can usually be rearranged back to their basic form. Try to delete expletives from your writing to achieve a spare, concise style (see chapter 17).

EXERCISE 1

Place a slash (/) between the subject and predicate parts of the following sentences. Identify the simple subject and simple predicate of each sentence with the abbreviations "ss" and "sp." Circle prepositions.

> *Example:*   The physics (of) particle behavior / is important (for) designing safe and efficient processing plants.

1. Farmers frequently store tons of grain in large metal silos.

EXERCISE 1

1. Farmers/frequently store tons *of* grain *in* large metal silos.

   ss · · · · sp

2. Unlike silos *for* liquids, grain silos/ occasionally collapse.

   ss · · · sp

3. We/do not know exactly the cause *of* this failure.

   ss · sp

4. Simple fluid dynamics applied *to* sand flow/does not predict the instability *of* grain particles.

   ss · · sp

5. Silo manufacturers/still must include some details *of* the physics design criteria.

   ss · · sp

2. Unlike silos for liquids, grain silos occasionally collapse.
3. We do not know exactly the cause of this failure.
4. Simple fluid dynamics applied to sand flow does not predict the instability of grain particles.
5. Silo manufacturers still must include some details of the physics of particle flows in their design criteria.

7b Understanding basic sentence patterns

There are five basic sentence patterns in English, from which virtually all of the sentences you read in this and other books are built. Each of the five sentence patterns consists of a subject and predicate. Depending on the sentence's structure, the predicate may contain a **direct object,** an **indirect object,** or a (subject or object) **complement.** The basic pattern diagrams that follow include definitions of these key terms and concepts.

		⌐ *Predicate* ⌐
Pattern 1:	Subject	verb
	We	*look.*

SUBJECT: a noun or noun-like word group that produces the main action of the sentence or is described by the sentence.

PREDICATE: a verb, and other words associated with it, that state the action undertaken by the subject or the condition in which the subject exists.

		⌐——— *Predicate* ———⌐
Pattern 2:	Subject	verb (tr.) direct object
	Stories	*excite the imagination.*

DIRECT OBJECT: a noun, or group of words substituting for a noun, that receives the action of a transitive verb (tr.). A direct object answers the question *What or who is acted upon?*

		⌐———— *Predicate* ————⌐
Pattern 3:	Subject	verb (tr.) indirect object direct object
	Stories	*offer us relief.*

INDIRECT OBJECT: a noun, or group of words substituting for a noun, that is indirectly affected by the action of a verb. Indirect objects typically follow transitive verbs such as *buy, bring, do, give, offer, teach, tell, play,* or *write.* The indirect object answers the question *To whom or for whom has the main action of this sentence occurred?*

		⌐————— *Predicate* —————⌐
Pattern 4:	Subject	verb (tr.) direct object object complement
	They	*make us tense.*

OBJECT COMPLEMENT: an adjective or noun that completes the meaning of a direct object by renaming or describing it. Typically, object complements follow verbs such as *appoint, call, choose, consider, declare, elect, find, make, select,* or *show.*

```
                       ┌────────── Predicate ──────────┐
Pattern 5:  Subject    verb (linking) subject complement
            We         are readers.
```

SUBJECT COMPLEMENT: a noun or adjective that completes the meaning of a subject by renaming or by describing it. Subject complements follow linking verbs such as *appear, feel, seem, remain,* as well as all forms of *be.*

EXERCISE 2

Working with a topic of your choice, write a paragraph in which you use each of the five basic sentence patterns.

> *Example:* The trumpeter played music. [Sentence Pattern 2] The couple listened. [Sentence Pattern 1] A waiter brought them a drink. [Sentence Pattern 3] The trumpeter was sizzling. [Sentence Pattern 5] The couple found the music excellent. [Sentence Pattern 4]

7c   Expanding sentences with single-word modifiers

Principles of sentence expansion can be found at work in virtually any paragraph you read. The first technique for expanding sentences is to add modifiers—descriptive, modifying information. The nouns and verbs in the five basic sentence patterns can be modified by adjectives and adverbs.

1   Modifying nouns and verbs with adjectives and adverbs

VERB MODIFIED   I read *thoroughly.*
BY ADVERB

NOUN MODIFIED   A novel will engage an *active* imagination.
BY ADJECTIVE

2   Positioning modifiers

The position of an adverb can be shifted in a sentence from beginning to middle to end. Depending on its location, an adverb will change

REFERENCES

LUNSFORD, ANDREA. "Cognitive Development and the Basic Writer." *CE* 41 (1979): 38–48. With appropriate assignments, basic writing students can develop skills in sentence development.

HERRINGTON, ANNE J. "Grammar Recharted: Sentence Analysis for Writing." *Writing Exercises from "Exercise Exchange."* Vol. 2. Urbana: NCTE, 1984. 276–87. Using a simplified chart, students can become more adept at recognizing sentence patterns.

STERNGLASS, MARILYN. "Composition Teacher as Reading Teacher." *CCC* 27 (1976): 378–82. Students who read analytically can develop an understanding of sentence structure.

EXERCISE 2

Individual responses

FOR DISCUSSION

After students have completed Exercise 2, ask for volunteers to have their paragraphs analyzed by the class. Reproduce sample paragraphs on the board or on an overhead projector, and ask the class to identify the sentence patterns within the paragraph. When there is disagreement over certain sentences, students should explain the reasons for their decisions. The ensuing discussion will reinforce students' understanding of the five basic sentence patterns.

the meaning of a sentence or the rhythm. When placing an adverb, take care that it modifies the word you intend it to modify.

SHIFTED
MEANING
I am *only* moving my bed (that is, doing nothing more important than moving).

I am moving *only* my bed (that is, no other furniture).

SHIFTED
RHYTHM
Sometimes, stories can provide emotional relief.
Stories *sometimes* can provide emotional relief.

Stories can provide emotional relief *sometimes.*

A single-word adjective is often positioned directly before the noun it modifies, although writers make many variations on this pattern. When more than one noun in the sentence could be described by the adjective, take particular care to place the adjective closest to the noun it modifies. See chapter 15 on editing to correct misplaced modifiers and section 44b for the sequence of adjective modifiers in a typical English sentence.

A *good* story will excite a reader.   [*Story* is the word modified.]
A story will excite a *good* reader.   [*Reader* is the word modified.]

EXERCISE 3

Use one-word adjectives or adverbs to modify the nouns and verbs in the following sentences.

>*Example:* A man walked down a street.
>An *old* man walked *slowly* down a *tree-lined* street.

1. The moon rose. [Sentence Pattern 1]
2. The earth eclipsed the moon. [Sentence Pattern 2]
3. Motion brings us eclipses. [Sentence Pattern 3]
4. Shadows make the moon disappear. [Sentence Pattern 4]
5. The moon is hidden. [Sentence Pattern 5]

EXERCISE 4

Take the paragraph you wrote for Exercise 2 and modify its nouns and verbs as you have done in Exercise 3.

7d Modifying and expanding sentences with phrases

A **phrase** does not express a complete thought, nor can it stand alone as a sentence. Phrases consist of nouns and the words associated with them, or verb forms not functioning as verbs (called *verbals*) and the words associated with them. Phrases function in a sentence as modifiers and as objects, subjects, or complements. As such, they can be integrated into any of the five sentence patterns (see 7b) to add detail.

EXERCISE 3

Underlined words are modifiers.
1. The <u>full</u> moon rose <u>slowly</u>. [Sentence Pattern 1]
2. The earth <u>completely</u> eclipsed the moon. [Sentence Pattern 2]
3. <u>Celestial</u> motion brings us <u>partial</u> and <u>total</u> eclipses. [Sentence Pattern 3]
4. <u>Earth's</u> shadows make the moon disappear. [Sentence Pattern 4]
5. The moon is <u>fully</u> hidden. [Sentence Pattern 5]

GROUP ACTIVITY

Exercise 4 adapts well to group work. Ask students to meet in groups of three or four and share responses. The group will then decide, for each sentence, which is the best response and offer reasons for their decision. Since a primary purpose for studying sentence structure is to expand the writer's ability to compose, sharing responses to this exercise and weighing the relative merits of the chosen modifiers can offer students some initial insight into style.

EXERCISE 4

Individual responses

1 Adding prepositional phrases

A preposition links nouns and pronouns to other words in a sentence. (See 7a-8 for a list of commonly used prepositions.) Together with its noun, called an *object,* a preposition forms a **prepositional phrase,** which functions in a sentence as a modifier—such as an adjective or an adverb.

ADJECTIVE   Stories can excite the imaginations *of young people.*

ADVERB   Paul reads *in the evening.*

2 Adding verbals: Infinitive phrases

A verbal is a verb form functioning not as a verb but instead as a noun, adjective, or adverb. An infinitive—the base form or dictionary form of a verb—often is preceded by the word *to.* Infinitives function as adjectives, adverbs, or nouns, but behave as verbs in that they can be modified with adverbs and can be followed with direct and indirect objects. Infinitives and the various words associated with them form **infinitive phrases.**

NOUN SUBJECT   *To read in the evening* is a great pleasure.

NOUN OBJECT   Some children start *to read at an early age.*

ADJECTIVE   Stories offer us a chance *to escape dull routines.*

ADVERB   We read *to gain knowledge.*

3 Adding verbals: Gerund and participial phrases

When appearing without its helping verbs, the *-ing* form of the verb functions as a noun and is called a *gerund.* Without its helping verb, the present or past participle can function as an adjective. Like infinitives, both gerunds and participles form phrases by taking objects and modifiers. A noun or pronoun appearing before a gerund is often called the subject of the gerund; this pronoun or noun must be written in its possessive form. In the following sentences, the gerund phrase functions as the object of the preposition *of.*

GERUND   We did not approve of *Paul's* reading all night. [The gerund phrase functions as the object of the preposition *of.* A noun in the possessive case is used before the gerund.]

FAULTY   We did not approve of *him* reading all night. [The pronoun before the gerund does not use the possessive case.]

REVISED   We did not approve of *his* reading all night.

4 Adding noun phrases

A **noun phrase** consists of a noun accompanied by all of its modifying words. A noun phrase can be quite lengthy, but it always functions as a single noun—as the subject of a sentence, as the object of a verb or preposition, or as a complement.

SUBJECT *Even horror stories with their gruesome endings* can delight readers.

DIRECT OBJECT A tale of horror will affect *anyone who is at all suggestible.*

COMPLEMENT Paul is *someone who likes to read horror stories.* [The phrase is a subject complement.]

5 Adding absolute phrases

Unlike other phrases, **absolute phrases** consist of both a subject and a predicate—although an incomplete predicate. Absolute phrases modify entire sentences, not individual words. When you use an absolute phrase, set it off from your sentence with a comma or pair of commas (see chapter 25). An absolute phrase is formed by deleting the linking verb *be* from a sentence.

SENTENCE His hands were weak with exhaustion.

ABSOLUTE PHRASE his hands weak with exhaustion

NEW SENTENCE His hands weak with exhaustion, Paul lifted the book off its shelf. [The phrase modifies the basic sentence, *Paul lifted.* . . .]

An absolute phrase may also be formed by changing the main verb of a sentence to its *-ing* form, without using an auxiliary.

SENTENCE His hands trembled with exhaustion.

ABSOLUTE PHRASE his hands trembling with exhaustion

NEW SENTENCE His hands trembling with exhaustion, Paul lifted the book off its shelf.

6 Adding appositive phrases

Appositive phrases rename nouns. The word *appositive* describes the positioning of the phrase *in apposition to,* or beside, the noun. Appositives are actually "clipped" sentences—the predicate part (minus the verb) of Sentence Pattern 5.

		Predicate	
Pattern 5:	Subject	linking verb	subject complement
	Paul	*is*	*an old college friend.*

ESL ALERT

Most ESL students will never have been introduced to absolutes, will find them most puzzling, and will tend to equate them with comma splice problems, especially when the central verb is a passive form so it looks more complete than it is: "Their work completed, they went home." Marcella Frank's *Modern English, Part II* has a clear explanation of how and when to use absolutes.

APPOSITIVE PHRASE   an old college friend

NEW SENTENCE   Paul, an old college friend, is an avid reader.

EXERCISE 5

In the sentences that follow, circle all single-word modifiers and underline all modifying phrases.

> *Example:* (Recently) Stephen W. Hawking <u>published</u> a (popularized)
>
> <u>version</u> of his ideas about space and time.

- *Recently* is an adverb and modifies the verb *published.*
- *Popularized* is an adjective and modifies the noun *version.*
- Two prepositional phrases—*of his ideas about space and time*—function as an adjective by modifying the noun *version.*
- The second prepositional phrase, *about space and time,* functions as an adjective by modifying the object of the preceding phrase, *ideas.*

1. On a clear, moonless night, he says, the brightest objects in the sky are the planets nearest Earth.
2. Looking more closely, we can see that the stars near Earth appear to be fixed, but they are not.
3. To measure the distance of a star from Earth, scientists calculate the number of years it takes the star's light to reach us.
4. His calculations having proved it, Sir William Herschel confirmed that our galaxy (the Milky Way) forms a spiral.
5. We now know our galaxy is only one of some hundred thousand million galaxies.
6. Each of those hundred thousand million galaxies contains a hundred thousand million stars.

7e Modifying and expanding sentences with dependent clauses

A **clause** is any grouping of words that has both a subject and a predicate. There are two types of clauses. An **independent** (or **main**) **clause** can stand alone as a sentence. Any sentence fitting one of the five structural patterns reviewed in 7b is an independent clause. A **dependent** (or **subordinate**) **clause** cannot stand alone as a sentence because it is usually introduced either with a subordinating conjunction (e.g., *while*) or with a relative pronoun (e.g., *who*). There are four types of dependent clauses: adverb, adjective, noun, and elliptical clauses.

1 Adding dependent adverb clauses

Dependent **adverb clauses** that modify verbs, adjectives, and other adverbs begin with subordinating conjunctions and answer the question

---

EXERCISE 5

1. *On a clear, moonless night,* he says, the *brightest* objects *in the sky* are the planets *nearest Earth.*
   The prepositional phrase *On a clear, moonless night* functions as an adverb modifying the entire sentence. (Within this phrase *clear* and *moonless* are adjectives and modify the noun *night.*)
   Brightest is an adjective and modifies the noun *object.*
   The prepositional phrase *in the sky* functions as an adjective by modifying the noun *objects.* The phrase *nearest Earth* functions as an adjective by modifying the noun *planets.*

2. *Looking more closely,* we can see *that the stars near Earth appear to be fixed,* but they are not.
   The participial phrase *looking more closely* functions as an adverb modifying the entire sentence. (Within this phrase *more closely* functions as an adverb modifying the verbal *looking.*)
   The noun phrase *that the stars near Earth appear to be fixed* functions as direct object of the verb *see.* (Within this phrase *near Earth* functions as an adjective modifying the noun *stars,* and the infinitive phrase *to be fixed* functions as a subject complement to the linking verb *appears.*)

3. *To measure the distance of a star from Earth,* scientists calculate the number *of years* it takes the star's light *to reach us.*
   The infinitive phrase *To measure the distance of a star from Earth* functions as an adverb modifying the verb *calculate.* (Within this phrase *of a star* functions as an adjective modifying the noun *distance.*)
   The prepositional phrase *of years* functions as an adjective by modifying the noun *numbers.*
   The prepositional phrase *to reach us* functions as an adverb modifying *takes.*

4. *His calculations having proved it,* Sir William Herschel confirmed *that our galaxy (the Milky Way) forms a spiral.*
   The participial phrase *His calculations having proved it* functions as an adverb modifying the entire sentence.
   The noun phrase *that our galaxy (the Milky Way) forms a spiral* functions as the direct object of the verb *confirmed.* (Within this phrase the phrase *the Milky Way* functions as an appositive to the noun *galaxy.*)

(continued)

5. We *now* know *our galaxy is only one of some hundred thousand million galaxies.*

   Now is an adverb and modifies the verb *know.* The noun phrase *our galaxy is only one of some hundred thousand million galaxies* functions as the direct object of the verb *know.* (*That* is implied at the beginning of the phrase.) (Within this phrase the prepositional phrase *of some hundred thousand million galaxies* functions as an adverb by modifying the adjective *one,* and *some hundred thousand million* functions as an adjective by modifying the noun *galaxies.*)

6. Each *of those hundred thousand million galaxies* contains *a hundred thousand million stars.*

   The prepositional phrase *of those hundred thousand million galaxies* functions as an adjective by modifying the pronoun *each.* (Within this phrase *those hundred thousand million* functions as an adjective by modifying the noun *galaxies.*)

   A hundred thousand million functions as an adjective by modifying the noun *stars.*

LOOKING AHEAD

Just as phrases and subordinate clauses sometimes transform themselves into fragments, sentences beginning with conjunctive adverbs sometimes latch onto adjoining sentences to become comma splices or fused sentences. As with phrases and subordinate clauses, paying careful attention to dependent clauses as modifiers here may make it easier for students to understand their treatment in chapter 13 (Comma Splices and Fused Sentences).

LOOKING AHEAD

Dependent clauses, like some of the phrases in 7d, sometimes end up as sentence fragments. As with phrases, paying careful attention to dependent clauses as modifiers here may make it easier for students to understand their treatment in chapter 12 (Sentence Fragments).

when, how, where, how often, to what extent, or *to what degree.* Subordinating conjunctions establish a distinct logical relationship between the clauses joined.

Subordinating Conjunctions and the Logical Relationships They Establish

To show condition: *if, even if, unless,* and *provided that*

To show contrast: *though, although, even though,* and *as if*

To show cause: *because* and *since*

To show time: *when, whenever, while, as, before, after, since, once,* and *until*

To show place: *where* and *wherever*

To show purpose: *so that, in order that,* and *that*

Placed at the head of a clause, a subordinating conjunction makes one sentence grammatically dependent on another. When the subordinating conjunction *if,* for example, is placed at the head of a sentence, it renders that sentence grammatically dependent, unable to stand alone.

MAIN CLAUSE PLUS SUBORDINATING CONJUNCTION	*if* + Food is repeatedly frozen and thawed.
DEPENDENT CLAUSE	if food is repeatedly frozen and thawed

Although it consists of a subject and predicate, this last grouping of words is no longer a sentence. To make sense, this clause must be set in a dependent relationship with an independent clause.

If food is repeatedly frozen and thawed, it will spoil.

For guidance on punctuating sentences with subordinating conjunctions, see 25a-1.

2 Adding dependent adjective clauses

Like adjectives, **adjective clauses** modify nouns. The clauses usually begin with the relative pronoun *which, that, who, whom,* or *whose.* The following examples show an adjective clause modifying the subject of a sentence.

People *who lived through the Depression of the 1930s* remember it well.

A country *that had prospered in the first two decades of the century* now saw massive unemployment and hardship.

For a discussion of when to use which relative pronoun, see 8f.

3 Adding dependent noun clauses

Noun clauses function exactly as single-word nouns do in a sentence: as subjects, objects, complements, and appositives. Noun clauses are introduced with the pronoun *which, whichever, that, who, whoever, whom, whomever,* or *whose* and with the word *how, when, why, where, whether,* or *whatever.*

SUBJECT   *That ozone holes have already caused blindness and skin cancer in grazing animals* suggests the need for immediate legislative action.

OBJECT   Apparently, few inhabitants of populous northern cities are aware of *how the depletion of ozone in the upper atmosphere can harm living organisms—humans included.*

COMPLEMENT   The looming danger that ozone depletion poses is *why researchers have sounded an alarm.*

4 Working with elliptical clauses

An **elliptical clause** is one in which a word or words have been omitted, though the sense of the clause remains clear. Often, the words omitted are relative pronouns and the logically parallel second parts of comparisons. An elliptical clause functions exactly as a clause would, were all its words restored. In the following example, the words in parentheses are usually omitted.

English speakers, with their verb tenses and numerous words for divisions of years, weeks, and days, have a far different concept of time than the Hopis do (have a concept of time).

EXERCISE 6

Combine each of the sentence pairs that follow by using a subordinating conjunction.

Example: Colonial America could support its many needs with its own population. It could not so much as hope for independence.
Unless colonial America could support its many needs with its own population, it could not so much as hope for independence.

1. One hundred years of colonization had passed. Seventeenth-century America held only 250,000 people.
2. In the eighteenth century, America's population exploded. Immigration and birth rates increased.
3. So many white settlers had come from England. It was not surprising that the English language, English customs, and English ways of government dominated the land.

REFERENCES

O'HARE, FRANK. *Sentence-Combining: Improving Student Writing without Formal Grammar Instruction.* Urbana: NCTE, 1973. Through sentence combining, students can develop mature style even without grammar instruction.

STRONG, WILLIAM. "Creative Approaches to Sentence Combining." Urbana: ERIC Clearinghouse on Reading and Communication Skills, 1986. ERIC ED 274 985. A discussion of the history of sentence combining, with suggestions for classroom use.

DAIKER, DONALD, ANDREW KEREK, and MAX MORENBERG. "Sentence Combining and Syntactic Maturity in Freshman English." *CCC* 29 (1978): 36–41. A report on the results of a successful experiment in sentence combining.

———. *Sentence Combining: A Rhetorical Perspective.* Carbondale: Southern Illinois UP, 1985. A collection of essays on sentence combining techniques and classroom use.

CROWHURST, MARION. "Sentence Combining: Maintaining Realistic Expectations." *CCC* 34 (1983): 62–72. The claims made by advocates of sentence combining need to be examined with scrutiny.

SOLOMON, MARTHA. "Teaching the Nominative Absolute." *CCC* 26 (1975): 356–61. A practical discussion of teaching students to recognize and use the nominative absolute.

EXERCISE 6

1. After one hundred years of colonization had passed, seventeenth-century America held only 250,000 people.
2. In the eighteenth century, America's population exploded as immigration and birth rates increased.
3. It was not surprising that the English language, English customs, and English ways of government dominated the land after so many white settlers had come from England.
4. When Britons moved, they faced the challenges of living with Africans, Scots, Scotch-Irish, Irish, Portuguese, Jews, Swedes, Finns, Swiss, and even a few Austrians and Italians.
5. Conflict had to give way to cooperation so that new communities might flourish.

4. Britons moved. They faced the challenges of living with Africans, Scots, Scotch-Irish, Irish, Portuguese Jews, Swedes, Finns, Swiss, and even a few Austrians and Italians.
5. Conflict had to give way to cooperation. New communities might flourish.

7f   Classifying sentences

1   Functional definitions

Sentences are classified by structure and by function. There are four functional types: statements, questions, exclamations, and commands. Statements, called **declarative** sentences, are by far the most common of the four types and make direct assertions about a subject. A question, or **interrogative** sentence, is formed either by inverting a sentence's usual word order (*She did sing./Did she sing?*) or by preceding the sentence with words such as *who, whom, which, when, where, why,* and *how.* An exclamation, or **exclamatory** sentence, used rarely in academic writing, serves as a direct expression of a speaker's or writer's strong emotion. Commands, or **imperative** sentences, are an expression of an order or urgent wish addressed to a second person.

DECLARATIVE   The driver turned on the ignition.

INTERROGATIVE   Was the engine flooded?

EXCLAMATORY   What an awful fire! How terrible!

IMPERATIVE   Get back! Don't you go near that!

2   Structural definitions

As you expand sentences by adding phrase- and clause-length modifiers, or by combining two or more sentences, you change the structural relationships within sentences. There are four structural classes of sentences in English: simple, compound, complex, and compound-complex. Good stylistic sense dictates that you vary sentence types and lengths. See the discussion in chapter 20.

Each of the five basic sentence patterns discussed in 7b qualifies as a **simple sentence:** Each has a single subject and a single predicate. The designation "simple" refers to a sentence's structure, not its content. A simple sentence, with all its modifying words and phrases, can be long.

For thousands of years, waves of migrating people had moved slowly across the great Eurasian steppes down into the Mediterranean. [This sentence consists of one subject, *waves,* and one simple predicate, *had moved.*]

Then again, a simple sentence can be brief.

> Migrating peoples moved slowly into Europe.

Compound sentences have two subjects and two predicates. They are created when two independent clauses are joined with a coordinating or correlative conjunction or with a conjunctive adverb. Coordinating conjunctions express specific logical relations between the elements they join. *Or* and *nor* suggest choice, one positive and the other negative. *And* joins elements by addition. *But* and *yet* join elements by establishing a contrast. *For* and *so* are the only coordinating conjunctions that must join entire sentences. The others may join sentence elements and entire sentences. *For* suggests a cause of an occurrence. *So* suggests a result of some action. Correlative conjunctions such as *either/or* and conjunctive adverbs such as *however* can also be used to create compound sentences. For details on how coordination can be used to create sentence emphasis, see 19a.

> In the second century A.D. the Goths moved southward from the Baltic regions, and they settled on the north shore of the Black Sea. [The conjunction *and* joins two independent clauses.]

Complex sentences consist of an independent clause and one or more dependent clauses. As shown in 7e, the four kinds of dependent clauses can be introduced with subordinating conjunctions (see 7a-9) or relative pronouns (see 7a-7). For details on how complex sentences help to create sentence emphasis, see 19b.

> The Goths met and defeated the Vandals, who retreated toward central Europe. [The relative pronoun *who* signals a dependent adjective clause in this complex sentence.]

> After they met and defeated the Vandals, the Goths forced that tribe to retreat toward central Europe. [The subordinating conjunction *after* signals a dependent adverb clause.]

Compound-complex sentences consist of at least two independent clauses and one subordinate, dependent clause.

> Rome had for centuries been able to withstand migratory incursions along its northern borders, but in A.D. 376 the Emperor Valens and nearly two-thirds of his army were killed in a battle with the Visigoths at Adrianople, which marked the last real Roman resistance to the barbarian nations. [The coordinating conjunction *but* here signals a compound sentence, and the relative pronoun *which* signals a dependent clause in a complex sentence.]

EXERCISE 7

Use the clauses and phrases provided to build up the core sentence. Add conjunctions when they are necessary to the logic of your expanded sentence.

ESL EXERCISE

Choose a grammatical interference problem between your first language and English. "Grammatical interference" means that the mental habit involved in the grammatical form in the first language causes mistakes or confusion in the second language, English. In one well-organized paragraph, explain the grammatical interference problem, providing numerous examples to make it clear to your audience, which is teachers who do not speak your language and who do not understand why you make so many mistakes.

The order of your paragraph should be as follows: a clear topic sentence at the beginning expressing the problem and the reason for the problem; at least two supporting examples with explanations of each; and a concluding sentence or two clearly aimed at the teacher who is your audience.

Remember that your strategy is to make your mistakes part of a general pattern, not a personal or private problem that other speakers of your language do not share.

FOR DISCUSSION

A discussion of the various ways in which sentences can be combined may make students more aware of style. Collect students' responses to this exercise, and (with permission, of course) distribute several successful versions. Ask students to discuss not only why these versions represent good writing, but also the effects of the different stylistic choices the students made. (You could also make this a small group activity along the lines of the group activity outlined for Exercise 4.)

EXERCISE 7

1. A common thread connects Fugard's work: the respect for humanity, the search for dignity, and the struggle to cultivate trust and hope in a demeaning world.
2. Fugard's tenacious, weathered looks reflect his struggles.
3. In this computer age, Fugard uses a tortoise-shell Parker pen to write his plays, which include *A Lesson from Aloes, The Road to Mecca, "Master Harold" . . . and the Boys,* and *My Children, My Africa,* all successfully produced in America.
4. For Fugard, there are signs that South Africa is changing: the freeing of Nelson Mandela, the lifting of the ban on the African National Congress, and the government's willingness to negotiate.
5. During the mid-1960s, Fugard continued writing and staged classic plays with the Serpent players, the country's first non-white theater troupe.

ADDITIONAL EXERCISE F

Expand the paragraph you composed for Additional Exercise E to include at least one example of each structural type of sentence (simple, compound, complex, compound-complex). You may use existing sentences in the paragraph to represent a structural type. Identify each sentence type with an abbreviation (s-simple, cd-compound, cx-complex, cd-cx-compound-complex). [NOTE: This exercise would also work well as a group activity.]

Example: Athol Fugard is a South African playwright.
       plays confront difficulties
       interracial relations
       his troubled country

Athol Fugard is a South African playwright whose plays confront the difficulties of interracial relations in his troubled country.

1. A common thread connects Fugard's work.
respect for humanity
search for human dignity
struggle to cultivate trust and hope in a demeaning world.
2. Fugard's looks reflect his struggles.
tenacious
weathered
3. Fugard handwrites his plays.
in this computer age
with a tortoise-shell Parker pen
which include *A Lesson from Aloes, The Road to Mecca, "Master Harold" . . . and the Boys,* and *My Children, My Africa,* all successfully produced in America
4. South Africa is changing.
for Fugard there are signs
the freeing of Nelson Mandela
the lifting of the ban on the African National Congress
the government's willingness to negotiate
5. Fugard continued writing.
during the mid-1960s
he staged classic plays with the Serpent players
the country's first non-white theater troupe

Case in Nouns and Pronouns

The term **case** refers to a noun or pronoun's change in form, depending on its function in a sentence. Nouns do not change their form when their function changes from subject to object. Especially when revising, you may change a pronoun's function—say, from object to subject. By understanding how a pronoun's function changes, you will be prepared to make a corresponding change to the pronoun's form. There are eight classes of pronouns. Most troublesome are the **personal pronouns,** which refer to people and things, and these will be the focus of discussion.

8a Using pronouns in the subjective case

 Use the subjective case when a pronoun functions as a subject, as a subject complement, or as an appositive that renames a subject.

She speaks forcefully. The speaker is *she.*
The executive officers—and only *they*—can meet here.

SUBJECT OF AN INDEPENDENT CLAUSE	Abigail Adams was brilliant and much admired; *she* ran the family farm and business while her husband attended the Continental Congress.
SUBJECT OF A DEPENDENT CLAUSE	While *she* lived in the capital, Abigail Adams repeatedly approached her husband on behalf of American women.
SUBJECT COMPLEMENT	John Adams was a pacifist, and *he* was largely the one who kept the country from going to war with France in 1798.
APPOSITIVE THAT RENAMES A SUBJECT	Adams retired from public life in 1801; only one President of the United States—*he, alone*—has lived to see a son elected president.

Pronouns Used as Subjects

	Singular	*Plural*
1st person	I	we
2nd person	you	you
3rd person	he, she, it	they

SPOTLIGHT ON COMMON ERRORS—CASE FORMS

These are the errors most commonly associated with a pronoun's case. For full explanations and suggested revisions, follow the cross-references to chapter sections.

CASE FORM ERRORS occur when writers misunderstand a pronoun's function in a sentence as a subject, object, or indicator of possession. These common situations lead to errors.

- **When a noun or an indefinite pronoun (such as *one, anyone, somebody*) shows possession, use an apostrophe (see 27a–b).**

FAULTY	REVISED
This is Alberts signature.	This is Albert's signature.
Rondas team is impressive.	Ronda's team is impressive.
The families decision was final.	The family's decision was final.
Somebodies book is here.	Somebody's book is here.
This is nobodies business.	This is nobody's business.

- **A personal pronoun that shows possession (such as *his, her, mine, ours*) uses NO apostrophe (see 8c-1 and 27a).**

FAULTY	REVISED
This coat is her's.	This coat is hers. (This is her coat.)
Give the cat it's food.	Give the cat its food.
These coats are their's.	These coats are theirs. (These are their coats.)
Your's are the first hands to touch this.	Yours are the first hands to touch this. (Your hands are the first hands to touch this.)

- **After a form of the verb *be* (*is, are, was, were*), use a pronoun's subjective form (*I, you, he, she, we, they*) or its possessive form (*mine, yours, his, hers, theirs, ours*) with *no* apostrophe (see 8a-2, 8c-1).**

FAULTY		REVISED	
This is her.	This is him.	This is she.	This is he.
Is that her?	It is me.	Is that she?	It is I.
This is our's.	That is her's.	This is ours.	That is hers.

- **When a personal pronoun (such as *I, me, you, he, she, it*) follows the word *and,* choose the pronoun's form as if the pronoun were alone in the sentence (see 8d and 8b-1).**

FAULTY	REVISED
Sally and me went to the movies.	Sally and **I** went to the movies. [TEST: I went to the movies alone.]
She and me went. Her and me went. Tom went with Sally and I.	She and **I** went. [TEST: She went. I went.] Tom went with Sally and **me.** [TEST: Tom went with me.]
It's a secret between you and I.	It's a secret between you and **me.** [TEST: It's a secret between me and a friend.]
That's between he and Sally.	That's between **him** and Sally. [TEST: That's between him and a friend.]

- **Use *its* to show possession; use *it's* ONLY for a contraction of *it is* (see 27a-2).**

FAULTY	REVISED
A dog hates it's fleas.	A dog hates **its** fleas.
Its raining.	**It's** raining. (It is raining.)

- **For a contraction with the verb *be* (*is, are*), use an apostrophe (see 27a-2).**

FAULTY	REVISED
Its a difficult position.	It**'s** a difficult position. (It is a difficult position.)
Their coming home.	They**'re** coming home. (They are coming home.)
There coming home.	They**'re** coming home. (They are coming home.)
Shes home.	She**'s** home. (She is home.)
Your home.	You**'re** home. (You are home.)
Whos there?	Who**'s** there? (Who is there?)

ESL ALERT

Vietnamese students might have major problems with pronouns, commonly confusing "he" and "she," which sound almost identical to their ears. Part of the problem is that pronouns of person (*he, she, we, they, you*) are mainly reserved for "rude" street slang and are replaced in polite Vietnamese with special nouns to identify personal relationships precisely.

Speakers of Spanish and other gender-based languages will tend to use "he" or "she" where English speakers would say "it."

Because in many languages the verb form differs according to subject, ESL students might insert unnecessary pronouns equal to the sentence subject, especially when a lengthy series of modifiers separates subject from verb:

"The room that they had just finished remodeling ~~it~~ was lovely."

REFERENCE

SHAUGHNESSY, MINA P. *Errors and Expectations: A Guide for the Teacher of Basic Writing.* New York: Oxford UP, 1977. Chapter 4. Some students have difficulty with plural and possessive nouns regardless of their use of the forms in speech.

TEACHING IDEAS

MULTICULTURAL DIFFERENCES This book stresses the importance of writers' choices with regard to style and meaning. The first of those choices with respect to pronoun use is whether to use standard English. This issue is particularly relevant to speakers of certain dialects, especially black English vernacular, where the apostrophe *s* possessive is not used. If appropriate for your classroom, you might want to call attention to some of the differences between standard edited English and other dialects, as well as the difference between formal academic prose and what is known as "imaginative literature." A case in point is Alice Walker, whose frequently anthologized essay "In Search of Our Mothers' Gardens" is written in standard edited English, but whose highly respected novel *The Color Purple* is written primarily in black English vernacular, complete with apostrophe-*s*-less possessives. The relative demands of the two

2 **Use the subjective case for pronouns with the linking verb *be*.**

The speaker is *she*.   These are *they*.   It is *I*.

The linking verb *be* in a sentence serves as a grammatical "equals" sign (see 11d); it links the subject of the sentence to a completing or "complement" word that is made identical to the subject. When pronouns are involved in this equation, they too are made identical to the subject and are also used in the subjective form.

Clinton *was* President.   It was *he*, the President, who spoke.

The use of subjective pronoun forms is quite clear in sentences with normal word order (subject + *be* + complement), but writers need to remember that subjective forms are used in the same equation when sentence order is reversed.

In nonstandard or informal usage it is fairly common to hear a linking-verb construction using an objective form: as in "It's me" or "This is her." But in academic English these constructions should be revised using a subjective pronoun that maintains sentence logic and consistency: "It's I" and "This is she."

INFORMAL OR   It isn't *me* in the White House; the decision makers are never
NONSTANDARD   *us* ordinary folks.

REVISED   It isn't *I* in the White House; the decision makers are never
we ordinary folks. [These linking-verb constructions require the same subjective form they would have required in a sentence with normal word order.]

To some writers, the word order in this revised sentence sounds stilted. If this is your view, the best remedy is to reorder the sentence in question.

REORDERED   *I* am not in the White House; *we* ordinary folks never make decisions. [Use normal order and subjective-case pronouns.]

The decision makers don't consult *us*. [Use normal word order and an objective-case pronoun.]

8b Using pronouns in the objective case

1 **Use the objective forms for pronouns functioning as objects.**

The governor handed *her* the report. The job appealed to *me*. We enjoyed taking *them* to dinner.

Pronouns Used as Objects		
	Singular	*Plural*
1st person	me	us
2nd person	you	you
3rd person	him, her, it	them

Pronouns functioning as the object of a preposition, as the object or indirect object of a verb, or as the object of a verbal take the objective form.

Object or indirect object of verb (see 7b)

Babe Ruth started as a pitcher in 1915, when the Boston Red Sox gave *him* a contract. [*Him* is the indirect object of *gave.*]

Ruth so impressed *them* with his hitting that between the games he pitched he was asked to play first base and outfield. [*Them* is the direct object of *impressed.*]

Object of preposition (see 7d-1)

Ruth pitched 25 games in 1916 and won 23 of *them.*

Appositive that renames the object (see 7d-6)

Hank Aaron eventually broke Ruth's home run record of 714; a place in the Hall of Fame has been reserved for both legends—Aaron and *him.*

Object of verbal (see 7a-4)

Even though teams opposing *him* could not hit his pitching, Ruth gave up the pitcher's mound to concentrate on hitting. [*Him* is the direct object of the participle *opposing.*]

For twelve years Ruth either led the American League in hitting home runs or was tied for hitting *them.* [*Them* is the object of the gerund *hitting.*]

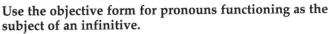

2 **Use the objective form for pronouns functioning as the subject of an infinitive.**

Study enabled *us* to reach the goal.

When a pronoun appears between a verb and an infinitive, the pronoun takes the objective form. In this position, the pronoun is called the subject of the infinitive.

forms of prose, and the reasons for acknowledging the place of standard and nonstandard English, could provoke a meaningful discussion.

GROUP ACTIVITY

Ask students to form groups of three or four and compose a paragraph in which they use pronouns serving the following functions:

> object of verb
> indirect object of verb
> object of preposition
> appositive that renames object
> object of verbal
> subject of infinitive

Then ask groups to exchange paragraphs. The second task of each group will be to identify and explain the function of each of the objective case pronouns in the other group's paragraph.

TEACHING IDEAS

This advice is sure to confuse weaker writers: Why should the *objective case* be used for a pronoun that's a *subject?* Of course, it's a good question. If students think of the pronoun as doing double duty as the subject of the infinitive phrase but as the object of the verb in the main clause, then they can justify using the objective case.

ESL ALERT

Expect confusion about noun-noun formations like "table top" and "car engine" as opposed to "table's top" and "car's engine." The students may have learned the rule that people and animals appear in the possessive form ("John's car"; "her dog's bone") but that inanimate objects take the "of" formation ("the center of the room"; "top of the desk"). They might ask why we can say "desk top" but not "room center," and how "center room" differs from "room center."

WITH INFINITIVE   His 60 home runs in 1927 helped *him* to reach a level of stardom unmatched by other athletes of his era. [The objective-form pronoun appears between the verb *helped* and the infinitive *to reach.*]

His home runs helped *him* reach stardom. [The subject of the infinitive *reach* uses the objective form, *him.*]

8c   Using nouns and pronouns in the possessive case

Use a possessive noun or pronoun before a noun to indicate ownership of that noun (or noun substitute).

Eleanor Roosevelt gave the Civil Works Administration *her* enthusiastic support for hiring 100,000 women by the end of 1933.

ESL NOTE   Many English nouns are made possessive either with the possessive case form (*a woman's voice*) or with the noun as object of the preposition *of* (*voice of a woman*). With some inanimate nouns the prepositional form is standard and the possessive case form is seldom used (NOT *a house's color* BUT *color of a house*). See 42c-1.

	Possessive Forms of Pronouns	
	Singular	*Plural*
1st person	my, mine	our, ours
2nd person	your, yours	your, yours
3rd person	his, her, hers, its	their, theirs

1   Certain possessive pronouns are used as subjects or subject complements to indicate possession.

Yours are the first hands to touch this. These are *theirs.*

The possessive pronouns *mine, ours, yours, his, hers, theirs* are used in place of a noun as subjects or subject complements.

Ours is a country of opportunity for both men and women, Eleanor Roosevelt argued. This opportunity is *ours.* (*mine, yours, his, hers, theirs*)

2   Use a possessive noun or pronoun before a gerund to indicate possession.

The group argued for *her* getting the new position.

When appearing before a gerund, an *-ing* word that functions as a noun, a pronoun should use the possessive form.

GERUND   *Her* lobbying helped to legitimize the role of women in government. [The pronoun before the gerund specifies whose *lobbying*.]

Problems with pronouns before gerunds occur when the *-ing* word is confused with a participle, which has the same *-ing* form but functions as an adjective. A participle is often preceded by an objective pronoun.

OBJECT PLUS PARTICIPLE   In Babe Ruth's most famous game, fans saw *him pointing* to the spot where, moments later, he hit a home run. [*Him*, a direct object of *saw*, is modified by the participle *pointing*, which functions as an adjective.]

In a similar construction, *pointing to the spot* . . . can be preceded by the possessive *his*.

POSSESSIVE WITH GERUND   Fans saw *his pointing* to a spot in the left-field bleachers as a sign of confidence, not arrogance. [The gerund phrase *pointing to a spot* . . . functions as the object of *saw*; the possessive *his* indicates Ruth's ownership of this act.]

The focus in this last sentence is no longer on *him* (on Ruth) but on *his pointing*—a difference in meaning. Since gerunds and participles both have distinctive uses in sentences, be sure to choose the correct pronoun form to help convey your meaning. Confusion between an *-ing* word's function—as a gerund or as a participle—can create errors.

FAULTY   Hard work resulted in *them* getting government jobs. [*Getting* is mistakenly treated as a participle and is incorrectly preceded by an objective pronoun.]

REVISED   Hard work resulted in *their* getting government jobs. [*Their* indicates possession of the gerund *getting . . . jobs*.]

EXERCISE 1

Based on your analysis of each of the following sentences, fill in the blanks with an appropriate subjective, objective, or possessive pronoun: *I/we, you, he/she/it/they; me/us, you, him/her/it/them; my/mine/our/ours, your/ yours, his/her/hers/its/their/theirs.*

> *Example:* _____ changing costumes, mid-performance, amused the audience.
>
> *Changing costumes* is a gerund phrase and takes a possessive pronoun. *His* (or *her*) changing costumes, mid-performance, amused the audience.

1. Delegates to the convention watched _____ changing positions on important issues and deserted the candidacy.
2. Delegates wanted _____ to remain steadier under challenges from contenders.

EXERCISE 2

1. they
2. she/he
3. I/you/we/they
4. her/his/their/our/my
5. he

3. After _____ left the convention, the delegates searched for a restaurant.
4. The newly elected president arrived and said the delegates had worked so effectively that she wanted to give _____ a banquet.
5. " _____ is an organization that recognizes honest effort," the president said.

EXERCISE 2

Complete the sentences that follow by filling in the blanks with pronouns or nouns of the appropriate form.

1. Presenting the newly discovered evidence—the intruder's gloves—to the district attorney, the chief inspector said: "These are _____ ."
2. It is _____ who has won.
3. It is _____ who have won.
4. This is _____ contest.
5. Mark answered the phone and, listening to a person asking for him, said: "Yes, this is _____ ."

8d **In a compound construction, use pronouns in the objective or subjective form according to their function in the sentence.**

Sally and *I* went to the movies. Tom went with Sally and *me.*

The coordinating conjunction *and* can create a compound construction—a doubled subject or object. These can sometimes mask how a pronoun functions in a sentence. When you have difficulty choosing between a subjective or objective pronoun in a compound construction, try this test: *Create a simplified sentence by dropping out the compound;* then *try choosing the pronoun.* With the compound gone in the simpler construction, you should be able to tell whether the pronoun operates as a subject or an object.

Compound subject

Pierre and Marie Curie worked collaboratively; together Marie and *he* discovered polonium and radium. [The subjective pronoun forms the second part of a compound subject.]

CONFUSED   Marie and *him* received the Nobel Prize in physics in 1903. [The pronoun subject is mistakenly put in the objective form.]

SIMPLIFIED   Marie received the Nobel Prize; *he* also received it. [In the simplified construction the need for the subjective pronoun is clear.]

REVISED   Marie and *he* received the Nobel Prize in 1903.

Compound object

The 1903 Nobel Prize in physics was awarded to Pierre and *her* for their work on radioactivity. [The objective pronoun is the object of a preposition in a compound construction.]

CONFUSED   An award was presented to Pierre and *she* in 1903, for their work on radioactivity. [In this construction, the pronoun functions as part of the preposition's compound object. Mistakenly, the pronoun is made subjective.]

SIMPLIFIED   The award was presented to Pierre; it was also presented to *her.*

REVISED   An award was presented to Pierre and *her* in 1903.

8e Pronouns paired with a noun take the same case as the noun.

1   For first-person plural pronouns (*we, us*) paired with a noun use the same case as the noun.

We first-year students face important challenges.
Transitions can be challenging for *us* first-year students.

The first-person plural pronoun *we* or *us* is sometimes placed before a plural noun to help establish the identity of the noun. Use the subjective-case *we* when the pronoun is paired with a noun subject and the objective-case *us* when the pronoun is paired with an object of a verb, verbal, or preposition. To test for the correct pronoun, simplify the sentence and *drop out* the paired noun. In the simpler sentence, you should be able to determine which pronoun case is required.

NONSTANDARD   *Us* strikers demand compensation. [*Strikers* is the subject of the sentence and the pronoun paired with it should be the subjective-case *we.*]

SIMPLIFIED   *We . . .* demand compensation. [The need for subjective-case *we* is now clear.]

REVISED   *We* strikers demand compensation.

NONSTANDARD   Give *we* strikers a fair share. [*Strikers* in this sentence is the indirect object of the verb *give,* and the pronoun paired with it should be the objective-case *us.*]

SIMPLIFIED   Give *us . . .* a fair share. [The need for objective-case *us* is now clear.]

REVISED   Give *us* strikers a fair share.

2 **In an appositive, a pronoun's case should match the case of the noun it renames.**

The executive officers—and only *they*—can attend.
Give this report to Linda—**her** and no one else.

Pronouns may occur in an **appositive**—a word or phrase that describes, identifies, or renames a noun in a sentence. If so, the pronoun must take the same case as the noun being renamed. Once again you can test for pronoun choice by simplifying the sentence: *Drop the noun being renamed out of the sentence.* The simpler sentence that remains will usually reveal what pronoun case is required.

RENAMED SUBJECT   For years Babe Ruth held the home run record; only one player—*he* alone—had hit the magic 714 home runs.

CONFUSED   Only one player—*him* alone—had hit the magic number.

SIMPLIFIED   *He* alone had hit the magic number.

8f **Choose the appropriate form of the pronouns *whose, who, whom, whoever,* and *whomever* depending on the pronoun's function.**

The basic forms of the relative pronouns *whose, who, whom, whoever,* and *whomever* are shown in the following table. A relative pronoun's form depends on its function within its own clause.

Forms of the Relative Pronoun "Who(m)/Who(m)ever"

Subjective	Objective	Possessive
who	whom	whose
whoever	whomever	—

1 **In a question, choose a subjective, objective, or possessive form of *who(m)* or *who(m)ever* according to the pronoun's function.**

Who is going? To *whom* are you writing? *Whose* birthday is it?

To test the correct choice for these pronouns at the beginning of a question, mentally *answer* the question, substituting the personal pronouns *I/me, we/us, he/him,* or *she/her* for *the relative pronoun.* Your choice of the subjective or objective form in the answer sentence will likely be quite clear, and it will be the same choice to make for the form of *who(m)* or *who(m)ever.*

QUESTION   (Who/whom) are you addressing?

ANSWER   You are addressing (he/*him*). [The choice of the objective form is clear.]

REVISED   *Whom* are you addressing? [The objective form is correct.]

QUESTION   For (who/whom) are you writing?

ANSWER   You are writing for (she/*her*). [The choice of the objective form is clear.]

REVISED   For *whom* are you writing? [The objective form is correct.]

The possessive form *whose* can begin a question if the pronoun must show possession of the noun that immediately follows. To determine whether a possessive pronoun is correct for a sentence, replace the initial pronoun in the question with *what* and then mentally answer that question: If the answer requires that you use *his, her, their,* or *its* in place of the relative pronoun, then choose the possessive form, *whose*.

QUESTION   What name goes on the envelope? [Is a pronoun in the possessive case—his/her/their/its—needed?]

POSSESSIVE   *Whose* name goes on the envelope?

2   **In a dependent clause, choose the subjective, objective, or possessive form of *who(m)* or *who(m)ever* according to the pronoun's function within the clause.**

Henry Taylor, *who* writes poems, lives in Virginia. Taylor, *whom* critics have praised, has a new book. The poet, *whose* book won a prize, lives quietly.

To choose the correct case for a relative pronoun in a dependent clause, eliminate the main clause temporarily; consider the pronoun's function *only* in the dependent clause. When deciding between the subjective or objective forms, apply the following tests.

Determine whether the relative pronoun functions as the subject of a dependent clause.

If the relative pronoun is followed immediately by a verb, you should probably use the subjective-case *who* or *whoever.* To be sure that the choice of pronouns is correct, substitute the word *I, we, you, he,* or *she* for *who* or *whoever.* Does this yield a legitimate sentence? If so, the choice of the subjective case is correct.

SUBJECTIVE   Your request will be of concern to (whoever/whomever) gets it.

SIMPLIFIED   (Whoever/whomever) gets it. [The pronoun is followed by a verb, *gets,* so the likely choice of pronouns will be *whoever.*]

REVISED   Your request will be of concern to *whoever* gets it.

Determine whether the relative pronoun functions as an object in the dependent clause.

If the relative pronoun is followed immediately by a noun or by the pronoun *I, we, you, he, she, few, some, many, most, it,* or *they,* you should probably use the objective-case *whom* or *whomever.* To be sure of the choice, consider the dependent clause as if it were a sentence by itself (without the main clause). Rearrange the clause into normal word order and then substitute the word *him, her,* or *them* for the relative pronoun. If one of these newly substituted pronouns fits into the sentence as an object of a verb, verbal, or preposition, then the choice of the objective-case *whom* or *whomever* is correct.

OBJECTIVE   Please send this to *whomever* it might interest. [The relative pronoun is followed by the pronoun *it,* so the choice of pronoun will likely be objective form. A second test: The objective-case *them,* substituted for *whomever,* yields a rearranged sentence, "It might interest *them.*"]

Determine whether the relative pronoun needs to show possession.

If the relative pronoun beginning a dependent clause needs to show possession, then you should use the possessive-case *whose.* Confirm the choice by substituting the word *his, her, their,* or *its* for the relative pronoun. A sentence should result when the dependent clause is considered by itself.

POSSESSIVE   Daly, *whose* theories on urban wildlife have generated heated discussion, believes that we can profit by finding nature in our cities. [The possessive-case *his* yields a sentence: "*His* theories on urban wildlife. . . ."]

 Choose the case of a pronoun in the second part of a comparison depending on the meaning intended.

I studied Keats more than *him* (more than I studied Arnold—him).
I studied Keats more than *she* (more than Margo—she—studied Keats).

The words *than* and *as* create a comparison.

Calcutta is more densely populated than New York.

The new magneto engines are as efficient as traditional combustion engines.

For brevity's sake, writers and speakers often omit the second part of a comparison. Written in their complete form, the preceding examples would read as follows.

CRITICAL DECISIONS

Challenge your sentences: Apply a test for *who* and *whom*

In a clause the relative pronouns *who* and *whom* take the place of nouns (or pronouns) that function as subjects or objects. Choosing the correct relative pronoun requires that you see that pronoun in relation to the words immediately following. You must examine the broader context of the clause in which the pronoun is located. Two questions should help you to choose between *who* and *whom* correctly.

■ Is the relative pronoun followed by a verb?

—"Yes": choose the subjective-case *who* or *whoever.*

A relative pronoun followed by a verb indicates the pronoun occupies the subject position of the clause. To confirm this choice, substitute *I, we, you, he,* or *she* for the pronoun.

Clinton, *who* won by a landslide in the electoral college, did not win as convincingly in the popular vote. [*Who* is followed by a verb, and when it is converted to *he* it yields a sentence: "*He* won by a landslide. . . ."]

—"No": choose the objective-case *whom* or *whomever.* See the next test.

■ Is the relative pronoun followed by a noun or by any of these pronouns: *I, we, you, he, she, few, some, many, most, it, they?*

—"Yes": choose the objective-case *whom* or *whomever.*

A relative pronoun followed by a noun or one of the listed pronouns indicates that the normal order of the clause (subject-verb-object) has been rearranged, suggesting the need for a pronoun in its objective form. To confirm your choice of *whom* or *whomever,* consider the pronoun and the words immediately following. Rearrange these words and substitute *him, her,* or *them* for the relative pronoun.

Clinton, *whom* most analysts counted out of the presidential race, surprised supporters and detractors alike. [*Whom* is followed by *most,* and when it is converted to *him* it yields a sentence: "Most analysts counted *him* out."]

ADDITIONAL EXERCISE C

Compose ten sentences, each of which includes either *who* or *whom.* Then review each sentence, applying the test for proper use of the pronouns. In which cases did you use the correct form? If you made an error, how can you make sure that you use the correct form in the future?

Calcutta is more densely populated than New York is densely populated.

The new magneto engines are as efficient as traditional combustion engines are efficient.

A comparison links two complete clauses. The brief form of a comparison is its "clipped" form; the fully expressed comparison, its "complete" form. When you compare people and use pronouns in the second part of your comparison, be sure to express your exact meaning. At times, the pronoun in the second part of a comparison will take the place of a noun functioning as a subject, in which case use the subjective form: *he, she, we.*

COMPLETE J. M. Synge is not as famous as James Joyce is famous. [*James Joyce* functions as a subject in the second part of the comparison. A pronoun replacement for *Joyce* would take the subjective form.]

COMPLETE J. M. Synge is not as famous as *he* is famous.

CLIPPED J. M. Synge is not as famous as *he*.

At times, the pronoun in the second part of a comparison will take the place of a noun functioning as an object, in which case use the objective form: *him, her, us.*

COMPLETE We know James Joyce better than we know J. M. Synge. [*J. M. Synge* functions as the object of the verb *know* in the second part of the comparison. A pronoun replacement for *Synge* would take the objective form.]

COMPLETE We know James Joyce better than we know *him*.

CLIPPED We know James Joyce better than *him*.

Avoid "clipping" the second part of a comparison unless all its parts are obvious. If you do clip the comparison, mentally recreate the full comparison to determine the function of the noun your pronoun is replacing. When that noun functions as a subject, use pronouns in the subjective form; when that noun functions as an object, use pronouns in the objective form.

EXERCISE 3

1. I
2. he
3. Who   she
4. Whom
5. *you*   her
6. *You*   *she*
7. we
8. *Whomever*   whom
9. *who*
10. His   *our*

EXERCISE 3

In the following sentences, correct the usage of the italicized pronouns. If a pronoun choice is correct, circle the pronoun.

Example: Anne told me it was Simon's fault; but between you and *I,* she's as much to blame as *him.*

Anne told me it was Simon's fault; but between you and *me,* she's as much to blame as *he.* [Pronouns that follow a preposition must be objective case: thus, between you and me. The second part of the comparison requires a subjective-case pronoun: She is to blame as much as *he is to blame.*]

1. It was *me* who asked Helen to go to the museum.
2. It was not *him* who called.
3. "*Whom* may I ask is calling? Yes, this is *her.*"
4. "To *Who* It May Concern" is not an especially effective opening for a business letter.
5. He gave the present to both *you* and *she.*
6. *You* and *she* have been friends for many years.
7. A group that can't afford cutbacks in health care is *us* salaried employees.
8. *Whomever* the people elect is the person *who* we depend upon.
9. Richard Nixon, *who* was elected, resigned from office.
10. *Him* resigning was the first presidential abdication in *our* history.

CHAPTER 9

Verbs

The verb forms you select will convey three important messages that are the focus of this chapter: *tense*—an indication of when an action or state of being occurs; *mood*—your judgment as to whether a statement is a fact, a command, or an unreal or hypothetical condition contrary to fact; and *voice*—your emphasis on the actor of a sentence or on the object acted on.

VERB FORMS

9a   Using the principal parts of regular verbs consistently

All verbs other than *be* have two basic forms and three principal parts; these five forms and parts are the foundation for all the varied uses of verbs. A full dictionary entry may present these forms and parts: base form, -s form, past tense, past participle, and present participle.

The Principal Parts of Regular Verbs

Base form	Present tense (-s form)	Past tense	Past participle	Present participle
share	shares	shared	shared	sharing
start	starts	started	started	starting
climb	climbs	climbed	climbed	climbing

Most verbs in the dictionary are **regular** in that they follow the simple, predictable pattern shown in the box, in which the past tense and past participle are identical. (For regular verbs, only base forms appear in most dictionaries.)

1   Recognizing the forms of regular verbs

Alison *walks* to the theater.   Yesterday, she *walked* there.
She *has walked* often.   She *is walking* there now.

KEY FEATURES

This chapter takes a practical approach to verbs, opening with a discussion of the principal parts of regular verbs. As in chapter 3 (Case in Nouns and Pronouns), the question of nonstandard forms is addressed in terms of accepted use in formal academic prose. In fact, early in the chapter the point is made that even among speakers of standard English, rapid conversation eliminates the *-s* and *-ed* endings. This approach is consistent with Part II (Writing as a Process), placing the writer's choices in the context of the purpose of the discourse and the needs of the audience: In everyday speech, endings are eliminated without consequence, while in formal discourse the appropriate use of endings is essential. A list of irregular verbs is provided for quick reference in case of confusion over appropriate forms. In discussing auxiliaries and modals, the chapter provides only as much information as students need to make appropriate choices. The section on intransitive verbs contains a brief discussion of three of the more troublesome pairs of words in the language: *sit/set, lie/lay*, and *rise/raise*. All of the above topics are covered in such a way that the chapter can be used as an easy reference tool; the student will not become bogged down with extensive linguistic analysis. Tense, voice, and mood are dealt with similarly, paying particular attention to sequencing tenses within a sentence, a problem many students face in written discourse. Exercises provide practice in choosing, identifying, and correcting verb forms, as well as in commenting on the meaning of a passage with respect to the tense used by the writer.

SPOTLIGHT ON COMMON ERRORS—VERBS

These are errors commonly associated with verb use. For full explanations and suggested revisions, follow the cross-references to chapter sections.

TENSE ERRORS: Keep clear the time relationships among two or more verbs in closely linked clauses or sentences.

- **If you refer to *past events occurring at roughly the same time,* use past-tense verbs (see 9f):**

  FAULTY

  Tom *had traveled* where jobs *presented* themselves. [past perfect/past]
  Tom *traveled* where jobs *had presented* themselves. [past/past perfect]
  [The different tenses wrongly suggest that the events happened at different times.]

  REVISED

  past event   past event
  Tom *traveled* where jobs *presented* themselves. [past/past].
  [The sentence refers to events that occurred at the same time.]

- **If you refer to *past events occurring one before the other,* use the past tense for the more recent event and the past perfect for the earlier event.**

  FAULTY

  I remembered Mrs. Smith, who showed me kindness. [past/past]
  [The tenses wrongly suggest that actions occurred at the same time.]

  REVISED

  later event   earlier event
  I *remembered* Mrs. Smith, who *had shown* me kindness. [past/past perfect]
  [Mrs. Smith's "showing" occurred before the remembering.]

  BUT if a key word (such as *before* or *after*) establishes a clear time relation, then the past perfect form of the verb is not used.

  earlier event   later event
  I *was* unable to follow current events, *before* Mrs. Smith *showed* me how to read. [past/past]

- **Avoid abrupt tense shifts between closely linked sentences (see 16b).**

  FAULTY TENSE SHIFT

  The problem started when Fred forgot his appointment. Today he comes in late again.

FOR DISCUSSION

Since most students have problems with only a few of these common errors, you might want to initiate a class discussion of errors most relevant to your students. Ask students to identify from the Spotlight on Common Errors examples of usage familiar to them and to make their own list of common errors. Students can then discuss the function of verb tense and form in sentences, thereby reinforcing their understanding of verb use. (In large classes, this activity might begin with small groups: The groups will identify their common errors, and then the class as a whole will discuss the list of errors compiled from each group's report.)

REVISED

The problem started when Fred forgot his appointment. Today he came in late again.
[All action is in the past tense.]

ERRORS OF VERB FORM occur when writers confuse regular verbs with irregular verbs; the moods of verbs; and transitive verbs like *lay* with intransitive verbs like *lie*.

■ **Regular/irregular : Know whether a verb is regular or irregular (see 9b).**

FAULTY	REVISED
I begun the story.	I began the story.
I had drank three full glasses.	I had drunk three full glasses.

■ **Mood: When writing about an event that is unreal or hypothetical, use a verb's subjunctive forms. Expressions such as *recommend, suggest*, and *it is important* signal an unreal or hypothetical event (see 9h).**

FAULTY	REVISED
I recommend that Sarah builds a playhouse.	I recommend that Sarah *build* a playhouse.

In sentences expressing unreal conditions and beginning with *if,* use *were* in the first part of the sentence and *would* as a helping verb in the second part (see 9h).

FAULTY	REVISED
If it was any colder, the pipes will freeze.	*If it were* any colder, the pipes *would freeze.*

■ **Transitive/intransitive: Use a transitive verb (*set, lay, raise*) to show an action transferred from an actor to an object. Use an intransitive verb (*sit, lie, rise*) to limit action to the subject (see 9d).**

FAULTY	REVISED
Sit the books on the table.	*Set* the books on the table. [Transitive]
It hurts only when I set.	It hurts only when I *sit*. [Intransitive]
I think I'll lay down.	I think I'll *lie* down [Intransitive]
Lie the blanket in the corner.	*Lay* the blanket . . . [Transitive]

The forms of *lie* and *lay* are particularly tricky. (See page 238.)

FAULTY	REVISED
Yesterday, I laid down to rest.	Yesterday, I *lay* down to rest.
I had lain the book on the table.	I had *laid* the book on the table.

TEACHING IDEAS

In order to acquaint students with using the dictionary, ask them to look up and list the principal parts of five regular verbs. In addition to revealing one of the features of a dictionary, this activity will also reinforce the distinctions between the principal parts.

Base form + the *-s form* = *present tense*

The **base** (or infinitive) **form** of a verb—often called its **dictionary form**—is the base from which all changes are made. Use the base form of a verb with *no* ending for occasions when the action of a verb is present for plural nouns or for the personal pronouns *I, we, you,* or *they.*

Alaska's Pacific mountains *create* a region of high peaks, broad valleys, and numerous island fjords.

The *-s form* of a verb (creates, tries, loves) occurs with third-person, singular subjects when an action is in the present. A verb's *-s* form (add *-s* or *-es* to a verb) is used in three instances: with the personal pronouns *he, she,* or *it;* with any noun that can be replaced by these pronouns; and with a number of indefinite pronouns (such as *something* or *no one*), which are often considered singular.

Alaska's north slope *consists* of the plateaus and coastal regions north of the Brooks mountain range.

Difficulties with subject-verb agreement occur when a writer is unsure whether to use a verb's base form or *-s* form in a sentence. For a discussion of subject-verb agreement, see chapter 10.

Past-tense form

The **past tense** of a verb indicates that an action has been completed in the past. The regular verbs follow a predictable pattern in forming the past tense by taking the suffix *-ed* or *-d.*

Secretary of State William H. Seward *arranged* for the purchase of Alaska from Russia in 1867.

Irregular verbs follow no such pattern: Their base forms change their root spelling to show the past tense (see 9b).

Two participle forms

For regular verbs, the form of the **past participle** is identical to that of the past tense. A verb's past participle is used in three ways: paired with *have,* the past participle functions as a main verb; paired with *be,* the past participle forms a passive construction; and, paired with a noun or pronoun, the past participle functions as an adjective.

With the Russian treasury *depleted* [adjective] after the Crimean War, the Tsar *had decided* [main verb] to sell the western-most part of his empire, which *was colonized* [passive construction] very sparsely by Russians.

ESL NOTE Both past and present participles have uses as adjective modifiers, usually placed before the nouns or pronouns modified—as in *a confused speaker* or *a confusing speaker.* Note that while the past and present participles from this verb are related in meaning, they work in opposite directions on the word modified (see 44a-1).

The **present participle,** the *-ing* form of the verb, has three uses: it functions as a main verb of a sentence and shows continuing action when paired with a form of *be* (*am, are, is, was, were*); it functions as an adjective when paired with a noun or pronoun; or it functions as a noun, in which case it is called a *gerund* (see 7a).

The *decimating* [gerund] of seal herds *was proceeding* [main verb] at an *alarming* [adjective] rate.

ESL NOTE The role of a gerund in a sentence is determined by the verb being used. Certain verbs pair idiomatically with gerunds, as in *go swimming* or *enjoy swimming* (see 43e-2). Gerunds can be objects of certain prepositions that are idiomatically determined by the preceding verb: *I have reasons for coming* versus *I decided on walking.* Certain other verbs are paired idiomatically with the other verbal noun form, the infinitive (see 43e-2).

2 Revising nonstandard verb forms by using standard *-s* and *-ed* forms

NONSTANDARD	He walk home.
REVISED	He walked home.

In rapid conversation, many people skip over *-s* and *-ed* endings. In some dialects the base (or infinitive) form of the verb is used in place of verbs with *-s* and *-ed* endings. Writers of standard academic English, however, need to observe the regular forms.

NONSTANDARD   She was *ask* to read this assignment. She *like* to stay up late and she *be* still wide awake.

REVISED   She was *asked* to read it. She *likes* to stay up late and she *is* still wide awake. [Base forms have been replaced by standard verb forms with *-s* and *-ed* endings.]

9b Learning the forms of irregular verbs

Most verbs are regular in that they form the past tense and past participle with the suffixes *-ed* or *-d*. An irregular verb will form its past tense and past participle by altering the spelling of the base verb, as in *build/built* or *bring/brought.* A dictionary entry for an irregular verb shows the principal parts and basic forms of a verb as the first information in the entry. This will show you when a verb is irregular—when it does not take an *-ed* ending in its past tense and past participle forms. Because irregular verbs are some of the most commonly used words in the language, most speakers and readers are accustomed to, and expect, them. You should take care to use correct irregular forms. Memorize troublesome forms or look them up as necessary.

the reasons for acknowledging the place of standard and nonstandard English, could provoke a meaningful discussion.

ESL ALERT

A common ESL mistake is to omit the *-s* in the third-person singular, present tense. Be sure to warn that verbs of perception ("see," "hear") and verbs of stasis or state of being ("be," "appear," "seem," "remember," "forget," "love") require the simple present or simple past and cannot be progressive. Discussing the difference between "I think he should be president" (an intellectual position) as opposed to "I am thinking about what to do this summer" (a temporary thought) should help clarify the problem. Also compare "I drink coffee" (a consistent preference) and "I am drinking coffee" (a current action).

ESL ALERT

Certain English verbs are troublesome because English has several verbs where the ESL student's native language has only one. For example, Japanese, Spanish, Italian, and French have only one word for the English "do" and "make." It helps to note that "do" often, though not always, involves mechanical activity, whereas "make" is creative: The teacher *makes* up the exercise, but the student *does* the exercise. There are also a number of confusing idiomatic "do" and "make" expressions, such as "do the right thing," "do someone a favor," "do good," "do away with," as opposed to "make a speech," "make mistakes," "make a living," "make arrangements," "make an impression," "make progress," "make up one's mind," and so forth. "Make" can be confused with "create" as well: We "make (or create) a mess" but "create (but never "make") disorder," with "make" having more physical and conventional applications than its more formal equivalent. We create poetry, confusion, progeny, and discord. In general, students whose languages have "all purpose" verbs (a word like "make" used for many activities) should be advised to choose a specific English verb if a familiar "make" construction does not come to mind: not "make" but "cook a meal," "write a paper," "build a house."

"Say" and "tell" cause the same confusion for the same reason. It might help to give a series of examples of usage: tell time, tell a story or joke,

Be

The most frequently used verb in our language, *be*, is also the only verb with more than five forms. It functions both as the main verb in a sentence and as a frequently used auxiliary verb (see 9c and 7a-3). The eight forms of *be* are shown in the box.

The Principal Parts of *be*

Base form	*Present tense*	*Past tense*
(to) be	he, she, it *is*	he, she, it, *was*
	I *am*	I *was*
	we, you, they *are*	we, you, they *were*
	Past participle	*Present participle*
	been	being

The following box contains the principal parts for a partial list of irregular verbs. Remember that the past participle is the form of the verb used with the auxiliary *have*. Without the auxiliary, it functions as an adjective.

Some Irregular Verb Forms

Base form	*Past tense*	*Past participle*
bear	bore	borne, born
beat	beat	beaten
become	became	become
begin	began	begun
bend	bent	bent
bind	bound	bound
bite	bit	bit, bitten
bleed	bled	bled
blow	blew	blown
break	broke	broken
bring	brought	brought
build	built	built
burn	burned, burnt	burned, burnt
burst	burst	burst

(continued)

Base form	Past tense	Past participle
buy	bought	bought
catch	caught	caught
choose	chose	chosen
cling	clung	clung
come	came	come
cost	cost	cost
cut	cut	cut
dig	dug	dug
dive	dove, dived	dived
do (does)	did	done
draw	drew	drawn
drink	drank	drunk
drive	drove	driven
eat	ate	eaten
fall	fell	fallen
feed	fed	fed
feel	felt	felt
fight	fought	fought
find	found	found
flee	fled	fled
fling	flung	flung
fly	flew	flown
forbid	forbade, forbad	forbidden *or* forbid
forget	forgot	forgot *or* forgotten
freeze	froze	frozen
get	got	got, gotten
give	gave	given
go	went	gone
grow	grew	grown
hang[1]	hung	hung
have (has)	had	had
hear	heard	heard
hide	hid	hidden
hit	hit	hit
keep	kept	kept
know	knew	known
lead	led	led
leave	left	left
lend	lent	lent
lose	lost	lost
make	made	made
mean	meant	meant
pay	paid	paid
prove	proved	proved *or* proven
read	read	read

(continued)

[1]*Hang* as an irregular verb means to *suspend*. When *hang* means to *execute*, it is regular: *hang, hanged, hanged.*

tell me, tell the difference, but say hello, say grace, say that we should go, say "Let's go!," but never "say me" or "explain me." ESL students also tend to confuse verbs of perception with verbs of action, as in "hear" and "listen to," "see" and "watch," a distinction that may be made differently in other languages.

Both Japanese and Spanish speakers tend to use the past tense inappropriately, not for the historical past, but for regular, repeated behavior.

The present perfect tense does not exist in many Asian languages, so the idea of a verb that connects the past with the present, either because of action started in the past and continuing to the present ("I have lived here for many years") or because of action completed in the past but affecting a present course of action ("I have already eaten"), needs special attention.

Greeks will tend to overuse the present progressive, treating it as equivalent to a simple present tense. Indians and Pakistanis will tend to use the present progressive tense for all situations: present, future, and maybe even past. Slavic language speakers will use the simple present in the same way.

ADDITIONAL EXERCISE A

Choose five of the irregular verbs (other than *be*) from the list provided and construct three sentences with each: one using the base form, one using the past tense form, and one using the past participle form. (If you have difficulty using the past participle form, consult the sections on tense and voice below.)

REFERENCES

SHAUGHNESSY, MINA P. *Errors and Expectations: A Guide for the Teacher of Basic Writing.* New York: Oxford UP, 1977. Chapter 4. Some students have difficulty with inflections because of the absence of inflection in their own speech.

FARR, MARCIA, and HARVEY DANIELS. *Language Diversity and Writing Instruction.* New York: ERIC Clearinghouse on Urban Education and Urbana: NCTE, 1986. Nonstandard dialects present specific challenges to educators; appropriate teaching strategies can help students master standard forms.

(continued)

EPES, MARY. "Tracing Errors to the Sources: A Study of the Encoding Processes of Adult Basic Writers." *Journal of Basic Writing* 41 (1985): 4–33. Speakers of nonstandard English can benefit from traditional grammar instruction.

SMITHERMAN, GENEVA. *Talkin and Testifyin.* Boston: Houghton, 1977. Speakers of Black English use an abbreviated inflection system, and sometimes transfer that use to their writing.

WOLFRAM, WALT, and RALPH W. FASOLD. *The Study of Social Dialects in American English.* Englewood Cliffs NJ: Prentice, 1974. Contains an extensive analysis of verb forms in Black English, including a discussion of problems related to education.

TEACHING IDEAS

Most students will recognize in this list several verbs that pose problems for them. It might be useful to ask students to cull from these pages a personal list of problem irregular verbs. For each verb, have students write out the base, past, and past participle forms of the verb, followed by three sentences using each form. This list can be used both for study and for reference as students edit their papers.

ESL ALERT

ESL students will need to be encouraged to simply memorize a list like the one in 9b in order to master irregular verbs. Spanish speakers frequently confuse "fall/fell" with "feel/felt". "Lie/lay/lain" versus "lay/laid/laid" versus "lie/lied/lied" confuse all. The fact that "lie" "sit," and "rise" do not take objects, while "lay," "set," and "raise" do helps facilitate use, as in "She lay in the sun" (location) versus "She laid *her books* on the floor" (first object, then location); "She sat in the chair" (location) versus "She set *the table* for four" (object) or "His words set *her mind* at rest" (object); "The sun rises every morning" (time) versus "They raised *the flag*" (object) or "They raised *chickens*" (object).

ESL ALERT

There is little logic to English speakers' use of prepositions, and such use differs in British and American English. In fact, American usage can vary as well ("stand on line"—East Coast; "stand in line"—other regions). ESL students may *never* master English prepositions com-

Some Irregular Verb Forms (continued)

Base form	Past tense	Past participle
ride	rode	ridden
ring	rang	rung
run	ran	run
say	said	said
see	saw	seen
seek	sought	sought
send	sent	sent
shake	shook	shaken
shine[2]	shone	shone
sing	sang	sung
sink	sank	sunk
sleep	slept	slept
speak	spoke	spoken
spend	spent	spent
spring	sprang, sprung	sprung
stand	stood	stood
steal	stole	stolen
stick	stuck	stuck
strive	strove	striven
swear	swore	sworn
swim	swam	swum
swing	swung	swung
take	took	taken
teach	taught	taught
tear	tore	torn
tell	told	told
think	thought	thought
throw	threw	thrown
wake	woke, waked	waked, woken
wear	wore	worn
wind	wound	wound
wring	wrung	wrung
write	wrote	written

[2]*Shine* as an irregular verb means to *emit light.* When *shine* means to *polish,* it is regular: *shine, shined, shined.*

9c   Using auxiliary verbs

An **auxiliary** (or helping) **verb** is combined with the base form of a verb or the present or past participle form to establish tense, mood, and voice in a sentence. This combination of verbs creates a **verb phrase.** The most frequently used auxiliaries are *be, have,* and *do. Be* functions as an auxiliary when it combines with the *-ing* form of a verb to create the progressive tenses (as in I *am going*). *Have* functions as an auxiliary when it combines with the past participle form of a verb to create the perfect tenses (as in I *have gone*). *Do* functions as an auxiliary when it combines with the base form of a verb to form questions, to show emphasis, and to show negation. (*Do you care? I do care. I don't care.*)

ESL NOTE   For illustrations of the varied uses for auxiliary verbs in English, see 43c–d.

1   **Use modal auxiliaries to refine meaning.**

> The producers *should* agree to this.   They *must* agree.
> They *might* agree to these terms.

When paired with the base form of a verb, a **modal auxiliary** expresses urgency, obligation, likelihood, possibility, and so on: *may, might, must, ought to, should, would.* Unlike the auxiliaries *be, have,* and *do,* most of these modal auxiliaries do not change form. They follow singular or plural subjects in the first, second, or third person. Modal auxiliaries can follow the pronouns *I, we, you, he, she, one, it, they.* Observe how meaning in a sentence changes depending on the choice of modal auxiliary.

> I must resign.   I ought to resign.   I would resign.
> I could resign.   I can resign.   I might resign.

Modal auxiliaries can combine with other auxiliaries to create complex verbal phrases that require careful use.

> I ought to have resigned.   I might have been resigning.

The auxiliaries *will* and *shall* establish the future tense.

> When shall I resign?   She will resign then.

ESL NOTE   For illustrations of how modal auxiliaries affect word order and verb constructions, see 43c.

2   **Revise nonstandard auxiliaries by using standard forms of *be.***

> **FAULTY**   She going to class.   **REVISED**   She is going to class.

Some dialects form present-tense auxiliary constructions with variations on the base form of *be.* For written academic English, these forms must be revised.

NONSTANDARD   She *be* singing beautifully. [The base form of *be* is a nonstandard usage here. The *-s* form of the verb is needed.]

NONSTANDARD   She singing a beautiful melody. [The *be* form has been dropped.]

REVISED   She *is* singing a beautiful melody. [The base form of *be* in the auxiliary has been replaced by the standard *-s* form.]

pletely and *should not be expected to.* There are some rules to help with prepositions of location, but even a seemingly bilingual student can be recognized as a non-native speaker by occasional preposition abuse.

Multiword prepositions will be the hardest ones for non-native speakers to recognize as prepositions, and prepositions used in two- and three-part verbs—called *particles* (see 43f)—will confuse every non-native speaker of English.

ESL EXERCISE

Write down as many two- and three-part verbs as you can using (1) get (2) check (3) look. Go over these in class, discussing the way the preposition or particle changes the meaning.

ESL students can *never* get enough practice with these forms, and not knowing them or misusing them can create confusion and misunderstanding.

ADDITIONAL EXERCISE B

When is an auxiliary not an auxiliary? In the following sentences, identify the verbs *be, have,* and *do* as auxiliary verbs or main verbs.

1. Melinda *has* gone to school already.
2. She *did* not complete her homework last night.
3. Christine *is* a senior in high school this year.
4. Both girls *have* regularly scheduled study hours each evening.
5. Melinda *was* planning to finish her homework in the morning.

Answers:

1. auxiliary; 2. auxiliary; 3. main; 4. main; 5. auxiliary

ESL ALERT

Spanish speakers tend to misuse "should" as an equivalent of "expect to" in sentences where native speakers would mean obligation, saying, for example, "I should see him," when they mean "I expect to see him" rather than "I have an obligation or need to see him." However, they may not use "should" properly for expectation, saying "He would be here any minute" instead of "He should be here any minute."

Students trained in British English might end to avoid "do have" formations, particularly in questions: "Have you any potatoes?"

(continued)

Most ESL students find the distinction between "have" as a verb and "have" as an auxiliary difficult to make, especially in the perfect forms ("has had"/"had had"), and the use of "could" for ability, possibility, and politeness confusing:

"He could play the piano well."
"You could be right about that."
"Could you please help me with this?"

There may be some confusion of contractions, especially the use of "-s" inappropriately: "She's some eggs" for "She has some eggs."

EXERCISE 1

1. *Had* is the auxiliary; *let* is the main verb.
2. *Showed* is the verb.
3. *Consists* is the verb.
4. *Will* is the auxiliary; *bend* is the main verb.
5. *Believed* is the verb.

EXERCISE 2

1. left
2. go
3. will be forbidden
4. has gotten
5. is
6. seek
7. have arisen

GROUP ACTIVITY

The different meanings achieved through the use of auxiliaries and modal auxiliaries make for an interesting group activity. Assign each group a main verb, and ask them first to compose a sentence using that verb in its base form. Then have groups alter the sentence by pairing the verb with as many modal auxiliaries as possible and then combining the modals with other auxiliaries, creating a new sentence each time. For each sentence, ask students to explain the shifts in meaning as they use different modals and auxiliaries.

ESL ALERT

List the request forms in English from the least polite (the command form) to the most polite.
   This activity should allow teachers to discuss the differences between such forms as "Might I help you?" and "Would you be so kind as to . . . ?" Note in particular how the choice of form relates

EXERCISE 1

Identify the main verb and any auxiliary verb associated with it in the sentences that follow.

> *Example:* Almost 300 years ago, Isaac Newton separated visible light into a spectrum of colors. (The verb is *separated*.)

1. Newton had let light pass through a prism.
2. The experiment showed the following.
3. White light consists of different colors, ranging from violet at one end of the spectrum to red at the other.
4. Light of different colors will bend at different angles in passing through a prism.
5. Newton believed that light was a stream of particles.

EXERCISE 2

In the sentences that follow, use the appropriate form of the irregular verb.

> *Example:* Today, many businesses have (grow) _____ to recognize the importance of preparing workers for assignments in other nations. [grown]

Cultural differences have (leave) __1__ many workers feeling adrift in foreign countries. When employees (go) __2__ abroad, they cannot be sure if behaviors considered appropriate at home will be (forbid) __3__ in the host country, and vice versa. Such uncertainty has (get) __4__ some younger employees into embarrassing situations. Most managers agree that it (be) __5__ better to (seek) __6__ advice before traveling abroad than to react to problems after they have (arise) __7__ .

9d   Using transitive and intransitive verbs

Action verbs are classified as *transitive* and *intransitive*. A **transitive verb** (marked with the abbreviation **tr.** in the dictionary) transfers an action from a subject to an object; the action of an **intransitive verb** is limited to the subject of a sentence.

1   Distinguish between verbs that take direct objects and those that do not.

Sharon studied.   Sharon studied her lecture notes.

A large number of verbs regularly take a direct object and are always transitive; others never take an object and are always intransitive.

TRANSITIVE   The politician kissed the baby. [The transitive verb *kissed* transfers action from *politician* to *baby*.]

INTRANSITIVE   The politician smiled. [An action is performed, but no object is acted on.]

Many verbs can have both a transitive and an intransitive sense. Such "two-way" verbs will take a direct object or not depending on their use.

INTRANSITIVE   She runs every day. [The verb takes no object.]

TRANSITIVE   She runs a big business. [The verb has changed meaning and now takes an object.]

ESL NOTE   Note that a transitive verb is the *only* type that can be made passive (see 9g); neither intransitive nor most linking verbs can take a passive form in modern English. For specifics on transitive verbs and passive constructions, see 43a-1.

2   **Avoid confusion between the verbs *sit/set, lie/lay, rise/raise*.**

Set the books on the table.
It hurts only when I *sit*.
I think I'll *lie* down for a rest.
Lay the blanket in the corner.

Difficulties in distinguishing between transitive and intransitive verbs lead to misuse of *sit/set, lie/lay,* and *rise/raise*. The forms of these verbs are shown in the box on page 238. Because the meaning of the verbs in each pairing is somewhat similar, the verbs are sometimes used interchangeably in speech. In formal writing, however, careful distinctions should be maintained: the first verb in each pair is intransitive—it takes no object—while the second verb is transitive.

Sit is normally an intransitive verb; its action is limited to the subject.

>   adverb
> You sit *on the bench.*

Set is a transitive verb. It transfers action to an object, which must be present in the sentence.

>   object   adverb
> You set <u>*the papers*</u> *on the bench.*

Lie is an intransitive verb; its action is limited to the subject.

>   adverb
> I lie *on the couch.*

Lay is a transitive verb. It transfers action to an object, which must be present in the sentence.

>   object   adverb
> I lay <u>*the pillow*</u> *on the couch.*

Rise is an intransitive verb; its action is limited to the subject.

>   adverb
> I rise *in the morning.*

not simply to the degree of formality and of politeness but to the type of relation between the people involved. Would it be correct to ask a roommate with whom one is very close, "Might I help you?" Would it be correct to tell a university president to whom one wishes to show respect, "Come help me!"?

ESL EXERCISE

Write two letters to a friend.
1. The first should use hypothetical forms like "if," "unless," and "suppose" as well as advice forms like "should," "had better," and "have to" to give suggestions to a friend who is coming from your country to visit you at your school.
2. The second should follow the same pattern as the first, but should explain that your friend did not have a good time because of a failure to follow your advice and suggestions. Use past tense advice forms like "should have" and unreal conditionals like "if you had."

REFERENCE

HALLIDAY, M. A. K. *System and Function in Language.* Ed. Gunther Kress. London: Oxford UP, 1976. Chapter 11. Traditional definitions of transitive verbs are incomplete.

ADDITIONAL EXERCISE C

Compose six sentences, one each for the verbs *sit/set, lie/lay,* and *rise/raise.* If you need help in distinguishing between any of the pairs, consult the explanations provided in the text.

Raise is a transitive verb. It transfers action to an object, which must be present in the sentence.

object   adverb
I raise *the flag each morning.*

The Principal Parts of *sit/set, lie/lay,* and *rise/raise*

Base form	Present tense	Past tense	Past participle	Present participle
sit	sits	sat	sat	sitting
set	sets	set	set	setting
lie	lies	lay	lain	lying
lay	lays	laid	laid	laying
rise	rises	rose	risen	rising
raise	raises	raised	raised	raising

EXERCISE 3

1. set
2. sat
3. lay
4. raised
5. rose

EXERCISE 3

Choose the appropriate form of *sit/set, lie/lay,* or *rise/raise* in these sentences.

> *Example:* A squirrel was (*sit/set*) _____ on a picnic table.
> A squirrel was *sitting* on a picnic table.

1. A man walked by and (*sit/set*) _____ a newspaper on a nearby table.
2. He then (*sit/set*) _____ down and unfolded the paper.
3. From one pocket he produced a tomato, which he (*lie/lay*) _____ on the paper.
4. From another pocket came a salt shaker, which he (*rise/raise*) _____ ceremoniously.
5. The squirrel (*rise/raise*) _____ at the scent of food.

EXERCISE 4

1. hoped   left
2. was
3. fought   be
4. transferred   battering   were
5. had expanded

EXERCISE 4

In the following sentences, fill in the blanks with the appropriate form of the verb indicated in parentheses.

> *Example:* The First World War _____ (begin) as an Old World War.
> The First World War *began* as an Old World War.

1. Everything about the war expressed the world that Americans _____ (hope) they had _____ (leave) behind.
2. That Old World _____ (be) a battlefield of national ambitions, religious persecutions, and language barriers.
3. European armies had _____ (fight) over whether a nation's boundary should _____ (be) on one side or the other of a narrow river.

4. Old World monarchs had _____ (transfer) land from one flag to another, _____ (barter) people as if they _____ (be) mere real estate.
5. In the 1800s, the English, French, and German empires _____ (expand) across the globe.

TENSE

9e   Understanding the uses of verb tenses

A verb's tense indicates when an action has occurred or when a subject exists in a given state. There are three basic tenses in English: *past*, *present*, and *future*. Each has a **perfect** form, which indicates a completed action; each has a **progressive** form, which indicates ongoing action; and each has a **perfect progressive** form, which indicates ongoing action that will be completed at some definite time.

1   The varied uses of the present tense

Present: I start the engine.
  Present perfect: I have started the engine.
  Present progressive: I am starting the engine.
  Present perfect progressive: I have been starting the engine.

The simple present

A verb's base form is the present-tense form for first- and second-person subjects, singular or plural (*I, we, you* play), as well as plural third-person subjects (*they* play). A present-tense verb for a third-person, singular noun or pronoun ends with the suffix *-s* (*he* plays). The **simple present tense** indicates an action taking place in the writer's present time: *You see these words.* But the present tense in combination with other time-specific expressions (such as *after, before, when,* or *next week*) indicates other time references, such as ongoing action or future action (see 9f-1).

> After I arrive, I will *call.*
>
> Before I arrive, I will *call.*
>
> When I arrive, *pretend* you don't know me.
>
> Next week, Nelson *dances* at the White House.

The historical present

The so-called **historical present tense** is used when referring to actions in an already existing work: a book, a report, an essay, a movie, a

ESL ALERT

There may be some confusion of progressives that depend on shifts in verb meaning. For example, the word "think" in "He is thinking about what to do next" emphasizes mental activity, while "think" in "He thinks she spoke the truth" emphasizes a conclusion or opinion reached through past processes. In general, verbs expressing a completed mental process (believe, consider, forget, know, remember, think, understand) or states of being (am, appear, have, seem) or perceptions (feel, hear, see, taste) do not take progressive forms. A few of these verbs may be made progressive, but doing so changes their meaning.

"I am considering buying a car [a decision-making process]
versus
"I consider my choice the best" [an already completed decision]

television show, an article, and so on. Action in an existing work is always present to a reader or viewer.

In *The Songlines*, Bruce Chatwin *explores* the origins and meanings of Aboriginal "walkabouts" in Australia.

The historical present tense is also used when referring to movies.

In *Blade Runner*, Harrison Ford *plays* a world-weary detective whose job it *is* to disable renegade, human-like robots.

Additionally, the present tense is used to express information that, according to current scientific knowledge or accepted wisdom, is true or likely to be true.

Evidence *indicates* that Alzheimer's patients *show* a decrease in an important brain transmitter substance.

Absence *makes* the heart grow fonder.

She *is* an excellent dentist.

The present tense is also used to indicate a generalized time or a customary, repeated action.

Time *flies*.

Each Tuesday I *walk* to the bakery.

The present perfect tense

The **present perfect tense** is formed with the auxiliary *have* or *has* and the verb's past participle. This tense indicates an action completed at an indefinite past time.

I *have returned* and she *has left*.

The present perfect tense also indicates an action that, although begun at some past time, continues to have an impact in the present.

He *has* recently *given* support to museums.

ESL NOTE   Expressions for duration of time, such as *since* and *for*, require the use of the perfect tense.

FAULTY   I *was* here *since* four o'clock and *waited* here *for* many hours. [The simple past is not used with these expressions showing duration of time.]

REVISED   I *have been* here *since* four o'clock and *have waited* here for many hours. [The present perfect is used.]

In constructions that indicate a specific past time using phrases or clauses (with *when, after, before, while*), the simple past is required.

FAULTY   I have met him at eight o'clock and I have left after he arrived. [These expressions for a specific past time or event do not use the perfect.]

Revised   I met him at eight o'clock and I left after he arrived.

For more information on the use of tenses with time expressions, see 43b-2.

The present progressive tense

The **present progressive tense** is formed with the auxiliary *is, am,* or *are* and the verb's present participle. This tense indicates a present, ongoing action that may continue into the future.

>   She *is considering* a move to Alaska.

ESL Note   Certain verbs such as *have* are generally not used in a progressive tense, except with some idioms: *having a good time; having a baby* (see 43b-1).

The present perfect progressive tense

The **present perfect progressive tense** is formed with the auxiliary *has been* or *have been* and the verb's present participle. This tense indicates an action that began in the past, is continuing in the present, and may continue into the future.

>   She *has been studying* English for a year.

2   The past and future tenses

PAST TENSES

Past: I started the engine.
> **Past perfect:** I had started the engine.
> **Past progressive:** I was starting the engine.
> **Past perfect progressive:** I had been starting the engine.

The simple past tense

Regular verbs form the **simple past tense** by adding *-d* or *-ed* to the infinitive of the verb; irregular verbs form the past tense in less predictable ways and are best memorized or verified in a dictionary. The simple past tense indicates an action completed at a definite time in the past.

>   In 1867, the United States *bought* Alaska from Russia for $7.2 million.

The past perfect tense

The **past perfect tense** is formed with the auxiliary *had* and the verb's past participle. This tense indicates a past action that has occurred prior to another action.

>   Relatively few Americans *had visited* Alaska.

FOR DISCUSSION

Among future tenses, the most problematic seems to be future perfect progressive—perhaps simply because of the number of auxiliaries required to produce it correctly. But students also may need to discuss specific situations in which it should be used. Ask students to generate sentences using future perfect progressive, and then ask them to explain why that tense is appropriate in those sentences. If students can explain the use of future perfect progressive in terms of a time line, they should come to understand more clearly the role played by the auxiliaries. It is the existence of the specific future time reference that necessitates the use of *have* as an auxiliary. Without *have*, the future action's relationship to that time reference would be unclear.

ESL EXERCISE

Describe what you plan to be doing exactly ten years from today in the future. Be specific about your location, your career, your family status, and your financial situation.

The past progressive tense

The **past progressive tense** is formed with the auxiliary *was* or *were* and the verb's present participle. This tense indicates an ongoing action conducted—and completed—in the past.

Britain, France, and Russia *were vying* for control of Alaska.

The past perfect progressive tense

The **past perfect progressive tense** is formed with the auxiliary *had been* and the verb's present participle. This tense indicates a past, ongoing action completed prior to some other past action.

Before the first Russian settlers, native Americans *had been living* in Alaska.

FUTURE TENSES

Future: I will start the engine.
   Future perfect: I will have started the engine.
   Future progressive: I will be starting the engine.
   Future perfect progressive: I will have been starting the engine.

The future tense

The **future tense** consists of the base form of the verb along with the auxiliary *will* for all nouns and pronouns. This tense indicates an action or state of being that will begin in the future. In very formal writing, the first person *I* and *we* have traditionally taken the auxiliary *shall*; increasingly, this word is reserved for opening (first-person) questions implying obligation: "Shall I?"

Alaska *will celebrate* fifty years of statehood in the year 2009. I think I *will* attend the celebration. Shall I go? I *shall* attend. (This last sentence is reserved for the most formal writing.)

ESL NOTE English has no simple future tense but expresses future events with a variety of constructions, including some uses of the present tense (described above), as well as auxiliaries and such expressions as *going to* or *about to* (see 43b-3).

The future perfect tense

The **future perfect tense** is formed with the verb's past participle and the auxiliary *will have*. This tense indicates an action occurring in the future, prior to some other action.

By the time the cleanup of the *Exxon Valdez* spill is completed, the federal government *will have spent* hundreds of millions of dollars.

The future progressive tense

The **future progressive tense** is formed with the auxiliary *will be* (or *shall be)* and the verb's present participle. This tense indicates an ongoing action in the future.

> Government officials in Alaska *will be monitoring* oil shipments very carefully.

The future perfect progressive tense

The **future perfect progressive tense** is formed with the auxiliary *will have been* and the verb's present participle. This tense indicates an ongoing action in the future that will occur before some specified future time.

> By the year 2000, the Alaska pipeline *will have been transporting* crude oil for twenty-three years.

9f Sequencing verb tenses

Although it will always have a main verb located in its independent clause, a sentence may have other verbs as well: a complex sentence will have a second verb in its dependent clause, and a sentence with an infinitive or participle (verb forms that function as adjectives, adverbs, and nouns) will also have at least two verbs or verb forms. Since every verb shows tense, any sentence with more than one verb may indicate actions that occur at different times. Unless the sequence of these actions is precisely set, confusion will result.

UNCLEAR   Before I leave, I reported on my plans. [The logic of this sentence suggests that two events (one in each clause) are related, but the time sequencing of the events—one future, the other past—makes the relationship impossible.]

CLEAR   Before I leave, I will report on my trip. [The two actions take place in the future, one action earlier than the other.]

CLEAR   Before I left, I reported on my plans. [The two actions take place in the past, one action earlier than the other.]

1 Sequence the events in complex sentences with care.

Jones *attacked* Representative Kaye, who *had proposed* the amendment. Jones *has spent* months preparing for the trial that *will begin* next week.

A complex sentence joins an independent clause with a dependent clause. Generally, look to the logical relationship between events in the two clauses and choose verb tenses that clarify that relationship.

ESL ALERT

ESL students will need a lot of practice with sequencing verb tenses. Their grammar classes will have taught them the tenses as separate entities, and so they will have had little practice with the mix of tenses common in most writing.

Common tense sequence mistakes include using the future instead of the present or present perfect tense in a subordinate clause whose main clause is future ("After I will finish the dishes, I will go to the movies"); failing to use the past perfect to indicate time earlier than another past tense time ("The thief took everything the students brought home from school"); forgetting that wishes and unreal conditionals take a tense one step further into the past than the time they refer to ("I wish I took that course last year"); or using the past perfect with a present, a present perfect, or a future ("After I had finished the work, I will go to Caracas").

ADDITIONAL EXERCISE D

In the following sentences, write out the verb in parentheses in a tense appropriate to the meaning of the sentence:

1. For years before the girls in Salem Village (begin) accusing local people of witchcraft, disputes over land boundaries (plague) the town.
2. In 1691 the village (be) without a minister for years, but when Samuel Parris (arrive) he (proclaim), "Before the year (be) out, I (sweep) the devil from your midst!"
3. In the winter of that year, while his daughter and his niece (study) Scripture, they (begin) to shake and scream.
4. By the time the doctor (arrive), the girls (behave) strangely for days.
5. His conclusion (be) chilling: "The girls (be) bewitched."
6. Thus an episode (begin) that (baffle) us now and (baffle) others in years to come.

Answers:

1. For years before the girls in Salem Village began accusing local people of witchcraft, disputes over land boundaries had plagued the town.
2. In 1691 the village had been without a minister for years, but when Samuel Parris arrived he proclaimed, "Before the year is out, I will have swept the devil from your midst!"

(continued)

3. In the winter of that year, while his daughter and his niece were studying Scripture, they began to shake and scream.
4. By the time the doctor arrived, the girls had been behaving strangely for days.
5. His conclusion was chilling: "The girls are bewitched."
6. Thus an episode began that baffles us now and will baffle others in years to come.

GROUP ACTIVITY

Students will better understand how to sequence verb tenses if they practice with their own sentences. Divide students into groups of three or four and ask each group to generate additional sentences that exemplify the relationships outlined in this section. When finished, each group will report to the class as a whole, reading their sentences and explaining the reasons why they have sequenced tenses as they have. (If it's possible for groups to write their sentences on transparencies, all the better. Then the class can see as well as hear the sentences.) As students explain their choices, they will gain a firmer grasp of the concept of sequencing verb tenses.

Establishing a relationship between two events, both of which occur in the past

Use the simple past for one past event—and any of the four past tenses for the other event.

If the two past events happened at the same time, use the simple past tense for both or combine the simple past with the past progressive tense.

> The settlers *lived* where the land *supported* them. [A simple past tense is followed by another simple past.]

> Shelley *wrote* her letters while she *was traveling* to Moscow. [A simple past is followed by a past progressive.]

If the two past events happened one before the other, use the simple past (or past progressive) for the more recent event, and use the past perfect (or past perfect progressive) to establish the earlier event.

> We *understood* that she *had been working* on the solution for years. [The past perfect progressive establishes that her work occurred earlier than our understanding.]

> Frank *called* the doctor who *had operated* on him. [The past perfect established that the operation came before the call.]

> Frank *had called* the doctor who *operated* on him yesterday. [The past perfect established that the call came before the operation.]

If key expressions establish that one past event happened before the other, the simple past tense is used for both events.

> Last Wednesday Frank *called* the doctor who *operated* on him. [The key expression *last Wednesday* establishes that the call came before the operation.]

ESL NOTE Indirect quotation or reported speech is a common case of tense sequence involving two verbs. A main verb such as *says* makes the report while another makes the indirect quotation in a *that . . .* clause—often occurring at a different time from the report: *She says that she will go.* When one event occurs before another, the verb sequence requires careful attention (see 43b-4).

Establishing a relationship between a past event and a future event

Use the simple past tense for the past event and the simple future or the future progressive for the future event.

> We *reserved* tickets for the play that *will open* on Saturday. [The reservations were made in the past for a play that opens in the future.]

> We *reserved* tickets for the play that *will be opening* on Saturday. [The reservations were made in the past for a play that opens in the future.]

Establishing a relationship between a past event and an acknowledged fact or condition

Use the simple past tense for the past event and the simple present tense for the acknowledged fact or condition.

The study *concluded* that few people *trust* strangers. [The study has been completed and has reached a conclusion about human nature.]

Helen *contacted* the lawyer who *has* the best reputation. [The contact was made in the past with someone who has an ongoing reputation.]

We *found* evidence that the theory *is* correct. [The finding in the past is that the theory was and continues to be correct.]

Use the past perfect tenses for the past event and the simple present tense for the acknowledged fact or condition.

Smith *had argued* that everyone *needs* basic services. [The argument occurred in the past concerning an ongoing need.]

2 Choose verb tense in an infinitive phrase based on your choice of verb in the main clause.

Ellen hoped to get rich.   To have voted was critical.

An **infinitive phrase** begins with the word *to* placed before a verb such as *see, want, watch, wish, need, go, like,* and *hope.* A present infinitive shows an action that occurs at the same time as or later than the action of the main verb. In the following sentences, the main verb is underlined.

Once Hull House became known as a center of social reform, admiring visitors from all over the world <u>arrived</u> *to see* the work of Jane Addams and her colleagues. [*To see* shows an action at the same time as *arrived.*]

A number of people <u>wanted</u> *to see* Addams properly recognized for her work—perhaps with a Nobel Prize. [*To see Addams . . .* shows a possible action in the future, later than *wanted.*]

A perfect infinitive is formed by placing the auxiliary *have* between the word *to* and the past participle of the verb. A perfect infinitive phrase shows an action that occurs before the action of the main verb.

To have participated in the programs at Hull House profoundly <u>changed</u> the lives of Jane Addams and her co-residents—Julia Lathrop and Florence Kelley. [The *change* in people is past; their *participation* occurred earlier than, and encouraged, the change.]

ESL Note   Certain transitive verbs take an infinitive or infinitive phrase as their object (as in the examples above), while other verbs (such as *enjoy*) take a gerund as object (see 43e-2).

3   **Choose the verb tense of a participle based on your choice of verb in the main clause.**

Arriving early, the speaker <u>had</u> time to relax.
Having thoroughly *studied* the matter, the judge <u>made</u> her decision.
Impressed with the novel, Marie <u>recommended</u> it to friends.

Participles, past and present, function as adjectives in a sentence. A participle in its present (*-ing*) form indicates an action that occurs at the same time as the action of the sentence's main verb. The main verb in each of the following examples is underlined.

> *Starting with efforts to improve the immediate neighborhood,* the Hull House group <u>became</u> involved with a city- and state-wide campaign for better housing. [The efforts at improvement occurred at the same time as the involvement in another campaign. Both actions occur in the past.]

A participle's present perfect form (the past participle preceded by the auxiliary *having*) shows an action that occurs before that of the main verb.

> *Having given twenty-five years of her life to Hull House,* Addams <u>turned</u> in 1915 to the peace movement. [Addams gave of her time to Hull House before turning to the peace movement. Both actions occur in the past.]

A participle in its past form (the base form + *-ed* for regular verbs) shows an action that occurs at the same time as or earlier than the action of the main verb.

> *Resented for her pacifist views,* Addams nonetheless <u>lobbied</u> for an end to international conflict and founded the Women's International League for Peace and Freedom. [Addams was likely resented for her pacifist views both before and during her efforts to end war.]

EXERCISE 5

In each sentence that follows, identify the tense of the italicized verb. Then choose the appropriate tense for subsequent verbs in each sentence.

> *Example:* Personality *is* the unique but stable set of characteristics and behavior that _____ (set) each individual apart from all others.
>
> *is*   present tense   *sets*   present tense

1. Most people *have accepted* the view that human beings _____ (possess) specific traits that _____ (be) fairly constant over time.
2. You *may be* surprised _____ (learn) that until recently a heated debate _____ (exist) in the behavioral sciences over the definition's accuracy.
3. On one side of this debate *were* scientists who _____ (contend) that people _____ (do) not _____ (possess) lasting traits.

EXERCISE 5

1. *have accepted*	present perfect
possess	present
are	present
2. *may be*	modal present
to learn	infinitive
existed	past
3. *were*	past
contended	past
do	present
possess	present
4. *will term*	future
is	present
5. *were*	past
held	past
do	present

4. According to these researchers (whom we *will term* the "anti-personality" camp), behavior _____ (be) shaped largely by external factors.
5. On the other side of the controversy *were* scientists who _____ (hold), equally strongly, that stable traits _____ (do) exist.

VOICE

9g Using the active and passive voices

Voice refers to the emphasis a writer gives to the actor in a sentence or to the object acted upon. Because only transitive verbs (see 9d) transfer action from an actor to an object, these verbs exhibit the active and passive voices. The **active voice** emphasizes the actor of a sentence.

Brenda scored the winning goal.

Thomas played the violin.

In each case, an actor, or agent, is *doing* something. In a **passive-voice** sentence, the object acted on is emphasized.

The winning goal was scored by Brenda.

The violin was played by Thomas.

The emphasis on the object of a passive-voice sentence is made possible by a rearrangement of words—the movement of the object, which normally follows a verb, to the first position in a sentence. A passive-voice construction also requires use of the verb *be* (*is, are, was, were, has been, have been*) and the preposition *by*.

| Brenda | **was** | scored | the winning goal | by |

The winning goal was scored by Brenda.

In a further transformation of the active-voice sentence, you can make the original actor/subject disappear altogether by deleting the prepositional phrase.

The winning goal was scored.

1 Use a strong active voice for clear, direct assertions.

Stronger   A guidance counselor recommended the book.
Weaker   A book was recommended.

In active-voice sentences, people or other agents *do* things. Active-voice sentences attach ownership to actions and help create a direct, lively

REFERENCE

WILLIAMS, JOSEPH M. *Style: Ten Lessons in Clarity and Grace*. Glenview: Scott, 1981. 8–32. Discusses voice from the perspective of style.

GROUP ACTIVITY

Students often have difficulty with the passive voice; many of them seem to think it's always taboo, while others use it far too often. In order to put the issue into perspective, ask groups to compose a brief story written entirely in passive voice. When they've finished, they can edit out any passives that seem inappropriate, keeping those that seem to work. When they write the story in the passive voice, they should get a sense of how wordy and awkward it can be, and when they justify their revisions, they should begin to understand the appropriate place of the passive voice in written discourse.

attitude toward the subject and the reader. By contrast, passive-voice sentences are inherently wordy and reliant on the weak verb *be*. Unintended overuse of the passive voice makes prose dull. Unless you have a specific reason for choosing the passive voice (see the following discussion), use the active voice.

You can make a passive-voice sentence active by restoring a subject/verb sequence. Rewording will eliminate both the preposition *by* and the form of *be*. Note that if an actor of a passive-voice sentence is not named, you will need to provide a name.

PASSIVE (WEAK)	In 1858, Stephen Douglas was challenged to a series of historic debates. [The "challenger" is not named.]
ACTIVE (STRONGER)	In 1858, Abraham Lincoln challenged Stephen Douglas to a series of historic debates.
PASSIVE (WEAK)	The senate race was won by Douglas, but a national reputation was established by Lincoln.
ACTIVE (STRONGER)	Douglas won the senate race, but Lincoln established a national reputation.

 2 Use the passive voice to emphasize an object or to deemphasize an unknown subject.

OBJECT EMPHASIZED	The funding goal was reached earlier than expected.
ACTOR(S) EMPHASIZED	We reached the funding goal earlier than expected.

While you should generally prefer the active voice for making direct statements, you will find the passive voice indispensable on two occasions: to emphasize an object and to deemphasize an unknown subject/actor.

Emphasize an object with a passive construction.

When the subject/actor of a sentence is relatively unimportant compared to what is acted on, use the passive voice both to deemphasize the subject/actor and to emphasize the object. The passive voice will shift the subject/actor to a prepositional phrase at a later position in the clause. You may then delete the phrase.

ACTIVE	We require twelve molecules of water to provide twelve atoms of oxygen.
PASSIVE (ACTOR RETAINED)	Twelve molecules of water are required by us to provide twelve atoms of oxygen.
PASSIVE (ACTOR DELETED)	Twelve molecules of water are required to provide twelve atoms of oxygen.

Deemphasize an unknown subject with the passive voice.

You may deemphasize or delete an *unknown* subject/actor by using the passive voice. Instead of writing an indefinite subject/actor (such as *someone* or *people*) into a sentence, use the passive voice to shift the subject/actor to a prepositional phrase. You may then delete the phrase.

ACTIVE	People mastered the use of fire some 400,000 years ago.
PASSIVE (ACTOR RETAINED)	The use of fire was mastered by people some 400,000 years ago.
PASSIVE (ACTOR DELETED)	The use of fire was mastered some 400,000 years ago.

EXERCISE 6

Change the passive-voice sentences that follow to the active voice and change active-voice sentences to passive. Invent a subject if need be for the active-voice sentences.

> *Example:* Stocks and securities are bought by an arbitrageur and then quickly sold for a profit. [The passive voice involves two verbs: "*are bought* . . . and . . . *sold.*"]

An arbitrageur buys stocks and securities and then quickly sells them for a profit. [changed to active voice]

1. In the 1980s, an increase in the number of stock broker arbitrageurs was seen.
2. Originally, companies were invested in by arbitrageurs after a merger was announced.
3. Investments were based on the relationship between the stock prices of the two firms involved and the probabilities that the two firms would merge.
4. In the mid-1980s, investments were made in firms that *might* be candidates for mergers.
5. Arbitrageurs hoped to make a profit on the price increases at the time of the merger announcement.

MOOD

9h Understanding the uses of mood

The **mood** of a verb indicates the writer's judgment as to whether a statement is a fact, a command, or an unreal or hypothetical condition contrary to fact. In the **indicative mood,** a writer states a fact, opinion, or question. Most of our writing and speech is in the indicative mood.

The mayor has held office for eight years. [fact]

The mayor is not especially responsive. [opinion]

Did you vote for the mayor? [question]

EXERCISE 6

1. In the 1980s we saw an increase in the number of stock broker arbitrageurs.
2. Originally, arbitrageurs invested in companies after a merger was announced.
3. Arbitrageurs based investments on the relationship between the stock prices of the two firms involved and the probabilities that the two firms would merge.
4. In the mid-1980s, arbitrageurs made investments in firms that *might* be candidates for mergers.
5. It was hoped by arbitrageurs that they would make a profit on the price increases at the time of the merger announcement.

ESL ALERT

All of the discussion on mood will be confusing for ESL students, whose language texts do not use the word "subjunctive." For *if* forms and "wishes," ESL texts use terms like "real" versus "unreal," "conditionals" and "*if*-clauses contrary to fact" to help distinguish when to use past tense forms. ESL practice with *urge, recommend, suggest, command,* and so forth focuses on these terms' being equivalents of *must* or *should* and therefore on taking the short forms of the verb common with use of *should* and *must* to avoid redundancy, as in "I suggest that he ~~should~~ see a doctor." The *if* formation will be familiar, but the use of *as though* or *as if* to express the hypothetical will probably be new territory.

To avoid confusion, remind ESL students that the *would* form cannot be used with *I* because if the *I* wishes to do something, the question is not one of *will* but of *ability*: "I would if I could" not "I would if I would." The sentence "I would if I could but I can't" is a socially useful mantra to practice.

TEACHING IDEAS

To help students understand the use of subjunctive mood with *if* constructions, you may want to offer the following quotations:

Subjunctive:
If it were in my power to forgive you for your reckless cruelty, I would do so. (Joseph Nye Welch)

I truly wish there were some sort of badge of dishonor that a non-voter would have to wear. (India Edwards)

Indicative:
If the human race wants to go to hell in a basket, technology can help it get there by jet. (Charles M. Allen)

If you rest, you rust. (Helen Hayes)

Ask students to explain the distinction between the two pairs of quotations. Their responses should help them understand the idea that subjunctive mood is used to indicate conditions contrary to fact.

In the **imperative mood,** a writer gives a command, the subject of which is "you," the person being addressed. In this book, for example, the imperative addresses readers with specific guidelines for writing or making revisions. An imperative uses the verb in its base form. Often, the subject of a command is omitted, but occasionally it is expressed directly.

> Follow me!
>
> Do not touch that switch.
>
> Don't you touch that switch!

By using the **subjunctive mood,** a writer shows that he or she believes an action or situation is unreal or hypothetical. With a subjunctive verb, a writer can also make a recommendation or express a wish or requirement, usually preceded by such a verb construction as *recommend, suggest, insist, it is necessary,* or *it is important.* The **present subjunctive** uses the base form (infinitive) of the verb, for all subjects.

> I recommend that he *develop* his math skills before applying.
>
> I recommend that they *develop* their skills.

The **past subjunctive** uses the past-tense form of the verb—or, in the case of *be*—the form *were.*

> If management *assumed* traveling costs, the team would be happier.
>
> He wished he *were* four inches taller.

ESL NOTE *If* constructions require a subjunctive verb form only when they express a condition that is considered unreal or hypothetical. Section 43b-5 demonstrates differences between real and unreal conditions with *if* constructions.

 1 **Use the subjunctive mood with certain *if* constructions.**

If I owned a dog, I would walk it every day.

When an *if* clause expresses an unreal or hypothetical condition, use the subjunctive mood. In a subjunctive *if* construction, the modal auxiliary *would, could, might,* or *should* is used in the main clause. (See 9c for a discussion of modals.)

FAULTY	If Tom was more considerate, he would have called. [Clearly, Tom was not considerate (he did not call), and so the indicative or "factual" mood is at odds with the meaning of the sentence.]
SUBJUNCTIVE	If Tom *were* more considerate, he would have called.
SUBJUNCTIVE	If I *were* elected, I might raise taxes.

NOTE: When an *if* construction is used to establish a cause-and-effect relationship, the writer assumes that the facts presented in a sentence either are true or could very possibly be true; therefore the writer uses an indicative ("factual") mood with normal subject-verb agreement.

FAULTY   If I were late, start without me.

REVISED   If I am late, start without me. [The lateness is assumed to be a likely or possible fact.]

2 **Use the subjunctive mood with *as if* and *as though* constructions.**

He dances as though he were weightless.

When an *as if* or *as though* construction sets up a purely hypothetical comparison that attempts to explain or characterize, use the subjunctive mood.

FAULTY   She swims as if she *was* part fish. [But since the speaker knows she is not, the indicative ("factual") mood is inconsistent.]

REVISED   She swims as if she *were* part fish.

SUBJUNCTIVE   He writes quickly, as though he *were* running out of time. [The sentence assumes that he is not running out of time.]

3 **Revise to eliminate auxiliary *would* or *could* in subjunctive clauses with *if*, *as if*, or *as though*.**

CLEAR   If I had listened, I would have avoided the problem.
CONFUSING If I would have listened, I would have avoided the problem.

In subjunctive constructions like those shown previously, the modal auxiliary verbs *would*, *could*, or *should* may appear in the main clause to help indicate that its action is unreal or is conditional. The auxiliaries *would* and *could* cannot appear in the *if* clause, however, since this creates a kind of "double conditional"; these auxiliaries must be replaced with the appropriate subjunctive form.

FAULTY   If the mate at the wheel *would have* been alerted, the oil spill would have been avoided.

REVISED   If the mate at the wheel *had* been alerted, the oil spill would have been avoided.

FAULTY   He could have acted as though he *could have* seen the reef.

REVISED   He could have acted as though he *had* seen it.

4 **Use the subjunctive mood with a *that* construction.**

I think it is important that he arrive early.

Use the subjunctive mood with subordinate *that* constructions expressing a requirement, request, urging, belief, wish, recommendation, or doubt. In each of these constructions, the word *that* may be omitted.

TEACHING IDEAS

Students who frequently misuse *would* and *could* in subjunctive clauses might be advised to use the following strategy to edit their papers: After identifying subjunctive structures in the paper, check to see if the auxiliaries are used twice in the same sentence. If they are, then the sentence probably needs to be revised.

Example: If I *would* have known that the storm was coming, I *would* have stocked up on supplies.

The appearance of the auxiliary twice in the same sentence should alert the writer to the error.

The rules require that we *be* present.

I wish that I *were* a painter.

We recommend that he *accept* the transfer.

We recommend he *accept* it.

ESL NOTE　*That* clauses can occur in a variety of sentences not requiring a subjunctive form. See 43b-6 for special rules in constructions involving *wish that.* . . .

EXERCISE 7

Use the subjunctive mood, as appropriate, in revising the sentences that follow.

> *Example:* If more Americans studied foreign languages, they will be more sensitive to cultural issues abroad.
>
> If more Americans studied foreign languages, they would be more sensitive to cultural issues abroad.

1. If language study was to begin in American schools in the second or third grade, American students will be better prepared for international business.
2. A bipartisan committee of Congress should review the language curriculum in this country and recommend that America improves its commitment to language instruction.
3. Our historical refusal to take language instruction seriously is based on a naive, isolationist view that Americans do not need anyone besides themselves to flourish. If this is true, then indices like the annual trade deficit do not matter.
4. But the trade deficit does matter and if America will sell goods and services overseas, it must understand its overseas customers. We must understand their languages and their cultures.
5. If this country is to remain competitive internationally, we must explain to every American the necessity that he or she is literate in two, and preferably more than two, languages.

EXERCISE 7

1. If language study *were* to begin in American schools in the second or third grade, American students *would* be better prepared for international business.
2. A bipartisan committee of Congress should review the language curriculum in this country and recommend that America *improve* its commitment to language instruction.
3. Our historical refusal to take language instruction seriously is based on a naive, isolationist view that Americans don't need anyone besides themselves to flourish. If this *were* true, then indices like the annual trade deficit *would* not matter.
4. But the trade deficit does matter and if America *would* sell goods and services overseas, it must understand its overseas' customers. We must understand their languages and their cultures.
5. If this country is to remain competitive internationally, we must explain to every American the necessity that he or she *be* literate in two, and preferably more than two, languages.

CHAPTER 10

Agreement

Agreement is a term that describes two significant relationships in a sentence: between a subject and a verb and between a pronoun and an antecedent. These elements occur in pairs. The subject of a sentence must be paired with a verb to make a complete statement. A subject and its verb are either *both* singular or *both* plural.

A pronoun derives meaning from its relation to the noun, or antecedent, that it renames. A pronoun and its antecedent are also either *both* singular or *both* plural.

SUBJECT-VERB AGREEMENT

Subjects and verbs must agree in both number and person. The term **number** indicates whether a noun is singular (denoting one person, place, or thing) or plural (denoting more than one). The term **person** identifies the subject of a sentence as the same person who is speaking (the first person), someone who is spoken to (the second person), or someone or something being spoken about (the third person). Pronouns differ according to person.

	First-person subject	*Second-person subject*	*Third-person subject*
Singular	I	you	he, she, it
Plural	we	you	they

Agreement between a verb and first- or second-person pronoun subject does not vary. The pronouns *I, we,* and *you* take verbs *without* the letter *s*.

I walk. We walk. You walk.
I scream, you scream, we scream—for ice cream.

Problems of confusion sometimes occur, however, in the forms of agreement for third-person subjects and verbs.

10a Make a third-person subject agree in number with its verb.

The suffix *-s* or *-es*, affixed to a present-tense verb, indicates an assertion about a singular third-person subject (A frog do*es* this.); the suffix *-s* or *-es*, affixed to most nouns or third-person pronouns, indicates a plural (Frog*s* do this.).

SPOTLIGHT ON COMMON ERRORS—AGREEMENT

These are the errors most commonly associated with agreement between subject and verb or pronoun and antecedent. For full explanations and suggested revisions, follow the cross-references to chapter sections.

AGREEMENT ERRORS occur when the writer loses sight of the close link between the paired subjects and verbs, or between pronouns and the words they refer to (antecedents). Paired items should both be singular (referring to *one* person, place, or thing) or both be plural (referring to *more than one* person, place, or thing).

- **A subject and its verb should both be singular or both be plural (they should agree), whether or not they are interrupted by a word or word group (see 10a-1). Match subject and verb. Disregard interrupting words.**

FAULTY	REVISED
Some people, when not paying attention, easily *forgets* names.	Some **people,** when not paying attention, easily *forget* names.

- **A sentence with a singular subject needs a singular form of the verb *be* (*am, is, was*); a sentence with a plural subject needs a plural form of the verb *be* (*are, were*) (see 10a-7). To ensure agreement in sentences beginning with the subject, ignore words following the verb *be*.**

FAULTY	REVISED
The reason for her success *are* her friends.	The **reason** for her success *is* her friends.

When the subject comes after the verb in sentences beginning with *it* or *there,* verb and subject must still agree. Ignore the word *it* or *there.*

FAULTY	REVISED
There *is* seven hills in Rome.	There **are seven hills** in Rome. [The subject, *hills,* needs a plural verb.]

- **When *and* joins words to create a two-part subject or a two-part pronoun referent, the sense is usually plural and so the matching verb or pronoun is plural (see 10a-2–3). When *or/nor* creates a two-part subject or pronoun referent, the nearer word determines whether the matching verb or pronoun is singular or plural (see 10b-1–2).**

FAULTY	REVISED
A cat and a dog often *shares* **its** food.	A cat and a dog often *share* **their** food. [Here, *cat and dog* serve as a two-part subject and as a two-part referent.]
Neither the rats nor the dog *chase* **their** tail.	Neither the rats nor the dog *chases* **its** tail. [The verb and pronoun match the nearer singular subject, *dog.*]

FOR DISCUSSION

Since most students have problems with only a few of these common errors, you might want to initiate a class discussion of errors most relevant to your students. Ask students to identify from the Spotlight on Common Errors examples of usage familiar to them and to make their own list of common errors. Students can then discuss the function of agreement in sentences, thereby reinforcing their understanding of the concept. (In large classes, this activity might begin with small groups. The group will identify their common errors, and then the class as a whole will discuss the list of errors compiled from each group's report.)

The "tradeoff" technique

To remember the basic forms of third-person agreement for most verbs in the present tense, you may find it helpful to visualize something like a balanced tradeoff of -s endings between most noun subjects and their verbs: If one ends with an -s, then the other does not. Thus if the noun subject is singular and lacks an -s or -es ending, then the singular verb takes the -s ending. If the subject is a plural noun with an -s ending, then it takes the -s and the plural verb does not.

SINGULAR   A boy__ hikes. A girl__ swims. A kid__ does it.

PLURAL   The boys hike__. The girls swim__. Kids do__ it.

If a noun or pronoun has a plural sense, even if it does not end with an -s (e.g., children, oxen, geese, they, these), then the tradeoff technique still applies. Since the noun or pronoun is plural (just as it would be if it were a word made plural with an -s ending), the verb is also plural—that is, the verb now lacks its -s ending.

SINGULAR   A child plays. He plays. He does it.

PLURAL   Children play__. They play__. They do__ it.

NOTE: The "tradeoff" technique does not apply when a verb is paired with an auxiliary (or helping) verb (see 9c). Verbs so paired do *not* use -s.
A child will play.   He may play.   He might do it.
Children should play.   They could play.   They must do it.

Revising nonstandard verb and noun forms to observe -s and -es endings

In rapid conversation people sometimes skip over the -s or -es endings of verbs that are paired with singular nouns. In some English dialects, the base (or infinitive) form of the verb is used for singular nouns. Standard academic English, however, requires that writers observe subject-verb agreement.

NONSTANDARD   He read the book.   NONSTANDARD   She do it.

STANDARD   He reads the book.   STANDARD   She does it.

1 A subject agrees with its verb regardless of whether any phrase or clause separates them.

The *purpose* of practicing daily for several hours is to excel.

Often a subject may be followed by a lengthy phrase or clause that comes between it and the verb, confusing the basic pattern of agreement. To clarify the matching of the subject with the verb, mentally strike out or

---

ESL ALERT

Common ESL agreement problems include the following: a plural "a number" versus a singular "the number"; a singular form for "everyone/everybody/every man, woman, and child/each of them/none of them"; a singular form for quantities like "five dollars/two quarts/four pounds/twenty minutes"; words that end in "s" but take a singular like "mathematics/news/mumps/billiards/athletics"; words that are one item but take a plural like "scissors/jeans/pants/eyeglasses"; words that may be singular or plural depending on meaning like "ethics/acoustics/barracks/chicken/fish"; indefinite pronouns that depend on an "of" phrase, as in "half of the class" versus "half of the students"; and plural group nouns formed from adjectives ("the poor/the good/the bad/the ugly/the inconsiderate").

Discussing the difference between count and mass (noncount) nouns ("cars" versus "sugar"; "luggage/baggage" versus "suitcases/bags") is a must, as is a focus on verb agreement with whatever comes after the "or" or "nor" in an "either/or" or "neither/nor" sequence. Marking out prepositional phrases helps ESL students decide on agreement.

ESL students need a great deal of practice with consistency of pronoun reference since it will be a new concept for many of them.

ESL ALERT

Chinese and Vietnamese nouns have no singular or plural forms, so the concept of agreement is difficult for speakers of these languages to understand.

LOOKING BACK

MULTICULTURAL DIFFERENCES If a discussion of the -s ending and nonstandard dialects is relevant to your classroom, refer also to sections 9a-2 and 9c-2.

MULTICULTURAL DIFFERENCES If you find that students have difficulty with plurals not formed by adding *-s,* you can ask the class to generate a list of such words, writing them on the board and having students write them in their notebooks. Then they'll have a list handy whenever they're in doubt. This activity is especially useful for non-native speakers.

ADDITIONAL EXERCISE A

ACROSS THE CURRICULUM Peruse the books you're reading for your classes to find three examples of sentences in which subject and verb are separated by lengthy clauses or phrases. Copy the sentences, and then rewrite them so that subject and verb are closer together. (You'll probably need more than one sentence to replace each original.) In comparing the two versions, answer the following questions: Which seems clearer, the original or your rewrite? Why? Which *sounds* better? Why? Which seems more effective overall? Why?

ignore phrases or clauses separating them. Verbs in the following examples are underlined; subjects are italicized.

> *Downward mobility*—a swift plunge down America's social and economic ladders—<u>poses</u> an immediate and pressing problem. [The verb *poses* agrees with its singular subject, *downward mobility,* not with the plural *ladders* in the interrupting phrase.]

> *One* of my friends in a nearby town <u>has</u> heard this. [The prepositional phrases must be ignored to make the singular *one* agree with *has.*]

The words *each* and *every* have a singular sense. When either of these words precedes a compound subject joined by *and,* use a singular verb.

> *Every* city and county in Massachusetts <u>has</u> struggled with the problem of downward mobility.

EXCEPTION: When *each* follows a compound subject, the sense is plural and the plural verb is used.

> Boston and New York *each* <u>are</u> launching programs to reeducate workers.

NOTE: Phrases beginning with "in addition to," "along with," "as well as," "together with," or "accompanied by" may come between a subject and its verb. Although they add material, these phrases do *not* create a plural subject; they must be mentally stricken out to determine the correct number of the verb.

FAULTY *The anthropologist,* as well as social researchers such as statisticians and demographers, <u>are</u> always looking for indicators of change in status. [The interrupting phrase before the verb gives a false impression of a plural subject.]

REVISED *The anthropologist,* as well as social researchers such as statisticians and demographers, <u>is</u> always looking for indicators of change in status. [The singular subject *anthropologist* agrees with the singular verb.]

2 **A compound subject linked by the conjunction *and* is in most cases plural.**

> *UPS and Federal Express* <u>compete</u> with the U.S. postal system.

When a compound subject linked by *and* refers to two or more people, places, or things, it is usually considered plural.

PLURAL *Statistical information* and *the analysis based upon it* <u>allow</u> an anthropologist to piece together significant cultural patterns. [The compound subject has a plural sense. Thus the verb, *allow,* is plural.]

EXCEPTION: When a compound subject refers to a single person, place, or thing, it is considered singular.

SINGULAR   Whatever culture she studies, *this anthropologist* and *researcher* <u>concerns</u> herself with the relations among husbands, wives, children, kin, and friends. [The compound subject has a singular sense—it refers to one person and can be replaced by the singular pronoun *she.* Thus the verb, *concerns,* is singular.]

3   **When parts of a compound subject are linked by the conjunction *or* or *nor*, the verb should agree in number with the nearer part of the subject.**

Neither the crew members nor the *captain* <u>speaks</u> Arabic.

When all parts of the compound subject are the same number, agreement with the verb is fairly straightforward.

Either John or *Maria* <u>sings</u> today.

Either the Smiths or the *Taylors* <u>sing</u> today.

When one part of the compound subject is singular and another plural there can be confusion; the subject nearest the verb determines the number of the verb. If the nearest subject is singular, the verb is singular.

SINGULAR   According to popular wisdom, either poor habits or *ineptitude* <u>is</u> responsible when an individual fails to succeed in American culture. [The singular subject, *ineptitude,* is nearest to the verb; therefore the verb, *is,* is singular.]

When the subject nearest the verb is plural, the verb is plural.

PLURAL   Neither the downwardly mobile individual nor the *people* surrounding him <u>realize</u> that losing a job is often due to impersonal economic factors. [The plural subject, *people,* is nearer to the verb; therefore the verb, *realize,* is plural.]

NOTE: Subject/verb agreement in this situation may appear to be mismatched unless the plural part of the compound subject is placed closest to the verb. Avoid such awkwardness by revising to place the plural part closest to the verb.

4   **Most indefinite pronouns have a singular sense and take a singular verb.**

Virtually *everybody* in developed countries <u>travels</u> by bus.
Many who live elsewhere <u>have</u> no choice but to walk.

Indefinite pronouns (such as *any* and *each*) do not have specific antecedents—they rename no particular person, place, or thing and thus raise questions about subject-verb agreement.

TEACHING IDEAS

One of the most common "errors" in English usage is the *"everyone . . . their"* construction. You may want to discuss the idea of *convention* with students, letting them know that of course many people use this construction, but the conventions of formal academic discourse dictate that pronouns replacing *everyone* be singular. You may also want to read for yourself the Kolln article listed in the references. She is not alone in her opposition to labeling this usage an error.

ESL ALERT

Remind ESL students that "each," "every," "-body," "-thing," "one," and "none" will *always* take a singular verb, even when used to encompass a group and when followed by a list, as in "Every man, woman, and child in the group *is* here."

ADDITIONAL EXERCISE B

In the following sentences, determine whether the collective noun has a singular or a plural meaning, and choose the verb accordingly.

1. After the loss, the team bickered among (itself, themselves).
2. The crowd booed heartily, expressing (its, their) disapproval.
3. A Brownie troop could have forged (its, their) way around the field more effectively than this team.
4. The press corps shook (its, their) heads in disbelief.
5. A couple who had both bet against the team happily collected (its, their) winnings.

Answers:

1. plural—themselves
2. singular—its
3. singular—its
4. plural—their
5. plural—their

The following indefinite pronouns have a singular sense:

another	each one	more	one
any	either	much	other
anybody	every	neither	somebody
anyone	everybody	nobody	someone
anything	everyone	none, no one	something
each	everything	nothing	

SINGULAR   For every five men working in America, *one* <u>skids</u> down the occupational ladder sometime during his career.

SINGULAR   While our culture provides stories that give meaning and shape to the lives of the upwardly mobile, *nothing* of this sort <u>is</u> available to once-prosperous individuals who suddenly lose their positions.

The indefinite pronouns *both, ones,* and *others* have a plural sense and take a plural verb.

PLURAL   Occasionally, the downwardly mobile are heroes who find ways to rise above their circumstances; *others* <u>are</u> lost souls, wandering the social landscape without direction.

The indefinite pronouns *all, any, more, many, enough, none, some, few,* and *most* have a singular or plural sense, depending on the meaning of a sentence.

Try substituting *he, she, it, we,* or *they* for the indefinite pronoun. The context of a sentence will give you clues about the number of its subject.

PLURAL   After losing their jobs, *some* people <u>are</u> highly self-critical. [*Some* (people) has a plural sense. It can be replaced by the pronoun *they,* and thus it takes a plural verb, *are.*]

SINGULAR   Self-doubt is a common reaction among the downwardly mobile; at least *some* of this reaction <u>is</u> unwarranted. [*Some* can be replaced by *it,* has a singular sense, and thus takes a singular verb, *is.*]

 5   **Collective nouns have a plural or a singular sense, depending on the meaning of a sentence.**

At this school, the *faculty* <u>meets</u> as a group with the President.

When a collective noun, such as *audience, band, bunch, crew, crowd, faculty, family, group, staff, team,* and *tribe,* refers to a single unit, the sense of the noun is singular and the noun takes a singular verb. The context of a sentence will give you clues about the number of its subject.

SINGULAR   *The tribe of the downwardly mobile* <u>consists</u> *of four subgroups.* [*Tribe* is a single unit, subdivided; thus, it has a singular sense and takes a singular verb.]

When the collective noun refers to individuals and their separate actions within a group, the sense of the noun is plural and the noun takes a plural verb.

PLURAL   *The tribe* of the downwardly mobile <u>have</u> diverse reactions to losing their jobs, depending on their subgroup membership. [*Tribe* here emphasizes the action of individual members; thus, it has a plural sense and takes a plural verb.]

 6 **Nouns plural in form but singular in sense take singular verbs.**

Economics <u>depends</u> heavily on mathematics.

The nouns *athletics, economics, mathematics, news, physics,* and *politics* all end with the letter *-s*, but they nonetheless denote a single activity. NOTE: *Politics* can be considered plural, depending on the sense of a sentence.

News of a layoff <u>causes</u> some people to feel alone and blame themselves.

Politics often <u>comes</u> into play. [*Politics* has a singular sense and takes a singular verb.]

 7 **A linking verb agrees in number with its subject, not with the subject complement.**

One *reason* for his success **<u>is</u>** his friends.
His *friends* **<u>are</u>** one reason for his success.

In a sentence with a linking verb, identify the singular or plural subject when deciding the number of the verb. Disregard any distracting phrase or clause that interrupts the subject and verb; also disregard the subject complement *following* the linking verb.

SINGULAR   *The cause* of downward mobility <u>is</u> market conditions. [The singular verb, *is*, agrees in number with the singular subject, *the cause*, not with the plural subject complement, *market conditions*.]

PLURAL   *Market conditions* <u>are</u> the cause of downward mobility. [The plural verb, *are*, agrees in number with the plural subject, *market conditions*, not with the singular subject complement, *the cause*.]

 8 **In sentences with inverted word order, a verb should agree in number with its subject.**

Here *is* Michael.   Here *are* Janice and Michael.   There *is* a strategy.

ADDITIONAL EXERCISE C

Rearrange the following sentences to eliminate *here* or *there*, expletives, and questions, choosing the verb that agrees with the subject.

1. There (is, are) a property tax cut planned for next year.
2. (Do, Does) the mayor support it?
3. It (is, are) the city council members who don't want the cut.
4. The reporter stated, "Here (is, are) the woman who proposed the cut."
5. There (is, are) several strong arguments against tax cuts.

Answers:

1. A property tax cut *is* planned for next year.
2.. The mayor *does* support it.
3. It *is* the city council members who don't want the cut.
4. The reporter stated, "Here *is* the woman who proposed the cut."
5. There *are* several strong arguments against tax cuts.

ESL ALERT

Some romance language speakers (Spanish, Italian, Portuguese) will have difficulty with the concept of the expletive since it does not exist in their language. Their tendency will be to leave out the "there" or "it" and to simply begin with a "be" verb as they would in their language: "Is hot." "Is over there." Calling attention to the problem often helps the student self-correct.

ESL ALERT

A general distinction between the expletive "there" and the expletive "it" is that "there" is normally followed by a noun while an "it" is normally followed by an adjective, except in cases of identification, time, and distance.

ESL ALERT

Students should be reminded that, because gerunds serve the functions of nouns and may appear wherever a noun appears, one gerund equals one noun and therefore takes a singular verb.

The subject of an English sentence is normally placed before a verb. When this order is rearranged, the subject and verb continue to agree in number. Most errors with rearranged sentences occur with the verb *be*.

Here and *there* as adverbs

When inverted sentences begin with *here* and *there* as adverbs, the verb will agree in number with the subject (which follows the verb), not with the adverb.

NORMAL   The adviser said, "The Pattersons are here." [The plural subject, *Pattersons,* needs a plural verb.]

REARRANGED   The adviser said, "Here *are* the Pattersons."

SINGULAR   The adviser said, "Here *is* David Patterson."

Expletives

The words *it* and *there* often function as **expletives,** words that fill gaps in a sentence when normal word order is reversed (see 7a-11). *There* can never serve as the subject of a sentence. Disregard it when determining whether the sentence has a singular or plural subject.

PLURAL   There <u>are</u> *two reasons* for helping the downwardly mobile. [*There* is disregarded; the plural subject, *reasons,* needs to agree with a plural verb, *are.*]

SINGULAR   There <u>is</u> at least *one* good *reason.*

Notice that the expletive *it* is always followed by a singular verb.

SINGULAR   It <u>is</u> a very good *idea* to help them.

ESL NOTE   Some languages do not use *expletives.* In this very common form, a "dummy subject" or filler word *it* or *there* occupies a position normally filled by the subject, followed by the verb *be* or any linking verb: *There were children inside.* The real subject, *children,* is on the other side of the linking verb "equation" (see 11d). See 43a-2 and 7a-11 for ways to use this construction; see 14e and 17a for ways to avoid wasting words with expletives.

Questions

Inverting a sentence's word order is one method of forming a question. The relocated verb must still agree in number with the subject.

STATEMENT   <u>He</u> really *wants* to hold on to that idea.

QUESTION   <u>Does</u> he really <u>want</u> to hold on to that idea? [The verb *does want* agrees with the subject *he.*]

Many questions are formed with *wh* words (*what, where, when, why*), with a verb following the *wh* word and a noun following that. The verb and noun should agree in number.

SINGULAR   What <u>is</u> *the cost* to him of abandoning it?

PLURAL   What <u>are</u> *the costs* aside from that?

9 **The verb of a dependent clause introduced by the pronoun *which, that, who,* or *whom* should agree in number with the pronoun's antecedent.**

The *books, which* <u>are</u> old, <u>are</u> falling apart.   *Which book* <u>is</u> mine?

In such a dependent clause, both the pronoun subject (*which, that,* etc.) and verb are dependent for their number on an antecedent in the main clause.

PLURAL   The *costs* of downward mobility, *which* <u>are</u> measured in more than dollars and cents, can be fearfully high. [The relative pronoun, *which*, renames the plural antecedent, *costs*; the relative pronoun has a plural sense and the verb following must be plural.]

SINGULAR   The American workplace, *which* in many ways <u>is</u> the American psyche, will be undermined if workers and employers no longer trust one another. [The relative pronoun, *which*, renames the singular antecedent, *workplace*; the relative pronoun has a singular sense and the verb following must be singular.]

10 **Phrases and clauses that function as subjects are treated as singular and take singular verbs.**

To swim well <u>is</u> the first prerequisite for scuba diving.
That the child is able to cough <u>is</u> a good sign.

Often a noun clause, or a phrase with a gerund or infinitive, will act as the subject of a sentence. Such a construction is always regarded as a singular element in the sentence.

SINGULAR   *To live in a society that closely connects occupation to self-worth* <u>places</u> us at emotional risk when we lose our jobs. [The long infinitive phrase that functions as the subject of this sentence has a singular sense. It therefore takes a singular verb, *places*.]

SINGULAR   *That honest effort and ability can go unrewarded* <u>strikes</u> many as unfair. [The noun clause introduced by *that* functions as the subject of this sentence and takes a singular verb, *strikes*.]

ADDITIONAL EXERCISE D

ACROSS THE CURRICULUM Photocopy a passage from a textbook in one of your other courses. Underline clauses introduced by the pronouns *which, that, who,* and *whom,* and circle the verbs in these clauses. Then underline phrases and clauses functioning as subjects and circle the main verbs in those sentences. This activity should help you better understand subject-verb agreement.

11 **Titled works, key words used as terms, and companies are treated as singular in number and take singular verbs.**

Classics is an overused word.   "The Killers" is a Hemingway story.

Titles of works, names of companies or corporations, underlined or italicized words referred to as words, numbers, and units of money are regarded as singular entities in a sentence and take singular verbs.

SINGULAR *Falling from Grace: The Experience of Downward Mobility in the American Middle Class* is the title of Katherine Newman's book.

SINGULAR *Savage dislocation* is the term Newman uses to describe the experience of the downwardly mobile.

SINGULAR *Fifty thousand dollars* per year <u>provides</u> for a solidly middle-class lifestyle; unemployment checks do not.

EXERCISE 1

1. is
2. is   assures   seem
3. is
4. has
5. work

EXERCISE 1

In the following sentences, determine whether a subject is singular or plural. Choose the correct form in parentheses and be able to explain your choice.

Example: How (do/does) we get other people to agree with us?

How *do* we get other people to agree with us? [The subject of the sentence is the plural pronoun, *we.* Even though the auxiliary part of the verb, *do,* is placed before the subject to form a question, the full verb (including the auxiliary) and the subject must agree in number.]

1. One reason for making a purchase (is/are) a buyer's emotional needs.
2. There (is/are) no single method that (assure/assures) success in persuading others; still, several methods (seem/seems) helpful.
3. One effective way of getting a "yes" from other people (is/are) to get them to like us.
4. Flattery, an extremely common tactic for gaining compliance, (has/have) a long history.
5. Both flattering people and getting them to talk about themselves (work/works) in surprisingly consistent ways.

PRONOUN-ANTECEDENT AGREEMENT

An **antecedent** is a word—usually a noun, sometimes a pronoun—that is renamed by a pronoun. Pronouns in the following examples are underlined and antecedents are italicized.

antecedent   pronoun
Van Leeuwenhoek called the microorganisms that <u>he</u> found everywhere in vast numbers "little animals."

A pronoun's antecedent must be clearly identified in order for the pronoun itself to have a meaningful reference (see chapter 14 on pronoun reference). A pronoun and antecedent must agree in *number, person,* and *gender.* **Gender** refers to whether a noun or pronoun is feminine, masculine, or neuter.

> *Mary* flies planes. <u>She</u> flies planes. (feminine)
>
> *Bob* rides trolleys. <u>He</u> rides trolleys. (masculine)
>
> *A trolley* runs on tracks. <u>It</u> runs on tracks. (neuter)

In most cases, as in the preceding examples, a pronoun is easily matched to its antecedent in terms of person (first, second, or third), number (plural or singular), and gender (masculine or feminine). At times, however, the choice of the right pronoun requires careful attention.

10b Pronouns and their antecedents should agree in number.

Of the three components that determine pronoun selection, agreement in number causes the most difficulty—for the same reason that subject-verb agreement is sometimes difficult: the *number* of a noun (either as subject or antecedent) is not always clear. The following conventions will help you to determine whether an antecedent is singular or plural.

1 A compound antecedent linked by the conjunction *and* is usually plural.

Watson and Crick were awarded a Nobel prize for <u>their</u> achievement.

PLURAL In all early attempts at classification, living things were separated into two major groups—*the plant kingdom* and *the animal kingdom.* <u>These</u> were then subdivided in various ways. [The compound antecedent has a plural sense; therefore the pronoun renaming it is plural in form.]

PLURAL In the 4th century B.C., *Aristotle* made a study of the animal kingdom and *Theophrastus* studied the plant kingdom; <u>their</u> systems for classifying animals and plants began the scientific effort of classifying all living things. [The compound antecedent has a plural sense; therefore the pronoun renaming it is plural in form.]

EXCEPTIONS: When a compound antecedent with parts joined by the conjunction *and* has a singular sense, use a singular pronoun.

SINGULAR *An English naturalist* and *writer,* Thomas Blythe, used <u>his</u> classification scheme to identify more than 18,000 different types of plants. [The compound antecedent refers to one person—Thomas Blythe; therefore the pronoun renaming it is singular.]

The words *each* and *every* have a singular sense. When either of these words precedes an antecedent joined by *and,* use a singular pronoun.

REFERENCES

SKLAR, ELIZABETH S. "The Tribunal of Use: Agreement in the Indefinite Constructions." *CCC* 39 (1988): 410–22. Indefinite pronouns sometimes take on singular, sometimes plural, meanings.

KOLLN, MARTHA. "Everyone's Right to Their Own Language." *CCC* 37 (1986): 100–02. Argues from a common usage standpoint that constructions like "everyone ... their" should not be called errors.

SINGULAR   Every *visible organism* and *microscopic organism* has <u>its</u> own distinctive, two-word Latin name according to the system designed by Carolus Linnaeus in the early eighteenth century.

EXCEPTION: When *each* follows an antecedent joined by *and*, the sense is plural and the plural pronoun is used.

PLURAL   Daly and Blythe have *each* contributed to our understanding of classification systems.

2   When parts of a compound antecedent are linked by the conjunction *or* or *nor*, a pronoun should agree in number with the nearer part of the antecedent.

Neither the captain nor the *crew members* understood *their* predicament.

This pattern of agreement with *or* or *nor* follows the same convention as does subject-verb agreement (10a-3).

SINGULAR   Neither the traditional two-kingdom systems nor the recent five-kingdom *system* is complete in <u>its</u> classification of organisms. [The pronoun is nearer to the singular "system" and so agrees in the singular.]

NOTE: Avoid awkward pronoun use by revising to place the plural part of the compound antecedent nearer to the pronoun.

REVISED   Neither the five-kingdom system nor the traditional two-kingdom *systems* are complete in <u>their</u> classifications. [The plural part of the antecedent is revised to fall nearer to the pronoun; the sentence is no longer awkward in its agreement.]

3   Make pronouns agree in number with indefinite pronoun antecedents.

Each one has <u>her</u> own job.   *Both* have begun <u>their</u> research.

Indefinite pronouns (such as *each, anyone,* and *everyone*) do not refer to particular persons, places, or things. Most often, an indefinite pronoun used as an antecedent will have a singular sense. When it does, rename it with a singular pronoun.

SINGULAR   *Each* of the millions of organisms now living has <u>its</u> own defining features.

When an indefinite pronoun (such as *both* or *others*) functions as an antecedent and has a plural sense, rename it with a plural pronoun.

PLURAL   Some organisms are readily classified as animal or plant; *others,* most often the simplest single-cell organisms, find <u>themselves</u> classified in different ways, depending on the classification system used.

A few indefinite pronouns (such as *some, more,* or *most*) can have a singular or a plural sense, depending on the context of a sentence. Determine the number of an indefinite pronoun antecedent before selecting a pronoun replacement.

PLURAL   *Some* of the simplest living organisms defy classification, by virtue of <u>their</u> diversity. [*Some* has a plural sense.]

SINGULAR   *Some* of the recent research made possible by microscopes is startling in <u>its</u> findings that certain unicellular organisms like the euglena have both plantlike and animal-like characteristics. [*Some* has a singular sense.]

 4   Make pronouns agree in number with collective noun antecedents.

A well-informed group, the *faculty* is outspoken in <u>its</u> opinions.
The *faculty* at the gathering shared <u>their</u> thoughts on the issue.

Collective nouns will be singular or plural depending on the meaning of a sentence. When a collective noun such as *audience, band, group,* or *team* refers to a *single unit,* the sense of the noun as an antecedent is singular and takes a singular pronoun.

SINGULAR   A *group* of similar organisms that interbreed in nature is called a species and is given <u>its</u> own distinct Latin name. [*Group* has a singular sense.]

When a collective noun refers to individuals and their *separate actions* within a group, the sense of the noun as an antecedent is plural and takes a plural pronoun.

PLURAL   Human beings are the only *group* of primates who walk on two legs, without the aid of <u>their</u> hands. [*Group* has a plural sense.]

 10c   Rename indefinite antecedents with gender-appropriate pronouns.

A lawyer serves *his or her* clients.   Lawyers serve *their* clients.

Indefinite pronouns that have a singular sense and refer to people (as opposed to places or things) will likely refer to both males *and* females. Traditionally, the **generic *he*** or ***his*** was used to rename an indefinite antecedent, such as *each* or various nouns without specific gender identity. Today, many find this generic use offensive.

OFFENSIVE   To some extent, *a biologist* must decide for <u>himself</u> which system of classification <u>he</u> will use.

The use of *himself* and *he* in this sentence would exclude female biologists, of whom there are many. In addition to being inaccurate, this exclusion will offend anyone sensitive to the ways in which language can inflict harm. Be aware of the gender content of your pronoun choice.

FOR DISCUSSION

SEXIST LANGUAGE   While the generic masculine has been out of favor in academe for quite some time, it's alive and kicking elsewhere in society. Thus many students may consider this section much ado about nothing. It might be useful to ask students to discuss their feelings about the subject, particularly the traditional explanation that the masculine pronoun was inclusive of females. Of course, if this were completely true, then why the need to preface professional titles for women ("woman doctor," "woman lawyer") or to change suffixes of generic terms to accommodate females ("actress," "heroine")? If no student offers this line of argument, you may want to offer it yourself to see what kind of response it receives.

REFERENCE

BRYONY, SHANNON. "Pronouns: Male, Female, and Undesignated." *ETC.: A Review of General Semantics* 45 (Winter 1988): 334–36. To avoid using the generic masculine, a plural pronoun should be acceptable.

CRITICAL DECISIONS

Set issues in a broader context: Understand the gender messages implied by your pronouns

Gender-specific pronoun use can be inaccurate and offensive. Be aware, when choosing a pronoun, of the larger social setting in which you work. To avoid unintentional sexism, use five techniques, either alone or in combination. For more discussion on gender reference, see 21g.

1. **Use the constructions *he or she, his or her,* and *him or her* in referring to an indefinite pronoun or noun.** Choose this option when the antecedent of a pronoun must have a singular sense. Realize, however, that some readers object to the *he or she* device as cumbersome. The variants *(s)he* and *he/she* are considered equally cumbersome. The *he or she* device can work, provided it is not overused.

   AWKWARD To some extent, *a biologist* must decide for <u>him- or herself</u> which system of classification <u>he or she</u> will use.

   REVISED To some extent, *a biologist* must decide which system of classification <u>he or she</u> will use.

   REVISED To some extent, *a biologist* must decide which system of classification to use. [The infinitive *to use* avoids the *he or she* difficulty.]

2. **Make a pronoun's antecedent plural.** If the accuracy of a sentence will permit a plural antecedent, use this device to avoid unintentional sexism in pronoun selection.

   PLURAL To some extent, *biologists* must decide for <u>themselves</u> which system of classification *they* will use. [Note the possible shift in meaning: *biologists* may imply a group discussion.]

3. **Use the passive voice to avoid gender-specific pronouns—but only if it is appropriate to deemphasize a subject.** Note, however, that using the passive voice creates its own problems of vague reference. (See 9g-2 and 17b-1.)

   NEUTRAL It is every biologist's responsibility to specify which system of classification *is being used.*

4. **Reconstruct the entire statement so as to avoid the problem.** Often it is easier to rewrite sentences to avoid pronouns altogether.

   NEUTRAL When choosing among competing systems of classification, the biologist makes a choice that greatly affects later work both in the field and in the lab. [*Later work* is left without a limiting, gender-specific modifier.]

5. **Link gender assignments to specific indefinite antecedents.** Some writers will arbitrarily assign a masculine identity to one indefinite antecedent and a feminine identity to another. The gender assignments are then maintained throughout a document.

   ALTERNATE GENDER ASSIGNMENTS A *biologist* must decide which system of classification <u>she</u> will use. An *anthropologist* must also choose when selecting the formal, stylistic, and technological attributes <u>he</u> will use in distinguishing ancient objects from one another.

EXERCISE 2

Revise the following sentences to ensure agreement between pronouns and antecedents. Eliminate the generic *he*. Place a check before the sentences in which a pronoun agrees in number with its antecedent.

Example: Like land mammals, marine mammals have ears that it uses to receive impressions of its environment.

Like land mammals, marine mammals have ears that *they use* to receive impressions of *their* environment.

1. The clicks, groans, and creaking of whales have impressed researchers with its variations.
2. A dolphin produces his sound by blowing air through the nasal passageway and over two flap-like structures in his blowhole.
3. Anyone who wants to communicate with dolphins must turn his attention to patterns of whistles, squeaks, and yelps that constitute his vocabulary.
4. When dolphins are angry, they bark.
5. The neurophysiologist and marine mammal specialist John Lilly has spent a great deal of their time attempting to communicate with dolphins.

EXERCISE 3

Revise the following gender-biased sentences so that they do not stereotype males or females or restrict references to males. When you make singular nouns plural, other words in the sentence will change.

Example: The behaviorist theory in psychology assumes that man's response to his environment is similar to the response of other animals.

The behaviorist theory in psychology assumes that humans respond to their environment in the same ways that other animals do.

1. Each operator answers her phone.
2. As part of her job, a nurse prepares injections for her patients.
3. A miner would take a canary below ground to make sure the air was safe for him to breathe.
4. A pilot, today, takes much of his training in flight simulators.
5. Recent research has suggested a relationship between the amount of time a child watches television and his later performance in school.

EXERCISE 4

Revise the following paragraph to ensure agreement between subject and verb and between pronoun and antecedent. Also, revise any sentence in which the generic *he* is used.

A manager or others who delivers bad news performs two functions. First, he delivers the news and makes certain the message is received and understood. To accomplish this task require an ability to be both blunt and supportive. This trait allows the giver of news to fulfill his responsibilities to management and at the same time protect workers when he or she is about to be laid off. Either the person delivering bad news or his colleagues has as one of his responsibilities the job of helping the worker cope with the event.

EXERCISE 2

1. The clicks, groans, and creaking of whales have impressed researchers with their variations.
2. Dolphins produce their sound by blowing air through their nasal passageways and over two flap-like structures in their blowholes.
3. Anyone who wants to communicate with dolphins must turn his or her attention to patterns of whistles, squeaks, and yelps that constitute their vocabulary.
4. Correct
5. The neurophysiologist and marine mammal specialist John Lilly has spent a great deal of his time attempting to communicate with dolphins.

EXERCISE 3

Suggested revisions:

1. Each operator answers his or her phone.
2. As part of their job, nurses prepare injections for their patients.
3. Miners would take a canary below ground to make sure the air was safe for them to breathe.
4. A pilot, today, takes much of his or her training in flight simulators.
5. Recent research has suggested a relationship between the amount of time children watch television and their later performance in school.

EXERCISE 4

Suggested revisions:

Managers or others who deliver bad news perform two functions. First, they deliver the news and make certain the message is received and understood. To accomplish this task requires an ability to be both blunt and supportive. This trait allows the giver of news to fulfill his or her responsibilities to management and at the same time protect workers when they are about to be laid off. Either those delivering bad news or their colleagues have as one of their responsibilities the job of helping the worker cope with the event.

Adjectives and Adverbs

The first example presented here illustrates the focus of the entire chapter: The function of adjectives and adverbs is to make sentences clearer and more vivid. As in other chapters on sentence elements, the approach is straightforward and relatively traditional. A chart shows the distinctive functions of the two parts of speech, and the forms are clearly described. Nonstandard usage is treated with tact. The treatment of problem words such as *good/well* and *bad/badly* includes a number of examples to guide students, and a chart lists irregular forms of comparison for easy reference. Exercises focus on editing sentences.

TEACHING IDEAS

Regardless of what they see in their reading, some students have the idea that in their own writing, adjectives and adverbs are designed simply to emphasize the *qualities* of a noun or a verb rather than to more clearly define those words. When you ask for more modifiers in an essay, you get a few words like *beautiful, quickly, strong*. To give students a sense of the distinction between modifiers that clarify and those that simply emphasize qualities, write the following revision of the opening example on the board: "Nicholas II, the strong and handsome leader, fearlessly ruled beautiful Russia." (Granted, the sentence is a little silly, but an extreme example is often useful.) Ask students about the difference in *information provided* between the two sentences. What function do the modifiers serve in each sentence? What do we know about Nicholas, his rule, and Russia from each sentence? Given the apparently historical importance of the sentence, what do we need to know? Finally, which sentence provides more information about the historical situation?

Adjectives and adverbs are **modifiers**—*descriptive* words, phrases, or clauses that enliven sentences with vivid detail. In chapter 7 you learned how phrases and clauses function as modifiers. But even when dealing with one-word modifiers, as in this chapter, you can see that the effectiveness of modifiers depends on keeping straight the two main types: adjectives and adverbs.

11a Distinguishing between adjectives and adverbs

Some basic distinctions between the use of adjectives and adverbs are summarized in the following box.

Distinguishing Adjectives from Adverbs

An **adjective** modifies a noun or pronoun and answers these questions:
  Which: The *latest* news arrived.
  What kind: An *insignificant* difference remained.
  How many: The *two* sides would resolve their differences.
An **adverb** modifies a verb and answers these questions:
  When: *Tomorrow,* the temperature will drop.
  How: The temperature will drop *sharply*.
  How often: Weather patterns change *frequently*.
  Where: The weather patterns *here* change frequently.
An **adverb** also modifies adjectives, adverbs, and entire clauses:
  Modifying an adjective: An *especially* large group enrolled.
  Modifying a clause: *Consequently,* the registrar closed the course.
  Modifying an adverb: Courses at this school *almost* never get closed.

When choosing between an adjective and adverb form for a sentence, identify the word being modified and determine its part of speech. Then follow the conventions presented in this chapter.

1   Identifying and using adjectives

An **adjective** modifies a noun or pronoun by answering these questions: **which?** the *tall* child; **what kind?** the *artistic* child; **how many?** *five* children. Pure adjectives are not derived from other words: *large, small, simple, difficult, thick, thin, cold, hot.* Many adjectives, however, are derived from nouns.

Base noun	Suffix	Adjective
science	-ic	scientific
region	-al	regional
book	-ish	bookish

Adjectives are also derived from verbs.

Base verb	Suffix	Adjective
respect	-ful	respectful
respect	-ed	respected (past participle)
respect	-ing	respecting (present participle)
demonstrate	-ive	demonstrative
hesitate	-ant	hesitant

Writers frequently build up their desired meanings by taking a word and adapting its base form, thereby converting the word into the part of speech needed for a new sentence.

The audience maintained a (respect + ful) silence.

The (region + al) conference was about to begin.

ESL NOTE   The past and present participles formed from the same basic verb are related in meaning. Consider, though, how two forms derived from a transitive verb (such as *confuse*) may work in opposite directions on the word modified: *a confused speaker* experiences confusion, while *a confusing speaker* gives others this experience (see 44a-1).

Placement

A single-word adjective is usually placed before the word it modifies. Occasionally an adjective will appear after a noun or pronoun—usually when the adjective is formed by a phrase or clause.

The speaker was received with *enthusiastic* applause.

The speaker, *bookish* and *hesitant*, approached the podium.

ESL NOTE   In most English sentences, two or more adjectives that accumulate as modifiers before a noun or pronoun are typically given a standard order or sequence. For example, adjectives describing nationality and color are typically placed nearer than others to the noun or pronoun.

ESL ALERT

ESL trouble spots will be distinguishing between "hard" and "hardly," "a few" and "few," "a little" and "little," "some" and "any," and using "well" and "good" correctly. The distinction between "I have *a* little time/money" and "I have little time/money" is *not* self-evident, even to many fluent second-language speakers, and may have damaging social consequences.

ESL ALERT

Spanish speakers tend to have difficulty with "too," using it as an equivalent of "very" instead of as a negative form involving an explanation: "He is too tall to enter without bending over" or "She is too tired to work any longer." Try to have students articulate what it means to have "too much money" or "too much love." Also contrast the following:

"She is very hungry."
"She is too hungry to wait for us."
"She is hungry enough to eat a horse."

ESL ALERT

Marcella Frank's *Modern English, Part I* has a complete chapter on adverbs, and the final section of the chapter practices distinguishing between adverbs and adjectives, as in "He felt bad" as opposed to "He did that badly."

ADDITIONAL EXERCISE A

GROUP ACTIVITY   In groups of three or four, modify the following sentences by adding single-word adjectives and adverbs. Then compare your responses to those of other groups. How does the meaning of each sentence change as a result of the modifiers used?

1. A skier sped down the slope.
2. The boxer danced around his opponent.
3. The colonel inspected her office.
4. The child cried.
5. An artist contemplated the scene.

LOOKING BACK

If any students need to refresh their memories with regard to the role of parts of speech in a sentence, refer them to chapter 7 (Constructing Sentences).

ADDITIONAL EXERCISE B

ACROSS THE CURRICULUM Make a photocopy of a brief passage from one of your textbooks. Circle the adjectives and adverbs and draw arrows to the words they modify. Then, for each sentence in the passage, explain how the adjectives enhance meaning.

REFERENCES

CHRISTENSEN, FRANCIS. "A Generative Rhetoric of the Sentence." CCC 14 (1963): 155–61. Use of modifiers improves students' prose style.

SHAUGHNESSY, MINA P. *Errors & Expectations: A Guide for the Teacher of Basic Writing.* New York: Oxford UP, 1977. Chapter 6. Building vocabulary can help students break away from standard, overused modifiers.

ESL ALERT

Initial emphatic negative adverbial phrases requiring reversed word order will prove difficult and confusing for most ESL students: "Never in a million years will I marry you" or "Not once did she try to help." Confusing also are the rules for word order with initial adverbial phrases of place: "In the center of the room was an ornate table" or "Near the fireplace stood an antique lamp." Many ESL students will tend to put the subject before the verb with these patterns.

ESL ALERT

Adverb placement is not treated clearly in most ESL texts. Such texts do not explain well the shifts in meaning and emphasis possible through shifts in placement, so the examples in this section require close attention. Students will have trouble with placement of adverbs in three-part verbs: frequency/time between the first two parts, manner/degree between the last two, as in "She had *rarely* been so *completely* enchanted" or "*Yesterday* she had *nearly* been *completely* convinced." This is because native speakers have an instinctual sense of when a variation of this standard pattern is necessary, as in "She has *recently* been advancing *more slowly*," but cannot always articulate clearly why this variation must occur (in this case the extra word makes the final two words a phrase of manner, and phrases of manner follow the verb just as phrases of frequency follow phrases

CONFUSING   *a blue Japanese cheerful flower*

TYPICAL   *a cheerful blue Japanese flower*

Section 44f-1–2 describes typical patterns for placement of English adjective modifiers.

2   Identifying and using adverbs

An **adverb** modifies a verb by answering several questions: **When?** *Yesterday,* the child sang. **How?** The child sang *beautifully.* **How often?** The child sings *regularly.* **Where?** The child sang *here.* Adverbs modify adjectives: The child sang an *extremely* intricate melody. Adverbs can modify other adverbs: The child sings *almost* continuously. Certain adverbs can modify entire sentences: *Consequently,* the child's voice has improved.

Pure adverbs are not derived from other words: *again, almost, always, never, here, there, now, often, seldom, well.* Many adverbs, however, are formed from adjectives. These adverbs may be formed simply by adding the suffix *-ly* to adjectives.

Adjective	*Add -ly*	*Adverb*
beautiful		beautifully
strange		strangely
clever		cleverly
respectful		respectfully

However, an *-ly* ending alone is not sufficient to establish a word as an adverb, since certain adjectives show this ending: a friend*ly* conversation, a love*ly* afternoon. In any standard dictionary look for the abbreviations **adj.** and **adv.,** which will distinguish between the forms of a word.

Thousands of words in our language have both adjective and adverb forms. Consider the noun *grace,* defined by the *American Heritage Dictionary* as "seemingly effortless beauty or charm of movement, form, or proportion." *Graceful* and *gracious* are adjectives, and *graciously, gracefully,* and *gracelessly* are adverbs.

Placement

The location of an adverb may be shifted in a sentence, depending on the rhythm and emphasis a writer wants to achieve. An adverb (as a word, phrase, or clause) can appear in the sentence's beginning, middle, or end.

> *Formerly,* Zimbabwe was known as Rhodesia.

> Zimbabwe was *formerly* known as Rhodesia.

> Zimbabwe was known as Rhodesia, *formerly.*

A note of caution: Lengthy adverb phrases and clauses should not split sentence elements that occur in pairs, such as a subject and verb or a verb and its object (see 15d). Also, limiting modifiers such as *only, al-*

most, or *nearly* must be carefully placed close to the word they modify (see 15b).

ESL Note   While the placement of most English adverbs is flexible, limiting adverbs and others require specific positions in the sentence, as described in 44c-1–2.

EXERCISE 1

Identify the single-word adjectives and adverbs in the following sentences; also identify the words being modified.

adj   adj

Example: As night began to fall on the *Russian* Empire's *western*

adv   adj

borders, day was *already* breaking on the *Pacific* coast.

1. Through the depth of Russian winters, millions of tall pines stood silently in heavy snows.
2. In summer, clusters of white-trunked birches gently rustled in the slanting rays of the afternoon sun.
3. Rivers, wide and flat, flowed peacefully through the grassy plains of European Russia.
4. Eastward, in Siberia, mightier rivers rolled northward to the Arctic.
5. Here and there, thinly scattered across the broad land, lived one hundred and thirty million subjects of the Tsar.

EXERCISE 2

Convert the following nouns and verbs to adjectives and adverbs; convert the adjectives to adverbs. (Use a dictionary for help, if necessary.) Then use each newly converted word in a sentence.

Example: courtesy (noun)   courteous (adjective)   courteously (adverb)

A courteous driver will signal before turning.

substance	wonderful
reason	colossal
argue	

11b   **Use an adverb (not an adjective) to modify verbs as well as verbals.**

Adverbs are used to modify verbs even when a direct object stands between the verb and its modifier.

FAULTY   If you measure an object in Denver *precise*, it will weigh somewhat less than the same object measured in Washington. [The adjective *precise*—following a direct object—is used incorrectly to modify the verb *measured*.]

of manner: "I understand him more and more fully each time I see him").

EXERCISE 1

adj

1. Through the depth of *Russian* winters,

   adj   adv   adj
   millions of *tall* pines stood *silently* in *heavy* snows.

   adj
2. In summer, clusters of *white-trunked* birches

   adv   adj
   gently rustled in the *slanting* rays of the

   adj
   afternoon sun.

   adj   adj   adv
3. Rivers, *wide* and *flat*, flowed *peacefully*

   adj   adj
   through the *grassy* plains of *European* Russia.

   adv   adj
4. *Eastward*, in Siberia, *mightier* rivers rolled

   adv
   northward to the Arctic.

   adv   adv
5. *Here and there, thinly* scattered across the

   adj   adj
   broad land, lived *one hundred and thirty million* subjects of the Tsar.

EXERCISE 2

(individual responses for sentence portion)

1. substance (noun)   substantive (adj)   substantively (adv)
2. reason (noun)   reasonable (adj)   reasonably (adv)
3. argue (noun)   arguable (adj)   arguably (adv)
4. wonderful (adj)   wonderfully (adv)
5. colossal (adj)   colossally (adv)

REVISED   If you measure an object in Denver *precisely*, it will weigh somewhat less than the same object measured in Washington.

FAULTY   A *precise* measured object in Denver will weigh somewhat less than the same object measured in Washington. [The adjective *precise* incorrectly modifies the participle *measured*.]

REVISED   A *precisely* measured object in Denver will weigh somewhat less than the same object measured in Washington.

FAULTY   An object's weight can be determined by measuring it *careful* against a known weight. [The adjective *careful* incorrectly modifies the gerund *measuring*.]

REVISED   An object's weight can be determined by measuring it *carefully* against a known weight.

11c   Use an adverb (not an adjective) to modify another adverb or an adjective.

Although informal or nonstandard usage occasionally finds adjectives like *real* or *sure* functioning as adverbs ("a real bad time," "it sure was good"), standard academic usage requires that adverbs modify adjectives and other adverbs.

NONSTANDARD   A *reasonable* accurate scale can measure hundredths of a gram. [The adjective *reasonable* incorrectly modifies the adjective *accurate*.]

REVISED   A *reasonably* accurate scale can measure hundredths of a gram.

FAULTY   An object on the Moon weighs *significant* less than it does on Earth. [The adjective *significant* incorrectly modifies the adverb *less*.]

REVISED   An object on the Moon weighs *significantly* less than it does on Earth.

11d   Use an adjective (not an adverb) after a linking verb to describe a subject.

The following verbs are linking verbs: forms of *be* (*is, are, was, were, has been, have been*), *look, smell, taste, sound, feel, appear, become, grow, remain, seem, turn,* and *stay.* A sentence with a linking verb establishes, in effect, an equation between the first part of the sentence and the second:

$$\underline{\quad A \quad} \text{ LINKING VERB } \underline{\quad B \quad}, \text{ or } \underline{\quad A \quad} = \underline{\quad B \quad}.$$

In this construction, the predicate part, *B*, is called the *subject complement*. The function of a **subject complement** is to rename or modify the subject of a sentence, which is a noun. The subject complement may be a noun, pronoun, or adjective—but **not** an adverb. In these examples, the linking verbs are followed by adjectives that describe a subject.

LINKING   The dessert looks *delicious.*
          The crowd turned *violent.*
          The pilots were *thirsty.*

IMPORTANT EXCEPTIONS: Several linking verbs, especially those associated with the five senses, can also express action. When they do, they are considered *action* (not linking) *verbs* and are modified by adverbs.

ACTION   Palmer looked *menacingly* at the batter. [*Looked* is an action verb with an adverb modifier.]

LINKING   Palmer looked angry and *menacing.* [*Looked* is a linking verb, with the adjective *menacing* describing the subject's apparent attitude.]

ACTION   The storm turned *violently* toward land. [*Turned* is an action verb with an adverb modifier.]

LINKING   The storm turned *violent.* [*Turned* is now a linking verb meaning "became." The adjective *violent* is linked as a modifier to *storm.*]

Good, well, bad, badly

The words *good* and *well, bad* and *badly* are not interchangeable in formal writing (though they tend to be in conversation). The common linking verbs associated with well-being, appearance, or feeling—*looks, seems, appears, feels*—can cause special problems. The rules of usage follow.

1 Good and well

Good is an adjective, used either before a noun or after a linking verb to describe the condition of a subject.

ACCEPTABLE   Kyle looks good. [After a linking verb, *good* describes the subject's appearance.]

              Kyle is a good dancer. [*Good* modifies the noun *dancer.*]

NONSTANDARD   Susan drives good. [*Drives* is an action verb and requires an adverb as modifier.]

REVISED   Susan drives well.

The word *well* can be used as either an adjective or an adverb. It has limited use as an adjective only after certain linking verbs (*looks, seems, be/am/is/are*) that describe the subject's good health.

TEACHING IDEAS

Like the pronoun *whom* and the phrase *you and I*, *well* and *badly* are often mistakenly identified as signals of "cultured" speech; people frequently use these adverbs inappropriately, assuming that *well* and *badly* are "proper" English while *good* and *bad* are not. You might want to remind students that although "He looks *well*" is appropriate, a statement such as "That tie looks *well* on him" is actually incorrect, and should be revised to read "That tie looks *good* on him."

ACCEPTABLE Robert looks well. [*Looks* is a linking verb. The sense of this sentence is that Robert seems to be healthy.]

Well functions as an adverb whenever it follows an action verb.

NONSTANDARD Janet sings good. [*Sings* is an action verb and requires an adverb as modifier.]

REVISED Janet sings well.

2 Bad and badly

Bad is an adjective, used before a noun and after a linking verb to describe a subject. Again, the linking verbs that involve appearance or feeling—*looks, seems, appears, feels*—can cause special problems.

FAULTY Marie feels badly. [*Feels* is a linking verb and must tie the subject, *Marie*, to an adjective.]

REVISED Marie feels bad. [As an adjective, *bad* is linked to the subject to describe *Marie* and her mental state.]

EXCEPTION: The verb *feels* could possibly be an action verb indicating a sense of touch rather than a linking verb indicating well-being: "The blind reader feels braille letters carefully and well." Only in this limited meaning would the phrases "feels badly" or "feels well" be used properly to show how that sense is operating.

Badly is an adverb, used after an action verb or used to modify an adjective or adverb.

NONSTANDARD John cooks bad. [*Cooks* is an action verb and must be modified by an adverb.]

REVISED John cooks badly.

EXERCISE 3

Individual responses

EXERCISE 4

1. Tom has been looking bad.
2. If he were under a doctor's supervision, he might look well.
3. He certainly sleeps well.
4. A good sleeper can put in eight hours a night.
5. Sleeping badly can make one feel old in a hurry.

EXERCISE 3
Browse through a dictionary and locate five words that have both adjective and adverb forms. Write a sentence for the two uses of each word—ten sentences in all. Draw an arrow from each adjective or adverb to the word modified.

Example: patient   The people in the waiting room were patient.

patiently The people waited patiently.

EXERCISE 4
Fill in the blank in each sentence with *good, well, bad,* or *badly* and draw an arrow from the word chosen to the word modified.

Example: The team's prospects are _____ .

The team's prospects are *good.*

1. Tom has been looking _____ .
2. If he were under a doctor's supervision, he might look _____ .
3. He certainly sleeps _____ .
4. A _____ sleeper can put in eight hours a night.
5. Sleeping _____ can make one feel old in a hurry.

11e Using comparative and superlative forms of adjectives and adverbs

Both adjectives and adverbs change form to express comparative relationships. The base form of an adjective or adverb is called its **positive** form. The **comparative** form is used to express a relationship between two elements, and the **superlative** form is used to express a relationship among three or more elements. Most single-syllable adverbs and adjectives, and many two-syllable adjectives, show comparisons with the suffix *-er* and superlatives with *-est.*

	Positive	*Comparative*	*Superlative*
Adjective	crazy	crazier	craziest
	crafty	craftier	craftiest
Adverb	near	nearer	nearest
	far	farther	farthest

Adverbs of two or more syllables and adjectives of three or more syllables change to the comparative and superlative forms with the words *more* and *most.* Adjectives and adverbs show downward (or negative) comparisons with the words *less* and *least* placed before the positive form. If you are uncertain of an adjective's or adverb's form, refer to a dictionary.

	Positive	*Comparative*	*Superlative*
Adjective	elegant	more/less elegant	most/least elegant
	logical	more/less logical	most/least logical
Adverb	beautifully	more/less beautifully	most/least beautifully
	strangely	more/less strangely	most/least strangely

1 Use irregular adjectives and adverbs with care.

A number of adjectives and adverbs are irregular in forming comparatives and superlatives, and they must be memorized. Consult the following box for these basic forms.

ADDITIONAL EXERCISE C

Add adjectives and adverbs to the sentences below to make them clearer and more lively. (Remember that adjectives and adverbs can be phrases and clauses as well as single words.)

1. Martin planted a garden.
2. The plants grew.
3. Martin took a vacation.
4. Sherry looked after the garden.
5. Everything in the garden died.

ADDITIONAL EXERCISE D

Rewrite all of the incorrect sentences below, revising for accuracy, completeness, and logic of adjective forms

1. Suellen and Marc ran a race to see who was the fastest.
2. That was the most nearly perfect performance I've ever seen.
3. Our chocolate chip cookies are chewier.
4. Of all the children, the youngest is more favored by the parents.
5. We saw the most unique necklace at the flea market.

Answers:

1. Suellen and Marc ran a race to see who was faster.
2. Correct
3. Our chocolate chip cookies are chewier *than yours.* (suggested revision)
4. Of all the children, the youngest is *most* favored by the parents.
5. We saw *a nearly* unique necklace at the flea market. (suggested revision)

Irregular Forms of Comparison

	Positive	*Comparative*	*Superlative*
Adjective	good	better	best
	bad	worse	worst
	little	less	least
	many	more	most
	much	more	most
	some	more	most
Adverb	well (also adj.)	better	best
	badly	worse	worst

2 Express comparative and superlative relationships accurately, completely, and logically.

Accuracy

Use the comparative form of adverbs and adjectives to show a relationship between two items; use the superlative form when relating three or more items.

TWO ITEMS John is funnier than his brother Frank.

TWO ITEMS Walking is less strenuous than running.

MULTIPLES IBM is the world's largest manufacturer of computers.

Completeness

If the elements of a two- or three-way comparison are not being mentioned explicitly in a sentence, be sure to provide enough context so that the comparison makes sense.

INCOMPLETE John is funnier. [Funnier than what? whom?]

REVISED John is the funnier brother. [Two brothers are being compared.]
or
John is funnier than his brother Frank.

Logic

Certain adjectives have an absolute meaning—they cannot be logically compared. It makes no sense, for instance, to discuss greater or lesser degrees of *perfect* (although in advertising and in conversation, people often try). *Perfect* represents a logical endpoint of comparison, as do the words *unique, first, final, last, absolute, infinite,* and *dead.* Note, though,

CRITICAL DECISIONS

Be alert to differences: Apply a test for choosing comparative forms—few/fewer/fewest, little/less/least, many, much

When making comparisons, note the differences between elements that can be counted and those that cannot (see 7a-2 and 42a-1). Then choose the appropriate form for your comparison.

- For nouns that can be counted, downward comparisons must be made with *few, fewer,* or *fewest.*

  FAULTY   Frozen yogurt has *less* calories than ice cream. [Since *calories* can be counted, *less* is the wrong comparative term.]

  REVISED   Frozen yogurt has *fewer* calories than ice cream.

- For mass nouns, which cannot be counted (see 7a-2), downward comparisons must be made with *little, less,* or *least.*

  FAULTY   "Drinker's Delight" coffee has *fewer* caffeine than regular coffee. [Since *caffeine* is a mass noun and cannot be counted, *fewer* is the wrong comparative term.]

  REVISED   "Drinker's Delight" coffee has *less* caffeine than regular coffee.

- For nouns that can be counted, use the adjective *many,* not *much.*

  FAULTY   Ice cream has *much* calories. [Since *calories* can be counted, *much* is the incorrect adjective form.]

  REVISED   Ice cream has *many* calories.

TEACHING IDEAS

"Less Calories!" is a claim seen all too frequently in product advertising today. Since the claim is so familiar, you may want to call particular attention to it in order to acquaint students with the appropriate use of adjectives with count nouns and with mass nouns.

that a concert performance might be *nearly* perfect or a patient on an operating table *almost* dead. Once *perfection* or *death* is reached, comparisons literally make no sense.

ILLOGICAL   The story was submitted in its most final form.

REVISED   The story was submitted in its final form.
or
The story was submitted in nearly final form.

11f Avoid double comparisons, double superlatives, and double negatives.

Double comparisons/superlatives

Adjectives and adverbs show comparative and superlative relationships either with a suffix (-er/-est) *or* with the words *more, most, less, least.* It is redundant and awkward to use the -er/-est suffix with *more/most* or *less/least.*

ESL ALERT

The double comparison and double superlative are common ESL mistakes because students have learned the "more/most" pattern and will use it in all situations.

FAULTY	The World Trade Center is more taller than the Chrysler Building.
REVISED	The World Trade Center is taller than the Chrysler Building.
FAULTY	That is the least likeliest conclusion to the story.
REVISED	That is the least likely conclusion to the story.

Double negatives

Double negatives—the presence of two modifiers that say "no" in the same sentence—are redundant and sometimes confusing, though fairly common in nonstandard usage. A clear negation in a sentence should be expressed only once. Combine the negatives *not, never, neither/nor, hardly,* or *scarcely* with *any, anything,* or *anyone.* Do not combine these negatives with the negatives *no, none, nothing,* or *no one.*

NONSTANDARD	I didn't have none. I didn't have no cash. [These double negatives risk the implication that the speaker in fact has cash.]
REVISED	I had none. I didn't have any cash.
NONSTANDARD	I hardly had none.
REVISED	I hardly had any.
NONSTANDARD	I never had nothing.
REVISED	I never had any. I had nothing.

11g Avoid overusing nouns as modifiers.

A noun can modify another noun and thus function as an adjective. A few examples include *gate* keeper, *toll* booth, *cell* block, *beauty* parlor, *parlor* game, *finger* puppet, and *tax* collector. Noun modifiers provide handy shortcuts, but when two or more nouns are stacked before a third noun to function as adjectives, the result is logically and stylistically disastrous.

| UNCLEAR | The textbook Civil War chapter review questions are due tomorrow. |

The sentence falters because we are given five seemingly unrelated nouns from which to choose a subject: *textbook, Civil War, chapter, review,* and *questions.* Unstack noun modifiers by moving the subject to the beginning of the sentence and arranging modifying nouns into phrases.

        subject   **prep. phrase with possessive**   **prep. phrase**

| REVISED | The *review questions from the textbook's chapter on the Civil War* are due tomorrow. |

ESL NOTE With noun modifiers, sequence and placement are more critical than with adjectives or adverbs (see 44a-2 on noun modifiers). Some of the conventions for ordering cumulative adjective modifiers may also apply to nouns (see 44f).

EXERCISE 5

Correct the problems with comparative and superlative forms in the following sentences.

> *Example:* Of three books I read recently on life in nineteenth-century England, Hardy's *Far from the Madding Crowd* is the more engaging.
>
> Of the three books I read recently on life in nineteenth-century England, Hardy's *Far from the Madding Crowd* is the <u>most</u> engaging. [The superlative is needed for differentiating three or more items.]

1. Hardy is better known for *Tess of the d'Urbervilles.*
2. Hardy is sometimes called the most last of the Victorians.
3. He was one of the prolifickest writers of the nineteenth century, with several major novels and more than one thousand poems to his credit.
4. Scholarship on Hardy's life and work is so bountiful that no one should have no trouble in finding ample analyses of his works.
5. Of the many editions of Hardy's work now available, the more notable is the Macmillan Wessex edition.

CHAPTER 12

Sentence Fragments

KEY FEATURES

Since many students really aren't sure what a fragment is, this chapter begins with a brief, clear definition of the error, followed by a detailed strategy to check for completeness of sentences. The examples of each type of fragment focus on the major culprits, especially verbals, subordinate conjunctions, and relative pronouns. With a wealth of examples to study, students should be able to recognize the type(s) of fragments they produce, thereby simplifying the editing of their papers. After categorizing fragments, the chapter moves immediately to strategies for eliminating them. Methods of editing for fragments are clearly delineated; again, if students are aware of the specific types of fragments they produce, they can make use of the chart to correct their errors. The chapter also acknowledges the intentional fragment, with the warning that the effectiveness of this construction hinges on the fact that it is indeed a breach of the rules, and thus should be used rarely. As in preceding chapters, the material here is presented in a straightforward, traditional manner, with an emphasis on clear, effective communication rather than rules and errors. Exercises require identification and correction of fragments, as well as identification of types of fragments. The latter exercises should help students classify their own errors.

One important goal of writing is to keep readers focused on clearly stated ideas. Few errors are more disruptive of this goal than the **sentence fragment,** a partial sentence punctuated as if it were a complete sentence. Because it is only a partial sentence, a fragment leaves readers confused, trying to guess at what claims or statements are being made. To be a sentence, a group of words must first have a subject and a predicate (see 7a-1). A sentence fragment may lack either a subject or a predicate—and sometimes both. A fragment may also be a dependent clause (see 7e) that has not been joined to an independent (or main) clause.

FRAGMENT   Emphasizing a focused, single effect as the story's main feature. [The clause lacks both a subject and a verb, since *emphasizing* is a verbal. (See 12c.)]

REVISED   *Edgar Allan Poe emphasized* a focused, single effect as the story's main feature. [A subject and verb are added to create a sentence.]

FRAGMENT   Although storytelling is one of the oldest arts. [This unit is a dependent clause.]

REVISED   Although storytelling is one of the oldest arts, *the short story* as a narrative form *is* comparatively new in literature. [The clause is joined to an independent clause.]

 12a   **Check for completeness of sentences.**

Avoid writing fragments by checking your sentences for grammatical completeness. There are three tests you can conduct:

1. Locate a verb.
2. Locate the verb's subject.
3. Check for subordinating conjunctions or relative pronouns.

SPOTLIGHT ON COMMON ERRORS—SENTENCE CONSTRUCTION AND FRAGMENTS

These are the errors most commonly associated with sentence construction and fragments. For full explanations and suggested revisions, follow the cross-references to chapter sections.

FRAGMENT ERRORS arise when writers incorrectly mark a group of words as a sentence. Apply a three-part test to confirm that a grouping of words can stand alone as a sentence (see 12a).

Test 1:   **Locate a verb: A sentence must have a verb.**

Churchill *was* a leader.
[Verb—*was*]

A leader of great distinction.
[No verb—this grouping of words cannot be a sentence; it is a FRAGMENT.]

When he *became* Prime Minister.
[Verb—*became*—BUT this word grouping fails Test 3 below, so it is still a FRAGMENT.]

REVISED   Churchill was *a leader of great distinction.*

NOTE: Be sure the word selected as a verb is not a verbal, which looks like a verb but actually serves as a subject, object, or modifier (see 7a-4).

After *serving* his country in the first World War.
[Verbal: *serving* looks like a verb but is actually an object in the prepositional phrase beginning with *after.* This grouping of words is therefore a FRAGMENT.]

REVISED   **After serving his country in the first World War,** he became Prime Minister.

Test 2:   **Locate the verb's subject: A sentence must have a subject.**

Churchill was a leader.
[Subject—*Churchill*]

When he became Prime Minister.
[Subject—*he*—BUT this word grouping fails Test 3 so it is still a FRAGMENT.]

Test 3:   **Be sure that words such as *when, while, because* or *who, which, that* do not prevent the word group from being a sentence (see subordinating conjunctions and relative pronouns, 19b-1–2).**

SENTENCE   Churchill *was* a leader.
[No words prevent the grouping from being a sentence.]

FRAGMENTS   *When* he became Prime Minister.   *Who* became Prime Minister.
[*When* (a subordinating conjunction) and *who* (a relative pronoun) prevent these word groups from standing alone as sentences.]

REVISED   **He became Prime Minister.**

See 12b–12d for ways to correct fragments once you have identified them.

FOR DISCUSSION

Since most students have problems with only certain types of fragments, you might want to initiate a class discussion of errors most relevant to your students. Ask students to identify from the Spotlight on Common Errors examples of fragments familiar to them and to make a personal list of common types of fragments. Students can then discuss how fragment errors arise, thereby reinforcing their understanding of sentence completeness. (In large classes, this activity might begin with small groups: The groups will identify their common types of fragments, and then the class as a whole will discuss the list of types compiled from each group's report.)

ESL ALERT

Most ESL students will have difficulty recognizing as fragments phrases containing a passive participle, confusing, for example, the past tense, as in "His style bored her," with the passive participle, as in "His work finished more rapidly than he expected."

LOOKING BACK

References to chapter 7 (Constructing Sentences) appear throughout this chapter. Section 7b (Understanding basic sentence patterns) could be especially helpful to students with a need for more basic instruction. If chapter 7 has not been covered yet, or if some time has passed since it was covered, you may want to spend a little time on that material now.

First test: Locate a verb.

Every sentence has a verb. To be sure you've written a sentence, find the verb. Be sure that the word you settle on as the verb of the sentence is not a verbal (see 7a-4). There are three types of verbals you should disqualify when looking for sentence verbs: verb forms ending in *-ing*, verb forms ending in *-ed* (when not paired with a subject), and verb forms introduced with the infinitive *to*.

Verb forms ending in *-ing* must be preceded by a form of *be* (e.g., *is, are, were, was, has been*, etc.) in order to function as sentence verbs.

FRAGMENT His arguing a long and tiresome case without any sensitivity to his readers. [*Arguing* is a verbal since it is not preceded by a form of *be*.]

REVISED *He was* arguing a long and tiresome case without any sensitivity to his readers. [*Was arguing* is a verb. The subject of the revised sentence is *he*.]

Verb forms ending in *-ed* may be called *participles* and function as adjectives, not as verbs, when they are preceded by an article (*a, an,* or *the* [see 7a-2]), by a noun or pronoun in its possessive form (e.g., *Paul's, his*), or by a preposition (*of, by, for,* etc.). To function as a verb, such a form must be paired with a subject.

FRAGMENT The calculated, high risk. [*Calculated* functions as a participle describing *risk*.]

REVISED *Susan calculated* the high risk. [*Calculated* is paired with a subject, *Susan*, to become a verb.]

REVISED Susan's *calculated risk* paid off. [*Calculated* is a participle describing the subject *risk*. A verb, *paid*, has been added.]

FRAGMENT A series of legislated revolutionary reforms. [*Legislated* is a participle describing reforms.]

REVISED *Congress legislated* revolutionary reforms. [*Legislated* is a verb with a subject, *Congress*.]

Verb forms introduced with the infinitive marker *to* never function as sentence verbs; another verb must be added to make a sentence.

FRAGMENT To appreciate the alternative.

REVISED *Frank failed* to appreciate the alternative. [The verb *failed* has been added along with the subject *Frank*.]

Second test: Locate the verb's subject.

Once you have located a verb, ask *who* or *what* makes its assertion or action and you will find the subject.

FRAGMENT   Separated visible light into a spectrum of colors.

REVISED   *Isaac Newton* separated visible light into a spectrum of colors.
            [The subject, *Isaac Newton*, is needed to answer the question
            Who separated?]

FRAGMENT   First attempted an analysis of the short story.

REVISED   *Edgar Allan Poe* first attempted an analysis of the short story.
            [A subject, *Edgar Allan Poe*, is added to answer the question
            Who first attempted an analysis?]

Imperative sentences—commands—often lack a subject; still, they are considered sentences since the implied subject is understood to be *you*.

IMPERATIVE SENTENCE	UNDERSTOOD AS
Open the door!	You open the door.
Come here, please.	You come here, please.

ESL NOTE   The subject of a sentence in English, unlike that in many other languages, is expressed directly as a separate word in one location only. Because the subject is not implied in the form of a verb (other than the imperative) or other sentence part, identifying the subject with a specific word is critical to the structure of an English sentence (see 7a-1 and 7b).

Third test: Check for subordinating conjunctions or relative pronouns.

Be certain that a subject and verb are not preceded by a subordinating conjunction or that a relative pronoun taking the place of a subject does not make the clause dependent. If a word grouping consists of a subject and predicate, it is a sentence *unless* it contains a subordinating word, either an opening subordinating conjunction or a relative pronoun taking the place of its subject.

SUBORDINATING CONJUNCTIONS

after	although	as if	assuming that
because	before	how	if
provided that	since	though	unless
until	whenever	where	while

A subordinating conjunction placed at the beginning of an independent clause renders the clause dependent, so that it cannot stand alone as a complete sentence. If the conjunction is eliminated, the clause will stand as a sentence. If the clause is combined with another sentence, the new dependent clause will function as if it were an adverb.

FRAGMENT   Though people may have a personality disorder. [The conjunction *though* makes the clause dependent on another assertion.]

REVISED   ~~Though~~ People may have a personality disorder. [Dropping the conjunction makes a simple sentence.]

REVISED Though people may have a personality disorder, *they may see their behavior as normal.* [The dependent clause now functions as an adverb.]

RELATIVE PRONOUNS

that	which	whichever	who
whoever	whom	whomever	

A relative pronoun taking the place of a subject in a clause signals that the clause is dependent and cannot stand alone as a complete thought. If the pronoun is eliminated, the clause will stand as a sentence. If it is combined with another sentence, the dependent clause will function as if it were an adjective.

FRAGMENT People who have a personality disorder. [*Who* takes the place of the subject *people,* creating a dependent clause.]

REVISED People ~~who~~ have a personality disorder. [Eliminating *who* leaves a simple sentence.]

REVISED People who have a personality disorder *see their behavior as acceptable.* [*People* is the subject of a verb, *see,* with a *who* clause as adjective modifier.]

EXCEPTION: When one of the above-listed relative pronouns introduces a question, it becomes an interrogative (questioning) pronoun. The resulting construction is not considered to be a fragment: *Who has a personality disorder?*

EXERCISE 1

1. Fragment—fails test 2 (no subject)
2. Correct
3. Correct
4. Fragment—fails test 1 (no verb)
5. Fragment—fails test 1 (verbal)
6. Correct
7. Fragment—fails test 1 (verbal)

EXERCISE 1

Use the three-part test to identify fragments and to explain the cause of each fragment. Place a check before complete sentences, and circle the numbers of items that are fragments.

Example: In the Near East, five thousand years of history.

Fragment—fails test 1 (no verb)

1. Recorded in government archives in inscriptions and on thousands of clay tablets.
2. The lists of kings and genealogies in Egyptian archives record dates in years that go back to at least 3000 B.C.
3. Recorded history starts in about 750 B.C. in the central Mediterranean.
4. About 55 B.C. the start of historical records in Britain.
5. The first historical records for the New World long thought to begin with the Spanish conquest.
6. Parts of Africa entered "history" in A.D. 1890.
7. Historical records covering but the very smallest fraction of the human experience.

Eliminate fragments: Revise dependent clauses set off as sentences.

A dependent clause functions as a modifier—either as an adverb (see 19b-1) or as an adjective (see 19b-2). A dependent clause that has been set off incorrectly as a sentence can be corrected in one of two ways: by converting the clause to an independent clause or by joining the clause to a new sentence.

 1   Convert the dependent clause to an independent clause.

FRAGMENT   Even though the president attended the meeting.
CLEAR   The president attended the meeting.

If the dependent clause begins with a subordinating conjunction, delete the conjunction and you will have an independent clause—a sentence.

FRAGMENT   After Teddy Roosevelt was hit in the eye while boxing.

REVISED   ~~After~~ Teddy Roosevelt was hit in the eye while boxing. [The conjunction is deleted.]

If a dependent clause uses a relative pronoun, eliminate the relative pronoun, replacing it with a noun or personal pronoun, and you will have an independent clause.

FRAGMENT   The president, who went blind in his left eye from the incident.

REVISED   The president ~~who~~ went blind in his left eye from the incident. [The eliminated relative pronoun leaves the noun as subject.]

REVISED   ~~The President, who~~ *He* went blind in his left eye from the incident. [The eliminated relative pronoun is replaced by a personal pronoun.]

 2   Join the dependent clause to a new sentence.

FRAGMENT   Though the president attended.
CLEAR   Though the president attended, she did not speak.

The dependent clause introduced by a subordinating conjunction can be made to function as an adverb by joining it to an independent clause. When the dependent clause introduces a sentence, set it off with a comma (see 25a-1). When the clause ends a sentence, do not use a comma (but see 25a-3).

REFERENCE

HARRIS, MURIEL. "Mending the Fragmented Free Modifier." *CCC* 32 (1981): 175–82. Free modifiers, although they risk producing sentence fragments, should not be discouraged in student writing.

ESL ALERT

Many Japanese students have been trained to believe that beginning an English sentence with "and" or "but" or "so" is a way to make their writing seem more natural and will have difficulty giving up this practice, while European students might feel that fragments make their writing seem more creative. Vietnamese writing style and punctuation precludes the idea of fragments, comma splices, or fused sentences: they simply do not exist. Instead, the sentences flow much like conversation, with few formal regulations.

FRAGMENT   When Teddy Roosevelt had his first chance to show how a president should lead.

REVISED   *Teddy Roosevelt hardly had moved into the White House* when he had his first chance to show how a president should lead.

A dependent clause fragment that uses a relative pronoun can be made to function as an adjective (a relative clause) by attaching it to an independent clause. If the new relative clause is not essential to defining the noun it modifies, set the clause off with a *pair* of commas. If the new relative clause *is* essential to the definition, do not use commas (see 25d-1).

FRAGMENT   Roosevelt, the champion of the ordinary American, who had gotten striking coal miners a "square deal." [The noun and modifying clause have no verb.]

REVISED   Roosevelt, who had gotten striking coal miners a "square deal," *became* the champion of the ordinary American. [The *who* clause functions as an adjective in a sentence with a new verb, *became.*]

FRAGMENT   Powerful business interests that controlled all rail traffic in the Northeast. [The noun and its modifying clause have no verb.]

REVISED   He showed respect for the ordinary American *by busting powerful business interests that controlled all rail traffic in the Northeast.* [The noun and its modifying clause become part of a new sentence (as objects of the verbal *busting*).]

EXERCISE 2

Identify fragments in the following pairs. Combine pairs to make complete sentences.

> *Example:* Even though Anheuser-Busch, Miller, G. Heileman, Coors, and Pabst brew 95 percent of the 200 million barrels of beer produced annually in the United States. These companies are not the only producers of American beer.
>
> Even though Anheuser-Busch, Miller, G. Heileman, Coors, and Pabst brew 95 percent of the 200 million barrels of beer produced annually in the United States, these companies are not the only producers of American beer.

1. While only eight microbreweries existed in the United States a decade ago. Today seventy microbreweries are brewing more than 65,000 barrels of specialty beers a year.
2. Microbreweries are winning awards for the tastiness of their products. Which has caused the large producers to alter their production and advertising techniques.
3. Because microbrewery beer is often free of additives. It must be sold locally.

EXERCISE 2

1. While only eight microbreweries existed in the United States in a decade ago, today seventy microbreweries are brewing more than 65,000 barrels of specialty beers a year.
2. Microbreweries are winning awards for the tastiness of their products, which has caused the large producers to alter their production and advertising techniques.
3. Because microbrewery beer is often free of additives, it must be sold locally.
4. Local production, distribution, and advertising has become a key to microbrewery success, which depends on creating the perception among buyers of a freshness and healthfulness not available in mass-market beers.
5. Even though image is important, quality product is what has convinced an increasing number of American beer drinkers to buy from local, smaller breweries.

4. Local production, distribution, and advertising has become a key to microbrewery success. Which depends on creating the perception among buyers of a freshness and healthfulness not available in mass-market beers.

5. Even though image is important. Quality of the product is what has convinced an increasing number of American beer drinkers to buy from local, smaller breweries.

Eliminating Fragments from Your Writing

1. **Revise dependent clauses set off as sentences.**
   Convert the dependent clause to an independent clause.

   FRAGMENT   Although computers may be revolutionizing the world.

   REVISED   ~~Although~~ Computers may be revolutionizing the world.

   Join the dependent clause to a new sentence.

   FRAGMENT   Although computers may be revolutionizing the world.

   REVISED   Although computers may be revolutionizing the world, *relatively few people understand how they function.*

2. **Revise phrases set off as sentences.**
   There are various kinds of phrases: verbal, prepositional, absolute, and appositive (see 7d). None can stand alone as a sentence.

   FRAGMENT   After years of drought.

   REVISED   ~~After~~ Years of drought *can devastate a national economy.*

   REVISED   After years of drought, *a nation's economy can be devastated.*

3. **Revise repeating structures or compound predicates set off as sentences.**
   Repeating elements and compound predicates cannot stand alone. Incorporate such structures into an existing sentence or add words to construct a new sentence.

   FRAGMENT   College sports has long been conducted as a business. A profitable business. [The repeating element is a fragment.]

   REVISED   College sports has long been conducted as a business—*a* profitable business. [The repeating element has been incorporated into an existing sentence.]

   FRAGMENT   Some coaches achieve legendary status on campus. And are paid legendary salaries. [The second element is part of a compound verb.]

   REVISED   Some coaches achieve legendary status on campus *and* are paid legendary salaries. [The second verb and its associated words are incorporated into an existing sentence.]

GROUP ACTIVITY

Once students have completed this exercise, have them discuss their responses in groups. The inevitable differences between various correct responses will help students understand the number of possible ways to construct sentences without falling into error. The discussion should also help students who have yet to master the concept of the fragment. (This activity can be used for all subsequent exercises in the chapter.)

TEACHING IDEAS

You may want to use this box to reinforce in students a sense of responsibility for correcting their own mistakes. Ask students to check their personal lists of fragment types (from the Spotlight on Common Errors note, p. 281) against the types enumerated in the box. If they can find that they frequently produce fragments similar to those listed here, they can make a checklist for use when revising and editing their papers.

12c Eliminate fragments: Revise phrases set off as sentences.

Phrases consist of nouns and the words associated with them or verb forms not functioning as verbs (called *verbals*) and the words associated with them. Phrases function as sentence parts—as modifiers, subjects, objects, and complements—but never as sentences. The various kinds of phrases are defined in 7d. As with dependent clauses that form fragments, you may either convert phrases to complete sentences by adding words, or you may join phrases to independent clauses.

1 Revising verbal phrases

Participial and gerund phrases (functioning as modifiers or nouns)

FRAGMENT   Reviving the Sherman Antitrust Act.

REVISED   *Roosevelt* ~~reviving~~ *revived* the Sherman Antitrust Act. [The phrase is rewritten as a sentence.]

REVISED   Reviving the Sherman Antitrust Act, *Roosevelt brought suit against the Northern Securities Company.* [The participial phrase, functioning as an adjective, is joined to an independent clause.]

REVISED   Reviving the Sherman Antitrust Act *was one way to fight Northern Securities Company.* [The phrase is used as a gerund, functioning as a noun, to become the subject of an independent clause.]

Infinitive phrases (functioning as nouns)

FRAGMENT   To sue Northern Securities rather than deal.

REVISED   *Roosevelt decided* to sue Northern Securities rather than deal. [The phrase is rewritten as a sentence.]

2 Revising prepositional phrases (functioning as modifiers)

FRAGMENT   In 1904 by a very narrow vote of 5 to 4.

REVISED   In 1904 by a very narrow vote of 5 to 4, *the Supreme Court held that the Northern Securities Company did violate the Sherman Antitrust Act.* [The phrase is joined to an independent clause.]

3 Revising absolute phrases (modifying an entire sentence)

FRAGMENT   Roosevelt's instincts leaning to public protection.

REVISED   His instincts ~~leaning~~ *leaned* to public protection. [The phrase is rewritten as a sentence.]

REVISED   His instincts leaning to public protection, *Roosevelt tolerated trusts that benefited ordinary Americans.* [The phrase is joined as modifier to an independent clause.]

4 Revising appositive phrases (renaming or describing other nouns)

FRAGMENT   A bill designed to give federal officials the right to inspect all meat shipped in interstate commerce.

REVISED   *The Meat Inspection Act was* a bill designed to give federal officials the right to inspect all meat shipped in interstate commerce. [The phrase is rewritten as a sentence.]

REVISED   *Roosevelt went on to advocate the Meat Inspection Act,* a bill designed to give federal officials the right to inspect all meat shipped in interstate commerce. [The phrase is joined to an independent clause.]

EXERCISE 3

Identify the numbered units that are fragments, and correct them by joining them to independent clauses. Then specify what type of phrase the fragment has become in the new sentence. Place a check before any sentence needing no revision.

Example: (1) In order to comprehend the nature of stress, we must consider three related issues. (2) *Physiology, the nature of stressors, and personality.*

(1) In order to comprehend the nature of stress, we must consider three related issues: physiology, the nature of stressors, and personality. [The fragment is joined with the independent clause to become an appositive renaming *issues.*]

(1) Physiologically, the body prepares itself for stress. (2) By eliciting an immediate and vigorous alarm reaction. (3) Alarm is soon replaced by resistance. (4) A state in which activation remains relatively high but at levels a person can sustain over a long period of time. (5) If stress persists, the body's resources may become depleted. (6) Exhaustion occurs. (7) The ability to cope decreasing sharply over time. (8) A person risks severe biological damage by remaining exhausted for too long. (9) *Stres-*

EXERCISE 3

1. and 2. Join fragment (2) with (1) as a participial phrase.
2. and 4. Join fragment (4) with (3) as an appositive.
3. A correct sentence.
4. A correct sentence.
5. and 8. Join fragment (7) with (8) as an absolute phrase.
6. and 10. Join fragment (10) with (9) as an infinitive phrase.

sors can be defined as those elements in the environment that produce an urge in the individual to approach a stressful activity. (10) To flee from it as well.

12d Eliminate fragments: Revise repeating structures or compound predicates set off as sentences.

FRAGMENT   As large as the capitol's rotunda
CLEAR   The foyer was large, as large as the capitol's rotunda.

Repetition can be an effective stylistic tool (see 19c-2). Repeated elements, however, are not sentences but sentence parts and should not be punctuated as sentences. Use a comma or dashes to set off repeated elements.

FRAGMENT   Children begin for the first time to differentiate themselves from others as they enter adolescence. *As they begin to develop a personal identity.* [The subordinate *as* clause cannot stand alone.]

REVISED   Children begin for the first time to differentiate themselves from others as they enter adolescence, as they begin to develop a personal identity. [The clause is subordinated.]

FRAGMENT   Adolescents want to know they belong in the social order. An order shaped by forces they barely understand. [The phrase and clause need a connection.]

REVISED   Adolescents want to know they belong in the social order— an order shaped by forces they barely understand. [The structure repeats and expands the term *social order*.]

Compound predicates consist of two sentence verbs (and their associated words) joined with a coordinating conjunction, such as *and* or *but*. The two predicates share the same subject and are part of the same sentence. When one half of the compound predicate is punctuated as a sentence, it becomes a fragment. To correct the fragment, join it to a sentence that contains an appropriate subject or provide the fragment with its own subject.

FRAGMENT   The process of maturation is lifelong. *But is most critical during the adolescent years.* [The last unit has no subject.]

REVISED   The process of maturation is lifelong. But *the process* is most critical during the adolescent years. [The unit is given its own subject.]

REVISED   The process of maturation is lifelong but is most critical during the adolescent years. [The phrase is joined to the preceding sentence as a compound predicate.]

EXERCISE 4

Identify which of the following units are fragments. Correct each by writing a new sentence or by joining the fragment to an independent clause.

> *Example:* At very low temperatures, many materials behave in unfamiliar ways. *And display properties much different from those we expect.* [The second unit lacks a subject.]
>
> At very low temperatures, many materials behave in unfamiliar ways and display properties much different from those we expect. [The second unit is attached as a compound verb to the preceding sentence.]

1. When cooled in liquid nitrogen, a banana becomes extremely hard. So hard that it can be used as a hammer.
2. A rubber ball becomes brittle. And will shatter like glass when dropped onto the floor.
3. When certain metals are cooled to low temperatures, they gain the ability to conduct electric currents with no resistance at all. And are called superconductors.
4. Once the current is set up, a superconducting ring can carry current for a long time. For thousands of years with no further source of energy.

12e   Use fragments intentionally on rare occasions.

Whose business was it? No one's.
The speaker made his point. Barely.

Experienced writers will occasionally use sentence fragments by design. These intentional uses are always carefully fitted to the context of a neighboring sentence, sometimes answering an implied question or completing a parallel structure that has been separated for emphasis. Such intentional uses occur mainly in personal or expressive essay writing or in fiction, when writers want to alter the rhythm of paragraphs and thereby call attention to fragments or to reproduce the staccato rhythms of speech or thought. A fragment should be used rarely if at all in academic prose, where it will probably be regarded as a lapse, not as a stylistic flourish.

INTENTIONAL USE OF FRAGMENTS

> Dick and Elsie backed the skiff in to the little island beach. Joxer helped Miss Perry and Sally and the baby. The other guests took off their shoes and went over the sides, calling heartily to Joxer and Joxer's wife. They were as cheerful as Joxer. *Amused too.*
>
> —JOHN CASEY, *Spartina*

EXERCISE 4

1. When cooled in liquid nitrogen, a banana becomes extremely hard, so hard that it can be used as a hammer.
2. A rubber ball becomes brittle and will shatter like glass when dropped onto the floor.
3. When certain metals called superconductors are cooled to low temperatures, they gain the ability to conduct electric currents with no resistance at all.
4. Once the current is set up, a superconducting ring can carry current for thousands of years with no further source of energy.

FOR DISCUSSION

Reproduce several brief passages with intentional fragments, including one or two that aren't particularly effective. (These can be from published prose or from your own pen.) Ask students to edit the passages to eliminate the fragments, and decide which version is more effective. In class discussion, students can defend their positions, thereby clarifying for them the function of the intentional fragment.

REFERENCES

KLINE, CHARLES R., JR., and W. DEAN MEMERING. "Formal Fragments: The English Minor Sentence." *Research in the Teaching of English* 11 (1977): 97–110. In certain circumstances, fragments are not only acceptable but effective.

ELBOW, PETER. *Writing without Teachers.* New York: Oxford UP, 1973. 30–31. Fragments should not be viewed as errors but rather as specific stylistic devices.

Democrats favored bureaucratic delivery of education and other services because bureaucracies serve everyone equally. Badly, perhaps, but equally.

—GEORGE F. WILL

We are lucky in that the central fact of our country is both inspiring and true: America is the place formed of the institutionalization of miracles. Which made it something new in the history of man, something— better.

—PEGGY NOONAN

EXERCISE 5

Correct each sentence fragment either by joining it with an independent clause or by rewriting it as an independent clause.

> *Example:* When the influential scholar Ulrich B. Phillips declared in 1918 that slavery in the Old South had impressed upon African savages the glorious stamp of civilization. He set the stage for a long and passionate debate. [The first unit is a dependent clause.]
>
> When the influential scholar Ulrich B. Phillips declared in 1918 that slavery in the Old South had impressed upon African savages the glorious stamp of civilization, he set the stage for a long and passionate debate. [The dependent clause is connected to the sentence that follows it.]

1. As the decades passed and the debate raged on. One historian after another confidently professed to have deciphered the real meaning of slavery. That "peculiar institution."
2. The special situation of the female slave remained unexamined. Amidst all this scholarly activity.
3. Because the ceaseless arguments about her "sexual promiscuity" or her "matriarchal" proclivities obscured the condition of Black women during slavery.
4. If and when a historian sets the record straight on the experiences of enslaved Black women. She (or he) will have performed an inestimable service.
5. It is not for the sake of historical accuracy alone that such a study should be conducted. For lessons can be gleaned from the slave era. That will shed light upon Black women's and all women's current battle for emancipation.
6. The enormous space that work occupies in Black women's lives today. Follows a pattern established during the very earliest days of slavery.
7. Compulsory labor overshadowed every other aspect of women's existence. The slave system defined Black people. As chattel. Since women, no less than men, were viewed as profitable labor units. They might as well have been genderless as far as the slaveholders were concerned.

EXERCISE 5

1. As the decades passed and the debate raged on, one historian after another confidently professed to have deciphered the real meaning of slavery, that "peculiar institution."
2. The special situation of the female slave remained unexamined amidst all this scholarly activity.
3. The ceaseless arguments about her "sexual promiscuity" or her "matriarchal" proclivities obscured the condition of Black women during slavery.
4. If and when a historian sets the record straight on the experiences of enslaved Black women, she (or he) will have performed an inestimable service.
5. It is not for the sake of historical accuracy alone that such a study should be conducted, for lessons can be gleaned from the slave era that will shed light upon Black women's and all women's current battle for emancipation.
6. The enormous space that work occupies in Black women's lives today follows a pattern established during the very earliest days of slavery.
7. Compulsory labor overshadowed every other aspect of women's existence. The slave system defined Black people as chattel. Since women, no less than men, were viewed as profitable labor units, they might as well have been genderless as far as the slaveholders were concerned.

ADDITIONAL EXERCISE A

Look through your graded papers to find instructor's comments regarding fragments. Reread the papers, identifying the fragments as you read by using the three-part test. Then identify the cause of the fragment and correct it. (If you don't have any graded papers handy, look through any body of writing you've done recently.)

CHAPTER 13

Comma Splices and Fused Sentences

Sentence grammar is built on the fundamental rule that independent clauses—complete sentences—are the basic units for making a statement. Sentences must be kept distinct from one another. When sentence boundaries are blurred, statements become confused; readers must turn away from the content of a paper and struggle to decipher which combinations of words might form meaningful units.

To keep your statements distinct and clear, remember: independent clauses must be separated with a period, a semicolon, or a colon, or they must be carefully linked with a conjunction and appropriate punctuation.

Five Ways to Mark the Boundary between Sentences

Mark a sentence boundary with punctuation.

1. Use a period: He laughed. He danced. He sang.
2. Use a semicolon: He laughed; he danced and sang.

Mark a sentence boundary with a conjunction and punctuation.

3. Use a coordinating conjunction: He laughed, and he danced.
4. Use a subordinating conjunction: While he laughed, he danced.
5. Use a conjunctive adverb: He laughed; moreover, he danced.

Sentence boundaries can become blurred in two ways: with comma splices or with fused (run-on) sentences. In the **fused (or run-on) sentence**, the writer fails to recognize the end of one independent clause and the beginning of the next.

FUSED SENTENCE   The blurring of sentence boundaries can create a comprehension problem readers must often stop to decipher which combinations of words form meaningful units. [*Readers* is a new subject of a new independent clause; a period or semicolon should precede it.]

The writer of a **comma splice** recognizes the end of one independent clause and the beginning of the next, but marks the boundary between the two incorrectly—with a comma.

KEY FEATURES

The emphasis in this chapter, as in previous revising and editing chapters, is on producing clear, lively prose. Approached from this standpoint, correcting comma splices and fused sentences becomes not an exercise in following rules but rather a courtesy extended from the writer to the reader. In fact, few comma splices and fused sentences render an essay incoherent; they do, however, distract the reader from the content of the essay. Learning to identify and correct these errors, then, becomes one more way to refine a piece of written discourse. In dealing with the topic, this chapter remains consistent with previous chapters in its straightforward approach. Beginning on a positive note, the chapter identifies five acceptable ways to mark sentence boundaries, and then explains the two ways in which those boundaries can be blurred. The chapter acknowledges that a comma splice indicates that the writer recognizes the need for some sort of break, but chooses punctuation that isn't up to the job. Errors are dealt with by looking at the common reasons why writers make them (e.g., fusing or splicing sentences of explanation to sentences being explained, confusing conjunctive adverbs and conjunctions). Strategies for correcting comma splices and fused sentences are explained with clear examples. Exercises, using sentences and paragraphs, provide students with practice in identifying and correcting errors.

SPOTLIGHT ON COMMON ERRORS—SENTENCE CONSTRUCTION AND SENTENCE BOUNDARIES

These are the errors most commonly associated with sentence construction and sentence boundaries. For full explanations and suggested revisions, follow the cross-references to chapter sections.

RECOGNIZING SENTENCE BOUNDARIES: The end of a sentence is usually marked with a period. Not marking the end clearly will result in a FRAGMENT (see 12a), a FUSED SENTENCE (see 13b-1), or a COMMA SPLICE (see 13b-1).

> CORRECT: Winston Churchill became a leader. He served his country in the first World War. Churchill was a leader of distinction.

> FUSED SENTENCES: Winston Churchill became a leader he served his country in the first World War Churchill was a leader of distinction.

> COMMA SPLICES: Winston Churchill became a leader, he served his country in the first World War, Churchill was a leader of distinction.

REVISING ERRORS OF SENTENCE CONSTRUCTION: Learn to recognize sentence boundaries (see 12a). Link sentences with these strategies:

- **Link by combining parts of two sentences into one (see 12c).**

  Winston Churchill became a leader. Churchill was a leader of distinction.

  Winston Churchill became a leader of distinction.

- **Link by using a comma plus one of these conjunctions—*and, but, or, nor* (see coordinating conjunctions, 13b-2, 19a-1).**

  Winston Churchill served his country in the first World War, *and* he became a leader of distinction.

- **Link by using a semicolon (see 13b-3, 26a–c).**

  Winston Churchill served his country in the first World War; he became a leader of distinction.

- **Link by using a semicolon (or period) and a word like *however, consequently,* or *therefore* (see conjunctive adverbs, 13b-4, 19a-3).**

  Winston Churchill served his country in the first World War; *subsequently,* he became a leader of distinction.

- **Link by using a word like *when, while,* or *because* (see subordinating conjunctions, 13b-5, 19b).**

  After he served his country in the first World War, Winston Churchill became a leader of distinction.

13a   Identify fused sentences and comma splices.

FUSED	Winston Churchill served in World War I he became a leader of great distinction.
COMMA SPLICE	Winston Churchill served in the World War I, he became a leader of great distinction.
CLEAR	Winston Churchill served in World War I. He became a leader of great distinction.

Before submitting a draft of your work to be read or reviewed by others, read your sentences aloud. When you listen to your writing, you can often catch errors that go undetected when you read silently. Look for long sentences that seem to consist of two or more separate statements, or those that seem so long they force you to stop midway to take a breath. Be on the alert, especially, for the following three circumstances in which fused sentences and comma splices are found.

1. **A sentence of explanation, expansion, or example** is frequently fused to or spliced together with another sentence that is being explained, expanded on, or illustrated. Even if the topics of the two sentences are closely related, the sentences themselves must remain distinct.

FUSED SENTENCE	Tobacco smoking is an ancient habit of humankind studies on the effects of smoking have appeared in medical journals over the last 100 years.
COMMA SPLICE	Tobacco smoking is an ancient habit of humankind, studies on the effects of smoking have appeared in medical journals over the last 100 years.
REVISED	Tobacco smoking is an ancient habit of humankind. Studies on the effects of smoking have appeared in medical journals over the last 100 years. [The sentences are separated.]

2. **The pronouns** *he, she, they, it, this,* and *that,* when renaming the subject of a sentence, can signal a comma splice or a fused sentence. Even when the subject named or renamed in adjacent sentences is identical, the sentences themselves must be kept distinct.

FUSED SENTENCE	Raphael was a painter he was also a muralist.
COMMA SPLICE	Raphael was a painter, he was also a muralist.
REVISED	Raphael was a painter, and he was a muralist.

3. **Conjunctive adverbs** (words such as *however, furthermore, thus, therefore,* and *consequently*) **and transitional expressions** (phrases such as *for example* and *on the other hand*) are commonly found in fused or spliced clauses. Conjunctive adverbs and transitions always link complete sentences. Writers must reflect this linkage with appropriate punctuation: a period or semicolon. (For a complete list of conjunctive adverbs, see 19a-3.)

LOOKING BACK

References to chapter 7 (Constructing Sentences) appear throughout this chapter. If chapter 7 has not been covered yet, or if some time has passed since it was covered, you may want to spend a little time on that material now.

ESL ALERT

Romance-language speakers (especially of Spanish) will persist in making comma faults because of a very different conception of comma use. The Spanish sentence can easily run to eighty or more words, with clauses, joined snugly by commas; there is no "fault" or "splice" involving commas, but rather a comfortable sense of fullness and continuity, a sense missing in the seemingly (to Spanish speakers) attenuated English version. Thus native Spanish speakers will require reminders to keep sentences short and tightly connected, and perhaps, some confidence building that their English prose is not "too simple." Vietnamese experience some of the same difficulty.

TEACHING IDEAS

Comma splices are more common than fused sentences, and they often reflect punctuation problems rather than problems understanding sentences. Therefore, you may want to ask students who produce comma splices to actually memorize the five ways of marking sentence boundaries.

TEACHING IDEAS

Some students have trouble understanding what the terms "comma splice" and "fused sentence" mean. Some may have to unlearn the term "run-on" and learn "fused." You can explain that "run-on" was often misused to characterize overly long sentences that were in fact grammatically correct. "Fused" is a more accurate term, relying on the image of joining two separate things together. "Comma splice" is more easily understood if students think of splicing film—also creating an image of joining two pieces together.

TEACHING IDEAS

Conjunctive adverbs and transitional expressions account for a significant percentage of comma splices in student writing; many students treat these words as if they were conjunctions. Put two columns on the board, one labeled "conjunctive adverbs/transitional expressions," the other "coordinating/subordinating conjunctions." Ask students to name all the words they can to fill in the lists (refer to chapter 7 [Constructing Sentences] if necessary). They can copy the lists for easy reference.

EXERCISE 1

1. They were accustomed to the wooded lands of the East, / some had become acquainted with the flat prairies that stretched from Illinois to Iowa and from Canada to Texas / the prairies were known for rich soil, regular rainfall, and tall grass.
2. The Great Plains were different, however, / out there trees were rare.
3. The grass was short / worst of all there was very little rain, / it is not surprising that for a while the farmer had gladly left the West to others.
4. Finally farmers decided to move onto the plains, / they faced new problems.
5. Since there was no wood for houses, they had to learn to make houses of sod, / to their astonishment they found that sod houses could be warm and cozy in winter / they could be cool in summer.

FUSED SENTENCE	Ninety percent of the Hispanic vote is concentrated in nine states that cast seventy-one percent of all electoral ballots consequently Hispanics have emerged as a nationally influential group of voters in presidential politics.
COMMA SPLICE	Ninety percent of the Hispanic vote is concentrated in nine states that cast seventy-one percent of all electoral ballots, consequently, Hispanics have emerged as a nationally influential group of voters in presidential politics.
REVISED	Ninety percent of the Hispanic vote is concentrated in nine states that cast seventy-one percent of all electoral ballots. Consequently, Hispanics have emerged as a nationally influential group of voters in presidential politics. [*Consequently* starts a new main clause.]

EXERCISE 1

Use a slash mark (/) to identify the points at which the following sentences are fused or spliced together.

> *Example:* The American farmer and his family had avoided the Great Plains, it was a strange place at first they did not like it.
>
> The American farmer and his family had avoided the Great Plains, / it was a strange place / at first they did not like it.

1. They were accustomed to the wooded lands of the East, some had become acquainted with the flat prairies that stretched from Illinois to Iowa and from Canada to Texas the prairies were known for rich soil, regular rainfall, and tall grass.
2. The Great Plains were different, however, out there trees were rare.
3. The grass was short worst of all there was very little rain, it is not surprising that for a while the farmer had gladly left the West to others.
4. Finally farmers decided to move onto the plains, they faced new problems.
5. Since there was no wood for houses, they had to learn to make houses of sod, to their astonishment they found that sod houses could be warm and cozy in winter they could be cool in summer.

13b Correct fused sentences and comma splices in one of five ways.

1 Separate independent clauses with a period (and sometimes a colon).

COMMA SPLICE	Cotton was once the lead farm product in Alabama, today poultry has replaced it.

CLEAR   Cotton was once the lead farm product in Alabama. Today, poultry has replaced it.

Using a period is the most obvious way to repair a fused or spliced construction, especially when the first independent clause is not very closely related in content to its neighbor, and when you do not want to link the two with a conjunction. But when using a period to repair faulty constructions, take care that your paragraphs do not become choppy. See the discussion on sentence variety in chapter 20.

Occasionally, writers use a colon between independent clauses when the first sentence is a formal and emphatic introduction to an explanation, example, or appositive in the second sentence.

FUSED SENTENCE   Logging is often the first step in deforestation it may be followed by complete clearing of trees and a deliberate shift to unsound land uses.

COMMA SPLICE   Logging is often the first step in deforestation, it may be followed by complete clearing of trees and a deliberate shift to unsound land uses.

REVISED   Logging is often the first step in deforestation. It may be followed by complete clearing of trees and a deliberate shift to unsound land uses.

REVISED   Logging is often the first step in deforestation: it may be followed by complete clearing of trees and a deliberate shift to unsound land uses. [The colon gives the opening clause an emphatic introductory function.]

2   Link clauses with a comma and a coordinating conjunction.

FUSED   January may be the coldest month it is a month of great productivity.

CLEAR   January may be the coldest month, but it is a month of great productivity.

Use a comma placed *before* a coordinating conjunction—*and, but, or, nor, for, so,* and *yet*—to link sentences that are closely related in content and that are equally important. Like all conjunctions, coordinating conjunctions establish clear and definite logical relationships between the elements joined, so choose conjunctions with care. (See 19a for a detailed discussion of coordinating conjunctions.)

FUSED SENTENCE   Deforestation has a severe environmental impact on soil in heavy tropical rains soil erodes quickly.

COMMA SPLICE   Deforestation has a severe environmental impact on soil, in heavy tropical rains soil erodes quickly.

REVISED   Deforestation has a severe environmental impact on soil, for in heavy tropical rains soil erodes quickly.

GROUP ACTIVITY

Exercise 1 and subsequent exercises are ideal for group work. Have students either complete the exercises in groups or compare their responses after completing the exercises individually. Either way, as they negotiate responses or defend their choices, they'll understand more clearly the appropriate punctuation of sentences.

ESL ALERT

Most ESL students will never have been introduced to absolutes, will find them most puzzling, and will tend to equate them with comma splice problems, especially when the central verb is a passive form so it looks more complete than it is: "Their work completed, they went home." Marcella Frank's *Modern English, Part II* has a clear explanation of how and when to use absolutes.

REFERENCES

SHAUGHNESSY, MINA P. *Errors and Expectations: A Guide for the Teacher of Basic Writing.* New York, Oxford UP, 1977. 16–43. Comma splices reflect larger problems with written discourse, and should be addressed accordingly.

BAMBERG, BETTY. "Periods Are Basic: A Strategy for Eliminating Comma Faults and Run-on Sentences." *Teaching the Basics—Really!* Ed. Ouida Clapp. Urbana: NCTE, 1977. 97–99. Teaching punctuation as an integral part of sentence structure helps students avoid problems with comma splices and fused sentences.

MEYER, EMILY, and LOUISE Z. SMITH. *The Practical Tutor.* New York: Oxford UP, 1987. 177–201. A thorough analysis of the causes of sentence errors, with guidelines for helping students overcome them.

TEACHING IDEAS

Many comma splices (and a few fused sentences) are actually the result of sound thinking on the part of student writers. For example, the student who joins two sentences with a comma often recognizes that the sentences are linked; the problem arises when the student doesn't understand the options open to him or her. Careful attention in class to the Critical Decisions box may help those who know that two sentences should be closely linked but don't know how to link them. You may want to ask students to compare their papers to the box and identify types of errors they make frequently. The box will provide them with the strategies they need to follow through on their hunches about relationships between sentences.

CRITICAL DECISIONS

Challenge and be challenged: Choosing a method to link independent clauses

Sentence boundaries clearly marked with a period help readers focus on, and understand, one thought at a time. When you want to show the relationship *between* sentences and get readers to consider one thought in light of another, then you should link clauses. You have various options for doing so; which option you choose depends on the relationship you want to establish between independent clauses.

- Do you want one independent clause to announce another? If so, use a colon to make the announcement (see 13b-1).

  SEPARATED   The race was postponed for one reason. The sponsors withdrew their support.

  LINKED   The race was postponed for one reason: the sponsors withdrew their support.

- Do you want to relate but maintain equal emphasis between two independent clauses? If so, use a coordinating conjunction with a comma, a conjunctive adverb with a semicolon or period, or a semicolon to link the clauses (see 13b-2–4 and 19a).

  Coordinating conjunction with a comma

  SEPARATED   Runners had already arrived. They were angry with the postponement.

  LINKED   Runners had already arrived, **and** they were angry with the postponement.

  Conjunctive adverb with a semicolon or a period

  SEPARATED   The sponsors cited financial worries. They had political concerns as well.

  LINKED   The sponsors cited financial worries; **however,** they had political concerns as well.

  Semicolon

  SEPARATED   One faction of runners wanted to boycott all future races in that city. Another faction wanted to stage a protest march.

  LINKED   One faction of runners wanted to boycott all future races in that city; another faction wanted to stage a protest march.

- Do you want to link two independent clauses but emphasize one more than the other? If so, use a subordinating conjunction to link the clauses (see 13b-5 and 19b).P

  SEPARATED   The press was embarrassing. The sponsors canceled the race permanently.

  LINKED   **Because** the press was embarrassing, the sponsors canceled the race permanently.

3 Link clauses with a semicolon.

FUSED	Wind is one cause of erosion water is another cause.
COMMA SPLICE	Wind is one cause of erosion, water is another cause.
CLEAR	Wind is one cause of erosion; water is another cause.

Use a semicolon in place of a comma and a coordinating conjunction to link sentences that are closely related and equally important. The semicolon links independent clauses without making the relationship between them explicit. You might choose a semicolon to repair a fused or spliced construction either when the relationship between clauses is crystal clear and a conjunction would be redundant or when you wish to create anticipation—leaving your readers to discover the exact relationship between clauses.

FUSED SENTENCE	Experience reinforces the argument that deforestation has not been a path to economic development in most tropical countries it has instead been a costly drain on resources.
COMMA SPLICE	Experience reinforces the argument that deforestation has not been a path to economic development, in most tropical countries it has instead been a costly drain on resources.
REVISED	Experience reinforces the argument that deforestation has not been a path to economic development; in most tropical countries it has instead been a costly drain on resources.

4 Link clauses with a semicolon (or period) and a conjunctive adverb.

COMMA SPLICE	John Ciardi is a poet, he is a radio commentator and translator of Dante.
CLEAR	John Ciardi is a poet; he is, **moreover,** a radio commentator and translator of Dante.

Use conjunctive adverbs—words such as *however, furthermore, thus, therefore,* and *consequently*—to link closely related, equally important clauses. (See 19a-3 for a complete list of conjunctive adverbs.) Conjunctive adverbs establish the same relationships, such as addition, contrast, and cause, as do coordinating conjunctions. The conjunctive adverbs, however, are more formal and a little stiffer, but also more rigorous and forceful than coordinating conjunctions. As well, conjunctive adverbs and coordinating conjunctions create different rhythms in the sentences you are linking. Choose conjunctions based on the relationships you wish to establish in your paragraphs.

Place a period between clauses when you want a full separation of ideas. Place a semicolon between clauses when you want to emphasize the link between ideas. As with most adverbs, a conjunctive adverb can shift its location in a sentence. If placed at the beginning, the conjunctive adverb is followed (usually) by a comma. If placed in the middle, it is usually set off by a pair of commas. And if placed at the end, it is preceded by a comma. Wherever you place the adverb, be sure to use a period or a semicolon between the two clauses you have linked.

FUSED SENTENCE	Deforestation is not irreversible once a forest is cleared regeneration takes a lifetime.
COMMA SPLICE	Deforestation is not irreversible, once a forest is cleared regeneration takes a lifetime.
REVISED	Deforestation is not irreversible; however, once a forest is cleared, regeneration takes a lifetime. [The semicolon emphasizes the link between ideas.]
REVISED	Deforestation is not irreversible. However, once a forest is cleared, regeneration takes a lifetime. [The period makes a full separation.]
REVISED	Deforestation is not irreversible. Once a forest is cleared, however, regeneration takes a lifetime.

5   Link clauses with a subordinating conjunction or construction.

COMMA SPLICE	Hannibal crossed the Alps, he defeated the Romans in the Po Valley.
CLEAR	**After** Hannibal crossed the Alps, he defeated the Romans in the Po Valley.

Use a subordinating conjunction or construction to join fused or spliced independent clauses. By placing a subordinating conjunction at the beginning of an independent clause, or by using a relative pronoun such as *who, whom, which,* or *that,* you render that clause dependent, unable to stand alone as a complete thought. The new dependent clause will function as a modifier. Be aware of comma use with these constructions: when the clause begins a sentence, a comma often follows it to signal the reader that the main point of the sentence, the independent clause, is being delayed. By the same logic, when an independent clause begins a sentence, the dependent clause that follows very often does not use a comma. (See 19b for a discussion of subordination.)

FUSED SENTENCE	International development-assistance agencies have begun to lend help a number of governments are now strengthening their forest-management programs.
COMMA SPLICE	International development-assistance agencies have begun to lend help, a number of governments are now strengthening their forest-management programs.
REVISED	Because international development-assistance agencies have begun to lend help, a number of governments are now strengthening their forest-management programs. [A dependent clause begins the sentence.]

Conjunctions and Punctuation

Coordinating Conjunctions

and but so or for nor yet

Use coordinating conjunctions with punctuation in this pattern:

Independent clause **,** CONJUNCTION independent clause

FUSED SENTENCE   Newton developed calculus he discovered laws of gravity.

COMMA SPLICE   Newton developed calculus, he discovered laws of gravity.

REVISED   Newton developed calculus, and he discovered laws of gravity.

Conjunctive Adverbs

however furthermore thus therefore consequently

Use conjunctive adverbs with punctuation in these patterns:

Independent clause **;** CONJUNCTION **,** independent clause

Independent clause **.** CONJUNCTION **,** independent clause

REVISED   Newton developed calculus; moreover, he discovered laws of gravity.

REVISED   Newton developed calculus. Moreover, he discovered laws of gravity.

Subordinating Conjunctions

after although because once since though while

Use subordinating conjunctions with punctuation in these patterns:

CONJUNCTION clause **,** independent clause

Independent clause CONJUNCTION clause

REVISED   After Newton developed calculus, he discovered laws of gravity.

REVISED   Newton discovered laws of gravity after he developed calculus.

REVISED   A number of governments are now strengthening their forest-management programs because international development-assistance agencies have begun to lend help. [A dependent clause ends the sentence.]

REVISED   A number of governments are now strengthening the forest-management programs that have begun to get help from international development-assistance agencies. [A dependent relative clause ends the sentence, creating a different meaning.]

EXERCISE 2

Using any of the strategies discussed in this chapter, correctly punctuate the following word groupings in which you find fused sentences or comma splices. In each case, name the error (or errors) you are correcting.

ADDITIONAL EXERCISE B

Look through your graded papers to find instructors' comments regarding fused sentences and/or comma splices. Reread the papers, identifying the errors as you read by using the three guidelines in 13a. Then revise the errors. (If you don't have any graded papers handy, look through any body of writing you've done recently.)

EXERCISE 2

1. Fused sentence, comma splice
   Genetic engineering is the technique by which scientists alter or combine hereditary materials. Genes are part of all living material: they carry chemical information that determines every organism's characteristics.

2. Fused sentence

The movement of creating genetically engineered organisms began in the early 1900s based on the earlier experiments of the Austrian monk Gregory Mendel. He laid the foundation for future experiments with his work on cross-breeding in plants.

3. Fused sentence

Scientists have discovered the benefits and uses of genetically engineered organisms in agriculture. One of the first examples is the ice-minus bacterium created by Steve Lindow and Nicholas Panopoulos.

4. Comma splice

Lindow and Panopoulos realized that a bacterium commonly found in plants produces a protein that helps ice to form causing damaging frost. They removed this unfavorable gene, and they prevented ice from forming on greenhouse plants.

5. Fused sentence, comma splice

Researchers hope in 20 to 30 years to create corn and wheat plant that can fix their own nitrogen. In this way the plants would not need to be fertilized, and this would save anywhere from $3 to $14 billion annually.

6. Fused sentence, comma splice

Geneticists have found beneficial uses of engineered organisms in agriculture. They have also found ways to use these organisms to clean up environmental hazards: for instance, Dr. Anandra M. Chakrabarty has engineered an organism that breaks up oil spills.

EXERCISE 3

Suggested revisions:

We primates are very social animals. Watch a troop of baboons crossing the African savanna, or a group of gorillas preparing their overnight bivouac, and you soon realize the importance of communal living. Human behavior centers on the social group, too; the profusion of modern and extinct societies offers a bewildering variety of ways and means of ordering social relations. These have spawned an anthropological jargon that tries to divide and place other cultures into neat groupings.

Example: Genetic engineering has been called the great scientific breakthrough of the century there are still many doubts concerning its potential effects on our environment.

Fused sentence. Genetic engineering has been called the great scientific breakthrough of the century. **However,** there are still many doubts concerning its potential effects on our environment.

1. Genetic engineering is the technique by which scientists alter or combine hereditary materials, genes are part of all living material they carry chemical information that determines every organism's characteristics.
2. The movement of creating genetically engineered organisms began in the early 1900s based on the earlier experiments of the Austrian monk Gregory Mendel he laid the foundation for future experiments with his work on cross-breeding in plants.
3. Scientists have discovered the benefits and uses of genetically engineered organisms in agriculture one of the first examples is the ice-minus bacterium created by Steve Lindow and Nicholas Panopoulos.
4. Lindow and Panopoulos realized that a bacterium commonly found in plants produces a protein that helps ice to form causing damaging frost, they removed this unfavorable gene, they prevented ice from forming on greenhouse plants.
5. Researchers hope in 20 to 30 years to create corn and wheat plants that can fix their own nitrogen in this way the plants would not need to be fertilized, this would save anywhere from $3 to $14 billion annually.
6. Geneticists have found beneficial uses of engineered organisms in agriculture, they have also found ways to use these organisms to clean up environmental hazards for instance, Dr. Anandra M. Chakrabarty has engineered an organism that breaks up oil spills.

EXERCISE 3

Correct the fused sentences and comma splices in the following paragraphs, making use of all five strategies discussed in this chapter. One consideration governing your choice of corrections should be sentence variety. Vary methods for correcting fused and spliced clauses to avoid repeating sentence structures in consecutive sentences.

We primates are very social animals watch a troop of baboons crossing the African savanna, or a group of gorillas preparing their overnight bivouac, and the importance of communal living soon becomes apparent. Human behavior centers on the social group, too, the profusion of modern and extinct societies offers a bewildering variety of ways and means of ordering social relations. These have spawned an anthropological jargon that tries to divide and place other cultures into neat groupings.

CHAPTER 14

Pronoun Reference

A **pronoun** substitutes for a noun, allowing you to talk about something without having to repeat its name over and over (see 7a-7). To serve this function, a pronoun must take on meaning from a specific noun; the pronoun must make a clear and unmistakable reference to the noun for which it substitutes—called its **antecedent.** When the reference is not clearly made to a specific noun, the meaning of the whole sentence can become vague or confused.

UNCLEAR   Michelangelo had a complex personality, as did Raphael, though *his* was the more complex. *His* art was not nearly so typical of the High Renaissance, and *he* was frequently irascible—as impatient with the shortcomings of others as with *his* own.

To whom do the pronouns *he* and *his* refer in these sentences? No one can tell. The sentences need to be revised, and the pronouns and antecedents must be placed with care to keep readers moving forward.

REVISED   Michelangelo had a complex personality, as did Raphael, though *Michelangelo's* was the more complex. *His* art was not nearly so typical of the High Renaissance, and *he* was frequently irascible—as impatient with the shortcomings of others as with *his* own. [The proper noun replaces an unclear pronoun, providing a reference point for all the pronouns that follow.]

14a   Make pronouns refer clearly to their antecedents.

CONFUSING   When Mark and Jay return home, *he* will call.
CLEAR   When Mark and Jay return home, *Mark* will call.

Revise a sentence whenever a pronoun can refer to more than one antecedent. Use a noun in place of a pronoun, if needed for clarity; or reposition a pronoun so that its antecedent is unmistakable.

CONFUSING   In 1806, Andrew Jackson dueled with Charles Dickinson, a successful lawyer who had learned his profession from Chief Justice John Marshall. *He* was a fine southern gentleman—and a crack shot, too. [Does the pronoun *he* refer to Jackson, Dickinson, or Marshall?]

REVISED   Dickinson was a fine southern gentleman—and a crack shot, too. [In the second sentence a noun is substituted for the unclear pronoun.]

KEY FEATURES

Unclear pronoun reference, a common error among student writers, is treated extensively. Rather than emphasize errors, however, the chapter sections approach the topic from a positive perspective, classifying the various strategies a writer can use to assure clear pronoun reference. Among these strategies are keeping pronouns close to their antecedents, making certain that the antecedent is stated in the sentence, and avoiding indefinite antecedents. The use of the latter in casual, everyday speech is acknowledged, but as in previous chapters, the need for more clarity in formal written discourse is emphasized. Specific pronouns that often cause problems are dealt with in separate sections: *it* as an expletive and pronoun, as well as the inappropriate use of *who, which,* and *that.* As in previous chapters, exercises provide ample practice in identifying and correcting errors.

SPOTLIGHT ON COMMON ERRORS—
PRONOUN REFERENCE

FOR DISCUSSION

Since most students have problems with only certain types of pronoun reference errors, you might want to initiate a class discussion of errors most relevant to your students. Ask students to identify from the Spotlight on Common Errors examples of reference errors familiar to them and to characterize their own errors accordingly. Students can then discuss how pronoun reference errors can occur, thereby reinforcing their understanding of the need for clarity in pronoun use. (In large classes, this activity might begin with small groups: The groups will identify their errors, and then the class as a whole will discuss the types compiled from each group's report.)

These are the errors most commonly associated with pronoun reference. For full explanations and suggested revisions, follow the cross-references to chapter sections.

PRONOUN REFERENCE ERRORS arise when a sentence leaves readers unable to link a pronoun with an *antecedent*—a specific noun that the pronoun refers to and renames (see 7a-7). If the identity of this antecedent is unclear, readers may miss the reference and become confused. Four error patterns lead to problems with pronoun reference.

- **A pronoun should refer clearly to a single noun. When the pronoun can refer to either of two (or more) nouns within a sentence or between sentences, revise sentences for clarity (see 14a).**

Within a sentence

FAULTY	REVISED
When Mark and Jay return home, *he* will call. [To whom does *he* refer?]	When Mark and Jay return home, *Mark* will call.

Between sentences

FAULTY	REVISED
The conversation between Clara and Nancy lasted two hours. At the end, *she* was exhausted. [Which one is *she*?]	The conversation between Clara and Nancy lasted two hours. At the end, *Clara* was exhausted.

- **A pronoun should be located close to the noun it renames. When a pronoun is too far from its antecedent, revise the sentence to narrow the distance and clarify meaning (see 14b).**

Within a sentence

FAULTY	REVISED
The statement that Dr. Parker made about a city water fountain and that she issued as a formal warning infuriated the mayor, who knew *it* would alarm the public. [Does *it* clearly refer to the faraway *statement* and not to something else?]	Issued as a formal warning, Dr. Parker's *statement* about a city water fountain alarmed the public, and *it* infuriated the mayor. [Less distance between the pronoun and antecedent makes the reference clear.]

Between sentences

FAULTY	**REVISED**
Major oil spills have fouled coastlines in Alaska, France, and England and have caused severe ecological damage. *Some* could almost certainly be avoided. [Does *some* refer to faraway *spills* or to *coastlines*?]	Major oil spills have fouled coastlines in Alaska, France, and England and have caused severe ecological damage. *Some spills* could almost certainly be avoided. [*Spills* is added to clear up the reference.]

■ The pronouns <u>this</u> and <u>that</u> should refer to specific words. When either is used as a one-word summary of a preceding sentence, revise to clarify the reference between sentences by adding an additional word or phrase of summary (see 14c-3).

FAULTY	**REVISED**
The purpose of the conference was to explore the links between lung cancer and second-hand smoke. *This* was firmly established. [What was established?]	The purpose of the conference was to explore the links between lung cancer and second-hand smoke. *This connection* was firmly established. [A summary word added makes the reference clear.]

■ Once you establish a pattern of first-person (*I/we*), second-person (*you*), or third-person pronouns (*he/she/it/they*) in a sentence or paragraph (see 8a, 8b), keep references to your subject <u>consistent.</u> Prevent confusion by avoiding shifts and revising sentences for consistency (see 16a-1).

Within a sentence

FAULTY	**REVISED**
Students generally fare better when *you* are given instruction on taking lecture notes. [Confusion arises between third-person *students* and second-person *you*. Who is the subject?]	*Students* generally fare better when *they* are given instruction on taking lecture notes. [Consistent third person] OR As a student *you* will generally fare better when *you* are given instruction on taking lecture notes.

Between sentences

FAULTY	**REVISED**
Students fare better when given instruction on basic skills. *You* can improve *your* note taking after getting help with the techniques. [Have *students* suddenly become *you*?]	*Students* fare better when given instruction on basic skills. *They* can improve *their* note taking after getting help with the techniques.

Describing a person's speech indirectly can lead to unclear pronoun reference. Occasionally, if you can document what was said, you can convert indirect quotations to direct ones in order to clarify a pronoun's reference. Otherwise, you can restate the sentence carefully to avoid confusion among the nouns.

CONFUSING   First Dickinson, then Jackson, fired. Jackson later told a friend *he* thought *he* had been killed.

DIRECT STATEMENT   Jackson later told a friend, "I thought I had been killed."

RESTATEMENT   As he later told a friend, Jackson at that moment felt mortally wounded.

ESL NOTE   In a standard English sentence, the subject is not repeated elsewhere in the sentence with an unnecessary pronoun. Pronouns are also involved when the subject is renamed in a dependent clause (see 7e-2). Repeated subjects must be avoided in sentences with long dependent clauses separating subjects from verbs (see 14e-1 and 44d-1).

14b Keep pronouns close to their antecedents.

CONFUSING   The *statement* that Dr. Parker made and that she issued as a formal warning infuriated the mayor, who knew *it* would alarm the public.

CLEAR   Issued as a formal warning, Dr. Parker's *statement* alarmed the public, and *it* infuriated the mayor.

Even when pronoun choice is correct, too many words between a pronoun and its antecedent can confuse readers. If in a long sentence or in adjacent sentences several nouns appear between a pronoun and its proper antecedent, these nouns will incorrectly claim the reader's attention as the word renamed by the pronoun.

CONFUSING   *Prehistoric peoples* used many organic substances, which survive at relatively few archaeological sites. Bone and antler were commonly used, especially in Europe some fifteen thousand years ago. *They* relied heavily on plant fibers and baskets for their material culture. [The pronoun *they* must refer to *prehistoric peoples,* since only people can *rely,* but the intervening nouns distract from this reference.]

CLOSER ANTECEDENT   *Prehistoric peoples* used many organic substances, which survive at relatively few archaeological sites. *They commonly used* bone and antler, especially in Europe some fifteen thousand years ago. *They* also relied heavily on plant fibers and baskets for their material culture. [The pronoun subject, *they,* is added to the second sentence in order to maintain a clear antecedent. The pronoun subject of the third sentence is thereby made clear.]

PRONOUN REPLACED

Prehistoric peoples used many organic substances, which survive at relatively few archaeological sites. Bone and antler were commonly used, especially in Europe some fifteen thousand years ago. *The desert peoples of western North America* relied heavily on plant fibers and baskets for their material culture. [A new subject replaces the confusing pronoun.]

The relative pronouns *who, which,* and *that,* when introducing a modifying adjective clause, should be placed close to the nouns they modify (see 19b-2).

CONFUSING

Prehistoric peoples used many organic substances difficult to find at archaeological sites, which included bone and antler. [Does *which* refer to *sites* or *substances*?]

CLOSER ANTECEDENT

Prehistoric peoples used many organic substances, including bone and antler, which survive at relatively few archaeological sites.

EXERCISE 1

Rewrite the sentences that follow so that pronouns are replaced or are close to and refer clearly to the nouns they rename. Place a check beside the sentences that need no revision.

Example: Edmund Halley as well as Isaac Newton studied the motions of comets, and in 1705 he published calculations relating to 24 cometary orbits. [Is Halley the clear antecedent, or could *he* refer to Newton?]

Edmund Halley as well as Isaac Newton studied the motions of comets, and in 1705 Halley published calculations relating to 24 cometary orbits. [The pronoun is replaced with a noun.]

1. In particular, he noted that the elements of the orbits of the bright comets of 1531, 1607, and 1682 were so similar that a single comet could have produced all of them.
2. Halley predicted that only one object existed and it should return about 1758.
3. Alexis Clairaut calculated the variations a comet should experience in passing near the planet Jupiter and also near Saturn and predicted that it should first make its appearance very late in 1758.
4. The comet that Clairaut identified was first sighted by an amateur astronomer, George Palitzsch, on Christmas night, 1758, exactly in accordance with his calculations.
5. The comet has been named *Halley's comet* in honor of the man who first recognized it to be a permanent member of the solar system.

EXERCISE 1

1. In particular, he noted that the elements of the orbits of the bright comets of 1532, 1607, and 1682 were so similar that a single comet could have produced all of the orbits.
2. Correct
3. Alexis Clairaut calculated the variations a comet should experience in passing near the planet Jupiter and also near Saturn and predicted that the comet should first make its appearance very late in 1758.
4. The comet that Clairaut identified was first sighted by an amateur astronomer, George Palitzsch, on Christmas night, 1758, exactly in accordance with Clairaut's calculations.
5. Correct

GROUP ACTIVITY

This and subsequent exercises are ideal for group work. Have students either complete the exercises in groups or compare their responses after completing the exercises individually. Either way, as they negotiate responses or defend their choices, they'll understand more clearly the appropriate punctuation of sentences.

14c State a pronoun's antecedent clearly.

To be clear, a pronoun's antecedent should be stated directly, either in the sentence in which the pronoun appears or in an immediately preceding sentence. If the antecedent is merely implied, the pronoun's meaning will be weak or imprecise and the reader will probably be confused.

1 Make a pronoun refer to a specific noun antecedent, not to a modifier that may imply the antecedent.

CONFUSING   From films like *Fantasia* in 1940 to *Aladdin* in 1992, Disney studios have raised <u>it</u> to an art form.

CLEAR   From films like *Fantasia* in 1940 to *Aladdin* in 1992, Disney studios have raised <u>animation</u> to an art form.

Although an adjective may imply the antecedent of a pronoun, an adjective is not identical to and thus cannot serve as that antecedent. Revise sentences so that a *noun* provides the reference for a pronoun.

CONFUSING   Two glass rods will repel each other when they are electrified. *It* is created from a buildup of positive and negative charges in the rods. [What does *it* refer to?]

NOUN
ANTECEDENT   Two glass rods will repel each other when they carry *electricity*. *It* is created from a buildup of positive and negative charges in the rods.

NOUN
ANTECEDENT   Two glass rods will repel each other when they carry *electricity*, *which* is created from a buildup of positive and negative charges in the rods.

PRONOUN
REPLACED   Two *electrified* glass rods will repel each other. *Electricity* arises from the buildup of positive and negative charges in the rods.

2 Make a pronoun refer to a noun, not the possessive form of a noun.

CONFUSING   *Sally's* case is in trouble. Does *she* know that?

CLEAR   *Sally* is in trouble with this case. Does *she* know that?

Although the possessive form of a noun may imply the noun as the intended antecedent of a pronoun, this form is not identical to, and thus is not clear enough to serve as, that antecedent. Revise sentences so that a *noun* provides the reference for a pronoun. Alternately, change the pronoun so that it, too, is in the possessive form.

CONFUSING   The *Greeks'* knowledge of magnetic forces was evident before 600 B.C. *They* observed how certain minerals, such as loadstone, have the ability to attract pieces of iron.

NOUN ANTECEDENT	The *Greeks* had knowledge of magnetic forces before 600 B.C. *They* observed how certain minerals, such as loadstone, have the ability to attract iron. [The possessive form—*Greeks'*—is eliminated to provide an antecedent for the pronoun *they*.]
PRONOUN REPLACED	The *Greeks'* knowledge of magnetic forces was evident before 600 B.C. *Their scientists* observed how certain minerals, such as loadstone, have the ability to attract pieces of iron.

3 Give the pronouns *that, this, which,* and *it* precise reference.

CONFUSING	The paper proposed to link cancer and secondary smoke. *This* was established.
CLEAR	The paper proposed to link cancer and secondary smoke. *This connection* was established.

The pronouns *that, this, which,* and *it* should refer to specific nouns. Avoid having them make vague reference to the overall sense of a preceding sentence.

CONFUSING	Magnets have two poles—called north and south poles—and these poles obey the same kind of rule as electric charges: like poles repel each other and unlike poles attract each other. *This* was not well understood until the twentieth century. [What, exactly, does *this* refer to?]
ANTECEDENT PROVIDED	Magnets have two poles—called north and south poles—and these poles obey the same kind of rule as electric charges: like poles repel each other and unlike poles attract each other. *This phenomenon* was not well understood until the twentieth century.
CONFUSING	Knowledge of atomic structure was advanced in the late nineteenth century by British scientist J. J. Thomson, *which* established that one component of the atom, electrons, are negatively charged. [The pronoun *which* does not refer to a particular noun.]
ANTECEDENT PROVIDED	Knowledge of atomic structure was advanced in the late nineteenth century by British scientist J. J. Thomson, *who* established that one component of the atom, electrons, are negatively charged.
CONFUSING	Thomson believed atoms of matter contain two kinds of particles, intermingled: negatively charged electrons and positively charged protons. *That* was the impetus other physicists needed to refine even further the structural model of the atom. [No single word serves as the antecedent of *that*.]
PRONOUN REPLACED	Thomson believed atoms of matter contain two kinds of particles, intermingled: negatively charged electrons and positively charged protons. *Thomson's theory* was the impetus other physicists needed to refine even further the structural model of the atom.

ESL ALERT

ESL students find sentences in which the relative clause pronoun has been omitted most confusing and have trouble separating subordinate clauses from main clauses in such situations. With adjective clauses in which the verb takes a preposition, ESL students might add an extraneous "it"; they do so most frequently if the relative clause pronoun is omitted.

> "He soon caught up with the car which his girlfriend was riding in ~~it~~."

> "He soon caught up with the car his girlfriend was riding in ~~it~~."

REFERENCES

LAKOFF, GEORGE. "Pronouns and Reference." *Notes from the Linguistic Underground.* Ed. James D. McCawley. New York: Academic Press, 1976. 275–335. A thorough discussion of various issues involved in pronoun reference.

SLOAN, GARY. "Relational Ambiguity Between Sentences." *CCC* 39 (1988): 154–65. Comparing written and spoken discourse can be beneficial when studying pronoun reference.

MOSKOVIT, LEONARD. "When is Broad Reference Clear?" *CCC* 34 (1983): 454–69. At times, broad pronouns without specific antecedents are indeed clear.

GROUP ACTIVITY

Because students are more likely to learn rules when working with their own writing, analysis of pronoun reference errors in their papers can be beneficial. Ask students to bring in several papers in order to take part in this activity. When you divide students into groups, try to mix strong with weak writers. Then have each group work together on one student's writing at a time, identifying unclear pronoun references, particularly those involving *that, this, which, it, they,* and *you.* The group's attempts to determine which references are unclear and how to revise them should generate healthy discussion. This discussion will help strong writers to articulate their implicit understanding of grammatical rules and weak writers to gain an understanding of such rules.

4 Avoid indefinite antecedents for the pronouns *it*, *they*, and *you*.

NONSTANDARD   *It* will rain tomorrow.
STANDARD   *We* are expecting rain tomorrow.

Expressions such as "you know," "they say," and "it figures" are common in speech and informal writing. The pronouns in these expressions do not refer to particular people—or, in the case of *it*, to a particular object. These pronouns are said to have *indefinite* reference. In academic writing, pronouns should refer to specific antecedents. *You* should be used either to address the reader directly or for a direct quotation; *it* and *they* should refer to particular things, ideas, or people.

NONSTANDARD   Today, *they say* that an atom has a nucleus with neutrons and protons.

STANDARD   Today, *physicists believe* that an atom has a nucleus with neutrons and protons.

NONSTANDARD   Because physicists work with abstract models and mathematical languages, *you* must almost take what physicists say as an item of faith.

STANDARD   Because physicists work with abstract models and mathematical languages, *nonscientists* must almost take what physicists say as an item of faith.

How to Revise Unclear Pronoun Reference

1. Provide a clear, nearby antecedent.
2. Replace the pronoun with a noun and thereby eliminate the problem of ambiguous reference.
3. Totally recast the sentence to avoid the problem of ambiguous reference.

5 Avoid using a pronoun to refer to the title of a paper in the paper's first sentence.

A pronoun should have a reference in the sentence in which it appears or in an immediately preceding sentence. A title, while directly related to a paper or essay, does not occur *within* the paper or essay and thus cannot function appropriately as an antecedent.

A TITLE   "Eliot's Desert Images in *The Waste Land*"

A FIRST SENTENCE   They are plentiful, and their cumulative effect is to leave readers thirsty—in both body and soul.

FIRST SENTENCE REVISED | Desert images in T. S. Eliot's *The Waste Land* are plentiful, and their cumulative effect is to leave readers thirsty—in both body and soul.

14d Avoid mixing uses of the pronoun *it*.

CONFUSING | *It* will be a successful experiment if the computer doesn't overload *its* memory.

CLEAR | The experiment will succeed if the computer doesn't overload *its* memory.

The word *it* functions both as a pronoun and as an expletive (see 7a-11)—that is, as a space filler in a rearranged sentence.

AS AN EXPLETIVE | *It* is clear that the committee is resisting the initiative. [The entire "that . . . " clause is the subject.]

AS A PRONOUN | Although the committee voted, *it* [i.e., the committee] showed no leadership.

Avoid using the word *it* both as an expletive and as a pronoun in the same sentence.

CONFUSING | *It* is clear that *it* is shirking *its* responsibilities.

WEAK | *It* is clear that the committee is shirking *its* responsibilities.

CLEAR | Clearly, the committee is shirking *its* responsibilities.

14e Use the relative pronouns *who*, *which*, and *that* appropriately.

1 Selecting relative pronouns

Relative pronouns (see 7e-2) introduce dependent clauses that usually function as adjectives. The pronouns *who*, *which*, and *that* rename and refer to the nouns they follow. The pronoun *who* can refer to people or to divinities or personified animals.

Nobel laureate Gabriel García Márquez, *who* was born in 1929 in Colombia, one of sixteen children of an impoverished telegraph operator, is among the most eminent of living Latin American writers.

That refers to animals, things, or people (when not referring to a *specific* person, in which case the pronoun *who* is used).

At 19, he began to write stories *that* were rich in myth.

Which refers to animals and things.

His books, *which* are translated into more than a dozen languages, have made Márquez a respected literary figure throughout the world.

TEACHING IDEAS

If you're aware of students whose writing lacks clarity because of overuse of *it*, then you may find the following exercise useful. Ask those students to gather three or four of their papers and circle every use of *it*, labeling the word as either an expletive or a pronoun. Above each pronoun use of *it* (or in the margin) they are to name the pronoun's antecedent. An inability to determine the antecedent and/or an overabundance of expletives should alert the student that there is a problem with clarity in his or her writing. Such students might be advised to use this exercise with every future draft until the problem is alleviated.

ESL ALERT

Some romance-language (Spanish, Italian, Portuguese) speakers will have difficulty with the concept of the expletive since it does not exist in their language. Their tendency will be to leave out the "there" or "it" and to simply begin with a *be* verb as they would in their language: "Is hot." "Is over there." Calling attention to the problem often helps the student self-correct.

ADDITIONAL EXERCISE B

ACROSS THE CURRICULUM This exercise should reinforce your understanding of the use of relative pronouns in essential and nonessential clauses. Photocopy a long passage from a textbook used in one of your other classes, and underline all of the relative clauses. Based on the guidelines in this box, identify each of the clauses as essential or nonessential. Then, for each clause, explain why the author chose to use the relative pronoun he or she did.

Be alert to differences: Apply a test for choosing *who, which,* or *that*—with or without commas.

Writers can be unsure of themselves when choosing relative pronouns (*who, which,* and *that*) and when using commas with relative clauses. Relative pronouns begin relative clauses, and these function in a sentence as if they were adjectives: they modify nouns. You can apply three tests for deciding which pronoun to use and whether or not to use commas.

Identify the noun being modified.

■ Is this a proper noun—the name of a *specific* person (Larry), place (Baltimore), or thing (Levis)? If yes, then use the pronoun *who, whom,* or *whose* (for a person) or *which* (for a place or thing) *with* commas. The noun does not need the modifying clause to specify its meaning. This clause is *nonessential* (see 25d).

My friend George, *who* is constantly angry, has developed a stress disorder.

The harbor area in Baltimore, *which* is the largest city in Maryland but not the capital, has changed significantly in the last twenty years.

The Levis, *which* fit me well, were on sale.

■ Is the noun being modified a common noun—an unspecified person (man), place (city), or thing (pants)? If yes, then it is quite likely that the modifying information of the clause is essential for specifying the noun's identity. Use *who, whom,* or *whose* (for a person) and *which* or *that* (for a place or thing) *without commas.* The modifying clause is *essential* (see 25d).

People *who* are constantly angry often develop stress disorders.

The cities *that* are of greatest interest to me are all accessible by train.
The cities *which* are of greatest interest to me are all accessible by train.

The pants *that* fit me best were on sale.

■ If, in the context of a paragraph, the identity of the common noun being modified is made clear and specific to the reader, then treat the common noun in the same way that you would a proper noun: use a relative clause, with commas.

Over a year ago, I met the woman *who* is seated at that table in the corner. The woman, *whose* name I can't remember, is a friend of Joan's.

[In the first sentence, the relative clause *who is seated* . . . is needed to identify which woman, presumably in a roomful of people. In the second sentence, the reader knows who is being referred to, so the relative clause in that sentence (*whose name* . . .) is nonessential and takes commas.]

ESL NOTE Avoid repeating the subject of a sentence with an unnecessary pronoun, especially when a long dependent clause separates a subject from its verb (see 44d-1).

AVOID   The taller *man*, who ran away quickly, *he* recognized me.
           [An unnecessary pronoun repeats the subject.]

REVISED   The taller man, who ran away quickly, recognized me.

2 | Using relative pronouns in essential and nonessential clauses

ESSENTIAL   People who are constantly angry become stressed.
NONESSENTIAL   Jim, who is constantly angry, has become stressed.

Use either *that* or *which* depending on whether a clause begun by one of these words is essential or nonessential to the meaning of the noun being modified. Use *that* or *which* (with *no* commas around the dependent clause) to denote an **essential** (or restrictive) **modifier**—a word, phrase, or clause that provides information crucial for identifying a noun.

> As a young man, Márquez advocated many left-wing proposals for reform *that* were not in the end accepted.

> As a young man, Márquez advocated many left-wing proposals for reform *which* were not in the end accepted.

As the noun being modified becomes more specific (when it becomes a proper noun, for instance, that identifies a *particular* person, place, or thing), then a modifying clause is no longer essential since the core information of the noun is already established. Use *which* (*with* commas around the dependent clause) to denote a **nonessential** (or nonrestrictive) **modifier.**

> The celebrated *Cien años de soledad* (1967), *which* was published in English as *One Hundred Years of Solitude*, traces the history of a Colombian family through six generations. [Since the novel is titled, any modifying information is nonessential.]

Use *who* to denote either an essential or a nonessential modifier.

ESSENTIAL   One Latin American novelist *who* very effectively mixes elements of fantasy with reality is Gabriel García Márquez. [Since there are many Latin American novelists and none of them is named, the information in the modifying clause is essential.]

NONESSENTIAL   Nobel laureate Gabriel García Márquez, *who* was born in 1929 in Colombia, is among the most eminent of living Latin American writers. [Since a *particular* novelist is named, the modifying clause is nonessential.]

See 25d for a full discussion of essential and nonessential modifiers with commas.

TEACHING IDEAS

The concept of essential and nonessential is often difficult for students to grasp. Thus, although the focus of this section is on pronouns rather than punctuation, it may be useful to clarify the distinction between essential and nonessential for students at this point.

Write on the board a sentence that has two distinct meanings depending on whether or not the subordinate clause is essential. Write the sentence first with the comma, and then erase the comma. Ask students how the meaning changes when the comma is removed. A sentence like "Professor Shannon failed all her students, who had missed the exam" is a good example. Did all of Professor Shannon's students miss the exam? Did she fail only that group of students who missed the exam? As they work with sentences like this, students will gain a clearer understanding of how important it is to be able to distinguish essential from nonessential items.

EXERCISE 2

1. In recent years, the disorder has been called "bipolar affective disorder," because of the two opposite affects—or moods—involved. Researchers say the illness differs from depression, which is termed a "unipolar" illness.
2. The "blue moods" of manic depressives are characterized by feelings of discouragement, low energy level, and loss of interest in activities usually enjoyed. Manic depressives tend to think slowly and often have difficulty concentrating.
3. Characteristically, there are other distressing symptoms, such as insomnia, sleeping too much, restless sleep, poor appetite, and often a pervasive anxiety and tension. These symptoms usually last for weeks or months.
4. Correct
5. Researchers say you can recognize a person's manic phase by listening to his or her speech, which is usually fast and pressured, in an effort to keep pace with the rapid and shifting flow of ideas.
6. Correct

EXERCISE 2

Revise the following sentences so that pronouns refer clearly to their antecedents. Place a check beside the sentences that need no revision.

Example: Manic-depressive illness is a disorder characterized by extreme changes in mood between low (or depressed) and high (or manic). They usually are affected by the illness in the third or fourth decade of life.

Manic-depressive illness is a disorder characterized by extreme changes in mood between low (or depressed) and high (or manic). *Manic-depressives* usually are affected by the illness in the third or fourth decade of life.

1. In recent years, the disorder has been called "bipolar affective disorder," because of the two opposite affects—or moods—involved. They say the illness differs from depression, which is termed a "unipolar" illness.
2. The "blue moods" of manic-depressives are characterized by feelings of discouragement, low energy level, and loss of interest in activities usually enjoyed. They tend to think slowly and often have difficulty concentrating.
3. Characteristically, there are other distressing symptoms, such as insomnia, sleeping too much, restless sleep, poor appetite, and often a pervasive anxiety and tension. This usually lasts for weeks or months.
4. The opposite mood is the elated, euphoric, or manic mood, which gives one an abundance of energy and a diminished need for sleep.
5. They say you can recognize a person's manic phase by listening to his or her speech, that is usually fast and pressured in an effort to keep pace with the rapid and shifting flow of ideas.
6. It is common that expansive and grandiose plans preoccupy the manic mind, for it is full of itself and will even put into operation wild business ventures that can end in embarrassment or bankruptcy.

EXERCISE 3

The pronouns *this, that, these, which,* and *it* are often used ambiguously, especially when they refer to ideas, situations, or circumstances not previously identified or clearly explained. In the following sequence of sentences, avoid vagueness by rewriting sentences to provide clear references. Use information from adjoining sentences to provide references.

Example: Archaeology offers a unique approach to studying long-term change in human societies. This has characterized the study of humankind in North America.

Archaeology offers a unique approach to studying long-term change in human societies. *This approach* has characterized the study of humankind in North America.

1. Unfortunately, archaeologists have only recently undertaken it in the context of the European Contact Period.
2. In the past they somewhat rigidly saw it as the ending point of prehistory, when Native Americans came into the orbit of Western civilization.
3. This was apparent especially because archaeologists tended to be preoccupied with the classification of discrete periods in the past, rather than with the processes of cultural change.
4. These were given names such as Paleo-Indian, Archaic, Woodland, and so on.
5. In short, these narrowly constrained the interests of archaeologists.
6. Now they are taking a closer look at the phenomenon of European Contact as a part of long-term developments in that society.

EXERCISE 3

1. Unfortunately, archaeologists have only recently undertaken this approach [or such studies] in the context of the European Contact Period.
2. In the past archaeologists somewhat rigidly saw the European Contact Period as the ending point of prehistory, when Native Americans came into the orbit of Western civilization.
3. This rigidity was apparent especially because archaeologists tended to be preoccupied with the classification of discrete periods in the past, rather than with the process of cultural change.
4. These periods were given names such as Paleo-Indian, Archaic, Woodland, and so on.
5. In short, these categories narrowly constrained the interests of archaeologists.
6. Now archaeologists are taking a closer look at the phenomenon of European Contact as a part of long-term developments in that society.

ADDITIONAL EXERCISE C

Look through your graded papers to find instructors' comments regarding unclear pronoun reference. Reread the papers, identifying the errors as you read by using the strategies outlined in this chapter. Then revise the errors. (If you don't have any graded papers handy, look through any body of writing you've done recently.)

CHAPTER 15

Misplaced and Dangling Modifiers

KEY FEATURES

The joke opening this chapter is an indication of the unintentional humor that often results from misplaced or dangling modifiers. The chapter's value is established in the first paragraph: If you don't want to generate laughter at your own expense, or to leave your readers confused, learn how to position modifiers appropriately. As in previous chapters, the approach is positive, with each section of the chapter covering one strategy for assuring proper placement of modifiers. Limiting modifiers, squinting modifiers, lengthy modifiers between subject and verb, split infinitives, and the like are explained in clear, simple terms with extensive examples. In covering dangling modifiers, the chapter pays special attention to the role of passive voice in such constructions. Exercises provide extensive practice in identifying and correcting problems.

LOOKING BACK

References to chapter 7 (Constructing Sentences) appear throughout this chapter. If chapter 7 has not been covered yet, or if some time has passed since it was covered, you may want to spend a little time on that material now.

T*his chair was designed for weekend athletes with extra padding.* Who (or what) has extra padding: the chair or weekend athletes? Misplaced, awkward, or dangling modifiers can confuse readers. Recall that the function of a modifier is to describe a noun, verb, or other modifiers (see 7c). A modifier can be a single word: a *sporty* car; a phrase: Joanne drove *a car with racing stripes*; or a dependent clause: *After she gained confidence driving a sporty car,* Joanne took up racing.

In order to function most effectively, a modifier should be placed directly next to the word it modifies. If this placement disrupts meaning, then the modifier should be placed *as close as possible* to the word it modifies. These two principles inform the discussion that follows.

MISPLACED MODIFIERS

15a Position modifiers so that they refer clearly to the words they should modify.

CONFUSING	A truck rumbled down the street, gray with dirt.
CLEAR	A dirty, gray truck rumbled down the street.
	A truck rumbled down the gray, dirty street.

Readers expect a modifier to be linked clearly with the word the writer intended it to modify. When this link is broken, readers become confused or frustrated.

CONFUSING	This chair was designed for weekend athletes with extra padding.
REVISED	This chair with extra padding was designed for weekend athletes.

Here is a more complicated example of a sentence made confusing by a misplaced modifier.

CONFUSING	The behavior of a chemical compound in a laboratory that is put together is similar to the behavior of an identical compound obtained from plants and animals growing in nature.

SPOTLIGHT ON COMMON ERRORS—MODIFIERS

These are the errors most commonly associated with modifiers. For full explanations and suggested revisions, follow the cross-references to chapter sections.

MODIFIER ERRORS arise under two conditions: when the word being modified is too far from the modifier (a misplaced modifier); and when the word being modified is implied but does not appear in the sentence (a dangling modifier). Both errors will confuse readers.

- **Position a modifier near the word it modifies (see 15a).**

FAULTY	REVISED
A truck rumbled down the street, gray with dirt. [What is gray and dirty?]	A **dirty, gray** truck rumbled down the street. A truck rumbled down the **gray, dirty** street.

- **Make a modifier refer clearly to one word (see 15c).**

FAULTY	REVISED
The supervisor who was conducting the interview thoughtfully posed a question. [Was this a thoughtful interview or thoughtful question?]	The supervisor who was conducting the interview posed a final, **thoughtful question.** The supervisor, who was conducting a **thoughtful interview,** posed a final question.

- **Reposition a modifier that splits sentence elements (see 15d–15g).**

FAULTY	REVISED
Vigorous exercise—complemented by a varied diet that includes nuts, grains, vegetables, and fruits—is one key to fitness. [The "key to fitness" is unclear.] The agent signed, with her client seated beside her, the contract. [What is "signed" is unclear.]	Vigorous exercise, one key to fitness, should be complemented by a varied diet that includes nuts, grains, vegetables, and fruits. With her client seated beside her, the agent **signed the contract.**

- **Make introductory phrases refer clearly to a *specific* word in the independent clause (see 15h-1–2).**

FAULTY	REVISED
After considering his difficulty in the interview, the application was withdrawn. [Who withdrew the application?]	After considering his difficulty in the interview, **the candidate withdrew** his application.

FOR DISCUSSION

Since most students have problems with only certain types of common modifier errors, you might want to initiate a class discussion of errors most relevant to your students. Ask students to identify from the Spotlight on Common Errors examples of modifier errors familiar to them and to characterize their own errors accordingly. Students can then discuss how such errors occur, thereby reinforcing their understanding of the need for clarity in placement of modifiers. (In large classes, this activity might begin with small groups. The groups will identify their errors, and then the class as a whole will discuss the types compiled from each group's report.)

The example frustrates readers because key elements in the sentence do not seem to fit: Does *in a laboratory* modify *compound* or *behavior*? Is it really the *laboratory* that is *put together,* and if so, how or where? An analysis of the sentence suggests that the writer has misplaced the modifier *in the laboratory.* When the prepositional phrase is repositioned next to the words it should modify, the sentence becomes clear.

REVISED   The behavior of a chemical compound that is put together *in the laboratory* is similar to the behavior of an identical compound obtained from plants and animals growing in nature.

If a phrase or clause beginning a sentence functions as an adjective modifier, then the first words after the modifier—that is, the first words of the independent clause—should include the noun being modified.

CONFUSING   Still plunged in the darkness of superstition, legends of the mysterious East circulated widely among medieval Europeans. [Who or what is "plunged in the darkness of superstition"— certainly not *legends.*]

REWRITTEN   Still plunged in the darkness of superstition, *medieval Europeans* widely circulated legends of the mysterious East. [The original sentence, "*Legends . . . Europeans,*" has been given a new subject, *medieval Europeans,* that can be modified by the introductory phrase.]

ESL NOTE   In most English sentences, two or more adjectives that accumulate as modifiers before a noun or pronoun are typically given a standard order or sequence. Section 44f-1–2 describes typical patterns for placement of English adjective modifiers.

EXERCISE 1

1. Black rhythm and blues with its typical twelve-bar structure became rock 'n roll's most common format among white teenagers.
2. Organized in 1953 by a disc jockey in Cleveland, Ohio, a stage show featuring black rhythm and blues acts was seen by an audience of whom two-thirds were white.
3. Black and white members of the audience were separated by a rope that was strung down the center of the theater and that was often gone by the end of the performance.
4. Because rock 'n roll combined elements of black rhythm and blues and white country western music, American teenagers found it attractive.

EXERCISE 1

Reorganize or rewrite the following sentences so that the misplaced modifier is correctly placed. (You may need to add a word or two in some sentences and provide something specific for the modifier to describe.) Place a check mark beside any sentence in which modifiers are used clearly.

Example: Turning to black subculture as an alternative to homogenized mainstream culture, black slang and music became increasingly common among American teenagers after 1950.

Turning to black subculture as an alternative to homogenized mainstream culture, American teenagers after 1950 began using black slang and listening to black music. [The sentence is given a new subject, *American teenagers,* that can be modified by the introductory phrase.]

1. Black rhythm and blues with its typical twelve-bar structure among white teenagers became rock 'n roll's most common format.
2. Organized by a disc jockey in Cleveland, Ohio, two-thirds of the audience for a stage show featuring black rhythm and blues acts in 1953 were white.

3. Strung down the center of the theater, black and white members of the audience were separated by a rope that was often gone by the end of the performance.
4. Combining elements of black rhythm and blues and white country western music, American teenagers found rock 'n roll attractive.

15b Position limiting modifiers with care.

The children trusted only him.
Only the children trusted him.

In conversation, **limiting modifiers**—words such as *only, almost, just, nearly, even,* and *simply*—are often shifted within a sentence with little concern for their effect on meaning. When written, however, a limiting modifier is taken literally to restrict the meaning of the word placed directly after it. Observe how meaning changes as the position of a limiting modifier changes.

Nearly 90 percent of the 200 people who served in Presidential cabinets from 1897 to 1973 belonged to the social or business elite.

Ninety percent of the *nearly* 200 people who served in Presidential cabinets from 1897 to 1973 belonged to the social or business elite.

Placement of the limiting modifier *nearly* fundamentally alters the meaning of these sentences. To establish meaning clearly, position limiting modifiers with care.

EXERCISE 2

Use the limiting modifier in parentheses to rewrite each sentence two ways, giving each version a different meaning.

Example: The Greek astrolabe measured the elevation of the sun or a star. (only)

Only the Greek astrolabe measured the elevation of the sun or a star.

The Greek astrolabe measured *only* the elevation of the sun or a star.

1. When they market new musical trends, major record labels follow rather than lead. (usually)
2. The latest hot trend, "world music," is not an exception. (even)
3. "There is no one way to decide what to put out," says Roger Armstrong. (simply)
4. "By putting out titles you are developing a taste," he claims. (just)
5. Every record company takes a chance on every artist, unless that artist is a household name. (nearly)

GROUP ACTIVITY

Squinting modifiers are harder than other misplaced modifiers to catch when revising; the writer already knows the meaning of his or her sentences, and this type of error doesn't stand out the way some others do. To give students practice in recognizing these problems, have groups compose four or five sentences including squinting modifiers, and then pass the sentences on to another group for correction. This activity will give students practice in reading sentences closely for such errors.

ESL ALERT

Remind ESL students that single or phrasal participles may be placed before or after the noun they describe, but that adjective clauses are less versatile and must always go directly after the noun and preferably immediately adjacent to the noun. Note the contrast:

"Seeing the problem, the women agreed to . . ." and

"The women, seeing the problem, agreed to . . ."

in contrast to

"The women, who saw the problem, agreed to . . ."

but never

"Who saw the problem, the women agreed . . ."

or

"The women, standing near us, who saw the problem, agreed . . ."

EXERCISE 3

1. Sometimes going to the movies makes me wish I were an actress.
   Going to the movies makes me sometimes wish I were an actress.
2. The equation that Steven thought he had thoroughly analyzed confused him on the exam.
   The equation that Steven thought he had analyzed confused him thoroughly on the exam.
3. Reprimanding his son, the father angrily pushed the shopping cart down the supermarket aisle.
   Reprimanding his son angrily, the father pushed the shopping cart down the supermarket aisle.

15c Reposition modifiers that describe two elements simultaneously.

CONFUSING	The supervisor conducting the interview thoughtfully posed a final question.
CLEAR	The supervisor conducting the interview posed a final, thoughtful question.

A **squinting modifier** appears to modify two words in the sentence—the word preceding it and the word following it. To convey a clear meaning, the modifier must be repositioned so it can describe only a *single* word.

CONFUSING	The official being questioned aggressively shut the door. [What does *aggressively* describe—how the official was being questioned or how the official shut the door?]
REVISED	The official, who was being questioned aggressively, shut the door. [A clause is set off to become a nonessential modifier of *official.*]
REVISED	The official who was being questioned shut the door aggressively. [*Aggressively* is moved to an unambiguous position and modifies *shut.*]

EXERCISE 3

The following sentences are made awkward by squinting modifiers. Revise each sentence twice so that the modifier describes a different word in each revision.

Example: Sitting in the hot summer sun often accelerates the skin's aging process.

Sitting *often* in the hot summer sun accelerates the skin's aging process. [*Often* modifies *sitting*—the sense being that one must sit in the sun many times to accelerate the skin's aging.]

Often, sitting in the hot summer sun accelerates the skin's aging process. [The sense here is that sitting in the sun even once or a few times can accelerate the aging of the skin.]

1. Going to the movies sometimes makes me wish I were an actress.
2. The equation that Steven thought he had analyzed thoroughly confused him on the exam.
3. The father reprimanding his son angrily pushed the shopping cart down the supermarket aisle.
4. The suspect being questioned thoroughly believed his constitutional rights were being violated.
5. Taking long walks frequently helps me to relax.

CRITICAL DECISIONS

Challenge sentences: Question your placement of modifiers

Modifiers provide much of the interest in a sentence; but when misused, they undermine communication by forcing readers to stop and figure out your meaning. In every case, you should know precisely *which* word in a sentence you are modifying. Posing three questions should help you to be clear.

■ What modifiers am I using in this sentence? To use modifiers effectively and correctly, you should be able to recognize modifiers when you write them. Single words, phrases, and clauses can function as modifiers.

Modifying word (see 7c)

ADJECTIVE   The artist made a *deliberate* effort.

ADVERB   The artist succeeded *brilliantly*.

Modifying phrase (see 7d)

ADJECTIVE   The painting, *displayed on a dark wall*, glowed.

ADVERB   Patrons responded *with an unusual mix of excitement and nervousness.*

Modifying clause (see 7e)

ADJECTIVE   Many attended the opening, *which had become a much anticipated event.*

ADVERB   *After the gallery closed that evening,* the staff celebrated.

■ What word is being modified? (See 15a–c.)

The artist made a *deliberate* effort.   The artist succeeded *brilliantly*.
[The noun *effort* is being modified.]   [The verb *succeeded* is being modified.]

Several patrons who returned repeatedly called the young artist "a wonder."
[Confusing: The single-word modifier *repeatedly* seems to modify two words, *returned* and *called*.]

Having made a commitment of time and money, it was gratifying to see a successful show.
[Confusing: The phrase *having made a commitment of time and money* does not modify any specific word.]

■ Does the modifying word, phrase, or clause clearly refer to this word? (See 15a–c, 15h.)

On returning, several patrons repeatedly *called* the young artist "a wonder."
[The modifier *repeatedly* now clearly modifies the verb *called*.]

Having made a commitment of time and money, *the manager* was gratified to see a successful show.
[The modifying phrase now clearly modifies the noun *manager*.]

4. The suspect being questioned believed thoroughly his constitutional rights were being violated.
   The suspect being questioned believed his constitutional rights were being violated thoroughly.
5. Taking long walks helps me to relax frequently.
   Frequently, taking long walks helps me to relax.

GROUP ACTIVITY

Exercise 3 not only helps students understand the importance of avoiding lengthy modifiers that split subjects and verbs, but it also injects a bit of humor into the class. Provide students with three or four basic sentences, and ask groups to expand each sentence by placing a lengthy modifier between the subject and the verb. Upon completion of the task, groups can compete for the honor of having come up with the lengthiest, most obstructive modifiers. Possible sentences:

The *Enterprise* intercepted the Klingon vessel.
The Navajo Tribal Police awarded Jim Chee their highest honor.
The manager pulled Ice T's "Cop Killer" off the shelves.
Nelson Mandela was released from prison.

15d **Reposition a lengthy modifier that splits a subject and its verb.**

CONFUSING   One key to fitness—which should be complemented by a varied diet that includes nuts, grains, vegetables, and fruit—is exercise.

CLEAR   One key to fitness is vigorous exercise; another is by a varied diet that includes nuts, grains, vegetables, and fruit.

Meaning in a sentence depends on the link a writer establishes between a subject and its verb. We commonly interrupt or split these elements with adjective phrases and clauses; and provided these modifiers make a distinct modifying unit and do not suspend for too long the link between subject and verb, they need not confuse readers.

Handmade carpets, *woven in Iran by villagers and nomads for thousands of years*, have been exported to Europe since the sixteenth century.

Avoid Splitting Paired Sentence Elements with Lengthy Modifiers

Each of the five basic sentence patterns (see 7b) presents paired parts of speech that function together to create meaning. Avoid splitting the following elements with lengthy modifiers that disrupt meaning.

Pattern 1:   Subject   ⌐ *Predicate* ⌐
                 verb
           Sarah   *arrived.*

Pattern 2:   Subject   ⌐ *Predicate* ⌐
                 verb (tr.)   direct object
           Sarah   *embraced*   *her family.*

Pattern 3:   Subject   ⌐ *Predicate* ⌐
                 verb (tr.)   indirect object   direct object
           Sarah   *brought*   *them*   *presents.*

Pattern 4:   Subject   ⌐ *Predicate* ⌐
                 verb (tr.)   direct object   object complement
           Sarah   *considered*   *her family*   *a blessed sight.*

Pattern 5:   Subject   ⌐ *Predicate* ⌐
                 verb (linking)   subject complement
           She   *was*   *relieved.*

It is also common to find a one- or two-word adverb between a subject and verb.

> Groups of three or four weavers *normally* work seven days a week for anywhere between one and two years to produce a single carpet.

Lengthy modifiers, however, disrupt the link between subject and verb and should be repositioned to keep that link clear.

CONFUSING   Carpet production, *whether in the cities or in the tents of wandering tribes, or for that matter in the simple houses of villagers in small, isolated villages around the country,* has been labor intensive.

REVISED   *Whether in the cities or in the tents of wandering tribes, or for that matter in the simple houses of villagers in small, isolated villages around the country,* carpet production has been labor intensive. [An introductory modifier puts a repositioned subject next to its verb.]

REVISED   Carpets were produced *in the cities or in the tents of wandering tribes and in the simple houses of villagers in small, isolated villages around the country.* In all cases, the techniques of carpet production were labor intensive. [The lengthy original sentence has been split into two sentences.]

EXERCISE 4

Reposition modifiers in rearranged, rephrased, or divided sentences to establish clear links between subjects and verbs. Place a check before any sentence in which modifiers are used clearly. Try rewriting sentences in more than one way. Compare your revised sentences with those of other students, and decide on the preferable versions.

> *Example:* Heraldry, which includes the tracing of pedigrees and establishing the order of persons taking part in important ceremonies, as well as a familiarity with armorial bearings (or "emblems"), the rules regarding their design and use, and their technical description, in its broadest sense, comprises the skills and knowledge necessary to the occupation of *herald.*
>
> Heraldry, in its broadest sense, comprises the skills and knowledge necessary to the occupation of *herald.* These skills include the tracing of pedigrees and establishing the order of persons taking part in important ceremonies, as well as a familiarity with armorial bearings (or "emblems"), the rules regarding their design and use, and their technical description.

1. The origins of heraldry, first of all in clan totems and tribal and national emblems, and in Western civilization in the shield insignia used by Athenian families in the fifth and sixth centuries B.C., are perhaps as old as the human race.

TEACHING IDEAS

Not many elements of grammar and usage can be considered fun to study. Misplaced and dangling modifiers, however, are the exception. You might want to loosen things up a bit in class by writing a couple of humorous examples on the board—"After asking Eileen to the prom, the dog chewed up my tuxedo pants," for example. Students can then try to compose a few of their own. The student examples will represent a number of the possible errors covered in the chapter, and some may not even be dangling or misplaced modifiers. Rather than discussing those issues at the moment, however, have students keep a copy of the sentences generated; after completing the chapter they can try to match up the sentences with the types of errors represented here.

EXERCISE 4

Suggested revisions:

1. First appearing in clan totems and tribal and national emblems, and in Western civilization in the shield insignia used by Athenian families in the fifth and sixth centuries B.C., heraldry is perhaps as old as the human race.
2. Some of the older emblems were the eagle of Rome, which reappears as the eagle of the Austrian, German, and Russian emperors, and the white horse of Woden. These emblems eventually found their way into medieval heraldry.
3. Probably woven for Bishop Odo, who was himself present at Hastings, the Bayeux tapestry has no sign of any true armorial bearings. This absence of any sign seems to provide conclusive evidence that personal heraldry did not exist as early as the battle of Hastings (1066), pictured in detail in the tapestry.

2. Some of the older emblems, whether the eagle of Rome, which reappears as the eagle of the Austrian, German, and Russian emperors, or the white horse of Woden, eventually found their way into medieval heraldry.

3. The absence of any sign of true armorial bearings in the Bayeux tapestry, which was probably woven for Bishop Odo, who was himself present at Hastings, seems to provide conclusive evidence that personal heraldry did not exist as early as the battle of Hastings (1066), pictured in detail in the tapestry.

15e Reposition a modifier that splits a verb and its object or a verb and its complement.

CONFUSING   The agent signed, with her client seated beside her, the contract.

CLEAR   With her client seated beside her, the agent signed the contract.

A lengthy adverb phrase or clause can create an awkward sentence if it splits a verb and its object or a verb and its complement. Reposition these adverbs by placing them at the beginning or the end of a sentence.

AWKWARD   A number of presidents have emphasized *in foreign disputes* nonintervention. [The verb and object are split.]

REVISED   A number of presidents have emphasized nonintervention *in foreign disputes.*

AWKWARD   Millard Fillmore became, *after serving eight years as a U.S. representative from New York,* the elected vice president in 1848. [The verb and complement are split.]

REVISED   *After serving eight years as a U.S. representative from New York,* Millard Fillmore was elected vice president in 1848.

Note that one- or two-word adverbial modifiers commonly appear before a direct object or complement.

CLEAR   Zachary Taylor became *in 1848* the twelfth President.

However, when a modifier (or a combination of them) places too great a distance between a verb and its object or complement, the modifier should be repositioned.

AWKWARD   Millard Fillmore became, *on the death of Taylor in 1850,* the thirteenth President of the United States.

REVISED   Millard Fillmore became the thirteenth President of the United States *on the death of Taylor in 1850.*

EXERCISE 5

Reposition modifiers in order to restore clear links between verbs and objects or complements in these sentences. Place a check before any sentence in which modifiers are used correctly.

> *Example:* Heraldic devices became, once a particular design had been associated with a name and a lordship, hereditary.
>
> Heraldic devices became hereditary, once a particular design had been associated with a name and a lordship.

1. Armorial bearings once they became the fashion among the most influential aristocracy spread quickly throughout western Europe.
2. The use of coats of arms, as they became associated with military command and with the warlike games of joust and tourney, was at first confined to those who held their lands by force.
3. The surcoat and standard of a king or baron obviously had, like a modern army uniform, a practical military function, enabling soldiers to find and rally around their commander in the press of battle.
4. It is said that Henry IV had, at the Battle of Shrewsbury in 1403, several of his knights wear the royal surcoat, a dangerous honor because Henry's opponents were eager to kill him.
5. Today, families can pay researchers that want to impress people to manufacture a genealogy and create an impressive-looking, if bogus, coat of arms.

15f   Reposition a modifier that splits the parts of an infinitive.

CONFUSING	Her wish to boldly and decisively break the record won many supporters.
CLEAR	Her wish to break the record, boldly and decisively, won many supporters.

An **infinitive** is the dictionary or **base** form of a verb: *go, walk, see.* In a sentence, the infinitive form is often immediately preceded by the word *to: to go, to walk, to see.* Because the base word of the infinitive is a verb, the words that modify infinitives are adverbs. In conversation, emphasis on a short adverbial modifier sometimes interrupts the two parts of an infinitive: *"Please try to quickly move up."* Such an interruption in long or complex written sentences can be disruptive to the intended meaning.

Move an adverb to a position before or after an infinitive, or rewrite the sentence and eliminate the infinitive.

SPLIT	Many managers are unable *to* with difficult employees *establish* a moderate and reasonable tone.

EXERCISE 5

1. Once they became the fashion among the most influential aristocracy, armorial bearings spread quickly throughout western Europe.
2. As they became associated with military command and with the warlike games of joust and tourney, the use of coats of arms was at first confined to those who held their lands by force.
3. Like a modern army uniform, the surcoat and standard of a king or baron obviously had a practical military function, enabling soldiers to find and rally around their commander in the press of battle.
4. It is said that at the Battle of Shrewsbury in 1403 Henry IV had several of his knights wear the royal surcoat, a dangerous honor because Henry's opponents were eager to kill him.
5. Today, families that want to impress people can pay researchers to manufacture a genealogy and create an impressive-looking, if bogus, coat of arms.

TEACHING IDEAS

Gone (thank goodness) are the days when splitting an infinitive was the grammatical equivalent of fratricide. However, it's worth calling students' attention to the admonition to (closely) follow a safe course by eliminating the infinitive entirely. Unless they know their audience, they should assume that a split infinitive is unacceptable.

REVISED   Many managers are unable *to establish* a moderate and reasonable tone with difficult employees.

SPLIT   One of a manager's responsibilities is *to* successfully *manage* conflict.

REVISED   One of a manager's responsibilities is *to manage* conflict successfully.

Occasionally, a sentence with a split infinitive will sound more natural than a sentence rewritten to avoid the split. This will be the case when the object of the infinitive is a long phrase or clause and the adverbial modifier is short.

SPLIT   Some managers like to *regularly* interview a variety of workers from different departments so that potential problems can be identified and averted.

Avoiding the split may become somewhat awkward.

NO SPLIT   Some managers like to interview *regularly* a variety of workers from different departments so that potential problems can be identified and averted.

NO SPLIT   Some managers like *regularly* to interview a variety of workers from different departments so that potential problems can be identified and averted.

Some readers do not accept split infinitives, whatever the circumstances of a sentence. Others feel that the issue is one of style. The safe course for a writer is to avoid the split by eliminating the infinitive or changing the modifier.

MODIFIER CHANGED   *On a regular basis,* some managers like to interview a variety of workers from different departments so that potential problems can be identified and averted.

 ## 15g   Reposition a lengthy modifier that splits a verb phrase.

CONFUSING   The search for fairy tale origins has for over two centuries fascinated scholars.

CLEAR   The search for fairy tale origins has fascinated scholars for over two centuries.

A *verb phrase* consists of a main verb and its auxiliary or helping verb. Like an infinitive, a verb phrase is a grammatical unit. Unlike infinitives, verb phrases are commonly split with brief modifiers.

In developed countries, the commitment to children as a natural resource *has* long *been linked* to huge investments in education and health care.

The sense of a verb phrase is disrupted when it is split by a lengthy modifying phrase or clause. Repair the split by relocating the modifier.

CONFUSING   Despite severe economic limitations, many third-world countries *have* in efforts to improve the health, well-being, and education of children *invested* large sums.

REVISED   Despite severe economic limitations, many third-world countries *have invested* large sums in efforts to improve the health, well-being, and education of children.

EXERCISE 6

In the following sentences, reposition modifiers in order to repair split infinitives and restore clear links between auxiliary verbs and main verbs.

> *Example:* Coats of arms were in ensuing centuries used by bishops and abbots, who ranked as lords in the feudal hierarchy.
>
> Coats of arms were used in ensuing centuries by bishops and abbots, who ranked as lords in the feudal hierarchy.
>
> In ensuing centuries, coats of arms were used by bishops and abbots, who ranked as lords in the feudal hierarchy.

1. They were also, in municipalities and other corporations which held legal powers or lands, widely adopted.
2. The association of armorial bearings with nobility came, as evidence that the user and his descendants had acquired the social status of gentlemen, to symbolize rank.
3. The sporting and military uses of heraldry were with the appearance of both tournaments and closed helmets in the sixteenth century, becoming less important, while its other (social) uses were multiplying.
4. Coats of arms were within a very short span of time carved over doorways, placed in stained glass windows, engraved upon silver, and painted on porcelain dishes and other household articles of the upper class.

DANGLING MODIFIERS

15h   Identify and revise dangling modifiers.

CONFUSING   After considering these issues, the decision was postponed.

CLEAR   After considering these issues, the candidate postponed his decision.

A modifier is said to "dangle" when the word it modifies is not clearly visible in the same sentence. Correct the error by rewriting the sentence, making sure to include the word modified.

1. They were also widely adopted in municipalities and other corporations which held legal powers or lands.
2. The association of armorial bearings with nobility came to symbolize rank as evidence that the user and his descendants had acquired the social status of gentlemen.
3. With the appearance of both tournaments and closed helmets in the sixteenth century, the sporting and military uses of heraldry were becoming less important, while its other (social) uses were multiplying.
4. Within a very short span of time coats of arms were carved over doorways, placed in stained glass windows, engraved upon silver, and painted on porcelain dishes and other household articles of the upper class.

FOR DISCUSSION

The dangling modifier is one of those errors that students find very hard to understand. The word modified is usually *implied* in the sentence, so the error is sometimes difficult to spot. It's probably worthwhile to spend some time making sure that students understand what the problem is. One way to do this is to reproduce a passage with several dangling modifiers, and have the class as a whole identify and correct the errors. The discussion that ensues should clarify the problem for most students.

REFERENCES

WILLIAMS, JOSEPH. *Style: Ten Lessons in Clarity and Grace*. 2nd ed. Glenview: Scott, 1985. 145–48. Dangling modifiers are one of many problems encountered when students begin working with longer sentences.

CHAIKA, ELAINE. "Grammars and Teaching." *CE* 39 (1978): 770–83. Dangling modifiers can be explained from a linguistic standpoint.

PIXTON, WILLIAM H. "The Dangling Gerund: A Working Definition." *CCC* 24 (1973): 193–99. The dangling gerund can be defined separately from other dangling modifiers.

KOLNN, MARTHA. *Understanding English Grammar*. 2nd ed. New York: Macmillan, 1986. Chapter 2. Dangling participles often result from opening main clauses with *it* or *there*.

1 **Give introductory clauses or phrases a specific word to modify.**

An introductory phrase or clause will modify a specific word in a sentence, most often a subject or verb. First-draft sentences beginning with long introductory phrases or clauses often contain dangling modifiers, perhaps because complex openings lead a writer to assume that the word being modified is obvious. The modified word will *not* be obvious to a reader unless it appears in the sentence that follows the introductory remark. Revision involves asking what the opening clause or phrase modifies and rewriting the sentence to provide an answer.

DANGLING   Dominated though they are by a few artists who repeatedly get the best roles, millions of people flock to the cinemas. [Who or what are dominated? If the *millions* are not, the main clause lacks a visible word to be modified.]

REVISED   Dominated though they are by a few artists who repeatedly get the best roles, *movies* continue to attract millions of people. [With a rewritten main clause, the opening clause is immediately followed by a noun it can modify.]

DANGLING   After appearing in *The Maltese Falcon*, it was clear that Warner Brothers had a box-office star. [Who appeared in the film?]

REVISED   After appearing in *The Maltese Falcon*, <u>Humphrey Bogart</u> became Warner Brothers' box-office star.

2 **Rewrite passive constructions to provide active subjects.**

Often a modifying phrase that begins a sentence will dangle because the independent clause is written in the passive voice (see 9g). Missing from this passive-voice sentence is the original subject, which would have been modified by the introductory phrase or clause. Correct the dangling modifier by rewriting the independent clause in the active voice.

DANGLING   With his weary, sardonic style and his cigarettes lipped loosely, the persona of the private detective was etched into the American psyche. [The persona of the private detective was etched *by whom*?]

REVISED WITH ACTIVE VOICE   With his weary, sardonic style and his cigarettes lipped loosely, <u>Bogart</u> etched the persona of the private detective into the American psyche.

EXERCISE 7

Repair the dangling modifiers that follow by restoring the word modified to each sentence. (You will find this word in parentheses.) Place a check in front of any sentence in which modifiers are used correctly.

Example: Having conquered an area stretching from the southern border of Colombia to central Chile, civilian and military rule was maintained for two hundred years before the Spanish discovery of America. (the Incas)

Having conquered an area stretching from the southern border of Colombia to central Chile, *the Incas* maintained civilian and military rule for two hundred years before the Spanish discovery of America.

1. Centering on the city of Cuzco in the Peruvian Andes, the coastal and mountain regions of Ecuador, Peru, and Bolivia were included. (the empire)
2. As the only true empire existing in the New World at the time of Columbus, wealth both in precious metals and in astronomical information had been assembled. (the Inca empire)
3. Knitting together the two disparate areas of Peru, mountain and desert, an economic and social synthesis was achieved. (the Incas)
4. Growing and weaving cotton and planting such domesticated crops as corn, squash, and beans, Peru had been settled dating from before 3000 B.C. (the Incas)

EXERCISE 7

1. Centering on the city of Cuzco in the Peruvian Andes, the empire included the coastal and mountain regions of Ecuador, Peru, and Bolivia.
2. As the only true empire existing in the New World at the time of Columbus, the Inca empire had assembled wealth both in precious metals and in astronomical information.
3. Knitting together the two disparate areas of Peru, mountain and desert, the Incas achieved an economic and social synthesis.
4. Growing and weaving cotton and planting such domesticated crops as corn, squash, and beans, the Incas had settled Peru dating from before 3000 B.C.

ADDITIONAL EXERCISE A

Look through your graded papers to find instructors' comments regarding misplaced or dangling modifiers. Reread the papers, identifying the errors as you read by using the strategies outlined in this chapter. Then revise the errors. (If you don't have any graded papers handy, look through any body of writing you've done recently.)

Shifts and
Mixed Constructions

*C*onsistency is an essential quality of language, allowing us to learn and master vocabulary and sentence structure. When we open a book, we expect to read words from left to right; different, or suddenly shifting, positioning of sentences on the page would disorient us. Just so, we expect that within sentences writers will adhere to certain patterns or conventions. When these patterns are violated, clear communication suffers.

SHIFTS

Aside from the content it communicates, a sentence expresses other important information: whether a singular or plural subject is speaking or being spoken to; whether action takes place in the present, future, or past; whether a subject is acting or being acted on; whether the occasion for writing is formal or informal; and whether a subject is speaking directly or indirectly. Once a writer makes a decision about these matters, that decision should be followed conscientiously within any one sentence. To do otherwise will confuse readers.

16a Revise shifts in person and number.

The term **person** identifies whether the speaker of a sentence is the person speaking (the first person), the person spoken to (the second person), or the person spoken about (the third person). **Number** denotes whether a person or thing is singular or plural (see 7a-7 and 7a-2).

Pronoun Forms (Subjective Case)		
	Singular	*Plural*
First Person	I	we
Second Person	you	you
Third Person	he, she, it, one, a person	they, people

1 **Revise shifts in person by keeping all references to a subject consistent.**

A shift from one person form to another obscures a subject's identity, changing the reference by which the subject is known. Shifts in person often occur when a writer switches from the second person (you) to the first person (I, we) or to the third person (he, she, it). You can avoid this difficulty by recognizing the first-, second-, or third-person orientation of your sentences and by maintaining consistency.

INCONSISTENT	A person who is a nonsmoker can develop lung troubles when you live with smokers.
THIRD PERSON	A person who is a nonsmoker can develop lung troubles when he or she lives with smokers.
SECOND PERSON	If you are a nonsmoker, you can develop lung troubles if you live with smokers.

2 **Revise shifts in number by maintaining consistent singular or plural forms.**

Shifts in number can occur when a writer uses pronouns (see 10b and 14a). Pronouns should agree in number with the nouns they replace. You can avoid shifting number and confusing readers by maintaining a clear plural or singular sense throughout a sentence.

INCONSISTENT	At the turn of the century, it was common for a man to come to the United States alone and work to raise money so that family members could later join them.
REVISED	At the turn of the century, it was common for a man to come to the United States alone and work to raise money so that family members could later join him.

Any significant words related to a subject or object should match its number.

INCONSISTENT	The seven candidates for the judgeship have a liberal record.
REVISED	The seven candidates for the judgeship have liberal records.

When, in an effort to avoid sexist language, you change the number of a subject from singular to plural, be sure to change the number of subsequent pronouns that refer to the subject (see 10c).

SEXIST REFERENCE	Any candidate should file his papers by noon on December 1.
REVISED BUT INCONSISTENT	Any candidate should file their papers by noon on December 1.
REVISED	Any candidates should file their papers by noon on December 1.

LOOKING BACK

This would be an opportune time to review the material on pronoun-antecedent agreement, especially with regard to number. If you haven't covered chapter 10 (Agreement) yet, you may want to refer students to 10a on number agreement. Reviewing the cross-referenced material will reinforce students' understanding of the importance of consistency in number.

EXERCISE 1

1. Viking raids struck terror in the hearts of monks because, as peaceable men, they were ill-prepared to fend off attack.
2. Even Charlemagne reportedly feared the Vikings, and is said to have shed tears over their power to destroy the king's legacy for posterity.
3. For hit-and-run robbers the sea was the best avenue because they could strike their victims without warning, then make a quick getaway.
4. In a Viking invasion, news of their coming usually preceded them, giving victims time to hide their treasure and disappear.

LOOKING BACK

If you haven't covered chapter 9 (Verbs) in class, this would be a good time to refer students to the relevant sections, especially 9f on sequencing tenses. Even if the chapter has been studied, some students may need to refresh their memories.

EXERCISE 1

Correct shifts in person and number in the following sentences.

> *Example:* In the eighth century Vikings launched attacks on the peoples around the Baltic and the North Sea during which we raided churches and monasteries.
>
> In the eighth century Vikings launched attacks on the peoples around the Baltic and the North Sea during which *they* raided churches and monasteries.

1. Viking raids struck terror in the heart of a monk because, as peaceable men, they were ill-prepared to fend off attack.
2. Even Charlemagne reportedly feared the Vikings, and is said to have shed tears over their power to destroy his good works.
3. For a hit-and-run robber the sea was the best avenue because they could strike their victims without warning, then make a quick getaway.
4. In a Viking invasion, news of your coming usually preceded you, giving a victim time to hide their treasure and disappear.

16b Revise shifts in tense, mood, and voice.

Tense, mood, and *voice* denote important characteristics of main sentence verbs: when the action of the verb occurs, what a writer's attitude toward that action is, and whether the *doer* or *receiver* of the action is emphasized. When these characteristics are treated inconsistently, readers can be confused.

1 Revise shifts in tense by observing the appropriate sequence of verb tenses.

A verb's **tense** shows when an action has occurred or when a subject exists in a certain state of being (see 9e and 9f). The tenses are marked by verb endings and auxiliary verbs.

He walked home.	He *was* walking home.
He walks home.	He *is* walking home.
He *will* walk home.	He *will be* walking home.

Tenses are often changed within sentences in regular and consistent patterns, as shown in the box on the next page. (Section 9f shows examples of each pattern.) Shifts in tense that disrupt these patterns strike readers as illogical, especially when the shifts alter the logic or time sequencing within or between sentences.

INCONSISTENT   When the Civil War begins, only one American in five was living in a city. By 1915, cities hold half of all Americans. [The tense shifts from present to past and back again for no reason.]

GROUP ACTIVITY

Many students, even otherwise sophisticated writers, have difficulty with the historical present. If students are writing about literature in this or another class, the following exercise may help them grasp the concept of the historical present. Ask students to bring in one or two literary analyses in order to take part in this activity. When you arrange students in groups, try to include in each group one student who uses the historical present appropriately. Then have each group work together on one student's writing at a time, checking for consistent use of the historical present. As the groups attempt to determine when this tense is appropriate, they will become more comfortable with one of the conventions of academic writing.

Sequencing Verb Tenses in a Sentence

See the description and guidelines on tenses of verbs in 9e and 9f.

To establish a relationship between two events, both of which occur in the past:

- Use the simple past tense for one past event and any of the four past tenses for the other event (see 9f-1).

To establish a relationship between a past event and a future event:

- Use the past tense in the independent clause and the simple future, future progressive, or simple present tense in the dependent clause.

To establish a relationship between a past event and an acknowledged fact or condition:

- Use the simple past tense for the main clause and the simple present tense in the dependent clause.

- Use the past perfect tense for the main clause and the simple present tense in the dependent clause.

CONSISTENT   When the Civil War began, only one American in five was living in a city. By 1915, cities held half of all Americans. [The past tense is used consistently.]

The "historical present tense" is often used in academic writing to refer to material in books or articles or to action in a film (see 9e-1).

INCONSISTENT   In her article, Karen Wright referred to Marshall McLuhan's global village and asks rhetorically, "Who today would quarrel with McLuhan's prophecy?" [The reference to Wright's work should either be past or "historically" present, but not both.]

CONSISTENT   In her article, Karen Wright refers to Marshall McLuhan's global village and asks rhetorically, "Who today would quarrel with McLuhan's prophecy?"

Occasionally, a shift of tense in one sentence will be needed to establish a proper sequence of events.

ACCEPTABLE   After he *had read* of experiments in electricity, Nathaniel Hawthorne *observed* that the world *was becoming* "a great nerve." [The tenses change from past perfect to past to past progressive. See chapter 9 for a full discussion of tenses.]

2 Revise for shifts in mood.

A verb's **mood** indicates whether a writer judges a statement to be a fact, a command, or an occurrence contrary to fact (see 9h). Sentences in the **indicative mood,** by far the most common, are presented as fact. In the **imperative mood,** writers express commands—addressing them usually to an implicitly understood "you." In the **subjunctive mood,** writers express doubt or a condition contrary to fact (see 9h-1–4). When mood shifts in a sentence, readers cannot be sure of a writer's intended judgment about the information presented. You can avoid confusion by choosing a mood (most often the indicative) and using it consistently.

INCONSISTENT   If the writing process were easy, students will not need to take classes in composition. [The sentence shifts from the "doubtful" subjunctive to the "factual" indicative, leaving readers unsure about what is intended.]

CONSISTENT   If the writing process were easy, students would not need to take classes in composition. [Consistent use of the subjunctive makes the writer's judgment clear.]

3   Revise for shifts in voice.

A **transitive verb**—one that transfers action from a subject to an object—can be expressed in the active or passive voice. The natural state of a verb is the active voice. In the sentence *Mary kicked the ball,* the verb (*kicked*) transfers action from the subject (*Mary*) to the direct object (*the ball*). An **active-voice sentence** emphasizes the *doer* of an action. A rearrangement of words yields a **passive-voice sentence,** which emphasizes the *receiver* of an action: *The ball was kicked by Mary.*

Both the active and passive voices have their uses (see 9g-1–2). However, if writers shift from one voice to the other in a single sentence, both emphasizing and deemphasizing a subject (or *doer* of an action), then readers will be confused. Avoid the difficulty by choosing an active *or* a passive voice in any one sentence.

INCONSISTENT   Columbus arrived in the New World and it was believed he had found the coast of Asia. [The shift from active voice to passive leaves doubt about who believed this.]

CONSISTENT   Columbus arrived in the New World and believed he had found the coast of Asia.

EXERCISE 2

Correct the shifts in tense, voice, and mood in the following sentences.

Example: Gradually the Viking raiders became settlers; they find it more convenient to remain in the coastal villages they attack than to return to frigid Scandinavia.

Gradually the Viking raiders became settlers; they *found* it more convenient to remain in the coastal villages they *attacked* than to return to frigid Scandinavia.

1. Norsemen and Northmen became "Normans," and so would give their name to Normandy.

EXERCISE 2

1. Norsemen and Northmen became "Normans," and so gave their name to Normandy.
2. The Normans adapted readily to the variety of circumstances in which they found themselves, and fitted easily into the feudal hierarchy in France and Germany.
3. In England they helped catalyze the process of unification, while in Sicily they acted as mediators among the diverse groups who lived there.
4. A Norman, Tancred, led the First Crusade during which he captured Jerusalem and established a Norman kingdom in Syria.
5. Though adept at migration, the assimilation of peoples, and the cementing of nations, the Normans had no talent or appetite for exploration.

2. The Normans adapted readily to the variety of circumstances in which they found themselves, and were fitted easily into the feudal hierarchy in France and Germany.

3. In England they will help catalyze the process of unification, while in Sicily they acted as mediators among the diverse groups who live there.

4. A Norman, Tancred, led the First Crusade during which Jerusalem was captured and a Norman kingdom was established in Syria.

5. Though adept at migration, the assimilation of peoples, and the cementing of nations, the Normans would have no talent or appetite for exploration.

16c Revise for shifts in tone.

Tone refers to the writer's attitude toward the subject or the audience and is signaled by the qualities that make writing formal or informal, learned or breezy, measured or hysterical. Without doubt, tone is a difficult element to revise since so much determines it: choice and quality of description, verb selection, sentence structure, and sentence mood and voice. Tone changes depending on a writer's audience: You will adopt one tone in a letter to a friend and an altogether different tone when writing a paper for your art history professor. The level of diction used in a writer's choice of words is a major factor affecting tone. See 3a-4 and the box in 21e for more on matching the tone of a paper to your occasion for writing.

In papers that you prepare for your courses, your tone should be characterized by writing that is precise, logical, and formal, though not stuffy or filled with jargon (see 21e). Abrupt shifts from any established basic tone in a paper will be disconcerting to readers.

DISCONCERTING | In his famous painting *Persistence of Memory*, Salvador Dalí creates his most haunting allegory of empty space in which time is deader than a doornail. [The final slang expression creates an informal tone inconsistent with a formal analysis.]

CONSISTENT | In his famous painting *Persistence of Memory*, Salvador Dalí creates his most haunting allegory of empty space in which time is at an end. [A more formal expression is consistent with the analysis.]

EXERCISE 3

Correct any shifts in tone in the following sentences so that the sentences are consistent.

Example: Can you name a person who is always in a hurry, is extremely competitive, and blows his stack frequently?

Can you name a person who is always in a hurry, is extremely competitive, and is often angry?

ADDITIONAL EXERCISE A

ACROSS THE CURRICULUM Photocopy a brief passage from one of your textbooks, and pay close attention to the sequencing of tenses, consistency of mood, and use of voice. How does the writer's use of verbs help the reader understand the passage? Are there any apparent inconsistencies (in voice, for example)? If so, can you explain why the writer may have chosen to shift voice?

GROUP ACTIVITY

This exercise is ideal for group work. Identifying inappropriate words and phrases, as well as negotiating appropriate replacements, will provide students with useful practice in revising for consistent tone.

EXERCISE 3

Suggested responses:

1. Replace "couch potato" with "sedentary."
2. Replace *"homo sapiens"* with "people."
3. Replace "get frazzled" with "become agitated."
4. Replace "the patience of the blessed saints" with "great patience."
5. Replace "party animal" with "better social companion."

ADDITIONAL EXERCISE B

This exercise should help you understand the differences between indirect and direct discourse, making it easier for you to be consistent in your own writing. In the following sentences, change indirect discourse to direct discourse, and vice-versa.

1. In the *New York Times,* David Low wrote, "I have never met anybody who wasn't against war."
2. When faced with disclosures about the Watergate scandal, Richard Nixon told his aides, "I want you to stonewall it."
3. Martin Luther King, Jr., in his most famous speech, said that he had a dream.
4. Elizabeth Ray told the House Ethics Committee that she couldn't type. She couldn't file. She couldn't even answer the phone.
5. In a speech to her fellow senators, Margaret Chase Smith said that she thought it was high time that they remembered that they had sworn to uphold and defend the Constitution.

Answers:

1. In the *New York Times,* David Low wrote that he had never met anybody who wasn't against war.
2. When faced with disclosures about the Watergate scandal, Richard Nixon told his aides that he wanted them to stonewall it.
3. Martin Luther King, Jr., in his most famous speech, said, "I have a dream."
4. Elizabeth Ray told the House Ethics Committee, "I can't type. I can't file. I can't even answer the phone."
5. In a speech to her fellow senators, Margaret Chase Smith said, "I think is is high time that we remembered that we have sworn to uphold and defend the Constitution."

1. In contrast, can you think of someone who is so low key that he's a couch potato, not very competitive, and easy-going in relations with others?
2. You now have in mind two *homo sapiens* who could be described as showing Type A and Type B behavior patterns.
3. Type A individuals get frazzled by stress more easily and tend to suffer more coronary problems than Type Bs.
4. Type Bs have the patience of the blessed saints and perform well under high levels of stress and on tasks involving complex judgments and accuracy.
5. Who would make the better executive, the better spouse, the better party animal?

Maintain consistent use of direct or indirect discourse.

Direct discourse reproduces exactly, with quotation marks, spoken or written language. **Indirect discourse** approximately reproduces the language of others, capturing its sense, though not its precise expression (see 28a-1).

DIRECT   Lawrence asked, "Is that the telephone ringing?"

INDIRECT   Lawrence asked whether the telephone was ringing.

Mixing discourse in one sentence can disorient a reader by raising doubts about what a speaker has actually said. You can avoid the problem by making a conscious choice to refer to another's speech either directly or indirectly.

INCONSISTENT   In his inaugural speech, John F. Kennedy exhorted Americans to ask what they could do for their country, not "what your country can do for you." [The direct quotation following the indirect discourse raises unnecessary questions about what Kennedy actually said.]

CONSISTENT   In his inaugural speech, John F. Kennedy exhorted Americans to ask what they could do for their country, not what their country could do for them.

CONSISTENT   In his inaugural speech, John F. Kennedy exhorted Americans, "Ask not what your country can do for you, ask what you can do for your country."

EXERCISE 4

Correct the shifts in discourse in the following sentences by making direct quotations indirect.

> *Example:* As a boy in his teens, Albert Einstein asked how our view of the world would change if "I rode on a beam of light."
>
> As a boy in his teens, Albert Einstein asked how our view of the world would change if we rode on beams of light.

1. The great physicist Niels Bohr nailed a horseshoe on a wall in his cottage because "I understand it brings you luck whether you believe or not."
2. The mystery writer Agatha Christie believed that being married to an archaeologist, a man whose business it was to excavate antiquities, was a stroke of great good luck, because as she got older "he shows more interest in me."
3. In a feverish letter from a battlefield in Italy, Napoleon wrote Josephine that he had received her letters and that "do you have any idea, darling, what you are doing, writing to me in those terms?"

MIXED CONSTRUCTIONS

A **mixed construction** occurs when a sentence takes a reader in one direction by beginning with a certain grammatical pattern and then concludes as if the sentence had begun differently. The resulting mix of incompatible sentence parts invariably confuses readers.

16e   Establish clear, grammatical relations between sentence parts.

Mixed constructions are common in speech. We can compensate for grammatically inconsistent thoughts in speech with gestures or intonation, and listeners usually understand. But readers work at a disadvantage, for they cannot see or hear our attempts to correct jumbled expressions. More so than listeners, readers are likely to be sensitive to and confused by mixed constructions.

MIXED   If you do not understand a poem is when a lapse into singsong can become a problem as a reader.

This construction, imaginable as a spoken statement, is not a sentence but a fragment—actually two fragments (see 12a). The construction begins with a dependent clause—an *if* clause that readers expect to see followed by an independent *then* clause, which never appears. Instead, the *if* construction is followed by the verb *is* and by a second dependent clause, beginning with *when*. Revise mixed constructions by rearranging words until you create an independent clause.

REVISED   If you do not understand a poem, then the chances are good you will lapse into a singsong when reading it. [An independent clause beginning with *then* now completes the introductory *if* construction.]

REVISED   Lapsing into a singsong can become a problem if you read poems aloud before understanding them. [The mixed construction is avoided by rearranging words and by converting the *when* clause to a subject.]

REFERENCES

SHAUGHNESSY, MINA P. *Errors and Expectations: A Guide for the Teacher of Basic Writing.* New York: Oxford UP, 1977. 44–89. A lengthy discussion of underlying causes of and strategies for overcoming mixed constructions.

CARKEET, DAVID. "Understanding Syntactic Errors in Remedial Writing." *CE* 38 (1977): 682–86, 695. Mixed constructions occur when students lose track of how they began a sentence, and should be treated accordingly.

KRISHNA, VALERIE. "The Syntax of Error." *Journal of Basic Writing* 1 (1975): 43–49. Mixed constructions are a result of weakness in the core sentence.

D'ELOIA, SARAH. "The Uses—and Limits—of Grammar." Rpt. in *The Writing Teacher's Sourcebook.* Eds. Gary Tate and Edward P. J. Corbett. New York: Oxford UP, 1981. 225–43. Tangled syntax results from inexperienced writers trying to put complex ideas into acceptable prose form.

FREEMAN, DONALD C. "Linguistics and Error Analysis: On Agency." *The Territory of Language.* Ed. Donald A. McQuade. Carbondale: Southern Illinois UP, 1986. 165–73. Applying the concept of "agency" to an analysis of sentence structure can help students correct problems such as mixed constructions.

Proofread carefully to identify and correct mixed constructions, which tend to occur in predictable patterns.

"The fact that"

The expression "the fact that" and words immediately associated with it result in a mixed construction when writers forget that the expression begins a noun clause that functions as a subject or object. Writers see the subject and verb of the clause and mistakenly conclude that they have written a sentence.

MIXED   The fact that rhyming makes a poem memorable. [Even though *makes* is a verb, and *rhyming* functions as a noun, this string of words is not a sentence. It is a noun clause that takes the place of a noun, either as a subject or as an object.]

REVISED   The fact that rhyming makes a poem memorable is important to know when choosing poems to read aloud. [*The fact that* and its associated words now function as the subject of a sentence.]

REVISED   Rhyming makes a poem memorable. [Deleting the words *the fact that* converts the dependent noun clause into an independent clause. *Makes* now functions as the main verb.]

An adverb clause

Adverb clauses begin with subordinating conjunctions—words like *when, because,* and *although* (see the box in 19a). A mixed construction occurs when the final word of an introductory adverb clause also serves as the subject (or a word modifying the subject) of an independent clause.

MIXED   When a poem is rhymed words can stand out unnaturally if emphasized. [The last word of the adverb clause, *rhymed,* is also used to modify the subject, *words.*]

REVISED   When a poem is rhymed, the rhymed words can stand out unnaturally if emphasized.

REVISED   Rhymed words in a poem can stand out unnaturally if emphasized.

A prepositional phrase

A prepositional phrase consists of a preposition (*by, of, in,* etc.) and a noun—the object of the preposition (see 7d-1). A noun functioning as the object of a prepositional phrase cannot simultaneously function as the subject of an independent clause.

MIXED   By reading a poem slowly can help your listeners to concentrate. [*Reading a poem slowly* functions as both the object of the preposition *by* and (incorrectly) the subject of the independent clause.]

REVISED   Reading a poem slowly can help your listeners to concentrate.
           [Eliminating the preposition *by* allows the phrase *reading a poem
           slowly* to function as the subject of the independent clause.]

REVISED   By reading a poem slowly, you can help your listeners to
           concentrate. [The prepositional phrase is retained, and a new
           subject, *you*, is added.]

16f Establish consistent relations between subjects and predicates.

A second type of mixed construction occurs when the predicate
part of a sentence does not logically complete its subject. The error is
known as **faulty predication** and most often involves a form of the verb
be, a linking verb that connects the subject complement in the predicate
part of the sentence with the subject. You are familiar with the sentence
pattern ___A___ is ___B___ : *The child is happy* (see 7b, Pattern 5). In this sentence the verb functions as an equals sign. If the subject complement, *B*,
is logically inconsistent with the subject, *A*, then the predicate is faulty
and the sentence will confuse readers.

INCONSISTENT   The power of an electron microscope is keenly aware of life
                invisible to the human eye. [Can a microscope's power be
                keenly aware?]

REVISED   The resolving power of an electron microscope helps us to be
                keenly aware of life invisible to the human eye. [Now it is
                people (*us*) who have been made aware.]

REVISED   Aided by the resolving power of the electron microscope, we
                have grown keenly aware of life invisible to the human eye.

Faulty predication occurs in three other constructions involving the verb
be and sentence pattern ___A___ is ___B___ or ___A___ = ___B___ . If in writing a
definition you begin the subject complement (*B*) with the word *when* or
where, or if in giving a reason you begin the subject complement with *because*, you may create a mixed construction.

FAULTY   Electron illumination is when beams of electrons instead of light
          are used in a microscope. [In this sentence pattern, the subject
          (*electron illumination*) must be renamed by a noun or described by
          an adjective.]

FAULTY   The reason electron microscopes have become essential to research
          is because their resolving power is roughly 500,000 times greater
          than the power of the human eye. [In this sentence pattern, the
          subject (*reason*) must be renamed by a noun or described by an
          adjective.]

The sentence pattern of *subject / linking verb / subject complement* requires
an adjective or a noun to serve as subject complement. The words *when*,

where, and *because* begin adverb clauses and, thus, do not fit grammatically into the pattern. Revise a faulty predicate by changing the adverb clause to a noun clause or by changing the verb and reordering the sentence. Usually a revision requires adding and deleting words.

REVISED   Electron microscopes have become essential because their resolving power is roughly 500,000 times greater than the power of the human eye.

Verbs other than *be* can assert actions or states that are not logically consistent with a subject. Wherever you find faulty predication, correct it.

FAULTY   The rate of Native American enrollment in institutions of higher learning sees an improvement in the last ten years. [A *rate* cannot see.]

REVISED   The rate of Native American enrollment in institutions of higher learning has improved in the last ten years.

REVISED   Over the last ten years, educators have seen an improvement in the rate of Native American enrollment in institutions of higher learning.

EXERCISE 5

Suggested responses:

1. The fact that ancient Greeks and Romans as well as every other colonial power spread their languages as far as their armies maintained outposts is well known.
   Ancient Greeks and Romans as well as every other colonial power spread their languages as far as their armies maintained outposts.
2. The Nazi rise to power was established through military might in support of the Aryan myth.
   Through military might in support of the Aryan myth the Nazis rose to power.
3. Needs no revision.
4. One measure of loyalty to a nation is its citizens' willingness to speak a single language approved by the state.
   A nation's citizens express their loyalty by their willingness to speak a single language approved by the state.
5. Even a dialect of the state language is considered suspicious when local groups insist upon speaking their own way, in opposition to the rest of the country.
   There is suspicion of local groups who insist upon speaking their own way, in opposition to the rest of the county, even though their language is a dialect of the state language.

EXERCISE 5

Revise the sentences that follow in two ways, making each consistent in grammar or meaning. Place a check beside any sentence that needs no revision.

> *Example:* Language and the state that have been companions throughout history.
>
> Language and the state have been companions throughout history.
>
> Language and the state, which have been companions throughout history, have at last parted company in tonight's campaign speech.

1. The fact that ancient Greeks and Romans as well as every other colonial power spread their languages as far as their armies maintained outposts.
2. When the Nazis rose to power was established through military might in support of the Aryan myth.
3. The Aryans were not a race but rather a great variety of peoples who spoke the early Indo-European (also sometimes known as Indo-Aryan) languages.
4. One measure of loyalty is when a nation's citizens speak a single language approved by the state.
5. Even a dialect of the state language finds suspicion in local groups who insist upon speaking their own way, in opposition to the rest of the country.

INCOMPLETE SENTENCES

An **incomplete sentence,** as its name implies, is one that lacks certain important elements. A fragment (see chapter 12), the most extreme case of an incomplete sentence, has no subject or predicate. In less extreme cases, a sentence may lack a word or two, which you can identify and correct with careful proofreading.

16g   Edit elliptical constructions to avoid confusion.

Both in speech and in writing, we omit certain words in order to streamline communication. These "clipped" or shortened sentences are called **elliptical constructions,** and, when used with care, they can be concise and economical. But elliptical constructions may confuse readers if a writer omits words that are vital to sentence structure.

1   Use *that* when necessary to signal sentence relationships.

Often, *that* is the word omitted in an elliptical construction. If the omission of *that* does not confuse readers, then the omission is of no consequence.

> Closely related to the unequal treatment of a minority language by a majority language is the unequal treatment (that) many languages give to the two sexes.

If the omission of *that* alters the relationship among words in a sentence, then restore *that* to the sentence.

UNCLEAR   Who considers our scientific name for both sexes is the word for only one of them, "man"? [The wording incorrectly points to *our scientific name* as the object of *consider*.]

CLEAR   Who considers *that* our scientific name for both sexes is the word for only one of them, "man"? [It is now clear that the noun clause beginning with *that* and ending with *man* functions as the object of the verb.]

ESL NOTE   *That* clauses can occur in a variety of sentences. Notice that the noun clauses retain their structure even when the specific word *that* is omitted. For special rules in constructions involving *wish that . . . ,* see 43b-5.
Indirect quotation or reported speech is a very common special case of tense sequence involving two verbs in a *that* clause (see 43b-4).

ADDITIONAL EXERCISE C

ACROSS THE CURRICULUM Photocopy a long passage from one of your textbooks, and underline all of the parallel constructions that you can find. Examine the writer's use of parallelism, paying particular attention to completeness and use of appropriate prepositions. How does the effective use of parallelism help the reader understand the material? How does it contribute stylistically to the passage?

2 **Provide all the words needed for parallel constructions.**

Elliptical constructions are found in sentences where words, phrases, or clauses are joined by the conjunction *and* or are otherwise made parallel. Grammatically, an omission is legitimate when a word or words are repeated *exactly* in all compound parts of the sentence, as in the following examples. Words that could be omitted are placed in parentheses. (See the discussion of parallelism at 18a–b.)

PARALLEL　According to one widely accepted theory, humans possess sensory (memory), short-term (memory), and long-term memory. [A word is omitted.]

PARALLEL　Information moves from short- (term memory) to long-term memory when we think about its meaning or (when we think) about its relationship to other information already in long-term memory. [A clause is omitted.]

An incomplete sentence results when words omitted in one part of an elliptical construction do not match identically the words appearing in another part.

NOT PARALLEL　Sensory and short-term memory *last* seconds or minutes, while long-term memory years or decades.

PARALLEL　Sensory and short-term memory *last* seconds or minutes, while long-term memory *lasts* years or decades.

The omitted word, *lasts,* is not identical to the word in the first part of the parallel structure, *last.* One verb completes a singular subject and the other a plural subject, as in the following example.

NOT PARALLEL　One long-term memory *is triggered* by fleeting sight or smell and others by sounds.

PARALLEL　One long-term memory *is triggered* by fleeting sight or smell and others *are triggered* by sounds.

PARALLEL　One long-term memory *may be triggered* by fleeting sight or smell and others by sounds.

3 **Use the necessary prepositions with verbs in parallel constructions.**

Elliptical constructions also result from the omission of a preposition that functions idiomatically as part of a complete verb phrase: believe *in,* check *in,* handed *in,* hope *in,* hope *for,* looked *up,* tried *on,* turned *on.* When these expressions are doubled by the conjunction *and,* and you wish to omit the second preposition, be sure this preposition is identical to the one remaining in the sentence. (See 18a-2 and 18a-3 on parallel constructions.) In the following example, the doubled preposition is *on:* relied *on* and ultimately thrived *on.*

In 1914, Henry Ford opened an auto manufacturing plant that relied and ultimately thrived on principles of assembly-line production.

To be omitted from a parallel construction, a preposition must be identical to the one left remaining in the sentence. If the prepositions are not identical, then *both* must appear in the sentence so that the full sense of each idiomatic expression is retained.

FAULTY   Henry Ford believed and relied *on* the assembly line as a means to revolutionize American industry.

REVISED   Henry Ford believed *in* and relied *on* the assembly line as a means to revolutionize American industry.

16h   Make comparisons consistent, complete, and clear.

Writers have many occasions to devote sentences, paragraphs, and even entire essays to writing comparisons and contrasts. To make comparisons effective, you should compare logically consistent elements and state comparisons completely and clearly. (In chapter 11 you will find more on comparative forms of adjectives and adverbs.)

1   Keep the elements of a comparison logically related.

The elements you compare in a sentence must in fact be comparable—of the same logical class.

ILLOGICAL   Modern atomic theory provides for fewer types of atoms than Democritus, the ancient Greek philosopher who conceived the idea of atoms. [Atoms are being compared with Democritus, a person. The comparison must be made logical.]

LOGICAL   Modern atomic theory provides for fewer types of atoms than did Democritus, the ancient Greek philosopher who conceived the idea of atoms.

2   Complete all elements of a comparison.

Comparisons must be made fully, so that readers understand which elements in a sentence are being compared.

INCOMPLETE   Democritus believed there existed an infinite variety of atoms each of which possessed unique characteristics—so that, for instance, atoms of water were smoother. [Smoother than what?]

COMPLETE   Democritus believed there existed an infinite variety of atoms each of which possessed unique characteristics—so that, for instance, atoms of water were smoother than atoms of fire.

FOR DISCUSSION

Advertising is notorious for its use of incomplete comparative elements. Ask students to come up with examples of slogans including such incomplete comparisons as "creamier," "lighter," or "more robust." After writing the slogans on the board, ask students to speculate on the reasons advertisers might have for leaving comparisons incomplete. The ensuing discussion should alert students to the purpose of complete comparisons.

INCOMPLETE   The ideas of Democritus were based more on speculation. [More on speculation than on what?]

COMPLETE   The ideas of Democritus were based more on speculation than on the hard evidence of experimentation.

3 Make sure comparisons are clear and unambiguous.

Comparisons that invite alternate interpretations must be revised so that only one interpretation is possible.

UNCLEAR   Scientists today express more respect for Democritus than his contemporaries. [Two interpretations: (1) Democritus's contemporaries had little respect for him; (2) scientists respect the work of Democritus more than they respect the work of his contemporaries.]

CLEAR   Scientists today express more respect for Democritus than they do for his contemporaries.

CLEAR   Scientists today express more respect for Democritus than his contemporaries did.

EXERCISE 6

1. Since ancient times, fire has been regarded more as a transforming element than a sheer destructive power.
2. Medieval alchemists believed that in fire resided magical properties.
3. Alchemists would impress their patrons by heating the red pigment in cinnabar (a sulphide of mercury) to produce exquisite pearls of liquid mercury.
4. In legend, Prometheus's gift of fire made humans better than gods, and for this Prometheus was punished.
5. Needs no revision

EXERCISE 6

Revise the sentences that follow to eliminate problems with mixed constructions. Place a check beside any sentence that needs no revision.

> *Example:* We have a special reverence and fascination *with* fire.
>
> We have a special reverence *for* and fascination *with* fire.

1. Since ancient times, fire has been regarded more as a transforming element than sheer destructive power.
2. Medieval alchemists believed with fire they could transform lead into gold.
3. Alchemists would impress their patrons by heating the red pigment cinnabar (a sulphide of mercury) to produce exquisite pearls of liquid mercury.
4. In legend, Prometheus's gift of fire made humans better, and for this Prometheus was punished.
5. Although humans have used fire for about 400,000 years, not all people have known how to *make* fire.

CHAPTER 17

Being Clear, Concise, and Direct

I have made this letter longer than usual, only because
I have not had time to make it shorter.

—BLAISE PASCAL

Over three hundred years ago, the French mathematician and philosopher Pascal knew what writers know today: writing concisely is a challenge that takes time. Just like Pascal, you face a decision when rereading your first draft sentences: Should you revise? What will you get in return for your efforts at making sentences briefer? The answer is *clarity* and directness.

Revising sentences for clarity and directness means more than making a correct, complete expression. Revision at this level means making choices about wording that will help your audience to clearly understand your ideas. Your knowledge of an audience's readiness and level of understanding will strongly influence your choices.

17a Revise to eliminate wordiness.

There are many kinds of wordiness, including the use of empty words and phrases (see 21b-3, 21e-4, 21h-2); passive-voice constructions (see 9g); and buzzwords, redundancy, and unnecessary repetition. When you are revising a first draft, search out wordiness and eliminate it. Try to avoid saying things two different ways or with two words when one will do. Eliminating extra words is a reliable way to give your message direct impact; padded wording never makes writing sound more authoritative. If used as filler to meet the length requirement of an assignment, padded writing will backfire by obscuring your message to readers, causing them to be confused and annoyed.

KEY FEATURES

This part of the handbook shifts emphasis on revision from grammatical correctness to clarity and style. Students revising at this level will need to exercise good judgment. This chapter fosters the development of judgment by returning to the theme of earlier chapters, namely, that writers must make choices reflecting both the purpose of the paper and the obligation to the reader. In dealing with the major topics of conciseness and use of strong verbs, the chapter provides a number of strategies for revision. Students are reminded, however, that wordiness and weak verbs in early drafts are not indicative of poor writing skills. On the contrary, the chapter reiterates the notion that in the draft stage the writer concentrates on establishing the paper's purpose, organization, and development. Focusing on sentence-level revisions in early drafts tends to slow a writer's momentum. Thus the material covered in this chapter is presented as a stage of revision, not a correction of errors. Exercises reinforce this presentation; the sentences are not *wrong*; they're just *long*—and rather unclear in the bargain.

ESL ALERT

English is far more compact than many languages. Consequently, the concept of eliminating wordiness is vital for most non-native speakers, but difficult. They will confuse eliminating unnecessary words with eliminating discussion and detail, mainly because the acceptable writing style of many languages (like Spanish, Portuguese, and Italian) is far more discursive and abstract than that of English. Another difficulty in the move toward compact language is the student's paucity of synonyms to replace longer, explanatory phrases.

FOR DISCUSSION

The Pascal quotation provides an excellent opportunity to talk about length. The words probably sound strange to students accustomed to spending their time trying to make something long enough to satisfy an assignment. Ask students which takes longer to write, a five-page paper or a two-page paper? Chances are, most students will consider the two-page easier. Then ask them to speculate on why they often find themselves spending time lengthening their papers rather than shortening them. Chances are, the responses to this question will have something to do with not having enough to say about a subject. If you can remind students of what they've learned in Part II (Writing as a Process), you can steer discussion toward the responsibility of the writer to the audience—and to purpose. If a writer finds that she only has enough information to fill two pages of a five-page paper, then rather than hauling out the padding, she ought to be hauling herself to the library. If students can understand that the purpose is not to fill the pages but to make what's in the pages meaningful and clear, then they'll be in an appropriate frame of mind to approach this chapter.

1 Combine sentences that repeat material.

When writing a first-draft paragraph you are apt to string together sentences that repeat material. When revising your work, combine sentences to eliminate wordiness and to sharpen focus.

WORDY   In this era of Michael Jackson and Jaye Davison it might seem that we are moving toward *a unisex style of culture.* Jeans and track suits, normal wear for both men and women, are signs of *a unisex style of culture.* [Two sentences end by repeating the same point.]

COMBINED   In this era of Michael Jackson and Jaye Davison, when jeans and track suits are normal wear for both men and women, it might seem that we are moving toward a unisex style of culture.

2 Eliminate wordiness from clauses and phrases.

Eliminate wordiness by eliminating relative pronouns and by reducing adjective clauses to phrases or single words.

COMPLEX   Josephine Baker, *who was* the first black woman to become an international star, was born poor in St. Louis in 1906. [The clause creates some interruption in this complex sentence.]

CONCISE   Josephine Baker, the first black woman to become an international star, was born poor in St. Louis in 1906.

COMPLEX   Many were drawn by her vitality, *which was* infectious.

CONCISE   Many were drawn by her infectious vitality. [A simple sentence is created.]

OPTION   Her vitality was infectious; many were drawn by it. [Simple independent clauses are created.]

Wordiness can also be eliminated by shortening phrases. When possible, reduce a phrase to a one-word modifier (see 7c, d).

WORDY   *Recent revivals of* Baker's French films have included *re-releases of subtitled versions of* "Zou-Zou" and "Princess Tam-Tam."

CONCISE   *Recently* Baker's French films "Zou-Zou" and "Princess Tam-Tam" have been *re-released with subtitles.* [The phrases are reduced to simpler modifiers.]

3 Revise sentences that begin with expletives.

Expletive constructions (*it is, there is, there are, there were*) fill blanks in a sentence when a writer inverts normal word order (see 7a-11, 14d). Expletives are almost always unnecessary, and should be replaced with direct, active verbs, whenever possible.

WORDY	*There were many reasons why* Josephine Baker was more successful in Europe than in America. [The expletive is unnecessary here.]
DIRECT	Josephine Baker was more successful in Europe than in America for several reasons.
WORDY	*It is* because Europeans in the 1920s were interested in anything African *that* they so readily responded to Baker's outrageous style. [The expletive is indirect; it also sets up an unnecessary *that* clause.]
DIRECT	Because Europeans in the 1920s were interested in anything African, they readily responded to Baker's outrageous style.

4 Eliminate buzzwords.

Buzzwords are vague, often abstract expressions that sound as if they mean something but are only "buzzing" or adding noise to your sentence, without contributing anything of substance (see 21c, d). Buzzwords can be nouns: *area, aspect, case, character, element, factor, field, kind, sort, type, thing, nature, scope, situation, quality.* Buzzwords can be adjectives, especially those with broad meanings: *nice, good, interesting, bad, important, fine, weird, significant, central, major.* Buzzwords can be adverbs: *basically, really, quite, very, definitely, actually, completely, literally, absolutely.* Eliminate buzzwords. When appropriate, replace them with more precise expressions.

WORDY	*Those types of major* disciplinary problems are *really quite* difficult to solve. [None of these buzzwords has any meaning.]
CONCISE	Disciplinary problems are difficult to solve.
WORDY	*Basically,* she was *definitely* a *nice* person.
CONCISE	She was friendly. [*Kind, thoughtful, sweet, outgoing,* or any other more precise adjective could replace the vague *nice.*]

5 Eliminate redundant writing.

Occasional, intentional repetition can be a powerful technique for achieving emphasis (see 19c-2). Writers may not realize they are repeating themselves, and the result for readers is usually a tedious sentence. When you spot unintended repetition in your own writing, eliminate it.

REDUNDANT	In *Cinderella*, feminine, lady-like actions and behavior are praised and rewarded.
REVISED	In *Cinderella*, feminine behavior is rewarded.
REDUNDANT	Cinderella is a degraded household drudge and her household work demeans her.
REVISED	Cinderella is a degraded household drudge. Cinderella is a drudge degraded by housework. Housework degrades Cinderella.

REFERENCES

LANHAM, RICHARD. *Analyzing Prose.* New York: Scribner's, 1983. Extensive advice on revising for style.

WILLIAMS, JOSEPH. *Style: Ten Lessons in Clarity and Grace.* 2nd ed. Glenview: Scott, 1989. Provides guidelines for writers seeking to improve sentence style.

ESL ALERT

Some romance-language (Spanish, Italian, Portuguese) speakers will have difficulty with the concept of the expletive since it does not exist in their language. Their tendency will be to leave out the "there" or "it" and to simply begin with a "be" verb as they would in their language: "Is hot." "Is over there." Calling attention to the problem often helps the student self-correct.

ESL ALERT

Some language interference may result from direct translations of common expressions, such as "make groceries" instead of "buy groceries" in Spanish, Italian, and French. Sometimes a specific and a general meaning combine into one word which makes translation a peculiar kind of metaphorical synaesthesia, as in such common Ibo expressions as:

English	Ibo English
I smell it.	I hear the smell of it.
The soup tastes good.	The soup is sweet. (whether sour or salty)

Problems with reflexives may produce similar confusions:

The dress doesn't fit. (English)	The dress cannot enter me. (Ibo)

GROUP ACTIVITY

Playing with wordy passages can be both educational and enjoyable. Ask each group to compose an overly wordy paragraph, using the expressions listed here. (Of course, they can also add any of their own.) Then the paragraphs can be passed to another group, whose task it is to eliminate the excess. In composing the wordy passages students will be parodying what they do if they tend to pad their essays, and in revising they'll practice a skill that will come in handy when they start cutting the excess out of those essays.

Redundant phrases

A **redundant phrase** repeats a message unnecessarily. Redundant phrases include *small in size, few in number, continue to remain, green in color, free gift, extra gratuity, repeat again, combine together, add to each other, final end.* Make your sentences concise by omitting one part of a redundant phrase.

REDUNDANT Cinderella's stepsisters, two in number, continued to remain hateful toward her throughout the story.

CONCISE Cinderella's two stepsisters were hateful to her throughout the story.

REDUNDANT The fairy godmother's free gift of gown and carriage enables Cinderella to achieve a girl's final goal: marriage to the Prince.

CONCISE The fairy godmother's gift of gown and carriage enables Cinderella to achieve her goal: marriage to the Prince.

6 Eliminate long-winded phrases.

Long-winded phrases such as *at this point in time* do not enhance the meaning or elegance of a sentence. Such expressions are tempting because they come to mind ready-made and seem to endow writing with added formality, sophistication, and authority. But do not be fooled. Using such phrases muddies your sentences, making them sound either pretentious or like the work of an inexperienced writer. Eliminate these phrases and strive for simple, clear, direct expression.

Avoiding Wordy Expressions

Wordy	Direct
at this moment (point) in time	now, today
at the present time	now, today
due to the fact that	because
in order to utilize	to use
in view of the fact that	because
for the purpose of	for
in the event that	if
until such time as	until
is an example of	is
would seem to be	is
the point I am trying to make*	——
in a very real sense*	——
in fact, as a matter of fact*	——

* These expressions are fillers and should be eliminated.

WORDY   *Due to the fact that* Cinderella is a heroine in *what would appear to be* a fairy-tale world, she is, *in a very real sense,* "rewarded" with marriage to the Prince.

REVISED   Because Cinderella is a fairy-tale heroine, she is rewarded with marriage to the Prince.

As a fairy-tale heroine, Cinderella is rewarded with marriage to the Prince.

In fairy-tale worlds, heroines like Cinderella are rewarded with marriage to the Prince.

EXERCISE 1

Revise these sentences to eliminate wordiness by combining repeated material, reducing phrases and adjective clauses, and avoiding expletives.

> *Example:* What type of consumer do you want to advertise to? Specifying the target or consumer that you want to reach with your product is the main step in advertising.
>
> Effective advertising targets specific consumers.

1. When defining the purpose of advertising some experts admit that it is a manipulation of the public while others insist that advertising promotes the general well-being of its audience.
2. Advertising is one of the most eye-catching methods of selling a product. This is because advertising is a medium of information.
3. There are many consumers who are drawn to a product because the advertising campaign has been effectively utilized.
4. There are many qualities which an advertisement must have to lure the public to buy its product. The advertisement must be believable, convincing, informative, and persuasive. With these qualities in the ads, they will be the first ones to sell.
5. Like I mentioned before, it is not only women who are being portrayed sexually. Men are used in many advertisements also.
6. There exists a built-in sexual overtone in almost every commercial and advertisement around.
7. Advertising is one of several communications forces which performs its role when it moves the consumer through successive levels. These levels include unawareness, awareness, comprehension, conviction, and action.

EXERCISE 2

Revise the following sentences to eliminate wordiness.

> *Example:* Early forms of advertisements were messages to inform the consumers of the benefits and the availability of a product.
>
> Originally, advertisements informed consumers of a product's benefits and availability.

EXERCISE 1

Suggested responses:

1. Some experts admit that advertising manipulates the public; others insist that it benefits its audience.
2. Advertising is one of the most eye-catching sales methods because it imparts information.
3. Many consumers are drawn to a product by an effective advertising campaign.
4. To lure the public, the advertisement must be believable, informative, and persuasive.
5. Men as well as women are portrayed sexually.
6. Most commercials have built-in sexual overtones.
7. Advertising moves the consumer from unawareness, through comprehension and conviction, to action.

GROUP ACTIVITY

This and subsequent exercises are ideal for group work. Have students either complete the exercises in groups or compare their responses after completing the exercises individually. Either way, as they negotiate responses or defend their choices, they'll understand more clearly the value of clarity, conciseness, and directness.

1. The producer must communicate with the product's possible customers in a way that is quite personal and quite appealing to the customer.
2. By identifying the product you start to narrow down the range of people you want to buy the product.
3. Advertising is a complex, but not mysterious, business.
4. To summarize a successful advertiser in today's world in one word, it would have to be opportunistic.
5. From campaign to campaign there are many different objectives and goals ads are trying to accomplish.
6. It used to be that women were mainly portrayed in the kitchen or in other places in the home.
7. We find advertising on television, on the radio, in newspapers and magazines, and in the phone book, just to name a few places.

17b Use strong verbs.

A verb is like an engine. Strong verbs move sentences forward and precisely inform readers about the action a subject is taking or the condition or state in which the subject exists. One way to improve a draft is to circle all your verbs, revising as needed to ensure that each verb makes a crisp, direct statement.

1 Give preference to verbs in the active voice.

Sentences with verbs in the active voice emphasize the actor of a sentence rather than the object that is acted on (see 9g).

ACTIVE   The state legislature approved a tax hike.

PASSIVE   A tax hike was approved by the state legislature.

PASSIVE   A tax hike was approved. [The actor is not named.]

Unless a writer intends to focus on the object of the action, leaving the actor secondary or unnamed, the active voice is the strongest way to make a direct statement. When the actor needs to be named, a passive-voice sentence is wordier and thus weaker than an active-voice sentence.

PASSIVE   In 1947 the Hollywood Ten, writers and filmmakers, *were cited* for contempt of Congress, tried, and sentenced to prison. [The passive voice obscures the accusers, who are not named here.]

ACTIVE   In 1947 the House Un-American Activities Committee cited, tried, and sentenced the Hollywood Ten for contempt of Congress.

PASSIVE   The accused *were known as* "pinkos" while the prosecutors *were identified as* "red baiters." [The passive voice here conceals who promoted these labels.]

ACTIVE   Pro-Committee partisans identified the accused as "pinkos" while defenders of *the accused* identified the prosecutors as "red baiters."

2 **Use forms of *be* and *have* as main verbs only when no alternatives exist.**

The verb *be* is essential in forming certain tenses, as in a progressive tense.

> During the Red Scare of the early 1950s, the government *was prosecuting* anyone with suspected Communist sympathies.

In a sentence of definition, *be* functions as an equal sign.

> HUAC *is* an abbreviation for the House Un-American Activities Committee.

Beyond these uses, *be* is a weak verb. When possible, replace it with a strong, active-voice verb.

WEAK	Many people today *are* of the opinion that the government *was not right to have* its own citizens prosecuted for exercising their first amendment rights. [The verbs require weak and wordy constructions.]
STRONGER	Many people today *think* the government *should not have* prosecuted its own citizens for exercising their first amendment rights. [Stronger verbs make more direct, active statements here.]

The verb *have* functions as an auxiliary in forming the perfect tenses. This verb tends to make a weak and indirect statement when used alone as the main verb of a sentence. Replace forms of *have* with strong, active-voice verbs.

WEAK	The blacklist *had the effect of getting* people to inform on their friends and families. [The verb produces a vague statement.]
STRONGER	The blacklist *pushed* people to inform on their friends and families. [Replacement with another verb produces a definite statement.]

3 **Revise nouns derived from verbs.**

A noun can be formed from a verb by adding a suffix: dismiss/dismiss*al*, repent/repent*ance*, devote/devo*tion*, develop/develop*ment*. Often these constructions result in a weak, wordy sentence, since the noun form replaces what was originally an active verb and requires the presence of a second verb. When possible, restore the original verb form of a noun derived from a verb.

WORDY	Many people *found that cooperation* with HUAC *was necessary for survival*. [The noun form, the dependent clause, and the *be* verb make a weak, redundant sentence.]
DIRECT	Many people eventually *cooperated* with HUAC *to survive*. [The noun form is changed to a verb, producing a stronger statement.]

REFERENCES

O'HARE, FRANK. *Sentence-Combining: Improving Student Writing without Formal Grammar Instruction.* Urbana: NCTE, 1973. Through sentence combining, students can develop mature style even without grammar instruction.

STRONG, WILLIAM. "Creative Approaches to Sentence Combining." Urbana: ERIC Clearinghouse on Reading and Communication Skills, 1986. ERIC ED 274 985. A discussion of the history of sentence combining, with suggestions for classroom use.

DAIKER, DONALD, ANDREW KEREK, and MAX MORENBERG. "Sentence Combining and Syntactic Maturity in Freshman English." *CCC* 29 (1978): 36–41. A report on the results of a successful experiment in sentence combining.

———. *Sentence Combining: A Rhetorical Perspective.* Carbondale: Southern Illinois UP, 1985. A collection of essays on sentence combining techniques and classroom use.

FOR DISCUSSION

Since most students have problems in only a few of these areas, you might want to initiate a class discussion of errors most relevant to your students. Ask students to identify from the box examples of usage familiar to them and to make their own list of common flaws. Students can then discuss the function of clarity, conciseness, and directness in good writing, thereby reinforcing their understanding of the value of revising and "downsizing" their writing. (In large classes, this activity might begin with small groups: The groups will identify their common errors, and then the class as a whole will discuss the list of errors compiled from each group's report.)

EXERCISE 3

Suggested responses:

1. People understand that advertising is communication between the buyer and the seller.
2. Advertising aims to expose a certain product to a targeted audience.
3. Without catalogue viewership, consumers forget the product because they can't view it again.
4. Thomas R. Forrest's "Such a Handsome Face: Advertising Male Cosmetics" discusses effective marketing.
5. Today a man's appearance contributes to his success.
6. Several aspects of advertising are essential to successfully marketing a product.
7. Advertisers should ask five questions before implementing a successful advertising campaign.
8. Associating a product with something desirable increases its visibility.

WORDY   The government *was caught up in a period of intimidating* its own people.

DIRECT   The government intimidated its own people.

Write Clearly, Concisely, Directly

When revising a draft for clarity, conciseness, and directness, be critical of every sentence.

1. Combine repetitive sentences.
2. Reduce an adjective clause to a phrase or to one word.
3. Eliminate relative pronouns whenever possible.
4. Reduce adverbial and prepositional phrases to one word.
5. Eliminate expletives.
6. Eliminate buzzwords.
7. Eliminate redundant writing.
8. Eliminate long-winded phrases.
9. Use verbs in the active voice, not the passive.
10. Substitute strong verbs for *be* and *have.*
11. Convert nouns made from verbs back into verbs.

EXERCISE 3

Revise these sentences for clarity and directness by changing passive verbs to active verbs, replacing weak verbs with strong verbs, and converting nouns made from verbs back into verbs.

Example: Both positive and negative reactions to a product should be expected.

Consumers should expect both positive and negative reactions to products.

1. Advertising has always been generally understood as a form of communication between the buyer and the seller.
2. The aim of advertising is to give exposure of a certain product to a targeted audience.
3. Without catalogue viewership the product may be forgotten because the consumer will not have the ability to view it again.
4. There is a discussion of effective marketing in Thomas R. Forrest's article which is entitled "Such a Handsome Face: Advertising Male Cosmetics."
5. It has been noticed that in today's society a man's appearance is thought to be an important factor in his success.
6. There are several aspects of advertising that are seen to be essential to the successful marketing of a product.

7. Five questions should be asked before the implementation of a successful advertising campaign.
8. The association of a product with something that is desirable increases its visibility.

EXERCISE 4

Revise the following first draft of a student paper. Use all the techniques described in this and related chapters to achieve conciseness, clarity, and directness.

Advertising can be displayed in many different ways. One major way that advertisers try to sell their products is through the use of sexism. Sexism is portrayed in the majority of ads lately and it appears to be only getting worse.

It is now over twenty years after the feminist movement and sexism is as big of a problem as ever. Usually in the advertising industry it is the female that is used in the ad that portrays sexism: however, male sexism is found also. The latest problem occurred when Miller Beer tried to hook spring-break college bound kids with an ad insert for campus newspapers about annual trips to Florida that are often taken by college students. The ad included sketches of women in bikinis with hints of ways for these college kids to "pick up women." This ad insert drew a lot of attention from college students, mainly females that were outraged over it. There were even threats to boycott the product. However there were no results because the National Advertising Review Board has not issued guidelines on the use of women in ads since 1978. Also, there are very few agencies that have particular rules or regulations on sexism in ads. This could be due to the fact that the top managements are mostly male.

Everyone knows that sexism is used in advertisements all over the place but the question is, are they avoidable? Many advertising executives say no because they feel that advertisers have to address themselves to such a huge chunk of people that they are never going to be able to make everyone happy. This is why sexism and stereotyping in advertising is such a big problem today.

EXERCISE 4

Suggested revisions:

Although advertisers use many approaches, sexism appears in the majority of ads lately. And the problem appears to be getting worse.

Twenty years after the feminist movement, sexist ads still exploit females. Recently Miller Beer's insert in campus newspapers attempted to lure college kids on spring break with guidelines for picking up bikini-clad women. Outraged college females threatened to boycott the product. However, the protests failed because the National Advertising Review Board hasn't issued guidelines on using women in ads since 1978. In addition, few agencies enforce regulations on sexism in ads—probably because top management is male dominated.

Many advertising executives say that sexism in ads is unavoidable, stating that advertisers must appeal to such huge audiences that they can't keep everyone happy. Apparently sexism in advertising will remain a problem.

ADDITIONAL EXERCISE B

As you revise your drafts of any papers you're working on at present, concentrate on conciseness, clarity, and directness. Try to identify the specific kinds of problems you have in this area so that you can look out for them in future drafts. Compare your revision to the original: How much shorter is the revision? How much clearer?

Maintaining Sentence Parallelism

In writing, **parallelism** involves matching a sentence's structure to its content. When two or more ideas are parallel (that is, closely related or comparable), a writer can emphasize similarities as well as differences by creating parallel grammatical forms.

Parallel structures help sentences to cohere by establishing clear relationships among sentence parts. Through their closely matched word elements, parallel structures present ideas in a logical comparison or contrast. Parallelism in writing thus draws on your skills in creating a logical analogy, a comparison, or a parallel argument (see 6d-1). To use parallelism effectively, you must become consciously logical and systematic about how you present parallel ideas.

 18a Use parallel words, phrases, and clauses with coordinating conjunctions.

Whenever you use a coordinating conjunction (*and, but, for, or, nor, so, yet*), the words, phrases, or clauses joined form a *pair* or a *series* (a list of three or more related items) and become *compound* elements: compound subjects, objects, verbs, modifiers, and clauses. For sentence parts to be parallel in structure, the compound elements must share an equivalent, but not necessarily identical, grammatical form. If in one part of a parallel structure a verb is modified by a prepositional phrase, then a corresponding verb in the second part of the sentence should also be modified by a prepositional phrase—*but* that phrase need not begin with the same preposition.

 1 Using parallel words

NOT PARALLEL   The candidate was a visionary but insisting on realism.

PARALLEL   The candidate was <u>visionary</u> *but* <u>realistic.</u>

Words that appear in a pair or a series are related in content and should be parallel in form.

NOT PARALLEL   According to figures released by the Senate Judiciary Committee in 1991, the United States has the most violence and crime-ridden society in the industrialized world.

CRITICAL DECISIONS

Be alert to differences *and* similarities: Match parallel content with parallel phrasing

Words and word groups that refer to comparable content should show comparisons with parallel phrasing. The only indication of *faulty parallelism* may be that a sentence sounds "off" or illogical. Learn to recognize situations that call for parallel structures and to correct sentences with faulty parallelism.

Recognize situations that call for parallel structures.

Any time you use a coordinating conjunction (*and, but, or,* or *nor*), you are combining elements from two or more sentences into a single sentence.

The children are fond of ice cream.	The children are fond of salty pretzels.

Combined elements are logically comparable, and they should share a single grammatical form; otherwise, they are not parallel.

PARALLEL   The children are fond of ice cream and salty pretzels.
The children are fond of eating ice cream and salty pretzels.

NOT PARALLEL   The children are fond of ice cream and eating salty pretzels.

Correct faulty parallelism.

1. *Recognize a sentence that is not parallel.*

NOT PARALLEL   Before they had horses, Indians hunted buffalo by chasing them over blind cliffs, up box canyons, or *when they went* into steep-sided sand dunes.

To revise a sentence with faulty parallelism, *determine which elements should be parallel* (that is, logically comparable), and then *revise the sentence so that these elements share an equivalent grammatical form*. Think of parallel elements as word groupings that complete slots in a sentence. The same grammatical form that you use to complete any one slot in a parallel structure must be used to complete all remaining slots.

2. *Determine the parallel elements.*

by chasing them   Slot 1 ,   Slot 2 , and   Slot 3 .
by chasing them *over blind cliffs.*   Slot 2 , and   Slot 3 .

Because Slot 1 is completed with a prepositional phrase (*over blind cliffs*), Slots 2 and 3 should be filled with prepositional phrases. The series *over blind cliffs, up box canyons, or* when they went *into steep-sided sand dunes* lacks parallel structure because the third element in the series introduces a *when* clause, which is not consistent with the grammatical form of Slot 1.

3. *Revise so that parallel elements have equivalent grammatical form.*

PARALLEL   Before they had horses, Indians hunted buffalo by chasing them *over blind cliffs, up box canyons,* or *into steep-sided sand dunes.*

TEACHING IDEAS

Parallelism is a topic in which form and content seem to converge; both the structure and the idea establish a comparison or a contrast. It's worth pointing this out to students, whose view of the relevance of grammatical struc-tures is often obscured by rule-based understanding. Presenting a few additional parallel sentences at the beginning of the chapter can help students see that form really does follow function—in the case of parallelism, at least.

GROUP ACTIVITY

This activity can help students understand the need to recognize both correct and faulty parallel structures. Ask each group to generate five to ten sentences, using a variety of parallel structures. Completed sentences will then be passed on to another group for correction. As students compose the sentences, they will find themselves discussing the nature of parallel structures, and as they correct sentences, they will engage in a discussion of how to recognize problems in parallelism.

FOR DISCUSSION

Since most students have problems with only a few of these errors, you might want to initiate a class discussion of errors most relevant to your students. Ask students to identify from the Spotlight on Common Errors examples of usage familiar to them and to make their own list of common errors. Students can then discuss the function of effective parallel structures in good writing, thereby reinforcing their understanding of the relationship between style and content. (In large classes, this activity might begin with small groups: The groups will identify their common errors, and then the class as a whole will discuss the list of errors compiled from each group's report.)

SPOTLIGHT ON COMMON ERRORS—PARALLELISM

These are the errors most commonly associated with parallelism. For full explanations and suggested revisions, follow the cross-references to chapter sections.

FAULTY PARALLELISM occurs when writers compare or contrast sentence parts without using similarly constructed wordings. In the examples that follow, parallel structures are highlighted.

■ **Conjunctions suggest comparisons and require parallel structures.**

Conjunctions such as *and* and *but* require parallel structures (see coordinating conjunctions, 18a).

FAULTY	REVISED
The candidate was a visionary but insisting on realism. [The verb forms *was a visionary* and *insisting* are not parallel.]	The candidate was **visionary** but **realistic.** [Similarly worded adjectives are linked by the conjunction *but*.]
The candidate attended meetings, spoke at rallies, and she shook thousands of hands. [The candidate's three activities are not parallel.]	The candidate **attended meetings, spoke at rallies,** and **shook thousands of hands.** [The candidate's three activities are similarly worded.]

Paired conjunctions such as *either/or* and *both/and* require parallel structures (see correlative conjunctions, 18b).

FAULTY	REVISED
Explorers can be both afraid of the unknown and, when they encounter something new, they want to understand it. [The verb forms *can be afraid* and *want to understand* are not parallel.]	Explorers can be both **afraid of the unknown** and **curious about it.** [Similarly worded adjectives and phrases are joined by the conjunction *both/and*.]

■ **Direct comparisons and contrasts require parallel structures (see 18c).**

FAULTY

The staff approved the first request for funding, not the second presenter requesting funds. [The objects *request* and *presenter* are not parallel.]

REVISED

The staff approved **the first request for funding,** not **the second.** [Two types of *request* are being compared and share similar wording.]

■ **Lists require parallel structures (see 18e).**

FAULTY

Make sure you pack the following in your kit:
—an alcohol solution that will cleanse wounds
—bandages
—Remove splinters with a tweezers.
—matches
  [Items in the list are not parallel.]

REVISED

Make sure you pack the following in your kit:
—**alcohol**
—**bandages**
—**tweezers**
—**matches**
  [Items in the list are similarly worded.]

GROUP ACTIVITY

There is perhaps no stronger evidence of the staying power of parallel structures than children's fairy tales and nursery rhymes. Children remember the rhymes and lines from the fairy tales not only because of rhyming words but because of the parallel structures used. Offer students one or two examples ("All the king's horses and all the king's men," "I'll huff and I'll puff and I'll blow your house down," "Over the river and through the woods," etc.), and ask groups to come up with several more examples on their own. Then have them rewrite the lines without parallel structure ("All the king's horses and a full complement of the king's men," "I'll huff and by puffing I'll blow your house down," "Over the river and walking down the path in the woods," etc.). It won't take much discussion for students to recognize how powerful the parallel structure can be.

Determine the parallel elements.

> the United States has the most ___Slot 1___ and ___Slot 2___ society in the industrialized world.

In this sentence, the noun *violence* completes Slot 1 and the adjective *crime-ridden* completes Slot 2. In order for the sentence to be parallel, both slots must show the same part of speech. Both must be nouns or both must be adjectives. In this case, the words should be adjectives, since both are being used to modify the noun *society.*

Revise so that parallel elements have equivalent grammatical form.

PARALLEL   According to figures released by the Senate Judiciary Committee in 1991, the United States has the most *violent* and *crime-ridden* society in the industrialized world.

If the elements that should be logically parallel shift their function in a sentence, then they may well shift their part of speech. If the adjectives *violent* and *crime-ridden* are to become nouns—*violence* and *crime*—you should consider them as similar elements in a comparison and treat them as objects of the verb *has.*

PARALLEL   According to figures released by the Senate Judiciary Committee in 1991, the United States has the most *violence* and *crime* of any society in the industrialized world. [Two nouns are now comparable in a parallel structure.]

In parallel constructions, idiomatic terms must be expressed completely (see also 16g-3).

NOT   White people were called "Flop Ears" by some Indians who were
PARALLEL   both aghast and entertained *by* the way white parents grabbed their children by the ears to discipline them.

Determine the parallel elements.

> who were both ___Slot 1___ and ___Slot 2___ the way white parents grabbed their children by the ears to discipline them.

The preposition *at* is necessary for completing the first verb phrase, since the idiom is *aghast at*, not *aghast by.*

Revise so that parallel elements have equivalent grammatical form.

PARALLEL   White people were called "Flop Ears" by some Indians who were both aghast *at* and entertained *by* the way white parents grabbed their children by the ears to discipline them. [Each parallel item now has its proper idiomatic preposition.]

2   Using parallel phrases

NOT PARALLEL   The judge had an ability to listen to conflicting testimony and deciding on probable guilt.

PARALLEL   The judge had an ability <u>to listen to conflicting testimony</u> *and* <u>to decide on probable guilt.</u>

To echo the idea expressed in a phrase in one part of a sentence, use a phrase with the same grammatical structure in another part.

NOT
PARALLEL   Tumbleweeds' main function seems to be poetic, for they roll and bounce on the wind, *are flying through the air like weather balloons,* and pile up along fences.

Determine the parallel elements.

for they ___Slot 1___ , ___Slot 2___ , and ___Slot 3___ .

for they *roll and bounce on the wind,* ___Slot 2___ , and ___Slot 3___ .

Slot 1 is completed with two present-tense verbs and a modifying phrase. Slots 2 and 3 need at least one present-tense verb and a modifying phrase. Slot 2 is out of parallel because the verb appears in its *-ing* form with an auxiliary.

Revise so that parallel elements have equivalent grammatical form.

PARALLEL   Tumbleweeds' main function seems to be poetic, for they roll and bounce on the wind, *fly through the air like weather balloons,* and pile up along fences.

PARALLEL   Tumbleweeds' main function seems to be poetic, for they are always *rolling and bouncing* on the wind, *flying* through the air like weather balloons, and *piling* up along fences. [In this revision, all verbs appear in their *-ing* form and, thus, are parallel.]

3 Using parallel clauses

NOT PARALLEL   Before the storm's end but after the worst was over, the captain radioed the Coast Guard.

PARALLEL   <u>Before the storm had ended</u> *but* <u>after the worst was over</u>, the captain radioed the Coast Guard.

A *clause* is a grouping of words that has a complete subject and predicate. Both independent clauses (that is, sentences) and dependent clauses can be set in parallel, provided they are parallel in content. At times, brief sentences can be used to form items in a series. When choosing such a structure, make sure each sentence is parallel in form.

NOT
PARALLEL
(INDEPENDENT
CLAUSES)   Tumbleweeds are a signature of hundreds of old Westerns: the saloon doors swing back and forth, a tumbleweed rolls across a deserted street, the marshall and the bad guy *walking* slowly toward each other.

Determine the parallel elements.

Tumbleweeds are a signature of hundreds of old Westerns: ___Slot 1___ , ___Slot 2___ , and ___Slot 3___ .

the saloon doors swing back and forth, ___Slot 2___ , and ___Slot 3___ .

Slot 1 is completed with a clause that has the following structure: an article (*the, a*), noun, present-tense verb, modifying phrase: *the saloon doors swing back and forth.* The final element in the series is not a clause;

REFERENCES

WILLIAMS, JOSEPH M. "The Phenomenology of Error." *CCC* (1981): 152–68. When dealing with errors in parallelism, instructors must consider the student's stylistic choices.

LINDEMANN, ERIKA. *A Rhetoric for Writing Teachers.* 2nd ed. New York: Oxford UP, 1987. Chapter 9. Discussion of sentence combining includes treatment of parallelism.

WALKER, ROBERT L. "The Common Writer: A Case for Parallel Structure." *CCC* 21 (1970): 373–79. Argues that professional writers employ parallelism more than they do free modifiers.

CORBETT, EDWARD P. J. *Classical Rhetoric for the Modern Student.* New York: Oxford UP, 1965. 402–08, 429. Emphasizes the significance of parallelism in sentence style.

GRAVES, RICHARD L. "Symmetrical Form and the Rhetoric of the Sentence." *Rhetoric and Composition: A Sourcebook for Teachers and Writers.* Ed. Richard L. Graves. Upper Montclair, NJ: Boynton/Cook, 1984. 119–27. Parallelism in writing reflects a human way of looking at the world.

ADDITIONAL EXERCISE A

Complete the following sentences with your own words, filling in the slots with words, phrases, and clauses parallel to the italicized structures.

1. Colette *drove the children to school,* _____, and _____.

2. Colette drove *the children to school,* _____, and _____.

3. Colette drove the children *to school,* _____, and _____.

4. Colette drove the children to *school,* _____, and _____.

5. *Colette drove the children to school,* _____, and _____.

[Note: While the content of responses will vary, all students should recognize that in each sentence, the italicized structure is the one with which the responses should be parallel.]

specifically, the verb of the third element is not parallel with the two preceding verbs.

Revise so that parallel elements have equivalent grammatical form.

PARALLEL   Tumbleweeds are a signature of hundreds of old Westerns: the saloon doors *swing* back and forth, a tumbleweed *rolls* across a deserted street, the marshall and the bad guy *walk* slowly toward each other.

PARALLEL   Tumbleweeds are a signature of hundreds of old Westerns: the saloon doors *swinging* back and forth, a tumbleweed *rolling* across a deserted street, the marshall and the bad guy *walking* slowly toward each other. [In this revision, the verb of each slot is changed to its *-ing* form, making each element in the series a parallel phrase.]

In order to maintain parallel structure in sentences that have a pair or series of dependent relative clauses, you will need to repeat the relative pronouns *who, whom, which,* and *what.*

NOT PARALLEL (DEPENDENT CLAUSES)   Archimedes was the celebrated mathematician of antiquity *who* invented the Archimedean screw, *who* explained the theory of the lever, and *he* defended his native Syracuse against the Romans with great mechanical skill.

Determine the parallel elements.

Archimedes was the celebrated mathematician of antiquity ___Slot 1___, ___Slot 2___, and ___Slot 3___.

Archimedes was the celebrated mathematician of antiquity *who invented the Archimedean screw,* ___Slot 2___, and ___Slot 3___.

Slot 1 is completed with a relative clause beginning with the relative pronoun *who;* Slots 2 and 3 must have the same structure: each slot must be completed with a clause that begins with the word *who* (but see the variation immediately following).

Revise so that parallel elements have equivalent grammatical form.

PARALLEL   Archimedes was the celebrated mathematician of antiquity *who* invented the Archimedean screw, *who* explained the theory of the lever, and *who* defended his native Syracuse against the Romans with great mechanical skill.

VARIATION: Brief words that begin a series (for example, a relative pronoun such as *who,* a preposition such as *by* or *in,* and the infinitive *to*) may be written once at the beginning of the first item in the series and then omitted from all remaining items.

PARALLEL   Archimedes was the celebrated mathematician of antiquity *who* invented the Archimedean screw, explained the theory of the lever, and defended his native Syracuse against the Romans with great mechanical skill.

A CAUTION: If one of these introductory words appears in more than one part of the series but not in *all* parts, the use of parallelism will be faulty.

PARALLEL	I want *to* go home, *to* wash up, and *to* eat. I want *to* go home, wash up, and eat.
NOT PARALLEL	I want *to* go home, wash up, and *to* eat.

18b Use parallelism with correlative conjunctions.

NOT PARALLEL	Explorers can be both afraid of the unknown and, when they encounter something new, they want to understand it.
PARALLEL	Explorers can be *both* <u>afraid of the unknown</u> *and* <u>curious about it</u>.

Whenever you join parts of a sentence with pairs of words called *correlative conjunctions* (*either/or, neither/nor, both/and, not only/but also*), you must use the same grammatical form in both parts. Once again, think of the conjunction as creating parallel slots in the sentence. Whatever grammatical structure is used to complete the first slot must be used to complete the second.

NOT PARALLEL	After defeating Custer at Little Bighorn, Crazy Horse managed both to stay ahead of the Army and *escape*.

Determine the parallel elements.

managed both ___Slot 1___ and ___Slot 2___ .

managed both *to stay ahead of the army* and ___Slot 2___ .

Slot 2 must take the same form as Slot 1. Each must be a verb in its infinitive form: *to* _____ .

Revise so that parallel elements have equivalent grammatical form.

PARALLEL	After defeating Custer at Little Bighorn, Crazy Horse managed both *to stay* ahead of the Army and *to escape*.

VARIATION: By slightly modifying the sentence—by moving the word *to* outside of the parallel structure created by the correlative conjunction—you can eliminate the word *to* in both of the sentence's parallel slots.

managed *to* both ___Slot 1___ and ___Slot 2___ .

managed *to* both *stay ahead of the army* and ___Slot 2___ .

PARALLEL	After defeating Custer at Little Bighorn, Crazy Horse managed *to* both *stay ahead of the Army* and *escape*.

18c Use parallelism in sentences with compared and contrasted elements.

NOT PARALLEL	The staff approved the first request for funding, not the second presenter who requested funds.

TEACHING IDEAS

To help students understand the use of parallel constructions with correlative conjunctions, you may want to engage in the following class exercise: In succession, write on the board the pairs of correlative conjunctions (*either/or, neither/nor, both/and, not only/but also*). Then ask students to volunteer sentences using each of the constructions. After writing several sentences on the board, stop and ask for an evaluation of their effectiveness. Some students will be able to point out errors; others will need to have the errors explained to them. (In larger classes, you may start this activity with groups: Each group will generate sentences according to the selected patterns, and the entire class will evaluate the sentences' effectiveness.)

PARALLEL   The staff approved <u>the first request for funding</u>, *not* <u>the second request</u>.

When words, phrases, or clauses are compared or contrasted in a single sentence, their logical and grammatical structures must be parallel (see 16h). Expressions that set up comparisons and contrasts include *rather than, as opposed to, on the other hand, not, like, unlike,* and *just as/so too.*

NOT PARALLEL   Several experts explain the Loch Ness Monster as a survivor of an otherwise extinct reptile species rather than fulfilling people's need for a myth. [The noun *survivor* makes a mismatched contrast with the verbal *fulfilling.*]

Determine the parallel elements.

Several experts explain the Loch Ness Monster as __Slot 1__ rather than __Slot 2__ .

Several experts explain the Loch Ness Monster as *a survivor of an otherwise extinct reptile species* rather than __Slot 2__ .

Slot 1 consists of an article (*a*) and a noun that is modified (*survivor of an otherwise extinct reptile species*). Slot 2 should take the same basic form.

Revise so that parallel elements have equivalent grammatical form.

PARALLEL   Several experts explain the Loch Ness Monster as *a survivor of an otherwise extinct reptile species* rather than *a fulfillment of people's need for a myth.* [Two modified nouns are now matched in parallel contrast.]

EXERCISE 1

The following sentences contain coordinating or correlative conjunctions, or elements of comparison and contrast. Revise each to correct the faulty parallel structure.

Example: Native Americans have one of the highest unemployment rates in the nation, the lowest educational attainment of any U.S. minority group, and they fare worst in the area of health.

Native Americans have one of the highest unemployment rates in the nation, the lowest educational attainment of any U.S. minority group, and *the worst record of health care.* [Each slot in the series now begins with an adjective in its superlative form: *highest, lowest, worst.* Each adjective is followed by a noun and each noun by a prepositional phrase.]

1. Designating Asian Americans as the "model minority" is problematic not only because the term obscures the diversity of the group but they are represented in only a small percentage of top-ranking positions in the U.S.
2. Some sociologists say that racism is rooted in a preference for one's "own kind" rather than social causes.

3. Conflict theorists feel that racism results from competition for scarce resources and an unequal distribution of power and racial tension increases during periods of economic decline.
4. Corporate managers do not tend to wield the political power of professionals such as lawyers and doctors, nor workers whom they supervise.
5. Either the percentage of the elderly living below the poverty line has decreased or to underestimate the number of elderly living in poverty is prevalent.

18d Use parallelism among sentences to enhance paragraph coherence.

Like many other towns on the Great Plains, Nicodemus, Kansas *was founded* in the 1870s. *Unlike any other* that still survives, *it was founded* by black homesteaders.

Because parallel grammatical structures highlight parallel ideas among sentence parts, parallelism is an excellent device for organizing sentence content. But parallelism can also help to relate the parts of an *entire paragraph* by highlighting the logic by which a writer moves from one sentence to the next. Parallel structures bind a paragraph's sentences into a coherent unit.

PARALLEL SENTENCES WITHIN A PARAGRAPH

A house divided against itself cannot stand. I believe this government cannot endure, permanently half slave and half free. I do not expect the Union to be dissolved. I do not expect the house to fall. But I do expect it will cease to be divided. It will become all one thing, or all the other.
—ABRAHAM LINCOLN, 1858

In this famous passage, Lincoln uses parallel structures to show relationships not only among single words or phrases, but also among whole sentences. Elements of the first sentence (*house, divided*) are repeated near the end of the paragraph. Lincoln repeats the phrase *I do not expect* twice and then produces a parallel contrast with *But I do expect* in a third repetition. The final two sentences repeat *it will* with different verbs. The last sentence sets up a parallel opposition governed by *all*. These parallel repetitions of words, phrases, and structures help to make the paragraph coherent by highlighting relationships among sentences. Such relationships could be mapped in parallel "slot" diagrams similar to those used for sentences. Parallel structures also give the paragraph an emphatic, memorable rhythm.

18e Use parallel entries when writing lists or outlines.

A list or outline divides a single large subject into equal or coordinate elements. A grocery list is the simplest example: *grocery* is the subject,

ADDITIONAL EXERCISE D

As you revise drafts of any papers you're working on at present, look for places where parallel structure would make the paper more effective. A potential revision might be a series of words, or two phrases or clauses, or even a pair of sentences. Occasionally a paragraph can be arranged around parallel structures (as you saw in this section).

ADDITIONAL EXERCISE E

Using the information in the following paragraph, develop a list of parallel items.

> The Playground Committee has identified three major phases of the program. First, we'll have to raise funds by holding bake sales and doing things like raffling off prizes. Some other communities have had success with selling cookbooks too. Then we have to interview architects to find one who can do what we want in the space we have. He or she will also have to be affordable, and, of course, the plans that the architect comes up with will have to be attractive and imaginative. The last stage will involve mobilizing the townspeople to build the playground. We have to get volunteers to sign up to work. We'll also need people to donate and cook food for the volunteers. And there won't be enough tools, so people will have to lend us those.

Suggested responses:

Playground planning involves three major phases:

> raising funds (bake sales, raffles, cookbook sales)
>
> finding an architect (space, affordability, attractiveness)
>
> building the playground (construction help, food, tools)

and all the subdivisions appear as nouns (*steak, cheese, turnips, ketchup*). However, lists or outlines may also be written in phrases or clauses. When preparing a paper or taking notes from a book, keep the elements of lists and outlines in equivalent grammatical form. As with parallel elements in a sentence, parallel elements in a list or outline will highlight the logical similarities that underlie parallel content.

1 Making lists

A *list* is a displayed series of items that are logically similar or comparable and are expressed in grammatically parallel form. A list that is not parallel can be very confusing.

NOT PARALLEL

Those attending should be prepared to address these issues:
- morale of workers
- Why do we need so much overtime?
- getting more efficient
- We need better sales tools.

A list or outline can be a helpful way to organize your thoughts. To keep the logic of similar or comparable ideas in line, all items of a list should be expressed in equivalent grammatical form. The preceding example shows a list with four forms: a noun phrase, a question, a verb in its *-ing* form, and a sentence. Choosing any one of these forms as a standard for the list would make the list parallel.

PARALLEL

Those attending should be prepared to address these issues:
- morale of workers
- necessity of overtime
- need for efficiency
- need for better sales tools

PARALLEL

Those attending should be prepared to address these issues:
- improving worker morale
- reducing the need for overtime
- improving efficiency
- reevaluating sales tools

2 Making outlines

An **outline** is essentially a logically parallel list with further subdivisions and subsections under individual items in the list. To make an outline that will help you write a paper or take summarizing notes from a book, follow the guidelines shown in 3d-4. You should keep elements at the same level of generality in the outline parallel in form.

NOT PARALLEL

Chapter Title: Jefferson Takes Power [clause]

    A. The man and his policies [compound nouns]

    B. Buying Louisiana [-*ing* form of a verb]

    C. Jefferson, Marshall, and the courts [compound nouns]

    D. There's trouble on the seas [clause]

In this outline, the subdivisions within the chapter are written three different ways: as an independent clause, as a noun or noun phrase, and as a verb in its -*ing* form. You need to choose *one* of these grammatical structures to make a logically parallel outline. Any choice can be correct, but one may be preferable for your purposes. Often a compromise choice is to outline entries as nouns or noun phrases.

PARALLEL, WITH A SUBDIVISION

Chapter Title: Jefferson in Power

    A. The man and his policies

    B. The Louisiana Purchase

    C. Jefferson, Marshall, and the courts

    D. Trouble on the seas

        1. The benefits of neutrality

        2. The dangers of neutrality

As you expand the outline in greater detail, once again present each entry of the subdivision in parallel form. Within each subdivision, list all parallel items at the same level of generality. If you wanted to subdivide items in the outline to a still more particular level of detail, you would once again make the listed elements of the next subdivision parallel in form.

EXERCISE 2

Outline the major sections of any chapter in one of your textbooks, using the author's subheadings or your own. Then choose one section to outline in detail. Make parallel entries in your outline for every paragraph in that section, maintaining a consistent grammatical form.

EXERCISE 3

Repeat Exercise 2, using a paper you have recently written. Once you have outlined your paper, use the outline as a tool for evaluating the coherence of your work. Based on your outline, what observations can you make about the structure of your paper?

EXERCISE 2

Individual responses

EXERCISE 3

Individual responses

CHAPTER 19

Building Emphasis with Coordination and Subordination

KEY FEATURES

This chapter incorporates material found in several other chapters to offer students guidelines for achieving a desired *effect* in their writing. As in chapter 18, form is closely tied to content. In exploring various techniques for building emphasis, the chapter asks students to consider the nature of the ideas in the paper before deciding what and how to emphasize. The chapter treats techniques such as coordinate structures for equal ideas, conjunctive adverbs for balance, and subordinate structures to emphasize relationships between ideas, as well as specialized techniques such as punctuation, repetition, and specialized sentences. The chapter also presents the problems and trade-offs associated with certain techniques. Examples and exercises are plentiful; exercises offer practice with individual sentences and paragraphs. Throughout the chapter, students are provided with straightforward, practical advice for carrying revision beyond the stage of editing out errors.

LOOKING BACK/LOOKING AHEAD

As indicated in the introduction, this chapter makes use of material found in several other chapters. Students may want to reread the preceding chapters 17 and 18, and take a look at chapters 20 (Controlling Length and Rhythm) and 21 (Choosing the Right Word).

To emphasize a thought, a writer assigns special weight or importance to particular words in a sentence and to particular sentences in a paragraph. You are in the best position to make decisions about emphasis once you have written a draft and have your main points clearly in mind. Then you can manipulate words, phrases, and clauses to create the effects that will make your writing memorable.

Sentence emphasis does not exist independently of content. While your readers may admire the elegance and force of your writing, they must also be convinced that the content of your sentences and paragraphs is clear and logical as well as grammatical. As they consider what your sentences say, readers will appreciate any efforts you make to convert adequate, unemphatic writing into memorable prose.

Emphatic writing uses specific, concrete images (21c, d); is concise and direct (chapter 17); employs parallelism (chapter 18); and is varied (chapter 20). Your writing can improve immensely if you apply the techniques discussed here; but remember that no amount of emphasis can salvage sentences that are seriously flawed in content, grammar, usage, or punctuation.

COORDINATION

19a Use coordinate structures to emphasize equal ideas.

As a unit of thought, a sentence is naturally emphatic. Like a story, it has a beginning, middle, and end. One important and very common technique for both creating emphasis and eliminating wordiness is **coordination,** combining sentence elements by the use of coordinating and correlative conjunctions and conjunctive adverbs. Elements in a coordinate relationship share equal grammatical status and equal emphasis.

CRITICAL DECISIONS	GROUP ACTIVITY

Challenge sentences: Know when to coordinate or subordinate sentence elements

Coordination and subordination are methods of linking sentences and sentence parts. The following sentences can be joined in various ways to establish coordinate or subordinate relationships. Presently, each sentence—*because* it is a sentence—receives equal emphasis.

(1) A complete suit of armor consisted of some 200 metal plates. (2) The armor of the fifteenth century offered protection from cross bows. (3) Armor offered protection from swords. (4) Armor offered protection from early muskets. (5) A suit of armor weighed 60 pounds. (6) A suit of armor would quickly exhaust the soldier it was meant to protect.

Choosing when to link sentences with coordination or subordination requires that you be clear about (1) the level of emphasis you want to give particular information and (2) the specific logical relationships you want to establish.

Why choose coordinate relationships?

Coordinating Conjunctions and the Relationships They Establish

To show addition: *and*   **To show contrast:** *but, yet*
To show choice: *or, nor*   **To show cause:** *for*
To show consequences: *so*

Use coordinating conjunctions to link sentences by giving equal emphasis to specific words (in this case, words from sentences 2, 3, and 4).

The armor of the fifteenth century offered protection from cross bows, swords, *and* early muskets.

Use coordinating conjunctions to link sentences by giving equal emphasis to specific phrases (in this case, verb phrases from sentences 1 and 6).

A complete suit of armor consisted of some 200 metal plates *and* weighed 60 pounds.

Use coordinating conjunctions to link and give equal emphasis to whole sentences, in this case sentence 6 and the combination of sentences 2, 3, and 4.

The armor of the fifteenth century offered protection from cross bows, swords, and early muskets; *but* the armor would quickly exhaust the soldier it was meant to protect.

Conjunctive Adverbs and the Relationships They Establish

To show contrast: *however, nevertheless, nonetheless,* and *still*
To show cause and effect: *accordingly, consequently, thus,* and *therefore*
To show addition: *also, besides, furthermore,* and *moreover*
To show time: *afterward, subsequently,* and *then*
To show emphasis: *indeed*
To show condition: *otherwise*

Use conjunctive adverbs to link and give equal emphasis to two sentences. Conjunctive adverbs can be shifted from the beginning to the middle or to the end of the second sentence (which is not possible with coordinating conjunctions—see 19a-3).

(continued)

This activity can help students appreciate the distinction between and within coordinate and subordinate sentence elements. Ask each group to link two or more of the six sentences presented here to form a variety of coordinate and subordinate structures. (They can use the linked sentences in the box as guides.) Each group should produce five or six different sentences, which they will then present to the class. In general discussion, students can comment on the different effects of linking sentences through coordination and subordination.

Because the exercises in this chapter allow for a number of different responses, all but Exercise 5 would make ideal group activities. Whether students negotiate responses in groups or compare individual responses, they'll get a good sense of the various choices open to writers as they revise for emphasis.

ESL ALERT

Spanish speakers frequently confuse "after" with "afterwards" (as in, "After, they went home") because of translation models in Spanish-English pocket dictionaries.

Japanese students might consistently treat subordinate clauses as main clauses.

ADDITIONAL EXERCISE A

ACROSS THE CURRICULUM   Make three photocopies of several consecutive paragraphs from one of your textbooks. (You'll use the other two copies in subsequent exercises.) Underline all coordinate structures, and identify the words indicating equal ideas as coordinating conjunctions, correlative conjunctions, or conjunctive adverbs. How many times does the writer use coordination? How often are words joined? Phrases? Clauses? How does the use of coordination help the writer achieve emphasis in the passage?

ESL ALERT

ESL students will probably find coordination far easier than subordination, where the specialized connective words might confuse them. For example, they might understand that "despite/in spite of/although/even though/however/nevertheless" are all used for a contrast that is concessive, but they might also use such terms interchangeably. They might need help distinguishing which subordinators go with clauses ("although/even though/in spite of the fact that") and which words connect between sentences rather than subordinate ("however/nevertheless/nonetheless"). "Otherwise," "even if," and "unless" are particularly troublesome. Many ESL students cannot distinguish between "in addition" and "besides" because their grammar texts did not do so. Distinguishing between the coordinator "so" and the subordinator "so

---

CRITICAL DECISIONS (continued)

The armor of the fifteenth century offered protection from cross bows, swords, *and* early muskets; *however,* the armor would quickly exhaust the soldier it was meant to protect.

Conjunctive adverbs vs. coordinating conjunctions: Both conjunctive adverbs and coordinating conjunctions give equal emphasis to and establish similar logical relations between the sentences they join. Why choose one over the other? Differences are subtle and, if the sentences are punctuated correctly (see Critical Decisions box, page 471), both choices are correct. Because a conjunctive adverb's *only* function is to join whole sentences, it is the more emphatic choice. Use a conjunctive adverb when the sentences being joined are long or complicated (when the content requires a strong logical connection) or when you otherwise want to emphasize the relationship between sentences.

Why choose subordinate relationships?

Subordinating Conjunctions and the Relationships They Establish

    To show condition: *if, even if, unless,* and *provided that*
    To show contrast: *though, although, even though,* and *as if*
    To show cause: *because* and *since*
    To show time: *when, whenever, while, as, before, after, since, once,* and *until*
    To show place: *where* and *wherever*
    To show purpose: *so that, in order that,* and *that*

Subordinating conjunctions link whole clauses but, in the process, give one clause greater emphasis. Use a subordinating conjunction when you want one of the two sentences you are linking to modify (that is, to describe or to comment on) the other.

Because it weighed 60 pounds, a suit of armor would quickly exhaust the soldier it was meant to protect.

Designate one sentence as subordinate by placing a conjunction at its head; thereafter, the sentence is referred to as a *dependent clause* (in this example, *Because it weighed 60 pounds*). Emphasis in a sentence linked with subordination is given to the *independent clause* (in this example, to *a suit of armor . . . protect*). See the discussion on relative pronouns (14e, 19b-2, 25d-1&2), which also begin dependent clauses.

---

1   **Give equal emphasis to elements with coordinating conjunctions.**

The **coordinating conjunctions** *and, but, or, nor, so, for, yet* offer an efficient way of joining parallel elements from two or more sentences into a single sentence. The following sentences are parallel in content.

A market allows sellers of goods to interact with buyers.

A market allows sellers of services to interact with buyers.

By using the coordinating conjunction *or,* you can create a compound sentence in which each independent clause has equal grammatical status.

A market allows sellers of goods to interact with buyers, *or* a market allows sellers of services to interact with buyers.

If words are repeated in coordinate clauses, you can economize by coordinating sentence *parts,* in this case the objects of two prepositional phrases. In the following sentence, *goods* and *services* receive equal emphasis.

COMBINED   A market allows sellers of goods *or* services to interact with buyers. [The object of the preposition has been doubled with a coordinating conjunction.]

Coordinating conjunctions express specific logical relations between the elements they join. *Or* and *nor* suggest choice, one positive and the other negative. *And* joins elements by addition. *But* and *yet* join elements by establishing a contrast. *For* suggests a cause of an occurrence. *So* suggests a result of some action. *For* and *so,* when used as coordinating conjunctions, must join entire independent clauses. All other coordinating conjunctions may join sentence elements and entire sentences. Coordinating conjunctions must be used with appropriate punctuation to show that two ideas share the same emphasis.

To ESTABLISH EQUALITY BETWEEN WORDS

Darwin was a pioneer in biology *and* a thinker with an exceptionally fertile mind. [The coordinating conjunction *and* allows the writer to explain two aspects of Darwin in the same sentence.]

To ESTABLISH EQUALITY BETWEEN PHRASES

Darwin theorized that evolutionary changes proceed not in jumps *but* in leaps. [Here *but* contrasts two ideas in prepositional phrases of equal weight.]

To ESTABLISH EQUALITY BETWEEN CLAUSES

Darwin's theory of natural selection was his most daring, *for* it dealt with the mechanism of evolutionary change. [The independent clause after *for* permits the writer to give an explanation or reason for the first clause.]

Evolutionists from Darwin on have always emphasized the continuity of populational evolution, *yet* they have ignored the fact that even continuous evolution is mildly discontinuous. [The independent clause after *yet* permits the writer to establish an exception to the first clause.]

2 Give equal emphasis to elements by using correlative conjunctions.

Correlative conjunctions are pairs of coordinating conjunctions that emphasize the relationship between the parts of the coordinated construction. The following are the common correlative conjunctions:

either/or	*both/and*	*not only/but*
neither/nor	*whether/or*	*not only/but also*

that" and the use of "so" or "such" in adverbial clauses of result is also confusing.

> "He was tired so he went home."
> "He went home so that he could get some rest."
> "He was so tired that he went home."
> "He was such a tired man that he went home."

FOR DISCUSSION

To give students an idea of the stylistic capacity of coordinating conjunctions, present them with quotations such as the following and ask them to comment on how the structures serve to emphasize the content.

> "He had the air of a man who did not believe what he heard or what he himself was saying. He was the first cynic I had met." (Maya Angelou)

> "I believe by this time both of us began to realize we were leading two separate lives that no longer fitted together. . . . I was relieved when it was all over and glad we parted with a mutual affection and respect which still endures." (Margaret Bourke-White)

> "We stopped at the driving range. . . . I reared back and swung with all my might. I caught that ball square, but I came around so hard that the club hit the light post on the follow through and broke in two." (Babe Didrikson Zaharias)

> "I believe that I was the only one of my class of 150 who graduated without a definite plan for earning her living. . . . I did not want to teach school, nor had I taken the courses necessary for this occupation." (Margaret Morse Nice)

> "No one means all he says, and yet very few say all they mean, for words are slippery and thought is viscous." (Henry Adams)

ADDITIONAL EXERCISE B

ACROSS THE CURRICULUM Choose a topic from one of your courses, and compose a paragraph in which you use at least three pairs of different correlative conjunctions. (Make sure the topic is specific: e.g., the relationship between interest rates and economic growth, the role of sibling rivalry in family relationships, or the influence of Zora Neale Hurston on Alice Walker.) When you review your paragraph, try to determine how the correlative conjunctions contribute to its meaning.

The first word of the correlative is placed before the first element to be joined, and the second word of the correlative before the second element.

> *Both* supply *and* demand are theoretical constructs, not fixed laws.

3 Use conjunctive adverbs to give balanced emphasis to sentence elements.

Conjunctive adverbs, also called *adverbial conjunctions,* create compound sentences in which the independent clauses that are joined share a logically balanced emphasis. The following conjunctions (as well as others—see the box on page 367) provide logical linkages between sentences: *however, otherwise, indeed, nevertheless, afterward,* and *still.* (See 7a-9 and especially 13b-4 for uses of conjunctive adverbs.)

> *Linked sentences*
> As the price of a good or service increases, the quantity of the good or service demanded is expected to decrease. *Moreover,* as the price of a good or service decreases, the quantity of the good or service demanded is expected to increase.

Conjunctive adverbs, like most adverbs, can be moved around in a sentence.

> We almost take for granted that rain will replenish whatever amount of water we may use up. Water, *however,* is no longer the infinitely renewable resource that we once thought it was.

In the second sentence, the conjunctive adverb may be moved.

> *However,* water is no longer the infinitely renewable resource that we once thought it was.

NOTE: Because conjunctive adverbs have the force of transitional elements, they are usually set off in a sentence with commas. It is virtually automatic that with the use of a conjunctive adverb one of the joined independent clauses will contain a comma, as in all the preceding examples. (See 13b-4 for avoiding comma splices when using conjunctive adverbs.)

4 Revise sentences that use illogical or excessive coordination.

Problems with coordination arise when writers use conjunctions aimlessly, stringing unrelated elements together without regard for an equal or balanced relationship of ideas in the joined elements.

Faulty coordination

Two elements linked by a conjunction show faulty coordination when they are not logically related. Revise or reorganize sentences to establish groupings that make sense, using coordination for elements of closely related importance.

FAULTY   Newts are salamanders that live on the land and in the water, and they are characterized by a presence of lungs, well-developed eyes, and two rows of teeth on the roof of the mouth. [The writer coordinates these sentences improperly: the topic of the first sentence, the habitat of newts, is not shown to be logically related to the topic of the second sentence, physical characteristics.]

REVISED   Newts are salamanders that live on the land and in the water. They are characterized by a presence of lungs, well-developed eyes, and two rows of teeth on the roof of the mouth. [The first sentence now concerns only the habitat of newts. The second describes their physical characteristics.]

Excessive coordination

Readers look to a writer for signals about logical relationships among ideas, as well as for what is important in a paragraph. If a writer has aimlessly used coordinating conjunctions to join every statement to the next, readers will see no real connections among the ideas; no single idea will stand out. In reviewing first-draft writing, study your use of coordinating and correlative conjunctions and of conjunctive adverbs. Coordinate structures should be retained only when you have deliberately equated main ideas.

FAULTY   The tribe of Iks, a nomadic tribe in northern Uganda, have become celebrities and literary symbols for the ultimate fate of disheartened and heartless mankind at large, for two disastrous things happened to them, and they were compelled to give up hunting and become farmers on poor hillside soil, and an anthropologist detested them, and he wrote a book about them.

REVISED   The Iks, a nomadic tribe in northern Uganda, have become celebrities and literary symbols for the ultimate fate of disheartened and heartless mankind at large. Two disastrous things happened to them. They were compelled to give up hunting and become farmers on poor hillside soil. Also, an anthropologist detested them and wrote a book about them.

—LEWIS THOMAS, *LIVES OF A CELL*

The division into sentences is based on the writer's assessment of his most important ideas. The first sentence is a definition. The next three describe two events.

EXERCISE 1
Combine the following sets of sentences so that whole sentences or parts of sentences show equal emphasis. Use coordinating conjunctions, correlative conjunctions, or conjunctive adverbs.

EXERCISE 1

Suggested responses:

1. How and why living things evolve is only partly understood.
2. Monkeys, apes, and man are all good manipulators of hand-eye coordination. No mammal, however, can rival the chameleon for eye-tongue coordination.
3. Snake anatomy contains the most clever and intricately efficient feeding apparatus.
4. The snake opens its jaws and begins to engulf the monkey. It is not hurried, but deliberate and precise.
5. The Nunamiu Eskimo believe not only that wolves know where they are going when they set out to hunt caribou, but also that wolves learn from ravens where caribou might be. Moreover, they believe certain wolves in a pack never kill, and others specialize in killing small game.
6. When the wolves come together, they make squeaking noises and encircle each other. They also rub and push one another. They poke their noses into each other's fur, and back away to stretch. They not only chase each other but also stand quietly together. Then they are gone down a vague trail.
7. Mexico still has a small population of wolves, but large populations remain in Alaska and Canada.

EXERCISE 2

Suggested revision:

The word *dinosaur* conjures up a hazy picture of prehistoric creatures, but it is a far-from-accurate picture. They were thought to be cold-blooded; however, some scientists now believe that dinosaurs were warm-blooded, like birds and mammals. Popular imagination not only made them out to be slow, clumsy, and stupid, but also not very good at keeping themselves alive. Scientists now believe that some dinosaurs could run very fast. Indeed, they think that their legs were suitable for a very active life. Furthermore, they do not think that dinosaurs were any less intelligent than the reptiles of today. Their brains were not so small, but their bodies were unusually large by comparison.

Example: Ostriches grow from egg to 150-pound bird in nine months. A young python of five pounds requires ten to twenty years to reach 120 pounds.

Ostriches grow from egg to 150-pound bird in nine months, but a young python of five pounds requires ten to twenty years to reach 120 pounds.

1. Why living things evolve is only partly understood. How living things evolve is only partly understood.
2. Monkeys, apes, and man are all good manipulators of hand-eye coordination. No mammal can rival the chameleon for eye-tongue coordination.
3. Snake anatomy contains the most clever feeding apparatus. Snake anatomy also contains the most intricately efficient feeding apparatus.
4. The snake opens its jaws. It begins to engulf the monkey. It is not hurried. It is deliberate. It is precise.
5. The Nunamiu Eskimo believe that wolves know where they are going when they set out to hunt caribou. They believe that wolves learn from ravens where caribou might be. They believe certain wolves in a pack never kill. Others, they believe, specialize in killing small game.
6. When the wolves come together, they make squeaking noises. They encircle each other. They rub and push one another. They poke their noses into each other's neck fur. They back away to stretch. They chase each other. They stand quietly together. Then they are gone down a vague trail.
7. Mexico still has a small population of wolves. Large populations remain in Alaska and Canada.

EXERCISE 2

Rewrite the sentences in the following paragraph by using coordinating conjunctions, correlative conjunctions, or conjunctive adverbs along with appropriate punctuation. Remember that you want to show equality between ideas or parts of ideas. Be sure that the revised paragraph is cohesive and coherent.

The word *dinosaur* conjures up a hazy picture of prehistoric creatures. It is a far-from-accurate picture. They were thought to be cold-blooded. Some scientists now believe that dinosaurs were warm-blooded, like birds and mammals. Popular imagination made them out to be slow, clumsy, and stupid. They were not very good at keeping themselves alive either. Scientists now believe that some dinosaurs could run very fast. They think that their legs were suitable for a very active life. They do not think that dinosaurs were any less intelligent than the reptiles of today. Their brains were not so small. Their bodies were unusually large by comparison.

EXERCISE 3

Rewrite the following sets of sentences to correct problems of faulty co-ordination.

1. An intelligent dog can track a man across open ground by his smell and he can distinguish that man's tracks from those of others, and, more than this, the dog can detect the odor of a light human fingerprint on a glass slide, and he will remember that slide and smell it out from others for as long as six weeks when the scent fades.

2. Bats are obliged to make sounds almost ceaselessly and to sense, by sonar, all the objects in their surroundings, for they can spot with accuracy small insects, and they will home onto things they like with infallibility and speed, for they must live in a world of ultrasonic bat-sound.

SUBORDINATION

 19b   **Use subordinate structures to emphasize a main idea.**

Writers use **subordination** within sentences to give more emphasis to one idea than to another. The basic idea always appears in an **independent clause,** a core statement that can stand alone as a sentence in itself. To state another idea closely linked to that core statement writers add a **dependent clause,** which cannot stand by itself. A dependent clause begins with a subordinating conjunction, such as *if, although,* or *because* (see the Critical Decisions box in 19a for a complete list), or with a relative pronoun: *who, which,* or *that.* A sentence with both dependent and independent clauses is known as a **complex sentence.** (For more information on dependent clauses, see 7e.)

1   **Use subordinating conjunctions to form dependent adverb clauses.**

A subordinating conjunction placed at the beginning of an independent clause (a complete sentence) renders that clause *dependent.* Once dependent, this clause can be joined to an independent clause and will function like an adverb. In this new complex sentence, the independent clause will receive the primary emphasis, with the dependent clause closely linked to it in a subordinate relationship. To create a dependent adverb clause, begin with two sentences that you think could be combined.

Married women could not leave the home for the twelve-hour work days required in the mills.

Married women lost their ability to earn income.

ADDITIONAL EXERCISE C

Combine the following pairs of sentences, forming adjective clauses introduced by *that, which,* and *who.*

1. Muslims were adversely affected by the breakup of the Soviet Union.
   Muslims have been persecuted for centuries.
2. Bosnia fell victim to the "ethnic cleansing" perpetrated by Serbia.
   Bosnia was once a part of Yugoslavia.
3. Anti-Muslim violence also erupted in the former Burma.
   Anti-Muslim violence plagued Bosnia.
4. Islam was under siege in other parts of the world.
   Islam has enjoyed continued growth in Europe and North America.
5. One U.S. group is the African American community.
   The African American community has seen a significant conversion to Islam.

Suggested responses:

1. Muslims, who have been persecuted for centuries, were adversely affected by the breakup of the Soviet Union.
2. Bosnia, which was once a part of Yugoslavia, fell victim to the "ethnic cleansing" perpetrated by Serbia.
3. The anti-Muslim violence that plagued Bosnia also erupted in the former Burma.
4. Islam, which has enjoyed continued growth in Europe and North America, was under siege in other parts of the world.
5. One U.S. group that has seen a significant conversion to Islam is the African American community.

Place a subordinating conjunction at the head of the dependent clause, the clause that will function like an adverb in the new complex sentence.

> Because married women could not leave the home for the twelve-hour work days required in the mills,

Join the now dependent clause to the independent clause.

> Because married women could not leave the home for the twelve-hour work days required in the mills, they lost their ability to earn income.

Emphasis and logical sequence determine the placement of a dependent adverb clause.

AT THE BEGINNING

> When the first certain ancestor of man walked, it was with a foot almost indistinguishable from the foot of modern man. [The writer wants the reader to know immediately that the era is prehuman; the writer therefore places the dependent clause at the beginning of the sentence.]

IN THE MIDDLE

> Scientists concentrate, because it has undergone the most formative changes, on the head. [Here the emphasis is on the final word of the main clause, *head.* The dependent clause interrupts the independent clause to introduce tension or mystery, allowing the end of the sentence to resolve the tension.]

AT THE END

> *Australopithecus* or "Southern Ape" was the name given to a skull found in Africa, although it was actually the first non-ape skull ever uncovered. [Here the information in the dependent clause qualifies in a surprising way all the information presented in the main clause.]

2 Use *that, which,* and *who* to form dependent adjective clauses.

A dependent **adjective clause** modifies a noun in an independent clause. Adjective clauses are introduced by relative pronouns that rename and refer to the nouns they follow. The pronoun *who* can refer to people or to personified divinities or animals. *That* refers to people, animals, or things. *Which* refers to animals and things. To create a dependent adjective clause, begin with two sentences that you think could be combined.

> The ancient Turkic Khazars appeared in Transcaucasia in the 2nd century A.D.

> The ancient Turkic Khazars subsequently settled in the lower Volga region.

Substitute a relative pronoun for the subject of the dependent clause, the clause that will function like an adjective in the new complex sentence.

> who appeared in Transcaucasia in the 2nd century A.D.,

Join the now dependent clause to the independent clause.

> The ancient Turkic Khazars, who appeared in Transcaucasia in the 2nd century A.D., subsequently settled in the lower Volga region.

3 Use subordination accurately to avoid confusion.

Three errors are commonly associated with subordination: inappropriate and ambiguous use of subordinating conjunctions, illogical subordination, and excessive subordination.

Inappropriate and ambiguous use of subordinating conjunctions

The subordinating conjunction *as* is used to denote both time and comparison.

> As human beings became more advanced technologically, they learned to domesticate animals and plants rather than to forage and hunt.

As is occasionally used to indicate cause: *Mary didn't arrive this morning, as she missed her plane.* This usage is apt to confuse readers, who may expect *as* to indicate time or comparison. When you wish to establish cause and effect, use the subordinating conjunction *because.*

CONFUSING   *As* the plough is used as a wedge to divide the soil, it is the most powerful invention in all agriculture.

REVISED   *Because* the plough is used as a wedge to divide the soil, it is the most powerful invention in all agriculture. [The reason for the plough's being a powerful invention is given in the adverbial clause, requiring a conjunction that indicates *cause.*]

The preposition *like* is used as a subordinating conjunction in informal speech. In formal writing, use the subordinating conjunction *as* in place of *like* when a conjunction is needed.

NONSTANDARD   American agriculture did not have the plough and the wheel *like* Middle Eastern agriculture did.

REVISED   American agriculture did not have the plough and the wheel *as* Middle Eastern agriculture did.

Illogical subordination

The problem of illogical subordination arises when a dependent clause does not establish a clear, logical relationship with an independent clause. To correct the problem, reexamine the clauses in question and select a more accurate subordinating conjunction or, if the sentences warrant, a coordinating conjunction.

TEACHING IDEAS

If you are aware of students whose writing exhibits problems with inappropriate, ambiguous, illogical, or excessive subordination, you may want to suggest to them the following activity: After reading 19b-3, review several of your papers for evidence of this problem. Underline the offending sentences and on a separate sheet of paper, rewrite them to eliminate the problems. Now read the entire paper with the revised sentences. How do your revisions make your meaning clearer? How do they improve your writing stylistically?

ADDITIONAL EXERCISE D

Using the second photocopy you made for Exercise A, underline all subordinate structures and circle each subordinating conjunction. What kind of relationship does each subordinating conjunction establish? (Refer to the Critical Decisions box in 19a.) How many times does the writer use subordination? How often are subordinate clauses placed at the beginning of the sentence? In the middle? At the end? How does the use of subordination help the writer achieve emphasis in the passage?

FAULTY   *Although* she was agitated at being shut up in a matchbox for so long, the female scorpion seized the first opportunity to escape.

The subordinating conjunction *although* fails to establish a clear, logical relationship between the dependent and independent clauses. The content of the dependent clause gives no reason for the scorpion's wanting to escape.

REVISED   *Because* she was agitated at being shut up in a matchbox for so long, the female scorpion seized the first opportunity to escape. [The dependent clause explains the reason for the scorpion's escape and requires a subordinating conjunction denoting *cause*.]

Excessive subordination

As with coordination, a writer may overuse subordination. When all or most parts of a long sentence are subordinate in structure, readers may have trouble identifying points of particular importance. In your review of a first draft, study your use of subordinating conjunctions and relative pronouns. Retain subordinate structures when you have deliberately made the ideas of one clause dependent on another. Choose some other sentence structure when the clauses you are relating do not exist in a dependent/independent relationship.

FAULTY   As dawn suffuses the heavily shaded forest floor, the colony of army ants is in "bivouac," which means that it is temporarily camped in an exposed position, since the sites most favored for bivouacs are the relatively sheltered spots along the trunks of standing trees or beneath fallen trees, although most of the shelter for the queen is provided by the bodies of the workers themselves.

REVISED   As dawn suffuses the heavily shaded forest floor, the colony of army ants is in "bivouac," meaning that it is temporarily camped in an exposed position. The sites most favored for bivouacs are the relatively sheltered spots along the trunks of standing trees or beneath fallen trees, although most of the shelter for the queen is provided by the bodies of the workers themselves.

EXERCISE 4

Revise each pair of sentences that follow by creating a complex sentence with one dependent clause and one independent clause. Place the dependent clause in whatever position you think will best demonstrate the relationship of that clause to the main idea.

Example: The Viennese naturalist Konrad Lorenz took a degree in medicine. Later, Konrad Lorenz became director of the Max Planck Institute for behavioral physiology.

After he took a degree in medicine, the Viennese naturalist Konrad Lorenz became director of the Max Planck Institute for behavioral physiology. [A dependent adverb clause is joined to an independent clause to form a complex sentence.]

1. Social animals such as crows will attack or "mob" a nocturnal predator. The nocturnal predator sometimes appears during the day.
2. A fox is followed through the woods by a loudly screaming jay. The fox's hunting is spoiled.
3. Poisonous or foul-tasting animals have chosen the "warning" colors of red, white, and black. Predators associate these with unpleasant experiences.
4. Scent marks of cats act like railway signals. The scent marks prevent collision between two cats.
5. The surroundings become stranger and more intimidating to the animal. The readiness to fight decreases proportionately.

OTHER DEVICES FOR ACHIEVING EMPHASIS

19c   **Use special techniques to achieve emphasis.**

Coordination and subordination are fundamental to the structure of so many sentences that often they go unnoticed as devices for directing a reader's attention. Not so subtle are special stylistic techniques like repetition and contrast, which writers use to achieve highly visible and at times dramatic prose. Precisely because they are so visible, you should mix these techniques both with subordination and coordination and with less emphatic simple sentences in a paragraph.

1   **Punctuate, capitalize, and highlight to emphasize words.**

Punctuation, capitalization, and highlighting work *with* sentence content to create emphasis. *Capitalizing* a word, especially if it is not a proper name and hence is usually not begun with an uppercase letter, is one sure way to create emphasis. Capitalizing all the letters of a word, as in FIRE, will attract even more attention. So, of course, will **boldfacing** a word. In academic writing, strictly limit your use of these techniques and depend, instead, on the wording of your sentences to create emphasis. Occasionally, however, you might use uppercase letters for effect.

> There does not seem to be any point in my knowing for the rest of my life that, during 1964, 720 tons of soot fell on every square mile of New York City, yet there it is in my notebook, labeled "FACT."

Used sparingly, an exclamation point adds emphasis and will help a reader to share a writer's amazement, enthusiasm—or, in some cases, contempt (see 24c). Ending a sentence with a *colon* sets for your reader an expectation that important, closely related information will follow. The words after a colon are emphasized (see 29a). A *dash*, which you will

TEACHING IDEAS

In order to give students a sense of the power of repetition, you may want to add to the brief list of memorable lines printed here, and ask students to offer examples from their own reading.

"To the American people, it is inconceivable that military security can rest upon injustice, upon power, upon the ill-gotten fruits of imperialism and oppression." (Frank Tannenbaum)

"We don't eliminate the problems that people have simply by eliminating the people." (right-to-life pamphlet)

"I see one-third of a nation ill-housed, ill-clad, ill-nourished." (Franklin Delano Roosevelt)"

"Death? Why this fuss about death? Use your imagination, try to visualize a world *without* death! . . . Death is the essential condition of life, not an evil." (Charlotte Perkins Gilman)

"Blues are the songs of despair, but gospel songs are the songs of hope." (Mahalia Jackson)

REFERENCES

CORBETT, EDWARD P. J. "Approaches to the Study of Style." *Teaching Composition: 12 Bibliographical Essays.* 2nd ed. Ed. Gary Tate. Fort Worth: Texas Christian UP, 1987. 83–130. A survey of recent scholarship on style.

———. *Classical Rhetoric for the Modern Student.* New York: Oxford UP, 1965. 410–16. Analyzes characteristics of sentence style.

CHRISTENSEN, FRANCIS. "A Generative Rhetoric of the Sentence." *Notes Toward a New Rhetoric: Essays for Teachers.* 2nd ed. Eds. Francis Christensen and Bonniejean Christensen. New York: Harper, 1978. The cumulative sentence can be effective in achieving emphasis of ideas in sentences.

LANHAM, RICHARD. *Analyzing Prose.* New York: Scribner's, 1983. Extensive advice on revising for style.

WILLIAMS, JOSEPH. *Style: Ten Lessons in Clarity and Grace.* 2nd ed. Glenview: Scott, 1989. Provides guidelines for writers in pursuit of stylistic emphasis in their writing.

show on a typewriter or computer as a double hyphen (--), creates a pause in a sentence and the expectation that some significant comment will follow. Used sparingly, a dash is an excellent tool for emphasis. Overused, it creates a choppy effect and will annoy readers (see 29b).

Information set within *parentheses* will be viewed by readers as an aside—interesting, useful, but ultimately nonessential information. Parentheses give material special attention, but of a curious sort: parenthetical material limits its own emphasis and says in effect, pay attention, but not *too much.* Thus, material set off in parentheses is simultaneously emphasized and deemphasized (see 29c).

2   **Repeat words, phrases, and clauses to emphasize ideas.**

Intentional repetition is a powerful technique for creating emphasis. With repetition, words echo for a reader. Whatever is repeated, if it is repeated well, will be remembered. When using repetition, maintain parallel structure (see chapter 18) and avoid overuse. Our language and certain others seem naturally "tuned" to two and three repetitions in any one sentence. Words, phrases, and clauses doubled by coordinating conjunctions create by far the most typical instances of repetition. It is both more emphatic and less wordy to write

A market allows sellers of goods or services to interact with buyers.

instead of

A market allows sellers of goods to interact with buyers. A market allows sellers of services to interact with buyers.

Using repetition to triple sentence elements is more dramatic than doubling and will give a sentence an arresting, memorable rhythm. Think of Caesar's "I came, I saw, I conquered"; or the phrasing in the Declaration of Independence: "Life, Liberty and the pursuit of Happiness"; or Lincoln's lines at Gettysburg: "government of the people, by the people, for the people." (In each case, note the parallel structures.) One repetition too many can ruin a sentence, however, transforming a dramatic rhythm into a boring catalogue: *On arriving home, I folded the laundry, cooked dinner, read the paper, bathed my kids, finished the taxes, and went to sleep.*

To summarize, doubled sentence elements are commonplace and slightly emphatic; tripled elements are clearly emphatic; and quadrupled elements can tax a reader's patience, unless the sentence is carefully crafted. Generally, try not to follow one sentence that has a repeated structure with a second sentence of a similar structure. Too much repetition within a sentence or within a paragraph will create an unpleasant, overly balanced effect.

One special case of repetition concerns the *appositive phrase,* used to rename a noun. Although an appositive does not exactly repeat a word, in content the appositive is a technique based on repetition. In the following example, the phrase *a symbolic embodiment of its territorial status* renames (that is, repeats) the noun *flag.*

Today each nation flies its own flag, a symbolic embodiment of its territorial status.

3   Use contrasts to emphasize ideas.

Contrast, otherwise known as *antithesis* or *opposition*, creates emphasis by setting one element in a sentence off against another, in the process emphasizing both. When using this technique, be sure that the elements you set in contrast have parallel structures.

More ambiguous than other scientific inventions familiar to modern artists, but no less influential, are the psychoanalytic studies of Freud and his followers.

If the classroom now begins to seem a stale and flat environment for learning, the inventors of television itself are to blame, not the Children's Television Workshop.

4   Use specialized sentences to create emphasis.

Sentence length is variable and depends both on a writer's preferences and on an audience's needs; still, readers do not expect a steady diet of four- or five-word sentences. Nor do they expect one-sentence paragraphs. Purposefully violating these (and other) expectations regarding the sentence can create emphasis (see 20a and 20b).

The brief sentence

An especially brief sentence located anywhere in a paragraph will call attention to itself. The following paragraph concludes emphatically with a five-word sentence.

The Red Sox were winners of five of the first fifteen World Series but have not won one since 1918. They have been in Series since then but lost them all—in the seventh games. There have been two one-game playoffs in American League history. The Red Sox lost both.

The one-sentence paragraph

Because it is so rare, a one-sentence paragraph calls attention to itself. Often these emphatic paragraphs begin or conclude an essay. In the following example, the one-sentence paragraph appears mid-essay and is both preceded and followed by long paragraphs.

. . . Not only are fruit seeds dispersed in the coyote's scat, the seeds' pericarp dissolves in his digestive tract, increasing the chance of germination by 85 percent.

A coyote's breath is rumored to be so rank that he can stun his prey with it.

Most people may never see a coyote—especially if they go looking for one—but everyone can hear them at night. They're most vocal from December to February, during the mating season. . . .

The periodic sentence

Most sentences can be classified as *cumulative.* They begin with a subject and gather both force and detail as one reads, beginning to end. The advantage of a cumulative sentence is that it directly and emphatically announces its business by beginning with its subject.

CUMULATIVE | Most people may never see a coyote—especially if they go
SENTENCE | looking for one—but everyone can hear them at night.

A *periodic* sentence delays the subject and verb in an effort to pique the reader's interest. Information placed at the head of the sentence draws readers in, creating a desire to find out what happens. Emphasis is given to the final part of the sentence, where the readers' need to know is satisfied.

PERIODIC | Washing machines, garbage disposals, lawn mowers, furnaces,
SENTENCE | TV sets, tape recorders, slide projectors—all are in league with the automobile to take their turn at breaking down whenever life threatens to flow smoothly for their enemies.

EXERCISE 5

Read the sets of sentences that follow and underline the emphatic elements in each. Label the specific techniques each writer uses: coordination, subordination, punctuation, capitalization, repetition, contrast, or sentence length. Choose one set of sentences to analyze closely. Write your analysis in paragraph form.

[Robert E. Lee] embodied a way of life that had come down through the age of knighthood and the English country squire. America was a land that was beginning all over again, dedicated to nothing much more complicated than the rather hazy belief that all men had equal rights and should have an equal chance in the world. In such a land Lee stood for the feeling that it was somehow of advantage to human society to have a pronounced inequality in the social structure. There should be a leisure class, backed by ownership of land; in turn, society itself should be keyed to the land as the chief source of wealth and influence. It would bring forth (according to this ideal) a class of men with a strong sense of obligation to the community; men who lived not to gain advantage for themselves, but to meet the solemn obligations which had been laid on them by the very fact that they were privileged. From them the country would get its leadership; to them it could look for higher values—of thought, of conduct, or personal deportment—to give it strength and virtue.

—BRUCE CATTON

EXERCISE 5

Representative responses:

Coordination:

Paragraph 1: *had equal rights and . . .; in turn . . .; wealth and influence; strength and virtue*

Paragraph 2: *some reflecting . . .; others pointing . . .; Jane Eyre and Heathcliff's soul mate Cathy . . .; attractiveness or character. . . .*

Subordination:

Paragraph 1: *that had come down . . .; squire, that was beginning . . .; again, that all men . . .; world, who lived . . .; privileged. . . .*

Paragraph 2: *since I was young; who could . . . possibilities; that I am today; whose attractiveness . . . myself.*

Punctuation:

Paragraph 1: *(according to this ideal); —of thought, of conduct, or . . . deportment—. . . .*

Paragraph 2: *—some reflecting . . .; (if only she dared!).*

Repetition:

Paragraph 1: *equal rights . . . equal chance; to gain . . . to meet; from them . . . to them.*

Paragraph 2: *as ideals, as models, as possibilities; attractiveness or character or audacity; I still understand . . . I still understand.*

Contrast:

Paragraph 1: *not to gain . . . but to meet . . .; from them . . ., to them . . . .*

Paragraph 2: *some reflecting . . . others pointing. . . .*

Sentence Length:

Paragraph 1: Cumulative—*It would bring . . . .*

Paragraph 2: Brief sentence—*I still understand.*

Analyses will vary.

In books I've read since I was young I've searched for heroines who could serve as ideals, as models, as possibilities—some reflecting the secret self that dwelled inside me, others pointing to whole new ways that a woman (if only she dared!) might try to be. The person that I am today was shaped by Nancy Drew; by Jo March, Jane Eyre and Heathcliff's soul mate Cathy; and by other fictional females whose attractiveness or character or audacity for a time were the standards by which I measured myself.

I return to some of these books to see if I still understand the powerful hold that these heroines once had on me. I still understand.

—Judith Viorst

EXERCISE 6

Use the various techniques you have learned in this chapter to combine the short, choppy sentences that follow, rewording them to make an engaging paragraph.

The brain is a tissue. It is complicated. It is intricately woven. It is like nothing else we know of in the universe. It is composed of cells. These are highly specialized cells. They function according to laws. These same laws govern any other cells. The electrical and chemical signals of cells can be detected, recorded and interpreted. Their chemicals can be identified. For this reason, the brain can be studied systematically.

ADDITIONAL EXERCISE E

Using the third photocopy you made for Exercise A, underline and identify all special techniques for achieving emphasis. How many times does the writer use special techniques? How many different techniques does the author use? How does the use of special techniques help the writer achieve emphasis in the passage?

ADDITIONAL EXERCISE F

As you revise drafts of any papers you're working on at present, use the techniques covered in this chapter to achieve emphasis. Remember that the ideas you want to communicate will determine the specific technique you use. Compare the revision to the original. How has adding emphasis improved the effectiveness of your paper?

EXERCISE 6

Suggested revision:

The brain, a complicated and intricately woven tissue, is like nothing else we know of in the universe. It is composed of highly specialized cells that function according to the same laws that govern any other cells. Because the electrical and chemical signals of these cells can be detected, recorded, and interpreted, and their chemicals can be identified, the brain can be studied systematically.

CHAPTER 20

Controlling Length and Rhythm

KEY FEATURES

This final chapter on revising sentences focuses almost exclusively on style. At this stage of revision a paper should be grammatically correct and the ideas clearly presented; now is the time to consider how it sounds. The strategies presented in the chapter bear out the promise of the introduction: creating effective sentences *can* be learned. Students are reminded that content and commitment precede stylistic concerns; the pretty package doesn't matter if there's nothing of consequence in it, or if the giver doesn't care about it. If students do have significant content, and if they are committed to the paper, then they're ready to learn strategies for controlling sentence length and rhythm. The strategies presented follow a logical progression, with initial focus on monitoring length, then on varying length, and finally on controlling rhythm. In addition to extensive sample paragraphs, a paragraph from a student paper is analyzed for length and rhythm. Exercises also provide students with practice in revising and analyzing model paragraphs, along with ample opportunity to apply the material in the chapter to their own papers.

There is less art than you might think in creating effective sentences. A writer's intuition is built on very specific skills, which are used so often and are so familiar that they become automatic or intuitive. A writer's intuition has first to do with content and commitment. Effective sentences are always the work of someone who has something to say, who believes in that content, and who therefore will take time to revise so that the sentences are not only accurate and correct but also inviting.

Beyond content and commitment, good writing has much to do with timing: how long a sentence takes to read and what rhythmic effects are encountered along the way. Considerations of length and rhythm alone will not make a sentence memorable. But any significant content, once established, can be expressed with a more or less effective style, and effective style has a great deal to do with sentence length and rhythm (as well as conciseness, parallelism, and emphasis—see chapters 17, 18, and 19).

 20a Monitoring sentence length

1 Track the length of your sentences.

Often, without realizing it, writers will work with favorite sentence patterns. For reasons of personal preference and audience analysis, the average length of each writer's sentences will differ. Common sense dictates that when a sentence gets so long that readers forget important sentence parts (for instance, the subject), sentence length should be revised.

Track the length of your sentences. Especially in the late stages of revision, once you are certain of a paper's content, you are in a good position to monitor the length of sentences, which is the first step in varying length and rhythm. *Variety* means variation from an average. If you want to vary sentence length, you must be aware of the average length of your sentences. The information in the box on the next page will help you make that determination.

As you begin tracking sentence length, following a technique like the one suggested here will not be necessary for long. Soon you will develop a writer's intuition about sentence length; you will begin to vary the number of words from sentence to sentence because you *feel* the need. This *feeling* will be based on an analysis similar to the one shown here.

Tracking Sentence Length

Any given sentence in a paragraph is long or short in relation to the *average* number of words per sentence in that paragraph. A simple process of counting and dividing will reveal your average sentence length.

1. Number the sentences in a paragraph and write those numbers in a column on a piece of paper.

2. Count and record the number of words in each sentence.

3. Add the word counts for step 2 to obtain the total number of words in the paragraph.

4. Divide the number of words in the paragraph (step 3) by the number of sentences in the paragraph (step 1): this number is your average sentence length for the paragraph.

Consider a sentence to be *average* in length if it has *five words more or less* than your average. Consider a sentence *long* if it has six or more words more than your average and *short* if it has six or fewer words less than your average.

5. Return to the listing you made in step 2, and designate each sentence of your paragraph as *average* length, *short*, or *long*. These designations apply to your writing only. They are relative terms, representing different sentence lengths for different writers.

2 Vary sentence length and alternate the length of consecutive sentences.

Regardless of average sentence length, good writers will (1) write sentences in a paragraph that vary from their average and (2) avoid placing two or more very short or very long sentences consecutively (see 19c-4).

The paragraph below was written by a student, Jenafer Trahar. At twenty words, Trahar's average sentence length is slightly less than that of other stylistically strong writers. She is careful both to vary length and to alternate lengths in consecutive sentences.

(1) One major problem with the commercialization of college sports is the exploitation of student-athletes, many of whom come to school on athletic scholarships. (2) Frequently, student-athletes don't deserve to be admitted to a school. (3) Many colleges routinely lower admissions requirements for their ball players, and some schools will even waive requirements for that exceptional athlete, who without his sports abilities might not have had a place on a college campus. (4) Most kids not interested in academics would normally shun a college education. (5) But for gifted athletes, college appears to be a road that leads to the pros. (6) Or so they think. (7) According to Richard Lapchick of the Center for the Study of Sport in Society, twelve thousand high school

REFERENCES

CORBETT, EDWARD P. J. "Approaches to the Study of Style." *Teaching Composition: 12 Bibliographical Essays.* 2nd ed. Ed. Gary Tate. Fort Worth: Texas Christian UP, 1987. 83–130. A survey of recent scholarship on style.

———. *Classical Rhetoric for the Modern Student.* New York: Oxford UP, 1965. 410–16. Analyzes characteristics of sentence style and structure.

CHRISTENSEN, FRANCIS. "A Generative Rhetoric of the Sentence." *Notes Toward a New Rhetoric: Essays for Teachers.* 2nd ed. Eds. Francis Christensen and Bonniejean Christensen. New York: Harper, 1978. The cumulative sentence can be effective in achieving emphasis of ideas in sentences.

LANHAM, RICHARD. *Analyzing Prose.* New York: Scribner's, 1983. Extensive advice on revising for style.

WALPOLE, JANE R. "The Vigorous Pursuit of Grace and Style." *The Writing Instructor* 1 (1982): 163–69. An analysis of revision for style.

WILLIAMS, JAMES D. *Preparing to Teach Writing.* Belmont, CA: Wadsworth, 1989. 301–02, 306. A discussion of sentence style, including length.

WILLIAMS, JOSEPH. *Style: Ten Lessons in Clarity and Grace.* 2nd ed. Glenview: Scott, 1989. Provides guidelines for writers in pursuit of stylistic emphasis in their writing.

FOR DISCUSSION

To ease students into monitoring sentence length, you may want to have the class practice together on the paragraph below.

Because my mother was thrifty and talented, I had always worn handmade Heidi dresses or high-style outfits bought at Filene's Basement. When I wasn't dressing up, I was stripping down to bare bottom and marching down the neighbor's driveway. By comparison, the Academie clothing was boring and restrictive, two no-nos in my view. Every day we wore the same black uniform with a white stiff collar and clip-on black leatherette bow tie. Black serge bloomers covered white cotton panties, and a vest with attached garters held up long black cotton stockings. We even had black serge aprons to keep us clean. This unnatural attire cost twelve dollars for two complete sets, with the apron extra at a dollar twenty-five. My attempts at distinctive trim were always

(continued)

thwarted. The Sisters confiscated my dande-
lion chains and buttercup bracelets and
made me scrub clean the crayon embroidery
on my celluloid cuffs. (Gretchen Sentry)

1.	21	148 words ÷ 9 sentences = 16.4-
2.	18	word average sentence length
3.	14	*Paragraph has two long sen-
4.	19	tences, one short, two long, one
5.	19	short, one long, one short, one
6.	10	long.
7.	18	*No short sentences are placed
8.	8	consecutively.
9.	21	*Twice two long sentences are
		placed consecutively, in each case
		either preceded by or followed by
		short sentences.

TEACHING IDEAS

One of the most successful pedagogical techniques in composition is for the instructor to
share his or her writing with the class. Analysis
of sentence length provides an ideal opportunity for you to take this step. Find several paragraphs with which you are comfortable, and ask
the class to perform an analysis on them, noting
the variety of lengths as well as the placement of
sentences of different lengths within the paragraphs. (In large classes, you may want to begin
this exercise with small groups. When groups
report their findings to the class, a general discussion can follow.)

EXERCISE 1

Individual responses

GROUP ACTIVITY

Ask students to do this exercise in groups—
students who understand the concept can help
out those who aren't sure of what they're doing.
Then they can compare average sentence
lengths, proving for themselves that average
length is indeed different for different writers.
They can also compare the variety of sentence
lengths used by different writers in a single
paragraph.

athletes participate in sports in any one year, but only one will subsequently play for a professional team.

—JENAFER TRAHAR

Analysis of sentence length

(20 word avg.)
1. 24 words (average)
2. 11 words (short)
3. 36 words (long)
4. 12 words (short)
5. 15 words (average)
6. 4 words (short)
7. 36 words (long)
$138 ÷ 7 ≈ 20$

Trahar's sentence lengths are varied: three
short, two long, two average.
- No short sentences are placed
  consecutively.
- No long sentences are placed
  consecutively.
- No sentences of average length are placed
  consecutively.

Notice that Trahar varies sentence lengths in the paragraph, and at
no point does she write consecutive sentences of the same length. Trahar
regularly alternates short sentences with long or average-length ones.

Varying Sentence Length and Alternating the Length of Consecutive Sentences

While no precise formula exists for determining how many long or
short sentences should be used in a paragraph, you may find these general principles helpful:

- Determine the average length of sentences in a paragraph.
- Plan to vary from that average by using short and long sentences.
- Use short sentences to break up strings of longer ones.
- Avoid placing short sentences consecutively unless you are doing so
  for specific stylistic effect.
- Avoid placing more than two or three long sentences consecutively.
- Avoid placing more than three or four sentences of average length
  consecutively.

EXERCISE 1

Choose three paragraphs you have written recently (not necessarily
from the same paper) and analyze them for sentence length. Follow the
steps laid out in the preceding box. On finishing your analysis, you
should have figured your average sentence length for each paragraph
and designated each sentence in the paragraph as *short, average,* or *long*.
Write a brief paragraph in which you summarize your findings.

20b Strategies for varying sentence length

Once you have determined the average length of your sentences and the extent to which you vary from that average, you should become familiar with techniques for manipulating sentence length. The techniques discussed here will be helpful *only* if you are working with sentences that are already concise and direct. Sentence length can always be reduced by eliminating wordiness, and revising for conciseness should be your first strategy in managing sentence length. See chapter 17 for advice.

1 Control the use of coordination.

Coordination—the use of coordinating and correlative conjunctions and of conjunctive adverbs to compound sentence elements—is the principal means by which parts of two or more sentences are joined into a single sentence (see 19a). In its favor, coordination reduces the overall length of a paragraph by allowing a writer to combine sentence parts (or entire sentences) and eliminate redundancy. The following is a partial paragraph.

> In Puritan Massachusetts the town common had a dual function. It provided for the welfare of the needy. Somewhat incongruously, the town common was the place of public whippings and executions.

The cost of combining sentences with coordination is that the length of the revised sentence will increase. The first sentence in the preceding example has ten words and the set of sentences, thirty-one. In revision, three sentences are combined into one, but that one sentence now has twenty-five words.

> In Puritan Massachusetts the town common *both* provided for the welfare of the needy *and,* somewhat incongruously, was the place of public whippings and executions.

If you decided that the combined sentence made possible by coordination was too long (and you would only know this in relation to the sentences preceding and following it in an actual paragraph), you could break the combined sentence into two.

> In Puritan Massachusetts the town common provided for the welfare of the needy. Somewhat incongruously, it was also the place of public whippings and executions.

In this second revision, the first sentence has thirteen words and the set of sentences, twenty-five—still a reduction in length from the original.

2 Control the use of modifying phrases and clauses.

One way of controlling sentence length is to control the extent to which you use modifying phrases and clauses (see 7d, e). Two types of clauses and four types of phrases can function in sentences as adjectives or adverbs.

Infinitive phrases can function as adjectives or adverbs.

ADJECTIVE   Water is not a resource *to squander.*

ADVERB   Ranchers draw water from the Ogallala aquifer *in order to feed livestock.*

Prepositional phrases can function as adjectives or adverbs.

ADJECTIVE   We assume incorrectly that rain will replenish whatever amount *of water* we may use up.

ADVERB   Ranchers and farmers have begun arguing *over water rights.*

Participial phrases function as adjectives.

ADJECTIVE   *Alarmed by the diminishing supply of water,* rural and municipal leaders have begun serious attempts to find new sources.

Appositive phrases function as adjectives.

ADJECTIVE   In Los Angeles, *a city that has suffered through severe droughts,* engineers have considered building desalination plants.

Clauses with subordinating conjunctions function as adverbs.

ADVERB   *When a city is threatened with water shortages,* rationing often becomes necessary.

Clauses with relative pronouns function as adjectives.

ADJECTIVE   The melting of ice, *which would be towed south from the Arctic Ocean,* is one solution that would supply millions of gallons of fresh water.

Convert modifying clauses to phrases.

If you determine that a sentence is too long in relation to its neighbors, you can reduce sentence length by converting a modifying clause into a phrase.

When a city is threatened with water shortages, drastic actions become necessary.

In times of drought, drastic actions become necessary. [The dependent clause is shortened to two prepositional phrases.]

Move modifying phrases from one sentence to another.

If you determine that a sentence is too long in relation to its neighbors, you may be able to strip a sentence of a modifier, which you can then move to an adjacent sentence (where it may have a new function).

In Los Angeles, *a city that has suffered through severe droughts,* engineers have considered building desalination plants.

In Los Angeles, engineers have considered building desalination plants. Recently, *that city has suffered through severe droughts,* and municipal leaders are now ready to consider long-term solutions to a persistent problem. [The appositive phrase is converted to a subject and predicate in the new sentence.]

Substitute a single-word modifier for a phrase- or clause-length modifier.

If you determine that a sentence is too long in relation to its neighbors, you may be able to convert phrases or clauses to single-word adjectives or adverbs. In the following example an important detail (about towing icebergs) is lost in the conversion and would need to be added to some other sentence; still, the desired result, a briefer sentence, is achieved.

The melting of ice, *which would be towed south from the Arctic Ocean,* is one solution that would supply millions of gallons of fresh water.

The melting of *arctic* ice is one solution that would supply millions of gallons of fresh water.

3 Control the use of phrases and clauses used as nouns.

Sentences can be combined by converting the key words of one sentence into a phrase or clause that then functions as a noun (as a subject, object, or complement) in a second sentence. The disadvantage of the revision is that the newly combined sentence tends to be long.

Infinitive phrases can function as nouns:

Van Gogh painted peasants in their natural setting.

Van Gogh placed great importance in this painting.

COMBINED   *To paint peasants in their natural settings* was of great importance to Van Gogh. [The infinitive phrase functions as the subject.]

Gerund phrases can function as nouns.

At his uncle's art dealership in Paris, Vincent grew fond of *studying the work of French Barbizon landscapists, especially Millet.* [The gerund phrase functions as the object of a preposition.]

Noun phrases and clauses can function as nouns.

Personal awkwardness and a dislike of business turned Vincent away from dealing in art. [The noun phrase functions as the subject.]

Paris is *where Vincent met Paul Gauguin.* [The noun clause functions as a subject complement.]

If you determine that a sentence is too long in relation to its neighbors, try to identify a phrase or clause functioning as a noun. Revise

GROUP ACTIVITY

This activity will provide students with the opportunity to use clauses and phrases as nouns and to judge the effectiveness of such use within paragraphs. Ask each group to compose a paragraph of five or six sentences, in which several sentences use a clause or a phrase as a noun. Upon completing this task, each group will pass their paragraphs on to another group. The second group will determine which sentences in the paragraph seem too long and which seem to be a comfortable length. Students should discover that in a paragraph the appropriate length of a sentence will be determined not only by the sound of the sentence itself but also by its positioning in the paragraph. Some sentences that seem fine out of context may seem too long in relation to the surrounding sentences in the paragraph.

the sentence, possibly moving the noun phrase or clause into its own sentence.

SENTENCE WITH A NOUN CLAUSE The fact that Van Gogh's artistic career lasted only a decade astonishes most art historians who are familiar with his work.

REVISED Van Gogh's artistic career lasted only a decade. Art historians familiar with his work are astonished by this fact.

ESL Note Noun clauses in English have several uses. Notice the special rules in constructions involving *wish that* . . . (see 43b-6). Indirect quotation or reported speech is a very common special use involving *that* clauses. Section 43b-4 describes the tense sequences encountered in reported speech.

EXERCISE 2

Exercise 2 is a rewrite of a paragraph by Northrop Frye, from *The Educated Imagination*. Frye's original paragraph appears at the end of the chapter as the example to be analyzed in Exercise 5.

EXERCISE 2

Use any of the strategies discussed thus far in the chapter to combine the following sentences. Vary sentence length and alternate the length of consecutive sentences. Following is a brief listing of conjunctions you may want to use (see 19a, b). *Coordinating conjunctions:* and, but, or, nor, for, so, yet. *Correlative conjunctions:* not only/but also, either/or, both/and. *Conjunctive adverbs:* however, moreover, furthermore, therefore, consequently. *Subordinating conjunctions:* when, although, while, since, because, before. *Relative pronouns:* who, which, that.

I have been teaching English literature in a university. I have also been studying literature. I have been doing these things for twenty-five years. Certain questions stick in one's mind in this job; actually, they do in any job. They persist not only because people keep asking them. Such questions stick in one's mind because they are inspired by the very fact of being in a university. First one might ask what is the benefit of studying literature. Then one might ask whether literature helps us think more clearly, or whether it helps us feel more sensitively, or whether literature helps us live a better life than we could if we did not have it.

EXERCISE 3

Individual responses

GROUP ACTIVITY

This exercise, as well as Exercise 4, will work well with groups. Have students compare responses in small groups. After hearing all of the responses, the group can decide which is the most appealing, and explain why.

EXERCISE 3

Follow the instructions in Exercise 2 and revise the three paragraphs that you analyzed for sentence length in Exercise 1. The aim of your revision is to vary sentence length and to alternate the length of consecutive sentences.

20c Strategies for controlling sentence rhythm

1 Use modifying phrases and clauses to alter sentence rhythm.

Varying sentence openings is the most direct way of varying the rhythm of a sentence or the cadence with which the sentence is read. Sentences consist of a subject, followed by a verb and then an object (if the verb is transitive) or a complement (if the verb is linking). Any of these important elements can be modified, and it is primarily through placement of modifiers that sentences change rhythm. When you want to alter sentence rhythm, revise sentence structure by changing the extent and location of your modifiers. Writers often concentrate modifiers at the beginning, middle, or end of a sentence.

Modifiers concentrated at the *beginning* of a sentence:

> *For years when Andrew Carnegie might have chosen vast personal wealth for himself and his investors,* he funneled profits back into his steel works.

Modifiers concentrated in the *middle* of a sentence:

> Carnegie, *the first industrialist to transfer sophisticated methods of management to manufacturing,* built Carnegie Steel into the world's largest steel producer.

Modifiers concentrated at the *end* of a sentence:

> The United States became a great industrial power by 1900 *in part because of Carnegie, whose mills produced steel more cheaply than any in the world.*

Aside from being related to the extent and location of modifiers, rhythm is also a function of sentence length. A brief sentence with relatively few modifiers has a rhythm altogether different from the preceding sentences.

> Andrew Carnegie was born in Scotland in 1835.

Vary the position of phrases.

Phrases that function as adverbs (see 20b-2) may, like adverbs, be moved around in a sentence. Because such movement can change meaning as well as sentence rhythm, beware of altering the meaning of your sentences when revising for style.

> I reached our new home *on Monday,* wondering whether the movers would arrive.

SHIFTED RHYTHM	*On Monday,* I reached our new home, wondering whether the movers would arrive.
SHIFTED MEANING	I reached our new home, wondering whether the movers would arrive *on Monday.* [The timing of the movers' arrival has now become the issue.]

A phrase that functions as an adjective (see 20b-2) should be placed as close as possible to the noun it modifies to avoid confusion and faulty reference.

FAULTY	Zebulon Pike ventured west to the Rockies, *an explorer of the Mississippi.*

ADDITIONAL EXERCISE C

Revise the following sentences to smooth out the rhythm. If necessary, divide a sentence into two sentences.

1. Job dissatisfaction, a problem that affects workers at any point in their careers, because of its pervasiveness, costs American business billions.
2. In the past, when much of the workforce was blue collar, and white-collar jobs seemed meaningful, job dissatisfaction seemed confined to factory workers.
3. One cost to business, according to a study at the University of Louisville, is found in absenteeism, which results in lost productivity and high replacement expenses.
4. Inept managers, who often mistreat employees, or authoritarian bosses, who don't allow workers a say in how a business is run, can be a cause of negative employee attitudes, which result in absenteeism and poor performance.
5. Some companies, eager to change employee attitudes, now that they understand the problem better, have begun programs which seem successful.

Suggested responses:

1. Job dissatisfaction can affect workers at any point in their careers. Because of its pervasiveness, such dissatisfaction costs American business billions.
2. Job dissatisfaction seemed confined to factory workers in the past, when much of the workforce was blue collar and white-collar jobs seemed meaningful.
3. According to a University of Louisville study, absenteeism is one cost to business, resulting in lost productivity and high replacement expenses.
4. Negative employee attitudes resulting in absenteeism and poor performance can be caused by inept managers, who often mistreat employees, or by authoritarian bosses, who don't allow workers a say in how a business is run.
5. Some companies, now that they understand the problem better, are eager to change employee attitudes. They have begun programs which seem successful.

| REVISED | Zebulon Pike, *an explorer of the Mississippi,* ventured west to the Rockies. |
| SHIFTED RHYTHM | *An explorer of the Mississippi,* Zebulon Pike ventured west to the Rockies. |

Vary the position of clauses.

Like single-word adverbs and phrases functioning as adverbs, adverb clauses can be moved around in a sentence. An adverb clause that begins a sentence can be shifted to the interior or to the end of the sentence. The placement of the clause determines its punctuation.

After so many white settlers had come from England, it was not surprising that the English language, English customs, and English ways of government dominated America.

It was not surprising, *after so many white settlers had come from England,* that the English language, English customs, and English ways of government dominated America.

It was not surprising that the English language, English customs, and English ways of government dominated America *after so many white settlers had come from England.*

Place a dependent clause that functions as an adjective next to the word it modifies. Neglecting to do so may confuse readers. (See chapter 15 on revising to correct misplaced modifiers.)

FAULTY	The Berlin Wall was recently demolished which was 29 miles long.
REVISED	The Berlin Wall, which was 29 miles long, was recently demolished.
SHIFTED RHYTHM	Twenty-nine miles long, the Berlin Wall was recently demolished.

Vary the position of transitions.

Experienced writers make frequent use of **transitions,** words that like logical bridges help readers move from one idea to another within a sentence, between sentences, or between paragraphs (see 5d-3). Brief transitions include *for instance, for example, on the one hand, on the other hand, in addition,* and *additionally.* Conjunctive adverbs also serve as transitions: *however, moreover, consequently,* and *therefore.* Transitions like these can be moved around in a sentence; when their position changes, sentence rhythm changes.

Advertising is an ancient art. *For example,* some early advertisements appear about three thousand B.C. as stenciled inscriptions on bricks made by the Babylonians.

Advertising is an ancient art. Some early advertisements, *for example,* appear about three thousand B.C. as stenciled inscriptions on bricks made by the Babylonians.

2 Revise individual sentences with a disruptive rhythm.

As with the length of a sentence, the rhythm of a sentence should be evaluated both on its own terms and in relation to neighboring sentences. A sentence that starts and stops a reader repeatedly has a disruptive rhythm and should be revised.

DISRUPTIVE RHYTHM   The Boston Common, used originally as pasture land, at one point, early in the nineteenth century, because of excessive public drinking, turned into a site of rowdy and indecent exhibitions.

Because its erratic, bumpy rhythm interferes with understanding, this sentence needs revision. Revising in this case might lead to two sentences.

REVISED   The Boston Common has had a long history. Used originally as pasture land, it became in the early nineteenth century the site of excessive public drinking that led to rowdy and indecent exhibitions.

3 Revise groups of sentences to avoid a repetitive rhythm.

The rhythm of a sentence in isolation might be perfectly acceptable. Set in a paragraph, however, this same sentence may have a rhythm that too closely resembles the rhythm of other sentences. Unintentional repetition of sentence structures and rhythms usually results in a stylistically weak paragraph. Revise by restructuring one or more sentences.

UNINTENTIONALLY REPEATING RHYTHM
    Used originally as pasture land, the Boston Common became in the early nineteenth century the site of excessive public drinking that led to rowdy and indecent exhibitions. Because of the problem with public drinking, many temperance and drinking ordinances were put into effect. Arising from the needs of Boston's resident population, these ordinances and the Common itself embodied the city's ideals and aspirations.

The sentence structures and rhythms in this paragraph too closely resemble each other: every sentence begins with a modifying phrase or clause. For stylistic reasons, the structure of one or more sentences should be changed.

REVISED   Used originally as pasture land, the Boston Common became in the early nineteenth century the site of excessive public drinking that led to rowdy and indecent exhibitions. So bad was the problem that the city enacted many temperance and drinking ordinances. Boston's resident population was declaring its needs with these new laws. Over time, the Common and the rules that governed its use came to embody Boston's ideals and aspirations.

4 Vary sentence types.

Sentences are classified by structure and function. There are four functional types of sentences (7f-1). The direct statement is a *declarative* sentence: *The driver turned the ignition key.* The question is an *interrogative* sentence: *Was the engine flooded?* The exclamation, or *exclamatory* sentence, expresses emotion: *What an awful fire! How terrible!* The command, or *imperative* sentence, expresses an order or strong desire: *Get back! Don't go near that!*

Use occasional questions for variety and focus.

For the most part, academic writing is restricted to declarative and interrogative sentences. Researchers and writers pose questions, conduct investigations, and write responses. The occasional question posed in a paragraph will be important to the content, but a question also introduces a unique rhythm.

Vary the structure of sentences.

Varying sentence structure, as you have seen in 20c, will vary sentence rhythm. There are four structural types (see 7f-2). Writing that is strong stylistically tends to mix all four types of structure. A **simple sentence** has a single subject and a single verb or predicate. (In the examples that follow, simple subjects will be underlined once and simple predicates, twice.)

Before the rise of the railroad, most business <u>people</u> <u>based</u> decisions on experience, instinct, and information that was often guesswork.

A **compound sentence,** which has two subjects and two predicates, is created when a writer joins two independent clauses with a conjunction (see 7f-2 and 19a).

Textile <u>mills</u> <u>used</u> fairly complex methods of planning, but <u>they</u> still <u>relied</u> on preindustrial operations.

A **complex sentence** has one independent clause and one or more dependent clauses (see 7e and 19b). The dependent clause in this example is italicized.

<u>The system</u> of train control developed by American railroads <u>accomplished</u> a managerial revolution *that brought more change in busi-*

ness decision-making and operational methods in twenty-five years than had occurred in the preceding five centuries.

A **compound-complex sentence** has at least two independent clauses and one dependent clause. The dependent clause in this example is italicized.

When an employee performed badly in a well-managed shop, <u>the shop</u> <u>lost</u> only that employee's output; no great <u>harm resulted</u>.

Varying Sentence Rhythm

Variety in sentence structures and rhythms is the mark of stylistically strong writing. While no rules govern exactly how a writer should vary rhythm from sentence to sentence, you may find the following general principles helpful.

- Use phrases, clauses, and transitional expressions to vary sentence beginnings.
- Consciously shift the location of phrase- and clause-length modifiers in a paragraph: locate modifiers at the beginning of some sentences, in the middle of others, and at the end of others.
- Use short sentences to break up strings of long, heavily modified sentences.
- Limit your concentration of phrase- and clause-length modifiers to one and possibly two locations in a sentence. Heavily modifying a sentence at the beginning, middle, *and* end will create a burden stylistically.
- Vary sentence types.

Analyze sentence rhythm.

As an illustration of a student's effective use of sentence variety, consider again the paragraph by Jenafer Trahar in 20a-2. Here are the types of sentences she used:

(Structural) type of sentence	Sentence opens with
1. complex	noun phrase functioning as the subject
2. simple	single-word modifier
3. compound-complex	subject
4. simple	subject
5. simple	coordinating conjunction and modifying phrase
6. simple	coordinating conjunction
7. compound	modifying phrase

The preceding analysis may look technical, but peel away the numbers and structural descriptions and you have a paragraph that succeeds in both content and style. While her sentences are declarative (typical of academic writing), Trahar makes use of all four structural sentence types: simple, compound, complex, and compound-complex. What is more, she nicely varies the openings of her sentences, beginning twice with simple subjects, once with a long phrase that functions as a subject, and the remainder of the time with a modifier or a conjunction.

Jenafer Trahar's paragraph is stylistically sophisticated. Every technique she has used to gain that sophistication has been discussed in this chapter, and you can apply these same techniques to your own writing. Like Trahar, you will need to begin with a subject you care about. When revising for style, you may want to consult other chapters in this section on matters of conciseness (17), parallelism (18), and emphasis (19).

EXERCISE 4

Suggested revisions:

Although Vincent van Gogh was a very ordinary child, at the age of fifteen he abruptly left the school in which he had become an expert in several languages. His Uncle Cent, a partner in the eminent Paris-based art dealership Goupil and Company, offered him a position at the firm's branch in The Hague. While Vincent was working there, he saw the paintings created by some of the leading academic painters of the day. He was most impressed by the French Barbizon landscapists, especially Millet. However, it was years before Vincent would become an artist. He developed during this period the idealized image of peasant life that was to figure prominently in his early work, culminating in his first masterpiece, "The Potato Eaters." This painting of a rough-hewn family gathered around a dinner table epitomized van Gogh's attempt to crown the poor with a halo of sanctity.

EXERCISE 4

Revise the following paragraph to eliminate the choppiness created by too many short sentences. In your revision, use all the techniques you have learned in this chapter for varying sentence length and rhythm.

Vincent van Gogh was a very ordinary child. At the age of fifteen he abruptly left school. At this school he had become an expert in several languages. His Uncle Cent was a partner in Goupil and Company. Goupil's was the eminent Paris-based art dealership. Goupil's offered him a position at the firm's branch in The Hague. Vincent was working there. He saw the paintings. These were created by some of the leading academic painters of the day. He was most impressed by the French Barbizon landscapists. Millet impressed him especially. It was years before Vincent would become an artist. He developed during this period the idealized image of peasant life. This image was to figure prominently in his early work. It would culminate in his first masterpiece. His first masterpiece was "The Potato Eaters." This painting was of a family gathered around a dinner table. The family was rough-hewn. The painting epitomized van Gogh's attempt to crown the poor with a halo of sanctity.

EXERCISE 5

Read the paragraph that follows, and analyze the component sentences for length and rhythm. Structure your analysis like the analysis of Jenafer Trahar's paragraph in 20d. Be sure to include a paragraph that summarizes your observations.

For the past twenty-five years I have been teaching and studying English literature in a university. As in any other job, certain questions stick in one's mind, not because people keep asking them but because they're the questions inspired by the very fact of being in such a place. What good is the study of literature? Does it help us think more clearly, or feel more sensitively, or live a better life than we could without it?

—NORTHROP FRYE

EXERCISE 6

Reexamine the three paragraphs that you revised for sentence length in Exercise 3. Revise these paragraphs a final time for sentence rhythm, using the techniques you have learned in this chapter.

EXERCISE 5

This paragraph is the original version of the paragraph for analysis in Exercise 2. Frye's sentences average twenty words. The first and last sentence of the paragraph are of average length; the second sentence is long; the third sentence is short. No sentences of the same length are placed consecutively.

Sentence length	Sentence opens with	Sentence type
1. average	Modifying phrase	simple
2. long	Modifying phrase	complex
3. short	Interrogative marker—*what*	simple
4. average	Interrogative marker—verb	simple (implied compound)

EXERCISE 6

Individual responses

CHAPTER 21

Choosing the Right Word

Your purpose as a writer and your intended audience profoundly affect your **diction**—your choice of words. Like the overall tone of a document, diction can be high or low, formal or informal, or any register between (see 3a-4). The English language usually gives you options in selecting words. Readers have a certain attention span and a certain radar; they know when writers are invested in their work—when, for instance, writers have taken time to state a thought precisely or to render a description vividly. A document that shows little concern for word choice will quickly lose its readers.

21a Learning denotation and connotation

Your first concern in selecting a word is to be sure that its **denotation,** or dictionary meaning, is appropriate for the sentence at hand. A careless writer might, for instance, state that in performing their jobs diplomats should know when to *precede.* Is this the intended meaning (when to go first), or did the writer mean that diplomats should know when to *proceed* (when to go forward)? Although these words look similar and sound nearly the same, their denotations are very different. Once you are satisfied that you are using a word correctly according to its denotation, consider its **connotations**—its implications, associations, and nuances of meaning. Consider these sentences:

Thomas was *electrified* by the news.
Thomas was *exhilarated* by the news.
Thomas was *delirious* with the news.
Thomas was *delighted* with the news.

Electrified, exhilarated, delirious, and *delighted:* the dictionary meanings of these words, their denotations, are roughly the same. Each adjective describes excitement. Nonetheless, the adjectives differ in their connotations. Of the four adjectives, *electrified* and *delirious* suggest an excitement at the very edge of control. *Exhilarated* suggests excitement kept firmly in control, while *delighted* implies a happiness not so intensely felt that it could momentarily overwhelm a person. Your choice among these words with their different connotations will make a difference in how your readers react to what you write.

> **EXERCISE 1**
> Given the following set of words, state which word in each set you would prefer someone to use in describing you. Why? Choose one set of words and, in a paragraph, discuss what you understand to be the differences in connotation among the words. Use a dictionary, if necessary.
>
> 1. thrifty, economical, provident, frugal
> 2. reserved, inhibited, restrained, aloof
> 3. strange, bizarre, eccentric, peculiar, weird
> 4. lively, alert, enthusiastic, pert, spirited, sprightly
> 5. sentimental, emotional, maudlin, mushy

21b   Revising awkward diction

At times you may find the abbreviation *"AWK"* in the margins of your papers, with a line leading to a phrase or to a particular word. *Awkward diction*, or word choice, interrupts the process of communication. It momentarily stops an audience from reading by calling attention to a word that is somehow not quite right for a sentence. How can you avoid this difficulty? Until you have more experience with the ways of words, you will not be able to avoid it entirely. However, you can minimize awkward writing by guarding against four common errors: inappropriate connotation, inappropriate idiom, straining to sound learned, and unintentional euphony (rhyming, etc.).

1   Choosing words with an appropriate connotation

Frequently, *awkward diction* means that a word's connotation is inappropriate. The sentence in which the word appears is grammatical; the word in question is the right part of speech; but the word's meaning seems only partially correct for the sentence.

AWKWARD   The professor urged *abstinence* in times of emotional stress. [Does the writer mean to suggest the avoidance of alcohol only? The sentence seems to suggest something else.]

If you look at a dictionary's usage entry for *abstinence,* you will see that there are synonyms for this word with nearly the same denotation but which might have a less awkward and limited connotation.

example, Spanish speakers will automatically misuse words like "molest," "sympathize," "reunion," "actual," "real," "college," "contradictory" and "frontier." French, Greek, and Russian speakers will have similar translation difficulties. In fact, the modern Greek use of many words is totally different from the meanings of English words derived from ancient Greek. See C.W.E. Kirk-Greene, *French False Friends* (Boston: Routledge & Kegan Paul, 1981) for a helpful discussion of this type of problem.

Unlike English speakers, second-language students will *not* have a wide range of synonyms in their own languages. English has an estimated 500,000 total words, while Spanish and French have only 200,000 and Russian has only 100,000. Such languages depend more on context, innuendo, and multiple meanings than does English, whose multiple vocabularies derived from the Anglo-Saxon, French, and Greek/Latin are notoriously troublesome for second-language learners. What we gain in number of words, however, we perhaps lose in shades of connotation. Even the very best language-to-language dictionaries are 50 percent shorter than an equivalently bulky though pedestrian English-to-English dictionary, and thus stint connotation and subtlety. For home use, every ESL student should own a respectable English-to-English dictionary of at least 40,000 words.

Students who rely on dictionaries which translate from their language to English should be warned that such dictionaries may be dated or erroneous.

EXERCISE 1

Individual responses

GROUP ACTIVITY

To accustom students to differentiating between shades of meaning, provide groups with three or four common words for which there are several synonyms with different connotations (e.g., *crowd, angry, thin*). Ask groups to come up with as many synonyms as they can, and discuss the differences in connotations.

REFERENCE

ALTICK, RICHARD D., and ANDREA A. LUNSFORD. *Preface to Critical Reading.* 6th ed. New York: Holt, 1984. Chapter 1. Connotation is put to many uses in advertising, politics, and literature.

TEACHING IDEAS

Many college students rely heavily on the thesaurus when writing their papers. Of course, while the thesaurus can be an invaluable tool for the writer, it also can lead inexperienced writers into lexical trouble. You may want to advise students now (as well as at other times) that they should never use from a thesaurus a word with which they are unfamiliar. You may also want to introduce them to another, more useful tool for writers, the dictionary of usage. One of the more popular ones is *The Merriam Webster Dictionary of English Usage* (1989), available in paperback.

TEACHING IDEAS

Students, like the rest of us, rarely think about idioms. To help them become more aware of the many idioms in the language, use the list as a starting point and ask for additional idioms. If you have any non-native speakers in the class, you'll probably get quite a response from them. You may want to offer a few idioms of your own, such as *take in a show, stand up to someone, think it over,* to "prime the pump."

FOR DISCUSSION

Since you're probably covering this chapter after having covered the writing process and many of the revision chapters, students should be ready to discuss why some of them try to sound scholarly when they write. Now that they have more confidence in their writing, they may be able to recognize strategies—including trying to sound learned—that an insecure writer uses to cover up perceived failings.

REVISED The professor urged *sobriety* in times of emotional stress.

REVISED The professor urged emotional *restraint.* [The revisions do not limit the advice to avoiding alcohol.]

2 Following standard English idioms

An **idiom** is a grouping of words, one of which is usually a preposition, whose meaning may or may not be apparent based solely on simple dictionary definitions. Moreover, the grammar of idioms—particularly the choice of prepositions used with them—is a matter of customary usage and is often difficult if not impossible to explain. Native speakers of English know intuitively that "running *across* an old letter" is a legitimate phrase (often listed in the dictionary), while "running *in* an old letter" is not. The difference is very difficult to explain, even for native speakers. Often, our attempts at using idioms result in awkwardness.

NOT IDIOMATIC When the intruder left, the manager *got the courage* to call the police. [Idiomatically, we do not normally *get* courage; we either have it or we do not.]

IDIOMATIC When the intruder left, the manager *got up the courage* to call the police. [The standard idiom implies that courage is summoned from within when needed.]

To avoid awkwardness, memorize idioms or do not use them at all. You can refer to the detailed listings in a dictionary to find some idioms; for others, you must listen carefully to the patterns of common usage. The box on page 399 shows some common idiomatic expressions in English.

3 Writing directly rather than straining to sound learned

When you are new to an area of study, or for that matter new to a social group, it is natural to want to fit in and sound as if you know what you are talking or writing about. In academics, this desire shows when students strain to take on the learned diction of professors. Some students try so hard they will use words that do not exist in any dialect of English.

AWKWARD The character's grief and *upsetion* were extreme. [The word does not exist.]

AWKWARD *Disconcern* is common among the employees at that factory. [*Disinterest, indifference,* or *unconcern* could be used.]

At times, students straining at sophistication will choose lengthy, complicated phrasings when simpler ones will do; they will favor pretentious language because they believe this is the way learned people express themselves. The following sentence is *not* erudite.

AWKWARD The eccentricities of the characters could not fail to endear them to this reader.

REVISED I found the eccentric characters endearing.

Some Common Idioms in American English

We *arrived* <u>*at*</u> a conclusion.

We *arrived* <u>*in*</u> time.

We *arrived* <u>*on*</u> time.

We *brought* <u>*in*</u> the cake.

We *brought* <u>*up*</u> the rear of the parade.

Except <u>*for*</u> my close friends, no one knows of my plan.

Don't call, *except* <u>*in*</u> emergencies.

I often *get* <u>*into*</u> jams.

Get <u>*up*</u> the courage to raise your hand.

I *got* <u>*in*</u> just under the deadline.

Good friends will *make* <u>*up*</u> after they argue.

How did you *make* <u>*out*</u> in your interview?

We'll *take* <u>*out*</u> the trash later.

Next week, the Red Sox *take* <u>*on*</u> the Orioles.

The senate will *take* <u>*up*</u> the issue tomorrow.

A large crowd *turned* <u>*out.*</u>

At midnight, we will *turn* <u>*in.*</u>

The request was *turned* <u>*down.*</u>

---

4 Listening for unintentional euphony

In a poem, **euphony**—the pleasing sound produced by certain word combinations—is put to literary ends, and the effect can be memorable. A sentence in an essay or report, however, can be awkward when a writer unintentionally creates rhymes or alliterations (words that begin with the same consonant sound) that distract the reader from a sentence's meaning.

AWKWARD Particularly in poetry, euphony is put to literary ends. [The rhymes and alliterations distract from the meaning.]

SIMPLIFIED In a poem, euphony is used for literary ends.

The surest way to avoid unintentional rhymes or alliterations is to listen for them as you read your work aloud. Reading aloud forces you to slow down and hear what you have written. It can also help you to become aware of sentence rhythms. Finally, reading aloud can be an aid to proofreading—catching misspelled words, inadvertently misused homonyms (writing *affect* instead of *effect*), omitted words (often a preposition), and doubled words.

21c Using general and specific language

Specific details, illustrations, and observations are more vivid and more memorable than *general* remarks. To comment that a book about

GROUP ACTIVITY

In addition to illustrating the problems associated with unintentional euphony, this exercise can also inject a bit of humor into the class: Ask groups to come up with five or six sentences with too many rhyming words and/or too much alliteration. When groups report to the class, the class as a whole can determine which group has come up with the most outrageous examples. Such an exercise will help students recognize unintentional euphony in their own papers, but will spare them the embarrassment of public scrutiny of their work.

ESL ALERT

Idiomatic combinations with prepositions are treated in three categories in the ESL chapters; see 42c, 43f, and 44b. Other idiomatic combinations are also treated; see especially 43e-2 on idioms with gerunds and infinitives.

English places greater emphasis on specificity than do most languages; in fact, in some cultures the abstract is preferred to the concrete. As a consequence, the degree of specificity required in a given writing assignment will need to be illustrated with samples, and most ESL students will need particular instructions about how to generate such detail. In Farsi, for example, the broader and more encompassing your topic and your early treatment of it, the better; specifics are saved for endings.

Spanish speakers in particular will tend to use a high level of abstraction to sound sophisticated and serious. Furthermore, a Spanish locution such as *"la gente,"* or "the people," might have deep, almost mystical, associations for Spanish speakers, or it might change meaning in context, in one situation meaning "villagers," in another "the public," in still another "the downtrodden masses," but it sounds too general ("the people"—which people?) for English speakers. This use of a single abstraction for a series of different, more specialized meanings results in writing that in English sounds far too abstract.

Spanish, Italian, Russian, Greek, and French speakers have been taught to use overarching abstractions to write properly about literature and the arts, and will be surprised and disturbed by the degree of specificity asked of them by American teachers.

TEACHING IDEAS

Ask students to analyze several of their own papers for general and specific language. They can underline all of the general words, and circle all of the specific words. Have students ask themselves some questions about their writing as a result of their analyses: What is the ratio of general to specific words in their papers? Does one or the other seem to predominate? Does the topic influence the ratio? How might a better balance improve a given paper?

EXERCISE 2

Individual responses

fourteenth-century Europe was *interesting* is so general as to be meaningless. By contrast, to state that you were perplexed by your morbid fascination with Barbara Tuchman's description of bubonic plague in fourteenth-century Europe—*that* is a specific comment.

Successful writers shuttle back and forth between the general and specific, since to dwell at either end of this spectrum for too long will tax a reader's patience. The writer who concentrates on details and will not generalize gives the impression of being unable to see "the big picture." Conversely, the writer who makes nothing but general claims will leave readers restless for specific details that would support these claims. Read the following sets of sentences. One is specific, the other general. Consider the differences.

> Genetically engineered organisms can be of great benefit to agriculture. Scientists have discovered or are working on organisms that can make plants frost and herbicide resistant and can help plants produce their own nitrogen.

> Scientists have discovered the benefits and uses of genetically engineered organisms in agriculture. One important example is the ice-minus bacterium created by Steve Lindow and Nicholas Panopoulos. Realizing a bacterium commonly found in plants produces a protein that helps ice to form, these scientists removed the unfavorable gene and thereby prevented ice from forming on greenhouse plants. Others have manipulated genetic materials to create tobacco that kills attacking insects and to produce plants that resist herbicides. Geneticists hope in 20 to 40 years to produce plants such as corn and other grains that "fix" their own nitrogen—that will be able to extract nitrogen from the atmosphere without relying on nitrifying bacteria. If such a plant could be created, U.S. farmers would save $3 to $4 billion annually in fertilizer costs and could save one third of all crops lost each year to pests.

In the first example, the writer makes a claim and supports it with three general examples, each of which is named quickly and left undeveloped. In the second example, the writer makes the same claim; but this time, details are provided that give readers specific information about genetically engineered organisms. Details such as these help to establish the writer's authority and give readers reasons to accept the writer's claim as true or probable. To produce effective, academic writing, writers shuttle between general claims and specific, supporting details.

EXERCISE 2

Create three lists, the first item of each being a very general word, the next item somewhat less general, the next still less general, and so on. The completed list, top to bottom, will proceed from general to specific.

> *Example:* nation, state, county, city, neighborhood, street, house

EXERCISE 3

Choose a topic that you know well (sports, music, art, etc.) and write a general sentence about it. Then, in support of that sentence, write two additional sentences rich in specific detail.

Example: Topic—Cooking an omelette

General sentence:

Making omelettes is a delicate operation.

Specific sentences:

Use a well-seasoned omelette pan—cast iron, well greased, clean but never thoroughly scrubbed.

Scramble the eggs with a splash of water (not milk), blending lightly so as not to toughen the cooked eggs.

21d Using abstract and specific language

Like general words, **abstract** words are broad. They name categories or ideas, such as *patriotism, evil,* and *friendship.* **Concrete** expressions (a *throbbing* headache, a *lemon-scented* perfume) provide details that give readers a chance to see, hear, and touch—and in this way to understand how an idea or category is made real. Just as with general and specific language, you should seek a balance between the abstract and concrete. Writers who dwell on the concrete give readers the impression of literal mindedness, perhaps even denseness. Writers who dwell on the abstract give the impression of being vague or aloof.

As with the general and specific, balance is the key—and not just in literary writing or autobiography but in all disciplines where writers labor to give concrete meaning to their ideas. See, for example, the balanced use of abstract and concrete terms in the following paragraph on biological inheritance.

Among all the symbols in biology, perhaps the most widely used and most ancient are the hand mirror of Venus (♀) and the shield and spear of Mars (♂), the biologists' shorthand for male and female. Ideas about the nature of biological inheritance—the role of male and female—are even older than these famous symbols. Very early, men must have noticed that certain characteristics—hair color, for example, a large nose, or a small chin—were passed from parent to offspring. And throughout history, the concept of biological inheritance has been an important factor in the social organizations of men, determining the distribution of wealth, power, land, and royal privileges.

—HELENA CURTIS

Notice that the abstract term *symbol* is given two more concrete examples: the hand mirror of Venus and the shield and spear of Mars. The abstract term *characteristics* is given concrete examples: *a large nose, a small chin, hair color.* And the abstract phrasing *social organizations of men* is given more concrete examples: *power, wealth, land, social privileges.* Of these last examples, though, one can imagine more concrete cases (*what kinds of privileges?*); but Curtis does not provide these, and in any event the para-

EXERCISE 3

Individual responses

GROUP ACTIVITY

These exercises will work well with groups. It's almost always easier to generate ideas with others rather than individually, and students can challenge one another to come up with the most appropriate responses to Exercise 3. For Exercise 4, students can either generate the sentences together or share responses.

ADDITIONAL EXERCISE A

ACROSS THE CURRICULUM Photocopy a brief passage from one of your textbooks. Underline all of the general words, and circle all of the specific words. What is the proportion of general to specific words? How do the words relate to one another? How does the combination of both contribute to the effectiveness of the passage?

REFERENCE

OHMANN, RICHARD. "Use Definite, Specific, Concrete Language." *CE* 41 (1979): 390–97. Encouraging students to be specific is fine, but instructors should remember that abstract words are appropriate when identifying abstract ideas.

graph does not call for them. The important point is that Curtis *does* weave the abstract with the concrete (even if some of these examples could be made more concrete).

EXERCISE 4

Take an abstract word such as *honesty, truth, friendship,* or *chaos,* and, in two or three sentences, link that word with a specific person, place, or event. Then provide concrete, descriptive details that help give meaning to the abstraction.

21e   Using formal English as an academic standard

Academic writing is expected to conform to standards of **formal English**—that is, the English described in this handbook. There are many standards, or dialects, of English in this country, all of which are rich with expressive possibilities. Why formal English should be the acknowledged standard is, by some accounts, a purely political tactic orchestrated by the powerful to keep the less powerful disenfranchised. Those who grow up speaking formal English are born (so goes the argument) into an upper-range socioeconomic class that has a vested interest in maintaining its privileges. People who are privileged will admit into their circle only those who speak as they speak and who, presumably, share the same values because they share the same language.

In any case, it is clear that business, government, and academic communication would suffer if there were no accepted norm for language in a society. Some standard of communication is necessary, if only for the sake of efficiency. That the standard happens to be formal English has alienated some, and from a descriptive linguist's perspective it is certainly true that formal English is inherently no more *correct* than any other dialect of English. Linguists teach us that dialects—for instance, ones using the nonstandard *ain't*—are rule governed, just as formal English is rule governed. The diction of formal English is not better; it *is,* however, the only widely accepted standard for communicating among the many groups of English speakers. As a college student, you are learning communication skills that will enable you to reach the widest possible audience, and for that purpose you need to develop skill in formal English.

Academic writing avoids language that by virtue of its private references limits a reader's understanding or limits the audience. Slang, jargon, and regional or ethnic dialect language are examples of writing specific to particular groups. When you write to members of the *same* social group, profession, or region, there are two clear advantages to using in-group language: first, it is efficient, and second, it can help to cement a group's identity. When you address an audience *beyond* the group, slang, jargon, dialect, and regionalisms restrict what that audience can understand.

EXERCISE 4

Individual responses

FOR DISCUSSION

Most students have probably been taught that there's such a thing as "proper" English, and all other variations—including dialects—are "improper." This attitude, of course, is being reinforced at present by some state and federal efforts to make English an official language. While proponents of these movements don't specify standard edited English, their rhetoric makes clear that regional, racial, or ethnic dialects are not what they mean by English. Students need to be able to discuss this issue. For many of them, self-image is inextricably tied to their ability to produce standard academic prose. If there are racial or ethnic minorities in your class, or non-native speakers, that's all the more reason to discuss the concept of a standard. It's not necessary to "buy" the argument that language is a political weapon to discover that the ability to use standard English indeed separates the powerful from the less powerful.

ESL ALERT

Non-native English speakers will have no basis for judging between formal diction and slang and may use the two interchangeably; how formal or informal their usage is will depend on whether they learned English in a classroom setting or from daily use. If they learned from daily use, their English will include much slang and their instructor will have to call attention to its use regularly and consistently if they are to learn to hear the difference.

Vietnamese are used to distinguishing between formal and informal language mainly in terms of increased patterns of politeness for older generations.

CRITICAL DECISIONS

Set issues in a broader context: Choosing the right tone and register for your papers

Every sentence of every paper you write has a characteristic tone which, intended or not, communicates information about you: about your assumptions concerning the reader and about your knowledge of and attitude toward your topic. Choose a tone that helps you to meet the expectations of readers while satisfying your purpose as a writer. You will choose a formal, informal, or popular tone and register (3a-4).

Choosing an appropriate tone requires that you carefully analyze the writing occasion (see 3a-4)—the topic, your purpose, and your audience—and that you then make decisions about your document's level of content, language, and style.

■ Match the tone and register of your writing to the writing occasion—to your topic, your purpose, and the needs of your audience.

FORMAL: *Likely audience*—specialists or knowledgeable nonspecialists. *Content*—choose content that goes beyond introductory material. *Language*—to the extent that you understand and are comfortable with technical language, use it whenever needed for precision. *Style*—adhere to all the rules and conventions expected of writing in the subject area. Complicated and, if necessary, long sentences are acceptable if needed for precision. For guidance on format, see pieces similar to the one you are writing or consult a discipline-appropriate style guide (see 37e, 38e, 39e).

POPULAR: *Likely audience*—nonspecialists willing to follow a detailed presentation. *Content*—choose content similar to that of a formal presentation, but avoid any examples or explanations that require specialized understanding. Emphasize (but do not necessarily limit yourself to) content that intersects with the readers' experiences and will keep them engaged. *Language*—avoid specialized terms whenever possible, though if you must use them for precision, carefully prepare for and define them. *Style*—adhere to all conventions of grammar, usage, spelling, etc. Some slang or colloquial language is acceptable, but keep it to a minimum. Avoid specialized formats, but organize content in a sensible, orderly way. Closely monitor your sentences, alternating length and rhythm for best effect (see chapter 20).

INFORMAL: *Likely audience*—nonspecialists looking for general information. *Content*—choose content that closely intersects your readers' experiences; otherwise, readers will lose interest. Coverage of topic should be introductory. Draw only on the most accessible examples and cases. *Language*—do not use specialized terms. Generally, keep sentences brief. *Style*—adhere to conventions of grammar, usage, spelling, etc. Slang or colloquial language is accepted, especially when you are familiar with the local or in-group speech of your readers. A narrative, first-person format may be useful.

REFERENCES

LABOV, WILLIAM. *Language in the Inner City: Studies in Black English Vernacular*. Philadelphia: U of Pennsylvania P, 1972. Black English is a dialect governed by its own rules, consistent with the culture in which it is spoken.

BOLINGER, DWIGHT. "Stigma, Status, and Standard." *Language, the Loaded Weapon: The Use and Abuse of Language Today*. New York: Longman, 1980. 44–57. There is no objective justification for considering one dialect preferable to another.

GIANNASI, JENEFER M. "Language Varieties and Composition." *Teaching Composition: Twelve Bibliographic Essays*. Rev. ed. Ed. Gary Tate. Fort Worth: Texas Christian UP, 1987. A review of sociolinguistic studies of language varieties, with particular emphasis on classroom implications.

1 Revise most slang expressions into standard English.

Slang is the comfortable, in-group language of neighborhood friends, coworkers, teammates, or of any group to which we feel we belong. Assume for the moment you do not windsurf, and you happen to overhear a conversation between windsurfers in which someone says that she was *dialed in* or *completely powered*. What do these words mean? To someone not involved with the sport, nothing specific. Slang can be descriptive and precise for those who understand; it can just as readily be confusing and annoying to those who do not. In some cases, slang may mislead: the same expression can have different meanings for different groups. For example, *turbo charged* has distinctly different meanings for computer aficionados and for race-car enthusiasts and is likely to be vague and confusing when used outside of those settings. In the interest of writing accessibly to as many people as possible, avoid slang expressions in academic papers.

2 Replace regionalisms and dialect expressions with standard academic English.

Regionalisms are expressions specific to certain areas of the country. Depending on where you were born, you will use the word *tonic, soda, cola,* or *pop* to describe what you drink with your *sub, hoagie, grinder,* or *hero*. In a few states, when you are driving fast and a *smokey* catches up with you, your insurance rates will skyrocket. Words that have a clear and vivid reference in some areas of the country may lack meaning in others or have an unrelated meaning. For instance, *muss* means "to make messy" in some places and "to fight" in others. *Bad* means "good" in some places and "bad" in others.

Dialect expressions are specific to certain social or ethnic groups, as well as regional groups, within a country. Like regionalisms, dialects can use a specialized vocabulary and sometimes a distinctive grammatical system. Especially with respect to verbs (see chapter 9), regional and ethnic dialect usage may regularly differ from standard English in omitting auxiliary verb forms. ("I done everything I can" or "It taken him all day" omit the standard auxiliaries *have, had,* or *has*. "They be doing all right" replaces the standard *are* with the infinitive or base form *be*.) These are grammatically consistent and correct usages within the dialects they represent, but they address their language to a specific and restricted group rather than to a general audience. Like slang, regionalisms and dialect usages are appropriate for the audience that understands them; however, for general audiences in academic writing, they should be avoided.

3 Reduce colloquial language to maintain clarity and a consistent level of academic discourse.

Colloquial language is informal, conversational language. Colloquialisms do not pose barriers to understanding in the same way that slang, jargon, and regionalisms do; virtually all long-time speakers of English will understand expressions like *tough break, nitty-gritty,* and *it's a cinch.* In formal English, however, colloquialisms are rewritten or "translated" to maintain precision and to keep the overall tone of a document consistent. A few translations follow.

Colloquial	*Formal*
it's a cinch	it is certain
tough break	unfortunate
got licked	was beaten

Some colloquial expressions are also worn-out figures of speech whose meanings have become vague or obscure (see 21f-3).

4   Revise to restrict the use of jargon.

Jargon is the in-group language of professionals, who may use acronyms (abbreviations of lengthy terms) and other linguistic devices to take short cuts when speaking with colleagues. When writers in an engineering environment refer to RISC architecture, they mean machines designed to allow for **R**educed **I**nstruction **S**et **C**omputing. RISC is an easy-to-use acronym, and it is efficient—as long as one engineer is writing or speaking to another. (If the in-group that uses these expressions is a prestigious one, the use of jargon can become a form of false or pretentious writing—see 21h-2.) The moment communication is directed outside the professional group, a writer must take care to define terms. The following sentences illustrate highly technical, in-group language among biologists. The writers are addressing upper-division biology majors with language that nonbiologists will find difficult to follow.

Writing directed to an in-group audience:
Clostridia are ubiquitous, versatile, anaerobic flagellated microorganisms that generally form spores. As a group, they will ferment almost anything organic except plastics—sugars, amino acids and proteins, polyalcohols, organic acids, purines, collagen, and cellulose.
—Lynn Margulis and Kathlene V. Schwartz

By contrast, in this next passage biologists are addressing a general student population, only a fraction of whom are biology majors.

Writing directed to a general audience:
Historically, biology has been considered a "soft" science whose subject was more complex and "laws" less rigorous than disciplines such as chemistry and physics. This soft status, however, has been rapidly changing since the medical discovery of the role of microorganisms in disease, Darwin's theory of evolution by natural selection, Mendel's description of the rules by which traits are inherited, and the understanding of the way DNA both duplicates itself and determines the details for the manufacture of proteins that comprise all living things.
—Dorian Sagan and Lynn Margulis

REFERENCES

Bolinger, Dwight. "Another Case in Point: The Jargonauts and the Not-So-Golden Fleece." *Language, the Loaded Weapon: The Use and Abuse of Language Today.* New York: Longman, 1980. 125–37. An extensive analysis of the generation and perpetuation of jargon in contemporary English.

Barzun, Jacques. *Simple and Direct.* New York: Harper, 1976. Chapter 3. To avoid slipping into jargon, avoid nouns ending in *-tion* and verbs ending in *-ize.*

Language that is specialized by a particular group, for a particular purpose, is universal. Literary critics will speak of *deconstruction*, philosophers of *positivism*, sociologists of *dyads*, and mathematicians of *sigma functions*. When you become part of a group, academic or otherwise, you will be expected and will find it convenient to use in-group language. You will need to interpret that language for outsiders, of course; but even within the group, if you can communicate precisely without using jargon, do so.

EXERCISE 5

Individual responses

REFERENCES

CORBETT, EDWARD P. J. *Classical Rhetoric for the Modern Student.* New York: Oxford UP, 1965. Recognizing figures of speech in their reading opens up for students the possibility of using them.

PERRINE, LAURENCE. "Four Forms of Metaphor." *CE* 33 (1971): 125–38. Metaphors can be classified into four distinct forms, each of which has a variety of uses.

DEVET, BONNIE. "Bringing Back More Figures of Speech into Composition." *Journal of Teaching Writing* 6 (1987): 293–304. Current theories of composition lend credence to the notion that figures of speech should be taught.

LAKOFF, GEORGE, and MARK JOHNSON. *Metaphors We Live By.* Chicago: U of Chicago P, 1980. Metaphors influence both the expressive and conceptual components of language.

EXERCISE 5

Think of a group—social, geographic, or professional—to which you belong and which you know well. Write a paragraph on some subject using in-group language: slang, jargon, or regionalisms. When you are finished, translate your paragraph into formal English, rewriting in-group expressions so that the paragraph can be read and understood by a general audience.

21f   Using figures of speech with care

Similes, analogies, and *metaphors* are **figures of speech,** carefully controlled comparisons that clarify or intensify meaning. Perhaps your spirit *soars* when you read this line of poetry: "Come live with me and be my love." The figurative use of *soar* creates an image of birds in flight, of elevation and clear vision. Literally speaking, birds and planes soar; spirits do not. English allows for the pairing of unlikely, even totally opposite images to help readers feel and see as writers do. In academic writing, figurative language is used across disciplines, though in some disciplines more freely than in others.

Figurative language in the sciences

The author of one well-respected book on scientific writing advises caution in using figures of speech in the life sciences and physical sciences. "Use [them] rarely in scientific writing. If you use them, use them carefully."[1] Following the logic of this advice, a biologist who is writing to fellow biologists would not report that in the course of an experiment water turned *ice* cold. This figurative language, however suggestive to nonscientists, lacks precision (ice cold water *is* ice). Biologists reading the article will want to know the precise temperature of the water, and they expect that temperature to be given in degrees. However, scientists in control of their writing *do* use figurative language at times, when addressing colleagues but more often when attempting to convey to the

---

[1] Robert A. Day, *How to Write and Publish a Scientific Paper,* 3rd ed. (Phoenix: Oryx Press, 1988) 155.

general public complicated, specialized knowledge. Thus (as illustrated later) you will find physicists and physicians as well as philosophers and poets using figures of speech, all to the same end: to communicate in ways that literal language, alone, fails to do.

There are many techniques for using language figuratively. As you read in the disciplines, you will encounter three figures most often: *simile, analogy,* and *metaphor.*

1   Use similes, analogies, and metaphors.

A **simile** is a figure of speech in which two different things—one usually familiar, the other not—are explicitly compared. The properties of the thing known help to define what is unknown. Similes make comparison very explicit, often using the word *like* or *as* to set up the comparison.

> Plastic is the new protector; we wrap the already plastic tumblers of hotels in more plastic, and seal the toilet seats *like* state secrets after irradiating them with ultraviolet light.
>
> —LEWIS THOMAS
> Physician, researcher

> The wind whistled in the street and the music ghosted from the piano *as* leaves over a headstone and you could imagine you were in the presence of genius.
>
> —BRUCE CHATWIN
> Traveler, writer

> A particle of spin 2 is *like* a double-headed arrow: it looks the same if one turns it round half a revolution (180 degrees).
>
> —STEPHEN HAWKING
> Physicist

As with a simile, the purpose of an **analogy** is to make an explicit comparison that explains an unknown in terms of something known. Analogies most often use direct comparison to clarify a process or a difficult concept. An analogy can be developed in a single sentence; extended analogies can be developed over a paragraph or several paragraphs. The primary purpose of an analogy is to clarify.

> Just as a trained mechanic can listen to a ping in a car's engine and then diagnose and correct a problem, so too an experienced writer can reread an awkward sentence and know exactly where it goes wrong and what must be done to correct it.

Extended analogies usually begin and end with certain *cues,* or words that signal a reader that an analogy is about to be offered or concluded. Words that mark a transition to an analogy are *consider, by analogy,* and *just as.* The transition from analogy back to a main discussion is achieved with expressions like *similarly, just so, so too,* and *in the same way.* (See 6d-1 for use of analogies in building an argument.)

Just as with a simile and an analogy, a **metaphor** illustrates or intensifies something relatively unknown by comparison with something familiar. In the case of metaphor, however, the comparison is implicit: the thing or idea that is relatively unknown is spoken of in terms closely associated with a significant feature of the thing that is known. The key features of the "known" are attributed directly to the "unknown." In the expression *hand of time,* for instance, the abstract term *time* is given a physical attribute. *Like* and *as* or other signals of explicit comparison are not used in metaphors.

> In the mirror of his own death, each man would discover his individuality.
>
> —Philippe Ariès
> Historian

The metaphor suggests that contemplating death allows people to see themselves in revealing ways.

Metaphors are not restricted to poetry or academic writing; they are used everywhere in our daily speech when an abstract or unknown idea, thing, or activity is spoken of in terms associated with something else. When we say "round up everybody," we implicitly compare the activity to a cattle roundup. When we say "Walk the thin line between good and bad," we compare a moral dilemma to a tightrope act. By speaking of people who have been "jerked around" or "left hanging," we compare their general situation to those physical activities. At times, such metaphorical comparisons, if not well matched to the situation, can create more confusion for the reader than clarity.

2 Revise mixed metaphors.

Like all comparisons, metaphors need to match elements that can be compared logically (even if not explicitly). The metaphorical comparison must be consistent. Keep your language focused on a single metaphorical image throughout a sentence. Otherwise, you risk a **mixed metaphor,** which will stop your readers for a hearty laugh—at your expense. You would not, for instance, want to be the author of this.

| MIXED METAPHOR | This story weaves a web that herds characters and readers into the same camp. [The comparison mixes spider webs with cattle roundups.] |
| CONSISTENT | This story weaves a web that tangles characters and readers alike. |

3 Replace worn-out metaphors (clichés) with fresh figures.

In a famous essay, "Politics and the English Language," writer George Orwell warns against the *worn-out metaphor.*

A newly invented metaphor assists thought by evoking a visual image, while on the other hand a metaphor which is technically "dead" (e.g., *iron resolution*) has in effect reverted to being an ordinary word and can generally be used without loss of vividness. But in between these two classes there is a huge dump of worn-out metaphors which have lost all evocative power and are merely used because they save people the trouble of inventing phrases for themselves.

Orwell proceeds to offer his list of worn-out metaphors, which can also be termed **clichés**. These include *play into the hands of, no axe to grind, swan song,* and *hotbed.* These trite expressions, current when Orwell's essay was written in 1945, are with us still. Modern-day expressions that can be added to this list of clichés would include *the game of life, counting chickens before they hatch, water over the dam* or *under the bridge, crossing bridges,* and *burning bridges.* Work to create your own metaphors; keep them vivid; and keep them consistent.

EXERCISE 6

In a few sentences, use figurative language to describe the approach of a thunderstorm, the effect of a sunny morning on your mood, or the feeling of just having finished the last exam of a long and difficult semester.

21g   Eliminating biased, dehumanizing language

Language is a tool; just as tools can be used for building, so too they can be used to dismantle. You have heard and seen the words that insensitive people use to denigrate whole groups. Equally repugnant is language used to stereotype. In discussing the prevalence of crack cocaine in inner cities, the spread of AIDS, or the poverty endemic to certain areas of this country, some writers let creep into their language expressions such as *those people* or *they're the ones who . . .* or *can we really expect more from. . . .* Any language that explicitly or subtly characterizes an individual in terms of a group is potentially offensive. Writers must take care to avoid stereotyping.

Sexism in diction

Sexism in English is a particular problem when value judgments are linked with male or female reference. The issue can become a sensitive one in almost any sentence, since English has no gender-neutral pronoun in the third-person singular. Consider this sentence: *A doctor should wash _____ hands before examining a patient.* English demands that we choose the possessive pronoun *his* or *her* to complete this thought. Until recently, the designated "neutral" pronoun was usually masculine (*his*), but changing times have made this usage potentially offensive. It is obvious that women, along with men, are physicians, engineers, attorneys, construction workers, accountants, realtors, etc. Men, along with women,

REFERENCE

Nilsen, Don L. F. "Clichés, Trite Sayings, Dead Metaphors, and Stale Figures of Speech in Composition Instruction." *CCC* 27 (1976): 278–82. An exercise using clichés and dead metaphors can heighten students' appreciation of fresh figures of speech.

EXERCISE 6

Individual responses

FOR DISCUSSION

Few students should have trouble understanding why racial or ethnic slurs are offensive, but many still think the attention paid to sexist language is an overreaction. You may want to ask students if they've ever been in social or family situations where they've felt left out—perhaps they recall a family gathering at which conversation excluded the children, or they've felt ostracized at a party by the "in group." If they can make the analogy between these situations and the linguistic ostracism of women, they may be able to appreciate the move toward inclusive language. You also may want to ask what it means when you add a suffix or a qualifier to a word (*stewardess, woman doctor*)—the base word is the norm and the qualifier or suffix indicates an exception to the norm.

REFERENCES

Vardell, Sylvia M. " 'I'm No Lady Astronaut': Nonsexist Language for Tomorrow." Urbana: ERIC Clearinghouse on Reading and Communication Skills, 1985. ERIC ED 266 472. An extensive analysis of sexism in English, with suggestions for eliminating it.

Bolinger, Dwight. "A Case in Point: Sexism." *Language, the Loaded Weapon: The Use and Abuse of Language Today.* New York: Longman, 1980. 89–104. Evidence of the debasement of women in the English language abounds.

Miller, Casrey, and Kate Swift. *The Handbook of Non-Sexist Writing.* 2nd ed. New York: Harper, 1988. Sexism is inherent in the English language, but there are strategies for overcoming linguistic bias.

Cameron, Deborah. *Feminism and Linguistic Theory.* London: Macmillan, 1985. An extensive linguistic analysis of sexism in language, both explicit and implicit.

are elementary school teachers, nurses, cooks, tailors, receptionists, and secretaries. Given these circumstances, it is both offensive and inaccurate to imply by one's choice of a single pronoun that men or women, exclusively, inhabit one or another profession. (See 10c on gender pronouns.) Gender-offensive language can also be found in such expressions as chair*man*, *man*kind, *man*power, *mother*ing, etc. Reread late drafts of your writing to identify potentially gender-offensive language. Unless the context of a paragraph clearly calls for a gender-specific reference, follow the suggestions given in the box to avoid offending your readers.

Some Potentially Offensive Gender-Specific Nouns

Avoid: stewardess (and generally nouns ending with *-ess*)
Use: flight attendant

Avoid: chairman
Use: chair or chairperson

Avoid: woman driver; male nurse
Use: woman who was driving; driver; nurse; man on the nursing station

Avoid: mankind
Use: people; humanity; humankind

Avoid: workmen; manpower
Use: workers; work force; personnel

Avoid: the girl in the office
Use: the woman; the manager; the typist

Avoid: mothering
Use: parenting, nurturing

---

 1 **Rewrite gender-stereotyping nouns as neutral nouns.**

SEXIST   A cover letter, along with a résumé, should be sent to the *chairman* of the department. [The male suffix may be taken to imply that the writer expects this person to be male.]

NEUTRAL   A cover letter, along with a résumé, should be sent to the department *chair.*

SEXIST   *Man's* need to compete may be instinctive. [A generic male noun or pronoun referring to all of humanity is unacceptable.]

NEUTRAL   *The human* need to compete may be instinctive.

2 **Balance references to the sexes.**

SEXIST   The *men* and *girls* in the office contributed generously to the Christmas Fund. [A reference singling out females as children in an adult setting is demeaning.]

NEUTRAL   The *men* and *women* in the office contributed generously to the Christmas Fund. [In a school setting the reference might be to *boys* and *girls*.]

3 Make balanced use of plural and gender-specific pronouns.

See the Critical Decisions box in 10c for five strategies that will help you to correct gender problems with pronoun use.

SEXIST   A doctor should wash *his* hands before examining a patient. [Here the generic male pronoun implies that the writer expects most doctors to be male.]

NEUTRAL   *Doctors* should wash *their* hands before examining patients. [The plural strategy is used; see 10c.]

EXERCISE 7

Identify gender-offensive language in the following paragraph. Rewrite sentences in whatever way you feel is needed to make the gender references neutral.

> A teacher, like a parent, will maintain that she treats children fairly and equally regardless of their sex. Research demonstrates, however, that in practice a teacher typically interacts differently with her female and boy students. In elementary school, for example, a teacher routinely practices sex segregation in her classroom—e.g., by seating girls together and young men together; by having girls and young men form separate lines; and by organizing team competitions, such as spelling bees, by sex. At the other end of academic life, in college, girls—especially minorities—have few same-sex role models and mentors available to them on the faculty and administration. In the classroom, a professor will call on his male students more often than on girls and will interrupt girls more. Sexism, overt and covert, persists beyond college: in the workplace, in the home, and in the political arena.

21h Avoiding euphemistic and pretentious language

Sometimes writers betray an anxious, condescending, or self-inflated attitude through their word choices. These attitudes may arise from a variety of motives, but the result is almost always a loss of clear expression.

1 Restrict the use of euphemisms.

The **euphemism** is a polite rewording of a term that the writer feels will offend readers. Invariably, euphemisms are longer than the words

EXERCISE 7

Suggested revision:

Teachers, like parents, will maintain that they treat children fairly and equally regardless of their sex. Research demonstrates, however, that in practice a teacher typically interacts differently with female and male students. In elementary school, for example, a teacher routinely practices sex segregation in the classroom—e.g., by seating girls together and boys together; by having girls and boys form separate lines; and by organizing team competitions, such as spelling bees, by sex. At the other end of academic life, in college, women—especially minorities—have few same-sex role models and mentors available to them on the faculty and administration. In the classroom, a professor will call on male students more often than on females and will interrupt females more. Sexism, overt and covert, persists beyond college—in the workplace, in the home, and in the political arena.

GROUP ACTIVITY

Ask groups to compose a paragraph filled with euphemism and pretentious language. Not only will students have a good time doing it, but they'll also recognize how silly such language sounds. After the groups have completed the task, you may even want to have a contest to see which is the most outrageous paragraph.

REFERENCES

COE, RICHARD M. "Public Doublespeak—Let's Stop It." *English Quarterly* 19 (1986): 236–38. The variety of euphemism called "doublespeak" presents a danger that English teachers should address.

ENRIGHT, D. J., ed. *Fair of Speech: The Uses of Euphemism.* Oxford: Oxford UP, 1985. A collection of essays on the history, variety, and uses of euphemisms in the language.

they replace and by definition are less direct: instead of *dead* or *died*, you will find *passed on, passed away, mortally wounded.* You may also find these clichés: *kicked the bucket, bit the dust, didn't make it, met his/her Maker, caught the Last Train, went to the Great Beyond,* and so on. If you are concerned about using expressions that might offend readers, create a context within a sentence or paragraph that may soften a potentially harsh word choice.

EUPHEMISM	No one wanted to tell the child that his dog had gone to the Great Beyond.
REVISED	Breaking the news to the child that his dog had died was very painful.

In nonacademic writing, use discretion in selecting a euphemism. Debate with yourself your use of language and then make your choice.

2 Eliminate pretentious language.

Pretentious language is unnecessarily ornate, puffed-up with its own self-importance, and suggests a writer concerned more with image than with clear communication. See 17a-6 as well as 17a-2 and 4 on eliminating wordiness. Pretentious writers will often choose the windy version of everyday expressions that seem too common.

Pretentious	*Direct*
It appears to me that	I believe
In the final analysis	In conclusion
The individual who . . .	The person who . . .
utilize	use
demonstrate	show
functionality	function

Because many topics you will study are complex and technical, you should expect to encounter new and difficult vocabularies in your college career. In specialized areas of study, you will find that writers need technical terms to communicate precisely. Writing that requires specialized terms is very different from pretentious writing that is calculated to bolster a writer's ego. In your own work, you can distinguish between a legitimate technical term and a pretentious one by being both a concise and a precise writer.

Adhering to these two principles—the one helping you to cut wordiness and the other helping you to maintain precision—should make you aware of pretentious language, which can *always* be cut from a sentence.

PRETENTIOUS LANGUAGE	The Australian subcontinent was regarded by the leaders of the British policy-making establishment as the site of penal colonies that could optimize the expressed desire to rid the British Isles of its criminal elements.
DIRECT LANGUAGE	British politicians believed that they could resolve problems of crime at home by transporting criminals to penal colonies in Australia.

SPECIALIZED LANGUAGE
(NO REVISION NEEDED)

Index futures differ from other futures contracts in that they are not based on any underlying commodity or financial instrument that can be delivered; therefore, there is no cash market associated with them.

This passage on "index futures" comes from a book on investing. Students of finance would understand, or would be expected to understand, the terms *index futures, futures contracts, commodity, financial instrument,* and *cash market.* None of the words in this legitimately technical passage is calculated to bolster the writer's ego, as was the case in the preceding example.

Distinguishing Pretentious Language from Legitimate Technical Language

Bear in mind two principles when attempting to eliminate pretentious language:

- **Be concise:** Use as few words as possible to communicate clearly. Delete whole sentences or reduce them to phrases that you incorporate into other sentences; reduce phrases to single words; choose briefer words over longer ones. (See 17a for a full discussion of conciseness.)

- **Be precise:** Make sure your sentences communicate your *exact* meaning. If you need to add clarifying words, add as few words as possible. Use technical language for precision only when no other language will do.

EXERCISE 8

The following speech was generated by a computer as an example of empty political rhetoric. The professors of speech communication who programmed the computer with a list of set phrases had been alarmed by the growing dominance of style over substance in American political discourse. In the paragraphs of the speech excerpted here, identify what you feel are examples of euphemisms, clichés, and pretentious language. Find other samples of writing, perhaps from a current newspaper, and conduct a similar analysis.

The Middle East is again in a no-war, no-peace stalemate and is likely to remain so for some time. Step-by-step diplomacy, treating all parties with an even hand, is the only means for maintaining a delicate peace in the Middle East.

The United States must ground its China policy in morality. We should work to improve our relationships with her. The People's Republic of China is a sovereign state, but we must not forget to support our ally, The Republic of China, on Taiwan. I believe both governments can learn to live with the reality of each other.

ADDITIONAL EXERCISE C

Revise the following passage by eliminating pretentious language.

In point of fact, if any given individual of the male gender is to be in possession of respect for his essential self, then that individual, it would seem apparent, must hold knowledge of his talents or capabilities. Thus, one might be in agreement with the contention that of primary importance to the individual desirous of a self that can be the object of respect would be a full-fledged assessment of areas in which the individual exhibits strengths as well as those in which the individual reveals weaknesses. The individual in question is, by and large, in an exceedingly unlikely position to fall prey to confusion with regard to an overdeveloped sense of ego as opposed to a more genuine and valid appreciation for the true nature of the self if, in fact, that individual is in a state of comprehension regarding the essence of his being.

Suggested response:

If a man is to respect himself, he must know his talents and capabilities. An assessment of his strengths and weaknesses, then, should be a primary goal of the man seeking self-respect. A man is far less likely to confuse egotism with self-respect if he knows who he is.

EXERCISE 8

Representative responses:

Euphemisms: *a delicate peace; learn to live with the reality of each other.*

Clichés: *for some time; step-by-step; with an even hand; sovereign state.*

Pretentious language: *ground its China policy in morality.*

CHAPTER 22

Dictionaries and Vocabulary

KEY FEATURES

This chapter takes the historical approach to vocabulary, noting that language is a living, growing entity in a constant state of flux. Thus the contribution of dictionaries is established: they provide us not only with spellings and definitions for words, but also with roots, usage labels, and etymology, among other things. The introduction to dictionary use is thorough, drawing a clear distinction between the functions of abridged and unabridged dictionaries, and acquainting students with other types of dictionaries as well, such as specialized dictionaries, dictionaries of synonyms, and discipline-specific dictionaries. Throughout these sections examples are abundant and clearly explained. Exercises provide students with the opportunity to familiarize themselves with several kinds of dictionaries. The chapter addresses vocabulary in the context of language learning in general, admonishing students against rote vocabulary learning in favor of developing a vocabulary through encounters with new words. The advice in this section is practical: students learn how to make educated guesses about word meanings on the basis of roots, prefixes, suffixes, and context. Exercises provide practice in using strategies for making educated guesses and for consulting dictionaries. The chapter ends with guidelines for building a personal vocabulary file.

ESL EXERCISE

Look up the word *foreign* and make a list of synonyms. Discuss with your classmates how these words differ in connotations from each other and from the corresponding words in other languages. Then contrast the connotations of the most positive synonym with the connotations of the most negative synonym to illustrate the differences between them.

A living language is continually evolving; it is always shifting and changing; it is flexible and yet precise. English is just such a language. Two thousand years ago nobody spoke English; it did not exist. Today, in the last decade of the twentieth century, it is the first truly global language, more widely spoken and written than any language has ever been. English originally spread through British imperialism to such countries as the United States, Canada, Australia, New Zealand, India, and various African and Caribbean nations. But the demise of the British Empire in no way signaled the demise of English as an international language. Rather, as the novelist Salman Rushdie notes, "English, no longer an *English* language, now grows from many roots; and those whom it once colonized are carving out large territories within the language for themselves. The Empire is striking back." At the same time, the cultural dominance of American English, the international language of multinational corporations, science and technology, rock music, Hollywood films, television, and mass consumerism continues to further the dissemination of English world-wide.[1]

USING DICTIONARIES

The emergence of English as a constantly changing global language raises the question of what constitutes "English" and/or the various Englishes. It is the job, indeed often the life work, of the editors and compilers of dictionaries to help readers understand the most current usages of words in the language. The dictionary will tell you what forms and meanings have become widely used or are in restricted use. On the basis of this information, you must decide which forms and meanings are most precisely suited to your purpose. In the next sections you will find descriptions of what is included in a typical dictionary entry, followed by descriptions of the abridged and unabridged dictionaries which have best met the dual challenge of currency and comprehensiveness.

---

[1] This introduction is based on chapter 1, pages 19–48, of *The Story of English* by Robert McCrum, William Cran, and Robert MacNeil (New York: Elisabeth Sifton Books/Viking, 1986).

22a   Exploring dictionaries of the English language

Dictionaries give us far more than a list of words and their meanings. They not only define a given word, but also provide a brief description of its etymology, spelling, division, as well as pronunciation, and related words and forms. Here is a typical set of entries:

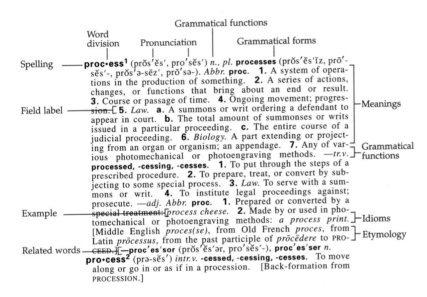

ADDITIONAL EXERCISE A

In order to get a rudimentary sense of the history of modern English, find an English "family tree" in an unabridged dictionary, and trace modern English back to its origins. In reverse order, list all of the other languages that evolved into modern English. List also the other modern languages that are "cousins" of English.

Answers:

Modern English, Middle English, Old English, West Germanic, Germanic, Indo-European. "Cousins" are Dutch, Afrikaans, Low German, German Yiddish, and Frisian.

REFERENCE

Markwardt, Albert H. "Dictionaries and the English Language." Rpt. in *Introductory Readings on Language.* Ed. Wallace L. Anderson and Norman Stageberg. New York: Holt, 1970. 114–28. A discussion of the two forms of dictionaries, the prescriptive (e.g., Johnson) and descriptive (e.g., OED).

1   Understanding standard entry information in dictionaries

Most dictionary entries include more information on words than many people expect. In a typical entry you can find:

- *Spelling* (including variations, especially British versus American spellings—see chapter 23 for more on rules of spelling)
- *Word division* indicating syllabication and where a word should be divided, if necessary
- *Pronunciation* (including variations)
- *Grammatical functions* (parts of speech)
- *Grammatical forms* (plurals, principal parts of irregular verbs, other irregular forms)
- *Etymology* (a given word's history/derivation)
- *Meanings* (arranged according to either currency or frequency of use, or earliest to most recent use)
- *Examples* of the word in context

- *Related words; synonyms* and *antonyms*
- *Usage labels* (see 22a-2)
- *Field labels* (for words that have discipline-specific meanings)
- *Idioms* that include the word

2   Usage labels

Usage refers to how, where, and when a word has been used in speech and writing. When preparing papers in an academic or business setting, use formal English as a standard (see 21e). That is, use words not otherwise labeled as nonstandard. There are several such nonstandard labels to be aware of. When you see the label *slang* assigned to the entry *prof*, for instance, the dictionary is indicating that in standard, formal English usage that word is not accepted. Aware of this *restriction* on the word, you would probably choose not to use it in formal writing. There are other categories of restricted usage, and these are generally listed and explained in the front matter of most dictionaries:

- *Colloquial:* used conversationally and in informal writing
- *Slang:* in-group, informal language; not standard
- *Obsolete:* not currently used (but may be found in earlier writing)
- *Archaic:* not commonly used; more common in earlier writing
- *Dialect:* restricted geographically or to social or ethnic groups; used only in certain places with certain groups
- *Poetic, literary:* used in literature rather than everyday speech

EXERCISE 1

Consult your dictionary to answer the following questions about grammatical function.

1. Which of the following nouns can be used as verbs: *process, counsel, dialogue, hamper, instance*?
2. How do you make these nouns plural: *annals, humanity, armor, accountancy, deer, analysis, medium, sister-in-law, knife*?
3. What are the principal parts of these verbs: *hang, begin, break, forbid, rise, set*?
4. What are the comparative and superlative forms of these adverbs and adjectives: *unique, bad, mere, initial, playful*?

EXERCISE 2

Using two different dictionaries, list and comment on the usage restrictions that are recorded for the following words:

1. awesome   3. celebrate   5. ere
2. mews   4. groovy   6. flunk

    Example: ain't

    Webster's New Collegiate Dictionary (Springfield, MA: G. & C. Merriam, 1974)

EXERCISE 1

1. process, counsel, hamper
2. annals, humanities, armors, accountancies, deer, analyses, media, sisters-in-law, knives
3. hang hung hung hanging hangs *or*
   hang hanged hanged hanging hangs
   begin began begun beginning begins
   break broke broken breaking breaks
   forbid forbade forbidden forbidding forbids
   rise rose risen rising rises
   set set set setting sets
4. _____ (*unique* is an absolute term)
   bad, worse, worst
   __ , merest
   _____ (*initial* is an absolute term)
   playful, more playful, most playful

EXERCISE 2

Responses depend on dictionary being used.

though disapproved by many and more common in less educated speech, used orally in most parts of the U.S. by many educated speakers esp. in the phrase *ain't I*

The American Heritage Dictionary, 2nd College Edition (Boston: Houghton Mifflin, 1982)

> *Ain't* has acquired such a stigma over the years that it is beyond rehabilitation, even though it would serve a useful function as a contraction for *am not* and even though its use as an alternate form for *isn't, hasn't, aren't,* and *haven't* has a good historical justification. In questions, the variant *aren't I* is acceptable in speech to a majority of the Usage Panel, but in writing there is no generally acceptable substitute for the stilted *am I not.*

Comment: *The American Heritage Dictionary* is clearly sympathetic to the word but seems resigned (even disappointed!) that *ain't* will never be acceptable as a standard word in the language. *Webster's* makes a class distinction between the "educated" and "less educated" and seems elitist about the word's usage.

22b   Choosing a dictionary

Because the English language is constantly changing and is used in so many environments around the world, no dictionary can ever claim to be the final authority on every possible current meaning or correct usage for the words it lists. A dictionary's authority rests mainly on its attempt to be reasonably comprehensive and linguistically accurate in recording the most frequently used meanings of a word. Dictionaries further try to be as balanced as possible in recording the kind of usage and the restrictions on usage that have been observed for each meaning. In addition, dictionaries record a time dimension for changes in meaning: some list the earliest meanings on record first, moving on to the more recent; others reverse the sequence to start with contemporary meanings. All dictionaries record the basic categories of information shown in the previous section.

1   Comparing abridged dictionaries

The most convenient and commonly used dictionaries in households, businesses, and schools are called "abridged"—or shortened. They do not try to be as exhaustive or complete as the "unabridged" dictionaries (described in 22b-2). An abridged dictionary tries to give as much information as possible in one portable volume. You will find that several dictionaries claim the name *Webster's,* after the early American lexicographer Noah Webster. Since his name is in the public domain and is not copyrighted, it appears in the titles of a number of dictionaries with vary-

TEACHING IDEAS

For two reasons it would be worthwhile for you to choose an abridged dictionary for the entire class to use: (1) It ensures consistency as students do these exercises and consult the dictionary for other reasons, and (2) It ensures that students have a dictionary *to* consult.

TEACHING IDEAS

If your library is equipped with a variety of abridged dictionaries, you may want to use the following activity to acquaint students with their use: Ask students, in teams perhaps, to examine two abridged dictionaries (not on the list here) in the library. They can then report to the class on the features of the dictionaries, offering advice on which is preferable. This exercise may even be used in order to decide on a dictionary for the class to use.

ing characteristics. The following list includes only some of the more widely used abridged dictionaries.[2]

The American Heritage Dictionary, 3rd ed. (Houghton Mifflin, 1992) includes about 200,000 entries. It differs from most other dictionaries in that it presents the most contemporary meaning of a word first, rather than proceeding historically. Guidance to good usage is provided by extensive usage-context indicators and "Usage Notes" which reflect the opinions of a panel of usage experts. The dictionary contains many photographs, illustrations, and maps. Foreign words and the names of mythological and legendary figures appear in the regular listings, while biographical and geographical entries and abbreviations are listed in the back.

The Concise Oxford Dictionary of Current English (Oxford University Press, 1982) is the briefest of the abridged dictionaries listed here. It is based on the work for the unabridged *Oxford English Dictionary* (see 22b-2) and includes current usage and illustrative quotations, scientific and technical terms, many colloquial and slang expressions, and both British and American spellings. There are no illustrations, and little front or back matter.

The Random House College Dictionary (Random House, 1975) is based on the unabridged *Random House Dictionary of the English Language* (see 22b-2). The dictionary contains about 155,000 entries, and it lists the most common usage of a word first. It indicates informal and slang usage and synonyms and antonyms, and lists recent technical words along with biographical and geographical names as part of its main entries. A manual of style is included as part of its back matter.

Webster's Ninth New Collegiate Dictionary (G. & C. Merriam, 1989) is based on *Webster's Third New International Dictionary of the English Language* (see 22b-2) and includes some 160,000 entries emphasizing "standard language." Labels indicating usage occur less frequently than in other desk dictionaries. Entries give full etymologies followed by definitions in chronological order, with the most recent meaning listed last. It includes extensive notes on synonyms and illustrative quotations. Foreign words and phrases, biographical and geographical names, and a manual of style are listed separately as back matter.

Webster's New World Dictionary of the American Language (Simon & Schuster, 1982) has a contemporary American emphasis and uses a star to indicate Americanisms—words that first became part of the

---

[2] The descriptions of abridged, unabridged, and discipline-specific dictionaries that follow are adapted from entries in Eugene Sheehy, *Guide to Reference Books,* 10th ed. (Chicago: American Library Association, 1986); Diane Wheeler Strauss, *Handbook of Business Information: A Guide for Librarians, Students and Researchers* (Englewood, CO: Libraries Unlimited, Inc., 1988); and Bohdan Wynar, *ARBA Guide to Subject Encyclopedias and Dictionaries* (Littleton, CO: Libraries Unlimited, 1986).

language in the United States. Definitions are listed in chronological order, with the earliest first, and extensive etymologies, synonyms, and usages are provided. Proper names, place names, abbreviations, and foreign phrases are included in the main listings.

EXERCISE 3

Look up the following words in one of the abridged dictionaries listed above. How many different meanings does each word have? From observing older meanings versus the more current meanings, how would you describe the overall shifts in meaning that some words have undergone over time?

1. immure
2. junk
3. obnoxious
4. heroic
5. luster
6. hide

2   Comparing unabridged dictionaries

The compilers of unabridged dictionaries attempt to be exhaustive both in recounting the history of a word and in describing its various usages. For quick reference—to check spelling, meaning, or commonplace usage, an abridged dictionary will serve you well. But when you are puzzled by or otherwise curious about a word and its history (for instance, if you want to know the route by which the word *farm* has made its way into the language), you will want to consult an unabridged dictionary where the principle for compiling an entry is *thoroughness*.

The second edition of *The Oxford English Dictionary* (Oxford: Clarendon Press), prepared by J. A. Simpson and E. S. C. Weiner, was published in 1989 and includes the text of the first edition (1933), the *Supplement* (1972–1986), and almost 5,000 new entries for a total of more than 500,000 words. It is the great dictionary of the English language, arranged chronologically to show the history of every word from the date of its entry into the language to its most recent usage, supported by almost two million quotations from the works of more than 5,000 authors since 1150. The *O.E.D.* is an invaluable source for scholars.

The Random House Dictionary of the English Language (Random House, 1987) is considerably briefer than the other unabridged dictionaries listed here, though it is particularly current, and includes extensive usage notes. The back matter includes several foreign word lists and an atlas with colored maps.

Webster's Third New International Dictionary of the English Language (G. & C. Merriam, 1986) includes about 450,000 entries, with special attention to new scientific and technical terms. The third edition of 1986 emphasizes the language as currently used (though entries are arranged chronologically, with the earliest uses first), with a descriptive approach to usage, construction, and punctuation. Many obsolete and rare words have been dropped. Although the third

EXERCISE 3

Responses depend on the dictionary being used.

GROUP ACTIVITY

Unabridged dictionaries are fascinating places to visit. Assign each group a specific unabridged dictionary that's in your library. (Depending on the size of your class and the number of dictionaries in the library, some dictionaries will be investigated by more than one group.) The group's task is simply to find out how many kinds of information—aside from the standard syllabication, pronunciation, and definition—can be found in the dictionary. Remind students to look not only at sample entries, but at front and rear appendices as well. Groups can then report to the class on what can be found in these dictionaries.

edition is widely used as a descriptive standard, some scholars prefer the more prescriptive approach of the second edition of 1959. Most college students will find that the third edition meets their needs and is convenient to use.

EXERCISE 4

Individual responses

EXERCISE 4

Choose two of the words you looked up in Exercise 3 and compare what you found with the entry for the same word in an unabridged dictionary, preferably *The Oxford English Dictionary.* Briefly characterize the history of each word, explaining how its meaning has shifted over time.

22c Using specialized dictionaries of English

Abridged and unabridged dictionaries of the English language can provide you with a wealth of general information about language. However, there will be times when you will need to consult a specialized dictionary which focuses on a specific kind of word or language information, such as slang, etymologies, synonyms, antonyms, and accepted usage. The following are some particularly useful specialized dictionaries.

1 Dictionaries of usage

When your questions regarding the usage of a word are not adequately addressed in a standard dictionary, consult one of the following dictionaries of usage:

> *A Dictionary of Contemporary American Usage,* ed. Bergen Evans and Cornelia Evans
>
> *Dictionary of Modern English Usage,* ed. H. W. Fowler
>
> *Dictionary of American-English Usage,* ed. Margaret Nicholson
>
> *Modern American Usage,* ed. Jacques Barzun

2 Dictionaries of synonyms

Dictionaries that present synonyms of words can be a great help for writers wanting to expand vocabulary. A caution, though: while synonyms have approximately the same denotation, their connotations (or nuances of meaning) differ. Before using a synonym, be sure that you thoroughly understand its connotation (see also 22e-3).

> *Webster's Dictionary of Synonyms*
>
> *The New Roget's Thesaurus of the English Language in Dictionary Form*

3 Other specialized dictionaries

The dictionaries listed here are specialized sources for the historical and social dimensions of word use.

Dictionaries of origins/etymologies

The information on word origins in basic dictionaries can be pursued in more detail in the following specialized references.

Dictionary of Word and Phrase Origins, ed. William Morris and Mary Morris

The Oxford Dictionary of English Etymology, ed. C. T. Onions

Origins: A Short Etymological Dictionary of Modern English, ed. Eric Partridge

Dictionaries of slang and idioms

Many terms omitted or given only brief notice in basic dictionaries are described in great detail in slang dictionaries.

The New Dictionary of American Slang, ed. Robert Chapman

Dictionary of Slang and Unconventional English, ed. Eric Partridge

Dictionary of American Slang, ed. Harold Wentworth and Stuart Berg Flexner

Dictionaries of regionalism or foreign terms

The *Dictionary of American Regional English,* compiled by linguist Frederic Cassidy, is the standard work on regional and dialect expressions in America.

Dictionary of American Regional English, ed. Frederic Cassidy

Dictionary of Foreign Phrases and Abbreviations, ed. Kevin Guinagh. 3rd ed.

Dictionary of Foreign Terms, ed. Mario Pei and Savatore Ramondino

Harper Dictionary of Foreign Terms, ed. C. O. Sylvester Mawson and Charles Berlitz. 3rd ed.

EXERCISE 5

Look up the following words in a dictionary of usage and a dictionary of origins. Based on information you find out about the meanings, origins, and uses of each word from these specialized sources, characterize the kind of writing or the kind of audience for which each term seems most appropriate.

1. awesome   3. celebrate   5. ere
2. mews   4. groovy   6. flunk

BUILDING VOCABULARY

You will need a good vocabulary to understand discussions in texts and to follow lectures. As you move from discipline to discipline, vocabularies will change: you will, in effect, learn new languages. As a writer,

REFERENCES

SCHWEIK, ROBERT, and DIETER RIESNER. *Reference Sources in English and American Literature: An Annotated Bibliography.* New York: Norton, 1977. Section XXII. "Dictionaries." A comprehensive list of specialized dictionaries.

SLEDD, JAMES, and WILMA R. EBBITT. *Dictionaries and That Dictionary.* Chicago, Scott, 1962. The usage policy of *Webster's Third New International Dictionary of the English Language* spurred controversy, much of it covered here.

EXERCISE 5

Suggested responses:

1. Standard American English or as current slang among young people.
2. Standard British English or for specialists referring to caged birds.
3. Standard American English or referring to a religious ceremony.
4. Sixties slang.
5. Formal, pretentious, or poetic language.
6. Current slang among young people.

you will need a good vocabulary to help you write precisely. This said, you should realize that *vocabulary power* alone, notwithstanding the promises of correspondence courses, does not a writer make. A modest but precise vocabulary will suffice in most cases, so long as you use it in sentences that are structured well, in paragraphs that are coherent, and in essays and reports that show a careful development of ideas. Vocabulary does not exist independently from any of these elements.

22d Learning root words, prefixes, and suffixes

Where applicable, the editors of college dictionaries will place in square brackets [ ] abbreviations of languages from which words are derived. Some of the abbreviations (and their spelled out versions) include: *F,* French; *Gk,* Greek; *LL,* Late Latin; *L,* Latin; *Heb,* Hebrew; *ME,* Middle English; *Dan,* Danish; *D,* Dutch; *G,* German; *LG,* Low German; *Flem,* Flemish; *Ital,* Italian; *OW,* Old Welsh; *Span,* Spanish; *Skt,* Sanskrit; and *OPer,* Old Persian. There are more than 100 languages from which the half-million words of English are derived. Modern words are often variants of earlier forms that have snaked their way through history, changing outward appearances for different peoples at different times—though retaining a recognizable core or root. The study of the history of words is called **etymology.** In the square brackets of dictionary entries you will usually find either the abbreviation **fr.** or the symbol <, meaning *derived from.*

Once a word enters the language, its core or *root* is often used as the basis of other words that are formed with *prefixes* and *suffixes*—letters coming before, or after, the root. When you can recognize root words, prefixes, and suffixes, often you will be able to understand the meaning of a new word without checking a dictionary.

EXERCISE 6

Using two unabridged dictionaries, research the etymology of a word. In four or five sentences, trace the word's use over time.

1 Becoming familiar with root words

A root anchors a plant or tree in the ground and provides a structural and nutritional base from which it can grow. The **root** of a word anchors it in language, providing a base from which meaning is built. When you encounter an unfamiliar word, try identifying its root; with help from the context of the surrounding sentence, you can often infer an appropriate definition. Consider the following sentence:

Beautiful and *beauteous* are paronymous words.

You have come upon an unfamiliar word, *paronymous.* You might say: "This reminds me of another word—*anonymous.*" Immediately, you sense that the similar sounding words share a root: *nymous*. You know that *anonymous* means "having an unknown name." It is not so tremendous a leap to conclude that the root *nymous* means *name*. Now you examine the sentence once more and make an educated guess, or inference. What do the words *beautiful* and *beauteous* have to do with *names*? The words themselves tell you—that they are built upon a single name: *beauty*. If you guessed that *paronymous* means "derived from the same word (or root)," you would be correct.

Whether you know a root word or make an educated guess about its meaning, your analysis will aid reading comprehension and, in the process, will improve your vocabulary. Many of the root words in English come from Latin and Greek. The following box contains a small sample of root words.

ADDITIONAL EXERCISE B

ACROSS THE CURRICULUM Make three photocopies each of passages from one of your textbooks. (The additional photocopies will be used for subsequent exercises.) Underline all words with roots recognizable from the box in 22d, and identify the language of the root. From which language do most of the roots seem to be taken? Based on your understanding of the discipline, why do you think this is so? Compare your findings to those of other students using textbooks from different disciplines. What are the similarities between disciplines? the differences?

Common Root Words

Root	Definition	Example
acus [Latin]	needle	acute, acumen
basis [Greek]	step, base	base, basis, basement, basic
bio- [Greek]	life	biography, biology, bionic
cognoscere [Latin]	to know	recognize, cognizant, cognition
ego [Latin]	I	ego, egocentric, egotistical
fleure [Latin]	flow	flow, fluid, effluence
grandis [Latin]	large	grandiose, aggrandize
graphein [Greek]	to write	graph, graphic
hypnos [Greek]	sleep	hypnosis, hypnotic
hydro [Greek]	water	hydraulic, dehydrate
jur, jus [Latin]	law	jury, justice
lumen [Latin]	light	illuminate, luminary
manu- [Latin]	hand	manage, management, manual, manipulate
mare [Latin]	sea	marine, marinate, marina, marinara
matr- [Latin]	mother	maternal, matrilineal
pathos [Greek]	suffering	empathy, sympathy
patr- [Latin]	father	paternal, patriarch
polis [Greek]	city	metropolis, police
primus [Latin]	first	primitive, prime, primary
psych [Greek]	soul	psychological, psyche
sentire [Latin]	to feel	sentiment, sentimental, sentient, sense, sensitive
scrib, script [Latin]	to write	describe, manuscript
sol [Latin]	sun	solstice, solar, solarium
solvere [Latin]	to release	solve, resolve, solution, dissolve, solvent
tele [Greek]	distant	telegraph, telemetry
therm [Greek]	heat	thermal, thermos
truncus [Latin]	trunk	trunk, trench, trenchant
veritas [Latin]	truth	verity, verify, veritable
vocare [Latin]	to call	vocal, vocation, avocation

ADDITIONAL EXERCISE C

Using the second photocopy from Additional Exercise B, circle all of the prefixes. (Use the chart in 22d-2 as your guide.) How dependent is the text on words with prefixes? What prefixes, if any, seem to predominate? Compare your findings to those of other students using textbooks from different disciplines. What are the similarities between disciplines? the differences?

2 **Recognizing prefixes**

A **prefix**—letters joined to the beginning of a root word to qualify or add to its meaning—illustrates its own definition: the root *fix* comes from the Latin *fixus,* meaning "to fasten"; *pre* is a prefix, also from Latin, meaning "before." The prefix joined to a root creates a new word, the meaning of which is "to place before." Recognizing prefixes can help you isolate root words. The prefix and the root, considered together, will allow you to infer a meaning. Prefixes can indicate number, size, status, negation, and relations in time and space. The following are some frequently used prefixes.

Prefixes indicating number

Prefix	Meaning	Example
uni-	one	unison, unicellular
bi-	two	bimonthly, bicentennial, bifocal
tri-	three	triangle, triumvirate
multi-	many, multiple	multiply, multifaceted
omni-	all, universally	omnivorous, omniscient
poly-	many, several	polytechnic, polygon

Prefixes indicating size

Prefix	Meaning	Example
micro-	very small	microscopic, microcosm
macro-	very large	macroeconomics
mega-	great	megalomania, megalith

Prefixes indicating status or condition

Prefix	Meaning	Example
hyper-	beyond, super	hyperactive, hypercritical
neo-	new	neonate, neophyte
para-	akin to	parachute, paramilitary
pseudo-	false	pseudoscience, pseudonym
quasi-	in some sense	quasi-official, quasi-public

Prefixes indicating negation

Prefix	Meaning	Example
anti-	against	antibiotic, antidote, anticlimax
counter-	contrary	counterintuitive, counterfeit
dis-	to do the opposite	disable, dislodge, disagree
mal-	bad, abnormal, inadequate	maladjusted, malformed, malcontent, malapropism
mis-	bad, wrong	misinform, mislead, misnomer
non-	not, reverse of	noncompliance, nonalcoholic, nonconformist, nonessential

Prefixes indicating spatial relations

Prefix	Meaning	Example
circum-	around	circumspect, circumscribe
inter-	between	intercede, intercept
intra-	within	intravenous, intramural
intro-	inside	introvert, intrude

Prefixes indicating relations of time

Prefix	Meaning	Example
ante-	before	antecedent, anterior
paleo-	ancient	Paleolithic, paleography
post-	after	postdate, postwar, posterior
proto-	first	protohuman, prototype

3 Analyzing suffixes

A **suffix**—letters joined to the end of a word or a root—will change a word's grammatical function. Observe how with suffixes a writer can give a verb the forms of a noun, adjective, and adverb.

VERB	impress
NOUN	impression
ADJECTIVE	impressive
ADVERB	impressively

The following are some frequently used suffixes.

Noun-forming suffixes

Verb	+	Suffix	(Meaning)	=	Noun
betray		-al	(process of)		betrayal
participate		-ant	(one who)		participant
play		-er	(one who)		player
construct		-ion	(process of)		construction
conduct		-or	(one who)		conductor

Noun	+	Suffix	(Meaning)	=	Noun
parson		-age	(house of)		parsonage
king		-dom	(office, realm)		kingdom
sister		-hood	(state, condition of)		sisterhood
strategy		-ist	(one who)		strategist
Armenia		-n	(belonging to)		Armenian
master		-y	(quality)		mastery

Adjective	+	Suffix	(Meaning)	=	Noun
pure		-ity	(state, quality of)		purity
gentle		-ness	(quality of, degree)		gentleness
active		-ism	(act, practice of)		activism

ADDITIONAL EXERCISE D

Using the second photocopy from Additional Exercise B, circle all of the suffixes. (Use the chart in 22d-3 as your guide.) How dependent is the text on words with suffixes? What suffixes, if any, seem to predominate? Compare your findings to those of other students using textbooks from different disciplines. What are the similarities between disciplines? the differences?

Verb-forming suffixes

Noun	+	Suffix	(Meaning)	=	Verb
substance		-ate	(cause to become)		substantiate
code		-ify	(cause to become)		codify
serial		-ize	(cause to become)		serialize
Adjective	+	*Suffix*	*(Meaning)*	=	*Verb*
sharp		-en	(cause to become)		sharpen

Adjective-forming suffixes

Noun	+	Suffix	(Meaning)	=	Adjective
region		-al	(of, relating to)		regional
claim		-ant	(performing, being)		claimant
substance		-ial	(of, relating to)		substantial
response		-ible	(capable of, fit for)		responsible
history		-ic	(form of, being)		historic
Kurd		-ish	(of, relating to)		Kurdish
response		-ive	(tends toward)		responsive
Verb	+	*Suffix*	*(Meaning)*	=	*Adjective*
credit		-able	(capable of)		creditable
abort		-ive	(tends toward)		abortive

EXERCISE 7

To be checked in the dictionary

ADDITIONAL EXERCISE E

Add a prefix and/or a suffix to each of the following words, and then write each new word in a sentence:

1. comfort
2. attend
3. impose
4. direct
5. lone

Possible new words:

1. comforting, comfortable, discomfort
2. attendance, attendant, attention
3. superimpose, imposing
4. direction, misdirected, directory
5. lonely, alone

EXERCISE 7

Identify and initially define, without using a dictionary, the roots, prefixes, and suffixes of the following sets of words. Then check your definitions against dictionary entries.

1. photometry
   photogenic
   photograph
   photoelectric

2. excise
   concise
   precise
   incisive

3. conduce
   reduce
   deduce
   produce

4. optometrist
   optician
   ophthalmologist
   optical

5. discourse
   recourse

6. diverge
   converge

7. convert
   pervert
   revert

8. tenable
   tenacious
   retain

9. memoir
   remember

10. remorse
    morsel

22e

Strategies for building a vocabulary

1 Use contextual clues and dictionaries.

In college, you will spend a great deal of your time reading, and reading provides the best opportunities for expanding your vocabulary.

When a new word resists your analysis of root and affix (prefix or suffix), reach for a dictionary or let the context of a sentence provide clues to meaning. Contextual clues will often let you read a passage and infer fairly accurate definitions of new words—accurate enough to give you the sense of a passage. Indeed, using a dictionary to look up *every* new word in the name of thoroughness can so fragment a reading that you will frustrate—not aid—your attempts to understand. Focus first on the ideas of an entire passage; circle or otherwise highlight new words, especially repeated words. Then, if the context has not revealed the meaning, reach for your dictionary.

In the passage that follows, possibly unfamiliar vocabulary is set in italics. Do not stop at these words. Note them, but then complete your reading of these paragraphs from an astronomy text by George O. Abell:

> Let us once again compare the *propagation* of light to the propagation of ocean waves. While an ocean wave travels forward, the water itself is *displaced* only in a *vertical* direction. A stick of wood floating in the water merely bobs up and down as the waves move along the surface of the water. Waves that propagate with this kind of motion are called *transverse* waves.
>
> Light also *propagates* with a transverse wave motion, and travels with its highest possible speed through a *perfect vacuum*. In this respect light differs markedly from sound, which is a physical vibration of matter. Sound does not travel at all through a vacuum. The *displacements* of the matter that carry a sound *impulse* are in a *longitudinal* direction, that is, in the direction of the propagation, rather than at right angles to it.

EXERCISE 8

Based on context alone, make an educated guess about the italicized words in the paragraphs on light and sound waves. Write down the definition you would give each word. Then look up each word in an unabridged dictionary. How do your definitions compare?

2   Collect words—and use them.

If a word is mentioned more than twice, you should know its formal definition since its repeated use indicates that the word is important. Look the word up if you are not sure of its meaning. When attempting to *increase* your vocabulary, proceed slowly when putting newly discovered words to use in your own writing and speech. As an aid to vocabulary building, you may want to create a file of new words, as described in the box on the next page.

3   Use the thesaurus with care.

A thesaurus (literally from the Greek word meaning "treasure") is a reference tool that lists the synonyms of words and, frequently, their antonyms. Because the thesaurus is found in many computerized word processing programs, its use has become dangerously easy. If you find

REFERENCES

PYLES, THOMAS. *Words and Ways of American English*. New York: Random, 1952. Chapters 1, 2, 7, 8. Many words in American speech are borrowed from other languages, or adapted from them.

Journal of Basic Writing 2 (1979). Special issue on teaching vocabulary.

EXERCISE 8

Individual responses

ADDITIONAL EXERCISE F

ACROSS THE CURRICULUM Locate in one of your textbooks a passage that includes several words that are new to you. Before looking them up in the dictionary, try to determine their meaning based on the context. Write out your tentative definition, and then check it with the dictionary definition. If the meanings are close, you've done a good job of making an educated guess.

LOOKING BACK

Students who tend to use a thesaurus in hopes of sounding more educated should follow the advice given in this section and take another look at chapter 21 (Choosing the Right Word).

A Personal Vocabulary File

- Make a set of flash cards with a new word and the sentence in which it appears on one side of each card; place the definition on the other side.

- Review the cards regularly. Categorize them by discipline or by part of speech. Practice changing the vocabulary word's part of speech with suffixes.

- Expand entries in your file when you find a previously filed word used in a new context.

- Consciously work one or two new words into each paper that you write, especially when the new words allow you to be precise in ways you could not otherwise be.

---

yourself turning to a thesaurus merely to dress up your writing with significant-sounding language, spare yourself the trouble. Unfortunately, sentences like the one that follows are too often written in a transparent effort to impress—and the effect can be unintentionally comical.

Pretentious The *penultimate* chapter of this novel left me *rhapsodic*.

This sentence shares many of the problems associated with pretentious diction (see 21h-2). It also suggests how the *diction* (the level) of the two italicized words chosen from the thesaurus is likely to contrast sharply with the diction that characterizes the rest of a paper. Often, the sense of the word (its denotation or connotation) may be slightly off the mark—not precisely what the meaning of the sentence requires (see 21a). In either case, a sentence with such "treasures" usually stands out as awkward (see 21b). A more restrained choice of words would produce a better sentence.

Revised I was overwhelmed by the next to last chapter of this novel.

By no means should you ignore the thesaurus; it is, in fact, a treasury of language. But when you find a word, make sure you are comfortable with it—that it is *your* word—before appropriating it for use in a paper.

4   Build discipline-appropriate vocabularies.

Each discipline has a vocabulary that insiders, or professionals, use when addressing one another; one of your jobs as you move from class to class will be to recognize important words and add them to discipline-specific vocabularies that you will develop. The longer you study in a discipline, and especially if you should major in it, the larger and more versatile your specific vocabulary will be. Discipline-specific vocabularies consist of two types of words: those that are unique to the discipline and those that are found elsewhere, though with different meanings. For example, the word *gravity* occurs in contexts outside of the physics classroom. In a newspaper article or essay you might find *gravity* used to suggest great seriousness: *The gravity of the accusations caused Mr. Jones to hire a famous attorney.* Present-day physicists use the word *gravity* in an altogether different sense.

Discipline-specific vocabularies also consist of words unique to a particular field of study. The sheer volume of these words makes it impossible to review them here; suffice it to say that as you see new terms repeated in texts or hear them recurring in the speech of your professors, you should note these words and learn their definitions. As you move from introductory courses in a subject to upper-level courses, the new terms will become more familiar.

EXERCISE 9

Take an informal survey to see if you can identify five words or phrases unique to a particular group of people. Listen to fraternity or sorority members on campus addressing members of their own houses; listen closely in a locker room to members of a team with which you have practiced; or sit in on a campus club meeting or a session of the student government. List the five words or phrases; then define each expression and illustrate its community-specific use in a sentence.

EXERCISE 10

Review your notes and text for one course and identify five words or phrases particular to that subject. The words or phrases might well occur in contexts beyond the course but will, as well, have a course-specific meaning. List the words or phrases; then define each expression and illustrate its discipline-specific use in a sentence.

EXERCISE 9

Individual responses

EXERCISE 10

Individual responses

CHAPTER 23

Spelling

English is an eclectic language derived from several different sources, including Old German, Scandinavian, and Norman French, as well as Latin and Greek. With such a mixed vocabulary, it is remarkable how closely most English spellings are associated with the sounds of words. Nevertheless, many words that look or sound alike may in fact derive from different sources, and thus be spelled or pronounced differently. With practice in writing and reading, certain basic patterns emerge that connect spelling to word sounds. Spelling can be mastered by learning a few rules and the exceptions to those rules. Spelling "demons" can be overcome by recognizing the words you most commonly misspell and remembering devices for memorizing their correct spelling.

KEY FEATURES

Spelling is rarely a pleasant subject to discuss, especially with students. But what we have to say is often judged by how well or poorly we spell the words. Regardless of how arbitrary the spelling rules for English words may be, and irrespective of the fact that some of the world's best writers can't spell, people still tend to judge a piece of writing by its spelling. The chapter begins on a historical note, explaining why English seems to have so many different spelling rules. After establishing the need to master spelling rules, the chapter goes on to discuss those rules clearly and thoroughly. All of the standard rules are covered, from "*i* before *e*" to irregular plurals. In addition, the final section of the chapter proposes a few strategies for developing spelling skills. Throughout the chapter, exercises provide students with valuable practice in learning and applying the rules.

FOR DISCUSSION

It's no secret that many students believe that when they "go out into the world" they won't need to know how to spell. It would be useful to question them about this belief at the beginning of the chapter. Among the reasons you're likely to hear is the availability of the computer spelling checker. Of course, spelling checkers don't spell the word for you. They also miss some of the most common misspellings, homonyms—only the most sophisticated programs are context-sensitive. Another argument is that the secretary will take care of the spelling. But who checks the secretary's spelling? How will you know that he or she is a capable speller if you're not? And what if the secretary gets mad at you on the day you're sending a letter to your most influential client and types exactly what you've written? A brief discussion of the importance of learning spelling rules should help students understand the need to study this chapter.

23a Overcoming spelling/pronunciation misconnections

Long-time speakers and readers of English have learned basic connections between sounds and letter combinations that help them spell a large number of words. However, for historical reasons certain combinations of letters are not always pronounced in the same way (for example: thou*gh*t, bou*gh*, throu*gh*, drou*gh*t, etc.). In addition, regional and dialect variations in pronunciation may drop or vary the pronunciation of certain endings of auxiliary verbs. It is safer to try to keep a visual image of a word in your mind, rather than to rely on what you hear to help you to spell a word correctly.

1 Recognizing homonyms and commonly confused words

One of the most common causes of spelling confusion is **homonyms**—words that sound alike, or are pronounced almost alike, but that have different spellings and meanings. The following box lists the most commonly confused homonyms and near homonyms.

Commonly Confused Homonyms and Near Homonyms

accept [to receive]	all ready [prepared]
except [to leave out]	already [by this time]
advice [recommendation]	bare [naked]
advise [to recommend]	bear [to carry, endure; an animal]
affect [to have an influence on]	board [piece of wood]
effect [result; to make happen]	bored [uninterested]

(continued)

Commonly Confused Homonyms and Near Homonyms (*continued*)

brake [stop, device for stopping]
break [to smash, destroy]
buy [purchase]
by [next to, through]
capital [city seat of government]
capitol [legislative or government building]
cite [quote, refer to]
sight [vision, something seen]
site [place, locale]
complement [something that completes]
compliment [praise]
conscience [moral sense, sense of right/wrong]
conscious [aware]
discreet [respectfully reserved]
discrete [distinct, separate]
dominant [controlling, powerful]
dominate [to control]
elicit [to draw out]
illicit [illegal]
eminent [distinguished]
immanent [inborn, inherent]
imminent [expected momentarily]
fair [just; light-complexioned; lovely]
fare [fee for transportation; meal]
gorilla [ape]
guerilla [unconventional soldier]
heard [past tense of *to hear*]
herd [group of animals]
hole [opening]
whole [entire, complete]
its [possessive form of *it*]
it's [contraction of *it is*]
lead [guide; heavy metal]
led [past tense of *to lead*]
lessen [decrease]
lesson [something learned]
loose [not tight, unfastened]
lose [misplace, fail to win]
moral [object-lesson, knowing right from wrong]
morale [outlook, attitude]
passed [past tense of *to pass*]
past [after; beyond; a time gone by]

patience [forbearance]
patients [those under medical care]
peace [absence of war]
piece [part or portion of something]
personal [private, pertaining to an individual]
personnel [employees]
plain [simple, clear, unadorned; flat land]
plane [carpenter's tool, flat surface, airplane]
presence [attendance, being at hand]
presents [gifts; gives]
principal [most important; school administrator]
principle [fundamental truth, law, conviction]
scene [setting, play segment]
seen [past participle of *see*]
shore [coastline]
sure [certain]
stationary [standing still]
stationery [writing paper]
straight [unbending]
strait [narrow waterway]
than [besides; as compared with]
then [at that time; therefore]
their [possessive form of *they*]
there [opposite of *here*]
they're [contraction of *they are*]
threw [past tense of *throw*]
through [by means of, finished]
thorough [complete]
to [toward]
too [also, in addition to]
two [number following *one*]
weak [feeble]
week [seven days]
weather [climatic conditions]
whether [which of two]
whose [possessive form of *who*]
who's [contraction of *who is*]
your [possessive form of *you*]
you're [contraction of *you are*]
yore [the far past]

ESL ALERT

Spanish speakers might persist in spelling "which" as "wich" since the "wh" sound does not exist for them, just as Japanese students frequently reverse the letters "*l*" and "*r*," as in "She lan down the rane" for "She ran down the lane" because Japanese does not distinguish between these two sounds. Arabic speakers might tend to leave out or confuse vowels because their lettering system focuses on consonants. Russians might use "*z*'s" in place of "*s*'s" because of their alphabet system, while Spanish speakers will add an initial "*e*" to words beginning with "*s*": estudy, estupid.

Students whose languages spell relatively phonetically, such as Spanish students, will have more trouble spelling correctly than, say, French students who are accustomed to more eccentric rules for spelling.

Spellings such as "*differes*" may derive from first language rules for syllabification requiring more vowels than English uses.

ADDITIONAL EXERCISE A

Choose six sets of words from the list of homonyms and near homonyms. If possible, choose sets that you have difficulty with. For each set, write one sentence incorporating all words in the set.

REFERENCES

BROWN, ALAN S. "Encountering Misspellings and Spelling Performance: Why Wrong Isn't Right." *Journal of Educational Psychology* 80 (1988): 488–94. An empirical study reveals that teaching or testing spelling by using incorrectly spelled words can be counterproductive; students retain the misspelling as well as the correct spelling.

CUMMINGS, D. W. *American English Spelling: An Informal Description.* Baltimore: Johns Hopkins UP, 1988. Chapters 1 & 11. A thorough and sometimes whimsical account of the development of English spelling rules, with particular attention to the hazards of phonetic spelling.

CHOMSKY, CAROL. "Reading, Writing, and Phonology." *Harvard Education Review* 40 (1970): 287–309. English spelling derives more from underlying lexical meaning than from pronunciation.

EXERCISE 1

1. you're sure your beer
2. they're through
3. eminent imminent
4. Your allusion illusion
5. devising device

EXERCISE 1

From each pair or trio of words in parentheses, circle the correct homonym. Then make up sentences using each of the other word[s] correctly.

1. If (your/you're) going to the store, make (shore/sure) you take (your/you're) shopping list and return the (bier/beer) bottles to get the deposit money back.
2. Jean's going to tell Gary (their/they're/there) (through/threw).
3. The (imminent/eminent) author's death was (immanent/imminent).
4. (Your/you're) (illusion/allusion) to Dave's preferring apple pie is an (illusion/allusion); he prefers cherry.
5. We're having trouble (devicing/devising) a (devise/device) to decode this code.

2 Recognizing words with more than one form

A subgroup of homonyms that many people find particularly troublesome consists of words that sometimes appear as one word and other times appear as two words.

We *always* work hard, in *all ways.*

By the time everyone was *all ready* to go, it was *already* too late to catch the early show.

It *may be* a question of etiquette, but *maybe* it's not.

Everyday attitudes are not always appropriate *every day.*

Walking *in to* the theater, he accidentally bumped *into* the usher.

Once we were *all together,* we were *altogether* convinced the reunion had been a wonderful idea.

Unlike *always/all ways* and *already/all ready, all right* and *a lot* do not vary: they can be written only as two words.

FAULTY   It's *alright* with me if Sally comes along.

REVISED   It's *all right* with me if Sally comes along.

FAULTY   James has *alot* of homework to do tonight.

REVISED   James has *a lot* of homework to do tonight.

3 Memorizing words with silent letters or syllables

Many words contain silent letters, such as the *k* and the *w* in *know* or the *b* in *dumb,* or letters that are not pronounced in everyday speech, such as the first *r* in February. The simplest way to remember the spelling of these words is to commit them to memory, mentally pronouncing the silent letters as you do so. Following is a list of frequently used words whose mispronunciation in everyday speech often leads to misspelling.

aisle	February	paradi*g*m
can*d*idate	foreign	*p*neumonia
clim*b*	gover*n*ment	privi*l*ege
condem*n*	int*e*rest	prob*a*bly

4 Distinguishing between noun and verb forms of the same word

Many spelling problems occur when noun and verb forms of a word have different spellings.

Verb	*Noun*
advise	advice
describe	description
enter	entrance
marry	marriage

5 Distinguishing American from British and Canadian spellings

The endings of various words differ depending on whether the American version or the British version of the word is being used. Though each is correct, when in America, do as the Americans do. Above all, you should be consistent. If you are not sure what the correct version of the word is, consult your dictionary, making sure you know whether the dictionary "prefers" English or American variations.

American	*British*
-or (humor, color)	-our (humour, colour)
-ment (judgment)	-ement (judgement)
-tion (connection)	-xion (connexion)
-ize (criticize, realize)	-ise (criticise, realise)
-er (center, theater)	-re (centre, theatre)
-led (traveled)	-lled (travelled)

Other American/British variations include gray/grey and check/cheque.

23b Learn basic spelling rules for *ie/ei*.

Despite the troublesome aspects of English spelling detailed previously, there are a number of general rules that greatly simplify the task of spelling words correctly.

The *i* before *e* rule you learned in grammar school still holds true: "*i* before *e* except after *c*, or when pronounced *ay*, as in n*ei*ghbor."

TEACHING IDEAS

Regardless of who won the Revolutionary War, many Americans still hold the belief that "British is better," and if not better, certainly classier. Thus we go to *theatres* in cultural *centres*. Students should be made aware that regardless of whether it's better, British spelling is *not* acceptable in American English writing.

EXERCISE 2

i before *e*

achieve	experience
belief/believe	field
brief	fiend/friend

Except after *c*

ceiling	receipt/receive
conceit	deceit/deceive
conceive	perceive

ei pronounced *ay*

beige	neighbor
eight(h)	heinous
freight	vein

Exceptions

ancient	foreign
height	seize
either	weird

Finally, if the *ie* is not pronounced as a unit, the rule does not apply: science, conscientious, atheist.

EXERCISE 2

Insert *ie* or *ei* in the following words. If necessary, use a dictionary to confirm your choice.

forf ____ t	s ____ zure	p ____ rce
financ ____ r	f ____ nt	pat ____ nce
consc ____ nce	h ____ ress	counterf ____ t
defic ____ nt	sl ____ ght	r ____ fy

23c Learn rules for using prefixes.

Prefixes are placed at the beginnings of words to qualify or add to their meaning. The addition of a prefix never affects the spelling of the root word: do not drop a letter from or add a letter to the original word.

un	+	usual	=	unusual
mis	+	statement	=	misstatement
under	+	rate	=	underrate
dis	+	service	=	disservice
anti	+	thesis	=	antithesis
de	+	emphasize	=	deemphasize

The following are also used as prefixes: *en, in, ante, inter, pre, per, pro,* and *over.*

23d Learn rules for using suffixes.

A **suffix** is an ending added to a word in order to change the word's function. For example, suffixes can change a present tense verb to a past tense verb (help, help*ed*); make an adjective an adverb (silent, silent*ly*); make a verb a noun (excite, excite*ment*); or change a noun to an adjective (force, forc*ible*). Spelling difficulties often arise when the root word must be changed before the suffix is added.

1 Learn rules for keeping or dropping a final *e.*

Many words end with a silent *e* (hav*e*, mat*e*, rais*e*, confin*e*, procur*e*). When adding a suffix to these words, you can use the following rules.

The basic rule: If the suffix begins with a vowel, drop the final silent *e.*

accuse + ation = accusation	sedate + ive = sedative
inquire + ing = inquiring	cube + ism = cubism
debate + able = debatable	pore + ous = porous

Exceptions

The silent *e* is sometimes retained before a suffix that begins with a vowel in order to distinguish homonyms (dyeing/dying); to prevent mispronunciation (*mileage,* not milage); and especially, to keep the sound of *c* or *g* soft.

courage + ous = courageous	embrace + able = embraceable
outrage + ous = outrageous	notice + able = noticeable

Rule: If the suffix begins with a consonant, keep the final silent *e.*

manage + ment = management	acute + ness = acuteness
sedate + ly = sedately	force + ful = forceful
blame + less = blameless	

Exceptions

When the final silent *e* is preceded by another vowel, the *e* is dropped (*argument,* not arguement; *truly,* not truely).
Other exceptions include:

judge + ment = judgment	awe + ful = awful
acknowledge + ment = acknowledgment	whole + ly = wholly

EXERCISE 3

1. investigative
2. malicious
3. duly
4. traceable
5. singeing
6. serviceable
7. completely
8. mistaken
9. grievance
10. binging

EXERCISE 3
Combine the following words and suffixes, retaining or dropping the final *e* as needed. Check your choices in the dictionary to make sure they are correct.

1. investigate + ive
2. malice + ious
3. due + ly
4. trace + able
5. singe + ing
6. service + able
7. complete + ly
8. mistake + en
9. grieve + ance
10. binge + ing

2 **Learn rules for keeping or dropping a final *y*.**

When suffixes are added to words that end in a final *y*, use the following rules.

Rule: When the letter immediately before the *y* is a consonant, change the *y* to *i* and then add the suffix.

beauty + ful = beautiful
breezy + er = breezier
worry + some = worrisome
comply + ant = compliant
busy + ness = business
study + ous = studious

Exceptions
Keep the final *y* when the suffix to be added is *-ing*.

study + ing = studying   comply + ing = complying

Keep the final *y* for some one-syllable root words.

shy + er = shyer   wry + ly = wryly

Keep the final *y* when the *y* is the ending of a proper name.

Janey/Janeys   Bobby/Bobbylike

Keep the final *y* when it is preceded by a vowel, and then add the suffix.

journey + ing = journeying
deploy + ment = deployment
spray + ed = sprayed
buoy + ant = buoyant
play + ful = playful
coy + ly = coyly

EXERCISE 4

1. supplier
2. stultifying
3. testier
4. rarefied
5. joyousness
6. conveyance
7. crier
8. Kennedys
9. plentiful
10. daily

EXERCISE 4
Combine the following root words and suffixes, changing the *y* to *i* when necessary.

1. supply + er
2. stultify + ing
3. testy + er
4. rarefy + ed
5. joy + ousness
6. convey + ance
7. cry + er
8. Kennedy + s
9. plenty + ful
10. day + ly

3 Learn rules for adding -ally.

Rule: Add -ally to make an adverb out of an adjective that ends with ic.

terrific   + ally = terrifically   emphatic + ally = emphatically
caustic   + ally = caustically   music   + ally = musically
fantastic + ally = fantastically

Exception
public + ly = publicly

4 Learn the rule for adding -ly.

Rule: Add -ly to make an adverb out of an adjective that does not end with ic.

hesitant + ly = hesitantly   fastidious   + ly = fastidiously
helpful   + ly = helpfully   conscientious + ly = conscientiously
fortunate + ly = fortunately

5 Learn the rule for adding -cede, -ceed, and -sede.

Words that sound like *seed* are almost always spelled *-cede*.

intercede   concede   precede
accede   recede   secede

Exceptions
Only supersede uses *-sede*.

Only exceed, proceed, and succeed use *-ceed*.

6 Learn rules for adding -able or -ible.

These endings sound the same, but there is an easy way to remember which to use.

Rule: If the root word is an independent word, use the suffix -able. If the root is not an independent word, use the suffix -ible.

comfort + able = comfortable   audible
advise + able = advisable   plausible
agree   + able = agreeable   compatible

Exceptions
culpable, probable, resistible

7 **Learn rules for doubling the final consonant.**

A word that ends in a consonant sometimes doubles the final consonant when a suffix is added.

Rule: Double the final consonant when a one-syllable word ends in a consonant preceded by a single vowel.

flip + ant = fli**pp**ant   slip + er = sli**pp**er
flat + en = fla**tt**en   split + ing = spli**tt**ing

Rule: Double the final consonant when adding a suffix to a two-syllable word if a single vowel precedes the final consonant and if the final syllable is accented once the suffix is added.

control + er = contro**ll**er   commit + ing = commi**tt**ing
concur + ence = concu**rr**ence

Rule: Do not double the final consonant when it is preceded by two or more vowels, or by another consonant.

sustain + ing = sustaining   insist + ent = insistent
comport + ed = comported

Rule: Do not double the final consonant if the suffix begins with a consonant.

commit + ment = commitment   fat + ness = fatness

Rule: Do not double the final consonant if the word is *not* accented on the last syllable, or if the accent shifts from the last to the first syllable when the suffix is added.

beckon + ing = beckoning   prefer + ence = preference

EXERCISE 5

Add the correct suffix to the following roots, changing the roots as necessary. Consult a dictionary as needed.

1. benefit   + ed   6. reverse + (-able or -ible?)
2. realistic + (-ly or -ally?)   7. allot   + ment
3. contempt + (-able or -ible?)   8. occur   + ence
4. parallel + ing   9. room   + mate
5. proceed + ure   10. control + (-able or -ible?)

EXERCISE 5

1. benefited   6. reversible
2. realistically   7. allotment
3. contemptible   8. occurrence
4. paralleling   9. roommate
5. procedure   10. controllable

23e Learn rules for forming plurals.

There are several standard rules for making words plural.

1 Learn the basic rule for adding -s/-es.

Adding -s

For most words, simply add -s.

gum/gums	automobile/automobiles
season/seasons	investment/investments

Adding -es

For words ending in -s, -sh, -ss, -ch, -x, or -z, add -es.

bus/buses	watch/watches
bush/bushes	tax/taxes
mistress/mistresses	buzz/buzzes

For words ending in -o, add -es if the o is preceded by a consonant.

tomato/tomatoes	hero/heroes
potato/potatoes	veto/vetoes

Exceptions
pro/pros, piano/pianos, solo/solos
soprano/sopranos

Add -s if the final o is preceded by a vowel.

patio/patios	zoo/zoos

2 Learn the rule for plurals of words ending in -f or -fe.

To form the plural of some nouns ending in -f or -fe, change the ending to -ve before adding the -s.

half/halves	leaf/leaves
elf/elves	yourself/yourselves

Exceptions

scarf/scarfs/scarves	hoof/hoofs/hooves	
belief/beliefs	proof/proofs	motif/motifs

3 **Learn the rule for plurals of words ending in -*y*.**

For words that end in a consonant followed by -*y*, change the *y* to *i* before adding -*es* to form the plural.

amenity/amenities	enemy/enemies
raspberry/raspberries	mystery/mysteries

Exceptions

proper names such as McGinty/McGintys; Mary/Marys
For words ending in a vowel followed by -*y*, add -*s*.

monkey/monkeys	delay/delays
alloy/alloys	buy/buys

4 **Learn the rule for plurals of compound words.**

When compound nouns are written as one word, add an -*s* ending as you would to make any other plural.

snowball/snowballs	mailbox/mailboxes
breakthrough/breakthroughs	

When compound nouns are hyphenated or written as two words, the most important part of the compound word (usually a noun that is modified) is made plural.

sister-in-law/sisters-in-law	head of state/heads of state
nurse-midwife/nurse-midwives	city planner/city planners

5 **Learn the irregular plurals.**

Some words change internally to form plurals.

woman/women	goose/geese
mouse/mice	tooth/teeth

Some Latin and Greek words form plurals by changing their final -*um*, -*on*, or -*us* to -*a* or -*i*.

curricul*um*/curricul*a*	criteri*on*/criteri*a*
syllab*us*/syllab*i*	medi*um*/medi*a*
dat*um*/dat*a*	stimul*us*/stimul*i*
alumn*us*/alumn*i*	

For some words, the singular and the plural forms are the same.

deer/deer	sheep/sheep	fish/fish
species/species	moose/moose	
elk/elk	rice/rice	

EXERCISE 6

Make the following words plural. Check your answers in the dictionary.

1. spoonful
2. phenomenon
3. monkey house
4. thesis
5. beauty
6. fish
7. apparatus
8. wolverine
9. attorney general
10. antenna

23f Developing spelling skills

In addition to learning the spelling rules detailed earlier, there are several ways to improve your spelling skills.

- Memorize commonly misspelled words.

- Keep track of the words that give you trouble. See if you can discern a pattern, and memorize the relevant rule.

- Use the dictionary. Check words whose spelling you are not sure of, and add them to your personal list of difficult-to-spell words. If you are not sure of the first few letters of a word, look up a synonym of that word to see if the word you need is listed as part of the definition.

- Pay attention when you read: your mind will retain a visual impression of a word that will help you remember how it is spelled.

- You may also develop mnemonic devices—techniques to improve memory—for particularly troublesome words. For instance, you might use the *-er* at the end of pap*er* and lett*er* as a reminder that station*er*y means writing pap*er*, while station*a*ry means st*a*nding still.

- Edit and proofread carefully, paying particular attention to how the words look on the page. You will find as you train yourself that you will begin to recognize spelling errors, and that you actually know the correct spelling but have made an old mistake in haste or carelessness.

- On word processors, use a spell-checker, but realize that this computer aid will only identify misspelled words: if you have used an incorrect homonym, but have spelled it correctly, the spell-checker will not highlight the word.

EXERCISE 6

1. spoonfuls
2. phenomena
3. monkey houses
4. theses
5. beauties
6. fish
7. apparatus/apparatuses
8. wolverine/wolverines
9. attorneys general/attorney generals
10. antennae/antennas

REFERENCES

SHAUGHNESSY, MINA P. *Errors and Expectations: A Guide for the Teacher of Basic Writing.* New York: Oxford UP, 1977. 160–86. If students can learn the causes of their spelling problems, they can take steps to improve.

CLARK, ROGER, and I. Y. HASHIMOTO. "A Spelling Program for College Students." *Teaching English in the Two-Year College* 11 (1984): 34–38. Students can improve their spelling through a program that involves keeping a personal spelling dictionary.

DOBIE, ANN R. "Orthographical Theory and Practice, or How to Teach Spelling." *Journal of Basic Writing* 5 (1986): 41–48. Various methods for helping students improve their spelling are presented here.

CLAPP, OUIDA., Ed. *Teaching the Basics—Really!* Urbana: NCTE, 1977. Includes articles by Muriel Harris and Ann Ruggles Gere on improving spelling skills.

CHAPTER 24

End Punctuation

REFERENCES

SHAUGHNESSY, MINA P. *Errors and Expectations: A Guide for the Teacher of Basic Writing.* New York: Oxford UP, 1977. Chapter 2. A practical discussion of students' difficulties with end punctuation.

LANHAM, RICHARD A. *Style: An Anti-Textbook.* New York: Yale UP, 1974. Chapter 6. Punctuation is a method of providing in written discourse the signals we hear in spoken discourse.

The ending of one sentence and the beginning of the next is a crucial boundary for readers. Sentences provide the primary medium for delivering isolatable, comprehensible chunks of information, and readers are highly sensitive to signals that show when they come to a full stop. When sentence boundaries are blurred, readers have trouble grouping a writer's words into meaningful segments. The end-of-sentence boundary in English is marked in three ways: with a period, a question mark, or an exclamation point.

THE PERIOD

 24a Using the period

The **period** is our workhorse mark of punctuation, the one used most often for noting a full stop—the end of a sentence.

 1 Placing a period to mark the end of a statement or a mild command

It is conventional to end statements or mild commands with a period.

> Carry that barrel over here.
>
> Four of the first five Presidents of the United States were Virginia men.
>
> We usually call them the "Virginia dynasty."

A restatement of a question asked by someone else is called an **indirect question.** Since it is really a statement, it does not take a question mark.

DIRECT QUESTION
These presidents asked, "Do Americans have faith in the people?"

STATEMENT
These presidents asked whether Americans have faith in the people.

2 Placing periods in relation to end quotation marks and parentheses

A period is always placed inside a quotation mark that ends a sentence.

These presidents basically asserted, "Americans should have faith in the people."

When a parenthesis ends a sentence, place a period outside the end parenthesis if the parenthetical remark is not a complete sentence (see 29c). If the parenthetical remark is a separate complete sentence, enclose it entirely in parentheses and punctuate it as a sentence—with its own period.

FAULTY   Four of the first five Presidents of the United States were Virginia men (Washington, Jefferson, Madison, and Monroe.).

REVISED   Four of the first five Presidents of the United States were Virginia men (Washington, Jefferson, Madison, and Monroe).

REVISED   Four of the first five Presidents of the United States were Virginia men. (These were Washington, Jefferson, Madison, and Monroe.)

3 Using a period with abbreviations

The following are considered abbreviations that conventionally end with a period:

Mr.   Mrs.   Ms. (even though this is not an abbreviation)

apt.   Ave.   St.   Dr.   Eccles.   mgr.

When an abbreviation ends a sentence, use a single period.

FAULTY   The lawyers addressed their questions to Susan Turner, Esq..

REVISED   The lawyers addressed their questions to Susan Turner, Esq.

When an abbreviation falls in the middle of a sentence, punctuate as if the word abbreviated were spelled out.

FAULTY   The award envelope was presented to Susan Turner, Esq. who opened it calmly.

REVISED   The award envelope was presented to Susan Turner, Esq., who opened it calmly.

See chapter 31a–e for a full discussion of abbreviations.

Use no periods with acronyms or certain long abbreviations.

A number of abbreviations do not take periods—most often *acronyms* (NATO for *North Atlantic Treaty Organization*), the names of

---

TEACHING IDEAS

Few students have difficulty using the period appropriately in ordinary sentences. However, the complications that arise with quotations, parentheses, and abbreviations make it more difficult to determine the exact placement of the period. Students should try to memorize the rules in these two sections; barring that, simply remind them that they now know where to look when they have questions.

Students who are familiar with British conventions may have questions about the period after abbreviations such as *Mr.* and *Mrs.* In British English those abbreviations do not call for a period.

LOOKING AHEAD

For more information on abbreviations, see chapter 31 a–e (Abbreviations and Numbers).

large organizations (IBM for *International Business Machines*), or government agencies (FTC for *Federal Trade Commission*). To be sure about the proper abbreviation of a word or organizational name, see the box at 31c and consult a standard dictionary for general purposes or specialized dictionaries when you are writing in a particular discipline. The following are some typical abbreviations:

ABC   CNN   AT&T   USA   ABM   FAA

EXERCISE 1

Add, delete, or reposition periods in these sentences as needed.

> *Example:* Organ transplants have increased since the development of immunosuppressive drugs such as cyclosporin
>
> Organ transplants have increased since the development of immunosuppressive drugs such as cyclosporin**.**

1. According to one expert, "roughly 5,000 patients are waiting at any given moment for replacement livers. Ten thousand wait for kidneys." (Thomas)
2. Modern transplant techniques have created a rush for human organs and have given rise to what is ghoulishly called the "meat market"
3. "The ethical dilemmas raised by organ transplants are enormous," says Dr. Philip Wier (an ethicist at the Longwood Institute.)
4. Some poor people, faced with the prospect of starving, sell off their kidneys (This practice is the subject of intense debate in some state legislatures)

THE QUESTION MARK

24b Using the question mark

1 Using a question mark after a direct question

Why do children develop so little when they are isolated from others**?**

Why is the crime rate higher in the city than the country, in impoverished areas more than other areas**?** Why do more males than females, more young people than older people, commit crimes**?**

NOTE: An indirect question restates a question put by someone else. The indirect question does not take a question mark.

Sociologists Eshleman and Cashion have asked why children develop so little when they are isolated from others**.**

Requests, worded as questions, are often followed by periods.

Would you pour another glass of wine**.**

Questions in a series inside a sentence will take question marks if each denotes a separate question.

EXERCISE 1

1. According to one expert, "roughly 5,000 patients are waiting at any given moment for replacement livers. Ten thousand wait for kidneys" (Thomas).
2. Modern transplant techniques have created a rush for human organs and have given rise to what is ghoulishly called the "meat market."
3. "The ethical dilemmas raised by organ transplants are enormous," says Dr. Philip Wier (an ethicist at the Longwood Institute).
4. Some poor people, faced with the prospect of starving, sell off their kidneys. (This practice is the subject of intense debate in some state legislatures.)

When an automobile manufacturer knowingly sells a car that meets government safety standards but is defective, what are the manufacturer's legal responsibilities? moral responsibilities? financial responsibilities? [Note that these three "clipped" questions—these incomplete sentences—do not require capitalization.]

When the sense of the questions in a series is not completed until the final question, use one question mark—at the end of the sentence.

Will the agent be submitting the manuscript to one publishing house, two houses, or more?

2 Using a question mark after a quoted question within a statement

Placing the question mark *inside* the end quotation mark

When the question mark applies directly to the quoted material, place it inside the quotation mark.

In a dream, Abraham Lincoln remembered a stranger asking, "Why are you so common looking?"

Place the question mark inside the end quotation mark when the mark applies to *both* the quoted material *and* the sentence as a whole.

Don't you find it insulting that a person would comment directly to a president, "Why are you so common looking?"

See 28a-7 for more on quotations with questions.

Placing the question mark *outside* the end quotation mark

When the sentence as a whole forms a question but the quoted material does not, place the question mark outside the quotation.

Was it Lincoln who observed, "The Lord prefers common-looking people; that's the reason he makes so many of them"?

NOTE: Do *not* combine a question mark with a period, a comma, or an exclamation point.

FAULTY   "Are you going with him?!" asked Joan.

REVISED   "Are you going with him?" asked Joan.

REVISED   "Are you going with him!" shouted Joan.

3 Using a question mark within parentheses to indicate that the accuracy of information is in doubt even after extensive research

The question mark can be used to indicate dates or numerical references known to be inexact. The following are equivalent in meaning:

TEACHING IDEAS

Unlike some other rules of English punctuation, the rule governing the order of question mark and end punctuation is simple and logical. You can call students' attention to the fact that this is a common-sense rule. You may want to emphasize the rule prohibiting the combination of question marks and other marks of punctuation. Especially tricky is the quoted question that doesn't end a sentence. Remind students that no comma is necessary in this situation. (This advice also applies to 24c, on exclamation points.)

Geoffrey Chaucer was born in 1340 **(?).**

Chaucer was born about 1340.

Chaucer was born c. 1340. (The c. is an abbreviation for *circa*, meaning "around.")

NOTE: Do *not* use the question mark in parentheses to make wry comments in your sentences.

FAULTY We found the play a stimulating **(?)** experience.

REVISED Martin fell asleep in the play's first act, and I persuaded him to leave at intermission.

See 29c for more on parentheses.

EXERCISE 2

Add or delete question marks as needed. If necessary, reword sentences.

> *Example:* The candidates' forum provided an illuminating **(?)** hour of political debate.
>
> The candidates' forum failed to provide an illuminating debate.

1. Many people are quick to complain about the quality of political discourse in American politics, so why is it that more thoughtful people aren't running for elected office.
2. When we find that it is polling information, not philosophical conviction, that shapes the public remarks of political figures, is it any wonder that Americans turn cynical, refuse to vote, bemoan the absence of leadership.
3. Political scientists ask why Americans have one of the lowest voter turnouts among democratic nations?
4. Was it Marie Thompson who asked, "Why do we have so much difficulty rising to the challenge of our democratic traditions"?
5. Thompson reaches no firm answers when she concludes, "If the framers of the Constitution assumed an educated, caring citizenry, then we must wonder aloud—have we failed to meet the challenges laid down 200 years ago"?

THE EXCLAMATION POINT

24c Using the exclamation point

In spoken conversation, exclamations are used freely, especially in moments of high passion. For some informal occasions, writers may be tempted to create with exclamation points what their tone of voice cannot show on paper. In academic writing, however, it is far more convincing to create emphasis by the force of your words, as opposed to the force of your punctuation.

EXERCISE 2

1. Many people are quick to complain about the quality of political discourse in American politics, so why is it that more thoughtful people aren't running for elected office?
2. When we find that it is polling information, not philosophical conviction, that shapes the public remarks of political figures, is it any wonder that Americans turn cynical? refuse to vote? bemoan the absence of leadership?
3. Political scientists ask why Americans have one of the lowest voter turnouts among democratic nations.
4. Was it Marie Thompson who asked, "Why do we have so much difficulty rising to the challenge of our democratic traditions?"
5. Thompson reaches no firm answers when she concludes, "If the framers of the Constitution assumed an educated, caring citizenry, then we must wonder aloud—have we failed to meet the challenges laid down 200 years ago?"

TEACHING IDEAS

A useful way to warn students against overusing the exclamation point is to remind them that if they feel the need to use an exclamation point to emphasize a sentence, then they probably haven't composed a sufficiently effective sentence to begin with. They should redirect their energies toward revising the sentence.

1 Using the exclamation point—sparingly—to mark an emphatic statement or command

Overused exclamation points create a none-too-flattering portrait of a "breathy" or "flaky" writer who is highly excitable and not too credible. Save the exclamation point to call special attention to a unique, memorable sentence, the content of which creates its own emphasis. The exclamation point will highlight the emphasis already present.

> Enterprising archaeologists visit their dentists regularly, if only to obtain supplies of worn-out dental instruments, which make first-rate fine digging tools!

> Please! Let me do it myself! [The use of exclamation points with this emphatic exclamation and command is appropriate for duplicating spoken dialogue.]

 2 Marking mild exclamations with periods or commas

Please, let me do it myself.

NOTE: Do not combine an exclamation point with a period, comma, or question mark.

FAULTY   "Leave this room!," demanded the judge.

REVISED   "Leave this room!" demanded the judge.

FAULTY   "Can't you give us some privacy?!" he snarled.

REVISED   "Can't you give us some privacy!" he snarled.

EXERCISE 3

Read the following paragraphs on the subject of blushing and provide periods, question marks, and exclamation points as needed.

> Occasionally you may find yourself blushing when you're being flattered The tendency is to interpret this as shyness Before interpreting it in this way, hold on Is your blush possibly saying, "I don't believe they mean it They're flattering me manipulatively" Trust the blush as an automatic aversion response that may be saying far more than just, "I'm shy"

> The next time you blush, try saying "I don't like . . . " and finish the sentence with the cause of the blushing (This may also keep you from being a constant target) In other words, "I don't like your asking me that question" See if that then makes sense in helping you understand your blushing problem

EXERCISE 3

Occasionally you may find yourself blushing when you're being flattered. The tendency is to interpret this as shyness. Before interpreting it in this way, hold on. Is your blush possibly saying, "I don't believe they mean it. They're flattering me manipulatively"? Trust the blush as an automatic aversion response that may be saying far more than just "I'm shy."

The next time you blush, try saying, "I don't like . . . " and finish the sentence with the cause of the blushing. (This may also keep you from being a constant target.) In other words, "I don't like your asking me that question." See if that then makes sense in helping you understand your blushing problem.

Commas

One important purpose of punctuation is to help readers identify clusters of related words, both between and within sentences. By far the most common mark used to distinguish one sentence from another is the period. *Within* sentences, the most common mark is the **comma,** and it is used primarily as a signal that some element, some word or cluster of related words, is being set off from a main sentence for a reason. Readers see the comma as a direct instruction from the writer on how to read and understand. Clear instructions will keep readers focused on the words in exactly the way the writer deems necessary. A well-used comma helps to move readers from the beginning of a sentence through to the end, effortlessly and with understanding. Poorly used, a comma will scatter meaning and create confusion. There is much to gain, therefore, in using commas precisely.

In this chapter you will find rules and guidelines for using the comma. Much of the logic of punctuating with commas is tied to the logic of a sentence's structure. See especially chapters 13, 15, and 19, as well as chapter 7.

25a Using commas with introductory and concluding expressions

1 Place a comma after a modifying phrase or clause that begins a sentence.

Yesterday, the faucet stopped working.
Once the weather turned cold, the faucet stopped working.

A sentence may begin with an opening phrase or clause that is neither the subject nor a simple modifier of the subject. If such an introductory element is longer than a few words, set it off from the main part of the sentence with a comma. The comma will signal the reader that the sentence's subject is being delayed.

> According to sociologist Herbert Gans, poverty's function is to provide a low-wage labor pool to do society's necessary dirty work.

> Because the poor seldom have a chance to buy desirable products, they in this way help merchants by purchasing leftovers—dilapidated cars or deteriorated housing.

OPTION: The comma after an introductory word or brief phrase is optional.

In fact, some will be surprised to find that sociologists consider poverty to have an economic function.

When an introductory element consists of two or more phrases, a comma is required.

Even with our understanding of poverty's root causes, we lack as a society the will to eliminate it. [With two prepositional phrases, the opening needs to be set off from the main sentence.]

NOTE: An opening verbal phrase or clause is set off with a comma if it is used as a modifier; an opening verbal used as a subject is *not* set off.

MODIFIER   Understanding what we do about the root causes of poverty, we lack as a society the will to eliminate it. [The opening modifier needs to be set off.]

SUBJECT   Understanding what we do about poverty does not help us gain the will to eliminate it. [The opening verbal functions as the subject of the sentence and is *not* set off.]

2 Place a comma after a transitional word, phrase, or clause that begins a sentence.

Actually, we've had this problem for years.

A transition is a logical bridge between sentences or paragraphs. As an introductory element, it is set off with a comma.

Once division of labor by sex arose, it must have produced several immediate benefits for the early hominids. *First of all,* nutrition would have improved owing to a balanced diet of meat and plant foods. *Second,* each male or female would have become expert in only part of the skills needed for subsistence and have increased his or her efficiency accordingly.

When a transitional element is moved to the interior of a sentence, set it off with a *pair* of commas. At the end of a sentence, the transitional element is set off with a single comma.

Lipid molecules, *of course,* and molecules that dissolve easily in lipids can pass through cell membranes with ease.

Lipid molecules and molecules that dissolve easily in lipids can pass through cell membranes with ease, *to cite two examples.*

3 Use a comma (or commas) to set off a modifying element that ends or interrupts a sentence *if* the modifier establishes a qualification, contrast, or exception.

The ships return to port at all hours, often at night.
The storm warning was broadcast on the A channel, not the B channel.

REFERENCES

SHAUGHNESSY, MINA P. *Errors and Expectations: A Guide for the Teacher of Basic Writing.* New York: Oxford UP, 1977. 14–43. A practical discussion of students' difficulties with commas.

LINDEMANN, ERIKA. *A Rhetoric for Writing Teachers.* 2nd ed. New York: Oxford UP, 1987. Chapter 9. In discussing sentences, Lindemann refers to problems students encounter with internal punctuation.

LANHAM, RICHARD A. *Style: An Anti-Textbook.* New York: Yale UP, 1974. Chapter 6. Punctuation is a method of providing in written discourse the signals we hear in spoken discourse.

MEYER, CHARLES F. "Teaching Punctuation to Advanced Writers." *Journal of Advanced Composition* 6 (1985–86): 117–29. More accomplished student writers can be taught to use punctuation for rhetorical effect.

MEYER, EMILY, and LOUISE Z. SMITH. *The Practical Tutor.* New York: Oxford UP, 1987. Chapter 9. Useful advice for helping students overcome punctuation problems.

THOMAS, LEWIS. "Notes on Punctuation." *The Medusa and the Snail: More Notes of a Biology Watcher.* New York: Viking, 1979. An imaginative and creative rumination on the joys and frustrations of punctuation.

It's worthwhile to ask students to keep in mind the guidelines presented in the Spotlight on Common Errors when they edit their papers. This outline can serve as a quick, easy reference for appropriate comma use.

FOR DISCUSSION

Since most students have problems with only a few of these common errors, you might want to initiate a class discussion of errors most relevant to your students. Ask students to identify from the list examples of usage familiar to them, and to make their own list of common errors. Students can then discuss the function of commas in sentences, thereby reinforcing their understanding of internal sentence punctuation. (In large classes, this activity might begin with small groups: The groups will identify their common errors, and then the class as a whole will discuss the list of errors compiled from each group's report.)

SPOTLIGHT ON COMMON ERRORS—COMMA USE

These are clues to the errors most commonly associated with comma use. For full explanations and suggested revisions, follow the cross-references to chapter sections.

COMMA ERRORS arise when the use—or absence—of commas leaves readers unable to differentiate between a main sentence and the parts being set off. Five error patterns account for most of the difficulty with comma use.

- **Use a comma to set off introductory words or word groupings from the main part of the sentence (see 25a).**

FAULTY
Yesterday the faucet stopped working.

REVISED
Yesterday, the faucet stopped working.

FAULTY
Once the weather turned cold the faucet stopped working.

REVISED
Once the weather turned cold, the faucet stopped working.

- **Do *not* use a comma to set off concluding words or word groupings from a main sentence (but see 25a-3 for exceptions).**

FAULTY
The faucet stopped working, yesterday.

REVISED
The faucet stopped working yesterday.

FAULTY
The faucet stopped working, once the weather turned cold.

REVISED
The faucet stopped working once the weather turned cold.

- **Place a comma before the word *and, but, or, for,* or *so* when it joins two sentences (see 25b).**

FAULTY
The faucet stopped working *and* the sink leaks.

REVISED
The faucet stopped working, *and* the sink leaks.

FAULTY
I'll fix them myself *and* I'll save money.

REVISED
I'll fix them myself, *and* I'll save money.

BUT use no comma if one key word, usually the subject, keeps the second grouping of words from being considered a sentence.

FAULTY
I'll fix them myself, and save money.

REVISED
I'll fix them myself and save money.

■ Use a comma to separate three or more items in a series (see 25c-1).

FAULTY
I'll need a washer a valve and a wrench.

REVISED
I'll need a washer, a valve, and a wrench.
or I'll need a washer, a valve and a wrench.

■ Use a *pair* of commas to set off from a sentence any word or word group that adds nonessential information (see 25d).

FAULTY
Ahorn Hardware which is just around the corner will have the materials I need.

REVISED
Ahorn Hardware, which is just around the corner, will have the materials I need.

[Since a specific hardware store is named and its identity is clear, the added information is nonessential and is set off with a pair of commas.]

BUT use *no* commas if a word or word group adds essential information needed for identifying some other word in the sentence.

FAULTY
The hardware store, which is just around the corner, will have the materials I need.

REVISED
The hardware store which is just around the corner will have the materials I need.

[Since the added information is essential for identifying *which* hardware store (perhaps there is more than one store in the area), no commas are used.]

GROUP ACTIVITY

All of the exercises in this chapter lend themselves to group activity. Have students respond to exercises individually, and then compare their responses with those of other group members. When the inevitable disagreement occurs, students will have to consult the handbook. Once they become accustomed to using the chapter, they'll likely continue to refer to it as they edit their papers.

A QUALIFICATION

The literary form *short story* is usually defined as a brief fictional prose narrative, *often involving one connected episode.*

A CONTRAST

The U.S. government located a lucrative project for an atomic accelerator in Texas, *not Massachusetts.*

AN EXCEPTION

The children of the rich are the group most likely to go to private preparatory schools and elite colleges, *regardless of their grades.*

When phrases or clauses of contrast, qualification, and exception occur in the middle of a sentence, set them off with a *pair* of commas.

The government chose Texas, *not Massachusetts,* as the site of a lucrative project for an atomic accelerator.

All seas, *except in the areas of circumpolar ice,* are navigable.

If a phrase or clause does *not* establish a qualification, contrast, or exception, do *not* use a comma to separate it from the sentence.

The faucet stopped working once the weather turned cold.

EXERCISE 1

1. In a second war over boundaries, Bulgaria attacked Serbia and Greece in 1913.
2. As a result of the 1913 war, Bulgaria was carved up by its former Balkan allies and Turkey.
3. The following year, the assassination of the Archduke Ferdinand of Austria brought on the First World War.
4. After the Austro-Hungarian Empire collapsed, a sprawling new nation, Yugoslavia, was formed.
5. Under the tenuous domination of the Serbs, the aspirations of Croats and other minorities in Yugoslavia were suppressed.
6. At the same time, the collapse of the Ottoman Empire left many ethnic Turks subject to their longtime foes the Bulgarians.
7. As a result of attempts at forging a new Turkish state in Anatolia, a million Armenians were slaughtered at the same time.
8. Parliamentary governments of southeastern Europe rose and fell, undermined by corrupt and meddling monarchs and by ethnic passions.

EXERCISE 1

The following sentences contain transitional expressions and modifying words or phrases. Rewrite each sentence so that the transition or modifier will come at the *beginning* of the sentence **or** at the *end*. Use commas as needed.

> *Example:* Some of the Balkan nations of southeastern and south central Europe declared war on the waning Ottoman Empire in 1912.
>
> In 1912, some of the Balkan nations of southeastern and south central Europe declared war on the waning Ottoman Empire.

1. Bulgaria attacked Serbia and Greece in 1913 in a second war over boundaries.
2. Bulgaria was carved up as a result of the 1913 war by its former Balkan allies and Turkey.
3. The assassination of the Archduke Ferdinand of Austria the following year brought on the First World War.
4. A sprawling new nation, Yugoslavia, was formed after the Austro-Hungarian Empire collapsed.
5. The aspirations of Croats and other minorities in Yugoslavia were suppressed under the tenuous domination of the Serbs.
6. The collapse of the Ottoman Empire at the same time left many ethnic Turks subject to their longtime foes the Bulgarians.
7. A million Armenians were slaughtered at the same time as a result of attempts at forging a new Turkish state in Anatolia.

8. Undermined by corrupt and meddling monarchs and by ethnic passions, parliamentary governments of southeastern Europe rose and fell.
9. The fall of Communist regimes in eastern Europe today has led to a resurgence of ethnic fighting.
10. "Ethnic cleansing" reminiscent of Nazi atrocities has annihilated whole villages.

9. Today, the fall of Communist regimes in eastern Europe has led to a resurgence of ethnic fighting.
10. Reminiscent of Nazi atrocities, "ethnic cleansing" has annihilated whole villages.

25b Using a comma before a coordinating conjunction to join two independent clauses

The faucet stopped working, and the sink leaks.
We can fix the problems ourselves, or we can call a plumber.

One of the principal ways to join two independent clauses is to link them with a comma and a coordinating conjunction: *and, but, or, nor* (see 19a-1).

The changes in *Homo erectus* are substantial over a million years, *but* they seem gradual by comparison with those that went before.

A computer's data and addressing information are stored in flip-flops within the various memory registers, *or* they take the form of an electrical signal that is moving through wires from one register to another.

OPTIONS: You have several options for linking independent clauses: (1) you can separate the clauses and form two distinct sentences—see 24a; (2) you can use a semicolon to link the clauses within one sentence—see 26a,b (and the Critical Decisions box there); (3) you can make one clause subordinate to another—see 19b (and the Critical Decisions box in 19a).

NOTE: When a coordinating conjunction joins two independent clauses, and when one or both of these clauses has internal punctuation, to prevent misreading change the comma appearing before the conjunction to a semicolon.

Several thousand years ago, probably some lines of Neanderthal man and woman died out; but it seems likely that a line in the Middle East went directly to us, *Homo sapiens*.

25c Using commas between items in a series

One major function of the comma is to signal a brief pause that separates items in a series—a string of related elements.

1 Place a comma between items in a series.

We'll need a washer, a valve, and a wrench.

TEACHING IDEAS

Some students have developed a habit of placing the comma *after* the coordinating conjunction. You may want to place particular emphasis on the precise placement of the comma in these structures.

Items joined in a series should be parallel (see chapter 18). Items can be single words, phrases, or clauses.

WORDS   A Central Processing Unit contains a large number of special-purpose registers for storing *instructions, addresses, and data.*

PHRASES   Booms and busts have plagued economic activity since the onset of industrialization, *sporadically ejecting many workers from their jobs, pushing many businesses into bankruptcy, and leaving many politicians out in the cold.*

OPTION: Some writers prefer to omit the final comma in a series—the comma placed before the coordinating conjunction *and.* The choice is yours. Whatever your preference, be consistent.

OPTION   Exercise appears *to reduce the desire to smoke, to lessen any tendency toward obesity and to help in managing stress.*

NOTE: When at least one item in a series contains a comma, use a semicolon to separate items and prevent misreading (see chapter 26). For the same reason, use semicolons to separate long independent clauses in a series.

I believe that the sun is about ninety-three million miles from the earth; that it is a hot globe many times bigger than the earth; and that, owing to the earth's rotation, it rises every morning and will continue to do so for an indefinite time in the future.

2   Place a comma between two or more coordinate adjectives in a series, if no coordinating conjunction joins them.

Getting under the sink can be a tricky, messy job.

A series of adjectives will often appear as a parallel sequence: the *playful, amusing* poet; an *intelligent, engaging* speaker. When the order of the adjectives can be reversed without affecting the meaning of the noun being modified, the adjectives are called **coordinate adjectives.** Coordinate adjectives can be linked by a comma or by a coordinating conjunction.

SERIES WITH COMMAS
The stomach is a thick-walled, muscular sac that can expand to hold more than 2 liters of food or liquid.

SERIES WITH *AND*
The stomach is a thick-walled *and* muscular sac that can expand to hold more than 2 liters of food or liquid.

SERIES WITH COMMAS
The left hemisphere of the brain thinks sequential, analytical thoughts and is also the center of language.

SERIES WITH *AND*
The left hemisphere thinks sequential *and* analytical thoughts and is also the center of language.

NOTE: The presence of two adjectives beside one other does not necessarily mean that they are coordinate. In the phrase "the wise old lady," the adjectives could not be reversed in sequence or joined by *and*; the adjective *wise* describes *old lady,* not *lady* alone. The same analysis holds for the phrase "the ugly green car." *Green car* is the element being modified by *ugly.* Only coordinate adjectives modifying the same noun are separated by commas.

EXERCISE 2

Combine the following sentences with the conjunction indicated in brackets, and decide whether you need to use a comma. Recall that unless a conjunction joins independent clauses, no comma is needed.

> *Example:* Anthropologists are currently investigating whether or not early hominids (proto-humans) ate meat. [and] Did they obtain meat by hunting or scavenging?
>
> Anthropologists are currently investigating whether or not early hominids (proto-humans) ate meat and whether they obtained it by hunting or scavenging.

1. Proto-humans did not walk as well on two feet as we do. They were better than we are at climbing trees and suspending themselves from branches.
2. Ancestors of present-day leopards were contemporary with early hominids. [and] Ancestors of present-day leopards shared the same habitats as early hominids.
3. Leopards cannot defend their kills from scavenging by lions. [so] They store their kills in trees.
4. Archaeologist John Cavallo thinks that early tree-climbing hominids may have fed off leopard kills stashed in trees. [since] Leopards don't guard the carcasses of their kills.

EXERCISE 3

In each sentence, place a comma as needed between items in a series.

> *Example:* Native American societies were based on notions of community mutual obligations and reciprocity and on close ties of kin.
>
> Native American societies were based on notions of community, mutual obligation, and reciprocity and on close ties of kin.

1. They possessed complex religious beliefs symbolic world views radically different from those of Europeans and cultural values Europeans did not understand.
2. Like other native populations "discovered" after them, Native Americans were exploited decimated by exotic diseases robbed of their lands and ultimately stripped of their traditional cultures.
3. Survivors became serfs slaves or subordinate and often tangential elements in the new social order.
4. Therefore, for centuries Native Americans continued to resist Catholic missionaries explorers and settlers from all over Europe.

EXERCISE 2

1. Proto-humans did not walk as well on two feet as we do, but they were better than we are at climbing trees and suspending themselves from branches.
2. Ancestors of present-day leopards were contemporary with early hominids and shared the same habitats.
3. Leopards cannot defend their kills from scavenging by lions, so they store their kills in trees.
4. Archaeologist John Cavallo thinks that early tree-climbing hominids may have fed off leopard kills stashed in trees, since leopards don't guard the carcasses of their kills.

EXERCISE 3

(In all sentences, the final comma in the series is optional.)

1. They possessed complex religious beliefs, symbolic world views radically different from those of Europeans, and cultural values Europeans did not understand.
2. Like other native populations "discovered" after them, Native Americans were exploited, decimated by exotic diseases, robbed of their lands, and ultimately stripped of their traditional cultures.
3. Survivors became serfs, slaves, or subordinate and often tangential elements in the new social order.
4. Therefore, for centuries Native Americans continued to resist Catholic missionaries, explorers, and settlers from all over Europe.

25d Using commas to set off nonessential elements

1 Identify essential (restrictive) elements that need no commas.

The hardware store which is just around the corner will have the materials I need.

When a modifier provides information necessary for identifying a word, then the modifier is said to be **essential** (or **restrictive**), and it appears in its sentence *without* commas.

> The Vatican theologian *charged with responding to scientific challenges* wanted to suppress the work of Galileo and Copernicus.

There have been many theologians in the Vatican. This sentence refers to the *one* theologian responsible for answering scientific challenges. Without the modifying phrase *charged with responding to scientific challenges,* the subject of this sentence, *the Vatican theologian,* could not be conclusively identified. Therefore, the modifying expression is essential, and no commas are used to set apart the phrase from the sentence in which it appears.

An essential modifier can also be a single word (or single name).

> The Apollo astronaut *Jim Irwin* has devoted a great deal of time and expense to proving the existence of Noah's Ark.

Without the name *Jim Irwin,* we would not know which of the Apollo astronauts has been hunting for Noah's Ark. By contrast, consider the following sentence.

> The first man on the moon, Neil Armstrong, was famous as a pilot who would stay with his craft until the last possible moment.

In this sentence, the modifying information—also the name of an astronaut—is no longer essential because there was only one *first* man on the moon. Thus *Neil Armstrong* is considered nonessential information and is set off by a pair of commas.

An essential modifier can also be a clause.

> The cyclotron is an instrument *that accelerates charged particles to very high speeds.*

The noun modified—*instrument*—could be *any* instrument, and the clause that follows provides information essential to the definition of *which* or *what kind* of instrument.

2 Use a pair of commas to set off nonessential (nonrestrictive) elements.

Ahorn Hardware which is just around the corner will have the materials I need.

If a word being modified is clearly defined (as, for instance, a person with a specific name is clearly defined), then the modifying element—though it might add interesting and useful information—is nonessential. When the modifier is not essential for defining a word, use commas to set the modifier apart from the sentence in which it appears.

NONESSENTIAL Cardinal Bellarmine, *the Vatican theologian charged with responding to scientific challenges,* wanted to suppress the work of Galileo and Copernicus.

The subject of the sentence has already been adequately defined by his name, *Cardinal Bellarmine.* The writer uses the modifying phrase not as a matter of definition but as an occasion to add nonessential information. The meaning of a sentence will change according to whether modifying elements are punctuated as essential or nonessential. The two pairs of sentences that follow are worded identically. Punctuation gives them different meanings.

Punctuating Modifying Clauses with *Who, Which,* and *That*

The relative pronouns *who, which,* and *that* begin modifying clauses that can interrupt or end sentences.

WHO

Who can begin a clause that is essential to defining the word modified.

Formal organizations designate managers *who help administrative units meet their specific goals.*

Who can also begin a nonessential clause. Note the presence of commas in this sentence.

Frank Smith, *who is an administrative manager,* helps his administrative unit meet its goals.

WHICH

Similarly, *which* can begin an essential or a nonessential modifying clause.

Two sites *which flourished in the dim yet documented past* are Saxon London and medieval Winchester. [essential]

Some historical archaeologists excavate sites like Saxon London or medieval Winchester, *which flourished in the dim yet documented past.* [nonessential]

THAT

That always denotes an essential clause. Do not use commas to set off a modifying clause beginning with *that.*

Two sites *that flourished in the dim yet documented past* are Saxon London and medieval Winchester. [essential]

LOOKING BACK

Students may find it helpful to review the discussion of relative pronouns in essential and nonessential clauses as they cover this material. If you believe that they may benefit from such a review, refer them to 14e.

ESSENTIAL	The miners *who went on strike* gained the support of local newspapers.
NONESSENTIAL	The miners, *who went on strike,* gained the support of local newspapers.
ESSENTIAL	The local newspapers supported the miners *who went on strike.*
NONESSENTIAL	The local newspapers supported the miners, *who went on strike.*

The essential modifiers precisely define *which* miners gained the support of the newspapers—*only* those who went on strike. The meaning, then, is that not all of the miners struck. The nonessential modifiers communicate that *all* of the miners struck, and all gained the support of the local newspapers.

3 Use commas to set off parenthetical or repeating elements.

The reasons she gave, all three of them, were convincing.

By definition, a parenthetical remark is not essential to the meaning of a sentence. The remark sometimes illuminates the sentence but by no means provides crucial information. Set off parenthetical expressions as you would any nonessential element.

Revolutionary Boston, *where it was easy to collect a crowd,* became a center of agitation.

OPTIONS: You have the choice of setting off parenthetical elements by using commas, parentheses, or dashes. Any of these options is correct, so base your decision on the level of emphasis you wish to give the parenthetical element. Dashes call the most attention to the element and parentheses the least attention.

Repeating elements

Repetition can both add useful information to a sentence and create pleasing sentence rhythms. By definition, a repeating element is nonessential, so the logic of setting off nonessential elements with commas applies. Set off a repeating element with a *pair* of commas if the element appears in the middle of a sentence. (You may also use a pair of dashes.) Use a comma or a dash and a period if the element concludes the sentence.

Samuel Adams, *a master of propaganda and mob tactics,* was clever at creating a sensation out of every incident and blaming it all on the British.

Archaeologists working underwater have exactly the same intellectual goals as their dry-land colleagues—*to recover, reconstruct, and interpret the past.*

These bare facts have become so familiar, *so essential in the conduct of an interlocking world society,* that they are usually taken for granted.

Appositives

One class of repeating element is called an **appositive phrase,** the function of which is to rename a noun. The phrase is called *appositive* because it is placed in *apposition* to—that is, *side by side* with—the noun it repeats. In the first example, the appositive *a master of propaganda and mob tactics* renames Samuel Adams. The sentence could be rewritten, and repunctuated, as follows:

A master of propaganda and mob tactics, Samuel Adams was clever at creating a sensation out of every incident and blaming it all on the British.

EXCEPTION: When a nonessential appositive phrase consists of a series of items separated by commas, set it off from a sentence with a pair of dashes—not commas—to prevent misreading.

CONFUSING   Motion sickness, nausea, dizziness, and sleepiness, is a dangerous and common malady among astronauts.

REVISED   Motion sickness—nausea, dizziness, and sleepiness—is a dangerous and common malady among astronauts.

CRITICAL DECISIONS

Form, and support, opinions: Within a sentence, distinguish essential from nonessential information

Comma placement regularly depends on a decision you make about whether certain qualifying (or additional) information is or is not essential to the meaning of a particular word. Your decision about this content determines how you punctuate your sentence.

A Test to Determine Whether Qualifying Information Is Essential or Nonessential

1. Identify the single word in the sentence being qualified by a word group.

2. Identify the qualifying word group.

3. Drop the qualifying word group from the sentence.

continued

CRITICAL DECISIONS (continued)

4. Ask of the single word from #1, above: Do I understand which one or who?

    a. If you can give a single answer to this question, the qualifying information is nonessential: Set the information off from the sentence with a *pair* of commas.

    b. If you cannot give a specific answer to the question, the qualifying information *is* essential: Include the information in the main sentence with *no* commas.

Example Sentences

Example 1:   The bill which placed a fifty cent tax on every pack of cigarettes was defeated.

1. Word being qualified: *bill*

2. Qualifying word group: *which placed a fifty cent tax on every pack of cigarettes*

3. New sentence: *The bill was defeated.*

4. Do I understand which one? *No.*

Therefore, the qualifying information is essential; include it in the sentence *without* commas.

    The bill which placed a fifty cent tax on every pack of cigarettes was defeated.

Example 2:   Bill 307 which placed a fifty cent tax on every pack of cigarettes was defeated.

1. Word being qualified: *Bill 307*

2. Qualifying word group: *which placed a fifty cent tax on every pack of cigarettes*

3. New sentence: *Bill 307 was defeated.*

4. Do I understand which one? *Yes.*

Therefore, the qualifying information is nonessential; set it off from the sentence with a *pair* of commas.

    Bill 307, which placed a fifty cent tax on every pack of cigarettes, was defeated.

EXERCISE 4

1. In the 1950s three films that influenced the "look" of rock 'n roll depicted youthful criminals as alienated loners and contributed to teenagers' sense of themselves as different.

2. The first film. *City Across the River* (1951), starring Tony Curtis as a hard but honest youth, dealt with youth gangs in Brooklyn.

EXERCISE 4

Combine the following pairs of sentences. Use commas to set off nonessential modifiers and omit commas when modifiers are essential.

    Example: Elvis Presley was a "white boy from across the tracks."

            Elvis Presley was a symbol of rebellion in popular music.

            Elvis Presley, a "white boy from across the tracks," was a symbol of rebellion in popular music.

1. In the 1950s three films depicted youthful criminals as alienated loners and contributed to teenagers' sense of themselves as different. These three films also influenced the "look" of rock 'n roll.

2. The first film, *City Across the River* (1951), dealt with youth gangs in Brooklyn. It starred Tony Curtis as a hard but honest youth.
3. Curtis's hairstyle started a major trend. Curtis wore his hair in a perfectly sculpted, swept back pompadour later copied by Elvis.
4. The second film, *The Wild One*, featured Marlon Brando as a laconic, distant, rebellious, but ultimately honorable motorcycle gang leader. Brando's character was infinitely more attractive than the ignorant, weak, or brutal adults he had to deal with.
5. James Dean starred in the last of the three films, *Rebel Without a Cause*. The film focused on an alienated teenager trying to find his own truth in a world where adults provide little guidance.
6. Dean's performance electrified the nation, especially teenagers. His performance derived its power from the same rebelliousness that fueled rock 'n roll.
7. Elvis saw *Rebel Without a Cause* more than a dozen times. Elvis could recite whole passages from *Rebel Without a Cause*.

3. Curtis's hairstyle, a perfectly sculpted, swept back pompadour later copied by Elvis, started a major trend.
4. The second film, *The Wild One*, featured Marlon Brando as a laconic, distant, rebellious, but ultimately honorable motorcycle gang leader who was infinitely more attractive than the ignorant, weak, or brutal adults he had to deal with.
5. James Dean starred in the last of the three films, *Rebel Without a Cause*, which focused on an alienated teenager trying to find his own truth in a world where adults provide little guidance.
6. Dean's performance, which derived its power from the same rebelliousness that fueled rock 'n roll, electrified the nation.
7. Elvis, who could recite whole passages from *Rebel Without a Cause*, saw the film more than a dozen times.

25e Using commas to acknowledge conventions of quoting, naming, and various forms of separation

1 Use a comma to introduce or to complete a quotation.

Tom said, "I'll be back in two hours."

Commas set a quotation apart from the words that introduce or conclude the quotation. Commas (and periods) are placed *inside* end quotation marks.

The prizefighter Rocky Graziano once said, "I had to leave fourth grade because of pneumonia—not because I had it but because I couldn't spell it."

Early in his career, Winston Churchill sported a mustache. At a fancy dinner, he argued with a woman who snapped, "Young man—I care for neither your politics nor your mustache."

"Madam," responded Churchill, "you are unlikely to come into contact with either."

(For more on using commas with quotations, see chapter 28.)

2 Use a comma to set off expressions of direct address. If the expression interrupts a sentence, set the word off with a *pair* of commas.

"Ed, did you bring your computer?"
"Our business, Ed, is to sell shoes."

You will most often encounter expressions of direct address when writing dialogue or when quoting speakers addressing their audiences.

"You, Sir, have the sense of a baboon."

"Paul, run to the exit."

"Run to the exit, Paul."

"My fellow citizens, I come before you with a heavy heart."

"I come before you, my fellow citizens, with a heavy heart."

 3 Use a comma to mark the omission of words in a balanced sentence.

The first train will arrive at 2 o'clock; the second, at 3 o'clock.

Sentences are balanced when identical clause constructions are doubled or tripled in a series. So that repeating words in the clauses do not become tedious to a reader, omit these words and note the omission with a comma.

Some southern novelists attribute the character of their fiction to the South's losing the Civil War; others, to the region's special blending of climate and race; and still others, to the salubrious powers of mint juleps.

In this example, the comma and the word *others* substitute for *some southern novelists attribute the character of their fiction.*

 4 Place a comma between paired "more/less" constructions.

The less you smoke, the longer you'll live.

Some constructions involve a paired comparison of "more" of one element contrasted against "more" or "less" of another. Separate these elements with a comma to maintain a clear relationship between them.

The more wires a data base contains, the greater the number of bits it can move at a time.

The more some people get, the less they are willing to give.

 5 Use a comma to set off tag questions that conclude a sentence.

This is the right house, isn't it?

A **tag question,** a brief question "tagged on" to a statement addressed to someone, should be set off from that statement. Tags are used for a variety of purposes, at times to suggest indecision or hesitancy.

You slipped into the office and read that letter, didn't you?

I have reached the only possible conclusion, haven't I?

6 Use a comma to set off yes/no remarks and mild exclamations.

"Yes, I'll call him right away."

"Oh well, I can put it off for another day."

7 Use commas according to convention in names, titles, dates, numbers, and addresses.

Commas with names and titles

Place a comma directly after a name if it is followed by a title.

Mr. Joe Smith, Executive Editor

Ms. Ann Jacobs, Senior Vice President

Lucy Turner, Ph.D.

Mr. Frank Reynolds, Esq.

Set off a title in commas when writing a sentence.

Mr. Joe Smith, Executive Editor, signed for the package.

Lucy Turner, Ph.D., delivered the commencement address.

Mr. Robert Jones, Sr., attended the ceremony.

Commas with dates

Place a comma between the day of the month and year. If your reference is to a particular month in a year and no date is mentioned, do not use a comma.

January 7, 1992   but   January 1992

When a date is written out, as in an invitation, use the following convention:

the seventh of January, 1992

No commas are used in the military convention for writing dates.

7 January 1992

If you include a day of the week when writing a date, use the following convention:

The package will be delivered on Thursday, January 7, 1992.

Commas with numbers

Place a comma to denote thousands, millions, and so forth.

543   5,430   54,300   543,000   5,430,000   5,430,000,000

Some writers place no comma in four-digit numbers that are multiples of fifty.

2550   1600   but   1,625

Do *not* use commas when writing phone numbers, addresses, page numbers, or years.

Commas with addresses

When writing an address, place a comma between a city (or county) and state.

Baltimore, Maryland   Baltimore County, Maryland

Place no comma between a state and zip code.

Baltimore, Maryland 21215

When writing an address into a sentence, use commas to set off elements that would otherwise be placed on separate lines of the address.

Mr. Abe Stein, Senior Engineer
Stein Engineering
1243 Slade Avenue
Bedford, Massachusetts 01730

The control boards were shipped to Mr. Abe Stein, Senior Engineer, Stein Engineering, 1243 Slade Avenue, Bedford, Massachusetts 01730.

8 Use commas to prevent misreading.

CONFUSING   To get through a tunnel will need to be dug.

REVISED   To get through, a tunnel will need to be dug.

Although no rule calls for it, a comma may be needed to prevent misreading. Misreading can occur when numbers are placed together.

CONFUSING   Down by twenty six members of the squad suddenly woke up.

REVISED   Down by twenty, six members of the squad suddenly woke up.

Misreading can occur when words that are often used as auxiliary verbs (e.g., *will, should,* forms of *be, do*) function as main verbs and occur before other verbs.

CONFUSING   Those who do know exactly what must be done.

REVISED   Those who do, know exactly what must be done.

Misreading can occur when a word that functions both as a preposition and as a modifier (e.g., *after, before, along, around, beneath, through*) is used as a modifier and is followed by a noun.

CONFUSING   Moments after the room began to tilt.

REVISED   Moments after, the room began to tilt.

Misreading can occur when identical words are placed together.

CONFUSING   To speak speak into the microphone and press the button.

REVISED   To speak, speak into the microphone and press the button.

EXERCISE 5

Decide whether commas are needed to clarify meaning in these sentences. Then make up three sentences of your own in which adding a comma will prevent misreading.

1. If you can come join us.
2. The doctor dressed and performed an emergency appendectomy.
3. The doctor dressed and sutured the wound.
4. From beneath the supports began to weaken.
5. By *twos* twenty children walked down the aisle.

25f Editing to avoid misuse or overuse of commas

1 Eliminate the comma splice.

CONFUSING   She climbed the ladder, she slid down the slide.

REVISED   She climbed the ladder. She slid down the slide.
She climbed the ladder, **and** she slid down the slide.

The most frequent comma blunder, the **comma splice,** occurs when a writer joins independent clauses with a comma.

FAULTY   Christopher Columbus is considered a master navigator today, he died in neglect.

To revise a comma splice, see the accompanying box and also chapter 13.

Four Ways to Avoid Comma Splices

1. Separate the two clauses with a period.
   Christopher Columbus is considered a master navigator today. He died in neglect.
2. Join the two clauses with a coordinating conjunction and a comma.
   Christopher Columbus is considered a master navigator today, but he died in neglect.
3. Join the two clauses with a conjunctive adverb and the appropriate punctuation.
   Christopher Columbus is considered a master navigator today; nevertheless, he died in neglect.
4. Join the two clauses by making one subordinate to the other.
   Although Christopher Columbus is considered a master navigator today, he died in neglect.

2 Eliminate commas misused to set off essential (restrictive) elements.

CONFUSING	Athletes, who use steroids, invite disaster. [The sense is that *all* athletes use steroids, which is not true.]
REVISED	Athletes who use steroids invite disaster. [Only those athletes who use steroids invite disaster.]

As noted in 25d-1, commas are not used with essential elements. The presence of commas can alter the meaning of otherwise identical sentences. Therefore, be sure of your meaning as you decide to punctuate (or not) a modifying element.

ESSENTIAL	The students who signed the petition are eligible. [The *who* clause is essential and restricts the meaning of students to those who signed the petition.]
NONESSENTIAL	The students, who signed the petition, are eligible. [The presence of commas signals that the *who* clause is nonessential. The sense of the sentence is that *all* the students signed the petition and are eligible.]

3 Eliminate commas that are misused in a series.

CONFUSING	For tomorrow, memorize the poem, and the song.
REVISED	For tomorrow, memorize the poem and the song.

A comma is not placed before a coordinating conjunction if it connects only two elements in a series.

FAULTY	You cannot learn much about prices, and the amounts of goods traded from demand curves alone.
REVISED	You cannot learn much about prices and the amount of goods traded from demand curves alone.

A comma is *not* used after a second coordinate adjective.

FAULTY	One reason individuals engage in various efforts at self-improvement is that they can imagine alternate, improved, selves.
REVISED	One reason individuals engage in various efforts at self-improvement is that they can imagine alternate, improved selves.

A comma is not placed before the first item in a series or after the last item, unless the comma is required because of a specific rule.

FAULTY	A Central Processing Unit (CPU) is designed with a fixed repertoire of instructions for carrying out a range of tests involving, data manipulation, logical decision making, and control of the computer. [The comma should be eliminated before the first item in this series.]

REVISED   A Central Processing Unit (CPU) is designed with a fixed repertoire of instructions for carrying out a range of tests involving data manipulation, logical decision making, and control of the computer.

4   Eliminate commas that split paired sentence elements.

CONFUSING   The police assisted, the emergency crew.

REVISED   The police assisted the emergency crew.

A comma is not placed between a subject and verb—even if the subject is a lengthy one.

FAULTY   What has sometimes been dramatically termed "the clash of civilizations," is merely the difference in the interpretation given by different societies to the same acts. [The noun clause subject should not be split from its verb *is*.]

REVISED   What has sometimes been dramatically termed "the clash of civilizations" is merely the difference in the interpretation given by different societies to the same acts.

A comma is not placed between a verb and its object or complement, nor between a preposition and its object.

FAULTY   One culture may organize, its social relations around rites of physical initiation. [The comma should not come between the verb and its object.]

REVISED   One culture may organize its social relations around rites of physical initiation.

FAULTY   The principle of mutual respect among, neighboring peoples requires flexibility and tolerance. [The comma should not come between the preposition and its object.]

REVISED   The principle of mutual respect among neighboring peoples requires flexibility and tolerance.

5   Eliminate misuse of commas with quotations.

CONFUSING   "Is anyone home?," he asked.

REVISED   "Is anyone home?" he asked.

A comma is not used after a quotation that ends with a question mark or an exclamation point.

FAULTY   "Get out!," cried the shopkeeper.

REVISED   "Get out!" cried the shopkeeper.

FAULTY   "Is this the way home?," asked Arthur.

REVISED   "Is this the way home?" asked Arthur.

A comma is not used to set apart words quoted (or italicized) for emphasis.

FAULTY   The list of, "exemplary," citizens the Governor referred to includes two convicted felons.

REVISED   The list of "exemplary" citizens the Governor referred to includes two convicted felons.

EXERCISE 6

I tugged Amah's sleeve and asked, "Who is the Moon Lady?"

"Chang-o," replied Amah, "who lives on the moon, and today is the only day you can see her and have a wish fulfilled."

"What is a secret wish?" I asked her.

"It is what you want but cannot ask," said Amah.

"Then how will the Moon Lady know my wish?" I wanted to know.

"Because she is not an ordinary person," Amah explained.

EXERCISE 7

1. Despite the fact that these people are so punctilious about the care of the mouth, this rite involves a practice which strikes the uninitiated stranger as revolting.
2. Correct
3. In addition to the private mouth-rite, the people seek out a holy-mouth-man once or twice a year.
4. These practitioners have an impressive set of paraphernalia, consisting of a variety of augers, awls, probes, and prods. (final comma is optional)
5. The use of these objects in the exorcism of the evils of the mouth involves almost unbelievable ritual torture of the client.
6. The holy-mouth-man opens the client's mouth and, using the above-mentioned tools, enlarges any holes which decay may have created in the teeth.
7. Magical materials are put into these holes.
8. If there are no naturally occurring holes in the teeth, large sections of one or more teeth are gouged out so that the supernatural substance can be applied.
9. In the client's view, the purpose of these ministrations is to arrest decay and to draw friends.
10. Correct

EXERCISE 6

Supply the commas for this dialogue between a young child and her nurse, adapted from Amy Tan's *The Joy Luck Club.*

I tugged Amah's sleeve and asked "Who is the Moon Lady?"

"Chang-o" replied Amah "who lives on the moon and today is the only day you can see her and have a secret wish fulfilled."

"What is a secret wish?" I asked her.

"It is what you want but cannot ask" said Amah.

"Then how will the Moon Lady know my wish?" I wanted to know.

"Because she is not an ordinary person" Amah explained.

EXERCISE 7

Correct the misuse of commas in the sentences that follow (from a parody of an anthropological study). Place a check before the sentences in which commas are used correctly.

Example: The daily body ritual, performed by the Nacirema people includes a mouth-rite.

The daily body ritual performed by the Nacirema people includes a mouth-rite.

1. Despite the fact that these people are so punctilious about the care of the mouth, this rite involves, a practice which strikes the uninitiated stranger as revolting.
2. It was reported to me that the ritual consists of inserting a small bundle of hog hairs into the mouth, along with certain magical powders, and then moving the bundle in a highly formalized series of gestures.
3. In addition to the private mouth-rite, the people seek out a holy-mouth-man once, or twice a year.
4. These practitioners have an impressive set of paraphernalia, consisting of a variety of, augers, awls, probes, and prods.
5. The use of these objects in the exorcism of the evils of the mouth involves, almost unbelievable ritual torture of the client.
6. The holy-mouth-man opens the client's mouth and, using the above mentioned tools, enlarges any holes which decay may have created in the teeth.
7. Magical materials are put into, these holes.
8. If there are no naturally occurring holes in the teeth, large sections of one or more teeth are gouged out so that the supernatural substance, can be applied.

9. In the client's view, the purpose of these ministrations is to arrest decay, and to draw friends.
10. The extremely sacred and traditional character of the rite is evident in the fact that the natives return to the holy-mouth-men year after year, despite the fact that their teeth continue to decay.

EXERCISE 8

Correct the misuse of commas in the following paragraph. In making your corrections, you may need to add or delete words. You should feel free to combine sentences.

> *Example:* The Arlmart Market which has been in operation for seventy years closed its doors last month.
>
> The Arlmart Market, which has been in operation for seventy years, closed its doors last month.

Neighbors and politicians wanted to know how an institution which many affectionately called their "temple of gossip" could close. Mayor Judith Flynn said "We should have supported them more" and she vowed to organize both formal and informal efforts to reopen the store. For those who are old enough to remember the store opened between the two world wars, "Pa" Lettelier handpainted the signs and served as butcher baker and stock manager. "Ma" Lettelier who kept books and arranged credit for mostly anyone in need could usually take a few minutes away from her desk to engage in neighborly talk. Their only son Frank says "They worked 18 hours most days." Frank Lettelier took over twenty years ago, he worked just as hard as his parents and he flourished until the large food chains opened stores in town. "They are interested in money not service" people often heard him complain. Customers even friends eventually abandoned the market, they felt guilty doing so but they had their own finances to worry about, the Arlmart Market couldn't compete. "I'm not bitter" Frank Lettelier says "only saddened."

EXERCISE 8

Neighbors and politicians wanted to know how such an institution, which many affectionately called their "temple of gossip," could close. Mayor Judith Flynn said, "We should have supported them more," and she vowed to organize both formal and informal efforts to reopen the store. For those who are old enough to remember, the store opened between the two world wars. "Pa" Lettelier handpainted the signs and served as butcher, baker, and stock manager. "Ma" Lettelier, who kept books and arranged credit for mostly anyone in need, could usually take a few minutes away from her desk to engage in neighborly talk. Their only son, Frank, says, "They worked 18 hours most days." Frank Lettelier took over twenty years ago. He worked just as hard as his parents, and he flourished until the large food chains opened stores in town. "They are interested in money, not service," people often heard him complain. Customers, even friends, eventually abandoned the market. They felt guilty doing so, but they had their own finances to worry about. The Arlmart Market couldn't compete. "I'm not bitter," Frank Lettelier says, "only saddened."

Semicolons

The main function of a **semicolon** is to separate elements. But as its name suggests, the semicolon serves to make only a "semi" or partial separation that maintains a relationship between independent elements. In its primary use, a semicolon can mark the end of one complete statement and the beginning of another. So can a period or a comma with a co-ordinating conjunction, of course. But whereas a period is chosen to make a full stop, a semicolon denotes a writer's decision to make a partial break. This chapter shows you the situations in which such a partial break is appropriate and gives you the tools for making such decisions as you write or revise your sentences.

26a Use a semicolon, not a comma, to join independent clauses that are intended to be closely related.

Secretariat won the race; Lucky Stars finished second.

Joining independent clauses with a semicolon is one of four basic ways to establish a relationship between clauses, ranging from full separation to subordination of one clause to another. (See the Critical Decisions box.) A comma should never be used to join independent clauses. (See chapter 13 on comma splices.)

FAULTY   Agriculture is one part of the biological revolution, the domestication and harnessing of village animals is the other.

REVISED   Agriculture is one part of the biological revolution; the domestication and harnessing of village animals is the other.

Use semicolons to join closely related independent clauses, not to string unconnected statements together.

Semicolons can be overused. By themselves, they are not enough to make close connections from a series of statements that are simply added together.

OVERUSED   Agriculture was the first part of the biological revolution; the development of crop rotation and irrigation contributed to it; another important part was the harnessing of village animals. [The semicolons add pieces together but do not make the statements closely related.]

REVISED   Agriculture, the first part of the biological revolution, was aided by the development of crop rotation and irrigation. There was also another part of the revolution; this was the harnessing of village animals. [The semicolon joins only closely related statements.]

CRITICAL DECISIONS

Challenge and be challenged: Using a period to separate sentences versus a semicolon or comma (with a conjunction) to link sentences

As a writer, you have options for separating or linking sentences by using coordination or subordination. (See chapter 19.) This discussion focuses on using punctuation to communicate degrees of linkage between sentences and suggests varieties of coordinate, or equal, relationships.

Why separate sentences with a period?

Use a period to show a full separation between sentences.

> Dante Alighieri was banished from Florence in 1302. He wrote the *Divine Comedy* in exile.

Why link sentences with a semicolon?

Use a semicolon, alone, to join sentences balanced in content and structure. Also use a semicolon to suggest that the second sentence completes the content of the first. The semicolon suggests a link but leaves it to the reader to infer how sentences are related.

BALANCED SENTENCE	Agriculture is one part of the biological revolution; the domestication of animals is the other.
SUGGESTED LINK	Five major books and many articles have been written on the Bayeux tapestry; each shows just how much the trained observer can draw from pictorial evidence.

Why link sentences with a conjunctive adverb and a semicolon or period?

Use a semicolon with a conjunctive adverb (*however, therefore,* etc.) to emphasize one of the following relationships: addition, consequence, contrast, cause and effect, time, emphasis, or condition. With the semicolon and conjunctive adverb, linkage between sentences is closer than with a semicolon alone. The relationship between sentences is made clear by the conjunctive adverb.

> Patients in need of organs have begun advertising for them; however, the American Medical Association discourages the practice.

Use a period between sentences to force a pause and then to stress the conjunctive adverb.

> Patients in need of organs have begun advertising for them. However, the American Medical Association discourages the practice.

(continued)

REFERENCES

SHAUGHNESSY, MINA P. *Errors and Expectations: A Guide for the Teacher of Basic Writing.* New York: Oxford UP, 1977. A practical discussion of students' difficulties with semicolons.

LINDEMANN, ERIKA. *A Rhetoric for Writing Teachers.* 2nd ed. New York: Oxford UP, 1987. Chapter 9. In discussing sentences, Lindemann refers to problems students encounter with internal punctuation.

THOMAS, LEWIS. "Notes on Punctuation." *The Medusa and the Snail: More Notes of a Biology Watcher.* New York: Viking, 1979. A whimsical but accurate description of the semicolon's function.

TEACHING IDEAS

This chart will help students understand the relationship between meaning and punctuation with regard to semicolon use. You may want to call their attention to the Critical Decisions box as a handy reference as they make decisions about appropriate use of semicolons in their own papers.

TEACHING IDEAS

It may enhance students' understanding of the uses of semicolons if they see more examples of the constructions described here. You may want to ask students to find examples of their own, providing the following as additional guidelines:

> With Jack Kennedy murdered, they had no hero to bind them, yet in memories of an idealized Camelot they had an image of a recent Golden Age to vivify the promise of liberalism. (Todd Gitlin)

> There must be, not a balance of power, but a community of power; not organized rivalries, but an organized common peace. (Woodrow Wilson)

> Perhaps our greatest responsibility is to repledge our continuing devotion to perpetuating a legacy of language in an age when the spoken word is suspected as "a glib and oily art," manipulative doublespeak; when the written word—badly written, of course—is unread; and when "vibrations" are alleged to be, not inarticulate throbbings, but true communication where every sentence begins with "I feel" and ends with "you know." (Paul Cubeta)

CRITICAL DECISIONS (continued)

Why link sentences with a comma and a coordinating conjunction?

Use a comma and a coordinating conjunction to join sentences in a coordinate relationship that shows addition, choice, consequence, contrast, or cause (see 19a-1). Since two sentences are fully merged into one following this strategy, linkage is complete. At the same time, this method offers the *least* emphasis in showing a coordinate relationship.

> Robotics has increased efficiency in the automobile industry, **but** it has put thousands of assembly-line employees out of work.

26b Use a semicolon, not a comma, to join two independent clauses that are closely linked by a conjunctive adverb.

> I had planned to call London; however, the circuits were busy. Eric arrived late the first day; thereafter, he was on time.

A conjunctive adverb is often used to establish a close connection between independent clauses. (See 19a and the Critical Decisions box on p. 471.) With conjunctive adverbs, use a semicolon (or a period) between the clauses, never a comma. (Refer to chapter 13.)

FAULTY Historical researchers cannot control the events they want to recreate, indeed, they often cannot find enough documentation to learn all the facts of an occurrence. [The comma after *recreate* makes a comma splice; a comma cannot be used to join independent clauses.]

REVISED Historical researchers cannot control the events they want to recreate; indeed, they often cannot find enough documentation to learn all the facts of an occurrence. [Here the conjunctive adverb creates a very close link between clauses.]

NOTE: When independent clauses are closely connected with a conjunctive adverb, the semicolon always falls between the clauses, no matter where the conjunctive adverb is located.

OPTION If chlorophyll is extracted from plant cells and exposed to light, it does momentarily absorb light energy; *however,* this energy is almost immediately reradiated as light.

OPTION If chlorophyll is extracted from plant cells and exposed to light, it does momentarily absorb light energy; this energy is almost immediately reradiated as light, *however.* [The semicolon falls between the independent clauses, even if the adverb is moved to the end of the sentence.]

NOTE: The use of a conjunctive adverb does not necessarily mean that there must be a semicolon between clauses. If you feel that the business of the first clause is finished, or that you do not need a sense of anticipation for the next clause, you can always make a full break between clauses with a period.

OPTION   If chlorophyll is extracted from plant cells and exposed to light, it does momentarily absorb light energy. This energy, however, is almost immediately reradiated as light, usually of a different wavelength. [Here the writer intends for the period to mark a sharp boundary between clauses.]

26c   Join independent clauses with a semicolon before a coordinating conjunction when one or both clauses contain a comma or other internal punctuation.

After the Shuttle landed, Perkins tried calling the President; but he didn't get through.

Short or uncomplicated independent clauses joined by coordinating conjunctions do not normally use a semicolon. However, internal commas or complicated subordinations within one of the independent clauses can create confusion and misreading; in such cases the clauses need stronger separation with a semicolon before the coordinating conjunction.

Gorbachev came to power relatively ill-prepared, both by personal temperament and by previous political experience, to deal with the nationalities in question; and he was clearly impatient that such intensely emotional, indeed irrational, sentiments could divert attention from the larger struggle over reform.

26d   Use a semicolon to separate items in a series when each item is long or when one or more items contain a comma.

I sent the letters to Baltimore, Maryland; Portland, Oregon; and Dallas, Texas.

Short or uncomplicated items in a series are normally separated only by commas (see chapter 25). However, when the units to be separated are further subdivided with internal punctuation or are made up of complex clauses, it is necessary to provide stronger separation with a semicolon.

Several issues have concerned Gorbachev: the extent to which the national republics in the Soviet federation should enjoy real sovereignty; the legal status of the Baltic republics, annexed as a result of the Molotov-Ribbentrop pact; and the criteria for allocating resources among the regions of the USSR.

26e Place semicolons *outside* of end quotation marks.

We read "Ode to the West Wind"; we then discussed the poem in detail.

A semicolon that separates independent clauses and other major elements is not part of a direct quotation.

According to political scientist Gail Lapidus, "Traditional assumptions about life in the Soviet Union are now being directly challenged in public debates"; such debates unquestionably complicate Gorbachev's efforts at political and economic reform.

26f Edit to avoid common errors.

1 Use a comma, not a semicolon, after an introductory subordinate clause.

Use semicolons to link independent clauses; never use them to link subordinate to independent clauses (see chapter 19).

FAULTY   When a writer begins a new project; the blank page can present a barrier.

REVISED   When a writer begins a new project, the blank page can present a barrier.

2 Use a colon, not a semicolon, to introduce a list.

FAULTY   The writing process consists of three stages; planning, drafting, and revision.

REVISED   The writing process consists of three stages: planning, drafting, and revision.

EXERCISE 1

Join the following pairs of sentences with a semicolon, with a semicolon and conjunctive adverb, or with a period and conjunctive adverb. Explain your decision.

Example: Politics and social realism have not been the hallmarks of the film industry in Hollywood.

Yet there was a time when liberal, conservative, and radical organizations made films for a mass audience aimed at politicizing millions of viewers.

Politics and social realism have not been the hallmarks of the film industry in Hollywood; yet there was a time when liberal, conservative, and radical organizations made films for a mass audience aimed at politicizing millions of viewers.

The sentences are closely enough related in meaning to warrant their being joined into a single, compound sentence. For this reason, the semicolon is appropriate. The conjunction *yet* is kept to establish the contrasting relationship between clauses. Without the conjunction this relationship might not be obvious to a reader.

1. During the early years of the twentieth century, leisure assumed an increasingly important role in everyday life.
   Amusement parks, professional baseball games, nickelodeons, and dance halls attracted a wide array of people anxious to spend their hard-earned cash.
2. Of all these new cultural endeavors, films were the most important.
   Even the poorest worker could afford to take his family to the local movie theater.
3. Cinemas took root in urban working-class and immigrant neighborhoods.
   They then spread to middle-class districts of cities and into small communities throughout the country.
4. As early as 1910 the appeal of movies was so great that nearly one-third of the nation flocked to the cinema each week.
   Ten years later, weekly attendance equalled fifty percent of the nation's population.
5. As is true today, early films were primarily aimed at entertaining audiences.
   But then, entertainment did not always come in the form of escapist fantasies.
6. Many of the issues that dominated Progressive-era politics were portrayed on the screen.
   While most of these films were produced by studios and independent companies, a significant number were made by what we might call today "special interest groups."
7. The modest cost of making one- or two-reel films allowed many organizations to make movies to advance their causes.
   Moreover, exhibitors' need to fill their daily bills with new films meant these films would be seen by millions.

EXERCISE 2

In very long sentences semicolons are used in place of commas to prevent misreading. Combine, repunctuate, or otherwise revise the following sentences by using semicolons.

Example: The traditional view of the diffusion of Indo-European languages over wide areas holds that as nomadic mounted warriors conquered indigenous peoples, they

show the relationship between the two sentences.]
2. Of all these new cultural endeavors, films were the most important; even the poorest worker could afford to take his family to the local movie theater. [The two sentences are closely related, but there isn't a logical connection between them requiring a conjunctive adverb.]
3. Cinemas took root in urban working class and immigrant neighborhoods; thereafter, they spread to middle-class districts of cities and into small communities throughout the country. [The conjunctive adverb is necessary to show the time sequence of the two sentences, and their meanings are related closely enough to warrant a semicolon.]
4. As early as 1910 the appeal of movies was so great that nearly one-third of the nation flocked to the cinema each week; moreover, ten years later, weekly attendance equalled fifty per cent of the nation's population. [The sentences are closely related, so a semicolon is preferable to a period. The conjunctive adverb emphasizes the importance of the second sentence.]
5. As is true today, early films were primarily aimed at entertaining audiences. Entertainment, however, did not always come in the form of escapist fantasies. [Separating the two sentences increases the drama of the second sentence. The conjunctive adverb is necessary to show the relationship between the two sentences.]
6. Many of the issues that dominated Progressive-era politics were portrayed on the screen; indeed, while most of these films were produced by studios and independent companies, a significant number were made by what we might call today "special interest groups." [The second sentence fulfills part of the promise of the first, so a semicolon is appropriate. The conjunctive adverb reveals the relationship between the two sentences.]
7. The modest cost of making one- or two-reel films allowed many organizations to make movies to advance their causes. Moreover, exhibitors' need to fill their daily bills with new films meant these films would be seen by millions. [The two reasons given here are quite different, so a period is appropriate. The conjunctive adverb shows the relationship between the two sentences.]

EXERCISE 2

Suggested responses:

1. Linguists divide the languages of Europe into families: the Romance languages include French, Italian, Spanish, Portuguese, and Romanian; the Slavonic languages include Russian, Polish, Czech, Slovak, Serbo-Croat, and Bulgarian; the Germanic languages include German, Norwegian, Danish, and Swedish.
2. Many archaeologists accept a theory of "Kurgan invasions" as an explanation of the spread of Indo-European languages, but others dispute it because the archaeological evidence is not convincing. The core words, which resemble each other from place to place, may have changed meaning over time; moreover, the hordes of mounted warriors would have had no obvious reason for moving west at the end of the Neolithic period.
3. There are four models of how language change might occur according to a process-based view: initial colonization, by which an uninhabited territory becomes populated; linguistic divergence arising from separation or isolation, which some think explains the development of the Romance languages in Europe; linguistic convergence, whereby languages initially quite different become increasingly similar to each other; and, finally, linguistic replacement, whereby indigenous languages are gradually replaced by the language of people coming from the outside.

EXERCISE 3

Suggested responses:

1. For Freud, what the dreamer remembers of a dream is not in itself important; it is a substitute for something not immediately available to the person dreaming, just as "slips of the tongue" are spoken for reasons not immediately understood by a speaker.
2. Freud chooses to refer to what is "hidden" in our psyches as that which is "inaccessible to the consciousness of the dreamer"; that is to say, what is hidden exists and is real but is unconscious at the moment.
3. Correct
4. Freud claims we should not concern ourselves with the surface meaning of a dream, whether it be reasonable or absurd, clear or

imposed their own proto-Indo-European language, *which*, in turn, evolved in local areas into the various languages we know today.

But many scholars have become dissatisfied with this explanation.

The traditional view of the diffusion of Indo-European languages over wide areas holds that as nomadic mounted warriors conquered indigenous peoples, they imposed their own proto-Indo-European language; *this language,* in turn, evolved in local areas into the various languages we know today. But many scholars have become dissatisfied with this explanation.

1. Linguists divide the languages of Europe into families: the Romance languages include French, Italian, Spanish, Portuguese, and Romanian.
   The Slavonic languages include Russian, Polish, Czech, Slovak, Serbo-Croat, and Bulgarian. The Germanic languages include German, Norwegian, Danish, and Swedish.
2. Many archaeologists accept a theory of "Kurgan invasions" as an explanation of the spread of Indo-European languages.
   But others dispute it because the archaeological evidence is not convincing, the core words, which resemble each other from place to place, may have changed meaning over time, and the hordes of mounted warriors would have had no obvious reason for moving west at the end of the Neolithic period.
3. There are four models of how language change might occur according to a process-based view: initial colonization, by which an uninhabited territory becomes populated, linguistic divergence arising from separation or isolation, which some think explains the development of the Romance languages in Europe, linguistic convergence, whereby languages initially quite different become increasingly similar to each other, and, finally, linguistic replacement, whereby indigenous languages are gradually replaced by the language of people coming from the outside.

EXERCISE 3

Correct the misuse of semicolons and, if necessary, the wording in the following sentences. Place a check by any sentence in which a semicolon is used correctly.

Example: Freud remarks in his lecture on the interpretation of dreams that dreams can tell us about the self hidden from conscious view; that they provide unique raw materials for analysis.

Freud remarks in his lecture on the interpretation of dreams that dreams can tell us about the self hidden from conscious view *and* that they provide unique raw materials for analysis.

1. For Freud, what the dreamer remembers of a dream is not in itself important; it is a substitute for something not immediately available to the person dreaming; just as "slips of the tongue" are spoken for reasons not immediately understood by a speaker.
2. Freud prefers to call what is "hidden" in our psyches as that which is "inaccessible to the consciousness of the dreamer;" that is to say, what is hidden exists and is real but is unconscious at the moment.
3. A dream as a whole is a distorted substitute for something else, something unconscious; and it is the task of dream interpretation to discover these unconscious thoughts.
4. Freud claims we should not concern ourselves with the surface meaning of a dream; whether it be reasonable or absurd, clear or confused; since it does not in any way constitute the unconscious thoughts of the dreamer; which is what the interpreter really seeks.

confused. The dream does not in any way constitute the unconscious thought of the dreamer, which is what the interpreter really seeks.

Apostrophes

The **apostrophe** (') is used to show possession, mark the omission of letters or numbers, and mark plural forms. In speech, keeping these matters straight poses no problem. In writing, however, the three uses of the apostrophe very nearly overlap with certain words, creating confusion for the reader. Therefore, try to distinguish carefully among the uses of the apostrophe.

27a Using apostrophes to show possession with single nouns

1 For most nouns and for indefinite pronouns, add an apostrophe and the letter *s* to indicate possession.

Bill's braces	the government's solution
history's verdict	somebody's cat
Susan's basketball	everyone's business

For singular nouns ending with the letter *s, show possession by adding an apostrophe and s if this new construction is not difficult to pronounce.*

Ellis's Diner   hostess's menu   Orson Welles's movie

NOTE: The possessive construction formed with *'s* may be difficult to read if it is followed by a word beginning with an *s* or *z* sound. If this is the case, you have the option of dropping the *s* after the apostrophe.

ACCEPTABLE   Ellis' zipper   or   Ellis's zipper

Whichever convention you adopt, be consistent.

2 Eliminate apostrophes that are misused or confused with possessive pronouns.

Personal pronouns have their own possessive case forms (see chapter 8); they *never* use apostrophes to show possession.

Possession with Personal Pronouns

its	the book's binding	*its* binding
whose	Who owns the book?	*Whose* book is this?
your	the book owned by you	*your* book
yours	the book owned by you	The book is *yours*.

their	a book owned by Bob and Sue	*their* book
theirs	a book owned by Bob and Sue	The book is *theirs*.
her	a book owned by Sue	*her* book
hers	a book owned by Sue	The book is *hers*.
our	a book owned by us	*our* book
ours	a book owned by us	The book is *ours*.
his	a book owned by Bob	*his* book
his	a book owned by Bob	The book is *his*.

Distinguish personal pronouns in their possessive form from personal pronouns that are contractions.

For readers, the most annoying possible mixup with apostrophes occurs when personal pronouns meant to show possession are confused with personal pronouns that are contractions formed with the verb *be,* as shown here. (See the guidelines for making contractions in 27c.)

Personal Pronouns: Contractions Formed with Be

it's	*It is* doubtful he'll arrive.	*It's* doubtful he'll arrive.
who's	*Who is* planning to attend?	*Who's* planning to attend?
you're	*You are* mistaken.	*You're* mistaken.
there's	*There is* little to do.	*There's* little to do.
they're	*They are* home.	*They're* home.

Edit to eliminate apostrophes from personal pronouns that are meant to show possession, not contraction.

FAULTY   You're order has arrived.

REVISED   Your order has arrived.

3   **For a plural noun ending with *s,* add only an apostrophe to indicate possession. For a plural noun not ending with *s,* add an apostrophe and the letter *s.***

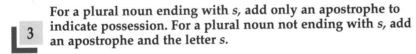

bricklayers' union	teachers' strike
dancers' rehearsal	men's locker
children's games	cattle's watering hole

EXERCISE 1

Read the following sentences. Use either an apostrophe or an apostrophe with the letter *s* to make possessive each noun or pronoun in parentheses.

EXERCISE 1

1. CE Software's
2. other's
3. computers'
4. Dow Jones's
5. owners'
6. file's
7. Microsoft Word's
8. IBM's
9. Macintosh's
10. systems'

GROUP ACTIVITY

All of the exercises in this chapter lend themselves to group activity. Have students respond to exercises individually, and then compare their responses with those of other group members. When the inevitable disagreement occurs, students will have to consult the handbook. Once they become accustomed to using the chapter, they'll likely continue to refer to it as they edit their papers.

Example: (Apple Corporation) Macintosh computers can transfer files with an IBM PC in a variety of ways.

Apple Corporation's Macintosh computers can transfer files with an IBM PC in a variety of ways.

1. You can connect a PC and a Mac with electronic mail software, such as (CE Software) QuickMail.
2. Networks are fast and convenient; they allow both camps access to the (other) hard disk.
3. But networks are rather expensive, and could tie up the linked (computers) memory systems.
4. Online information networks are another alternative. (Dow Jones) Desktop Express for the Macintosh can help download IBM files from a communications service.
5. Direct modem file transfers are inexpensive, but there needs to be an operator at both (owners) computers to ensure problem-free transfers.
6. Graphics files do not transfer as easily as text, so it is important to know your graphics (files) language codes.
7. (Microsoft Word) software can read documents written in both IBM and Mac formats on either computer.
8. Not too long ago it was thought that a Macintosh would never work with (IBM) programs.
9. Yet there are programs available today that can emulate and run almost any IBM software on a (Macintosh) configuration.
10. It is projected that over the next few years, the increased ease in transferring files from one computer system to another will help boost alternative (systems) sales.

27b Using apostrophes to show possession with multiple nouns

Multiple nouns showing possession can be tricky to punctuate, since the apostrophe and the letter *s* will indicate who—and how many people—own what, either separately or together. Because establishing possession is so important (especially in our culture), take care when using the apostrophe with multiple nouns. Punctuate so that your sentences express your exact meaning.

1 To indicate possession when a cluster of words functions as a single noun, add an apostrophe and the letter *s* to the last word.

Executive Vice President's role
brother-in-law's car

Chief Executive Officer's salary
First Deck Officer's watch

CRITICAL DECISIONS

Be alert to differences: Test your placement of apostrophes with nouns and with indefinite pronouns.

The personal pronouns *his, hers, ours, its, yours,* and *theirs* **never** use apostrophes. By contrast, nouns and indefinite pronouns (such as *somebody, other,* and *no one*) do use apostrophes to show possession. Nouns and indefinite pronouns also form plurals with the suffix *-s.* Apply the following tests to determine whether or not you should be using an apostrophe and *s* (*'s*) or the suffix *-s,* with no apostrophe.

Is the noun or indefinite pronoun followed by a noun? If so, then you probably intend to show possession. Use the possessive form *'s.*

<table>
<tr><td align="center">noun</td><td></td><td align="center">noun</td></tr>
<tr><td>government's <u>policy</u></td><td></td><td>hospital's <u>program</u></td></tr>
<tr><td align="center">noun</td><td></td><td align="center">noun</td></tr>
<tr><td>family's <u>holiday</u></td><td></td><td>other's <u>comment</u></td></tr>
</table>

Is a noun or indefinite pronoun followed by a verb or a modifying phrase? If so, then you probably intend to make the noun or indefinite pronoun plural. Use the suffix *-s,* with *no* apostrophe.

modifying phrase
government<u>s in that part of the world</u>

modifying phrase
famil<u>ies having two or more children</u>

modifying clause
hospital<u>s that have large staffs</u>

verb
other<u>s believe</u>

But if an omitted word is involved, you may need a possessive form.

Eric's friends attend Central High. Frank's attend Northern.

[In the second sentence, the omitted noun *friends* is clearly intended as the subject of the sentence. The *'s* is needed to show whose friends—*Frank's.*]

---

2 **To indicate possession of an object owned jointly, add an apostrophe and the letter *s* to the last noun (or pronoun) named.**

Smith and Thompson's interview notes are meticulous. [The notes belong jointly to, they were gathered jointly by, Smith and Thompson.]

Mary and Bill**'s** car needs a muffler. [The car belongs jointly to Mary and Bill.]

GROUP ACTIVITY

It may take some time for students to comprehend fully the intricacies of apostrophe use, so the following activity might be helpful: Ask groups to generate examples of phrases including nouns and indefinite pronouns, some of which require apostrophes and some of which do not. (They can use the examples in the Critical Decisions box as a guide.) However, no apostrophes should appear in any of the phrases. The completed phrases will then be passed on to other groups, whose task will be to determine which phrases require apostrophes and which do not. Discussion of where to use apostrophes should help students understand their use more clearly.

REFERENCE

FLESCH, RUDOLF. *The ABC of Style: A Guide to Plain English.* New York: Harper, 1964. 29–30. "Plain English" should include, not shun, contractions.

3 **To indicate individual possession by two or more people, add an apostrophe and the letter *s* to each person named.**

Judy's and Rob's interview notes are meticulous. [The reference is to two sets of notes, one belonging to Judy and the other to Rob.]

27c Using apostrophes in contractions to mark the omission of letters and numbers

When you join or compress words into a contraction, you omit letters to indicate a more rapid, informal pace of pronunciation. The omission *must* be marked in writing with an apostrophe. Similarly, when you omit numbers in a date, use an apostrophe. Because many readers consider contractions an informality, you may want to avoid using them in academic writing. When in doubt about the appropriateness of contractions and the register they indicate in a particular document, check with the professor who will be reading your work.

1 **Use an apostrophe to indicate the omission of letters in a contraction.**

can't = can not   won't = will not   you've = you have

2 **Use an apostrophe to indicate the omission of numbers in a date.**

the '60s   the '80s   the '90s

3 **Eliminate apostrophes from verbs in their -*s* form.**

The -*s* ending used in regular verb formation does *not* involve the omission of any letters (see 9a). Any apostrophe that creeps into such verb endings should be eliminated.

FAULTY   He walk's with a limp.   A cat eat's mice.

REVISED   He wal**ks** with a limp.   A cat eat**s** mice.

EXERCISE 2

1. your (crew's is correct)   6. your
2. they're   7. who's
3. It's   8. correct
4. correct   9. who's
5. your   10. who's

EXERCISE 2

Correct the use of apostrophes in the following sentences by adding or deleting apostrophes as needed. Place a check by the sentences in which apostrophes are used correctly.

Example: Rough weather sailing can be exciting, but only if you're crew is well prepared for it.

Rough weather sailing can be exciting, but only if your crew is well prepared for it.

1. Bad weather inevitably puts you're crew's lives in danger.
2. Obviously their likely to be wetter and colder; foul weather gear should be available and distributed *before* the first splash lands in the cockpit.
3. Its equally important to take precautions to prevent risk of injury to limbs and body.
4. Those who normally lead a sedentary life are much more liable to injuries than those whose muscles are well exercised to withstand rubs, bumps, and twists.
5. Inadequate footwear, or none at all if you're feet are not hardened to such treatment, can lead to real pain if a toe is stubbed against a deck bolt or stanchion.
6. Make sure you have a working man-overboard pole—you're attention to safety could save someone's life.
7. Bad weather is particularly tiring and can result in seasickness; keep a watch to see whose becoming sick.
8. Seasickness and exhaustion combined can lead to a state of not caring what happens next to your boat and crew.
9. An exhausted sailor huddled in a wave- and windswept cockpit, peering into the murk, can easily come to see Poseidon, whose lashing the waves to fury out of spite.
10. Perhaps the easiest precaution to avoid problems in raw weather is to bring a crew whose not afraid of the tense environment faced while sailing in rough seas.

27d   Using apostrophes to mark plural forms

As readers, we expect the letter *s* or letters *es* placed at the end of a word to show that the word is plural. Yet if we were to follow that convention with letters or symbols, we would quickly create a puzzle of pronunciation: *How many les in Lilliputian?* We avoid the confusion by adopting a different convention to form the plurals of letters, symbols, and so on.

1   **Use an apostrophe and the letter *s* to indicate the plural of a letter, number, or word referred to as a word.**

The letter, number, or word made plural should be underlined if typewritten or set in italics if typeset. Do *not* underline or italicize the apostrophe or the letter *s*.

Standard for Typewriter Usage

```
Mind your p's and q's.
How many 5's in sixty?
The frequent in's and with's reduced the effectiveness of
his presentation.
```

TEACHING IDEAS

The situations covered here are found only rarely in students' academic writing, but students will nevertheless encounter situations in which they'll need to know these rules. You may want to encourage them to keep handbooks like this available for easy reference later in their careers.

Standard for Typeset Usage

Mind your *p*'s and *q*'s.

How many 5's in sixty?

The frequent *in*'s and *with*'s reduced the effectiveness of his writing.

EXCEPTION: When forming the plural of a proper noun (e.g., someone's name), omit the apostrophe but retain the letter *s*.

Standard for Typewriter Usage

```
At the convention I met three Franks and two Maudes.
```

Standard for Typeset Usage

At the convention I met three *Frank*s and two *Maude*s.

Using an apostrophe in this case would mistakenly suggest possession and thus confuse a reader.

2 **Use an apostrophe and the letter *s* to indicate the plural of a symbol, an abbreviation with periods, and years expressed in decades.**

Do *not* underline or italicize the symbol, the abbreviation, or the decade.

Joel is too fond of using &'s in his writing.
With all the M.D.'s at this conference, I feel safe.
Computer assisted software engineering will be important in the 1990's.

OPTION: Some writers omit the apostrophe before the letter *s* when forming the plural of decades, abbreviations without periods, and symbols.

1900s   or   1900's

IBMs   or   IBM's

%s   or   %'s

Whichever convention you adopt, be consistent.

3 **Eliminate any apostrophes misused to form regular plurals of nouns.**

For a regular noun, an apostrophe is never used to create a plural form; rather, the apostrophe indicates possession (see 7a-2).

POSSESSIVE	the cat's meow	that idea's beginning
FAULTY PLURAL	Cat's eat meat.	Idea's begin in thought.
REVISED PLURAL	Cats eat.	Ideas begin.

EXERCISE 3

Follow the instructions in parentheses after each sentence to clarify possession.

> *Example:* The *governor office personnel* have formed some close friendships. (Use apostrophes to indicate that the people who have become friends work in the office of the governor.)
>
> The governor's office personnel have formed some close friendships.

1. Jane O'Leary works at the State House as the *governor spokesperson.* (Use apostrophes to indicate that the spokesperson for the governor is Jane O'Leary.)
2. *Mrs. O'Leary and her husband Bob house* is replete with pictures of government officials posing with the O'Leary family. (Use apostrophes to indicate that Mrs. O'Leary and Bob own their house together.)
3. The governor lives around the corner, in the *Governor Mansion.* (Use apostrophes to indicate that the governor lives in the mansion.)
4. *Jane O'Leary and the governor homes* are decorated similarly, both in a colonial style. (Use apostrophes to indicate that two different homes are being referred to.)
5. Often they'll have dinner together, cooked by *Jane and the governor husbands.* (Use apostrophes to indicate that two husbands cook together.)

EXERCISE 4

Decide whether an apostrophe is needed to form plurals for the following letters, numbers, or words.

> *Example:* b
>
> b's (or *b*'s if typeset)

1. &   2. 42   3. 7   4. j   5. d   6. Karen

EXERCISE 5

Read the following paragraph on Donald Duck. Provide apostrophes and rewrite words as needed.

Theirs one basic product never stocked in Disneys store: parents. Disneys is a universe of uncles and grand-uncles, nephews and cousins. The male-female relationships existence is found only in eternal fiancés. Donald Duck and Daisy relationship, like Mickey Mouse and Minnie relationship, is never consummated or even legitimized through the all-American institution of marriage. More troubling, though, is the origin of all of the nephews and uncles in the Disney Comics worlds. Huey, Dewey, and Louie Uncle Donald is never known to have a sister or sister-in-law. In fact, most of Donald relatives are unmarried and unattached males, like Scrooge

---

EXERCISE 3

1. governor's
2. Mrs. O'Leary and her husband Bob's
3. Governor's
4. Jane O'Leary's and the governor's
5. Jane's and the governor's

EXERCISE 4

1. &'s   4. *j*'s
2. 42's   5. *d*'s
3. 7's   6. *Karen*s

EXERCISE 5

There's one basic product never stocked in Disney's store: parents. Disney's is a universe of uncles and grand-uncles, nephews and cousins. The male-female relationship's existence is found only in eternal fiancés. Donald Duck and Daisy's relationship, like Mickey Mouse and Minnie's relationship, is never consummated or even legitimized through the all-American institution of marriage. More troubling, though, is the origin of all of the nephews and uncles in the Disney Comics' worlds. Huey, Dewey, and Louie's Uncle Donald is never known to have a sister or sister-in-law. In fact, most of Donald's relatives are unmarried and unattached males, like Scrooge McDuck. Donald's own parents are never mentioned, although Grandma Duck purports to be the widowed ancestor of the Duck family (again no husband-wife relationship). Donald's and Mickey's girlfriends, Daisy and Minnie, are often accompanied by nieces of their own. Since these women are not very susceptible to men or matrimonial bonds, Disney's "families" are necessarily and perpetually composed of bachelors accompanied by nephews, who come and go. A quick look at Walt Disney's own biography demonstrates a possible reason for his comics' anti-love, anti-marriage sentiments: Disney's mother is rarely mentioned, and his wife's role in his life was minimal at best. As for the future of the Magic Kingdom's demographic increases, it is predictable that they will be the result of extrasexual factors.

McDuck. Donalds own parents are never mentioned, although Grandma Duck purports to be the widowed ancestor of the Duck family (again no husband-wife relationship). Donald and Mickey girlfriends, Daisy and Minnie, are often accompanied by nieces of their own. Since these women are not very susceptible to men or matrimonial bonds, Disney's "families" are necessarily and perpetually composed of bachelors accompanied by nephews, who come and go. A quick look at Walt Disneys own biography demonstrates a possible reason for his comics anti-love, anti-marriage sentiments: Disney's mother is rarely mentioned, and his wifes role in his life was minimal at best. As for the future of the Magic Kingdoms demographic increases, it is predictable that they will be the result of extra-sexual factors.

CHAPTER 28

Quotation Marks

Quoting the words of others is a necessary, essential fact of academic life, both for professors and for students. As a writer you will make claims, cite the words and work of others, and then respond to those words. For the sake of both accuracy and fairness, your quotations must be managed precisely. (See 34g on quoting sources in research.) If you quote to help make a point, you must do so accurately since readers count on you for a faithful transcription of what another has written. (See chapter 36 for conventions on citing sources in various disciplines.) This chapter will discuss the conventions for quoting as well as the stylistic tricks for smoothly incorporating quoted language into your work.

28a Quoting prose

1 Use double quotation marks (" ") to set off a short direct quotation from the rest of a sentence.

Short quotations—those that span four or fewer lines of your manuscript—may be incorporated into your writing by running them in with your sentences as part of your normal paragraphing. When quoting a source, reproduce exactly the wording and punctuation of the quoted material. For the most part, when you enclose the material in quotation marks, you will do so to indicate **direct discourse,** the exact re-creation of words spoken or written by another person. Direct discourse places another person's language directly before readers as if you (the writer) were not present.

DIRECT   "To us," write scholars Douglas C. Wilson and William L. Rathje, "modern garbage deserves as much of our attention as does ancient garbage."

Indirect discourse occurs when you quote the words of someone inexactly, and from a distance.

INDIRECT   Douglas C. Wilson and William L. Rathje believe that modern garbage deserves as much archaeological attention as ancient garbage.

Indirect discourse inserts your voice into the quotation: You mediate the quotation, or create the frame through which your readers perceive it.

KEY FEATURES

This chapter will be a valuable reference tool for students who have trouble figuring out what to do with quotation marks. Use of quotation marks for direct quotations, dialogue, titles of short works, and emphasizing words, as well as other uses, is covered thoroughly. In addition, advice regarding quoted material within a quotation, placement of other punctuation with respect to quotation marks, and inappropriate use of quotation marks are all discussed. This material is especially pertinent to the proper uses of sources in the research paper, as discussed in 34g on quoting sources. Exercises allow students to use quotation marks in a number of ways, both in sentences and paragraphs.

TEACHING IDEAS

ACROSS THE CURRICULUM The introduction refers students to chapters that deal specifically with writing in various disciplines. Students should understand, however, that while *documentation* may vary by discipline, the rules for *punctuating a quotation* are the same in all disciplines.

ESL ALERT

Indirect discourse will be a problem area. ESL students might query why something that remains true must take a past tense form to agree: "He said that his name was John." ("Isn't it still John?" they will ask.) The rule is: Only unchanging facts of nature retain the present tense with an introductory past tense form.

> "He said that the sun rises in the east and sets in the west."
>   but
> "He said that the sun rose at six yesterday morning."

See 43b-4 on using verbs with reported speech.

REFERENCES

SUMMEY, GEORGE, JR. *American Punctuation.* New York: Ronald, 1949. Chapter 9. An extensive discussion on quotation marks that is still relevant today.

The following style sheets provide advice on using quotation marks:

The Chicago Manual of Style. 14th ed. Chicago: U of Chicago P, 1993.

GIBALDI, JOSEPH, and WALTER S. ACHTERT. *MLA Handbook for Writers of Research Papers.* 3rd ed. New York: MLA, 1988.

ALTERING A QUOTATION: **Quotation marks** denote the *exact* reproduction of words written or spoken by someone else. Changes that you make to quoted material (such as words omitted or added) must be announced as such—either with brackets or ellipses (see 29d and e).

2 **Use single quotation marks (' ') to set off quoted material or the titles of short works within a quotation enclosed by double (" ") marks.**

The use of single quotation marks can be shown by a comparison of original passages with quotations.

ORIGINAL PASSAGES

> Piecing through the ruins of our culture, anthropologists in the year 3000 will refer to our span of the twentieth century as the "mall era."

> Read Lukow's "Quest for Supremacy," an essay in this month's *Politics as Usual.*

QUOTATIONS

> Anthropologist Richard Marks believes that his colleagues 1000 years from now "will refer to our span of the twentieth century as the 'mall era.' "

> "Read Lukow's 'Quest for Supremacy,' " said Professor Lapidus.

If you find it necessary to quote material within single quotation marks, use double marks once again.

> Historian Beth Bailey cites popular magazines as one source of information. "In *Mademoiselle*'s 1938 college issue," writes Bailey, "a Smith college senior advised incoming freshmen to 'cultivate an image of popularity' if they wanted dates. 'During your first term,' the senior wrote, 'get "home talent" to ply you with letters, invitations, and telegrams.' "

3 **Use commas to enclose explanatory remarks that lie outside the quotation.**

A comma is placed after an explanatory remark that introduces a quotation.

> According to Bailey, "Competition was the key term in the formula—remove it and there was no rating, dating, or popularity."

When a remark interrupts a quotation, a pair of commas or a comma and a period should be used. The conventions for punctuation are as follows: The first comma enclosing an explanatory remark notes the (temporary) ending of the quoted material and is placed inside the quotation. If the sentence continues past the explanatory comment, a second comma is placed before the quote is reintroduced. If the sentence ends with an explanatory remark, a period is placed after that remark. In this case, when the quotation is resumed in a new sentence, the first letter of the quotation is capitalized.

> "Rating, dating, popularity, competition," writes Bailey, "were catch-words hammered home, reinforced from all sides until they seemed a natural vocabulary."

> "You had to rate in order to date, to date in order to rate," she adds. "By successfully maintaining the cycle, you became popular."

NOTE: When the word *that* introduces a direct quotation, or when an introductory remark has the sense of a "that" construction but the word itself is omitted, do not use a comma to separate the introduction from the quoted material. In addition, do not capitalize the first letter of the quotation.

FAULTY   Bailey discovered that, "The Massachusetts *Collegian* (the Massachusetts State College student newspaper) ran an editorial against using the library for 'datemaking.' "

REVISED   Bailey discovered that "the Massachusetts *Collegian* (the Massachusetts State College student newspaper) ran an editorial against using the library for 'datemaking.' "

See the Critical Decisions box on p. 492 for more information on incorporating quotations into your sentences.

4   **Display—that is, set off from text—lengthy quotations. Quotation marks are *not* used to enclose a displayed quotation.**

Quotations of five or more lines are too long to run in with sentences in a paragraph. Instead they are displayed in a block format in a narrower indentation, without being enclosed by quotation marks.

In his remarks, Bill Bradley spoke on the impressive economic growth of East Asia:

> East Asia is quickly becoming the richest, most populous, most dynamic area on earth. Over the last quarter century, the East Asian economies grew at an average real growth rate of 6 percent annually while the economies of the United States and the countries of the European Community grew at 3 percent. East Asia's share of gross world product has more than doubled during the last twenty years, rising from 8 percent to 20 percent.

Manuscript form

Double space the displayed quotation and indent ten spaces from the left margin. Punctuate material as in the original text. Quotation marks inside a displayed quotation remain double (" ") marks. If one paragraph is being displayed, do not indent the first word of the paragraph. If multiple paragraphs are being displayed, indent the first word of each paragraph three additional spaces (that is, thirteen spaces from the left). However, if you are quoting multiple paragraphs and the first sentence quoted does not begin a paragraph in the original source, then do not indent the first paragraph in your paper.

A displayed quotation is best introduced with a full sentence, ending with a colon. The colon provides a visual cue to the reader that a long quotation follows.

5   Place periods and commas inside the end quotation mark.

"The big question is whether this kind of growth is sustainable" says Bradley.

He adds, "Because American trade deficits must shrink in the years ahead, Asian nations can no longer count as heavily on expanding exports to the United States to fuel their growth."

EXCEPTION: When a pair of parentheses enclosing some comment or page reference appears between the end of the quotation and the end of the sentence, use quotation marks to note the end of the quoted text, place the parentheses, and then close with a period.

CONFUSING   He adds, "Because American trade deficits must shrink in the years ahead, Asian nations can no longer count as heavily on expanding exports to the United States to fuel their growth. (1)"

REVISED   He adds, "Because American trade deficits must shrink in the years ahead, Asian nations can no longer count as heavily on expanding exports to the United States to fuel their growth" (1).

6   Place colons, semicolons, and footnotes outside end quotation marks.

COLON   Bradley directly asserts that "the futures of Asia and the United States are inextricably intertwined": Asian countries profited by U.S. growth in the 1980s, and the U.S. must profit by Asian growth in the '90s and beyond.

SEMICOLON   Bradley believes that the United States must look to the East with the intention of forming a "strong, lasting partnership"; moreover, he states that we must do so without the condescension that has for so long characterized our relations with countries like Japan and South Korea.

FOOTNOTE   Bradley believes that the United States must look to the East with the intention of forming a "strong, lasting partnership."[4]

7 Place question marks and exclamation points inside or outside end quotation marks, depending on meaning.

Place a question mark or exclamation point *inside* the end quotation marks when it applies to the quoted material only or when it applies to both the quoted material and the sentence as a whole. Place the mark *outside* the end quotation mark when the sentence as a whole forms a question or exclamatory remark but the quoted material does not.

MARK APPLIES TO QUOTED MATERIAL ONLY

Naturalist José Márcio Ayres began his field work on the ukaris monkey of the upper Amazon with this question: "How do these primates survive almost exclusively on the pulp and seeds of fruit, when the forests in which they live are flooded much of the year?"

MARK APPLIES BOTH TO QUOTED MATERIAL AND TO SENTENCE AS WHOLE

How can we, sitting comfortably in living rooms and libraries, appreciate the rigors of field research when even Ayres remarks, "Is the relative protection of the ukaris habitat at all surprising in light of the enormous swarms of mosquitoes one encounters in all seasons and at all hours of the day?"

MARK APPLIES TO SENTENCE AS A WHOLE BUT NOT TO QUOTATION

Bachelor ukaris looking for mates behave as badly as hooligans at a soccer match. Ayres reports that fights are frequent and that "after all this trouble, copulation may last less than two minutes"!

 8 Place dashes inside quotations only when they are part of the quoted material.

PART OF QUOTED MATERIAL

Would-be competitors like "brocket deer, peccaries, agoutis, armadillos, and pacas—mammals common in upland habitats—"do not inhabit the ukaris forest, most likely because of the Amazon's annual flooding. This is one reason the ukaris has survived.

SEPARATE FROM QUOTED MATERIAL

Once the flood waters recede, each afternoon the ukaris descend from the upper canopy of trees—"where the temperature is uncomfortably high"—to forage for seedlings, which they dig up and eat.

EXERCISE 1

Use double quotation marks (" ") and single quotation marks (' ') to punctuate the sentences that follow. Words to be quoted are underlined.

Example: According to Carla Fernandez, <u>One third of all offenders are in prison because of property offenses such as larceny, car theft, and burglary.</u>

According to Carla Fernandez, "One third of all offenders are in prison because of property offenses such as larceny, car theft, and burglary."

GROUP ACTIVITY

All of the exercises in this chapter lend themselves to group activity. Have students respond to exercises individually, and then compare their responses with those of other group members. When the inevitable disagreement occurs, students will have to consult the handbook. Once they become accustomed to using the chapter, they'll likely continue to refer to it as they edit their papers.

EXERCISE 1

1. Half of the prison population has been incarcerated for "violent crimes such as assault, homicide, and rape."
2. The remaining 20 percent of offenders have been convicted of "offenses against public order, such as drug dealing."
3. In a speech on March 2, 1992, New York corrections official Stuart Koman voiced a widely held view: "Overcrowded prisons not only do not rehabilitate offenders, they teach offenders to reject the law-abiding life. One individual who has spent 13 of his 25 years behind bars said to me that 'I learned my techniques in jail. You know, the tools of my trade.' "
4. As sociologist Lauren Rose concludes, "Efforts to reform prisons and to make them real *penitentiaries*—institutions of penitence—have failed" (Jacobs 341).
5. "One dilemma that we now face," according to Rolf Hanson, "is to understand whether we want incarceration to correct criminal behavior or to punish it."

FOR DISCUSSION

No discussion of how to quote is complete without a focus on when to quote. Encourage students at this point to talk about their decisions to use quotations:

Have any of them ever chosen to quote on their own rather than in response to a teacher's instructions? If so, what contributed to the decision?

When assigned papers requiring quotations, how do students decide what and when to quote?

How often do students think the quotations they use really fit into their text?

What do they see as the relationship between the quotations and the text?

These and other similar questions should help students articulate their understanding of quotations as they ponder the advice found in the Critical Decisions box.

1. Half of the prison population has been incarcerated for <u>violent crimes such as assault, homicide, and rape</u>.
2. The remaining 20 percent of offenders have been convicted of <u>offenses against public order,</u> such as drug dealing.
3. In a speech on March 2, 1992, New York corrections official Stuart Koman voiced a widely held view: <u>Overcrowded prisons not only do not rehabilitate offenders, they teach offenders to reject the law-abiding life. One individual who has spent 13 of his 25 years behind bars said to me that "I learned my techniques in jail. You know, the tools of my trade."</u>
4. As sociologist Lauren Rose concludes, <u>Efforts to reform prisons and to make them real *penitentiaries*—institutions of penitence—have failed (Jacobs 341).</u>
5. <u>One dilemma that we now face</u>, according to Rolf Hanson, <u>is to understand whether we want incarceration to correct criminal behavior or to punish it</u>.

CRITICAL DECISIONS

Set issues in a broader context: Incorporating quotations into your writing

Knowing when to quote is something of an art, and you should see 34g for guidance on this matter. This discussion assumes you have decided to quote. The focus here is on determining *how much* to quote and on how to *incorporate* quoted materials into the logic and rhythm of your sentences.

The following examples draw on the following passage about shopping malls by the noted anthropologist Richard Marks (*The New American Bazaar*).

When they are successful, shopping malls in American cities fulfill the same function as *bazaars* did in the cities of antiquity. The bazaars of the ancient and medieval worlds were social organisms—if we mean by this term self-contained, self-regulating systems in which individual human lives are less important (and less interesting) than the interaction of hundreds, and sometimes thousands, of lives.

How much to quote

Quote other writers when you find their discussions to be particularly lively, dramatic, or incisive or especially helpful in bolstering your credibility (see 34g). In general, quote as little as possible so that you keep readers focused on *your* discussion.

- Quote a word or a phrase, if this will do.

  Anthropologist Richard Marks refers to the American shopping mall as a "social organism."

- Quote a sentence, if needed.

  Marks sees in shopping malls a modern spin on an ancient institution: "When they are successful, shopping malls in American cities fulfill the same function as *bazaars* did in the cities of antiquity."

(continued)

CRITICAL DECISIONS (continued)

■ Infrequently quote a long passage as a "block."

Long quotations of five or more lines are set off as a block (see 28a-4). Limit your use of block quotations, which tempt writers to avoid the hard work of selecting for quotation *only* the words or sentences especially pertinent to the discussion at hand. If you decide that a long quotation is needed, introduce the quotation with a full sentence and a colon. The following might introduce the passage previously quoted from *The New American Bazaar*.

> Various commentators have claimed that shopping malls serve a social function. Anthropologist Richard Marks compares the mall to the bazaar in cities of old:
>> When they are successful, shopping malls . . .

Using attributive phrases

■ Use attributive phrases.

By using attributive phrases like *Jones argues*, *Smith says*, or *according to Marks*, you alert readers to the fact that you are about to present someone else's words. (See the box in 34d-5 for a list of attributive verbs.) Tie these attributive phrases into the logic of your own sentences, linking the quotation with the content of your paper.

> Every American city now has its shopping malls. According to anthropologist Richard Marks, successful malls "fulfill the same function as *bazaars* did in the cities of antiquity."

■ Interrupt a quotation with an attributive phrase.

Place your attributive comment between a quotation's subject and verb or after an introductory phrase or clause in order to emphasize a key word. The word emphasized will come just before or after the interruption.

> "When they are successful," says Richard Marks, "shopping malls in American cities fulfill the same function as *bazaars* did in the cities of antiquity." [The interruption focuses attention on *shopping malls*.]

Split a quotation with an attributive remark to maintain the rhythm or continuity of your own paragraph. Compare these two versions of a quoted sentence.

ACCEPTABLE   Every American city has its shopping malls, its equivalents of the ancient bazaar. As anthropologist Richard Marks points out, "The bazaars of the ancient and medieval worlds were social organisms . . . "

PREFERRED   Every American city has its shopping malls, its equivalents of the ancient bazaar. "The bazaars of the ancient and medieval worlds," says anthropologist Richard Marks, "were social organisms . . . " [This version maintains paragraph coherence by keeping the reader's focus on the word *bazaar*.]

28b Quoting poetry, dialogue, and other material

> **Run-in brief quotations of poetry with your sentences. Indicate line breaks in the poem with a slash (/). Quote longer passages in displayed form.**

1

A full quotation of or a lengthy quotation from a poem is normally made in displayed form (see 28a-3).

The Black Riders

42

I walked in a desert.
and I cried:
"Ah, God, take me from this place!"
A voice said: "It is no desert."
I cried, "Well, but—
The sand, the heat, the vacant horizon."
A voice said: "It is no desert."

—STEPHEN CRANE

When quoting a brief extract—four lines or fewer—you can run the lines into the sentences of a paragraph, using the guidelines for quoting prose (see 28a); however, line divisions are shown with a slash(/) with one space before and one space after.

Stephen Crane's bleak view of the human condition is expressed in lyric 42 of his series "The Black Riders." Walking in a desert, his narrator cries: " 'Ah, God, take me from this place!' / A voice said: 'It is no desert.' "

2 Use quotation marks to quote or write dialogue.

When quoting or writing dialogue, change paragraphs to note each change of speaker. Explanatory comments between parts of the quotation are enclosed with two commas. The first, signaling the (temporary) ending of the quoted material, is placed *inside* the end quotation mark. The second comma, signaling the end of the explanatory remark, is placed before the quotation mark that opens the next part of the quotation. When the quotation resumes, its first letter may be capitalized only if a new sentence has been started (in which case the comma concluding the explanatory material is changed to a period).

"Nobody sees you any more, Helen," Nat began. "Where've you disappeared to?"

"Oh, I've been around," she said, trying to hide a slight tremble in her voice. "And you?"

TEACHING IDEAS

You may want to provide students with further examples of the use of quotation marks in dialogue. If the course includes a component in imaginative literature, you'll have a wealth of examples at your disposal. Here is one further example:

"Will you forgive me?"

She doesn't answer right away, which is fine, because I have to get used to the fact that I said it.

"Maybe," she says at last, "but I'm not the same girl."

I'm about to say she hasn't changed, and then I realize how much she has changed. She has gotten smarter than I am by a long shot, to understand she is different.

"I'm different now, too," I am able to admit.   (Louise Erdrich)

(This example illustrates all of the issues regarding quotation in dialogue covered in this section.)

"Is somebody there where you're talking that you sound so re-strained?"

"That's right."

"I thought so. So let me make it quick and clean. Helen, it's been a long time. I want to see you. What do you say if we take in a play this Saturday night? I can stop off for tickets on my way uptown tomorrow."

—BERNARD MALAMUD, *The Assistant*

In a speech of two or more paragraphs, begin each new paragraph with opening quotation marks to signal your reader that the speech continues. Use closing quotation marks *only* at the end of the final paragraph to signal that the speech has concluded.

3 | **Indicate the titles of brief works with quotation marks: chapters of books, short stories, poems, songs, sections from newspapers, essays, etc.[1]**

I read the "Focus Section" of the *Boston Sunday Globe* every week.

"The Dead" is, perhaps, Joyce's most famous short story.

"Coulomb's law" is the first chapter in volume two of Gartenhaus's text, *Physics: Basic Principles*.

Manuscript form

When placed on the title page of a paper you are submitting to a professor or your peers, the title of your work should *not* be put in quotation marks. Only when you are quoting a title (yours or anyone else's) *in* a paper do you use quotation marks. However, if a title itself contains a title—a reference to some other work, you must quote appropriately. If the title of your own paper included a reference to a poem, the title would look like this:

Images of the Quest in Tennyson's "Ulysses."

This same title, referred to *in* a sentence:

In her paper "Images of the Quest in Tennyson's 'Ulysses,'" Donna Smith defines heroism as a forward-looking state of mind, not as a series of great (but already accomplished) deeds.

When a title is included in any other quoted material, double quotation marks (" ") change to single marks (' ').

---

[1]The titles of longer works—books, newspapers, magazines, long poems—are underlined in typewritten text and italicized in typeset text. (See chapter 36.)

LOOKING BACK

Students should be told that use of quotation marks for the purpose of emphasis should be confined to rare occasions. You may want to remind them that it is far better to use precise diction than to resort to punctuation in order to achieve emphasis (see chapter 21).

4 Use quotation marks occasionally to emphasize words or to note invented words.

An uncommon usage of a standard term or a new term that has been invented for a special circumstance can be highlighted with quotation marks. Once you have emphasized a word with quotation marks, you need not use the marks again with that word.

> In the mid-1960s, when relaxed restrictions dramatically increased Asian immigration to the United States, the popular press, politicians, and others assigned Asian Americans the role of "model minority."

Words that will be defined in a sentence, or words that are referred to as words, are usually italicized, though they are sometimes set in quotations. Definitions themselves, especially if they provide a translation of a word or phrase in another language, are placed in quotation marks.

> The sense of the Latin *quid pro quo* is that "one thing is given in fair exchange for another."

> Some of the ancient literature (e.g., Ezekiel 31:1–18) places Eden, "the Garden of God," in the mountains of Lebanon.

28c Eliminating misused or overused quotation marks

1 Eliminate phrases using quotation marks to note slang or colloquial expressions.

If your use of slang is appropriate for and important (as slang) in your paper, then no quotation marks are needed. If, on the other hand, you are uncomfortable with slang or colloquial expressions and choose to show your discomfort by using quotation marks, then find another, more formal way to express the same thoughts.

OVERUSED   Kate promised she would "walk that extra mile" for Mark. [The quote does not excuse the use of a cliché here.]

REVISED   Kate promised to help Mark in any way she could.

2 Eliminate phrases using quotation marks to make ironic comments.

Express your thoughts as directly as possible through word choice.

MISUSED   Dean Langley called to express his "appreciation" for all I had done.

REVISED   Dean Langley called to complain about the accusations of bias I raised with reporters.

3 Eliminate quotation marks used to emphasize technical terms.

Assume your readers will note technical terms as such and will refer to a dictionary if needed.

MISUSED   "Electromagnetism" is a branch of physics.

REVISED   Electromagnetism is a branch of physics.

4 Eliminate quotation marks that are overused to note commonly accepted nicknames.

OVERUSED   "Bob" Dole is a powerful senator.

REVISED   Bob Dole is a powerful senator.

Reserve your use of quotation marks for unusual nicknames, which often appear in parentheses after a first name. Once you have emphasized a name with quotation marks, you need not use the marks again with that name.

Ralph ("The Hammer") Schwartz worked forty years as a longshoreman in San Francisco and was fond of saying, "Don't end your life face down at the bottom of a bird cage."

EXERCISE 2

Correct the use of quotation marks to emphasize specific words in the following paragraph. Two of the eight expressions in quotation marks are emphasized correctly.

"Don" Vito Corleone was a man to whom everybody came for help, and never were they disappointed. No matter how poor or powerless the supplicant, "Don" Vito Corleone would take that man's troubles to his heart. And he would let nothing stand in the way to a solution of that man's "woe." His reward? Friendship, the respectful title of "Don," and sometimes the more "affectionate" title of "Godfather." And perhaps, to show respect only, never for profit, some "humble gift"—a gallon of homemade wine or a basket of peppered taralles specially baked to grace his Christmas table. It was understood, it was mere "good manners," to proclaim that you were in his debt and that he had the right to call upon you at any time to redeem your debt by some small service.

—MARIO PUZO

EXERCISE 3

Following is a passage on Columbus by naval historian J.H. Parry. Quote from the paragraph, as instructed here.

1. Introduce a quotation with the word *that*.

1. Introduce a quotation with the word *that*.

   Naval historian J.H. Parry suggests that "Columbus was not concerned with theory for its own sake, but with promoting a practical proposal."

2. Introduce a quotation with a phrase and a comma. End the quotation with a page reference (which you will invent), noted in parentheses.

   According to J.H. Parry, "Columbus had to show that the westward distance from Europe to Asia was within the operating range of the available ships" (188).

3. Introduce a quotation with a sentence and a colon.

   In making his case to financial backers, Columbus faced one major task: "[He] had to show that the westward distance from Europe to Asia was within the operating range of the available ships" (188).

4. Interrupt a quotation with the phrase "Parry states."

   "Columbus was not concerned with theory for its own sake," Parry states, "but with promoting a practical proposal."

5. Follow a quotation with an explanatory remark.

   Parry believes that Columbus "combed the authorities known to him, and selected from them any assertion which supported his case," which suggests the confidence, and even arrogance, of the Great Navigator.

2. Introduce a quotation with a phrase and a comma. End the quotation with a page reference (which you will invent), noted in parentheses.
3. Introduce a quotation with a sentence and a colon.
4. Interrupt a quotation with the phrase "Parry states."
5. Follow a quotation with an explanatory remark.

Columbus was not concerned with theory for its own sake, but with promoting a practical proposal. He did not study the available authorities in order to draw conclusions; he began with the conviction—how formed, we cannot tell—that an expedition to Asia by a westward route was practicable and that he was the man destined to lead it. He then combed the authorities known to him, and selected from them any assertion which supported his case. The practicability of the voyage—assuming that no major land mass barred the way—depended partly on the pattern of winds and currents likely to be encountered, but mainly on the distance to be covered. Columbus had to show that the westward distance from Europe to Asia was within the operating range of the available ships. We can trace, from what is known of his reading, from his own later writings, and from biography written by his son Hernando, how he set about it.

CHAPTER 29

Other Marks

This chapter reviews the conventions for using colons, dashes, parentheses, brackets, ellipses, and slashes. Of these marks, the first three are the most frequently used. The colon, the dash, and parentheses are important marks for the writer concerned with style: They significantly alter and thereby vary the rhythm of sentence structures. Brackets and ellipses are marks you will need to know when incorporating quotations into your papers.

THE COLON

29a Using the colon

The **colon** is the mark of punctuation generally used to make an announcement. In formal writing, the colon follows only a *complete* independent clause and introduces a word, phrase, sentence, or group of sentences (as in a quotation). For readers, the colon gives an important cue about the relationship of one part of your text to another: The sentence before the colon leads directly to the word or words after, in the fashion of an announcement.

1 Edit to eliminate colons misused within independent clauses.

In formal writing, a colon must always follow a complete statement or independent clause. The mark must never be used as a break inside an independent clause.

FAULTY   For someone who is depressed, the best two things in life are: eating and sleeping.

REVISED For someone who is depressed, the best two things in life are eating and sleeping.

REVISED For someone who is depressed, only two things in life matter: eating and sleeping.

2 Use a colon to announce an important statement or question.

You create emphasis in a paragraph when you write one sentence to introduce another. Greater emphasis is created when you conclude that introduction with a colon.

KEY FEATURES

Another chapter designed primarily for reference, this chapter covers the remaining marks of punctuation in English: the colon, the dash, parentheses, brackets, ellipses, and slashes. Each of these punctuation marks is covered in careful detail, providing clear examples of virtually every possible use for them. Since the colon and the dash are more common than the others, their treatment is more extensive—especially with regard to stylistic choices. Throughout the chapter, exercises allow students to punctuate sample sentences and to create their own sentences, using the various marks discussed in the chapter.

REFERENCES

The following style sheets provide advice on using these marks:

The Chicago Manual of Style. 14th ed. Chicago: U of Chicago P, 1993.

GIBALDI, JOSEPH, and WALTER S. ACHTERT. *MLA Handbook for Writers of Research Papers*. 3rd ed. New York: MLA, 1988.

The mind's deepest desire, even in its most elaborate operations, parallels man's unconscious feeling in the face of the universe: it is an insistence upon familiarity, an appetite for clarity.

Dramatic changes now occurring in the !Kung culture are illuminating a major problem in anthropology: Why did most hunting and gathering societies disappear rapidly after coming in contact with societies that kept domesticated animals and plants?

3 Use a colon to introduce a list or a quotation.

If at the conclusion of an independent clause you want to introduce a list or a quotation, do so with a colon.

A LIST

According to Cooley, the looking-glass self has three components: how we think our behavior appears to others, how we think others judge our behavior, and how we feel about their judgments.

A QUOTATION

A New England soldier wrote to his wife on the eve of the First Battle of Bull Run: "I know how great a debt we owe to those who went before us through the Revolution. And I am willing, perfectly willing, to lay down all my joys in this life, to help maintain this government, and to pay that debt."

A colon can introduce either a list or a quotation that is set off and indented.

A New England soldier wrote to his wife on the eve of the First Battle of Bull Run:

I know how great a debt we owe to those who went before us through the Revolution. And I am willing, perfectly willing, to lay down all my joys in this life, to help maintain this government, and to pay that debt.

Chip designers use increased packing density of transistors in one of two ways:
1. They increase the complexity of the computers they can fabricate.
2. They keep the complexity of the computer at the same level and pack the whole computer into fewer chips.

NOTE: Both when lists and quotations are run in with sentences and when they are set off, the expression *as follows* or some variant often precedes the colon. If this expression is tagged onto a complete sentence, it is preceded by a comma.

There are three reasons to reject the theory of spontaneous generation, as follows:

4 Use a colon to set off an appositive phrase, summary, or explanation.

Appositive

Food sharing, in which individuals provision other members of a group, is extremely rare in mammals. In addition to bats, only a few species are known to display such behavior: wild dogs, hyenas, chimpanzees, and human beings.

Summary

A number of recent studies reveal that female vampire bats cluster together during the day but at night reassort themselves, creating a fluid social organization that is maintained for many years: vampire bats are remarkably social.

Explanation

When Calais surrendered, King Edward (of England) threatened to put the city to the sword, then offered the people a bargain: he would spare the city if six of the chief burghers would give themselves up unconditionally.

5 Use a colon to distinguish chapter from verse in Biblical citations, hours from minutes, and titles from subtitles or subsidiary material.

Biblical citation

It is an irony that almost none of the literature of the people who gave us the alphabet has been preserved. Fragments of Phoenician poetry have survived in the Psalms, where the mountains are described as "a fountain that makes the gardens fertile, a well of living water" (Song of Songs 4:15).

Hours from minutes

8:15 A.M.   12:01 P.M.

Titles from subtitles or subsidiary material

The New American Bazaar: Shopping Malls and the Anthropology of Urban Life

6 Use a colon after the salutation in a formal letter, and in bibliographic citations.

Dear Ms. King:
Dear Dr. Hart:
Bikai, Patricia. "The Phoenicians." *Archaeology* Mar./Apr. 1990: 30.

EXERCISE 1

1. A structural clue to the power elite today lies in the enlarged and military state: that clue becomes evident in the military ascendancy.
2. Virtually all political and economic actions are now judged in terms of military definitions: the higher warlords have ascended to a firm position within the power elite.
3. In part at least this has resulted from one simple historical fact, pivotal for the years since 1939: the focus of elite attention has been shifted from domestic problems, centered in the 1930s around slump, to international problems, centered in the '40s and '50s around war.

GROUP ACTIVITY

This exercise and Exercises 3, 5, and 6 all lend themselves to group activity. Have students respond to exercises individually, and then compare their responses with those of other group members. When the inevitable disagreement occurs, students will have to consult the handbook. Once they become accustomed to using the chapter, they'll likely continue to refer to it as they edit their papers.

EXERCISE 2

Individual responses

GROUP ACTIVITY

This exercise and Exercise 4 can be completed in groups. As they compose the sentences together, students will learn to articulate their perceptions of the appropriate use of the colon.

EXERCISE 1

Correct the use of colons in these sentences. Add or delete colons as needed.

> *Example:* The links between the military and national policy making continue to grow out of control the military budget of today resembles those of times when we are at war.
>
> The links between the military and national policy making continue to grow out of control: the military budget of today resembles those of times when we are at war.

1. A structural clue to the power elite today lies in the enlarged and military state that clue becomes evident in the military ascendancy.
2. Virtually all political and economic actions are now judged in terms of military definitions the higher warlords have ascended to a firm position within the power elite.
3. In part at least this has resulted from one simple historical fact: pivotal for the years since 1939: the focus of elite attention has been shifted from domestic problems, centered in the 1930s around slump, to international problems, centered in the '40s and '50s around war.

EXERCISE 2

Write brief sentences, as instructed.

1. Write a sentence with a colon that introduces a list.
2. Write a sentence with a colon that announces an emphatic statement.
3. Write a sentence with a colon that sets off an appositive phrase, summary, or explanation.

THE DASH

29b Using dashes for emphasis

On the typewritten page, the dash is written as two hyphens (--). The space between these hyphens closes when the dash is typeset (—).

1 Use dashes to set off nonessential elements.

Use dashes to set off brief modifiers, lengthy modifiers, and appositives. In contrast to pairs of commas and parentheses, dashes emphasize the nonessential element set off in a sentence (see 25d). If dashes are the most emphatic interrupting marks and parentheses the least emphatic, commas offer a third, middling choice—neither emphatic nor fully parenthetical.

When Do Writers Need Dashes?

Sentence constructions rarely *require* the use of dashes. The dash is a stylist's tool, an elective mark. It halts the reader within a sentence by creating a cha-cha, dance-like syncopation. On seeing the dash, readers pause; then they speed up to read the words you have emphasized. Then they pause once more before returning to the main part of your sentence:

EFFECTIVE   Zoologist Uwe Schmidt discovered that shortly after birth, vampire bat pups are given regurgitated blood—in addition to milk—by their mothers.

Use the single dash to set off elements at the beginning or end of a sentence and a pair of dashes to set off elements in the middle. When elements are set off at the end of a sentence or in the middle, you have the choice of using commas or parentheses instead of dashes. Whatever punctuation you use, take care to word the element you set off so that it fits smoothly into the structure of your sentence. For instance, in the following sentence the nonessential element would be awkward.

AWKWARD   Zoologist Uwe Schmidt discovered that shortly after birth, vampire bat pups are given regurgitated blood—they drink milk too—by their mothers.

BETTER   Bat pups are given regurgitated blood—in addition to milk—by their mothers.

Brief modifiers in mid-sentence

Seven to thirty percent of vampire bats in a cluster fail to obtain a sufficient blood meal on any given night. By soliciting regurgitated blood from a roostmate, a bat can fend off starvation—at least for one more night—and so have another chance to find a meal. [The phrase acts as an adverb, modifying *fend off*.]

Lengthy modifiers

Within the past ten years, a new generation of investigators—armed with fresh insights from sociobiology and behavioral ecology—have learned much about social organization in the birds of paradise. [The phrase acts as an adjective, modifying *investigators*.]

Appositives

We study history to understand the present. Yet sometimes the present can help us to clarify the past. So it is with a San-speaking people known as the !Kung—a group of what were once called African Bushmen. [The appositive phrase renames the noun *!Kung*.]

NOTE: Use dashes to set off appositives that contain commas. Recall that a nonessential appositive phrase can also be set off from a sentence by a

TEACHING IDEAS

Some students see the dash as a type of "free agent" that can be used anywhere in a sentence. You may need to remind these students that dashes have specific functions. They're not a substitute for careful punctuation, nor are they to be used when the writer isn't sure of what other punctuation to use.

pair of commas (see 25d). When the appositive is formed by a series, the items of which are already separated by commas, dashes prevent misreading.

CONFUSING   Since the turn of the century, the percentage of information workers, bankers, insurance agents, lawyers, science journalists, has gone from a trickle to a flood.

REVISED   Since the turn of the century, the percentage of information workers—bankers, insurance agents, lawyers, science journalists—has gone from a trickle to a flood.

2 Use dashes to set off a significant repeating structure or an emphatic concluding element.

Repeating structure

To me the vitality of the bird of paradise's mating display was—and continues to be—one of nature's most thrilling sights. [The verb is repeated.]

Emphatic concluding remark

Once disposed of in the landfill, garbage is supposed to remain buried for eternity. So it was in Collier County, Florida—until we found several good reasons to dig it up again. [The dash sets off a sharply contrasting element, in this case a subordinate clause that functions as an adverb.]

Use dashes—with care. [This brief qualifying tag, a prepositional phrase, functions as an adverb.]

3 Use a dash to set off an introductory series from a summary or explanatory remark.

Strategic spots on the Boston Common are occupied by regiments of lunch-hour workers, and the Common is still the preferred site for political rallies. Pocket change, ball-point pens, campaign buttons—humanity's imprint continues to be recorded on the grassy slopes of the Boston Common. [This sentence structure, which begins with a series, is relatively rare.]

4 Use a dash to express an interruption in dialogue.

A dash used in dialogue shows interruption—speakers interrupting themselves or being interrupted by others. The dash used in dialogue also shows a change of thought or an uncompleted thought, a change in tone, or a pause.

Adam studied his brother's face until Charles looked away. "Are you mad at something?" Adam asked.

"What should I be mad at?"

"It just sounded— "

"I've got nothing to be mad at. Come on, I'll get you something to eat."

—JOHN STEINBECK

5 Use a dash to set off an attribution (by name), following an epigram.

At blows that never fall you falter,
And what you never lose, you must forever mourn.

—GOETHE

Dashes used in this fashion often follow epigrams—succinct, provocative quotations placed at the beginning of a paper as a vehicle for the introduction. Typically, the writer opens such a paper with a direct reference to the epigram and its author: "In these lines from *Faust*, the main character laments his limited human powers. . . . "

EXERCISE 3

Add a dash or a pair of dashes to the following sentences.

Example: The emptiness of our middle-class futures made us willing to risk our lives to a degree in actions against racism, against repression, against the war.

The emptiness of our middle-class futures made us willing to risk our lives—to a degree—in actions against racism, against repression, against the war.

1. We had grown up in America's most seductive image of itself the suburban, consuming world you see on TV.
2. Most working people did not share the unusual source of our particular radicalism a privileged rejection of the middle-class life that Americans are supposed to strive for.
3. The early 1970s saw the end of this mass radical movement of white students and youth the end of great numbers of people self-consciously taking action as part of a group of people like themselves taking similar actions across the country.

EXERCISE 4

Write brief sentences, as instructed.

1. Write a sentence with a nonessential series placed mid-sentence, set off by a pair of dashes.
2. Write a sentence in which a nonessential element is set off at the end by a dash.
3. Write a sentence in which a dash or pair of dashes sets off a significant repeating structure or emphatic statement.

EXERCISE 3

1. We had grown up in America's most seductive image of itself—the suburban, consuming world you see on TV.
2. Most working people did not share the unusual source of our particular radicalism—a privileged rejection of the middle-class life that Americans are supposed to strive for.
3. The early 1970s saw the end of this mass radical movement of white students and youth—the end of great numbers of people self-consciously taking action as part of a group of people like themselves taking similar actions across the country.

EXERCISE 4

Individual responses

ADDITIONAL EXERCISE B

ACROSS THE CURRICULUM Academic writers make liberal use of parentheses. Look through your textbooks for other courses and try to identify examples of each of the uses of parentheses found in this section of the handbook. Copy the sentences to use as additional examples to refer to when you write academic papers.

PARENTHESES

29c   Using parentheses to set off nonessential information

Parentheses ( ) are used to enclose and set off nonessential dates, words, phrases, or whole sentences that provide examples, comments, and other supporting information. The remark enclosed by parentheses is the ultimate nonessential modifier; it presents the reader with an aside, an interesting but by no means crucial bit of information. To give nonessential remarks more emphasis, use commas or dashes. (See also the Critical Decisions box in 25d-3.)

1 **Use parentheses to set off nonessential information: examples, comments, appositives.**

Examples

The ground beetle *Pterostichus pinguedineus* vanished from Iowa 15,300 years ago, but today it survives in Alaska, in the Yukon, and in a series of isolated alpine refuges in the northern Appalachians (for example, the peak of Mt. Washington in New Hampshire).

Comments—explanatory or editorial

Beetles (especially those species that scavenge or that prey on other arthropods) are rapid colonizers and are among the first organisms to invade terrain opened up to them by changing climates.

Appositives

The information content of a slice of pizza (advertising, legal expenses, and so on) accounts for a larger percentage of its cost than the edible content does, according to Henry Kelley and Andrew W. Wyckoff of the Congressional Office of Technology Assessment.

2 **Use parentheses to set off dates, translations of non-English words, and acronyms.**

Dates

Thomas Aquinas (b. 1225 or 1226, d. 1274) is regarded as the greatest of scholastic philosophers.

Translations

The look on the faces of the Efe tribesmen made it clear that they could think of nothing worse than to have a *muzungu* (foreigner) living with them for even a day.

Acronyms

Lucy Suchman, staff anthropologist of Xerox's Palo Alto Research Center (better known as PARC), watches workers in an airline operations room at San Jose International Airport to learn how they extract particular information from a chaotic assortment of radio, telephone, text, and video feeds. [Typically, an acronym is placed in parentheses directly after the first mention of a term or title subsequently referred to by its acronym.]

TEACHING IDEAS

Students may need to be reminded that although acronyms are acceptable in academic writing, it is almost always necessary to identify the full name or title represented by the acronym. The first time the name or title is used, the acronym can be placed beside it in parentheses and used by itself thereafter.

3 **Use parentheses to set off numbers or letters that mark items in a series, when the series is run in with a sentence.**

Chip designers use increased packing density of transistors in one of two ways: (1) they increase the complexity of the computers they can fabricate, or (2) they keep the complexity of the computer at the same level and pack the whole computer into fewer chips.

When the series appears in list form, parentheses are omitted.

> Chip designers use increased packing density of transistors in one of two ways:
> 1. They increase the complexity of the computers they can fabricate.
> 2. They keep the complexity of the computer at the same level and pack the whole computer into fewer chips.

4 **Punctuate parentheses according to convention.**

Words enclosed by parentheses should be punctuated according to standard practice. When a parenthetical remark forms a sentence, the remark should begin with an uppercase letter and end with an appropriate mark (period, question mark, or exclamation point) placed *inside* the end parenthesis. In all other cases, end punctuation should be placed outside the end parenthesis, and punctuation that would normally be placed directly after a word should be placed directly after the parenthetical remark.

FAULTY   Like other nomads, the Bakhtiari think of themselves as a family, the sons of a single founding-father. (as did the ancient Jews)

REVISED   Like other nomads, the Bakhtiari think of themselves as a family, the sons of a single founding-father (as did the ancient Jews).

FAULTY   According to J. Bronowski, the Bakhtiari "think of themselves as a family, the sons of a single founding-father." (60)

REVISED   According to J. Bronowski, the Bakhtiari "think of themselves as a family, the sons of a single founding-father" (60).

EXERCISE 5

1. Because of their size and the "look down" viewing systems, twin-lens reflexes are not good for quick action candid shooting. (An SLR is best in these situations.)
2. The look-down viewing system is better for carefully composed photographs (in a studio or home, for example) when time is not of the essence.
3. For my money, the Canon AE-1 (originally designed in 1971) remains one of the best and most flexible workhorse cameras that an amateur photographer could want.
4. I still cannot understand why any amateur photographer would want anything besides a good, reliable, single-lens reflex camera (usually referred to as an SLR).

LOOKING AHEAD

Both this section and the next section on ellipses will come in handy when students work on research papers. You may want to refer them to the extensive discussion about using quotations in chapter 34 (Using Sources).

EXERCISE 5

Add parentheses to the following sentences to enclose nonessential information.

Example: Nearly all twin-lens reflex cameras and a few single-lens reflex SLR cameras are designed to accommodate roll film somewhat wider than 35 millimeters.

Nearly all twin-lens reflex cameras and a few single-lens reflex (SLR) cameras are designed to accommodate roll film somewhat wider than 35 millimeters.

1. Because of their size and the "look-down" viewing systems, twin-lens reflexes are not good for quick action candid shooting. An SLR is best in these situations.
2. The look-down viewing system is better for carefully composed photographs in a studio or home for example when time is not of the essence.
3. For my money, the Canon AE-1 originally designed in 1971 remains one of the best and most flexible workhorse cameras that an amateur photographer could want.
4. I still cannot understand why any amateur photographer would want anything besides a good, reliable, single-lens reflex camera usually referred to as an SLR.

BRACKETS

29d Using brackets for editorial clarification

Use brackets [ ] to clarify or insert comments into quoted material. Throughout this section the following passage will be altered to demonstrate the various uses of brackets. For an extended discussion of using quotations in a research paper, see 34g. Specifically, see 34g-3 for more on using brackets.

Elephant sounds include barks, snorts, trumpets, roars, growls, and rumbles. The rumbles are the key to our story, for although elephants can hear them well, human beings cannot. Many are below our range of hearing, in what is known as infrasound.

The universe is full of infrasound: It is generated by earthquakes, wind, thunder, volcanoes, and ocean storms—massive movements of earth, air, fire, and water. But very low frequency sound has not been thought to play much of a role in animals' lives. Intense infrasonic calls have been recorded from finback whales, but whether the calls are used in communication is not known.

Why would elephants use infrasound? It turns out that sound at the lowest frequency of elephant rumbles (14 to 35 hertz) has remarkable properties—it is little affected by passage through forests and grasslands. Does infrasound, then, let elephants communicate over long distances?

1 Use brackets to insert your own words into quoted material.

Recall that quotation marks denote an *exact* reproduction of someone else's writing or speech. When you alter the wording of a quotation either by adding or deleting words, you must indicate as much to your reader with appropriate use of punctuation.

Brackets to clarify a reference

When quoting a sentence with a pronoun that refers to a word in another, nonquoted sentence, use brackets to insert a clarifying reference into the quotation. Delete the pronoun and add bracketed information; or, if wording permits (as in this example), simply add the bracketed reference.

> According to Katherine Payne, "Many [elephant rumbles] are below our range of hearing, in what is known as infrasound."

Brackets to weave quoted language into your sentences

The stylistic goal of quoting material in your papers is to make the fit between quoted language and your language seamless. To do this, you will sometimes need to alter a quotation if its structure, point of view, pronoun choices, or verb forms differ from those of the sentence into which you are incorporating the quotation. Show any changes to quoted text in brackets.

> The human ear can discern a wide band of sounds, but there are animals we can't hear without special equipment. Elephants emit inaudible (that is, to humans), very low-frequency rumbles called infrasound. At frequencies of 14 to 35 hertz, elephant rumbles have "remarkable properties—[they are] little affected by passage through forests and grasslands" (Payne 67).

The bracketed verb and pronoun have been changed from their original singular form to plural in order to agree in number with the plural *elephant rumbles*. The original subject of the quoted sentence was singular (*sound*). Quoting without brackets would have resulted in an awkward construction: *Elephant rumbles have "remarkable properties—it is. . . ."*

Brackets to show your awareness of an error in the quoted passage

When you quote a sentence that contains an obvious error, you are still obliged to reproduce exactly the wording of the original source. To show your awareness of the error and to show readers that the error is the quoted author's, not yours, place the bracketed word *sic* (Latin, meaning "thus") after the error.

"Intense infrasonic calls have been recorded from finback whales, but weather [sic] the calls are used in communication is not known."

Brackets to note emphasis

You may wish to underline or italicize quoted words. To show readers that the emphasis is yours and not the quoted author's, add the bracketed expression *emphasis added, italics added,* or *italics mine.*

"The universe is *full* of infrasound: It is generated by earthquakes, wind, thunder, volcanoes, and ocean storms—massive movements of earth, air, fire, and water [italics mine]."

2 **Use brackets to distinguish parentheses inserted within parentheses.**

Katherine Payne reports that "sound at the lowest frequencies of elephant rumbles (14 to 35 hertz [cycles per second]) has remarkable properties—it is little affected by passage through forests and grasslands."

ELLIPSES

29e **Using an ellipsis to indicate a break in continuity**

Just as you will need to add words in order to incorporate quotations into your sentences, so too you will need to delete words. An **ellipsis,** noted as three spaced periods (. . .), shows that you have deleted either words or entire sentences from a passage you are quoting. Throughout this section the following passage will be altered to demonstrate the various uses of ellipses. For an extended discussion of using quotations in a research paper, see 34g. Specifically, see 34g-3 for more on using ellipses.

> First, for Americans, the human cost of the Civil War was by far the most devastating in our history. The 620,000 Union and Confederate soldiers who lost their lives almost equaled the 680,000 American soldiers who died in all the other wars this country has fought combined. When we add the unknown but probably substantial number of civilian deaths—from disease, malnutrition, exposure, or injury—among the hundreds of thousands of refugees in the Confederacy, the toll of the Civil War may exceed war deaths in all the rest of American history.

The ghastly toll gives the Civil War a kind of horrifying but hypnotic fascination. As Thomas Hardy once put it, "War makes rattling good history; but Peace is poor reading." The sound of drum and trumpet, the call to arms, the clashing of armies have stirred the blood of nations throughout history. As the horrors and the seamy side of a war recede into the misty past, the romance and honor and glory forge into the foreground.

1 **Know when *not* to use an ellipsis.**

Do *not* use an ellipsis to note words omitted from the beginning of a sentence. In the following example, three words are deleted.

FAULTY   James McPherson observes that " . . . the human cost of the Civil War was by far the most devastating in our history."

REVISED   James McPherson observes that "the human cost of the Civil War was by far the most devastating in our history."

Do *not* use an ellipsis if the passage you quote ends with a period and ends your sentence as well.

FAULTY   James McPherson believes that "the toll of the Civil War may exceed war deaths in all the rest of American history. . . . "

REVISED   James McPherson believes that "the toll of the Civil War may exceed war deaths in all the rest of American history."

2 **Use an ellipsis to indicate words deleted from the middle of a sentence.**

If you have deleted words mid-sentence from an original passage, indicate the deletion with an ellipsis. If the words omitted directly follow an internal mark of punctuation (comma, dash, colon, semicolon), retain that mark and then add the ellipsis.

"[T]he human cost of the Civil War was . . . the most devastating in our history," writes James McPherson.

"The sound of drum and trumpet, . . . [has] stirred the blood of nations throughout history."

3 **Use an ellipsis to indicate words deleted from the end of a sentence.**

You may delete the end of a sentence from a quoted passage while your own sentence continues. If so, retain any internal mark of punctuation (comma, dash, colon, semicolon) that directly follows the last quoted word. Then add the ellipsis.

Though the "6,500 men killed and mortally wounded in one day near Sharpsburg were nearly double the number of Americans killed and mortally wounded in combat in all the rest of the country's nineteenth-century wars combined—..." (McPherson 42), many in the twentieth century continue to view the Civil War as a romance.

You may want to end your sentence with a quotation that does not end a sentence in the original. If so, whatever mark of punctuation (if any) follows the last quoted word in the original should be deleted. Then add a period and an ellipsis, following one of two conventions. If you *do not* conclude your sentence with a citation, place the sentence period after the final letter of the quotation; place the ellipsis; and conclude with the end quotation mark.

Official mortality figures for the Civil War do not include the "probably substantial number of civilian deaths—from disease, malnutrition, exposure, or injury ... "

If you *do* conclude your sentence with a citation, skip one space after the final letter of the quotation; place the ellipsis and follow with an end quotation mark; skip one space and place the citation; and then place the sentence period.

Official mortality figures for the Civil War do not include the "probably substantial number of civilian deaths—from disease, malnutrition, exposure, or injury ... " (McPherson 42).

4 Use an ellipsis to show a pause or interruption.

In dialogue
"No," I said. I wanted to leave. "I ... I need to get some air."

In prose
When I left the seminary, I walked long and thought hard about what a former student of divinity might do. ... My shoes wore out, my brain wore thin. I was stumped and not a little nervous about the course my life would take.

THE SLASH

29f Using the slash

1 Use slashes to separate the lines of poetry run in with the text of a sentence.

Retain all punctuation when quoting poetry. Leave a space before and after the slash when indicating line breaks.

LOOKING BACK

You may want to remind students at this point that lengthy passages from poetry are normally set off from the text rather than incorporated into it with slashes. See 28b-1.

The "hermit" of Robert Bly's poem of the same name "is a man whose body is perfectly whole. / He stands, the storm behind him, / And the grass blades are leaping in the wind. / Darkness is gathered in folds / About his feet. / He is no one."

2 Use slashes to show choice.

Use slashes, occasionally, to show alternatives, as with the expressions *and/or* and *either/or*. With this use, do not leave spaces before or after the slash.

Either/Or is the title of a philosophical work by Kierkegaard.

As a prank, friends entered the Joneses as a husband/wife alternate entry in the local demolition derby.

If your meaning is not compromised, avoid using the slash; instead, write out alternatives in your sentence.

Send a telegram and/or call to let us know you're well.

The sense, here, is that there are three options: send a telegram, call, *or* send a telegram *and* call. If two options are intended, then the sentence should be rewritten one of two ways.

Send a telegram and call to let us know you're well.

Send a telegram or call to let us know you're well.

3 Use a slash in writing fractions or formulas to note division.

The February 1988 index of job opportunities (as measured by the number of help wanted advertisements) would be as follows:

$$(47,230/38,510) \times 100 = 122.6$$

1/2   5/8   20 1/4

EXERCISE 6

Construct sentences, as directed, in which you quote from the following passage by Sigmund Freud.

(1) As to the origin of the sense of guilt, the analyst has different views from other psychologists; but even he does not find it easy to give an account of it. (2) To begin with, if we ask how a person comes to have a sense of guilt, we arrive at an answer which cannot be disputed: a person feels guilty (devout people would say "sinful") when he has done something which he knows to be "bad." (3) But then we notice how little this answer tells us. (4) Perhaps, after some hesitation, we shall add that even when a person has not actually *done* the bad thing but has only recognized in himself an *intention* to do it, he may regard himself as guilty; and the question then arises of why the intention is regarded as equal to the deed. (5) Both cases,

EXERCISE 6

1. Freud believes that "a person feels guilty . . . when he has done something which he knows to be 'bad.' "
2. "Perhaps, after some hesitation, we shall add that even when a person has not actually *done* the bad thing but has only recognized in himself an *intention* to do it, he may regard himself as guilty. . . ."
3. "As to the origin of the sense of guilt, the analyst has different views from other psychologists; but even he does not find it easy to give an account of [the origin of the sense of guilt]."

4. "Both cases, however, presupose [sic] that one had already recognized that what is bad is reprehensible, is something that must not be carried out."

however, presupose that one had already recognized that what is bad is reprehensible, is something that must not be carried out. (6) How is this judgement arrived at?

Example: Quote sentence 1, but delete the phrase "As to the origin of the sense of guilt. . . . "

According to Sigmund Freud, "the analyst has different views from other psychologists; but even he does not find it easy to give an account of it."

1. Quote sentence 2, beginning with "a person feels. . . . " Delete the parenthetical note.
2. Quote sentence 4 but delete the end of the sentence, beginning with "and the question. . . . "
3. Quote sentence 1 and use a bracketed reference to clarify the second use of the pronoun *it.*
4. Quote sentence 5 and show your awareness of the spelling error.

CHAPTER 30

Capitals and Italics

Capitals and italics are primarily graphic devices that give readers cues on how to read: where to look for the beginning of a new thought, which words in a sentence are emphasized, which words form titles or proper names, and so on. Capitals and italics are also very useful for special designations that can only be shown in writing.

CAPITALS

Before the late nineteenth century, printers manually composed words by placing molded letters in type holders, taking letters from individual compartments, or type cases, set on a nearby wall. Letters used most often (vowels, for instance) were kept on the wall's lower cases, within easy reach. Letters used less often (capital letters, for instance) were kept in a slightly less convenient location in upper cases. In spite of innovations that have made manual typesetting obsolete, we still retain the printer's original designations, upper and lower case, when referring to the appearance of type on a page. Readers depend on capital (uppercase) letters, in contrast to lowercase letters, as cues to help recognize when sentences begin and when a noun refers to a particular person, place, or thing.

 30a **Capitalize the first letter of the first word in every sentence.**

The most basic use of capitals is to signal the start of sentences.

When a box of mixed-grain-and-nut cereal is shaken, large particles always rise to the top—for the same reason that, over time, stones will rise to the top of a garden lot or field.

KEY FEATURES

This chapter covers thoroughly the numerous uses of capitals and italics. Students will need to understand many of these uses as they write papers for various classes; the chapter can answer virtually any question they may have. Coverage of capitals includes everything from capitalizing the first word of a sentence to capitals in abbreviations, with clear examples of each specific use. The same extensive treatment is accorded italics, with particular attention to the restraint that writers must exercise in using italics for emphasis. The exercises provide students with ample practice in both areas.

TEACHING IDEAS

Although this chapter will probably be used for reference rather than for classwork, you may want to encourage students to read through it once. Students may not even be aware of some uses for capitals. You can also call attention to the many options in capitalization, encouraging students to be consistent once they've chosen an option.

ESL ALERT

Capitalization may be an alien concept to students whose script is not based on the English alphabet (Arabic, Chinese, Japanese, Korean, and so forth). They simply may not see the differences in size as meaningful and will tend to capitalize in odd places and rarely where they

(continued)

515

should. Greek capitalizes what are called "main nouns" and hence capitalization depends on a judgment about importance. Spanish and Italian use lowercase forms far more than does English.

REFERENCES

The following style sheets provide advice on using capitalization and italics:

The Chicago Manual of Style. 14th ed. Chicago: U of Chicago P, 1993.

GIBALDI, JOSEPH, and WALTER S. ACHTERT. *MLA Handbook for Writers of Research Papers.* 3rd ed. New York: MLA, 1988.

1 **Reproduce capitalization in a quoted passage.**

Capitalize the first word of quoted material when you introduce a quotation with a brief explanatory phrase.

> According to archaeologist Douglas Wilson, "Most of what archaeologists have to work with is ancient trash."

> "Most of what archaeologists have to work with is ancient trash," according to archaeologist Douglas Wilson.

Do not capitalize the first word of a quotation run into the structure of your sentence. When you change capitalization in a quoted text, indicate the change with brackets.

> Wilson says that archaeologists who dig through modern trash must come "[e]quipped with rubber gloves, masks, and booster shots."

2 **Capitalize the first word in a parenthetical statement if the remark is a sentence.**

> Once a sleepy suburban town whose workers commuted to Chicago every morning, Naperville, Illinois, has acquired its own employment base. (It has become an "urban village," a "technoburb.")

If the parenthetical remark forms a sentence but is placed inside another sentence (this is a relatively rare occurrence), *do not* capitalize the first word after the parenthesis and *do not* use a period. However, do use a question mark or exclamation point if the parenthetical remark requires it.

> Naperville grew robustly (the population nearly quadrupled!), as Amoco and companies large and small erected what Governor James R. Thompson would later term "The Illinois Research and Development Corridor."

3 **In a series of complete statements or questions, capitalize the first word of each item.**

When a series is formed by phrases or incomplete questions, capitalization of the first word is optional.

CAPITALS   What causes air sickness? Is it inner-ear disturbance? Is it brain waves?

OPTIONAL   Air Force scientists want to know what causes motion sickness. Is it inner-ear disturbance? brain wave anomalies? disorienting visual signals?

OPTIONAL   Air Force scientists want to know what causes motion sickness. Is it inner-ear disturbance? Brain wave anomalies? Disorienting visual signals?

In a series of phrases run in with a sentence, the phrases are *not* capitalized.

> The program for low-input sustainable agriculture that has emerged from a recent federal study has three objectives: (1) to reduce reliance on fertilizer, pesticide, and other purchased resources to farms; (2) to increase farm profits and agricultural productivity; and (3) to conserve energy and natural resources.

In a displayed series, capitalization of the first word is optional.

OPTIONAL   The program for low-input sustainable agriculture that has emerged from a recent federal study has three objectives:

1. To reduce reliance on fertilizer, pesticide, and other purchased resources to farms.
2. To increase farm profits and agricultural productivity.
3. To conserve energy and natural resources.

The word *to* could also be in lowercase letters in each number of the displayed series.

4   Capitalizing the first word of a sentence following a colon is optional.

OPTIONAL   The program has two aims: The first is to conserve energy.

OPTIONAL   The program has two aims: the first is to conserve energy.

30b   Capitalize words of significance in a title.

Capitalize all words of significance in the titles of books, journals, magazines, articles, and art works. *Do not* capitalize articles (*a, an, the*) or conjunctions and prepositions that have four or fewer letters, except at the title's beginning. *Do* capitalize the first and last words of the title (even if they are articles, conjunctions, or prepositions), along with any word following a colon or semicolon.

> *Pride and Prejudice*   *Great Expectations*
> *The Sound and the Fury*   *The Joy Luck Club*
> *Much Ado About Nothing*   *West with the Night*
> "The Phoenicians: Rich and Glorious Traders of the Levant"

Do not capitalize the word *the* if it is not part of a title or proper name.

> the Eiffel Tower   *The Economist*
> the Mediterranean Sea   *The Brothers Karamazov*

The first word of a hyphenated word in a title is capitalized. The second word is also capitalized, unless it is very short.

> "The Selling of an Ex-President"   *Engine Tune-ups Made Simple*
> "Belly-down in a Cave: A Spelunker's Weekend"

TEACHING IDEAS

Whenever students are presented with an option, as in the case of capitalizing the first word of a sentence following a colon, they should be reminded that whatever option they choose, they must remain consistent throughout their text.

30c Capitalize the first word in every line of poetry.

Lines of poetry are conventionally marked by initial capitals. The interjection *O*, restricted for the most part to poetry, is always capitalized. The word *oh* is capitalized only when it begins a sentence.

> Break, break, break,
> On thy cold gray stones, O Sea!
> And I would that my tongue could utter
> The thoughts that arise in me.
>
> —TENNYSON, from *"Break, Break, Break"*

NOTE: Some poets begin lines with lowercase letters—e. e. cummings, for instance. Others write verse that deliberately shifts some standard conventions. When quoting such poets, retain the capitalization of the original.

30d Capitalize proper nouns—people, places, objects; proper adjectives; and ranks of distinction.

Capitalizing the first letter of a noun helps to establish its identity. In general, capitalize any noun that refers to a *particular* person, place, object, or being that has been given an individual, or proper, name.

1 Capitalize names of people or groups of people.

Names of people are capitalized, as are titles showing family relationships *if* the title is part of the person's name.

George Bush	Martha Washington
Aunt Millie	Uncle Ralph

Names of family relations—brother, aunt, grandmother—are not capitalized if not used as part of a particular person's proper name.

> He phoned his grandmother, Bess Truman.
> I saw my favorite aunt, Janet, on a trip to Chicago.

Names of political groups and of formal organizations are capitalized.

Democrats	the Left
Republicans	the Right
Communists	Socialists

2 Capitalize religions, religious titles and names, and nationalities.

Religions, their followers, and their sacred beings and sacred documents are capitalized.

Judaism	Jew	the Bible
Catholicism	Catholic	the New Testament
Islam	Muslim	the Koran
God	Allah	Buddha

Nations and nationalities are capitalized.

America	Americans	Native Americans
Liberia	Liberians	Hispanic Americans
Czechoslovakia	Czechs	

NOTE: The terms *black* and *white*, when designating race, are usually written in lowercase, though some writers prefer to capitalize them (by analogy with other formal racial designations such as Mongolian and Polynesian).

 3 **Capitalize places, regions designated by points on the compass, and languages.**

Places and addresses

Cascades	Asia
Idaho	England
Joe's Diner	Philadelphia
Main Street	Elm Boulevard

NOTE: Capitalize common nouns such as *main* or *center* when they are part of an address.

Names of regions and compass points designating the names of regions

Appalachia	the frozen Northwest
the Great Lakes	the Sun Belt
the sunny South	Mid-Atlantic

NOTE: A compass point is capitalized only when it functions as a noun and serves as the name of a particular area of the country. As a direction, a compass point is not capitalized.

NO CAPITALS I'll be driving northeast for the first part of the trip. [The word *northeast* in this sentence is a modifier and indicates a direction, not a region.]

We made a course to the northeast, but soon turned to the north. [These are compass points, not the names of regions.]

CAPITALS I'll be vacationing in the Northeast this year. [The word *Northeast* is the name of an area of the country.]

Names of languages

English	Arabic	Swahili
Spanish	Greek	Italian

4 **Capitalize adjectives formed from proper nouns, and titles of distinction that are part of proper names.**

Proper adjectives formed from proper nouns

English tea	French perfume
Cartesian coordinates	Balinese dancer

NOTE: Both *Oriental* and *oriental* are considered correct, though the capitalized form is more common. Both *Biblical* and *biblical* are considered correct.

Titles of distinction

Capitalize a title of distinction when no words separate it from a proper noun. Do not capitalize most title designations if they are followed by the preposition *of*.

Governor Cuomo	Mario Cuomo, governor of New York
Mayor Giuliani	Rudolph Giuliani, mayor of New York

NOTE: When titles of the highest distinction are proper names for a specific office—President, Prime Minister—they often remain capitalized, even if followed by a preposition and even if not paired with a specific name.

Bill Clinton, President of the United States
John Major, Prime Minister of Great Britain
The President arrived at 2 o'clock.
The Secretary of State flew to Geneva.

The Prime Minister's role is to lead both party and government.
A prime minister may do as she pleases. [A specific office is not being named.]

Capitalize titles and abbreviations of titles when they follow a comma—as in an address or closing to a letter.

Martha Brand, Ph.D.	Fred Barnes, Sr.
Sally Roth, M.D.	David Burns, Executive Vice-President

5 **Capitalize the names of days, months, holidays, and historical events or periods.**

Monday	New Year's Day
Saturday	Columbus Day
December	Revolutionary War
January	Paleozoic Era
Christmas	Middle Ages

NOTE: When written out, centuries and decades are not capitalized.

the nineteenth century   the fifties   the twenty-third century

Seasons are capitalized only when they are personified.

spring semester   Spring's gentle breath
                    [The season is personified.]

6 Capitalize particular objects and name-brand products.

Mount Washington   USS *Hornet*
Jefferson Memorial   Sam Rayburn Building
Aswan Dam

Bic pen   Ford Taurus
Whopper   Apple computer
Sony television

7 Use capitals with certain abbreviations, prefixes, or compound nouns.

Capitalize abbreviations only when the words abbreviated are themselves capitalized.

Mister James Wolf   Mr. James Wolf
Apartment 6   Apt. 6
1234 Rockwood Avenue   1234 Rockwood Ave.
Silver Spring, Maryland   Silver Spring, Md.

Capitalize acronyms and abbreviations of companies, agencies, and treaties.

FAA (Federal Aviation Administration)
ABM Treaty (Anti-Ballistic Missile Treaty)
DEC (Digital Equipment Corporation)

The prefixes *ex, un,* and *post* are capitalized only when they begin a sentence or are part of a proper name or title.

a post-Vietnam event   the Post-Vietnam Syndrome
an un-American attitude   the Un-American Activities Committee

Capitalize a number or the first word in a compound number that is part of a name or title.

Third Avenue
the Seventy-second Preakness

EXERCISE 1

Correct the capitalization in these sentences. When needed, change lowercase letters to uppercase and change uppercase to lowercase.

> There are many allies for the historian. the law is one. Art is another. Obviously enough, the historian of all periods must draw upon purely Visual Evidence for some of his data, for man has chosen to Speak through Pictures from the age of pictographs to that of

TEACHING IDEAS

Occasionally students will need to be reminded that "Day" is capitalized only when it is part of the holiday's name. While "I took my mother to dinner on Mother's Day" is correct, "I had to work on Easter Day" is not.

EXERCISE 1

This paragraph was written by Robin W. Winks as an introduction to chapter 20 in *The Historian as Detective: Essays on Evidence* (New York: Harper Torchbooks, 1968), 420.

There are many allies for the historian. The law is one. Art is another. Obviously enough, the historian of all periods must draw upon purely visual evidence for some of his data, for man has chosen to speak through pictures from the age of pictographs to that of the camera and the comic book. It is true that one picture is worth a thousand words, if it is the right picture—Andrew Wyeth's "Christina's World" can tell us as much about the twentieth century as Michelangelo's Sistine Chapel tells us about the sixteenth. One of the most important records of the Norman Conquest of England in 1066 is not a document at all, nor is it a painting. I refer, of course, to the great Bayeux tapestry. In fact an embroidery, the tapestry records the conquest by William; it is preserved in the Bayeux Cathedral Museum in Normandy. Five major books and many articles have been written on the tapestry; each shows just how much the trained observer can draw from pictorial evidence.

GROUP ACTIVITY

Both exercises in this chapter lend themselves to group activity. Have students respond to exercises individually, and then compare their responses with those of other group members. When the inevitable disagreement occurs, students will have to consult the handbook. Once they become accustomed to using the chapter, they'll likely continue to refer to it as they edit their papers.

TEACHING IDEAS

It would be wise to call attention to underlining as the typewritten equivalent of italics. You may also want to remind students that writing a word in italics is *not* equivalent to putting it in quotation marks.

TEACHING IDEAS

You may want to call attention to the word *need* in the heading for 30e. As the note states, overreliance on typographical means of emphasis suggests that the writer's command of the language is weak.

the camera and the Comic Book. it is true that one picture is worth a thousand words, if it is the right picture—andrew wyeth's "christina's world" can tell us as much about the Twentieth Century as michelangelo's sistine chapel tells us about the sixteenth. One of the most important records of the Norman Conquest of england in 1066 is not a document at all, nor is it a Painting. I refer, of course, to the Great bayeux tapestry. In fact an embroidery, the tapestry records the conquest by william; it is preserved in the bayeux cathedral Museum in normandy. Five Major Books and many Articles have been written on the tapestry; each shows just how much the trained observer can draw from Pictorial Evidence.

ITALICS

A word set in italics calls attention to itself. On the typewritten (or handwritten) page, words that you would italicize are underlined. Italics have three principal uses: they give emphasis; they mark the plural forms of letters and numbers; and they denote titles of long works and certain names.

 ### 30e Underline or italicize words if they need a specific emphasis.

Words that you underline or set in italics are given particular emphasis. As a stylistic tool, italicizing will work well only if you do not overuse it.

Cultural relativity does *not* mean that a behavior appropriate in one place is appropriate everywhere.

Italicized words can be useful to create emphasis and change meaning in sentences, especially when writing attempts to duplicate the emphasis of speech.

"*You're* going to the movies with him?" [Why you and not Susan?]
"You're going to the movies with *him*?" [Why would you go with him?]
"You're going to the *movies* with him?" [Why aren't you going to the theater?]

NOTE: The best way to create emphasis in your writing is not to simulate emotion with punctuation or with typeface, but to make your point with words. Italics should be saved for rare occasions and for a specific purpose. Overuse devalues the emphasis of italics and makes your writing appear overexcited and unconvincing.

OVERUSED   The Phoenicians were *masters* of the sea and with the cities they founded, like Tyre and Carthage, they became commercial *giants*. But Rome *envied* the Phoenician wealth. The angry prophet Isaiah called the Phoenicians *sinners*, and the heroic poet Homer thought they were *sly*. Ultimately, these many hatreds *crushed* the Phoenicians.

REWORDED During the hundreds of years that they dominated the seas, the Phoenicians made enemies, the sort of enemies that are inevitable when you are commercially successful. Homer's heroic poems described the Phoenicians as slippery and as swindlers. Isaiah called Tyre a whore. The Romans depicted the Carthaginians as treacherous. In the end, the Phoenicians and Carthaginians lost to those enemies and were completely crushed, militarily and culturally.

30f Underline or italicize words, letters, and numbers to be defined or identified.

1 Use italics for words to be defined.

Words to be defined in a sentence are usually underlined or set in italics. Occasionally, such a word is set in quotation marks.

OPTION The *operating system* runs a computer as a sort of master organizer that can accept commands whenever no specific program is running.

OPTION The remarkable permanence of color in certain statues at the Acropolis is due, partly, to the technique of "encaustic," in which pigment is mixed with wax and applied to the surface while hot.

2 Use italics for expressions recognized as foreign.

Underline or italicize foreign expressions that have not yet been assimilated into English but whose meanings are generally understood. The following is a brief sampling of such words.

amore [Italian]	*Doppelgänger* [German]
enfant terrible [French]	*esprit de corps* [French]
e pluribus unum [Latin]	*hombre* [Spanish]
goyim [Hebrew]	*post hoc* [Latin]
pâté [French]	

No underlines or italics are used with foreign expressions that have been assimilated into English. The following is a brief sampling of such words.

alter ego [Latin]	blitz [German]
ex post facto [Latin]	fait accompli [French]
hoi polloi [Greek]	fellah [Arabic]
guru [Sanskrit]	kayak [Eskimo]
kibitz [Yiddish]	machete [Spanish]
maestro [Italian]	memorabilia [Latin]

TEACHING IDEAS

ACROSS THE CURRICULUM Many students will have difficulty determining whether or not a foreign word or phrase is indeed common in English. In particular, as they take courses in different disciplines, they'll encounter foreign terms that are common within the discipline but have not been assimilated into lay English. They should be advised to consult their instructors with regard to how to treat such terms.

3 Use italics to designate words, numerals, or letters referred to as such.

Underline or italicize words when you are calling attention to them as words.

Many writers have trouble differentiating the uses of *lie* and *lay.*

The word *the* is not capitalized in a title, unless it is the first word of the title or follows a colon or semicolon.

Italicize letters and most numerals when they are referred to as letters or numerals.

She crosses the *t* in *top.*

Shall I write a *1* or a *2*?

The combination of italics (or underlining) and an apostrophe with the letter *s* is used to make numbers and letters plural.

Cross your *t*'s and dot your *i*'s.

We saw *1*'s on the scoreboard each inning—a good sign.

Use underlining or italics for titles of book-length works separately published or broadcast, as well as 30g for individually named transport craft.

1 Use italics for books, long poems, and plays.

Love in the Ruins [novel]	*The Joy Luck Club* [novel]
A Discovery of the Sea [book]	*Twelfth Night* [play]
Antigone [play]	*The Odyssey* [long poem]
The Rime of the Ancient Mariner [long poem]	

The titles of sacred documents (and their parts) as well as legal or public documents are frequently capitalized (see 30d) but are not set in italics.

the Bible	the New Testament
the Magna Carta	the Bill of Rights
the Koran	Book of Exodus

2 Use italics for newspapers, magazines, and periodicals.

the *Boston Globe*	the *New York Times*
Brookline *Citizen*	*Times*
the *Georgia Review*	*Archaeology*

With newspapers, do not capitalize, underline, or set in italics the word *the,* even if it is part of the newspaper's title. Italicize or underline

LOOKING BACK

Students often become confused over which titles to underline and which to place in quotation marks. Refer students to 28b-3 for the appropriate presentation of short works.

the name of a city or town only if it is part of the newspaper's title. Titles of particular selections in a newspaper, magazine, or journal are set in quotation marks.

3 **Use italics for works of visual art, long musical works, movies, and broadcast shows.**

Rodin's *The Thinker*   *The Last Judgment*
Van Gogh's *The Starry Night*   the *Burghers of Calais*
Mozart's *The Magic Flute*   the *German Requiem*

NOTE: Underline or set in italics the article *the* only when it is part of a title.

Movies and television or radio shows are italicized.

As the World Turns   *A Prairie Home Companion*
Late Show with David Letterman   *All Things Considered*
The Firm   *Jurassic Park*

4 **Use italics for individually named transport craft: ships, trains, aircraft, and spacecraft.**

USS *Hornet* (a ship)   *Atlantis* (a spacecraft)
HMS *Bounty* (a ship)   the *Montrealer* (a train)
Apollo X (a spacecraft)   *Spirit of St. Louis* (an airplane)

Do not underline or italicize USS or HMS in a ship's name.

EXERCISE 2

Correct the use of italics in these sentences. Circle words that should not be italicized. Underline words that should be italicized. Place a check beside any sentence in which italics are used correctly.

Example: The most important tool of the navigator is an (accurate,) (current) chart, without which it is virtually impossible to navigate successfully.

1. Navigation is the art of staying *out* of trouble.
2. You can keep your charts as current as possible by subscribing to Local Notices to Mariners, a weekly publication of the U.S. Coast Guard.
3. The key to successful navigation is to navigate *continuously*, that is, *always* be able to determine the position of your boat on the chart.
4. *Landmarks* (smokestacks, water towers, buildings, piers, *etc.*) and *aids to navigation* (beacons, lighthouses, buoys) help relate what you see from your boat to items found on the chart.
5. Aids to navigation are installed and maintained by the Coast Guard *specifically* to help you relate your surroundings to the appropriate symbols on the chart.
6. A *beacon* will be denoted on the chart by a triangle and the letters *Bn.*

EXERCISE 2

1. circle: *out*
2. underline: Local Notices to Mariners
3. circle: *continuously, always*
4. circle: *Landmarks, aids to navigation*
5. circle: *specifically*
6. Correct

Abbreviations and Numbers

The root word of *abbreviation* is the Latin *breviare*, from which comes the familiar *brief, briefing*, and *brevity*. We use an **abbreviation**—the shortened form of a word followed (for the most part) by a period—only in restricted circumstances, as discussed below. Writers working in an unfamiliar discipline should consult the standard manuals of reference, style, and documentation for guidance in using abbreviations and numbers in the field. Many such reference works are listed in chapter 36, Documenting Research, with conventions shown in chapters 37–39 on writing in each of the major discipline areas.

ABBREVIATIONS

31a Abbreviating titles of rank both before and after proper names

The following titles of address are usually abbreviated before a proper name.

Mr.   Mrs.   Ms.   Dr.

Though not an abbreviation, *Ms.* is usually followed by a period. Abbreviations for titles of rank or honor are usually reserved for the most formal references and addresses in connection with a person's full name and title. Mention of a person's title or rank in a less formal context does not call for an abbreviation. Typically, the abbreviations *Gen., Lt., Sen., Rep.,* and *Hon.* precede a full name—first and last.

FAULTY	Gen. Eisenhower	Sen. Dole
REVISED	General Eisenhower	Senator Dole
REVISED	Gen. Dwight D. Eisenhower	Sen. Bob Dole

The following abbreviated titles or designations of honor are placed *after* a formal address or listing of a person's full name.

B.A.	M.A.	M.S.	Ph.D.	C.P.A.
Jr.	Sr.	M.D.	Esq.	

Place a comma after the surname, then follow with the abbreviation. If more than one abbreviation is used, place a comma between abbreviations.

Lawrence Swift, Jr., M.D.

Abbreviations of medical, professional, or academic titles are *not* combined with the abbreviations *Mr., Mrs.,* or *Ms.*

FAULTY	Ms. Joan Warren, M.D.	Ms. Mindy Lubber, Ed.D.
REVISED	Dr. Joan Warren *or* Joan Warren, M.D.	Mindy Lubber, Ed.D. *or* Dr. Mindy Lubber

Other than for direct reference to academic titles such as *Ph.D.* (Doctor of Philosophy), *M.A.* (Master of Arts), and *M.S.* (Master of Science), do not use freestanding abbreviated titles that have not been paired with a proper name in a sentence.

ACCEPTABLE	Jane Thompson earned her Ph.D. in biochemistry. [A degree is referred to separately.]
FAULTY	Marie Lew is an M.D. [The degree should either be referred to separately or attached to the person's title.]
REVISED	Marie Lew is a physician.
REVISED	Marie Lew was awarded an M.D. degree from Harvard.
FAULTY	John Kraft is a C.P.A.
REVISED	John Kraft is a certified public accountant.
REVISED	John passed the C.P.A. examination yesterday.

 ## 31b Abbreviating specific dates and numbers

With certain historical or archaeological dates, abbreviations are often used to indicate whether the event occurred in the last two thousand years.

Ancient times (prior to two thousand years ago)
B.C.   (before the birth of Christ)
B.C.E.   (before the common era)

Both abbreviations follow the date.

Modern times (within the last two thousand years)
C.E.   (of the common era)
A.D.   (*Anno Domini,* "in the year of the Lord," an abbreviation that precedes the date)

Augustus, the first Roman Emperor, lived from 63 B.C. (*or* B.C.E.) to A.D. 14 (*or* C.E.).

When the context of a paragraph makes clear that the event occurred in the last two thousand years—suppose you are writing on the

TEACHING IDEAS

For an interesting account of the history and use of abbreviations, you may want to refer students to Tom McArthur's *Oxford Companion to the English Language* (Oxford: Oxford UP, 1992). McArthur traces the practice of abbreviation back to the ancient Egyptians.

Industrial Revolution—it would be redundant, even insulting, to write "A.D. 1820."

Clock time, indicated as prior to noon or after, uses abbreviations in capitals or in lowercase.

> 5:44 P.M. (or p.m.)
>
> 5:44 A.M. (or a.m.)

When typeset, A.M./P.M. often appear in a smaller type size as capital letters: 5:44 P.M.

When numbers are referred to as specific items (such as numbers in arithmetic operations or as units of currency or measure), they are used with standard abbreviations.

> No. 23 or no. 23 $2 + 3 = 5$
> $23.01   99 bbl. [barrels]
> 54%

Abbreviations for time, numbers, units, or money should be used only with reference to specific dates or amounts.

Numerical concepts must be fully written out as part of a sentence, not given shortened treatment with abbreviations, unless they are attached to specific years, times, currencies, units, or items.

FAULTY   We'll see you in the A.M.

REVISED   We'll see you in the morning.

FAULTY   Let's wait until the nos. are in before we make a decision.

REVISED   Let's wait until the numbers are in before we make a decision.

FAULTY   This happened in the B.C. era.

REVISED   This happened almost three thousand years ago.

FAULTY   Please tell me the % of dropouts for the year.

REVISED   Please tell me the percentage of dropouts for the year.

31c Using acronyms, uppercase abbreviations, and corporate abbreviations

An **acronym** is the uppercase, pronounceable abbreviation of a proper noun—a person, organization, government agency, or country. Periods are not used with acronyms. If there is any chance that a reader might not be familiar with an acronym or abbreviation, spell it out on first mention, showing the acronym in parentheses.

> Medical researchers are struggling to understand the virus that causes Acquired Immune Deficiency Syndrome (AIDS).

The following are some familiar acronyms.

NATO   North Atlantic Treaty Organization

MADD   Mothers Against Drunk Driving

NASA   National Aeronautics and Space Administration

NOW   National Organization for Women

Helping Readers to Understand Acronyms

Unless an acronym or uppercase abbreviation is common knowledge, courtesy obligates you to write out the full word, term, or organizational name at its first mention. Then, in a parenthetical remark, you give the abbreviation. In subsequent references to the person, word, or organization, use the abbreviation—as is illustrated in the beginning of this article from the journal *Archaeology*.

> To the end of the Early Intermediate Period (EIP), the appearance of stunning, elaborately decorated ceramics . . . suggests that tribal leaders possessed and exchanged prestige items as a way of consolidating their claims to political power.

In lengthy documents where you will be using many uppercase abbreviations and acronyms, consider creating a glossary in addition to defining abbreviations the first time you use them. The glossary, which is placed at the end of the paper as an appendix, provides one convenient place to make identifications, sparing readers the trouble of flipping through pages and hunting for an abbreviation's first defined use.

Other uppercase abbreviations use the initial letters of familiar persons or groups to form well-known "call letter" designations conventionally used in writing.

JFK   John Fitzgerald Kennedy

SEC   Securities and Exchange Commission

ISBN   International Standard Book Number

NAACP   National Association for the Advancement of Colored People

MVP   Most Valuable Player

VFW   Veterans of Foreign Wars

USA (or U.S.A.)   United States of America

USSR (or U.S.S.R.)   Union of Soviet Socialist Republics

Abbreviations used by companies and organizations vary according to the usage of the organization. When referring directly to a specific organization, use its own preferred abbreviations for words such as *Incorporated (Inc.), Limited (Ltd.), Private Corporation (P.C.),* and *Brothers (Bros.).* Some companies will abbreviate the name of a city or state or the words *Apartment (Apt.), Post Office (P.O.) Box, Avenue (Ave.), Street (St.),* and *Boulevard (Blvd.)* in their formal return addresses; others will not. In a sentence that does not refer directly to a specific corporation, do not abbreviate such terms, but spell out all the pronounceable words.

FAULTY   I mailed it to a corp. out on the blvd.

REVISED   I mailed it to a corporation on the boulevard.
                I mailed it to The Impax Corp., Zero Wilshire Blvd.

ADDITIONAL EXERCISE A

ACROSS THE CURRICULUM Examine the textbooks you use in all of your courses for evidence
of the abbreviations listed in 31d. Make a list of
the abbreviations you find, and compare your
list to the ones in the book. Are all of the abbreviations you found covered here? If not, ask the
appropriate instructor to explain the meaning of
the abbreviation to you.

31d Using abbreviations for parenthetical references

From Latin, the traditional language of international scholarship,
we have inherited conventional expressions used in research to make
brief references or explanations. These are conventionally used in footnotes, documentation, and sometimes in parenthetical comments. All of
these Latin expressions should be replaced in a main sentence by their
English equivalents.

e.g. (*exempli gratia*)	for example
et al. (*et alii*)	and others
i.e. (*id est*)	that is
N.B. (*nota bene*)	note well
viz. (*videlicet*)	namely
cf. (*confer*)	compare
c. or ca. (*circa*)	about
etc. (*et cetera*)	and such things; and so on

The extremely vague abbreviation *etc.* should be avoided unless a
specific and obvious sequence is being indicated, as in *They proceeded by
even numbers (2, 4, 6, 8, etc.).* Even here the phrase *and so on* is preferable.
When used in parenthetical or bibliographical comments, these Latin abbreviations are not underlined or italicized since they are commonplace
in English. Typically, these expressions introduce a parenthetical remark
in an informal aside.

INFORMAL   A growing portion of our National Income is composed of
                  government transfer payments (e.g., welfare payments).

FORMAL   A growing portion of our National Income is composed of
                  government transfer payments (for example, welfare payments).

Bibliographical abbreviations are commonly used in documentation to provide short forms of reference citations, but they should not be
used in sentences of a paragraph. The following are some of the most frequently used abbreviations.

p.	page	Jan.	January
pp.	pages	Feb.	February
ed./eds.	editor(s)	Mar.	March
f./ff.	the following (pages)	Apr.	April
n.d.	no date (for a publication	Aug.	August
	lacking a date)	Sep./Sept.	September
ch./chs.	chapter(s)	Oct.	October
ms./mss.	manuscript(s)	Nov.	November
col./cols.	column(s)	Dec.	December
vol./vols.	volume(s)		

Each discipline has specific conventions for abbreviations in documentation, for example, the months May, June, and July are not abbreviated in MLA style; other conventions are discussed in chapter 36.

Writing in the Disciplines

Conventions differ in the disciplines about when and how much writers should use abbreviations—and about which abbreviations are common knowledge and need not be defined. Across disciplines, abbreviations are avoided in titles. For specific abbreviations lying beyond common knowledge, writers follow the convention of defining the abbreviation on first use. As a demonstration, a sketch of conventions for abbreviating in some of the science disciplines is provided here. For detailed information about conventions in a specific discipline, see the style manuals recommended in chapters 37–39, section e, or consult your professor.

- In scientific writing, courtesy dictates that writers define words that are later abbreviated.

  Some 800 species of bats live in diverse habitats and vary greatly in behavior and physical characteristics. Their biosonar pulses also differ, even among species within the same genus. Nevertheless, these pulses can be classified into three types: constant frequency (CF), frequency modulated (FM), and combined (CF-FM).

- Units of measure are generally abbreviated when they are paired with specific numbers. When not thus paired, the units are written out.

  In the next stage, 14 g were added.
  Several grams of the material were sent away for testing.

- Abbreviations of measurements in scientific writing need not be defined on first use.

- Symbol abbreviations are standardized, and you will find lists of accepted abbreviations in the *CBE Style Manual* published by the Council of Biology Editors. Generally, the use of abbreviations in titles is not accepted in science writing. Limited abbreviations—without definition—are accepted in tables.

31e Revise to eliminate all but conventional abbreviations from sentences.

In sentences, no abbreviations are used for the names of days or months, units of measure, courses of instruction, geographical names, and page/chapter/volume references. These abbreviations are reserved for specific uses in charts and data presentations that require abbreviated treatment in each discipline.

LOOKING AHEAD

Students can find a wealth of information on writing guidelines for specific disciplines in chapters 37 (Writing and Reading in the Humanities), 38 (Writing and Reading in the Social Sciences), and 39 (Writing and Reading in the Sciences). You may want to encourage students to get to know the chapter most relevant to their major.

GROUP ACTIVITY

Both exercises in this chapter lend themselves to group activity. Have students respond to exercises individually, and then compare their responses with those of other group members. When the inevitable disagreement occurs, students will have to consult the handbook. Once they become accustomed to using the chapter, they'll likely continue to refer to it as they edit their papers.

EXERCISE 1

1. These members decided to introduce shareholders' resolutions at the next annual stockholders' meeting of Texaco and SoCal that would require the companies and their affiliates to terminate operations in South Africa.
2. The effort to get Texaco out of South Africa was primarily directed by Tim Smith, project director of the Interfaith Center on Corporate Responsibility.
3. The management of Texaco and SoCal both opposed the resolution by citing their adherence to the Sullivan Principles, a code of conduct drafted by the Reverend Sullivan, a civil rights activist and minister of Philadelphia's large Zion Baptist Church.
4. South African blacks had in fact benefited from the presence of U.S. and other firms as evidenced by the dramatic 118% increase in black incomes between 1970 and 1975 followed by a 30% rise in the subsequent five year period.
5. In addition, the gap between black and white incomes had narrowed between 1970 and 1976.

FAULTY   Come see me on the first Mon. in Aug.

REVISED   Come see me on the first Monday in August.

FAULTY   He weighed 25 lbs.

REVISED   He weighed 25 pounds.

EXCEPTION: Abbreviations of standard, lengthy phrases denoting measurement are common in formal writing: miles per hour (mph or m.p.h.) and revolutions per minute (rpm or r.p.m.).

FAULTY   We enrolled in bio. and soc. next semester.

REVISED   We enrolled in biology and sociology next semester.

FAULTY   NYC is a haven for writers.

REVISED   New York City is a haven for writers.

FAULTY   The reference can be found in Vol. 6, sec. 5, p. 1. [These are used in bibliographies and documentation only.]

REVISED   The reference can be found in Volume 6, section 5, page 1.

EXERCISE 1

Correct the use of abbreviations in these sentences. When appropriate, write out abbreviations.

Example: In Apr. 1977, the Interfaith Ctr. on Corp. Responsibility announced that some of its subscribing members owned stock in Texaco and in SoCal (Standard Oil Company of California).

In April 1977, the Interfaith Center on Corporate Responsibility announced that some of its subscribing members owned stock in Texaco and in Standard Oil Company of California (SoCal).

1. These members decided to introduce shareholders' resolutions at the next annual stockholders' meeting of Texaco and SoCal that would require the companies and their affiliates to terminate operations in S. Africa.
2. The effort to get Texaco out of South Africa was primarily directed by Tim Smith, project dir. of the Interfaith Ctr. on Corp. Responsibility.
3. The managements of Texaco and SoCal both opposed the resolution by citing their adherence to the Sullivan Principles, a code of conduct drafted by the Rev. Sullivan, a civil rights activist and minister of Phila.'s large Zion Baptist Church.
4. S. African blacks had in fact benefited from the presence of U.S. and other firms as evidenced by the dramatic 118% increase in black incomes between 1970 and 1975 followed by a 30% rise in the subsequent five year period.
5. In addition, the gap between blk. and white incomes had narrowed between 1970 and 1976.

NUMBERS

31f **Write out numbers that begin sentences and numbers that can be expressed in one or two words.**

One to ninety-nine
nineteen	seventy-six
twenty-six	ninety-nine

Fractions
five-eighths	three-fourths
two and three-quarters	seven-sixteenths

Large round numbers
twenty-one thousand	fifteen hundred

Decades and centuries
the sixties	or	the '60s
the twenty-first century	or	the 21st century

Numbers that begin sentences should be written out.

FAULTY   57 percent of those attending the meeting fell asleep.

REVISED   Fifty-seven percent of those attending the meeting fell asleep.

REVISED   Of those attending the meeting, 57 percent fell asleep.

When it is awkward to begin a sentence by writing out a long number, re-arrange the sentence.

AWKWARD   Forty-two thousand eight hundred forty-seven was the paid attendance at last night's game.

REVISED   The paid attendance at last night's game was 42,847.

31g **Use figures in sentences according to convention.**

Numbers longer than two words
1,345   2,455,421

Units of measure

RATES OF SPEED	TEMPERATURE	LENGTH
60 mph	32° F	17.6 nanometers
33 rpm	0° C	24¼ in.

WEIGHT	MONEY	
34 grams	$.02 2¢	
21 pounds	$20.00	
	$1,500,000	$1.5 million

Amounts of money that can be written in two or three words can be spelled out.

two cents
twenty dollars
one and a half million dollars

Scores, statistics, ratios

The game ended with the score 2–1.

In the past presidential election, less than 50 percent of the eligible population voted.

The odds against winning the weekly lottery are worse than 1,000,000 to 1.

A mean score of 72 can be expected on the exam.

Addresses

Apartment 6   2nd Avenue
231 Park Avenue   East 53rd Street
New York, New York 10021

Telephone numbers
301-555-1212

Volume, page, and line references
Volume 6   act 1 scene 4 line 16
page 81   pages 120–133

Military units
the 41st Tactical Squadron   the 6th Fleet

Dates
70 B.C.   A.D. 70
from 1991 to 1992   1991–1992
1991–92

Time
Write out numbers when using the expression *o'clock.*

10:00 a.m.   but   ten o'clock in the morning
10:02 p.m.   but   two minutes past ten in the evening

31h **Edit to eliminate numbers and figures mixed together in one sentence, unless these have different references.**

FAULTY   A spacecraft orbiting Earth travels at seventeen thousand
            miles per hour; but because of the craft's distance from the
            planet, the images of continents and oceans seen through its
            window appear to be moving not much faster than images
            seen through the windshield of a car traveling 60 mph.

REVISED   A spacecraft orbiting Earth travels at 17,000 mph; but because of the craft's distance from the surface, the images of continents and oceans seen through its window appear to be moving not much faster than images seen through the windshield of a car traveling 60 mph.

ACCEPTABLE   For two months before its closing, the U-Trust Savings and Loan advertised wildly fluctuating interest rates in an effort to secure new cash: 9 percent one month and 15 percent the next. [Both numbers referring to advertised rates are presented as figures; the numbers *two* and *one*, referring to measures of time, are written out.]

EXERCISE 2

Correct the use of numbers in these sentences. Write out numbers in some cases; use figures in others.

> *Example:* 6,000,000 of its cars are sold annually, making Ford Motor Company the second largest automobile producer.
>
> Six million of its cars are sold annually, making Ford Motor Company the second largest automobile producer.

1. Ford was the subject of one of the most famous product liability controversies in the nineteen seventies as a result of problems with its Pinto.
2. Although the normal preproduction testing and development of an automobile takes about forty-three months, the Ford teams managed to bring the Pinto to production in a little over 2 years.
3. Styling preceded engineering, which resulted in the Pinto's gas tank being placed behind the rear axle, leaving only 9 or ten inches of crush space between the rear axle and rear bumper.
4. Subsequent crash-test results showed that striking a Pinto from the rear at twenty-one miles-per-hour caused the gas tank to be punctured, creating a fuel leak that could easily be ignited by any stray spark.
5. Other test results showed that design improvements needed to prevent the fuel leakage problem would have cost eleven dollars per vehicle.

EXERCISE 2

1. Ford was the subject of one of the most famous product liability controversies in the 1970s as a result of problems with its Pinto.
2. Although the normal preproduction testing and development of an automobile takes about forty-three months, the Ford teams managed to bring the Pinto to production in a little over two years.
3. Styling preceded engineering, which resulted in the Pinto's gas tank being placed behind the rear axle, leaving only nine or ten inches of crush space between the rear axle and the bumper.
4. Subsequent crash-test results showed that striking a Pinto from the rear at 21 mph caused the gas tank to be punctured, creating a fuel leak that could easily be ignited by any stray crash spark.
5. Other test results showed that design improvements needed to prevent the fuel leakage problem would have cost $11.00 per vehicle.

Hyphens

A small but important mark, the hyphen (-) has two uses: to join compound words and to divide words at the end of lines. You will find advice on word divisions in any dictionary, where each entry is broken into syllables. If you write on a computer, your word-processing software will probably suggest word divisions. As for compounds, these will require more discernment on your part, for relocating a simple hyphen can alter meanings entirely.

32a Using hyphens to make compound words

Compound words are created when two or more words are brought together to create a distinctive meaning and to function grammatically as a single word. Many compounds occur together so often that they have become one word, formed without a hyphen.

sandbox   outline   casework   aircraft

Many other words appearing in pairs remain separate. Two-word compounds often become one word over time, so consult a current dictionary when you are uncertain about spelling.

sand toys   out loud   case study   air conditioning

Use a hyphen to link words when a compound expression would otherwise confuse a reader, even if only momentarily.

CONFUSING   Helen's razor sharp wit rarely failed her. [Helen's *razor* is not the subject; Helen's *wit* is.]

CLEAR   Helen's razor-sharp wit rarely failed her. [With the hyphen, meaning is clear.]

Small as they are, hyphens make a difference. Each of the following sentences has a distinct meaning.

The cross reference helped me to understand the passage.

The cross-reference helped me to understand the passage.

The first sentence concerns a literary reference to a *cross;* the second, a note that refers readers to some other page in an article or text. The conventions for forming compounds with hyphens are as follows.

1 **Form compound adjectives with a hyphen to prevent misreading when they precede the noun being modified.**

The following hyphenations make compound or multiple-word modifiers out of words that might otherwise be misread.

low-interest loan   state-of-the-art technology   hoped-for success

Note that when a **compound adjective** is positioned *after* the noun it modifies, it does not need hyphenation. Placed after a noun, the first word of the adjective does not compete for the reader's attention as the subject or object in the sentence.

Helen's wit was razor sharp.

A compound modifier is not hyphenated when its first word ends with the distinctive suffix of a modifier.

Helen's impressively sharp wit rarely failed her.

Because of its ending, the first word in this compound modifier is not misread. In this case, the *-ly* suffix marks *impressive* as an adverb, and the reader knows that *impressively* will not function as the subject. Thus, the suffix in effect instructs the reader to move forward in search of the sentence's first noun—*wit,* which is in fact the subject. Because there is no possibility of misreading, no hyphen is used. The same analysis holds when the first word of the compound is a modifier ending with a comparative or superlative suffix *-er* or *-est* form (see 11e). In the following examples, the reader knows that *least* and *sweetest* are modifiers because of their endings.

The least expensive item in that store cost more than I could afford.
The sweetest sounding voice in the choir belonged to a child of ten.
[*By contrast:* The sweet-sounding voice belonged to a child of ten.]

2 **Form compound nouns and verbs with a hyphen to prevent misreading.**

Use a hyphen with **compound nouns** and **compound verbs** when the first word of the compound invites the reader to regard that word, alone, as a noun or verb. Hyphenated nouns and verbs are marked as such in a dictionary.

cross-reference (n)   cross-examine (v)   runner-up (n)   shrink-wrap (v)

Hyphenating the compound forms makes reading the following sentence easier.

CONFUSING   The runner up staged a protest. [What is intended: *runner-up* or *up-staged*?]

REVISED   The runner-up staged a protest.

REFERENCES

The following style sheets provide advice on hyphenation:

The Chicago Manual of Style. 14th ed. Chicago: U of Chicago P, 1993.

GIBALDI, JOSEPH, and WALTER S. ACHTERT. *MLA Handbook for Writers of Research Papers.* 3rd ed. New York: MLA, 1988.

3 Use hanging hyphens in a series of compound adjectives.

Hang—that is, suspend—hyphens after the first word of compound adjectives placed in a parallel series. In this usage, observe that the second word of the compound as well as the noun being modified is mentioned *once*.

The eighth-, ninth-, and tenth-grade classes went on the trip. [The second word of the compound, *grade*, and the noun modified, *classes*, are mentioned once.]

4 Follow conventions in hyphenating numbers, letters, and units.

Hyphenate fractions and the numbers twenty-one through ninety-nine.

Place a hyphen between the numerator and denominator of a fraction, unless one of these (or both) is already hyphenated.

one-fourth	seven-thousandths	seven one-thousandths
forty-six	seventy-one	

Hyphenate figures and letters joined with words to form nouns or modifiers.

4-minute mile   B-rated   U-turn

Hyphenate units of measure.

light-year   kilowatt-hour

5 Hyphenate compounds formed by prefixes or suffixes according to convention.

Use a hyphen with the prefixes *ex, quasi,* and *self,* with the suffix *elect,* and with most uses of *vice.* (Consult a dictionary for specifics.)

ex-President   quasi-serious   self-doubt

Use a hyphen with the prefixes *pro, anti,* and *pre* only when they are joined with proper nouns.

No hyphen	*Hyphen with proper noun*
prochoice	pro-Democracy
antimagnetic	anti-Maoist

But use a hyphen with a prefix or suffix that doubles a vowel or that triples a consonant.

No hyphen	*Hyphen with proper noun*
antiseptic	anti-intellectual
childlike	bell-like

6 **Hyphenate to avoid misreading.**

re-form (to form an object—such as a clay figure—again)
reform (to overhaul and update a system)

EXERCISE 1

Use hyphens in the sentences that follow to form compound adjectives; to mark prefixes or suffixes; to note fractions, numbers less than one hundred, or words formed with figures; and to prevent misreading. Place a check beside any sentence in which hyphens are used correctly.

> *Example:* Following WWII, Pepsi Cola Company succeeded in recruiting Alfred N. Steele, a tough talking, two fisted, pin-striped warrior with a unique grasp of the mood of the fifties.
>
> Following WWII, Pepsi Cola Company succeeded in recruiting Alfred N. Steele, a tough-talking, two-fisted, pin-striped warrior with a unique grasp of the mood of the fifties.

1. Steele was uniquely qualified to lead the Pepsi Cola Company when it began to falter because of its outdated marketing campaign; he had been educated at the world's greatest soft drink institution—the Coca-Cola Company.
2. Beginning his career running a circus, he moved into advertising and then jumped to a vice presidency at Coca Cola.
3. Subsequently, Steele accepted the more lucrative offer from Pepsi-Cola, though in his first quarter at the company it lost $100,000 as Coca-Cola pulverized the entire industry with a 67% stranglehold on the soft drink market.
4. Coca Cola was the darling of the ever expanding middle class, while Pepsi was a favorite of the downtrodden who couldn't afford to sacrifice Pepsi's extra ounces for Coke's prestige.
5. Thus, Steele set his sights on getting Pepsi into America's living rooms, and to that end redesigned Pepsi's standard 12 ounce bottle.

32b **Using hyphens to divide a word at the end of a line**

To the extent possible, avoid dividing words at the end of a line. For those times when you must divide words, do so only at syllable breaks (as indicated in a dictionary). Even when given suggestions for hyphenation by word-processing software, you often face a choice concerning hyphenation that could make a difference in clarity. The following conventions improve comprehension.

Divide compound words at the hyphen marking the compound.

When hyphens join compound words, it is unnecessary and confusing to divide the word at any place other than the compound. (See the discussion on writing compounds in 32a.)

UNNECESSARY   The mouthparts of many insects are exquisitely adapted to the nectaries (*nectar-hold-ing* organs) of special flowers.

CLEARER   The mouthparts of many insects are exquisitely adapted to the nectaries (*nectar-holding* organs) of special flowers.

Divide words at a prefix or suffix.

Hundreds of words are formed in English by adding prefixes and suffixes to root words (see 22d-2, 3). Divide these words, when possible, between prefix and root word or between suffix and root word. Thus, *un-necessary* would be preferable to *unne-cessary*.

A number of prefixes—such as *pro, anti, quasi, vice,* and *ex*—require the use of a hyphen. Divide these words at the hyphen.

AWKWARD   In the election of 1848, the "Free-Soil" party nominated Charles Francis Adams for *Vice-Presi-dent.*

REVISED   In the election of 1848, the "Free-Soil" party nominated Charles Francis Adams for *Vice-President.*

Eliminate hyphenations that hang a single letter at the beginning or end of a line.

To avoid misleading your readers, you would not divide these words: *e-nough* (it is misleading) or *tast-y.*

CONFUSING   Inflation creates fractures in the implicit and explicit *a-greements* that bind people together.

REVISED   Inflation creates fractures in the implicit and explicit *agree-ments* that bind people together.

Eliminate misleading hyphenations.

The first syllable of a word is sometimes itself a word (for instance, *break-fast, arch-angel, in-stall, match-less*). Confusion results when the first syllable, left hyphenated at the end of a line, fits a sentence's content and suggests one meaning while the full, undivided word suggests another.

Single-syllable words are never hyphenated.

To prevent misleading the reader, you would not, for example, divide any of these words; *ceased, doubt, friend, freeze, though.*

Abbreviations, contractions, or multiple-digit numbers are not hyphenated.

Abbreviations (*apt., IBM, NATO*) and contractions (*can't, won't, they're*) are already shortened forms. To shorten them further by a word division will confuse your readers. A multiple-digit number divided at the end of a line is also confusing.

CHAPTER 33

Understanding the Research Process

KEY FEATURES

This chapter presents an innovative approach to the research paper, describing research—appropriately—as a process of "making and revising knowledge." Students are asked to consider the research engaged in by their professors in order to better understand that process. This reference to professionals invites students to become a part of the process described above, treating them with a respect that can motivate them to take their own research seriously. Students are advised to find a "burning question" to stimulate their research rather than pursuing it solely for the purpose of fulfilling an assignment. To further assuage students' fears about research assignments, the chapter asks them to recall the writing wheel of chapter 3 (Planning, Developing, and Writing a Draft). Students are cautioned that research presents a different way of exploring questions than does the personal essay, and that particular way is explained in detail here. Using sample research assignments from across the curriculum, the chapter addresses such topics as the role of the research log, use of the library, consultation with faculty and other experts, and the movement toward developing a thesis. Throughout this discussion, the chapter emphasizes the self-generating nature of the research process, encouraging students to follow leads for their own satisfaction as well as for the benefit of the assignment. Extensive examples from student writers are presented.

Each discipline you study is based on a body of knowledge that is continually growing and changing. Your professors have a good deal to do with this change. In their own research they challenge assumptions; make discoveries about the physical world; and find meaningful patterns in human behavior and human artifacts, past and present. Researchers gain entrance into this world of making and revising knowledge gradually. At first their efforts focus on the library, where they develop habits of investigation important to all researchers, beginners and experts alike. In many of your courses you will be asked to write papers based on library research.

Four chapters constitute the section of this book devoted to research. The present chapter introduces you to a process of conducting library research that will lead you to pertinent sources on your topic. Chapter 34 is devoted to the ways in which you will *use* these sources: taking notes, summarizing, paraphrasing, and quoting. Chapter 35 will provide guidance on arranging materials and writing your paper. And chapter 36 will acquaint you with the process of documenting sources—acknowledging in your papers that you have drawn on the work of others.

33a Investigating the world through research

Your essential goal as a researcher is to learn: to discover information and ideas that will help answer one or more questions that seem important to you. An environmental studies course, for example, might motivate you to ask this question: What are the environmental effects of deforestation? Questions that might concern you in other courses include these: How are students on your campus dealing with the threat of AIDS? How did Malcolm X and the Black Muslims affect Martin Luther King, Jr.'s own civil rights movement? How effective, and legal, is drug testing in the workplace? As an active participant in your courses, you will start seeing critical differences and discrepancies in the material you encounter—differences that lead you to pose questions and challenges.

When you conduct research, you systematically seek answers to such questions. You may not find conclusive answers, but at the end of your research you should at least be able to express more informed opinions about your topic. But how do you develop questions in the first place? In some cases, your own experience may raise important questions that drive you to seek answers. A student whose grandfather was black-listed as a result of the McCarthy investigations of the 1950s may be impelled by a personal need to find out more about the anticommunist hysteria of the period and how it affected people like her grandfather. A less urgent but nonetheless provocative question may emerge from an informal discussion with a friend or a professor about politics or books or human behavior; some passing observation may set you thinking and stimulate you to investigate further. At each stage, your inquiries will lead to new questions, new ideas, and new priorities that challenge what you had assumed previously, leading to more inquiries.

Be a critical thinker.

In most cases research questions emerge when you apply the principles of *active reading* to your course texts or to the subject matter itself (see 1a). An active reader becomes alert to *differences* or inconsistencies in the material; for example, you may notice some interesting discrepancies between two or more textual treatments of General Grant or between one author's comments on schizophrenia and your own direct knowledge. As an active reader you *challenge* your text or your subject (see 1b-1); for example, considering the conflicting interpretations of this historical event, where does the truth lie? what are the reasons for this problem? how extensive is it? has the author fairly represented the situation? You would also ask questions of yourself (see 1b-2); for example, what do *I* believe about this issue? what do I think should be done? Before you can answer such questions, you need to locate and critically review more information than you currently have. As an active reader you try to set issues in a *broader context* (see 1c); for example, how is the problem of discovering a cure for AIDS tied up with the broader question of funding for disease research? You form *opinions* and try to support them (see 1d); for example, does evidence support the conclusion that dropping the atomic bomb on Japan was not necessary to bring about a Japanese surrender? And you devise *action plans*—in this case, research strategies to discover the answers. You will reflect this variety of thinking critically about texts in the writing of your paper. See chapter 2 on writing summaries, analyses, evaluations, and syntheses.

As your research progresses, you will *critically read* your sources. You will attempt to *understand* what others have said (see 1e); and you will *respond*, through questions and answers, to what they have said (see 1f).

TEACHING IDEAS

Embarking on the dreaded research paper journey can be daunting for many students, and downright paralyzing for some. It's possible, however, to help students maintain a positive attitude about the process. You can do this by telling them something about your own research—including your fears. Sharing your stories with students can help them in two ways: First, it lets them see that even professionals approach research with a certain amount of trepidation, and second, it treats student research seriously as an initial step into the literate community. Students will care more about their research if they see that their professors care.

REFERENCES

TOBIN, LAD. "Bridging Gaps: Analyzing Our Students' Metaphors for Composing." *CCC* 40 (1989): 444–58. Understanding students' metaphors for composing leads to less frustration in teaching the composing process.

BAZERMAN, CHARLES. *The Informed Writer: Using Sources in the Disciplines.* 2nd ed. Boston: Houghton, 1985. Chapters 11–15. A complete description of how the disciplines go about conducting research.

LUTZKER, MARILYN. *Research Projects for College Students: What to Write across the Curriculum.* Westport, CT: Greenwood, 1988. This librarian challenges teachers to design projects that are intellectually stimulating and eminently teachable (includes list of research topics and of periodical resources).

FLYNN, ELIZABETH A. "Composing 'Composing as a Woman': A Perspective on Research." *CCC* 41 (1990): 83–89. Feminist theory leads one to discuss students' writing and research in new, more fruitful ways.

McCARTNEY, ROBERT. "The Cumulative Research Paper." *Teaching English in the Two-Year College* 12 (1985): 198–202. Presents a way for students to thoroughly investigate one topic through several assignments.

WILLIAMS, NANCY. "Research as a Process: A Transactional Approach." *Journal of Teaching Writing* 7 (1988): 193–204. Discusses a set of assignments that illustrates the benefits of the research process.

(continued)

EMIG, JANET. "Writing as a Mode of Learning." *CCC* 28 (1977): 122–28. Writing is learning; researching, writing, and learning are interconnected.

LOOKING BACK

Not only will another examination of chapters 1–3 help students see the connections between research and critical thinking/essay writing, but it can also serve to allay some of the fears students may be harboring about research. There's nothing like the familiar to ease one's mind. You may want to ask students to review these early chapters, and then discuss in class what they recall that might be relevant in the research process.

REFERENCES

LANGER, JUDITH A. "Learning through Writing: Study Skills in the Content Areas." *Journal of Reading* 29 (1986): 400–406. Learning content is achieved best through writing, not through note-taking and answering test questions.

STRICKLAND, JAMES. "The Research Sequence: What to Do before the Term Paper." *CCC* 37 (1986): 233–36. A set of assignments starting with the generalized opinion paper—to which researched material may be added—ends with a thoroughly researched argument.

EXERCISE 1

Individual responses

FOR DISCUSSION

This exercise can foster valuable discussion about the research process. Select several students to read their paragraphs aloud to the class. (You can either rely on volunteers or read through responses and choose the most meaningful samples yourself.) As they hear different professors' reflections on research, students can begin to articulate their own questions about what research means (or will come to mean) to them. Discussing what research means to their professors can help students take their own research more seriously.

You will *evaluate* your sources, attempting to separate fact from opinion and to identify and take into account underlying assumptions (see 1g). Finally, you will *synthesize* the information and ideas that you have researched in ways that support your thesis—the statement that serves as your answer to your primary research question (see 1h). As you go through this process you will sift through all your questions, rearranging your research priorities until you have discovered the one key question that motivates you to find the most comprehensive and satisfying answer for your concerns. This may become the "burning question" for your research.

Using essay writing as a foundation for research writing

The process of writing a research paper is very similar to that of writing an essay. In chapter 3 of this book, a diagram was used to model the writing process (see 3a-1). This illustration shows writing and thinking as circular, recursive activities. *Recursive* means looping back on itself. The term as applied here suggests that although a writer will identify purpose and define audience, will generate ideas and organize information, and will produce a first draft, in no way will these activities represent a straight-line progression from the beginning of a paper to the end. For instance, well into developing the first draft of a research report, you may discover the need for new information. When this happens, you will need to interrupt your work on the draft and return to your notes, to the lab, or to the library for the necessary material. That is, to move forward you may sometimes need to pause and loop backward to an earlier stage in the process of writing and research.

EXERCISE 1

Interview two of your professors. Ask what kinds of research they do and why their research interests them personally. Ask what, if any, "burning questions" have directed their research. Why do these questions burn for them? Take notes during the interviews. Then review these notes and write three paragraphs: two paragraphs devoted to summarizing the interviews; and one paragraph in which you make observations about the research your professors do and their personal relationships to that research.

33b Defining the scope of your paper

1 Determining the research assignment

What you write about in your research paper—the kind of subjects you pursue—is determined primarily by the discipline in which you are working. A paper on the incidence of alcoholism among student athletes would be suitable for a sociology course, but not for a literature or business course. A paper on the genetic factor in crack cocaine addiction would be suitable for a biology course, but not for a sociology course. The following examples show some representative research assignments in the major disciplinary areas; they concern general topics that can be adapted to a wide variety of particular subjects.

Social science

Describe and discuss a particular behavioral pattern or syndrome among a definable social group. The group may be defined by social class, ethnicity, gender, occupation, age, or some other factor. You may also wish to compare the behaviors of this group with corresponding behaviors of one or more other groups.

Humanities

Examine several works by a particular playwright or novelist, focusing on a single feature or device characteristic of this artist. Explain how and why this feature manifests itself in different forms in various works and perhaps how it develops over the artist's career. Draw on the interpretations of critics and literary scholars to help illuminate your discussion.

Science

Scientists frequently find themselves drawn into controversies when their research tends either to support or to refute the views of particular groups or of social critics. For example, Darwin and his followers were embroiled in conflicts with creationists; physicists have been involved in controversies over the safety of nuclear power plants. Select a particular scientific discovery or line of research and explore the ways in which it has generated controversy among scientists and nonscientists alike.

Business

In recent years, much attention has been focused on the ethical aspects of business decisions. Research and discuss a particular business practice that has raised significant ethical questions. Show, by means of case studies, the kind of controversies and problems that have arisen as a result of such practices, and discuss and evaluate some of the recommended solutions to these problems.

2 Formulating initial questions

In preparing to write a paper on the general subject of drug abuse, what kind of questions might you ask? In most cases, questions will emerge from differences and discrepancies that you observe in your material (see 1a).

If you were writing a paper in the *social sciences*, you might ask, How do different cultures differ in their approach to drug abuse? How do drugs and alcohol affect the behavior and mental functioning of those who take them? If you were writing a paper in the *humanities*, you might

LOOKING AHEAD

ACROSS THE CURRICULUM The examples provided here represent assignments from several different disciplines. You may want to inform students at this point that they can find extended discussion of writing requirements in various disciplines in chapters 37 (Writing and Reading in the Humanities), 38 (Writing and Reading in the Social Sciences), and 39 (Writing and Reading in the Sciences).

REFERENCES

PAGE, MIRIAM DEMPSEY. " 'Thick Description' and a Rhetoric of Inquiry: Freshmen and the Major Fields." Urbana: ERIC Clearinghouse on Reading and Communication Skills, 1987. ERIC ED 279 020. Uses Clifford Geertz's theories to show the benefits of asking students to research career choices in the same way that anthropologists go about researching an unknown culture.

HORNING, ALICE S. "Advising Undecided Students through Research Writing." CCC 42 (1991): 80–84. Explains course designed around researching post-graduate options through writing experiences that move from self-exploration to career exploration.

LARSON, RICHARD L. "The 'Research Paper' in the Writing Course: A Non-Form of Writing." CE 44 (1982): 811–16. Rpt. in The Writing Teacher's Sourcebook. 2nd ed. Ed. Gary Tate and Edward P. J. Corbett. New York: Oxford UP, 1988. 361–66. Argues against teaching "the generic 'research paper' " as a form of writing, advocating instead that students cultivate their experiences as ways to inform the ideas they wish to develop.

PETERSON, BRUCE T., and JILL N. BURKLAND, "Investigative Reading and Writing: Responding to Reading with Research." CE 37 (1986): 236–40. Research is a way of thinking about our experiences with all texts; students can conduct research by tapping into their personal responses to texts.

REFERENCES

CAPOSSELA, TONI-LEE. "Students as Sociolinguists: Getting Real Research from Freshman Writers." *CCC* 42 (1991): 75–79. Research in sociolinguistics emphasizes aspects of language in which students are most expert and encourages students to engage in "real-life" issues.

COON, ANNE C. "Using Ethical Questions to Develop Autonomy in Student Researchers." *CCC* 40 (1989): 85–89. A set of assignments asks students to research an ethical problem, look at it in various ways, and then advance a hypothesis about it.

DELLINGER, DIXIE G. "Alternatives to Clip and Stitch: Real Research and Writing in the Classroom." *English Journal* 78 (1989): 31–38. Students may use different methods of inquiry (surveys, interviews, experiments) to generate their own research and to become engaged in writing about their results.

FORD, JAMES E. et al. "Research Paper Instruction: Comprehensive Bibliography of Periodical Sources, 1023–1980." *Bulletin of Bibliography* 39 (1981): 84–98. Provides resources and ideas for using sources and writing the research paper.

FOR DISCUSSION

ACROSS THE CURRICULUM This would be an ideal time to pause and ask students to consider the nature of disciplines. Many students have the idea that there's little connection between fields within a larger discipline, much less between the larger disciplines themselves. Here, however, they have an example of an issue that can be researched from a variety of perspectives. You may want to ask students to think of other issues that might lend themselves to a multi- or interdisciplinary approach. Students in different disciplines can then speculate on the direction research would take within those disciplines. (You may want to start the discussion off with a relatively general and easy topic to deal with, such as war.)

EXERCISE 2

Individual responses

---

ask, How has drug abuse been treated in works of art—novels, short stories, plays, films, poetry? To what extent do organized religions see drug use as a problem? If you were writing a paper in the *sciences*, you might ask, What are the physiological effects (long term, short term) of drugs and alcohol on the human body and its various systems and organs? Is alcoholism a disease? If you were writing a paper for a *business* course, you might ask, How is productivity affected by drug abuse? What are the costs of developing and implementing drug prevention and treatment programs in the workplace, and how effective are such programs?

Most of these questions are too broad as they now stand; you would have to narrow them down considerably to make them more suitable for a paper of ten to twenty-five pages. In looking at the question of how race is related to drug abuse, for example, you might focus on differences among alcohol consumption between Asians and Caucasians, or on drinking practices among Jews, or on substance abuse among Native American adolescents.

Before you narrow the focus too sharply, however, it would be wise to do some preliminary research on the subject. Otherwise, you may overlook aspects that you would have found particularly interesting. This preliminary research could involve reading an encyclopedia or magazine article, a section of a textbook, or possibly even a short book on the subject. Such reading may raise particular questions in your mind—"burning" questions that you feel compelled to pursue. Afterward, you will be in a better position to narrow your focus—and you will do this primarily by searching your sources to discover the answer to one primary *research question*. This research question may be one of the questions posed here, or it may be another question that was raised in the course of your preliminary reading. The advantage of a question, as opposed to a thesis, at this point, is that you are acknowledging that you still have to discover the answer(s), rather than just to find evidence to support a prematurely established conclusion.

EXERCISE 2
Select one question from each of the disciplinary groups covered in the previous section and narrow it down to a more particular question that you could deal with in a short research paper. Focus on *particulars*—particular social groups, artists, physical effects, companies, programs, and so on.

33c   Generating ideas for the paper

Perhaps you have selected a broad subject, which you may have already begun to narrow down. Or you may have started with a "burning question" and have begun to follow it up with further questions. Here, we will consider ways of further narrowing your focus and of searching for information sources about your topic (see 3a-1). Specifically, we will consider (1) how to keep a research log of your ongoing ideas; (2) how to develop a search strategy for preliminary reading; and (3) how to develop a search strategy for more focused reading, leading toward the development of your working thesis.

1 Keep a research log.

Many students find it valuable to keep track of their ideas in a research log. They write down their initial questions in this log and update it as often as possible. The log becomes a running record of all their inspirations, false starts, dead ends, second thoughts, breakthroughs, self-criticisms, and plans.

One technique that is particularly useful at the outset of a project is called *nonstop writing*. Nonstop writing (sometimes called *brainstorming* or *freewriting*) requires you to put pen to paper, consider your topic, and write down anything that occurs to you. Do not stop to revise, fix punctuation or spelling, or cross out bad ideas. Do not even stop to think what to say next—just write. The goal is to generate as many ideas as you possibly can within a limited period of time—say, ten or fifteen minutes. At the end of a session of nonstop writing, you may (or may not) have some useful ideas that you want to pursue.

Here, for example, are some initial ideas generated by nonstop writing sessions about alcohol and drugs. Note the difference in personal styles: the first is a stream-of-consciousness entry; the second is a list.

1. bad dangerous alcohol related accidents kill a lot of people drugs also kill and are one of the leading causes of violent crime alcohol is bad for the liver brain cells die with drugs, lungs, emotional problems, family problems begin because of alcohol and drug abuse, kids die, genetics are messed up miscarriage or deformations occur.

2. Cocaine, Crack, Heroin, Pot, Ludes, Sinsemilla
   Drugs can kill.
   Too many kids use drugs. Peer pressure
   AIDS from shared needles
   Alcohol is a drug
   Drinking and driving

Even though these ideas are in crude form, you can see some papers beginning to take shape here. As you proceed with your research, keep your log updated. You will want to do this not just to preserve a record of your research (often valuable in itself), but also to allow you to return to initially discarded ideas, which, at a later stage in the paper, may assume new relevance or importance.

Researchers use a log for other purposes, as well.

1. To jot down *sources* and possible sources—not only library sources, but also names and phone numbers of people to interview.

2. To freewrite their *reactions* to the material they are reading and to the people they are interviewing; these reactions may later find their way into the finished paper.
3. To jot down *questions* that occur to them in the process of research, which they intend to pursue later. (For example, how much money does the federal government allocate to drug education? What percentage of large U.S. companies have drug testing programs?)
4. To try out and revise ideas for *theses,* as their research progresses.

Do not use your log for actually taking notes on your sources; it is best to do this on note cards.

Generating Ideas for Your Paper

The following are three additional strategies for generating ideas. Each will help you consider ways in which to divide a broad topic into smaller, more manageable parts. You will probably be more specific and imaginative in thinking about *parts* of a topic than you will be in thinking about the topic as a whole.

- **Reading:** Read general works that survey your topic. The survey will suggest subdivisions. Some encyclopedia entries begin with an outline of the discussion. A research project appropriate for a term paper would focus on *part* of that outline.

- **Brainstorming:** Place your topic at the top of a page and, working for five or ten minutes continuously, list any related phrases or words that come to mind. Work quickly. After generating your list, group related items. Groups with the greatest number of items indicate areas that should prove fertile in developing your paper.

- **Listing attributes:** In a numbered list, jot down all of the attributes, or features, that a broad topic possesses. Then ask of every item on your list: What are its uses? What are its consequences?

---

2 Talk with your instructor or with other authorities.

Before you start your research, do not neglect another important resource: your professor. Schedule a conference or visit your professor during office hours. You may have little or no idea about what kind of paper you would like to write, but during the course of discussion, something may occur to your professor or to you that piques your curiosity, that becomes the equivalent of the "burning question." Your conference may turn into a kind of verbal freewriting session, with several unresolved questions remaining at the end of the session—one of which may become the focus of your paper.

3 Work toward a thesis.

You have now focused on a particular research question (3a-1); you have done some preliminary reading and perhaps have talked to one or two authorities on the subject; and you have begun generating some written ideas and have given some thought to your purpose and audience (3a-2, 3). At this point—having begun to formulate some informed opinions on the subject—you are ready to venture a thesis. If you had attempted to develop the thesis any earlier, you might not have been ready. You might have reached a conclusion that could not be supported by additional research. Or you might have proceeded to assemble a mass of supporting material without being sufficiently aware of whether or not you were missing sources in related areas that could enhance (or even refute) your thesis. On the other hand, do not wait too long to formulate a thesis. If you wait, your research is likely to be unfocused, and your supporting material may not provide a coherent answer to your central research question. Remember that having selected a thesis, you are under no obligation to zealously guard it against all changes. Quite possibly, you will need to adjust your focus—and therefore your thesis—as your research and your thinking on a subject develop.

> **EXERCISE 3**
>
> Choose a subject—either one of your own or one of the subjects discussed here—and develop some ideas about it, using one or more of the strategies discussed in this section. Read at least two relevant sources, and then develop a tentative thesis for a research paper on the subject.

33d Library research: Preliminary reading

Research logs and other strategies can be useful for getting down on paper ideas and information that you already have. Conferences with your professor can help get you thinking about a subject. Obviously, though, there are numerous aspects of that subject of which you are not yet aware, and one of these aspects may interest you enough to become your final topic. The best way to discover some of the possibilities is to use a systematic library search strategy.

1 Develop a preliminary search strategy.

A good search strategy begins with the most general reference sources: encyclopedias, bibliographic listings, biographical works, and dictionaries. The diagram on the next page shows a skeleton view of such a library search strategy. By consulting such sources at the outset, you will be able to narrow your subject to a manageable scope—that is, to one that you can cover in adequate depth within the length specified.

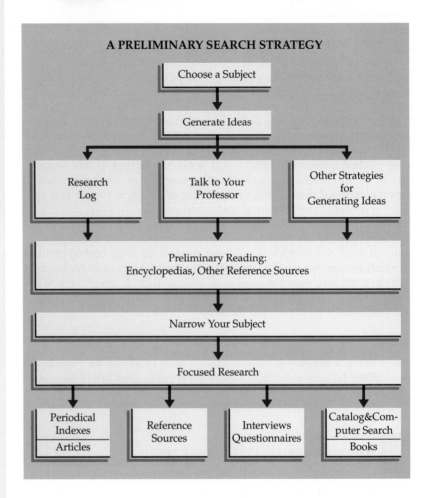

A PRELIMINARY SEARCH STRATEGY

Having narrowed your subject, you can then locate additional information, both from (1) periodicals and newspapers, which you locate through indexes and abstracts and/or computer search; and (2) books, which you locate through the card catalog and/or computer search. During this part of your search, you may further narrow your topic, and you can consult additional books and articles as necessary, along with additional reference sources such as biographical dictionaries, specialized dictionaries, and book reviews.

The second diagram illustrates how the narrowing down process might proceed. This diagram illustrates the process of a student who wants to write a paper on the drug problem. After some idea-generating strategies, she decides to focus on alcohol abuse. Since this subject is obviously still too broad for a relatively short paper, she does some preliminary reading and considers whether to focus on alcohol abuse among

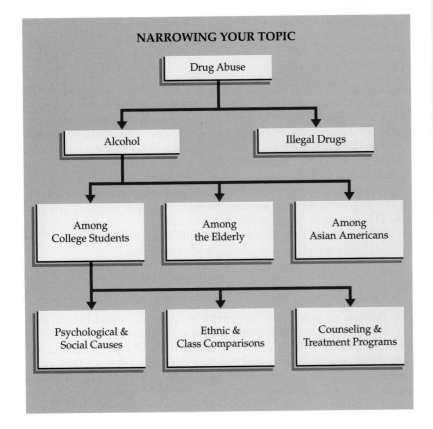

NARROWING YOUR TOPIC

Drug Abuse

Alcohol → Illegal Drugs

Among College Students | Among the Elderly | Among Asian Americans

Psychological & Social Causes | Ethnic & Class Comparisons | Counseling & Treatment Programs

REFERENCES

KLEINE, MICHAEL. "What Is It We Do When We Write Papers Like This One—and How Can We Get Students to Join Us?" *The Writing Instructor* 6 (1987): 151–61. Advances a "hunting and gathering" metaphor for the research process, affirming that writing the research paper is a discovery process that works best in a community of peers.

SCHMERSAHL, CARMEN B. "Teaching Library Research: Process, Not Product." *Journal of Teaching Writing* 6 (1987): 231–38. A set of assignments introduces students to how the library may be used for researching writing projects.

SCHWEGLER, ROBERT A., and LINDA K. SHAMOON. "THE AIMS AND PROCESSES OF THE RESEARCH PAPER." CE 44 (1982): 817–24. All research papers (academic and student) first "review" the research and then develop one of three patterns: work with a theory; "refute, refine, or replicate prior research"; or challenge a hypothesis.

TRYZNA, THOMAS N. "Research Outside the Library: Learning a Field." CCC 37 (1986): 217–23. A great deal of important, current information may not be discovered in using traditional library sources (provides useful lists of sources).

FORD, JAMES E. "The Research Loop: Helping Students Find Periodical Sources." CCC 37 (1986): 223–27. Offers a "research loop" that takes students (and their instructors) through a systematic research process.

college students, among the elderly, or among a particular ethnic group, such as Asian Americans. After some additional reading, she decides to concentrate on alcohol abuse among college students. But finding that even this narrowed-down topic is too broad, she finally decides on a paper dealing with the psychological and social causes of alcoholism among college students.

You should recognize that any diagram of the search strategy or of the narrowing-down procedure makes these processes look neater than they generally are. In practice, they are often considerably less systematic. What is crucial is to keep in mind the kinds of resources and procedures that are available to you, and—given the constraints on your time—to use as many as you can.

As you proceed, you will discover that research is to some extent a self-generating process. That is, one source will lead you—through references in the text, citations, and bibliographic entries—to others. Authors will refer to other studies on the subject; and frequently, they will indicate which ones they believe are the most important, and why. At some point you will realize that you have already looked at most of the key research on the subject. This is the point at which you can be reasonably assured that the research stage of your paper is nearing its end.

2 Use librarians as a resource.

We list "librarians" as a primary source, because they are a *major* resource too frequently overlooked both by harassed students *and* by professors. As one of our colleagues has remarked, "Librarians—especially reference librarians—are a *godsend*." Librarians have made it their career to know how to find information quickly and efficiently. This does not mean that they will do your research for you. It means they will be happy to direct you to the tools with which to do your own research. Frequently, the key to getting the information you need is simply knowing where to look. The next section will provide some assistance in this area. Your reference librarian will be able not only to supplement our list of sources, but also to tell you which ones are best for your purposes.

3 Look into the general sources.

General sources, such as general encyclopedias and biographical dictionaries, are designed for people who want to familiarize themselves relatively quickly with the basic information about a particular subject. Authors of general sources assume that their readers have little or no prior knowledge of the subjects covered and of the specialized terminology used in the field. Thus, if they use specialized terminology, they are careful to define it. General sources are also comprehensive in their coverage.

On the other hand, general sources tend to lack depth. They typically cover a subject in less detail than does a specialized source, such as an encyclopedia of music or a business periodical index. They also cover fewer subjects in a given field. Thus, while a student interested in a major film director such as Alfred Hitchcock would probably find an appropriate article in a general encyclopedia, someone beginning research on a less well-known director such as Leo McCarey would be better advised to consult a specialized encyclopedia of film. And, in fact, this specialized encyclopedia would probably have a more extensive article on Hitchcock than the general encyclopedia. In this section we will review some of the most useful general sources.

Encyclopedias

A general encyclopedia is a comprehensive, often multivolume work that covers events, subjects, people, and places across the spectrum of human knowledge. The articles, usually written by specialists, offer a broad overview of the subjects covered. From an encyclopedia you may

---

ADDITIONAL EXERCISE B

Having developed a tentative thesis, you're now ready to do some serious research. Bring your thesis and a few notes from your research log to the library and seek out a reference librarian. (If your library is a small one, you may want to call ahead and find out when the reference librarian is available.) Ask the librarian to help you decide where to look to find more information about your topic. Make sure to take notes in your research log so that you won't forget the directions you've received.

TEACHING IDEAS

Some students will have to be reminded more than once that encyclopedias should be used to provide background material only. Many students have been able to cite encyclopedias as sources in high school reports, and most students will be familiar with the ads for encyclopedias on MTV and VH1—ads that clearly present encyclopedias as the only source you'll need for a lengthy report.

be able to discover a particular aspect of the subject that interests you and to see how that aspect relates to the subject in general. Encyclopedia entries on major subjects frequently include bibliographies.

Keep in mind that encyclopedias—particularly general encyclopedias—are frequently not considered legitimate sources of information for college-level papers. Thus while you may want to use an encyclopedia article to familiarize yourself with the subject matter of the field and to locate specific topics within that field, you probably should not use it as a major source, or indeed, for anything other than background information.

One disadvantage of encyclopedias is that since new editions are published only once every several years, they frequently do not include the most up-to-date information on a subject. Naturally, this is of more concern in some areas than others: if you are writing on the American Revolution, you are on safer ground consulting an encyclopedia than if you are writing on whether doctors consider alcoholism a disease. Still, the nature of scholarship is that *any* subject—including the American Revolution—is open to reinterpretation and the discovery of new knowledge, so use encyclopedias with due caution.

Following are some of the most frequently used general encyclopedias:

American Academic Encyclopedia
Collier's Encyclopedia
Columbia Encyclopedia
Encyclopedia Americana
Encyclopædia Britannica

Biographical sources

Frequently you may have to look up information on particular people. Note that some biographical sources are classified according to whether the person is living or dead. The following are some of the most common biographical sources:

FOR PERSONS STILL LIVING

American Men and Women of Science
Contemporary Authors: A Biographical Guide to Current Authors and Their Works
Current Biography
Directory of American Scholars
International Who's Who

FOR PERSONS LIVING OR DEAD

American Novelists Since World War II
Biography Almanac
American Poets Since World War II

Contemporary American Composers: A Biographical Dictionary
McGraw-Hill Encyclopedia of World Biography
National Academy of Sciences, Biographical Memoirs
Webster's Biographical Dictionary

Dictionaries

Dictionaries enable you to look up the meaning of particular terms. As with encyclopedias, dictionaries may be either general or specialized in scope. Some of the more common dictionaries are listed in 22b-1.

Other sources of information

In addition to encyclopedias, biographical sources, and dictionaries, you may find the following sources useful:

Guides to the literature enable you to locate and use reference sources within particular disciplines. Here are five examples:
Reference Books: A Brief Guide
How and Where to Look It Up: A Guide to Standard Sources of Information
Sources of Information in the Social Sciences
Guide to Historical Literature
Business Information Sources

Handbooks provide facts and lists of data for particular disciplines. Here are several examples:
Handbook of Chemistry and Physics
The Allyn & Bacon Handbook (covers grammar and style)
Handbook of Basic Economic Statistics
Statistical Abstract of the United States
Gallup Poll: Public Opinion

Almanacs also provide facts and lists of data, but are generally issued annually:
Information Please Almanac (general)
The World Almanac (general)
Almanac of American Politics
Congressional Quarterly Almanac
Dow Jones Irwin Business Almanac

Yearbooks, issued annually, update data already published in encyclopedias and other reference sources:
Americana Annual
Britannica Book of the Year
Statesman's Yearbook

Atlases and gazetteers provide maps and other geographical data:

> *National Atlas of the United States of America*
> *Times Atlas of the World*

Citation indexes indicate when and where a given work has been cited *after* its initial publication; these are useful for tracing the influence of a particular work:

> *Social Science Citation Index*
> *Humanities Citation Index*
> *Science Citation Index*

Book review indexes provide access to book reviews; these are very useful for evaluating the scope, quality, and reliability of a particular source:

> *Book Review Digest* (includes excerpts from reviews)
> *Book Review Index*

Government publications are numerous and frequently offer recent and authoritative information in a particular field:

> *American Statistics Index*
> *Congressional Information Service*
> *The Congressional Record*
> *Government Manual*
> *Guide to U.S. Government Publications*
> *Information U.S.A.*
> *Monthly Catalogue of U.S. Government Publications*

Consult your librarian for information on guides to the literature, almanacs, and other reference guides relevant to your subject.

Bibliographic Index

Although we will cover periodical indexes in a later section of this chapter, it is appropriate here to mention the *Bibliographic Index* as an excellent research tool both for browsing through some of the subtopics of a subject and for directing you to additional sources. The *Bibliographic Index* is an annual bibliography of bibliographies (that is, a bibliography that lists other bibliographies), arranged by subject. On page 556, for example, is part of the listing under "Alcoholism" in the 1990 *Bibliographic Index*.

Each of these listings represents a bibliography that appears in another source—a book, a pamphlet, or an article. In most cases, the bibliography appears as a source of additional readings at the conclusion of the book, the chapter, or the article. In some cases, however, the bibliography stands by itself as an independent publication. If you browse through a few successive years of listings on a subject, you will probably discover some topics that interest you, as well as a source of readings on that topic.

TEACHING IDEAS

For a comprehensive, "user-friendly" reference book for general research (including some academic research), refer students to *The New York Public Library Book of How and Where to Look It Up* (Stonesong Press, 1992), edited by Sherwood Harris.

ADDITIONAL EXERCISE D

If you're still narrowing your topic, use this sample listing in the *Bibliographic Index* to guide you through a search for sources on possible topics for your research paper. Let the subheadings in the index help you narrow your topic, and make notes on sources that seem promising to you.

Main heading ——— **Alcoholism**
      See also

Entries under other main headings ⎡ Alcoholics
    Drinking of alcoholic beverages
    Korsakoff's syndrome
        See also subhead Alcohol use under classes of persons
        and ethnic groups

Ackerman, Robert J. Children of alcoholics; a bibliography and resource guide. 3rd ed Health Communications 1987 82p

Advances in alcohol and substance abuse. Haworth Press. See issues

Author ——— Ellis, R. J. and Oscar-Berman, M. Alcoholism, aging, and   Volume: Page
functional cerebral asymmetries. *Psychol Bull* 106:143–7 — numbers

Date of Periodical ——— Jl '89

Kline, R. B. The relation of alcohol expectancies to drinking patterns among alcoholics: generalization across gender and race. *J Stud Alcohol* 51:181–2 Mr '90

Title of Periodical ——— Room, R. Alcoholism and Alcoholics Anonymous in U.S. films, 1945–1962: the party ends for the "wet generations". *J Stud Alcohol* 50:382–3 Jl '89

Wallace, John. Alcoholism; new light on the disease. Edgehill Publs. 1990 p149–55

Wallace, John. John Wallace; writings. Edgehill Publs. 1989 — Publisher
incl bibl   and date

Subheading ——— **Genetic aspects**

Stabenau, J. R. Additive independent factors that predict risk for alcoholism. *J Stud Alcohol* 51: 172–4 Mr '90

Government policy
Great Britain

Preventing alcohol and tobacco problems; v. 2, Manipulating consumption: information, law and voluntary controls; edited by Christine Godfrey and David Robinson. Avebury 1990 incl bibl

History

Lender, Mark E., and Martin, James Kirby. Drinking in America; a history. rev & expanded ed Free Press; Collier Macmillan 1987   Entries are
p207–19 annot ——————————————— annotated

Cross-reference ——— **Physiological aspects**
——— *See* alcohol—Physiological effect

Prevention

Gonzalez, G. M. An integrated theoretical model for alcohol and other drug abuse prevention on the college campus. *J Coll Stud Dev* 30:501–3 N '89

Milgram, Gail Gleason. The facts about drinking; coping with alcohol use, abuse, and alcoholism; [assisted by] the editors of Consumer Reports Books. Consumers Union of U.S. 1990   Number of
p165–73 ——————————————————————— pages

O'Gorman, Patricia A., and Oliver-Diaz, Philip. Breaking the cycle of addiction; a parent's guide to raising healthy kids. Health Communications 1987 p155–62

Preventing alcohol and tobacco problems; v. 2, Manipulating consumption: information, law and voluntary controls; edited by Christine Godfrey and David Robinson. Avebury 1990 incl bibl

EXERCISE 4

Individual responses

EXERCISE 4

Select a subject you are interested in learning more about. Look up information about this subject in various general sources, keeping a record of (1) the *sources* used (give full bibliographic information); (2) the *location* of the relevant information (give page numbers); and (3) the *type* of information you find (give brief descriptions).

Using General Sources

- Use *encyclopedias* to get a broad overview of a particular subject.
- Use *biographical sources* to look up information about persons living or dead.
- Use *general dictionaries* to look up the meaning of particular terms.
- Use *guides to the literature* to locate reference sources in particular disciplines.
- Use *handbooks* to look up facts and lists of data for particular disciplines.
- Use *almanacs* to look up annually updated facts and lists of data.
- Use *yearbooks* to find updates of data already published in encyclopedias and other reference sources.
- Use *atlases* and *gazetteers* to find maps and other geographical data.
- Use *citation indexes* to trace references to a given work after its initial publication.
- Use *book review indexes* to look up book reviews.
- Use *government publications* to look up recent and authoritative information in a given field.
- Use *bibliographic sources* to locate books and articles on a particular subject.

33e Devising a working thesis

During your preliminary reading you began to focus on a *research question*. For example: should private companies require drug testing of their employees? As you continue to read about this subject—including arguments on both sides of the issue, anecdotal and statistical information about the experiences of certain individuals and certain companies—you should begin to develop your own ideas about your subject. Many of these ideas may have found their way into your journal (see 3b). Perhaps as you reflect on the experiences you have read about, and as you review your journal entries, one side's argument begins to seem considerably stronger than that of the other side. Or perhaps it is not a case of one argument being stronger than another, but a combination of various circumstances that makes testing advisable in some cases and inadvisable in others. Such observations and reflections on your part should eventually come into focus as a *working thesis* (see 3d). This thesis is, of course, subject to change as you come across new material and as your thinking about the subject develops further. For now, however, this working thesis is the main idea that shapes your thinking. The working thesis will also influence the focused reading of your subsequent research since, by defining relevant areas and eliminating irrelevant ones, it narrows the scope of your search for supporting evidence.

For the sake of example, let's consider four working theses. First, we will consider the narrower topics developed from the main subject:

> For a paper in the *social sciences,* the topic is alcoholism among college students.
>
> For a paper in the *humanities,* the subject is the motif of drug and alcohol abuse in the works of American playwright Eugene O'Neill.
>
> For a paper in *science,* the subject is whether alcoholism should be considered a disease.
>
> For a paper in *business,* the issue is drug testing in the workplace.

So far, these are only *topics*—not theses. To develop a working thesis from each of these topics, you will need to make a *statement* about the topic (after surveying a good deal of source material). Here are four statements that can be used as working theses:

> *Social Science:* Alcoholism among college students is an increasingly serious problem, but there are workable solutions.
>
> *Humanities:* Alcoholism and drug abuse are important elements of O'Neill's later plays; these elements are grounded in O'Neill's own life.
>
> *Science:* Alcoholism should be considered a disease, rather than an immoral behavioral syndrome.
>
> *Business:* For certain occupations drug testing is necessary to ensure public safety.

Note that while each thesis requires that the writer support his or her opinion, the first two theses tend to be *informative,* whereas the second two tend to be *argumentative.* That is, in each of the first two cases, the writer will attempt to describe a situation that she or he believes to be true. But the thesis itself is not a particularly controversial one; it is not a proposition that normally generates strong emotions. After considering the evidence, most people would probably agree with the thesis. In the latter two cases, however, the writer will argue one side of a fairly controversial issue. These are issues on which it is sometimes difficult to get people to change their minds, even after considering the evidence, because they have strong underlying feelings about them. The stand you take in the thesis may very well depend on your ambition for the paper (see 3d-3), as well as on the materials available and the conditions that apply to your argument (see 6d-1, 2, 3).

EXERCISE 5

Individual responses

EXERCISE 5

Based on your preliminary reading in general sources (Exercise 4), develop two working thesis statements about your topic: an *informative thesis* and an *argumentative thesis.* Make sure that each thesis takes the form of a *statement* about the topic.

33f Doing focused reading

If you have looked through a number of general sources, you have probably also developed a working thesis. At this point, you have some basic knowledge about your subject and some tentative ideas about it. But there are limits to your knowledge—which correspond to the limits of the kind of sources you have relied on so far. You need more specific information to pursue your thesis.

1 Looking for specific sources

General sources are not intended to provide in-depth knowledge, nor can they explore more than a few of the often numerous aspects of a subject. Refer back to the diagram on page 551. If you were researching the subject of alcoholism among college students, your general sources might be sufficient to get you down to the third level of the diagram, but the sources' inherent limitations would prevent them from taking you any further. For more detailed information about the kind of topics on the fourth level—the psychological and social causes of alcoholism among college students, ethnic and class comparisons, counseling and treatment programs—you would need to do more focused reading. You need a strategy for locating information in articles and books.

2 Finding what you need in focused sources

An overview of available sources will help you focus on the ones that best address your thesis. This overview will start with articles in order to emphasize the fact that periodical indexes are often preferable to the card catalogue as a first step in conducting focused research.

General periodical indexes: Magazines

Periodicals are magazines and newspapers published at regular intervals—quarterly, monthly, daily. Periodical articles often contain information available from no other source and are generally more up-to-date than books published during the same period. You are probably familiar with the *Readers' Guide to Periodical Literature* as a means of locating magazine articles, but there are numerous other periodical reference guides.

For example, consider *Ulrich's International Periodicals Directory*. This is not a periodical index, but rather a subject guide to periodicals, that is, it directs you to periodicals on a given subject. To find out more about the nature or scope of a particular magazine, check *Katz's Magazines for Libraries*. This reference tool lists the most commonly used magazines and offers basic descriptive and evaluative information about each.

Like encyclopedias, periodical indexes are of two types: *general* and *specialized.* The most commonly used general periodical index is, of course, the *Readers' Guide to Periodical Literature,* which indexes magazines of general interest such as *Time, Newsweek, U.S. News and World Report, The New Republic, Sports Illustrated, Commonweal.* Here, for example, is a recent *Readers' Guide* entry for "Drug Abuse."

DRUG ABUSE
  See also
  Alcoholics and alcoholism
  Children of drug addicts
  Cocaine
  Crack (Cocaine)
  Drug education
  Drugs and authors
  Drugs and blacks
  Drugs and infants
  Drugs and politicians
  Drugs and sports
  Drugs and the aged
  Drugs and women
  Drugs and youth
  Heroin
  Marijuana

The drug dilemma: manipulating the demand [cocaine] M. E. Jarvik. bibl f *Science* 250:387–92 O 19 '90 — **Title of article**

Drug policy: striking the right balance. A. Goldstein and H. Kalant. bibl f il *Science* 249:1513–21 S 28 '90 — **Includes picture**

The drug war [cover story; special section] il *The Humanist* 50:5–30+ S/O '90 — **Subject of article (if not clear from title)**

Just say whoa [J. Bennett resigns as drug czar] il por *Time* 136:91 N 19 '90 — **Volume: pages**

  Rehabilitation
  See also
  Church work with drug addicts

The cure: researchers say a nonaddictive painkiller stops cravings for cocaine and heroin [buprenorphine] K. McAuliffe. il *Omni* (*New York, N.Y.*) 13:20 D '90 — **Date of issue**

Meharry gets $2.8 million to treat drug-using moms. *Jet* 79:28 N 5 '90

Perinatal substance abuse and public health nursing intervention. B. A. Rieder. bibl f il *Children Today* 19:33–5 Jl/Ag '90 — **Title of Periodical**

  Testing — **Subheading**

Hairy problems for new drug testing method [Psychemedics Corp.'s use of radioimmunoassay] C. Holden. il por *Science* 249:1099–100 S 7 '90 — **Author**

Another useful general periodical index is the *Essay and General Literature Index,* which indexes (by subject, author, and sometimes by title) articles and essays that have been collected into books. The index is especially useful in that it gives you access to material that might not otherwise have surfaced in your search. These articles and essays generally would be classified under the humanities, but some deal with social science issues as well.

General periodical indexes: Newspapers

Most libraries have back issues of important newspapers on microfilm. The *New York Times Index* may be used to retrieve articles in the *Times* as far back as 1913. There are also indexes for the *San Francisco Chronicle,* the *Los Angeles Times,* and the *Wall Street Journal* (an important source of business news). The *Newspaper Index* lists articles from the *Chicago Tribune*, the *New Orleans Times-Picayune*, the *Los Angeles Times*, and the *Washington Post*. You can print out "hard copies" (from microfilm) of articles you need. If you're looking for articles in newspapers other than these, check dates of stories in the *New York Times Index*, or see whether the newspaper has a search service.

Here is a sample entry on "Drug Addiction and Alcohol Abuse" from a recent *New York Times Index*:

Major stories in boldface — **Brooklyn man who waged campaign against drug dealers in his Sunset Park neighborhood is run over and killed by furious van driver;** family and neighbors of victim, Ceferino Viera, say killing was in retaliation for his persistence in ordering drug dealers, addicts and prostitutes off block; note that Viera had refused to move even as crack dealing drove many of his neighbors away; police say they have no strong evidence that Viera was killed for his anti-crime stand, but his neighbors and friends are convinced that that was cause; photo (M), Ap 18,A1:1 — Date of story, section no., page no., column no.

Manhattan grand jury indicts defense lawyer Lynne F Stewart for criminal contempt for refusing to disclose source and amount of legal fees she got for defending drug dealer Donald Maldonado; her trial is expected to underscore growing legal battle in United States over lawyer-client confidentiality; special narcotics prosecutor Sterling Johnson sought unusual indictment; photo (M), Ap 18,B,1:5

Description of story — James J Dolan Jr, suspended police chief of Hudson,NY, is sentenced to five years probation and fined $8,000 for obstructing justice by interfering with drug investigations by other law-enforcement agencies (M), Ap 19,B,4:4 — Dates of relevant stories are in chronological order

Florida appeals court upholds first conviction in nation of woman charged with delivering cocaine to her newborn baby through umbilical cord; decision is first time state appeals court had approved prosecution strategy of charging new mothers whose babies are born with traces of cocaine in their blood under laws designed to punish drug dealers who give drugs to children under 18; mother, Jennifer Clarise Johnson, 25 years old, of Orlando, is sentenced to 14 years' probation and participation in drug-treatment program; photo (M), Ap 20,I,6:4

Computerized databases

During the past decade or so, library research has been revolutionized by the development of computerized databases—electronic indexes to vast numbers of articles, reports, and books. These electronic indexes, which may also provide abstracts (and in some cases the complete texts) of relevant sources, can make your research much more efficient and comprehensive than it would be if you were to rely exclusively on print indexes. An additional advantage of computerized databases is that they are much more current than print indexes, since they are updated every week, or even more frequently. You may read information from databases directly from the screen, or you may prefer to obtain printouts.

Computerized databases are generally of two types: *on-line* and *CD-ROM*. On-line databases originate from off-campus commercial information services (or "vendors"). The largest such service is DIALOG, which provides access to more than 100 million items in over 300 separate databases in the humanities, the social sciences, the natural sciences, and business. Among these specialized databases are PsycINFO, which references

TEACHING IDEAS

InfoTrac has become an immensely popular resource for students and faculty alike. But it's so easy to use that sometimes students don't bother to find out about its limitations. The index only lists articles that have appeared roughly within the last three years; thus, students will have to use other sources to find older material. Furthermore, students should be advised to always take down complete information on each relevant listing. Because the index is constantly updated, a three-year-old listing found during an initial search may well have been deleted by the time the paper is in the draft stages and the writer is checking source information.

items in psychological journals; ERIC, which references items in educational journals; and Arts and Humanities Search. Another important information service is WILSONLINE, which provides electronic access to the printed indexes published by the H. W. Wilson Co., including *Readers' Guide, Education Index,* and *Social Science Index.*

To use these databases, you must type in (or supply the librarian with) *key words* or *descriptors*—that is, subject headings—that focus your search on a particular area. Key words are terms or phrases that appear in the title of the item or that are used to categorize items in the database. (Many databases include a *thesaurus* or *dictionary* of key words.) The computer will search for all occurrences of the word, with no regard for word order or for connecting words. It is important that your key words be sufficiently narrow to make your search manageable. If you typed "alcoholism" into the terminal, for example, you would probably get a list of thousands of items. (On the other hand, if your key words are too narrow, your search may yield too few entries.) One way to narrow your search is to type in two or more key words; this will produce *only* items in which *both* terms occur. For example, a student using DIALOG to look for sources on alcoholism among the elderly used the key words "alcoholism" and "elderly" and located 37 items, including the following:

```
2059384.   88T5022
Research Issues concerning Alcohol Consumption among Aging
   Populations
   Stall, Ron
   Alcohol Research Group, 1816 Scenic Ave Berkeley CA 94709
   Drug and Alcohol Dependence     1987, 19, 3, May, 195-213.
   CODEN:DADEDV
   PUB. YEAR: 1987
   COUNTRY OF PUBLICATION: Switzerland
   LANGUAGE: English
   DOCUMENT TYPE: Abstract of Journal Article (aja)
   A review of literature concerning alcohol use & aging is
      presented highlighting reasons for change & stability in
      alcohol consumption during later life. Three categories of
      research are identified & analyzed—retrospective, cross-
      sectional, & prospective. Findings indicate that decreases
      in the prevalence of heavy & problematic drinking occur
      as a concomitant of the aging process. Hypotheses that
      have been offered to explain this association are
      identified & discussed, & those amenable to testing are
      suggested as subjects for future research. 65 References.
      Modified HA
   DESCRIPTORS: Alcohol Use (D022800); Elderly (D251100);
      Drinking Behavior (D231000)
   IDENTIFIERS: alcohol consumption, elderly; literature
      review;
   SECTION HEADINGS: sociology of health and medicine-
      substance use/abuse & compulsive behaviors (drug abuse,
      addiction, alcoholism, gambling, eating disorders, etc.)
      (2079)
```

One caution about on-line database searching: Since libraries have to pay for the use of such services, they frequently pass on the cost of an individual search to the user. You may pay by the item or by the amount of time on-line. Since these charges often range from $30 to $40 an hour or even higher, on-line searches are not always practical for the undergraduate researcher.

CD-ROM databases, as the name implies, are on compact disk (read only memory), and are more likely than on-line databases to be provided free to the user. Most periodical indexes available in print (*Readers' Guide, Humanities Index,* etc.) are also available on CD-ROM. Since one CD can store several years' worth of indexes, a CD-ROM search takes less time and effort than a search through several bound volumes.

One important compact disk index is InfoTrac, which provides access to articles in over 1,000 business, technological, and general-interest periodicals, as well as the *New York Times* and the *Wall Street Journal.*

A limitation of both on-line and CD-ROM databases is that they generally catalogue material that is only five or ten years old. If you needed sources published before that—contemporary material, for example, on the Watergate scandal of the early 1970s—you would need to rely on the print indexes for that period.

The card catalogue

Most libraries have now computerized their card catalogues; if this process is not yet complete, some of the older books may be accessible only through the traditional 3 × 5 card files. But whether on-line or on cards, a given item in the catalogue will be classified in three ways—by *author,* by *title,* and by *subject.* Browsing through some of the subject cards is a good way of locating books on your topic; but before you do this, you should have at least begun to narrow your subject. Otherwise, you could be overwhelmed with the sheer number of books available. (There may be several hundred books on various aspects of the drug problem.)

Notice the call number in the upper left-hand corner of the cards. One or more letters preceding the number indicates that the book has been catalogued according to the Library of Congress System, the most common cataloguing system for larger libraries. Smaller libraries use the Dewey Decimal System, which always begins with a number. If, for example, you are doing literary research in a library that uses the Library of Congress System, most of the books you will need will have call numbers beginning with "PR" (English literature) or "PS" (American Literature); if you are working on a political science paper, you will probably be looking in the "E" section. In a library using the Dewey Decimal System, literary books are in the 800 series and political science books are in the 300 series. Check the reference desk at your library for a key to the cataloguing system. The reference desk should also have a library map or shelving guide that will enable you to locate the books or bound periodicals that you need. Be certain that you accurately copy down the call numbers; a missing or incorrect letter or number may send you to the wrong section.

ADDITIONAL EXERCISE F

Whether your library has a computerized cataloging system or a card catalogue, this exercise should help you become familiar with the library: Record the call numbers and complete publishing information for the books listed under your topic. (You will probably find that most books share similar call numbers.) Now use the library's map or shelving guide to find the stacks where the books are located. After you have found the books you're interested in, browse the shelves for others that may be relevant. Make sure to take down all essential information on books you may use in your research.

Shown below are four catalogue entries for *Alcohol and Old Age* by Brian L. Mishara and Robert Kastenbaum: printed subject, author, and title cards, and an electronic display for author. One advantage of using the computerized catalogue, besides ease and speed of search, is that the displayed items may provide circulation information: You can see whether the book is on the shelf or checked out, and if so, when it is due back.

The miracle of electronic catalogue searching should not blind you to the old-fashioned advantages and pleasures of going into the stacks and browsing along the shelves in your area of interest. Browsing is not an efficient or comprehensive substitute for catalogue searching (some important books may be checked out; others may be shelved in another area). But pulling out promising titles and examining the contents may reveal to you valuable sources that you might otherwise have overlooked.

SUBJECT CARD

```
              ALCOHOLISM.
   RC
   451.4     Mishara, Brian L
   .A5         Alcohol and old age / by Brian L.
   M57       Mishara and Robert Kastenbaum. -- New
             York : Grune & Stratton, c1980.
               ix, 220 p. ; 24 cm. -- (Seminars in
             psychiatry)

               1. Geriatric psychiatry. 2. Aged--
             Psychology. 3. Alcohol--Physiological
             effect. 4. Alcohol--Psychological
             aspects. 5. Alcoholism.
```

AUTHOR CARD

```
   RC
   451.4     Mishara, Brian L.
   .A5         Alcohol and old age / by Brian L.
   M57       Mishara and Robert Kastenbaum. -- New
             York : Grune & Stratton, c1980.
               ix, 220 p. ; 24 cm. -- (Seminars in
             psychiatry)
               Includes bibliographies and index.

               1. Geriatric psychiatry. 2. Aged--
             Psychology. 3. Alcohol--Physiological
             effect. 4. Alcohol--Psychological
             aspects. 5. Alcoholism.
             I. Kastenbaum, Robert, joint author.
             II. Title
```

TITLE CARD

```
                Alcohol and old age
   RC
   451.4      Mishara, Brian L.
   .A5          Alcohol and old age / by Brian L.
   M57        Mishara and Robert Kastenbaum. -- New
              York : Grune & Stratton, c1980.
                ix, 220 p. ; 24 cm. -- (Seminars in
              psychiatry)
```

AUTHOR CARD—COMPUTER DISPLAY

```
  Search request: F PA MISHARA, BRIAN
  Search result:  5 records at all libraries

  Type HELP for other display options.

  1.
  Author:       Mishara, Brian L.
  Title:        Alcohol and old age / by Brian L. Mishara
                and Robert Kastenbaum.
                 New York : Grune & Stratton, c1980.
  Description:  ix, 220 p. ; 24 cm.

  Series:       Seminars in psychiatry.

  Notes:        Includes bibliographical references and
                index.

  Subjects:     Aged -- Alcohol use.
                Alcohol -- Physiological effect.
                Geriatric psychiatry.

  Other entries: Kastenbaum, Robert, joint author.
                 Seminars in psychiatry (New York, N.Y. :
                 1975)
                 (Record 1 continues on the next screen.)

  Press RETURN to see the next screen.
  -> f su aged alcohol use
```

Library of Congress Subject Headings

If you have not narrowed down your subject by the time you begin
your catalogue search, you should probably check the *Library of Congress
Subject Headings.* This is a set of volumes that indicates how the subjects
listed according to the Library of Congress System are broken down. For
example, drug abuse is broken down into such subtopics as "religious as-

TEACHING IDEAS

Students engaged in literary research will find yet another use for *Book Review Digest.* You may want to remind them that frequently book reviews, especially the extensive reviews found in the *New York Times,* the *Times Literary Supplement,* and the *New York Review of Books,* are at least in part literary analyses. Particularly with regard to contemporary works, students should not overlook the value of *Book Review Digest* as a resource for literature research papers.

FOR DISCUSSION

As students begin their research projects, it will be helpful to them (and to you in the long run) to review their progress periodically. A discussion of the value of the items in the box will allow students to assess their progress so far, to help one another with problem sources, and to fill in gaps in their research. Such a discussion will also alert you early on regarding potential problems in particular students' projects.

pects," "social aspects," and "treatment." You can use the *Library of Congress Subject Headings* as you used the encyclopedia entries or the *Bibliographic Index.* First, you can survey the main aspects of that subject. Second, you can select a particular aspect that interests you. Third, you can focus your subject search (in both the book and periodical indexes) on the particular aspect or subtopic that interests you, since these subtopics indicate the headings to look under in these indexes.

Book Review Digest

An invaluable source for determining the quality of books is the *Book Review Digest.* This publication, collected into annual volumes, indexes many of the most important books published during a given year by author, title, and subject. More important, it provides lists of reviews of those books, as well as brief excerpts from some of the reviews. Thus, you can use the *Book Review Digest* to quickly determine not only the scope of a given book (each entry leads off with an objective summary) but also how well that book has been received by reviewers. If the reviews are almost uniformly good, that book will be a good source of information. If they are almost uniformly bad, stay away. If the reviews are mixed, proceed with caution.

Trade bibliographies and bibliographies of books

For books too recent to have been acquired by your library or which the library does not have, you may wish to consult *Books in Print* and

---

Focused Reading

- To locate articles in general-interest magazines, use the *Readers' Guide to Periodical Literature,* the *Readers' Guide CD-ROM index, InfoTrac,* or another database index.

- To locate articles in newspapers, use the *New York Times Index* or other indexes for particular newspapers.

- To identify periodicals specializing in a given subject, use *Ulrich's International Periodicals Directory.*

- To determine the scope of a particular magazine, use *Katz's Magazines for Libraries.*

- To locate books and government publications, use the *card catalogue* or the library's *on-line catalogue.*

- To determine how a given subject is subclassified in card catalogues, use the *Library of Congress Subject Headings Index.*

- To locate reviews of books, see the *Book Review Digest.*

Paperbound Books in Print. These volumes, organized by author, title, and subject, are available in some libraries and in most bookstores. For books that your library does not have, but which may be in other libraries, consult the *Cumulative Book Index* and the *National Union Catalog.*

EXERCISE 6

Researching either the topic you selected in Exercise 4 or some other topic, locate at least five books and ten articles on the subject. Provide complete bibliographic information for these sources (see 34b). Locate several reviews of at least one of the books, and in a paragraph summarize the main responses.

3 Conducting interviews and surveys

Although you will probably conduct most of your research in the college library, remember that professional researchers do most of their work *outside* the library—in the field, in labs, in courthouses, and in government and private archives. Consider the possibilities of conducting original research for your own paper, by interviewing knowledgeable people and devising and sending out questionnaires. (Many subjects have been extensively discussed by experts on television news programs, talk shows, and documentaries. It may be possible to borrow videocassettes or to obtain printed transcripts of such programs.)

Interviews

Interviews allow you to conduct primary research and to acquire valuable information unavailable in print sources. By recounting the experiences, ideas, and quotations of people who have direct knowledge of a particular subject, you add considerable authority and immediacy to your paper. Those you select to interview may include business people, government officials, doctors, professors, community activists, or your own grandparent. If you would like to talk to a business executive or a government official but do not have a particular individual in mind, call the public relations office (in a business) or the public information office (in a government agency) and ask for the names of possible interviewees. Then, call the individual and try to schedule an appointment. Even busy people can usually find some time to give an interview; many will be glad to talk to someone about their experiences. But if you are turned down, as sometimes happens, try someone else.

It is important to prepare adequately for your interview. Devise most of your questions in advance; you can improvise with other questions during the interview, according to the turns it takes. Avoid *leading* questions that presume certain conclusions or answers:

Why do you think that American workers are lazier today than they were a generation ago?

What do you think of the fact that the present administration wants to burden small businesses with added health-care costs?

Ask *neutral* questions that allow the interviewee to express his or her own observations:

What changes, if any, have you noticed in the work habits of your present employees from those who worked here in the 1960s?

To what extent has government funding of genetic research changed during the present administration?

Also avoid *dead-end* questions that require yes/no answers or *forced choice* questions that impose a simplistic choice on the interviewee:

Do you think that this was an important experiment? (dead end)

What should take priority, in your view: jobs or the environment? (forced choice)

Instead, ask *open-ended* questions that allow the interviewee to develop her or his thoughts at some length:

In what way was this an important experiment for you?

How do you think it is possible to deal with the seemingly conflicting needs of jobs and the environment?

What were your impressions of Robert Kennedy when you met him?

Factual questions can be useful for eliciting specific information:

When did your restaurant begin offering a salad bar?

How many parade permits has the city denied during the past year?

Ask follow-up questions when appropriate, and be prepared to lead your respondent through promising, though unplanned, lines of inquiry. Throughout the interview show your interest in what your respondent is saying. On the other hand, keep in mind that your own reactions may unintentionally create cues that affect your subject's responses. Your subject, for instance, may begin to tell you what he or she thinks you want to hear (even if it is not quite accurate), based on how you have previously reacted. For this reason, trained interviewers try not to specifically respond to the interviewee's answers.

Surveys

Surveys are useful when you want to measure behavior or attitudes of a fairly large, identifiable group of people—provided that both the group and the measurements are carefully specified. An identifiable group could be freshmen on your campus, Democrats in town, Asian-Americans in a three-block area, or auto workers in two factories; measuring attitudes or behavior could mean obtaining records and comparing the frequency of responses made to specific and carefully worded questions. On the basis of measured comparisons among the re-

---

Checklist for Interviews

- Determine what kind of information you need from the person, based on the requirements of your paper and its thesis.

- Make an appointment, telling the person what your paper is about and how long the interview will take.

- Become knowledgeable about the subject so that you can ask informed questions. If the person has written a relevant article or book, read it.

- Prepare most of your questions in advance.

- Take pen, pencil, and a hardback notebook to the interview. If you take a tape recorder, ask the person's permission to record the interview. Even if you do record the conversation, take notes on especially important comments.

- At the end of the interview, thank the person for his or her time. Promise to send a copy of the finished paper. Soon afterwards, send a follow-up thank you note.

---

sponses to questions, a researcher might venture some broad claims about patterns of response as indicators of attitudes or behaviors within the population measured (it is not safe to generalize beyond the group actually measured without rigorous statistical procedures). Such generalizations are usually made in quantitative terms: "Fewer than two-thirds of the respondents said they feel threatened by the possibility of contracting AIDS."

To get honest answers to your questions, it is essential to guarantee your respondents' anonymity. Most frequently, questions and answers to surveys are written, though occasionally they may be oral (as when, for example, you ask students entering the library for their attitudes on American military activities in the Middle East). When devising questions for a survey, some of the same considerations apply as for interviews. For example, do not ask *loaded* questions that lead the respondent toward a particular answer ("Do you think that the money the university is spending to upgrade the president's residence would be better spent to reduce class size?"). For surveys, short-answer questions are better than open-ended questions, which are difficult to compare precisely or to quantify. It is relatively easy to quantify yes/no responses or responses on a five-point scale ("How concerned do you feel about the threat of AIDS? 5—extremely concerned; 4—very concerned; 3—moderately concerned; 2—somewhat concerned; 1—unconcerned").

Using Sources

Researchers in a college community work with written sources, and the library, home to these sources, is the hub of academic life. Each discipline has its specialized journals in which the latest research is reported, and each discipline has a multitude of specialized books devoted to its study. When researchers want to know what work has been done in an area, they conduct a search, or literature review, that reveals the varieties of inquiry into the area, the names of investigators, and the possibilities for further research. Without the benefit of prior work, researchers would be left to begin every inquiry from the beginning. Having to reinvent the wheel, so to speak, as if no one else had ever studied a particular problem, would be a wasted effort. The ability to read well, to *use* sources, is a crucial skill for researchers.

34a Reading with care

Your ability to write a research paper depends on your ability to use sources. And your ability to use sources, the subject of this chapter, depends *entirely* on your ability to read well. Because effective reading is a foundational skill on which the success of all research rests, you should turn to chapter 1 if you are not fully comfortable with the prospect of reading to understand, respond, and forge relationships. Close, strategic reading is a skill you can teach yourself; once learned, it will serve you well both in college and in your career.

34b Classifying sources: Primary and secondary

When attempting to determine the value and quality of a source, keep in mind the distinction between *primary* and *secondary* sources. Primary sources are written by people who have *direct* knowledge of the events or issues under discussion: they were participants in or observers of those events. Examples of primary sources are letters, diaries, autobiographies, oral histories, and historical documents. Authors of secondary sources have only *indirect* knowledge; they rely on primary or other secondary sources for their information. Examples of secondary sources include biographies, textbooks, historical surveys, and literary criticism.

For example, the following statements by President John F. Kennedy and Premier Nikita Khruschev of the Soviet Union serve as primary sources on the Cuban missile crisis of 1962:

This urgent transformation of Cuba into an important strategic base—by the presence of these large, long-range, and clearly offensive weapons of sudden mass destruction—constitutes an explicit threat to the peace and security of all the Americas.

—Kennedy

It was during my visit to Bulgaria that I had the idea of installing missiles with nuclear warheads in Cuba without letting the United States find out they were there until it was too late to do anything about them.

—Khruschev

The following statement by historian Louise FitzSimons, who was not a participant in the crisis, is a secondary source:

President Kennedy was moved to act because of his history of preoccupation with Cuba as an issue; because he feared that his prestige would suffer, that Khruschev would think him weak; because he permitted vestiges of cold war thinking to freeze his policy and prevent any flexibility in dealing with the Soviet Union; and because of his fear that the American public would respond to the missiles by removing his party or even himself from office.

A single source may be used either as a primary or as a secondary source, depending on what is being studied. A written piece that reacts to or interprets some previous event is a secondary source for anyone studying the original event or situation; however, for anyone studying typical ways of reacting to or thinking about that event, the same piece could be primary material. An editorial written during the Cuban missile crisis would be a secondary source for students seeking information on Soviet response to American actions, but it could be a primary source for students of contemporary popular reactions, images, or interpretations of the crisis.

Primary sources are not necessarily superior (or inferior) to secondary sources, but it is good to recognize the strengths and limitations of each. Primary sources provide facts and viewpoints that are generally not available from other sources; they often have immediacy and drama. On the other hand, primary sources may be colored by the bias or self-servingness of authors who want to inflate their own importance, justify questionable decisions, or willfully misrepresent the facts.

Secondary sources, by contrast, often have the opportunity to write from a different and broader perspective on the original events, to use hindsight and more varied information, or to be less affected by intense passions than those who experienced the original events. In spite of those opportunities, however, secondary sources can always be biased by their own agendas or be narrow-minded or unperceptive, while some primary writers close to original events might be quite reliable and unbiased. You will need to make your own determination of the reliability and credibility of every source, whether primary or secondary.

FOR DISCUSSION

To help students understand fully the distinction between primary and secondary sources, you may want to engage them in a discussion. Ask them to suggest possible primary and secondary sources for a given topic (Japanese-American internment camps, for example, or the psychological effects of growing up in a religious cult). As you list the sources on the board, ask students to explain why each source is classified as primary or secondary, and encourage discussion of questionable responses.

34c   Critically reading sources

Consider how the strategies described in chapter 1 for the critical reading of any text might work when applied to potential sources for your research paper. Suppose you are working on a paper on the progress of the Equal Rights Amendment, which was approved by Congress in 1972 but defeated by the deadline of 1982 when it fell three states short of ratification. If your *research question* asked why the amendment was defeated, your *thesis* would provide a summary answer to this question.

1   Reading to understand

Your main goal during this stage is to familiarize yourself with your sources and to determine their *relevance*. The previous section listed some of the best ways to do this. First, preview a source by skimming its contents: Read the table of contents, the introduction or preface, the conclusion, section headings, and selected topics. For example, you might locate a lengthy article that appeared in the *Yale Law Journal*: "The Equal Rights Amendment: A Constitutional Basis for Equal Rights for Women" (1971). Previewing this article, you might determine that about only four of its thirty-five pages (summarizing the rationale of the ERA) are directly relevant to your research question.

You might locate an anthology of essays on women's issues, Jane DeHart Matthews and Linda K. Kerber's *Women's America: Refocusing the Past* (1982), and quickly establish that at least three of its essays include material that may help answer your research question. A third source, an article by Andrew Hacker, "E.R.A.—R.I.P.," which appeared in *Harper's* in 1980, is devoted entirely to answering your research question. (Note, however, that the title of this article suggests that the author believes that the ERA *should* have been defeated, and so during later readings for response and evaluation, you will need to be alert to possible bias.)

2   Reading to respond

During this stage, your main goal is to read your source carefully enough to *react* and to *ask questions*. Check the credentials of the author and the critical reception of his or her work (see 33f). Does the author's background or professional affiliation suggest to you the point of view he or she will take? (For example, can you predict the likely viewpoint of an officer of the National Rifle Association on handgun control?) Identify the author's stance on the subject: Is she or he pro, con, or neutral? Relatively detached or passionately involved (or something in-between)? Is the tone angry, cynical, witty, solemn, or earnest? Does the author have a personal stake in the issue under discussion? If so, how might this affect your acceptance of her or his arguments?

Highlight important questions, particularly those most directly relevant to your research question; make marginal notations; take notes; look for important quotations you may be able to use in your paper. In an article called "The Woman Who Talked Back to God" by Mormon-turned-ERA activist Sonia Johnson, for example, you might highlight a section in which Johnson is questioned by a hostile senator during a congressional committee hearing. This interchange indicates the depth of anti-ERA feeling by some legislators, so it bears directly on your research question.

Reading about the testimony of Johnson might also stimulate you to ask questions about others who testified before this committee and to find out what arguments were made on both sides. In an attempt to answer this question, you would have to track down—perhaps in the government publications department of your library—the printed transcripts of the hearings of the Senate Subcommittee on Constitutional Rights during 1978–79.

Finally, be alert to *differences* between sources: for example, what Ann Scott (an official of the National Organization for Women) said of the ERA, and what Phyllis Schlafly (head of the conservative Eagle Forum) said about it. After critical reading and additional research, you will probably want to discuss such differences.

3   Reading to evaluate

During this stage, your goals are to determine the *reliability* of your sources. This involves attempting to separate fact from opinion in the source; identifying and assessing the author's assumptions; and evaluating both the evidence offered by the author in support of his or her argument and the logic by which the conclusions are reached (see 6h).

Reading to evaluate also involves considering the source of publication for an article or book. Was the article published in a popular magazine (intended for a general audience) or an academic or professional journal (intended for a specialized audience)? Articles in journals will probably be more difficult to read, but will tend to have more authority and credibility to your own readers. Is your book or pamphlet published by a commercial or academic publisher, or by a publisher with a special interest (a chemical company, for example, or a nonprofit agency like the pro-environmental Earth First! or the American Civil Liberties Union)? Special-interest publications should not necessarily be discounted, but you should consider the source and be aware of the potentiality for bias. For more specific advice, see the boxed information in 6d-2, "Using Authoritative Sources."

4   Reading to synthesize

During this stage, your main goal is to determine how the evidence from one source is related to evidence from other sources. You must compare what you find in your sources, evaluate the information and assumptions in each, and form your own ideas about the most important relationships among them. The skills for doing this are demonstrated in detail in chapters 1 and 2 (see 1h and 2d). Your discussion will require cross-references among sources, noting where one author refers to ideas discussed by any others. When possible, establish a relationship among them through comparing, contrasting, defining concepts or examples, or making connections by process or cause and effect. In this way you *synthesize* the sources to let them support your answers to the research question and your argument for the paper's provisional thesis. See example syntheses in the following student papers: 6g (based on reading selections in chapters 1 and 2); 35h, 37e, and 38d. In each case, student writers synthesized sources in order to answer research questions.

34d   Creating a working bibliography

Your **working bibliography** is a list of all of the sources you locate in preparing your paper. This includes books, articles, entries from biographical sources, handbooks, almanacs, and the various other kinds of sources cited in 33d and 33f. The bibliography should also include sources you locate in indexes that you intend to check later. Your working bibliography differs from your **final bibliography** in that it is more comprehensive: The final bibliography consists only of those sources that you actually use in writing the paper.

It is absolutely essential that you prepare your working bibliography *at the same time* that you are compiling and consulting your sources. That way you can be sure to have accurate and complete information when the time comes to return to your sources to obtain more information or to double-check information, and to compile your final bibliography. It is enormously frustrating to be typing your list of references (quite possibly the night before your paper is due!) and to suddenly realize that your notes do not contain all the information you need.

We recommend that you compile a working bibliography on 3" × 5" index cards. A card file allows you to easily alphabetize entries or to arrange them in any other order (such as by topic and subtopic order, or by sources you have already examined and ones you have not) that is most useful to you during the research and writing process. As you consult each new source, carefully record key information:

1. full name of author (last name first),
2. title (and subtitle),
3. publication information:
   a. place of publication
   b. name of publisher
   c. date of publication
4. inclusive page numbers

In case you have to relocate the source later, indicate the library call number (in the upper right-hand corner) and the name and date of the index where you located the source (at the bottom). It is also a good idea to include (either below the publication information or on the back of the card) a brief annotation, in which you describe the contents of that source or the author's main idea, and indicate your reaction to the source and how you might use it in your paper. By surveying your annotations as you proceed with your research, you will quickly be able to see how much you have already found on your subject and what else you still need to look up. Your annotations may also prevent you from wasting time looking up the same sources twice. Finally, you should assign a code number to each bibliographic entry. Then, when you are taking notes on the source (perhaps on 4" × 6" note cards), you can simply put that code number in the upper right-hand corner of the note card, which saves you from having to recopy your complete bibliographic information.

When the time comes to prepare your final bibliography, you can simply arrange the cards for the sources you used in alphabetical order and type up the pertinent information as a list. Here's a sample bibliography card for a book:

---

④ Berger, Gilda, _Drug Testing._ New York: HV58235
Franklin Watts, 1987.   U5 B&7
     1987

Considers the U.S. drug crisis and issues of drug testing in various public & private sectors. Chapter 7 deals with drug testing in private industry--includes several specific cases.

Here's a sample card for an article:

---

⑱ Gilmore, Thomas B. "_The Iceman Cometh_ and the   P1
Anatomy of Alcoholism" _Comparative Drama_, 18.4   C6184
(winter 1984–85): 335–47.

Focuses on Hickey. _Thesis:_ "Throughout the play the principles of AA [Alcoholics Anonymous] provide an excellent means of analysis for examining Hickey's salesmanship in order to determine the quality of his new product or line, sobriety"   (336)

1984 _MLA Bib._ 1:10436

TEACHING IDEAS

Another way to reduce the stress that inevitably accompanies the final stages of the research process is to ask students to present you with an annotated bibliography. This exercise provides students with the necessary incentive to get moving, and allows you the opportunity to evaluate not only their progress but their understanding of the research process as well. Requiring an annotated bibliography at this time might well prevent trouble later on.

TEACHING IDEAS

It is important for students to understand the difference between working and final bibliographies. To make the distinction clearer, you may want to use the analogy of the working and final theses for essays. By now students should have a clear sense of the tentative nature of the working thesis; it may help if they think of the working bibliography in the same way.

EXERCISE 1

Individual responses

Some instructors may ask for an **annotated bibliography** as an intermediate step between your working bibliography notes and the final bibliography. In effect, an annotated bibliography is a fully annotated working bibliography in manuscript form; it records the same information demonstrated above in card form, presenting it in alphabetical sequence on manuscript sheets for your review and for suggestions from collaborators, peers, or your instructor.

A note on *photocopying:* Frequently, you will not be able to check periodicals out of the library, so you may find yourself photocopying stacks of articles. In recent years many journals have begun to include complete bibliographic information at the bottom of the first page of each article. But if some or all of this information is not already there, *make sure you carefully and immediately record the bibliographic data on the first page of the photocopy.* To provide additional backup for documentation, you may find it useful to photocopy those pages of the bibliographic indexes from which you located sources; keep in mind, however, that these pages often indicate the authors' first names only by initials.

If you are photocopying a section of a book, it is a good idea to also photocopy the book's title page, which contains all the bibliographic information, except the date of publication (that is located on the reverse side of the title page). Whether copying articles or books, double-check to make sure that you have copied *all* of the text on each page—including the page number (you may have to write these in). Finally, if you are photocopying text that includes footnotes, remember to also copy the corresponding footnote references at the end of the article, the chapter, or the book. Again, taking the time to do all of this now—at the photocopy machine—may save you hours of time later if you have to relocate the item.

EXERCISE 1

Compile a working bibliography—both books and articles—of twenty to twenty-five items for one of the subjects you have been researching for the previous chapter. Or if you prefer, research a new subject. Record key information (as indicated above) on 3" × 5" cards or in your electronic database (if the latter, you will need a printout). Include content annotations for at least five items.

34e Taking notes

Use 4" × 6" cards for taking notes. You could use other materials, of course, but you will have difficulty sorting through and rearranging individual entries. Notecards solve this problem and allow you to add or drop entries with ease.

Researchers use various formats for notecards, but the following elements are most important:

1. a *code number* (corresponding to the code number on your bibliography card) *or* the bibliographic reference;
2. a *topic* or *subtopic* label (these enable you to easily arrange and rearrange the cards in topical order);
3. the *note* itself;
4. a *page reference*.

Do not attempt to include too much information on a single notecard. For example, do not summarize an entire article or chapter on one card, particularly if you are likely to use information from a single card in different places in your paper. By limiting each card to a single point or illustration, you make it easier to arrange your cards according to your outline, and to rearrange them later if your outline changes. A sample notecard for Gilda Berger's *Drug Testing* appears below. (For comparison's sake, it is placed directly after the bibliography card for the same source.)

---

④ Berger, Gilda, *Drug Testing*. New York: HV58235
Franklin Watts, 1987.   U5 B&7
                                                1987

Considers the U.S. drug crisis and issues of drug testing in various public & private sectors. Chapter 7 deals with drug testing in private industry--includes several specific cases.

Test Accuracy   ④
The accuracy of drug testing is open to serious question. Berger states that "out of every twenty people in a workplace tested for drugs, the chances are that one will get a false positive result" (p. 88). And while testing labs claim error rates of less than one percent, one study revealed that "known samples submitted to thirteen drug laboratories showed error rates as high as 100 percent for certain drugs." (p. 88)

There are three methods of notetaking: *summarizing, paraphrasing,* and *quoting*. These methods can be used either singly or in combination. *Summarizing* is used when there is a relatively long passage of text from which you need to extract one or two main points; these points would probably be used as background information for your own paper. *Paraphrasing* is used with a relatively brief passage of important material that is central to your discussion or argument. *Quoting* is used if the person being quoted has made a point in a particularly dramatic or incisive way, or if the reputation of this person would enhance the credibility of your presentation. The preceding notecard on drug testing used a combination of quotation and summary.

To illustrate how each of these methods of notetaking would show up in the final paper, we will use as an example the final two paragraphs of an article called "Jar Wars" by William Saletan, which appeared in the October 2, 1989, *New Republic*.

> Conyers's campaign chairman told reporters that he and other Conyers officials were "philosophically opposed" to the drug test but took it anyway just to quash the issue. "The conventional wisdom now is to acquiesce, to get it out of the arena right away," explains one GOP consultant. But in jar wars, like nuclear wars, everybody loses. Take Atlanta. In 1986 rumors of drug abuse by Bond provided at least a bare context for making testing an issue. In 1989 even that basis was lacking, but both candidates volunteered for the test anyway. Several other local officeholders have also begrudgingly taken the test to immunize themselves against suspicion. Local consultants say widespread capitulation has made the test, in effect, a mandatory ritual. Elsewhere consultants say more and more candidates are keeping test results at hand, just in case they're needed.
>
> Every politician who takes a drug test justifies it as a way to send a message to the public, particularly to the young. But the trouble is that it sends the wrong message: if you won't take the test, you're suspect. Not only are your agenda and your political record irrelevant, but so is your conduct, which is the only defensible basis for requiring a drug test of a political candidate. The only way to reverse this trend is to reverse the test. The message from voters to politicians must be: if you value substance above stunts, and if you respect yourself and your constituents, offer us your platform and your record, not your urine.

Here is how the information in that passage might turn up in the final paper. Markings indicate those sections summarized, paraphrased, and quoted from the original.

Summary	Many candidates for public office have been feeling pressure both from their political opponents and from the anti-drug atmosphere to submit to drug testing as a way of proving themselves drug free (Saletan 14). But self-imposed drug test-
Quotation	ing of politicians is not necessarily a good trend. As Saletan remarks, "in jar wars, like nuclear wars, everybody loses" (14). The message sent by these tests, notes Saletan, is if you
Paraphrase	don't agree to take one you may be guilty, and that your political philosophy and your past performance have no bearing on your qualifications for office.

1   Summarizing sources

A *summary* is a relatively brief, objective account, in your own words, of the main ideas in a source passage. As mentioned previously, you would summarize a passage when you wanted to extract the main ideas and use them as background material in your own paper. For details on the process of writing summaries, see 2a.

Suppose you were preparing the paper dealing with drug-taking among college students. You decided in the early part of this paper to do a brief survey of drug use in various cultures as one means of establishing the "normality" of such practices among college students. From an anthropology course you recall studying a tribe of Indians known as the Yanomamo who live in Venezuela and Brazil and for whom the regular taking of hallucinogenic drugs is an important part of tribal culture. Unfortunately you have sold your textbook, so you go to the library and check out a copy of *Yanomamo: The Fierce People* by Napoleon A. Chagnon (New York: Holt, 1968). You locate the following passage dealing with hallucinogenic drug-taking:

HALLUCINOGENIC DRUGS   Another useful plant provided by the jungle is the *ebene* tree. The inner bark of this tree is used in the manufacture of one kind of hallucinogenic drug. The bark is scraped from the trunk after the exterior layer of bark is removed, or is scraped from the inside of the bark surface itself. This material, which is fairly moist, is then mixed with wood ashes and kneaded between the palms of the hands. Additional moisture is provided by spitting periodically into the pliable wad of drug. When the drug has been thoroughly mixed with saliva and ashes, it is placed on a hot piece of broken clay pot and the moisture driven out with heat. It is ground into a powder as it dries, the flat side of a stone axe serving as the grinding pestle. The dried, green powder, no more than several tablespoons full, is then swept onto a leaf with a stiff feather. The men then gather around the leaf containing the drug, usually in the late afternoon, and take it by blowing the powder into each other's nostrils. . . . A small quantity of the powder is introduced into the end of a hollow cane tube some 3 feet long. The tube is then flicked with the forefinger to scatter the powder along its length. One end of the tube is put into the nostril of the man taking the drug, and his helper then blows a strong blast of air through the other end, emitting his breath in such a fashion that he climaxes the delivery with a hard burst of air. Both the recipient and the blower squat on their haunches to do this. The man who had the drug blown into his nostrils grimaces, groans, chokes, coughs, holds his head from the pain of the air blast, and duck-waddles off to some leaning post. He usually receives two doses of the drug, one in each nostril. The recipient usually vomits, gets watery eyes, and develops a runny nose. Much of the drug comes back out in the nasal mucus that begins to run freely after the drug has been administered. Within minutes after the drug has been blown into the man's nose, he begins having difficulties focusing his eyes and starts to act intoxicated. The drug allegedly produces colored

REFERENCES

SHERRARD, CAROL. "Summary Writing: A Topographical Study." *Written Communication* 3 (1986): 324–43. Inexperienced writers tend to copy when briefly summarizing a passage, but use more of their own words when writing longer summaries.

visions, especially around the periphery of the visual field, and permits the user to enter into contact with his particular *hekura*, miniature demons that dwell under rocks and on mountains. The man begins to chant to the *hekura* when the drug takes effect, inviting them to come and live in his chest.

Here is a sample summary from this source:

> *Drug use in primitive cultures*
> Among the Yanomamo Indians, hallucinogenic drug-taking is a regular and accepted habit. The drug is a powder derived from the bark of the ebene tree, and is administered through hollow, 3-foot long cane tubes. One man blows the powder with sharp bursts through the tube into the nostril of another. The man who has received the drug will stagger away, then vomit; and his nose will begin running with mucus containing the drug residue. He will begin to act intoxicated, to see visions, and to chant to his demons (pp. 23–24).

2   **Paraphrasing sources**

A *paraphrase* is a restatement, in your own words, of a passage of text. Its structure reflects the structure of the source passage. Paraphrases are sometimes the same length as the source passage, sometimes shorter. In certain cases—particularly if the source passage is written in densely constructed or jargon-laden prose—the paraphrase may be even longer than the original. You would paraphrase a passage when you want to preserve all of the points in the original, both major and minor, and when—perhaps for the sake of clarity—you want to communicate the ideas in your own words. Keep in mind that only an *occasional* word (but not whole phrases) from the original source appears in the paraphrase, and that a paraphrase's sentence structure does not reflect that of the source.

The following is a paraphrase of the first section of the passage on the hallucinogenic drugs taken by the Yanomamo:

> The Yanomamo make a hallucinogenic drug from the bark on the *ebene* tree. After scraping the outer bark off the tree trunk, they shave off the inner bark and mix it with wood ashes and saliva, while kneading the mixture in their hands. Then they place the mixture on a piece of hot clay pot, drying it and grinding it to a powder with the flat side of an ax, and finally depositing the dried powder onto a leaf. Next, the men gather around the leaf and take turns blowing the drug into each other's nostrils with a long, hollow tube.

The process as described here has almost as much detail as the original, but the wording is the student's own.

Sometimes you may wish to paraphrase a passage whose dense language makes it somewhat difficult to understand. Here, for example, is a paragraph from an article entitled "Cross-Cultural Perspectives on Developmental Stages in Adolescent Drug Use," by Israel Adler and Denise B. Kandel, which appeared in the *Journal of Studies on Alcohol* 42.9 (1981): 701–15.

The identification of a developmental sequence in adolescent drug use has important implications for understanding the phenomena of drug use and for policy making. A developmental sequence in drug use bridges the seeming gap between legal and illegal behaviors. Even though one cannot argue, as will be pointed out later, that there is a cause-and-effect relationship between the use of legal drugs and the use of illegal drugs, the link between the two types of behavior implies that they should be studied in conjunction with each other. Robins and Wish (3) go further, placing drug use within more general sequences of child development. They link drug behavior, through a series of cumulative events, to other behaviors that point to childhood deviance.

You might paraphrase this passage as follows:

The "developmental sequence"

```
It's important to understand that adolescents follow a regular
pattern in the way they progress from legal drugs to illegal
drugs. This pattern is called a "developmental sequence." It's
not necessarily true that if adolescents begin with wine or
beer, they will inevitably proceed to marijuana and then to
hard drugs. These behaviors are related, however, not only to
each other, but also to childhood development in general.
(p. 702)
```

EXERCISE 2
Write a 250–400 word summary of one of the sources you have located for your working bibliography (Exercise 1). Then write a paraphrase of several sentences from a section of text in the same source.

34f Quoting sources

You may decide to quote from a passage when the author's language is particularly well chosen, lively, dramatic, or incisive, and when you think you could not possibly express the same idea so effectively. Or you may decide to quote when you want to bolster the credibility of your argument with the reputation of your source. By the same token, you may occasionally decide to discredit an idea by quoting a discredited or notorious source.

1 Avoiding overquoting

Knowing how much to quote is an art in itself. If you underquote, your paper may come across as dry and secondhand. If you overquote, your paper may come across as an anthology of other people's statements ("a scissors-and-paste job"), rather than an original work. Some professors have developed rules of thumb on quoting. One such rule is that for a ten-page paper, there should be no more than two extended quotations (i.e., indented quotations of more than 100 words); and each page should contain no more than two short quotations. If this rule of thumb makes sense to you (or your professor), adopt it; otherwise, modify it to the extent you think reasonable.

2   How to quote

Suppose you are working on a paper on drug testing in certain occupations. Here is the concluding section from one source, "Testing for Drugs and Alcohol: Proceed with Caution," by Rusch O. Dees, Esq. (an attorney for management), which appeared in the magazine *Personnel* (Sep. 1986): 53–55.

> The precise legal status of drug and alcohol testing remains undefined. An employer's use of testing can be fraught with potential liabilities. The "quick fix" envisioned through random drug or alcohol testing intrudes too far into the area of individual privacy to be condoned. However, courts as well as arbitrators have upheld employee testing programs where such programs have fallen within the more limited framework and scope discussed above.
>
> To date, too many employers have begun testing without first making essential policy decisions on what standards must be met to warrant testing and deciding what action will be taken with the results. A drug-and-alcohol testing program must not be approached in a cavalier manner when an individual's career, a company's image, and legal liabilities are at stake.

The following note contains the most useful quotation:

```
          Cautions about drug testing

    "A drug-and-alcohol testing program must not be approached
in a cavalier manner when an individual's career, a company's
image, and legal liabilities are at stake." (p. 55)
```

Sometimes you may wish to quote a passage that has itself been quoted by your source author. For example, in researching the acceptability of alcohol in earlier periods of American history, you locate Jack H. Mendelson and Nancy K. Mello's *Alcohol: Use and Abuse in America* (Boston: Little, Brown, 1985). In a chapter on "Alcohol Use in Colonial Times," you find an interesting quotation concerning the extent to which the authorities frowned on excessive alcohol consumption:

> Almost nothing is known about alcohol use during the first years, but in a time of constant scarcity it is unlikely that alcohol was readily available in any form. However, the Colonists' concern with social order was soon extended to include alcohol intoxication. By 1633, in Plymouth Colony, a John Holmes was censured for drunkenness. His penalty—"to sit in the stocks, and was amerced forty shillings." In 1629, the gover-

nor of the Massachusetts colony was advised by his English superior that "We pray yow endeavor, though ther be much *strong waters* sent for sale, yett see to order it, as that the salvages may not for or lucre sake bee induced to excessive use or rather abuse of it, and, at any hand, take care or people give us ill example; and if any shall exceed in that inordinate kind of drinking as to become drunck, wee hope you will take care his punishment be made exemplary for all others."

If you decide to use only the quotation by the "English superior" (and not Mendelson and Mello's commentary), your notecard would look like this:

<u>Colonial attitudes toward excessive drinking</u>
[note #8]

Admonition to governor of Massachusetts colony from his English superior:

"We pray yow endeavor, though ther be much <u>strong waters</u> sent for sale, yett see to order it, as that the salvages may not for or lucre sake bee induced to excessive use or rather abuse of it, and, at any hand, take care or people give us ill example; and if any shall exceed in that inordinate kind of drinking as to become drunck, wee hope you will take care his punishment be made exemplary for all others." (pp. 7-8)

Note that these are the *exact* words from the original. The student has added nothing, omitted nothing, and changed nothing.

3 Using brackets and ellipses in quotations

Sometimes for the sake of clarity, conciseness, or smoothness of sentence structure, you will need to make additions, omissions, or changes to quotations. For example, suppose you wanted to quote a passage beginning with the following sentence: "In 1979, one week after receiving a 13.3% pay raise, she was called on the carpet." To clarify the pronoun *she*, you would need to replace it with the name of the person in question enclosed in a pair of brackets: "In 1979, one week after receiving a 13.3% pay raise, [Virginia Rulon-Miller] was called on the carpet." (See 29d.)

Suppose you also decided that the 13.3% pay raise was irrelevant for your purpose in quoting the material. You could omit this phrase, and indicate the omission by means of an *ellipsis*—three spaced dots: "In 1979 . . . [Virginia Rulon-Miller] was called on the carpet." (See 29e.) Note that, when using brackets, you do not need to use the ellipsis to indicate that the pronoun (*she*) has been omitted; brackets surrounding proper nouns imply that one word (or set of words) has replaced another. For more on altering quotations with ellipses and brackets, see chapters 28 and 29, and especially 29-d–e.

LOOKING BACK

You may want to refer students to chapter 29 (Other Marks) for additional advice on using brackets (29d), and ellipses (29e).

Sometimes you need to change a capital letter to a lowercase one in order to smoothly integrate the quotation into your own sentence. For example, suppose you want to quote the following sentence: "Privacy today matters to employees at all levels, from shop-floor workers to presidents." You could smoothly integrate this quotation into your own sentence by altering the capitalization, as follows.

> The new reality, as John Hoerr points out, is that "[p]rivacy today matters to employees at all levels, from shop-floor workers to presidents."

4 Smoothly integrating quotations into your text

Whether or not you alter quotations by means of ellipses or brackets, you should strive to smoothly integrate them into your own text. Suppose, for example, you decide to use the following sentence from *Heavy Drinking: The Myth of Alcoholism as a Disease* by Herbert Fingarette.

> The classic disease concept of alcoholism is unquestionably a hindrance rather than a help in addressing the broad problems of heavy drinking in our society (University of California Press, 1988).

You could integrate this quotation in any of several ways.

1. According to Fingarette, "The classic disease concept of alcoholism is unquestionably a hindrance rather than a help in addressing the broad problems of heavy drinking in our society" (4).
2. Fingarette puts it bluntly: "The classic disease concept of alcoholism is unquestionably a hindrance rather than a help in addressing the broad problems of heavy drinking in our society" (4).
3. "The classic disease concept of alcoholism," claims Fingarette, "is unquestionably a hindrance rather than a help in addressing the broad problems of heavy drinking in our society" (4).
4. "The classic disease concept of alcoholism is unquestionably a hindrance rather than a help in addressing the broad problems of heavy drinking in our society," claims Fingarette (4).
5. According to Fingarette, looking at alcoholism as a disease is "a hindrance rather than a help" (4).

After attributive phrases such as "According to Fingarette," a comma is inserted. In the second example, a colon is the appropriate punctuation (to avoid a comma splice or run-on sentence). The first, third, and fourth examples differ only in the location of the attributive phrase: at the beginning, the middle, or the end of the sentence. In the fifth example, the original sentence has been largely paraphrased, rather than quoted.

5 Using attributive phrases with quotations

Note that single, quoted sentences should never stand by themselves, without an attributive phrase like "According to Fingarette, . . ." For example, you would not write

---

Fingarette thinks this way of looking at alcoholism is part of the problem. "The classic disease concept of alcoholism is unquestionably a hindrance rather than a help in addressing the broad problems of heavy drinking in our society" (4).

Even though it ends with a citation, the quotation needs to be integrated with the previous material. You could do this by substituting a *colon* for the period after "part of the problem," or by inserting a phrase like "As he points out," before the quotation. (See the box below for other variations.)

Verbs That Help You Attribute Quotations

Attributive phrases use verbs in the present tense. To vary attributive phrases, you might consider verbs such as these:

adds	denies	relates
agrees	derides	reports
argues	disagrees	responds
asks	disputes	reveals
asserts	emphasizes	says
believes	explains	sees
claims	finds	shows
comments	holds	speculates
compares	illustrates	states
concedes	implies	suggests
concludes	insists	thinks
condemns	maintains	warns
considers	notes	writes
contends	observes	
declares	points out	
defends	rejects	

Note that all of the attributive verbs in the box are in the *present* tense (see 9e-1). Even though your source has already been written (and so technically, the author has already declar*ed* or stat*ed* or conclud*ed*), when quoting sources you should use the present tense (declares, states, concludes). This applies even if you are discussing a literary work; thus you would say that Hamlet ponder*s*: "To be or not to be. . . ." The only exception to the use of the present tense would be if you were reporting the historical progress of some development or debate and you wished to emphasize that certain things were said at a particular point in time. ("The Senator assert*ed*: 'I do not intend to dignify these scurrilous charges by responding to them.' ")

6 Using block quotations

You should integrate most quotations into your own text, using quotation marks. If a quotation runs longer than four lines, however, you should set it apart from the text by indenting it ten spaces from the left margin. Quotation marks are not required around block quotations. Block quotations should be double spaced, like the rest of the text (see 28a).

The following box reviews the discussion on summarizing, paraphrasing, and quoting sources.

When to Summarize, Paraphrase, or Quote a Source

Summarize

- to present the main points from a relatively long passage
- to condense information essential to your discussion

Paraphrase

- to clarify complex ideas in a short passage
- to clarify difficult language in a short passage

Quote

- when the language of the source is particularly important or effective
- when you want to enhance your credibility by drawing on the words of an authority on the subject

---

EXERCISE 3

Write a short section of a paper based on several of the sources you have located for exercises in the last two chapters. Summarize, paraphrase, and quote your sources. In particular, carefully select material that you believe deserves quotation, rather than summary or paraphrase. Your quotations should be of varying lengths: perhaps one block quotation, some sentence-length quotations, and others of phrase or clause length. In one or two cases, use ellipses and brackets to modify the quoted material. In all cases, smoothly integrate quotations into your own text, using a variety of attributive phrases.

34g   Eliminating plagiarism

Plagiarism is an unpleasant subject, but one that must be confronted in any discussion of research papers. In its most blatant form, **plagiarism** is an act of conscious deception: an attempt to pass off the ideas or the words of another as your own. To take an extreme example, a student who buys a research paper from a commercial "paper mill" and turns it in for academic credit is guilty of the worst kind of plagiarism. Only slightly less guilty is the student who copies into his paper passages of text from his sources without giving credit or using quotation marks.

The penalties for plagiarism can be severe—including a failing grade in the course or even a suspension from school. Graduate students guilty of plagiarism have been dropped from advanced degree programs. Even professionals no longer in school can see their reputations damaged or destroyed by charges of plagiarism. During the 1988 presidential campaign, a Democratic candidate was forced to drop out of the race when it was revealed that some of the material in his campaign speeches was copied from a speech by a prominent British politician.

Much plagiarism is unintentional. Students may not intend to pass off as their own the work of others; but either through ignorance of the conventions of quotation, attribution, and citation, or simply through carelessness, they may fail to distinguish adequately between their own ideas and words and those of their sources.

Here are two general rules to help you avoid unintentional plagiarism:

1. Whenever you *quote* the exact words of others, place these words within quotation marks and properly cite the source.

2. Whenever you *paraphrase* or *summarize* the ideas of others, do not use whole phrases, or many of the same words, or sentence structures similar to the original. You must identify the source of the paraphrased or summarized material: do not assume that you are under no obligation to credit your source if you simply change the wording of the original statement or alter the sentence structure.

1 Determining what is common knowledge

The only exception to the second rule just stated is if the information summarized or paraphrased is considered common knowledge. For example, you need not cite the source of the information that General Lee commanded the Confederate forces during the Civil War, or the fact that Mars is the fourth planet from the sun, or the fact that Ernest Hemingway wrote *The Sun Also Rises*. If, on the other hand, you are summarizing one particular theory of why Lee's forces faced almost certain defeat, or the geological composition of the Martian surface, or how the critical assessment of Hemingway's *The Sun Also Rises* has shifted over the years, then you are obliged to cite the sources of your information or ideas, whether or not you quote them directly.

Admittedly, it is not always easy for a nonspecialist to determine if a particular fact or idea is considered common knowledge. The course of Hemingway's shifting reputation is common knowledge among American literature professors, though not among most freshmen (or physics professors). And even the fact that Hemingway wrote *The Sun Also Rises* (or when it was first published) is unlikely to be common knowledge to the general population. It might be helpful to ask yourself whether the average, college-educated person is likely to be familiar with this particular fact or idea, or whether or not it would be readily available in any num-

REFERENCES

DRUM, ALICE. "Responding to Plagiarism." *CCC* 37 (1986): 241–43. The educational implications as well as the legal aspects of plagiarism should be stressed as a way to forestall the practice.

ST. ONGE, KEITH R. *The Melancholy Anatomy of Plagiarism*. Lanham, MD: UP of America, 1988. A "handbook on plagiarism" provides advice on how to avoid plagiarism and how to handle situations involving plagiarism.

KROLL, BARRY M. "How College Freshmen View Plagiarism." *Written Communication* 5 (1988): 203–21. In an extensive survey, 150 first-year students conceded that plagiarism is a grievous offense to "truthfulness, fidelity, and trust."

ADDITIONAL EXERCISE B

Once you've written a draft in which you've incorporated source material, it's time to evaluate the paper for plagiarism. Using the material in this section as a guide, ask yourself whether or not you've incorrectly assumed an idea to be common knowledge, inadvertently copied an author's words without quoting the author, or inadvertently rewritten the material so that it resembles the original too closely. Revise any possibly plagiarized sections of your paper now.

ber of easily accessible sources, such as a textbook or a one-volume encyclopedia. If the same fact is available in several sources, it is probably common knowledge. As you progress in your research, and later in your major field, you will gradually learn what is considered common knowledge in a subject area and what is not. In the meantime, if you remain unsure about the status of a particular idea or fact, the safest course is to cite it.

2 Identifying blatant plagiarism of a source

The sample passage below will illustrate what can happen when source ideas undergo several possible levels of intentional or unintentional plagiarism in the student examples that follow. The passage is from Steven F. Bloom's "Empty Bottles, Empty Dreams: O'Neill's Use of Drinking and Alcoholism in *Long Day's Journey into Night*," which appears in *Critical Essays on Eugene O'Neill*, edited by James J. Martine (Boston: G.K. Hall, 1984).

> In *Long Day's Journey Into Night*, O'Neill captures his vision of the human condition in the figure of the alcoholic who is constantly and repeatedly faced with the disappointment of his hopes to escape or transcend present reality. As the effects of heavy drinking and alcoholism increase, the alcoholic, in his attempt to attain euphoric forgetfulness, is repeatedly confronted with the painful realities of dissipation, despondency, self-destruction, and ultimately, death. This is the life of an alcoholic, and for O'Neill, this is the life of modern man.

Here is a plagiarized student version of this passage.

> *Long Day's Journey into Night* shows O'Neill's vision of the human condition in the figure of the alcoholic who is constantly faced with the disappointment of his hopes to escape. As the effects of heavy drinking and alcoholism increase, the alcoholic, in his attempt to attain forgetfulness, is repeatedly confronted with the painful realities of dissipation, self-destruction, and, ultimately, death. This is the life of an alcoholic, and for O'Neill, this is the life of modern man.

This is the most blatant form that plagiarism can take. The student has copied the passage almost word for word and has made no attempt to identify the source of either the words or the ideas. Even if the author *were* credited, the student's failure to use quotation marks around quoted material would render this version unacceptable.

3 Avoiding unintentional plagiarism of a source

Here is another version of the same passage.

> The figure of the disappointed alcoholic who hopes to escape reality represents the human condition in *Long Day's Journey into Night*. Trying to forget his problems, the alcoholic, while drinking more and more, is

confronted with the realities of his self-destructive condition, and, ultimately, with death. For Eugene O'Neill, the life of the alcoholic represents the life of modern man.

In this version, the writer has attempted (for the most part) to put the ideas in his own words; but the result still so closely resembles the original in sentence structure, in the sequence of ideas, and in the use of key phrases ("confronted with the realities") that it is also unacceptable. Note that this would hold true even if the author *were* credited; that is, had the first sentence begun, "According to Steven F. Bloom, . . . " The student may not have intended to plagiarize—he may, in fact, believe this to be an acceptable rendition—but it would still be considered plagiarism.

4 Making legitimate use of a source

Here is another version.

According to Steven F. Bloom, alcoholism in *Long Day's Journey into Night* is a metaphor for the human condition. The alcoholic drinks to forget his disappointments and to escape reality, but the more he drinks, the more he is faced with his own mortality. "This is the life of an alcoholic," asserts Bloom, "and for O'Neill, this is the life of modern man" (177).

This version is entirely acceptable because the student has carefully attributed both the paraphrased idea (in the first part of the passage) and the quotation (in the second part) to the source author, Steven Bloom. The student has also taken special care to phrase the idea in her own language.

Of course, you cannot avoid keeping *some* key terms: obviously, if you are going to paraphrase the ideas in this passage, you will need to use words and phrases like "alcoholic," "heavy drinking," "the human condition," and so on. However, what you say *about* these terms should be said in your own words.

It is crucial that you give your readers no cause to believe that you are guilty either of intentional or unintentional plagiarism. When you are summarizing or paraphrasing a particular passage, you must do more than change a few words. You must fully and accurately cite your source, by means of parenthetical citations or by means of attributive phrases, such as "According to Bloom, . . . "

5 Quoting accurately

When you do quote material directly, be certain that you quote it accurately. For example, consider a student quotation of the preceding passage (which follows the student's introduction).

Long Day's Journey into Night is O'Neill's "vision of the human condition," according to Steven F. Bloom:

As the effects of his heavy drinking and alcoholism increase, the alcoholic, attempting to achieve forgetfulness, is repeatedly confronted with all the painful realities of dissipation, self-destruction, and death. This is the life of an alcoholic for O'Neill and it is also the life of modern man.

At first glance, this quotation may seem to be accurate. But it is not. The student has *omitted* some words that were in the source passage (in the first sentence, "euphoric" and "despondency"; in the second sentence, "and"); has *changed* other words (in the first sentence, "attempting to achieve," instead of "in his attempt to attain"; in the second, "it," instead of "this"); has *added* some words that were not in the original (in the first sentence, "all"; in the second sentence, "also"); and has also omitted punctuation (in the second sentence, the comma after "O'Neill").

These changes may seem trivial and may not seem to essentially change the meaning of the passage, but once you place a passage within quotation marks, you are obligated to copy it *exactly*. Deleted material should be indicated by an ellipsis (. . .); your own insertions should be indicated by brackets ([ ]). Otherwise, the material within your quotation marks must be word for word, punctuation mark for punctuation mark, *identical* to the original.

EXERCISE 4

Individual responses

EXERCISE 4

Paraphrase a short passage from one of the sources you have located during your research. Then write a short paragraph explaining what you have done to eliminate all possibility of inadvertent plagiarism in your paraphrase.

CHAPTER 35

Writing the
Research Paper

Aside from the discussion on organizing notecards, the material in this chapter parallels that in chapters 3 and 4 on planning, writing, and revising an essay. Because the *process* of writing a research paper is in many (but not all) respects similar to that of writing an essay, the discussion here will be brief and will be cross-referenced with earlier sections of the book.

35a Refining the thesis

As you complete your research and prepare to write a paper, you probably will have more information than you can possibly absorb. How will you get from those stacks of 4″ × 6″ notecards to a finished paper? This is the moment—between generating sources and starting a first draft—when chaos begins coalescing into order. If you feel intimidated and overwhelmed by the quantity of your notes, rest easy: Probably every writer of research reports feels the same way at this particular moment in the process.

You will do well to remember the "burning question" that launched your project (see 33a-1). Ask yourself: What do I want to accomplish in this paper? Why write it in the first place? Why write on *this* subject, on this *aspect* of the subject? Such questions should help you to clear away extraneous details and refocus your attention. In 33e you saw the need for a researcher to devise a working thesis. The writer of any first draft needs a working thesis—a statement that will help to plan the first draft. With a working thesis, a writer has a principle on the basis of which to exclude or include information (see 3d).

In 33e you saw examples of working theses from four perspectives—the social sciences, the humanities, the sciences, and business—concerning the use of alcohol and drugs. For the purposes of the following discussion we will assume that you have decided to pursue one of these theses. The first thesis, for a course in the social sciences, was as follows.

INITIAL WORKING THESIS
Alcoholism among college students is an increasingly serious problem, but there are workable solutions.

KEY FEATURES

This chapter begins with an acknowledgment of the state many students find themselves in after finishing the "gathering" stage of the research process. Assuring students that this state of "cognitive overload" is natural, the chapter immediately presents students with a strategy for moving forward by returning to the "burning question" that spurred the research in the first place. The distinctive features of research as opposed to personal writing are highlighted and covered in depth. Students are advised to consider whether the thesis must be altered to accommodate the direction the research has taken; to facilitate drafting by arranging notecards; and to consider the relative merits of informal, flexible outlines or more rigid formal ones. The chapter acknowledges that moving from gathering material to composing the paper into which that material will be integrated is a daunting task, and that it is tempting to include everything from the notecards, but students are reminded that the paper is *their statement* and not simply a compilation of references. To that end, the chapter recommends that students compose a very rough draft of the paper without reference to any sources, and use that draft as a "scaffold" from which to build the fuller paper. This advice is followed by an extensive analysis of voice and audience considerations, allowing students to move through the planning and drafting stages not by adhering to a set of rules, but rather by considering both their purpose in writing the paper and the needs of their readers. At the end of the chapter a complete and extensively annotated student paper is reproduced, providing students with a clear working model for their own research papers.

ESL ALERT

Research and writing as a *process* will be an unfamiliar concept to many international students, though teachers in some cultures do in fact "intervene" with help in the stages of composition. Many students, however, may expect instructors to be uninterested in the process, focusing only on the final product. It may be worth explaining clearly (1) what a student's responsibility for original research, writing, and rewriting is supposed to be; (2) what the differing responsibilities of teacher and student entail in the evaluation of sources and the improvement of early drafts; and (3) what degree of dependency on the instructor (or tutors, peer editors, or other readers) is proper. The last point is crucial if plagiarism problems are to be forestalled.

GROUP ACTIVITY

This would be an ideal time for students to work together in small groups. Ask them to bring to the group a copy of their original working thesis, and to be prepared to discuss what their research revealed to them. As each student reads his or her working thesis to the group and highlights the research, others in the group can comment and ask questions to help the student decide whether the thesis needs alteration, and if so, how to alter it. This activity can help students see their research from a different perspective, as well as reminding them of their obligations to their audience.

Characteristics of a Working Thesis

- The subject of the thesis is *narrow* enough in scope that you can write a detailed paper without being constrained by the page limits of the assignment (3d-1).

- The predicate of the working thesis communicates a relationship you want to clarify about your subject, based on your understanding of the information you have generated (3d-2).

- The main statement of your thesis may involve one or more (but not many more) of the following relationships: sequential order, definition, classification, comparison, contrast, generalization, or causation.

- The thesis clearly suggests the patterns of development you will be pursuing in your paper. (The types of paragraphs you write in your paper will be directly tied to the relationships you develop in your thesis (3d-2, 3).

- The thesis will clearly communicate your intellectual ambitions for the paper (3d-3).

As you progressed in your notetaking, you probably proceeded to gather information on the seriousness of the problem of alcoholism among college students and on the workable solutions. Perhaps all of this information confirmed your working thesis and you see no reason to change it. You may still reserve the right to change it later, once you start writing the paper, but for now you leave your working thesis unchanged.

On the other hand, in the course of your research, you may have shifted direction, so that your working thesis is no longer accurate. Perhaps you discover that alcoholism among college students, while serious, is not increasing. Such a discovery would require only the deletion of "increasingly" from your provisional thesis. Or suppose you decide to focus exclusively on solutions to the problem of student alcoholism (you can deal with the seriousness of the problem in one or two paragraphs in the introduction), and then discover that these solutions are not as workable as you first suspected. You could consequently adjust your thesis to read as follows:

REFINED WORKING THESIS

Health care professionals have learned that while they can help some student alcoholics, there are no easy solutions to the problem.

The change of thesis may be even more dramatic. Recall from chapter 34 the passage dealing with the ritual use of the drug from the *ebene* tree from Napoleon A. Chagnon's book on the Yanomamo Indians. This subject may have fascinated you so much that you decided to shift your focus entirely from the problems of student alcoholism to a survey of drug use in various cultures. In this case, your working thesis would have to be abandoned and a new thesis would emerge from the results of your research.

The same process applies to the other working theses. For example, consider the thesis of a student taking a humanities course: "Alcoholism and drug abuse are important elements of O'Neill's later plays; these elements are grounded in O'Neill's own life." Such a thesis would require a consideration of O'Neill's most well known later plays, *The Iceman Cometh* and *Long Day's Journey into Night*. In the course of your research it may become obvious that you will have your hands full dealing with just *one* of these plays. So you change your thesis to include only one play—and regretfully, but decisively, put all of your notecards on the other play in the "inactive" file. (Do not discard them; they may come in handy for a subsequent paper.)

Or consider the working thesis of a student taking a science course: "Alcoholism should be considered a disease, rather than an immoral behavior syndrome." Suppose that a reading of Herbert Fingarette's *Heavy Drinking: The Myth of Alcoholism as a Disease* and several articles supporting Fingarette's position persuades you that alcoholism should not, in fact, be considered a disease—even if you still do not consider alcoholism an "immoral behavior syndrome." You would need to adjust your thesis accordingly.

The rest of this chapter will focus on the composition of a paper for a business course. The final provisional thesis for this paper reads: "For certain occupations drug testing is necessary to ensure public safety."

35b Developing a plan

At this point in your preparations for writing, your main task is to review the notes you have taken and to consolidate them into categories that will help you to refine your thesis and support it. If you have been conscientiously applying headings to each of your notecards, your task will be considerably easier. Stack the cards into piles according to their headings. For example, you may have devised this heading: "Extent of the Problem," referring to all cards that summarize, paraphrase, or quote material that provides numbers on how many employees are thought to have a drug problem and on how many major companies administer drug tests. You may have a heading, "Arguments for Drug Testing," to cover all the defenses commonly offered to justify the use of drug testing.

If you have not already written headings on your cards, write them as you review your notes. There are two ways to do this. Either you can draft a provisional outline and then write the appropriate headings and

GROUP ACTIVITY

As they develop outlines, students can "test" them on their classmates. Regardless of the format students choose or you require, it will be valuable for students to read each other's outlines. Advise them that they're not *criticizing* the outlines so much in this exercise as giving the writer *feedback* regarding what the outline seems to promise. Encourage students to ask each other questions that will help clarify the outlines, and to be frank about what they'd expect to see in the paper after having read the outline.

GROUP ACTIVITY

TEACHING IDEAS

Another reminder that the paper is at heart the student's own composition may be in order here. Not only is it difficult to let some of the notecards "fall to the cutting room floor," but it's also tempting to let the "experts" take over the paper. The student who turns her paper into a "memory dump" is probably not acting out of laziness so much as lack of confidence. A student who looks at any paper assignment and asks "What can I possibly have to say about this subject?" is all the more likely to slip into that response after researching what a collection of respected writers have to say. A word of encouragement that students have indeed learned a great deal and formed their own opinions through their research is in order here.

subheadings on the notecards, or you can write headings on the individual cards and then draft an outline based on groupings of cards.

Outlines and sketches for a paper come in all shapes and sizes (see 3d-4). Informal outlines generally have only two levels: one level for topics and another for subtopics. For example:

> Drug testing in the workplace
> —public sector
> —private sector

Formal outlines have several levels (3d-4). The most common type employs a combination of Roman and Arabic numerals and letters.

> I. Major topic
>   A. Subtopic
>   1. Minor subtopic
>   a. sub-subtopic (or illustration)
>   (a) illustration, example, explanation
>   (b) illustration, example, explanation
>   2. Minor subtopic
>   B. Subtopic
> II. Major topic

For more information on how to write outlines, see 3d-4 and 18e; for a discussion on how to work from outlines as you write a first draft, see 3e-2.

35c Drawing on your sources

After you have developed your outline and arranged notecards to correspond to the outline, you will probably discover that in some areas you have more information than you need, while in other areas you do not have enough. In the latter case, go back to the library to fill in the gaps or take another look at material you have already gathered. In the former case (too much information), you will have to make some hard decisions. After accumulating so much material, you may be tempted to use it *all*. Resist that temptation. Your goal is to fulfill the purpose you have set for yourself in writing the paper, not to overwhelm readers. Select information for your paper according to your purpose. Focus on your working thesis and bear in mind the ways in which a thesis limits the types of information in a paper. Once you have provided readers with enough explanation and examples of a particular point, move on.

As discussed in chapter 34, there are three ways of dealing with source material: summary, paraphrase, and quotation. However, your paper should not simply be a collection of summarized, paraphrased, and quoted material. After all, you are not compiling an anthology; you are presenting your own viewpoint on a particular subject, a viewpoint supported by evidence of various types from your sources. Keep in mind that you have conducted your research in an attempt to come to some understanding of the subject, and that you will use the sources to *support* that understanding.

To give your paper the feel of a coherent discussion, you need to establish the connections among various pieces of evidence by means of your own *commentary,* your own critical evaluations of your sources. You also need to establish *transitions* between ideas, both within paragraphs and from paragraph to paragraph. (See 5d-3 for a review of transitions.)

35d Determining your voice

How do you want to come across to your readers? As an authority, lecturing to the uninitiated? An old friend, casually discussing your observations on a subject? Serious? Cynical? Excited? Warm? Distant? The option you select determines the *voice* as well as the *tone* and *register* that comes across in the paper (see 3a-4 and the box in 21e).

Consider, for example, the voice of the following passage written by Jon D. Bible, a professor of business law, for an article that appeared in *Labor Law Review.*

> Most opponents of urine testing accept the employers' right to try to rid their workplaces of drugs. Their concerns focus on the appropriateness of urinalysis as a means to this end. Tests can be untrustworthy, they note, and even sound ones may produce erroneous results because of mistakes in the testing process. Tests may also yield positive results because of drug use occurring days or weeks earlier, which raises questions about an employer's right to proscribe usage that does not directly affect one's present ability to perform his job. Opponents also claim that tests compromise personal security and dignity, especially when given randomly or on a mass basis. Finally, they assert that urine testing violates the principle that people are to be presumed innocent of wrongdoing until proven guilty.

The voice of this passage is serious, systematic, somewhat dry, and impersonal. The author seems to make little attempt to engage his readers and certainly none to entertain them. But engagement and entertainment are not his purposes. This is a lawyer writing to other lawyers (or to management/labor professionals) who need to understand how the Fourth

REFERENCE

KANTZ, MARGARET. "Helping Students Use Textual Sources Persuasively." *CE* 52 (1990): 74–91. A research paper allows students to synthesize texts and to meet sophisticated writing aims.

LOOKING BACK

Reviewing chapters 3 and 4 should reassure students that in drafting this paper they can rely on many of the same strategies they've been using throughout the course.

TEACHING IDEAS

The advice presented here can be of immeasurable assistance to students who feel intimidated or overwhelmed by their sources. If they force themselves to write a rough draft without any sources, they'll discover what they have to say about the subject, and they'll have the framework they need to make sure they don't turn the paper over to the sources.

TEACHING IDEAS

Discuss with students why Jon Bible's paragraph on urinalysis contains no citations.

REFERENCE

DINITZ, SUSAN, and JEAN KIEDAISCH. "The Research Paper: Teaching Students to Be Members of the Academic Community." *Exercise Exchange* 31 (1986): 8–10. Rhetorical concerns such as purpose, audience, and voice should be addressed in writing the research paper.

Amendment applies to drug testing. Though it may be dry, Bible's writing is clear and to the point.

Now consider the following passage, by William Saletan, which first appeared in *The New Republic* on October 2, 1989:

> Jar wars are back. Three years ago, to dramatize their "Just Say No" campaign, President Reagan and Vice President Bush led the way to the water closet, and dozens of candidates for lower office followed. This year Bush is riding the drug issue again, and politicians campaigning in four major cities have already submitted to drug tests. In 1986 some politicians resisted this nonsense. This year resistance has disappeared. Drug testing has become almost a standard part of political campaigns.

The difference in voice between the two passages could hardly be greater. Saletan uses word play ("Jar wars"), off-color images ("led the way to the water closet"), and unusually blunt language ("nonsense"). Clearly, the audience for *The New Republic* (*TNR*) is quite different from the audience for *Labor Law Review*: While *TNR* readers also tend to be highly educated, they appreciate both witty language and plain speaking, and they are decidedly irreverent toward the powers-that-be. Saletan's voice, however, is not superior to Bible's—though more readers may prefer it. Each author's voice is suitable for its intended purpose and audience.

Think of your readers as intelligent people who are interested in the issue on which you are writing, but who still expect to be engaged, as well as informed, by what you have to say. Although they may *have* to read your paper, do not make them resent the effort. Be serious and informative, but not dull. A good academic paper should be like one side of an intelligent conversation—a conversation in which both participants take pleasure. (See 3a-4 for more on determining your own voice.)

35e Writing a draft

Sections 3b-e and 5a provide detailed discussions of strategies that will help you to write a first draft. You will need a method for working (or not working) from your outline, for writing a group of related paragraphs at a single sitting, and for recognizing and responding to obstacles as they arise.

You are finally ready to write. You have conducted systematic research on a subject in which you are interested; you have accumulated a stack of notecards, on which you have summarized, paraphrased, and quoted relevant material; you have developed and revised a thesis; and you have prepared an outline, on the basis of which you have organized your notecards: in short, you have become something of an expert on the subject. There is no reason to be anxious at this point: You are not writing

GROUP ACTIVITY

Although students may be quite comfortable right now with their writing process in general, the thought of writing a draft of a research paper can be intimidating. (Most instructors have faced the same anxiety many times.) You can ease some of the tension after the students have reviewed chapters 3 and 4 by asking groups to discuss the similarities and differences between their drafting processes. First ask students to outline the process they normally use when composing a draft, and then ask them to comment on the alterations they'll make to the process in order to accommodate the research paper. In groups, as they discuss their writing processes, they should come to realize that this writing process is not substantially different from the process they've used throughout the course.

the final draft; you are simply preparing a rough draft that will be seen by no one but yourself (and possibly some friends whose advice you trust). You will have plenty of opportunity to revise the rough draft.

To avoid overreliance on sources, as well as to clarify the main lines of a paper's argument, some researchers write their first draft referring only to their outlines—and not to their notecards. As they write, they note the places where source material (in summarized, paraphrased, or quoted form) will later be inserted. Drafts written in such a manner are simply scaffolds, of course. But by examining the scaffold, you can easily see whether your logic stands up. Does the argument make sense to you? Does one part logically follow from another? It should, even without the material on your notecards. The evidence, after all, is for your readers' benefit, not yours.

At some point in the drafting process, however, you will need to turn to your notecards. Arrange them in the order in which you intend to use them; but do not simply transcribe your notes onto your rough draft. Keep your mind on your purpose and on your audience: tell them—as if you were in conversation with them—what they should know about the subject and why you believe as you do. If you think you have made your point, move on, and skip any additional, unused notecards on the topic or subtopic (or substitute a particularly effective point from one of these unused notecards for a less effective point from a notecard already used).

To avoid having to transcribe lengthy quotations from the notecards onto your draft, you may want to consider taping or stapling these notecards (or photocopies of the quotations) directly onto the appropriate spots on the draft. When you do incorporate your quotations, summaries, and paraphrases, remember to transfer your bibliographic codes and page numbers as well, so that later you can enter the correct citations.

Many writers skip the introduction on the rough draft and get right into the body of the paper. These writers believe that they are in a better position to draft the introduction when they know exactly what they are introducing and when they have overcome the writer's block that frequently grips writers facing that first page. If this approach works for you, fine. However, if you believe that you must begin at the beginning and work systematically all the way through, then do that. Whichever approach you take (and neither one is inherently preferable), remember that this is only a *rough* draft; nothing at this stage is final.

35f Revising and editing

In sections 4a–d, you will find a discussion on strategies for revising and editing. You may wish to review this material after you compose your rough draft. Perhaps the main point to keep in mind is that revision literally means "re-seeing." You should not consider revision simply a matter of fixing up punctuation and spelling errors and improving a word or phrase here and there. It is, rather, a matter of looking at the whole essay, from top to bottom, and trying to determine whether you have presented your material in the most effective way possible. Some writers think of revision as a twofold process: *macro-revision*—concerning the essay as a whole (its purpose and its voice) and its larger component units, the section and the paragraph; and *micro-revision*—concerning sentence structure, grammar, punctuation, and mechanics. Others consider revision to be a four-stage process: (1) the essay as a whole; (2) individual paragraphs; (3) individual sentences; and (4) individual words. These strategies are means toward the same goal: ensuring that you consider *every* component of your essay, from the largest to the smallest, as you work to improve it.

When you begin to revise your paper, get as much feedback as possible from others. It is difficult even for professional writers to get perspective on what they have written immediately after they have written it. You are likely to be too close to the subject, too committed to your outline or to the particular words you have written to be very objective at this point. Show your draft to a friend or classmate whose judgment you trust and to your instructor. Obtain reactions on everything from the essay as a whole to the details of word choice.

35g Understanding the elements of documentation

Writers can use several systems of documentation to credit their sources (see chapter 36). The system used depends on the discipline in which they are writing—social sciences, humanities, science and technology, or business—or on the preferences of the person or persons to whom the writing is addressed.

Using documentation to give fair credit and to assist your reader

Why go to the trouble to document your sources? Perhaps the first reason is to avoid charges of plagiarism. You certainly do not want to give your readers the impression that you are claiming credit for ideas or words that are not yours. The second reason is to allow your readers to gauge the accuracy and reliability of your work. Any research paper will stand or fall according to how well (how resourcefully, perceptively, accurately, or selectively) you use sources. The third reason turns on the word *credit* itself—that is, you should give credit where it is merited. Your sources have done a great deal of work for you; by acknowledging them, you acknowledge the value of their work. The fourth reason for giving credit is to allow the reader who is interested in a particular point in your paper, or in a particular source that you have employed, to return to the original document.

Placing documentation references

Documentation is provided in two places: (1) *in the text*, to identify and credit a source immediately following its use; and (2) *following the text*, in the form of a list of references that readers can pursue in more detail. For the MLA, APA, and the CBE systems, in-text citations are usually placed within parentheses. In the footnote and endnote systems, in-text citations are made with a small superscript numeral, while references are listed in notes.

It is important that *all* information and ideas be documented—not simply the sources that you quote directly. Summaries or paraphrases also require source acknowledgment. The only exception to this rule is that *common knowledge* need not be documented (34g-1). For the particular documentation form in the discipline areas, see chapter 36.

35h A sample paper: "Drug Testing in the Workplace"

The following research paper demonstrates the process of research and writing discussed in these chapters. The student writer, Michael Arai, chose the topic of "Drug Testing in the Workplace" because a friend and his coworkers had recently been required to take periodic tests for substance abuse, even though no one at this particular job had ever manifested a drug a problem. In talking with his friend, Arai discovered a "burning question": Why should people who have never had problems with drugs be required to take drug tests as a condition of employment? Arai's paper conforms to Modern Language Association (MLA) documentation style.

TEACHING IDEAS/LOOKING AHEAD

This paper is consistent, in both form and content, with the typical research paper for a first-year composition course. You may want to refer students to it as a working model for their own papers. For additional sample papers, students can refer to chapters 37 (a literature paper), 38 (a sociology paper), and 39 (a chemistry lab report).

REFERENCE

JESKE, JEFF. "Borrowing from the Sciences: A Model for the Freshman Research Paper." *The Writing Instructor* 6 (1987): 62–67. Advocates a research paper form based on that of the sciences, including "Materials and Methods," "Results," and "Discussion" sections.

COVER-PAGE FORMAT

Drug Testing in the Workplace

by

Michael Arai

English 160, Section 8
Professor Gavis
April 3, 1994

Cover page: Center the title of your paper approximately one-third down the page. Skip four lines and center the preposition *by*. Skip another two lines and center your name. Skip approximately ten lines and center your course number and section. Then follow with your professor's name and the date submitted as shown.

Binding: Professors reading a stack of papers often find transparent folders to be a nuisance. Use a staple or paper clip to bind your paper at the upper-left corner.

ADDITIONAL EXERCISE A

Use this sample first page and the page shown in Appendix B2 as a model for your paper, and complete the following checklist:

_____ Name
_____ Instructor's name (spelled correctly)
_____ Course/section
_____ Date
_____ Page number and name
_____ Title

Arai 1

Michael Arai
Professor Gavis
English 160, Section 8
April 3, 1994

Drug Testing in the Workplace

In 1986 President Reagan's federal commission on organized crime called for widespread, random drug testing of American workers (Weiss 56). Two clear reasons prompted this call. The first was financial: in 1983 businesses lost up to $100 billion as a result of drug problems (Weiss 56). Concerns for public safety have also prompted the call for mandatory testing. On January 4, 1987, a Conrail locomotive near Baltimore collided with an Amtrak train, killing 16 people and wounding 176. Investigators later discovered that at the time of the accident the engineer was under the influence of marijuana (Sanders 10). Similarly infuriating stories abound of drug-dulled employees endangering an unsuspecting public. Advocates of drug testing claim that testing employees improves public safety. According to Peter Bensinger, former head of the Drug Enforcement Administration, "As a result of drug testing in American industry, the number of job-related incidents is beginning to go down. . . . It's saving lives" ("Interview" 58).

First-page format: Here is the first-page format for a paper *without* a cover page. Provide double-spaced information, flush with the left margin, as shown. (See Appendix B2 for exact measurements and margins.) Skip two lines and center your title. Skip four lines and begin your paper. Number the page, *with* your name, in the upper-right corner as shown. Beginning with page 2, place your name before the page number.

First page: See page 606 for the first-page format of a paper *with* a cover page. You will see that while the first page is numbered at the upper-right corner, no name appears. Your name and page number appear beginning with page 2. (If you are working on a computer, your word processing program probably has the capability to run "headers." Consult your user's manual.)

Outline (pages 604 and 605): Some professors will ask that you submit a formal outline with your completed paper—for two reasons. For professors, your outline is a previewing tool. Professors will read the outline and quickly gain a sense of your paper's scope and direction. For you, the outline serves as a final check that the paper is unified and coherent. Papers that do not outline easily may suffer from organizational problems.

> **Outline placement and form:** Papers with outlines should begin with a cover page. Place the outline immediately after the cover page. Number the outline in the upper-right corner with lowercase roman numerals, beginning with *i*.

> **Outline in sentences:** The following outline is written in sentences. If you choose not to write in sentences, your entries should be parallel (see chapter 18). Begin with a statement of your paper's thesis. Follow with major section headings (I, II), subsections (A, B), and supporting points (1, 2). Place your thesis first in the outline, regardless of its actual location in the paper. (In the sample paper—an argument with an inductive arrangement—the thesis and conclusion appear together at the end.)

GROUP ACTIVITY

Ask groups to evaluate this outline the way an instructor might—that is, to use it to get a sense of what to expect in the paper. When all groups have finished their evaluations, representatives from each will report to the class. If there are differences among groups' expectations, class discussion can clarify the reasons.

TEACHING IDEAS

If you wish students to turn in a non-sentence outline, then it might be worthwhile to have them practice on this sample. Ask students to transform this outline into one using parallel non-sentence structures (see 18e-2).

Arai i

Outline

Thesis statement: Random, sweeping drug testing as espoused by the government commission and proponents such as Peter Bensinger functions more as a propaganda tool in the overall "War on Drugs" than as a serious attempt to address the issues of productivity and safety in the workplace.

I. Review of the controversy: For the most part, experts disagree on the value and legality of mandatory drug testing.

   A. Proponent Peter Bensinger says that drug-related accidents are a major problem--but are decreasing because of drug testing.

   B. Opponents claim that mandatory tests violate an employee's civil rights.

      1. The Fourth Amendment to the Constitution protects citizens from "unreasonable searches and seizures."

      2. Ira Glasser and Norma Rollins of the American Civil Liberties Union emphasize the American tradition of fairness and of assuming innocence unless circumstances prove otherwise.

   C. Proponents and opponents of mandatory drug testing agree that in certain occupations tests are justified.

II. Drug testing is a bad idea: neither the extent of the problem of on-the-job drug use nor the benefits or accuracy of mandatory testing are clear.

   A. Statistics from different sources dramatically disagree about the cost of on-the-job drug use to American business.

   B. Companies that test employees cite gains in productivity and safety, but these gains are reported by the companies themselves, not by impartial researchers.

Arai ii

C. Tests are inaccurate and costly.

    1. First-round tests can be inaccurate by as much as 100 percent.

    2. Second-round tests are much more accurate but are very costly.

III. Drug testing is a bad idea: mandatory drug testing has created legal problems and may negatively affect worker productivity.

  A. Accusations of drug use against employees have led to court suits.

  B. The courts have generally ruled in favor of employees.

  C. Mandatory tests may negatively affect productivity in the workplace.

    1. One consultant predicts that testing will destroy employee morale.

    2. Another observer believes that companies that trust employees get more from them.

IV. Conclusion: manadatory drug testing is a flawed policy in any business where the work of employees does not directly affect public safety.

  A. Only people in high-risk jobs should be tested, and even then with more accurate and sensitive tests than are currently used.

  B. In all other cases, employees should be tested under two conditions.

    1. An employee should first demonstrate a drug-related problem.

    2. Tests should be administered to help that employee.

1

Drug Testing in the Workplace

In 1986 President Reagan's federal commission on
organized crime called for widespread, random drug
testing of American workers (Weiss 56). Two clear
reasons prompted this call. The first was financial:
in 1983 businesses lost up to $35 billion as a result
of drug problems (Weiss 56). Concerns for public
safety have also prompted the call for mandatory
testing. On January 4, 1987, a Conrail locomotive
near Baltimore collided with an Amtrak train, killing
16 people and wounding 176. Investigators later
discovered that at the time of the accident the
engineer was under the influence of marijuana (Sanders
62). Similarly infuriating stories abound of drug-
dulled employees endangering an unsuspecting public.
Advocates of drug testing claim that testing employees
improves public safety. According to Peter Bensinger,
former head of the Drug Enforcement Administration,
"As a result of drug testing in American industry,
the number of job-related incidents is beginning to go
down. . . . It's saving lives" ("Interview" 58).

Opponents of drug testing argue that testing vio-
lates American civil liberties, particularly the liberties guaranteed by the Fourth Amendment to the Constitution. This amendment guarantees that "[t]he right of
the people to be secure in their persons . . . against
unreasonable searches and seizures, shall not be violated." The Fourth Amendment also specifies that such
searches may only be conducted on the basis of "probable
cause" and under the authority of a signed warrant specifying the place to be searched and the items being
searched for.

Ira Glasser, executive director of the American
Civil Liberties Union, represents the opposition in
saying that "[t]he tradition in America is that you
don't hang them all to get the guilty. You can search
people . . . only if you have some reason to believe

A

B

C

Quoting and Paraphrasing Sources

Paragraph A (Excerpt from textual source of information: Weiss 56):
The private sector hardly needs the nudge. Businesses have been supporting drug testing in rapidly growing numbers: 25 percent of Fortune 500 companies, for example, now do some form of testing. The firms have been spurred on by studies showing huge productivity losses as a result of drug use ($33.3 billion in 1983). Georgia Power was worried about productivity. It was more than $6 billion above its original estimates for construction costs and years behind schedule on its Plant Vogthe nuclear plant, where Price and Register worked.

Paragraph A (Excerpt from textual source of quotation: "Interview" 58):
Mr. Bensinger, the President's Commission on Organized Crime has suggested that employers should consider testing their employees for drug use. Why do you favor the idea?

They should do it in the interest of safety, in the interest of health and in the interest of increased productivity.

As a result of drug testing in American industry, the number of job-related accidents is beginning to go down. Absenteeism is decreasing. Productivity is rising, and company medical costs are leveling off. It's saving money. It's saving lives.

Paragraph B (Quotation and paraphrase—common knowledge): The quotation in paragraph A, taken from the Fourth Amendment to the U.S. Constitution, is not cited because the amendment is common knowledge and is widely available in a variety of sources. Note the use of an ellipsis (. . .), three spaced dots, to indicate that some material has been omitted from the quotation. Following the quotation, Arai paraphrases material from the second part of the amendment ("under the authority of a signed warrant specifying the place to be searched and the items being searched for").

Paragraph C (Quotation—attributed and run in with text): In paragraph C, the quotation by Ira Glasser includes an ellipsis (. . .) (see pages 606 and 608). Note that the original text of this quotation began as follows: "The tradition in America is that you don't hang them all to get the guilty." Arai has changed the uppercase *T* in *The* to a lowercase *t* in order to integrate the quotation smoothly into his own sentence. Notice the use of brackets [ ] to indicate the change.

FOR DISCUSSION

Deciding upon a block quotation involves more than just counting lines: The reason for quoting at length must be valid. Ask students to comment on Arai's use of a block quotation here. Do they think the quotation is effective? Would a briefer quotation work as well? a paraphrase or a summary? Could Arai have used ellipses to eliminate unnecessary material in the quotation?

Arai 2

that a specific individual is committing an offense" ("Interview" 58). Norma Rollins, an official of the New York Civil Liberties Union, believes that drug testing should be directed only at the relatively few employees whose job performance suggests possible trouble with substance abuse (qtd. in Chapman 58). Opponents of drug **C** testing believe that mandatory testing is un-American and must be challenged at every opportunity. Even so, opponents say that in some cases--those involving public safety--drug testing is justified. George S. Odiorne, a professor of management at Eckard College, and an opponent of drug testing, defends the practice for high-risk jobs:

> Would I favor random testing for anybody? Yes. The kids in missile silos: two 19-year-old kids sitting 80 feet underground with their hands on the triggers of 12 Minuteman missiles that could blow up Minsk, Kapinsk and Moscow. (qtd. in Gordon 59)

Apparently, 6.6 million working Americans are alcoholics, and 6 million are regular drug users. Thirteen percent of American workers have abused drugs on the job--most of the 14 to 18 percent of Americans who abuse drugs or alcohol in general (Gordon 26). These statistics alone would seem to justify drug testing, even with the myriad problems associated with testing programs. But the statistics must be examined.

James Wrich, writing for the Harvard Business Review, claims that the cost of drug abuse to businesses is $100 billion annually (120). This astonishing figure appears less than exact, however, for research shows that no two authorities agree on the annual dollar cost of drug abuse. For instance, Philip Weiss, writing for Harper's, puts the cost at   **D** $33 billion (56). Another group, Research Triangle Institute (RTI), puts the annual cost of drug abuse at $25.7 billion (Gordon 26). RTI has been cited elsewhere as

Paragraph C (Paraphrase): Arai originally quoted a sentence from Rollins, as follows: "A fair program should focus on those individuals who exhibit drug dependence on the job, rather than forcing tests on thousands of innocent people . . . " (qtd. in Chapman 58). On rereading his draft, Arai decided that the paragraph had one too many quotations, and he therefore decided to paraphrase instead of quote Rollins. Here is the textual source of the Rollins quotation (qtd. in Chapman 58):

> "Mandatory urinalysis is an invasion of privacy that flies in the face of traditional U.S. values," says Norma Rollins, director of the privacy project for the New York Civil Liberties Union. "A fair program should focus on those individuals who exhibit symptoms of drug dependence on the job, rather than forcing tests on thousands of innocent people who will capitulate under the threat of immediate unemployment."

Paragraph C (Block quotation—attributed): At the end of paragraph C, the lengthy quotation of George Odiorne has been indented ten spaces from the left margin. Notice that the citation for a block quotation is set *outside* the final period. In this case, Arai found the quotation quoted by another author and has noted this in the citation.

Paragraph D (Excerpt from textual source of information): Note that the $100 billion figure provided by Wrich (in 1988) represents a significant increase over the corresponding figure of $33 billion provided by Weiss (citing 1983 statistics) in paragraph A. Weiss's figure, however, may relate only to Fortune 500 companies (see Weiss's quotation on page 607). Here is the source passage from Wrich:

> A recent estimate by the Alcohol, Drug Abuse and Mental Health Administration indicates that alcohol and drug abusers together cost the country more than $140 billion annually, including $100 billion in lost productivity. And these are only the direct costs. If we include family members in our calculation, the total will rise still higher.

Arai 3

putting the figure of drug _and_ alcohol abuse at $16
billion. Which authority is one to believe? The numbers
create anything but a clear picture of the extent of
the problem. Nobody really knows how much drug or
alcohol abuse costs business. Richard Bickerton of the   D
Employee Assistance Program believes that these
estimates are fictions and that "the figures you're
given often depend on the self-interest of the people
giving you the figures" (Gordon 26).

What, then, can one make of claims regarding the
benefits of drug testing? In support of their position,
proponents of testing on the one hand cite cost
estimates like $100 billion and on the other cite
success stories as evidence that drug testing works.
For instance, Southern Pacific Railroads has reported a
reduction in their accident rate by 67 percent and in
their "lost time" and injuries by 25 percent (Berger
94). Commonwealth Edison has reported 25 to 30 percent
lower absenteeism since they instituted their drug
testing program. Georgia Power has reported a sharp
drop in accidents (Kupfer 133).

Yet these figures on productivity and safety
advances due to testing are supplied largely by private
companies conducting the tests, not by impartial
research institutes. These companies might have an
interest in justifying their testing programs. These
same companies have admitted that their testing
programs are only _one_ part of an entire program of
managerial reforms (Kupfer 133). The fact is that no
conclusive relationship exists between drug testing and
productivity or safety gains.

Various accuracy studies conducted by independent
research groups have shown truly embarrassing rates of
error at testing centers across the country. One study
revealed that "known samples submitted to thirteen drug
laboratories showed error rates as high as 100 percent
for certain drugs" (Berger 88). Legal substances such

Revising the Paper

In revision, the following three rough-draft paragraphs were combined to yield the final paragraph (D):

~~Let's examine as an example one organization's claim that the annual cost of drug abuse to business is $100 billion (Gordon 26). The actual numbers or dources behind these claims provied inconclusive.~~ [The *~~impressive~~* *is astonishing figure* $100 billion price tag on workplace drug use appears ~~to be~~ *less than exact, however,* ~~little more than statistical fiction,~~ for ~~in my~~ research *shows* *annual dollar cost of drug abuse.* no two sources agreed on the ~~figure--in fact, the wide~~ ~~discrepencies called the concept of quantifying the cost~~ *Begin ¶ here* ~~into question.~~ James Wrich, writing for the Harvard Business Review, quoted $100 billion *annually* (120). *For instance,* ~~but~~ Philip Weiss, writing for Harper's, found the cost more like $33 billion (56).

o confusing: eep focus on various dollar amounts.

Furthermore, from where do these statistics come? The $100 billion was attributed to an organization called the Research Institute of America (RIA). It, ~~in~~ turn, cited "varrious estimates" for iits numbers (Gordon 26). But RIA puts out inconsistent and cnofusing reports. For example, it has also stated flatly that alcohol presents the greatest threat to productivity and safety in the workplace. However, in the same report RIA estimated that the annual cost of alcohol abuse was only $10 billion.

Another ~~research~~ group, Research Triangle Institute (RTI), *puts* ~~estimated~~ the annual coast of drug abuse at $25.7 billion, ~~"about half of what alcohol abuse costs"~~ (Gordon 26). ~~But~~ RTI has been cited elsewhere *as* putting the ~~the~~ figure of drug and alcohol *gbr* use combined at $16 billion. ~~The point?~~ *Which authority is one to believe?* Nobody really knows how much drug or alcohol abuse costs business. ~~Says~~ Richard Bickerton of the Employee Assistance Program: *believes that these estimates are* ~~"The truthy is, nobody~~ *fictions and that* ~~knows . . .~~ "the figures you're given often depend on the self-interest of the people giving you the figures" (Gordon 26). ~~Fortune magazine concurs, concluding that the figures "rely on a lot of guesswork. Pinning down the cost more precisely is almost impossible" (Chapman 59).~~ *one note is enough*

TEACHING IDEAS

Before commenting on the revisions that produced this page, you may want to ask students to evaluate the writer's style. These paragraphs illustrate the smooth, clear, vivid writing discussed in chapter 5 and part V. You may want to ask students what specific components of effective paragraphs and sentences are illustrated in this section of the paper.

GROUP ACTIVITY

After dividing the class into groups, ask each group to compare Arai's draft to his revision. On what basis did he seem to make his decisions? How closely does his revising process mirror those of students in the group? How effective does the group consider his revision to be?

TEACHING IDEAS

Ask students to paraphrase the topic sentence or main point of paragraphs D, E, F, and G.

Arai 4

as Contac, Sudafed, diet pills, asthma medications, cough syrup, antibiotics, painkillers, poppy seeds, and herbal teas will all register as illegal drugs (O'Keefe 35). Testing proponents like Bensinger agree that drug-testing companies must double-check their results, and to their credit the confirmation tests boast a 95 percent accuracy rate. But they also cost up to $100--five times as much as the initial tests. The Centers for Disease Control (CDC) has reported that most companies are failing to double-check tests that initially are positive for drug use (Chapman 60). Even though some companies do follow up with accuracy checks, nationally companies will falsely accuse one employee of every twenty tested (Berger 88). Companies are firing their employees and ruining careers on the basis of test results that are as scattershot as if the testers had simply flushed the samples down the toilet and flipped a coin--as one CDC doctor put it.

E

Predictably, less-than-reliable testing procedures have resulted in legal problems. The jury is still out regarding the current legal status of drug testing in the private workplace. Urine testing has been pronounced "search and seizure," but Fourth Amendment restrictions apply only to governmental drug testing. "Private employers currently have an unfettered right to test, but do have limits on disciplinary actions based on test results," report Brian Heschizer and Jan Muczyk (356). Firing somebody because of a failed drug test is almost certain to bring down a lawsuit upon a company.

The courts have in most cases ruled in favor of employees. Management lawyer Rusch O. Dees advises extreme caution concerning the drug testing of an ordinary worker: "The further removed from the public safety concerns a particular job may be, the more difficult it becomes to establish the reasonableness of the test program" (54). A management law firm

F

Incorporating Your Notes into the Paper

Paragraph E: Following are an excerpt from Gilda Berger's *Drug Testing*, and then two cards that Michael Arai made as he read this book. The first card is his bibliography card; the second, one of several notecards. The first time Arai refers to this note on test accuracy, he quotes Berger. In his second reference, he paraphrases her.

Paragraph E (Excerpt from textual source of information: Berger 88):

That means that positive indications of drugs are not double-checked. Even though the results say "tested positive," they might be false positives.

Out of every twenty people in a workplace tested for drugs, the chances are that one will get a false positive result.[14] The result may be dismissal or a blemish on that person's employment record for using drugs.

Laboratories that do industrial drug screening claim an error rate of less than one percent. But critics say that the error rates are much higher. An article in the *Journal of the American Medical Association* in April 1985 says that there is a "crisis in drug testing." Known samples submitted to thirteen drug laboratories showed error rates as high as 100 percent for certain drugs. "The results reflect serious shortcomings in the laboratories," the authors write.

---

④ Berger, Gilda, *Drug Testing*. New York: HV 58235
    Franklin Watts, 1987.   U5 B&7
                                                       1987

Considers the U.S. drug crisis and issues of drug testing in various public & private sectors. Chapter 7 deals with drug testing in private industry--includes several specific cases.

Test Accuracy   ④
The accuracy of drug testing is open to serious question. Berger states that "Out of every twenty people in a workplace tested for drugs, the chances are that one will get a false positive result" (p. 88). And while testing labs claim error rates of less than one percent, one study revealed that "known samples submitted to thirteen drug laboratories showed error rates as high as 100 percent for certain drugs." (p. 88)

Arai 5

survey revealed that jury verdicts in invasion of privacy cases are increasing--and averaging $316,000
(Hoerr 62). These large awards are in part the result
of several cases in which employers used drug testing
as a weapon against whistle-blowers. In Philadelphia,   F
companies have tested "trouble-some" union leaders as
often as five times in three months. Clearly, testing
has the potential to be misused.

Drug and alcohol use <u>have</u> caused problems for American companies. Debates may exist over the extent of
the problem and the accuracy of the tests, but no one
can deny the fact that thousands of employees show up
to work every day impaired and not fit to work at full
productive capacity. Surely a company has the right to
be concerned with employee productivity. The difficult
question is how this concern should be translated into   G
action. Should drug tests be mandated for all employees? Based on a review of the findings just presented,
the answer is <u>no</u>. Proponents of drug testing prop their
arguments on guesswork, hazy statistics, and blind
faith in an extremely inexact science. No conclusive
relationship has been established between drug testing
and gains in productivity or safety. Moreover, the
tests themselves are notoriously unreliable, and testing can too readily become a weapon in the hands of un-
scrupulous employers.

Granting for the moment that these serious objections to drug testing could be overcome, there remains
a final, compelling reason to reject mandatory testing:
a possible <u>decline</u> in worker productivity. A consultant
in Raleigh, North Carolina, predicts that testing will
destroy employee morale. "I imagine it would be a matter of [employees] not putting themselves out," he says
(Gordon 24-25). In other words, if management all but
admits its distrust of employees by requiring drug
tests, why should employees give an extra measure of
effort to meet management's objectives?

Ultimately, the decision of whether or not to test   H
rests on a philosophy of management and involves two

Paragraph F (Citation logic): In paragraph F, Arai cites two sources. In the first case, he mentions the author's name in preparing for a quotation, since he thinks it useful for the reader to know that the quotation's originator is a lawyer for management. With Rusch O. Dees mentioned in the sentence, there is no need to cite him again in the parenthetical note. The reader has enough information to locate the source of the quotation in the "Works Cited." In the sentence that ends with the second citation, Arai makes no mention of the author (Arai is focusing on information); therefore, he must note the author's last name in the parentheses.

Paragraph F (Textual source of information: Hoerr 62):

These aren't isolated stories. A survey by Ira Michael Shepard and Robert L. Duston, members of a management law firm in Washington, turned up 97 jury verdicts against employers in privacy cases from 1985 to mid-1987. Damage awards averaged $316,000. Before 1980 employee suits for invasion of privacy rarely reached a jury.

Paragraph G (First explicit mention of the thesis): Until this point in the paper, Arai has discussed several ways in which the arguments favoring mandatory drug testing are flawed. In paragraph G, he summarizes his arguments and draws them together in a conclusion: that drug testing should not be mandated for all employees. The paragraph serves as a preparation for a final, compelling argument that Arai believes will sway his readers.

FOR DISCUSSION

After having students read Arai's paper through, ask them to comment on his choice of placement for the thesis. Is the delay effective? Why, or why not? How would a different placement have altered the effect of the essay?

CRITICAL THINKING

Ask students to identify and list Arai's conclusions. How does he support his conclusions: with fact? assumptions? analysis? Ask students to write out or explain their responses and, in doing so, to refer to specific sentences in Arai's paper when evaluating his persuasiveness.

TEACHING IDEAS

This discussion allows students to see firsthand the purpose of a research paper—not to rehash the ideas of all the sources, but instead to use those ideas to further the writer's own purpose. You may want to lead the class through an analysis of this section of the paper, pointing out specifically how Arai is able to make the material his own.

Arai 6

opposing views on how a company achieves higher productivity from its employees. Some employers prefer to crack the whip, telling their employees exactly how to do their jobs, establishing strict rules, and imposing harsh disciplinary measures for infractions. Other employers prefer to motivate their employees by treating them decently and fairly, by giving them autonomy in doing their jobs, and by praising them for work well done. Jack Gordon, summarizing management theory, calls the first approach "Theory X" and the second, "Theory Y" (27-28). According to Gordon, who is editor of the journal <u>Training</u>, Theory Y management results in greater productivity than Theory X management. If Gordon is correct, then companies that impose drug testing programs to achieve greater productivity may in fact be operating counterproductively.

Random, sweeping drug testing as espoused by the government commission and test proponents such as Peter Bensinger functions more as a propaganda tool in the overall "War on Drugs" than as a serious attempt to address the issues of productivity and safety in the workplace. The only cases for which I would recommend random drug testing are the so-called "high risk" jobs of airline pilot, Secret Service agent, nuclear reactor operator, and so on. And even then I would demand more appropriate and sensitive tests than are usually given.

In all other cases, I would recommend a management program of training and encouragement that better evaluates employee performance. Following the reasoning that "you don't need a chemist to tell you to fire somebody who spends ten or twenty weeks a year in bed," I advise reaction to specific problems, not a near-futile search for drug use that may or may not be causing those problems ("Your Boss" 8). Responsibly applied drug testing serves only one purpose in the case of the problem employee: pinpointing the problem in order to offer that employee treatment. To conclude more specifically, I suggest several guidelines regarding testing:

H

Using Sources—But Ensuring That Your Voice Predominates

Paragraph H is based on the following material, found in Jack Gordon's "Drug Testing as a Productivity Booster?" (in *Training*, 22 Mar. 1987).

Theory X and Theory Y are, of course, terms coined by Douglas McGregor in the 1950s to represent two basic philosophies by which managers may view their subordinates. In a nutshell, the Theory X manager assumes that workers are untrustworthy—they won't show up for work, do their jobs properly, refrain from robbing the company fund, control their dark urges to turn into dope fiends, etc.— unless and until they prove otherwise. The Theory Y manager assumes the opposite—that unless a worker proves otherwise, he or she probably is honest, at least semi-competent, and willing to do a good job.

The body of management theory rooted in Theory Y says basically that while it's true the Egyptians got the pyramids built with Theory X methods, they would have gotten better, faster, and even cheaper pyramids had they 1) dropped their whips and 2) enlisted the hearts and minds of the labor force in the project by giving them well-targeted praise, rewards, responsibility, authority, training, and not least, trust.

Another theory comes into play here. It's called the Pygmalion Effect. In essence, it says that if you treat employees as if you believe they are honest, trustworthy people who want to do a good job, most of them will behave like honest, trustworthy people who want to do a good job. If you treat them as if you believe they're thieves, incompetents and malingerers, constantly on the lookout for ways to abuse their positions, many will, indeed, start looking for ways to abuse their positions.

Participative management techniques and other methods grounded in a Theory Y view of employees have been consistently pushed forward as responses to virtually every "workplace crisis" of the '80s: the productivity crisis, the international-competition crisis, the "How in the world are we going to cope with the accelerating pace of change?" crisis, the "declining loyalty toward employers" crisis, and so on. Theory Y techniques are strongly recommended for managers who want to keep their companies "union-free." Without Theory Y assumptions, there is no such thing as "intrapreneuring." Theory Y is the basis for the HRD emphasis on team building. To a large extent, it's the basis for the popular view that "leadership" is something different from "management," and that effective leaders draw their power not from their rank in the company hierarchy but from their ability to win the hearts and minds of their peers and subordinates.

If management theory for the past two decades tells us nothing else, it tells us that if we want productivity, Theory Y is the way to go.

If you say nothing else about a policy stating that employees under no particular suspicion of anything will be subjected to urine inspections to prove that they aren't dope fiends, you have to say that it is, by definition, a Theory X policy. And a pretty dramatic one at that.

While most of paragraph H summarizes the passage here, the first and the last sentences serve as the writer's own critical commentary which sets the summarized material in the context of a larger issue (first sentence) and also provides the writer's own viewpoint (last sentence). This viewpoint is consistent with the writer's thesis, stated directly in the paragraph following. Michael Arai uses his summaries (as well as paraphrases and quotations) for his own purpose and ensures that his voice, not the voices of his sources, predominates in the paper.

TEACHING IDEAS

You may want to inform students of the different types of entries here. In order, they represent the following:

a book with one author

an article in a weekly magazine

an article in a monthly magazine

an article without consecutive pagination

an article in a journal paginated continuously throughout the volume

a multi-authored article

an unsigned article

an unsigned article

an article in a weekly magazine

an article in a monthly magazine

an article in a weekly magazine

an article in a monthly magazine

an article in a journal paginated continuously throughout the volume

an unsigned article

Arai 7

Employees must have demonstrated a clear job-performance problem before any tests are administered; all positive tests must be confirmed; results must remain confidential; and use of urinalysis must be accompanied by drug rehabilitation (Berger 99).

Arai 8

Works Cited

Berger, Gilda. <u>Drug Testing</u>. New York: Franklin Watts, 1987.

Chapman, Fern Schumer. "The Ruckus Over Medical Testing." <u>Fortune</u> 19 Aug. 1985: 57–62.

Dees, Rusch O. "Testing for Drugs and Alcohol: Proceed with Caution." <u>Personnel</u> Sept. 1986: 53–55.

Gordon, Jack. "Drug Testing As a Productivity Booster?" <u>Training</u> 22 Mar. 1987: 22–28+.

Heschizer, Brian, and Jan P. Muczyk. "Drug Testing at the Workplace: Balancing Individual, Organizational, and Societal Rights." <u>Labor Law Journal</u> 39 (1988): 342–57.

Hoerr, John, Katherine M. Hafner, Gail DeGeorge, Anne R. Field, and Laura Zinn. "Privacy." <u>Business Week</u> 28 Mar. 1988: 61–68.

"Interview with Ira Glasser." <u>U.S. News & World Report</u> 17 Mar. 1986: 58.

"Interview with Peter Bensinger." <u>U.S. News & World Report</u> 17 Mar. 1986: 58.

Kupfer, Andrew. "Is Drug Testing Good or Bad?" <u>Fortune</u> 19 Dec. 1988: 133–39.

O'Keefe, Anne Marie. "The Case Against Drug Testing." <u>Psychology Today</u> June 1987: 34–38.

Sanders, A. L. "Boost for Drug Testing." <u>Time</u> 3 Apr. 1989: 62.

Weiss, Peter. "Watch Out: Urine Trouble." <u>Harper's</u> June 1986: 56–57.

Wrich, James T. "Beyond Testing: Coping with Drugs at Work." <u>Harvard Business Review</u> 66 (1988): 120–30.

"Your Boss Is Not a Cop." <u>The New Republic</u> 6 June 1988: 7–9.

Format for the list of references (Works Cited). See chapter 36 for explanations and examples of the proper form for each entry. The entries are alphabetical and double-spaced; the heading is centered an inch from the top of the page. Each new entry begins at the left margin; subsequent lines in the entry are indented five spaces.

Business Periodicals Index (1986–87) listing for "Drug Testing" (includes two items—Hoerr and Dees—cited in research paper):

> **Drug abuse—Testing**—*cont.*
> Major chemical producers toughen stance on drug abuse. M. S. Reisch graph il tab *Chem Eng News* 65:7–12 Ag 3 '87
> The medical case against drug testing. D. Bearman. *Harv Bus Rev* 66:126 Ja-F '88
> NLRB nips drug testing. *ENR* 219:93–4 O 1 '87
> Oil and drugs [drug testing] P. Crow. *Oil Gas J* 85:17 Ag 31 '87
> Paper companies begin drug testing of new applicants, problem workers. P. J. Tombaugh. il tab *Pulp Pap* 61:165–9 S '87
> Plan for drug testing of federal workers firming [proposed rules published] D. Hanson tab *Chem Eng News* 65:13–14 Ag 31 '87
> ✓ Privacy [workplace issue; special report] J. Hoerr and others. *Bus Week* p61–8 Mr 28 '88
> The right to be tested. M. I. Finney. *Pers Adm* 33:74–5 Mr '88
> Screening for drugs is becoming routine for American employers. *Pers Manage* 19:8 Ag '87
> Static risks demand equal time: Hall exec [T. V. Hallett] *Natl Underwrit (Prop Casualty Employee Benefits Ed)* 91:65+ S 14 '87
> Straight dope on drug testing [BNA Communications video] *Mod Off Technol* 32:38+ Jl '87
> Test workers for drugs? [survey] M. A. Verespej. graphs *Ind Week* 235:17–18 D 14 '87
> Testing for drug use: handle with care [employee privacy issue] K. Hafner and S. Garland. *Bus Week* p65 Mr 28 '88
> ✓ Testing for drugs and alcohol: proceed with caution. R. O. Dees. *Personnel* 63:53–5 S '86
> Testing: forearmed may not be advantageous [testing for drug use and AIDS] *Empl Benefit Plan Rev* 42:53–4 Mr '88

Documenting Research

Any time you use material derived from specific sources, whether quoted passages or summaries or paraphrases of fact, opinion, explanation, or idea, you are ethically obligated to let your reader know who deserves the credit. Further, you must tell your readers precisely where the material came from so that they can locate it for themselves. Often readers will want to trace the facts on which a conclusion is based, or to verify that a passage was quoted or paraphrased accurately. Sometimes readers will simply want to follow up and learn more about your subject.

There are basically two ways for a writer to show a "paper trail" to sources. The format most used today is the parenthetical reference, also called an *in-text citation.* This is a telegraphic, short-hand approach to identifying the source of a statement or quotation. It assumes that a complete list of references appears at the end of the paper. Each entry in the list of references includes three essential elements: authorship, full title of the work, and publication information. In the references, entries are arranged, punctuated, and typed to conform to the bibliographic style requirements of the particular discipline or of the instructor. With this list in place, the writer is able to supply the briefest of references—a page number or an author's name—in parentheses right in the text, knowing that the reader will be able to locate the rest of the reference information easily in the list of references. The second method for showing a paper trail is the footnote style—which is less often used today than the parenthetical system.

For more detailed information on the conventions of style in the humanities, social sciences, business disciplines, and sciences, refer to the style manuals listed below.

- Gibaldi, Joseph, and Walter S. Achtert. *MLA Handbook for Writers of Research Papers.* 3rd ed. New York: MLA, 1988.
- *Publication Manual* (of the American Psychological Association). 3rd ed. Washington, DC: APA, 1983.
- *Chicago Manual of Style.* 14th ed. Chicago: University of Chicago Press, 1993.
- *CBE Style Manual.* 5th ed. Bethesda, MD: CBE, 1983.

36a Using the MLA system of documentation

The Modern Language Association (MLA) publishes a style guide that is widely used for citations and references in the humanities. This

An Overview of the Four Documentation Systems Presented in This Chapter

section gives detailed examples of how the MLA system of parenthetical references provides in-text citation. In addition, a later section (36c) will show how to use the footnote or endnote system of documentation, where complete information on each source is given every time a source is cited.

In a research paper, either of these systems of source citation is followed at the end by a list of references. In the MLA system, the list of references is called "Works Cited." Keep in mind that the complete infor-

REFERENCE

GIBALDI, JOSEPH, and WALTER S. ACHTERT. *MLA Handbook for Writers of Research Papers.* 3rd ed. New York: MLA, 1988. Extensive advice on documenting sources.

mation provided in the list of references will be the basis of your in-text citations. The parenthetical form provides minimal information and sends the reader to the list of references to find the rest. By contrast, the footnote or endnote system virtually duplicates the information in the list of references but uses a slightly different arrangement of the elements in the entry. Following is an index to this section on the MLA system of documentation.

1 Making in-text citations in the MLA format

When you make a parenthetical in-text citation, you assume that your reader will look to the list of "Works Cited" for complete references. The list of references at the end of your paper will provide three essential pieces of information for each of your sources: author, title, and facts of publication. Within your paper, a parenthetical citation may serve either of two purposes: to point to a source considered as a whole, or to point to a specific page location in a source. Here is an example of an MLA in-text citation referring to a story as a whole.

```
In "Escapes," the title story of one contemporary author's
book of short stories, the narrator's alcoholic mother makes a
public spectacle of herself (Williams).
```

The next example refers to a specific page in the story. In the MLA system, no punctuation is placed between a writer's last name and a page reference.

```
In "Escapes," a story about an alcoholic household, a key
moment occurs when the child sees her mother suddenly appear
on stage at the magic show (Williams 11).
```

Here is how the references to the Williams story would appear as described in the list of references or "Works Cited."

```
Williams, Joy. "Escapes." Escapes: Stories. New York: Vintage,
     1990. 1-14.
```

Deciding when to insert a source citation and what information to include is often a judgment call rather than the execution of a mechanical system. Use common sense. Where feasible, incorporate citations smoothly into the text. Introduce the parenthetical reference smoothly at a pause in your sentence, at the end if possible. Place it as close to the documented point as possible, making sure that the reader can tell exactly which point is being documented. When the in-text reference is incorporated into a sentence of your own, always place the parenthetical reference *before* any enclosing or end punctuation.

```
In Central Africa in the 1930s, a young girl who comes to town
drinks beer with her date because that's what everyone does
(Lessing 105).
```

```
In a realistic portrayal of Central African city life in the
1930s (Lessing), young people gather daily to drink.
```

When a quotation from a work is incorporated into a sentence of your own, the parenthetical reference *follows* the quotation marks, yet precedes the enclosing or end punctuation.

```
At the popular Sports Club, Lessing's heroine finds the
"ubiquitous glass mugs of golden beer" (135).
```

EXCEPTION: When your quotation ends with a question mark or exclamation point, keep these punctuation marks inside the end quotation marks, then give the parenthetical reference, and end with a period.

```
Martha's new attempts at sophistication in town prompted her
to retort, "Children are a nuisance, aren't they?" (Lessing
115).
```

Naming an author in the text

When you want to emphasize the author of a source you are citing, incorporate that author's name into your sentence. Unless you are referring to a particular place in that source, no parenthetical reference is necessary in the text.

```
Biographer Paul Mariani understands Berryman's alcoholism as
one form of his drive toward self-destruction.
```

Naming an author in the parenthetical reference

When you want to emphasize information in a source but not especially the author, omit the author's name in the sentence and place it in the parenthetical reference.

```
Biographers have documented alcohol-related upheavals in John
Berryman's life. Aware, for example, that Dylan Thomas was in
an alcohol-induced coma, dying, Berryman himself drank to
escape his pain (Mariani 273).
```

When you are referring to a particular place in your source and have already incorporated the author's name into your sentence, place only the page number in parentheses.

Biographer Paul Mariani describes how Berryman, knowing that
his friend Dylan Thomas was dying in an alcohol-induced coma,
himself began drinking to escape his pain (273).

Documenting a block quotation

For block quotations, set the parenthetical reference—with or without an author's name—*outside* of the end punctuation mark.

The story graphically portrays the behavior of Central African
young people gathering daily to drink:

> Perry sat stiffly in a shallow chair which looked
> as if it would splay out under the weight of his
> big body . . . while from time to time--at those
> moments when laughter was jerked out of him by
> Stella--he threw back his head with a sudden
> dismayed movement, and flung half a glass of
> liquor down his throat. (Lessing 163)

A work by two or three authors

If your source has two or three authors, name them all, either in
your text or in a parenthetical reference. Use last names, in the order they
are given in the source, connected by *and*.

Critics have addressed the question of whether literary
artists discover new truths (Wellek and Warren 33-36).

One theory claims that the alcoholic wants to "drink
his environment in" (Perls, Hefferline, and Goodman
193-94).

A work by four or more authors

For a work with four or more authors, name all the authors, or use
the following abbreviated format with *et al.* to signify "and others."

Some researchers trace the causes of alcohol dependence to
"flawed family structures" (Stein, Lubber, Koman, and Kelly
318).

Some researchers trace the causes of alcohol dependence to
"flawed family structures" (Stein et al. 318).

Stein et al. trace the causes of alcohol dependence to "flawed
family structures" (318).

Reference to two or more sources with the same authorship

When you are referring to one or two or more sources written by the same author, include in your in-text citation a shortened form of each title so that references to each text will be clear. The following example discusses how author Joy Williams portrays the drinking scene in her fiction. Note that a comma appears between the author's name and the shortened title.

```
She shows drinking at parties as a way of life in such stories
as "Escapes" and "White Like Midnight." Thus it is matter of
course that Joan pours herself a drink while people talk about
whether or not they want to survive nuclear war (Williams,
"White" 129).
```

Distinguishing two authors with the same last name

Use one or more initials to supplement references to authors with the same last name.

```
It is no coincidence that a new translation of Euripides' The
Bacchae should appear in the United States (Williams, C. K.)
at a time when fiction writers portray the use of alcohol as a
means of escape from mundane existence (Williams, J.).
```

Two or more sources in a single reference

Particularly in an introductory summary, you may want to group together a number of works that cover one or more aspects of your research topic. Separate one source from another by a semicolon.

```
Studies that confront the alcoholism of literary figures
directly are on the increase (Mariani; Dardis; Gilmore).
```

A corporate author

A work may be issued by an organization or government agency with no author named. Cite the work as if the name given is the author's. Since the name of a corporate author is often long, try incorporating it into your text rather than using a parenthetical note. In this example the corporate author of the book is Alcoholics Anonymous. The book will be listed alphabetically under "Alcoholics" in Works Cited.

```
Among publications that discuss how to help young people cope
with family problems, Al-Anon Faces Alcoholism, put out by
Alcoholics Anonymous, has been reissued frequently since 1974
(117-24).
```

A multivolume work

When citing a page reference to a multivolume work, specify the volume by an arabic numeral followed by a colon and the page number. The Trevelyan history is in four volumes.

```
Drunkenness was such a problem in the first decades of the
eighteenth century that it was termed "the acknowledged
national vice of Englishmen of all classes" (Trevelyan 3: 46).
```

A literary work

Well-known literary works, particularly older ones now in the public domain, may appear in numerous editions. When referring to such a work or a part of one, give information for the work itself rather than for the particular edition you are using, unless you are highlighting a special feature or contribution of the edition.

For a play, supply act, scene, and line number in arabic numerals, unless your instructor specifies using Roman numerals for act and scene (II. iv. 118–19). In the following example, the title of the literary work includes numerals referring to the first of two plays that Shakespeare wrote about Henry IV, known as parts 1 and 2.

```
Shakespeare's Falstaff bellows, "Give me a cup of sack, rogue.
Is there no virtue extant?" (1 Henry IV 2.4.118-19).
```

To cite a modern editor's contribution to the publication of a literary work, adjust the emphasis of your reference. The abbreviation *n.* stands for *note.*

```
Without the editor's footnote in the Riverside Shakespeare
explaining that lime was sometimes used as an additive to make
wine sparkle, modern readers would be unlikely to understand
Falstaff's ranting: "[Y]et a coward is worse than a cup of
sack with lime in it. A villainous coward!" (1 Henry IV
2.4.125-26n.).
```

Material quoted in your source

Often you will want to quote and cite material that you are reading at second hand—in a work by an intermediate author. Quote the original material and refer to the place where you found it.

```
Psychoanalyst Otto Fenichel included alcoholics within a
general grouping of addictive personalities, all of whom use
addictive substances "to satisfy the archaic oral longing, a
need for security, and a need for the maintenance of self-
esteem simultaneously" (qtd. in Roebuck and Kessler 86).
```

An anonymous work

A work with no acknowledged author will be alphabetized in a list of references by the first word of its title. Therefore cite the anonymous work in the same way in your parenthetical reference. The title in this example is *The Hidden Alcoholic in Your Midst.*

```
People who do not suffer from addiction often can be
thoughtless and insensitive to the problems of those around
them. That is the message of an emotional and thought-
provoking pamphlet (Hidden), whose author writes anonymously
about the pain of keeping his alcoholism secret.
```

2   Preparing a list of references in the MLA format

In research papers following MLA format, the list of references is called "Works Cited" when it includes those sources you have referred to in your paper. Be aware that some instructors request a more comprehensive list of references—one that includes every source you consulted in preparing the paper. That list would be titled "Bibliography."

The examples in this section show how entries in the "Works Cited" list consist of three elements essential for a list of references: authorship, full title of the work, and publication information. The basic format for each entry requires the first line to start at the left margin, with each subsequent line to be indented five typed spaces from the left margin.

Not every possible variation is represented here. In formatting a complicated entry for your own list, you may need to combine features from two or more of the examples. The MLA "Works Cited" list begins on a new page, after the last page of your paper, and continues the pagination of your paper. Entries in the list are alphabetized by the author's last name. An anonymous work is alphabetized by the first word in its title (but disregard *A, An,* and *The*).

Listing books in the MLA "Works Cited" format

The MLA "Works Cited" list presents book references in the following order:

1. Author's name: Put the last name first, followed by a comma and the first name (and middle name or initial) and a period. Omit the author's titles and degrees, whether one that precedes a name (Dr.) or one that follows (Ph.D.). Leave two typed spaces after the period.
2. Title of the book: Underline the complete title. If there is a subtitle, separate it from the main title by a colon and one typed space. Capitalize all important words, including the first word of any subtitle. The complete title is followed by a period and two typed spaces.

3. Publication information: Name the city of publication, followed by a colon and one typed space; the name of the publisher followed by a comma; the date of publication followed by a period. This information appears on the title page of the book and the copyright page, on the reverse side of the title page.

If the city of publication is not well known, add the name of the state, abbreviated as in the zip code system. Shorten the name of the publisher in a way that is recognizable. "G. P. Putnam's Sons" is shortened to "Putnam's." For university presses use "UP" as in the example "U of Georgia P." Many large publishing companies issue books under imprints that represent particular groups of books. Give the imprint name first, followed by a hyphen and the name of the publisher: Bullseye-Knopf.

Any additional information about the book goes between author and title or between title and publication data. In the examples that follow, you will notice the kinds of information that can be added to an entry. Observe details of how to organize, abbreviate, and punctuate this information.

A book with one author

The basic format for a single-author book is as follows:

Mariani, Paul. Dream Song: The Life of John Berryman. New

York: Morrow, 1990.

A book with two or three authors

For a book with two or three authors, follow the order of the names on the title page. Notice that first and last name are reversed only for the lead author. Notice also the use of a comma after the first author.

Roebuck, Julian B., and Raymond G. Kessler. The Etiology of

Alcoholism: Constitutional, Psychological and Sociological

Approaches. Springfield: Thomas, 1972.

A book with four or more authors

As in the example under in-text citations (see 36a-1), you may choose to name all the authors or to use the abbreviated format with *et al.*

Stein, Norman, Mindy Lubber, Stuart L. Koman, and Kathy Kelly.

Family Therapy: A Systems Approach. Boston: Allyn, 1990.

Stein, Norman, et al. Family Therapy: A Systems Approach.

Boston: Allyn, 1990.

A book that has been reprinted or reissued

In the following entry, the date 1951 is the original publication date of the book, which was reprinted in 1965.

Perls, Frederick, Ralph F. Hefferline, and Paul Goodman.
  <u>Gestalt Therapy: Excitement and Growth in the Human
  Personality</u>. 1951. New York: Delta-Dell, 1965.

A dictionary or encyclopedia

If an article in a reference work is signed (usually by initials), include the name of the author, which is spelled out elsewhere in the reference work (usually at the beginning). The first example is unsigned. The second article is signed (F.G.H.T.).

"Alcoholics Anonymous." <u>Encyclopaedia Britannica: Micropaedia</u>.
  1991 ed.

Tate, Francis G. H. "Rum." <u>Encyclopaedia Britannica</u>. 1950 ed.

A selection from an edited book or anthology

For a selection from an edited work, name the author of the selection and enclose the selection title in quotation marks. Underline the title of the book containing the selection, and name its editor(s). Give the page numbers for the selection at the end of your entry.

Davies, Phil. "Does Treatment Work? A Sociological Perspective." <u>The Misuse of Alcohol</u>. Ed. Nick Heather et al. New
  York: New York UP, 1985. 158-77.

When a selection has been reprinted from another source, include that information too, as in the following example. State the facts of original publication first, then describe the book in which it has been reprinted.

Bendiner, Emil. "The Bowery Man on the Couch." <u>The Bowery Man</u>.
  New York: Nelson, 1961. Rpt. in <u>Man Alone: Alienation in
  Modern Society</u>. Ed. Eric Josephson and Mary Josephson. New
  York: Dell, 1962. 401-10.

Two or more works by the same author(s)

When you cite two or more works by the same author(s), you should write the author's full name only once, at first mention, in the reference list. In subsequent entries immediately following, substitute three hyphens and a period in place of the author's name.

Heilbroner, Robert L. <u>The Future as History</u>. New York: Harper
  Torchbooks-Harper, 1960.

---. <u>An Inquiry into the Human Prospect</u>. New York: Norton,
  1974.

A translation

When a work has been translated, acknowledge the translator's name after giving the title.

Kufner, Heinrich, and Wilhelm Feuerlein. <u>In-Patient Treatment</u>
    <u>for Alcoholism: A Multi-Centre Evaluation Study</u>. Trans. F.
    K. H. Wagstaff. Berlin: Springer, 1989.

A corporate author
    If authorship is not individual but corporate, treat the name of the
organization as you would the author. This listing would be alphabetized
under "National Center."

National Center for Alcohol Education. <u>The Community Health</u>
    <u>Nurse and Alcohol-Related Problems: Instructor's Curriculum</u>
    <u>Planning Guide</u>. Rockville: National Institute on Alcohol
    Abuse and Alcoholism, 1978.

Signaling publication information that is unknown
    If a document fails to state place or date of publication or the name
of the publisher, indicate this lack of information in your entry by using
the appropriate abbreviation.

Missing, Andrew. <u>Things I Forgot or Never Knew</u>. N.p.: n.p.,
    n.d.

In the above example, the first *n.p.* stands for "no place of publication."
The second *n.p.* means "no publisher given," and *n.d.* stands for "no date."

An edition subsequent to the first
    Books of continuing importance may be revised substantially before
reissue. Cite the edition you have consulted just after giving the title.

Scrignar, C. B. <u>Post-Traumatic Stress Disorder: Diagnosis,</u>
    <u>Treatment, and Legal Issues</u>. 2nd ed. New Orleans: Bruno,
    1988.

A book in a series
    If the book you are citing is one in a series, include the series name
(no quotation marks or underline) followed by the volume number and a
period before the publication information. You need not give the name of
the series editor.

Schuckit, Marc A., ed. <u>Alcohol Patterns and Problems</u>. Series
    in Psychological Epidemiology 5. New Brunswick: Rutgers UP,
    1985.

An introduction, preface, foreword, or afterword
    When citing an introductory or concluding essay by a "guest au-
thor" or commentator, begin with the name of that author. Give the type
of piece—Introduction, Preface—without quotation marks or underline.
Name the author of the book after giving the book title. At the end of the

listing, give the page numbers for the essay you are citing. If the author of the separate essay is also the author of the complete work, repeat that author's last name, preceded by *By,* after the book title.

Fromm, Erich. Foreword. <u>Summerhill: A Radical Approach to</u>
    <u>Child Rearing</u>. By A. S. Neill. New York: Hart, 1960. ix-
    xiv.

In this book, the editors also wrote the introduction to their anthology.

Josephson, Eric, and Mary Josephson. Introduction. <u>Man Alone:</u>
    <u>Alienation in Modern Society</u>. Ed. by Josephson and
    Josephson. New York: Dell, 1962. 9-53.

An unpublished dissertation or essay

An unpublished dissertation, even of book length, has its title in quotation marks. Label it as a dissertation in your entry. Naming the university and year will provide the necessary publication facts.

Reiskin, Helen R. "Patterns of Alcohol Usage in a Help-Seeking
    University Population." Diss. Boston U, 1980.

Listing periodicals in the MLA "Works Cited" format

A *periodical* is any publication that appears regularly over time. A periodical can be a daily or weekly newspaper, a magazine, or a scholarly or professional journal. As with listings for books, a bibliographical listing for a periodical article includes information about authorship, title, and facts of publication. Authorship is treated just as for books, with the author's first and last names reversed. Citation of a title differs in that the title of an article is always enclosed in quotation marks rather than underlined; the title of the periodical in which it appears is always underlined. Notice that the articles *a, an,* and *the,* which often begin the name of a periodical, are omitted from the bibliographical listing.

The facts of publication are the trickiest of the three elements because of the wide variation in how periodicals are dated, paginated, and published. For journals, for example, the publication information generally consists of journal title, the volume number, the year of publication, and the page numbering for the article cited. For newspapers, the listing includes name of the newspaper, full date of publication, and full page numbering by both section and page number(s) if necessary. The following examples show details of how to list different types of periodicals. With the exception of May, June, and July, you should abbreviate the names of months in each "Works Cited" entry (see 31d).

A journal with continuous pagination through the annual volume

A continuously paginated journal is one that numbers pages consecutively throughout all the issues in a volume instead of beginning with page 1 in each issue. After the author's name (reversed and followed by a period and two typed spaces), give the name of the article in quotation marks. Give the title of the journal, underlined and followed by two typed spaces. Give the volume number, in arabic numerals. After a typed space, give the year, in parentheses, followed by a colon. After one more space, give the page number(s) for the article, including the first and last pages on which it appears.

Kling, William. "Measurement of Ethanol Consumed in Distilled
    Spirits." <u>Journal of Studies on Alcohol</u> 50 (1989): 456-60.

In a continuously paginated journal, the issue number within the volume and the month of publication are not included in the bibliographical listing.

A journal paginated by issue

Latessa, Edward J., and Susan Goodman. "Alcoholic Offenders:
    Intensive Probation Program Shows Promise." <u>Corrections</u>
    <u>Today</u> 51.3 (1989): 38-39+.

This journal numbers the pages in each issue separately, so it is important to identify which issue in volume 51 has this article beginning on page 38. The plus sign following a page number indicates that the article continues after the last-named page, but after intervening pages.

A monthly magazine

This kind of periodical is identified by month and year of issue. Even if the magazine indicates a volume number, omit it from your listing.

Waggoner, Glen. "Gin as Tonic." <u>Esquire</u> Feb. 1990: 30.

Some magazines vary in their publication schedule. *Restaurant Business* publishes once a month or bimonthly. Include the full date of publication in your listing. Give the day first, followed by an abbreviation for the month.

Whelan, Elizabeth M. "Alcohol and Health." <u>Restaurant Business</u>
    20 Mar. 1989: 66+.

A daily newspaper

In the following examples, you see that the name of the newspaper is underlined. Any introductory article (*a, an,* and *the*) is omitted. The complete date of publication is given—day, month (abbreviated), year. Specify the edition if one appears on the masthead, since even in one day an article may be located differently in different editions. Precede the page number(s) by a colon and one typed space. If the paper has sections designated by letter (A, B, C), include the section before the page number.

If the article is unsigned, begin your entry with the title, as in the second example ("Alcohol Can Worsen . . . ").

Welch, Patrick. "Kids and Booze: It's 10 O'Clock--Do You Know
    How Drunk Your Kids Are?" <u>Washington Post</u> 31 Dec. 1989: C1.

The following entry illustrates the importance of including the particular
edition of a newspaper.

"Alcohol Can Worsen Ills of Aging, Study Says." <u>New York Times</u>
    13 June 1989, natl. ed.: 89.

"Alcohol Can Worsen Ills of Aging, Study Says." <u>New York Times</u>
    13 June 1989, late ed.: C5.

A weekly magazine or newspaper
    An unsigned article listing would include title, name of the publi-
cation, complete date, and page number(s). Even if you know a volume
or issue number, omit it.

"A Direct Approach to Alcoholism." <u>Science News</u> 9 Jan. 1988:
    25.

A signed editorial, letter to the editor, review
    For these entries, first give the name of the author. If the piece has
a title, put it within quotation marks. Then name the category of the
piece—Letter, Rev. of (for Review), Editorial—without quotation marks
or underline. If the reference is to a review, give the name of the work
being reviewed with underline or quotation marks as appropriate.

Fraser, Kennedy. Rev. of <u>Stones of His House: A Biography of</u>
    <u>Paul Scott</u>, by Hilary Spurling. <u>New Yorker</u> 13 May 1991:
    103-10.

James, Albert. Letter. <u>Boston Globe</u> 14 Jan. 1992: 61.

Stein, Norman. "Traveling for Work." Editorial. <u>Baltimore Sun</u>
    12 Dec. 1991: 82.

Listing other sources in the MLA "Works Cited" format

An abstract of an article
    Libraries contain many volumes of abstracts of recent articles in
many disciplines. If you are referring to an abstract you have read rather
than to the complete article, list it as follows.

Corcoran, K. J., and M. D. Carney. "Alcohol Consumption and
    Looking for Alternatives to Drinking in College Students."
    <u>Journal of Cognitive Psychotherapy</u> 3 (1989): 69-78. Abstr.
    in <u>Excerpta Medica</u> Sec. 32 Vol. 60 (1989): 40.

A government publication
    Often, a government publication will have group authorship. Be
sure to name the agency or committee responsible for writing a document.

United States Cong. Senate. Subcommittee to Investigate
    Juvenile Delinquency of the Committee on the Judiciary.
    <u>Juvenile Alcohol Abuse: Hearing</u>. 95th Cong., 2nd sess.
    Washington: GPO, 1978.

An unpublished interview

A listing for an unpublished interview begins with the name of the person interviewed. If the interview is untitled, label it as such, without quotation marks or underlining. Name the person doing the interviewing only if that information is relevant.

Bishop, Robert R. Personal interview. 5 Nov. 1987.

An unpublished letter

Treat an unpublished letter much as you would an unpublished interview. Designate the recipient of the letter. If you as the writer of the paper were the recipient, refer to yourself as "the author."

Bishop, Robert R. Letter to the author. 8 June 1964.

If a letter is housed in a library collection or archive, provide full archival information.

Bishop, Robert R. Letter to Jonathan Morton. 8 June 1964.
    Carol K. Morton papers. Smith College, Northampton.

A film or videotape

Underline the title, and then name the medium, the distributor, and the year. Supply any information that you think is useful about the performers, director, producer, or physical characteristics of the film or tape.

<u>Alcoholism: The Pit of Despair</u>. Videocassette. Gordon Jump.
    AIMS Media, 1983. VHS and Beta. 20 min.

A television or radio program

If the program you are citing is a single episode with its own title, supply the title in quotation marks. State the name and role of the foremost participant(s). Underline the title of the program, identify the producer and list the station on which it first appeared, the city, and the date.

"The Broken Cord." Interview with Louise Erdrich and Michael
    Dorris. Dir. and prod. Catherine Tatge. <u>A World of Ideas
    with Bill Moyers</u>. Exec. prod. Judith Davidson Moyers and
    Bill Moyers. Public Affairs TV. WNET, New York. 27 May
    1990.

A live performance, lecture

Identify the "who, what, and where" of a live performance. If the "what" is more important than the "who," as in a performance of an opera, give the name of the work before the name of the performers or director. In the following example, the name of the speaker, a cofounder of AA, comes first.

```
Wilson, Bill. "Alcoholics Anonymous: Beginnings and Growth."
    Presented to the NYC Medical Society. New York, 8 Apr.
    1958.
```

A work of art

Underline the title of a work of art referred to, and tell the location of the work. The name of the museum or collection is separated from the name of the city by a comma.

```
Manet, Edouard. The Absinthe Drinker. Ny Carlsberg Glyptotek,
    Copenhagen.
```

Electronic material

Information services. Listings in indexes, volumes of abstracts, and bibliographies on computer often have identification numbers. If you are citing such a listing, whether you located it in print or in a computer database, add the name of the source and the identification number of your entry. The "ED" number for each item in ERIC (Educational Resources Information Center) will represent one document.

```
Weaver, Dave. "Software for Substance Abuse Education: A
    Critical Review of Products." Portland: Northwest Regional
    Educational Lab, 1988. ERIC ED 303 702.
```

Computer software. Like a printed book, computer software has authorship, a title, and a publication history. Include this in any bibliographical listing, along with relevant information for your reader about the software and any hardware it requires. Underline the title of the program. Identify the title as computer software. In the example, the name of the author and the location of the company would be added if they were known.

```
Alcohol and Pregnancy: Protecting the Unborn Child. Computer
    software. Student Awareness Software, 1988. 48K Apple II
    and 256K IBM PC.
```

A separately issued map, chart, or graph

Even a free-standing map or poster generally tells something about who published it, where, and when. Give the title, underlined, and any identifying information available. Use the abbreviation *n.d.* any time a date is lacking in publication information.

```
Roads in France. Map. Paris: National Tourist Information
    Agency, n.d.
```

36b   Using the APA system of documentation

The American Psychological Association's *Publication Manual* has set documentation style for psychologists. Writers in other fields, especially those in which researchers report their work fairly frequently in periodicals and edited collections of essays, also use the APA system of documentation. Whichever style of documentation you use in a given research paper, use only one; do not mix features of APA and MLA (or any other format) in a single paper.

APA documentation is similar to the MLA system in coupling a brief in-text citation, given in parentheses, with a complete listing of information about the source at the end of the paper. In the APA system this list of references is called "References." In the in-text citation itself, APA style differs by including the date of the work cited. The publication date is often important for a reader to have immediately at hand in psychology and related fields, where researchers may publish frequently, often modifying conclusions reached in prior publications. Date of publication also serves to distinguish readily among publications for authors who have many titles to their name. Following is an index to this section on the APA system of documentation.

TEACHING IDEAS

As with MLA format, students should be encouraged to check with individual instructors regarding documentation requirements. You may also want to point out the rationale behind highlighting the publication date—this explains one of the differences between MLA and APA formats.

REFERENCE

Publication Manual (of the American Psychological Association). 3rd ed. Washington, DC: APA, 1983. Extensive advice on documenting sources.

1   Making in-text citations in the APA format

For every fact, opinion, or idea from another source that you quote, summarize, or otherwise use, you must give credit. You must also give just enough information so that your reader can locate the source. Whether in the text itself or in a parenthetical note, APA documentation calls for you to name the author and give the date of publication for every work you refer to. When you have quoted from a work, you must also give the page or page numbers (preceded by *p.* or *pp.,* in APA format). When you summarize or paraphrase, as well, it is often helpful to supply exact location of the source material by page number as part of the parenthetical reference. Supply the page number(s) immediately following a quotation or paraphrase, even if the sentence is not at a pause point.

In the sample paragraphs that follow, you will find variations on using APA in-text citation. Notice that, wherever possible, reference information is incorporated directly into the text and parentheses are used as a supplement to information in the text. Supply the parenthetical date of publication immediately after an author's name in the text. If you refer to a source a second time within a paragraph, you need not repeat the information if the reference is clear. If there is any confusion about which work is being cited, however, supply the clarifying information. If in your entire paper you are citing only one work by a particular author, you need give the date only in the first reference. If the page number for a subsequent reference differs from the earlier page number, supply the number. Separate items within a parenthetical reference by commas.

```
    Dardis's study (1989) examines four twentieth-century
American writers--three of them Nobel Prize winners--who were
alcoholics. Dardis acknowledged (p. 3) that American painters
too include a high percentage of addicted drinkers. Among
poets, he concludes (p. 5) that the percentage is not so high
as among prose writers.
    However, even a casual reading of a recent biography of
poet John Berryman (Mariani, 1990) reveals a creative and
personal life dominated by alcohol. Indeed, "so regular had
[Berryman's] hospital stays [for alcoholism] become . . . that
no one came to visit him anymore" (Mariani, p. 413). Berryman
```

himself had no illusions about the destructive power of
alcohol. About his friend Dylan Thomas he could write, "Dylan
murdered himself w. liquor, tho it took years" (qtd. in
Mariani, p. 274). Robert Lowell and Edna St. Vincent Millay
were also prominent American poets who had problems with
alcohol (Dardis, p. 3).

A work by two authors

To join the names of two authors of a work, use *and* in text but use
the ampersand (&) in a parenthetical reference. Notice how the parenthetical information immediately follows the point to which it applies.

Roebuck and Kessler (1972) summarized the earlier research
(pp. 21-41).

A summary of prior research on the genetic basis of alcoholism
(Roebuck & Kessler, 1972, pp. 21-41) is our starting point.

Two or more works by the same author

If the work of the same author has appeared in different years, distinguish references to each separate work by year of publication. If, however, you refer to two or more works published by the same author(s)
within a single year, you must list the works in alphabetical order by title
in the list of references, and assign each one an order by lowercase letter.
Thus,

(Holden, 1989a)

could represent Caroline Holden's article "Alcohol and Creativity," while

(Holden, 1989b)

would refer to the same author's "Creativity and Craving," published in
the same year.

A work by three to five authors

Use names of all authors in the first reference, but subsequently give
only the first of the names followed by *et al.* Use the *et al.* format for six
or more authors.

Perls, Hefferline, and Goodman (1965) did not focus on the
addictive personality. Like other approaches to the study of
the mind in the '50s and '60s, Gestalt psychology (Perls et
al.) spoke of addiction only in passing.

A work by a corporate author

Give a corporate author's whole name in a parenthetical reference. If the name can be readily abbreviated, supply the abbreviation in brackets in the first reference. Subsequently, use the abbreviation alone.

<u>Al-Anon Faces Alcoholism</u> (Alcoholics Anonymous [AA], 1974) has been reissued many times since its initial publication.

One of the books most widely read by American teenagers (AA, 1974) deals with alcoholism in the family.

Distinguishing two authors with the same last name

Distinguish authors with the same last name by including first and middle initials in each citation.

(J. Williams, 1990)

(C. K. Williams, 1991)

Two or more sources in a single reference

Separate multiple sources in one citation by a semicolon. List authors alphabetically within the parentheses.

We need to view the alcoholic in twentieth-century America from many perspectives (Bendiner, 1962; Dardis, 1989; Waggoner, 1990) in order to understand how people with ordinary lives as well as people with vast creative talent can appear to behave identically.

TEACHING IDEAS

You may want to inform students that some instructors prefer that the more comprehensive list of references be called "Works Consulted." Students should always ask the instructor for the preferred reference form.

2 Preparing a list of references in the APA format

In research papers following the APA system, the list of references (which is alphabetized) is called "References." Within an entry, the date is separated from the other facts of publication. The APA list of references includes only those works referred to in your paper.

Listing books in the APA format

Leave two typed spaces to separate items in an entry. Double-space the list throughout. Start each entry at the left margin; if the entry runs beyond one line, indent subsequent lines three typewriter spaces. The following order of presentation is used:

1. Author's name(s): Put the last name first, followed by a comma. Use first—and middle—initial instead of spelling out a first or middle name.

2. Date: Give the year of publication in parentheses followed by a period. If your list includes more than one title by an author in any one year, distinguish those titles by adding a lowercase letter (a, b, etc.) to the year of publication (as in 1989a and 1989b).

3. Title of the book: Underline the complete book title. Capitalize only the first word in a title or subtitle, in addition to proper names.

4. Publication information: Name the city of publication, followed by a colon. Give the full name of the publisher, but without the "Co." or other business designation.

Dardis, T. (1989). <u>The thirsty muse: Alcohol and the American</u>
    <u>writer</u>. New York: Ticknor & Fields.

A book with two authors
    Invert both names; separate them by a comma. Use the ampersand (&).

Roebuck, J. B., & Kessler, R. G. (1972). <u>The etiology of</u>
    <u>alcoholism: Constitutional, psychological and sociological</u>
    <u>approaches</u>. Springfield, IL: Charles C. Thomas.

A book with three or more authors
    List *all* authors, treating each author's name as in the case of two authors. Use the ampersand before naming the last. (This book was first published in 1951, then reissued without change.)

Perls, R., Hefferline, R. F., & Goodman, P. (1965). <u>Gestalt</u>
    <u>psychology: Excitement and growth in the human</u>
    <u>personality</u>. New York: Delta-Dell. (Originally published
    1951)

A selection from an edited book or anthology
    Underline the title of the book. The selection title is not underlined or enclosed in quotation marks. (In APA style, spell out the name of a university press.)

Davies, P. (1985). Does treatment work? A sociological
    perspective. In N. Heather (Ed.), <u>The misuse of alcohol</u>
    (pp. 158-177). New York: New York University Press.

A corporate author
    Alphabetize the entry in the references list by the first significant word in the name, which is given in normal order.

```
National Center for Alcohol Education. (1978). The community
     health nurse and alcohol-related problems: Instructor's
     curriculum planning guide. Rockville, MD: National
     Institute on Alcohol Abuse and Alcoholism.
```

An edition subsequent to the first

Indicate the edition in parentheses, following the book title.

```
Scrignar, C. B. (1988). Post-traumatic stress disorder:
     Diagnosis, treatment, and legal issues (2nd ed.). New
     Orleans: Bruno.
```

A dissertation

In contrast with MLA style, the title of an unpublished dissertation or thesis is underlined.

```
Reiskin, H. R. (1980). Patterns of alcohol usage in a help-
     seeking university population. Unpublished doctoral
     dissertation, Boston University.
```

If you are referring to the abstract of the dissertation, the style of the entry differs because the abstract itself appears in a volume (volume number underlined).

```
Reiskin, H. R. (1980). Patterns of alcohol usage in a help-
     seeking university population. Dissertation Abstracts
     International, 40, 6447A.
```

Listing periodicals in the APA format

A journal with continuous pagination through the annual volume

The entry for a journal begins with the author's last name and initial(s), inverted, followed by the year of publication in parentheses. The title of the article has neither quotation marks nor underline. Only the first word of the title and subtitle are capitalized, along with proper nouns. The volume number, which follows the underlined title of the journal, is also underlined. Use the abbreviation *p.* or *pp.* when referring to page numbers in a magazine or newspaper. Use no abbreviations when referring to the page numbers of a journal.

```
Kling, W. (1989). Measurement of ethanol consumed in distilled
     spirits. Journal of Studies on Alcohol, 50, 456-460.
```

A journal paginated by issue

In this example, the issue number within volume 51 is given in parentheses. Give all page numbers when the article is not printed continuously.

```
Latessa, E. J., & Goodman, S. (1989). Alcoholic offenders:
     Intensive probation program shows promise. Corrections
     Today, 51(3), 38-39, 45.
```

A monthly magazine

Invert the year and month of a monthly magazine. Write the name of the month in full. (For newspapers and magazines use the abbreviations *p.* and *pp.*)

```
Waggoner, G. (1990, February). Gin as tonic. Esquire, p. 30.
```

A weekly magazine

If the article is signed, begin with the author's name. Otherwise, begin with the article's title. (You would alphabetize the following entry under *d*.)

```
A direct approach to alcoholism. (1988, January 9). Science
     News, p. 25.
```

A daily newspaper

```
Welch, P. (1989, December 31). Kids and booze: It's 10
     o'clock--Do you know how drunk your kids are? Washington
     Post, p. C1.
```

A review or letter to the editor

Treat the title of the review or letter as the title of an article, without quotation. Use brackets to show that the article is a review or letter. If the review is untitled, place the bracketed information immediately after the date.

```
Fraser, K. (1991, May 13). The bottle and inspiration [Review
     of Stones of his house: A biography of Paul Scott]. New
     Yorker, pp. 103-110.
```

Two or more works by the same author in the same year

If you refer to two or more works published by the same author(s) within a single year, list the works in alphabetical order by title in the list of references, and assign each one an order by lowercase letter.

```
Chen, J. S., & Amsel, A. (1980a). Learned persistence at 11-12
     days but not at 10-11 days in infant rats. Developmental
     Psychobiology, 13, 481-492.
Chen, J. S., & Amsel, A. (1980b). Retention under changed-
     reward conditions of persistence learned by infant rats.
     Developmental Psychobiology, 13, 469-480.
```

Listing other sources in the APA format

An abstract of an article
Show where the abstract may be found, at the end of the entry.

Corcoran, K. J., & Carney, M. D. (1989). Alcohol consumption
and looking for alternatives to drinking in college
students. <u>Journal of Cognitive Psychotherapy</u>, <u>3</u>, 69-78.
(From <u>Excerpta Medica</u>, 1989, <u>60</u>, Abstract No. 1322)

A government publication

Senate subcommittee to investigate juvenile delinquency of the
committee on the judiciary. (1978). [Hearing, 95th
Congress, 2nd sess.] <u>Juvenile Alcohol Abuse</u>. Washington,
DC: U.S. Government Printing Office.

A film or videotape
For nonprint media, identify the medium in brackets just after the
title.

Jump, G. (1983). <u>Alcoholism: The pit of despair</u> [Video-
cassette, VHS and Beta]. New York: AIMS Media.

A television or radio program

Erdrich, L., & Dorris, M. (1990, May 27). The broken cord
[Interview]. <u>A world of ideas with Bill Moyers</u> [Television
program]. New York: Public Affairs TV. WNET.

An information service

Weaver, D. (1988). <u>Software for substance abuse education: A
critical review of products</u>. Portland, OR: Northwest
Regional Educational Lab. (ERIC Document Reproduction
Service No. ED 303 702)

Computer software
Begin your reference to a computer program with the name of the
author or other primary contributor, if known.

Cohen, L. S. (1989). <u>Alcohol testing: Self help</u> [Computer
program]. Baltimore, MD: Boxford Enterprises.

36c   Using the footnote style of documentation

The parenthetical reference mode of in-text citation is neat and easy to use. The physical and biological sciences, as well as the social sciences, have used it for decades. In the humanities and some social sciences, as well as in business-related disciplines, some writers prefer to make their citations by means of the note—whether a footnote at the bottom of the page containing the cited material, or an endnote placed at the end of the chapter or of the entire work. Check with your instructor regarding use of notes. He or she may prefer the in-text citation form or may prefer endnotes to footnotes. Some instructors may not require a separate list of references if you use footnotes or endnotes.

In the discussion that follows, basic information for preparing notes is presented. For more detailed information, see the pertinent sections of *The Chicago Manual of Style*, 14th edition, and the *MLA Handbook for Writers of Research Papers*, 3rd edition. To use footnotes or endnotes, signal a citation in the text by a raised numeral (superscript) at the appropriate point, preferably just after a comma or period. Place the citation information that you have signaled in a separate note with matching number. Place a footnote at the bottom of the page; collect endnotes at the end of your paper, just before the list of references.

To type a footnote, leave two double spaces below the text. Single-space the note, but double-space between notes. Indent the start of each note five typewriter spaces. Begin with the superscript numeral, followed immediately by the first word of the note. To continue the note on subsequent lines, return to the left margin, as in this example.

[3]Paul Mariani, <u>Dream Song: The Life of John Berryman</u> (New York: Morrow, 1990) 45-49.

A citation note contains essentially the same information—author, title, publication facts—as an entry in a list of references, but there are differences in order and punctuation between the two. Notice that the note, unlike an entry in a list of references, concludes with a page reference. A note need not tell the span of pages of a source article or essay because that information is provided in the list of references.

There are two key features of the footnote and endnote format: (1) An author's name appears in normal (not inverted) order and is followed by a comma; and (2) publishing information is contained in parentheses and follows the book title with no intervening period.

Here is an index to this section:

1 Making the first and subsequent references in notes

The first time you cite a source in your paper, you will give complete information about it. If you refer to that source again, you need give only the briefest identification. Usually, this is the author's name and a page reference.

In the following sample paragraph, the first note refers to an entire book. The second note cites a particular passage in a review, and refers to that page only. The third note refers to a work already cited in note 2.

Alcohol has played a destructive, painful role in the lives of numerous twentieth-century writers. Among poets, Dylan Thomas is often the first who comes to mind as a victim of alcoholism. John Berryman, too, suffered from this affliction.[1] Among novelists who battled alcohol was the great British writer Paul Scott, author of the masterpiece <u>The Raj Quartet</u>. A reviewer of a new biography of Scott faults the biographer for not understanding fully the effect of alcoholism on Scott and his wife and daughters.[2] Scott's own mother, out of a kind of bravado, encouraged Paul to drink gin at the age of six.[3]

[1]Paul Mariani, <u>Dream Song: The Life of John Berryman</u> (New York: Morrow, 1990).

[2]Kennedy Fraser, rev. of <u>Stones of His House: A Life of Paul Scott</u>, by Hilary Spurling. <u>New Yorker</u> 13 May 1991: 110.

[3]Fraser 108.

Compare the format of these footnotes with their corresponding entries in the "Works Cited" list.

Fraser, Kennedy. Rev. of <u>Stones of His House: A Biography of</u>
   <u>Paul Scott</u>, by Hilary Spurling. <u>New Yorker</u> 13 May 1991:
   103-110.

Mariani, Paul. <u>Dream Song: The Life of John Berryman</u>. New
   York: Morrow, 1990.

2   Following the note style in citing books

A book with two or three authors

[1]Julian B. Roebuck and Raymond G. Kessler, <u>The Etiology of</u>
<u>Alcoholism: Constitutional, Psychological and Sociological</u>
<u>Approaches</u> (Springfield, IL: Thomas, 1972) 72.

A book with four or more authors
      Name each author, or use the *et al.* format.

[2]Norman Stein et al., <u>Family Therapy: A Systems Approach</u>
(Boston: Allyn, 1990) 312.

A corporate author

[3]National Center for Alcohol Education, <u>The Community</u>
<u>Health Nurse and Alcohol-Related Problems: Instructor's</u>
<u>Curriculum Planning Guide</u> (Rockville: National Institute on
Alcohol Abuse and Alcoholism, 1978) 45-49.

A multivolume work

[4]G. M. Trevelyan, <u>Illustrated English Social History</u>, vol.
3 (Harmondsworth: Pelican-Penguin, 1964) 46.

Two sources cited in one note

[5]Joy Williams, <u>Escapes</u> (New York: Vintage, 1990) 57-62; C.
K. Williams, <u>The Bacchae of Euripides: A New Version</u> (New
York: Farrar, 1990) 15.

An edition subsequent to the first

[6]C. B. Scrignar, <u>Post-Traumatic Stress Disorder: Diagnosis,</u>
<u>Treatment, and Legal Issues</u>, 2nd ed. (New Orleans: Bruno,
1988) 23-28.

A selection in an edited book or anthology

[7]Emil Bendiner, "The Bowery Man on the Couch," <u>Man Alone:</u>
<u>Alienation in Modern Society</u>, ed. Eric Josephson and Mary
Josephson (New York: Dell, 1962) 408.

An introduction, preface, foreword, or afterword

[8]Erich Fromm, foreword, <u>Summerhill: A Radical Approach to Child Rearing</u>, by A. S. Neill (New York: Hart, 1960) xii.

Following the note style in citing periodicals and other sources

A journal with continuous pagination through the annual volume

[9]William Kling, "Measurement of Ethanol Consumed in Distilled Spirits," <u>Journal of Studies on Alcohol</u> 50 (1989): 456.

A monthly magazine

[10]Glen Waggoner, "Gin as Tonic," <u>Esquire</u> Feb. 1990: 30.

A weekly magazine

[11]"A Direct Approach to Alcoholism," <u>Science News</u> 9 Jan. 1988: 25.

A daily newspaper

[12]"Alcohol Can Worsen Ills of Aging, Study Says," <u>New York Times</u> 13 June 1989, late ed.: C5.

A dissertation abstract

[13]Helen R. Reiskin, "Pattern of Alcohol Usage in a Help-Seeking University Population," <u>DAI</u> 41 (1983): 6447A (U of Vermont).

Computer software

[14]<u>Alcohol and Pregnancy: Protecting the Unborn Child</u>, computer software, Student Awareness Software, 1988.

A government document

[15]United States Senate, Subcommittee to Investigate Juvenile Delinquency of the Committee on the Judiciary, <u>Juvenile Alcohol Abuse: Hearing</u>. 95th Cong., 2nd sess. (Washington: GPO, 1978) 3.

36d Using the CBE systems of documentation

The Council of Biology Editors (CBE) systems of documentation are standard for the biological sciences and, with minor or minimal adaptations, are also used in many of the other sciences. You will find many similarities between the CBE styles of documentation and the APA style, which was derived from the conventions used in scientific writing. As in APA and MLA styles, any in-text references to a source are provided in shortened form in parentheses. For complete bibliographic information, readers expect to consult the list of references at the end of the document. Following is an index to this section on the CBE systems for documentation.

1 Making in-text citations in the CBE formats

The CBE Style Manual presents three formats for citing a source in the text of an article. Your choice of format will depend on the discipline in which you are writing. Whatever format you choose, remain consistent within any one document.

The name-and-year system

The CBE convention that most closely resembles the APA conventions is the name-and-year system. In this system a writer provides in parentheses the name of an author and the year in which that author's work was published. Note that, in contrast to the APA system, no comma appears between the author's name and the year of publication.

```
Slicing and aeration of quiescent storage tissues induces a
rapid metabolic activation and a development of the membrane
systems in the wounded tissue (Kahl 1974).
```

If an author's name is mentioned in a sentence, then only the year of publication is set in parentheses.

```
Jacobsen et al. found that a marked transition in respiratory
substrate occurs in sliced potato tissue that exhibits the
phenomenon of wound respiration (1974).
```

If your paper cites two or more works published by the same author in the same year, assign a letter designation (a, b, etc.) to inform the reader of precisely which piece you have cited. This form of citation applies both to journal articles and to books.

```
Chen and Amsel (1980a) obtained intermittent reinforcement
effects in rats as young as eleven days of age. Under the same
conditions, they observed that the effects of intermittent
reinforcement on perseverance are long lived (Chen and Amsel
1980b).
```

When citing a work by an organization or government agency with no author named, use the corporate or organizational name in place of a reference to an individual author. Provide the year of publication following the name as indicated previously.

```
Style guides in the sciences caution that the "use of nouns
formed from verbs and ending in -tion produces unnecessarily
long sentences and dull prose (CBE Style Manual Committee
1983).
```

The number systems

The briefest form of parenthetical citation is the number system, a convention in which only an Arabic numeral appears in parentheses to identify a source of information. There are two variations on the number system. With references *in order of first mention*, you assign a reference number to a source in the order of its appearance in your paper. With references *in alphabetized order*, you assign each source a reference number that identifies it in the alphabetized list of references at the end of the paper.

Citation for a reference list in order of first mention

According to Kahl et al., slicing and aeration of quiescent
storage tissues induces a rapid metabolic activation and a
development of the membrane systems in the wounded tissue (1).
Jacobsen et al. found that a marked transition in respiratory
substrate occurs in sliced potato tissue that exhibits the
phenomenon of wound respiration (2).

Citation for a reference list in alphabetized order

According to Kahl et al., slicing and aeration of quiescent
storage tissues induces a rapid metabolic activation and a
development of the membrane systems in the wounded tissue (2).
Jacobson et al. found that a marked transition in respiratory
substrate occurs in sliced potato tissue that exhibits the
phenomenon of wound respiration (1).

These numbered text citations are linked to corresponding entries in a list
of references. The reference list may be numbered either in the order of
first mention or alphabetically.

2   Preparing a list of references using CBE systems

In the sciences the list of references appearing at the end of the
paper is often called "Literature Cited." If you adopt the name-and-year
system for in-text citation (see 36d-1), the entries in your list of references
are alphabetized, much as with the APA system, rather than numbered.
Like the list of references in the APA system, the "Literature Cited" list is
double-spaced; each entry starts at the left margin and the second or subsequent lines are indented three typewriter spaces.

If you adopt one of the numbered systems for in-text citation (see
36d-1), you will either number entries alphabetically or in order of appearance in the paper. A numbered entry, beginning with the numeral,
starts at the left margin. Place a period after the number, skip two spaces,
and list the author's last name followed by the rest of the entry. For the
spacing of the second or subsequent lines of a numbered entry, there are
two conventions: either align the second line directly beneath the first letter of the author's last name, or indent the second and subsequent lines
five spaces from the left margin. Select a convention depending on the
preference of your professor. For style guides in the specific sciences, see
39e. The following are some of the basic formats for listing sources in the
CBE systems.

Listing books in the CBE format

In preparing a list of references in the CBE format, leave two typed spaces between each item in an entry. Sequence the items in an entry as follows:

- Number: Assign a number to the entry if you are following a numbered system.
- Author's name: Put the last name first, followed by a comma and the initials of the first and middle names.
- Title of the book: Do not use underlining or italics. Capitalize the first letter of the first word only. End the title with a period. If the work is a revised edition, abbreviate the edition as 2d, 3d, 4th, etc.
- Publication information: Name the city of publication (and state, if needed to clarify). Place a colon and give the full name of the publisher. Place a semicolon, and give the year of publication followed by a period.

If you refer to more than one work published by the same author(s) in the same year, list the works in alphabetical order by title in the list of references, and assign each one a lowercase letter according to its order.

Books by individual or multiple authors

For a book with one author follow the conventions immediately above. For a book with multiple authors, place a semicolon after each coauthor.

1. Beevers, H. Respiratory metabolism in plants. Evanston, IL: Row, Peterson and Company; 1961.

2. Goodwin, T. W.; Mercer, E. I. Introduction to plant biochemistry. Elmsford, NY: Pergamon Press; 1972.

Books by corporate authors

3. CBE Style Manual Committee. CBE style manual. 5th ed. Bethesda, MD: Council of Biology Editors; 1983.

Books by compilers or editors

4. Smith, K. C., editor. Light and plant development. New York: Plenum Press; 1977.

Dissertation or thesis

5. Reiskin, H. R. Patterns of alcohol usage in a help-seeking university population. Boston: Boston Univ.; 1980. Dissertation.

Listing periodicals in the CBE format

Leave two typed spaces between each item in an entry. Sequence the items as follows:

- Number: Assign a number to the entry if you are using a numbered system.
- Author's name: Put the last name, followed by a comma and the initials of the first and middle names. If there are multiple authors, see the convention for books above.
- Title of the article: Do not use underlining or quotation marks. Capitalize the first letter of the first word only.
- Journal name: Abbreviate the name, unless it is a single word, without underlining. For example, The Journal of Molecular Evolution would be abbreviated as J. Mol. Evol.
- Publication information: Put the volume number, followed by a colon, followed by page numbers (use no abbreviations), followed by a semicolon and the year of publication.

Articles by individual and multiple authors

6. Kling, W. Measurement of ethanol consumed in distilled spirits. J. Stud. Alcohol. 50:456-460; 1989.

7. Coleman, R. A.; Pratt, L. H. Phytochrome: immunological assay of synthesis and destruction in plants. Planta 119:221-231; 1974.

Newspaper articles

8. Welch, P. Kids and booze: it's 10 o'clock--do you know how drunk your kids are? Washington Post. 1989 Dec. 21:C1.

Listing other references in the CBE format

Media materials

9. Jump, G. Alcoholism: the pit of despair [Videocassette]. New York: AIMS Media; 1983. VHS; Beta.

Electronic materials

10. Alcohol and pregnancy: protecting the unborn child [Computer program]. New York: Student Awareness Software; 1988.

CHAPTER 37

Writing and Reading in the Humanities

KEY FEATURES

The first of three chapters on academic writing and reading in the disciplines, this chapter establishes the pattern for the subsequent chapters. It approaches the humanities from the perspective of modes of inquiry, arguing that literature, history, and philosophy are united more by questions than by answers. Humanities are "text-centered" and "reactive" in that they explore questions by analyzing, interpreting, and evaluating sources. The chapter is divided into five major sections: writing, reading, types of assignments, responding to literature, and research papers. Writing in the humanities is addressed in terms of the purposes for writing and the methods of argument employed; in the first section a single text is analyzed for different purposes by a literary critic, a philosopher, and an historian. Reading is covered by considering the nature of sources (primary and secondary). The third section discusses various writing assignments students can expect to receive in these disciplines. Relying heavily on chapter 2 (Critical Thinking and Writing) for its methodology, clear guidelines for writing analyses are presented. Section four guides the student through the process of responding to and writing about literature. Section five reproduces a heavily annotated sample research paper, a literary analysis of James Joyce's "Counterparts." The paper, consistent with the other samples in this part and Part IX (The Research Paper), deals with the general subject of drugs and alcohol. The chapter ends with a comprehensive list of reference materials in the humanities.

The *humanities*—traditionally considered as the disciplines of literature, history, and philosophy—address many puzzles of life and human nature, frequently by posing "large," difficult questions to which there are seldom definite answers. Those who study the humanities ask in distinctive ways such questions as these: Who are we? What are our responsibilities to ourselves? To others? What is a *good* life? How do we know what we know? Difficult questions like these lend themselves to difficult and varied answers, and answers in the humanities change from one culture to the next and from one generation to the next. Even within generations and cultures, answers vary: Ask two philosophers *how do we know what we know?* and you will likely get different responses. The same would hold if you approached two historians about the causes of the Civil War or two critics about the literary merit of Kate Chopin's novel *The Awakening*. Indeed, historians, philosophers, and literary critics may fiercely debate among themselves exactly which "large" questions should be asked and how one should go about investigating them.

Still, whatever their specific character, the large questions remain. Philosophers from Plato in ancient times to Richard Rorty today have continued to ask what it means to be an educated human. Two thousand years ago Homer's *Odyssey* told of a Mediterranean hero's search for identity and fulfillment, while James Joyce set his *Ulysses* on the same theme in modern-day Dublin. Thucydides in ancient Greece and Barbara Tuchman today have asked the historian's questions of how we as humans can interpret the events of the past. Such quests for meaning require readers and writers to judge evidence, to develop responsible opinions, to interpret events, and above all to appreciate the value of multiple perspectives.

Students of humanities are concerned with discovering or recreating relationships among (1) the world as it has been observed by or commented on by someone; (2) a *text* that somehow reflects the facts about or the observer's impressions of that world; and (3) an audience—a reader, listener, or viewer. Texts provide the occasion to learn how others have investigated the large questions and to investigate these questions ourselves. A text could be a novel, a philosophical treatise, a letter, a film, a symphony, a song, a poem, a sculpture, or a painting—any creation that records one person's response to or accounting of what is seen and that, later, can be read, viewed, or listened to by someone else.

In this formulation, history is the discipline in which readers question texts to learn what is revealed about a past event and what about that event might be pertinent to the present. Philosophy is the discipline in which readers study the articles and books (the *texts*) of those who, with rigorous and careful reasoning, have reflected on ideas important to understanding human nature. Literature is the discipline in which readers read a work of drama, poetry, or fiction to gain entry into an imaginative world and to learn how this text and its world is constructed, how it might reflect circumstances of the author's experience, and how it might comment on and force questions about the *reader's* experience. For the historian, philosopher, and student of literature, texts are the point of entry into the three-way relationship of text, creator/author, and audience. For a student in the humanities there is always the relationship; there is always the implicit understanding that texts are important and that as we read, view, listen to, and write about them, we create meaning ourselves. In the humanities, we *create* new texts as we study older ones. We carry on a tradition of raising and investigating difficult questions and, through our efforts, seek to grow more aware of who we are and what we have done (Frankel 8–9).*

37a   Writing in the humanities

1   Expressing and informing in the humanities

Students in the humanities write for many purposes, two of which are to inform and to express. Expressive writing, often beginning as a personal response to an individual text, discusses questions like these: What do I feel when reading this material? Why do I feel this way? How am I changed in response to this text? How can I account for differences I have observed between this text and others, or between this text and my own experience? Readers may find themselves so involved with a text that they want to respond in writing. You might consider keeping a reading journal in which you record responses to texts and, based on your entries, develop ideas for papers. Much of what is best about writing in the humanities begins as a personal response.

All writing in literature, history, and philosophy courses is, at least in part, informative. Working as an historian, you may need to sift

* In-text citations in this chapter refer to the Works Cited list at the end of the book.

ADDITIONAL EXERCISE A

Interview a professor of history, literature, or philosophy on the subject of the writing he or she does in the profession. Pose questions such as the following: What kinds of text do you study? What kinds of questions do you ask about texts? What forms does your writing usually take? What is your purpose in writing in these forms? What kind of audience do you usually address? Try to think of some additional questions as well. Use your notes from the interview to write a paragraph describing the nature of writing in this particular discipline.

LOOKING BACK

Students may want to review patterns of development in chapter 3 as they study this material. It's important that they recognize how the patterns of development cross disciplinary lines.

REFERENCES

BARTHOLOMAE, DAVID. "Inventing the University." In *When a Writer Can't Write*. Ed. Mike Rose. New York: Guilford, 1985: 134–65. Essential to being a college student is the mastering of discipline-specific discourses, but such achievement is the result of a gradual process with multiple stages.

RUSSELL, DAVID R. "Writing Across the Curriculum in Historical Perspective: Toward a Social Interpretation." *CE* 52 (1990): 52–73. Looks at WAC in its historical, social context, arguing that such a perspective will provide new ways of "integrating students, instead of excluding them."

YOUNG, ART, and TOBY FULWILER, eds. *Writing Across the Disciplines: Research into Practice.* Upper Montclair, NJ: Boynton, 1986. Collection of essays discussing a writing-across-the-curriculum program, including essays on writing in the humanities.

MCLEOD, SUSAN D. "Writing Across the Curriculum: The Second Stage, and Beyond." *CCC* 40 (1989): 337–43. Overview of the changes in WAC that argues for continued reform in thinking, learning, and writing across the disciplines.

BEYER, BARRY K. "Using Writing to Learn in History." *The History Teacher* 13 (1980): 167–78. Writing may be used not only as an aid to students seeking information, but also as a method for their developing "historical-mindedness."

MARTIN, BRUCE K. "Teaching Literature as Experience." *CE* 51 (1989): 377–85. While it may be disturbing, recent renunciations of the formalist tendency to find single, determinate meanings of literary texts may actually liberate teachers who wish to discuss literature openly with their students.

through documents in order to establish a *sequence* to events on which to base a narrative—perhaps the story of how your grandparents came to this country. As a student of literature, you may *compare* and *contrast* works of the same author, responding to assignments such as this: *Choose two of Hawthorne's short stories and discuss his treatment of the origins and consequences of sin.* In a philosophy course, you might be asked to *classify* discussions on a topic, such as education, according to the types of argument authors are making. In informing readers, you will often *define* and illustrate a term by referring to specific passages in a text.

2   Making arguments

Frequently in the humanities, you will use informative writing to make arguments. The purpose of making arguments in literature, history, and philosophy is to *interpret* texts and to *defend* interpretations as reasonable.[1] No one will expect your arguments to end all discussion of a question, but as in any discipline, your arguments should be compelling and well supported. The purpose of reading stories, of retelling the past, or of puzzling through large questions is not to arrive at agreement (as in the sciences), but to deepen individual perception and to realize that we are part of a larger human community. The goal of an argument in the humanities is reached when readers can make this or a similar acknowledgment: "I understand your point of view, and I find it reasonable." You should therefore not expect to read—or write—a single, correct interpretation of a play. History professors will urge you to reject single, apparently definitive versions of the past. Philosophy professors will urge you to reject the notion that any one answer to the question *What is a good life?* could satisfy all people.

Consensus is not the goal of arguments in the humanities. But this is not to say that all arguments are equally valid. Arguments must be supported and well reasoned. They can be plainly wrong and they can be irresponsible, as when someone insists: "Since discussions in this course are based on personal opinions, my opinion is as good as anyone else's." Not true. One interpretation, argued well, can be clearly superior to and more compelling than another. In each of the humanities this is so, notwithstanding the fact that students of literature, history, and philosophy pose different questions and examine texts using different methods. As a student of literature, you might investigate living conditions during the Great Depression by reading novels like *The Grapes of Wrath*. In a history class, you might work with oral accounts such as the one compiled by

---

[1] This discussion is based directly on the work of Stephen Toulmin, Richard Rieke, and Allan Janik in *Introduction to Reasoning* (New York: Macmillan, 1979). See chapter 12, their "Introduction" to fields of argument, 195–202; and chapter 15, "Arguing about the Arts," 265–82. For a related discussion, see Richard D. Rieke and Malcolm O. Sillars, *Argumentation and the Decision Making Process*, 2nd ed. (Glenview: Scott, 1984).

Studs Terkel in *Hard Times: An Oral History of the Great Depression.* In a philosophy course, you might read and debate discussions of a society's obligations to its poor. You would in every case be arguing for an interpretation, and in every case your argument would be more or less convincing, in light of the conventions for arguing in that discipline. You can help yourself focus on the purpose of argumentation in your humanities classes by posing these questions:

- What sorts of questions will I investigate in this course?
- How do the texts I study help to focus my attention on these questions?
- How do students in this discipline make claims about a text? How do they support these claims?

Claims and evidence

In making a *claim* in the humanities, a writer usually interprets a text. That is, the writer attempts to explain how the text is meaningful—how, for instance, a poem's images direct the reader's attention to certain themes, how an essay confirms or contradicts our understanding of a particular problem, how the content of a letter or diary suggests a revised understanding of some historical event. One much-relied-on process for making and supporting claims in the humanities goes something like this: During the process of reading, you begin to see a pattern emerge—you notice certain details and forge a link between them. (See the discussion of "thesis" at 3d and of "argumentative thesis" at 6b.) At first the pattern may not be well defined; but as you read and reread, the pattern becomes increasingly clear until you can express it as a formal claim. Your claim becomes the basis of an argument that says, in effect: Here is one way in which this text is meaningful. You then provide *evidence* for your claim by pointing readers to the same passages in the text that helped you to detect a pattern, explaining why these passages are significant and how they confirm the reasonableness of your claim. The process of claim and support, then, looks like this:

1. Read a text and discover in it certain patterns that help to make the text meaningful (see 37d for hints on detecting patterns in literary works).
2. Reread and confirm that the pattern exists, and then make a claim: a formal statement in which you interpret some element of the text, its relationship to the reader, or its relationship to the writer and the times in which it was written.
3. Refer to the text as evidence for your claim.
4. Comment on or discuss these references (optional).

Consider the following examples of how claims are made and supported in major areas of the humanities.

A literary study. In a paragraph from an essay entitled "The Greatness of *Huckleberry Finn*," the literary critic Lionel Trilling claims that

LOOKING BACK

All of the chapters in this part of the handbook rely heavily on ideas discussed in chapter 6 (Writing and Evaluating Arguments), especially the material on modes of inquiry in various disciplines. If you haven't yet covered chapter 6 in class, it would be useful to do so now. Otherwise, students should review the chapter on their own in order to make better use of the information in this part of the handbook.

Huck Finn is a character who sympathizes with the misfortunes of others. As you read the paragraph, you will be watching Trilling make his claim *after* he had discovered it for himself. Trilling is persuasive, and you might find yourself thinking "This isn't an interpretation; it's a fact." But Trilling *is* interpreting the novel, and he is trying to convince you that his interpretation is both accurate and useful:

> [Huckleberry Finn's] sympathy is quick and immediate. When the circus audience laughs at the supposedly drunken man who tries to ride the horse, Huck is only miserable: "It wasn't funny to me . . . ; I was all of a tremble to see his danger." When he imprisons the intending murderers on the wrecked steamboat, his first thought is of how to get someone to rescue them, for he considers "how dreadful it was, even for murderers, to be in such a fix. I says to myself, there ain't no telling but I might come to be a murderer myself yet, and then how would I like it?" But his sympathy is never sentimental. When at last he knows that the murderers are beyond help, he has no inclination to false pathos. "I felt a little bit heavy-hearted about the gang, but not much, for I reckoned that if they could stand it I could." His will is genuinely good and therefore he has no need to torture himself with guilty second thoughts.

Notice that Trilling makes two related claims in this paragraph: first, that Huck's "sympathy is quick and immediate," and second, that this "sympathy is never sentimental." He refers the reader to specific passages that support his claims and, after a final quoted passage, makes a comment: "His [Huck's] will is genuinely good and therefore he has no need to torture himself with guilty second thoughts." With this comment, Trilling cements the relationship between the claims he has made and the evidence he has offered. He has made an *argument.* Be assured that Trilling's awareness of Huck's sympathies did not always exist. There must have been some point before which Trilling simply did not think about Huck's "quick and immediate" sympathy. We can assume that Trilling has read the novel many times; we can imagine that on one rereading he began to see a pattern emerging in various passages. We can further imagine that on noticing this pattern, Trilling was able to confirm and refine it by *re*reading various passages. At this point, he was prepared to write: to convert the pattern he had detected (then confirmed) into a claim, which he then used as the basis for an argument.

In one brief paragraph, Lionel Trilling demonstrates the cycle of claim, reference, and comment that is basic to writing about literature. *To make a claim about literature, first find a pattern of meaning in a text. Confirm and refine that pattern and then make a claim. To support this claim, return to the text and discuss specific passages.* An analysis of a literary text is built by linking many such cycles according to an overall plan or thesis. (See 37d for more on writing about literature.)

An historical study. The historian Joanna Stratton supports a claim in the following passage by referring to a source (information from a letter or journal) but does not comment on the source in the same way Trilling does for a literary text. In her book on pioneer women of the American Frontier, Stratton worked with interviews, letters, and journals that her great-grandmother had collected in the 1920s.

> For the most part, the cavelike dugout provided cramped and primitive quarters for the pioneering family. Damp and dark year round, it was practically impossible to keep clean, for dirt from the roof and the walls sifted onto everything. Although its thick earthen walls did afford warm insulation from the cold and strong protection from the wind, in rain the dugout became practically uninhabitable.
> "Father made a dugout and covered it with willows and grass," wrote one settler, "and when it rained, the water came through the roof and ran in the door. After the storms, we carried the water out with buckets, then waded around in the mud until it dried up. Then to keep us nerved up, sometimes the bull snakes would get in the roof and now and then one would lose his hold and fall down on the bed, then off on the floor. Mother would grab the hoe and there was something doing and after the fight was over Mr. Bull Snake was dragged outside. Of course there had to be something to keep us from getting discouraged."
>
> JOANNA L. STRATTON, *Pioneer Women*

Often in an historical account the writer wants to maintain focus on the narrative or story, and so withholds immediate comment on a source quotation except in footnotes or in specialized analysis. *To make a claim in history, writers make interpretations of available records from the past and try to reconstruct them into a meaningful pattern.*

Sometimes the presentation of a claim in historical writing may seem not to be an interpretation at all:

> [I]n the rain the dugout became practically uninhabitable.

This claim reads as a fact, but actually it is a generalization Joanna Stratton has reached based on available evidence, one example of which she provides with a supporting quotation. Other historians examining the same or different evidence might reach a different conclusion. The importance of an historian's interpretations becomes obvious when you read the conflicting accounts of the events immediately before and after Lincoln's assassination. If these conflicting accounts were based on eyewitness testimony, you would realize that historians must interpret evidence as well as gather it. While Lincoln *was* shot at Ford's Theatre on April 14, 1865, the precise circumstances of and reason for the shooting are subject to historical debate—or interpretation.

A philosophical study. The philosopher Ludwig Wittgenstein makes a claim in the following passage without reference to any written text, but rather to the meaning that is attached to a word and to the patterns of human activity that can be observed in connection with that word. In the process, Wittgenstein himself created a philosophical text, one that later became the subject of interpretation and claim by other philosophers. In

TEACHING IDEAS

Students may understand the nature of historical interpretation more clearly if you remind them of the various interpretations of the circumstances surrounding John F. Kennedy's assassination. Popular speculation aside, for over thirty years historians have been arguing about the event, interpreting the medical record, the movements of relevant individuals, the accounts of eyewitnesses, and the historical record of possibly related events.

this passage, Wittgenstein examines the difficulty of defining the word "game." He does so in the larger context of discussing the complexities of defining "language." Just as "family resemblances" describes the relationship between various games, so too does this term describe what is common to various languages—that is, there is no single feature but rather an array of features.

> Consider for example the proceedings that we call "games". I mean board-games, card-games, ball-games, Olympic games, and so on. What is common to them all?—Don't say: "There *must* be something common, or they would not be called 'games' "—but *look and see* whether there is anything common to all.—For if you look at them you will not see something that is common to *all*, but similarities, relationships, and a whole series of them at that. To repeat: don't think, but look!—Look for example at board-games, with their multifarious relationships. Now pass to card-games; here you find many correspondences with the first group, but many common features drop out, and others appear. When we pass next to ball-games, much that is common is retained, but much is lost.—Are they all "amusing"? Compare chess with noughts and crosses. Or is there always winning and losing, or competition between players? Think of patience. In ball games there is winning and losing; but when a child throws his ball at the wall and catches it again, this feature has disappeared. Look at the parts played by skill and luck; and at the difference between skill in chess and skill in tennis. Think now of games like ring-a-ring-a-roses; here is the element of amusement, but how many other characteristic features have disappeared! And we can go through the many, many other groups of games in the same way; can see how similarities crop up and disappear.
>
> And the result of this examination is: we see a complicated network of similarities overlapping and criss-crossing: sometimes overall similarities, sometimes similarities of detail.
>
> I can think of no better expression to characterize these similarities than "family resemblances"; for the various resemblances between members of a family: build, features, colour of eyes, gait, temperament, etc. etc. overlap and criss-cross in the same way.—And I shall say: 'games' form a family.

—LUDWIG WITTGENSTEIN, *Philosophical Investigations*

This passage has generated enormous discussion on the meaning and significance of "family resemblances." For example, some might argue that "amusement" is common to all games and might proceed to define that concept. As a student of philosophy, you will sometimes generate your own evidence for arguments; but more often, you will refer to and build on the work of the philosophers you are studying. Learning to make claims in philosophy can be especially demanding for those with little experience in the discipline. In literature and history, sources and what one writes about them are connected in concrete ways to a story, imagined or actually lived. Philosophy has no elements of story as such. *To support a claim in philosophy, you will focus on ideas and their relation to other ideas.* (Wittgenstein discusses specific games in order to develop his idea of "family resemblance.") Arguments, consequently, can become quite abstract.

The three examples of claims made by Trilling, Stratton, and Wittgenstein do not begin to represent the variety of claims you will encounter in your study of literature, history, and philosophy. These examples are meant to suggest that variety; they suggest, as well, a common concern in the humanities: interpretation. As you read and study in your courses, try to identify the specific types of claims that are made and the methods of evidence used to support them. To aid this process, pose these questions: What sorts of claims (interpretations) do people make in this subject? In what ways do writers use sources (books, films, works of art, or pieces of music) to support their claims?

37b Reading in the humanities

When you read a poem, a story, a letter, or an autobiography, you are working with a **primary source**. Of the preceding examples, only the one by Wittgenstein is a primary source. The writings of Trilling and Stratton are examples of **secondary sources,** the work of scholars who themselves have interpreted particular poems, stories, or letters. If you were writing a paper on *Huckleberry Finn,* you might refer to Trilling's interpretations. In doing so, you would need to read with care in order to understand and evaluate his ideas and to distinguish them from your own. In deciding whether to cite Trilling in your paper, you might ask: What point is he making? How well does he make it? Is his observation well grounded in the text that he quotes? On what basis do I agree or disagree with him?

A given source or text in the humanities can be studied from several perspectives within a discipline or across disciplines. Some writers look at a work as a whole, in a broad context of events or ideas surrounding it; others look closely at individual parts of the source, analyzing it independently of its original surroundings. For example, consider how differently Benjamin Franklin's *Autobiography* is studied in the following examples: as a literary expression, as political philosophy, or as an historical event.

Literary critic Joseph Fichtelberg (Fordham University) sees in the *Autobiography* a conscious effort by Franklin to sift through his life's work and beliefs in order to present himself as an "exemplar" to the world, a model of American virtue. The following constitutes one segment of Fichtelberg's argument, which appeared in the journal *Early American Literature.* Numbers in parentheses are page references to sources noted below:

> That the correspondent—the reader—is crucial to Franklin's self-conception is evident throughout the *Autobiography.* Part One, readers have often noted, appears to be a fatherly homily to an ambitious young man. "Now imagining it may be equally agreable to you to know the

LOOKING BACK

Students may want to review chapter 1 (Critical Thinking and Reading) for a general discussion of the subject before reading this section.

TEACHING IDEAS

Since the distinction between primary and secondary sources is an important one, you may want to call students' attention to it here. If they are to make legitimate observations and interpretations of primary sources, then they must spend some time analyzing those sources themselves in addition to evaluating the secondary sources.

REFERENCES

HOLMAN, C. HUGH, and WILLIAM HARMON. *A HANDBOOK TO LITERATURE.* 5th ed. New York: Macmillan, 1986. Complements any classroom discussion of literary criticism, terms, and genres, and offers students accessible discussions concerning the difficulties of approaching literature.

SWOPE, JOHN W., and EDGAR H. THOMPSON. "Three R's for Critical Thinking about Literature: Reading, 'Riting, and Responding." *Activities to Promote Critical Thinking: Classroom Practices in Teaching English.* Urbana: NCTE, 1986. 75–79. ED 2273 985. Presents assignments that offer alternatives to teaching literature in a lecture format.

COMMEYRAS, MICHELLE. "Using Literature to Teach Critical Thinking." *Journal of Reading* 32 (1989): 703–7. Studying literature advances critical thinking skills (emphasis is on younger students).

DRAGGA, SAM. "Collaborative Interpretation." *Activities to Promote Critical Thinking: Classroom Practices in Teaching English.* Urbana: NCTE, 1986. 84–87. ED 273 985. Offers a method for creating a student-centered literature classroom based on collaborative learning as an alternative to the traditional teacher-led class.

BOOTH, WAYNE C. *The Rhetoric of Fiction.* 2nd ed. Chicago: U of Chicago P, 1983. Study of narration that is indispensable to students of literature.

(continued)

CHAMBERLAIN, LORI. "Bombs and Other Exciting Devices, or the Problem of Teaching Irony." *CE* 51 (1989): 29–40. Teachers need to emphasize the importance of irony as a device and to encourage its use in student writing, because it establishes a political relationship between writer and reader.

Circumstances of *my* Life," Franklin begins, alluding to his spectacular success, "I sit down to write them for you" (I). But as Governor of New Jersey in 1771, William Franklin was successful in his own right, hardly in need of counsel, and, at forty-four, hardly a young man. Rather, Franklin seems to be writing for the "Posterity" he addresses several lines later, indeed, for all American readers, who may find his narrative "suitable to their own Situations, & therefore fit to be imitated" (I). Hence his character, as Mitchell Breitwieser notes, would "liv[e] on in the person of the emulating reader, and . . . gai[n] a wider circulation than it otherwise would have" (265, 270). As he announces his intention to recount the "conducing Means"—the process—by which he achieves eminence, so Franklin's prose emphasizes the reader's own immersion in that process. The fourth sentence in this introductory paragraph (a revision, incidentally, of an earlier draft) is resonantly ungrammatical:

> Having emerg'd from the Poverty & Obscurity in which I was born & bred, to a State of Affluence & some Degree of Reputation in the World, and having gone so far thro' Life with a considerable Share of Felicity, the conducing Means I made Use of, which with the Blessing of God, so well succeeded, my Posterity may like to know, as they may find some of them suitable to their own Situations, & therefore fit to be imitated. (I)

As Tatham notes, the two dangling participial phrases[2] shift the emphasis from the grammatical subject to "my Posterity," as if "future Americans in general" had taken Franklin's course to affluence and were now eager to understand the "Means," the particular process of their ascent (228).

WORKS CITED [BY FICHTELBERG]

Breitweiser, Mitchell. *Cotton Mather and Benjamin Franklin: The Price of Representative Personality.* Cambridge: Cambridge UP, 1984.

Franklin, Benjamin. *The Autobiography of Benjamin Franklin: A Genetic Text.* Ed. J. A. Leo Lemay and P. M. Zall. Knoxville: U of Tennessee P, 1981.

Tatham, Campbell. "Benjamin Franklin, Cotton Mather, and the Outward State." *Early American Literature* 6 (Winter 1971–72): 223–33.

This analysis focuses on Franklin's *Autobiography* as a work of literature. Joseph Fichtelberg is interested in the relationship between Franklin and the readers he presumably had in mind when composing the *Autobiography*. Fichtelberg begins with a claim: The reader is crucial to the way Franklin thinks of and presents himself in the *Autobiography*. As evidence for this claim, Fichtelberg quotes from the obvious *primary* source, and he refers to *secondary* sources, the work of two literary critics

---

[2] Fichtelberg assumes readers will follow the reference here to the following phrases: "Having emerg'd . . . in the World, and having gone so far . . . so well succeeded." The obvious grammatical subject of these phrases is "I"—Franklin is the one who emerged from poverty and who went through life with such success. In the *Autobiography,* however, Franklin dangles these phrases (see 15h) and places "my Posterity" where the grammatical subject, "I," should occur. Both Fichtelberg and the writer he cites (Tatham) find this significant.

also interested in Franklin. These references, it should be added, place Fichtelberg's own investigation in a tradition of literary criticism. Writers in *every* discipline similarly refer to the work of others in that discipline to benefit from previous research and to become members of a scholarly community. What identifies Fichtelberg's writing as specifically *literary* criticism is not only his references to secondary sources who are themselves literary critics but also his method of arguing: He relies on a cycle of claim and text-based support that is common to literary studies (see 37a-2). Most important, Fichtelberg assumes that the *Autobiography* is a work of literature: He wants to investigate the role that readers played in the creation of a text.

Philosopher Ralph Ketchem approaches the *Autobiography* with an entirely different set of concerns. He sees in Franklin's work an expression of the author's philosophy on the power of individual initiative in politics:

> As a public philosopher, Franklin assumed that the traditional personal values have political relevance. He shared the Aristotelian belief that government exists for the sake of the good life and that its powers can be used to that end. A good citizen, guided by the virtues Franklin encouraged in *Poor Richard's Almanack* and in his *Autobiography,* would undertake civic improvement and participate disinterestedly in government. In an expanding country filled with opportunity, Franklin saw individual initiative as the essential engine of progress, but he did not hesitate to seek whatever seemed required for the public good through government. His confidence in the virtue of the citizens of the United States caused him to favor government by consent, but he was not a simple democrat who believed majority will should be omnipotent. He accepted democracy because he thought it would yield good government; if it did not, he readily rejected it.

Ketchem shows how the *Autobiography* was part of Franklin's overall ambition to promote the role of the individual and of personal values as a force in political life. He supports his claims by focusing on Franklin's ideas about individual values in relation to other ideas about the role of government.

Still another viewpoint, from Franklin's biographer Carl Van Doren, looks at how parts of the *Autobiography* were written and read in their own time and afterward. While literary or philosophical analysts see the work as a self-contained expression of current or ongoing American ideas, the historian looks at the concrete events of the work's arrival and reception.

> The two copies went off to England and France to set in train the complex textual history of this simple book: of which three parts appeared first in French, and of which the earliest English editions were retranslations from the French, and of which [the author's son] Temple Franklin published as authorized in 1818, the copy sent to Le Veillard instead of Franklin's original, which was not published entire, as Franklin wrote it, till 1868. At some time after the copies [of the origi-

FOR DISCUSSION

Students will probably need to talk about this section in order to grasp it. If the chapter is to be understood at all, then students will need to know not only how scholars in different disciplines approach a work, but also how the uses to which a source is put influence the ways in which it is interpreted. You may want to begin by writing the names of the three disciplines on the board and ask students to describe how, based on this example, each discipline approaches a text. If students are able to work through this discussion, you may then want to ask what the text *represents* to scholars in the different disciplines. The discussion should clarify for students many of the points covered in the chapter.

nal manuscript] were made, Franklin, in the six painful months left to him, wrote the fragmentary fourth part and then broke off. It seems likely that he himself had made the revisions which in the copy tamed the original. He could no longer trust his taste and could now and then prefer round academic phrases to his own natural sharp, homely ones. He had lived too long, and put off writing too late, to be able to do justice to himself in a book. His greatest years would have to stay unwritten. He might truly have reflected that this was not altogether the loss it seemed. Plenty of other men could find materials for the story of his latest years. Only he had known about his obscure youth, which could never again be obscure. (767–68)

Van Doren's claims and interpretations try to establish how and where the work came into existence, and the extent to which it reflected Franklin's public versus private personality. The argument follows the pattern of interpreting records to reconstruct a meaningful pattern of events for Franklin's life.

Fichtelberg, Ketchem, and Van Doren interpret a single text differently, according to their separate disciplinary perspectives. Each makes a claim—a statement that expresses the pattern of meaning each author had found in the work he was examining.

FICHTELBERG   That the correspondent—the reader—is crucial to Franklin's self-conception is evident throughout the *Autobiography.*

KETCHEM   As a public philosopher, Franklin assumed that the traditional personal values have political relevance.

VAN DOREN   [The *Autobiography* has a] complex textual history.

If all three writers were literary critics, philosophers, or historians, they might just as likely offer different interpretations, since each of the humanities has its subdisciplines or subfields, each of which in turn is guided by a unique perspective. (For examples of this variety in literary studies, see 37d-4.) The more experienced you become in any of these disciplines, the more you will differentiate among perspectives *within* disciplines. *Perspective* determines how you will read, what questions you will pursue, and what interpretations you will make—both between and within disciplines.

37c Types of writing assignments in the humanities

The assignments you will most often write in your humanities courses—close analyses of texts, research papers, and book reviews—have in a general way been addressed in chapter 2, "Critical Thinking and Writing." The discussion here will introduce the special requirements of these assignments in the humanities and will refer you to pertinent sections in chapter 2.

1   The analysis

An **analysis** is an investigation that you conduct by applying a principle or definition to an activity or to an object in order to see how that activity or object works, what it might mean, or why it might be significant. As a writer, your job is to identify and discuss particular parts, or features, of the text that you feel are especially meaningful. In analyzing a short story or novel, for instance, you might focus on characters, themes, plot, or structure. You might analyze a poem for its rhymes, meter, or symbols (see 37d). These features, which are mutually reinforcing, give literary texts their meaning—though the meaning of a work will never be a simple sum of its analyzed parts. Good literature invites and can sustain multiple analyses without ever being "explained away."

Historical events similarly invite a variety of analyses. As one teacher of history has put it, "[H]istorians like to argue [for differing interpretations of events]. In fact, they disagree to a greater or lesser extent in their views of personalities and events in every major period in United States History, from Captain John Smith to William Westmoreland, from the American Revolution to the computer revolution" (O'Reilly 281). Historians present conflicting interpretations in order to understand as fully as possible the causes of events. These causes are usually complex and resist (as mature works of literature resist) a single, definitive explanation.

As a student of literature, philosophy, and history, you will use features specific to these disciplines in conducting your analyses. You have seen previously (in 37b) that one text can be analyzed as a work of literature, philosophy, or history, depending on a writer's perspective. Perspective determines the way in which a writer divides a text into analyzable parts. The more you study in a discipline, the more you will learn which features of a text are important to that discipline and, hence, which are worth analyzing.

The following general pattern serves as a model for writing an analysis, regardless of discipline. Placement of one or more of these elements in a paper may vary according to discipline; but when writing an analysis you can expect to touch on the following:

- Introduce the work being analyzed and the interpretation you will make (your claim).
- Introduce the features you will use to analyze the text. Your choice of features will depend on the discipline in which you are writing.
- Conduct your analysis by discussing one feature of a text (or idea) at a time. For literary texts, quote specific passages and *comment* on the ways the passage supports your interpretation (see 37a-3).
- Conclude by summing up the evidence for your interpretation. Show how the features you have discussed separately reinforce one another in creating the effect or quality you have argued for.

Section 2c discussed analysis as an investigation conducted by systematically applying a set of *principles*. In introductory courses to literature, this set of principles will be general if you are interpreting a poem or story according to standard features such as *theme*. (Other standard features are suggested in 37d-4.) In advanced literature courses, and also in philosophy and history courses, you may be asked to analyze a text or some situation by applying a much-discussed theory. In a philosophy course, for example, you might be asked to apply Wittgenstein's notion of "family resemblances" to some activity other than games. In this instance, your professor would be asking that you analyze a situation, based on principles laid out in a specific source.

2 The book review

You may be asked to read and review a book for your courses, both inside and outside of the humanities. The purpose of a review is to make a judgment about the worth of a text and to communicate and justify that judgment to a reader. See 2b for an extended discussion on preparing and writing a review (which in 2b is called an *evaluation*). Before writing to evaluate you should *read* to evaluate. That is, you should understand what an author has written so that you can summarize main points; you should distinguish an author's facts from opinions; and you should distinguish your assumptions from those of the author. Your overall assessment of a book will rest largely on the extent to which you and the author share assumptions about the subject being discussed.

3 The research paper

A research paper calls on you to investigate some topic, using both primary and secondary sources. Often, a research paper in the humanities is an analysis (see 37c-1) that you set in a broader context. In writing an analysis, you typically read and interpret a single text—in the paper that follows, it is a short story ("Counterparts") by James Joyce. Broadening your effort into a research paper, you would analyze the story and also draw on available scholarship as an aid to your analysis. A second reason to draw on available scholarship is to provide a context for your thesis. By reviewing the literature on your topic, you tap into the conversation that has taken place concerning it. Aware of what others have written, you can add your voice (through your paper) and contribute to the conversation.

For her paper on "Counterparts," Sarika Chandra turned to the work of a Joyce scholar, Richard Ellman, and to the work of a sociologist who has investigated patterns of drinking among Irish men. Chandra also consulted Joyce's nonfiction writing, compiled by Ellman into a collection called *Critical Writings*. In a research paper, you remain responsible for developing and supporting an interpretation. You draw on sources, as needed, to help make your points.

Gathering sources on a topic and using them judiciously, according to a plan, is the activity central to writing a research paper. In 2d you will find a discussion on writing a synthesis based on multiple sources. To write an effective research paper in the humanities, you must be able to read multiple sources on a topic, understand the main points of each, and then link these points to one another and to your own guiding interpretation, or thesis. In short, you must read source materials effectively. (See chapter 1, "Critical Thinking and Reading.") If you are uncertain of your ability to draw on and refer to multiple sources, also see chapters 33, 34, and 35 on the research process. In chapter 36, you will find a discussion on how to cite sources when writing a paper. In the humanities, you will generally follow the MLA form for documenting sources.

37d Writing about literature[3]

To write knowledgeably about a literary work—about a poem, a play, a short story, or a novel—you need to understand, generally, how arguments are made in the humanities. In 37a-2 you saw that arguments in the humanities depend on a cycle of claim, reference to a text, and comment. In that same discussion and in 37b you found examples of such arguments about literary texts (about *Huckleberry Finn* and Franklin's *Autobiography*). The cases illustrated a cycle of claim, reference, and comment. If you have not already done so, read these sections of the chapter. The discussion here assumes your familiarity with the terms *claim, text, refer/reference,* and *comment.*

1 First reading: Respond

> On a *first* reading, respond to the text.

Personal response is fundamental to the critical reading of *any* text. See chapter 1 for a discussion of critical reading, generally, and of the importance of responding. Pose these questions to a text: *What can I learn from this selection? What is my background on the subject that this selection concerns? What is the origin of my views on the topics of this text? What new interest, or what new question or observation, does this text spark in me?* These questions, which you can ask of any text, can be refined somewhat when applied to literary texts.

---

[3] In this discussion, the term *literature* refers to works of art *in writing:* poems, plays, and fiction. The expression "review of the literature," common in the humanities, social sciences, and sciences, refers to a writer's presentation of prior research on a topic. Such a presentation is usually meant to set a broader context for a paper and to demonstrate the need for additional research.

TEACHING IDEAS

If you're using this handbook in conjunction with a literature anthology, the guidelines listed here can be of great help to students as they plan their papers. You may want to emphasize that the guidelines offer questions designed only to suggest a focus for a literary analysis, and that only one or two questions from each section would be included in a single paper. Nevertheless, these questions can help students through the often difficult steps of getting started on an analysis.

Developing a personal response requires that you read a text closely, in such a way that you are alert to details that make the text meaningful. At the risk of stating the obvious, you should prepare for a close reading by finding a block of uninterrupted time when you are feeling alert and able to concentrate on what you read. Realize that close reading involves *multiple* readings. Expect that you will read a full text twice and selected parts of the text three or more times. On your first reading, disregard for the moment the paper you intend to write and read to be engaged, even moved. Read for the same reasons people have read or listened to stories and poetry or watched dramas for centuries: to be fascinated, to learn something of other lives, to wonder, and to question. Writing about literature is premised on the belief that the text you are examining *is* worthy of your extended reflection. If you have not thought about what you have read, if you have not responded to it personally, you can hardly expect to write about it with conviction.[4]

Questions to prompt a personal response on a first reading

- What do I feel when reading this material? Why do I feel this way?
- Does this text make me *want* to read? Why or why not?
- What about this text is worth reading a second time?
- How am I challenged by or changed in response to this text?
- With what questions does this text leave me?
- What differences do I see between the author's observations of the world and my observations? How can I explain these differences?

Personal responses based on these and related questions can make you want to know more about what you have read. For instance, if on completing a story, drama, or poem you find yourself *moved, offended, challenged, saddened, confused, needled,* or *intrigued,* you will have an

---

[4] Which specific features of a text merit our calling it *literature* is a matter of some controversy. There is the traditional "canon," the body of works that for generations scholars (and an obedient public) have regarded as important texts in Western culture: Shakespeare, Keats, Brontë, Shelley, Melville, and many more. But a difficulty arises: Given that authors are forever creating new texts, why are some texts added to the canon, the "important" list worthy of study, while other texts are excluded? Applied historically, this same question has caused a revolution in literary studies: What makes Shakespeare, Shelley, and the others canonical—that is, examples of what we call literature? Why were *they* included in the canon and not more women writers, more minorities, or more representatives of less industrial nations? Who made, and who makes, decisions about what texts are to be called literature? What assumptions about art and culture guide these decision makers, and might not different assumptions lead us to create a different canon? These explosive questions may well become guiding concerns in one of your literature courses. Suffice it to say that what counts as "literature" is under intense scrutiny at the moment.

immediate and even pressing reason to return for a second reading. And it is the second reading in which you will discover the patterns that will enable you to write a worthwhile paper. Sometimes, you may need to brainstorm after a first reading in order to understand your particular response to a text (see 3b-2). What follows is a demonstration of such a brainstorming session. Sarika Chandra, whose paper you will read in 37d-5, spent five minutes writing out her response to "Counterparts," a short story by James Joyce. Read the concluding paragraphs of "Counterparts" (and Chandra's marginal notes). The story concerns a man named Farrington, who in this scene returns home from a night of heavy drinking—paid for by pawning his watch and prompted by a disagreement with his boss.

A very sullen-faced man stood at the corner of O'Connell Bridge waiting for the little Sandymount tram to take him home. He was full of smouldering anger and revengefulness. He felt humiliated and discontented; he did not even feel drunk; and he had only twopence in his pocket. He cursed everything. He had done for himself in the office, pawned his watch, spent all his money; and he had not even got drunk. He began to feel thirsty again and he longed to be back again in the hot reeking public-house. He had lost his reputation as a strong man, having been defeated twice by a mere boy. His heart swelled with fury and, when he thought of the woman in the big hat who had brushed against him and said *Pardon!* his fury nearly choked him.

At this pt., Farrington's lost his name

F's defeated, powerless in his job & in the bar

His tram let him down at Shelbourne Road and he steered his great body along in the shadow of the wall of the barracks. He loathed returning to his home. When he went in by the side-door he found the kitchen empty and the kitchen fire nearly out. He bawled upstairs:

—Ada! Ada!

His wife was a little sharp-faced woman who bullied her husband when he was sober and was bullied by him when he was drunk. They had five children. A little boy came running down the stairs.

This miserable? Is there any joy in this man's life?

—Who is that? said *the man* peering through the darkness.

—Me, pa.

—Who are you? Charlie?

—No, pa. Tom.

—Where's your mother?

—She's out at the chapel.

—That's right. . . . Did she think of leaving any dinner for me?

—Yes, pa. I—

Again, no name.

FOR DISCUSSION

After reading the example of Chandra's marginal notes, you might initiate a discussion of annotating a text. Ask students what they think of the notes she makes—do they sound like the musings of a literary scholar? How similar are they to notes students in the class make? Why do students think she commented as she did? What other notes would members of the class make?

—Light the lamp. What do you mean by having the place in darkness? Are the other children in bed?

The man sat down heavily on one of the chairs while the little boy lit the lamp. He began to mimic his son's flat accent, saying half to himself: *At the chapel. At the chapel, if you please!* When the lamp was lit he banged his fist on the table and shouted:

—What's for my dinner?

—I'm going . . . to cook it, pa, said the little boy.

The man jumped up furiously and pointed to the fire.

I'd be terrified, too! The bully.

—On that fire! You let the fire out! By God, I'll teach you to do that again!

He took a step to the door and seized the walking-stick which was standing behind it.

—I'll teach you to let the fire out! he said, rolling up his sleeve in order to give his arm free play.

Is this the only way he can feel good about himself—by beating a kid?

The little boy cried *O, pa!* and ran whimpering round the table, but the man followed him and caught him by the coat. The little boy looked about him wildly but, seeing no way of escape, fell upon his knees.

—Now, you'll let the fire out the next time! said the man, striking at him viciously with the stick. Take that, you little whelp!

The boy uttered a squeal of pain as the stick cut his thigh. He clasped his hands together in the air and his voice shook with fright.

The man could use some salvation. What a grim life.

—O, pa! he cried. Don't beat me, pa! And I'll . . . I'll say a *Hail Mary* for you. . . . I'll say a *Hail Mary* for you, pa, if you don't beat me. . . . I'll say a *Hail Mary* . . . .

Sarika Chandra wrote for several minutes on completing these final paragraphs of Joyce's story. Here is her response:

```
Farrington is a lost, desperate man. His powerlessness
depresses me. He's so powerless that he grabs the only power
left to him by beating his young son. It's a sick thing to do
and it's cowardly and it gets me mad, a father taking out his
troubles on a boy this way. I'd hate Farrington if his
situation at work weren't so miserable. He's trapped and
doesn't have a clue about what's trapping him. His son is
trapped, living in a house with this man. Although I don't see
her, I bet his wife is feeling trapped, too. Husband and wife
bully each other. There's no happiness in this world.
```

2 Second reading: Analyze the text—find patterns of meaning in it based on your response

> Ask *why* or *how* of your personal response, and you will have a specific, guiding question to lead you through a second reading. Your goal with this question is to understand your response by finding a pattern that makes the text meaningful.

In chapter 2, you will find an extended discussion on the ways in which thoughtful writing is based on a close, critical reading of a text. Certainly, thoughtful writing about literature is based on your reading of the literary work. *Response* is the first component of this reading; *analysis,* based on that response, is the second. See 2c for a general discussion on writing analyses. The principles established there apply to this discussion as well.

You can approach a second reading of a text by working with the response that most interested you in your first reading. Convert that response into a pointed question by asking *Why? How? What are some examples?* Guided by this question, return to the text and analyze it (see 2c-2). If your analysis succeeds, it will yield insights into how the text works, how you think it achieves its meaning in one particular way (with respect to your question). As you read a second time, make notes in the margin wherever you feel the text provides details that can help you answer your guiding question. These notes, considered in light of your question, can suggest a pattern that makes the text meaningful. You can write a successful paper by presenting this same pattern to your reader.

Following is an illustration of a second reading—selected paragraphs from the conclusion of "Counterparts," accompanied by Sarika Chandra's notes. The question that she used to guide her second reading was as follows: *In what way do characters show power or powerlessness in this short story?* Note how the question builds directly on the response she made in her five-minute brainstorming session, in which her main concern was with power and powerlessness. Observe how she uses her question to tease out details in the text that will, subsequently, provide her with material for a paper. If you have trouble deciding on a question to guide your second reading, reflect again on your response to the text. See also 37d-4 for a discussion of how you can pose specific questions based on one or another theory of literary criticism.

He cursed everything. He had done for himself in the office, pawned his watch, spent all his money; and he had not even got drunk. He began to feel thirsty again and he longed to be back again in the hot reeking public-house. He had lost his reputation as a strong man, having been defeated twice by a mere boy.

Defeated & powerless at the office

Defeated & powerless at the bar

FOR DISCUSSION

In this discussion students will continue their commentary on annotating a text. Questions to consider now include the following: How did Chandra come up with her controlling question? How is the question reflected in her annotations? Do students see anything else in the selection that is relevant to the question?

His wife was a little sharp-faced woman who bullied her husband when he was sober and was bullied by him when he was drunk. They had five children. A little boy came running down the stairs.

—Who is that? said the man, peering through the darkness.

—Me, pa.

—Who are you? Charlie?

—No, pa. Tom.

—Where's your mother?

—She's out at the chapel.

—That's right. . . . Did she think of leaving any dinner for me?

—Yes, pa. I—

—Light the lamp. What do you mean by having the place in darkness? Are the other children in bed?

The man sat down heavily on one of the chairs while the little boy lit the lamp. He began to mimic his son's flat accent, saying half to himself: *At the chapel. At the chapel, if you please!* When the lamp was lit he banged his fist on the table and shouted:

—What's for my dinner?

Powerless at home, unless he's drunk

The chapel: the one place F's wife can go to get beyond his abuse. God is more powerful than F.

F knows it (↑) too; she's beyond his reach.

—I'll teach you to let the fire out! he said, rolling up his sleeve in order to give his arm free play.

The little boy cried *O, pa!* and ran whimpering round the table, but the man followed him and caught him by the coat. The little boy looked about him wildly but, seeing no way of escape, fell upon his knees.

—Now, you'll let the fire out the next time! said the man, striking at him viciously with the stick. Take that, you little whelp!

The boy uttered a squeal of pain as the stick cut his thigh. He clasped his hands together in the air and his voice shook with fright.

—O, pa! he cried. Don't beat me, pa! And I'll . . . I'll say a *Hail Mary* for you. . . . I'll say a *Hail Mary* for you, pa, if you don't beat me. . . . I'll say a *Hail Mary.* . . .

F: pathetic grab for power by beating his son

The boy: as w/his mother, some measure of power over F, through the church

3   Construct a pattern of meaning: Making claims and providing evidence

Refine the pattern you have found and make a claim. Locate passages in the text that support this claim.

Based on your first and second readings of a text, you are ready to make a claim: to state for your readers the pattern you have found and your reasons for believing this pattern is worth your time pursuing and your reader's time considering. With her first and second readings of Joyce's short story in mind, Sarika Chandra developed this claim:

"Counterparts" is a story about how otherwise powerless people
seek to gain control over their lives.

Chandra has found a pattern that helps make Joyce's story meaningful to her, and she formally expresses this pattern as a claim. That Chandra found this pattern and not another is not to say that other patterns do not exist. Many do. "Counterparts" is a story rich with meaning and, like any enduring work of literature, yields itself to countless interpretations. The point to remember is that whatever pattern a student of literature finds in a text, she or he is obliged to show readers why, given all the patterns that *could* be found, this one is reasonable and worth the reader's consideration. A writer demonstrates the worthiness of a pattern, or claim, by repeatedly referring the reader to the text—a primary source, and when pertinent, to secondary sources. (See 37a and b). Again, you have seen in examples in this chapter (37a-2) how claims in the humanities in general, and claims about literary texts in particular, are supported. Often, before planning an argument in support of a claim, the writer will prepare a sketch. Here is how Chandra planned to support the claim above, based on her reading of the text and on her reading of secondary sources:

Plot summary of basic situation--Farrington's powerlessness

Reference to secondary source--Farrington and Joyce, connection

Farrington buying drinks--buys power

Farrington abusing son--grasps for power

Farrington's wife and child going to Church--pray for power
(or endurance?)

Reference to secondary source--women not welcome in Irish
pubs, no power that way for F's wife

When you read the paper in 37e, you will see that Chandra used this sketch as a guide to selecting passages in "Counterparts" and in secondary sources that helped her support the claim that Joyce had written a story about how "otherwise powerless people seek to gain control over their lives." You will find on reading the paper that Chandra adheres closely to her sketch; that her sketch is built directly from the notes she made in her second reading; and that her second reading followed directly from the question that evolved from her first, personal response to the story.

TEACHING IDEAS

This section provides an ideal opportunity for you to discuss another mistaken notion about literary analysis: that it's all opinion, and therefore everybody's opinion counts. The care with which Chandra chooses and plans to support her claim indicates that she is not merely offering an opinion. Instead, she is making a claim whose worthiness will be demonstrated by her careful reference to primary and secondary sources. The sketch she uses can become a model for students, keeping them from making unsubstantiated claims about the works they're studying.

TEACHING IDEAS

You may want to emphasize here that the plot summary is presented for a specific purpose and not as an end in itself. Chandra only includes enough of the plot to allow the reader to follow her argument. And she certainly doesn't attempt to pass off a plot summary as a literary analysis.

REFERENCES

LYNN, STEVEN. "A Passage into Critical Theory." *CE* 52 (1990): 258–71. Illustrates various critical approaches (from formalism to feminism) by submitting a sample text to analysis.

Plot summaries

Chandra's planned use of the plot summary should be noted here because it is a feature common to so many papers written about literature. A **plot summary** is a brief description of characters and events that provides readers, some of whom may be unfamiliar with the story, context enough to follow a discussion. Plot summaries are written in the historical present tense. Consider these sentences from Chandra's paper (present-tense verbs are underlined):

```
"Counterparts" tells the story of a man named Farrington, who
will not do his job right and takes abuse from his boss for
that. . . . The story opens with a scene in which Farrington
is being summoned to the office of Mr. Alleyne, his boss.
```

Variations from the present tense may be needed from time to time (as above—"who will not do his job" and "is being summoned") to clarify sequences of events; but plot summaries are written predominantly in the present tense because the events of a text are always present to a reader—the same actions occur in the same order in the text no matter how many times that text is read. Remember that the purpose of the plot summary is to allow the writer to refer to a text and in this way support a claim. Typically, the writer's observation about the text immediately follows the plot summary, sometimes in the same sentence:

```
Frustrated by his loss at arm wrestling, Farrington returns
home, where yet another attempt to gain power fails.
```

The clause "where yet another attempt to gain power fails" is not part of Chandra's summary but is rather one of her observations about the story, an observation that followed from her guiding question (*In what ways do characters show power or powerlessness?*) and that she makes in her paper to support her claim. To ensure that readers can follow her discussion, Chandra summarizes portions of "Counterparts" throughout her paper so that her observations will have a specific reference and will make sense to her readers.

4 Literary criticism: More formal readings of texts

What counts as a detail worth noting in a poem, story, or play? What counts as a pattern of details worth discovering? Answers depend on the questions a reader poses. You will see (in 37d-5) that Sarika Chandra observed details of "Counterparts" and fit them together in a pattern based on a question built from her *personal response* to the story. There are other, more formal questions that can be put to a literary text, and these are based on the philosophies of various "schools" of literary criticism, each of which regards texts differently and, based on its approach, poses distinctive questions.

Scholars who write professionally about and teach poetry, plays, and fiction are called *literary critics;* and critics affiliate themselves with one of several approaches to literature. Some critics read *Moby Dick*, for instance, and ask: What is the psychological basis of the relationship between Ishmael and Queequeg? Some read the novel with this question: What echoes can we find of Melville's years at sea? Some look at the public's initial reaction to the novel (they disliked it) and ask: Why and when did this work come to be regarded as an American classic? The possible angles from which to study a literary work are many; and each angle suggests its own set of questions, its own set of problems worth investigating, and its own rules about what counts as acceptable evidence in support of an argument. Fundamentally, readers find in a text what they look for: pose one question, and you will focus on the relationship between Ishmael and Queequeg; pose another, and you will concern yourself with the readers' changing responses to *Moby Dick* over the years.

The questions that guide your reading, then, are of paramount importance. People who make a profession of literary studies insist that their questions be based on sound, carefully thought through philosophical principles. From one school to the next, these principles differ. Differences notwithstanding, all literary critics believe in the abiding value of literature, and believe that we can learn about ourselves and others by reading it. All critics and all teachers of literature accept as a general model of argumentation the cycle of claim, reference to a text, and comment.

It is impossible to say that one approach to a literary text is ultimately correct. There are *many* approaches, and each can show us patterns of meaning in a text that make the text more understandable. If you major in literature, and especially if you go on to graduate school, you will learn about schools of literary criticism. For the moment, even without the benefit of a literary critic's carefully prepared questions (some of which will be presented below), you can gain lasting insights into a poem, play, or work of fiction by finding in it a pattern based on your own personal responses.

Posing more formal questions for a second reading

You may find yourself writing papers for literature courses in which you approach the study of literature according to the viewpoints of various schools of literary criticism. Without naming these schools here and introducing you to complicated terminologies and methods, following are some additional questions you might pose to a text. These questions assume that you have already completed a first close reading.

- What circumstances of the author's life does the text reflect?
- In what ways does the text exist in a relationship with other texts by the same author and with other texts from the same time period?
- How might the text shift its meaning from one reader to the next? from one audience to the next, over time?
- What is the reader's role in making this text meaningful?
- How does the text reflect certain cultural assumptions (about gender or culture, for instance) in the author's and the readers' times?

- What psychological motives underlie the characters' actions?
- What are the economic or power relationships among the characters?

When you want to maintain your focus on a poem, play, or work of fiction itself (as opposed to considering the readers' responses or various influences on the author), then you can pose the following questions, arranged by category. These questions are often appropriate for introductory survey courses in literature.

Characterization Who are the main characters? What are their qualities? Is each character equally important? Equally well developed?

Language What devices such as rhyme (identical sounds), meter (carefully controlled rhythms), and pauses does the author use to create special emphasis? How does the author use metaphors and choose words to create visual images? In what ways are these images tied to the meaning of the text?

Narrator, Point of View Who is speaking? What is the narrator's personality and how does this affect the telling? Is the narrator omniscient in the sense that he or she can read into the thoughts of every character? If not, how is the narrator's vision limited?

Plot How does the writer sequence events so as to maintain the reader's attention? Which actions are central? How are other, subsidiary actions linked to the central ones? What patterning to the plot do you see? Are there ways in which the plot's structure and theme are related?

Structure In what ways can you (or does the author) divide the whole poem or story into component parts—according to theme? plot? setting? stanza? How are these parts related?

Setting Where does the story take place? How significant is the setting to the meaning of the text?

Symbolism Are any symbols operating, any objects that (like a flag) create for readers emotional, political, religious, or other associations? If so, how do these symbols function in the poem, story, or play?

Theme What large issues does this text raise? Through which characters, events, or specific lines are the questions raised? To what extent does the text answer these questions?

LOOKING BACK

As students prepare to write literary analyses, it might be worthwhile to review chapter 2 in class, especially the material on synthesis (2d).

 5

Write the paper: Synthesize the details you have assembled

Demonstrate the reasonableness of your claim by making observations about the text; if appropriate, refer to secondary sources and the observations of others. Synthesize these observations into a coherent argument.

The goal of a paper in a literature course is to show that your interpretation, the pattern of meaning you have found, is reasonable and can help others understand the text. Your observations about the text and, if you use them, the observations of others, are the details that you will *synthesize* into a coherent argument. See 2d for a discussion on writing syntheses. The principles reviewed there apply here.

37e Sample student paper: "The Power of Alcohol and the Church in Joyce's 'Counterparts' "

In the following paper, Sarika Chandra examines the ways in which the character Farrington, in a short story by James Joyce, uses alcohol in virtually the same way his wife uses the Church—both of them to gain power. Throughout the paper, you will find Chandra following the pattern of claim and support common in literary criticism: Chandra makes a claim, refers to a passage, and then comments on the passage in order to cement its relationship to the claim. She carefully develops an interpretation of the story and, when she finds a broadening of the context useful, draws on secondary sources. This paper is one of three discipline-specific papers relating to the topic of alcohol. See 38d for a lab report on the fermentation of wine and 39d for a sociological paper on women alcoholics.

TEACHING IDEAS

The sample research paper presented here is heavily annotated so that students can use it as a guide in writing their own research papers. You may want to call particular attention to specific features peculiar to humanities papers—arrangement, documentation, method of supporting claims, and the like.

↕ 1/2"
Chandra 1

↓ 1"

Sarika Chandra

Dr. Robert Crooks

English 204

15 May 1991   ⌐ Double space

     The Power of Alcohol and the Church

Indent 5 spaces   in Joyce's "Counterparts"   1"

← → "Counterparts" tells the story of a man named ← →

1" Farrington, who will not do his job right and takes abuse from his boss for that. Farrington spends a long time drinking after work and when he gets home beats his son. However, Joyce tells much more in eleven pages than just another story about an abusive alcoholic. "Counterparts" is a   The thesis
story about how otherwise powerless people seek to gain control over their lives.

    The story opens with a scene in which Farrington is being summoned to the office of Mr.   Plot summary (present tense)
Alleyne, his boss. Farrington copies documents for a living, and this element of the story ap-

GROUP ACTIVITY

Ask students to read Chandra's paper in its entirety, and then divide the class into groups of three or four. Each group will then analyze the effectiveness of Chandra's argument based on the material presented in the chapter. You may want to offer the following guidelines for the analysis:

How clearly does Chandra state her claim?

How do her references to the text support her claim?

How does she use secondary sources to support her claim?

How effectively does she synthesize her observations?

1/2"
Chandra 2

1"

1" pears to have some basis in Joyce's childhood. Richard Ellman notes that "calligraphy enabled [Joyce's father, John] to work for a solicitor named Aylward" (39). Calligraphy is similar in nature to Farrington's job of copying documents. Further, Ellman points out that "Aylward's office is probably that described in 'Counterparts,' where his name is changed to Alleyne" (39). However, nothing in Joyce's biography explains the complexity of "Counterparts."

Farrington sits in Alleyne's office, powerless, listening to this man berate him for some job poorly done. Apparently, mistakes and the resulting humiliation are regular occurrences in this office. Aside from the abuse that he must take from Alleyne, Farrington is made powerless by the very nature of his profession. As a copyist, not even his work is his own: he must labor all day at copying someone else's words. Farrington is trapped, immediately by his boss and more generally by his job.

After work, Farrington looks forward to drinking, which he does every time he is humiliated. After the scene in Alleyne's office, he wants to go to the pub but he realizes that he has no money. Suddenly, he thinks of his watch and pawns it for six shillings. Now nothing else matters, for he is in the position to buy himself some power. At the pub, Farrington relates the incident in Alleyne's office to his companions. He claims that he looked coolly at Mr. Alleyne and said, "I don't think that that's a fair question to put to me" (93). Nosey Flynn and Davy Byrne say that this was the smartest thing they have heard. Farrington is pleased and he "[stands] a drink in his turn" (93). He repeats the same story to O'Halloran and Paddy Leonard

1"

Reference to a secondary source, in support of the thesis.

1"

Observation #1 about the story, in support of the thesis.

Plot summary (present tense)

and they too agree that the story was smart. Farrington stands another round of drinks. Higgens comes to the bar and praises Farrington for being cool in front of Mr. Alleyne.

Here Farrington is trying to get himself some power by buying people drinks and repeating his story in order to believe that he had some control at the office (which he didn't) and that he has control at the pub. But buying drinks leads to no real power or respect, since people take interest in Farrington for only so long as he pays for the whiskey. Nevertheless, interest for whatever reason pleases Farrington very much. Later, when the conversation strays away from his story, he buys another round. At the end of the evening, when all his money is gone, he is defeated at arm wrestling by Weathers. Again, Farrington is humiliated: "He had lost his reputation as a strong man, having been defeated twice by a mere boy" (97).

Frustrated, he goes home, where yet another attempt to gain power fails. He walks into a dark room in his house and "a little boy [comes] running down the stairs" (97). It is one of his five children, Tom, who says that his mother is at the chapel. Farrington responds, "That's right. . . . Did she think of leaving any dinner for me?" (97). Again, Farrington feels out of control, and this makes him nervous. He wants his wife home to serve him since a "servant" gives service to someone who by definition is powerful. But his wife is not home. Worse, he has to be informed of her absence by his young son. Farrington becomes a mimic and grows enraged: "At the chapel. At the chapel, if you please!" (97-98) and then tries to assert control by beating Tom, who cries "O pa! . . . Don't

---

Marginal annotations:

Observation #2 about the story, in support of the thesis.

Plot summary (present tense, woven throughout paragraph.)

Observation #3 about the story, in support of the thesis.

TEACHING IDEAS

This page provides some excellent examples of the use of quotations. You may want to call attention to such features as the use of ellipses, the smooth integration of quotations into the text, and the appropriate use of parenthetical references.

TEACHING IDEAS

This page contains some particularly impressive stylistic features. You may want to ask students to make note of especially vivid diction, effective sentence structures, and cohesive paragraphs.

beat me, pa! And . . . I'll say a <u>Hail Mary</u> for you . . . " (98).

Tom's attempt to save himself by offering a false prayer shows the influence of the church and of Farrington's wife on the home. Whereas Farrington escapes to a pub to gain power, his wife has only the chapel as a means of escape and a path to power. The Catholic church is extremely influential in Irish life. As Joyce put it, "Ireland has been . . . the most faithful daughter of the Catholic church. . . . Its faith was never once shaken seriously" (<u>Critical Writings</u> 169). In Joyce's day, women were welcome in church but certainly not in a pub. Married men were expected to socialize. According to one sociologist, pub life "was a means of enforcing the religiously inspired segregation of men and women that even marriage did not break down" (Stivers 86). Ability to drink was not only a display of manliness but also of a solidarity among men that excluded women:

> The men drink heavily. . . . The public
> houses are drab and uncomfortable. There
> is no provision but for hard drinking, and
> a respectable woman would not set foot in-
> side one of these places. (Stivers 87)

Indent 10 spaces

Farrington's wife, unable to go to a pub, turns to the church both as a source of strength and as a source of control over her husband. Evidence for this control can be found in the story even though Farrington's wife is not directly present. Tom offers to say a prayer for his father, the implication being that his father needs help. A helper is someone in control, someone who has power and is willing to use it. In this case, power flows from the church, not from a bottle. Farrington's wife has done well in teaching her children how to combat a brutish father. As a

Observation #4 about the story, in support of the thesis.

Reference to source outside the text, in support of the thesis.

Reference to a secondary source, in support of the thesis.

Observation #5 about the story, in support of the thesis.

Chandra 5

child, Tom has only one weapon to fend off this man who has hit him "viciously" with a stick. Tom has the church, which he uses in an effort to save himself. This offer to make a prayer is false in the sense that it is motivated by self defense. But we see also that Farrington is a man whose soul in fact needs help, so perhaps a prayer--any prayer--is legitimate.

In attempting to get power, Farrington uses alcohol and his wife and children use the chapel. It is hard to say which is more powerful from Joyce's point of view. In "Counterparts," alcohol is generally ineffective, but still it is strong enough an influence to evoke Tom's cry. Yet the story also shows that the chapel is effective in that it frustrates Farrington's desire for authority in his own home. But <u>effective</u> is not quite the right word, for Joyce has created a man who is powerless in his job and a home in which the wife "bullied her husband when he was sober and was bullied by him when he was drunk" (97). The characters in "Counterparts" are locked in a struggle for power, a struggle that everyone seems to be losing.

[margin note: Conclusion]

[margin note: Conclusion argues for the thesis and reflects this writer's personal response to the story (see 37d-1).]

---

‡1/2"
1"
Chandra 6

Works Cited

1"

Ellman, Richard. <u>James Joyce</u>. Oxford: Oxford UP, 1982.

Joyce, James. "Counterparts." <u>Dubliners</u>. Ed. Robert Scholes and A. Walton Litz. New York: Cornell UP, 1989.

[margin note: Indent 5 spaces]

---. <u>The Critical Writings</u>. Ed. Ellsworth Mason and Richard Ellman. New York: Cornell UP, 1989.

Stivers, Richard. <u>A Hair of the Dog: Irish Drinking and American Stereotype</u>. University Park, PA: Pennsylvania State UP, 1976.

GROUP DISCUSSION

Chandra has summarized "Counterparts" effectively. Identify the place in the penultimate paragraph where she begins her conclusion. Does her conclusion adequately use the facts she marshals earlier? Does it explain everything about the dynamics between the characters she describes? (For example, how effectively in fact has Mrs. Farrington taught her children to deal with their father?)

FOR DISCUSSION

Chandra's conclusion is lucid and persuasive. This might be a good place to talk with your students about the purposes served by a concluding paragraph in different kinds of papers.

TEACHING IDEAS

Students should note that the "Works Cited" page includes an example of a second reference to the same author. Especially when one is working with literary analysis, such references are common.

REFERENCES

LYNN, STEVEN. "A Passage into Critical Theory." *CE* 52 (1990): 258–71. Illustrates various critical approaches (from formalism to feminism) by analyzing a sample text.

LENTRICCIA, FRANK, and THOMAS McLAUGHLIN, eds. *Critical Terms for Literary Study.* Chicago: U of Chicago P, 1990. Collection of essays that provides current, clear, and comprehensive discussions of twenty-two common terms such as "author," "figurative language," and "structure."

BIDDLE, ARTHUR W., and TOBY FULWILER, eds. *Reading, Writing, and the Study of Literature.* New York: Random, 1989. An introduction to different ways students may approach literature (includes chapters, with bibliographies, authored by different scholars on genres and literary criticism).

EAGLETON, TERRY. *Literary Theory: An Introduction.* Minneapolis: U of Minnesota P, 1983. Surveys and critiques twentieth-century literary theory (chapter "The Rise of English" is indispensable to anyone involved in literary study).

CULLER, JONATHAN. *The Pursuit of Signs: Semiotics, Literature, Deconstruction.* Ithaca: Cornell UP, 1981. Important discussion about the influence of poststructuralist criticism on the interpretation of literary texts.

TOMPKINS, JANE P., ed. *Reader-Response Criticism: From Formalism to Post-Structuralism.* Baltimore: Johns Hopkins UP, 1980. Selection of representative essays on poststructuralist criticism (Tompkins' introduction includes insightful discussion of reader-response criticism).

GOULD, CHRISTOPHER. "Literature in the Basic Writing Course: A Bibliographic Survey." *CE* 49 (1987): 558–74. Integrates theory and practice for teachers of basic writing who want to use literature in their classes (includes list of helpful texts).

REILLY, JILL M., et al. "The Effects of Prewriting on Literary Interpretation." ERIC, 1986. ED 276058. Presents results of a study that show how focused prewriting exercises lead students to compose more effective analytical papers.

TUCHMAN, BARBARA W. *Practicing History: Selected Essays.* New York: Knopf, 1981. Provides recommendations for the analysis of works in history.

37f Reference materials in the humanities

Style guides

The following sources offer discipline-specific guidance for writing in the humanities.

Barnet, Sylvan. *A Short Guide to Writing About Literature.* 5th ed. Glenview: Scott, 1985.

Blanshard, Brand. *On Philosophical Style.* Bloomington: Indiana UP, 1954.

Daniels, Robert V. *Studying History: How and Why.* 3rd ed. Englewood Cliffs, NJ: Prentice, 1981.

Specialized references

The following specialized references will help you to assemble information in a particular discipline or field within a discipline.

Encyclopedias provide general information useful when beginning a search.

Cassell's Encyclopedia of World Literature rev. ed.
Encyclopedia of American History
Encyclopedia of Art
Encyclopedia of Bioethics
Encyclopedia of Dance and Ballet
Encyclopedia of Philosophy
Encyclopedia of Religion and Ethics
Encyclopedia of World Art
An Encyclopedia of World History: Ancient, Medieval, and Modern
International Encyclopedia of Film
International Standard Bible Encyclopedia
The New College Encyclopedia of Music
Oxford Companion to Art
Oxford Companion to Film
Oxford Companion to Canadian Literature (there are also *Oxford Companion* volumes for Classical, English, French, German, and Spanish Literature)
Oxford Companion to Music
Penguin Companion to American Literature (there are also *Penguin Companion* volumes for English, European, Classical, Oriental, and African Literature)
Princeton Encyclopedia of Poetry and Poetics

Dictionaries provide definitions for technical terms.

A Handbook to Literature
Concise Oxford Dictionary of Ballet
Dictionary of American History
Dictionary of Films
Dictionary of Philosophy
Harvard Dictionary of Music
Interpreter's Dictionary of the Bible
McGraw-Hill Dictionary of Art
New Grove Dictionary of Music and Musicians

Periodical indexes list articles published in a particular discipline over a particular period. *Abstracts,* which summarize the sources listed and involve a considerable amount of work to compile, tend to be more selective than indexes.

Abstracts of English Studies
America: History and Life
Art Index
Arts and Humanities Citation Index
British Humanities Index
Cambridge Bibliography of English Literature and *New Cambridge Bibliography of English Literature*
Essay and General Literature Index
Film Literature Index
Historical Abstracts
Humanities Index
Index to Book Reviews in the Humanities
International Index of Film Periodicals
MLA International Bibliography of Books and Articles on Modern Languages and Literatures
Music Index
New York Times Film Reviews
Philosopher's Index One: Periodicals
Religion Index
Year's Work in English Studies

CHAPTER 38

Writing and Reading in the Social Sciences

KEY FEATURES

While the humanities ask questions about the meaning of human existence, the social sciences seek to find patterns to help explain human behavior. This chapter approaches the social sciences from the perspective of common underlying theories of human behavior as well as distinctive modes of inquiry. Like the preceding chapter on the humanities, this chapter is divided into four major sections: writing, reading, types of assignments, and research papers. Writing in the social sciences is addressed in terms of patterns of informative writing and methods of argumentative writing; in this section the two primary methods of investigation, the laboratory experiment and the field (or case) study, are represented. Reading is addressed by considering the difference between quantitative and qualitative reports. The third section discusses various writing assignments students can expect to receive in these disciplines, relying on chapter 2 (Critical Thinking and Writing) and chapter 39 (Writing and Reading in the Sciences) for methodology; clear guidelines for manuscript form and contents of reports are presented in this section. Section four reproduces an annotated sample research paper, a sociological study of women alcoholics. The paper, consistent with the other samples in this part and Part IX (The Research Paper), deals with the general subject of drugs and alcohol. The chapter ends with a comprehensive list of reference materials in the social sciences.

"Socially, as well as individually, organization is indispensable to growth," observed Herbert Spencer, a nineteenth-century pioneer of social science (59).* Today, the inheritors of that view—psychologists, sociologists, economists, political scientists, and anthropologists—attempt to discover patterns in human behavior that illuminate the ways in which we behave as members of groups: as members of family or community groups; as members of racial, ethnic, or religious groups; and as members of political or economic groups.

The belief that behavior is patterned suggests that a person's actions in his or her social setting are not random but instead are purposeful—whether or not the actor explicitly understands this. Social scientists do not claim that human behavior can be known absolutely—that, for instance, given enough information we can plot a person's future. They speak, rather, in terms of how and why a person or group is likely to behave in one set of circumstances or another. Social science is not mathematically precise in the manner of the natural sciences, and yet it is similar to those disciplines in the way that claims are based on what can be observed. Social scientists share the following broad theories:

- Human behavior is patterned, rule-governed behavior that can be described and explained.
- Individuals exist in a complex array of social systems, large and small. Individuals within systems interact; systems themselves interact and are dynamic, evolving entities.
- Individuals and social systems evolve—they change over time. Present behaviors can be traced to prior causes.

At any given moment, each of us exists in a broad constellation of systems: economic, political, cultural, psychological, and familial. The fabric of our lives is so complex that, in order to speak meaningfully and in detail about how we interact, social scientists carve up the social world according to the separate systems that constitute it. But no one of the social sciences is dominant: each contributes a partial understanding to what we know of human society.[1]

---

* In-text citations refer to the Works Cited list at the end of the book.

[1] To the extent that historical inquiry is based on an interpretation of texts, history is regarded as one of the humanities. Many historians, though, consider themselves to be social scientists in that they use procedures like statistical analysis to find meaningful patterns in the past. In this book, history is discussed as one of the humanities. See chapter 37.

38a Writing in the social sciences

1 Writing to inform

Before significance can be found in social behavior, behavior must be accurately described and, when appropriate, objectively measured. A great deal of what social scientists do when they write is to *inform* readers with precise descriptions. Consider, for instance, an anthropologist's account of ritual drug-taking among the Yanomamo Indians of Venezuela and Brazil. (For a fuller description of the practice, see 34f-1.)

> Another useful plant provided by the jungle is the *ebene* tree. The inner bark of this tree is used in the manufacture of one kind of hallucinogenic drug. The bark is scraped from the trunk after the exterior layer of bark is removed, or is scraped from the inside of the bark surface itself. This material, which is fairly moist, is then mixed with wood ashes and kneaded between the palms of the hands. Additional moisture is provided by spitting periodically into the pliable wad of drug. When the drug has been thoroughly mixed with saliva and ashes, it is placed on a hot piece of broken clay pot and the moisture driven out with heat. It is ground into a powder as it dries, the flat side of a stone axe serving as the grinding pestle. The dried, green powder, no more than several tablespoons full, is then swept onto a leaf with a stiff feather. The men then gather around the leaf containing the drug, usually in the late afternoon, and take it by blowing the powder into each other's nostrils.

As in other disciplines, informative writing in the social sciences is built on recognizable patterns, one such pattern being a *process* by which some activity takes place. Napoleon Chagnon's account of the process by which a hallucinogenic drug is prepared is precise and authoritative—in a word, informative. Similarly informative accounts can be found in any of the disciplines in the social sciences. A psychologist, for instance, might *compare* and *contrast* the different motivations people have for joining groups. In the course of this discussion, the psychologist might *classify* types of people according to their need for group identity. Such a discussion might begin or end with an attempt to *define* the term *group*. All of the techniques discussed in chapter 3 for informing writers are put to use in social science writing.

2 Making arguments

When social scientists report their findings in journals, they make arguments. Achieving general agreement about the causes of human behavior may be a distant goal of researchers, but achieving this goal is unlikely inasmuch as the subjects that social scientists study—humans—are willful beings whose behavior is determined by numerous, overlapping causes. Researchers acknowledge the complexity of human behavior by

TEACHING IDEAS

Students unfamiliar with writing outside the humanities may need to spend some time sifting through this material. While critical approaches differ within the humanities, the essential method of investigation—analyzing a text—remains the same. This is not so in the social sciences. You may want to reinforce the material here by cautioning students to be aware of the connections between type of claim and method of investigation. (The two sample arguments outlined below should help students see the difference between methods.)

avoiding cause-and-effect explanations. They prefer, instead, to express findings in terms of their *probability* of being correct—in terms of their "significance level." A level of .05, for instance, signifies that there is a less than 5 out of 100 possibility that the researcher's findings occurred by chance.

Arguments are the means by which knowledge is built in the social sciences. Various subdisciplines within each discipline carry on these arguments, and each one frames questions differently, uses distinctive methods, and subscribes to different theories. For instance, the discipline of anthropology is broadly understood as the study of humankind in its physical and cultural setting. There are two broad divisions of anthropology: physical anthropology and cultural anthropology. Physical anthropologists study humans as a biological species that evolved in certain environments from earlier forms (such as *Australopithecus*) to its present form (*Homo sapiens*). Cultural anthropologists investigate the artifacts of civilization in an effort to understand how various peoples have organized their lives socially, economically, technologically, or linguistically. Ethnographers, ethnologists, geographers, linguists, archaeologists, and other specialists in the discipline can all be termed anthropologists in that they share basic assumptions—for instance, about the value of studying the physical and/or cultural development of humankind. Nonetheless, both within and between subfields of anthropology, researchers will disagree on how to study human culture or biology. As a student in one of the social sciences, you will learn to read, think, and write in the context of arguments made in a particular field. The more courses you take in a discipline, the more you will learn how to produce arguments and to think like researchers in that discipline.

Claims and evidence

A *claim* is an arguable statement that a writer is obliged to support with evidence. *Claims in the social sciences will often commit you to observing the actions of individuals or groups and to stating how these actions are significant, both for certain individuals and for the people responding to them* (Braybrooke 11). The variety of human behavior is, of course, vast, and researchers have developed methods for gathering data both in controlled laboratory settings and in field settings. The interview and the survey are two widely used techniques that allow researchers to observe aspects of behavior that remain largely invisible such as attitudes, beliefs, and desires. Researchers carefully develop questionnaires, trying not to skew responses by the way questions are framed. If successfully developed and administered, questionnaires yield information about behavior that can be quantified and grouped into categories. These categories, in turn, can be analyzed statistically so that logical and reliable comparisons or contrasts can be drawn. Statistics can then be used as *evidence* in social scientific arguments to show whether a proposed connection between behaviors is significant.

The logic by which social scientists argue and connect evidence to claims (see 3d and 6d-1) will also depend on the method of investigation. Following is a sketch of two social scientific arguments, excerpts of which you will read in 38b-1. You will see in each the interplay of method of observation, type of evidence, and logic that connects evidence to a claim.

Study 1: "Factors Influencing the Willingness to Taste Unusual Foods"

PURPOSE   Psychologist Laura P. Otis investigates the factors that influence a person's willingness to taste unusual foods.

METHOD   Laboratory experiment—Otis showed students at a Canadian university various unusual foods (e.g., octopus), which they were led to believe they might eat. At various points during the experiment, subjects responded to questionnaires.

EVIDENCE   Statistical, based on frequency of responses to a questionnaire.

LOGIC   An argument from correlation or sign (see 6d-1); one pattern of responses is shown to be closely associated with another pattern—one pattern indicates the presence of another.

CLAIM   The older a person is, the more likely it is that he or she will experiment with unusual foods. Food preference is generally unrelated to an individual's willingness to engage in novel or risky activities.

Study 2: "The Story of Edward: The Everyday Geography of Elderly Single Room Occupancy Hotel Tenants"

PURPOSE   Ethnographer Paul A. Rollinson "seeks to provide a rich description of the everyday geography of an often overlooked population in contemporary urban America: elderly tenants of Single Room Occupancy Hotels" (188).

METHOD   Participant observation—Rollinson spends extended periods of time visiting run-down hotels in a section of Chicago where elderly tenants rent rooms. He tape records his conversations with tenants and forms a close and trusting relationship with one such man, 70-year-old Edward.

EVIDENCE   Personal observations

LOGIC   An argument from generalization (see 6d-1); the observations made are shown to form a pattern. The observer suggests that this pattern may form a general principle describing conditions for other individuals in similar circumstances.

CLAIM   "The problems faced by elderly tenants of SRO hotels are numerous and often life-threatening. Their treasured independence is encumbered by their poverty-level incomes, their wide range of chronic disabilities, and their inappropriate housing environ-

REFERENCES

GRIFFIN, C. W., ed. *New Directions for Teaching and Learning: Teaching Writing in All Disciplines.* San Francisco: Jossey-Bass, 1982. Collection of essays that examines how writing may lead students to learn about the content of the various disciplines.

DAEMMRICH, INGRID. "A Bridge to Academic Discourse: Social Science Research Strategies in the Freshman Composition Course." *CCC* 40 (1989): 343–48. Presents three strategies (family stories, observation reports, and case studies) that introduce inexperienced writers to the methodological and discourse conventions of the social sciences.

YOUNG, ART, and TOBY FULWILER, eds. *Writing Across the Disciplines: Research into Practice.* Upper Montclair, NJ: Boynton, 1986. Collection of essays discussing a writing-across-the-curriculum program, including essays on writing in the social sciences.

REFERENCES

ABRAHAMSON, MARK. *Social Research Methods.* Englewood Cliffs, NJ: Prentice, 1983. Discusses research methods in the social sciences, including surveys and interviews.

MACDONALD, SUSAN PECK. "Problem Definition in Academic Writing." *CE* 49 (1987): 315–33. Argues that different ways of composing are demanded by the different disciplines of the college or university.

SHAMOON, LINDA K., and ROBERT A. SCHWEGLER. "Sociologists Reading Student Texts: Expectations and Perceptions." *The Writing Instructor* 7 (1988): 71–81. Asserts that there are significant differences in the ways sociology and composition instructors perceive the features of a paper.

PITTENDRIGH, ADELE S., and PATRICK C. JOBES. "Teaching Across the Curriculum: Critical Communication in the Sociology Classroom." *Teaching Sociology* 11 (1984): 281–96. Discusses a set of writing assignments designed to help students develop the critical thinking and communications skills required in the sociology profession.

BEERS, SUSAN E. "Questioning and Peer Collaboration as Techniques for Thinking and Writing About Personality." *Teaching of Psychology* 13 (1986): 75–77. Describes an assignment sequence that leads students to inquire and to write about the topic of personality.

SNODGRAS, SARA E. "Writing as a Tool for Teaching Social Psychology." *Teaching of Psychology* 12 (1985): 91–94. Argues that implementing writing assignments (journals, analyses of published articles, observational studies, and formal research reports) enhances students' learning of social psychology.

LOOKING BACK

Students may want to review chapter 1 (Critical Thinking and Reading) for a general discussion of the subject before reading this section. While chapter 1 focuses primarily on reading texts other than reports, the general principles are still relevant.

ments." [The generalization of this particular field study extends only to elderly tenants in SRO hotels. While still a generalization, the claim is kept relatively narrow. As you will see, Rollinson is seeking to inform with his discussion as much as to argue.]

These two studies, excerpts of which follow, represent two distinct strains of social scientific research—one quantitative (a researcher's number-based analysis of experiments in a laboratory setting) and the other qualitative (a researcher's perceptions of life lived in its natural social setting). Social scientists have developed methods for investigating human behavior and, accordingly, many types of evidence are used in a variety of arguments. You can help orient yourself to your courses in the social sciences by understanding the special characteristics of arguments. Pose these questions in each of your courses:

- What questions about human behavior are studied in this discipline?
- What methods of investigation do researchers in this discipline use to study these questions?
- How are claims that researchers make related to methods of investigation?
- In this discipline, what types of information count as evidence in support of a claim?

Expect a variety of answers to these questions, even when you ask them of a single discipline. Given the many subspecialties in the social sciences, you are likely to find researchers using several methods to investigate a particular question. For instance, sociologists wanting to clarify the relationship between violence on television and the activities of children might set up several studies. One might be a lab experiment in which a group of children, closely monitored for their reactions, watch violent and nonviolent programs; a second study might take researchers into the field to videotape children watching television programs at home; a third study might collect, analyze, and draw conclusions about the state of published research on television violence and behavior of children (Rieke and Sillars 245–46). Each of these studies would properly be described as "sociological," but each would have its own distinct method and would, accordingly, lead to different claims and different sorts of evidence offered in support of these claims.

38b Reading in the social sciences

The sources you read in the social sciences will represent the variety of investigations carried out by researchers. Aside from textbooks and other general surveys of the disciplines, you will read reports of carefully controlled laboratory experiments as well as field and case studies. These two broad categories of source types parallel two major strategies for generating information in the social sciences: quantitative (number-based) and qualitative (observation-based) research.

Experimental (quantitative) reports

One method that social scientists have developed for studying human behavior is to conduct controlled experiments in a laboratory. Experimental researchers seek evidence for their claims by making careful observations and measurements in a lab. Based on statistical evidence (often questionnaire responses represented numerically), researchers are able to argue that the relationships they claim exist among various behaviors in fact *do* exist and are very likely not due to chance. Equally important can be the finding that no relationship exists between variables. For example, in the following report of a laboratory experiment, psychologist Laura Otis makes the claim displayed previously in Study #1 (38a-2).

Otis began her study with a specific question about human behavior: "Why do some people apparently prefer to eat novel or unusual foods?" Her report represents a particular instance of a social scientist observing the actions of individuals and stating how these actions are significant. Note that whenever Otis makes a direct statement concerning preferences for food, she reviews the literature—that is, she reviews previous research and theories—and thereby situates herself in a tradition of experimental research. Her opening section and the Methods section are reproduced entirely. Most of her highly technical Results and Discussion section has been omitted (as well as her References section), although it is in this technical discussion that Otis conducts her statistical analysis, which she then uses as evidence in support of her claims.

Factors Influencing the Willingness to Taste Unusual Foods

LAURA P. OTIS

York University

Summary.—Factors associated with willingness to taste 12 unusual foods were examined among 42 mature university students in a realistic taste testing situation. Low or nonsignificant correlations were found between subjects' willingness to taste the different foods and their scores on personality measures of sensation seeking as well as their ratings of familiarity with each food. Unexpectedly, age was a significant factor, with the older subjects being somewhat more willing to taste the unusual foods. Only a scale of items dealing specifically with food habits was highly correlated with subjects' willingness to try the unusual foods. The results suggest that food adventurousness is best accounted for by highly specific attitudes about food rather than general personality measures.

FOR DISCUSSION

You may want to initiate a class discussion of this model, particularly the opening summary. Some students may have declared social science majors already and understand quantitative reports; others will need the format explained to them. If students can discuss the features of the report themselves, they are more likely to understand the chapter.

Context-setting introduction

Both humans and animals have strong preferences for familiar rather than novel foods (Barnett, 1956; Domjan, 1977; Hall & Hall, 1939; Hill, 1978; Maslow, 1933, 1937; Meiselman & Waterman, 1978; Peryam, 1963; Pliner, 1982; Rozin, 1976). Typically, the animal research on this topic has been interpreted in terms of the "learned safety" hypothesis (Kalat & Rozin, 1973) while research with humans has been interpreted in terms of the "familiarity breeds liking" hypothesis (Zajonc, 1968).

Review of the literature—of existing research and theories on the topic.

However, neither hypothesis is sufficient to explain the full range of human selection of food. For example, why do some people apparently prefer to eat novel or unusual foods? One possibility is that the desire for novelty in food is a consequence of the negative effects of monotony (Balintfy, Duffy, & Sinha, 1974; Brickman & D'Amato, 1975; Kamen & Peryam, 1961; Siegel & Pilgrim, 1958). Further, it may be that preference for unfamiliar food is a reflection of some personality trait which predisposes some people toward novelty or sensation seeking. In fact, the item "I like to try new foods that I have never tasted before" is included in Zuckerman's Sensation Seeking Scale (Zuckerman, Kolin, Price, & Zoob, 1964) on the assumption that trying new foods reflects a general preference for engaging in risky and exciting kinds of activities.

All statements supported with references to social science literature.

Only a very few studies have actually investigated the relationship between sensation seeking and food preferences. Kish and Donnenwerth (1972) found a significant, although very modest relationship between sensation seeking and preference for sour, crunchy, and spicy foods. Similarly, Brown, Ruder, Ruder, and Young (1974) report a low but significant correlation between scores on the Change Seeker Index and preference for spicy food. But Rozin and Schiller (1980) conclude that sensation seeking is not related to preference for hot chili pepper. The only other evidence of a relationship between sensation seeking and food preference is provided by Back and Glasgow (1981) who noted that self-proclaimed gourmets scored significantly higher than vegetarians on measures of the General Sensation Seeking Scale and the Experience Seeking subscale of the Sensation Seeking Scale.

Gaps in existing research leave room for additional research.

It is difficult to draw any clear conclusions regarding the relationship between sensation seeking and food preferences from the existing literature. An obvious omission in the research to date is that no study has looked specifically at the relationship between sensation seeking and preference for *novel* foods. The purpose of

Present study designed to address gaps in existing research.

the present study was to look specifically at the relationship between personality measures of sensation seeking and preference for unfamiliar and unusual foods. Also, since most previous studies used only verbal measures of acceptance of food, the present study employed a realistic food-choice situation. Finally, the Neary-Zuckerman Sensation Seeking and Anxiety State Scale (Zuckerman, 1979) was included to assess the contribution of situational reactions to preference for unusual foods.

Method

Subjects

The subjects were 42 students enrolled in a summer session Introductory Psychology class at Glendon College, York University, Toronto. Their ages ranged from 17 to 50 yr., with a mean age of 30 yr. Many of the subjects were public school teachers.

Questionnaire described—research results to be based on data obtained from questionnaire.

Materials and Procedures

As part of a special class exercise, students were given a brief introduction to the present study which was described as research about attitudes towards foods. Questionnaires were distributed and students were asked to fill in the first two sections of the questionnaire. Section one, entitled "General Interest and Preference Survey" was made up of three subscales of Zuckerman's Sensation Seeking Scale (Form V), the Experience Seeking subscale, the Boredom Susceptibility subscale, and the Thrill and Adventure Seeking subscale (Zuckerman, 1979). The second section, entitled "Food Preference Survey" was made up of 13 items dealing specifically with attitudes towards trying new foods. These items were developed and pretested in an earlier pilot study. The survey included statements such as "I consider myself an adventurous eater," "I don't like eating unusual food because it might upset my stomach," and "I often try new brands of food on the chance of finding something different or better." Each statement was answered on a five-point scale going from 1 (not at all) to 5 (very much) according to how much each statement reflected the respondent's own eating habits.

Physical setting of experiment.

While these sections of the questionnaire were being completed, the food display table in the front of the room was set up. Bite-size pieces of 12 different foods (octopus, hearts of palm, seaweed, soya bean milk, blood sausage, Chinese sweet rice cake, pickled watermelon rind, raw fish, quail egg, star fruit, sheep milk cheese, and black beans) were placed on separate paper

TEACHING IDEAS

Although the format may seem intimidating to students accustomed to writing in the humanities, the practice of spelling out method actually makes for a clear, forthright presentation. You may want to ask students to compare this material to the types of writing they're accustomed to reading. Which seems easier to comprehend? Why?

plates. Each plate was clearly labeled and the product container or intact fresh example of the product was placed beside the food sample plate. When students had finished the Sensation Seeking Scale and the Food Preference Survey they were instructed to leave their seats and walk around the display table where they were to look at but not yet taste the different foods. Students were led to believe that they would be tasting some of the samples at a later time. They were asked not to talk or communicate their feelings about the foods in any way. Students then returned to their seats and completed the third section of the questionnaire, the Sensation Seeking and Anxiety State Scale. The last section of the questionnaire asked students for three kinds of food evaluation. First, they actually ate and then rated the appearance, taste, and preference for an unfamiliar Japanese snack food. Next, they indicated their willingness to try each of the 12 different food items. These two evaluations were made on a five-point scale going from 1 (not at all) to 5 (very much). They then rated their familiarity with each of the 12 foods on a five-point scale from 1 ("I have never heard of it or seen it before") to 5 ("I have tasted it often"). Finally, students were asked to indicate their age, sex, and whether or not they followed any special diet. At the end of the study, students were given a complete explanation of the purpose of the research and were told that they would not be required actually to eat any of the food samples. Of the 42 participants in the study, 32 indicated at this point that they fully believed that they would be expected to taste some of the food items.

Results and Discussion

Various statistical tests conducted (discussion omitted here).

The data are discussed in terms of the relationship between each of the main predictor variables (familiarity, trait and state measures of Sensation Seeking, the Food Preference Survey, and age) and the subjects' willingness to taste the unusual foods. A multiple regression analysis showing the relative contribution of each of these factors is also described.

• • •

Conclusions

Conclusion, based on statistical evidence, is presented and set in context of existing research.

In exploring a number of factors associated with food adventurousness, several surprises were found. An expected positive relationship between familiarity and food adventurousness was not confirmed. On the other hand, an unanticipated positive relationship between food adventurousness and age was noted. Consistent with previous research, personality measures did not appear to play a very significant role in individual food selections. In conclusion, this study suggests that willingness to taste unusual foods is best predicted by specific attitudes about food and is largely unrelated to preferences for engaging in other kinds of novel or risky activities.

Field (qualitative) studies

Quite different from experimental research, which takes place in the controlled conditions of a laboratory and generates quantifiable data, field studies situate researchers among people in a community in order to observe life as it is lived in its natural social context. The result is a *qualitative* study built on an observer's descriptions and interpretations of behavior. Based on observations, the field worker writes reports and discusses the possible general significance of the behavior he or she has seen, offering what in many cases is a fascinating glimpse into exotic cultures both foreign and local.

Following are excerpts from a field study of an elderly population living in Single Room Occupancy (SRO) hotels in Chicago. You will notice that author Paul Rollinson bases his claims either on prior participant-observer research or on his own observations. Rollinson maintains a distance from his subject that allows him an analytical stance, yet at the same time he is able to enter into the lives of the population he has observed. His report is qualitative, based on personal observations that he then interprets in the context of scholarly work in his discipline. (The References section has been omitted here.) As testament to the impact field studies can have on a researcher, Rollinson dedicates his article to the principal subject of his study, Edward, who (says Rollinson) "taught me infinitely more valuable lessons than my formal academic training."

The Story of Edward

The Everyday Geography Of Elderly Single Room Occupancy (SRO) Hotel Tenants

PAUL A. ROLLINSON

This article seeks to provide a rich description of the everyday geography of an often overlooked population in contemporary urban America: elderly tenants of Single Room Occupancy (SRO) hotels. The term SRO is a recent one, originally coined to describe apartment dwellings that had been subdivided into single rooms in New York City (Shapiro 1966). SRO's have also been described as "flophouses" and "fleabag hotels" (Eckert 1979). These buildings, originally designated as transient facilities, have evolved into largely permanent residences for the single poor of all ages. Today, SRO hotels, which are typically

FOR DISCUSSION

Social science writing, especially the field study report, is sometimes erroneously considered dry and objective. You may want to initiate a discussion to dispel this notion by asking the class to characterize Rollinson's attitude toward his subjects, based on the introduction to his study. Ask students to explain their characterizations and to comment on how they think Rollinson's attitude affects his work.

located in dilapidated and deteriorating inner city areas, have been characterized as the nation's least desirable housing (Kasinitz 1984).

• • •

The problem to be studied is defined and set in context of existing research.

The scope of the problem facing the elderly living in these SRO hotels throughout the nation is great; at least 400,000 are estimated to live in such accommodations (Eckert 1983). Previous ethnographic studies have brought attention to the unique socio-demographic characteristics of this population. Elderly tenants of SRO's are overwhelmingly single males (Eckert 1980; Mackelman 1961; Stephens 1976) who exist in a state of poverty (Tissue 1971). They are not newcomers to the inner city (Erickson and Eckert 1977; Lally et al. 1979), and Shapiro (1971), Siegal (1978), and Sokolovsky et al. (1978) have all found evidence to suggest the presence of considerable ties among elderly SRO tenants. However, little attention has been paid to this population's involvement in the built environment, their geographical movement, the places that are vital to these men and women, and the barriers that constrain them (Stutz 1976). It is the purpose of this description to pay attention to the elderly tenants' involvement in the built environment within a framework of the geography of everyday experience, defined as "the sum total of a person's first-hand involvements with the geographical world in which he or she typically lives" (Seamon 1979, 15–16). The primary focus of this framework is on understanding and conveying the everyday geographical experience in a "lived" form with as little a priori structuring as possible (Reinharz and Rowles 1988). SRO hotels have, in the past, been portrayed romantically as allowing this population to live independent lives (Eckert 1979; Stephens 1976). In reality, the findings of this exploration suggest that these hotels offer anything but independence. The elderly men and women in this study were caught in an environment that exacerbated their isolation and withdrawal from society. In this research, I portray this unique and vulnerable elderly population's everyday geography.

Purpose of present research.

Framework (or point of view) from which observations will be made.

Methods

Method of observation set in context of a tradition of observation.

The methodology I used aligns itself with a lengthy tradition of participant-observation studies in exploratory social science research (Clark 1965; Gans 1962; Hill 1986; Jackson 1980; Ley 1974; Rowles 1978; Suttles 1968; Whyte 1943; Zorbaugh 1929).

• • •

The Everyday Geography of Edward

This is the story of Edward, an elderly SRO tenant. I compare Edward to the other elderly tenants in the study, briefly describe his life history, how he viewed the SRO hotel and the neighborhood environment, and I discuss his everyday geography and concerns about the future. I met Edward in the lobby of one of the four hotels in August of 1985. Initially, he simply agreed to answer some of my questions. Later, he invited me to his room and subsequently to spend time with him traveling around the neighborhood.

Description of the subject in the subject's world.

Edward was similar to the majority of the elderly SRO tenant population I saw. The elderly SRO tenant population in the study had a mean age of 70 years, was predominantly white (92%), and male (58%). Edward was a 62-year-old white male. Overall, the elderly tenants had a low educational attainment; almost three-quarters (73%) had achieved education levels of high school or lower. Edward, in contrast, had completed two years of college. Elderly SRO tenants were extremely poor; Edward's yearly income ($4,620 in 1986) was even less than the mean of the elderly tenants in the study ($5,559) and well below the mean poverty level ($5,360). Accompanying his low income was a higher than average rent burden of 69% (compared to the already high mean of 46% for all those I interviewed), which exacerbated the tenuousness of Edward's already critical financial status. Nationally, the accepted normal rent-to-income ratio was 30%. Like 62% of his fellow elderly tenants, Edward received most of his income from Social Security. He was fortunate in that he had some savings to rely upon in times of financial need, as only 10% of all the elderly tenants interviewed had any savings.

• • •

Conclusions

Graphic review of conditions observed.

The elderly tenants of SRO hotels had few resources or alternatives, and they lived there out of necessity. The SRO hotel environments were largely unsuited to the needs of this population. These hotels were deteriorating, dirty, and dangerous. In the winter, the heating systems were nonfunctional for days at a time. In the summer, the hotels were unbearably hot. The rooms, bathrooms, hallways, and elevators were not designed to accommodate the functionally impaired elderly tenants. It is very important to remember that the hotels in this study represented the least dilapidated and more conscientiously managed of the hotels, both in the study neighborhood and in the city of Chicago. The elderly tenants were overlooked by social scientists, social service providers, and planners because the majority were trapped inside their hotels and not visible to the wider society. This isolation should not be confused with independence. . . .

Claims made based on observations.

The problems faced by elderly tenants of SRO hotels are numerous and often life-threatening. Their treasured independence is encumbered by their poverty-level incomes, their wide range of chronic disabilities, and their inappropriate housing environments. Their desire to make choices and remain independent is all-important to these men and women. Their residence in the SRO hotels was not a genuine choice. Policymaker and social service agencies must strive to create a genuine choice for these men and women and they must also honor the right of this population to choose their unique and independent life-style. Given the fact that this elderly population had few resources and alternatives, the current and rapid decline in the SRO housing stock poses a serious threat to their ability to secure shelter. SRO hotels were inappropriate to the needs of the elderly tenants, but they did provide shelter at a time when homelessness was on the rise throughout the nation. Tenants of SRO hotels are labelled both deviant and undesirable, as "bums" or "derelicts." These men and women suffer greatly as a result of these inaccurate labels and they are consequently left in isolation, and the hotels are allowed to be removed from the housing stock. Edward noted: "[To] whoever is out there I'd like to say that one day you are going to be old. You will never know what it's like until it happens. A lot of us thought that there would always be someone to look out for us. It's a shock to us all to be in this situation."

38c   Types of writing assignments in the social sciences

The assignments you will most often be given in your social sciences courses have in a general way been addressed in chapter 2, "Critical Thinking and Writing," as well as in other chapters. The discussion here will introduce the special requirements of assignments in the social sciences and will provide references to other sections of the book.

1   The lab report (quantitative research)

Experimental researchers in the social sciences have patterned their writing of lab reports on those done in the sciences. Section 39c-1 discusses the general requirements of each section of the standard lab report: introduction, methods, results, and discussion. In the social sciences, you will encounter more variability than in the sciences in titling the various sections of a research report.

The opening

Depending on the conventions in a discipline (check with your professor), a paper's first section may be titled "Introduction," "Theoretical Background," or "Previous Work," or may appear with no heading at all, as is the case of the example report you read by Laura Otis on pages 689–693. Whatever you call your introduction, make sure it orients your reader to the perspective from which you are conducting research and that it situates your thesis, or claim, in relation to the claims of other scholars. You will need to review the literature on your topic to suggest gaps in existing research and to provide a rationale for your own study. This can be done by reviewing the history of the question you are investigating and by citing pertinent sources.

Methods

This section describes how you conducted your study. In the social sciences, the Methods section is divided into subsections as needed to provide a full and accurate accounting of an experiment. Standard subsections include "Subjects," "Measures," "Apparatus," "Procedures," and "Design." In the Methods section, the researcher discusses any instruments that were used, such as questionnaires, in generating data for the experiment.

Results

This section presents the data generated by your research. If you have used surveys in your research, you will probably compress your results numerically and run one or more statistical programs, the results of which will provide the evidence for whatever claims you are making.

Discussion

This section calls a reader's attention to significant patterns that emerge from your statistical analysis. Your discussion will interpret your results for the reader and lead to a statement of your claims. The discussion will often end with a note on the significance of your research and, if appropriate, suggestions for future research.

TEACHING IDEAS

The guidelines for manuscript form will be invaluable to students preparing lab reports in their social science classes. Students should be encouraged to mark this page for future reference.

Manuscript Form for Research Reports in the Social Sciences

- A research paper should have its own (unnumbered) title page. One-third of the way down the page, center your title. Do *not* place it in quotation marks. Center a line below the title and then center your name: first name, middle initial, last name. Below your name, center the name of the department in which you are taking the course. On the next line, center the name of your college or university. On the next line, center the address of your college or university (Solomon 19, 31).

- Give the abstract its own numbered page following the title page. (The abstract is the first numbered page of the report.) Center the word Abstract, skip a line, and begin, writing the abstract as a single paragraph.

- The heading, Method, is given its own line and is centered. Skip a line to begin the first subsection, Subjects. Each subheading—such as Subjects, Measures, Apparatus, Procedure, and Design—is given its own line, is underlined, and is placed flush to the left margin.

- Each table or figure should be numbered and titled and placed on its own page at the end of the report, after the Reference list. (In a published article, tables and figures appear in the body of the report.) When referring in your report to a particular table or figure, capitalize the *T* and *F*.

- Observe APA (American Psychological Association) citation form. (See 36b, and see 36a and 36c for citation forms in the humanities and sciences, respectively.)

2 The field report and case study (qualitative research)

Many inquiries in the social sciences do not lend themselves to statistical analysis but rather to observations of social interactions in the communities where they occur. Researchers who conduct qualitative research go into the "field," a closely defined area of study that may be as exotic as the Trobriand Islands or as commonplace as an urban pool hall. The investigator, informed by a particular disciplinary point of view, collects data by directly observing and in many cases participating in social life. Then the researcher sifts through notes and conducts an analysis (see 2c). At the beginning of research, an observer or participant-observer may purposely try *not* to make predictions, as quantitative researchers do, so as to approach the novel social environment with as few preconceived ideas as possible (Richlin-Klonsky and Strenski 90–91; Rollinson 189). One outcome of field research is the field report, which provides a rich and detailed description of the behaviors observed as well as an analysis that discusses the possible significance of those behaviors. In Paul Rollinson's "Story of Edward," you read a field report—which is also called an *ethnography*.

A set of field observations may be put to other uses. When they concern a "relatively short, self-contained episode or segment of a person's life," field notes may be used in a *case study*, a focused narrative account that becomes the occasion for an analysis (Bromley 1). The case may provide the basis for making a recommendation: for example, concerning the placement of a drunk driver in a rehabilitation program (as opposed to jail) or concerning the placement of a child in an appropriate class. You will find case studies used as the basis of recommendations in most disciplines, but especially in the social sciences and the business and medical professions. You may also be given cases to analyze. In this instance, your professor will present a snapshot narrative of some behavior in its social context: perhaps observations of a child in a daycare setting or observations about employee morale at a business. Your job will be to sort through the information presented just as if you had made and recorded the observations yourself. Then you select the most important information to include in your case analysis, based on a theoretical approach recently read or reviewed in class.

If you go into the field to conduct research, you will keep a notebook or journal in which to record observations. Your professor will review particular methods for observing and making field notes. One challenge of writing your report will involve choosing and organizing the particular observations you want to discuss. The following categories of information often appear in case or field reports, and the categories can be useful for notetaking. (In brief reports, the researcher may not write on each of these categories.)

- An introduction that sets the question or problem you have studied in a context of prior research and that establishes your question or problem as *worthy* of research
- Information on the subjects studied and the environment in which you observed them
- Your theoretical perspective
- Your method of making observations
- Your analysis of significant behaviors
- Your conclusions

3 The library research paper

Just as in other disciplines, your library research paper in the social sciences should be guided by a central "burning" question. (See 33a-1 and, generally, chapter 33, "Understanding the Research Process.") You will base your library research on secondary sources of the sort you found illustrated in 38b. Depending on your topic, you will read journal articles

REFERENCES

BARTHOLOMAE, DAVID. "Inventing the University." In *When a Writer Can't Write*. Ed. Mike Rose. New York: Guilford, 1985. 134–65. Essential to being a college student is the mastering of discipline-specific discourses, but such achievement is the result of a gradual process with multiple stages.

RUSSELL, DAVID R. "Writing Across the Curriculum in Historical Perspective: Toward a Social Interpretation." *CE* 52 (1990): 52–73. Looks at WAC in its historical, social context, arguing that such a perspective will provide new ways of "integrating students, instead of excluding them."

YOUNG, ART, and TOBY FULWILER, eds. *Writing Across the Disciplines: Research into Practice*. Upper Montclair, NJ: Boynton, 1986. Collection of essays discussing a writing-across-the-curriculum program, including essays on writing in the humanities.

MCLEOD, SUSAN H. "Writing Across the Curriculum: The Second Stage, and Beyond." *CCC* 40 (1989): 337–43. Overview of the changes in WAC that argues for continued reform in thinking, learning, and writing across the disciplines.

and books that are both qualitative and quantitative in their method. As you choose a topic, be aware that you will need to narrow it so that you can reasonably manage your discussion in an allotted number of pages. Also, be aware that professors will want you to use sources to support a thesis, or claim, of your own design (see 33c-3). In a research paper, you will read sources and relate them to each other and to your thesis. As you synthesize material, try to arrange your discussion by *topic* or *idea*, not by source (see 2d). If you need help in conducting your library research, consult chapters 33, 34, and 35 on writing research papers. For suggestions of discipline-specific sources you might turn to when conducting library research, see 38e. And for the conventions of documenting sources in the social sciences, see 36b.

38d Sample student paper: "Women Alcoholics: A Conspiracy of Silence"

The following library research paper, written by a student for her sociology class, investigates why women alcoholics in this country are largely an unrecognized population. Kristy Bell read several sources in order to support her thesis that the denial surrounding the problems of women alcoholics "amounts to a virtual conspiracy of silence and greatly complicates the process of diagnosis and treatment." Notice that Bell organizes her material by *idea*, not by source—one clear indication of which is her use of headings in the paper. Each heading develops one part of her thesis. Notice as well her use of the American Psychological Association's (APA's) format for documenting sources. This paper is one of three discipline-specific papers relating to the topic of alcohol. See 37e for a paper on the uses of alcohol in a short story by James Joyce, and see 39d for a lab report on the fermentation of wine.

Women Alcoholics: A Conspiracy of Silence

Kristy Bell
Behavioral Sciences Department
Bentley College
Waltham, Massachusetts
November 4, 1991

Information centered on title page

Bell 1

Currently, in the United States, there are at least two million women alcoholics (Unterberger, 1989, p. 1150). Americans are largely unaware of the extent of this debilitating disease among women and the problems it presents. Numerous women dependent on alcohol remain invisible largely because friends, family, coworkers and the women themselves refuse to acknowledge the problem. This denial amounts to a virtual conspiracy of silence and greatly complicates the process of diagnosis and treatment.

Silence: The Denial of Family, Friends and Employers

Although the extent of the problem of alcoholism among women is slowly being recognized, a tremendous stigma still accompanies the disease for women. The general public remains very uncomfortable in discussing the topic. A primary reason that women alcoholics remain invisible is that they are so well protected. Family and friends, even if aware of the seriousness of the addiction, suffer pain and embarrassment and generally protect their loved one rather than suggesting that she seek professional counseling. By not confronting the issue, family and friends hope the problem will correct itself. According to Turnbull (1988), "The initial response of those close to the alcoholic woman is usually to deny the problem right along with her" (p. 366). Spouses, friends, relatives and even employers tend to protect the alcoholic rather than help her initiate treatment. "A husband will nervously protect his wife's illness from friends and neighbors" (Sandmaier, 1980, p. 8). Family and friends

Side annotations:

Introduction: women alcoholics will be studied in their social context.

Thesis

Denial by others.

Claims supported by references to social science literature.

APA format for documenting sources.

TEACHING IDEAS

You may want to call students' attention to the difference between in-text citations in APA and MLA styles. Note the importance of the date of publication in APA style.

FOR DISCUSSION

Just as Rollinson does in his study of Edward, Bell allows her own attitude to come through in her writing. You may want to ask students to point out evidence of her sympathies in the paper, and explain how her writing reflects her feelings in addition to laying out her reasoned argument.

Bell 2

experience a great deal of guilt and responsibility that, in turn, causes them to deny or hide the problem (Grasso, 1990, p. 32).

The needs of women dependent on alcohol are also ignored by employers, who are unable to confront the problem, in part, due to their having no prior experience with alcoholic women. The conspiracy of silence thus extends to the workplace. Employers tend generally to dodge confrontation by simply firing the alcoholic woman on an unrelated charge rather than steering her to an employee assistance program (Sandmaier, p. 131).

Silence: Self-Denial Among Women Alcoholics

Women not only fail to seek treatment because they are ignored and abandoned, but also because they deny the extent of the problem themselves. Sandmaier believes that in "responding to survey questions, women may be more likely than men to minimize alcohol-related problems because of more intense guilt and shame" (p. 73). Thus, statistics published concerning women's dependence upon alcohol understate the extent of the problem. Once again, guilt and pain can be directly related to unfamiliarity with the issue--this time the woman alcoholic's own awareness that alcoholism among women is a debilitating and growing problem. Women alcoholics suffer from the same feelings of guilt and embarrassment felt by family members and friends. Obviously, these feelings are incredibly more intense in the actual alcoholic and tend to force the woman to be driven underground by her drinking problem. Unterberger observes that "[m]ore often than men, female alcoholics turn their anger on themselves rather than others, with anxiety and guilt being the result" (p. 1150).

Denial by alcoholic, herself.

At second and subsequent references to an author, no date needed in citation.

Bell 3

A common feeling among women alcoholics is that
they are disrupting their lives and that any
wrongdoing is their fault. More so than the male,
claims Sandmaier, they tend to feel guilty about
their drinking habits because they realize the
effects it can have on family, home and career:
"Both recovered alcoholic women and treatment
specialists attest to the intense guilt and self-
hatred borne by alcoholic women because of
society's judgement that they have failed as wives
and mothers" (p. 17). <u>Specialists in the field</u>
<u>of alcoholism believe that there is an inherent</u>
<u>trait among women to ignore the value of their</u>
<u>own lives.</u> Unfortunately, a woman today is
rarely taught nor is she able to properly take
care of herself first (Grasso, p. 40). As soon as
she marries, in most cases, she is expected to
"take care" of her husband. With the arrival of
children she is required to take care of them.
Often, if parents are aged, she will feel
responsible for their well-being. Grasso firmly
believes that women not only ignore and deny their
problem, but never really think enough about
themselves to realize that they are in trouble with
and becoming very dependent on alcohol. Sandmaier
says this feeling is especially true among
housewives due to the close identification with
their dual roles of wife and mother.

Examination
of reasons
alcoholic
women deny
their prob-
lems

Difficulties in Treatment and Diagnosis

Many women avoid treatment because of concern for the well-being of their children. A
rehabilitation program including hospital care
cannot be considered because the woman is unable to
be absent from home for an extended period.
Feelings of obligation to a husband and children
are extremely powerful for a woman, especially one
whose emotions are intensified by alcohol. Turnbull

New head-
ing signals
development
of second
part of thesis

FOR DISCUSSION

While these chapters spend a good deal of time
emphasizing the differences in writing and
thinking between disciplines, this section of
Bell's paper illustrates similarities. Ask students
to analyze how Bell supports her argument in
this section, and to compare her use of outside
sources to those used by Chandra in the previous chapter.

(1988) believes that "child-care services need to be provided to allow women to seek and remain in treatment" (p. 369). Treatment would be considerably easier and progress much more quickly if the woman was confident that her children would receive proper care.

Professionals in the field of social work are not yet experienced enough to recognize alcoholism by its preliminary characteristics. Because female alcoholism has never really been a well-defined problem, health specialists do not have the experience needed to detect it when a woman approaches them with an alcohol-related problem. Frequently, the alcoholic woman is dismissed as being "just depressed" or under stress (Turnbull, 1989, p. 291). Moreover, she is not likely to announce the problem directly:

> An alcoholic woman is unlikely to come into her doctor's office announcing her drinking problem, but she is apt to seek medical attention for a wide range of problems commonly associated with alcohol abuse, including depression, anxiety, stomach trouble, and injuries from alcohol-related accidents or physical abuse. (Sandmaier, p. 207)

On numerous occasions, many alcoholic women have had personal contacts with health professionals during which opportunities for intervention went unobserved or ignored (Turnbull, 1988, p. 369).

Conclusion

Society is now realizing that there is and has been a definite alcohol problem among women. The problem now lies in learning to recognize the symptoms and help women to seek treatment. Many

---

Date continues to be cited in this reference since Turnbull has written two articles that are referred to in this paper

Social work professionals need help in detecting alcoholism among women.

Extended block quotation

Conclusion: the paper *has* established that a problem exists.

TEACHING IDEAS

You may want to call attention to a similarity and a difference between social science and humanities: The block quotation is treated in essentially the same way in both disciplinary styles, while the conclusion is highlighted in social science writing.

Bell 5

believe that women should be screened routinely at the onset of any kind of treatment program. This would allow for identification of alcohol problems much earlier and would facilitate treatment before problems grow out of control. Social workers, as well, should include screening for drinking problems in all female clients. Some specialists believe that routine screening for substance abuse should become a mandatory part of all gynecological examinations as well as job orientations (Turnbull, 1988, pp. 366-68).

Two solutions explored

As the recognition of alcoholism among women grows, changes are being initiated to help make these women more visible to themselves, to health care professionals and to society at large. "Public education programs must be strengthened to counter the fear of social stigma that inhibits women from seeking treatment" (Turnbull, 1988, p. 369). The public must be made aware of the severity of the problem of alcoholism.

Self-perception of women alcoholics encouraged

Bell 6

References

Grasso, A. (1990). Special treatment needs of the chemically dependent woman. Syracuse: Crouse-Irving Memorial School of Nursing.

Sandmaier, M. (1980). The invisible alcoholics. New York: McGraw-Hill.

Turnbull, J. (1988). Primary and secondary alcoholic women. Social Casework: The Journal of Contemporary Social Casework, 36, 290-298.

Turnbull, J. (1989). Treatment issues for alcoholic women. Social Casework: The Journal of Contemporary Social Casework, 47, 364-370.

Unterberger, G. (1989, December 6). Twelve steps for women alcoholics. The Christian Century, pp. 1150-1152.

FOR DISCUSSION

It would be helpful for students to recognize the differences in format between APA and MLA style with regard to references. Ask students to note the differences, and to explain why they think the date is highlighted in APA style.

38e   Reference materials in the social sciences

Style guides

The following sources offer general or discipline-specific guidance for writing in the social sciences.

Bart, Pauline, and Linda Frankel. *The Student Sociologist's Handbook.* 4th ed. New York: Random House, 1986.

Becker, Howard S. with a chapter written by Pamela Richards. *Writing for Social Scientists: How to Start and Finish Your Thesis, Book, or Article.* Chicago: University of Chicago Press, 1986.

Cuba, Lee J. *A Short Guide to Writing About Social Science.* Glenview: Scott, Foresman, 1988.

Jolley, Janina M., Peter A. Keller, and J. Dennis Murray. *How to Write Psychology Papers: A Student's Survival Guide for Psychology and Related Fields.* Sarasota: Professional Resource Exchange, 1984.

McCloskey, Donald. *The Writing of Economics.* New York: Macmillan, 1987.

Publication Manual of the American Psychological Association. 3rd ed. Washington: American Psychological Association, 1983 (Revisions, 1984).

Richlin-Klonsky, Judith, and Ellen Strenski, coordinators and eds. *A Guide to Writing Sociology Papers.* New York: St. Martin's, 1986.

Specialized references

The following specialized references will help you to assemble information in a particular discipline or field within a discipline.

Encyclopedias provide general information that is useful when beginning a search.

Editorial Research Reports (current events)

Encyclopedia of Crime and Justice

Encyclopedia of Education

Encyclopedia of Human Behavior

Encyclopedia of Psychology

Encyclopedia of Social Work

Encyclopedia of Sociology

Guide to American Law

International Encyclopedia of Higher Education

International Encyclopedia of Psychiatry, Psychology, Psychoanalysis and Neurology

International Encyclopedia of the Social Sciences

Dictionaries provide definitions of technical terms.

Black's Law Dictionary
Dictionary of the Social Sciences
McGraw-Hill Dictionary of Modern Economics: A Handbook of Terms and Organizations
The Encyclopedic Dictionary of Psychology
The Prentice-Hall Dictionary of Business, Finance and Law

Periodical indexes and abstracts list articles published in a particular discipline over a particular period. *Abstracts,* which summarize the sources listed and involve a considerable amount of work to compile, tend to be more selective than indexes.

Abstracts in Anthropology
Current Index to Journals in Education (CIJE)
Education Index
Key to Economic Science
Psychological Abstracts
Public Affairs Information Service (PAIS)
Social Sciences Citation Index
Social Science Index
Social Work Research and Abstracts
Sociological Abstracts
Women's Studies Abstracts

Writing and Reading in the Sciences

Scientists work systematically to investigate the world of nature—at scales so small that they are invisible to the naked eye and at scales so vast that they are equally invisible. A scientist's investigations are always built on observable, verifiable information, known as **empirical** evidence. Scientific investigations often begin with questions like these:

- What kinds of things are there in the world of nature?
- What are these things composed of, and how does this makeup affect their behavior or operation?
- How did all these things come to be structured as they are?
- What are the characteristic functions of each natural thing and/or its parts? (Toulmin, Rieke, and Janik 231)*

At one point or another, we have all asked these questions and speculated on answers. Scientists do more than speculate. They devise experiments in order to gather information and, on the basis of carefully stated predictions, or **hypotheses,** they conduct analyses and offer explanations. All scientists share two fundamental assumptions about the world and the way it works: that "things and events in the universe occur in consistent patterns that are comprehensible through careful, systematic study" and that "[k]nowledge gained from studying one part of the universe is applicable to other parts" (American Association 25). On the strength of these assumptions, scientists pose questions and conduct experiments in which they observe and measure. Then they make claims (usually) of fact or definition, about *whether* a thing exists and, if it does, *what* it is or *why* it occurs. Questions that cannot be answered by an appeal to observable, quantifiable fact may be important and necessary to ask (for example, "What makes *Moby Dick* a great novel?" or "What are a society's responsibilities to its poor?"), but these are not matters for scientific investigation.

39a Writing in the sciences

1 Writing to inform

A major function of scientific writing is to *inform;* and scientists try to be precise in their descriptions of the world, writing, when possible,

---

*In-text citations in this chapter refer to the Works Cited list at the end of the book.

with *mathematical* or *quantifiable* precision. A researcher would report the temperature of water as 4°C, not as "near freezing"—an inexact expression, the meaning of which would change depending on the observer. Precise measurements taken from a thermometer or some other standard laboratory instrument help readers of scientific literature to know exactly what has been observed or what procedures have been followed so that, if necessary, experiments can be repeated.

As in other disciplines, informative writing in science is built on recognizable patterns. One of the ways in which a scientist may inform is by writing a precise *description*—for example, of experimental methods and materials or of observations made in the lab or field. A description may involve presenting a *sequence* of events—perhaps the sequence by which volcanic islands are born. Presenting information can also take the form of a *comparison and contrast*—for example, between the organization of the human brain and that of a computer. Scientists also *classify* the objects they study. When entomologists report on newly discovered insects, they identify each discovery with respect to a known species of insect. If no closely related species exists, researchers may attempt to *define* a new one.

When contributors bring different specialties to a project, researchers very often work and write collaboratively. Look in any journal and you will find a number of multiauthored articles. The great advantage of working collaboratively is that researchers can put the power of several minds to work on a particular problem. The challenge in writing collaboratively is to make a final report read as though *one* person had written it, even if several people have had a hand in its creation. If you are part of a group assigned to write a paper, be sure to meet with group members before any writing takes place. Agree on a structure for the document and then assign parts to individual group members. (See 4d for details on how to manage the logistics of collaborative writing.)

2 Arguing in the sciences

A scientist's efforts to inform readers are very often part of a larger attempt to *persuade*. In every discipline arguments are built on claims, evidence, and the logical relationships that connect them. But the characteristics of these elements change from one discipline to the next and also *within* disciplines as theoretical perspectives change.[1] Geneticists working on techniques of tissue analysis argue differently from astronomers. Each discipline uses different methods and different tools of investigation. Each asks different questions and finds meaning in different sorts of

---

[1] This discussion is based directly on the work of Stephen Toulmin, Richard Rieke, and Allen Janik in *Introduction to Reasoning* (New York: Macmillan, 1979). See chapter 12, their "Introduction" to fields of argument, 195–202; and chapter 14, "Argumentation in Science," 229–263. For a related discussion, see Richard D. Rieke and Malcolm O. Sillars, *Argumentation and the Decision Making Process*, 2nd ed. (Glenview: Scott, Foresman, 1984).

background; if they can articulate the nature of scientific argument, while other students articulate humanistic or social scientific arguments, the class should be better able to distinguish between different types of argument.

ADDITIONAL EXERCISE A

Interview a professor of biology, chemistry, or physics on the subject of the writing he or she does in the profession. Pose questions such as the following: What kinds of questions do you ask? What kinds of investigations do you conduct? What forms does your writing usually take? What is your purpose in writing in these forms? What kind of audience do you usually address? Try to think of some additional questions as well. Use your notes from the interview to write a paragraph describing the nature of writing in this particular discipline.

LOOKING BACK

Students may want to review the appropriate sections of chapter 3 as they study this material. It's important that they recognize how the patterns of development cross disciplinary lines.

TEACHING IDEAS

Students unfamiliar with writing outside the humanities may need to spend some time sifting through this material. In particular, the concept of replication may be difficult for students to grasp: Why would anyone want to repeat an experiment that's already been done? You may want to actually "walk students through" this section of the chapter.

LOOKING BACK

All of the chapters in this part of the handbook rely heavily on ideas discussed in chapter 6 (Writing and Evaluating Arguments), especially the material on modes of inquiry in various disciplines. If you haven't yet covered chapter 6 in class, it would be useful to do so now. Otherwise, students should review the chapter in order to make better use of the information in this part of the handbook.

REFERENCES

BARTHOLOMAE, DAVID. "Inventing the University." In *When a Writer Can't Write*. Ed. Mike Rose. New York: Guilford, 1985. 134–65. Essential to being a college student is the mastering of discipline-specific discourses, but such achievement is the result of a gradual process with multiple stages.

RUSSELL, DAVID R. "Writing Across the Curriculum in Historical Perspective: Toward a Social Interpretation." *CE* 52 (1990): 52–73. Looks at WAC in its historical, social context, arguing that such a perspective will provide new ways of "integrating students, instead of excluding them."

YOUNG, ART, and TOBY FULWILER, eds. *Writing Across the Disciplines: Research into Practice*. Upper Montclair, NJ: Boynton, 1986. Collection of essays discussing a writing-across-the-curriculum program.

MCLEOD, SUSAN H. "Writing Across the Curriculum: The Second Stage, and Beyond." *CCC* 40 (1989): 337–43. Overview of the changes in WAC that argues for continued reform in thinking, learning, and writing across the disciplines.

information. Within any one discipline you will find that multiple perspectives give rise to competing communities or schools of thought. Within any one scientific community the purpose of argument will be to achieve agreement about the way in which some part of the universe works.

The process of scientific inquiry generally goes like this: Once investigators make their observations in a laboratory or in a natural setting, they report their findings to colleagues in articles written for scientific and technical journals. The scientific community will not accept these reports as dependable until independent researchers can recreate experiments and observe similar findings. As scientists around the world try to replicate the experiments and confirm results, a conversation—an argument—develops in which researchers might publish a challenge or addition to the original findings. In this way, a body of literature—of writing on a particular topic—grows.

As in other disciplines, debates in science can grow heated—for instance, when one person attempts to demonstrate why a particular theory is flawed and should be replaced. Revolutions in scientific thinking may upend whole schools of thought and threaten careers of those who have built reputations on outmoded theories. At any one moment, agreement (if it exists) is provisional and will last only until some new challenge is put to conventional thinking—perhaps by a researcher who has observed some new fact that cannot be explained by existing knowledge. As an undergraduate student in the sciences, you will be introduced to scientific thinking and to the ways in which scientists argue. In each of your science classes, try to identify the purposes of argumentation. Pose these questions:

- In this area of science, what are the particular issues around which researchers seek to gain agreement?
- What questions do researchers pose and why are these questions useful?

Claims

Scientific arguments often involve two sorts of claims. The first takes the form *X is a problem* or *X is somehow puzzling*. This claim establishes some issue as worthy of investigation, and it is on the basis of this claim (which must be supported) that experiments are designed. Recognizing what counts as a problem or a puzzle requires both experience and creativity. Assume it is early October. One evening the temperature drops and you have the first hard frost of the season. The following day you notice that most of the flowers and vegetables in your garden have wilted—but one particular grouping of flowers (your mums) and one vegetable (your turnips) seem as healthy as ever. You and your neighbor both notice this fact. Your neighbor passes it by with a shrug, but you wonder *why*. You have noticed a *difference*, an anomaly (see 1a). If you were scientifically inclined, you might begin an investigation into why a certain plant or flower is frost resistant.

Tense in Scientific Writing

There is one special convention of writing scientific papers that is very sticky. It has to do with *tense,* and it is important because proper usage derives from scientific ethics.

When a scientific paper has been validly published in a primary journal, it thereby becomes knowledge. Therefore, whenever you quote previously published work, ethics requires you to treat that work with respect. You do this by using the *present* tense. It is correct to say "Streptomycin inhibits the growth of *M. tuberculosis* (13)." Whenever you quote or discuss previously published work, you should use the present tense; you are quoting established knowledge.

Your own present work must be referred to in the *past* tense. Your work is not presumed to be established knowledge until *after* it has been published. If you determined that the optimal growth temperature for *Streptomyces everycolor* was 37°C, you should say "*S. everycolor* grew best at 37°C." If you are citing previous work, possibly your own, it is then correct to say "*S. everycolor* grows best at 37°C."

In the typical paper, you will normally go back and forth between the past and present tenses. Most of the Abstract should be in the past tense, because you are referring to your own present results. Likewise, the Materials and Methods and the Results sections should be in the past tense, as you describe what you did and what you found. On the other hand, most of the Introduction and much of the Discussion should be in the present tense, because these sections usually emphasize previously established knowledge.

Source: Robert Day. *How to Write and Publish a Scientific Paper.* 3rd ed. (Phoenix: Oryx Press, 1988) 158–59.

Recognizing a difference or anomaly often begins the process of scientific investigation. The process continues when you make a second claim that attempts to explain the anomaly. Such a claim takes this form: *X can be explained as follows.* If in a book on horticulture you did not find an answer to your puzzle about frost heartiness, you might conduct a study in which you examined the leaf and root structures of the various plants in your garden. Based on your research you might develop an educated guess, or hypothesis, to explain why certain plants are frost resistant. To test your hypothesis you might design an experiment in which you exposed several plants to varying temperatures. Based on your results, you might claim that frost resistance in plants depends on two or three specific factors. Generally, when you are reading or writing in the sciences, these questions will help you to clarify how arguments are made:

- What is the question being investigated? What problem or anomaly is said to exist?

- What explanation is offered in response to this problem or anomaly?

LOOKING BACK

If students have difficulty understanding this discussion of tense, you may want to refer them to the treatment of "historical present tense" in 9e-1.

REFERENCES

OLMSTED, JOHN III. "Teaching Varied Technical Writing Styles in the Upper Division Laboratory." *Journal of Chemical Education* 61 (1984): 798–800. Discusses in detail twelve types of reports, each with a different style, that students must write on experiments they conduct.

VARGAS, MARJORIE FINK. "Writing Skills for Science Labs." *The Science Teacher* (1986): 29–33. Discusses a classroom exercise to show students how choices in voice are predicated on the demands of report writing.

GOODMAN, W. DANIEL, and JOHN C. BEAN. "A Chemistry Laboratory Project to Develop Thinking and Writing Skills." *Journal of Chemical Education* 60 (1983): 483–84. Discusses a way to integrate laboratory projects and research writing in a collaborative setting, the end result being the approximation of a professional research paper.

MALACHOWSKI, MITCHELL R. "Honing Observational Skills by the Use of Writing Exercises." *Journal of Chemical Education* 63 (1986): 497. Assigning short, in-class writing assignments helps students to consolidate their chemistry lab findings.

STRAUSS, MICHAEL J., and TOBY FULWILER. "Interactive Writing and Learning Chemistry." *Journal of College Science Teaching* 15 (1987): 256–62. Informal writing deposited into "Questions/Concerns/Critiques" boxes at the exits of a lecture hall led students to work through their chemistry problems in writing, thereby beginning the process of solving them.

AMBRON, JOANNA. "Writing to Improve Learning in Biology." *Journal of College Science Teaching* 15 (1987): 263–66. Discusses three writing assignments (journals, freewriting, short essays [microthemes]) that develop analytical skills and improve learning biology.

NAHRGANG, CYNTHIA L., and BRUCE T. PETERSEN. "Using Writing to Learn Mathematics." *Mathematics Teacher* 79 (1986): 461–65. Describes how journal writing assists students in organizing

(continued)

their thoughts about mathematics and improves their writing ability.

WINSOR, DOROTHY A. "Engineering Writing/Writing Engineering." *CCC* 41 (1990): 58–70. Attempts to show what engineers' writing looks like through the lens of "contemporary views about the textual shaping of knowledge," suggesting that such writers reveal "both their knowledge and themselves."

MOGER, SUSAN, and ROBERT G. WLEZIEN. "Using Current Technological Issues in a Writing Course for Engineers." *Engineering Education* 73 (1983): 316–18. Offers an alternative approach to teaching traditional technical writing by designing employment-related and socially important topics and by emphasizing revision and collaboration.

POTVIN, JANET H., and ROBERT L. WOODS. "Technical Communication and the Non-Native Speaker." *Engineering Education* 74 (1983): 171–73. Argues that teaching communication skills in the technological disciplines must entail sensitivity to linguistic, stylistic, and grammatical differences of non-native speakers.

Logic and evidence

As in any discipline, writers in science use various principles of logic to examine raw data and to select *particular* information as significant. The variety of logical principles that scientists have available to them in trying to make sense of their research is vast and complex, and if you major in a science it will be the purpose of your entire undergraduate career to train you to understand which principles of logic are appropriately applied in which circumstances. For purposes of demonstration, observe the application of one common logical principle—concerning *types*. Watch how certain kinds of evidence are assembled on the basis of this logic.

Investigations begin with a puzzle or anomaly.

All the flowers and vegetables in my garden—except for mums and turnips—have wilted after the first hard frost. Why weren't these harmed?

A variety of information is available.

This is an above-ground garden, 3 feet deep, 5 feet wide, and 10 feet long. The garden gets full morning sun but is largely shaded each afternoon. I grow tomatoes, beans, peas, cucumbers, turnips, table flowers, geraniums, mums, and morning glories. The soil tests slightly acidic, and it is well fertilized. Turnips are my sweetest crop, high in sugar. All the plants except the turnips grow above ground. The mums differ from the other above-ground plants in that their crown is located below ground. I water the garden twice daily, morning and evening.

The investigator applies a logical principle as an aid to sifting through the available information.

A frost-resistant plant is a type of plant that exhibits two or three of these features: (1) The plant is high in sugar content; solutions high in sugar resist freezing. (2) The cell walls of the leaves are thick and fibrous and are not easily punctured by ice crystals. (3) The crown—the portion of the plant from which the above-ground plant grows—is located below ground and is not harmed until the temperature drops to 25° F.

The investigator uses the principle to distinguish meaningful information—potential evidence—from meaningless information.

Based on the principle above, I see that mums exhibit features 2 and 3, while turnips exhibit features 1 and 3.

Working with an inference and carefully selected evidence, a writer can support a claim (or conclusion).

Of all the *types* of plants in my garden, only mums and turnips can be classified as frost resistant in that only they exhibit two of the three features characteristic of frost-resistant plants.

Each different logical pattern an investigator might use prompts him or her to look for a certain patterning among available information. You can better understand the workings of a science by identifying the varieties of logical principles researchers use in making arguments. As a student reading or writing in a scientific discipline, pose these questions:

- What logical principles are used in this discipline to make meaningful, supportable connections between observed facts and claims?
- What observable, measurable evidence can help to support a scientific claim?

39b Reading in the sciences

Scientists work with written sources all the time. Accurate written records of experiments are essential in the process of reaching consensus about questions of scientific interest. As a student of science, you will read journal articles and textbooks, and you will do well to establish a strategy for reading both. First of all, adopt the general strategies suggested in chapter 1 of this book, especially in 1e, "Reading to understand."

Journal articles

Journal articles are written by researchers for colleagues, not for students, and you can expect the language, concepts, and methodologies in journals to be challenging. The use of equations and sophisticated statistical techniques in a study's results section may leave you baffled. But you can still develop a general, useful understanding of an article (if not a critical response to the author's research methodology) by reading as follows: Read the article's Abstract, the Introduction, and the Discussion—in this order. If these sections prove interesting, then read the middle sections (the Materials and Methods, and the Results), which will probably contain the article's most technical elements. As you read, pose these questions:

- What is the purpose of this study?
- What is the researcher's perspective—for instance, biologist, chemist, or electrical engineer—and how does this influence the study?
- What is the researcher's claim or conclusion?
- What seems significant about this research?

The following Abstract, Introduction, and Discussion are sections of a scientific report on mummified human tissue. The authors employ a sophisticated DNA analysis in their study—techniques far too complicated for anyone but specialists to follow. But by reading selected sections of the article, any persistent reader can gain a good sense of how the study develops and why the authors think their work is significant. Written by Ingolf Thuesen and Jan Engberg, "Recovery and Analysis of Human Genetic Material from Mummified Tissue and Bone" appeared in the *Journal of Archaeological Science* 17 (1990): 679–89.

LOOKING BACK

Students may want to review chapter 1 (Critical Thinking and Reading) for a general discussion of the subject before reading this section. While chapter 1 focuses primarily on reading texts other than reports, the general principles are still relevant.

TEACHING IDEAS

Students accustomed to reading through a journal article from start to finish may have trouble understanding the advice given here. If you focus on the questions listed and ask students where in the sample those questions are answered, you should be able to reinforce the advice to read the middle sections of scientific reports last.

FOR DISCUSSION

Some of your students will probably be enrolled simultaneously in introductory science classes. Ask them to bring their textbooks to class and to comment on how they differ from texts in humanities and social sciences. With a little prodding from you, this activity should lead to a class discussion on the different purposes and expectations of textbooks in various disciplines.

ABSTRACT

Using sensitive techniques of molecular biology, we have been able to demonstrate the presence of genomic material of human origin in samples of mummified human tissue and bone from selected archaeological sites in Greenland. This result has far-reaching consequences for both evolutionary and archaeological studies of past human populations.

INTRODUCTION

Using sensitive techniques of molecular biology, we have investigated the possibility of recovering and analyzing genetic materials (deoxyribonucleic acid, DNA) from mummified human tissue and bone from selected archaeological sites in Greenland. Simple extraction procedures of both skin and bone samples yielded DNA material in purified form. Using human specific probes, we demonstrated that a minor, but distinct, portion of the purified DNA material was of human origin. Further analysis showed the remaining portion of the isolated DNA to consist mainly of DNA of fungal origin. The findings of DNA of human origin in mummified skin and bone samples, in particular, opens up the possibility for detailed anthropological genetic studies.

DISCUSSION

Recovery and analysis of ancient tissue and bone of human origin has long been intensively investigated. With the rapid advances within molecular biology in recent years, we have seen the first successful extraction of DNA from archaeological and anthropological materials (Higuchi *et al.*, 1984; Pääbo 1985*a*, *b*; Doran *et al.*, 1986). The perspective arising from those results and results of the reported work are indeed fascinating. The potential in establishing libraries of ancient DNA is obvious and prepares the road not only for the study of biological evolution (Thomas *et al.*, 1989), but also for research into human cultural history.

Within the archaeological discipline the information that may be recovered from survived fragments of DNA may concern inherited diseases, ethnic or racial associations and even sex and lineage. With the successful extraction of DNA from bones, we are also stabilizing and expanding the interpretative basis of the method. Bones are much more abundant in museum magazines and excavations than soft tissue fragments whether from artificially or naturally mummified bodies. According to our results bones are not contaminated in the same way as is skin tissue. An example of future research topics generated by the present project would be a search for the Eskimo–Norseman ethnic relationship and/or the occurrence of inherited diseases, based on successful extraction of DNA from bone material, which is abundantly available in the collections.

Despite being a time-consuming task, the extraction and identification of relevant fragments of ancient DNA should be a challenge for many anthropologists or evolutionists. In particular, after the appearance of the PCR technique, this task no longer seems out of reach (Pääbo & Wilson, 1988). The study of ancient DNA has already been suggested as a subdiscipline to paleoanthropology (Perizonius *et al.*, 1989). As a curiosity we may mention, that during our work, which has also involved other mummified tissues such as Danish bog people, Nubian cemetery samples (natural mummification) and artificially mummified Egyptians, the project was nicknamed GAP, Genetic Archaeology Project.

The lengthy and highly technical Materials and Methods section, and Results section (omitted here) are detailed, and other molecular biologists could repeat the authors' DNA analysis. As a student in an introductory course, surely replication will not be your purpose for reading journal articles. Read for other reasons: to see issues important to particular scientists raised and addressed from a particular perspective; to see the process of scientific inquiry at work; and to share in a researcher's excitement.

Textbooks

In introductory courses your reading will be primarily in textbooks, where the writing is directed to students and should, therefore, be more accessible than the writing in journal articles. In the sciences, textbooks play a special role in synthesizing available knowledge in an area and presenting it, with explanations, to students. The material in texts will grow increasingly technical as you move from introductory to specialized courses. Read your texts in science courses closely (see 1e), monitoring your progress frequently to ensure that you understand the material. Highlight any concepts or terms that confuse you, and seek clarification from classmates or a professor.

39c Types of writing assignments in the sciences

As an undergraduate, you will most often be assigned two kinds of writing: a report of a laboratory experiment and a literature review. The purpose of writing in both cases will be to introduce you to methods of scientific thinking and ways that scientists argue.

1 The lab report

A laboratory experiment represents a distinct (empirical) strategy for learning about the world. Experimental researchers agree on this basic premise: that research must be *replicable*—that is, repeatable. Knowledge gained through experiment is based on what can be *observed*; and what is observed, if it is going to be accepted universally as a fact, must be observed by others: hence the need for *reporting on* and *writing* original research. Reports of experimental research usually consist of four parts: Introduction, Methods, Results, and Discussion. Even when scientific papers do not follow this structure, they will mirror its problem-solution

FOR DISCUSSION

You may want to ask students to explain why they think these guidelines are necessary for a laboratory notebook. Those who have already taken laboratory science courses may be able to help the uninitiated understand the purpose of the notebook.

Keeping a Laboratory Notebook

The notebook should reflect a daily record of work. It is best to make entries explaining the results expected from each stage of the investigation. Entries should be in chronological order, and so thorough and comprehensive that they can be understood by the corroborating witnesses. Each page should be signed by the inventor or researcher below the last entry, and by one or preferably two witnesses. Full names should be used and the signatures dated.

• • •

1. Use a *bound* notebook, if possible.

2. If a loose leaf notebook is preferred, the pages should be numbered in advance and a record kept of the numbered pages given to each laboratory worker. The point is to rebut any inference that a worker may have inserted a page at a later date.[1]

3. Do not remove any pages or any part of a page. Pages missing from a notebook will seriously weaken a case in the Patent Office, or in cases that go to court for litigation.

4. Record all entries directly and legibly in solvent-resistant black ink.

5. Define the problem or objective concisely. Make entries consistently as the work is performed.

6. All original work, including simple arithmetical calculations, should be performed in the notebook. If you make a mistake, recalculate—**do not erase.**

7. Never use correction fluid or paste-overs of any kind. If you decide to correct an error, place a single line through the mistake, sign and

(continued)

---

approach. Robert A. Day, author of a highly readable and authoritative guide to writing scientific papers, characterizes the logic of the four-part form this way:

> What question (problem) was studied? The answer is the Introduction. How was the problem studied? The answer is the Methods. What were the findings? The answer is the Results. What do these findings mean? The answer is the Discussion. (7)

Introduction

The Introduction of a scientific paper should clearly define the problem(s) or state the hypothesis you are investigating, as well as the point of view from which you will be investigating it. Establishing your point of view will help readers to anticipate the type of experiment you will be reporting on, as well as your conclusions. Your Introduction should also state clearly your reasons for investigating a particular subject. This is

Keeping a Laboratory Notebook *(continued)*

date the correction, and give a reason for the error. Take care the underlying type can still be read. However, even the practice of drawing a line through numbers entered in error is discouraged in many companies. Instead, workers are asked simply to make a new entry, correcting the error when possible.

8. Do not leave blank spaces on any page. Instead, either draw diagonal lines or a cross through any portion of the page you don't use.

9. Date and sign what you have written on the day of entry. In addition, have each notebook page read, signed, and dated by a qualified witness—someone who is not directly involved in the work performed, but who understands the purpose of the experiment and the results obtained.

10. Extra materials such as graphs and charts should be inserted, signed, and witnessed in the same way as other entries.

11. All apparatus should be identified. Schematic sketches should be included.

12. Head each entry with a title. If you are continuing on the next page, say so at the bottom of the page before you continue.

These rules have received a popular formulation as, "Record it. Date it. Sign it. Have it witnessed."

[1]1976 Patent Institute. "A Continuing Seminar of New Developments in Law and Practice," College of Business Administration, Fairleigh Dickinson University, Madison, NJ.

Source: Anne Eisenberg, "Keeping a Laboratory Notebook," *Journal of Chemical Education* 59 (1982): 1045–46.

common practice in journal articles, where researchers will cite pertinent literature in order to set their current project in a context. In referring to prior work in which the same or similar problems or processes have been reported, you will cite sources. (See 36d for the conventions on citing and documenting sources in the sciences.) These references will help you to establish a context as well as a need for the present experiment.

Materials and methods

The Methods section of the lab report is given slightly different names in different discipline areas: Experimental Details, Experimental Methods, Experimental Section, or Materials and Methods (American Chemical Society [ACS] 6); and Subjects, Materials, and Methods (CBE 21). Whatever heading your professor prefers, it is in the Materials and Methods section that you provide readers with the basis on which to reproduce your experimental study. Unless you have some reason for not doing so, describe your experimental methods chronologically. When reporting on the Materials and Methods of *field studies* (investigations carried out beyond the strictly controlled environment of the lab), describe precisely *where* you conducted your study, *what* you chose to study, the *instruments* you used to conduct the study, and the *methods of analysis* you employed.

As you set up and conduct your experiment, keep detailed records that will allow you to report precisely on your work when the time comes for writing. Both student and professional experimenters keep a *lab notebook* for this purpose. Even though you may be tempted to make quick, shorthand entries, write in precise and complete sentences that will allow you to retrace your steps. The notebook should be complete, containing the information necessary to write your lab report.

Results

The Results section of your paper should precisely set out the data you have accumulated in your research. The statements you make in this section will provide the basis on which you state conclusions in the Discussion section to follow; your presentation of results, therefore, must be both clear and logically ordered. (Professors will usually review in class what constitutes clear and logical ordering of results in their disciplines.) As in the Materials and Methods section, when your discussion of results is lengthy, use subheadings to organize the presentation.

Discussion

The purpose of the Discussion section in your report is to interpret experimental findings and to discuss their implications. In the Discussion, your main task is to address the *So what?* question. Readers should know, clearly, what you have accomplished (or failed to accomplish) and why this is significant. Directly address the question or problem that prompted the experimental study, and state the extent to which your data adequately answer the initial question(s). If you believe your research findings are significant, say so and give your reasons. If appropriate, suggest directions for future study. As in the Introduction, set your experimental findings in a context by relating them to the findings of other experiments. When your results differ from those you expected or from results reported by others, explain the difference.

The Abstract

The Abstract is the *briefest possible* summary of an article (see 2a). In some journals, articles conclude with a Summary (marked as such). It is more common to find the Abstract appearing at the beginning. An article published in a scientific journal will usually have the complete text of its Abstract reproduced on an electronic database. Researchers scanning the database will read the Abstract to determine whether an article is related to their own work and, thus, worth retrieving in its entirety. Abstracts must therefore be concise and self-contained. Typically, they include the following:

- The subject of the paper, its purpose and objectives
- The experiment's materials and methods, including the names of specific organisms, drugs, and compounds
- Experimental results and their significance

Most often, the Abstract excludes the following:

- References to literature cited in the paper
- Any reference to equations, figures, or tables (AIP 5; CBE 20)

When writing the Abstract of your lab report, consider devoting one sentence of summary to each of the major headings (Introduction, Materials and Methods, Results, and Discussion). If necessary, follow your four-sentence Abstract with a concluding sentence.

Title page and manuscript form

Every research report should have a precise, descriptive title. The title, along with the Abstract, will be read first, so if you want to pique interest, this is the place to begin. Check with your professor about the form your lab report should take. All text—including the Abstract, footnotes, and the reference list—should be double spaced. Generally, all pages of a manuscript are numbered consecutively, *beginning* with the title page. The Abstract page follows, then the body of your report. Each major heading—Introduction, Materials and Methods, Results, and Discussion—should be centered on its own line. (Some professors will want to see each major section begin on a new page.) Subheadings should be placed flush to the left margin; after each, skip one line and begin your text. Place the reference list at the end of the report and follow with your tables and figures if you do not incorporate them into the text of your paper. Each table and figure should be titled and placed on a separate page.

2   The Literature Review

The Literature Review, a prominent and important form of writing in science, synthesizes current knowledge on a topic. Unlike a term paper, which draws on a limited number of sources in order to support a thesis, a literature review covers and brings coherence to the range of studies on a topic. A review may also evaluate articles, advising readers pressed for time about which articles merit attention. While every experimental report begins with a review of pertinent literature, only the Literature Review makes this discussion its main business.

Professors assigning review papers will not ask that you conduct an exhaustive search of literature on a topic. Your search should be limited

LOOKING BACK

Students preparing to write a Literature Review would do well to review thoroughly the sections of chapters 1 and 2 mentioned here. Proper evaluation of a source is crucial to the Literature Review, as is making inferences about relationships among sources and synthesizing a number of sources in one paper.

in such a way that it will both introduce you to a topic and acquaint you with scientific ways of thinking. Your topic should not be so broad that you overwhelm yourself with vast amounts of reading material. For general advice on the skills necessary for conducting a Literature Review, see "Reading to evaluate" (1g), "Reading to synthesize" (1h), and "Writing a synthesis" (2d). (These same principles apply to writing Literature Reviews in the social sciences and the humanities. In both discipline areas, scholars periodically write articles in which they bring their colleagues up to date on research concerning one topic.)

Writing the paper

Writing a Literature Review in the sciences involves several steps. Once you have a topic in mind, you will need to read widely so as to learn enough that you can ask a pointed question and can begin to conduct more focused library research. Reading scholarly review articles is an excellent place to begin, since by definition they survey a great many potential sources for you and, better still, point out themes and raise questions that you can take up in your own review. Review articles are published for most of the sciences. Locate them by searching for the word *review* in the various publications that abstract and index journal articles, such as *Microbiological Abstracts, Chemical Abstracts, Engineering Index Annual, Physics Abstracts,* and *Science Abstracts.*

If you are unfamiliar with the process of conducting research, then before attempting a Literature Review you might skim chapter 33, where you will find general strategies for writing a research paper. A Literature Review, like any good synthesis or research paper, is usually organized by *ideas,* not by sources. (See the discussion in 2d, on "Ensuring that your voice is heard.") In Literature Reviews, you will not find a simple listing of summaries: These are the substance of annotated bibliographies, which are themselves useful tools to researchers. The review should represent your best effort at inferring themes, problems, trends, and so on. When referring to sources, use the citation form appropriate to your discipline. See 36d for information on citing and documenting sources in the sciences.

39d Sample student paper: "Comparison of Two Strains of Wine-Producing Yeasts"

Following is a lab report on the fermentation of wine. The microbiological processes involved in wine production have been known for nearly 150 years, and the student writing this report has added no new knowledge to our understanding of how wine is made. But creating new knowledge was not the purpose of the assignment. Clarence S. Ivie met his professor's objectives by successfully planning and carrying out an experiment, by making careful observations, and by thinking and writing like a biologist. This paper is the third of three discipline-specific papers relating to the topic of alcohol. (See 37e for a literary analysis of alcohol use in a short story by James Joyce and 38d for a sociological paper on women alcoholics.)

Here are several features you might look for when reading Clarence Ivie's paper.

- The writer assumes an audience of experts, and it is clear that the occasion for writing is formal. Ivie does not define scientific terms—he assumes his readers will understand all references. (This same observation accounts for the difficulty you might have in reading the paper.)

- The writer demonstrates the logic of a scientific investigation. Ivie bases claims on measurable observations—with an important exception at the end of the paper, in which he makes what he calls "subjective observations" of the two wines he is comparing. In the context of a laboratory experiment, Ivie is careful to distinguish subjective impressions from objective measurements. He follows a standard format for reporting lab results.

- The writer uses graphs and a table to show the relationship among three different sets of information. For those who can read graphs and tables (the assumed reader *can*), these are useful tools for communicating experimental results.

- In sections of the paper where technical language is not needed, the writer avoids such language. See especially the Introduction (the first paragraph) and the Discussion.

TEACHING IDEAS

The sample lab report presented here is heavily annotated so that students can use it as a guide in writing their own reports. You may want to call particular attention to specific features peculiar to lab reports—format, presentation of results, use of tables and graphs, and the like.

Comparison of Two Strains of
Wine-Producing Yeasts

Clarence S. Ivie III

Microbiology 314
Department of Biological Sciences
University of South Alabama
Mobile, Alabama 36688
Professor Burke Brown
4 March 1993

1

Comparison of Two Strains of Wine-Producing Yeasts

The purpose of this experiment was to determine which strain of yeast produced the most favorable wine. Wine yeast, <u>Saccharomyces cerevisiæ</u> var. <u>ellipsoideus</u> and Fleishman's baker's yeast, <u>Saccharomyces cerevisiæ,</u> were used to make two samples of wine. The wines were then compared with one another to determine which yeast created the best wine based on smell, taste, and alcohol content. The results of the experiment indicated that the wine yeast produced a better wine.

The abstract consists of one-sentence summaries of the report's major sections.

Fermentation is a process whereby a strain of yeast metabolizes sugar to produce alcohol. Wine is most commonly produced from grape juice by the process of fermentation. Grapes are crushed to acquire the juice. Sugar is then added to the grape juice. The grape juice, or <u>must</u>, is then inoculated with yeast and allowed to ferment, a process that takes around fourteen days. <u>The end product is an alcoholic beverage which has been valued for centuries. It is not known when the first wines were created. However, throughout the history of wine making, people have constantly made attempts at improving the quality of the wine (2).</u> In this experiment, the strain of yeast that produced the best wine was determined on the basis of smell, taste, and alcohol content.

In some disciplines, "Introduction," as a heading, is omitted from the lab report.

The introduction sets the study in a larger context and establishes the research perspective: microbiology.

Materials and Methods

Two 1.9L bottles were used in this experiment. Each bottle contained 1.7L of grape juice. Two hundred thirty (230) grams of table sugar was

The author provides exact information so that readers can replicate the study.

Ivie 2

added to each bottle of grape juice. Bottle #1 was then inoculated with one package of Saccharomyces var. ellipsoideus. Bottle #2 was inoculated with one package of Fleishman's baker's yeast. The mixtures were then shaken to dissolve their contents. Initial measurements were immediately taken, including: pH, specific gravity, and temperature. Subjective observations, such as the mixture's color, were also made. A pH meter was used to measure pH, a hydrometer was used to measure specific gravity, and a thermometer was used to measure temperature. After the initial measurements were taken, both bottles were then sealed and allowed to ferment. Periodically CO_2 gas production rates were measured for each experimental wine fermentation procedure. This was done by measuring the volume of displacement, due to the gas production. As the wine continued to ferment, these measurements were made daily throughout the 20 day duration of the experiment. On the eighteenth day of the experiment, both bottles were inoculated with a bisulphite to stop the fermentation process.

Results

After the fermentation process was halted, the specific gravity changes of bottles 1 and 2 were compared. The specific gravities of both wine experiments decreased, but the most substantial decrease occurred in bottle #1. These results indicated that the wine yeast metabolized the sugar more efficiently than the Fleishman's baker's yeast (Fig. 1).

The results of the pH change, in each case, fluctuated daily. There was, however, an overall increase in both samples.

The author provides a specific criterion, or test, by which to analyze the two samples.

FOR DISCUSSION

Students should recognize immediately the stylistic differences between a scientific lab report and a social science field study report. Even more striking should be the differences between a lab report and a literary analysis. Ask students to cite the differences among the discipline-specific forms of writing, explaining why they think such differences exist.

FOR DISCUSSION

After they have read the entire lab report, students should discuss the function of the graphs. What purpose do the graphs serve? How do they support the narrative portion of the report? What effect would you expect them to have on an audience of scientists? How would the impact of the report be altered if the graphs were eliminated?

Ivie 3

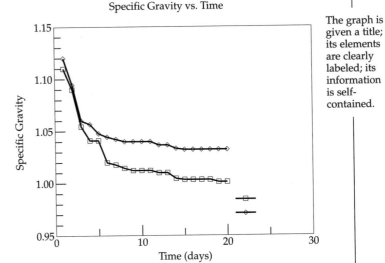

Fig. 1. Comparison of specific gravity versus time between <u>Saccharomyces</u> var. <u>ellipsoideus</u>, the wine yeast, and <u>Saccharomyces cerevisiæ</u>, the baker's yeast.

The graph is given a title; its elements are clearly labeled; its information is self-contained.

<u>The temperatures of both samples remained more or less constant at 22.5 degrees Celsius throughout the entire fermentation process.</u>
       <u>The gas production measurements showed that the wine yeast produced more carbon dioxide than the baker's yeast.</u> Gas production is directly related to yeast growth. Because of this fact, it was not a surprise to find that the graph of the gas production rate of the yeast was quite similar to a typical growth curve (Fig. 2).

The author provides three additional criteria by which to analyze the samples.

       To calculate the % alcohol content of wine, data from table 1 was used in the following equation (1): % alc. = (Initial % potential alc.) − (Final % potential alc.)

       The wine produced from <u>Saccharomyces</u> var. <u>ellipsoideus</u> was 14.9% alcoholic, while the wine produced from <u>Saccharomyces cerevisiæ</u> was only 12.3% alcoholic.

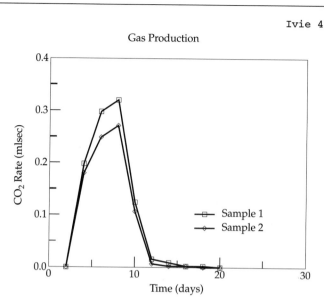

Ivie 4

Fig. 2. Comparison of CO_2 production between <u>Saccharomyces</u> var. <u>ellipsoideus</u> and <u>Saccharomyces cerevisiæ</u>.

<u>Subjective observations of smell and taste favored the wine yeast.</u> The wine made from the baker's yeast smelled like bread and tasted bitter. The wine made from the wine yeast smelled like wine and tasted sweet.

Discussion

Wine is the product of yeast fermentation. The purpose of this experiment was to determine which type of yeast produced the best wine. The basis by which the wines made in the experiment were judged included taste, smell, and alcohol content. It was clearly evident that the wine yeast created a more pleasant smelling and tasting wine than did the baker's yeast. The wine produced by the baker's yeast had a harshly over powering smell which resembled the smell of bread. Its taste was extremely bitter. Overall,

---

The graph is given a title; its elements are clearly labeled; its information is self-contained.

Subjective observations are clearly distinguished from objective measurements.

The discussion does more than merely repeat results: it reviews the purpose of the experiment, sets the results in relation to the purpose, and succinctly states a conclusion.

TEACHING IDEAS

You may want to ask students to read the Discussion carefully and comment on how it fulfills the function of the Discussion described earlier in the chapter.

Ivie 5

Table 1. Relations between specific
gravities and % potential alcohol

Specific Gravity	% Potential Alcohol
1.000	0
1.010	0.9
1.020	2.3
1.030	3.7
1.040	5.1
1.050	6.5
1.090	7.8
1.080	10.6
1.090	12.0
1.100	13.4
1.110	14.9
1.120	16.3
1.130	17.7

The information in the table is clearly displayed and is self-contained. The table provides the standards by which alcohol percentages are determined in the experiment.

on the basis of taste and smell, the baker's yeast
created an undesirable wine while the wine yeast
created a pleasant smelling and more desirable
tasting wine. On the basis of alcohol content, it
is clearly seen from the results of this experiment that the wine yeast produced a more alcoholic
wine than the baker's yeast. The wine yeast proved
to be more efficient in the metabolism of sugar
than the baker's yeast. Evidence of this is seen
in the specific gravity measurements. The wine
yeast also achieved a greater rate of fermentation
as seen in the gas production measurement. From
this experiment, it can be concluded that the use
of wine yeast, Saccharomyces var. ellipsoideus,
is far more advantageous than the use of baker's
yeast in making wine.

Each of the author's claims is supported by evidence gathered during the experiment.

```
                                          Ivie 6
                    Literature Cited
    1. Case, J.; Johnson, L. Laboratory experi-
       ments in microbiology. Reading, MA: The
       Benjamin/Cummings Publishing Company;
       1984.
    2. Prescott, A.; Harley, J.; Klein, P. Micro-
       biology, Dubuque, IA: Wm. C. Brown Pub-
       lishers; 1990.
    3. Stryer M.; Lubert, A. Biochemistry. New
       York: W. H. Freeman and Company; 1988.
```

39e Reference materials in the sciences

Style guides

A source of excellent general advice for writing papers in the sciences is Robert Day's *How to Write and Publish a Scientific Paper,* 3rd ed. (Phoenix: Oryx Press, 1988). For discipline-specific advice on writing, consult the following works:

AIP [American Institute of Physics] Style Manual. 4th ed. New York: AIP, 1990.

CBE [Council of Biology Editors] *Style Manual.* 5th ed. Bethesda: CBE, 1983.

Dodd, Janet S., et al. *The ACS [American Chemical Society] Style Guide: A Manual for Authors and Editors.* Washington: ACS, 1986.

Michaelson, Herbert B. *How to Write and Publish Engineering Papers and Reports.* 2nd ed. Philadelphia: ISI Press, 1986.

Specialized references

The following specialized references will help you to assemble information in a particular discipline or field within the discipline.

Encyclopedias provide general information useful when beginning a search.

Cambridge Encyclopedia of Astronomy
Encyclopedia of Biological Sciences
Encyclopedia of Chemistry

FOR DISCUSSION

It would be helpful for students to recognize the differences in format among CBE, APA, and MLA style with regard to references—in particular the order of references in CBE style.

TEACHING IDEAS

Students who plan to major or minor in the sciences should be encouraged to consult faculty in their chosen discipline regarding the preferred style guide. With so many from which to choose, it is important that students know which guide their instructors use.

Encyclopedia of Computer Science and Engineering
Encyclopedia of Computer Science and Technology
Encyclopedia of Earth Sciences
Encyclopedia of Physics
Grzimek's Animal Life Encyclopedia
Grzimek's Encyclopedia of Ecology
Harper's Encyclopedia of Science
Larousse Encyclopedia of Astronomy
McGraw-Hill Encyclopedia of Environmental Science
McGraw-Hill Yearbook of Science and Technology
Stein and Day International Medical Encyclopedia
Universal Encyclopedia of Mathematics
Van Nostrand's Scientific Encyclopedia

Dictionaries provide definitions of technical terms.

Computer Dictionary and Handbook
Condensed Chemical Dictionary
Dictionary of Biology
Dorland's Medical Dictionary
Illustrated Stedman's Medical Dictionary
McGraw-Hill Dictionary of Scientific and Technical Terms

Periodical indexes list articles published in a particular discipline over a particular period. *Abstracts*, which summarize the sources listed and involve a considerable amount of work to compile, tend to be more selective than indexes.

Applied Science and Technology Index
Biological Abstracts
Biological and Agricultural Index
Cumulative Index to Nursing and Allied Health Literature
Current Abstracts of Chemistry and Index Chemicus
Engineering Index
General Science Index
Index Medicus
Index to Scientific and Technical Proceedings
Science Citation Index

Computerized periodical indexes are available for many specialized areas and may be faster than leafing through years of bound periodicals. Access to these databases may be expensive.

Science and Technology Databases
Agricola (agriculture)
Biosis Previews (biology, botany)
CA Search (chemistry)
Compendix (engineering)
NTIS (National Technical Information Search)
ORBIT (science and technology)
SciSearch
SPIN (physics)

CHAPTER 40

Writing in a Business Environment

KEY FEATURES

In discussing the various types of business writing, this chapter maintains the emphasis introduced in the first chapters of the handbook: Good writing takes into consideration both the purpose of the document and the audience to which it is addressed. In business this translates into the importance of getting to the point in an environment where time is of the essence. Business writing is characterized in the chapter as being direct, concise, and clearly organized. Referring to chapters 3 and 4, this chapter presents a "distilled" process of preparation, drafting, and revision. Many forms of business writing are covered, including letters, résumés, and memoranda. Students are advised on matters of form and content, and are provided with clearly annotated examples.

LOOKING BACK

Most students should be able to appreciate the audience concerns expressed in this chapter. Nevertheless, you may want to ask them to review chapter 3 on audience awareness.

In a business environment, much is accomplished—meetings are attended, information is shared, agendas are set, arguments are settled—based on writing alone. When you enter this environment by writing a letter or memo, you must understand that people are not obligated to answer you (rude as this might seem). Business people have many demands placed on them simultaneously. When reading, they must know a writer's purpose and they must be given a motivation for continuing to read. Lacking either of these qualities, a document will not represent itself as *important* enough to merit attention, and the reader will simply turn to more pressing concerns.

You will significantly improve your chances of readers acting on your letters and memos if you begin by appreciating the constraints on their time. Think of your readers as busy people inclined to help if your writing is direct, concise, and clearly organized. A *direct* letter or memo will state in its opening sentence your purpose for writing. A *concise* letter or memo will state your exact needs in as few words as possible. A *well-organized* letter or memo will present only the information that is pertinent to your main point, in a sequence that is readily understood.

The writing process in a business environment

Direct, concise, and clearly organized writing takes time, of course, and is seldom the effort of a single draft. Writing a document in a business setting involves a process, just as your writing a research paper in an academic setting involves a process. It may seem counterintuitive, but you will spend less time writing a letter twice (producing both rough and revised drafts) than you will trying to do a creditable job in a single draft. Generally, you will do well to follow the advice in chapters 3 and 4 on planning, developing, drafting, and revising a paper. For every document that you write, aside from the simplest two- or three-line notes, you should prepare to write, write a draft, and then revise.

40a Standard formats, spacing, and information in a business letter

Standard formats

Use unlined, white bond paper ($8\frac{1}{2} \times 11$) or letterhead stationery for your business correspondence. Prepare your letter on a typewriter or word processor, and print on one side of the page only. Format your letter according to one of three conventions: full block, block, and semi-block—terms describing the ways in which you indent information. The six basic elements of a letter—return address, inside address and date, salutation, body, closing, and abbreviated matter—begin at the left margin in the *full block* format. Displayed information such as lists begins five spaces from the left margin. In the *block* format, the return address and the closing are aligned just beyond the middle of the page, while the inside address, salutation, new paragraphs, and abbreviated matter each begin at the left margin. (See the "Letter of Inquiry" in 40b for an example of block format.) The *semi-block* format is similar to the block format except that each new paragraph is indented five spaces from the left margin and any displayed information is indented ten spaces. (See the "Letter of Application" in 40d for an example of a semi-block format.)

Standard spacing

Maintain a one-inch margin at the top, bottom, and sides of the page. Single-space the document for all but very brief letters (two to five lines), the body of which you should double-space. Skip one or two lines between the return address and the inside address; one line between the inside address and the salutation (which is followed by a colon); one line between the salutation and opening paragraph; one line between paragraphs; one line between your final paragraph and your complimentary closing (which is followed by a comma); four lines between your closing and typewritten name; and one line between your typewritten name and any abbreviated matter.

Standard information

RETURN ADDRESS AND DATE
Unless you are writing on letterhead stationery (on which your return address is preprinted), type as a block of information your return address—street address on one line; city, state, and zip code on the next; the date on a third line. If you are writing on letterhead, type the date only, centered one or two lines below the letterhead's final line.

REFERENCES

KEENE, MICHAEL L. "Technical Information in the Information Economy." Rpt. in *Perspectives on Research and Scholarship in Composition.* Ed. Ben W. McClelland and Timothy R. Donovan. New York: Modern Language Association, 1985. A look at recent scholarship in business communication.

ODELL, LEE, and DIXIE GOSWAMI, eds. *Writing in Nonacademic Settings.* New York: Guilford, 1986. Essays by Paul V. Anderson and Janice C. Redish. Indispensable collection of essays for teaching writing in business.

BARNETT, MARVA T. *Writing for Technicians.* Albany: Delmar, 1982. Includes chapters on types of letters, résumés, and application inquiries.

SHENK, ROBERT. "Ghost-Writing in Professional Communities." *Journal of Technical Writing and Communication* 18 (1988): 377–87. Writers can effectively compose materials to which their department heads may attach signatures.

MENDELSON, MICHAEL. "Business Prose and the Nature of the Plain Style." *Journal of Business Communication* 24 (Spring 1987): 3–18. Students should be oriented to various stylistic possibilities as a way of making their content more persuasive.

STERKEL, KAREN S. "The Relationship between Gender and Writing Style in Business Communication." *Journal of Business Communication* 25 (Fall 1988): 17–38. An evaluation of business letters written by students of both sexes revealed "no significant [gender] differences"; students do not write as themselves.

LANHAM, RICHARD A. *Revising Business Prose.* New York: Scribner's, 1981. Offers writers the successful methods for business writing (including his plea for writing in plain English) he developed for academic writing in *Revising Prose.*

INSIDE ADDRESS

Provide as a block of information the full name and address of the person to whom you are writing. Be sure to spell all names—personal, company, and address—correctly. Use abbreviations only if the company abbreviates words in its own name or address.

SALUTATION

Begin your letter with a formal greeting, traditionally *Dear* _____: Unless another title applies, such as *Dr.* or *Senator,* address a man as *Mr.* and a woman as *Miss* or *Mrs.*—or as *Ms.* if you or the person addressed prefer this. When in doubt about a woman's marital status or preferences in a salutation, use *Ms.* If you are not writing to a specific person, avoid the gender-specific and potentially insulting *Dear Sirs.* Many readers find the generic *Dear Sir or Madam* and *To whom it may concern* to be equivocal, and you may want to open instead with the company name, *Dear Acme Printing,* or with a specific department name or position title: *Dear Personnel Department* or *Dear Personnel Manager.* See the discussion at 31a for the conventions on abbreviating titles in a salutation or an address.

BODY OF THE LETTER

Develop your letter in paragraph form. State your purpose clearly in the opening paragraph. Avoid giving your letter a visually dense impression. When your content lends itself to displayed treatment (if, for instance, you are presenting a list), indent the information. You may want to use bullets, numbers, or hyphens. (See, for example, the "Letter of Inquiry" in 40b.)

CLOSING

Close with some complimentary expression such as *Yours truly, Sincerely,* or *Sincerely yours.* Capitalize the first word only of this closing remark and follow the remark with a comma. Allow four blank lines for your signature, then type your name and, below that, any title that applies.

ABBREVIATED MATTER

Several abbreviations may follow at the left-hand margin, one line below your closing. If someone else has typed your letter, abbreviate initials as follows: Capitalize your initials, place a slash, then place the typist's initials in lowercase—*LR/hb.* If you are enclosing any material with your letter, type *Enclosure* or *Enc.* If you care to itemize this information, place a colon and align items as in the example letter in 40d. If you are sending copies of the letter to other readers (known as a *secondary audience*), write *cc:* (for *carbon copy*) and list the names of the recipients of the copies, as in the example letter in 40f.

THE SECOND PAGE

Begin your letter's second page with identifying information so that if the first and second pages are separated the reader will easily be able to match them again. The blocked information should consist of your name, the date, and the page number presented in a block at the upper left-hand corner of the page.

```
Jon Lipman
January 7, 1993
Page 2

and in the event of your coming to Worcester, I
would be happy to set up an interview with you here.
Perhaps the week of May 20 would be convenient,
since I will be traveling to eastern Massachusetts.
```

ENVELOPE

Single-space all information. If you are not using an envelope with a preprinted return address, type your return address at the upper left-hand corner. Center between the right- and left-hand sides the name and address of the person to whom you are writing. Vertically, type the address just below center.

```
Jon Lipman
231 Gray Street
Worcester, Massachusetts 01610



            Ms. Hannah Marks
            Equipment Design, Inc.
            1254 Glenn Avenue
            Arlington, Massachusetts 02174
```

FOR DISCUSSION

Some of your students probably have had experience with business letters; some may work in the business world, some may have taken business courses, and some may have written letters of inquiry or complaint. Ask these students to discuss the reasons why the guidelines for business letters are so precise. What purpose does the letter serve in business communications?

American-style business writing is not standard internationally. In many places a typed letter indicates an impersonal lack of concern while a handwritten letter indicates an attempt to make personal contact and to show personal consideration.

By the standards of most cultures, American-style business letters are rude; they get down to business too quickly and they don't take time for the amenities. For example, a Japanese business letter must make some comment about the beauty of the season: "It is cherry-blossom time in Tokyo today," and introduce the serious business concerns with a casual "by the way . . ." Latin American, Greek, and Arab writers might ask about the reader's family or health, and their greetings will be much more effusive and "flowery" by our standards than our simple "Dear sir." In many cultures personal statements and questions (about health, family, etc.) provide a friendly, personal touch before getting down to business.

ADDITIONAL EXERCISE B

Following the guidelines provided in this chapter, write a letter of inquiry, complaint, or application. Use either full block, block, or semi-block format as illustrated in the sample letters.

GROUP ACTIVITY

Ask students to use the model business letter as a guide for this activity. In groups of three, have students give each other editorial advice (on both form and content) on the letters composed for Additional Exercise B. Then ask students to discuss the comments and make revisions based on their readers' advice.

40b Letters of inquiry

A letter of inquiry is based on a question you want answered. Presumably, you have done enough research to have identified a person knowledgeable in the area concerning you. Do not ask for too much information or for very general information that you could readily find in a library. Avoid giving your reader the impression that you are asking him or her for basic information that you should have managed to locate yourself. If you are inquiring about price or product information, simply ask for a brochure.

- Begin the letter with a sentence that identifies your need. State who you are, what your general project is (if the information is pertinent), and the reason for your writing.
- Follow with a sentence devoted to how you have learned of the reader or the reader's company and how this person or company could be of help to you.
- Pose a few *specific* questions. Frame these questions in such a way that you demonstrate you have done background research.
- State any time constraints you may have. Do not expect your reader to respond any sooner than two or three weeks.
- Close with a brief statement of appreciation. If you feel it would expedite matters, you might include a self-addressed, stamped envelope.

Block Format

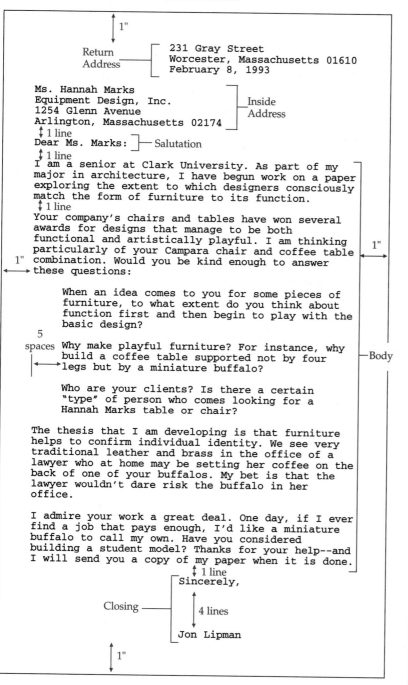

Return Address

231 Gray Street
Worcester, Massachusetts 01610
February 8, 1993

Ms. Hannah Marks
Equipment Design, Inc.
1254 Glenn Avenue
Arlington, Massachusetts 02174

Inside Address

↕ 1 line
Dear Ms. Marks: — Salutation
↕ 1 line
I am a senior at Clark University. As part of my major in architecture, I have begun work on a paper exploring the extent to which designers consciously match the form of furniture to its function.
↕ 1 line
Your company's chairs and tables have won several awards for designs that manage to be both functional and artistically playful. I am thinking particularly of your Campara chair and coffee table combination. Would you be kind enough to answer these questions:

When an idea comes to you for some pieces of furniture, to what extent do you think about function first and then begin to play with the basic design?

Why make playful furniture? For instance, why build a coffee table supported not by four legs but by a miniature buffalo?

5 spaces

Who are your clients? Is there a certain "type" of person who comes looking for a Hannah Marks table or chair?

The thesis that I am developing is that furniture helps to confirm individual identity. We see very traditional leather and brass in the office of a lawyer who at home may be setting her coffee on the back of one of your buffalos. My bet is that the lawyer wouldn't dare risk the buffalo in her office.

I admire your work a great deal. One day, if I ever find a job that pays enough, I'd like a miniature buffalo to call my own. Have you considered building a student model? Thanks for your help--and I will send you a copy of my paper when it is done.

— Body

↕ 1 line
Sincerely,

Closing

4 lines

Jon Lipman

ESL ALERT

The letter of complaint was unimaginable and is still relatively unknown in Russia and former USSR nations; students from those areas will not understand the rationale for them and will have no models or standards for such a letter other than the ones provided in the text or by the instructor. Indonesians and other Asians from a similar tradition will understand the concept, but will instinctively be more indirect and polite in such letters because of their culture's emphasis on avoiding direct confrontation.

REFERENCES

HALL, DEAN G., and BONNIE A. NELSON. "Initiating Students into Professionalism: Teaching the Letter of Inquiry." *Technical Writing Teacher* 14 (Winter 1987): 86–89. Argues for using the letter of inquiry in a set of assignments that may include a current research topic or a career option.

NORMAN, ROSE. "Résumés: A Computer Exercise for Teaching Résumé-Writing." *Technical Writing Teacher* 15 (1988): 162–66. Offering questions may lead students to discover ways for revising résumés; the computer can illustrate how stylistic changes affect résumés.

ANDERSON, W. STEVE. "The Rhetoric of the Résumé." ERIC, 1984, ED 249 537. Applies James Kinneavy's communication triangle and asserts that students need to attend to the relationship of the writer, text, and reader in order to compose effective résumés.

40c   Letters of complaint

When you have a problem that you want remedied, write a letter of complaint. No matter how irate you may be, keep a civil but firm tone and do not threaten. If the time comes to take follow-up action, write a second letter in which you repeat your complaint and state your intentions. Your letter of complaint should be clear on the following points:

- Present the problem.
- State when and where you bought the product in question (if this is a consumer complaint). Provide an exact model number. If this is a complaint about poor service or ill treatment, state when and where you encountered the unacceptable behavior.
- Describe precisely the product failure or the way in which a behavior was unsatisfactory.
- Summarize the expectations you had when you bought the product or when you engaged someone's services. State succinctly how your expectations were violated and how you were inconvenienced (or worse).
- State exactly how you want the problem resolved.

40d   Letters of application

Whether you are applying for summertime work or for a full-time job after graduation, your first move probably will be to write a letter of application in which you ask for an interview. A successful letter of application will pique a prospective employer's interest by achieving a delicate balance: On the one hand you will present yourself as a bright, dependable, and resourceful person while on the other you will avoid sounding like an unabashed self-promoter. Your goal is to show a humble and earnest confidence. As you gather thoughts for writing, think of the employer as someone in need of a person who can be counted on for dependable and steady work, for creative thinking, and for an ability to function amiably as a member of a team. Avoid presenting yourself merely as someone who has a particular set of skills. You are more than this. Skills grow dated as new technologies become available. You want to suggest that your ability to learn and to adapt will never grow dated.

- Keep your letter of application to one typewritten page.
- Open by stating which job you are applying for and where you learned of the job.
- Review your specific skills and work experience that make you well suited for the job.
- Review your more general qualities (in relation to work experience, if appropriate) that make you well suited for the job.

- Express your desire for an interview and note any constraints on your time: exams, jobs, and other commitments. Avoid statements like "you can contact me at...." You will provide your address and phone number on your résumé.

- Close with a word of appreciation.

When you have written a second draft of your letter, seek out editorial advice from those who have had experience applying for jobs and particularly from those who have been in a position of reading letters of application and setting up interviews. Here are a few questions you can put to your readers: What sort of person does this letter describe? Am I emphasizing my skills and abilities in the right way? How do you feel about the tone of this letter? Am I direct and confident without being pushy? Based on editorial feedback, revise. Proofread two or three times so that your final document is direct, concise, well organized, and letter-perfect with respect to grammar, usage, and punctuation. Write your letter in a block or semi-block format on bond paper that has a good, substantial feel to it. Use paper with at least a twenty-five percent cotton fiber content, which you will find at any stationery store. Use an envelope of matching bond paper.

Semi-Block Format

231 Gray Street
Worcester, Massachusetts 01610
March 30, 1993

Ms. Hannah Marks
Equipment Design, Inc.
1254 Glenn Avenue
Arlington, Massachusetts 02174

Dear Ms. Marks:
5 spaces

I would like to apply for the marketing position you advertised in <u>Architectural Digest</u>. As you know from our previous correspondence, I am an architecture major with an interest in furniture design. As part of my course work I took a minor in marketing, with the hope of finding a job similar to the one you have listed.

For the past two summers I have apprenticed myself to a cabinet maker in Berkshire County, Massachusetts. Mr. Hiram Stains is 70 years old and a master at working with cherry and walnut. While I love working in a shop, and have built most of the furniture in my own apartment (see the photographic enclosures), I realize that a craftsman's life is a bit too solitary for me. Ideally, I would like to combine in one job my woodworking skills, my degree in architecture, and my desire to interact with people.

Your job offers precisely this opportunity. I respect your work immensely and am sure I could represent Equipment Design with enthusiasm. Over time, if my suggestions were welcomed, I might also be able to contribute in terms of design ideas.

I would very much like to arrange an interview. Final exams are scheduled for the last week of April. I'll be preparing the week before that, so I'm available for an interview anytime aside from that two-week block. Thank you for your interest, and I hope to hear from you soon.

Sincerely,

Jon Lipman

Jon Lipman

enc.: photographs   ⎤ Align
      writing sample   ⎥ itemized
                       ⎦ enclosures

40e   Résumés

A résumé highlights information that you think employers will find useful in considering you for a job. Typically, résumés are written in a clipped form. Although word groups are punctuated as sentences, they are, strictly speaking, fragments. For instance, instead of writing "I supervised fund-raising activities" you would write "Supervised fund-raising activities." Keep these fragments parallel: Keep all verbs either in the present or in the past tense; begin all fragments with either verbs or nouns.

NOT PARALLEL   Supervised fund-raising activities. Speaker at three area meetings on the "Entrepreneurial Side of the Art World." [The first fragment begins with a verb; the second begins with a noun.]

PARALLEL   Supervised fund-raising activities. Spoke at three area meetings on the "Entrepreneurial Side of the Art World." [Both fragments begin with a verb in the past tense.]

A résumé works in tandem with your job application. The letter of application establishes a direct communication between you and your prospective employer. Written in your voice, the letter will suggest intangible elements such as your habits of mind and traits of character that make you an attractive candidate. The résumé, by contrast, works as a summary sheet or catalogue of your educational and work experience. The tone of the résumé is neutral and fact-oriented. The basic components are these:

- Your name, address, and telephone number—each centered on its own line at the top of the page.

Provide headings, as follows:

- *Position Desired* or *Objective*. State the specific job you want.
- *Education*. Provide your pertinent college (and graduate school) experience. List degrees earned (or to be earned); major; classes taken, if pertinent; and your grade point average, if you are comfortable sharing this information.
- *Work Experience*. List your jobs, including titles, chronologically, beginning with your most recent job.
- *Related Activities*. List any clubs, volunteer positions, or activities that you feel are indicative of your general interests and character.
- *References*. Provide names and addresses if you expect the employer to contact references directly. If you are keeping references on file at a campus office, state that your references are available upon request.

TEACHING IDEAS

Students can benefit from seeing a variety of résumés. Gather a collection—from business writing texts, from friends in business, or from other sources—to distribute to students. In comparing the effectiveness of various forms, students will get a better idea of how to prepare their own résumés.

ADDITIONAL EXERCISE D

Using this résumé as a model, compose one of your own. Be sure that you emphasize your skills and that you pay close attention to layout. Ask for editorial advice from other students, and revise your résumé accordingly.

Jon Lipman
231 Gray Street
Worcester, Massachusetts 01610
508-555-8212

Objective: Marketing position in an arts-related
                 company

Education: Clark University, Worcester,
                 Massachusetts
                 Bachelor of Arts in Architecture, May
                 1993
                 Minor in Marketing, May 1993
                 Grade point average (to date) 3.3/4.0

Work   September 1992-present: Directed
Experience: marketing campaign for campus-based
                 artists' collective and supervised fund
                 raising. Spoke at three area meetings
                 on the "Entrepreneurial Side of the Art
                 World." Generated community interest in
                 the work of campus artists by
                 organizing a fair and a direct mail
                 program.

                 May 1992-August 1992: Studied cabinet
                 making with Hiram Stains, master
                 cabinetmaker in Berkshire County,
                 Massachusetts. Prepared wood for
                 joining, learned dove-tail technique,
                 and applied design principles learned
                 in school to cabinet construction.

                 September 1991-April 1992: Organized
                 artists' collective on campus and
                 developed marketing plan.

                 May 1991-August 1991: Studied cabinet
                 making with Hiram Stains. Learned tool
                 use and maintenance.

Related   Supervised set design for theater
Activities: productions on campus. Donated services
                 as carpenter to local shelter for the
                 homeless. Designed and built virtually
                 all furniture in my apartment.

References: Mr. Hiram Stains
                 Route 16
                 Richmond, Massachusetts 01201

                 Ms. Amanda Lopez
                 Center Street Shelter
                 Worcester, Massachusetts 01610

                 Dr. Edward Bing
                 Department of Architecture
                 Clark University
                 Worcester, Massachusetts 01610

40f Memoranda

Memoranda, or memos, are internal documents written from one employee to another in the same company. The reasons for writing memos are many: You may want to announce a meeting, summarize your understanding of a meeting, set a schedule, request information, define and resolve a problem, argue for funding, build consensus, and so on. Because they are written "in-house," memos tend to be less formal in tone than business letters; still, they must be every bit as direct, concise, and well organized, or readers will ignore them. When writing a memo longer than a few lines, follow the process discussed earlier of preparing to write, writing, and revising. A memo will differ from a business letter in the following ways:

- The memo has no return address, no inside address, and no salutation. Instead, the memo begins with this information:

    (Date)
    To:
    From:
    Subject:

- The memo follows a full block format, with all information placed flush to the left margin.

- The memo is often divided into headings that separate the document into readily distinguished parts.

- Portions of the memo are often displayed—that is, set off and indented when there are lists or other information lending itself to such treatment.

- Some companies highlight the information about distribution of memo copies to others, either placing the *cc:* line under the *To:* line or adding a subsection titled *Distribution:* with the opening section.

If your memo is three-quarters of a page or longer, consider highlighting its organization with headings, as in the example memo below. Headings work in tandem with the memo's subject line and first sentence to give readers the ability to scan the memo and quickly—within thirty seconds—understand your message. Once again, realize that your readers are busy; they will appreciate any attempt to make their job of reading easier.

ADDITIONAL EXERCISE G

This exercise will help students further fine-tune their evaluation skills. In groups of three or four, students should evaluate the effectiveness of the model memo, based on the material covered in the book. Ask students to consider such issues as the purpose of the memo, the clarity of information presented, and the layout.

February 14, 1993

TO: Linda Cohen

FROM: Matthew Franks

SUBJECT: Brochure production schedule

Thanks for helping to resolve the production schedule for our new brochure. Please review the following production and distribution dates. By return memo, confirm that you will commit your department to meeting this schedule.

Production dates

Feb. 19	1993	First draft of brochure copy
March 1	1993	First draft of design plans
March 8	1993	Second draft of brochure copy and design
March 15	1993	Review of final draft and design
March 17	1993	Brochure to printer

Distribution dates

April 4	1993	First printing of 10,000 in our warehouse
April 11	1993	Mailing to Zone 1
April 14	1993	Mailing to Zone 2
April 17	1993	Mailing to Zones 3 and 4

Please let me hear from you by this Friday. If I haven't, I'll assume your agreement and commitment. It looks as though we'll have a good brochure this year. Thanks for all your help.

cc: Amy Hanson

CHAPTER 41

Writing Essay Exams

Increasingly, professors across the curriculum are using essay exams to test student mastery of important concepts and relationships. A carefully conceived exam will challenge you not only to recall and organize what you know of a subject but also to extend and apply your knowledge. Essay exams will require of you numerous responses; but the one response to *avoid* is the so-called information dump in which at first glimpse of a topic you begin pouring onto the page *everything* you have ever read or heard about it. A good answer to an essay exam question requires that you be selective in choosing the information you discuss. What you say about that information and what relationships you make with it are critical. As is often the case with good writing, less tends to be more—provided that you adopt and follow a strategy.

41a A strategy for taking essay exams

Prepare

Ideally, you will have read your textbooks and assigned articles with care *as* they were assigned during the period prior to the exam. If you have read closely, or "critically" (see 1e–1h), your preparation for an exam will amount to a *review* of material you have already thought carefully about. Skim assigned materials and pay close attention to notes you have made in the margins or have recorded in a reading log. Take new notes based on your original notes: highlight important concepts from each assignment. Then reorganize your notes according to key ideas that you think serve as themes or focus points for your course. List each idea separately, and beneath each, list any reading that in some way comments on or provides information about that idea. In an American literature course this idea might be "nature as a character" or "innocence lost." In a sociology course the idea might be "social constructions of identity." Turn next to your class notes (you may want to do this *before* reviewing your reading assignments), and add information and comments to your lists of key ideas. Study these lists. Develop statements about each idea that you could, if asked, support with references to specific information. Try to anticipate your professor's questions.

Read the entire exam before beginning to write.

Allot yourself a certain number of minutes to answer each essay question, allowing extra time for the more complex questions. As you write, monitor your use of time.

KEY FEATURES

This chapter advises students to apply the basic principles of reading and writing presented in chapters 1 through 4 when they write essay exams. Focusing on the importance of critical thinking in preparing for and writing essay exams, the chapter advises students to begin with notes and general ideas, and to move through a compressed writing process as they compose their responses. Reference is also made to chapters 37 through 39 in advising students to be aware of the specific requirements of different disciplines. Strategies for managing time, for reading exam questions, and for drafting and revising responses are explained in detail. A list of key verbs found in essay questions is reproduced at the end of the chapter, providing students with a valuable reference to guide them in formulating responses.

LOOKING BACK

Advice in this chapter relies on a number of previous chapters in the handbook. In particular, students should refer to chapters 1–2 on critical reading and writing, chapters 3–4 on the writing process, chapter 5 on paragraphs, and chapters 37–39 on writing in the disciplines.

REFERENCES

BERLIN, JAMES A. *Rhetoric and Reality: Writing Instruction in American Colleges, 1900–1985.* Carbondale and Edwardsville, IL: Southern Illinois UP, 1987. Provides history of the essay examination, arguing that it proliferated as a result of a shift in emphasis from rhetoric to poetics.

BARTHOLOMAE DAVID, and ANTHONY PETROSKY. *Facts, Artifacts, and Counterfacts: Theory and Method for a Reading and Writing Course.* Upper Montclair, NJ: Boynton, 1986. Discusses the implications of essay examinations in a process-oriented writing course, cautioning that the emphasis may shift from global to local concerns.

BIDDLE, ARTHUR W., and TOBY FULWILER, eds. *Reading, Writing, and the Study of Literature.* New York: Random, 1989. Useful chapter discussing the writing of essay exams (includes bibliography).

GREENBERG, KAREN, HARVEY S. WEINER, and RICHARD A. DONOVAN, eds. *Writing Assessment: Issues and Strategies.* New York: Longman, 1986. Collection of twelve essays on assessment (includes annotated bibliography).

OTTENS, ALLEN J. *Coping with Academic Anxiety.* New York: Rosen Pub. Group, 1984. Provides suggestions for overcoming "test anxiety."

Adopt a discipline-appropriate perspective.

Essay exams are designed in part to see how well you understand particular ways of thinking in a discipline. If you are writing a mid-term exam in chemistry, for instance, appreciate that your professor will expect you to discuss material from a chemist's perspective. That is, you will need to demonstrate not only that you know your information but also that you can *do* things with it: namely, think and reach conclusions in discipline-appropriate ways.

Adapt the writing process according to the time allotted for a question.

Assuming that you have thirty minutes to answer an essay question, spend at least five minutes of this allotted time in plotting an answer.

- Locate the assignment's key verb and identify your specific tasks in writing. (See the box that follows.)
- Given these tasks, list information you can draw on in developing your answer.
- Examine the information you have listed and develop a thesis (see 3d), a statement that directly answers the question and that demonstrates your understanding and application of some key concept associated with the essay topic.
- Sketch an outline of your answer. In taking an essay exam, you have little or no time for writing to discover. Know before you write what major points you will develop in support of your thesis and in what order.

Spend twenty minutes of your allotted time on writing your answer. When you begin writing, be conscious of making clear, logical connections between sentences and paragraphs. Well-chosen transitions (see 5d-3) not only will help your professor follow your discussion but also will help you to project your ideas forward and to continue writing. As you do in formal papers, develop your essay in sections, with each section organized by a section thesis (see 5a). Develop each section of your essay by discussing *specific* information.

Save five minutes to reread your work and ensure that its logic is clear and that you address the exam question from a discipline-appropriate point of view. Given the time constraints of the essay exam format, professors understand that you will not submit a polished draft. Nevertheless, they will expect writing that faces the question and that is coherent, unified, and grammatical. Again, avoid an information dump. Select information with care and write with a strategy.

41b The importance of verbs in an essay question

In reading an essay assignment, you will need to identify a specific topic and purpose for writing. Often, you can identify exactly what a professor expects by locating a key verb in the assignment such as *illustrate, discuss,* or *compare.* Following is a guide to students on "Important Word Meanings" in assignments. Developed by the History Department at UCLA, this guide was intended to help students develop effective responses to essay questions. The guide will serve you well in any of your courses.

Important Word Meanings

Good answers to essay questions depend in part upon a clear understanding of the meanings of the important directive words. These are the words like *explain, compare, contrast,* and *justify,* which indicate the way in which the material is to be presented. Background knowledge of the subject matter is essential. But mere evidence of this knowledge is not enough. If you are asked to *compare* the British and American secondary school systems, you will get little or no credit if you merely *describe* them. If you are asked to *criticize* the present electoral system, you are not answering the question if you merely *explain* how it operates. A paper is satisfactory only if it answers directly the question that was asked.

The words that follow are frequently used in essay examinations:

summarize sum up; give the main points briefly. *Summarize the ways in which man preserves food.*

evaluate give the good points and the bad ones; appraise; give an opinion regarding the value of; talk over the advantages and limitations. *Evaluate the contributions of teaching machines.*

contrast bring out the points of difference. *Contrast the novels of Jane Austen and William Makepeace Thackeray.*

explain make clear; interpret; make plain; tell "how" to do; tell the meaning of. *Explain how man can, at times, trigger a full-scale rainstorm.*

describe give an account of; tell about; give a word picture of. *Describe the Pyramids of Giza.*

define give the meaning of a word or concept; place it in the class to which it belongs and set it off from other items in the same class. *Define the term "archetype."*

compare bring out points of similarity and points of difference. *Compare the legislative branches of the state government and the national government.*

discuss talk over; consider from various points of view; present the different sides of. *Discuss the use of pesticides in controlling mosquitoes.*

criticize state your opinion of the correctness or merits of an item or issue; criticism may approve or disapprove. *Criticize the increasing use of alcohol.*

justify show good reasons for; give your evidence; present facts to support your position. *Justify the American entry into World War II.*

(continued)

ESL ALERT

Native speakers have grown up interpreting the terms standard to class assignments; non-native speakers have not. They will benefit from the explanatory list in this section and from practice interpreting assignment requirements. For example, what do you *do* when you "discuss" or "evaluate" on an essay exam? European exams reward eloquent style and more abstract and philosophical language over specificity.

REFERENCES

BRUCE, BERTRAM, SARAH MICHAELS, and KAREN WATSON-GEGEO. "How Computers Can Change the Writing Process." *Language Arts* 62 (1985): 143–49.

COSTANZO, WILLIAM. "Language, Thinking, and the Culture of Computers." *Language Arts* 62 (1985): 516–23.

KIEFER, KATHLEEN. "Revising on the Word-Processor: What's Happened, What's Ahead." *ADE Bulletin* 87 (1987): 24–27.

———. "Writing: Using the Computer as Tool." *Computer-Aided Instruction in the Humanities.* Ed. Solveig Olsen. New York: MLA, 1985.

MARCUS, STEPHEN. "Computers and English: Future Tense, Future Perfect?" *English Journal* 76 (1987): 88–90.

OLSEN, SOLVEIG. *Computer-Aided Instruction in the Humanities.* New York: MLA, 1985.

ROSS, DONALD, and LILLIAN S. BRIDWELL. "Computer-Aided Composing: Gaps in the Software." *Computer-Aided Instruction in the Humanities.* Ed. Solveig Olsen. New York: MLA, 1985.

Important Word Meanings (continued)

trace   follow the course of; follow the trail of; give a description of progress. *Trace the development of television in school instruction.*

interpret make plain; give the meaning of; give your thinking about; translate. *Interpret the poetic line, "The sound of a cobweb snapping is the noise of my life."*

prove   establish the truth of something by giving factual evidence or logical reasons. *Prove that in a full-employment economy, a society can get more of one product only by giving up another product.*

illustrate use a word picture, a diagram, a chart, or a concrete example to clarify a point. *Illustrate the use of catapults in the amphibious warfare of Alexander.*

Source: Andrew Moss and Carol Holder, *Improving Student Writing: A Guide for Faculty in All Disciplines* (Dubuque, IA: Kendall/Hunt, 1988) 17–18.

PART XII
ESL REFERENCE GUIDE

The next three chapters are designed to supplement the rest of the *Handbook*. They provide basic information on structural and idiomatic features of the English language that students from an English as a Second Language (ESL) background may need for reference.

These chapters assume that ESL students are now working in a basic English composition course alongside native speakers, and that they have already completed a college-level course of instruction (or its equivalent) in using English as a Second Language. The role of this material is not to provide primary ESL instruction but to give students help in three ways: (1) to identify key topics and problems that persistently cause difficulties for ESL students from many different backgrounds; (2) to propose standard usage guidelines and remedies for such problems (with the assistance of exercises); and (3) to refer ESL students to sections of chapters 1–41 that will give particular help with difficult language and usage issues in English. Students should also notice that chapters 7–33 have been furnished with topical "ESL Note" references, which briefly describe key issues and refer readers to pertinent sections of these supplementary chapters.

The following chapters cover topics in the three functional areas of English language usage: chapter 42—nouns and noun-related structures (including articles and determiners); chapter 43—verbs, verbals, and related structures (including particles with phrasal verbs); and chapter 44—usage for modifiers and modifying structures. Prepositions—perhaps the most troublesome feature of English—are treated in connection with the structures that determine them in each chapter of this part. (Prepositions determined by nouns are discussed in 42c; those determined by phrasal verbs are discussed in 43f; and those governed by adjectives are discussed in 44b.)

CHAPTER 42

Using English Nouns, Pronouns, and Articles

KEY FEATURES

Teaching ESL students to write well in English in the face of grammatical and cultural interference complicates the already difficult task of the writing instructor, but can also bring unanticipated pleasures and rewards. The former involve helping students face a monumentally difficult task; the latter come from new understandings by the instructor of grammar and rhetoric derived most effectively from contrasts with a radically different system. The ESL Alerts in this Instructor's Edition are based on teacher experiences with students at particular schools, and are backed by panels of native speakers at those schools. A caveat is necessary: that all such experiences are shaped and distorted by individual differences and differences *within* cultures. *Your* Chinese students may not experience the problems described in these notes. The task of an ESL teacher, however, is not to lay down certitudes, but rather to generate explanations and "rules" in response to student difficulty.

42a Using the different classes of English nouns

English nouns name things or people that are considered either countable or not countable in English. English also distinguishes whether a noun names a person or thing that is specific, or something that is generic.

1 Identifying and using count nouns

In English, **count nouns** name things or people that are considered countable. They identify one of many possible individuals or things in the category named. Count nouns have three important characteristics.

- Singular count nouns can be preceded by *one,* or by *a/an*—the indefinite articles that convey the meaning "one (of many)."

  one car   a rowboat   a truck   an ambulance

Singular count nouns can also be preceded by demonstrative pronouns (*this, that*), by possessive pronouns (*my, your, their*), and often by the definite article (*the*).

- Plural count nouns can be preceded by expressions of quantity (*two, three, some, many, a few*) and can use a plural form.

  two cars   some rowboats   many trucks   a few ambulances

- A count noun used as a singular or plural subject must agree with a singular or plural verb form.

  This *car stops* quickly. [A singular subject and verb agree.]
  Other *cars stop* slowly. [A plural subject and verb agree.]

  (See 10a for guidelines on subject-verb agreement.)

2 Forming plurals with count nouns

Plural count nouns are either regular or irregular. Regular nouns form the plural with *-s* or *-es*. Irregular plural forms—such as *man/men, tooth/teeth, wolf/wolves, medium/media*—follow the models shown in 23e. (See rules for plural forms in 10a and in the spelling sections in 23e-1, 3, and 5.)

3   Identifying and using noncount (mass) nouns

In English, **noncount (mass) nouns** name things that are being considered as a whole, undivided group or category that is not being counted. Noncount (mass) nouns name various kinds of individuals or things that are considered as group categories in English, such as these:

abstractions: courage, grammar

fields of activity: chemistry, tennis

natural phenomena: weather, dew, rain

whole groups of objects: rice, sand, oxygen, wood, oil

Objects considered too numerous or shapeless to count are often treated as noncount nouns, as with the word *rock* in this sentence.

We mined dense *rock* in this mountain.

As such objects become individually identifiable, the same word may be used as a count noun.

Four *rocks* fell across the road.

Some nouns name things that can be considered either countable or noncountable in English, depending on whether they name something specific or something generic.

COUNTABLE (AND SPECIFIC)	A *chicken* or two ran off. A *straw* or two flew up.
NONCOUNTABLE (AND GENERIC)	*Chicken* needs a lot of cooking. *Straw* can be very dry.

Nouns that name generalized or generic things often occur in noncountable form, but may also occur in singular form in scientific usage (see 42a-5).

Three characteristics distinguish noncount (mass) nouns:

- Noncount nouns never use the indefinite article *a/an* (or *one*). (Articles are discussed in detail in 42b.)
- Noncount nouns are never used in a plural form.
- Noncount nouns always take singular verbs. (See 10a for guidelines on subject-verb agreement.)

4   Using expressions of quantity with count and noncount nouns

Expressions of quantity—such as *many, few, much, little, some,* and *plenty*—are typically used to modify nouns. Some expressions are used to quantify count nouns; some are used with noncount nouns; and others are used with both kinds of nouns.

COUNT NOUNS	NONCOUNT NOUNS	BOTH COUNT AND NONCOUNT NOUNS
many potatoes	*much* rice	*lots of* potatoes and rice
few potatoes	*little* rice	*plenty of* potatoes and rice
		some, any potatoes and rice

When the context is very clear, these expressions can also be used alone as pronouns.

Do you have *any* potatoes or rice?
I have *plenty* if you need *some.*

5 Using nouns in specific and generic senses

English nouns show differences in usage between nouns that name specific things or people and nouns that name generalized or generic things.

A DEFINITE NOUN	The whale migrated thousands of miles. The whales migrated thousands of miles. [When a noun names something very specific, either singular or plural, it is preceded by the **definite article** (or by demonstrative pronouns *this/that*).]
AN INDEFINITE NOUN	A whale surfaced nearby; then several whales surfaced. [When a noun names something indefinite but countable, the **indefinite article** is used.]
GENERIC USAGE	Whales are migratory animals. A whale is a migratory animal. [When the reference is to a general group, nouns often use either the **plural with no article** or the **singular with an indefinite article.**]
SCIENTIFIC USAGE	The whale is a migratory animal. Whales are migratory animals. [A generic noun may also be singular or plural with a definite article (see 42b-3).]

6 Distinguishing pronouns in specific and indefinite or generic uses

Most pronouns, including personal pronouns, rename and refer to a noun located elsewhere that names a specific individual or thing. However, indefinite pronouns, such as *some, any, one, someone,* or *anyone,* may refer to a noun in an indefinite or generic sense.

PERSONAL PRONOUN	Where are my pencils? I need *them.* [Meaning: I need specific pencils that are mine.]
INDEFINITE PRONOUN	Where are my pencils? I need *some.* [Meaning: I need generic, indefinable pencils; I will use any I can find.]

(The list in 7a-7 gives terms that describe various classes of pronouns.)

42b Using articles with nouns

Articles are the most important class of words used in English to show whether nouns are being used as count or noncount nouns, or as specific or generic nouns. There are three articles in English: *a*, *an*, and *the*. *Some*, the indefinite pronoun, is occasionally used as if it were an indefinite article.

1 Nouns sometimes take the indefinite articles *a* and *an*.

The indefinite articles *a* and *an* are grammatically the same: They are singular indefinite articles that mean "one (of many)," and they are used only with singular count nouns. Pronunciation determines which to use: *A* precedes a noun beginning with a consonant or a consonant sound (a bottle, a hotel, a youth, a user, a xylophone). *An* precedes a noun beginning with a vowel or vowel sound (an egg, an hour, an undertaker).

A is sometimes used with the quantifiers *little* and *few*. Note the differences in the following examples.

EXAMPLE	MEANING
a little, a few a few onions a little oil	a small amount of something
little, few few onions little oil	a less-than-expected amount of something

A and *an* are rarely used with proper nouns, which usually identify a unique individual rather than one of many. The indefinite article occasionally appears with a proper noun in a hypothetical statement about one of many possible persons or things in the category named, as in this sentence.

Dr. King dreamed of *an America* where children of all colors would grow up in harmony. [We may dream of more than one possible "America."]

2 Nouns sometimes take the definite article *the*.

Use *the* with specific singular and plural count nouns and with noncount nouns.

SPECIFIC NOUNS

I need *the tool* and *the rivets*. [one singular and one plural noun]

I need *the equipment*. [a noncount noun]

I need *the tool* on *the top shelf*. I need *the tools* that are painted orange. I need *the smallest tool* on *that shelf*.	[Note the modifiers, clauses, and phrases that make the nouns specific.]

GENERIC NOUNS

> I need tools for that work. [In this case, no article is used.]

(For varieties of usage with generic nouns, see 42a-5.)

Use *the* in a context where a noun has previously been mentioned, or where the writer and the reader both know the particular thing or person being referred to.

> I saw a giraffe at the zoo. *The giraffe* was eating leaves from a tree.

> I stopped at an intersection. When *the light* turned green, I started to leave. [The sentence assumes the existence of a particular traffic light at the intersection.]

Other uses of the definite article

- Use *the* with items that are to be designated as one of a kind (*the* sun, *the* moon, *the* first, *the* second, *the* last).

- Use *the* with official names of countries when it is needed to give specific meaning to nouns like *union, kingdom, state(s), republic, duchy,* and so on (*the* United States, *the* Republic of Cyprus, *the* Hashemite Kingdom of Jordan). No article is needed with certain other countries (Cyprus, Jordan, Japan, El Salvador).

- Use *the* when a noun identifies institutions or generic activities *other than sports,* and in certain usages for generic groups (see 42a-5).

  > We called *the* newspapers, *the* radio, and *the* news services.

  > Sergei plays *the* piano, *the* flute, and *the* guitar.

  > *The* whales are migratory animals. *The* birds have feathers.

  > **WITHOUT AN ARTICLE**   Nadia plays basketball, hockey, and volleyball.

- Use *the* with names of oceans, seas, rivers, and deserts.

  > *the* Pacific   *the* Amazon   *the* Himalayas   *the* Sahara

  > **WITHOUT AN ARTICLE**   Lake Michigan   Mt. Fuji

- Use *the* to give specific meaning to expressions using the noun *language,* but not for the proper name of a language by itself.

  > He studied the Sanskrit language, not the Urdu language.

  > **WITHOUT AN ARTICLE**   He studied Sanskrit, not Urdu.

- Use *the* with names of colleges and universities containing *of.*

  > He studied at *the* University *of* Michigan.

  > **WITHOUT AN ARTICLE (TYPICALLY)**   He studied at Michigan State University.

3   Nouns sometimes take no article.

Typically no article is needed with names of unique individuals, because they do not need to be made specific and they are not usually counted as one among many. In addition, nouns naming generalized persons or things in a generic usage commonly use no article: *Managers often work long hours. Whales are migratory animals.* (See 42a-5.)

Some situations in which no article is used are shown in 42b-2. Here are some others.

- Use no article with proper names of continents, states, cities, and streets, and with religious place names.

  Europe   Alaska   New York   Main Street   heaven   hell

- Use no article with titles of officials when accompanied by personal names; the title effectively becomes part of the proper noun.

  President Truman   King Juan Carlos   Emperor Napoleon

- Use no article with fields of study.

  Ali studied literature. Juan studied engineering.

- Use no article with names of diseases.

  He has cancer. AIDS is a very serious disease.

- Use no article with names of magazines and periodicals, unless the article is part of the formal title.

  Life   Popular Science   Sports Illustrated

  BUT: *The New Yorker* [The article is part of the proper name.]

42c   Using nouns with prepositions

Some of the complex forms of prepositions in English are determined by their use with nouns. Nouns that follow prepositions are called **objects of prepositions** (see 7a-8 and 8b-1); this grouping forms a modifying **prepositional phrase** (7d-1). The distinctive function of such modifying phrases often determines which preposition to choose in an English sentence.

1   Using the preposition *of* to show possession

The preposition *of* is often widely used to show possession as an alternative to the possessive case form (*I hear a man's voice. I hear the voice of a man*). It is also widely used to show possession for many nouns that do not usually take a possessive form. For example, many inanimate nouns, as well as some nouns naming a large group of people (*crowd, mob, company*) or a location (*place, center*), are not typically used with a possessive case form, and are likely to show possession with the preposition *of.*

FAULTY   I washed the *car's hood.*

CORRECT   I washed the *hood of her car.*

FAULTY   *The Information Center's* location is unknown.

CORRECT   The location *of the Information Center* is unknown.

The preposition *of* is not used with proper nouns.

FAULTY   I washed the *car of Luisa.*

CORRECT   I washed *Luisa's car.*

2 Using prepositions in phrases with nouns or pronouns

The distinctive function of a modifying prepositional phrase often determines which preposition to choose in an English sentence. Here are a few typical functions for prepositional phrases, with distinctive prepositions in use.

Function	Preposition	Example/Explanation
Passive voice (9g)	*by* the cook	He was insulted *by* the cook.
	with a snowball	I was hit *with* a snowball.
Time expressions	*on* January 1	use for specific dates
	on Sundays	use for specific days
	in January	use for months
	in 1984	use for years
	in spring	use for seasons
	at noon, *at* 5 P.M.	use for specific times
	by noon, *by* 5 P.M.	use to indicate *before* a specific hour
	by April 15	use to indicate *before* a specific date
Locations	*at* 301 South Street	use for an address
	in the house	
	on the floor	
Directions	*onto* the floor	
	beside the library	
	through the window	
	into the air	

For information on verbs with prepositions, see 43f; for information on adjectives with prepositions, see 44b.

EXERCISE 1

Complete the following sentences with *a, an, the,* or *some,* or write *X* for no article.

1. Please pass me _____ butter. I usually eat _____ bread with lunch.
2. Today we watched _____ policeman arguing with _____ driver. _____ driver didn't understand _____ English.
3. You need _____ furniture. You should buy _____ chair and borrow _____ round green table in my house.

Choose the correct form.

4. He admired (Sam's motorcycle) (the motorcycle of Sam) where it stood in the (driveway's center) (center of the driveway).
5. Meet me (on) (in) (at) March 15 (on) (at) the theater (on) (in) (at) six o'clock.

CHAPTER 43

Using English Verbs

43a Distinguishing different types of verbs and verb constructions

A verb, the main word in the predicate of an English sentence, asserts the action undertaken by the subject or else the condition in which the subject exists. The four types of verbs include transitive verbs (which take direct objects), intransitive verbs (which do not take direct objects), linking verbs, and helping or auxiliary verbs (which show tense or mood). Although only transitive verbs can show passive voice, most verbs can show various tenses and mood. (See chapter 9 for a discussion of verb usage.)

1 Transitive and intransitive verbs work differently.

A **transitive verb** can take an object. Examples of transitive verbs include *throw* and *take.*

subject	verb	object	subject	verb	object
He	throws	a pass.	They	took	the ball.

Because transitive verbs can take an object, most of them can operate in both the active and passive voices.[1] The active and the passive forms of the verb may be similar in meaning, but the emphasis changes with the rearrangement of the subject and object, as well as with changes in the verb form (to the past participle with *be*).

subject	verb	object	subject	verb	modifiers
Workers in Ohio make Hondas.			Hondas are made (by workers) in Ohio.		
active voice			passive voice		

Notice how the active-voice object *Hondas* in the first sentence becomes the passive-voice subject in the second. In a passive-voice sentence the original performer of the action (*workers* in the example) is not emphasized and may even be omitted. (See 9g on the uses of passive constructions.)

By contrast, an **intransitive verb** never takes an object and can never be used in the passive voice. Examples of intransitive verbs include *smile* and *go.*

subject	verb	subject	verb
The politician smiled.		He went into the crowd.	

---

[1]**Exceptions:** Transitive verbs *have, get, want, like,* and *hate* are seldom used in passive voice.

2 Linking verbs are used in distinctive patterns.

Linking verbs, the most common example of which is *be,* serve in sentences as "equals signs" to link a subject with an equivalent noun or adjective. Some other linking verbs are *appear, become,* and *seem.* (See 11d for a full list and description of linking verbs; see also 7b, Pattern 5.)

Things *seem* unsettled.
Shall I *become* a doctor?

Expletives

Linking verbs also serve in a distinctive English construction that uses changed word order with an **expletive** word, *there* or *it.* Expletives are used only with linking verbs, as in these sentences.

It *is* important to leave now.   It *appears* unnecessary to do that.
There *seems* to be a problem.   It *seems* important.

There and *it* form "dummy subjects" or filler words that occupy the position of the subject in a normal sentence; the true subject is elsewhere in the sentence, and the verb agrees with the true subject (see 10a-8).

EXPLETIVE IN SUBJECT POSITION	TRUE SUBJECT
There is a cat in that tree.	*A cat* is in that tree.
There are some cats in the tree.	*Some cats* are in the tree.
It is convenient to use the train.	*To use the train* is convenient.

The expletive *it* also has a unique role in expressing length of time with *take* followed by an infinitive.

It takes an hour to get home by car. *It took* us forever.

Expletive constructions are important and useful for length-of-time expressions and for short or emphatic statements.

It is a tale of great sorrow. There were no survivors.

However, in complex and formal English sentences, the "dummy subject" expletive becomes an unnecessary word obscuring the true subject. The expletive also encourages using linking verbs instead of more direct, active verbs—transitive or intransitive verbs. To eliminate wordiness and promote the clear, direct style that is preferred in English academic prose, try to avoid expletives; revise sentences to restore normal word order (see 17a-3).

43b Changing verb forms

Verb forms express *tense,* an indication of when an action or state of being occurs. The three basic tenses in English are the past, the present, and the future. (See 9a for a discussion of the forms of English verbs, and 9e-1, 2 for a basic discussion of tenses.)

1   **Not all verbs use progressive tense forms.**

Each of the three basic tenses has a progressive form, made up of *be* and the present participle (the *-ing* form of the verb). The progressive tense emphasizes the *process* of doing whatever action the verb asserts. The tense is indicated by a form of *be*: present progressive (I *am going*), past progressive (I *was going*), past perfect progressive (I *had been going*), future progressive (I *will be going*). For examples, see 9e and 9f.

Certain verbs are generally *not* used in the progressive form; others have a progressive use only for process-oriented or ongoing meanings of the verb.

Words that are rarely seen in a progressive form

Think (in the sense of "believe"): "I think not."

EXCEPTION: The progressive form can be used for a process of considering something.

FAULTY   I *am thinking* it is wrong.

CORRECT   I *am thinking* about changing jobs. [considering]

Believe, understand, recognize, realize, remember: "You believe it."

EXCEPTION: The last four can sometimes use the progressive form if a process of recognition or recollection is meant: "He is slowly realizing the truth." "He is gradually remembering what happened."

Belong, possess, own, want, need: "We want some." "We once owned it."

Have: "You have what you need."

EXCEPTION: The progressive form can be used in the sense of "experiencing."

FAULTY   Maria *is having* a car.

CORRECT   Mary *is having* a baby. [experiencing childbirth]
           Maria *is having* success in her project.

Be, exist, seem: "This seems acceptable."

EXCEPTION: The progressive form is used only with an abstract emphasis on a process of "being" or "seeming": "Just existing from day to day is enough."

Smell, sound, and **taste** as intransitive verbs, as in "It smells good"; "it sounds funny"; "it tastes bad."

Appear in the sense of "seem": "It appeared to be the right time."

EXCEPTION: Sometimes the progressive form is used in the sense of presenting itself/oneself over a time period. "She's appearing nightly as the star actress."

See. "I can never see why you do it."

EXCEPTION: The progressive form is used in the sense of interviewing someone or witnessing or experiencing something.

FAULTY   I *am seeing* an airplane now.

REVISED   I *am seeing* a new patient. [interviewing]

Surprise, hate, love, like: "It surprises me"; "I hate lima beans."

2 Using the perfect forms

The perfect tense is made up of *have* and the past participle (the *-ed* form of the verb). The form of *have* indicates the tense: present perfect (*has* worked), past perfect (*had* worked), and future perfect (*will have* worked). (See 9e and 9f; also 9b, irregular past participles.)

Sometimes students confuse the use of the simple past with the use of the present perfect. The present perfect is used when an action or state of being that began in the past continues to the present; it is also used to express an action or state of being that happened at an indefinite time in the past.

PRESENT PERFECT   Linda has worked in Mexico since 1987.

PRESENT PERFECT   Ann has worked in Mexico. [The time is unspecified.]

By contrast, the simple past is used when an action or state of being began *and ended* in the past.

SIMPLE PAST   Linda worked in Mexico last year. [She no longer works there.]

Since or *for* with perfect tenses in prepositional phrases of time

A phrase with *since* requires using the present perfect (*has worked*) or past perfect tenses (*had worked*); it indicates action beginning at *a single point in time* and still continuing at the time shown by the verb tense.

She [has/had worked]   *since* noon
since July
since 1991
since the end of the school year
since the last storm
since the baby was born

A time phrase with *since* cannot have a noun object that shows plural time; *since* phrases must indicate a single point in time.

FAULTY   He lived here since three months.
I am here since May.

REVISED   He has lived here *for* three months.
I have been here since May.

ESL ALERT

ESL students may need help distinguishing between "since," which takes a specific initial time (since 3 P.M.; since July 3) and "for," which takes a length or period of time (for two hours; for 10 days).

Also, a time phrase with *since* cannot modify a simple past tense or any present tense.

FAULTY   He lived here since three months.
                I am here since May.

REVISED   He *had lived* here since February.
                I *have been* here since May.

The perfect tenses can have a time modifier with a prepositional phrase formed either with *since* or *for*.

He has worked since noon.
He had worked for a month.

A modifying phrase with *for* indicates action *through a duration of time*.

He [has/had worked] *for* three hours
                          for a month and a half
                          for two years
                          for a few weeks

When a phrase uses a plural noun, thus showing duration of time, this signals that the preposition in the modifier must be *for*, not *since*.

FAULTY   I had worked on it since many years.

REVISED   I had worked on it for many years.

3   **Using the varied forms of English future tenses**

The following list shows different ways of expressing the future.

VERB FORM	EXPLANATION
She *will call* us soon. She *is going to* call us soon.	These examples have the same meaning.
The movie *arrives* in town tomorrow. The next bus *leaves* in five minutes. The bus *is leaving* very soon.	The simple present and the present progressive are used to express definite future plans, as from a schedule.
Your flight *is taking off* at 6:55. The doctor *is operating* at once. I *am calling* them right now.	The present progressive is sometimes used to make strong statements about the future.
Hurry! The movie *is about to* begin. Finish up! The bell *is about to* ring.	The "near" future is expressed by some form of *be* plus *about to* and a verb.
It's cold. *I'm going to* get a sweater. It's cold. *I'll lend* you a sweater.	This suggests a plan. This suggests a willingness.

Verbs expressing thoughts about future actions, such as *intend* and *hope,* are not used in any future tense, and the verb *plan* uses a future tense only in the idiomatic *plan on* (to make or follow a plan).

FAULTY   I will intend to meet my friends tomorrow.

REVISED   I intend to meet my friends tomorrow.
        I plan to attend college.

See 43b-5 for guidelines on expressing future time in conditional sentences.

4   Using verb tenses in sentences with a sequence of actions

In complex sentences that have more than one verb, it is important to adjust the sequence of verb tenses to avoid confusion. See the discussion on verb tense combinations in 9f.

Verb tenses with reported speech

Reported speech, or indirect discourse, is very different from directly quoted speech, which gives the exact verb tense of the original.

DIRECT SPEECH   Ellie said, "He is taking a picture of my boat."

Indirectly quoted speech may occasionally be reported immediately.

REPORTED SPEECH   Ellie just said [that] he is taking a picture of her boat.

Some kinds of reported speech can be summarized with verbs like *tell, ask, remind,* and *urge,* followed by an infinitive:

REPORTED SPEECH   Ellie asked him to take a picture of her boat.

Most often, however, reported speech has occurred sometime before the time of the main verb reporting it. In English, the indirect quotation then requires changes in verb tense and pronouns.

REPORTED SPEECH   She said [that] he had taken a picture of her boat.

In this situation, the reported speech itself takes the form of a *that* noun clause (although the word *that* is often omitted); its verb tense shifts to past tense, following the guidelines shown in 9f-1 for tense sequences.

The following table shows the patterns for changing verb tenses, verb forms, and modal auxiliaries in reported speech or indirect discourse.

Direct Speech	Reported Speech
Tenses:	
present $\rightarrow$ **past**	
Ellie said, "I like horses."	Ellie said [that] she liked horses.
past $\rightarrow$ **past perfect**	
Ellie said, "I rode the horse."	Ellie said [that] she had ridden the horse.

Direct Speech	Reported Speech

Tenses:

present progressive → **past progressive**
Ellie said, "I'm going riding."   Ellie said [that] she was going riding.

present perfect → **past perfect**
Ellie said, "I have ridden there."   Ellie said [that] she had ridden there.

past progressive → **past perfect progressive**
She said, "I was out riding."   She said [that] she had been out riding.

*past perfect → **past perfect**
She said, "I had ridden there."   She said [that] she had ridden there.

Auxiliary verbs:

can → **could**
She said, "I can show him."   She said [that] she could show him.

will → **would**
She said, "I will ride again."   She said [that] she would ride again.

*could → **could**
She said, "I could ride."   She said [that] she could ride.

*would → **would**
She said, "I would go."   She said [that] she would go.

Note: The asterisked verbs do not change form as they undergo tense shifts.

Conventions for maintaining consistency with direct and indirect discourse in English are discussed in 16d; punctuation is discussed in 28a-1.

5 Using verb tenses in conditional and subjunctive sentences

Conditional sentences talk about situations that are either possible in the future or else unreal or hypothetical (contrary to fact) in the present or past. Conditional sentences typically contain the conjunction *if* or a related conditional term (*unless, provided that, only if, (only) after, (only) when,* etc.). The following are guidelines for using verb forms in conditional sentences.

Possible or real statements about the future

Use the present tense to express the condition in possible statements about the future; in the same sentence, use the future to express the result of that condition.

	conditional + present	future (*will* + base form)
REAL STATEMENT	*If I have* enough money,	*I will go* next week.
	When I get enough money,	*I will go.*
	[**Meaning:** The speaker may have enough money.]	

Hypothetical or unreal statements about the future

Use the past subjunctive form (which looks like a past tense) with sentences that make "unreal" or hypothetical statements about the future; in the same sentence, use the past form of a modal auxiliary (usually *would, could,* or *might*) to express an unreal result of that stated condition.

	If + past	past form of modal (*would*)
UNREAL STATEMENT	*If you found* the money,	*you would go* next week.

[**Meaning:** The speaker now is fairly sure you will not have the money.]

Hypothetical or unreal statements about the past

Use the subjunctive with appropriate perfect tense verb forms with sentences that make hypothetical or unreal statements about the past. Use the past perfect tense for the unreal statement about the past. In the same sentence, use the past form of the modal auxiliary plus the present perfect to express the unreal result.

	If + past perfect (*had made*)	past modal + present perfect (*would*) (*have gone*)
UNREAL STATEMENT	*If I had made* money,	*I would have gone* last week.

[**Meaning:** At that time the speaker did not have the money.]

For more on the subjunctive, see 9h-1; for more on modal auxiliaries, see 43d.

6   Expressing a wish or suggestion for a hypothetical event

In stating a wish in the present that might hypothetically occur, use the **past subjunctive** (which looks like the past tense) in the clause expressing the wish. (The object of the wish takes the form of a *that* clause, although the word *that* is often omitted.)

present	[that]	past subjunctive (like past tense)
He *wishes*	[that]	she *had* a holiday.
I *wish*	[that]	I *were* on vacation.

The auxiliaries *would* and *could* (which have the same form in the present and past tenses) are often used to express the object of a wish.

present	[that]	*would/could* + base form
I *wish*	[that]	she *would stay.*
We *wish*	that	we *could take* a vacation day.

In stating a wish made in the past or present for something that hypothetically might have occurred in the past, use the past perfect in the *that* clause. (The verb *wish* may be expressed either in the past or in the present tense.)

present OR past [that]   past perfect [*had worked*]
    I wished   [that]   I *had* not *worked* yesterday.
    I wish   [that]   it *had been* a holiday.

See 9h-4 for guidelines on using the subjunctive mood with *that* clauses.

Expressing a recommendation, suggestion, or urgent request

In stating a recommendation, suggestion, or urgent request, use the **present subjunctive**—the base form of the verb (*be, do*)—in the *that* clause (see 9h).

    present   [that]   present subjunctive = base form
We *suggest*   that   he *find* the money.
We *advise*   [that]   you *be* there on time.

(See 9h-5 for comments on the subjunctive in this form.)

EXERCISE 1

Write the appropriate verb form in the space provided:

1. Sam insisted that she (wants)(wanted) _____ something to drink.
2. For some reason it (smelled)(was smelling) _____ very strange.
3. Many years ago I (heard)(have heard) _____ an unusual story.
4. Perhaps if you (had wanted)(would have wanted) _____ the job, you (would have gotten)(had gotten) _____ some money.
5. She wishes that she (could do)(can do) _____ a good job.

EXERCISE 1

1. wanted
2. smelled
3. heard
4. had **wanted**; would have gotten
5. could do

43c   Changing word order with verbs

1   Invert the subject and all or part of the verb to form questions.

The subject and verb are inverted from normal order to form questions. The following patterns are used with the verb *be*, with modal auxiliaries, with progressive forms, and with perfect forms.

	Normal Statement Form	Question Form
Be	He *is* sick today.	*Is he* sick today?
Modals	She *can* help us.	*Can she* help us?
Progressive	They *are* studying here.	*Are they* studying here?
Perfect	It *has* made this sound before.	*Has it* made this sound before?

Questions (and negatives) with the auxiliary *do/does*

Verbs other than those shown above use the auxiliary verbs *do/does* to form questions, and also to form negatives with *not*. In this form, when the auxiliary verbs *do/does* are added, the verb changes to the base form (the dictionary form). Use this pattern for the simple present and simple past:

Question Form / Negative Form: Do + Base Form

STATEMENT	He *gets on* this bus.
QUESTION	*Does* he *get on* this bus?
NEGATIVE	He *does not get on* this bus.
AVOID	Does he *gets on* this bus? [Needs a base form.]
STATEMENT	She *finishes* at noon.
QUESTION	*Does* she *finish* at noon?
NEGATIVE	She *does not finish.*
AVOID	Does she *finishes* at noon? [Needs a base form.]
STATEMENT	It *ran* better yesterday.
QUESTION	*Did* it *run* better yesterday?
NEGATIVE	It *did not run* better.
AVOID	Did it *ran* better yesterday? [Needs a base form.]
STATEMENT	They *arrived* at noon.
QUESTION	When *did* they *arrive?*
NEGATIVE	They *did not arrive.*
AVOID	When do they *arrived?* [Needs a base form.]

For more on auxiliary verbs, see the listings in 9c and in 43d.

2   Invert the subject and verb in some emphatic statements.

The question form is also used with auxiliaries or expletives in some emphatic statements that begin with adverbs such as *never, rarely,* and *hardly,* producing a negative meaning.

NORMAL	EMPHATIC
There is never an easy answer.	Never *is there* an easy answer to that.
They have rarely come to check.	Rarely *have they* come to check the work.

43d   Using the helping verbs: Auxiliaries and modal auxiliaries

1   Auxiliary verbs, or helping verbs, are part of basic grammar.

The basic auxiliary verbs (*be, will, have, do*) are used to show tense, to form questions, to show emphasis, and to show negation.

To show tense, or aspect (*be, will, have*): He is driving. She has driven.

To form questions (*do/does*): Do they drive? Why do you drive?

To show negation (*do + not*): I do not drive there.

To show emphasis (*do/does*): She does drive sometimes.

2   Use modal auxiliaries for a wide range of meanings.

Modal auxiliaries include *can, could, may, might, should, would,* and *must,* as well as the four modals that always appear with the particle *to: ought to, have to, able to,* and *have got to.* The base form of the verb (the dictionary form) is always used with a modal auxiliary, whether the time reference is to the future, present, or past. For a past time reference, use the modal plus the past perfect (*have* + the past participle).

Meaning Expressed	Present Time or Past Time	Modal + Past Perfect
ability and permission	She can drive.	
	She could drive.	She could have driven.
possibility	She may drive.	
	She might drive.	She might have driven.
advisability	She should drive.	She should have driven.
	She ought to drive.	She ought to have driven.
	She had better drive.	
necessity	She must drive.	
	She has to drive.	She had to drive.
negative necessity versus prohibition*	She does not have to drive. [she need not]	
	She must not drive. [she is not allowed]	

*Note that the two negatives above have very different meanings.

Some idiomatic expressions with modals

Some other idiomatic expressions with modals are expressed in the following list.

EXAMPLE	MEANING
I *would rather* drive than fly.	I prefer driving to flying.
We *would talk* for hours.	We always talked for hours then.
She has car keys, so she *must* drive.	[must = probably does]
Shall we dance again?	I'm inviting you to dance again.
Would you mind turning the heat up?	[would you mind = would you object to]
Do you mind turning it off?	Please turn it off.

43e   Choosing gerunds and infinitives with verbs

There are three types of verbals: infinitives, gerunds, and participles (see 7a-4).

ESL ALERT

Students should be reminded that because gerunds serve the function of nouns and may appear wherever a noun appears, one gerund equals one noun and therefore takes a singular verb. Gerunds often, though not always, refer to action in the past or action from the past to the present (in contrast to infinitives, which refer to the future). When gerunds are placed as objects of the verb, this distinction is vital to clear communication, as in the following.

He stopped seeing her. / He stopped to see her.
He remembered going there. / He must remember to go there.

Also, gerunds take the possessive pronoun:

his book / his having done that.

Another helpful rule is that two- and three-part verbs always take a gerund instead of an infinitive object: "look forward to going" not "look forward to go."

Recognizing gerund and infinitive subjects may be difficult for ESL students, who might benefit from practice underlining subjects, as in *"Getting to know you* will be fun" and *"To be or not to be* was Hamlet's question."

1 ### Using infinitives and gerunds as nouns

Use an infinitive or a gerund to function either as a subject or as an object.

As SUBJECTS   *To be one of the leaders here* is not really what I want.
His being one of the leaders here is unacceptable.

As OBJECTS   I don't really want *to be one of the leaders here.*
I don't accept *his being one of the leaders here.*

NOTE: The possessive case is used with gerunds; see 8c-2. (See 7a-4 and 7d-2, 3 for basic definitions and examples of verbals. See 44a-1 for participles that function as modifiers, and 43b-1 for participles in the progressive form of English verbs.]

2 ### Learning idiomatic uses of verb/verbal sequences

Sometimes it is difficult to determine which verbs are followed by a gerund, which are followed by an infinitive, and which can be followed by either verbal. This usage is idiomatic and must be memorized; there are no rules to govern these forms. Note in the following examples that verb tense does not affect a verbal.

Verb + Gerund	Verb + Infinitive	Verb + Either Verbal
enjoy	**want**	**begin**
I enjoy swimming.	I want to swim now.	Today I begin swimming.
		Today I begin to swim.
go	**agree**	**continue**
I went swimming	I agreed to swim.	I continued swimming.
		I continued to swim.
enjoy + gerund	want + infinitive	begin + either verbal
go + gerund	agree + infinitive	continue + either verbal
finish + gerund	decide + infinitive	like + either verbal
recommend + gerund	need + infinitive	prefer + either verbal
risk + gerund	plan + infinitive	start + either verbal
suggest + gerund	seem + infinitive	love + either verbal
consider + gerund	expect + infinitive	hate + either verbal
postpone + gerund	fall + infinitive	can't bear + either verbal
practice + gerund	pretend + infinitive	can't stand + either verbal

NOTE: There is no difference in meaning between *I begin to swim* and *I begin swimming.* However, sentences with other verbs differ in meaning depending on whether a gerund or an infinitive follows the verb. This difference in meaning is a function of certain verbs. See the following examples.

EXAMPLE	MEANING
I always remember *to lock* the car.	I always remember to do this.
I remember *locking* the car.	I remember that I did this.
They stop *to drink* some water.	They stopped in order to drink.
They stopped *drinking* water.	They didn't drink anymore.

Information on idiomatic usage is provided in ESL dictionaries such as the *Longman Dictionary of American English: A Dictionary for Learners of English,* 1983.

EXERCISE 2

1. I am certain that you (have to)(might) _____ walk to town.
2. They all need (doing)(to do) _____ some daily exercise.
3. You might consider (walking)(to walk) _____ to town.
4. Doesn't she (get)(gets) _____ angry sometimes?
5. We can postpone (doing)(to do) _____ the hard work till later.

EXERCISE 2

1. have to
2. to do
3. walking
4. get
5. doing

43f Using two- and three-word verbs, or phrasal verbs, with particles

Phrasal verbs consist of a verb and a **particle.** Note that a particle can be one or more prepositions (off, up, with) or an adverb (away, back). English has many phrasal verbs, often built on verbs that have one basic meaning in their simple one-word form, but different meanings when particles are added.

> The coach *called off* the game because of the storm.
> He *left out* some important details.

The meaning of a phrasal verb is idiomatic; that is, the words as a group have a different meaning from each of the words separately. Most of these varied meanings are found in a standard English dictionary. Here are some examples of sentences with two-word and three-word verbs.

> I *got ready* for work.
> She didn't go to the party because she didn't *feel up to* it.
> The doctor told him to *cut down on* red meat.
> They *did without* a television for a few years.

1 Some phrasal verbs are separable.

With separable phrasal verbs, a noun object either can separate a verb and particle or follow the particle.

	noun object		noun object
CORRECT	I *made out* <u>a check</u> to the IRS.		I *made* <u>a check</u> *out* to the IRS.

However, a pronoun object always separates the verb and the particle. A pronoun never follows the particle.

               pronoun object

FAULTY   I *made out* <u>it</u> to the IRS.

REVISED   I *made* <u>it</u> *out* to the IRS.

Other separable phrasal verbs include the following:

call off	hand out	prevent from
check out	leave in, out	set up
divide up	look up [research]	sign on, up
find out	pick up	start over, up
fill in	put over	take on
fit in	[present	throw out
give back, up	deceptively]	turn on, off,
hang out, up	put up to [promote]	up, down
[suspend:	put back	wake up
trans.]	put off	write down

2 **Some phrasal verbs are nonseparable.**

With nonseparable phrasal verbs, a noun or pronoun object always follows the particle. For these verbs it is not possible to separate the verb and its particle with a noun or pronoun object.

	noun object		pronoun object
FAULTY	I ran Mary into	**FAULTY**	I ran her into.
REVISED	I ran into Mary	**REVISED**	I ran into her.

Other nonseparable phrasal verbs include the following:

bump into	call on	do without
get into	get over	get through
keep on	keep up with	hang out [= stay]
refer to	stop by	see about

Several verbs in their basic form are intransitive, but can become transitive phrasal verbs when a nonseparable prepositional particle is added to them.

INTRANSITIVE   The politician *smiled* sheepishly, then quickly apologized.

TRANSITIVE   He *smiled at* me sheepishly, then *apologized* quickly for being late.

Other examples of this kind of verb include the following:

complain about	laugh at	participate in
feel up to	look at, into	run into
insist on	object to	walk around, down, up, into etc.

NOTE: An adverb, but not a noun or pronoun, may separate the verb from its particle.

He *apologized* quickly *for* being late.

The following are nonseparable two-word verbs that are intransitive, but that can be made transitive if still another particle is added to them:

run around with	*get ready* for	*get by* with
get away with	*drop out* of	*look out* for
read up on		

3 Some phrasal verbs can be either separable or nonseparable.

Some phrasal verbs can be either separable or nonseparable. The meaning of a phrasal verb will change, depending on whether or not the phrase is separated by an object. Note the difference in meaning that appears with the placement of the object in the similar verbs below.

EXAMPLES	MEANING
I *saw through* it. [nonsep.]	I found it transparent.
I *saw* it *through*. [sep.]	I persisted.
She *looked over* the wall. [nonsep.]	She looked over the top of it.
She *looked* the wall *over*. [sep.]	She examined or studied it.
I *turned on* him. [nonsep.]	I turned to attack him.
I *turned* it *on*. [sep.]	I flipped a switch.
I *turned* him *on*. [sep.]	I aroused his passion.
They *talked to* us. [nonsep.]	They spoke to us.
They *talked* us *into* staying. [sep.]	They convinced us to stay.

NOTE: Standard dictionaries usually list verbs with the meanings of most particles (indicating whether or not they are transitive), but they usually do not indicate whether a phrasal verb is separable or nonseparable. However, this information is provided in ESL dictionaries such as the *Longman Dictionary of American English: A Dictionary for Learners of English,* 1983.

EXERCISE 3

1. Can you (fit in it)(fit it in) _____ to your busy schedule?
2. If you (call on her)(call her on) _____, she may not be home.
3. We may want to (wake up her)(wake her up) _____ early today.
4. I forgot to tell you something; I (left out it)(left it out) _____ of my note yesterday.
5. Will you (set up him)(set him up) _____ to do the job?

EXERCISE 3

1. fit it in
2. call on her
3. wake her up
4. left it out
5. set him up

CHAPTER 44

Using Modifiers and Connectors in English Sentences

Modifiers expand sentences in a variety of ways. The two types of modifiers are adjectives and adverbs, as well as phrases and clauses that function as adjectives or adverbs. There are two types of adverbs, descriptive and conjunctive. For basic discussions of the types of modifiers, how they function, and how they are placed or located in sentences, see 7a-5 and 6, and 7c. (For more on adjectives, see 11a-1 and 11e. For more on descriptive adverbs, see 11e and f. For more on conjunctive adverbs, see 19a-3.)

44a Using single-word adjectives and nouns as modifiers of nouns

A modifier of a noun must be placed as close to the noun modified as possible (11a-1; 15a). Single-word adjectives are normally placed before a noun or after a linking verb.

BEFORE A NOUN   The *bored student* slept through the *boring lecture.*

AFTER A LINKING VERB   Jack *is bored.* The lecture he heard *was boring.*

1 Using the present and past participle forms of verbs as adjectives

The present participle and the past participle forms of verbs are often used as single-word adjectives. The choice of form has an important impact on meaning. In the following examples, notice that these forms can be very different—almost opposite—in meaning.

PAST PARTICIPLE	MEANING
a tired student	Something tired this student.
damaged buildings	Something damaged these buildings.
a frightened passenger	Something frightened this passenger.
excited tourists	Something excited the tourists.
an accredited school	Some group accredited the school.

PRESENT PARTICIPLE	MEANING
a tiring lecture	The lecture causes a feeling of being tired.
a damaging explosion	The explosion caused the damage.
a frightening storm	The storm causes the fright.
an exciting tour	The tour caused excitement.
an accrediting board	This group gives accrediting status.

2   Using nouns as modifiers

When two nouns are combined in sequence, the last is considered to be the noun modified; the first is the modifier. (This follows the pattern for single-word adjectives mentioned earlier.) The importance of sequence is evident in the following examples, where the same nouns are combined in different order to produce different meanings.

MODIFIER	+ NOUN MODIFIED	MEANING
a car	company	a company whose business involves cars
a company	car	a car provided to someone by the business
a light	truck	a small truck
a truck	light	a light attached to a truck
a game	parlor	a place where indoor games are played
a parlor	game	a type of game, like chess, played indoors

When more than two nouns are combined in sequence, it is increasingly difficult to determine which noun is modified and which is a modifier; see 44f-2. For this reason, it is best to avoid overusing nouns as modifiers (see 11g).

44b   Using adjectival modifiers with linking verbs and prepositions

Adjectives and past-participle adjectives in sentences with linking verbs are often followed by a modifying prepositional phrase.

We are *ready*. We are *ready for* the next phase of training.
Jenny seems an *involved* person. She is *involved with* a boyfriend.

The preposition to be used in such phrases is determined by the adjective or participle adjective. With each such adjective, the choice of preposition is idiomatic, not logical; therefore, adjective/preposition combinations must be memorized. Sometimes the same adjective will change its meaning with different prepositions, as in this example.

Jenny was *involved in* planning from the start. Meanwhile, she was *involved with* a new boyfriend.

ESL ALERT

There is little logic to English speakers' use of prepositions, and such use differs in British and American English. See the comments at 42c.

Past-participle adjective examples include the following:

excited about	acquainted with	divorced from
composed of	opposed to	scared of/by
involved in	interested in	cautioned to/against
exhausted from	done with	angry at/with

Single-word adjective examples include the following:

absent from	afraid of	mad at
bad for	clear to	sure of
crazy about	familiar with	cruel to
excited about	capable of	accustomed to
guilty of	responsible for	

NOTE: Standard dictionaries may not indicate which preposition is typically used with a given adjective. However, this information is provided in ESL dictionaries such as the *Longman Dictionary of American English: A Dictionary for Learners of English,* 1983.

44c Positioning adverbial modifiers

1 Observe typical locations for adverbs in English sentences.

Adverbs have typical or standard locations in English sentences, although these patterns can be varied for special emphasis. Adverbs are typically located immediately before a transitive or intransitive verb.

FAULTY   She finishes cheerfully her homework.

REVISED   She cheerfully finishes her homework.

EMPHATIC   She finishes her homework—cheerfully.

Common adverbs expressing frequency or probability typically come after the verb *be* and helping verbs. In questions, such adverbs can come after the subject.

He was frequently at the gym on Fridays.
She may often discuss politics.
Does she often come here?

However, when sentences are inverted for negatives, these adverbs are usually placed before the helping verb.

FAULTY   They don't frequently talk. It doesn't sometimes matter.

REVISED   They frequently don't talk. It sometimes doesn't matter.

2 Limiting modifiers cannot move without changing meaning.

Although many adverbs can be located at a number of different places in a sentence without changing the meaning, positioning is quite critical with certain **limiting modifiers** such as *only, almost, just, nearly, even, simply* (see 15b).

NO CHANGE IN MEANING	SIGNIFICANT CHANGE IN MEANING
Generally it rains a lot in April.	*Only* Leonid sings those songs.
It *generally* rains a lot in April.	Leonid *only* sings those songs.
It rains a lot in April, *generally*.	Leonid sings *only* those songs.
	[OR . . . sings those songs *only*.]

See 15a–g and 44d-3 for more on positioning modifiers. See also 43c-2 for inverted word order with adverbs—such as *rarely, never, seldom*—located at the beginning of a sentence.

44d Using phrases and clauses to modify nouns and pronouns

See the guidelines for modifier placement in 15a–h.

1 Positioning adjective phrases and clauses

Unlike single-word adjective modifiers (which are placed before a noun and after a linking verb; 44a), clauses and most phrases functioning as adjectives must immediately *follow* the noun or pronoun they modify in order to avoid confusion with adverbial modifiers in the sentence.

FAULTY   I brought the tire to the garage *with the puncture.*
          I brought the tire to the garage *that had a puncture.*
          [The modifier next to *garage* is very confusing.]

REVISED   I brought the tire *with the puncture* to the garage.
           I brought the tire *that had a puncture* to the garage.

If two or more adjective phrases or clauses modify the same noun, typical patterns of sequence operate, as shown in 44f-1. (See 25d-1–3 for rules on punctuating adjective clauses.)

2 Avoid adding unnecessary pronouns after adjective clauses.

The subject in an English sentence can be stated only once; pronouns in the sentence refer to the subject (or to other nouns) but they do not repeat it. When a lengthy adjective clause follows the subject as a modifier, it is important not to repeat the subject with an unnecessary pronoun before the verb.

FAULTY   The *person* who works in office #382 *she* decides. [The subject is repeated with an unnecessary pronoun.]

REVISED   The person who works in office #382 decides.

This error is likely to occur because of a failure to observe the steps in forming a dependent clause. Here is the process for forming an adjective

ESL ALERT

ESL students may need to note how single or phrasal participles may be placed before or after the noun they describe. Adjective clauses are less versatile and must always go directly after the noun and preferably immediately adjacent to the noun. Note the contrast:

"Seeing the problem, the women agreed to . . . " and
"The women, seeing the problem, agreed to . . . "

in contrast to
"The women, who saw the problem, agreed to . . . "

but never
"Who saw the problem, the women agreed . . . "

or
"The women, standing near us, who saw the problem, agreed . . . "

clause, using *who, which,* or *that* to replace the noun or pronoun of the dependent clause:

TWO SENTENCES	The person decides. *She* works in office #382.
TRANSFORM TO A CLAUSE	[*she = who*] *who* works in office #382
PLACE THE CLAUSE	The person <u>*who works in office #382*</u> decides.

The correct form for the relative pronouns *who* or *whom* in a dependent clause is discussed in 8f-2.

3 Use the relative pronoun *whose* for a clause showing possession.

An adjective clause is often constructed with the relative pronoun *whose* to show possession by the person or thing modified. Students sometimes omit a step in transforming a separate possessive statement into an adjective clause with *whose.*

FAULTY	The person whom her office was locked called security.
REVISED	The person whose office was locked called security.

Here is the pattern for transforming a sentence showing possession to a relative clause showing possession, using *whose* to replace the possessive noun or pronoun.

TWO SENTENCES	The person called security. *Her* office was locked.
REPLACE POSSESSIVE SUBJECT WITH *WHOSE*	*whose office was locked* [Her = *whose*]
PLACE THE CLAUSE	The person *whose* <u>office was locked</u> called security.

The same process is used for a clause showing possession of a thing.

TWO SENTENCES	The government made a protest. *Its* ambassador was insulted.
TRANSFORM: REPLACE WITH *WHOSE*	[*its = whose*] ambassador was insulted
PLACE THE CLAUSE	The government *whose* <u>ambassador was insulted</u> made a protest.

44e Combining phrases and clauses with connecting words

As writers combine phrases and clauses, they choose between two basic relationships: a coordinate or a subordinate connection. Elements that have a **coordinate** connection emphasize a balance or equality between elements. (See 19a for a discussion of coordinate relationships.) Elements can also have a **subordinate** or **dependent** connection that emphasizes that the elements are unequal, with one having a dependent link to another. (See 7e and 19b for a discussion of subordinate relationships.)

Phrases and clauses are often logically linked with connecting words, **conjunctions** and **conjunctive adverbs,** that require careful consideration of the kind of connection students wish to establish.

1 Choose the right connecting word for coordinate structures.

Connecting words for a coordinate, or balanced, relationship include **coordinating conjunctions** (*and, but, or, nor, so, for, yet*), **correlative conjunctions** (*either/or, neither/nor, both/and, not only/but, whether/or, not only/but also*), and many **conjunctive adverbs** (*however, nevertheless, accordingly, also, besides, afterward, then, indeed, otherwise*). These words show relationships of contrast, consequence, sequence, and emphasis; they are discussed in 19a-1, 2, 3.

After deciding on the desired relationship among sentence parts, select a *single set of connecting words.* Avoid a mixture of words that may cancel out the meaning.

MIXED   They were *both* competitive, *but however* they were well matched. [The mixed connecting words show similarity and contrast at the same time.]

BALANCED   They were *both* competitive, *and* they were well matched.
They were competitive; *however,* they were well matched.

See 25a-1 and 25f-1 for appropriate rules on punctuation.

2 Choose the subordinating conjunction that establishes the desired dependent relationship.

Subordinating conjunctions establish different relationships, including conditional relationships and relationships of contrast, cause and effect, time and place, purpose, and outcome (see chapter 19). In your writing, choose a single coordinating conjunction, and avoid combinations that are contradictory or confusing.

MIXED   *Because* she was sick, *so* she went to the clinic. [A relation of cause and effect is confusingly combined with one of purpose or outcome.]

CLEAR   *Because* she was sick, she went to the clinic. [cause/effect]
She was sick, *so* she went to the clinic. [outcome]

See 19b for a full discussion on establishing clear subordinate relationships among sentence parts. See 25a-1 and 25f-1 for rules on punctuation.

ESL ALERT

For Americans, correct adjective order is intuitive; for ESL students it must be learned consciously. Both Marcella Frank's *Modern English, Part I* and Betty Azar's *Understanding and Using English Grammar* have excellent charts detailing the logic behind our adjective order system.

Spanish, Korean, and Vietnamese, as well as a number of other languages, place the adjective after the noun: *the house red.* This accounts for what may seem to be peculiar constructions, even in highly fluent students who occasionally "forget" and revert to the deep structure of the mother tongue. The surface error rarely causes confusion except in one of the few cases of English reversible adjectives and nouns: house cat/cat house, ice free/free ice, etc.

Another troubling adjective problem is with number. Many languages make nouns and adjectives agree in number, while English adjectives take only the singular or nonnumbered form; thus the fairly common habit of Spanish speakers writing in English of adding a number inflection to adjectives: *the reds houses.*

44f Arranging cumulative modifiers

1 Observing typical order of cumulative adjectives

Single-word adjective modifiers are placed close to a noun, immediately before a noun, or after a linking verb (44a).

Cumulative adjectives are groups of adjectives that modify the same noun. There is a typical order of modifiers and cumulative adjectives in an English sentence. A major disruption of typical order can be confusing.

FAULTY	a beach French gorgeous tent	red light my small bulb
REVISED	a gorgeous French beach tent	my small red light bulb

Although some stylistic variations from typical order in the location of cumulative adjectives are possible for emphasis, typical locations in an English sentence provide a very strong normal pattern. Here are some guidelines.

Possessives precede numbers. Ordinal numbers follow cardinal numbers.

Jill's first car   my first nine drafts

The typical order of descriptive adjectives is shown below:

(1)	*(2)*	*(3)*	*(4)*	*(5)*	*(6)*	*(7)*	*(8)*
Opinion	*Size*	*Shape*	*Condition*	*Age*	*Color*	*Origin*	*Noun*
ugly		round			green		fenders
	huge		muddy				spots
lovely				old	red	Turkish	slippers
comfortable			sunny				room

2 Arranging cumulative phrases, clauses, or noun modifiers*

A single phrase or clause functioning as an adjective immediately follows the noun or pronoun it modifies to avoid confusion with any adverbial phrases in the same sentence (44b).

When accumulated adjective phrases or clauses modify the same noun, their flexible emphasis creates an extremely varied sequence, especially for issues of opinion. In a neutral context some of the same typical sequences may be observed as for single-word adjectives (above), except that the modifying phrases follow the noun.

---

*We owe this discussion on order of modifiers to Jean Praninskas, *Rapid Review of English Grammar* (Englewood Cliffs, NJ: Prentice-Hall, 1975).

I found *spots* that are *huge* and that are also very *muddy.*
We saw that the *rooms* were very *narrow* and yet they seemed *bright.*

When two adverbial phrases or clauses are accumulated, place phrases typically precede time phrases.

NOT TYPICAL   They lived in the 1970s in Japan.

TYPICAL   They lived in Japan in the 1970s.

Two-word modifiers of nouns

Three nouns are often combined, with the first two forming a two-word modifier for the last noun. When this happens, nouns fall into a typical arrangement somewhat comparable with that of adjectives.

NOT TYPICAL   a file steel cabinet

TYPICAL   a steel file cabinet

The sequence of two nouns to modify a third noun may be classified and arranged in this sequence.

Material, Number, or Location	Origin, Purpose, or Type	Noun Modified
chapter	review	questions
two-word	noun	modifier
slate	roofing	tile
steel	file	cabinet

However, the categories of meaning for nouns are less clear than for adjectives and the opportunity for confusion is much greater. Students are therefore advised to avoid accumulating noun modifiers beyond this limit, and to rewrite combinations as phrases and clauses (see 11g).

EXERCISE 1

Choose the correct form.

1. The girls thought the ride was (excited)(exciting) and they were (interested)(interesting) in the things they saw.
2. These gang members seemed capable (of)(in) any kind of violence and were cruel (at)(to) their enemies.
3. Luisa (walks usually)(usually walks) to her studio (even when)(when even) she feels tired.
4. The famous preacher (he spoke)(who spoke) at our meeting was inspiring.
5. I have lost my (yellow beautiful)(beautiful yellow) umbrella with the (large Japanese)(Japanese large) designs.

EXERCISE 1

1. exciting; interested
2. of; to
3. usually walks; even when
4. who spoke
5. beautiful yellow; large Japanese

Writing
with a Computer

If a computer's word processing software only relieved writers of tedium, this benefit in itself would be enormous. In the bad old days, only fifteen years ago, a student would need to retype an entire page for the sake of some small correction, like a spelling error. Today, only a few keystrokes are needed to enter changes and command a printer to reproduce a corrected page. Of greater significance than this ease of correction is the difference a computer can make in the composing and revising process. If you have written much at all, and if you have followed the advice in this handbook, you know that good writing is the result of *rewriting*. In brief, the view that writing is a process suggests that a first draft is never complete and that refinements in a writer's thinking come as a consequence of revision. First drafts are created to be revised: Paragraphs will be restructured and sentences reworked until they are direct and concise. Here are some ways computers can help you become a more efficient writer:

- Computers can help you assemble ideas quickly and transfer your best ones electronically to an outline or sketch.
- Computers can help you create multiple outlines with ease.
- Computers can help you produce a first draft quickly, with the knowledge that your first draft, once entered onto an electronic file, can be reworked.
- Computers can help you revise repeatedly, maintaining your focus on your document, not on the tedium of retyping.
- Computers can help you edit your document with the aid of spell checkers and other programs.
- Computers, ultimately, can help engender in you a positive attitude toward writing.

A computer is a machine, referred to as *hardware*, that uses silicon chip technology to process information. Without instructions, a computer can do nothing at all. It relies on commands from a user, who will use *software* (a computer program) to instruct the machine to perform various tasks. Of the hundreds of thousands of software programs available, *word processing programs* are among the most widely used. A word processor combines with a computer to create a tool of extraordinary power.

⬛ A1 Word processing commands

If you are working in an IBM environment, you will execute word processing commands by using a mouse or by keystroking some combination of your keyboard's *control, shift,* or *alternate keys* along with one of the computer's ten or twelve *function keys.* The *block* command will highlight a set of words that you can then *cut* (or delete) and *paste* (move to a new location). The *search* command enables you to search a document forward or backward to find a particular word or string of words. The *retrieve* or *load* command allows you to call up to the screen your documents, which are called *files.* The *save* command saves your work on a *floppy disk,* which you store outside of the computer, or on a *hard disk,* a disk with large storage capacity located within the computer. The *print* command will print any part or all of a document.

In learning to work with a word processor, you will repeatedly use several keys: the *arrow* keys will move the *cursor* around the screen. The cursor is the blinking line or block that shows you where on the screen letters or numbers will appear as you type them. The *backspace* key will move the cursor from right to left and erase characters. Some combination of keys will move the cursor to the top or bottom of a page or to the beginning or end of a document. The *cancel* key will instruct the computer to ignore a command—such as *delete*—that you have given inadvertently.

If you are working in a Macintosh or IBM Windows environment with a *mouse,* many of the commands otherwise achieved with keystrokes can be accomplished using the mouse and the menus at the top of the screen. Consult your software manual for instructions.

ALERT: Save your work often! When working on a document, use the *save* command every fifteen minutes or so to ensure that in the event of a computer failure your work will not be lost. At the end of a work session, print a copy of your paper and create a *backup file* so that you always have one paper copy and two electronic copies, each on a separate disk.

⬛ A2 Computers and the writing process

1 Preparing to write

The computer can be enormously helpful in preparing to write. As you read a writing assignment, focus on two key questions: What do you know about your topic? What do you want to say to your audience? Subsequent decisions will depend on your answers, and you can use the power of word processing to make flexible entries and notes that can be rearranged to suit your changing purpose.

Generating ideas and organizing your thoughts

If you use the computer to generate ideas and to keep notes, you can put your word processing software to work by creating an outline of your paper and then moving into that outline all the pertinent information you have generated or collected. With the computer's *block move* or *cut/paste* commands you can rearrange material and sketch your paper in any number of ways, allowing you to compare possible strategies. In this way, the computer can help free you from any inclination to think that only one plan for a paper exists. Any paper can be structured in a variety of ways. The more flexible you are in experimenting with different outlines, the more likely it is you will arrive at one that represents a strong, creative synthesis of possible approaches.

Writing collaboratively

If your computer is hooked into a network, you can share your ideas for a paper with classmates and friends. Send them an electronic letter in which you describe the general approach you want to take in the paper and ask for reactions. As you work through the writing process, use a network for conducting research, revising, and editing. (See A2-3.)

Conducting library research

If you are writing a research paper, you can take your "to do" list with you to the library as you begin the general search process (see chapter 33). If your computer is hooked into a network, you may not need to travel to the library to check its holdings since these may exist on file in the college's main computer, which you can access over the phone lines. Some colleges will even have general references on a mainframe computer, and you will be able to peruse these references and do your initial reading while seated at your own computer. You can take notes at the computer, too, by creating files that divide your research topic into important categories. If categories get too large or ill defined, you can split them into separate files. When the time comes for sketching a plan for your paper, you can print out your notes, laying before you all the information that you have to work with.

2 Writing a first draft

Some people need the physical connection of hand to pen to paper when writing. Some can draft certain sorts of documents—say, business correspondence—on a computer but must write longer efforts by hand. Whatever your preferences, remember that the purpose of a first draft is to get a version of your document written—quickly. If you can work on a computer, all the better. Even if you are a poor typist, a computer keyboard encourages speed. Once you are open to the idea of writing a first draft, making large and small refinements later, you free yourself to write quickly, even furiously. The clear advantage of working on a computer at this stage is having your draft on file, ready and waiting for the work of revision.

3 Revising

Computers greatly facilitate the process of revision. One strategy that many writers find effective is to work consistently from a *hard copy*, or printed page. Read and make changes to words on a page, using a pencil or pen to do so. Once you are satisfied with your changes, turn to the computer and transfer them to your file. Then print your revised document and reread—again with a pen in hand. By making several such passes through your document, you will work steadily toward a final draft.

Revising for purpose, content, and structure

The first order of business in revising is to determine whether you have written the paper you intended (see 4a). Working from hard copies of your paper, revise your working thesis; use your final thesis to revise for unity and coherence; and revise for balance, making sure that the structure of your paper is sound and that parts are developed according to their importance. After you make one or more passes through your paper and revise for content, logic, and balance, enter your changes onto the computer and create a solid second draft.

Writing collaboratively

Writers are always in need of good, critical readers who can offer advice; and certainly writing on a computer facilitates the author/editor relationship. Once you have a complete second draft of your paper, consider sending it over a network or providing both a hard copy and an electronic copy (on floppy disk) to a classmate. Some word processing programs have a feature that allows an editor to suggest deletions and additions without destroying any of your text. When your editor returns the document, suggestions will show up on your screen marked in two distinctive ways. In some programs, additions are shaded and deletions are underlined. Similar markings will also appear on a printed copy. Working from a draft that has been edited in this way, you can get the full benefit of a colleague's close reading of your paper. Of course you have the prerogative to accept or reject editorial advice: you can alter the suggested additions or deletions and then, with a few keystrokes, enter into your work those suggestions you find most helpful. Once again, print out the document so that you can review it with pen in hand.

Revising to achieve concise and direct expression

Having settled on the content and structure of your paper, turn to sentence-level clarity. You probably will have stopped to revise particular sentences during prior stages of writing, but you will not have devoted systematic, document-wide attention to the construction of your sentences. A word processor encourages you to be a wordsmith—to quibble with word choices and to experiment with alternate phrasings. Ultimately, the goal is to achieve a concise, spare style (see chapter 17) that allows you to communicate your content in as few words as possible.

Editing for grammar, punctuation, and style

Toward the final stages of writing, when you have assured yourself that the content of your paper is solid and that the writing is direct, your word processor provides an opportunity to rework small matters that can make a big difference to readers: grammar, usage, and punctuation. Make your changes and, again, enter them into the computer and print out a clean draft. You may want to work collaboratively at this stage, asking a colleague to read your work for matters of punctuation, grammar, and usage.

Proofreading

You have worked too hard on your paper to let trivial errors of spelling, doubled words, or inadvertently used homonyms mar the end product. Now is the time to engage your word processor's *spell check program*. If your software package does not include such a program, you are sure to find a reasonably priced one at a local retailer's or in a catalog of public domain software. With its dictionary of 200,000 words or more, a spell checker compares every word of your paper against the words in its memory. When no match can be found, the computer highlights the word and prompts you to make a decision regarding possible replacements. Remember that a computer cannot identify the word or meaning that is right for a sentence. The best a computer can do is call attention to apparent inconsistencies between its word database and what is shown on the screen. No computer will highlight as incorrect the contraction *it's*, even when the context of your sentence requires using the possessive pronoun *its*. Once again, you must rely on your good judgment as a writer.

Printing

When you have proofread your document, print two final copies: one each for you and your instructor. Word processors have *formatting commands* that allow you to set the margins and spacing for a paper. Generally, conform to the guidelines for manuscript preparation in Appendix B.

NOTE: Save your drafts as proof of your hard work. When the paper is graded and returned, collect your drafts and take them to a recycling center.

A3   Specialized software for writers

Aside from spell checkers, several types of computer programs are available to writers. *Database programs* can prove very useful to researchers who take a great many notes or who constantly arrange and rearrange notes. If you have a portable computer that you can carry with you to the library, these programs allow you to take notes electronically while researching and then to call on these notes, later, while writing. *Prewriting* programs can prompt you to think about a topic in multiple ways and then to organize your thoughts into an outline. *Style checkers* will count the number of words in sentences and sentences in paragraphs, advising you with prompts on the screen to vary sentence length and rhythm. Style checkers will also highlight prepositions and uses of *to be* as a main verb, in both cases prompting you to consider revisions. *Thesaurus* programs are sometimes helpful for locating synonyms; see 22e-3. *Grammar checkers* will analyze the text of your papers and highlight word sequences that apparently do not match its programs for identifying normal or correct sentences. The programs will then suggest with a prompt that you reread these apparently incorrect sentences for any errors that may be present. As with spelling programs, all that such "checker" programs can do is count occurrences and identify patterns that do not precisely match data in the program; they are never a substitute for even the most casual reading for meaning. For instance, a grammar checker would regard the following sentence as correct: *Running down the street, the book dropped out of her hands.* You know perfectly well that books do not run down streets. Yet the computer does *not* know this, primarily because the software is not programmed to distinguish between animate nouns (that can do things like run) and inanimate ones. When sophisticated artificial intelligence becomes available on personal computers, such distinctions may become possible. Even if that day arrives, you will have to rely on your own knowledge to make important decisions about writing and revising. The computer is a tool, and a powerful one. But the computer is no match, and was never meant to be a substitute, for your own sound judgment.

Manuscript Form and Preparation

Before readers register a word of your writing, they form an impression based on your paper's appearance. If you are committed enough to a paper to have revised it several times, surely you will want to give it a crisp appearance. A clean, well-prepared, typed manuscript is a sign of an attentive attitude taken toward all the stages of writing. Careful manuscript preparation implicitly shows respect for your readers, who will certainly appreciate any efforts to make their work easier.

Style guides in the disciplines recommend slightly different conventions for preparing manuscripts, and you should consult the specialized guides listed in 37f, 38e, and 39e when writing in the humanities, social sciences, and sciences. Consult your professor as well. The recommendations here follow the guide commonly used in the humanities, the *MLA [Modern Language Association] Handbook for Writers of Research Papers*, 3rd ed.

B1 Paper and binding

Prepare your work on plain white, twenty-pound paper that measures $8\frac{1}{2} \times 11$ inches. For economy's sake, you might consider buying a ream (500 sheets) if you are typing the manuscript or are preparing it on a laser printer. If you are working with a dot matrix printer, buy a box of 500 or 1000 sheets of fanfold paper. Unless your professor advises otherwise, avoid onion skin or erasable paper, both of which will easily smudge. (For ease of preparation, though, you might type your work on erasable paper and submit a photocopy, which will not smudge.) Make a copy of your final paper to keep for your files, and submit the original to your professor. In binding pages, affix a single paper clip to the upper left-hand corner. To ease your reader's handling of your paper, do *not* place multiple staples along the left margin, and avoid plastic folders unless otherwise directed.

B2 Page layout

Whether you adopt conventions for page layout suggested by the *MLA Handbook* or by other style guides, maintain consistent margins and spacing. Your paper's first page, subsequent pages, and reference-list page(s) should be designed according to standard practice in a discipline.

Margins and line spacing

Type on one side of a page, double-spacing all text (including footnotes and endnotes). Maintain double-spacing between paragraphs and between lines of text and any displayed quotations. Leave a one-inch margin on the top and bottom of a page and a one-inch margin on both sides of a page. If you are working on a computer, set the margins as well as the running head (your last name and a page number) automatically. With each new paragraph, indent five spaces (on a computer, press the Tab key). For displayed quotations (see 28a-4), indent ten spaces and maintain that indentation for the length of the quotation.

Design of first page

Following the MLA format, you do not need to prepare a separate title page for your research papers. (This convention differs in the sciences and social sciences. See the box on page 698 as well as the example research paper on 721.) Observe the spacing of headings and title in the following example.

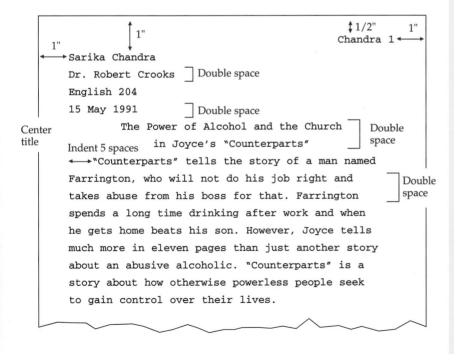

Design of subsequent pages

Observe the position of the running head and the first line of text on a paper's second or subsequent page.

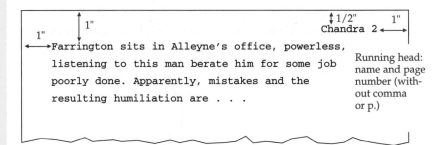

Design of "Works Cited" page

Observe the position of the running head, the title "Works Cited," and the indentation of the reference entry's second line.

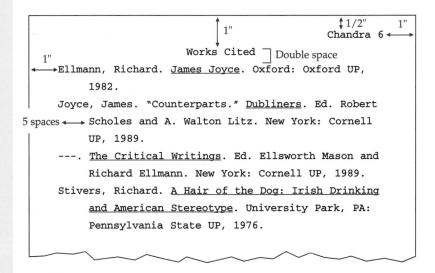

B3   Text preparation

Printing a manuscript on a word processor

Print on one side of the page and, if possible, use a laser printer. If none is available, use a dot matrix printer with a fresh enough ribbon that readers will have no trouble reading your text. Keep the right-hand edge of your text ragged, or *un*justified. If your dot matrix machine is printing a light page, you may be able to improve the product by photocopying the page with the photocopier adjusted to a darker than normal setting.

Printing a manuscript on a typewriter

Type on one side of a page with standard typewriter fonts. Avoid typefaces giving the appearance of script, since these are difficult to read. Use a fresh ribbon with black ink.

Handwriting a manuscript

Very few professors accept handwritten papers. If yours does, use lined, white 8½× 11 inch paper. Do not use spiral-bound notebook paper with its ragged edges. Write neatly and legibly in pen, on one side of the page, using dark blue or black ink. Consult your professor, who may ask you to skip every other line to allow room for editorial comments.

B4   Alterations

In a final review of your paper, when you are working away from your typewriter or word processor, you may find it necessary to make minor changes to your text—perhaps to correct a typographical error or to improve your wording. Make corrections *neatly*. When striking out a word, do so with a single line. Use a caret (^) to mark an insertion in the text, and write your correction or addition above the line you are altering. If time permits and you have worked on a word processor, enter the changes into your file and reprint the affected pages. Retype or reprint a page when you make three or more handwritten corrections on it. If your typewriter or computer keyboard lacks a particular symbol or mark that you need, handwrite that symbol on the page.

```
                                   named Farrington
  "Counterparts" tells the story of a man who will not do

  his job right and takes abuse from his boss for that.
```

B5   Punctuation and spacing

Observe the following standard conventions for spacing before and after marks of punctuation.

ONE SPACE BEFORE
  beginning parenthesis or bracket
  beginning quotation mark
  period in a series denoting an omission—see ellipses, 29e

No space before (except as noted)

comma	question mark	semicolon
period[1]	apostrophe	end quotation mark
exclamation point	colon	hyphen or dash

No space after (except as noted)

hyphen[2] or dash
beginning parenthesis or bracket
apostrophe[3]

One space after (except as noted)

comma

semicolon

colon[4]

apostrophe denoting the possessive form of a plural

end parenthesis or bracket that does not end a sentence

end quotation within a sentence

period in a series denoting an omission—see ellipses, 29e

period marking an abbreviated name or an initial

Two spaces after the following marks when they conclude a sentence

period	closing quotation
question mark	end parenthesis or bracket
exclamation	

Exceptions (as noted above)

[1]Unless the period occurs in a series denoting omission—see 29e.

[2]Unless the hyphen denotes one in a pair or series of delayed adjectives, as in *a first-, second-, or third-place finish.*

[3]Unless the apostrophe denotes the possessive form of a plural, as in *boys',* in which case skip one space.

[4]Unless the colon denotes a ratio, as in *3:2.*

Glossary of Usage

This glossary is intended to provide definitions and descriptions of selected word usages current in formal academic writing. In consulting this kind of glossary, writers should be prepared to make informed decisions about the meaning and the level of diction that is most appropriate to their writing project.

Many entries in this glossary consist of commonly confused homonyms—words that are pronounced almost alike but have different meanings and spellings. A comprehensive listing of often-confused homonyms appears in section 23a-1 in the spelling chapter.

a, an Use *a* when the article precedes a noun beginning with a consonant. For example, *At last we found a hotel.* Use *an* when the article precedes a word beginning with a vowel or an unpronounced *h. It was an honor to receive an invitation.* (See 7a.)

accept, except Use *accept* when your meaning is "to receive." Use *except* when you mean an exception, as in *He invited everyone except Thuan.* You can also use *except* as a verb that means "to leave out," as in *The report excepted the two episodes of misconduct.*

adverse, averse Use *averse* when you mean a person's feelings of opposition. Use *adverse* when you refer to a thing that stands in opposition or is opposed to someone or something, as in *I was not averse to taking the roofing job, but the adverse circumstances of a tight deadline and bad weather almost kept me from it.*

advice, advise Use *advice* as a noun meaning "a recommendation," as in *Longfellow gave excellent military advice.* Use *advise* as a verb meaning "to recommend," as in *Many counselors advise students to declare a double major.*

affect, effect If your sentence requires a verb meaning "to have an influence on," use *affect.* If your sentence requires a noun meaning "result," use *effect. Effect* can also be a verb, however. Use *effect* as a verb when you mean "to make happen," as in *He was able to effect a change in how the city council viewed the benefits of recycling.*

aggravate, irritate In formal writing, use *aggravate* when you mean "to make worse," as in *The smoke aggravated his cough.* Use *irritate* when you mean "to bother," as in *He became irritated when the drunken driver said the accident was not her fault.*

ain't Do not use *ain't* in formal writing. Use *is not, are not,* or *am not* instead.

all ready, already Use *all ready* when you mean "prepared" as in *He was all ready for an expedition to Antarctica.* Use *already* when you mean "by this time," as in *The ushers at Symphony Hall will not seat you if the concert has already started.*

all right Do not use *alright.* It is simply a misspelling.

all together, altogether   Use *all together* when you mean "as a group" or "in unison," as in *Once we got the family all together, we could discuss the estate.* Use *altogether* when you mean "entirely," as in *Some of the stories about Poe's addictions and personal habits are not altogether correct.* (See 23a.)

allude, elude   Use *allude* when you mean "to refer indirectly to." Use *elude* when you mean "to avoid or escape."

allusion, illusion   Use *allusion* when you mean "an indirect reference," as in *The children did not understand the allusion to Roman mythology.* Use *illusion* when you mean "false or misleading belief or appearance," as in *Smith labored under the illusion that he was a great artist.*

a lot   Do not use *a lot* in formal writing. Use a more specific modifier instead. When you use *a lot* in other contexts, remember that it is always two words.

among, between   Use *between* when you are expressing a relationship involving two people or things, as in *There was general agreement between Robb and Jackson on that issue.* Use *among* when you are expressing a relationship involving three or more separable people or things, as in *He failed to detect a link among the blood cholesterol levels, the red blood cell counts, and the T-cell production rates.*

amongst   Do not use *amongst* in formal writing. Instead, use *among.*

amount, number   Use *amount* when you refer to a quantity of something that cannot be counted, as in *The amount of effort put into finding the cure for AIDS is beyond calculation.* Use *number* when you refer to something that can be counted, as in *The number of people who want to run the Boston Marathon increases yearly.*

an, and   Use *an* when the article precedes a noun beginning with a vowel or an unpronounced *h.* Use *and* when your sentence requires a conjunction that means "in addition to."

and etc.   Avoid using *etc.* in formal writing. When you must use *etc.* in nonformal writing, do not use *and. Etcetera* means "and so forth"; therefore, *and etc.* is redundant.

and/or   Use *and* or *or,* or explain your ideas by writing them out fully. But avoid *and/or,* which is usually too ambiguous to meet the demands of formal writing.

anxious, eager   Use *anxious* when you mean "worried" or "nervous." Use *eager* when you mean "excited or enthusiastic about the possibility of doing something."

anybody, any body; anyone, any one   Use *anybody* and *anyone* when the sense of your sentence requires an indefinite pronoun. Use *any body* and *any one* when the words *body* and *one* are modified by *any,* as in *The teacher was careful not to favor any one student* and *Any body of knowledge is subject to change.*

any more, anymore   Use *any more* to mean "no more," as in *I don't want any more of those plums.* Use *anymore* as an adverb meaning "now," as in *He doesn't work here anymore.*

anyplace   Do not use *anyplace* in formal writing. Use *anywhere* instead.

anyways, anywheres   Do not use *anyways* and *anywheres* in formal writing; use *anyway* and *anywhere* instead.

apt, likely, liable   Use *apt* when you mean "having a tendency to," as in *Khrushchev was apt to lose his temper in public.* Use *likely* when you mean "probably going to," as in *We will likely hear from the Senator by Friday.* Use *liable* when you mean "in danger of," as in *People who jog long distances over concrete surfaces are liable to sustain knee injuries.* Also use *liable* when you are referring to legal responsibility, as in *The driver who was at fault was liable for the damages.*

as, like   Use *as* either as a preposition or as a conjunction, but use *like* as a preposition only. If your sentence requires a preposition, use *as* when you are making an exact equivalence, as in *Edison was known as the wizard of Menlo Park.* Use *like* when you are referring to likeness, resemblance, or similarity, as in *Like Roosevelt, Reagan was able to make his constituency feel optimism.*

as, than   When you are making a comparison, you can follow both *as* and *than* with a subjective- or objective-case pronoun, depending on meaning. For example, *We trusted O'Keeffe more than him [we trusted Smith]* and *We trusted O'Keeffe more than he [Jones trusted O'Keeffe]. O'Keeffe was as talented as he [was talented]* and *We found O'Keeffe as trustworthy as [we found] him.* (See 8g.)

as to   Do not use *as to* in formal writing. Rewrite a sentence such as *The president was questioned as to his recent decisions in the Middle East* to read *The president was questioned about his recent decisions in the Middle East.*

assure, ensure, insure   Use *assure* when you mean "to promise" as in *He assured his mother that he would return early.* Use *ensure* when you mean "to make certain," as in *Taking a prep course does not ensure success in the SATs.* Use *insure* when you mean "to make certain" in a legal or financial sense, as in *He insured his boat against theft and vandalism.*

at   Do not use *at* in a question formed with *where.* For example, rewrite a sentence such as *Where is the class at?* to read *Where is the class?*

a while, awhile   Use *awhile* when your sentence requires an adverb, as in *He swam awhile.* If you are not modifying a verb, but rather want a noun with an article, use *a while*, as in *I have not seen you in a while.*

bad, badly   Use *bad* as an adjective, as in *Bad pitching changed the complexion of the game.* Use *badly* as an adverb, as in *The refugees badly needed food and shelter.* Use *bad* to follow linking verbs that involve appearance or feeling, as in *She felt bad about missing the party.* (See 11d.)

being as, being that   Do not use either *being as* or *being that* to mean "because" in formal writing. Use *because* instead.

beside, besides   Use *beside* as a preposition meaning "next to." Use *besides* as an adverb meaning "also" or "in addition to" as in *Besides, I needed to lose the weight.* Use *besides* as an adjective meaning "except" or "in addition to," as in *Rosa Parks seemed to have nothing besides courage to support her.*

better, had better; best, had best   Do not use *better, had better, best,* and *had best* for *should* in formal writing. Use *ought* or *should* instead.

between, among   See *among, between.*

breath, breathe   Use *breath* as a noun; use *breathe* as a verb.

bring, take Use *bring* when you are referring to movement from a farther place to a nearer one, as in *The astronauts were asked to bring back rock samples.* Use *take* for all other types of movement.

broke Use *broke* only as the past tense, as in *He broke the Ming vase.* Do not use *broke* as the past participle; for example, instead of writing *The priceless vase was broke as a result of careless handling,* write *The priceless vase was broken as a result of careless handling.*

bunch Use *bunch* to refer to "a group or cluster of things growing together." Do not use *bunch* to refer to people or a group of items in formal writing.

burst, bust Use *burst* when you mean "to fly apart suddenly," as in *The pomegranate burst open.* (Notice that the example sentence doesn't say *bursted;* there is no such form of the verb.) (See 9b.)

but however, but yet When you use *however* and *yet,* do not precede them with *but* in formal writing. The *but* is redundant.

but that, but what When you use *that* and *what,* do not precede them with *but* in formal writing. The *but* is unnecessary.

calculate, figure, reckon If your sentence requires a word that means "imagine," use *imagine.* Do not use *calculate, figure,* or *reckon,* which are colloquial substitutes for "imagine."

can, may Use *can* when you are writing about the ability to do something, as in *He can jump six feet.* Use *may* when you are referring to permission, as in *He may rejoin the team when the period of probation is over.*

can't hardly, can't scarcely See *not but, not hardly, not scarcely.*

can't help but Use *can't help* by itself; the *but* is redundant.

can't, couldn't Do not use these contractions in formal writing. Use *cannot* and *could not* instead.

censor, censure Use *censor* when you mean editing or removing from the public eye on the basis of morality. Use *censure* when you mean "to give a formal or official scolding or verbal punishment."

center around Do not use *center around* in formal writing. Instead, use *center on.*

chose, choose Use the verb *choose* in the present tense for the first and second person and for the future tense, as in *They choose [or will choose] their teams carefully.* Use *chose* for the past tense, as in *The presidential candidate chose a distinguished running mate.*

compare to, compare with Use *compare to* to note similarities between things, as in *He compared the Chinese wine vessel to the Etruscan wine cup.* Use *compare with* to note similarities and contrasts, as in *When comparing market-driven economies with socialist economies, social scientists find a wide range of difference in the standard of living of individuals.*

complement, compliment Use *complement* when you mean "something that completes," as in *The wine was the perfect complement for the elegant meal.* Use *compliment* when you mean "praise," as in *The administrator savored the compliment on her organizational skills.*

conscience, conscious   Use *conscience* when your sentence requires a noun meaning "a sense of right or wrong." Use *conscious* as an adjective to mean "aware of" or "awake."

consensus of opinion   Do not use *consensus of opinion* in formal writing. Use *consensus* instead to avoid redundancy.

continual, continuous   Use *continual* when you mean "constantly recurring," as in *Continual thunderstorms ruined their vacation days at the beach.* Use *continuous* when you mean "unceasing," as in *The continuous sound of a heartbeat, unceasing and increasing in volume, haunted the narrator.*

could of, would of, should of, might of, may of, must of   In formal writing, avoid combining modal auxiliaries (*could, would, should, might, may,* and *must*) with *of.* Instead, write *could have, would have, should have, might have, may have,* and *must have.*

couple, couple of   Do not use *couple* or *couple of* to mean "a few" in formal writing. Instead, write *a few.*

criteria   Use *criteria* when you want a plural word referring to more than one standard of judgment. Use *criterion* when you are referring to only one standard of judgment.

data   Use *data* when you are referring to more than one fact, statistic, or other means of support for a conclusion. When you are referring to a single fact, use the word *datum* in formal writing, or use *fact, figure,* or another term that is specific to the single means of support.

different from, different than   Use *different from* when an object or phrase follows, as in *Braque's style is different from Picasso's.* Use *different than* when a clause follows, as in *Smith's position on the deficit was <u>different</u> when he was seeking the presidency <u>than</u> it was when he was president.*

differ from, differ with   Use *differ from* when you are referring to unlike things, as in *Subsequent results of experiments in cold fusion differed radically from results first obtained in Utah.* Use *differ with* to mean "disagree," as in *One expert might differ with another on a point of usage.*

discreet, discrete   Use *discreet* to mean "respectfully reserved," as in *He was always discreet when he entered the synagogue.* Use *discrete* to mean "separate" or "distinct," as in *The essay was a discrete part of the examination and could be answered as a take-home assignment.*

disinterested, uninterested   Use *disinterested to mean "impartial,"* as in *An umpire should always be disinterested in which team wins.* Use *uninterested* to mean "bored" or "not interested."

doesn't, don't   Do not use *doesn't* and *don't* in formal writing; instead, use *does not* and *do not.* In other contexts, use *don't* with the first and second person singular, as in *I don't smoke* and with the third person plural, as in *They don't smoke.* Use *doesn't* with the third person singular, as in *He doesn't ride the subway.*

done   Use *done* when your sentence requires the past participle; do not use done as the simple past. For example, rewrite a sentence such as *Van Gogh done the painting at Arles* to read *Van Gogh did the painting at Arles.*

due to, due to the fact that   Use *due to* to mean "because" only when it follows a form of the verb *be,* as in *The sensation of a leg falling asleep is due to pooling of the blood in the veins.* Do not use *due to* as a preposition, however. Also, do not use *due to the fact that* in formal writing because it is wordy. (See 17a.)

eager, anxious   See *anxious, eager.*

effect, affect   See *affect, effect.*

elicit, illicit   Use *elicit* to mean "to draw out," as in *The social worker finally elicited a response from the child.* Use *illicit* to mean "illegal," as in *Illicit transactions on the black market fuel an underground Soviet economy.* (See 23a.)

emigrate, immigrate, migrate   Use *emigrate* to mean "to move away from one's country." Use *immigrate* to mean "to move to another country." Use *migrate* to mean "to move to another place on a temporary basis."

ensure, assure, insure   See *assure, ensure, insure.*

enthused, enthusiastic   Use *enthusiastic* when you mean "excited about" or "showing enthusiasm." Do not use *enthused* in formal writing.

especially, specially   Use *especially* when you mean "particularly," as in *Maria Mitchell was especially talented as a mathematician.* Use *specially* when you mean "for a specific reason," as in *The drug was intended specially for the treatment of rheumatism.*

et al., etc.   Do not use *et al.* and *etc.* interchangeably. *Et al.* is generally used in references and bibliographies and is Latin for "and others." *Etcetera* is Latin for "and so forth." Like all abbreviations, *et al.* and *etc.* are generally not used in formal writing, except that *et al.* is acceptable in the context of a citation to a source.

etc.   Do not use *etc.* in formal writing. Use *and so forth* instead. Or, preferably, be as specific as necessary to eliminate the phrase.

everybody, every body   Use *everybody* when you mean "everyone." Use *every body* when you are using *body* as a distinct word modified by *every,* as in *Is every body of water in Canada contaminated by acid rain?*

every day, everyday   Use *everyday* when your sentence requires an adjective meaning "common" or "daily," as in *Availability of water was an everyday problem in ancient Egypt.* Use *every day* when you are using the word *day* and modifying it with the adjective *every,* as in *Enrico went to the art gallery every day.*

everywheres   Do not use *everywheres* in formal writing. Use *everywhere* instead.

except, accept   See *accept, except.*

except for the fact that   In formal writing prefer the less wordy *except that.*

explicit, implicit   Use *explicit* when you mean "stated outright," as in *The Supreme Court rules on issues that are not explicit in the Constitution.* Use *implicit* when you mean "implied," as in *Her respect for the constitution was implicit in her remarks.*

farther, further Use *farther* when you are referring to distance, as in *He was able to run farther after eating carbohydrates.* Use *further* when you are referring to something that cannot be measured, such as *Further negotiations are needed between the central government and the people of Azerbaijan.*

fewer, less Use *fewer* when you are referring to items that can be counted, as in *There are fewer savings accounts at the branch office this year.* Use *less* when you are referring to things that cannot be counted, as in *The East German people have less confidence in the concept of unification than they had one year ago.* (See 11e.)

figure See *calculate, figure, reckon.*

fixing to Do not use *fixing to* in formal writing. Use *intend to* instead.

former, latter Use *former* and *latter* only when you are referring to two things. In that case, the former is the first thing, and the latter is the second. If you are referring to more than two things, use *first* for the first and *last* for the last.

get Do not overuse *get* in formal writing. Prefer more precise words. For example, instead of *get better*, write *improve;* instead of *get,* write *receive, catch,* or *become;* instead of *get done,* write *finish* or *end.*

good and Do not use *good and* in formal writing. Use *very* or, preferably, a more precise modifier instead.

good, well Use *good* as an adjective, as in *Astaire gave a good performance, but not one of his best.* Use *well* as an adverb, as in *He danced well.* You can also use *well* as an adjective when you refer to good health, as in *She felt well* or *She is well today.* (See 11d.)

gone, went Use *gone* when your sentence requires the past participle of *to go,* as in *They had gone there several times.* Use *went* when your sentence requires the past tense of *to go,* as in *They went to the theater Friday.*

got, have; has/have got to Do not use *got* in place of *have* in formal writing. For example, rewrite a sentence such as *I got to lose weight* to read *I have to [or I must] lose weight.*

had better, better; had best, best See *better, had better.*

had ought Do not use *had ought* in formal writing. Use *ought* by itself instead.

half When you refer to half of something in formal writing, use *a half* or *one-half,* but do not use *a half a.* For example, rewrite a sentence such as *He had a half a sandwich for dinner* to read *He had a half sandwich for dinner.*

hanged, hung Use *hanged* for the action of hanging a person, as in *The innocent man was hanged by an angry mob.* Use *hung* for all other meanings, such as *The clothes were hung on the line* and *The chandelier hung from a golden rope.* (See 9b.)

he, she; he/she; his, her; his/her; him, her; him/her When you are using a pronoun to refer back to a noun that could be either masculine or feminine, you might use *he or she* in order to avoid language that is now considered sexist. For example, instead of writing *A doctor must be constantly alert; he cannot make a single mistake* to refer generally to doctors, you could write *A doctor* *must be constantly alert; he or she cannot make a single mistake.* Or you could re-cast the sentence in the plural to avoid this problem: *Doctors must be constantly alert; they cannot make a single mistake.* (See 10c and 21g for specific strategies on avoiding gender-offensive pronoun references.)

herself, himself, myself, yourself   Use pronouns ending in *-self* when the pronouns refer to a noun that they intensify, as in *The teacher himself could not pass the test.* Do not use pronouns ending in *-self* to take the place of subjec-tive- or objective-case pronouns. Instead of writing, for example, *Joan and my-self are good friends,* write *Joan and I are good friends.* (See 7a.)

himself   See *herself, himself, myself, yourself.*

his/her   See *he/she.*

hisself   Do not use *hisself* in formal writing. In a context such as *He hisself or-ganized the picnic,* recast the sentence to read *He himself organized the picnic.*

hopefully   Use *hopefully* when you mean "with hope," as in *Relatives watched hopefully as the first miners emerged after the fire.* Avoid using *hopefully* as a mod-ifier for an entire clause or to convey any other meaning. For example, avoid *Hopefully, a cure for leukemia is not far away.*

hung, hanged   See *hanged, hung.*

if, whether   Use *if* to begin a subordinate clause when a stated or implied result follows, as in *If the court rules against the cigarette manufacturers, [then] thousands of lawsuits could follow.* Use *whether* when you are expressing an al-ternative, as in *Economists do not know whether the dollar will rebound or fall against the strength of the yen.*

illicit, elicit   See *elicit, illicit.*

illusion, allusion   See *allusion, illusion.*

immigrate   See *emigrate, immigrate, migrate.*

impact   Use *impact* when you are referring to a forceful collision, as in *The impact of the cars was so great that one was flattened.* Do not use *impact* as a verb meaning "to have an effect on." Instead of writing *Each of us can positively im-pact waste reduction efforts,* write *Each of us can reduce waste.*

implicit, explicit   See *explicit, implicit.*

imply, infer   Use *imply* when you mean "to suggest without directly stat-ing," as in *The doctor implied that being overweight was the main cause of my prob-lem.* Use *infer* when you mean "to find the meaning of something," as in *I inferred from her lecture that drinking more than two cups of coffee a day was a health risk.*

in, into   Use *in* when you are referring to location or condition. Use *into* to refer to a change in location, such as *The famous portrait shows a man going into a palace.* (See 23a.) In formal writing, do not use *into* for "interested in." For example, avoid a statement such as *I am into repairing engines.*

incredible, incredulous   Use *incredible* to mean "unbelievable," as in *Some of Houdini's exploits seem incredible to those who did not witness them.* Use *incredu-lous* to mean "unbelieving," as in *Many inlanders were incredulous when they* *heard tales of white people capturing men, women, and children who lived on the coast.*

individual, person, party   Use *individual* when you are referring to a single person and when your purpose is to stress that the person is unique, as in *Curie was a tireless and brilliant individual.* Use *party* when you mean a group, as in *The party of eight at the next table disturbed our conversation and ruined our evening.* The word *party* is also correctly used in legal documents referring to a single person. Use *person* for other meanings.

infer, imply   See *imply, infer.*

in regards to   Do not use *in regards to* in formal writing. Generally, you can substitute *about* for *in regards to.*

inside of, outside of   Use *inside* and *outside,* without *of,* when you are referring to location, as in *The roller blades were stored inside the garage.* In formal writing, do not use *inside of* to replace *within* in an expression of time. For example, avoid a sentence such as *I'll have that report inside of an hour.*

insure, assure, ensure   See *assure, ensure, insure.*

irregardless, regardless   Do not use *irregardless.* Use *regardless* instead.

is when, is where   Do not use *is when* and *is where* when you are defining something. Instead of writing *Dinner time is when my family relaxes,* write *At dinner time, my family relaxes.*

its, it's   Use *its* when your sentence requires a possessive pronoun, as in *Its leaves are actually long, slender blades.* (See 8c-1 and 27a-2.) Use *it's* only when you mean "it is." (See 23a.)

-ize   Do not use the suffix *-ize* to turn a noun into a verb in formal writing. For example, instead of writing *He is finalizing his draft,* write *He is finishing his draft* or *He is working on his final draft.*

kind of, sort of   Do not use these phrases as adjectives in formal writing. Instead, use *rather* or *somewhat.*

kind, sort, type   Do not precede the singular words *kind, sort,* and *type* with the plural word *these.* Use *this* instead. Also, prefer more specific words than *kind, sort,* and *type.* (See 17a.)

later, latter   Use *later* when you refer to time, as in *I will go to the concert later.* Use *latter* when you refer to the second of two things, as in *The latter of the two dates is better for my schedule.* (See also *former, latter.*)

latter, former   See *former, latter.*

lay, lie   Use *lay* when you mean "to put" or "to place," as in *She lays the present on the table.* Use *lie* when you mean "recline," as in *She lies awake at night,* or when you mean "is situated," as in *The city lies between a desert and a mountain range.* Also, remember that *lay* is a transitive verb that takes a direct object. (See 9d.)

learn, teach   Do not use *learn* to mean "teach." For example, rewrite a sentence such as *Ms. Chin learned us Algebra* to read *Ms. Chin taught us Algebra.*

leave, let Use *leave* to mean "depart." Use *let* to mean "allow." You can use either *leave* or *let* when the word is followed by *alone*, as in *Leave her alone* or *Let him alone*.

less, fewer See *fewer, less*.

liable See *apt, liable, likely*.

lie, lay See *lay, lie*.

like, as See *as, like*.

like, such as Use *like* to make a comparison, as in *Verbena is like ageratum in size and color*. Use *such as* when you are giving examples, as in *Many small flowers, such as verbena, ageratum, and alyssum, can be combined to create decorative borders and edgings*.

likely See *apt, liable, likely*.

lose, loose Use *lose* as a verb meaning "to misplace" or "to fail to win." Use *loose* as an adjective meaning "not tight" or "unfastened." You can also use *loose* as a verb meaning "to let loose," as in *They loosed the enraged bull when the matador entered the ring*. (See 23a.)

lots, lots of Do not use *lots* or *lots of* in formal writing. Use *many, very many, much*, or choose a more precise word instead.

man, mankind Do not use *man* and *mankind* to refer to all people in general. Instead, consider using *people, men and women, humans*, or *humankind*. (See 21g.)

may be, maybe Use *maybe* to mean "perhaps." Use *may be* as a verb (or auxiliary verb), as in *William may be visiting tomorrow*. (See 23a.)

may, can See *can, may*.

may of See *could of, would of, should of, might of, may of, must of*.

media Use a plural verb with *media*, as in *The media are often credited with helping the consumer win cases against large companies*. *Medium* is the singular form.

might of See *could of, would of, should of, might of, may of, must of*.

migrate See *emigrate, immigrate, migrate*.

moral, morale Use *moral* when you mean "an object lesson" or "knowing right from wrong." *What is the moral to the story?* Use *morale* when you mean "outlook" or "attitude." *The team's morale was high*. (See 23a.)

Ms. Use *Ms.* to refer to a woman when a title is required and when you either know that she prefers this title or you do not know her marital status. An invented title, *Ms.* was intended to address the issue of discrimination or judgment based on marital status. In research writing, use last names alone, without any title, as in *Jenkins recommends. . . .* In this case, do not use a title for either a man or a woman.

must of See *could of, would of, should of, might of, may of, must of*.

myself See *herself, himself, myself, yourself*.

nor, or   Use *nor* and *or* to suggest a choice. Use *nor* when the choice is negative; use *or* when the choice is positive. (See 7f.)

not but, not hardly, not scarcely   Do not use *not* to precede *hardly, scarcely,* and *but* in formal writing. Because *but, hardly,* and *scarcely* already carry the meaning of a negative, it is not necessary or correct to add another negative.

nothing like, nowhere near   Do not use *nothing like* and *nowhere near* in formal writing. Instead, use *not nearly.*

nowheres   Do not use *nowheres* in formal writing. Use *nowhere* instead.

number, amount   See *amount, number.*

off of   Do not use *off of* in formal writing. Use *off* or *from* alone instead, as in *She jumped off the bridge* or *He leaped from the rooftop.*

Ok, okay, O.K.   Do not use *Ok, okay,* or *O.K.* in formal writing as a substitute for *acceptable.*

on account of   Do not use this as a substitute for *because.* Use *because* instead.

on, upon   Use *on* instead of *upon* in formal writing.

or, nor   See *nor, or.*

outside of, inside of   See *inside of, outside of.*

party, individual, person   See *individual, person, party.*

people, persons   Use *people* to refer to a general group, as in *The people will make their voices heard.* Use *persons* to refer to a (usually small) collection of individuals, as in *The persons we interviewed were nearly unanimous in their opinion.*

per   Do not use *per* in formal writing. For example, instead of writing *The package was sent per your instructions,* it is better to write *The package was sent according to your instructions. Per* is acceptable in technical writing or when used with data and prices, as in *Charging $75 per hour, the consultant earned a handsome salary.*

percent (per cent), percentage   Use *percent* (or *per cent*) with a specific number. Use *percentage* with specific descriptive words and phrases, such as *A small percentage of the group did not eat meat.* Do not use *percentage* as a substitute for *part;* for example, rewrite a sentence such as *A percentage of my diet consists of complex carbohydrates* to read *Part of my diet consists of complex carbohydrates.*

person, party, individual   See *individual, person, party.*

plenty   Do not use *plenty* as a substitute for *quite* or *very.* For example, instead of writing *The Confederate troops were plenty hungry during the winter of 1864,* write *The Confederate troops were hungry [or starving] during the winter of 1864.*

plus   Avoid using *plus* as a conjunction joining independent clauses or as a conjunctive adverb. For example, rewrite *Picasso used color in a new way plus he experimented with shape; plus, he brought new meaning to ideas about abstract painting* to read *Picasso used color in a new way and he experimented with shape;*

moreover, he brought new meaning to ideas about abstract painting. It is acceptable to use *plus* when you need an expression meaning "in addition to," as in *The costs of day care, plus the costs of feeding and clothing the child, weighed heavily on the single parent's budget.*

practicable, practical   Use *practicable* when you mean "capable of putting into practice," as in *Although it seemed logical, the plan for saving the zoo was very expensive and turned out not to be practicable.* Use *practical* when you mean "sensible," as in *Lincoln was a practical young man who studied hard, paid his debts, and dealt with people honestly.*

precede, proceed   Use *precede* when you mean "come before," as in *The opening remarks precede the speech.* Use *proceed* when you mean "go forward," as in *The motorists proceeded with caution.*

pretty   Do not use *pretty,* as in *pretty close,* to mean "somewhat" or "quite" in formal writing. Use *somewhat, rather,* or *quite* instead.

previous to, prior to   Avoid these wordy expressions. Use *before* instead.

principal, principle   Use *principal* when you refer to a school administrator or an amount of money. Use *principle* when you are referring to a law, conviction, or fundamental truth. You can also use *principal* as an adjective meaning "major" or "most important," as in *The principal players in the decision were Sue Marks and Tom Cohen.*

quotation, quote   Use *quotation* when your sentence requires a noun, as in *The quotation from Nobel laureate Joseph Goldstein was used to lend credence to the theory.* Use *quote* when your sentence requires a verb, as in *She asked Goldstein whether she could quote him.*

raise, rise   Use *raise* when you mean "to lift." Use *rise* when you mean "to get up." To help you understand the difference, remember that *raise* is transitive and takes a direct object; *rise* is intransitive. (See 9d.)

rarely ever   Do not use *rarely ever* in formal writing. Use *rarely* or *hardly ever* instead.

real, really   Use *real* as an adjective and use *really* as an adverb.

reason is because   Do not use *reason is because* in formal writing. Rewrite your sentence to say, for example, *The real reason that the bomb was dropped was to end the war quickly* or *The bomb was dropped because Truman wanted to prevent Soviet influence in the Far Eastern settlement.*

reckon   See *calculate, figure, reckon.*

regarding, in regard to, with regard to   In formal writing that is not legal in nature, use *about* or *concerning* instead of these terms.

regardless, irregardless   See *irregardless, regardless.*

respectfully, respectively   Use *respectfully* when you mean "with respect," as in *He respectfully submitted his grievances.* Use *respectively* when you mean "in the given order," as in *The chief of police, the director of the department of public works, and the director of parks and recreation, respectively, submitted their ideas for budget cuts.*

right   Do not use *right* as an intensifier in formal writing. For example, instead of writing that *The farmer was right tired after milking the cows,* write *The farmer was tired [or exhausted] after milking the cows.*

rise, raise   See *raise, rise.*

seen   Do not use *seen* without an auxiliary such as *have, has,* or *had.* For example, rewrite a sentence such as *I seen the film* to read *I have seen the film.*

set, sit   Use *set* when you mean "to place." *Set* is a transitive verb that requires an object, as in *I set the book on the table.* Do not use *set* to mean "to sit" in formal writing. (See 9d.)

shall, will   Use *shall* instead of *will* for questions that contain the first person in extremely formal writing, as in *Shall we attend the meeting?* In all other cases, use *will.*

should of   See *could of, would of, should of, might of, may of, must of.*

should, would   Use *should* when you are referring to an obligation or a condition, as in *The governor's mansion should be restored.* Use *would* when you are referring to a wish, as in *I would like to see it repainted in its original colors.*

sit, set   See *set, sit.*

so   Do not use *so* in formal writing to mean "very" or "extremely," as in *He is so entertaining.* Use *very, extremely,* or, preferably, a more specific intensifier instead. Or follow *so* with an explanation preceded by *that,* as in *The reaction to the Freedom Riders was <u>so</u> violent* that *Robert F. Kennedy ordered a military escort.*

some   Do not use *some* to mean either "remarkable" or "somewhat" in formal writing. For example, rewrite a sentence such as *Babe Ruth was some hitter* to read *Babe Ruth was a remarkable hitter,* or use another more precise adjective to modify *hitter.* Also, rewrite a sentence such as *Wright's mother worried some about the kinds of building blocks her young child used* to read *Wright's mother worried a bit [or was somewhat worried about] the kinds of building blocks her young child used.*

somebody, some body; someone, some one   Use the indefinite pronouns *somebody* and *someone* when referring to a person, such as *There is someone I admire.* Use *some body* and *some one* when the adjective *some* modifies the noun *body* or *one,* as in *We will find the answer in some body of information.*

sometime, sometimes, some time   Use *sometime* when you mean "an indefinite, later time." Use *sometimes* when you mean "occasionally" or "from time to time." Use *some time* when *some* functions as an adjective modifying *time,* as in *His eyes required some time to adjust to the darkened room.*

sort   See *kind, sort, type.*

specially, especially   See *especially, specially.*

stationary, stationery   Use *stationary* to mean "standing still." Use *stationery* to mean "writing paper."

such   Do not use *such* to mean "very" or "extremely" unless *such* is followed by *that.* For example, rewrite a sentence such as *It had such boring lyrics* to read *It had extremely boring lyrics* or *It had <u>such</u> boring lyrics* that *I almost fell asleep half way through the song.*

such as, like   See *like, such as.*

supposed to, used to   Do not use *suppose to* or *use to* in formal writing. Use *supposed to* or *used to* instead.

sure and, sure to; try and, try to   Do not use *sure and* and *try and* in formal writing. Instead, use *sure to* and *try to*. For example, rewrite the sentence *Be sure and bring your computer* to read *Be sure to bring your computer*.

sure, surely   Use *surely* instead of *sure* when your sentence requires an adverb. For example, rewrite a sentence such as *Robert Fulton was sure a genius* to read *Robert Fulton was surely [or certainly] a genius*.

take, bring   See *bring, take*.

than, as   See *as, than*.

than, then   Use *than* when you mean "as compared with," as in *The violin is smaller than the cello*. Use *then* when you are stating a sequence of events, as in *First, he learned how to play the violin. Then he learned to play the cello*. Also use *then* when you mean "at that time" or "therefore." (See 23a.)

that there   See *this here, these here, that there, them there*.

that, which   Use *that* or *which* in an essential (or restrictive) clause, or a clause that is necessary to the meaning of the sentence, as in *This is the book that explains Locke's philosophy*. Use *which* in a nonessential (nonrestrictive) clause, or one that is not necessary to the meaning of the sentence, as in *My library just acquired Smith's book on Locke, which is not always easy to find*. (See 14e.)

their, there, they're   Use *their* as a possessive pronoun, as in *Their father prevented William and Henry James from being under the control of any one teacher for more than a year*. (See 8c-1.) Use *there* to refer to a place, as the opposite of *here*. Use *they're* to mean "they are." (See 27a-2.)

theirselves   Do not use *theirselves* in formal writing. Rewrite a sentence such as *They treated theirselves to ice cream* to read *They treated themselves to ice cream*.

them there   See *this here, these here, that there, them there*.

then, than   See *than, then*.

these here   See *this here, these here, that there, them there*.

these kind   See *kind, sort, type*.

this here, these here, that there, them there   Do not use *this here, these here, that there*, and *them there* in formal writing. Use *this, that, these*, and *those* instead.

thru   Do not use *thru* in formal writing. Use *through* instead.

thusly   Do not use *thusly* in formal writing. Use *thus* instead. (*Thus*, which is already an adverb, does not need an *-ly* ending.)

till, until, 'til   Do not use *'til* or *till* in formal writing. Prefer *until*.

to, too, two   Use *to* as a preposition meaning "toward"; use *too* to mean "also" or "excessively"; and use *two* as a number. (See 23a.)

toward, towards   Use *toward* instead of *towards* in formal writing. *Towards* is the British form.

try and, try to   See *sure and, sure to; try and, try to*.

type of   Do not use *type* in formal writing when you mean "type of." For example, rewrite a sentence such as *He is an anxious type person* to read *He is an anxious type of person*. (See also *kind, sort, type*.)

uninterested, disinterested   See *disinterested, uninterested*.

unique   Do not modify *unique* in formal writing. Because *unique* is an absolute, you should not write, for example, *most unique* or *very unique*.

until   See *'til, till; until;* is the preferred form in formal writing.

use, utilize   When you need a word that means "use," prefer *use*. *Utilize* is a less direct choice with the same meaning. (See 17a.)

used to   See *supposed to, used to*.

very   Avoid using *very* as an intensifier. Sometimes you will want to replace more than one word in order to eliminate *very*. For example, in the sentence *It was a very nice painting*, you could substitute more precise language, such as *It was a colorful [or provocative or highly abstract] painting*. (See 17a.)

wait for, wait on   Unless you are referring to waiting on tables, use *wait for* instead of *wait on* in formal writing. For example, rewrite *We grew tired as we waited on Sarah* to read *We grew tired as we waited for Sarah*.

ways   Do not use *ways* in formal writing to mean "way." Use *way* instead.

well, good   See *good, well*.

where at   See *at*.

whether, if   See *if, whether*.

which, that   See *that, which*.

which, who   Use *which* when you are referring to things. Use *who* when you are referring to people.

who, whom   Use *who* when a sentence requires a subject pronoun, as in *Who can answer this question?* Use *whom* when a sentence requires an object pronoun, as in *Whom did you invite?* (See 8f.)

who's, whose   Do not use *who's* in formal writing. Use *who is* instead. (See 27a-2.) Use *whose* to show possession, as in *Whose computer did you use?* (See 8f.)

will, shall   See *shall, will*.

-wise   Do not attach the suffix *-wise* to nouns or adjectives to turn them into adverbs in formal writing. For example, instead of writing *I am not doing well grade-wise*, you could recast the sentence to read *My grades are falling* or *My grades are low*.

would of   See *could of, would of, should of, might of, may of, must of*.

would, should   See *should, would*.

your, you're   Do not use *you're* in formal writing. Use *you are* instead. (See 27a-2.) Use *your* to show possession, as in *Your CD player is broken*. (See 8f.)

yourself   See *herself, himself, myself, yourself*.

Glossary of Terms: Grammar and Composition

abbreviation   The shortened form of a word, usually followed by a period.

absolute phrase   See *phrase.*

abstract expression   An expression that refers to broad categories or ideas (*evil, friendship, love*).

abstract noun   See *noun.*

acronym   The uppercase, pronounceable abbreviation of a proper noun—a person, organization, government agency, or country. Periods are not used with acronyms (*ARCO, WAVES*). (See 31c.)

active voice   See *voice.*

adjective   A word that modifies or describes a noun, pronoun, or group of words functioning as a noun. Adjectives answer the questions: which, what kind, and how many. A single-word adjective is usually placed before the word it modifies. Pure adjectives are not derived from other words. (See 7a-5; chapter 11).

adjective clause   See *clause.*

adjective forms   Adjectives change form to express comparative relationships. The **positive form** of an adjective is its base form. The **comparative form** is used to express a relationship between two elements. The **superlative form** is used to express a relationship between three or more elements. Most single-syllable adjectives and many two-syllable adjectives show comparisons with the suffix *-er* (tall*er*) and superlatives with the suffix *-est* (tall*est*). Adjectives of three or more syllables change to the comparative and superlative forms with the words *more* and *most,* respectively (*more beautiful, most beautiful*). Negative comparisons are formed by placing the words *less* and *least* before the positive form (*less interesting, least interesting*). (See 11e.)

adverb   A word that modifies a verb, an adjective, another adverb, or an entire sentence. Adverbs describe, define, or otherwise limit the words they modify, answering the questions when, how, where, how often, to what extent, and to what degree. Adverbs (as words, phrases, or clauses) can appear in different places in a sentence, depending on the rhythm the writer wants to achieve. Most adverbs are formed by adding the suffix *-ly* to an adjective. (See 7a-6; chapter 11.)

adverb clause   See *clause.*

adverb forms   The change of form that adverbs undergo to express comparative relationships. The **positive form** of an adverb is its base form. The **comparative form** is used to express a relationship between two elements. The **superlative form** is used to express a relationship among three or more elements. Most single-syllable adverbs show comparisons with the suffix *-er* (*nearer*) and superlatives with the suffix *-est* (*nearest*). Adverbs of two or more syllables change to comparative and superlative forms with *more* and *most*, respectively (*more beautifully, most beautifully*). Negative comparisons are formed by placing the words *less* and *least* before the positive form (*less strangely, least strangely*). (See 11e.)

adverbial conjunctions   See *conjunctive adverbs.*

agreement   The grammatical relationship between a subject and a verb, and a pronoun and its antecedent. If one element in these pairs is changed, the other must also be changed. Subjects and verbs must agree in number and person; pronouns and antecedents must agree in number, person, and gender. (See chapter 10.)

analogy   A figure of speech that makes a comparison between two apparently unrelated people, objects, conditions, or events in order to clarify a process or a difficult concept. The unknown entity is explained in terms of the more familiar entity. (See 5e-7; 6d-1; 21f-1.)

analysis   A close, careful reading of a text in which parts are studied to determine how the text as a whole functions. In a written analysis, in most instances the author is obliged to support his or her interpretation with direct evidence to a text. (See 37c-1.)

antecedent   A noun (or occasionally a pronoun) that a pronoun refers to and renames. A pronoun and its antecedent must agree in number, person, and gender. (See 10b; chapter 14.)

antonym   A word whose denotation (dictionary meaning) is opposite that of another word.

apostrophe   A punctuation mark used to show possession, mark the omission of letters or numbers, and mark plural forms. (See chapter 27.)

appositive   A word or phrase that describes, identifies, or renames a noun in a sentence. (See 8e-2.)

appositive phrase   See *phrase.*

article   The words *a, an,* or *the.* The **indefinite articles,** *a* or *an,* introduce a generalized noun. *A* appears before nouns beginning with a consonant; *an* is placed before nouns beginning with a vowel or an unpronounced *h.* The **definite article,** *the,* denotes a specific noun. Also called *determiners.*

assumption   A core belief, often unstated, that shapes the way people perceive the world. (See 1h.)

audience   The person or people who will be reading a piece of writing. Writing that takes a particular audience's needs and experience into consideration is most effective.

auxiliary verb   The verbs *be, will, can, have, do, shall,* and *may,* combined with the base form of another verb, or its present or past participle. Such auxiliary verbs are used to establish tense, mood, and voice in a sentence. Also called *helping verbs.* (See 7a-3; chapter 9.)

base form The infinitive form of a verb (*to be, to go*) from which all changes are made. Also called the *dictionary form.*

bibliography The list of sources used in writing a paper. An **annotated bibliography** is a fully annotated working bibliography in manuscript form. A **working bibliography** includes all of the sources located in researching a paper. A **final bibliography** consists of only those sources used in the actual writing of a paper. In Modern Language Association (MLA) format, the bibliography is titled *Works Cited;* in American Psychological Association (APA) format, it is called *References;* and in Council of Biology Editors (CBE) format it is called *Literature Cited.* (See 34b; chapter 36.)

brackets Punctuation marks used to clarify or insert remarks into quoted material. (See 29d.)

brainstorming A technique of idea generation in which the writer quickly jots down words or phrases related to a broad subject. When the time limit (five or ten minutes) is reached, related items are grouped; groupings with the greatest number of items indicate potential topics for composition. (See 3b-2.)

buzzwords Vague, often abstract expressions that sound as if they have meaning, but do not contribute anything of substance to a sentence. (See 17a-4.)

case The change in form of a noun or pronoun, depending on its function in a sentence. The three cases are the subjective, objective, and possessive forms. Nouns and indefinite pronouns take all three cases, but change form only when they show possession (with the addition of an apostrophe and *s*). Pronouns change form in all three cases. The **subjective case** is used when a pronoun functions as a subject, subject complement, or as an appositive that renames a subject. The **objective case** is used when a pronoun functions as the object of a preposition, as the object or indirect object of a verb, as the object of a verbal, or as the subject of an infinitive. The **possessive case** of a noun or pronoun indicates possession or ownership. (See chapter 8.)

chronological arrangement A method of organizing a paper in which the writing begins at one point in time and proceeds in sequence, forward or backward, to some other point. (See 5d-1.)

clause A grouping of words that has a subject and a predicate. An **independent clause** (or *main clause*) is a core statement that can stand alone as a sentence. A **dependent clause** (or *subordinate clause*) cannot stand alone as a sentence; it is joined to an independent clause by either a subordinating conjunction or a relative pronoun. There are four types of dependent clauses. **Adverb clauses** begin with subordinating conjunctions (*when, because, although*) and modify verbs, adjectives, and other adverbs. **Adjective clauses** begin with relative pronouns (*which, that, who, whom, whose*) and modify nouns or pronouns. **Noun clauses** are introduced by pronouns (*which, whichever, who, whoever, whom, whomever, whose*) and the words *how, when, why, where, whether,* and *whatever* and function as subjects, objects, complements, or appositives. **Elliptical clauses** have an omitted word or words (often relative pronouns or the logically parallel second parts of comparisons), but the sense of the sentence remains clear. (See 7e; 16e.)

cliché A trite expression that has lost its impact. (See 21f-3.)

coherence The clarity of the relationship between one unit of meaning and another. (See 4b-2.)

collective noun See *noun.*

colloquial Informal, conversational language. (See 21e-3.)

colon A punctuation mark (:) generally used to make an announcement. In formal writing, the colon follows only a complete independent clause and introduces a word, phrase, sentence, or group of sentences. (See 29a.)

comma A punctuation mark (,) used to signal that some element, some word or cluster of related words, is being set off from a main clause for a reason. (See chapter 25.)

comma splice The incorrect use of a comma to mark the boundary between two independent clauses. (See chapter 13; 25f-1.)

common noun See *noun.*

comparative form See *adjective forms, adverb forms.*

complement A word or group of words that completes the meaning of a subject or direct object by renaming it or describing it. A **subject complement** follows a linking verb and can be a noun, pronoun, adjective, or group of words substituting for an adjective or noun. An **object complement** typically follows verbs such as *appoint, call, choose, make,* and *show* and can be a noun, adjective, or group of words substituting for a noun or adjective.

complete predicate See *predicate.*

complete subject See *subject.*

complex sentence See *sentence.*

compound adjective Two or more words that are combined to modify a given noun. Often, when a compound adjective precedes a noun it is hyphenated to prevent misreading; when it follows the noun it modifies, it does not need hyphenation. (See 32a-1; 32a-3.)

compound-complex sentence See *sentence.*

compound noun Two or more words that are combined to function as a single noun. Hyphens are used when the first word of the compound could be read alone as a noun (*cross-reference*). (See 32a-2.)

compound predicate Two or more verbs and their objects and modifiers that are joined with a coordinating conjunction to form a single predicate.

compound sentence See *sentence.*

compound subject Two or more nouns or pronouns and their modifiers that function as a single subject.

compound verb Two or more verbs that are combined to function as a single verb. Hyphens are used when the first word of the compound could be read alone as a verb (*shrink-wrap*). (See 32a-2.)

compound words Nouns, adjectives, or prepositions created when two or more words are brought together to form a distinctive meaning and to function grammatically as a single word. (See 32a.)

concrete expression A vivid, detailed expression (*a throbbing headache*).

concrete noun See *noun.*

conjunction A word that joins sentence elements or entire sentences by establishing a coordinate or equal relationship among combined parts, or by establishing a subordinate or unequal relationship. **Coordinating conjunctions** (*and, but, or, nor, for, so, yet*) join complete sentences or parallel elements from two or more sentences into a single sentence and express specific logical relationships between these elements. **Correlative conjunctions** (*both/and, neither/nor, either/or, not only/but also*) are pairs of coordinating conjunctions that place extra emphasis on the relationship between the parts of the coordinated construction. The parts of the sentence joined by correlative conjunctions must be grammatically parallel. **Subordinating conjunctions** (*when, while, although, because, if, since, whereas*) connect dependent clauses to independent clauses. (See 7a-9; 18b; 19a-1, 2.)

conjunctive adverb An adverb (such as *however, therefore, consequently, otherwise,* or *indeed*) used to create a compound sentence in which the independent clauses that are joined share a logically balanced emphasis. Also called *adverbial conjunction.* (See 7a-9; 19a-3; 26b.)

connotation The implications, associations, and nuances of a word's meaning. (See 21a.)

coordinate adjectives Two or more adjectives in a series, whose order can be reversed without affecting the meaning of the noun being modified. Coordinate adjectives are linked by a comma or by a coordinating conjunction (*an intelligent, engaging speaker*). (See 25c-2.)

coordinating conjunction See *conjunction.*

coordination The combining of sentence elements by the use of coordinating and correlative conjunctions and conjunctive adverbs. Elements in a coordinate relationship share equal grammatical status and equal emphasis. (See 19a; 20b-1.)

correlative conjunction See *conjunction.*

count noun See *noun.*

cues Words and phrases that remind readers as they move from sentence to sentence that (1) they continue to read about the same topic and (2) ideas are unfolding logically. Four types of cues are pronouns, repetition, parallel structures, and transitions. (See 5d-2.)

cut To delete sentences because they are off the point or because they give too much attention to a subordinate point. (See 4b-3.)

dangling modifier A word, phrase, or clause whose referent in a sentence is not clearly apparent. (See 15h.)

dash A punctuation mark (—) used to set off and give emphasis to brief or lengthy modifiers, appositives, repeating structures, and interruptions in dialogue. (See 29b.)

dead metaphor   A metaphor that has been used so much it has become an ordinary word.

declarative sentence   See *sentence.*

definitional assumption   See *assumption.*

demonstrative pronoun   See *pronoun.*

denotation   The dictionary meaning of a word. (See 21a.)

dependent clause   See *clause.* Also called *subordinate clause.*

descriptive assumption   See *assumption.*

determiner   See *article.*

dialect   Expressions specific to certain social or ethnic groups as well as regional groups within a country. (See 21e-2.)

diction   A writer's choice of words. (See chapter 21.)

dictionary form   See *base form.*

direct discourse   The exact recreation, using quotation marks, of words spoken or written by a person. Also called *direct quotation.* (See 28a-1; 34g.)

direct object   See *object.*

direct quotation   See *direct discourse.*

documentation   The credit given to sources used in a paper, including the author, title of the work, city, name of publisher, and date of publication. There are different systems of documentation for various disciplines; three frequently used systems include the Modern Language Association (MLA), American Psychological Association (APA), and the Council of Biology Editors (CBE) systems of documentation. (See chapter 36.)

double comparative   An incorrect method of showing the comparative form of an adverb or adjective by adding both the suffix *-er* to the word and placing the word *more* before the adverb or adjective. Only one form should be used. (See 11f.)

double negative   An incorrect method of negation in which two negative modifiers are used in the same sentence. Only one negative should be used. (See 11f.)

double superlative   An incorrect method of showing the superlative form of an adverb or adjective by adding both the suffix *-est* to the word and placing the word *most* before the adverb or adjective. Only one form should be used. (See 11f.)

drafting   The stage in the composition process in which the writer generates the first form of a paper from a working thesis or outline. (See 3e; 35e.)

editing   The stage in the composition process in which the writer examines and, if necessary, alters the work's style, grammar, punctuation, and word choice. (See 4c-1; 35f.)

ellipses   Punctuation marks (. . .) consisting of three spaced periods that indicate the writer has deleted either words or entire sentences from a passage being quoted. (See 29e.)

elliptical clause   See *clause.*

elliptical construction   A shortened sentence in which certain words have been omitted deliberately in order to streamline communication. (See 16g.)

essential modifier   A word, phrase, or clause that provides information crucial for identifying a noun; this type of modifier appears in its sentence without commas. The relative pronoun *that* is used only in essential clauses (*who* or *which* may also be used). Also called a *restrictive modifier.* (See 14e-2; 25d-1.)

etymology   The study of the history of words. (See 22c.)

euphemism   A polite rewording of a term that the writer feels will offend readers.

euphony   The pleasing sound produced by certain word combinations.

exclamation point   A punctuation mark (!) used to indicate an emphatic statement or command. (See 24c.)

exclamatory sentence   See *sentence.*

expletive   A word that fills the space left in a sentence that has been re-arranged. The words *it* and *there* are expletives (filler words without meaning of their own) when used with the verb *be* in sentences with a delayed subject.

faulty parallelism   An error in a sentence where elements that should be grammatically equivalent are not. Faulty parallelism is indicated in a sentence when the use of a coordinating conjunction makes part of the sentence sound out of place or illogical. (See 18a.)

faulty predication   An error in a sentence indicated when the predicate part of a sentence does not logically complete its subject. Faulty predication often involves a form of the linking verb *be.*

figure of speech   A carefully controlled comparison that intensifies meaning. See *simile, analogy,* and *metaphor.*

final thesis   See *thesis.*

first person   See *person.*

formal English   The acknowledged standard of correct English. (See 21e.)

formal register   The writing of professional and academic worlds. Formal writing is precise and concise, avoids colloquial expressions, is thorough in content, and is highly structured. (See 3a-4.)

freewriting   A technique of idea generation in which the writer chooses a broad area of interest and writes for a predetermined amount of time or in a prescribed number of pages, without pausing to organize or analyze thoughts. In *focused freewriting,* the same process is followed, but a specific topic is prescribed. (See 3b-3.)

fused sentence   The joining of two independent clauses without a coordinate conjunction or proper punctuation. Also called a *run-on sentence.* (See chapter 13.)

future perfect progressive tense   See *tense.*

future perfect tense   See *tense.*

future progressive tense   See *tense.*

future tense   See *tense.*

gender   The labeling of nouns or pronouns as masculine, feminine, or neuter.

generalization   A statement about a group that applies to individual members of that group. (See 6d-1.)

gerund   The *-ing* form of a verb without its helping verbs; gerunds function as nouns.

gerund phrase   See *phrase.*

helping verbs   See *verbs.*

historical present tense   The present tense form used when referring to actions in an already existing work (a book, a movie). (See 9e-1.)

homonyms   Words that sound alike or are pronounced alike but that have different spellings and meanings. (See 23a-1.)

hyphen   A punctuation mark (-) used to join compound words and to divide words at the end of lines.

hypothesis   A carefully stated prediction.

idiom   A grouping of words, one of which is usually a preposition, whose meaning may or may not be apparent based solely on simple dictionary definitions. The grammar of idioms is often a matter of customary usage and is often difficult to explain. (See 21b-2.)

imperative mood   See *mood.*

imperative sentence   See *sentence.*

indefinite pronoun   See *pronoun.*

independent clause   See *clause.*

indicative mood   See *mood.*

indirect discourse   The inexact quotation of the spoken or written words of a person. Indirect discourse inserts the writer's voice into the quotation. Also called *indirect quotation.* (See 28a-1.)

indirect object   See *object.*

indirect question   A restatement of a question asked by someone else. An indirect question uses a period as punctuation, not a question mark.

indirect quotation   See *indirect discourse.*

infinitive   The base form of a verb, which is often preceded by the word *to.* Also called the *dictionary form.*

infinitive phrase   See *phrase.*

informal register The more colloquial, casual writing of personal correspondence and journals. (See 3a-4.)

intensive pronoun See *pronoun.*

interjection An emphatic word or phrase. When it stands alone, an interjection is frequently followed by an exclamation point. As part of a sentence, an interjection is usually set off by commas. (See 7a-10.)

interrogative pronoun See *pronoun.*

interrogative sentence See *sentence.*

intransitive verb See *verb.*

irregular verb A verb that changes its root spelling to show the past tense and form the past participle, as opposed to adding *-d* or *-ed.*

jargon The in-group language of professionals, who may use acronyms and other linguistic devices to take short-cuts when speaking with colleagues. (See 21e-4.)

limiting modifier A word that restricts the meaning of another word placed directly after it (*only, almost, just, nearly, even, simply*).

linking verb See *verb.*

list A displayed series of items that are logically similar or comparable and are expressed in grammatically parallel form.

logical arrangement A method of organizing a paper in which the topic is divided into its constituent parts, and the parts are discussed one at a time in an order that will make sense to readers. (See 5d-1.)

main clause See *independent clause.*

mapping A visual method of idea generation. The topic (word or phrase) is circled and from the circle are drawn spokes labeled with the "journalist's questions" (*who, what, where, when, how, why*). The answer to each question is then queried with the journalist's questions again. This method groups and subordinates ideas, thus assisting in generating main ideas and supporting information. (See 3b-7.)

mass noun See *noun.*

metaphor A figure of speech that illustrates or intensifies something relatively unknown by comparing it with something familiar. (See 21f-1.)

misplaced modifier A word, phrase, or clause whose position confuses the meaning of a sentence. A misplaced modifier is not placed next to the word(s) it is meant to modify. (See 15a.)

mixed construction A confused sentence structure that begins with a certain grammatical pattern and then abruptly changes direction with another grammatical pattern.

mixed metaphor An illogical comparison of two elements. (See 21f-2.)

modal auxiliary A verb that is paired with the base form of a verb to express urgency, obligation, likelihood, or possibility (*can, could, may, might, must, ought to, should, would*). (See 9c-1.)

modifier   An adjective or adverb, in the form of a single word, phrase, or clause, that adds descriptive information to a noun or verb. A single-word adjective is often positioned directly before the noun it modifies. Adverbs can be shifted to any part of a sentence. Depending on its location, an adverb will change the meaning or rhythm of a sentence, so care must be taken to ensure that an adverb modifies the word intended. (See 7c.)

mood   The form of a verb that indicates the writer's attitude about an action. The **indicative mood** expresses facts, opinions, or questions. The **imperative mood** expresses commands. The **subjunctive mood** expresses a recommendation, a wish, a requirement, or a statement contrary to fact. (See 9h.)

narrative   Writing that recounts for readers a story that will have a point pertinent to the larger essay. Narratives are often sequenced chronologically. (See 5e-1.)

nonessential modifier   A word, phrase, or clause that provides information that is not essential for defining a word. Commas are used to set the clause apart from the sentence in which it appears. The relative pronouns *who* and *which* may be used in nonessential clauses. Also called *nonrestrictive modifier*. (See 14e-2; 25d-2.)

nonrestrictive modifier   See *nonessential modifier*.

noun   A noun names a person, place, thing, or idea. Nouns change their form to show number; the plural is usually formed by adding *-s* or *-es*. Possession is indicated with the addition of an apostrophe and usually an *s*. **Proper nouns,** which are capitalized, name particular persons, places, or things. **Common nouns** refer to general persons, places, or things. **Mass nouns** denote items that cannot be counted. **Count nouns** denote items that can be counted. **Concrete nouns** name tangible objects. **Abstract nouns** name intangible ideas, emotions, or qualities. **Animate** versus **inanimate nouns** differ according to whether they name something alive. **Collective nouns** are singular in form and have either a singular or plural sense, depending on the meaning of the sentence. (See 7a-2; 10a-5.)

noun clause   See *clause*.

noun phrase   See *phrase*.

number   A change in the form of a noun, pronoun, or verb that indicates whether it is singular or plural. (See 16a.)

object   A noun, pronoun, or group of words substituting for a noun that receives the action of a transitive verb (**direct object**); is indirectly affected by the action of a transitive verb (**indirect object**); or follows a preposition (**object of a preposition**). (See 7b.)

object complement   See *complement*.

objective case   See *case*.

object of a preposition   See *object*.

outline   A logically parallel list with further subdivision and subsections under individual items in the list. (See 18e-2.)

paragraph   A group of related sentences organized by a single, controlling idea. (See chapter 5.)

parallel case An argument that develops a relationship between directly related people, objects, events, or conditions.

parallelism The use of grammatically equivalent words, phrases, and sentences to achieve coherence and balance in writing. (See 5d-2; chapter 18.)

paraphrase A restatement of a passage of text. The structure of a paraphrase reflects the structure of the source passage. (See 34f-2.)

parentheses Punctuation marks used to enclose and set off nonessential dates, words, phrases, or whole sentences that provide examples, comments, and other supporting information. (See 29c.)

participial phrase See *phrase.*

participle A verb form. The **present participle** (the *-ing* form) functions as a main verb of a sentence and shows continuing action when paired with *be;* functions as an adjective when paired with a noun or pronoun (*the loving parent*), and functions as a noun when used as a gerund (*studying takes time*). (See *gerund.*) The **past participle** (the past tense *-d, -ed, -n,* or *-en* forms) functions as the main verb of a sentence when paired with *have* (*I have studied for days*); forms a passive construction when paired with *be* (*The rock was thrown*); and functions as an adjective when paired with a noun or pronoun (*the contented cow*).

parts of speech The categories into which words are grouped according to their grammatical function in a sentence: nouns, verbs, verbals, adjectives, adverbs, pronouns, prepositions, conjunctions, interjections, and expletives. (See glossary entries for each category and 7a-2–11.)

passive voice See *voice.*

past participle See *participle.*

past perfect progressive tense See *tense.*

past perfect tense See *tense.*

past progressive tense See *tense.*

past tense See *tense.*

perfect progressive tense See *tense.*

period A punctuation mark (.) that denotes a complete stop—the end of a sentence. (See 24a.)

person The form of a pronoun or a noun that identifies whether the subject of a sentence is the person speaking (the **first person**); the person spoken to (the **second person**); or the person spoken about (the **third person**). (See 16a.)

personal pronoun See *pronoun.*

phrase A grouping of words that lacks a subject and predicate and cannot stand alone as a sentence. **Verbal phrases** consist of infinitive phrases, gerund phrases, and participial phrases—all of which are built on verb forms not functioning as verbs in a sentence, along with associated words (objects and modifiers). **Infinitive phrases** consist of the infinitive form, often preceded by *to*; they function as adjectives, adverbs, or nouns. **Gerund phrases** consist of the *-ing* form of a verb and function as nouns—as subjects, objects, or complements. **Participial phrases** consist of the present or past participle of a verb and function as adjectives. **Verb phrases** consist of the combination of an auxiliary and the base form, or present or past participle, of a verb. **Noun phrases** consist of a noun accompanied by all of its modifying words. A noun phrase may be quite lengthy, but it always functions as a single noun—as a subject, object, or complement. **Absolute phrases** consist of a subject and an incomplete predicate; they modify entire sentences, not individual words. **Appositive phrases** rename or further identify nouns and are placed directly beside the nouns they refer to. (See 7d; 12c; 29a-4; 29b-1.)

plagiarism   A conscious attempt to pass off the ideas or the words of another as one's own. (See 34h.)

popular register   The writing typical of most general-interest magazines. The language is more conversational than formal writing, but all conventions of grammar, usage, spelling, and punctuation are adhered to. (See 3a-4.)

positive form   See *adjective forms, adverb forms.*

possessive case   See *case.*

predicate   A verb, and other words associated with it, that states the action undertaken by a subject or the condition in which the subject exists. A **simple predicate** consists of the verb and its auxiliaries. A **complete predicate** consists of the simple predicate and its modifiers and objects. A **compound predicate** consists of two verbs and their associated words which are joined with a coordinating conjunction and share the same subject. (See 7a-1.)

prefix   A group of letters joined to the beginning of a root word to form a new, derived word. Prefixes indicate number, size, status or condition, negation, and relations in time and space. (See 22d-2; 23c.)

preposition   A word (*in, at, of, for, on, by, above, under*) that links a noun, pronoun, or word group substituting for a noun to other words in a sentence—to nouns, pronouns, verbs, or adjectives. (See 7a-8.)

prepositional phrase   See *phrase.*

present participle   See *participle.*

present perfect progressive tense   See *tense.*

present perfect tense   See *tense.*

present progressive tense   See *tense.*

present tense   See *tense.*

primary source   An original document or artifact that may be referred to in a paper, such as a story, letter, or autobiography.

principal parts   The forms of a verb built from the infinitive, from which the tenses are formed: past tense, present participle, and past participle.

pronoun   A word that takes on the meaning of and substitutes for a noun (referred to as the pronoun's *antecedent*). Pronouns show number (singular or plural) and change case depending on their function in a sentence. **Personal**

pronouns (*I, me, you, us, his, hers . . .*) refer to people or things. **Relative pronouns** (*who, which, that . . .*) introduce dependent clauses that usually function as adjectives. The pronouns *who, which,* and *that* rename and refer to the nouns they follow. **Demonstrative pronouns** (*this, that, these, those*) point to the nouns they replace. **Interrogative pronouns** (*who, which, what, whose*) form questions. **Intensive pronouns** (*herself, themselves*) are formed with the suffix *-self* or *-selves* to repeat and emphasize a noun or pronoun. **Reflexive pronouns** (*herself, ourselves*) are formed with the suffix *-self* or *-selves* and rename or reflect back to a preceding noun or pronoun. **Indefinite pronouns** (*one, anybody*) refer to general or nonspecific persons or things. **Reciprocal pronouns** (*one another, each other*) refer to the separate parts of a plural noun. (See 7a-7; chapter 8; chapter 14.)

proofreading   The final stage in the composition process in which the writer rereads the final paper to identify and correct misspelled words; words (often prepositions) omitted from sentences; words that have been doubled; punctuation that may have been forgotten; and homonyms. (See 4c-2.)

proper noun   See *noun.*

quotation   See *direct discourse.*

reciprocal pronoun   See *pronoun.*

redundant phrase   An expression that repeats a message unnecessarily.

reflexive pronoun   See *pronoun.*

regionalism   An expression whose meaning is specific to certain areas of the country. Use of such expressions is inappropriate in formal writing. (See 21e-2.)

register   The level of language or tone used in a paper. (See *formal register, informal register, popular register.*)

regular verbs   Verbs that change form in predictable ways, taking the suffix *-ed* to show the past tense and the past participle.

relative pronoun   See *pronoun.*

restrictive modifier   See *essential modifier.*

revision   A stage in the composition process in which the writer examines the first draft to clarify the purpose or thesis; rewrites to achieve unity and coherence; and adjusts to achieve balance by expanding, condensing, or cutting material. (See chapter 4; 35f.)

root word   The base form of a word that contains its core meaning. Suffixes and prefixes are added to a root word to form additional words.

run-on sentence   See *fused sentence.*

secondary source   The work of scholars who have interpreted the writings of others.

second person   See *person.*

section   A grouping of paragraphs that constitutes part of the larger document. (See 5a-1.)

section thesis   See *thesis.*

semicolon   A punctuation mark (;) used to denote a partial separation between independent elements. (See chapter 26.)

sentence   A fully expressed thought consisting of a complete subject and a complete predicate. A sentence begins with a capital letter and ends with a period, question mark, or exclamation point. The four functional types of sentences include declarative, interrogative, exclamatory, and imperative sentences. A **declarative sentence** makes a statement or assertion about a subject. An **interrogative sentence** poses a question and is formed either by inverting a sentence's usual word order or by preceding the sentence with words such as *who, which, when, where,* and *how.* An **exclamatory sentence** is used as a direct expression of a speaker's or writer's strong emotion. An **imperative sentence** expresses a command. The four structural types of sentences are simple, compound, complex, and compound-complex sentences. A **simple sentence** has a single subject and a single predicate. A **compound sentence** has two subjects and two predicates. A **complex sentence** has an independent clause and one or more dependent clauses. A **compound-complex sentence** has at least two independent clauses and one dependent clause.

sentence fragment   A partial sentence punctuated as if it were a complete sentence, with an uppercase letter at its beginning and a period, question mark, or exclamation point at its end. A sentence fragment lacks either a subject or a predicate, and sometimes both. It can also be a dependent clause that has not been joined to an independent clause.

sexism   In writing, the use of inappropriate gender-specific words (*a biologist in his lab*) that creates biased or inaccurate characterizations linked with a male or female reference. (See 21g.)

simile   A figure of speech in which two different things, one usually familiar, the other not, are explicitly compared. The properties of the known thing help to define the unknown thing. Similes often use the words *like* or *as* to set up the comparison. (See 21f-1.)

simple future tense   See *tense.*

simple past tense   See *tense.*

simple predicate   See *predicate.*

simple present tense   See *tense.*

simple sentence   See *sentence.*

simple subject   See *subject.*

slang   The informal language peculiar to a culture or subculture; inappropriate for formal writing.

slash   A punctuation mark (/) used to separate lines of poetry run in with the text of a sentence; to show choice, as in *either/or;* and to note division in fractions or formulas. (See 29f.)

spatial arrangement   A method of organizing a paper in which the subjects are described according to their relative positions; for example, for a photograph, the foreground, middle ground, and background might be described. (See 5d-1.)

split infinitive   The insertion of an adverbial modifier between the two parts of an infinitive—the word *to* and the base form—which can disrupt the intended meaning (. . . *to* successfully *attempt*). (See 15f.)

squinting modifier   A word, phrase, or clause that ambiguously appears to modify two words in a sentence—both the word preceding and following it.

subject   A noun, pronoun, or group of words substituting for a noun, that engages in the main action of a sentence or is described by the sentence. A **simple subject** consists of a single noun or pronoun. A **complete subject** consists of a simple subject and its modifiers. A **compound subject** consists of a multiple subject created by using the coordinating conjunction *and.*

subject complement   See *complement.*

subjective case   See *case.*

subjunctive mood   See *mood.*

subordinate clause   See *clause, dependent clause.*

subordinating conjunction   See *conjunction.*

subordination   A method for linking words, phrases, or clauses that is used to give more emphasis to one idea than to another in a sentence. The words in a dependent (subordinate) clause cannot stand alone as a sentence. (See 19b.)

suffix   A group of letters joined to the end of a root word. Suffixes change the grammatical function of words and can be used to indicate tense.

summary   A brief, objective account of the main ideas of a source passage. (See 34f-1.)

superlative form   See *adjective forms, adverb forms.*

synonym   A word that has approximately the same denotation (dictionary meaning) as another word.

synthesis   A presentation that draws together material from several sources. (See 2d.)

tag question   A brief question attached to a statement, set off by a comma. Tag questions consist of a helping verb, a pronoun, and frequently the word *not* (*He won the match, didn't he?*). (See 25e-5.)

tense   The change in form of a verb that shows when an action has occurred or when a subject exists in a certain state of being. Tenses are marked by verb endings and auxiliary verbs. (See 9e, f; 16b-1.) The **simple present tense** indicates an action taking place at the writer's present time. The verb's base form is used for singular or plural first- and second-person subjects, as well as for plural third-person subjects (*I go, you go, they go*). The verb for a third-person singular subject ends with the suffix -*s* (*she goes*). The **simple past tense** indicates an action completed at a definite time in the past. Regular verbs form this tense by adding -*d* or -*ed* to the base form. The **simple future tense** indicates an action or state of being that will begin in the future. All other tenses build on these basic tenses by using auxiliaries. See chapter 9 for more information on the present, past, and future perfect tenses; the present, past, and future progressive tenses; and the perfect progressive tenses.

thesis A general statement about a topic that crystallizes the main purpose of a writing and suggests its main parts. A **section thesis** explicitly announces the point to be addressed in a section and either directly or indirectly suggests what will be discussed relating to this point. (See 5a-2.) A **working thesis** is a statement that should prove to be a reasonably accurate summary of what will be written. A **final thesis** is an accurate, one-sentence summary of a work that will appear in the final draft. (See 3d; 33e; 35a.)

third person See *person.*

tone The expression of a writer's attitude toward the subject or audience. Tone is determined by word choice and quality of description, verb selection, sentence structure, and sentence mood and voice. The tone of a piece changes depending on the audience. (See 3a-4; 16c.)

topic The subject of a piece of writing. (See 3a.)

topical development The expansion of statements about a topic announced in the opening sentence of a paragraph. After its opening announcement, the topic is divided into two or three parts, each of which is developed at a different location in the paragraph. (See 5c–d.)

topic sentence A paragraph's central, controlling idea. (See 5c.)

transition A word, sentence, or paragraph devoted to building a smooth, logical relationship between ideas in a sentence, between sentences, between paragraphs, or between whole sections of an essay. (Phrases include *for example, on the other hand, in addition.*) (See 4b-2; 5d-3; 20c-1.)

transitive verb See *verb.*

usage The prevailing, customary conditions describing how, where, and when a word is normally used in speech and writing. Usage labels in a dictionary, such as *colloquial, slang, archaic,* and *dialect,* indicate special restrictions on the conditions for using a particular meaning or form of a word.

value assumption See *assumption.*

verb The main word in the predicate of a sentence expressing an action or occurrence or establishing a state of being. Verbs change form to demonstrate tense, number, mood, and voice. **Transitive verbs** (*kick, buy*) transfer the action from an actor—the subject of the sentence—to a direct object—a person, place, or thing receiving that action. **Intransitive verbs** (*laugh, sing, smile*) show action that is limited to the subject; there is no direct object that is acted upon. (*The rock fell.*) The same verb can be transitive in one sentence and intransitive in another. (*She runs a good business. She runs every day.*) **Linking verbs** (*is, feel, appear, seem*) allow the word or words following the verb to complete the meaning of the subject. (*Joan is a lawyer.*) (See 7a-3; chapter 9.)

verbal A verb form that functions in a sentence as an adjective, an adverb, or a noun. Verbals include infinitives, participles, and gerunds. (See *infinitive, participle, gerund;* 7a-4; 7d-2.)

verbal phrase See *phrase.*

verb phrase See *phrase.*

voice The form of a transitive verb in a sentence that shows whether emphasis is given to the actor or to the object acted upon. **Active-voice** sentences emphasize the doer of an action. **Passive-voice** sentences emphasize the object acted upon or deemphasize an unknown subject. In passive-voice sentences the words are rearranged so that the object occupies the first position. This construction requires the use of a form of the verb *be* and the preposition *by.* (*The house was designed by Frank Lloyd Wright.*)

working thesis See *thesis.*

REFERENCES *and* WORKS CITED

CHAPTER 1: REFERENCES FOR JEAN KILBOURNE, "THE CHILD AS SEX OBJECT"

Bayer, Alan E. and Daniel H. Baker. "Adolescent Eating Disorders: Anorexia and Bulimia." *Family Life Educator* 3:2 (1984): 4–9.

Broverman, I. K., D. M. Broverman, F. E. Clarkson, P. S. Rosenkrantz and S. R. Vogel. "Sex-Role Stereotypes and Clinical Judgments of Mental Health." *Journal of Consulting and Clinical Psychology* 34:1 (1970): 1–7.

Brownmiller, S. *Against Our Will: Men, Women and Rape.* New York: Simon and Schuster, 1975.

Butler, M., and W. Paisley. *Women and the Mass Media.* New York: Human Sciences Press, 1980.

Cagan, E. "The Selling of the Women's Movement." *Social Policy* 9:1 (1978): 4–12.

Comstock, G. "The Impact of Television on American Institutions." *Journal of Communication* 28:2 (1978): 12–28.

Courtney, A. and T. Whipple. *Sex Stereotyping in Advertising.* Lexington, MA: D.C. Heath & Co., 1983.

Elkind, D. *The Hurried Child: Growing Up Too Fast, Too Soon.* Reading, MA: Addison-Wesley, 1981.

Ewen, S. *Captains of Consciousness: Advertising and the Social Roots of the Consumer Culture.* New York: McGraw-Hill, 1976.

Fore, W. "The Role of Mass Communication in Society: A Theological Perspective." In B. Logan (Ed.), *Television Awareness Training.* New York: Parthenon Press, 1977.

Gerbner, G. "Communication and Social Environment." *Scientific American* 26:3 (1972): 152–160.

Goffman, E. *Gender Advertisements.* New York: Harper & Row, 1979.

"Judge Blames Sex Assault on 5-Year-Old Victim." *National Now Times.* January 2, 1982, p. 2.

Leymore, V. L. *Hidden Myth: Structure and Symbolism in Advertising.* New York: Basic Books, Inc., 1975.

Lindsey, K. "Towards a New Recognition of Reality." *Sojourner* (January 1980): 5, 22.

Malamuth, N., and E. Donnerstein. *Pornography and Sexual Aggression.* Chicago: Academy Press, 1984.

Miller, J. B. *Toward a New Psychology of Women.* Boston: Beacon Press, 1976.

Nabokov, V. *Lolita.* New York: Putnam Publishing Group, 1955.

Price, J. *The Best Thing on TV: Commercials.* New York: Penguin Books, 1978.

Rush, Florence. (Quoted in "Advertising and the Lolita Image.") *The Christian Science Monitor.* January 30, 1981, p. B4.

Sontag, S. "The Double Standard of Aging." *Saturday Review of the Society* 55: 39 (1972): 29–38.

Williamson, J. *Decoding Advertisements: Ideology and Meaning in Advertising.* London: Marion Boyars Publishers, Ltd., 1978.

Wynn, M. *Children Without Childhoods.* New York: Pantheon, 1983.

821

CHAPTER 5: REFERENCES

The illustrative paragraphs in this chapter are attributed in the text as they occur; they are drawn from the following sources:

Boorstin, Daniel, and Brooks Mather Kelley. *A History of the United States.* Englewood Cliffs, NJ: Prentice, 1989. 499.

Bronowski, J. *The Ascent of Man.* Boston: Little, Brown, 1973. 115.

Carson, Rachel. *Silent Spring.* Boston: Houghton, 1962. 39, 105, 136.

Catton, Bruce. "Grant and Lee: A Study in Contrasts." Rpt. in *The Longwood Reader.* Ed. Edward A. Dornan and Charles W. Dawe. Boston: Allyn and Bacon, 1991. 236.

Chang, Semoon, *Modern Economics.* Boston: Allyn and Bacon, 1990. 38, 39.

Clarke, Arthur C. "Electron Tutors." *Omni Magazine* 1980. Rpt. in *Writing and Reading Across the Curriculum.* Ed. Laurence Behrens and Leonard Rosen. Boston: Little, Brown, 1982. 273.

Cohen, Paul S., and Milton A. Rothman. *Basic Chemistry.* Boston: Allyn and Bacon, 1986. 45.

Costello, Kevin. "Long Odds: How a Bill Becomes Law." Student essay. *Aims of the Essay.* Ed. Don Knefel. Boston: Allyn and Bacon, 1991. 154.

Curtis, Helena. *Biology.* 2nd ed. New York: Worth, 1975. 47.

Daniels, Robert V. *Studying History: How and Why.* 3rd ed. Englewood Cliffs: Prentice, 1981.

Dillard, Annie. *An American Childhood.* New York: Harper, 1987. 53–54.

Farb, Peter. *Humankind.* Boston: Houghton, 1978. 53.

Farber, Stephen. *The Movie Rating Game.* Public Affairs Press, 1972. Rpt. in *Writing and Reading Across the Curriculum.* 3rd ed. Ed. Laurence Behrens and Leonard Rosen. Glenview: Scott, 1987. 177.

Fagan, Brian M. *Archaeology: A Brief Introduction.* 3rd ed. Glenview: Scott, 1988. 37–38.

Gardner's Art Through the Ages. 5th ed. Revised edition by Horst de la Croix and Richard Tansey. New York: Harcourt, 1970. 40.

Huneven, Michelle. "Living Well Is the Best Revenge—Just Ask the Urban Coyote." Rpt. in *The Longwood Reader.* Ed. Edward A. Dornan and Charles W. Dawe. Boston: Allyn and Bacon, 1991. 19.

Janis, Irving L. "Groupthink." Rpt. in *Writing and Reading Across the Curriculum.* 3rd ed. Ed. Laurence Behrens and Leonard Rosen. Glenview: Scott, 1987. 266.

Jones, Beau Fly, Annemarie Sullivan Palincsar, Donna Sederburg Ogle, and Eileen Glynn Carr. *Strategic Thinking and Learning: Cognitive Instruction in the Content Areas.* Alexandria: ASCD, 1987. 22–23.

Jones, Rachel L. "What's Wrong with Black English." *Newsweek,* "My Turn," 27 Dec. 1982: 7. Rpt. in *Effective Argument.* Ed. J. Karl Nicholas and James R. Nicholl. Boston: Allyn and Bacon, 1991. 157, 159.

Keller, Helen. *The Story of My Life.* New York: Doubleday, 1954. 35–37.

Morreall, John. *Taking Laughter Seriously.* New York: State University of New York Press, 1983. Rpt. in *Writing and Reading Across the Curriculum.* 3rd ed. Ed. Laurence Behrens and Leonard Rosen. Glenview: Scott, 1987. 365–366.

Nilsen, Alleen. "Sexism in English: A 1990s Update." *The Longwood Reader.* Ed. Edward A. Dornan and Charles W. Dawe. Boston: Allyn and Bacon, 1991. 209.

Roddy, Jim. "Images of America in Doctorow's *Ragtime*." Student essay. *Aims of the Essay.* Ed. Don Knefel. Boston: Allyn and Bacon, 1991. 256.

Sagan, Carl. *The Dragons of Eden: Speculations on the Evolution of Human Intelligence.* New York: Random, 1977. 45–46.

Shanahan, Daniel. "We Need a Nationwide Effort to Encourage, Enhance, and Expand Our Students' Proficiency in Language." *The Chronicle of Higher Education,* 31 May 1989: 40. Rpt. in *Effective Argument.* Ed. J. Karl Nicholas and James R. Nicholl. Boston: Allyn and Bacon, 1991. 244.

Sheils, Merril, et al. "And Man Created the Chip." *Newsweek*, 30 June 1980. Rpt. in *Writing and Reading Across the Curriculum*. Ed. Laurence Behrens and Leonard Rosen. Boston: Little, Brown, 1982. 256.

Shapiro, David. *Neurotic Styles*. New York: Basic Books, 1965. 44–45.

Singer, Peter. "Animal Liberation." Rpt. in *Elements of Argument*. 2nd ed. Ed. Annette E. Rottenberg. New York: Bedford, 1988. 250.

Stratton, Joanna L. *Pioneer Women: Voices from the Kansas Frontier*. New York: Simon and Schuster–Touchstone, 1981. 45.

Trachtenberg, Alan. *Brooklyn Bridge: Fact and Symbol*. Chicago: Chicago UP, 1979. Preface.

Trahar, Jenafer. "Athletes and Education." Student essay. Quoted by permission of the author.

Watts, James, and Allen F. Davis, eds. *Your Family in Modern American History*. 2nd ed. New York: Knopf, 1978. Rpt. in *Writing and Reading Across the Curriculum*. Ed. Laurence Behrens and Leonard Rosen. Boston: Little, Brown, 1982. 136.

CHAPTER 6: WORKS CITED

Berger, Arthur Asa. "Sex as Symbol in Fashion Advertising." *Media Analysis Techniques* (Vol 10, The Sage COMMTEXT Series), 1982. Rpt. in *Reading Culture*. Ed. Diana George and John Trimbur. New York: HarperCollins, 1992. 257.

Carson, Rachel L. "The Obligation to Endure." *Silent Spring*. Rpt. in *The Shape of this Century*. Ed. Diana Wyllie Rigden and Susan S. Waugh. New York: Harcourt, 1990. 393.

Smith, Adam. "Fifty Million Handguns." *Esquire* 1981. Rpt. in *The Informed Argument*. Ed. Robert K. Miller. New York: Harcourt, 1986. 36.

Gary Turbak. "60 Billion Pounds of Trouble." *American Legion Magazine* Nov. 1989. Rpt. in *Effective Argument*. Ed. J. Karl Nicholas and James R. Nicholl. Boston: Allyn and Bacon, 1991, 135–136.

CHAPTER 37: WORKS CITED

Fichtelberg, Joseph. "The Complex Image: Text and Reader in the *Autobiography* of Benjamin Franklin." *Early American Literature* 23.2 (1988): 206.

Frankel, Charles. "Why the Humanities?" *The Humanist as Citizen*. Ed. John Agresto and Peter Riesenberg. Chapel Hill: N. Carolina UP, 1981.

Franklin, Benjamin. *The Autobiography and Other Writings*. New York: Penguin, 1987.

Joyce, James. "Counterparts." *Dubliners*. Ed. Robert Scholes and A. Walton Litz. Viking Critical Library. New York: Viking, 1969.

Ketchem, Ralph. "Benjamin Franklin." *Encyclopedia of Philosophy*. Rpt. 1972 ed.

Oates, Joyce Carol. *The Edge of Impossibility: Tragic Forms in Literature*. New York: Vanguard, 1972.

———. *On Boxing*. Garden City: Dolphin, 1987.

———. "Where Have You Been? Where Are You Going?" *The Wheel of Love*. New York: Vanguard, 1970.

O'Reilly, Kevin. "Teaching Critical Thinking in High School History." *Social Education* Apr. 1985: 281.

Rieke, Richard D., and Malcolm O. Sillars. *Argumentation and the Decision Making Process*. 2nd ed. Glenview: Scott, 1984.

Stratton, Joanna L. *Pioneer Women*. New York: Touchstone, 1981.

Toulmin, Stephen, Richard Rieke, and Allan Janik. *An Introduction to Reasoning*. New York: Macmillan, 1979.

Trilling, Lionel. "The Greatness of *Huckleberry Finn*." *Adventures of Huckleberry Finn*. By Samuel Langhorn Clemens. Ed. Sculley Bradley, et al. 2nd ed. Norton Critical Edition. New York: Norton, 1977.

Van Doren, Carl. *Benjamin Franklin*. New York: Viking, 1938.

Wittgenstein, Ludwig. *Philosophical Investigations*. 3rd ed. Trans. G.E.M. Anscombe. New York: Macmillan, 1968.

CHAPTER 38: WORKS CITED

Braybrooke, David. *Philosophy of Social Science*. Prentice-Hall Foundations of Philosophy Series. Englewood Cliffs: Prentice, 1987.

Bromley, D. B. *The Case-study Method in Psychology and Related Disciplines*. Chichester, Great Britain: John Wiley, 1986.

Otis, Laura P. "Factors Influencing the Willingness to Taste Unusual Foods." *Psychological Reports* 54 (1984): 739–45.

Richlin-Klonsky, Judith, and Ellen Strenski, coordinators and eds. *A Guide to Writing Sociology Papers*. New York: St. Martin's, 1986.

Rieke, Richard D., and Malcolm O. Sillars. *Argumentation and the Decision Making Process*. 2nd ed. Glenview: Scott, 1984.

Rollinson, Paul A. "The Story of Edward: The Everyday Geography of Elderly Single Room Occupancy (SRO) Hotel Tenants." *Journal of Contemporary Ethnography* 19 (1990):" 188–206.

Skinner, B. F. "Two Types of Conditioned Reflex and a Pseudo-type." *The Journal of General Psychology* 12 (1935): 66–77. Rpt. in B.F. Skinner, *Cumulative Record: A Selection of Papers*. 3rd ed. New York: Appleton, 1972, 479.

———. "How to Teach Animals." *Scientific American* 185 (1951): 26–29. Rpt. in B.F. Skinner, *Cumulative Record: A Selection of Papers*. 3rd ed. New York: Appleton, 1972, 539.

Solomon, Paul R. *A Student's Guide to Research Report Writing in Psychology*. Glenview: Scott, 1985.

Spencer, Herbert. *The Study of Sociology*. Ann Arbor: U of Michigan P, 1961.

CHAPTER 39: WORKS CITED

AIP [American Institute of Physics] Style Manual. 4th ed. New York: AIP, 1990.

American Association for the Advancement of Science. *Project 2061: Science for All Americans*. Washington: AAAS, 1989.

CBE [Council of Biology Editors] Style Manual. 5th ed. Bethesda: CBE, 1983.

Day, Robert. *How to Write and Publish a Scientific Paper*. 3rd ed. Phoenix: Oryx Press, 1988.

Gould, Stephen Jay. *Hen's Teeth and Horse's Toes: Further Reflections on Natural History*. New York: Norton, 1983.

Thuesen, Ingolf, and Jan Engberg. "Recovery and Analysis of Human Genetic Material from Mummified Tissue and Bone." *Journal of Archaeological Science* 17 (1990): 679–89.

Toulmin, Stephen, Richard Rieke, and Allan Janik. *An Introduction to Reasoning*. New York: Macmillan, 1979.

Woodruff, David S., and Stephen Jay Gould, "Fifty Years of Interspecific Hybridization: Genetics and Morphometrics of a Controlled Experiment on the Land Snail *Cerion* in the Florida Keys." *Evolution* 41 (1987): 1026.

INDEX

REVISION SYMBOLS

The symbols below indicate a need to make revisions in the areas designated. Boldface numbers and letters refer to handbook sections.

ab	abbreviation **31 a–e**
ad	form of adjective/adverb **7c, 11**
agr	agreement **10**
awk	awkward diction or construction **7b, 15, 21**
ca	case form **8**
cap	capitalization **30a–d**
coh	coherence **4b, 5d**
coord	coordination **7f, 18a, 19a**
cs	comma splice **13**
d	diction, word choice **21, 22**
dm	dangling modifier **15h**
dev	development needed **3, 4, 18d**
emph	emphasis needed **19, 20**
frag	sentence fragment **7b, 12**
fs	fused sentence **13**
hyph	hyphen **32**
inc	incomplete construction **7b, 16g–h**
ital	italics **30e–g**
k	awkward diction or construction **7b, 15, 21**
lc	lower-case letter **30a–d**
log	logic **6, 37a, 38a, 39a**
mm	misplaced modifier **7d, 15**
ms	manuscript form **35h, Appx. B**
mix	mixed construction **16e–f**
no ¶	no paragraph needed **5**
num	number **31f–h**
¶	paragraph **5**
¶ dev	paragraph development needed **5**

ref	unclear pronoun reference **14**
rep	unnecessary repetition **17a**
sp	spelling error **23**
shift	inconsistent, shifted construction **16**
sub	sentence subordination **7e–f, 19b**
t	verb tense error **9e–f**
trans	transition needed **5a, 5d, 5f**
var	sentence variety needed **19, 20**
vb	verb form error **9, 17b**
w	wordy **17a**
ww	wrong word; word choice **21, 22**
//	faulty parallelism **18**
. ? !	end punctuation **24**
:	colon **29a**
∨̓	apostrophe **27**
—	dash **29b**
( )	parentheses **29c**
[ ]	brackets **29d**
. . .	ellipsis **29e**
/	slash **29f**
;	semicolon **26**
" "	quotation marks **28**
∧̦	comma **25**
⁀‿	close up
∧	insert a missing element
℘	delete
⊔⊓	transpose order

SPOTLIGHT ON COMMON ERRORS

I. FORMS OF NOUNS AND PRONOUNS   See the SPOTLIGHT (page 214), Chapter 8.

Apostrophes can show possession or contraction. Never use an apostrophe with a possessive pronoun.

FAULTY FORMS	REVISED
The scarf is *Chris*. It is *her's*.	The scarf is *Chris's*. It is *hers*.
Give the dog *it's* collar.	Give the dog *its* collar.
Its a difficult thing.	*It's* [it is] a difficult thing.

Choose a pronoun's form depending on its use. For pronouns connected by *and*, or with forms of the verb *be (is/are/was/were)*, decide which forms to use (*I/he/she/they* OR *me/him/her/them*).

FAULTY FORMS	REVISED
This is *him*. It was *me*. Is that *her*?	This is *he*. It was *I*. Is that *she*?
The ball landed between *she* and *I*.	The ball landed between *her* and *me*.
Her and *me* practice daily.	*She* and *I* practice daily.

II. VERBS   See the SPOTLIGHT (page 228), Chapter 9.

Keep verb tenses consistent when describing two closely connected events.

INCONSISTENT	REVISED
She *liked* the work. Still, she *keeps* to herself.	She *likes* the work. Still, she *keeps* to herself.

(a) Choose the right verb forms with an *if* clause expressing an unreal or hypothetical condition.
(b) Decide on which of these verb forms to use: *sit* or *set, lie* or *lay, rise* or *raise*.

FAULTY VERB FORM	REVISED
(a) If it *would be* any colder, the pipes *would* freeze.	(a) If it *were* any colder, the pipes *would* freeze.
(b) *Lie* the books here. Then *lay* down.	(b) *Lay* the books here. Then *lie* down.

III. AGREEMENT   See the SPOTLIGHT (page 254), Chapter 10.

Match subjects with verbs. Make sure both are either singular or plural.

NOT IN AGREEMENT	REVISED
The *reason* she wins *are* her friends.	The *reason* she wins *is* her friends.

Match pronouns with the words they refer to. (a) Words joined by *and* require a plural pronoun and verb. (b) For words joined by *or/nor*, match the pronoun and verb to the nearer word.

NOT IN AGREEMENT	REVISED
(a) My friends **and** Sue *likes her* pizza hot.	(a) My friends **and** Sue *like their* pizza hot.
(b) Neither her friends **nor** Sue *like their* pizza cold.	(b) Neither her friends **nor** Sue *likes her* pizza cold.

IV. SENTENCE STRUCTURE: FRAGMENTS   See SPOTLIGHT (page 281), Chapter 12.

Recognize sentence boundaries. Mark where sentences should end, usually with a period (or sometimes with a semicolon). Avoid a FRAGMENT—a word group that will not stand alone with a full subject and predicate. See the test for fragments in Chapter 12.

FAULTY	REVISED
If our cousins arrive today. [Fragment]	Our cousins may arrive today.

V. SENTENCE STRUCTURE: BOUNDARIES   See SPOTLIGHT (page 294), Chapter 13.

Recognize boundaries. (a) Avoid a FUSED SENTENCE: two sentences with no connecting word or punctuation. (b) Avoid a COMMA SPLICE: two sentences with only a comma between them.

FAULTY	REVISED
(a) He's here now later he'll go to Iowa. [Fused]	He's here now. Later he'll go to Iowa.
(b) He's here now, later he'll go to Iowa. [Splice]	He's here now; later he'll go to Iowa.